# Bradford's Crossword Solver's Dictionary

### Third Edition

# Bradford's Crossword Solver's Dictionary

### Third Edition

Anne R. Bradford

PETER COLLIN PUBLISHING

First published in Great Britain 1986
as Longman Crossword Solver's Dictionary

Second edition 1993
Third edition first published 1997
Reprinted 1998
Reprinted twice 1999

by Peter Collin Publishing Ltd
1 Cambridge Road, Teddington, Middlesex TW11 8DT

**British Library Cataloguing-in-Publication Data**

A catalogue record for this book is available from the
British Library

ISBN 1-901659-03-8

Text computer typeset by PCP, Teddington, Middlesex
Printed by WSOY, Finland
Cover design by Gary Weston

## Author's preface

Every word has a definition - an identity. If it has only one definition we can look at it and know it for what it is, but some words are like cut stones with many facets; they can mean different things according to the way in which we use them. These are the words which add spice to the cryptic crossword puzzle - the setter plays with them and tries to deceive his solvers into believing he means what he does not. They are the basis of puns and word-play.

Introduced to crossword puzzles at an early age, it soon became clear to me that some words are beloved of setters - rivers Po and Dee; the town of Diss in Norfolk; the diocesan 'see' of Ely, these and many more quickly became familiar, but now and again the odd one would elude the memory. It seemed logical then to write these down, and by a natural progression to start to turn the normal dictionary inside out - if 'flummery' is defined as a blancmange, then why not list it under 'blancmange' alongside other words which can be defined as such? Not a new idea, of course, but why stop at synonyms? There are words which have recognised associations with other words, descriptive words or words with literary connections, foreign words, archaic words, technical words and even folkloric words - all highly collectable. And so this crossword dictionary began to evolve. Every puzzle I have laid hands on in the past forty years has been scrutinised, the clues broken down into definitions and cryptic parts; words indicating anagrams, reversals, puns, etc., all carefully recorded and stored.

## Preface to the new edition

Since publication of the second edition in 1993, a further four years' material has been added. Some alterations have been made, and the work now contains further headwords and entries.

I appreciate the continual support and encouragement I receive from fellow crossword addicts and am glad that they find the work so useful.
*ARB. 1997*

## Solving crossword clues

Crossword puzzles tend to be basically 'quick' or 'cryptic'. A 'quick' crossword usually relies on a one or two-word clue which is a simple definition of the answer required. As has been stated, many words have different meanings, so that the clue 'ball' could equally well lead to the answer 'sphere', 'orb' or 'dance'. The way to solve 'quick' crosswords is to press on until probable answers begin to interlink, which is a good sign that you are on the right track

'Cryptic' crosswords are another matter. Here the clue usually consists of a basic definition, given at either the beginning or end of the clue, together with one or more definitions of parts of the answer. Here are some examples taken from all-time favourites recorded over the year:

*1. 'Tradesman who bursts into tears' (Stationer)*
Tradesman is a definition of stationer. Bursts is cleverly used as an indication of an anagram, which into tears is of stationer.

*2. 'Sunday school tune' (Strain)*
Here Sunday is used to define its abbreviation S, school is a synonym for train, and put together they give strain, which is a synonym of tune

*3. 'Result for everyone when head gets at bottom' (Ache)*
(used as a 'down' clue)
This is what is known as an '& lit' clue, meaning that the setter has hit on a happy composition which could literally be true. Everyone here is a synonym for each, move the head (first letter) of the word to the bottom, and the answer is revealed, the whole clue being the definition of the answer in this case.

*4. 'Tin out East' (Sen)*
In this example, tin, implying 'money', requires its chemical symbol Sn to go out(side) East, or its abbreviation, E, the whole clue being a definition of a currency (sen) used in the East.

*5. 'Information given to communist in return for sex' (Gender)*
Information can be defined as gen; communist is almost always red, in return indicates 'reversed', leading to gen-der, a synonym for sex.

6. 'Row about no enclosure of this with sardines' (Tin-opener)
Row is a synonym for tier, about indicates 'surrounding' no enclosure can be no pen, leading to ti-no pen-er, and another '& lit' clue.

7. *'Cake-sandwiches-meat, at Uncle Sam's party' (Clambake)*
Meat here is lamb, sandwiches is used as a verb, so we have C-lamb-ake, which is a kind of party in America. Uncle Sam or US is often used to indicate America.

8. *'Initially passionate meeting of boy and girl could result in it' (Pregnancy)*
Initially is usually a sign of a first letter, in this case 'p' for passionate + Reg (a boy) and Nancy (a girl), and another clever '& lit'.

With 'cryptic' clues the solver needs to try to analyse the parts to see what he or she is looking for - which word or words can be the straight definition, and which refer to the parts or hint at anagrams or other subterfuges. Whilst it would be unreal to claim total infallibility, practice has shown that in most crosswords some 90% of the answers are to be found in this work.

*Anne R Bradford*

## How to use the dictionary

This dictionary is the result of over thirty-five years analysis of some 300,000 crossword clues, ranging from plain 'quick' crosswords requiring only synonyms to the different level of cryptic puzzles. Therefore the words listed at each entry may be connected to the keyword in various ways, such as

- a straightforward synonym
- a commonly associated adjective
- an associated proper noun
- a pun or other devious play on words

Keywords marked with the symbol > give leads to anagrams and other ploys used by crossword setters.

Keywords are listed alphabetically, in cases where the heading consists of more than one keyword taking the first of these words and in cases where the end of a word is bracketed taking the material up to the bracket.

If the keywords found in the clue do not lead directly to the required answer, the solver should look under the words that are listed. Those in small capitals point to entries where additional information will be found.

# Aa

**A, an** Ack, Ae, Alpha, Angstrom, Argon, D, Ein, Her, If, L, One, Per, They

**A1** Tiptop

**AA** Milne

**Aardvark** Ant-bear, Ant-eater, Ground-hog

**Aaron's Rod** Hagtaper

**Aba, Abba** Patriarch

**Abacus** Counter, Soroban

**Abaft** Astern, Sternson

**Abalone** Ormer, Paua

**Abandon(ed)** Abnegate, Cancel, Castaway, Corrupt, Defect, Derelict, DESERT, Disown, Dissolute, Ditch, Dump, Elan, Flagrant, Forhoo(ie), Forlend, Forsake, Gomorra, Immoral, Jack(-in), Jettison, Jilt, Louche, Maroon, Old, Orgiastic, Profligate, Quit, Rat, Renounce, Reprobate, Scrap, Shed, Sink, Strand, Waive

**Abase** Degrade, Demean, Disgrace, Grovel, HUMBLE, Kotow, Lessen

**Abash** Daunt, Discountenance, Mortify

**Abate(ment)** Allay, Appal, Decrescent, Diminish, Lyse, Lysis, Reduce, Remit, SUBSIDE

**Abattoir** Knackery, Slaughterhouse

**Abbey** Abbacy, Bath, Buckfast, Cloister, Downside, Glastonbury, Medmenham, Melrose, Nightmare, Northanger, Priory, Tintern, Westminster, Whitby, Woburn

**Abbot** Archimandrite, Brother, Friar

**Abbreviate, Abbreviation** Abridge, Ampersand, Compendium, Condense, Curtail, SHORTEN, Sigla

**ABC** Absey

**Abdicate** Cede, Disclaim, Disown, Resign

**Abdomen** Belly, Gaster, Paunch, Pleon, STOMACH, Tummy, Venter

**Abduct(ed), Abduction** Enlèvement, Kidnap, Rapt, Ravish, Shanghai, Steal

**Aberrant, Aberration** Abnormal, Aye-aye, Deviant, Idolon, Perverse

**Abet(tor)** Aid, Back, Candle-holder, Second

**Abeyance, Abeyant** Dormant, Shelved, Sleeping, Store

**Abhor(rent)** DETEST, HATE, Loathe, Shun

**Abide** Dwell, Inhere, LAST, Lie, Live, Observe, Remain, Stand, Tarry

**Abigail** Maid, Masham

**Ability** Aptitude, Capacity, Cocum, COMPETENCE, ESP, Faculty, Ingine, Lights, Savey, Savv(e)y, Skill

**Abject** Base, Craven, Grovel, Humble, Servile, Slave

**Abjure** Eschew, Forswear, Recant, Renege, Reny

**Ablaze** Afire, Ardent

**Able** Ablins, ADEPT, Aiblins, Apt, Capable, COMPETENT, Fere, Seaman, Yibbles

**Abnormal(ity)** Atypical, DEVIANT, Erratic, Etypical, Freakish, Odd, Preternatural, QUEER, Sport, Unnatural

**Aboard** On

**Abode** Domicile, Dwelling, Habitat, HOME, Lain, Libken, Remain

**Abolish, Abolition(ist)** Annihilate, Annul, Axe, BAN, D, Delete, Destroy, Eradicate, Erase, Extirpate, John Brown, Nullify, Repeal, Rescind

**Abomasum** Read

**Abominable, Abominate, Abomination** Bane, Cursed, HATE, Nefandous, Nefast, Revolting, Snowman, Vile, Yeti

**Aborigine, Aboriginal** Adivasi, Aranda, Autochthon, Binghi, Boong, Bushmen, Carib, Evolué, Indigenous, Koori, Lubra, Maori, Mary, Motu, Myall, Sakai, Sican, Vedda

**Abort(ion), Abortive** Apiol, Cancel, Ecbolic, Miscarry, Moon-calf, Slip, Sooterkin, Teras

**Abound(ing)** Bristle, Copious, Enorm, Rife, Teem

**About** A, Almost, Anent, Around, C, Ca, Circa, Concerning, Encompass, Environs, Going, Near, Of, On, Over, Re, Regarding

> **About** may indicate one word around another

**Above** Abune, Over, Overhead, Overtop, Owre, Sopra, Superior, Upon

**Abracadabra** Cantrip, Heypass

**Abrade, Abrasive** Carborundum, Emery, Erode, File, GRATE, Rub, Sand, Scrape, Scrat

**Abraham** Lincoln, Urite

**Abreast** Alongside, Beside, Level, Up

**Abridge(ment)** Audley, Compress, Condense, Cut, Digest, Dock, Epitome, Pot, Shorten, Trim

**Abroad** Away, Distant, Forth, Out, Overseas

> **Abroad** may indicate an anagram

**Abrogate** Abolish, Repeal, Replace

> **Abrupt** may indicate a shortened word

**Abrupt(ly)** Bold, Brusque, Curt, Gruff, Offhand, Premorse, Prerupt, Short, Staccato, Terse

**Abscess** Gumboil, Impost(h)ume, Ulcer, Warble

**Abscond** Absquatulate, Decamp, Desert, Elope, Flee, Leg-bail, Levant, Welch

**Abseil** Rappel

**Absence, Absent(ee), Absent-minded** Abstracted, Away, Distant, Distracted, Distrait, Exile, Skip, Truant, Vacuity, Void

**Absolute(ly)** Bang, Complete, Downright, Ipso facto, Mere, Plumb, Real, Sheer, Total, Unqualified, Utter

**Absolve** Clear, Exculpate, Excuse, Pardon, Shrive

**Absorb(ed), Absorbing, Absorption** Assimilate, Autism, Blot, Consume, Devour, Digest, Dope, Drink, ENGROSS, Imbibe, Ingest, Intent, Merge(r), Occlude, Occupy, Porous, Preoccupation, Rapt

**Absquatulate** Skedaddle

**Abstain(er), Abstemious, Abstinence** Continent, Desist, Eschew, Forbear, Forgo, Maigre, Nazarite, Nephalism, Rechabite, Refrain, Resist, Sober, Temperate, TT

**Abstract(ed), Abstraction** Abrege, Abridge, Academic, Appropriate, Brief, Deduct, Digest, Discrete, Epitome, Essence, Metaphysical, Notional, Précis, Prepossessed, Prescind, Resumé, Reverie, Stable, Steal, Tachism

**Abstruse** Deep, Esoteric, Obscure, Recondite

**Absurd(ity)** Alician, Apagoge, Fantastic, Folly, Inept, Irrational, Laputan, Ludicrous, Nonsense, Paradox, Preposterous, Ridiculous, Silly, Solecism, Stupid, Toshy, Whim-wham

**Abundance, Abundant** A-gogo, Bounty, Copious, Flood, Fouth, Fowth, Fruitful, Galore, Lashings, Mine, Mint, Oodles, Over, PLENTIFUL, Pleroma, Prolific, Replete, Rich, Rife, Routh, Rowth, Sonce, Sonse, Store, Tallents, Uberous

**Abuse** Assail, Blackguard, Flak, Fustilarian, Fustil(l)irian, Hail, Insult, Invective, Limehouse, Maltreat, Miscall, MISTREAT, Misuse, Obloquy, Opprobrium, Philippic, Rail, Rampallian, Rate, Rayle, Revile, Satire, Scarab(ee), Scurrilous, Slang, Slate, Snash, Tirade, Violate, Vituperation

**Abut** Adjoin, Border, Touch

**Abysm(al), Abyss** Avernus, Barathrum, Barranca, Chasm, Deep, Gulf, Swallet, Tartarean, Tartarus

**AC** Current, Erk

**Acacia** Bablah, Boree, Brigalow, Gidgee, Gidjee, Koa, Mimosa, Mulga, Myall, Sallee, Shittim, Wattle

**Academic(ian)** A, Della-Cruscan, Don, Erudite, Fellow, Hypothetic(al), Immortals, Literati, Master, Pedantic, PRA, RA, Rector

**Academy** Athenaeum, Dollar, Loretto, Lyceum, Sandhurst, Seminary, St Cyr, West Point

**Acanthus** Blankursine, Ruellia

**Accelerate, Accelerator** Antedate, Betatron, Bevatron, Festinate, Gal, Gun, Hasten, Increase, Linac, Linear, Rev, Speed, Stringendo

**Accent(ed), Accentuate** Acute, Beat, Brogue, Bur(r), Doric, Drawl, Enclitic, Enhance, Grave, Hacek, Intonation, Long, Macron, Nasal, Orthotone, Oxytone, Pitch, Rhythm, Stress, Tone, Twang

**Accentor** Dunnock

**Accept(able) Acceptance, Accepted** A, Accede, Admit, Adopt, Agree, Allow, Bar, Believe, Buy, Common, Consent, Done, Grant, Obey, On, Pocket, Stand, Swallow, Take, U, Wear

**Access** Avenue, Card, Credit, Door, Entrée, ENTRY, Key, Recourse, Wayleave

**Accessory, Accessories** Abettor, Addition, Aide, Ally, Ancillary, Appendage, Appurtenance, Attribute, Bandanna, Cribellum, Findings, Staffage, Trimming

**Accident(al)** Adventitious, Bechance, Blunder, Calamity, CHANCE, Circumstance, Contingency, Contretemps, Crash, Disaster, Fall, Fluke, Hap, Hit and run, Mischance, Mishap, Promiscuous, Smash, Spill, Stramash, Wreck

**Accidie** Acedia, Sloth, Torpor

**Acclaim** Accolade, Applaud, Brava, Bravo, Cheer, Eclat, Fame, Hail, Kudos, Ovation, Praise, Salute

**Accolade** Award, Honour, Token

**Accommodate, Accommodation** Adapt, B and B, Bedsit, Berth, Board, Camp, Crashpad, Gite, Hotel, House, Lend, Loan, Lodge, OBLIGE, Parador, Pension, Quarters, Rapprochement, Recurve, Room, Sorehon, Stabling, Stateroom, Steerage, Storage, Wharepuni

> **Accommodating** may indicate one word inside another

**Accompany(ing), Accompanied (by), Accompaniment, Accompanist** Accessory, Alberti, And, Attend, Chaperone, Chum, Concomitant, Consort, Descant, ESCORT, Harmonise, Obbligato, Obligate, Trimmings, Vamp

**Accomplice** Abettor, Aide, ALLY, Confederate, Federarie, Partner, Shill

**Accomplish(ed)** ACHIEVE, Arch, Attain, Clever, Complete, Done, Effect, Master, Perform, Polished, Realise, Ripe, Savant

**Accord(ingly), According to** After, Agree, Ala, Allow, As per, Attune, Chime, Give, Grant, Harmony, Meet, Sort, Thus

**According to nature** SN

**Accost** Abord, Approach, Greet, Hail, Importune, Molest, Solicit, Tackle

**Account(s)** AC, Audit, Battels, Behalf, Bill, Cause, Charge, Chronicle, Current, Deposit, Expense, Explain, Exposition, Ledger, Long, Memoir, Reason, Recital, Regest, Register, REPORT, Repute, Sake, Tab, Tale, Thesis, Version

**Accountant** Auditor, CA, Hyde, Reckoner, Vestry-clerk

**Accumulate, Accumulation** Aggregate, AMASS, Augment, Collect, Gather, Hoard, Lodg(e)ment, Pile, Uplay

**Accuracy, Accurate(ly)** Cocker, CORRECT, Fair, Fidelity, Minute, Precise, Right, Spot-on, True

**Accursed** Argued, Sacred

**Accusation, Accuse(d)** Allege, Arraign, Attaint, Bill, Blame, Censure, Challenge, Charge, Criminate, Denounce, Dite, Gravamen, Impeach, Panel, Suspect, Tax, Threap, Threep, Traduce

**Accustom(ed)** Acquaint, Attune, Enure, General, Habituate, Inure, Woon

**Ace(s)** Basto, Dinger, EXPERT, Jot, Master, Mournival, One, Quatorze, Spadille, Spadill(i)o, Spot, Tib, Wonderful

**Ache, Aching** Aitch, Die, Long, Mulligrubs, Nag, Otalgia, Pain, Stitch, Yearn, Yen

**Achieve(ment)** Accomplish, Attain, Come, Compass, EFFECT, Exploit, Feat, Fulfil, Hatchment, Realise, Stroke, Succeed, Triumph, Trock, Troke, Truck

**Acid(ity)** Abietic, Acrimony, Adipic, Alanine, Amide, Amino, Aquafortis, Aqua-regia, Arginine, Ascorbic, Asparagine, Aspartic, Auric, Barbituric, Boric, Capric, Caprylic, Caproic, Carbolic, Corrosive, DNA, Dopa, Drop, Ellagic, Erucic, Folacin, Folic, Formic, Gallic, HCL, Hippuric, Iodic, Lactic, Lauric, Leucin(e), Linoleic, LSD, Lysergic, Maleic, Malic, Meconic, Mucic, Niacin, Nucleic, Oleic, Orcin(ol), Oxalic, Persulphuric, PH, Phenol, Phthalic, Picric, Proline, Propionic, Prussic, Pyro, Pyruvic, Racemic, Reaction, RNA, Sassolite, Serine, Silicic, Solvent, Sour, Stannic, Suberic, Succinic, Sulphonic, Sulphuric, Tannic, Tart, Tartaric, Threonine, Tiglic, Titanic, Trona, Tryptophan, Tyrosine, Uric, Valine, Vinegar, Vitriol, Xylonic

**Acknowledge(ment)** Accept, Admit, Allow, Answer, Avow, Confess, Grant, Own, Receipt, Recognise, Respect, Salute, Ta, Touché, Wilco

**Acme** Apex, Apogee, Climax, Comble, Crest, Peak, Summit, Top, Zenith

**Acolyte** Nethinim, Novice, Server, Thurifer

**Acorn(s), Acorn-shell** Balanus, Glans, Mast, Rac(c)ahout

**Acoustic(s)** Harmonic, Sonics

**Acquaint(ance), Acquainted** Advise, Cognisant, Enlighten, Familiar, INFORM, Knowledge, Nodding, Notify, Tell, Versed

**Acquiescence, Acquiescent** Accept, Bow, Conform, Resigned, Roger, Wilco

**Acquire, Acquisition** Acquest, Earn, Ern, Gain, GET, Land, Procure, Purchase, Steal

**Acquit(tal)** Assoil, Cleanse, Clear, Exonerate, Free, Loose, Loste, Pardon

**Acre(s)** A, Area, Hide, Rival, Rood

**Acrid, Acrimony** Bitter(ness), Empyreuma, Rough, Sour, Surly

**Acrobat(ic)s** Gymnast, Splits, Trampoline, Tumbler

**Acropolis** Citadel, Parthenon

**Across** A, Ac, Athwart, Opposite, Over

**Act(ing), Action** A, Antic, Assist, Assumpsit, Auto, Barnstorm, Behave, Bit, Camp, Campaign, Case, Cause, Come, Conduct, Daff, Deal, DEED, Deputise, Do, DORA, Enclosure, Excitement, Exert, Exploit, Feat, Feign, Forth-putting, Function, Incident, Industrial, Lance-jack, Litigate, Measure, Movement, Pas, Perform(ance), Play, Pp, Practice, Pretence, Procedure, Process, Qua, Reflex, Represent, Rising, Routine, Sasine, Serve, Simulate, Stanislavski, Statute, Steps, Suit, Synergy, Test, Thing, Thellusson, Treat, Trover, Turn, Twig, Uniformity, Union, Vicegerent, War

**Actinium** Ac

**Activate** Goad, Spark, Spur, Stur, Styre, Trigger

**Active, Activitist, Activity** A, Alert, At, Athletic, Brisk, Busy, Deedy, Do(ing), Dynamited, Effectual, Energetic, Energic, Extra-curricular, Fluster, Go-go, Hum, Leish, Licht, Live, Mobile, Motile, Nimble, Ongo, Sprightly, Springe, Spry, Voice, Wimble

**Actor(-like)** Agent, Alleyn, Artist, Ashe, Barnstormer, Benson, Betterton, Burbage, Cast, Character, Company, Donat, Gable, Garrick, Gielgud, Guiser, Ham, Hamfatter, Heavy, Histrio(n), Jay, Kean, MacReady, Mime, Mummer, Olivier, Performer, Player, Playfair, Roscian, Roscius, Savoyard, Sim, Stager, Strolling, Super, Thespian, Tragedian, Tree, Tritagonist, Trouper, Understudy

**Actress** Bankhead, Duse, Ingenue, Pierrette, Siddons, Terry, West

**Actual(ity), Actually** De facto, Entelechy, Literal, Live, Material, Real, True, Very

**Acumen** Insight

**Acute** Astute, Fitché, INTENSE, Keen

**Adage** Aphorism, Gnome, Maxim, Motto, Proverb, Saw, Saying, Truism

**Adam** Bede, Delved

**Adamant** Obdurate, Rigid, Unbending

**Adapt(er), Adaptable** Bushing, Ecad, Versatile

**Add(ed), Addendum** Accrue, Adscititious, APPENDIX, Attach, Cast, Dub, Ech(e), Eik, Eke, Elaborate, Embroider, Enhance, Fortify, Insert, Lace, Reckon, Score, Spike, Sum, Tot(e), Total

**Addict(ion)** Acidhead, Buff, Devotee, Etheromaniac, Fan, Fiend, Freak, Hophead, Hype, Junkie, Mania, Shithead, Slave, User

**Addison** Spectator

**Addition(al)** Addend, Additive, Accession, Adscititious, Adulterant, And, Annexure, (As an) in, Codicil, Eik, Eke, Encore, Epithesis, Etc, Extender, EXTRA, IN ADDITION, Increment, Makeweight, New, Odd, On, On top, Other, Paragog(u)e, Plus, PS, Rider, Ripieno, Spare, Suffect, Suffix, Supplementary, Thereto, Verandah

**Address** Accost, Adroit, Allocution, Apostrophe, Apostrophise, Appellation, Art, Ave, Call, Compellation, Dedication, Delivery, Den, Diatribe, Direction, Election, Epilogue, Epirrhema, Esquire, Hail, Home, Lecture, Ode, Orate, Parabasis, Prelection, Rig, Salute, Sermon, Speech,

Stance, Tact, Tannoy

**Adelphic** Adam

**Adept** Able, Adroit, Dab, Don, EXPERT, Handy, Mahatma

**Adequate** Condign, Does, Due, Egal, Equal, Ere-now, Proper, SUFFICIENT, Tolerable, Valid

**Adhere(nt), Adhesive** Allegiance, Ally, Araldite, Burr, Cling, Conform, Dextrin, Disciple, Epoxy, Follower, Glue, Guebre, Gum, Hot-melt, Jain(a), Partisan, Resin, Servitor, Supporter, Sticker, Synechia

**Adjacent** Bordering, Conterminous, Handy, Nigh

**Adjective** Epithet, Gerundive

**Adjourn(ment)** Abeyance, Delay, POSTPONE, Prorogate, Recess, Suspend

**Adjudicate, Adjudicator** Judge, Jury, Referee, Try, Umpire

**Adjunct** Addition, Aid, Rider

**Adjust(able)** Accommodate, Adapt, Attune, Coapt, Dress, Fit, Gang, Gauge, Modify, Modulate, Orientate, Regulate, Scantle, Sliding, Suit, Trim, True, Tune

> **Adjust** may indicate an anagram

**Adjutant** Argala, Officer, Stork

**Adler** Irene

**Administer, Administration, Administrator** Adhibit, Anele, Control, DIRECT, Dispence, Dispense, Executive, MANAGE, Regime, Run, Steward

**Admirable, Admiration, Admire(d), Admirer** Clinker, Clipper, Crichton, Esteem, EXCELLENT, Flame, Fureur, Ho, Idolater, Partisan, Regard, Ripping, Toast, Tribute, Venerate, Wonder

**Admiral** Adm, Anson, Beatty, Beaufort, Benbow, Blake, Boscawen, Butterfly, Byng, Drake, Effingham, Fisher, Hood, Hornblower, Howard, Jellicoe, Keyes, Marrowfat, Navarch, Nelson, Raeder, Rodney, Spee, Sturdee, Togo, Vanessa, Van Niemen, Van Tromp

**Admission, Admit(ting), Admittance** Access, Agree, Allow, Avow, Concede, CONFESS, Enter, Entrée, Entry, Estoppel, Grant, Ingress, Initiate, Owe, Own, Recognise, Tho(ugh), Yield

**Admonish, Admonition** Chide, Lecture, Rebuke, SCOLD, Tip, Warn

**Ado** Bother, Bustle, Fuss

**Adolescent** Developer, Grower, Halflin, Juvenile, Neanic, Teenager, Veal, Youth

**Adonais** Keats

**Adonis** Pheasant's Eye

**Adopt** Accept, Affiliate, Assume, Embrace, Espouse, Father, Foster, Mother

**Adoration, Adore** Homage, Love, Pooja(h), Puja, Revere, Venerate, Worship

**Adorn(ed), Adornment** Attrap, Banderol, Bedeck, Bedight, Bejewel, Caparison, Clinquant, Deck, Dight, Drape, Embellish, Emblaze, Emblazon, Embroider, Equip, Festoon, Furnish, Garnish, Grace, Graste, Ornament, Riband, Tattoo, Tatu, Tinsel

**Adrenaline** Epinephrine

**Adroit** Adept, Dextrous, Expert, Skilful

**Adulate, Adulation** Flatter(y), Praise, WORSHIP

**Adullam** Cave

**Adult** Grown-up, Man, Mature, Upgrown, X

**Adulterant, Adulterate** Cut, Debase, Impurify, Lime, Mix, Multum, POLLUTE, Sophisticate, Weaken

**Adulterer, Adultery** Avoutery, Cuckold, Fornication, Francesca, Lenocinium

**Advance(d)** A, Abord, Accelerate, Anabasis, Ante, Approach, Assert, Charge, Develop, Extreme, Fore, Forward, Haut(e), Impress, Imprest, Incede, Late, Lend, LOAN, March, Mortgage, Overture, Pass, Piaffe, Posit, Postulate, Precocious, Prefer, Prest, Process, Progress, PROMOTE, Propose, Propound, Ripe, Rise, Sub

**Advantage(ous)** Accrual, Aid, ASSET, Avail, Batten, Benefit, Bisque, Boot, Edge, Emolument, Expedient, Exploit, Favour, Fruit, Gain, Grouter, Handicap, Handle, Help, Interess, Interest, Lever(age), Odds, Percentage, Plus, Privilege, Prize, Purchase, Strength, Use, Van, Whiphand

**Advent(ist)** Coming, Shaker

**Adventure(r), Adventuress** Assay, Buccaneer, Casanova, Enterprise, Escapade, EXPLOIT, Filibuster, Gest, Lark, Mata Hari, Mercenary, Merchant, Picaresque, Picaro, Risk, Routier, Rutter, Vamp, Voyage

**Adversary** Cope(s)mate, Enemy, Foe

**Adverse, Adversity** Calamity, Cross, Down, Harrow, Misery, Reversal, Setback, Untoward, Woe

**Advert(ise), Advertisement** Ad, Allude, Bark, Bill, Circular, Classified, Coign(e), Coin, Commercial, Display, Dodger, Hype, Jingle, Noise, NOTICE, Parade, Placard, Plug, POSTER, Promo, Promote, Promulgate, Prospectus, Puff, Quoin, Refer, Splash, Stunt, Throwaway, Tout, Trailer, Trawl

**Advice** Conseil, Counsel, GUIDANCE, Information, Invoice, Read, Recommendation, Re(e)de

**Advise(r), Advisable** Acquaint, CAB, Egeria, Enlighten, Expedient, Genro, Induna, Inform, Instruct, Mentor, Oracle, Peritus, RECOMMEND, Tutor, Urge, Wise

**Advocate(d)** Agent, Argue, Attorney, Back, Exponent, Gospel, Lawyer, Move, Paraclete, Peat, Peddle, Pleader, Preach, Pragmatist, Proponent, Syndic, Urge

**Aerial** Aeolian, Antenna, Dipole, Dish, Ethereal, Yagi

**Aerobatics** Stunt

> **Aeroplane** see AIRCRAFT

**Aerosol** Atomiser

**Aesir** Loki

**Aesthetic** Arty, Tasteful

**Affable** Amiable, Avuncular, Benign, Suave, Urbane

**Affair** Amour, Business, Concern, Effeir, Effere, Event, Fight, Go, Indaba, Intrigue, Matter, Pash, Res, Romance, Shebang, Subject, Thing

**Affect(ed), Affectation, Affection** Air, Alter, Breast, Camp, Chi-chi, Concern, Crazy, Euphuism, Foppery, Hit, Ladida, Mimmick, Minnick, Minnock, Mouth-made, Phoney, POSE, Poseur, Precieuse, Pretence, Prick-me-dainty, Spoilt, Storge, Sway, Twee, Unction, Unnatural

**Affiliate, Affiliation** Adopt, Associate, Merge, Unite

**Affinity** Bro, Kin(ship), Rapport, Tie

**Affirm(ative)** Assert, Attest, Maintain, Predicate, Uh-huh, VERIFY

**Affix(ed)** Ascribe, Append, ATTACH, Connect, Fasten, On

**Afflict(ed), Affliction** Cross, Cup, Curse, Harass, Hurt, Lumbago, Molest, Nosology, Palsy, Persecute, Pester, Plague, Scourge, Smit, Sore, SORROW, Stricken, Teen, Tene, Tic, Tribulation, TROUBLE, Unweal, Visitation, Woe

**Affluence** Abundance, Fortune, Opulence, Wealth

**Afford** Bear, Manage, Offer, Provide, Spare

**Affray** Brawl, Fight, Mêlée, Scuffle, Skirmish

**Affront** Assault, Defy, Facer, INSULT, OFFEND, Outrage, Scandal, Slight, Slur

**Afghan** Dard, Hound, Kaf(f)ir, Pakhto, Pakhtu, Pashto, Pashtu, Pathan, Pushto(o), Pushtu

**Afloat** Abroach, Adrift, Natant

**Afoot** Astir, Up

**Aforesaid** Same

**Afraid** Adrad, Alarmed, Chicken, Fearful, Funk, Rad, Regretful, Scared, Timorous, Windy, Yellow

**Africa(n)** Abyssinian, Ashanti, Bantu, Barotse, Basuto, Beento, Berber, Biafran, Bintu, Black, Boer, Botswana, Cairene, Carthaginian, Congolese, Cushitic, Dyula, Efik, Ethiopian, Ewe, Fang, Fanti, Fingo, Gambian, Ganda, Griqua, Hamite, Hausa, Herero, Hottentot, Ibibi, Ibo, Igbo, Kaffer, Kaffir, Kenyan, Kongo, Lesotho, Liberian, Libyan, Lowveld, Luba, Maghreb, Malawi, Mandingo, Masai, Mashona, Matabele, Moor, Munt(u), Namibian, Negro, Nguni, Nilot(e), Nuer, Nyanja, Ovambo, Pondo, Rastafarian, Rhodesian, Shona, Somali, Sotho, Sudanese, Susu, Swahili, Swazi, Transkei, Transvaal, Tshi, Tswana, Tutsi, Twi, Venda, Yoruban, Zulu

**Afrikaans** Taal

**After(wards)** About, At, Behind, Beyond, Eft, LATER, On, Past, Rear, Since, Sine

**Afterbirth** Sooterkin

> **After injury** may indicate an anagram

**Aftermath** Consequence, Mow(ing), Rawing, Rawn, Rowan, Rowen, Rowing, Sequel(a)

**Afternoon** A, Arvo, PM, Undern

**Afterpiece, Afterthought** Addendum, Codicil, Epimetheus, Exode, Footnote, PS, Supplement

**Again** Afresh, Anew, Back, Bis, De novo, Ditto, Do, Eft, Encore, Iterum, More, Moreover, Re-, Recurrence, Reprise, Than, Then

**Against** A, Anti, Beside, Con, Counter, Nigh, On, Opposing, To, V, Versus

**Agape** Feast, Hiant, Ringent, Yawning

**Agate** Onyx

**Agave** Henequen, Lily, Maenad, Maguey

**Age(d), Aging** Ae, Aeon, Alcheringa, Antique, Archaise, Azilian, Calpa, Century, Chellean, Cycle, Day, Doddery, Eld, Eon, Epact, Epoch(a), Era, Eternity, Generation, Grey, Hoar, Hore, Jurassic, Kaliyuga, Kalpa, La Tene, Lias, Maglemosian, Mature, Millenium, Neolithic, Of, Oligocene, Paleolithic, Passé, Period, S(a)eculum, Saros, Senescence, Yellow, Yonks, Yug(a)

**Agency, Agent** Agitator, Ambassador, Bailiff, Barm, Bond, Broker, Catalyst, Cat's paw, Cause, Commis, Comprador(e), Consul, Delcredere, Doer, Emissary, Enzyme, Factor, Fed, Finger, Flack, G-man, Go-between, Hand, Instrument, Kinase, Legate, Man, Means, Medium, Mole, Mutagen, Narc, Ninja, -or, Pinkerton, Procurator, Proxy, Rep(resentative), Resident, Runner, Secret (service), Setter, Sleeper, Solvent, Spy, Syndic, Tass, Vakeel, Vakil, Voice

**Agenda** Business, Programme, Schedule

**Aggie** Agnes, Nessa, Nesta

**Aggravate** Annoy, Inflame, Irk, Provoke, Try, Vex

**Aggregate, Aggregation** Ballast, Congeries, Detritus, Granulite, Gravel, Omnium, Ore, Sum

**Aggression, Aggressive, Aggressor** Attack, Belligerent, Butch, Defiant, Enemy, Feisty, Foe, Hawk, Invader, Militant, On-setter, Pushing, Rambo, Rampant, Truculent, Wild

**Agile** Acrobatic, Deft, Lissom(e), Nifty, Nimble, Quick, Spry, Supple, Swank

**Agitate(d), Agitation, Agitator** Activist, Ado, Agitprop, Betoss, Boil, Bolshie, Bother, Chartist, Churn, Commotion, Commove, Convulse, Demagogue, Discompose, Distraught, DISTURB, Doodah, Ebullient, Emotion, Excite, Extremist, Ferment, Firebrand, Flurry, Fluster, Flutter,

Fuss, Goad, Heat, Hectic, Jabble, Lather, Militant, Pedetic, Perturb, Poss, Rattle, Restless, Rouse, Seethed, Sod, Stir(-up), Swivet, Taking, Tizzy, Toss, Tremor, Trouble, Turmoil, Tweak, Twitchy, Welter, Whisk, Ytost

> **Agitate** may indicate an anagram

**Agley** Awry, Unevenly

**Aglow** Alight, Tipsy

> **Agnes** see AGGIE

**Agnostic** Laodicean

**Agog** Athirst, Eager, Keen

**Agony** Ache, Anguish, Ecstasy, Heartache, PAIN, Torture

**Agree(ing), Agreement** Accede, Accord, Acquiescence, Allow, Amen, Analog(ue), Analogy, Apply, Assent, Assort, Atone, Aye, Bilateral, Bipartite, Bond, Chime, Closing, Coincide, Comart, Community, Compact, Comply, Comport, Concert, Concord(at), Concur, Conform, Congruent, Consension, Consensus, CONSENT, Consonant, Contract, Contrahent, Cotton, Covenant, Deal, Deign, Done, Entente, Equate, Escrow, Fadge, Gatt, Indenture, Jibe, League, Nod, Pact, Placet, Rabat(te), Roger, Sanction, Sortance, Square, Suit, Syntony, Sympathy, Synchronise, Tally, Threshold, Treaty, Union, Unison, Unspoken, Wilco, Yea, Yes

**Agreeable** Amene, Harmonious, Pleasant, Sapid, Sweet, Willing, Winsome

**Agriculture, Agricultural(ist)** Arval, Geoponic, Georgic, Inari, Tull

**Aground** Ashore, Beached, Sew, Stranded

> **Ague(ish)** may indicate an anagram

**Ah** Ach, Ay

**Ahead** Anterior, Before, Foreship, Frontwards, Up

**Aiblins** Perhap, Yibbles

**Aid, Aide** Accessory, Adjutant, Assist, Decca, DEPUTY, Galloper, Grant, Help, Key, Lend-lease, Monitor, Optophone, PA, Serve, Slim, Succour, Support

**Ail(ment)** Affect, Afflict(ion), Complaint, Croup, Disease, Malady, Narks, Pink-eye, Pip, Sickness

**Aim** Approach, Aspire, Bead, Bend, End, Ettle, Eye, Goal, Hub, Intent, Level, Mission, Plan, Plank, Point, Purpose, Reason, Sake, Seek, Sight(s), Target, Tee, Telos, Train, View, Visie

**Aimless** Drifting, Erratic, Haphazard, Random, Unmotivated

**Air(s), Airy** Aerate, Aerial, Ambiance, Ambience, Aquarius, Arietta, Allure, Atmosphere, Attitude, Aura, Bearing, Calypso, Canzona, Canzone, Cavatina, Demaine, Descant, Ditty, Draught, Dry, Ether(eal), Expose, Fan, Front, Gemini, Inflate, Libra, Lift, Look, Lullaby, Madrigal, Manner, Melody, Mien, Nitre, Ozone, Parade, Pneumatic, Radio, Serenade, Serenata, Serene, Shanty, Side, Sky, Solo, Swank, Trigon, TUNE, Vent, Wake, Wind

**Aircraft, Airship** Aerodyne, Auster, Autogiro, Autogyro, Aviette, Avion,

Biplane, Blimp, Brabazon, Camel, Canard, Chopper, Comet, Concorde, Crate, Dirigible, Doodlebug, Fokker, Galaxy, Glider, Gotha, Harrier, Heinkel, Helicopter, Hunter, Hurricane, Jumbo, Jump-jet, Kite, Lancaster, Liberator, Microlight, Messerschmitt, MIG, Mirage, Monoplane, Mosquito, Moth, Oerlikon, Ornithopter, Orthopter, Parasol, Penguin, Ramjet, Rigid, Sopwith, Spitfire, Swing-wing, STOL, Stuka, Trident, Tube, Turbo-jet, Turbo-prop, Viscount, VTOL, Zeppelin

**Aircraftsman, Airman** AC, Aeronaut, Erk, Kiwi, LAC, RAF

**Aircraftswoman** Penguin, Pinguin

> **Airfield** see AIRPORT

**Airlift** Thermal

**Airline, Airway** Aeroflot, Anthem, BAC, BEA, Duct, Larynx, Lot, S(ch)norkel, SAS, TWA

> **Airman** see AIRCRAFTSMAN

**Airport** Drome, Entebbe, Faro, Gander, Heliport, Idlewild, Kennedy, Landing strip, Lod, Luton, Lympne, Orly, Runway, Shannon, Stolport, Vertiport, Wick

**Air-raid** Blitz, Mission

**Air-tight** Hermetic, Indisputable, Sealed

**Aitch** Ache, Aspirate, H

**Ajax** Loo

**Akin** Alike, Cognate, Congener, Kindred

**Alarm** Alert, Arouse, Bell, Caution, Dismay, Fricht, Fright, Ghast, Larum, Panic, Perturb, Rouse, Siren, Startle, Tirrit, Tocsin, Warn, Yike(s)

**Alas** Ah, Alack, Ay, Eheu, Ha, Haro, Harrow, Io, Lackadaisy, Lackaday, O, Oh, Ohone, O me, Waesucks, Waly, Well-a-day, Wel(l)away, Woe

**Alaskan** AK, Sourdough

**Alban** Berg

**Albanian** Arna(o)ut

**Albatross** Alcatras, Gooney(-bird), Golf, Omen, Onus

**Albeit** Tho(ugh)

**Albert** Chain, Chevalier, Consort, Hall, Herring, Slang

**Album** Looseleaf, Record

**Albumen, Albumin** Chalaza, Mucin, Protein, Ricin, White

**Alchemic, Alchemist, Alchemy** Brimstone, Hermetic, Multiplier, Orpiment, Paracelsus, Quicksilver, Sal ammoniac, Sorcery, Spagyric, Spagyrist, Witchcraft

**Alcides** Hercules

**Alcohol(ic)** Acrolein, Aldehyde, Bibulous, Booze, Catechol, Cholesterol, Choline, Cresol, Dipsomaniac, Drinker, Ethal, Ethanol, Ethyl, Farnesol, Feni, Fenny, Geraniol, Glycerin(e), Hard, Inebriate, Inositol, Linalool, Mahua, Mahwa, Mannite, Mannitol, Mercaptan, Methanol, Meths,

Mow(r)a, Rotgut, Sorbitol, Spirits, Sterol, Wino, Xylitol

**Alcove** Apse, Bay, Bole, Dinette, Lunette, Niche, Recess

**Alcyonarian** Sea-feather

**Aldehyde** Acrolein, Aldol

**Alder** Fothergilla

**Alderman** Bail(l)ie, CA

**Alderney** CI, Cow

**Ale, Alehouse** Audit, Barleybree, Beer, Humpty-dumpty, Lamb's wool, Light, Morocco, Nappy, Nog, October, Purl, Stout, Swats, Tiddleywink, Tipper, Whitsun, Wort, Yard, Yill

**Alert** Arrect, Astir, Attentive, Aware, Gleg, Gogo, Intelligent, Qui vive, Scramble, Sharp, Sprack, Sprag, Stand-to, Vigilant, Wary, Watchful

**Alewife** Gaspereau

**Alexander, Alexandrine** Alex, Arius, Macedonian, Pope, Sandy, Sasha, Sawn(e)y, Selkirk, Senarius

**Alfalfa** Lucern(e), Luzern

**Alfred** Dreyfus, Garnet, Jingle

**Alfresco** Barbecue, Plein-air

**Alga(e)** Chlorella, Conferva, Desmid, Diatom, Heterocontae, Isokont, Jelly, Nostoc, Protococcus, Spirogyra, Star-jelly, Stonewort, Ulothrix, Ulotrichales, Valonia, Volvox

**Algebra** Boolean

**Algerian** Kabyle, Nimidian

**Alias** Epithet, Moni(c)ker, Pen-name, Pseudonym

**Alibi** Excuse, Watertight

**Alien(ate), Alienation** A-effect, Amortise, Ecstasy, Estrange, ET, Exotic, External, Foreign, Hostile, Martian, Metic, Philistine, Strange(r)

**Alight** Alowe, Availe, Detrain, Disembark, Dismount, In, Lambent, Land, Lit, Perch, Pitch, Rest, Settle

**Align** Arrange, Associate, Collimate, Dress, Marshal, Orient

> **Alike** see LIKE

**Aliquot** Submultiple

**Alive** Alert, Animated, Breathing, Extant, Quick

**Alkali(ne), Alkaloid** Antacid, Apomorphine, Base, Bebeerine, Berberine, Betaine, Borax, Brucine, Codeine, Colchicine, Ephedrine, Gelsemin(in)e, Harmaline, Lye, Narceen, Narceine, Nicotine, Papaverine, Piperine, Potash, Quinine, Reserpine, Rhoeadine, Soda, Sparteine, Thebaine, Theobromine, Veratrin(e), Vinblastine, Vincristine, Yohimbine

**All** A, ENTIRE, Entity, Finis, Omni, Pan, Sum, TOTAL, Toto, Tutti, Whole

**Allah** Bismillah, God

**Allay** Calm, Lessen, Quieten

**Allegation, Allege** Assert, Aver, Claim, Obtend, Represent, Smear

**Allegiance** Faith, Foy, Loyalty

**Allegory** Fable, Myth, Parable

**Allergy** Atopy, Aversion

**Alleviate** Allege, Calm, Mitigate, Mollify, Palliate, RELIEVE, Temper

**Alley** Aisle, Bonce, Corridor, Ginnel, Lane, Laura, Passage, Tinpan, Walk, Wynd

**Alliance** Agnation, Axis, Bloc, Cartel, Coalition, Combine, Compact, Federacy, LEAGUE, Marriage, NATO, Syndicate, Union

**Alligator** Al(l)igarta, Avocado, Cayman

**Allocate, Allocation** Allot, Earmark, Placement, Ration, Share, Zone

**Allot(ment), Allow(ance), Allowed, Allowing** Admit, Affect, Alimony, Allocation, Although, Assign, Aret(t), Award, Batta, Beteem(e), Budget, Charter, Cloff, Confess, Cor(r)ody, Diet, Discount, Dole, Excuse, Feod, Grant, House-bote, Latitude, Legit(imate), Let, Licit, Mag, Palimony, Parcel, Pension, PERMIT, Pittance, Plot, Portion, Quota, Ratio, Ration, Rebate, Rood, Sanction, Sequel, Share(-out), Sizings, Stint, Stipend, Suffer, Tare, Teene, Tolerance, Tolerate, Tret, Weighting, Yield

**Allotment-holder** Cleruch

> **Allow** see ALLOT

**Alloy** Babbit, Bell-metal, Brass, Britannia metal, Bronze, Cermet, Compound, Constantan, Duralumin, Electron, Electrum, Invar, Latten, Magnalium, Marmem, Mischmetal, Mix, Nicrosilal, Nimonic, Occamy, Oreide, Orichalc, Ormolu, Oroide, Pewter, Pinchbeck, Potin, Shakudo, Shibuichi, Similor, Solder, Steel, Terne, Tombac, Tombak, Tutenag

> **Alloy** may indicate an anagram

**All-right** A1, Assuredly, Fit, Hale, Hunky(-dory), OK, Safe, Well

**All-round** Overhead, Versatile

**Allude, Allusion** Hint, Imply, Innuendo, Mention, Refer, Reference, Suggest

**Allure, Alluring** Agaçant(e), Charm, Circe, Decoy, Glam, Magnet(ic), SA, Seduce, Seductive, Tempt, Trap, Trepan, Vamp

**Ally, Allied** Accomplice, Agnate, Aide, Alley, Backer, Belamy, Cognate, Colleague, German(e), Marble, Marmoreal, Partner, Plonker, Related, Taw

**Almanac** Calendar, Clog, Ephemeris, Nostradamus, Whitaker's, Wisden, Zadkiel

**Almighty** Dollar, God, Jehovah, Omnipotent

**Almond** Amygdal, Emulsion, Jordan, Marchpane, Marzipan, Orgeat, Praline, Ratafia, Sugared, Valencia

**Almost** Anear, Anigh, Most, Near, Nigh(ly), Ripe, Une(a)th, Virtually, Well-nigh, Welly

**Alms** Awmous, Charity, Dole, Handout

**Aloe** Agave, Pita

**Alone** Hat, Jack, Lee-lane, Onely, Secco, Separate, Single, Singly, Solo, Solus, Unaided, Unholpen

**Along, Alongside** Abeam, Aboard, Abreast, Apposed, Beside, By, Parallel

**Aloof** Abeigh, Apart, Cool, Detached, Distant, Offish, Reticent, Stand-offish

**Alpaca** Paco

**Alphabet** ABC, Brahmi, Braille, Cyrillic, Devanagari, Estrang(h)elo, Futhark, Futhorc, Futhork, Glagol, Glossic, Grantha, Horn-book, ITA, Katakana, Nagari, Og(h)am, Pangram, Pinyin, Romaji

**Alpine** Gentian, Laburnum, Tyrol

**Also** Add, And, Eke, Item, Likewise, Moreover, Too, Und

**Altar, Altar-cloth** Dossal, Dossel, Shrine

**Alter** Adapt, Adjust, Bushel, Change, Correct, Lib, Modify, Recast, Revise, Transpose, VARY

**Altercation** Barney, Brawl, Fracas, Row, Words, Wrangle

**Alternate, Alternation, Alternative** Boustrophedon, Bypass, Exchange, Instead, Metagenesis, OPTION, Ossia, Other, Rotate, Variant

> **Alter(native)** may indicate an anagram

> **Alternately** may indicate every other letter

**Althaea** Mallow, Malva

**Although** Admitting, Albe(e), All-be, Even, Howsomever, Whereas, While

**Altitude** Elevation, Height

**Altogether** Algate(s), All-to-one, Completely, Entirely, Holus-bolus, Idea, Nude, Nudity, Purely, Slick, Tout, Uncut, Wholly

> **Altogether** may indicate words to be joined

**Altruistic** Heroic, Humane, Philanthropic, Unselfish

**Aluminium, Alumino-silicate** Al, Bauxite, Sillimanite, Stilbite

**Alumnus** Graduate, OB

**Always** Algate(s), Ay(e), Constant, E'er, Eternal, Ever(more), Forever, I, Immer, Sempre, Still

**Amalgamate** Coalesce, Consolidate, Fuse, Merge, Unite

**Amalthea** Cornucopia

**Amarylli(d)s** Leocojum, Lily, Polianthes

**Amass** Accumulate, Assemble, Collect, Heap, Hoard, Pile, Upheap

**Amateur(s)** A, AA, Armchair, Beginner, Corinthian, Dilettante, Diy, Ham, Inexpert, L, Lay, Novice, Tiro, Tyro

**Amatory** Eros, Erotic, Fervent

**Amaze(d), Amazement, Amazing** Astound, Awhape, Cor, Dumbfound, Gobsmack, Goodnow, Grace, Magical, Monumental, O, Perplex, Stagger, Stupefaction, Stupendous, Thunderstruck

**Amazon** Ant, ATS, Brimstone, Britannia, Dragon, Hippolyta, Orellana, Penthesilea, Thalestris, Tupi, Virago

**Ambassador** Diplomat, Elchee, Elchi, Eltchi, Envoy, HE, Ledger, Legate, Leiger, Minister, Nuncio, Plenipo

**Amber** Lammer, Ligure, Resin, Succinum

**Ambience** Aura, Milieu, Setting

**Ambiguous, Ambiguity** Amphibology, Delphic, Double, Enigmatic, Epicene, Equivocal, Loophole

**Ambition, Ambitious** Aim, Aspiring, Emulate, Goal, Keen, Office-hunter, Purpose, Rome-runner

**Amble** Meander, Mosey, Pace, Saunter, Stroll

**Ambrose** Emrys

**Ambrosia(l)** Beebread, Fragrant, Odorant, Ragweed, Savoury

**Ambulance** Blood-wagon, Pannier, Van, Yellow-flag

**Ambulatory** Stoa

**Ambush(ed)** Ambuscade, Embusque, Latitant, Lurch, Perdu(e), Trap, Waylay

**Amelia** Bloomer

**Ameliorate** Amend, Ease, Improve, Remedy

**Amen** Ammon, Approval, Inshallah, Verify

**Amend(ment)** Alter, Change, Fifth, Redress, Reform, Restore, REVISE

> **Amend** may indicate an anagram

**Ament** Catkin, Idiot

**American** Am, Cajun, Carib, Chicano, Doughface, Down-easter, Federalist, Gringo, Jonathan, Norteno, Stateside, Statesman, Statist, Tar-heel, US(A), Yankee

**Americium** Am

**Amiable** Friendly, Genial, Gentle, Inquiline, Sweet, Warm

**Amid(st)** Among, Atween, Between, Inter, Twixt

**Amide** Asparagine

**Amino-acid** Dopa, Tyrosine, Valine

**Amiss** Awry, Ill, Up, Wrong

**Ammonia(c)** Amide, Amine, Ethylamine, Hartshorn, Oshac

**Ammonite** Serpent-stone

**Ammunition** Ammo, Bandoleer, Bandolier, Buckshot, Bullets, Chain-shot, Dum-dum, Grenade, Round, Shot, Slug

**Amnesia** Fugal, Fugue, Lethe

**Amnesty** Oblivion

**Among** Amid(st), In, Within

**Amorous(ly)** Casanova, Erotic, Fervent, Lustful, Smickly, Warm

**Amorphous** Formless, Shapeless, Vague

**Amount** Come, Dose, Element, Figure, Lot, Number, Pot(s), Price, Quantity, Quantum, Span, Stint, Whale

**Amour** Affair(e), Intrigue, Love

**Amphetamine** Benzedrine, Speed

**Amphibian, Amphibious** Amblystoma, Amtrack, Anura, Axolotl, Caecilia, Eft, Frog, Guana, Hassar, Mermaid, Newt, Olm, Proteus, Rana, Salamander, Seal, Tadpole, Urodela(n), Urodele, Weasel

**Amphipod** Sand-screw, Shrimp

**Amphitheatre** Bowl, Coliseum, Colosseum, Ring, Stage

**Ample** Bellyful, Copious, Enough, Generous, Large, Profuse, Rich, Roomy, Uberous

**Amplifier, Amplify** Booster, Double, Eke, Enlarge, Hailer, Maser, Push-pull, Solion, Transistor, Treble

**Amulet** Abraxas, Charm, Churinga, Fetish, Greegree, Grigri, Grisgris, Haemon, Periapt, Phylactery, Sea-bean, Talisman, Tiki, Token

**Amuse(ment), Amusing(ly)** Caution, Cottabus, Disport, Diversion, Divert, Divertimento, Drole, Droll, Game, Gas, Giocoso, Glee, Hoot, Killing, Light, Occupy, Pleasure, Popjoy, Priceless, Rich, Scream, Slay, Solace, SPORT, Tickle

**Amy** Johnson, Robsart

> **An** see A

**Ana(s)** Story, Teal

**Anabaptist** Abecedarian, Dipper, Dopper, Hutterite, Knipperdolling

**Anableps** Four-eyes

**Anachronism** Archaism, Solecism

**Anacreon** Te(i)an

**Anaemia** Favism, Sickle-cell

**Anaesthetic, Anaesthetise, Anaesthetist** Analgesic, Cocaine, Epidural, Ether, Eucain(e), Freeze, Gas, General, Halothane, Jabber, Lignocaine, Local, Metopryl, Novocaine, Number, Opium, Orthocaine, Procaine, Stovaine, Trike, Urethan(e)

**Anagram** Jumble

**Anal** Proctal

**Analgesic** Codeine, Disprin, Menthol, Pethidine, Quina, Sedative

**Analogous, Analogy** Akin, Corresponding, Like, Parallel, Similar

**Analyse(r), Analysis** Alligate, Anagoge, Anatomy, Assess, Breakdown, Construe, Eudiometer, Examine, Parse, Rundown, Scan(sion), Semantics, Sift, Spectral

> **Analysis** may indicate an anagram

**Analyst** Alienist, Jung, Shrink, Psychiatrist, Trick cyclist

**Anarchist, Anarchy**  Bolshevist, Chaos, Kropotkin, Provo, Rebel, Revolutionary, Trotskyite

**Anathema**  Ban, Curse, Execration, Oath, Warling

**Anatole, Anatolian**  France, Hittite

**Anatomy**  Bones, Framework

**Ancestor, Ancestral, Ancestry**  Adam, Avital, Descent, Extraction, For(e)bear, Gastraea, Lin(e)age, Parent, Proband, Profectitious, Propositus, Roots, Sire, Tree

**Anchor(age)**  Atrip, Bower, Cell, Drag, Eremite, Grapnel, Hawse, Hermit, Kedge, Killick, Killock, Laura, Mud-hook, Nail, Roads(tead), Sheet, Spithead, Stock

**Anchovy**  Fish, Pear

**Ancient**  Archaic, Auld-warld, Early, Gonfanoner, Hoary, Iago, Immemorial, Lights, Ogygian, OLD(en), Old-world, Primeval, Primitive, Pristine, Ur, Veteran

**Ancient city**  Carthage, Ur

**Ancillary**  Adjunct, Secondary, Subservient

**And**  Als(o), Ampassy, Ampersand, Amperzand, Ampussyand, Besides, Et, Furthermore, 'n', Plus, Und

**Andalusite**  Macle

**Andiron**  Chenet, Dog, Firedog

**Andrew(es)**  Aguecheek, Lancelot

**Android**  Automaton, Golem, Robot

**Anecdote(s)**  Ana, Story, Tale, Yarn

**Anemometer**  Wind-sleeve, Windsock

**Angel(s)**  Abdiel, Adramelech, Apollyon, Ariel, Arioch, Asmadai, Backer, Banker, Beelzebub, Belial, Benefactor, Cherub, Clare, Deva, Eblis, Gabriel Guardian, Hierarchy, Host, Investor, Israfel, Ithuriel, Lucifer, Raphael, Recorder, Rimmon, Seraph, Spirit, St, Throne, Uriel, Uzziel, Watcher, Zadkiel, Zephiel

**Angel's wings**  Begonia

**Angela**  Brazil

**Anger, Angry**  ANNOY, Bristle, Choler(ic), Conniption, Cross, Dander, Enrage, Exasperation, Face, Fury, Gram, Heat, Horn-mad, Incense, Iracund, Irascible, Ire, Kippage, Livid, Monkey, Moody, Nettle, Pique, Radge, Rage, Rampant, Ratty, Renfierst, Rile, Roil, Rouse, Sore, Steam, Tantrum, Teen(e), Tene, Vex, Vies, Waxy, Wrath, Wroth

**Angina**  Sternalgia

**Angle(d), Angular**  Acute, Altitude, Argument, Aspect, Axil, Azimuthal, Canthus, Cast, Catch, Chiliagon, Coign, Contrapposto, Corner, Cos, Diedral, Deidre, Elbow, Elevation, Ell, Fish, Fish-hook, Fork, Geometry, Gonion, Hade, Hip, L, Laggen, Laggin, Mitre, Obtuse, Pediculate, Perigon, Piend, Quoin, Radian, Rake, Re-entrant, Sine, Sinical, Steeve, Steradian,

Viewpoint, Washin, Weather

**Angler** Peterman, Rodster, Walton, Wide-gab

**Anglesey** Mona

**Anglican(s)** CE-men, Conformist, Episcopal

**Anglo-Catholic** High-church

**Anglo-Indian** Topi-wallah

**Angora** Goat, Mohair, Rabbit

**Anguish** Agony, Distress, Gip, Gyp, Heartache, Misery, PAIN, Pang, Sorrow, Throes, TORMENT, Torture, Woe

**Angus** Aberdeen

**Animal(s)** Acrita, Anoa, Armadillo, Atoc, Bag, Bandog, Barbastel, Beast, Bestial, Brute, Cariacou, Carnal, Chalicothere, Coati, Creature, Criollo, Critter, Fauna, Felis, Gerbil, Herd, Ichneumon, Jacchus, Jerboa, Kinkajou, Klipdas, Mammal, Marmoset, Marmot, Menagerie, Moose, Noctule, Oribi, Pet, Pudu, Quagga, Rac(c)oon, Rhesus, Sloth, Stud, Teledu, Urson, Waler, Xenurus, Yapock, Zerda, Zoo

**Animal-catcher** Utricularia

**Animate(d), Animation** Activate, Arouse, Ensoul, Excite, Fire, Hot, Inspire, Live, Mosso, Rouse, Spritely, Verve

**Animosity** Enmity, Friction, Hostility, Malice, Pique, Rancour

**Ankle** Coot, Cuit, Cute, Hock, Knee, Malleolus

**Ankle(t), Ankle covering** Cootikin, Cuitikin, Cutikin, Gaiter, Jess

**Anna, Anne, Annie** Boleyn, Hathaway, Laurie, Oakley, Page, Pavlova, Sewell, Sister

**Annal(s)** Acta, Archives, Chronicles, Register

**Annex(e)** Acquire, Add, Affiliate, Attach, Codicil, Extension, Subjoin

**Annihilate** Destroy, Erase, Exterminate, Slay

**Anniversary** Birthday, Feast, Jubilee, Obit, Yahrzeit

**Annotate, Annotator** Comment, Interpret, Note, Postil, Scholiast

**Announce(r), Announcement** Banns, Bellman, Bill, Blazon, Bulletin, Communiqué, Decree, Herald, Hermes, Inform, Intimate, Meld, Post, Preconise, Proclaim, Promulgate, Publish, Release, REPORT, Speaker(ine), State, Trumpet

**Annoy(ance), Annoyed, Annoying** Aggrieve, Anger, Antagonise, Badger, Bother, Bug, Bugbear, Chagrin, Disturb, Frab, Fumed, Gall, Harass, Hatter, Hector, Hip, Huff, Hump, Incense, Irk, IRRITATE, Miff, Mischief, Molest, Nag, Nark, Nettle, Peeve, Pesky, Pique, Rats, Ride, Rile, Rub, Shirty, Tracasserie, Try, Vex

**Annual, Annuity** Book, Etesian, FLOWER, Half-hardy, Hardy, Pension, Perpetuity, Rente, Tontine, Yearly

**Annul(ment)** Abolish, Abrogate, Cassation, Irritate, Negate, Repeal, Rescind, Revoke, Vacatur, VOID

**Anodyne** Balm, Narcotic, Paregoric, Sedative

**Anoint** Anele, Cerate, Embrocate, Grease, Hallow, Nard, Smear

> **Anomaly** may indicate an anagram

**Anon** Again, Anew, Later, Soon

**Anonymous** Adespota, Anon, A.N.Other, Faceless, Grey, Somebody, Unnamed

**Another** Extra

**Answer(ing)** Acknowledge, Amoebaean, Ans, Antiphon, Because, Comeback, Defence, Echo, Key, Lemon, Light, Oracle, Rebuttal, Rebutter, Rein, Rejoin(der), Repartee, Reply, Rescript, Respond, Response, Retort, Return, Riposte, Serve, Sol, Solution, Verdict

**Ant(s)** Amazon, Emmet, Ergataner, Ergates, Formic, Myrmecoid, Myrmidon, Nasute, Neuter, Pharaoh, Pismire, Sauba, Soldier, Termite

**Antacid** Magnesia

**Antagonist, Antagonize** Estrange, Peare, Peer

**Ant-bear** Tamanoir

**Ante** Bet, Punt, Stake

**Ant-eater** Aardvark, Echidna, Edental, Manis, Numbat, Pangolin, S(e)ladang, Tamandua, Tapir

**Antelope** Addax, Antilope, Blaubok, Blesbok, Bloubok, Bongo, Bontebok, Bubalis, Bushbuck, Chamois, Chikara, Dikdik, Duiker, Duyker, Dzeren, Eland, Elk, Gazelle, Gemsbok, Gerenuk, Gnu, Goral, Grysbok, Hartbees, Hartebeest, Impala, Inyala, Kaama, Kid, Klipspringer, Kob, Kongoni, Koodoo, Kudu, Lechwe, Madoqua, Nagor, Nilgai, Nilgau, Nyala, Nylghau, Oribi, Oryx, Ourebi, Pale-buck, Pallah, Pronghorn, Pudu, Pygarg, Reebok, Reedbuck, Rhebok, Sable, Saiga, Sasin, Sassaby, Serow, Sitatunga, Situtunga, Steenbok, Steinbock, Stembok, Thar, Topi, Tragelaph

**Antenna** Aerial, Dipole, Horn, Sensillum

**Anterior** Anticous, Earlier, Front, Prior

**Anthelmintic** Worm

**Anthem** Hymn, Introit, Marseillaise, Motet(t), National, Psalm, Song, Theme, Tract

**Anthology** Album, Ana, Digest, Divan, Florilegium, Garland, Pick, Spicilege

**Anthony** Absolute, Adverse, Trollope

**Anthrax** Sang

**Anthropoid** Sivapithecus

**Anthropologist** Mead

**Anti** Against, Agin, Con, Hostile

**Anti-aircraft** AA

**Antibiotic** Bacitracin, Bacteriostat, Drug, Erythromycin, Gramicidin, Griseofulvin, Interferon, Lineomycin, Neomycin, Nystatin, Penicillin,

Streptomycin, Wide-spectrum

**Antibody** Amboceptor, Blocker, Lysin, Precipitin, Reagin

**Antic** Caper, Dido, Frolic, Gambado, Hay, Prank, Stunt

**Anti-carlist** Queenite

**Anticipate, Anticipation** Antedate, Augur, Await, Drool, EXPECT, Forecast, Foresee, Forestall, Foretaste, Hope, Intuition, Prevenancy, Prolepsis, Prospect

**Anticlimax** Bathos, Deflation, Letdown

**Anticoagulant** Heparin, Hirudin, Warfarin

**Anticyclone** High

**Antidote** Adder's wort, Alexipharmic, Angelica, Bezoar, Contrayerva, Cure, Emetic, Guaco, Mithridate, Nostrum, Orvietan, Remedy, Senega, Theriac(a), (Venice)-Treacle

**Anti-freeze** Lagging

**Anti-imperialist** Guelf, Guelph

**Antimacassar** Tidy

**Antimony** Sb, Stibium

**Anti-parliamentarian** Poujadist

**Antipathy** Allergy, Aversion, Detest, DISLIKE, Enmity, Repugnance

**Anti-perfectionist** Cobden

**Antipodean** Abo, Antarctic, Antichthon, Enzed, Underworld

**Antipope** Novatian

**Anti-protectionist** Cobden

**Antiquated, Antique, Antiquarian** Ancient, Archaic, A(u)stringer, Bibelot, Curio, Dryasdust, FAS, Fog(e)y, Fogram(ite), Ostreger, Relic

**Anti-revolutionary** White

**Anti-Roman** Ghibel(l)ine

**Anti-royalist** Whig

**Anti-semitic** Pamyat

**Antiseptic** Cassareep, Creosote, Disinfectant, Eupad, Eusol, Formaldehyde, Iodine, Phenol, Sterile, Thymol, Tutty

**Anti-slavery** Free-soil, Wilberforce

**Anti-smoker** ASH, Misocapnic

**Antisocial** Hostile, Ishmaelitish, Misanthropic

**Antithesis** Contrary, Converse, Opposite

**Anti-three** Noetian

**Antitoxin** Antibody, Antivenin, Guaco, Serum, Vaccine

**Anti-union** Secesher

**Antler(s)** Horn, Rights, Staghorn, Surroyal, Tine

**Ant-proof** Bilian

**Anus** Tewel

**Anvil** Bick-iron, Block, Incus, Stiddie, Stithy

**Anxiety, Anxious** Angst, Brood, Care(ful), Cark, Concern, Dysthymia, Fanteeg, Fantigue, Fraught, Grave, Jimjams, Reck, Restless, Scruple, Suspense, Sweat, Tension, Unease, Upset

**Any** Arrow, Ary, Some

**Anybody, Anyone** One, Whoso, You

**Anyhow** Anyway, Leastways

**Anything** Aught, Whatnot

> **Anyway** may indicate an anagram

**Apache** Arizona, AZ

**Apart** Aloof, Aside, Asunder, Atwain, Beside, Separate

**Apartheid** Racism

**Apartment** Ben, Condominium, Digs, Duplex, Flat, Insula, Mansion, Paradise, Penthouse, Quarters, Room, Solitude, Suite, Unit

**Apathetic, Apathy** Accidie, Acedia, Incurious, Languid, Listless, Torpid

**Ape(-like)** Barbary, Catarrhine, Copy, Dryopithecine, Gelada, Gibbon, Gorilla, IMITATE, Magot, Mimic, Orang, Paranthropous, Pongo, Proconsul, Simian, Simulate

**Aperient** Cascara, Laxative, Senna

**Aperitif** DRINK, Pernod

**Aperture** Balistraria, Chink, Hole, Osculum, Spiracle, Window

**Apex** Acme, Culmen, Keystone, Knoll, Knowe, Summit

**Aphorism** Adage, Epigram, Proverb, Sutra

**Aphrodisiac, Aphrodite** Cytherean, Erotic, Idalian, Paphian, Philter, Philtre, Urania

**Aplomb** Cool, Equanimity, Poise, Sangfroid, Serenity

**Apocryphal** Spurious, Tobit

**Apograph** Roneo

**Apollo** Belvedere, Pythian, Sun

**Apology** Excuse, Pardon, Scuse

**Apostate** Citer, HERETIC, Pervert, Rat, Recreant, Renegade, Runagate, Turncoat

**Apostle, Apostolic** Cuthbert, DISCIPLE, Evangelist, Johannine, Matthew, Pauline, Spoon, Twelve

**Apostrophe, Apostrophise** O(h), Soliloquy, Tuism

**Apothegm** Dictum, Maxim, Motto

**Appal(ling)** Abysmal, Affear(e), Dismay, Frighten, Horrify, Piacular, Tragic

> **Appallingly** may indicate an anagram

**Apparatus** Alembic, Appliance, Coherer, Cosmotron, Davis, Device, Eprouvette, Equipment, Fixings, Gadget, Graith, Instrument, Jacquard, Kipps, Masora(h), Retort, Rounce, Set, Tromp(e)

**Apparel** Attire, Besee, COSTUME, Garb, Raiment, Wardrobe, Wardrop

**Apparent** Detectable, Ostensible, Outward, Overt, Plain, Visible

> **Apparent** may indicate a hidden word

**Apparition** Dream, Fetch, Ghost, ILLUSION, Phantom, Shade, Spectre

**Appeal(ing)** Ad, Beg, Cachet, Charisma, Charm, Cry, Entreat, Entreaty, Epirrhema, Fetching, Invocation, It, O, Plead, SA, Screeve, Solicit, SOS, Suit

**Appear(ance)** Advent, Air, Apport, Arrival, Aspect, Broo, Brow, Burst, Compear, Debut, Emerge, Enter, Eye, Facade, Facies, Far(r)and, Farrant, Fa(s)cia, Feature, Guise, Hue, Image, Kithe, Kythe, Loom, MANNER, Mien, Occur, Ostensibly, Outward, Person, Phase, Phenomenon, Presence, Prosopon, Represent, Rig, Seem, Semblance, Show, Spring, Theophany, View, Wraith

**Appease(ment)** Allay, Calm, Danegeld, Mitigate, MOLLIFY, Pacify, Placate, Propitiate, Satisfy, Soothe, Sop

**Appendage** Aglet, Allantois, Aril, Arista, Cercus, Codpiece, Ctene, Hanger-on, Lobe, Lug, Paraglossa, Suffix, Tail, Uropod, Uvula

**Appendix** Addendum, Apocrypha, Codicil, Grumbling, Label, Pendent, Rider, Schedule

**Appetite, Appetitive, Appetize(r)** Antepast, Antipasto, Aperitif, Appestat, Bhagee, Bhajee, Bulimia, Bulimy, Canapé, Concupiscence, Concupy, Crudités, Dim-sum, Entremes(se), Entremets, Flesh, Hunger, Limosis, Malacia, Meze, Nacho, Orectic, Orexis, Passion, Pica, Relish, Titillate, Twist, Yerd-hunger, Yird-hunger

**Applaud, Applause** Bravo, CHEER, Clap, Claque, Eclat, Encore, Extol, Kentish fire, Olé, Ovation, Praise, Root, Ruff, Tribute

**Apple** Alligator, Baldwin, Biffin, Blenheim orange, Charlotte, Codlin(g), Cooker, Costard, Crab, Discord, Eater, Greening, Jenneting, John, Jonathan, Mammee, Nonpareil, Pearmain, Pippin, Pomace, Pome(roy), Pomroy, Pyrus, Quarantine, Quarenden, Quar(r)ender, Quarrington, Redstreak, Reinette, Rennet, Ribston(e), Ruddock, Russet, Seek-no-further, Snow, Sops-in-wine, Sturmer, Sweeting, Windfall, Winesap

**Apple Juice** Malic

**Apple-picker** Atalanta

**Applicant** Postulant

**Application, Apply, Appliance** Address, Adhibit, Appeal, Appose, Assiduity, Barrage, Devote, Diligence, Dressing, Exercise, Foment, Inlay, Lay, Lotion, Ointment, Petition, Plaster, Poultice, Put, Resort, Rub, Sinapism, Stupe, Truss, USE

**Appoint(ed), Appointment** Advowson, Assign, Berth, Date, Delegate, Depute, Designate, Dew, Due, Induction, Installation, Make, Name,

NOMINATE, Nominee, Office, Ordain, Position, Post, Rendezvous, Room, Set, Tryst

> **Appointed** may indicate an anagram

**Apportion(ment)** Allocate, Allot, Mete, Parcel, Ration, Share, Weigh

**Apposite** Apt, Cogent, Germane, Pat, Pertinent, Relevant, Suitable

**Appraise, Appraisal** Analyse, EVALUATE, Gauge, Judge, Tape, VALUE, Vet

**Appreciate, Appreciation** Cherish, Clap, Dig, Endear, Esteem, Gratefulness, Increase, Prize, Realise, Regard, Relish, Sense, Treasure, VALUE

**Apprehend, Apprehension** Afears, Alarm, Arrest, CATCH, Grasp, Insight, Perceive, See, Take, Unease, Uptake

**Apprehensive** Jumpy, Nervous, Uneasy

**Apprentice(ship)** Article, Cub, Devil, Improver, Indent(ure), Jockey, Learner, L, Lehrjahre, Novice, Noviciate, Novitiate, Pupillage, Trainee, Turnover

**Approach(ing)** Abord, Access, Accost, Advance, Anear, Appropinquate, Avenue, Close, Come, Converge, Cost(e), Drive, Feeler, Gate, Imminent, Line, Near, Nie, Overture, Procedure, Verge

**Appropriate** Abduct, Annex, Apposite, Apt, Asport, Assign, Bag, Borrow, Collar, Commandeer, Confiscate, Convenient, Due, Embezzle, Expedient, Fit, Germane, Good, Happy, Hijack, Hog, Jump, Just, Nick, Pilfer, Pocket, Pre-empt, Proper, Right, Seize, Sequester, Snaffle, Steal, Suit, Swipe, Take, Timely, Usurp

**Approval, Approve** Adopt, Allow, Amen, Applaud, Attaboy, Aye, Blessing, COUNTENANCE, Dig, Endorse, Imprimatur, Kitemark, Laud, Nod, Okay, Olé, Plaudit, Ratify, Rubber-stamp, Sanction, Tick, Tribute, Yes

**Approximate(ly), Approximation** Almost, Circa, Close, Estimate, Guess, Imprecise, Near, Roughly

**Apricot** Mebos

**April** Apr

**Apron** Barm-cloth, Bib, Blacktop, Brat, Bunt, Canvas, Dick(e)y, Ephod, Fig-leaf, Gremial, Pinafore, Placket, Stage, Tablier, Tier

**Apse** Concha, Exedra, Niche, Recess, Tribune

**Apt(ly)** Apposite, Appropriate, Apropos, Ben trovato, Capable, Evincive, Fit, Gleg, Happy, Liable, Prone, Suitable, Tends

**Aptitude** Ability, Bent, Faculty, Flair, Gift, Skill, Talent, Tendency

**Aqua(tic)** Euglena, Lentic, Lotic, Regia, Zizania

**Aqualung** Scuba

**Aqueduct** Canal, Channel, Conduit, Hadrome, Xylem

**Arab(ian), Arabia** Abdul, Algorism, Ali, Baathist, Bedouin, Druse, Druz(e), Effendi, Fedayee(n), Gamin, Geber, Hashemite, Himyarite, Horse, Iraqi, Lawrence, Mudlark, Nabat(h)ean, Omani, PLO, Rag(head), Saba,

Sab(a)ean, Saracen, Semitic, Sheikh, UAR, Urchin, Yemen

**Arachnid** Podogona, Ricinulei, SPIDER

**Arbiter, Arbitrator** Censor, Judge, Ombudsman, Ref(eree), Umpire

**Arbitrary** Despotic, Random, Wanton

**Arboreal, Arbour** Bower, Dendroid, Pergola, Trellis

**Arc** Azimuth, Bow, CURVE, Octant, Quadrant, Rainbow, Trajectory

**Arcade** Amusement, Burlington, Cloister, Gallery, Loggia, Triforium

**Arcadia** Idyllic

**Arcane** Obscure, Occult, Recherché, Rune, Secret

**Arch(ed)** Admiralty, Arblaster, Arcuate, Camber, Chief, Coom, Crafty, Crown-green, Ctesiphon, Counterfort, CUNNING, Curve, Elfin, Embow, Espiegle, Fornicate, Fornix, Hance, Haunch, Hog, Instep, Intrados, Keystone, Lancet, Leery, Marble, Ogive, Order, Parthian, Proscenium, Roach, Roguish, Saucy, Soffit, Span, Squinch, Trajan, Triumphal, Vault, Zygoma

**Archaeological, Archaeologist** Dater, Evans, Layard, Mycenae, Pothunter, Wheeler

**Archangel** Azrael, Gabriel, Israfel, Jerahmeel, Michael, Raguel, Raphael, Sariel, Satan, Uriel

**Arch-binder** Voussoir

**Archbishop** Anselm, Cosmo, Cranmer, Davidson, Dunstan, Ebor, Elector, Hatto, Lanfranc, Lang, Langton, Laud, Metropolitan, Primate, Temple, Trench, Tutu

**Archdeacon** Ven

**Archduke** Trio

**Archer** Acestes, Bow-boy, BOWMAN, Cupid, Eros, Hood, Philoctetes, Tell, Toxophilite

**Archetype** Avatar, Model, Pattern

**Archibald, Archie, Archy** Ack-ack, Cockroach, Oerlikon, Rice, Roach

**Archilochian** Epode

**Archipelago** Alexander, Bismarck, Fiji, Marquesas, Sulu

**Architect** Adam, Bramante, Creator, Designer, Gropius, Hawkmoor, Inigo (Jones), Kent, Lutyens, Mackintosh, Nash, Nervi, Nissen, Palladio, Piranesi, Planner, Pugin, Soane, Spence, Trophonius, Vanbrugh, Wren, Wright

**Architecture, Architectural** Baroque, Bauhaus, Brutalism, Byzantine, Composite, Corinthian, Decorated, Doric, Flamboyant, Gothic, Ionic, Macquarie, Norman, Palladian, Perpendicular, Romanesque, Tectonic, Tuscan

**Architrave** Epistyle, Platband

**Archive(s)** Muniment, PRO, Records, Register

**Archon** Draco

**Arch-villain** Ringleader

**Arctic** Estotiland, Frigid, Polar, Tundra

**Ardent, Ardour** Aglow, Boil, Broiling, Burning, Fervent, Fervid, Fiery, Flagrant, Heat, Het, HOT, In, Mettled, Mettlesome, Passion(ate), Perfervid, Rage, Spiritous, Vehement, Zealous, Zeloso

**Arduous** Uphill

**Are** A

**Area** Acre, Are, Belt, Bovate, Carucate, Catchment, Centiare, Dec(i)are, District, Endemic, Extent, Farthingland, Gau, Hectare, Hide, Husbandland, Imperium, Landmass, Lathe, Latitude, Lek, Locality, Manor, Milieu, Morgen, Oxgang, Oxgate, Oxland, Place, Plot, Precinct, Province, Quad, Range, REGION, Rood, Sector, Shire, Terrain, Theatre, Tie, Tract, Tye, Yard, Zone

**Arena** Circus, Cockpit, Dohyo, Field, Maidan, Olympia, RING, Stadium, Venue

**Argent** Ag, Silver

**Argentina** RA

**Argon** Ar

**Argonaut** Acastus, Jason, Lynceus, Meleager, Nautilus

**Argot** Flash, Idiom, Jargon, Lingo

**Argue, Argument** Altercation, Antistrophon, Argie-bargie, Argle-bargle, Argy-bargy, Bandy, Beef, Brush, Casuism, Conflict, Contend, Debate, Deprecate, Diallage, Difference, Dilemma, Dispute, Elenctic, Enthymeme, Exchange, Forensic, Logic, Moot, Ob and soller, Patter, Plead, Polemic, Premiss, Quibble, Quodlibet, REASON, Run-in, Sophism, Sorites, Spar, Stickle, Syllogism, Theme, Thetic, Tiff, Trilemma, Wrangle, Yike

**Argyle** Argathelian

**Aria** Ballad, Melody, Song

**Ariel** Peri

**Arise** Appear, Develop, Emanate, Emerge, Upgo, Wax

**Aristocracy, Aristocrat(ic)** Blood, Boyar, Classy, Debrett, Duc, Elite, Gentry, Grandee, High-hat, Junker, Noble, Optimate, Patrician, U-men, Upper-crust

**Aristotle** Peripatetic, Stagirite, Stagyrite

**Arithmetic(ian)** Algorism, Algorith, Arsmetrick, Cocker, Euclid, Logistic, Sums

**Arkwright** Noah

**Arly** Thicket

**Arm(ed), Arms** Akimbo, Arsenal, Bearing, Brachial, Branch, Cove, Crest, Embattle, Equip, Escutcheon, Fin, Firth, Frith, Halbert, Hatchment, Heel, Heraldic, Inlet, Limb, Loch, Member, Olecranon, Quillon, Radius, Ramous, Rotor, SAA, Tappet, Tentacle, Transept, Ulnar, WEAPON, Whip

**> Arm** may indicate an army regiment, etc.

**Armadillo** Dasypod, Dasypus, Pangolin, Peba, Pichiciago, Tatou(ay), Xenurus

**Armenian** Haikh

**Armistice** Truce

**Armour(ed)** Ailette, Armet, Beaver, Besagew, Bevor, Brasset, Brigandine, Buckler, Byrnie, Camail, Cannon, Cataphract, Chaffron, Chain, Chamfrain, Chausses, Corium, Cors(e)let, Couter, Cuirass, Curiet, Cuish, Cuisse, Culet, Curat, Cush, Defence, Fauld, Garniture, Gear, Genouillère, Gere, Gorget, Greave, Habergeon, Hauberk, Jack, Jambeau, Jazerant, Jesserant, Lamboys, Loricate, Mail, Male, Mentonnière, Panoply, Panzer, Pauldron, Petta, Placcat, Placket, Poitrel, Poleyn, Pouldron, Sabaton, Secret, SHIELD, Solleret, Spaudler, Tace, Taslet, Tasse(t), Thorax, Tuille, Vambrace, Vantbrass, Visor, Weed

**Armpit** Axilla, Oxter

**Armstrong** Satchmo

**Army** Arrière-ban, BEF, Colours, Crowd, Federal, Fyrd, Horde, Host, IRA, Landwehr, Legion, Line, Military, Militia, Multitude, Para-military, SA, Sabaoth, Salvation, Sena, Service, Soldiers, Swarm, TA, War

**> Army** may indicate having arms

**Aroma(tic)** Allspice, Aniseed, Aryl, Balmy, Coriander, Fenugreek, Fragrant, Odorous, Pomander, Spicy, Wintergreen

**Around** About, Ambient, Circa, Near, Peri-, Skirt, Tour

**> Around** may indicate one word around another

**Arouse, Arousal** Alarm, EXCITE, Fan, Fire, Incite, Inflame, Must(h), Needle, Provoke, Urolagnia, Waken

**Arrange(r), Arrangement** Adjust, Array, Attune, Bandobast, Bundobust, Concert, Design, Dispose, Do, Edit, Engineer, Foreordain, Formation, Grade, Ikebana, Layout, Marshal, Orchestrate, Orchestration, Ordain, ORDER, Ordnance, Organise, Pack, Pattern, Perm, Plan, Prepare, Prepense, Quincunx, Redactor, Regulate, Run, Scheme, Set, Settle, Sort, Stow, Straighten, System, Tactic, Taxis, Transcribe

**> Arrange** may indicate an anagram

**Arras** Tapestry

**Array(ed)** Attire, Bedight, Deck, Marshal, Muster, Panoply

**Arrear(s)** Aft, Ahint, Backlog, Behind, Debt, Owing

**Arrest(ed), Arresting** Abort, Alguacil, Alguazil, Ament, Apprehend, Attach, Attract, Blin, Bust, Caption, Capture, Cardiac, Catch, Check, Collar, Hold, Knock, Nab, Nail, Nip, Pinch, Pull, Restrain, Retard, Riveting, Round-up, Run-in, Sease, Seize, Stop, Sus(s)

**Arrival, Arrive** Accede, Advent, Attain, Come, Get, Happen, Hit, Influx, Land, Natal, Nativity, Reach

**Arrogance, Arrogant** Assumption, Bold, Bravado, Cavalier, Cocksure,

Disdain, Dogmatic, Haughty, Haut(eur), Hogen-mogen, Imperious, Presumption, Proud, Surquedry, Toploftical, Uppity, Upstart

**Arrogate** Appropriate, Assume, Claim, Impute, Usurp

**Arrow, Arrow-head** Acestes, Any, Ary, Bolt, Dart, Filter, Missile, Pheon, Quarrel, Reed, Shaft, Sheaf

**Arrowroot** Maranta, Pia

**Arsenal** Ammo, Armo(u)ry, Depot, Magazine, Side

**Arsenate, Arsenic(al)** As, Realgar, Resalgar, Rosaker, Salvarsan, Scorodite, Skutterudite, Speiss, Zarnich

**Arson** Pyromania

**Art(s), Arty, Art school, Art style** Abstract, Ars, Bauhaus, Bloomsbury, Chiaroscuro, Clair-obscure, Clare-obscure, Cobra, Constructivism, Craft, Cubism, Cunning, Dada, Daedal(e), Deco, Dedal, Diptych, Earth, Es, Feat, Fine, Finesse, Fugue, Futurism, Genre, Guile, Impressionist, Jugendstil, Kano, Kitsch, Knack, Mandorla, Mystery, Norwich, Nouveau, Perigordian, Primitive, Relievo, Sienese, SKILL, Still-life, Surrealism, Synchronism, Trecento, Trivium, Trouvé, Virtu, Vorticism

> **Art** may indicate an -est ending

**Artefact** Neolith, Xoanon

> **Artefact** may indicate an anagram

**Artemis** Selene

**Artemus** Ward

**Artery** Aorta, Carotid, Duct, Femoral, Iliac, M1, Route

**Artful** Cute, Dodger, Foxy, Ingenious, Quirky, Sly, Subtle, Tactician

**Artichoke** Cardoon

**Article(s)** A, An, Apprentice, Column, Commodity, Definite, Feature, Indenture, Item, Leader, Paper, Piece, Pot-boiler, Specify, The, Thing, Thirty-nine, Treatise, Ware

**Articulation, Articulate(d)** Clear, Coudé, Diarthrosis, Distinct, Eloquent, Enounce, Express, Fluent, Gimmal, Gomphosis, Hinged, Jointed, Jymold, Lenis, Limbed, Lisp, Pronounce, Schindylesis, Trapezial, Utter, Vertebrae, Voice

**Artifice(r), Artificial** Bogus, Chouse, Dodge, Ersatz, Finesse, Guile, Hoax, Logodaedaly, Man-made, Mannered, Opificer, Pretence, Prosthetic, Reach, Ruse, Sell, Sham, Spurious, Stratagem, STRATEGY, Synthetic, Theatric, TRICK, Unnatural, Wile, Wright

**Artillery** Battery, Cannon, Fougade, Fougasse, Guns, Mortar, Ordnance, RA, Rafale, Ramose, Ramus, Train

**Artiodactyl** Chevrotain, Deerlet

**Artisan** Craftsman, Joiner, Mechanic, Pioner, Pyoner, Workman

**Artist(ic)** Aiken, Alma-Tadema, Beardsley, Bellini, Bernini, Bohemian, Bonington, Bonnard, (Hieronymus) Bosch, Burne-Jones, Canaletto,

Cartoonist, Cézanne, Chagall, Chardin, Claude, Collier, Constable, Corot, Correggio, Courbet, Cranach, Crome, Cubist, Cuyp, Dadaist, Daedal(e), Dali, Degas, Derain, Doré, D'Orsay, Dulac, Dürer, Epstein, Ernst, Etcher, Etty, Fine, Fragonard, Fuseli, Gainsborough, Gentle, Giotto, Goya, Guardi, Hals, Hobbema, Hogarth, Holbein, ICA, Ingres, John, Klee, Kneller, Landseer, Leech, Léger, Lely, Leonardo, Linear, Lowry, Madox Brown, Maestro, Manet, Masaccio, Master, Matisse, Millais, Millet, Miró, Mondrian, Monet, Morland, Munch, MUSICIAN, Nattier, Nazarene, Nevinson, Opie, Orpen, Oeuvre, Orphism, PAINTER, Phiz, Poussin, RA, Raeburn, Raphael, Rembrandt, Ribera, Rivera, Rodin, Rothko, Rouault, Rousseau, Rowlandson, Screever, SCULPTOR, Sickert, Spencer, Stubbs, Tachisme, Tatum, Tiepolo, Tintoretto, Tissot, Titian, Toulouse-Lautrec, Trapeze, Trecentist, Turner, Uccello, Utrillo, Van Eyck, Velasquez, Vermeer, Virtuose, Virtuoso, Warhol, Watteau, Watts, Winterhalter

**Artless**  Candid, Ingenuous, Innocent, Naive, Open, Seely

**Arturo**  Toscanini

**Arum**  Green-dragon, Lily, Taro

**As**  Aesir, Als, Arsenic, Coin, Eg, Forasmuch, Qua, Ridge, 's, Since, Thus, Ut, While

**As above**  US

**Asafoetida**  Hing

**As before**  Anew, Ditto, Do, Stet

**Asbestos**  Amiant(h)us, Amosite, Chrysolite, Earthflax, Fireproof

**Ascend(ant), Ascent**  Climb, Dominant, Escalate, Gradient, Pull, Ramp, Rise, Sclim, Sklim, Slope, Up, Upgang, Uphill, Uprise, Zoom

**Ascertain**  Determine, Discover, ESTABLISH, Prove

**Ascetic**  Agapetae, Anchor(et), Anchorite, Ancress, Austere, Dervish, Diogenes, Encratite, Eremital, Essene, Fakir, Faquir, Hermit, Monk, Nazarite, Sad(d)hu, Stylite, Therapeutae, Yogi(n)

**Ascidian**  Chordate

**Asclepiad**  Stapelia

**Ascribe**  Assign, ATTRIBUTE, Blame, Imply, Impute

**Asdic**  Sonar

**As far as**  Quoad

**As good as**  Equal, Tantamount

**Ash(es), Ashy**  Aizle, Cinders, Cinereal, Clinker(s), Easle, Embers, Kali, Pallor, Pozz(u)olana, Rowan, Ruins, Sorb, Tephra, Urn, Varec, Wednesday, Yg(g)drasil(l)

**Ashamed**  Abashed, Embarrassed, Hangdog, Mortified, Repentant, Shent

**Ashore**  Aland, Beached, Grounded, Stranded

**Ash-pan**  Backet

**Asia(n), Asiatic**  Balinese, Bengali, E, Gook, Indian, Korean, Kurd, Lao, Mongol, Pushtu, Samo(y)ed, Siamese, Tibetan

**Asia Minor**  Anatolia, Ionic

**Aside**  Apart, By, Despite, Private, Separate, Shelved, Sotto voce

**Asinine**  Crass, Dull, Idiotic, Puerile, Stupid

**Ask**  Beg, Beseech, Cadge, Demand, Entreat, Enquire, Evet, Implore, Intreat, Invite, Newt, Petition, Prithee, Pump, Request, Rogation, Seek, Speer, Speir, Touch

**Askance**  Asconce, Askew, Oblique, Sideways

**Askew**  Agee, Aglee, Agley, Ajee, Aslant, Awry, Crooked, Skivie

**Asleep**  Dormant, Inactive, Napping

**Asparagus**  Asperge, Sparrow-grass, Spear, Sprue

**Aspect**  Angle, Bearing, Brow, Face, Facet, Facies, Feature, Look, Mien, Nature, Outlook, Perspective, Side, VIEW, Visage, Vista

**Aspersion**  Calumny, Innuendo, Libel, Slander, Slur, Smear

**Asphalt**  Bitumen, Pitch, Uinta(h)ite

**Aspirant, Aspirate, Aspiration, Aspire**  Ambition, Breath, Desire, Dream, Ettle, Goal, H, Hope(ful), Pretend, Pursue, Rough, Spiritus

**Ass**  Buridan, Burnell, Burro, Cardophagus, Clot, Couscous, Cuddie, Dick(e)y, Donkey, Dziggetai, Funnel, Golden, Hemione, Hinny, Jack, Jenny, Kiang, K(o)ulan, Kourbash, Kourmiss, Kouskous, Kumiss, Kurbash, Kyang, Liripoop, Liripipe, Moke, Neddy, Nitwit, Onager, Quagga, Sesterce, Simp, STUPID PERSON

**Assail**  Assault, Batter, Bego, Belabour, Bepelt, Beset, Bombard, Impugn, Oppugn, Ply, Revile

**Assassin(ation)**  Booth, Brave, Bravo, Brutus, Casca, Frag, Highbinder, Hitman, Killer, Ninja, Sword, Thuggee

**Assault**  Assail, Assay, Attack, Battery, Bombard, Hamesucken, Invasion, Mug, RAID, Stoor, Storm, Stour, Stowre

**Assay**  Cupel, Examine, Proof, Test

**Assemble, Assembly**  Agora, Audience, Ball, Bundestag, Chapter, Chatuaqua, Cho(u)ltry, Co, COLLECTION, Comitia, Company, Conclave, Concourse, Congeries, Congress, Consistory, Constituent, Convene, Convention, Convoke, Cortes, Council, Curia, Dail Eireann, Dewain, Diet, Donnybrook, Ecclesia, Eisteddfod, Erect, Feis(anna), Folkmoot, Force, Gather(ing), Gemot, Gorsedd, Group, Hoi polloi, Kgotla, Knesset, Landtag, Levee, Majlis, Make, Mass, MEETING, Mejlis, Moot, Muster, Parliament, Patron, Pattern, Plenum, Pnyx, Powwow, Presence, Quorum, Rally, Rechate, Recheate, Repair, Resort, Sanhedron, Senate, Skupshtina, Sobranje, Soc, Society, Stort(h)ing, Synedrion, Synod, Thing, Tribunal, Troop, Volksraad, Wapens(c)haw, Wapins(c)haw, Wappens(c)haw, Wardmote, Weapon-s(c)haw, Witan, Witenagemot, Zemstvo

**Assent**  Accede, Acquiesce, Agree, Amen, Aye, Comply, Concur, Nod, Placet, Sanction, Yea, Yield

**Assert(ing), Assertion**  Affirm, Allege, Constate, Contend, DECLARE,

Ipse-dixit, MAINTAIN, Pose, Predicate, Proclaim, Protest, Thetical

**Assess(ment)** Appraise, Estimate, Gauge, JUDGE, Levy, Measure, Rating, Referee, Scot and lot, Tax, Value, Weigh

**Asset(s)** Advantage, Chattel, Goodwill, Liquid, Plant, Property, Talent, Virtue

**Assiduous** Attentive, Busy, Constant, Diligent, Studious, Thorough

**Assign(ation), Assignment** Allocate, ALLOT, Aret, Ascribe, Attribute, Award, Date, Dedicate, Duty, Fix, Grant, Point, Quota, Refer, Transfer, Tryst

**Assimilate(d)** Absorb, Blend, Digest, Esculent, Fuse, Imbibe, Incorporate, Merge

**Assist(ance), Assistant** Acolyte, Adjunct, Aid(e), Ally, Alms, Attaché, Cad, Collaborate, Counterhand, Counter-jumper, Dresser, Factotum, Famulus, Gofer, HAND, Help, Relief, Reinforce, Second, Server, Stead, Subsidiary, Suffragan, SUPPORT, Usher

**Assize** Botley, Circuit, Oyer

**Associate, Association** Accomplice, Affiliate, Alliance, Ass, Attach, Bedfellow, Brotherhood, Cartel, Chapel, Chum, Club, Cohort, Combine, Compeer, Complice, Comrade, Confrère, CONNECT, Consort(ium), Co-partner, Correlate, Crony, Enclisis, Fellow, Fraternise, Gesellschaft, Guild, Hobnob, Intime, Join, League, Liaison, Member, Mix, Moshav, Pal, Partner, Relate, Ring, Sidekick, Sodality, Symbiosis, Union

> **Assorted** may indicate an anagram

**Assuage** Allay, Appease, Beet, Calm, Ease, Mease, Mitigate, Mollify, Slake, Soften

**As Such** Qua

**Assume, Assuming, Assumption** Adopt, Affect, Arrogate, Attire, Axiom, Believe, Don, Donné(e), Feign, Hypothesis, Lemma, Occam's Razor, Posit, Postulate, Premise, Premiss, Presuppose, Pretentious, Saltus, Suppose, Surmise, Take

> **Assumption** may mean attire

**Assure(d), Assurance** Aplomb, Aver, Belief, Calm, CERTAIN, Confidence, Confirm, Earnest, Gall, Pledge, Poise, Warranty

**Assuredly** Indeed, Perdie, Verily, Yea

**Astatine** At

**Astern** Abaft, Apoop, Rear

**Asteroid** Eros, Star, Starfish

**Astir** Afoot, Agate, Agog

**Astonish(ed), Astonishing, Astonishment, Astound** Abash, Amaze, Banjax, Bewilder, Confound, Corker, Daze, Flabbergast, Rouse, Singular, Stagger, Startle, Stupefy, Surprise, Thunderstruck, Wow

**Astray** Abord, Amiss, Errant, Lost, Will, Wull

**Astride**  Athwart, Spanning, Straddle-back

**Astringent**  Alum, Gambi(e)r, Harsh, Kino, Rhatany, Sept-foil, Severe, Sour, Styptic, Tormentil, Witch-hazel

**Astrologer**  Archgenethliac, Chaldean, Faust, Figure-caster, Genethliac, Lilly, Moore, Nostradamus, Soothsayer

**Astronaut**  Cosmonaut, Spaceman, Spacer

**Astronomer, Astronomy**  Almagest, Bessel, Brahe, Callipic, Celsius, Copernicus, Eddington, Flamsteed, Galileo, Halley, Herschel, Hipparchus, Hoyle, Hubble, Jeans, Kepler, Laplace, Ptolemy, Reber, Tycho Brahe, Urania

**Astrophel**  Penthia

**Astute**  Acute, Canny, Crafty, Cunning, Downy, Shrewd, Subtle, Wide, Wily

**As usual**  Solito

**As well**  Additionally, Also, Both, Even, Forby, Too

**Asylum**  Bin, Bughouse, Frithsoken, Girth, Grith, Haven, Magdalene, Refuge, Retreat, Sanctuary, Shelter

**Asymmetric**  Skew

**At all events**  Algate

**At**  Astatine, To

**Atahualpa**  Inca

**At all**  Ava, Ever, Oughtlings

**Atavistic**  Reversion, Throw-back

**Atheist**  Doubter, Godless, Infidel, Sceptic

**Athenian, Athene**  Attic, Pallas, Solon, Timon

**Athlete, Athletic**  Agile, Agonist, Blue, Coe, Discobolus, Gymnast, Jock, Leish, Miler, Milo, Nurmi, Pacemaker, Runner, Sportsman, Sprinter

**Athodyd**  Ram-jet

**Athwart**  Across, Awry, Oblique, Traverse

**Atlantic**  Pond

**Atlas**  Maps, Range

> **At last**  may indicate a cobbler

**Atmosphere**  Air, Ambience, Aura, Elements, Epedaphic, Ether, Miasma, Ozone, Tropopause

**Atoll**  Bikini, Eniwetok, Motu

**Atom(ic)**  Boson, Electron, Ion, Iota, Isobare, Isotone, Isotope, Ligand, Molecule, Muonic, Nuclide, Particle, Pile, Steric

**At once**  Ek dum, Immediate, Instanter, Presto, Swith, Tight, Tit(e), Titely, Tyte

**Atone(ment)**  Aby(e), Acceptilation, Appease, Expiate, Redeem, Redemption, Yom Kippur

**Atop**  Upon

> **At random** may indicate an anagram

**Atrocious, Atrocity** Abominable, Brutal, Diabolical, Heinous, Horrible, Monstrous, Outrage, Vile

**Atrophy** Marasmus, Sweeny, Wasting

**Attach(ed), Attachment** Accessory, Adhesion, Adhibition, Adnate, Adnation, Adscript, Affix, Allonge, Bolt, Devotement, Devotion, Distrain, Glue, JOIN, Obconic, Snell, Stick, Tie, Weld

**Attack(ing)** Access, Alert, Anti, Apoplexy, Asperse, Assail, Assault, At, Bego, Belabour, Beset, Bestorm, Blitz(krieg), Bodrag(ing), Bombard, Bordraging, Broadside, Camisade, Camisado, Cannonade, Charge, Clobber, Descent, Feint, Fit, Fleche, Foray, Get, Handbag, Impugn, Incursion, Inroad, Invade, Inveigh, Mug, Offensive, Onding, Onrush, Onset, Onslaught, Pillage, Pre-emptive, Push, Quart(e), Raid, Rough, Savage, Siege, Sortie, Storm, Strafe, Swoop, Thrust, Vilify, Wage, Warison, Zap

**Attain(ment)** Accomplish, Arrive, Earn, Fruition, Get, Land, Reach

**Attempt** Bash, Bid, Burl, Crack, Debut, Effort, Endeavour, Go, Mint, Seek, Shot, Shy, Stab, Strive, TRY, Venture, Whack, Whirl

**Attend(ant)** Accompany, Apple-squire, Await, Batman, Bearer, Be at, Behold, Cavass, Chasseur, Courtier, Custrel, Entourage, Equerry, Escort, Esquire, Famulus, Gillie, Harken, Hear, HEED, Hello, Holla, Iras, Kavass, LISTEN, Maenad, Marshal, Note, Outrider, Page, Panisc, Panisk, Paranymph, People, Presence, Pursuivant, Respect, Satellite, Second, Sowar, Steward, Valet, Varlet, Visit, Wait, Watch, Whiffler, Zambuck

**Attention, Attentive** Achtung, Court, Dutiful, Ear, Gallant, Gaum, Gorm, Heed, Mind, Notice, Present, Punctilio, Qui vive, REGARD, Tenty, Thought

**Attenuate, Attenuation** Lessen, Neper, Rarefy, Thin, Weaken

**Attest** Affirm, Certify, Depose, Guarantee, Swear, WITNESS

**Attic** Garret, Greek, Koine, Loft, Muse, Salt, Solar, Soler, Sollar, Soller, Tallat, Tallet, Tallot

**Attila** Etzel, Hun

**Attire** Accoutre, Adorn, Apparel, Clobber, DRESS, Garb, Habit

**Attitude** Air, Aspect, Behaviour, Demeanour, Light, MANNER, Pose, Posture, Sense, Stance

**Attorney** Advocate, Counsellor, DA, Lawyer, Proctor

**Attract(ion), Attractive** Attrahent, Bait, Bewitch, Bonny, Catchy, CHARM, Cheesecake, Cute, Cynosure, Dipolar, Dish, Draught, DRAW, Duende, Engaging, Entice, Epigamic, Eyeful, Fascinate, Feature, Fetching, Gravity, Hunky, Inducement, Inviting, It, Loadstone, Lodestone, Lure, Magnes, Magnet(ism), Pull, Sematic, Soote, Stotter, Taking, Tasteful, Weber, Winning, Winsome, Zaftig, Zoftig

**Attribute** Accredit, Allot, Ap(p)anage, Ascribe, Asset, Credit, Gift, Impute, Owe, Refer

**Attune**  Accord, Adapt, Temper

**Aubergine**  Brinjal, Brown Jolly, Egg-plant, Mad-apple

**Aubrey**  Beardsley

**Auburn**  Abram, Chestnut, Copper, Vill(age)

**Auction(eer)**  Barter, Bridge, Cant, Dutch, Hammer, Outcry, Outro(o)per, Roup, Sale, Sub hasta, Tattersall, Vendue

**Audacious, Audacity**  Bold, Brash, Cheek, Der-doing, Effrontery, Face, Hardihood, Indiscreet, Insolence, Neck, Nerve, Sauce

**Audience, Auditorium**  Assembly, Court, Durbar, Gate, House, Interview, Sphendone, Tribunal

**Audiovisual**  AV

**Audit(or)**  Accountant, Check, Ear, Examine, Inspect, Listener

**Auditory**  Acoustic, Oral

**Audrey**  Hoyden

**Augment**  Boost, Eche, Eke, Increase, Supplement, Swell

**August**  Awe-inspiring, Grand, Imperial, Imposing, Majestic, Noble, Solemn, Stately, Stern

**Augustine, Augustus**  Austin, Hippo, John

**Auk**  Ice-bird, Roch, Rotch(e)

**Aunt(ie)**  Augusta, Beeb, Giddy, Naunt, Tia

**Aura**  Aroma, Odour, Vibrations

**Aureole**  Coronary, Halo, Nimbus

**Auricle**  Ear, Otic

**Aurora**  Eos, Leigh, Matutinal

**Auspice(s)**  Aegis, Patronage

**Auster**  S-wind

**Austere, Austerity**  Astringent, Bleak, Dantean, Hard, HARSH, Moral, Plain, Rigour, Stern, Stoic, Strict, Vaudois, Waldensian

**Austin**  Friar

**Australia(n)**  Alf, Antipodean, Aussie, Balt, Banana-bender, Bananalander, Billjim, Canecutter, Cobber, Darwinian, Digger, Gin, Larrikin, Myall, Ocker, Oz, Roy, Sandgroper, Strine, Wallaby, Yarra-yabbies

**Austrian**  Cisleithan, Tyrolean

**Authentic(ate)**  Certify, Echt, Genuine, Honest, Official, Real, Sign, True, Validate

**Author(ess)**  Addison, Auctorial, Aymé, Buchan, Cervantes, Colette, Constant, Crane, Cranmer, Daudet, Defoe, Dramatist, Dumas, Forester, Genet, Gide, Gissing, Gogol, Gosse, Grimm, Hand, Hawthorne, Hope, Hugo, Inventor, James, Joyce, Kafka, Kingsley, Le Fanu, Loti, Maker, Malory, Mandeville, Marryat, Me, NOVELIST, Orwell, Parent, Pasternak, Pater, Peacock, Pen, Pliny, Proust, Pushkin, Rabelais, Racine, Rattigan,

Reade, RLS, Sapper, Smollett, Sterne, Surtees, Thoreau, Trollope, Turgenev, Volumist, Ward, Wells, Whitman, Wordsmith, WRITER, Zola

> **Author** may refer to author of puzzle

**Authorise(d), Authorisation** Accredit, Empower, Enable, Imprimatur, Legal, LICENCE, Official, OK, Passport, PERMIT, Sanction, Sign, Stamp, Warrant

**Authority, Authoritarian** Canon, Charter, Circar, Cocker, Commune, Dominion, Expert, Jackboot, Licence, Mandate, Mastery, Name, Oracle, Permit, POWER, Prefect, Prestige, Pundit, Remit, Right, Rod, Say-so, Sceptre, Sircar, Sirkar, Source, Warrant

**Autocrat(ic)** Absolute, Caesar, Cham, Despot, Neronian, Tsar, Tyrant

**Autograph** Signature

**Autolycus** Scrapman

**Automatic, Automaton** Android, Aut, Browning, Instinctive, Machine, Mechanical, Pistol, Robot, RUR, Zombi

**Auto-pilot** George

**Auto-suggestion** Coueism

**Autumn(al)** Fall, Filemot, Philamot

**Auxiliary** Adjunct, Adminicle, Aide, Be, Feldsher, Have, Helper, Ido

**Avail(able)** Benefit, Dow, Going, Handy, On call, Open, READY, Serve, Use, Utilise

**Avalanche** Deluge, Landfall, Landslide, Landslip, Lauwine, Slide, Slip, Snowdrop

**Avant-garde** Modernistic

**Avarice, Avaricious** Cupidity, Golddigger, Greed, Sordid

**Avatar** Epiphany, Incarnation, Rama

**Avaunt** Away, Go

**Avenge(r)** Eriny(e)s, Eumenides, Goel, Punish, Redress, Requite, REVENGE, Wreak

**Avenue** Alley, Arcade, Channel, Corso, Cradle-walk, Hall, Mall, Passage, Vista, Way, Xyst(us)

**Aver** Affirm, Asseverate, Depose, Swear, Vouch

**Average** Adjustment, Av, Mean, Middling, Norm, Par, Run, Soso, Standard

**Averse, Aversion** Against, Antipathy, Apositia, Disgust, Distaste, Hatred, Horror, Opposed, Phobic

**Avert** Avoid, DEFLECT, Forfend, Parry, Ward

**Aviator** Airman, Flier, Icarus, Lindbergh, Pilot

**Avid** EAGER, Greedy, Keen

**Avifauna** Ornis

**Avignon** Pont

**Avocado** Aguacate, Guac(h)amole, Pear

**Avocet** Scooper

**Avoid(er), Avoidance** Baulk, Boycott, Bypass, Cut, Dodge, Duck, Elude, Escape, Eschew, Evade, Evitate, Evite, Fly, Forbear, Gallio, Hedge, Miss, Parry, Scutage, Secede, Shelve, Shun, Sidestep, Skirt, Spare, Spurn

**Avoirdupois** Size, Weight

**Avow(ed)** Acknowledged, Affirm, Declare, Own, Swear

**Await** Abide, Bide, Expect, Tarry

**Awake(ning)** Aware, Conversion, Fly, Rouse, Vigilant

**Award** Accolade, Addoom, Allot, Alpha, Aret(t), Bestow, Bursary, Cap, Clasp, Clio, Crown, Emmy, Exhibition, Grammy, Grant, Medal, Meed, Mete, Oscar, Premium, Present(ation), PRIZE, Scholarship, Tony, Trophy, Yuko

**Aware(ness)** Alert, Cognisant, Conscious, Conversant, ESP, Hep, Informed, Onto, Samadhi, Sensible, Sensitive, Sentience, Vigilant, Wot

**Away** Absent, Afield, Apage, Avaunt, By, Fro(m), Go, Hence, Off, Out, Past

> **Away** may indicate a word to be omitted

**Awe(d)** Dread, D(o)ulia, Fear, Intimidate, Loch, Overcome, Popeyed, Regard, Respect, Reverent, Scare, Solemn

**Awe-inspiring** Numinous

**Awful(ly)** Alas, Deare, Dere, Dire, Fearful, O so, Piacular, Terrible

> **Awfully** may indicate an anagram

**Awkward** Angular, Bumpkin, Complicated, Clumsy, Corner, Crabby, Cumbersome, Embarrassing, Farouche, Fix, Gauche, Gawky, Howdy-do, Inconvenient, Inept, Lanky, Loutish, Lurdan(e), Lurden, Mauther, Mawr, Nasty, Slummock, Spot, Sticky, Stroppy, Stumbledom, Uneasy, Ungainly

**Awl(-shaped)** Brog, Els(h)in, Nail, Stob, Subulate

**Awn(ing)** Barb, Beard, Canopy, Ear, Shade, Velarium

**Awry** Agley, Askew, Cam, Kam(me), Wonky

**Axe** Adz(e), Bill, Celt, Chop(per), Cleaver, Eatche, Gisarme, Gurlet, Halberd, Halbert, Hatchet, Jethart-staff, Labrys, Mattock, Partisan, Palstaff, Palstave, Piolet, Retrench, Sax, Sparth(e), Sperthe, Spontoon, Thunderbolt, Tomahawk, Twibill

**Axiom** Adage, Motto, Peano, Proverb, Saw, Saying

**Axis** Alliance, Anorthic, Axle, Caulome, Chital, Cob, Henge, Myelon, Pivot, Rachis, Spindle, Sympodium

**Axle, Axle-shoulder** Axis, Fulcrum, Hurter, Journal, Mandrel, Mandril, Pivot

**Ay** I

**Aye** Eer, Ever, Yea, Yes

**Ayesha** She

**Azo-dye** Para-red

**Aztec** Nahuatl

# Bb

**B**  Bachelor, Black, Book, Born, Boron, Bowled, Bravo

**Babble(r)**  Blather, Chatter, Gibber, Haver, Lurry, Prate, Prattle, Runnel, Tonguester, Twattle, Waffle

**Babel**  Charivari, Confusion, Din, Dovercourt, Medley

**Baboon**  Ape, Chacma, Dog-ape, Drill, Gelada, Hamadryad, Mandrill, Sphinx

**Baby**  Bairn, Bub, Bunting, Duck, Grand, Infant, Jelly, Nursling, Pamper, Papoose, Sis, Small, Sook, Suckling, Tar, Tot, Wean

**Babylonian**  Semiramis, Sumerian

**Bacchantes**  Maenads

**Bacchus**  Ivied

**Bachelor**  BA, Bach, Benedict, Budge, Celibate, Pantagamy, Parti, Single, Stag

**Bacillus**  Comma, Germ, Virus

**Back(ing), Backward**  Abet, Addorse, Again, Ago, Antimacassar, Arear, Arrière, Assist, Baccare, Backare, Buckram, Consent, Defender, Dorsal, Dorse, Dos, Ebb, Empatron, Endorse, Finance, Frae, Fro, Gaff, Help, Hind, La-la, Late, Notaeum, Notum, On, Patronise, Poop, Pronotum, Punt, Rear(most), Retral, Retro(grade), Retrogress, Retrorse, Return, Rev, Ridge, Root, Spinal, Sponsor, Stern, SUPPORT, Tail, Telson, Tergum, Third, Thrae, Tonneau, Uphold, Vie

> **Back(ing)**  may indicate a word spelt backwards

**Back and forth**  Boustrophedon

**Backbiter, Backbiting**  Catty, Defame, Detract, Libel, Molar, Slander

**Backbone**  Chine, Grit, Guts, Mettle

**Backchat**  Lip, Mouth

**Backer**  Angel, Benefactor, Patron, Punter, Seconder, Sponsor

**Backgammon**  Acey-deucy, Lurch, Tick-tack, Tric-trac, Trick-track, Verquere

**Background**  Antecedence, Fond, History, Horizon, Setting, Ulterior

**Backhander**  Payola

**Backroom**  Boffin, Boy, Moor

**Backslide(r), Backsliding**  Apostate, Lapse, Regress, Relapse, Revert

**Backwash**  Rift

**Backwater**  Bogan, Ebb, Retreat, Slough, Wake

**Backwoods**  Boondocks, Boonies, Hinterland

**Backyard**  Court, Patio

**Bacon**  Danish, Essayist, Flitch, Francis, Gammon, Pig, Pork, Rasher, Roger, Speck, Verulam

**Bacteria, Bacterium**  Aerobe, Bacteriological, Bacilli, Clostridia, Cocci, Escherichia, GERM, Klebsiella, Microbe, Mother, Packet, Pasteurella, Proteus, Salmonella, Schizomycete, Serotype, Serum, Shigella, Spirilla, Staph, Strep(tococcus), Treponemata, Vibrio, Vinegar-plant, Yersinia

**Bad(ly), Badness**  Addled, Chronic, Crook, Defective, Diabolic, Dud, Duff, Egregious, Execrable, Faulty, Heinous, Ill, Immoral, Inferior, Injurious, Lither, Mal, Naughty, Nefandrous, Nefarious, Off, Ominous, Oncus, Onkus, Piacular, Poor, Rank, Ropy, Scampish, Scoundrel, Sinful, Spoiled, Turpitude, Useless, Wick, WICKED

> **Bad(ly)**  may indicate an anagram

**Badge**  Brassard, Brooch, Button, Cockade, Crest, Emblem, Ensign, Epaulet, Episemon, Flash, Garter, Gorget, Insignia, Kikumon, Mark, Mon, Rosette, Scallop, SIGN, Symbol, Token

**Badger**  ANNOY, Bait, Bedevil, Beset, Brock, Browbeat, Bug, Bullyrag, Cete, Dassi(e), Gray, Grey, HARASS, Hassle, Nag, Provoke, Ratel, Ride, Roil, Sow, Teledu, Wisconsin

**Bad habit**  Cacoethes, Vice

**Badinage**  Banter, Chaff, Raillery

**Bad luck**  Ambs-ace, Ames-ace, Deuce-ace, Hoodoo, Jinx, Shame, Voodoo

**Bad-tempered**  Carnaptious, Curnaptious, Curst, Grouchy, Grum(py), Irritable, Moody, Patch

**Bad woman**  Harridan, Loose, Mort

**Baffle(d), Baffling**  Anan, Balk, Bemuse, Bewilder, Confound, Confuse, Elude, Evade, Floor, Flummox, Foil, Fox, Get, Mate, Muse, Mystify, Nark, Nonplus, Pose, Puzzle, Stump, Throw, Thwart

**Bag(s), Baggage**  Alforja, Allantois, Ascus, Amaut, Amowt, Besom, Bladder, Bulse, Caba(s), Caecum, Callet, Capture, Carpet, Cecum, Cly, Cod, Corduroy, Crone, Crumenal, Cyst, Dilli, Dilly, Dorothy, Dunnage, EFFECTS, Flannels, Follicle, Galligaskins, GEAR, Gladstone, Grip, Holdall, Impedimenta, Jelly, Jiffy, Kill, Lithocyst, Marsupium, Minx, Mixed, Nap, Net, Overnight, Oxford, Pantaloons, Pochette, Pock(et), Pockmanky, Pockmantie, Poke, Port(manteau), Portmantle, Portmantua, Pot, Pouch, Purse, Rake, Reticule, Ridicule, Rucksack, Sabretache, Sac(cule), Sachet, Sack, Saddle, Satchel, Scrip, Scrotum, Slattern, Sporran, Stacks, Strossers, TRAP, Trews, Trollop, Trouse(r), Unmentionables, Utricle, Valise, Win

**Bagatelle**  Bauble, Fico, Trifle, Trinket

**Bagpipe**  Chorus, Cornemuse, Drone, Musette, Pibroch, Piffero, Skirl, Sourdeline, Uillean, Zampogna

**Bahamas**  BS

**Bail(er), Bailment**  Bond, Ladle, Mainpernor, Mainprise, Mutuum, Scoop

**Bailey** Bridge, Ward

**Bailiff** Adam, Bandog, Bum, Factor, Foud, Huissier, Land-agent, Nuthook, Philistine, Shoulder-knot, Steward, Tipstaff

**Bairn** Baby, CHILD, Infant, Wean

**Bait** Badger, Berley, Brandling, Burley, Capelin, Chum, Dap, Decoy, Entice, Gentle, Harass, Hellgram(m)ite, Incentive, Lobworm, Lug(worm), Lure, Mawk, RAG, Ragworm, Sledge, Teagle, Tease

**Bake(r), Baked, Baking** Alaska, Batch, Baxter, COOK, Fire, Kiln-dry, Roast, Scorch

**Baker's daughter** Own

**Baker Street** Irregular

**Balance(d)** Account, Beam, Counterpoise, Equate, Equilibrium, Equipoise, Equiponderate, Even, Gyroscope, Gyrostat, Isostasy, Launce, Libra, Librate, Meet, Otolith, Peise, Perch, Poise, REMAINDER, Remnant, Residual, Rest, Scale, Steelyard, Symmetry, TOTAL, Trial, Trim, Tron(e)

**Balcony** Circle, Gallery, Loggia, Mirador, Moucharaby, Porch, Tarras, Terrace, Veranda(h)

**Bald(ing), Baldness** Alopecia, Apterium, Awnless, Barren, Calvities, Coot, Crude, Egghead, Fox-evil, Glabrous, Hairless, Madarosis, Open, Peelgarlic, Pilgarlic(k), Pollard, Psilosis, Tonsured

**Balderdash** Drivel, Nonsense, Rot

**Baldmoney** Emeu, Meu, Spignel

**Bale** Bl, Bundle, Pack, Truss

**Baleful** Evil, Malefic, Malignant

> **Balk** see BAULK

**Balkan** Albanian, Bulgarian, Macedon, Rumanian

**Ball(s)** Aelopile, Aelopyle, Agglomerate, Alley, Ally, Ammo, Aniseed, Bead, Beamer, Bolus, Bosey, Break, Caltrap, Caltrop, Cherry, Chinaman, Clew, Cotill(i)on, Croquette, Crystal, Daisy-cutter, DANCE, Delivery, Eolopile, Eolopyle, Falafel, Felafel, Gazunder, GLOBE, Googly, Gool(e)ys, Goolies, Grub, Gutta, Hop, Inswinger, Ivory, Knur(r), Leather, Lob, Long-hop, Marble, Masque(rade), Medicine, Moth, Nur(r), O, Pea, Pellet, Pill, Poi, Pompom, Prom, Puck, Quenelle, Rissole, Rover, Rundle, Seamer, Sliotar, Sneak, Sphere, Spinner, Thenar, Tice, Witches, Wood, Yorker

**Ball-boy** Dry-bob

**Ballad(ist)** Bab, Calypso, Carol, Lay, Lillibullero, Lilliburlero, SONG, Torch-song

**Ballast** Kentledge, Makeweight, Stabiliser, Trim, Weight

**Ballerina** Coryphee, Dancer, Pavlova

**Ballet** Bolshoi, Checkmate, Giselle, Kirov

**Ballet-interlude** Divertimento

**Balloon(ist)** Aeronaut, Aerostat, Airship, Bag, Barrage, Billow, Blimp, Bloat, Dirigible, Dumont, Fumetto, Montgolfier, Rawinsonde, Zeppelin

**Ballot** Election, POLL, Referendum, Suffrage, Ticket, Vote

**Ballot-box** Urn

**Balm(y)** Anetic, Arnica, Balsam, Calamint, Fragrant, Garjan, Gilead, Gurjun, Lenitive, MILD, Mirbane, Myrbane, Nard, Oil, Opobalsam, Ottar, Redolent, Remedy, Soothe, Spikenard, Tolu, Unguent

**Baloney** Bunk, Hooey

**Balmoral** Bonnet

**Balsam** Copaiba, Copaiva, Nard, Resin, Spikenard, Tamanu, Tolu(ic), Touch-me-not, Tous-les-mois, Turpentine

**Balt** Esth, Lett

**Bamboozle(d)** Cheat, Dupe, Flummox, Hoodwink, Mystify, Nose-led, Perplex, Trick

**Ban** Abolish, Accurse, Anathema, Black(ing), Censor, Debar, Embargo, Excommunicate, For(e)say, For(e)speak, Gate, Moratorium, No, Prohibit, Proscribe, Taboo, Tabu, Veto

**Banal** Corny, Flat, Hackneyed, Mundane, TRITE, Trivial

**Banana(s)** Abaca, Hand, MAD, Musa, Plantain, Scitamineae, Split, Strelitzia

**Band(s)** Alice, Ambulacrum, Anadem, Armlet, Barrulet, Belt, Border, Braid, Brassard, Brassart, Caravan, CB, Channel, Circlet, Cohort, Collar, Combo, Company, Corslet, Coterie, Crew, Elastic, Endorse, Enomoty, Facia, Falling, Fascia, Fasciole, Ferret, Ferrule, Filament, Fillet, Frieze, Frog, Gamelan, GANG, Garter, Gasket, Gaskin, Gird, Girth, HOOP, Hope, Iron, Kitchen, Label, Laticlave, Mariachi, Massed, Myrmidon, Noise, Orchestra, Orchestrina, Pack, Parral, Parrel, Parsal, Parsel, Patte, Plinth, Purfle, Puttee, Retinaculum, Rib, Rigwiddie, Rigwoodie, Rim, Ring, Robbers, Rubber, Sash, Scarf, Screed, Shallal, Shash, Strake, Strap, Stratum, Stripe, Swath(e), Tape, Tendon, Tippet, Torques, Train, Troop, Troupe, Turm, Tyre, Unite, Virl, Vitta, Wanty, Weeper, Welt, With(e), Zona, Zone

**Bandage** Bind, Capeline, Dressing, Fillet, Ligature, Lint, Pledget, Roller, Scapula, Sling, Spica, Suspensor, Swaddle, Swathe, T, Tape, Truss, Wadding

**Bandicoot** Pig-rat

**Bandit** Apache, Bravo, Brigand, Fruit-machine, Klepht, Moss-trooper, Outlaw, Pirate, Rapparee, ROBBER

**Bandsman, Band-leader** Alexander, Bugler, Conductor, Maestro, Miller

**Bane** Curse, Evil, Harm, Poison

**Bang(er)** Amorce, Cap, Chipolata, Clap, Cracker, Explode, Flivver, Fringe, Haircut, Heap, Implode, Jalopy, Maroon, Report, Sausage, Sizzler, Slam, Thrill, Wurst

**Bangle** Anklet, Armlet, Bracelet, Kara

**Banish** Ban, Deport, Exile, Expatriate, Expel, Forsay, Maroon, Ostracise, OUTLAW, Relegate, Rusticate

**Banjo** Ukulele

**Bank(s)** An(n)icut, Asar, Backs, Bar, Bay, Bk, Bluff, Brae, Brim, Bund, Camber, Clearing, Cloud, Depend, Deposit, Dogger, Down, Dune, Dyke, Earthwork, Escarp, Glacis, Gradin(e), Hele, Hill, Levee, Link, Mound, Nap, Nore, Overslaugh, Parapet, Piggy, Rake, Ramp, Rampart, Reef, RELY, Rivage, Rodham, Row, Shallow, Shelf, Side, Sunk, Terrace, Terreplein, Tier, Vault

**Banker** Agent, Financial, Fugger, Gnome, Lombard, Medici, RIVER, Rothschild, Shroff

**Banknote** Greenback

**Bankrupt(cy)** Break, Broke, Bust, Cadaver, Carey Street, Crash, Debtor, Deplete, Duck, Dyvour, Fail, Fold, Insolvent, Ruin, Rump, Scat, Sequestration, Smash

> **Bankrupt** may indicate 'red' around another word

**Bank System** Giro

**Bann(s)** Out-ask

**Banner** Banderol(e), Bandrol, Bannerol, FLAG, Gumphion, Labarum, Oriflamme, Sign, Streamer

**Banquet** Beanfeast, Dine, Feast, Junket, Spread

**Banquette** Firestep

**Bant** Diet, Reduce

**Banter** Badinage, Borak, Chaff, Jest, JOKE, Persiflage, Picong, Rag, RAILLERY, Rally, Roast, Tease

**Bantu** Herero, Sotho, Tutsi, X(h)osa

**Bap** Bread, Roll, Tommy

**Baptise(d), Baptism, Baptist** Amrit, Christen, Dip, Dopper, Dunker, Illuminati, Sprinkle, Tinker

**Bar(s)** Bail, Ban, Baulk, Beam, Bilboes, Billet, Bistro, Black(ball), Block(ade), Bloom, Bolt, Boom, Bottega, Brasserie, Buffet, But, Buvette, Café(-chantant), Café-concert, CAGE, Came, Cantina, Capo, Counter, Cramp(on), Crow, Dive, Double-tree, Espresso, Estop(pel), Except, Exclude, Fen, Fid, Forbid, Foreclose, Forestall, Gad, Gemel, Grate, Grid, Hame, Handspike, Heck, HINDRANCE, Impediment, Ingoes, Ingot, Ingowes, Inn, Latch, Let, Lever, Line, Local, Mandrel, Mandril, Measure, No-go, Norman, Obstacle, Onely, Orgue, Overslaugh, Parallel, Pile, Pinch, Pole, Prohibit, Pub, Rabble, Rack, Rail, Ramrod, Rance, Randle-balk, Randle-perch, Randle-tree, Restrict, Rib, Rod, Rung, Saloon, Sans, Save, Saving, Semantron, Shaft, Shanty, Shet, Shut, Skewer, Slot, Snug, Spacer, Spar, Speakeasy, Sperre, Spina, Spit, Stancher, Stanchion, Stave, Sternson, Stick, Stirre, Stretcher, Stripe, Swee, T, Tael, Tap(-room), Tapas, Tavern(a), Temple, Toll, Tombolo, Tommy, Torsion, Trace, Trangle,

Transom, Trapeze, Triblet, Vinculum, Ward, Whisker, Z, Zed, Zygon

**Barabbas** Robber

**Barb(ed)** Bur(r), Fluke, Harl, Herl, HOOK, Jag(g), Jibe, Pheon, Prickle, Ramus, Tang

**Barbados** Bim(m)

**Barbara** Allen, Major

**Barbarian, Barbaric** Boor, Fifteen, Foreigner, Goth, Heathen, Hottentot, Hun, Inhuman, Lowbrow, Outlandish, Philistine, Rude, Savage, Tatar(ic), Tartar

**Barbary** Ape, Roan

**Barbecue** Cook-out, Flame-grill, Grill, Hangi, Hibachi, Roast, Spit

**Barbel** Beard

**Barber** Epilate, Figaro, Scraper, Shaver, Strap, Todd, Tonsor, Trimmer

**Bard** Ariosto, Griot, Heine, Minstrel, Muse, Ossian, Scald, Skald, Taliesin

**Bare, Bare-headed** Adamic, Aphyllous, Bald, Barren, Blank, Bodkin, Cere, Décolleté, Denude, Hush, Lewd, Marginal, Moon, NAKED, Open, Plain, Scant, Sear, Stark, Uncase, Uncover, Unveil

**Barefoot** Discalced, Unshod

**Barely** Just, Merely, Scarcely, Scrimp

**Bargain** Barter, Chaffer, Champerty, CHEAP, Coup, Deal, Dicker, Find, Go, Haggle, Higgle, Horse-trade, Huckster, Option, PACT, Scoop, Snip, Steal, Trade, Trock, Troke, Truck, Wanworth

**Barge** Birlinn, Bucentaur, Budgero(w), Gabbard, Gabbart, Hopper, Intrude, Keel, Nudge, Obtrude, Pra(a)m, Scow, SHIP, Wherry

> **Barge** may indicate an anagram

**Bargee, Bargeman** Keeler, Legger, Lighterman, Ram, Trow

**Barium** Ba, Witherite

**Bark(ing)** Angostura, Ayelp, Bass, Bast, Bay, Bowwow, Calisaya, Cascara, Cascarilla, China, Cinchona, Cinnamon, Cork, Cortex, Cusparia, Honduras, Kina, Latration, Liber, Myrica, Peel, Pereira, Peruvian, Quebracho, Quillai, Quina, Quinquina, Rind, Salian, Sassafras, Scrape, Ship, Skin, Tan, Tap(p)a, Totaquine, Waff, Waugh, Woof, Wow, Yaff, YAP, Yelp, Yip

**Bar-keeper, Barmaid, Barman** Advocate, Ale-wife, Bencher, Hebe, Luckie, Lucky, Tapster, Underskinker

**Barley** Awn, Bear, Bere, Bigg, Hordeum, Malt, Truce, Tsamba

**Barmecide, Barmecidal** Imaginary

**Barn** Byre, Cowshed, Grange, Skipper

**Barnaby** Rudge

**Barnacle** Cypris, Limpet

**Barometer** Aneroid, Glass, Sympiesometer, Torricellian

**Baron** B, Corvo, Munchausen, Noble, Thyssen, Tycoon

**Baronet** Bart

**Baronne Dudevant** Sand

**Baroque** Gothic, Ornate, Rococo

> **Baroque** may indicate an anagram

**Barrack(s), Barracking** Asteism, Boo, Casern(e), Cat-call, Garrison, Heckle, Irony, Quarters

**Barrage** Balloon, Fusillade, Salvo

**Barred** Banned, Edh, Trabeculated

**Barrel(-stand)** Bl, Butt, Cade, Capstan, Cascabel, Cask, Clavie, Drum, Hogshead, Keg, Morris-tube, Organ, Run(d)let, Thrall, Tierce, Tun, Wood

**Barrel-organ** Hurdy-gurdy

**Barren** Addle, Arid, Blind, Blunt, Dry, Eild, EMPTY, Farrow, Sterile, Waste, Yeld, Yell

**Barricade, Barrier** Bail, Barrage, Bayle, Block, Cauld, Cheval de frise, Chicane, DAM, Defence, Fence, Fraise, Gate, Hedge, Hurdle, Mach, Obstruct, Rail(-fence), Rampart, Roadblock, Spina, Stockade, Turnpike, WALL

**Barrister** Advocate, Attorney, Counsel, Devil, Lawyer, Rumpole, Serjeant, Silk, Templar, Utter

**Barrow** Dolly, Handcart, Henge, Hurley, Kurgan, Molehill, Mound, Pushcart, Tram, Trolley, Truck, Tumulus

**Barrow-boy** Coster, Trader

**Bar-tail** Scamel, Staniel, Stannel

**Barter** Chaffer, Dicker, EXCHANGE, Haggle, Hawk, Niffer, Sco(u)rse, Swap, TRADE, Traffic, Truck

**Basalt** Wacke

**Base(ness)** Adenine, Alkali, Beggarly, Billon, Bottom, Caitiff, Camp, Codon, Degenerate, Degraded, Down, E, Erinite, ESTABLISH, Foot, Found, Fundus, Harlot, Ignoble, Infamous, Install, LOW, MEAN, Nefarious, Nook, Partite, Patten, Platform, Plinth, Podium, Premise, Radix, Rests, Ribald, Root, Rosaniline, Servile, Shameful, Shand, Sheeny, Socle, Soda, STAND, Station, Substrate, Torus, Turpitude, Vile

**Baseball** Nine

**Baseless** Idle, Unfounded, Ungrounded

**Base-line** Datum

**Bash** Belt, Clout, Go, Hit, Shot, Slog, Strike, Swat, Swipe

**Bashful** Awed, Blate, Coy, Modest, Retiring, Shamefast, Sheep-faced, Sheepish, SHY

**Basic(s), Basis** ABC, Abcee, Alkaline, Aquamanale, Aquamanilc, ESSENTIAL, Fond, Fundamental, Ground(work), Gut, Integral, Intrinsic, Logic, Principle, Radical, Staple, Substance, Underlying, Uracil

**Basilisk** Cannon, Lizard

**Basin** Aquamanale, Aquamanile, Bidet, Bowl, Dish, Dock, Impluvium, Lavabo, Laver, Monteith, Pan, Playa, Porringer, Reservoir, Scapa Flow, Stoop, Stoup, Tank

**Bask** Apricate, Revel, Sun, WALLOW

**Basket, Basket-work** Baalam, Bass, Bassinet, Bread, Buck, Cabas, Calathus, Canephorus, Cob, Coop, Corbeil(le), Corbicula, Corf, Creel, Cresset, Dosser, Fan, Flasket, Frail, Gabion, Hamper, Hask, Junket, Kago, Kajawah, Kipe, Kit, Leap, Maund, Mocock, Mocuck, Moses, Murlain, Murlan, Murlin, Osiery, Pannier, Ped, Petara, Pitara(h), Pottle, Punnet, Rip, Scull, Scuttle, Seed-lip, Skep, Skull, Trug, Van, Wagger-pagger(-bagger), Wattlework, Whisket, Will(e), Wisket

**Basket-bearer** Canephor(a), Canephore, Canephorus

**Basket-maker** Alfa, Cane, Halfa, Wicker

**Basque** Euskarian

**Bass** Ale, Alfie, Continuo, Deep, El-a-mi, Fish, Low, Serran

**Bast** Liber

**Bastard, Bastard-wing** Alula, Base, By-blow, Git, Illegitimate, Mongrel, Sassaby, Side-slip, Slink, Spuriae, Spurious, Whoreson

> **Bastard** may indicate an anagram

**Baste** Enlard, Sew, Stitch, Tack

**Bastion** Citadel, Lunette, Moineau

**Bat(ter), Bats, Batting, Batsman, Batty** Aliped, Ames, Assail, Barbastelle, Baton, Blink, Chiroptera, Close, Cosh, Crackers, Dad, Eyelid, Flittermouse, Grace, Hatter, Haywire, Hit, Hobbs, Hook, In, Kalong, Language, Leisler, Maul, May, Mormops, Myopic, Nictate, Night, Nightwatchman, Noctilio, Opener, Pinch-hit, Poke, Pummel, Racket, Racquet, Ram, Rearmouse, Reremice, Reremouse, Roussette, Ruin, Sauch, Saugh, Serotine, Stick, Stonewall, Striker, Swat, Vampire, Viv, Whacky, Willow, Wood

**Batch** Bake, Bunch

**Bath(room)** Aeson's, Bagnio, Bain-marie, Caldarium, Cor, En suite, Epha, Hammam, Hip, Hummaum, Hummum, Jacuzzi, Laver, Mustard, Piscina, Sauna, Stew, Tepidarium, Therm, Tub, Tye, Wife

**Bathe, Bathing** Balneal, Balneation, Balneology, Bay(e), Beath, Bogey, Bogie, Dip, Dook, Embay, Foment, Immerse, Lave, Lip, Souse, Splash, Stupe, SWIM, Tub, WASH

**Batman** Valet

**Baton** Mace, Rod, Sceptre, Staff, Truncheon

**Batrachian** Frog, Toad

> **Bats, Batting** may indicate an anagram

**Battalion** Bn, Corps, Troop

**Batten** Fasten, Tie

**Batter(ed)** Bombard, Bruise, Decrepit, Pound

**Battery** Artillery, Drycell, Henhouse, Nicad, Pra(a)m, Troop, Waffle

**Battle, Battleground** Aboukir, Accra, Action, Actium, Affair, Agincourt, Alamein, Alamo, Allia, Alma, Arcot, Ardennes, Argyle, Armageddon, Arnhem, Arras, Balaclava, Bannockburn, Beaches, Ben, Blenheim, Borodino, Bosworth, Boyne, Britain, Bulge, Bull Run, Bunkers Hill, Cambrai, Camlan, Camperdown, Cannae, Caporetto, Clash, Cockpit, Colenso, Combat, CONFLICT, Coronel, Corunna, Crecy, Culloden, Dunkirk, Edgehill, Encounter, Engagement, Field, FIGHT, Flanders, Flodden, Flowers, Fray, Front, Gallipoli, Gettysburg, Glencoe, Hastings, Hohenlinden, Inkerman, Issus, Ivry, Jena, Joust, Jutland, Kut, Laon, Lepanto, Lewes, Loos, Magenta, Maldon, Marathon, Marengo, Marne, Marston Moor, Mons, Naseby, Nations, Navarino, Nile, Omdurman, Otterburn, Oudenarde, Parma, Passchendaele, Pharsalia, Philippi, Picardy, Plassey, Poitiers, Prestonpans, Ragnarok, Ramillies, Royal, Salamis, Sarah, Saratoga, Sciamachy, Sedan, Sedgemoor, Senlac, Shiloh, Skiamachy, Solferino, Somme, Spurs, Stoor, Stour, Stowre, Talavera, Theatre, Trafalgar, Ulm, Varese, Verdun, Vigrid, Wage, Wagram, WAR, Warburg, Waterloo, Wipers, Worcester, Ypres, Zama

**Battle-axe** Amazon, Bill, Gorgon, Halberd, Ogress, Sparth(e), Termagent, Turmagent

**Battlement** Barmkin, Crenellate, Merlon, Rampart

**Battle-order** Phalanx

**Battleship** Carrier, Destroyer, Dreadnought, Gunboat, Man-o'-war, Potemkin

**Bauble** Bagatelle, Gaud, Gewgaw, Trifle

**Bauhaus** Gropius

**Baulk** Demur, Gib, Hen, Impede, Jib, Shy, Thwart

**Bavardage** Fadaise

**Bawdy** Raunchy, Sculdudd(e)ry, Skulduddery

**Bawl** Bellow, Gollar, Howl, Weep

**Bay** Arm, Baffin, Bantry, Bark, Bell, Bengal, Bight, Biscay, Botany, Cardigan, Cove, Covelet, Creek, Daphne, Fleet, Harbour, Herne, Horse, HOWL, Hudson, Inlet, Laura, Laurel, MA, Massachusetts, Niche, Oleander, Oriel, Pigs, Recess, Red, Roan, Sligo, Suvla, Tampa, Tralee, Vae, Voe, Waff, Wash

**Bayonet** Jab, Skewer, Stab

**Bazaar** Alcaiceria, Emporium, Fair, Fete, Market, Pantechnicon, Sale, Sook, Souk

**BBC** Auntie

**Be** Exist, Live

**Beach** Bondi, Coast, Ground, Hard, Lido, Littoral, Machair, Miami, Plage, Sand, Seaside, Shingle, Shore, Strand

**Beachcomber** Arenaria

**Beacon** Belisha, Fanal, Need-fire, Pharos, Racon, Signal

**Bead(s)** Aggri, Aggry, Baily's, Bauble, Blob, Bugle, Chaplet, Crab-stones, Drop, Gadroon, Gaud, Moniliform, Ojime, Paternoster, Poppet, Poppit, Rosary, Tear, Wampum(peag), Worry

**Beadle** Apparitor, Bederal, Bedral, Bumble, Herald, Paritor, Verger

**Beak** AMA, Bill, Cad, Cere, Gar, JP, Kip(p), Magistrate, Master, Metagnathous, Mittimus, Nasute, Neb, Nose, Pecker, Prow, Ram, Rostellum, Rostrum

**Beak-shaped** Coracoid

**Beaker** Cup, Goblet

**Beakless** Erostrate

**Beam(ing)** Arbor, Bar, Boom, Breastsummer, Bressummer, Broadcast, Bum(p)kin, Cantilever, Cathead, Girder, Grin, Herisson, Holophote, I, Irradiate, Joist, Laser, Lentel, Needle, Outrigger, Principal, Purlin, RAFTER, RAY, Rayon, Refulgent, Rident, Scantling, Shaft, Shine, Sleeper, Smile, Solive, Stemson, Streamer, Stringer, Summer, Support, Tie, Timber, Trabeate, Transom, Trave, Yard

**Beamish** Galumphing, Nephew

**Bean** Abrus, Adsuki, Arabica, Berry, Borlotti, Cacao, Calabar, Cocoa, Cow-pea, Fabaceous, Flageolet, Frijol(e), Haricot, Harmala, Head, Lablab, Lentil, Lima, Locust, Molucca, Mung, Nelumbo, Nib, Noddle, Ordeal, Pichurim, Soy(a), Tonga, Tonka, Tonquin, Urd

**Beanfeast** PARTY, Spree, Wayzgoose

**Bear(er), Bearish** Andean, Arctic, Baloo, Balu, Beer, Bigg, Breed, Brook, Bruin, Brunt, CARRY, Churl, Coati-mundi, Coati-mondi, Demean, Dree, Ean, ENDURE, Engender, Exert, Fur-seal, Gonfalonier, Hack, Ham(m)al, Have, Hold, Humf, Hump(h), Jampani, Koala, Kinkajou, Kodiak, Koolah, Lioncel(le), Lionel, Lug, Mother, Nandi, Owe, Paddington, Panda, Polar, Pooh, Rac(c)oon, Rupert, Russia, Sackerson, Seller, Shoulder, Sit, Sloth, Stand, Stay, Stomach, SUFFER, Sustain, Targeteer, Teddy, Teem, Throw, Tolerate, Tote, Undergo, Upstay, Ursine, Whelp, Wield, Yield

**Bearberry** Manzanita

**Beard(ed)** Arista, Awn, Balaclava, Barb, Beaver, Charley, Charlie, Confront, Defy, Face, Fungus, Goatee, Hair(ie), Hairy, Hear(ie), Imperial, Mephistopheles, Outface, Peak, Rivet, Vandyke, Whiskerando, Whiskery, Ziff

**Beardless** Callow, Clean, Tahr, Tehr

> **Bearhug** may indicate Teddy or similar around a word

**Bearing(s)** Air, Amenaunce, Armorial, Aspect, Azimuth, Ball, Bush, Carriage, Deportment, Direction, E, Endurance, Gait, Hatchment, Manner, Mascle, Mien, N, Nor, Pheon, Port, Presence, Reference, Relevant, S, Tenue, W, Yielding

> **Bearing** may indicate compass points

**Beast** ANIMAL, Behemoth, Brute, Caliban, Caribou, CREATURE, Dieb, Dragon, Gayal, Genet, Grampus, Hippogriff, Hog, Hy(a)ena, Jumart, Kinkajou, Lion, Mammoth, Marmot, Mastodon, Oliphant, Opinicus, Oryx, Panda, Potto, Quagga, Rac(c)oon, Rhytina, Rother, Sassaby, Steer, Sumpter, Tarand, Teg, Triceratops, Wart-hog, Whangam, Yahoo, Yak, Zizel

**Beat(er), Beaten, Beating** Anoint, Arsis, Athrob, Bandy, Baste, Bastinado, Batter, Battue, Belabour, Belt, Bepat, Best, Blatter, Bless, Cadence, Cane, Chastise, Clobber, Club, Clump, Conquer, Curry, Debel, DEFEAT, Ding, Dress, Drub, Excel, Fatigue, Faze, Feeze, Fibbed, Flagellate, Flail, Flam, Float, Flog, Floor, Flush, Fly, Fustigate, Hollow, Horsewhip, Ictus, Inteneration, Knock, Knubble, Lace, Laldie, Lambast(e), Laveer, Lay, Lick, Lilt, Lounder, Mall, Malleate, Nubble, Outclass, Outflank, Outstrip, Paik, Palpitate, Pash, Paste, Pommel, Pound, Prat, Pug, Pulsate, Pulse, Pulsedge, Pummel, Pun, Quop, Raddle, Ram, Ratten, Resolve, Retreat, Rhythm, Round, Rowstow, Ruff(le), Scourge, Slat, Smight, Smite, Soak, Sock, Strak, Strike, Swinge, Taber, Tabrere, Tact, Tala, Tattoo, Thesis, Thrash, Thresh, Throb, Thud, Thump, Thwack, Tick, Tired, Top, Trounce, Tuck, Tund, Verberate, Vibrate, Wallop, Wappend, Welt, Wham, Whip, Whisk, Whitewash, Wraught, Ybet, Yerk, Yirk

> **Beaten-up** may indicate an anagram

**Beat it** Skedaddle, Vamo(o)se

**Beatitude** Macarism

**Beau** Admirer, Blade, Brummel, Cat, Damoiseau, Dandy, Flame, Geste, Lover, Masher, Nash, Spark, Tibbs

**Beaufort** Scale, Windscale

**Beaut(y)** Advantage, Belle, Camberwell, Charmer, Colleen, Corker, Dish, Glory, Houri, Hyperion, Lana, Picture, Pulchritude, Purler, Sheen, Smasher, Stunner

**Beautiful, Beautify** Bonny, Bright, Embellish, Enhance, Fair, Fine, Ornament, Pink, Smicker, Specious, To kalon

**Beauty spot** Patch, Tempe, Tika

**Beaver** Beard, Castor, Eager, Grind, Oregon, Rodent, Sewellel

**Because (of)** As, Forasmuch, Forwhy, In, Sens, Since

**Beckon** Gesture, Nod, Summons, Waft, Wave

**Become, Becoming** Besort, Decent, Decorous, Enter, Fall, Fit, Get, Go, Grow, Happen, Occur, Seemly, Suit, Wax

**Bed(ding), Bedstead** Air, Allotment, Amenity, Arroyo, Base, Bassinet, Berth, Bottom, Bunk, Charpoy, Cill, Cot, Couch(ette), Cradle, Crib, Cul(t)ch, Cott, Divan, Doss, Duvet, Erf, Flying, Four-poster, Futon, Greensand, Hammock, Inlay, Kang, Kip, Layer, Litter, Mat, Matrix, Mattress, Nest, Nookie, Pad, Paillasse, Pallet, Palliasse, Pan, Parterre, Plant, Plot, Procrustean, Quilt, Sack, Scalp, Shakedown, Sill, Sitter, Sleep,

Stratum, Stretcher, Thill, Trough, Truckle, Wadi, Wady, Ware, Water, Wealden

**Bedaub** Cake, Deck, Smear

**Bed-bug** B, B flat, Chinch, Flea, Louse, Vermin

**Bedchamber, Bedroom** Chamber, Cubicle, Dormer, Dorm(itory), Dorter, Ruelle, Ward

**Bedcover** Palampore, Palempore

**Bedeck** Adonise, Adorn, Array, Festoon

> **Bedevilled** may indicate an anagram

**Bedjacket** Nightingale

**Bedlam** Chaos, Furore, Madness, Nuthouse, Tumult, Uproar

**Bed-rest** Dutch-wife

**Bee** Athenia, Bumble, Deseret, Drone, Drumbledor, Dumbledore, Group, Hiver, Honey, Humble, King, Lapidary, Leaf-cutter, Mason, Queen, Spell, Spell-down, Swarm, Worker

**Beech** Hornbeam, Mast, Tree

**Bee-eater** Merops

**Beef(y)** Baron, Brawny, Bull(y), Bullock, Charqui, Chuck, Complain, Corned, Groan, Grouse, Jerk, Liebig, Mart, Mice, Mousepiece, Ox, Pastrami, Peeve, Porterhouse, Rother, Sey, Silverside, Sirloin, Stolid, Tournedos, Tranche, Undercut, Vaccine

**Beefeater** Billman, Exon, Gin, Oxpecker, Warder, Yeoman

**Bee-glue** Propolis

**Beehive** Alveary, Ball, Gum, Skep

**Beelzebub** Devil

**Beer** Ale, Alegar, Bitter, Bock, Chaser, Drink, Entire, Gill, Granny, Grog, Heavy, Kvass, Lager, Lush, Malt, Mild, Mum, Nog, October, Pils(e)ner, Pint, Pony, Porter, Root, Saki, Scoobs, Sherbet, Skeechan, Spruce, Stingo, Stout, Swanky, Swats, Swipes, Switchel, Taplash, Tinnie, Tipper, Tube, Wallop, Zythum

**Beer garden** Brasserie

**Bee's nest** Bink

**Beet** Blite, Chard, Fat-hen, Goosefoot, Mangel(wurzel), Spinach

**Beetle** Ambrosia, Anobiid, Batler, Bug, Bruchid, Bum-clock, Buprestidae, Buprestus, Bustle, Buzzard-clock, Cadelle, Cantharis, Carabus, Chafer, Cicindela, Clock, Cockchafer, Cockroach, Coleoptera, Colorado, Coprophagan, Dermestid, Dor(r), Dor-fly, Dumbledore, Dyticus, Dytiscus, Elater, Elytron, Elytrum, Firefly, Goliath, Hammer, Hangover, Hercules, Hornbug, Huhu, Humbuzz, Impend, Ladybird, Ladybug, Lamellicorne, Longhorn, Longicorn, Mall(et), Maul, May-bug, Meloid, Overhang, Project, Roach, Rosechafer, Rove, Scarab(ee), Scurry, Skelter, Sledge(-hammer), Stag, Tenebrio, Toktokkie, Turnip-flea, Typographer, Vedalia, VW, Weevil, Whirligig, Wireworm, Woodborer, Wood-engraver

**Beetle-crushers** Cops

**Befall** Happen, Occur

**Before(hand)** A, Advance, Ante, Avant, By, Coram, Earlier, Early, Ere, Erst(while), FORMER, Or, Pre, Previously, Prior, Sooner, Till, To, Until, Van

**Before food** Ac

**Befriend** Assist, Fraternise, Support

**Befuddle** Bemuse, Inebriate, Stupefy

**Beg(gar), Begging** Abr(ah)am-man, Ask, Badgeman, Beseech, Besognio, Bey, Bezonian, Blighter, Blue-gown, Cadge, Calendar, Clapper-dudgeon, Crave, ENTREAT, Exoration, Fleech, Gaberlunzie, Hallan-shaker, Implore, Impoverish, Irus, Jarkman, Lackall, Lazar, Lazzarone, Maund, Mendicant, Mump, Palliard, Panhandle, Pauper, Penelophon, Penniless, PLEAD, Pled, Pray, Prig, Prog, Ptochocracy, Rag, Randie, Randy, Ruffler, Sadhu, Schnorr(er), Skelder, Skell, Solicit, Sue, Supplicate, Thig(ger), Toe-rag, Touch, Undo, Whipjack

**Beggar rule** Ptochocracy

**Begging bowl** Clackdish, Clapdish

**Begin(ning), Begun** Ab ovo, Alpha, B, Cause, Clapdash, Commence, Daw, Dawn, Debut, Embryo, Enter, Exordium, Fall-to, Go, Inaugural, Inception, Inchoate, Incipient, Initial, Initiate, Intro, Lead, Learn, Logos, Nascent, Onset, Ope(n), Ord, ORIGIN, Pose, Prelim(inary), Seed, Set, START, Yearn

**Beginner** Author, Black, Greenhorn, L, Learner, Neophyte, NOVICE, Primer, Rookie, Tiro, Tyro

**Begonia** Elephant's-ear(s)

**Begone** Aroint, Aroynt, Avaunt, Scram, Shoo, Vamo(o)se

**Begorrah** Bedad, Musha

**Begrudge** Envy, Resent

**Beguile(r)** Charm, Divert, Ensnare, Flatter, Gull, Intrigue, Jack-a-lantern, Wile

**Behalf** For, Part, Sake

**Behave, Behaviour** Act, Conduct, Demean, Do, Etepimeletic, Ethics, Horme, MANNER, Obey, Quit, React, Response

**Behead** Decapitate, Decollate

**Behind(hand)** Abaft, Aft(er), Ahind, Ahint, Apoop, Arear, Arere, Arrear, Astern, Bottom, Bum, Buttocks, Croup, Derriere, Fud, Late, Prat, REAR, Slow, Tushie

**Behold(en)** Affine, Ecce, Eye, Indebted, La, Lo, Look, Observe, See, View

**Being** Creature, Ens, Entia, Entity, Esse, Essence, Existence, Human, Man, Metaphysics, Mode, Nature, Omneity, Ontology, PERSON, Saul, Soul, Subsistent, Substance, Wight

**Bejabers** Arrah

**Belch** Brash, Burp, Emit, Eruct, Rift, Spew, Yex

**Belcher** Foulard, Handkerchief, Toby

**Beldam(e)** Crone, Hag, Harridan, Scold

**Belfry** Campanile, Tower

**Belgian** Flemish, Walloon

**Belief, Believe(r), Believing** Accredit, Ativism, Bigot, Buy, Conviction, Credence, Credit, Creed, Cult, Deist, Doctrine, Doxastic, Faith, Gnostic, Hold, Holist, Islam, Methink, OPINION, Pantheism, Persuasion, Presumption, Seeing, Solfidian, Superstition, Tenet, Theist, Think, Trow, Trust, Wear, Wis(t)

**Belittle** Cheapen, Decry, Depreciate, Derogate, Discredit, Disparage, Humble, Slight

**Bell(s)** Angelus, Ben, Bob, Bow, Bronte, Cachecope, Carillon, Chime, Crotal, Curfew, Daisy, Gong, Grandsire, Jar, Low, Lutine, Passing, Pavilion, Peal, Peter, Pinger, Ring, Roar, Sacring, Sanctus, Tailor, Tantony, Tenor, Tent, Tintinnabulum, Toll, Tom, Triple, Vair

**Bell-bird** Arapunga, Campanero

**Belle** Beauty, Starr, Toast, Venus

**Bell-founder** Belleter

**Bellicose, Belligerent** Combatant, Hostile, Jingoist, Martial, Militant, Truculent, Warmonger

**Bellow(s)** Buller, Holla, Holler, Moo, Rant, Rave, Roar, Saul, Thunder, Troat, Tromp(e), Trumpet, Windbag

**Bell-ringer, Bell-ringing** Bob, Campanology, Changes, Clapper, Course, Quasimodo, Rope, Sally, Tocsin, Toller

**Belly** Abdomen, Alvine, Bag, Bunt, Calipee, Celiac, Coeliac, Kite, Kyte, Pod, STOMACH, Swell, Tum(my), Venter, Wame, Weamb, Wem(b), Womb

**Belonging(s)** Apply, Appurtenant, Chattels, Effects, Inhere, Intrinsic, Paraphernalia, Pertain, PROPERTY, Relate, Traps

**Beloved** Dear, Esme, Inamorata, Joy, Lief, Pet, Popular, Precious

**Below** Beneath, Inf(erior), Infra, Nether, Sub, Under, Unneath

**Belt(ed)** Baldric(k), Band, Bandoleer, Bandolier, Baudric(k), Bible, Clitellum, Clobber, Conveyor, Equator, Gird(le), Girt, Inertial, Larrup, Lonsdale, Orion, Polt, Pound, Sash, Speed, Strap, Surcingle, Stratosphere, Swipe, Taiga, Tear, Tore, Van Allen, Wanty, Webbing, Wing, Zodiac, Zone, Zoster

**Belt up** Sh

**Belvedere** Gazebo, Mirador

**Bemoan** LAMENT, Mourn, Sigh, Wail

**Bemuse** Infatuate, Stonn(e), Stun, Stupefy, Throw

**Ben** Battle, Hur, Jonson, Mountain, Nevis, Spence

**Bench**  Banc, Bink, Counter, Court, Exedra, Form, Knifeboard, Magistrates, Pew, Rusbank, SEAT, Settle, Siege, Stillage, Thoft, Thwart, Trestle

**Benchmark**  Yardstick

**Bend(er), Bending, Bends**  Angle, Arc, Arch, Articular, Bight, Binge, Buck(le), Bust, Camber, Carrick, Circumflect, Chicane, Corner, Crank(le), Cringe, CROOK, Curl, Curve, Dog-leg, Engouled, Epinasty, Es(s), Falcate, Fawn, Flex(ural), Fold, Geller, Geniculate, Genu, Genuflect, Grecian, Hairpin, Hinge, Hook, Horseshoe, Hunch, Knee(cap), Kneel, Kowtow, Mould, Nutant, Ox-bow, Plash, Plié, Recline, Reflex, Retorsion, Retortion, Retroflex, Riband, S, Scarp, Souse, Spree, Spring, Stoop, Swan-neck, Twist, U, Ups(e)y, Uri, Wale, Warp, YIELD, Z

> **Bendy**  may indicate an anagram

**Beneath**  Below, Sub, Under, Unworthy

**Benedict(ine)**  Cluniac, Dom, Eggs, Olivetan, Tironensian, Tyronensian

**Benefactor**  Angel, Backer, Barmecide, Carnegie, Donor, Maecenas, PATRON, Promoter

**Benefice, Beneficial, Beneficiary, Benefit**  Avail, Behalf, Behoof, Behove, Boon, Boot, Charity, Commendam, Commensal, Devisee, Dole, Donee, Enure, Fringe, Incumbent, Inure, Living, Ménage, Neckverse, Pay, Perk, Perquisite, Portioner, Prebend, Profit, Sake, Salutary, Sanative, Sinecure, Spin-off, Stipend, Use, Usufruct

**Benevolence, Benevolent**  Charitable, Clement, Humanitarian, Kind, Liberal, Philanthropy

**Benighted**  Ignorant

**Benign**  Affable, Altruistic, Gracious, Kindly, Trinal

**Benito**  Duce, Mussolini

**Benjamin**  Franklin

**Bennett**  Alan, Phil

**Bent**  Akimbo, Bowed, Brae, Coudé, Courb, Crooked, Curb, Determined, Falcate, Flair, Heath, Inclination, Ingenium, Intent, Leant, Peccant, Penchant, Ply, Reclinate, Scoliotic, Talent, Taste

> **Bent**  may indicate an anagram

**Bent grass**  Fiorin, Redtop

**Bentham**  Utilitarian

**Benzine**  Kinone, Phene, Toluene, Toluol

**Bequeath, Bequest**  Bestow, Chantr(e)y, Endow, Heirloom, LEAVE, Legacy, Mortification, Transmit, Will

**Berate**  Censure, Chide, Jaw, Reproach, Scold, Slate, Vilify

**Berber**  Kabyle, Riff, Tuareg

**Bereave(d), Bereavement**  Deprive, Loss, Mourning, Orb, Sorrow, Strip, Widow

**Berg** Alban, Floe

**Bermuda** Shorts

**Bernard** Levin, Shaw

**Bernini** Baroque

**Berry** Allspice, Bacca, Cubeb, Fruit, Goosegog, Haw, Pepo, Pottage, Rhein, Rhine, Sal(l)al, Slae, Sloe, Sop

**Berserk** Amok, Baresark, Frenzy, Gungho, Rage

**Berth** Anchorage, Bunk, Cabin, Couchette, Dock, Moor, Seat, Space

**Beryl** Aquamarine, Emerald, Heliodor, Morganite, Silica

**Beryllium** Be

**Beseech** Beg, Crave, Entreat, Implore, Invoke, Obsecrate

**Beset** Assail, Assiege, Badger, Bego, Environ, Harry, Perplex

**Beside(s)** Adjacent, Alone, And, At, Else, Forby, Moreover, Next, On, Withal

**Besiege(d)** Best(ed), Blockade, Gherao, Girt, Invest, Plague, Surround

> **Besiege** may indicate one word around another

**Besmirch** Smear, Soil, Sully

**Besot(ted)** Dotard, Infatuate, Intoxicate, Lovesick, Stupefy

**Bespangle** Adorn, Gem

**Bespeak, Bespoken** Address, Bee, Beta, Engage, Hint

**Best** A1, Ace, Aristocrat, Beat, Choice, Cream, Creme, Damnedest, Elite, Eximious, Finest, Flower, Foremost, Greatest, Ideal, Optima, Outdo, Outwit, Overcome, Peak, Peerless, Pick, Pink, Plum, Ream, Super, The, Tiptop, Top, Topper, Transcend, Wale

**Best man** Paranymph

**Bestow** Accord, Bequeath, Donate, GIVE, Impart, Present

**Bestride** Cross

**Bet, Betting System** Ante, Back, Double, Flutter, Gaff, Gamble, Go, Hedge, Impone, Lay, Martingale, Mise, Note, Pari-mutuel, Perfecta, Punt, Quadrella, Quinella, Ring, Risk, Saver, Set, Spec, Sport, Stake, Tattersalls, Tatts, Treble, Triella, Trifecta, WAGE(R), Yankee

**Betel** Catechu, Pan, Pawn, Siri(h)

**Betimes** Anon, Early, Soon

**Betise** Solecism

**Betray(al), Betrayer** Abandon, Abuse, Belewe, Cornuto, Desert, Divulge, Dob, Grass, Judas, Renegade, Renege, Rumble, Sell, Shop, Sing, Sinon, Traditor, Traitor, Treason, Turncoat

**Betroth(ed), Betrothal** Engage, Ensure, Espouse, Fiancé(e), Pledge, Subarrhation

**Better** Abler, Amend, Apter, Bigger, Buck, Cap, Gambler, Imponent, Improve, Meliorate, Mend, Outdo, Outpoint, Preponderate, Race-goer,

Reform, Superior, Surpass, Throw, Top, Turfite, Worst

**Between** Amid, Betwixt, Inter, Linking

**Bevel** Angle, Cant, Oblique, Slope, Splay

**Beverage** Ale, Cocoa, Coffee, Cordial, Cup, DRINK, Nectar, Tea

**Bevy** Flock, Group, Herd, Host

**Beware** Cave, Fore, Heed, Mind, Mistrust

**Bewilder(ment)** Amaze, Baffle, Buffalo, Confuse, Daze, Flummox, Mate, Maze, Perplex, Stun, Will, Wull

**Bewitch(ing)** Charm, Delight, Enchant, Ensorcell, Glam(orous), Hex, Jinx, Obeah, Obiah, Strike

**Beyond** Above, Ayont, Besides, Farther, Over, Thule, Trans, Ulterior

**Bias(ed)** Angle, Bent, Imbalance, Partial, Partisan, Penchant, Predilection, PREJUDICE, Prepossess, Skew, Slope, Tendency, Warp

**Bib, Bibulous** Apron, Beery, Feeder, Pout, Tope, Tucker

**Bibelot** Objet d'art

**Bible** Alcoran, Alkoran, Antilegomena, AV, Avesta, Bamberg, Book, Breeches, Coverdale, Cranmer, Cromwell, Douai, Douay, Gemara, Geneva, Gideon, Goose, Gospel, Hexapla, Itala, Italic, Leda, Mazarin, Midrash, Missal, Murderer, NT, Omasum, OT, Pentateuch, Peshito, Peshitta, Peshitto, Polyglot, RV, Scriptures, Stomach, Talmud, Tanach, Tantra, Targum, Taverners, Vinegar, Vulgate, Whig, Wyclif(fe), Zurich

**Biblical scholar** Rechabite, USPG, Wycliffe

**Bibliophagist, Bibliophile** Bookworm

**Bicker** Argue, Bowl, Brawl, Coggie, Dispute, Tiff, Wrangle

**Bicycle, Bike** Bone-shaker, Coaster Dandy-horse, Draisene, Draisine, Hobby, Mixte, Moped, Mount, Ordinary, Pedal, Penny-farthing, Raleigh (tdmk), Roadster, Safety, Scooter, Spin, Tandem, Velocipede

**Bid** Apply, Call, Canape, Command, Contract, Declare, Double, Gone, Invite, Misère, Nod, NT, OFFER, Order, Pass, Pre-empt, Proposal, Redouble, Summon, Take-over, Tell, Tender, Vied

**Biddy** Gammer

**Biennial** Trieteric

**Bier** Hearse, Litter

**Big** Beamy, Bulky, Bumper, Burly, Cob, Enormous, Fat, Gross, LARGE, Loud, Massive, Mighty, Obese, Skookum, Slockdoliger, Slockdologer, Soc(k)dologer, Sogdolager, Sogdoliger, Thumping, Tidy, Vast, Whacker, Whopper

**Bigamy, Bigamist, Bigamous** Bluebeard, Diandrous

**Bigot(ed)** Chauvinist, Fanatic, Hide-bound, Intolerant, Racialist, Wowser, Zealot

**Bigshot, Bigwig** Cheese, Nob, Oner, Oneyer, Oneyre, Swell, VIP

**Bijou** Doll-like

**> Bike** see BICYCLE

**Bikini** Atoll, Tanga

**Bile, Bilious(ness)** Cholaemia, Choler, Gall, Icteric, Melancholy, Scholaemia, Venom

**Bilge** Leak, Pump, Rot, Waste

**Bilingual** Diglot

**Bill(y)** Ac(c), Accompt, Account, Act, Ad, Addition, Barnacle, Beak, Becke, Budd, Buffalo, Can, Carte, Chit(ty), Cody, Coo, Coronoid, Dixy, Docket, Exactment, Fin, Goat, Invoice, Kaiser, LAW, Lawin(g), Legislation, Liam, Liar, List, Measure, Menu, Neb, Ness, Nib, NOTE, Notice, Poster, Programme, Reckoning, Remanet, Rhamphotheca, Rostral, Rostrum, Score, Shot, Sickle, Silly, Spoon, Sticker, Tab, Tomium, Willy

**Billet** Berth, Casern, Chit, Note, Quarter

**Billet doux** Capon, Valentine

**Billiards, Billiards player, Billiards stroke** Bar, Cueist, Jenny, Massé, Pool, Potter, Pyramids, Snooker

**Billion** Gillion, Milliard, Tera

**Bill of sale** Bs

**Billow** Roil, Roller, Rule, Surge, Swell, Wave

**Bin** Bing, Box, Container, Crib, Hell, Receptacle, Snake-pit, Stall

**Binary** ASCII

**Bind(er), Binding** Adherent, Akedah, Apprentice, Astrict, Astringent, Bale, Bandage, Bandeau, Bias, Bibliopegist, Brail, Calf, Chain, Cinch, Clamp, Colligate, Complain, Cord, Cummerbund, Deligation, Drag, Edge, Embale, Enchain, Engage, FASTEN, Fetter, Galloon, Gird, Girdle, Grolier, Hay-wire, Hold, Incumbent, Indenture, Iron, Keckle, Lash(er), Leash, Ligament, Ligature, Mail, Morocco, Muslin, Obligate, Oblige, Oop, Organdie, Oup, Pinion, Raffia, Restrict, ROPE, Roxburghe, Sheaf, Strap, Stringent, Swathe, Syndesis, Tether, Thirl, Thong, Tie, Tree-calf, Truss, Twine, Valid, Whip, Withe, Yapp, Yerk, Yoke

**Bindweed** Bearbine, Convolvulus, With(y)wind

**Bing** Crosby, Go, Heap

**Binge** Bat, Beano, Bend(er), Carouse, DRINK, Drinking-bout, Party, Riot, Soak, Souse, Spree, Toot, Tout

**Bingo** Beano, Housey-housey, Lotto, Tombola

**Binoculars** Glasses, OO

**Biochemical** DNA

**Biographer, Biography** Boswell, CV, Hagiography, History, Life, Memoir, Plutarch, Potted, Prosopography, Suetonius, Vita

**Bioscope** Kinema

**Birch** Birk, Cane, Cow, Flog, Hazel, Kow, Larch, Reis, Rice, Rod, Swish, Twig, Whip, Withe

**Bird** Aasvogel, Aberdevine, Accentor, Adjutant, Aepyornis, Agami,
Aigrette, Albatross, Alcatras, Al(l)erion, Altrices, Amadavat, Anhinga, Ani,
Apteryx, Aquiline, Arapunga, Archaeopteryx, Ardea, Ariel, Auk, Aves,
Avian, Avocet, Avoset, Aylesbury, Babbler, Baldicoot, Baltimore, Bantam,
Barb, Barbet, Barnacle, Becasse, Beccaccia, Beccafico, Bennu, Bergander,
Bertram, Bishop, Bittern, Bitto(u)r, Bittur, Blackbird, Blackcap, Blackhead,
Bluecap, Blue-eye, Blue jay, Bluethroat, Blue-wing, Boatbill, Boattail,
Bobolink, Bob-white, Boo(book), Booby, Bosun, Bower-bird, Brambling,
Bronze-pigeon, Brood, Bubbly-jock, Budgerigar, Bulbul, Bullbat,
Buln-buln, Bunting, Buphaga, Bush-tit, Bustard, Butter-bump, Buzzard,
Campanero, Capon, Caracara, Cargoose, Cariama, Cassowary, Chaffinch,
Chat, Che(e)wink, Chickadee, Chiff-chaff, Chirn-owl, Chough, Chukar,
Cirl, Coal-tit, Cob(b), Cockatiel, Cockatoo, Cole-tit, Colibri, Colin, Colly,
Condor, Coot, Corbie, Corella, Cormorant, Corncrake, Cotinga, Coucal,
Courlan, Courser, Cow-bird, Crane, Crax, Creeper, Cross-bill, Crow,
Cuckoo, Curassow, Curlew, Currawong, Cushat, Dabchick, Damsel, Darter,
Demoiselle, Dickcissel, Didapper, Didunculus, Dikkop, Dip-chick, Dipper,
Diver, Dobchick, Dodo, Doll, Dott(e)rel, Dove, Dovekie, Dowitcher,
Drongo(-cuckoo), Drongo-shrike, Dunlin, Dunnock, Early, Egret, Elanet,
Ember-goose, Emeu, Emu(-wren), Erne, Estreldid, Estridge, Evejar,
Eyas(-musket), Falcon, Fantail, Fauvette, Fieldfare, Finch, Fire-crest,
Fish-hawk, Flamingo, Fledgling, Fleet, Flier, Fly-catcher, Fowl, Francolin,
Fringillid, Frogmouth, Fulmar, Fum, Fung, Gal, Galah, Gallinule, Gambet,
Gander, Gannet, Garefowl, Garganey, Garuda, Gentle, Gerfalcon,
Gier-eagle, GIRL, Gled(e), Goatsucker, Gobemouche, Goburra, Godwit,
Goldfinch, Goosander, Goose, Gorcrow, Goshawk, Goura, Gra(c)kle,
Grallae, Grallatores, Grebe, Greenlet, Greenshank, Grenadier, Grip,
Grosbeak, Guacharo, Guan, Guga, Guillemot, Gull, Hackbolt, Hacklet,
Hagbolt, Hagden, Hagdo(w)n, Haglet, Halcyon, Hangbird, Hangnest,
Hawk, Hen, Hermit, Hern, Heron, Her(o)nshaw, Hoa(c)tzin, Hobby,
Homer, Honey-sucker, Hoopoe, Hornbill, Houdan, Huia, Huma,
Humming(-bird), Ibis, Ice-bird, Icteridae, Impundulu, Isaac, Iynx, Jabiru,
Jacamar, Jacana, Jack-snipe, Junco, Jynx, Ka(e), Kaka(po), Kamichi, Kea,
Kestrel, Kight, Killdee(r), Kingfisher, Kinglet, Kiskadee, Kite, Kittiwake,
Kiwi, Knot, Kookaburra, Kora, Landrail, Lanner(et), Lapwing, Lark,
Laverock, Leatherhead, Leghorn, Leipoa, Limpkin, Linnet, Lintie,
Lintwhite, Liver, Loon, Lorikeet, Loriot, Lory, Lourie, Lowan, Lungie,
Lyre, Macaw, Madge, Magotpie, Magpie, Mallemuck, Manakin, Manch,
Maribou, Martin, Martlet, Mavis, Maw, Megapode, Menura, Merganser,
Merle, Merlin, Merops, Mesites, Mina, Minivet, Mire-drum, Missel, Moa,
Mollymawk, Monal, Monaul, Monk, Mopoke, Morepork, Moss-bluiter,
Moss-cheeper, Mossie, Motmot, Murre(let), Musket, Myna(h), Nandoo,
Nandu, Nelly, Noddy, Notornis, Nun, Nutcracker, Nuthatch, Nutjobber,
Oriole, Ornis, Ortolan, Oscires, Osprey, Ossifraga, Ossifrage, Ostrich, Otis,
Ousel, Ovenbird, Ox-eye, Oxpecker, Oyster-catcher, Pandion, Paradise,
Pardalote, Parrot, Pavo(ne), Peacock, Peahen, Peaseweep, Pecker, Peewee,
Peetweet, Peewit, Peggy, Pekan, Pelican, Pen, Penguin, Percolin, Peregrine,
Pern(is), Petchary, Petrel, Pettichaps, Pettychaps, Pewit, Phalarope,
Pheasant, Philomel, Phoebe, Phoenix, Pickmass, Pictarnie, Picus, Pie, Piet,

Pigeon, Pink, Pinnock, Pintado, Pintail, Piper, Pipit, Plover, Poaka, Pochard, Pockard, Podargus, Poe-bird, Poker, Poorwill, Potoo, Poultry, Pouter, Poy-bird, Pratincole, Prion, Progne, Ptarmigan, Puffin, Pukeko, Pullet, Pyot, Quail, Quaker-bird, Quarrian, Quarrion, Queest, Quelea, Quest, Quetzal, Qu(o)ist, Rafter-bird, Rail, Rainbird, Rallidae, Raptor, Rasores, Raven, Razorbill, Redcap, Redpoll, Redshank, Redstart, Redwing, Ree, Reedling, Reed-warbler, Reed-wren, Reeler, Reeve, Regulus, Rhampastos, Rhea, Ring-dotterel, Ringtail, Riroriro, Roaster, Robin, Roc, Roch, Rook, Rooster, Rosella, Rotch(ie), Roller, Ruc, Ruddock, Ruff, Ruru, Rype(r), Sage-thrasher, Saker(et), Salangane, Sanderling, Sandpeep, Sandpiper, Sapsucker, Sawbill, Scamel, Scansores, Scape, Scart(h), Scaup, Scaury, Scolopar, Scooper, Scops, Scourie, Screamer, Scray(e), Sea-cob, Sea-mell, Sea-mew, Seapie, Sea-turtle, Serin, Serpent-eater, Shag, Shake-bag, Shama, Shearwater, Sheldrake, Shoebill, Shoveller, Shrike, Silktail, Silverbill, Simara, Simurg(h), Sirgang, Sis, Siskin, Sitella, Sitta, Skart(h), Skimmer, Skirt, Skua-gull, Skunk-bird, Smeath, Smee, Snipe, Snow-cap, Solan(d), Solitaire, Sora, Sorage, Soree, Spadger, Sparrow, Spatchcock, Spink, Sprug, Squab, Standard-wing, Standgale, Stan(n)iel, Stare, Stilt, Stint, Stonechat(ter), Stone-curlew, Stone-snipe Stork, Strich, Struthio, Sturnus, Stymphalian, Sultan, Swallow, Swift, Sword-bill, Sylph, Sylvia, Taha, Takahe, Talegalla, Tanager, Tanagridae, Tantalus, Tapacolo, Tapaculo, Tarcel, Tarrock, Tassel, Tattler, Teal, Terek, Tern, Teru-tero, Teuchat, Tew(h)it, Thickhead, Thornbill, Thrasher, Thresher, Throstle(-cock), Thunderbird, Tiercel, Tinamou, Tit(lark), Titmouse, Tody, Tokahea, Tom-noddy, Tom-tit, Topaz, Totanus, Toucan(et), Touraco, Towhee, Tragopan, Tree-creeper, Trembler, Trochilus, Trogon, Troopial, Troupial, Trumpeter, Tui, Tuli, Turbit, Turnstone, Tweeter, Twite, Tyrant, Tystie, Umber, Umbre(tte), Urubu, Veery, Verdin, Vireo, Volucrine, Vulture, Vulturn, Wader, Wagtail, Walker, Warbler, Water-hen, Waxbill, Waxeye, Waxwing, Whaup, Whimbrel, Whinchat, Whippoorwill, Whisky-jack, Whisky-john, Whitecap, White-eye, Whitethroat, Widgeon, Willet, Wimbrel, Wind-hover, Witwall, Wonga(-wonga), Woodcock, Woodpecker, Woodwale, Woosel(l), Wren(-tit), Wrybill, Wryneck, Xanthoura, Xema, Yaffa, Yaffingale, Yaffle, Yale, Yang-win, Yellow-yowley, Yite, Ynambu, Yoldring, Yucker, Zoozoo

**Bird-catcher**  Avicularia, Fowler

**Bird-like**  Hirundine, Sturnine

**Bird's nest(ing)**  Caliology, Monotropa, Soup

**Bird-watcher**  Augur, Twitcher

**Birkenhead**  F.E.Smith

**Birmingham**  Brum(magem)

**Birth**  Burden, Delivery, Drop, Extraction, Genesis, Jataka, Lineage, Nativity, Origin, Parage

**Birthday**  Anniversary, Genethliac

**Birthmark**  Blemish, Mole, Mother-spot, Naevus, Stigmata

**Birthright**  Heritage, Mess, Patrimony

**Birthwort** Aristolochia

**Biscuit** Abernethy, Bath-oliver, Bourbon, Butterbake, Charcoal, Cookie, Cracker, Cracknel, Dandyfunk, Digestive, Dunderfunk, Fairing, Flapjack, Florentine, Garibaldi, Gingersnap, Hardtack, Kiss, Macaroon, Marie, Mattress, Nut, Oliver, Osborne, Parkin, Perkin, Petit four, Pig's ear, Poppadom, Poppadum, Pretzel, Ratafia, Rusk, Tack, Wafer, Zwieback

**Bisexual** AC/DC, Freemartin

**Bishop** Aaronic, Abba, Aidan, Ambrose, Bench, Bp, Cambrensis, Cantuar, Chad, Coverdale, Diocesan, Dunelm, Ely, Eparch, Episcopate, Eusebian, Exon, Golias, Hatto, Henson, Latimer, Lord, Magpie, Metropolitan, Norvic, Odo, Ordainer, Patriarch, Peter, Piece, Polycarp, Pontiff, Prelate, Priest, Primate, Primus, Proudie, RR, Sleeve, Suffragan, Titular, Tulchan, Weed

**Bismarck** Otto

**Bismuth** Bi

**Bison** Bonas(s)us, Buffalo, Ox, Wisent

**Bit(s)** Cantle(t), Chad, Cheesecake, Chip, Crumb, Curb, Curn, Drib, Excerpt, Fraction, Haet, Hate, Ion, Jaw, Jot, Mite, Modicum, Morsel, Mote, Mu, Nit, Ort, Ounce, Pelham, Peni, Penny, PIECE, Port, Rap, Rare, Ratherish, Scintilla, Scrap, Section, Shaving, Shiver, Shred, Snaffle, Snatch, Snippet, Soupcon, Spale, Speck, Splinter, Spot, Suspicion, Tad, Tait, Tate, Threepenny, Trace, Unce, Whit

**Bite(r), Biting, Bitten** Caustic, Chelicera, Chew, Eat, Engouled, Erose, Etch, Gnash, Gnat, Incisor, Knap, Masticate, Midge, Molar, Mordacious, Mordant, Morsel, Morsure, Nibble, Nip(py), Occlude, Pium, Rabid, Remorse, Sarcastic, Sharp, Shrewd, Snap, Tart

**Bitter(ness)** Absinth, Acerb, Acid, Acrimonious, Ale, Aloe, Angostura, Bile, Caustic, Eager, Ers, Fell, Gall, Keen, Marah, Maror, Myrrh, Pique, Rancorous, Rankle, Resentful, Sarcastic, Sardonic, Snell, Sore, Spleen, Tart(aric), Venom, Virulent, Vitriolic, Wormwood

**Bittern** Boomer, Bull-of the-bog, Butterbump, Heron, Sedge, Siege

**Bittersweet** Dulcamara

**Bitumen** Albertite, Asphalt, Pissasphalt, Pitch, Tar

**Bivalve** Clam, Cockle, Mollusc, Muscle, Mussel, Oyster, Piddock, Scallop, Whelk

**Bivouac** Camp

**Bizarre** Curious, Eccentric, Exotic, Fantastic, Gonzo, Grotesque, Odd, Outlandish, Outre, Pythonesque, Queer, Strange, Surreal, Weird

**Blab** Babble, Gossip, Squeal

**Black(ness), Blacken(ing), Black-out** Amadoda, Atramental, B, BB, Bess, Blac, Charcoal, Cilla, Coloured, Coon, Cypress, Death, Denigrate, Dwale, Ebon(y), Eclipse, Ethiop, Gladwellise, Graphite, Heben, Hole, Ink(y), Japan, Jeat, Jet, Kohl, Lepidomelane, Malign, Market, Melanic, Melano, Moke, Moor, Myall, Negritude, Negro, Niello, Niger, Nigrescent,

Nigritude, Obliterate, Obscure, Outage, Oxford, Piceous, Pitch, Pongo, Prince, Pudding, Raven, Sable, Scab, School, Sheep, Slae, Sloe, Solvent, Sombre, Soot, Spode, Spook, Stygian, Swart(y), Swarth(y), Tar

**Blackball**   Ban, Exclude, Pip, Reject

**Blackberry**   Acini, Bramble, Mooch, Mouch

**Blackbird**   Crow, Jackdaw, Ousel, Raven

**Black eye(d)**   Half-mourning, Mouse, Shiner, Susan

**Blackguard**   Leg, Nithing, Raff, Rotter, Scoundrel, Sweep

**Blackhead**   Comedo

**Black hole**   Collapsar

**Blackjack**   Billie, Billy, Vingt(-et)-un

**Blackleg**   Fink, Scab, Snob

**Black magic**   Goety

**Blackmail(er)**   Bleed, Chantage, Chout, Exact, Extort, Ransom, Strike, Vampire

**Blackout**   ARP, Eclipse, Faint, Swoon

**Black Sea**   Pontic

**Black sheep**   Neer-do-well, Reprobate

**Blacksmith**   Brontes, Burn-the-wind, Farrier, Forger, Harmonious, Shoer, Vulcan

**Blackthorn**   Sloe

**Bladder(y)**   Balloon, Blister, Cyst, Isinglass, Sac, Sound, Utricle, Varec(h), Vesica

**Blade**   Acrospire, Bilbo, Brand, Brown Bill, Cleaver, Co(u)lter, Cutlass, Dandy, Espada, Foible, Forte, Gleave, Guillotine, Hydrofoil, Lance, Leaf, Man, Oar, Peel, Rachilla, Rapier, Razor, Rip, Scimitar, Scull, Skate, Spade-bone, Spatula, Spatule, Spear, Spoon, Stiletto, Stock, SWORD, Symitar, Toledo, Vane, Vorpal, Web

**Blame**   Accuse, Censure, Condemn, Confound, Fault, Guilt, Inculpate, Odium, Rap, Reprove, Stick, Thank, Wight, Wite, Wyte

**Blameless**   Innocent, Irreproachable

**Blanch**   Bleach, Etiolate, Whiten

**Blancmange**   Flummery, Mould, Shape, Timbale

**Bland**   Anodyne, Mild, Pigling, Sleek, Smooth, Suave, Unctuous

**Blandish(ment)**   Agremens, Agrement, Cajole, COAX, Flatter, Treacle, Wheedle

**Blank**   Cartridge, Empty, Flan, Lacuna, Planchet, Shot, Tabula rasa, VACANT

**Blanket**   Afghan, Bluey, Counterpane, Cover, General, Kaross, Mackinaw, Manta, Obscure, Overall, Poncho, Quilt, Rug, Serape, Shabrack, Smog, Stroud, Wagga, Whittle

**Blare**   Horn, Trumpet

**Blarney**   Cajolery, Flattery, Nonsense, Sawder, Taffy

**Blasé**   Worldly

**Blaspheme**   Abuse, CURSE, Defame, Revile

**Blast(ed)**   Blight, Blore, Bombard, Dang, Darn, Dee, Drat, Dynamite, Explode, Fanfare, Flaming, Flurry, Fo(e)hn, Gale, Gust, Parp, Pryse, Scarth, Scath(e), Sere, Shot, Sideration, Skarth, Toot, Tromp(e), Trump(et), Volley

**Blatant**   Flagrant, Hard-core, Strident, Vulgar

**Blather**   Baloney, Gabble

**Blaze(r)**   Beacon, Bonfire, Burn, Cannel, Conflagration, FLAME, Flare, Glare, Jacket, Low(e), Lunt, Palatinate, Race, Ratch, Star, Sun, Tead(e)

**Bleach(er)**   Blanch, Chemic, Chloride, Decolorate, Etiolate, Keir, Kier, Peroxide, Whiten

**Bleak**   Ablet, Bare, Blay, Bley, Dour, Dreary, Dreich, Raw, Wintry

**Bleary**   Blurred, Smudged

**Bleat**   Baa, Blat, Bluster

**Bleed(er), Bleeding**   Cup, Epistaxis, Fleam, Haemorrhage, Leech, Menorrh(o)ea, Milk, Root-pressure

**Bleep**   Earcon, Pager

**Blefuscudian**   Big-endian, Little-endian

**Blemish**   Birthmark, Blot, Blotch, Blur, Defect, Flaw, Mackle, Mark, Mote, Scar, Smirch, Spot, Sully, Taint, Vice, Wart, Wen

**Blench**   Flinch, Recoil, Wince

**Blend(ing)**   Amalgam, Coalesce, Commix, Contemper, Contrapuntal, Counterpoint, Electrum, Go, Harmonize, Hydrate, Liquidise, Meld, Melt, MERGE, Mingle, Mix, Osmose, Scumble

> **Blend**   may indicate an anagram

**Blenny**   Eel-pout, Gunnel, Shanny

**Bless(ed), Blessedness, Blessing**   Amen, Approval, Beatitude, Benediction, Benison, Benitier, Boon, Consecrate, Cup, Damosel, Darshan, Elysium, Ethereal, Felicity, Gesundheit, Gwyneth, Holy (dam), Luck, Macarise, Mercy, Sain, Saint, Sanctity, Xenium

**Bless me**   Lawk(s)

**Blight**   Afflict, Ague, Bespot, Blast, Destroy, Eyesore, Rot, RUIN, Rust, Shadow, Viticide, Wither

**Blighter**   Cuss, Perisher, Varment, Varmint

**Blimey**   Coo, Cor, Crimini, O'Riley, Strewth

**Blimp**   Airship, Colonel

**Blind(ness), Blind spot**   Amaurosis, Amblyopia, Artifice, Beesome, Bisson, Blend, Blotto, Carousal, Cecity, Chi(c)k, Cog, Concealed, Dazzle,

Eyeless, Feint, Hemeralopia, Hood, Jalousie, Legless, Mole, Meropia, Onchocerciasis, Persiennes, Pew, Prestriction, Rash, Scotoma, Seel, Shade, Shutter, Stimie, Stimy, Stymie, Teichopsia, Venetian, Yblent

**Blindfish**  Amblyopsis

**Blindfold**  Bandage, Hoodwink, Muffle, Seal, Wimple

**Blindworm**  Anguis

**Blink(er), Blinkered, Blinking**  Bat, Bluff, Broken, Flash, Haw, Idiot, Insular, Nictate, Owl-eyed, Owly, Twink, Wapper, Wink

**Bliss(ful)**  Bouyan, Delight, ECSTASY, Eden, Happy, Ignorance, Millenium, Nirvana, Paradise, Rapture, Sion, Tir-na-nog, Valhalla, Walhalla, Wedded

**Blister(ed), Blistering**  Blab, Blain, Bleb, Bubble, Bullate, Epispastic, Herpes, Pemphigus, Phlyctena, Scorching, Tetter, Vesicle

**Blitz**  Attack, Bombard, Onslaught, Raid

**Blizzard**  Buran, Gale, Snowstorm

**Bloat**  Puff, Strout, Swell, Tumefy

**Blob**  Bead, Bioblast, Drop, Globule, O, Spot, Tear

**Bloc**  Alliance, Cabal, Cartel, Party

**Block(ade), Blockage**  Altar, Anvil, Ashlar, Atresia, BAR, Barricade, Barrier, Breeze, Briquette, Bung, Bunt, Catasta, Choke, Chunk, Clint, Clog, Clot, Cloy, Compass, Congest, Cylinder, DAM, Dead-eye, Debar, Dentel, Dentil, Dit, Electrotint, Encompass, Euphroe, Fipple, Hack-log, High-rise, Hunk, Ileus, Impede, Impost, Insula, Interrupt, Interclude, Investment, Jam, Lodgment, Log-jam, Mutule, Oasis, Obstacle, OBSTRUCT, Occlude, Oppilate, Pad, Parry, Plinth, Prevent, Scotch, Sett, Siege, Stenosis, Stimie, Stimy, Stone, Stonewall, Stop, Stymie, Tamp, Tower, Tranche, Trig, Triglyph, Uphroe, Upping-stock, Zinco, Zugzwang

**Blockbuster**  Epic

**Blockhead**  Jolterhead, Mome, Nitwit, Noodle, Stupid

**Bloke**  Beggar, Chap, Cove, Fellow, Gent, Man, Oik

**Blonde**  Fair, Goldilocks, Platinised, Strawberry, Tallent, Towhead

**Blood(y)**  Ancestry, Bally, Blut, Claret, Clot, Cruor, Ecchymosis, Epigons, Factor, GORE, Haemal, Ichor, Introduce, Kin, Knut, Nut, Opsonin, Persue, Pigeon's, Plasma, Properdin, Pup, Race, Rare, Red, Rh negative, Rh positive, Ruby, Sang, Stroma, Toff, Welter

**Blood disease, Blood-poisoning**  Hypinosis, Pyaemia, Spanaemia, Toxaemia, Uraemia

**Bloodhound**  Lime, Lyam, Sleuth, Spartan

**Bloodless**  Anaemic, Isch(a)emic, Wan, White

**Blood-letter**  Leech, Phlebotomist, Sangrado

> **Blood-poisoning**  see BLOOD DISEASE

**Blood-sport**  Hunting, Shooting, Venery

**Biood-sucker** Asp, Dracula, Flea, Gnat, Ked, Leech, Louse, Mosquito, Parasite, Reduviid, Sponger, Tick, Vampire(-bat)

**Bloom(er), Blooming** Bally, Blossom, Blow, Blush, Boner, Dew, Film, Florescent, Flowery, Flush, Gaffe, Glaucous, Heyday, Knickers, Out, Pruina, Reh, Remontant, Rosy, Underwear

> **Bloomer** may indicate a flower

**Blossom** Blow, Burgeon, Festoon, Flourish, Flower, May, Orange, Pip

**Blot** Atomy, Blob, Cartel, Delete, Disgrace, Eyesore, Obscure, Smear, Smudge, Southern, Splodge, Splotch

**Blotch(y)** Blemish, Giraffe, Monk, Mottle(d), Spot, Stain

**Blotto** Legless

**Blouse** Choli, Garibaldi, Guimpe, Middy, Smock, Tunic, Windjammer

**Blow(er)** Appel, Bang, Bash, Bellows, Biff, Billow, Blip, Bloom, Brag, Breeze, Buckhorse, Buffet, Burst, Calamity, Clat, Claut, Clip, Clout, Clump, Conk, Coup, Cuff, Dad, Daud, Dev(v)el, Dinnyhayser, DintDouse, Dowse, Estramacon, Etesian, Facer, Fan, Gale, Grampus, Gust, Haymaker, Hit, Hook, Ictus, Impact, Insufflate, Karate, Kibosh, KO, Lame, Lander, Lick, Muff, Neck-herring, Northerly, Noser, Oner, One-two, Paik, Pash, Phone, Plague, Plug, Polt, Pow, Puff, Punch, Purler, Rattler, Sas(s)arara, Scat, Settler, Sideswipe, Side-winder, Sis(s)erary, Skiff, Slat, Slog, Snot, Sock, Sockdolager, Sockdologer, Southwester, Spanking, Spat, Spout, Squander, Stripe, Stroke, Strooke, Stunning, Supercharger, Swash, Swat, Swinger, Telephone, Thump, Tingler, Tootle, Trump(et), Upper-cut, Waft, Wallop, Wap, Waste, Welt, Whample, Whang, Whap, Wheeze, Wherret, Whirret, WIND, Wipe, Wuther

**Blown-up** Elated, Enlarged, Exploded

**Blow-out** Binge, Bloat, Exhale, Feast, Feed, Flat, Lava, Nosh-up, Snuff, Spiracle, SPREAD

**Blowpipe** Hod, Peashooter, Sarbacane, Sumpit(an)

**Blub(ber)** Cry, Fat, Snotter, Sob, Speck, WEEP, Whimper

**Bludgeon** Bully, Club, Cosh, Cudgel, Sap

**Blue** Abattu, Accablé, Anil, Aquamarine, Azure, Beard, Berlin, Bice, Bleuâtre, Bottle, C, Caesious, Cantab, Celeste, Cerulean, Cobalt, Cyan, Danish, Danube, Dejected, Dirty, Disconsolate, Doldrums, DOWN, Eatanswill, Electric, Facetiae, Firmament, Germander, Glum, Hauyne, Hump, Indecent, Indigo, Indol(e), Isatin(e), Lavender, Lewd, Lionel, Mazarine, Midnight, Monastral, Mope, Morose, Nattier, Naughty, Navy, Oxford, Perse, Porn, Prussian, Rabbi, Ribald, Riband, Right, Royal, Sad, Sapphire, Saxe, Scurrilous, SEA, Shocking, Sky, Slate, Smalt(o), Smutty, Sordid, Splurge, Stafford, Stocking, Teal, Tony, Trist, True, Turnbull's, Ultramarine, Unhappy, Verditer, Watchet, Wedgwood, Welkin, Woad, Zaffer, Zaffre

> **Blue** may indicate an anagram

**Bluebell** Blawort, Blewart, Campanula, Harebell

**Bluebottle**  Blawort, Blewart, Blowie, Brommer, Brummer, Fly, Policeman

**Blue-legged, Bluestocking**  Basbleu, Carter, Erudite, Hamburg(h), Mrs Montagu, Précieuse, Sheba

**Blueprint**  Cyanotype, Draft, Plan, Recipe

> **Bluestocking**  see BLUE-LEGGED

**Bluff**  Blunt, Cle(e)ve, Cliff, Clift, Crag, Fake, Flannel, Frank, Hal, Headland, Height, Hoodwink, Pose, Precipice, Steep, Trick

**Blunder(er), Blundering**  Bévue, Bish, Bloomer, Boob, Bull, Bumble, Clanger, Clinker, Err, Faux pas, Floater, Flub, Fluff, Gaff(e), Goof, Howler, Inexactitude, Irish, Josser, Malapropism, MISTAKE, Mumpsimus, Slip, Solecism, Stumble, Trip

**Blunt(ed)**  Abrupt, Alleviate, Bate, Bayt, Candid, Disedge, Forthright, Hebetate, Mole, Morned, Obtund, Obtuse, Outspoken, Pointblank, Rebate, Retund, Retuse, Snub, Stubby

**Blur(ring)**  Cloud, Confuse, Fog, Fuzz, Halation, Mackle, Macule, SMUDGE

**Blurb**  Ad, Puff

**Blush(ing)**  Colour, Cramoisy, Crimson, Erubescent, Erythema, Incarnadine, REDDEN, Rouge, Ruby, Rutilant

**Bluster(er), Blustery**  Arrogance, Bellow, Blore, Hector, Rage, Rant, Rodomontade, Roister, Sabre-rattler, Swagger, Vapour, Wuthering

**Boar**  Barrow, Calydonian, Erymanthian, Hog, Sanglier, Sounder, Tusker

**Board(s), Boarding**  Abat-voix, Admiralty, Billet, Bristol, Cheese, Committee, Contignation, Dart, Deal, Directors, Embark, Embus, Enter, Entrain, Fare, Fascia, Fibro, Hack, Hawk, Hoarding, Lag, Lodge, Malibu, Notice, Otter, Ouija, Palette, Panel, Particle, Planchette, Plank, Ply(wood), Quango, Sandwich, Sarking, Shelf, Shingle, Side-table, Sign, Skirting, Stage, Surf, TABLE, Theatre, Trencher, Wainscot

> **Board**  may refer to chess or draughts

**Boarder**  Interne, PG, Roomer

**Boarding house**  Digs, Lodgings, Pension

**Boast(er), Boasting**  Blow, Blew, Blowhard, Bluster, Bobadil, Bounce, Brag, Braggadocio, Breeze, Crake, Crow, Fanfaronade, Gas, Gascon(nade), Glory, Line, Ostent(atious), Prate, Rodomontade, Scaramouch, Skite, Swagger, Swank, Tall, Thrasonic, Vainglory, Vaunt, Yelp

**Boat**  Gravy, Jolly, SHIP, Slogger, Swing, Torpid, VESSEL

**Boater**  HAT, Punter, Straw

**Boatman**  Bargee, Charon, Cockswain, Coxswain, George, Gondolier, Harris, Hoveller, Phaon, Waterman, Wet-bob

**Boat population**  Tank(i)a

**Boat-shaped**  Carina, Scaphoid

**Boatswain**  Bosun, Serang, Smee

**Bob**  Beck, Curtsey, Deaner, Dip, Dock, Dop, Duck, Float, Hod, Hog, Jerk, Page-boy, Peal, Plummet, Popple, Rob, S, Shingle

**Bobbin**  Reel, Shuttle, Spindle, Spool

**Bobble**  Pompom

**Bobby**  Bluebottle, Busy, Copper, Flatfoot, Patrolman, Peeler, Pig, POLICEMAN

**Bobby-dazzler**  Dinger, Stunner

**Bock**  Stein

**Bode**  Augur

**Bodice**  Basque, Bolero, Chemise, Choli, Corsage, Gilet, Halter, Jirkinet, Polonie, Polony, Spencer

**Bodkin**  Eyeleteer, Needle, Poniard, Stilet(to)

**Body, Bodies, Bodily**  Administration, Amount, Anatomic, Board, Bouk, Buik, Buke, Bulk, Cadaver, Cadre, Carcase, Carcass, Carnal, Caucas, Centrosome, Chapel, Chapter, Chassis, Chondriosome, Clay, Coccolite, Cohort, Column, Comet, Committee, Cormus, Corpor(e)al, Corps, Corpse, Corpus, Corse, Cytode, Detail, Earth, Flesh, Frame, Fuselage, Gazo(o)n, Golgi, Goner, GROUP, Hull, Lich, Like, Lithites, MASS, Militia, Moit, Mote, Mummy, Nacelle, Nucleole, Nucleolus, Pack, Plant, Platelet, Platoon, Politic, Posse, Purview, Quango, Relic(t), Ruck, Soma, Soredium, Soyle, Spinar, Spore, Squadron, Square, Stiff, Thallus, Torse, Torso, Trunk, Turm, Ulema

> **Body**  may indicate an anagram

**Body builder**  Steroid

**Bodyguard**  Amulet, ESCORT, Gentleman-at-arms, House-carl, Minder, Praetorian, Protector, Retinue, Schutzstaffel, SHIELD, SS, Varangian, Ycomen

**Body segment**  Arthromere, Metamere

**Boer**  Afrikaner, Kruger

**Bog(gy)**  Allen, Can, Carr, Clabber, Fen, Gents, Glaur, Hag, Lair, Loo, Machair, Marsh, Mire, Morass, Moss(-flow), Mud, Muskeg, Peat, Petary, Quag, Serbonian, Slack, Slade, Slough, Spew, Spouty, Stodge, Sump, Vlei, WC, Yarfa, Yarpha

**Bog(e)y**  Boggart, Bug(aboo), Bugbear, Chimera, Eagle, Mumbo jumbo, Par, Poker, Scarer, Spectre, Troll

**Boggle**  Astonish, Bungle, Demur, Hesitate, Perplex, Shy

**Bog-trotter**  Tory

**Bogus**  Counterfeit, False, Histrionic, Phoney, SHAM, Snide, Snobbish, Spoof, Spurious

**Bohemian**  Arty, Beatnik, Gypsy, Hippy, Mimi, Taborite

**Boil(er), Boiled, Boiling point**  Anthrax, Blain, Brew, Bubble, C, Cook, Cree, Dartre, Decoct, Ebullient, Feruncle, Foam, Hen, Herpes, Kettle, Leep, Ligroin, Pimple, Poach, Rage, Samovar, Seethe, Simmer, Sod, Sore, Stew,

Stye, Tea-kettle

**Boister(ous)**  Gilp(e)y, Gusty, Noisy, Rambunctious, Randy, Riotous, Rough, Stormy, Termagant, Turbulent, Wild

**Bold(ness)**  Assumptive, Brash, Brass, Bravado, Bravery, Bravura, Brazen, Caleb, Crust, Daredevil, Defiant, Derring-do, Diastaltic, Familiar, Free, Gallus, Hardihood, Impudent, Intrepid, Outspoken, Pert, Plucky, Presumptive, Rash, Unshrinking

**Bole**  Stem, Trunk

**Bolivar**  Liberator

**Bollard**  Kevel

**Bolshevik**  Communist, Maximalist, Soviet

**Bolster**  Cushion, Pillow, PROP

**Bolt**  Arrow, Cuphead, Dash, Elope, Flee, Gobble, Gollop, Gulp, Latch, Levant, Levin, Lightning, Lock, Missile, Pig, Pintle, Rivet, Roll, Scoff, Slot, Snib, Sperre, Thunder, U

**Bolus**  Ball

**Bomb(er), Bombing**  Atom, Attack, Blockbuster, Carpet, Deterrent, Doodlebug, Egg, Flop, Fusion, Grenade, H, Lancaster, Liberator, Megaton, Mills, Minnie, Mint, Napalm, Nuke, Petar, Pineapple, Plaster, Prang, Ransom, Shell, Stealth, Stuka, Tactical, Terrorist, Torpedo, Turkey, V1

**Bombard(ment)**  Attack, Battery, Blitz, Cannonade, Drum-fire, Pelt, Shell, Stone, Stonk, Strafe, Straff

**Bombardon**  Tuba

**Bombast(ic)**  Euphuism, Fustian, Grandiose, Magniloquence, Orotund, Pomp, Rant, Timid, Turgent

**Bombay**  Nasik

**Bombay duck**  Bum(m)alo

> **Bomber**  see under Bomb

**Bonanza**  Luck, Windfall

**Bonaparte**  Boney, NAPOLEON, Plon-plon

**Bond(age)**  Adhesive, Agent, Assignat, Cedula, Cement, Chain, Compact, Connect, Copula, Duty, Escrow, Gilt, Hyphen, James, Knot, Liaise, Ligament, Link(age), Manacle, Mortar, Nexus, Noose, PLEDGE, Rapport, Shackle, Starr, Thral(l)dom, TIE, Valence, Vinculum, Yearling, Yoke

**Bond(s)man**  Ernie, Esne, Fleming, Serf, Slave, Thete, Vassal

**Bone(s), Bony**  Apatite, Astragalus, Calcaneus, Catacomb, Chine, Clavicle, Cly, Coccyx, Columella, Condyle, Coral, Costa, Crane, Cranium, Diaphysis, Dib, Dice, Ethmoid, Femur, Fibula, Fillet, Funny, Gaunt, Horn, Humerus, Ilium, Incus, Ischium, Ivory, Jugal, Knuckle, Luez, Luz, Malleus, Manubrium, Medulla, Metacarpal, Metatarsal, Napier's, Nasal, Occipital, Olecranon, Omoplate, Os, Ossicle, Patella, Pecten, Pelvis, Pen, Perone, Phalanx, Pubis, Rachial, Rack, Radialia, Radius, Rib, Sacrum, Scaphoid, Sclere, Skeleton, Skull, Squamosal, Stapes, STEAL, Sternebra, Sternum,

Stirrup, T, Talus, Tarsus, Temporal, Tibia, Tot, Trapezium, Ulna, Vertebrae, Vomer, Wish, Zygomatic

**Bone-head**  Capitellum, Capitulum

**Bonehouse**  Ossuary

**Boneshaker**  Dandy-horse, Draisene, Draisine

**Bonfire**  Bale-fire, Beltane, Blaze, Clavie

**Boniface**  Inn-keeper, Landlord, Taverner

**Bonne-bouche**  Cate

**Bonnet**  Balmoral, Bongrace, Cap, Glengarry, Hood, Kiss-me, Mobcap, Mutch, Poke, Toorie

**Bonny**  Blithe, Gay, Merry, Sonsy, Weelfar'd

**Bonus**  Bounty, Bye, Dividend, Hand-out, No-claim, PREMIUM, Reward, Scrip, Spin-off, Windfall

**Boob**  Gaffe, Nork, Simpleton, Stumer

**Booby**  Dunce, Hick, Patch, Patchcocke, Patchoke, STUPID

**Boojum**  Snark

**Book(ish), Bookwork**  Academic, Acts, Album, Amos, Antilegomena, Apocalypse, Apocrypha, Atlas, B, Bestiary, Bible, Breviary, Chrestomathy, Classic, Corinthians, Cyclopedia, Daniel, Deuteronomy, Diary, Dictionary, Digest, Directory, Domesday, Eccles, Edda, Ench(e)iridion, Encyclopedia, Engage, Enter, Eph, Ephesians, Erudite, Esdras, Esther, Exercise, Exeter, Exodus, Ezra, Facetiae, Folio, Genesis, Gradual, Grimoire, Grolier, Heptameron, Herbal, Hitopodesa, Hosea, I Ching, Imprint, Incunabula, Isaiah, Jashar, Jasher, John, Joshua, Jude, Judges, Kells, Kings, Lam(entations), Ledger, Leviticus, Lib, Liber, Libretto, Literary, Log, Luke, Manual, Mark, Martyrs, Matthew, Micah, Missal, Nahum, NT, Numbers, Octavo, Octodecimo, Omnibus, Open, Orarium, Order, Ordinal, OT, Paperback, Pedantic, Pharmacopoeia, Plug, Primer, Proverbs, Psalter, Quair, Quarto, Quire, Ration, Reader, Remainder, RESERVE, Revelations, Romans, Scroll, Sixteenmo, Snobs, Studious, Study, Sutra, Tablet, Text(ual), Thriller, Title, Titule, To-bit, Tome, Triodion, Twelvemo, Vade-mecum, Veda, Vercelli, Vol(ume), Work, Year

**Bookbinding**  Grolier

**Book-case**  Credenza, Press, Satchel

**Bookie(s), Bookmaker**  John, Layer, Librettist, Luke, Mark, Matthew, Printer, Ringman, To-bit

**Booking**  Reservation

**Bookkeeper**  Clerk, Librarian, Recorder, Satchel

**Booklet**  B, Brochure, Folder

**Book-like**  Solander

**Book-lover**  Incunabulist

**Bookmark**  Tassel

**Book-scorpion**  Chelifer

**Bookseller(s)**  Bibliophile, Colporteur, Conger, Sibyl

**Bookworm**  Sap, Scholar

**Boom(ing)**  Beam, Boost, Bowsprit, Bump, Increase, Jib, Orotund, Prosper, Roar, Sonic, Spar, Thrive

**Boomer**  Bittern, Bull-of-the-bog, Mire-drum

**Boomerang**  Backfire, Kiley, Kyley, Kylie, Recoil, Ricochet, Woomera

**Boon**  Benefit, Blessing, Bounty, Cumshaw, Gift, Godsend, Mills, Mitzvah, Prayer, Windfall

**Boor(ish)**  Bosthoon, Churl, Clodhopper, Crass, Goth, Grobian, Hog, Ill-bred, Jack, Keelie, Kern(e), Kernish, Kill-courtesy, Lob, Lout, Ocker, Peasant, Philistine, Trog, Yahoo, Yob

**Boost(er)**  Bolster, Encourage, Fillip, Help, Hoist, Impetus, Increase, Injection, Promote, Raise, Reheat, Reinforce, Reinvigorate, Spike, Supercharge, Tonic

**Boot(s)**  Addition, Avail, Balmoral, Benefit, Blucher, Bottine, Brogan, Brogue, Buskin, Cerne, Chukka, Concern, Cothurn(us), Cracowe, Denver, Derby, Dismiss, Finn(e)sko, Finsko, Fire, Galage, Galosh, Gambado, Hessian, Jack, Jemima, Kamik, Larrigan, Last, Mitten, Muchie, Muc(k)luc(k), Mukluk, Profit, Sabot, SACK, SHOE, Tonneau, Tops, Trunk, Vibs, Wader, Weller, Wellie, Wellington, Welly

**Booth**  Assassin, Crame, Kiosk, Stall, Stand

**Bootlegger**  Cooper, Coper, Runner

**Bootless**  Futile, Idle, Vain

**Booty**  Haul, Loot, Prey, Prize, Spoil, Spolia optima, Swag

**Booze**  DRINK, Liquor, Spree, Tipple

**Borage**  Bugloss, Comfrey, Gromwell

**Borax**  Tincal

**Border(line)**  Abut, Adjoin, Bed, Bind, Checkpoint, Coast, Cot(t)ise, Dado, Dentelle, EDGE, Engrail, Frieze, Fringe, Frontier, Furbelow, Head-rig, Hem, Impale, Kerb, Lambrequin, Limb, Limbo, Limen, Limes, Limit, Limitrophe, Lip, List, March, MARGIN, Mat, Mattoid, Meith, Mete, Mount, Neighbour, Orle, Pand, Pelmet, Perimeter, Purlieu, Rand, Rim, Roadside, Roon, Royne, Rund, Rymme, Selvage, Selvedge, Side, Skirt, Strand, Strip, Surround, Swage, Trench, Tressure, Valance, Valence, VERGE

> **Borders** may indicate first and last letters

**Bore(d), Boredom, Borer, Boring**  Aiguille, Apathy, Aspergillum, Aspergillus, Aspersoir, Auger, Awl, Beetle, Bind, Bit, Brog, Bromide, Calibre, Deadly, Drag, DRILL, Dry, Eagre, Eat, Eger, Elshin, Elsin, Ennui, Ennuye, Foozle, Gim(b)let, Gouge, Gribble, Grind, Had, Ho-hum, Irk, Listless, Longicorn, Miser, Mole, Noyance, Nudni(c)k, Nuisance, Nyaff, Pall, Penetrate, Perforate, Pest, Pholas, Pierce, Pill, Probe, Punch,

Ream(ingbit), Rime, Sat, Schmoe, Scolytus, Screw, Snooze, Sondage, Spleen, Sting, Stob, Tediosity, Tedious, Tedisome, Tedium, Tedy, Terebra, Teredo, Termes, Termite, Thirl, Tire, Trocar, Tunnel, WEARY, Well, Wimble, Woodworm, Xylophoga, Yawn

**Borgia** Cesare, Lucretia

**Boric** Sassolin, Sassolite

**Born** B, Free, Great, Nascent, Nat(us), Né(e)

**Boron** B

**Borough** Pocket, Port, Quarter, Rotten, Township, Wick

**Borrow(ed), Borrowing** Adopt, Appropriate, Cadge, Copy, Eclectic, George, Hum, Scunge, Straunge, TAKE, Touch

**Bosh** Humbug, Nonsense, Rot

**Bosom** Abraham's, Breast, Close, Gremial, Inarm, Intimate

**Boss(ed), Bossy** Burr, Cacique, Director, Dominate, Gadroon, Headman, Honcho, Hump, Inian, Inion, Jewel, Knob, Knop, Knot, Maestro, MANAGER, Massa, Netsuke, Noop, Nose-led, Omphalos, Overlord, Overseer, Owner, Pellet, Protuberance, Ruler, Run, Stud, Superintendent, Taskmaster, Umbo(nate)

**Boston** Hub

**Bot** Oestrus

**Botanist** Banks, Dendrologist, Herbist, Linnaeus, Weigel

**Botch** Bungle, Clamper, Flub, Fudge, Mismanage, Spoil, Tink

**Both** Together, Two

**Bother** Ado, Aggro, Care, Deave, Deeve, Disturb, Drat, Fash, Fluster, Fuss, Get, Hector, Incommode, Irritate, Nuisance, Perturb, Pest(er), Pickle, Reke, Todo, TROUBLE

**Bottle(s)** Ampul(la), Bacbuc, Balthasar, Balthazar, Belshazzar, Borachio, Bundle, Carafe, Carboy, Cock, Costrel, Courage, Cruse, Cucurbital, Cutter, Dead-men, Decanter, Demijohn, Fearlessness, Fiasco, Flacket, Flacon, Flagon, Flask, Goatskin, Gourd, Hen, Jeroboam, Klein, Lachrymal, Lagena, Magnum, Marie-Jeanne, Matrass, Medicine, Methuselah, Mettle, Nebuchadnezzar, Phial, Pitcher, Pooter, Rehoboam, Resource, Retort, Salmanazar, Split, Vial, Vinaigret(te), Wad, Winchester, Woulfe

> **Bottle(d)** may indicate an anagram or a hidden word

**Bottom** Aris, Arse, Ass, Base, Bed, Benthos, Bilge, Breech, Buttocks, Croup(e), Croupon, Demersal, Doup, Fanny, Floor, Foot, Foundation, Fud, Fundus, Haunches, Hunkers, Hurdies, Keel(son), Kick, Nadir, Podex, Posterior, Pottle-deep, Prat, Pyramus, Root, Rump, Sill, Ship, Sole, Staddle, Tail, Tush, Weaver

**Botulism** Limberneck

**Boudoir** Bower, Room

**Bouffant** Pouf

**Bough** Branch, Limb

**Boulder**  Gibber, Rock, STONE

**Boule**  Senate

**Bounce(r), Bouncy**  Bang, Blague, Bound, Caper, Dap, Doorman, Dop, Dud, Eject, Evict, Lie, Resilient, Ricochet, Spiccato, Spring, Stot, Tale, Tamp, Verve, Vitality, Yorker, Yump

> **Bouncing**  may indicate an anagram

**Bound(er), Boundary**  Adipose, Apprenticed, Articled, Bad, Barrier, Border, Bourn(e), Bubalis, Cad, Cavort, Certain, Circumference, Curvet, Decreed, Dool, Engirt, Entrechat, Exciton, Fence, Four, Galumph, Gambado, Gambol, Girt, Harestane, Hedge, Heel, Held, Hoarstone, Hops, Hourstone, Jump, Kangaroo, LEAP, Limes, Limit, Linch, Lollop, Lope, Meare, Meer, Meith, Mere, Mete, Muscle, Obliged, Outward, Pale, Parameter, Perimeter, Periphery, Prance, Precinct, Prometheus, Purlieu, Redound, Ring-fence, Roller, Roo, Roped, Rubicon, Scoup, Scowp, Side, Six(er), Skip, Spang, Spring, Sten(d), Stoit, T(h)alweg, Tied, Touchline, Upstart, Vault, Verge, Wallaby

> **Bounds**  may indicate outside letters

**Bountiful, Bounty**  Aid, Bligh, Boon, Christian, Generosity, GIFT, Goodness, Grant, Honorarium, Largess(e), Lavish

**Bouquet**  Aroma, Attar, Aura, Compliment, Corsage, Fragrancy, Garni, Nose, Posy, Spray

**Bourbon**  Alfonso

**Bourgeois**  Common, Pleb(ian)

**Bout**  Bender, Bust, Contest, Dose, Go, Jag, Match, Spell, Spree, Turn, Venery, Venewe, Venue

**Boutique**  Shop

**Bow(er), Bowman**  Alcove, Arbour, Arc, Arch, ARCHER, Arco, Arson, Beck, Bend, Boudoir, Congé(e), Crescent, Crook, Cupid, CURVE, Defer, Drail, Droop, Duck, Eros, Eye, Fiddle(r), Foredeck, Halse, Hawse, Kneel, Kotow, Laval(l)ière, Lean, Lout, Moulinet, Nod, Nutate, Obeisance, Obtemper, Paganini, Pergola, Quarrel, Reverence, Salaam, Seamer, Shelter, Slope, Stick, SUBMIT, Tie, Yew

**Bowdler(ize)**  Edit(or), Water

**Bowels**  Entrails, Guts, Innards, Viscera

> **Bower**  may indicate using a bow

**Bowl(er), Bowling, Bowls**  B, Basin, Bicker, Bocce, Bocci(a), Boccie, Bodyline, Bool, Bosey, Bouncer, Calabash, Cap, Caup, Chalice, Cheese, Chinaman, Christie, Christy, Cog(g)ie, Coolamon, Crater, Cup, Derby, DISH, Dome, Drake, Ecuelle, End, Googly, Grub, Hog, Hoop, Jack, Jeroboam, Jorum, Kegler, Krater, Lavabo, Laver, Leg-spin, Lightweight, Lob, Locke, Monteith, Night, Offbreak, Old, Over-arm, Pan, Pétanque, Piggin, Pot-hat, Raku, Rink, Roll, Seamer, Skip, Skittle(s), Spare, Spinner, Spofforth, Stadium, Stagger, Stummel, Ten-pin, Tom, Underarm, Underhand, Underwood, Voce, Wood, York(er)

**Box(ing)** Baignoire, Bijou, Binnacle, Bonk, Buist, Bunk, Bush, Caddy, Camera, Canister, Case, Cassolette, Chest, Christmas, Coffer, Coffret, Crate, Cuff, Drawer, Enclose, FIGHT, File, Fist, Fund, Hedge, Hutch, Jury, Kiosk, Kite, Knevell, Ladle, Locker, Lodge, Loge, Mill, Mocock, Mocuck, Package, Pandora's, Pew, Pix, Ring, Saggar(d), Sagger, Savate, Scrap, Seggar, Sentry, Shoe, Skip(pet), Solander, SPAR, Telly, Tube, TV, Yakhdan

**Boxer** Ali, Amycus, Bantamweight, Bruiser, Canine, Carnera, Carpentier, Carthorse, Chinaman, Cooper, Crater, Dog, Eryx, Farr, Featherweight, Flyweight, Ham, Heavyweight, McCoy, Pandora, Pollux, Pug, Pugil(ist), Rebellion, Rocky, Shadow, Welterweight, Wilde

**Boxing-glove** Hurlbat, Muffle, Whirlbat, Whorlbat

**Boy(s)** Apprentice, Blue-eyed, Breeches, Bub(by), Cabin, CHILD, Chummy, Cub, Callant, Catamite, Champagne, Galopin, Garçon, Gorsoon, Gossoon, Groom, Ha, Jack, Kid, Klonkie, Knave, Lackbeard, LAD, Loblolly's, Loon(ie), Minstrel, Nibs, Nipper, Page, Prentice, Principal, Putto, Roaring, Son, Spalpeen, Sprig, Stripling, Tad, Ted(dy), Tiger, Urchin, YOUTH

> **Boy** may indicate an abbreviated name

**Boycott** Avoid, Bat, Black, Exclude, Hartal, Isolate, Shun

**Boyfriend** Beau, Date, Steady

**Boyle** Juno

**Bp** Bishop, DD, RR

**Brace(s), Bracing** Accolade, Couple, Gallace, Gallows, Gallus, Gird, Hound, Invigorate, Pair, Pr, Rear-arch, Rere-arch, Skeg, Splint, Steady, Stiffener, Strut, SUPPORT, Tauten, Tone, Tonic, Two

**Bracelet** Armil(la), Bangle, Cuff, Darbies, Handcuff, Manacle, Manilla

**Brachiopod** Ecardines, Spirifer

**Bracken** Brake, Fern, Pteridium, Tara

**Bracket(s)** Angle-iron, Bibb, Brace, Cantilever, Corbel, Couple, Cripple, Misericord(e), Modillion, Mutule, Parenthesis, Sconce, Straddle, Strata, STRUT, Trivet, Truss

**Bract** Glume(lla), Leaf, Palea, Palet, Phyllary, Spathe

**Brad** Nail, Pin, Rivet, Sprig

**Brag(gart), Bragging** Basilisco, Birkie, Bluster, Boast, Bobadil, Braggadocio, Bull, Crow, Fanfaronade, Gab, Gascon, Hot-air, Loudmouth, Parolles, Puckfist, Puff, Rodomontader, Skite, Slam, Swagger, Thrason, Tongue-doubtie, Tongue-doughty, Vainglorious, Vaunt

**Brahma(n)** Sannyasi(n)

**Braid** A(i)glet, Aiguillette, Frog, Galloon, Lacet, Plait, Plat, Ricrac, Rick-rack, Seaming-lace, Sennet, Sennit, Sinnet, Soutache, Tress, Trim, Twist, Weave

> **Brain(s)** may indicate an anagram

**Brain(y), Brain-power**  Bean, Bright, Cerebrum, Diencephalon, Encephalon, Epencephalon, Fornix, Genius, Gyrus, Harn(s), Head, Intelligence, IQ, Limbic, Loaf, Lobe, Mater, Mind, Noddle, Noesis, Nous, Peduncle, Pia mater, Pons, Pontile, Sconce, Sense, Striatum, Subcortex, Tectum, Vermis, Wetware

**Brainless**  Anencephaly, Stupid, Thick

**Brain-washing**  Menticide, Propaganda

**Brake**  Adiantum, Bracken, Curb, Drag, Fern, Grove, Nemoral, Ratchet, Rein, Shoe, SLOW, Spinney, Sprag, Tara, Thicket

**Bramble, Brambly**  Batology, Blackberry, Brier, Cloudberry, Rubus, Thorn, Wait-a-bit

**Bran**  Cereal, Chesil, Chisel, Oats, Pollard

**Branch(ed), Branching, Branch Office**  Affiliate, Antler, Arm, BO, Bough, Cladode, Cow, Dendron, Diverticulum, Divide, Filiate, Fork, Grain, Kow, Lateral, Limb, Lobe, Loop, Lye, Lylum, Offshoot, Olive, Raguly, Ramate, Ramulus, Reis, Rice, Shroud, Spray(ey), Sprig, Spur, Tributary, Twig, Yard

**Branch-rib**  Lierne

**Brand**  Broadsword, Buist, Burn, Cauterise, Chop, Class, Denounce, Earmark, Ember, Excalibur, Falchion, Faulchin, Faulchion, Idiograph, Label, Line, MARK, Marque, Sear, Stigma, Sweard, Sword, Torch, Wipe

**Brandish**  Bless, Flaunt, Flourish, Waffle, Wampish, Wave

**Brandy**  Aguardiente, Armagnac, Bingo, Calvados, Cape smoke, Cold without, Dop, Fine, Framboise, Grappa, Marc, Mampoer, Nantes, Nantz, Napoleon, Quetsch, Slivovic(a), Slivovitz, Smoke

**Bras**  Arms

**Brash**  Impudent, Pushy, Rain, Rash

**Brass(ware), Brassy**  Benares, Brazen, Cheek, Corinthian, Cornet, Dinanderie, Face, Front, Harsh, Horn, Latten, Lip, Lota(h), Loud, Matrix, MONEY, Oof, Oricalche, Orichalc, Pyrites, Snash, Talus, Trombone

**Brassard**  Armlet

**Brass hat**  Brig

**Brassica**  Brussels (sprout), CABBAGE, Colza

**Brat**  Bairn, Gait(t), Gamin, Geit, Git, Gyte, Imp, Lad, Terror, Urchin

**Brave(ry)**  Amerind, Apache, Bold, Conan, Corragio, Courage, Creek, Dare, DEFY, Doughty, Dress, Face, Gallant, Game, Gamy, Gutsy, Hardy, Heroism, Indian, Injun, Intrepid, Manful, Manly, Nannup, Plucky, Prow(ess), Sannup, Stout, Uncas, Valiant, Valour, Wight

**Bravo**  Acclaim, Bandit, Bully, Desperado, Euge, Murderer, Olé, Spadassin, Villain

**Brawl**  Affray, Bagarre, Bicker, Brabble, Donnybrook, Dust, Fight, Flite, Flyte, Fracas, Fray, Prawl, Rammy, Roughhouse, Scuffle, Set-to, Stoush, Tar, Wrangle

**Brawn(y)**  Beef, Burliness, He-man, Muscle, Power, Sinew

**Bray**  Cry, Heehaw, Stamp, Vicar, Whinny

**Brazen**  Bold, Brassy, Flagrant, Impudent, Shameless, Unabashed

**Brazier**  Brasero, Fire, Hibachi, Mangal, Scaldino

**Brazilian**  Carioca, Para

**Breach**  Assault, Break, Chasm, Cleft, Gap(e), Infraction, Redan, Rupture, Saltus, Schism, Solution, Trespass, Violate

**Bread**  Azym(e), Baguette, Bap, Barmbrack, Batch, Brewis, Brioche, Brownie, Bun, Cash, Chal(l)ah, Chapati, Cheat, Coburg, Corn, Corsned, Croute, Crouton, Crust, Damper, Dibs, Doorstep, Elephant's-foot, French, Gluten, Graham, Guarana, Host, Injera, Jannock, Laver, Leavened, Loaf, Manchet, MONEY, Na(a)n, Panada, Panary, Paneity, Pit(t)a, Pone, Poultice, Pumpernickel, Ravel, Roll, Rooty, Roti, Rusk, Rye, Shive, Stollen, Sugar, Sweet, Tartine, Tommy, Tortoise-plant, Wastel, Zwieback

**Breadfruit**  Ja(c)k

**Breadwinner**  Earner, Pa

**Break(ing), Break-down, Break-in, Break-up, Broken**  Adjourn, Aposiopesis, Breach, Caesura, Caesure, Cark, Cesure, Chinaman, Chip, Cleave, Comb, Comma, Comminute, Compost, Crack, Crumble, Deave, Debacle, Deeve, Demob, Destroy, Diffract, Disintegrate, Disperse, Disrupt, Erupt, Exeat, Fault, Four, FRACT(URE), Fritter, Frush, Gaffe, Greenstick, Half-term, Hernia, Holiday, Infringe, Interim, Interlude, Intermission, Interrupt, INTERVAL, Irrupt, Knap, Lacuna, Lapse, Lysis, Nooner, Polarise, Recess, Recrudescent, Relief, Rend, Respite, Rest, Rift, Ruin, Saltus, Schism(a), Secede, Shatter, Shiver, Smash, Smokeho, Smoko, Snap, Stave, Stop, Stove, Sunder, Tame, Tea-ho, Tear, Torn, Transgress, Truce, Vacation, Violate

**Breakable**  Brittle, Delicate, Fissile, Frail, Friable

**Breakdown**  Analyse, Autolysis, Cataclasm, Collapse, Conk, Glitch, Lyse, Lysis, Ruin

**Breaker**  Billow, Comber, Ice, Roller, Smasher, Surf

**Breakfast**  B, Brunch, Chota-hazri, Disjune, Kipper

**Breakwater**  Groyne, Jetty, Mole, Pier, Tetrapod

**Bream**  Fish, Porgy, Sar(gus), Tai

**Breast(bone), Breastwork**  Bazuma, Blob, Bosom, Brave, Brisket, Bust, Counter, Duddy, Dug, Garbonza, Gazunga, Heart-spoon, Jubbies, Knockers, Nork, Rampart, Redan, Sangar, Sungar, Stem, Sternum, Tit

**Breastplate**  Armour, Byrnie, Curat, Curiet, Pectoral, Plastron, Rational, Rest, Shield, Thorax, Xiphiplastron

**Breath(ing), Breathe(r)**  Aerobe, Aspirate, Branchia, Cypress-knee, Flatus, Gasp, Gill, H, Halitosis, Hauriant, Haurient, Hobday, Inhale, Lung, Nares, Nostril, Oxygenator, Pant, Pneuma, Prana, Pulmo, Rale, Respire, Respite, Rest, Rhonchus, Scuba, Snorkel, Snortmast, Spiracle, Spirit, Wheeze, Whiff, Whisper, Whift, Whist, Wind, Windpipe

**Breathlessness**  Anhelation, Apnoea, Asthma, Orthopnoea, Wheezing

**Breathtaking**  Amazing, Asphyxia

**Breech(es)**  Bible, Buckskin, Chaps, Flog, Galligaskins, Hose, Jodhpurs, Kneecords, Knickerbockers, Plushes, Smalls, Trews, Trouse(rs)

**Breed(ing), Breeding-place**  Bear, Beget, Cleck, Endogamous, Engender, Engend(r)ure, Eugenics, Gentrice, Lineage, MANNERS, Origin, Procreate, Pullulate, Race, Rear, Seminary, Species, Stock, Strain, Stud, Telegony, Tribe, Voltinism

**Breeze, Breezy**  Air, Breath, Brisk, Catspaw, Chipper, Doctor, Gust, Slant, Sniffler, Tiff, Zephyr

**Brethren**  Kin, Darbyite, Plymouth

**Breton**  Armoric, Brezonek

**Breve**  Minim, Note, O

**Breviary**  Portesse, Portous

**Brew(er)y, Brewing**  Ale, Billycan, Brose, Browst, Bummock, CONCOCT, Contrive, Dictionary, Ferment, Infusion, Liquor, Malt, Steep, Yeast, Yill, Zymurgy

**Briar**  Bramble, Canker, Lawyer

**Bribe(ry)**  Backhander, Bonus, Boodle, Dash, Get at, Graft, Grease, Hush-money, Insult, Kickback, Oil, Palm, Payola, Schmear, Slush, Soap, Sop, Square, Suborn, Sweeten(er), Tempt, Tenderloin, Vail, Vales

**Bric-a-brac**  Bibelot, Curio, Smytrie, Tatt, Virtu

**Brick(s), Brickwork**  Adobe, Bat, Bath, Boob, Bur(r), Clanger, Clinker, Closer, Course, Fletton, Gaffe, Gault, Header, Ingot, Klinker, Lego, Nogging, Red, Soldier, Sport, Stalwart, Terra-cotta, Testaceous, Tile, Trojan, Trump

**Brickbat**  Missile

**Bricklayer**  Churchill

**Bride**  Bartered, Ellen, Spouse, Wife, Ximena

**Bridesmaid**  Paranymph

**Bridge, Bridge player**  Acol, Aqueduct, Auction, Bailey, Barre, Bascule, Bestride, Bifrost, Biritch, Cantilever, Capo, Capodastro, Capotasto, Catwalk, Chevalet, Chicago, Chicane, Clapper, Clifton, Contract, Cross, Cut-throat, Declarer, Duplicate, Gangway, Gantry, Hog's back, Humpbacked, Jigger, Link, London, Menai, Ponceau, Ponticello, Pontoon, Rialto, Rubber, Sighs, Sinvat, SPAN, Spanner, Stamford, Straddle, Swing, Tay, Viaduct, Vint, Waterloo, Wheatstone

**Bridge pair**  EW, NS, SN, WE

**Bridge protector**  Ice-apron

**Bridge system**  Acol

**Bridle**  Bit, Branks, Bridoon, Bristle, Curb, Hackamore, Halter, Headstall, Musrol, Noseband, Rein

**Bridle path**  Orbit, Track

**Brief(s), Briefing, Briefly**  Awhile, Bluette, Breviate, Cape, Compact, CONCISE, Curt, Dossier, Instruct, Laconic, Nearly, Pants, Pithy, Prime, Scant, SHORT(EN), Sitrep, Summing, Tanga, Terse, Transient, Undies, Update

**Brig**  Br, Jail, Nancy Bell, SHIP, Snow

**Brigade**  Corps, Red, Troop

**Brigand**  Bandit, Bandolero, Cateran, Haiduck, Heiduc, Heyduck, Klep(h)t, Pillager, Pirate, ROBBER, Trailbaston

**Bright(en), Brightness**  Afterglow, Alert, Breezy, Brilliant, Brisk, Cheery, Clever, Effulgent, Elaine, Fair, Floodlit, Florid, Gay, Glad, Glow, Hono(u)r, Light, Loud, Luculent, Lustre, Net(t), Nit, Radiant, Rosy, Scintillating, Sharp, Sheeny, Sheer, Shere, Skyre, Smart, Stilb, Sunlit, Sunny, Vive, Vivid, White

**Bright spot**  Facula

**Brilliance, Brilliant**  Blaze, Brainy, Def, Effulgent, Flashy, Galaxy, Gay, Gemmy, Glossy, Inspired, Lambent, Lustre, Meteoric, Nitid, RADIANT, Refulgent, Resplendent, Shiny, Spangle, Splendour, Star, VIVID, Virtuoso, Water

**Brimstone**  Hellfire, S, Sulphur

**Brindisi**  Skolion, Toast

**Brindled**  Piebald, Tabby, Tawny

**Brine**  Ozone, Pickle, Salt

**Bring(ing)**  Afferent, Bear, Carry, Cause, Conduct, Convey, Earn, Fet, Fetch, Hatch, Induce, Land, Produce, Wreak

**Bring up**  Breed, Educate, Exhume, Foster, Nurture, Raise, REAR

**Brink**  EDGE, Lip, Rim, Shorc, VERGE

**Brisk(ness)**  Active, Alacrity, Alert, Allegro, Breezy, Busy, Chipper, Crank, Crisp, Fresh, Gaillard, Galliard, Jaunty, Kedge, Kedgy, Kidge, Lively, Perk, Pert, Rattling, Roaring, Scherzo, Sharp, Smart, Snappy, Spirited, Vivace, Yare, Zippy

**Bristle(d), Bristling, Bristly**  Arista, Awn, Barb, Birse, Bridle, Campodeiform, Chaeta, Flurry, Fraught, Frenulum, Hair, Herissé, Horrent, Horripilation, Nereid, Polychaete, Seta, Setose, Striga, Strigose, Stubble, Whisker, Vibraculum, Villus

**Bristle-tail**  Campodea

**Britain**  Alban(y), Albion

**Britannia, Britannia metal**  Tutania

**British, Briton(s)**  Anglo, Iceni, Insular, Isles, Limey, Pict, Pom, Saxon, Silurian, UK

**Brittany**  Armorica

**Brittle**  Bruckle, Crackly, Crimp, Crisp, Delicate, FRAGILE, Redshort, Spall, Spalt

> **Brittle**  may indicate an anagram

**Broach**  Approach, Open, Raise, Spit, Suggest, Tap, Widen

**Broad(ly)**  Crumpet, Dame, Doll, Doxy, Drab, General, Largo, Loose, Outspoken, Pro, Roomy, Thick, Tolerant, Wide, Woman

**Broad-beaked**  Latirostrate

**Broadcast(er), Broadcasting**  Ad(vertise), Air, Announce, Breaker, CB, Disperse, Disseminate, Emission, Ham, IBA, On, Pirate, Programme, Promulgate, Radiate, Radio, Relay, SCATTER, Screen(ed), Seed, Sow, Sperse, Spread, Sprinkle, Transmission, Ventilate

**Broad-nosed**  Platyrrhine

**Broadside**  Barrage, Criticism, Salvo, Tire

**Broadway**  Boulevard, Esplanade, Motorway

**Brocade**  Arrasene, Baldachin, Baldaquin, Baudekin, Bawdkin, Kincob

**Brochure**  Leaflet, Pamphlet, Tract

**Brogue**  Accent, SHOE

**Broke(n)**  Bankrupt, Bust(ed), Duff, Evans, Insolvent, Kaput, Shattered, Skint, Stony, Stove, Strapped

> **Broken**  may indicate an anagram

**Broken off**  Prerupt

**Broker**  Agent, Banian, Banyan, Jobber, Go-between, Mediator, MERCHANT, Uncle

**Bromide**  Halide, Haloid

**Bromine**  Br

**Bronchitic**  Chesty

**Bronte(s)**  Bell, Cyclops

**Brontosaurus**  Apatosaurus

**Bronze**  Bras(s), Brown, Gunmetal, Ormolu, Schillerspar, Sextans, Talos, Tan, Third

**Brooch**  Cameo, Clasp, Fibula, Ouch, Owche, Pin, Prop, Spang

**Brood**  Clock, Clutch, Cogitate, Covey, Eye, Eyrie, Hatch, Incubate, Introspect, Kindle, Litter, Meditate, Mill, Mull, Nest, Nid, Perch, Pet, PONDER, Roost, Sit, Sulk, Team

**Brook**  Babbling, Beck, Branch, Burn, Countenance, Creek, Endure, Ghyll, Gill, Kerith, Kill, Purl, Rill(et), River, Rivulet, Runlet, Runnel, Stand, Stomach, Stream, Suffer, Tolerate

**Broom**  Besom, Brush, Cow, Genista, Gorse, Greenweed, Knee-holly, Kow, Orobranche, Retama, Spart, Whisk

**Broth**  Bouillon, Brew(is), Cullis, Kail, Kale, Muslin-kale, Pottage, Skilly, SOUP, Stock

**Brothel**  Bagnio, Bordel(lo), Cathouse, Corinth, Den, Honkytonk, Kip, Seraglio, Stew

**Brother**  Ally, Billie, Billy, Brethren, Bro, Bud, Comrade, Fellow, Fra, Freemason, MONK, Moose, Sib(ling), Theatine, Trappist, Worker

**Brow**  Crest, Forehead, Glabella, Ridge, Sinciput, Tump-line

**Browbeat**  Badger, Bully, Hector

**Brown**  Abram, Adust, Amber, Auburn, Bay, Bister, Bistre, Bole, Br, Braise, Brunette, Burnet, Capability, Caramel, Cook, Coromandel, Dun, Fallow, Fusc(ous), Grill, Hazel, Ivor, John, Khaki, Liver, Mocha, Rugbeian, Russet, Rust, Scorch, Sepia, Sienna, Soare, Sore, Sorrel, Tan, Tawny, Tenné, Toast, Tom, Umber, Vandyke, Windsor

**Browne**  Sam

**Brownie**  Dobbie, Dobby, Goblin, Hob, Kobold, Leprechaun, Nis(se), Sprite

**Browse**  Graze, Pasture, Read, Scan, Stall-read

**Bruce**  Robert

**Bruise**  Contund, Contuse, Crush, Damage, Ding, Ecchymosis, Frush, Golp(e), Hurt, Intuse, Lividity, Mark, Mouse, Pound, Purpure, Rainbow, Shiner, Ston(n), Stun, Surbate

**Brummagen**  Tatty

**Brunette**  Dark, Latin

**Brush (off), Brushwood**  Bavin, Brake, Broom, Chaparral, Clash, Dismiss, Dust, Encounter, Firth, Fitch, Frith, Grainer, Hag, Kiss, Loofah, Paint, Pig, Pope's head, Putois, Rebuff, Rice, Sable, Scrub, Skim, Thicket, Touch

**Brusque**  Abrupt, Blunt, Curt, Downright, Pithy, Short

**Brussels**  Carpet, Lace

**Brutal, Brute**  Animal, Beast, Bête, Caesar, Caliban, Cruel, Hun, Iguanodon, Inhuman, Nazi, Nero, Ostrogoth, Pitiless, Quagga, Ruffian, Thresher-whale, Yahoo

**Brutus**  Wig

**Bryophyte**  Moss, Tree-moss

**Bubble(s), Bubbly**  Air-bell, Air-lock, Bead(ed), Bell, Bleb, Blister, Boil, Buller, Champagne, Effervesce, Embolus, Enthuse, Espumoso, Foam, FROTH, Gassy, Globule, Gurgle, Head, Mississippi, Popple, Reputation, Seed, Seethe, Simmer, South Sea, Vesicle, Widow

**Bubble and squeak**  Colcannon

**Buccaneer**  Corsair, Dampier, Drake, Freebooter, Morgan, Picaroon, Pirate

**Buck (up)**  Bongo, Brace, Cheer, Dandy, Deer, Dollar, Elate, Encheer, Hart, Jerk, Leash, Male, Ourebi, Pitch, Pricket, Ram, Rusa, Sore, Sorel(l), Sorrel, Spade, Spay(a)d, STAG, Staggard, Stud, Wheel

**Buckaroo**  Cowboy, Cowpoke

**Bucket(s)**  Bail, Bale, Kibble, Noria, Pail, Piggin, Scuttle, Situla, Stoop(e), Stope, Stoup, Tub

**Buckeye**

---

**Buckeye** Ohio

**Buckle** Clasp, Contort, Crumple, Dent, Fasten, Warp

> **Buckle** may indicate an anagram

**Buckle-beggar** Patrico

**Buckler** Ancile, Rondache, SHIELD, Targe

> **Bucks** may indicate an anagram

**Buckshee** Free

**Buckthorn** Cascara, Wahoo

**Buckwheat** Brank, Sarrasin, Sarrazin

**Bucolic** Aeglogue, Eglogue, Idyllic, Pastoral, Rural, Rustic

**Bud(ding), Buddy** Bulbil, Burgeon, Clove, Cobber, Deb, Eye, Gem(ma), Germinate, Knosp, Knot, Nascent, Pal, Scion, Serial, Shoot, Sprout, Turion

**Buddha, Buddhism, Buddhist** Abhidhamma, Arhat, Asoka, Bodhisattva, Dalai Lama, Gautama, Hinayana, Jain, Jodo, Mahatma, Mahayanali, Maya, Pali, Pitaka, Sakya-muni, Theravada, Tripitaka, Zen(o)

**Budge** Jee, Move, Stir, Submit

**Budget** Estimate, Plan, Programme, Shoestring

**Buff** Beige, Birthday suit, Eatanswill, Fan, Fawn, Nankeen, Nude, Polish, RUB, Streak

**Buffalo** Anoa, Arna, Bison, Bonasus, Bugle, Cap, Carabao, Ox, Perplex, Takin, Tamarao, Tamarau, Zamouse

**Buffer** Fender

**Buffet** Bang, Blow, Box, Counter, Cuff, Hit, Lam, Maltreat, Perpendicular, Shove, Sideboard, Strike, Strook(e)

**Buffoon(ery)** Antic, Clown, Droll, Goliard, Harlequin, Horseplay, Jester, Mime(r), Mome, Mummer, Pantaloon, Pickle-herring, Pierrot, Scaramouch, Scogan, Scoggin, Scurrile, Slouch, Tomfool, Vice, Wag, Zany

**Bug(s)** Anoplura, Arthropod, Bacteria, Beetle, Capsid, Chinch, Cimex, Coccidae, Cockchafer, Dictograph, Eavesdrop, Hemiptera, INSECT, Jitter, Mike, Mite, Tap, Vex, Wiretap

**Bugbear** Anathema, Bogey, Bogle, Bogy, Eten, Ettin, Poker, Rawhead

**Buggy** Car, Cart, Shay, Tipcart, Trap

**Bughouse** Fleapit, Loco

**Bugle, Bugle call** Chamade, Clarion, Cornet, Hallali, Last post, Ox, Reveille, Taps, TRUMPET, Urus

**Build(ing), Building site** Anabolism, Ar(a)costyle, Accrue, Assemble, Big, Colosseum, Cot, CREATE, Cruck, Develop, Dipteros, Drystone, Edifice, Edify, Erect, Fabric, Hut, Insula, Kaaba, Minaret, Mould, Outhouse, Phalanx, Pile, Raise, Rotunda, Skyscraper, Stance, Structure, Synthesis, Tectonic, Temple, Tenement, Tower

**Builder** Brick, Constructor, Engineer

> **Building**   may indicate an anagram

**Bulb**   Camas(h), Chive, Cive, Corm, Globe, Lamp, Light, Scallion, Set, Shallot, Squill

**Bulge, Bulging**   Astrut, Bag, Bias, Biconvex, Bug, Bulbous, Bunchy, Cockle, Entasis, Expand, Exsert, Inion, Protrude, Relievo, Rotund, Strout, Strut, SWELL, Tumid

**Bulk(y)**   Aggregate, Ample, Big, Body, Corpulent, Extent, Gross, Hull, Massive, Preponderance, Roughage, Scalar, SIZE, Stout, Vol(ume), Weight

**Bull(y)**   Anoa, Apis, Bakha, Beef, Blarney, Bluster, Bovine, Brave, Browbeat, Buchis, Bucko, Despot, Dragoon, Drawcansir, Englishman, Eretrian, Fancyman, Farnese, Flashman, Flatter, Gold, Gosh, Hapi, Harass, Hawcubite, Haze(r), Hector, Hoodlum, Huff, Intimidate, Investor, Iricism, Irishism, John, Killcow, Lambast, Maltreat, Merwer, Mick(e)(y), Mistake, Mithraism, Mohock, Nandi, Neat, Papal, Piker, Pistol, Placet, Rhodian, Roarer, Rot, Ruffian, Sitting, Souteneur, Stag, Strong-arm, Swash-buckler, Taurine, Taurus, Toitoi, Tosh, Tyran(ne), Tyrannise, Tyrant, Unigenitus, Zo(bo)

**Bulldog**   Marshal, Tenacious

**Bulldoze(r)**   Coerce, Leveller, Overturn

**Bullet**   Balata, Ball, Biscayan, Dumdum, Fusillade, Minié, Missile, Pellet, Round, Shot, Slug, Tracer

**Bulletin**   Memo, Newsletter, Report, Summary

**Bull-fight(er)**   Banderillo, Corrida, Cuadrilla, Escamillo, Matador, Picador, Rejoneador, Toreador, Torero

**Bull-head**   Cottoid, Father-lasher, Pogge, Sea-poacher

**Bull-rider**   Europa

**Bull-roarer**   Rhombos

**Bull's eye**   God, Humbug, Target

**Bulrush**   Reed, Tule

**Bulwark**   Bastion, Defence, Rampart

**Bum**   Ass, Beg, Prat, Sponge, Thumb, Tramp, Vagabond

**Bumble**   Beadle, Bedel(l)

> **Bumble**   may indicate an anagram

**Bumboat woman**   Buttercup

**Bump(er)**   Big, Blow, Bradyseism, Bucket, Clour, Collide, Dunch, Encephalocele, Fender, Hillock, Immense, Inian, Inion, Joll, Jo(u)le, Jowl, Keltie, Kelty, Knar, Knock, Mamilla, Mogul, Organ, Reveille, Rouse, Thump

**Bumpkin**   Bucolic, Clodhopper, Hayseed, Hick, Jock, Lout, Oaf, Put(t), Rube, Rustic, Yokel, Zany

**Bumptious**   Arrogant, Brash, Randie, Randy, Uppity

**Bun**   Barmbrack, Chelsea, Chignon, Chou, Huffkin, Mosbolletjie, Roll,

Teacake, Toorie, Wad

**Bunch**  Acinus, Anthology, Bob, Botryoid, Cluster, Fascicle, Finial, Flock, GROUP, Hand, Lot, Lump, Panicle, Raceme, Spray, Tee, Truss, Tuft

**Bundle**  Bale, Bavin, Bluey, Bottle, Byssus, Desmoid, Dorlach, Drum, Fag(g)ot, Fascicle, Knitch, Matilda, PACK(AGE), Parcel, Sack, Sheaf, Shiralee, Shock, Shook, Stook, Swag, Tie, Truss, Wad, Wadge, Wap

**Bung**  Cork, Dook, Obturate, Plug, Stopgap, Stopper

**Bungalow**  Dak

**Bungle(r)**  Blunder, Blunk, Bodge, Boob, Botch, Bumble, Bummle, Duff, Fluff, Foozle, Foul, Goof, Mess, Mis(h)guggle, Muddle, Muff, Mull, Prat, Screw, Spoil

**Bunk(er), Bunkum**  Abscond, Absquatulate, Balderdash, Baloney, Berth, Blah, Bolt, Casemate, Claptrap, Clio, Guy, Hazard, History, Hokum, Humbug, Rot, Scuttle, Tosh, Trap, Tripe

**Bunter**  Billy, Owl

**Bunthorne**  Aesthete, Poet

**Bunting**  Bird, Cirl, Flag, Ortolan, Streamer, Yellow-hammer, Yowley

**Buoy**  Dan, Daymark, Float, Marker, Nun, Raft, Seamark, Sonar, Sustain

**Buoyant**  Blithe, Resilient

**Burble**  Blat, Gibber

**Burden(ed)**  Beare, Bob, Cargo, Cark, Chant, Chorus, Cross, Cumber, Drone, Droore, Encumber, Encumbrance, Fa-la, Fardel, Folderol, Fraught, Freight, Gist, Handicap, Hum, Lade, LOAD, Millstone, Monkey, Oercome, Onus, Oppress, Refrain, Rumbelow, Saddle, Shanty, Substance, Tax, Tenor, Torch, Trouble, Weight, Woe, Yoke

**Burdensome**  Irksome, Onerous, Oppressive, Weighty

**Burdock**  Clote(-bar), Clothur, Cockle-bar, Weed

**Bureau**  Agency, Cominform, Davenport, Desk, Interpol, Kominform, OFFICE

**Bureaucrat(ic)**  CS, Impersonal, Jack-in-office, Mandarin, Tapist, Wallah

**Burgeon(ing)**  Asprout, Bud, Grow, Sprout

**Burgess, Burgher**  Citizen, Freeman

**Burglar, Burgle**  Area-sneak, Cat, Crack(sman), Intruder, Peterman, Picklock, Raffles, Robber, Thief, Yegg

**Burgundy**  Macon, Vin

**Burial, Burial place**  Catacomb, Charnel, Committal, Crypt, Darga, Funeral, Golgotha, Grave, Interment, Lair, Tomb, Vault, Zoothapsis

**Burin**  Graver

**Burlesque**  Caricatura, Caricature, Comedy, Farce, Heroicomical, Hudibrastic(s), Hurlo-thrumbo, Lampoon, Parody, Satire, Skit, Spoof, Travesty

**Burlington**  RA

**Burly**  Bluff, Stout

**Burmese**  Karen(ni), Naga, Shan

**Burn(er), Burning, Burnt**  Adust, Afire, Alow(e), Ardent, Argand, Ash, Auto-da-fé, Bats-wing, Beck, Bishop, Blaze, Blister, Brand, Bren(ne), Brook, Bunsen, Cauterise, Char, Chark, Cinder, Coal, Coke, Combust, Conflagration, Cremate, Crucial, Deflagrate, Eilding, Ember, Emboil, Fervid, Fircone, FIRE, Fishtail, Flagrant, Flare, Gleed, Gut, Holocaust, Ignite, In, Incendiary, Inure, Inust(ion), Kill, Lunt, Offering, On, Oxidise, Rill, Sati, Scald, Scorch, Sear, Sienna, Sike, Singe, Smoulder, Suttee, Swale, Thurible, Umber, Urent, Ustion, Weeke, Wick

**Burr(ing)**  Clote, Croup, Dialect, Knob, Rhotacism

**Burrow(er), Burrowing**  Dig, Earth, Fossorial, Gopher, Hole, How, Mole, Nuzzle, Sett, Tunnel, Viscacha, Warren, Worm

**Bursar**  Camerlengo, Camerlingo, Purser, Treasurer

**Bursitis**  Beat

**Burst(ing)**  Brast, Break, Dehisce, Disrupt, Dissilient, Ebullient, Erumpent, Erupt, EXPLODE, Fly, Implode, Pop, Sforzato, Shatter, Spasm, Spirt, Split, Spurt, Sprint, Stave, Tetterous

**Bury**  Cover, Eard, Engrave, Enhearse, Graff, Graft, Imbed, Inhearse, Inhume, Inter, Inurn, Repress, Sink, Ye(a)rd, Yird

**Bus**  Aero, Bandwagon, Car, Charabanc, Coach, Hondey, Mammy-wagon, Rattletrap, Tramcar, Trolley

**Bus conductor**  Cad, Clippy

**Bush(y)**  Bramble, Brier, Bullace, Busket, Clump, Dumose, Hawthorn, Hibiscus, Mallee, Mulberry, Outback, Shepherd, Shrub, Thicket, Tire, Tod(de)

**Bush-baby**  Nagapic

**Bushel**  Bu, Co(o)mb, Cor, Ephah, Fou, Homer, Peck, Weight, Wey

**Business**  Affair, Agency, Biz, Cerne, Co, Commerce, Company, Concern, Craft, Duty, Enterprise, Ergon, Establishment, Exchange, Fasti, Firm, Game, Gear, Industry, Line, Métier, Monkey, Palaver, Pi(d)geon, Pidgin, Practice, Professional, Shebang, Shop, To-do, Trade, Traffic, Tread, Turnover, Vocation

**Businessman**  Babbitt, City, Realtor, Trader, Tycoon

**Busk(er)**  Bodice, Corset, Entertainer, German-band

**Buskin(s)**  Brod(e)kin, Cothurn(us), Shoe

**Buss**  Kiss, Osculate, Smack

**Bussu**  Troelie, Troely, Troolie

**Bust**  Beano, Brast, Boob, Break, Chest, Falsies, Herm(a), Sculp, Shatter(ed), Spree, Statue, Term(inus), To-tear, To-torne, Ups(e)y

> **Bust**  may indicate an anagram

**Bustard**  Bird, Otis, Turkey

**Buster** Keaton

**Bustle** Ado, Do, Flap, Pad, Scurry, STIR, Swarm, Tournure, Whew

**Busy** Active, At (it), Deedy, Detective, Dick, Eident, Employ, Ergate, Eye, Hectic, Hive, Humming, Occupied, Ornate, Prodnose, Tec, Throng, Worksome

**Busybody** Bustler, Meddler, Noser, Snooper, Trout, Yenta

**But** Aber, Bar, Except, However, Merely, Nay, Only, Save, Sed, Simply, Tun

**Butch** He-man, Macho

**Butcher(y)** Cumberland, Decko, Dekko, Flesher, Kill, Killcow, Look, Massacre, Ovicide, Sever, Shambles, Shochet, Shufti, Slaughter, Slay

**Butler** Bedivere, Bread-chipper, RAB, Rhett, Samuel, Servant, Sewer, Sommelier, Steward

**Butt (in)** Aris, Barrel, Bunt, Clara, Enter, Geck, Goat, Header, Horn, Jesting-stock, Laughing-stock, Mark, Outspeckle, Pipe, Push, Ram, Roach, Scapegoat, Snipe, STOOGE, Target, Tun, Ups

**Butter** Adulation, Billy, Butyric, Flatter, Galam, Garcinia, Ghee, Ghi, Goat, Illipi, Illupi, Kokum, Mahua, Mahwa, Mow(r)a, Nutter, Pat, Peanut, Print, Ram, Scrape, Shea, Spread

**Buttercup** Crow-foot, Crow-toe, Ranunculus, Reate, Thalictrum

**Butterfingers** Muff

**Butterfly** Apollo, Argus, Blue, Brimstone, Cleopatra, Comma, Dilettante, Eclosion, Fritillary, Gate-keeper, Grayling, Hair-streak, Heath, Hesperid, Kallima, Lycaena, Monarch, Morpho, Nerves, Nymphean, Orange-tip, Papilionidae, Pieris, Psyche, Rhopalocera, Ringlet, Satyr(idae), Satyrinae, Skipper, Stamper, Sulphur, Swallow-tail, Thecla, Vanessa

**Buttermilk** Bland

**Butternut** Souari

**Butter-tree** Mahua, Mahwa, Mow(r)a

**Buttock(s)** Arse, Bottom, Coit, Derrière, Doup, Duff, Fundament, Hinderlan(d)s, Hurdies, Jacksy, Keister, Nates, Prat, Quoit, Seat

**Button(s)** Barrel, Bellboy, Fastener, Frog, Knob, Netsuke, Olivet, Page(boy), Stud, Switch, Toggle

**Buttonhole** Accost, Detain, Eye, Flower

**Buttress** Brace, Pier, Prop, Stay, Support

**Buxom** Bonnie, Busty, Plump

**Buy(er), Buying** Bribe, Coff, Corner, Customer, Emption, Engross, Monopsonist, Purchase, Shop, Shout, Spend, Trade, Vendee

> **Buyer** may indicate money

**Buzz(er)** Bee, Button, Fly, Hum, Rumour, Scram, Whirr, Whisper, Zed, Zoom

**Buzzard** Bee-kite, Bird, Hawk, Pern, Puttock, Vulture

**By**   At, Gin, Gone, In, Near, Nigh, Of, Past, Per, Through, With, X

**By Jove**   Egad

**By so much**   The

**By the way**   Incidentally, Obiter

**Bye-bye**   Adieu, Farewell, Tata

**Bygone**   Dead, Departed, Past, Yore

**Bypass**   Avoid, Circuit, DETOUR, Evade, Ignore, Omit, Shunt, Skirt

**By-product**   Epiphenomenon, Spin-off

**Byre**   Cowshed, Manger, Stable, Trough

**Byway**   Alley, Lane, Path

**Byword**   Ayword, Phrase, Proverb, Slogan

**Byzantine**   Complicated, Intricate, Intrince

# Cc

**C** Around, Caught, Celsius, Cent, Centigrade, Charlie, Conservative, San

**Cab** Boneshaker, Crawler, Drosky, Fiacre, Growler, Hackney, Hansom, Mini, Noddy, Taxi, Vettura

**Cabal(ler)** Arlington, Ashley, Buckingham, Clifford, Clique, Conspiracy, Coterie, Faction, Junto, Lauderdale, Party, Plot

**Cab(b)alistic** Abraxis, Mystic, Notarikon, Occult

**Cabaret** Burlesque, Floorshow

**Cabbage(-head), Cabbage soup** Borecole, Castock, Cauliflower, Cole, Collard, Crout, Custock, Kohlrabi, Kraut, Loaf, Loave, Pamphrey, Pe-tsai, Sauerkraut, Savoy, Shchi, Shtchi, Thieve, Wort

**Caber** Fir, Janker, Log, Sting

**Cabin** Berth, Bibby, Box, Cabana, Caboose, Coach, Cottage, Crannog, Cuddy, Den, Gondola, Hovel, Hut, Lodge, Log, Long-house, Room, Saloon, Shanty

**Cabin-boy** Grummet

**Cabinet** Bahut, Cabale, Case, Closet, Commode, Console, Cupboard, Kitchen, Ministry, Shadow, Shrinal

**Cabinet maker** Ebeniste, Joiner, PM

**Cable(way)** Coax(ial), Flex, Halser, Hawser, Junk, Lead, Outhaul, Rope, Slatch, Téléférique, TELEGRAM, Telpher(age), Wire

**Cache** Deposit, Hidlin(g)s, HOARD, Inter, Stash, Store, Treasure

**Cackle** Cluck, Gaggle, Gas, Haw, Snicker, Titter

**Cacography** Scrawl

**Cacophony** Babel, Caterwaul, Charivari, Discord, Jangle

**Cactus, Cactus-like** Alhagi, Cereus, Cholla, Dildo, Echino-, Jojoba, Maguey, Mescal, Nopal, Ocotillo, Opuntia, Peyote, Retama, Saguaro, Torch-thistle, Tuna, Xerophytic

**Cad** Base, Boor, Bounder, Churl, Cocoa, Heel, Oik, Rascal, Rotter, Skunk

**Cadaver(ous)** Body, Corpse, Ghastly, Haggard, Stiff

**Caddy** Porter, Teapoy

**Cadence** Beat, Fa-do, Flow, Lilt, Meter, Plagal, Rhythm

**Cadenza** Fireworks

**Cadet(s)** Junior, OTC, Scion, Syen, Trainee

**Cadge(r)** Bot, Bum, Impose, SCROUNGE, Sponge

**Cadmium** Cd

**Caesar** Nero

**Caesium** Cs

**Cafe(teria)** Automat, Brasserie, Bistro, Buvette, Canteen, Commissary, Diner, Dinette, Estaminet, Filtré, Greasy spoon, Pizzeria, Tearoom, Transport

**Cage** Bar, Battery, Box, Cavie, Confine, Coop, Corf, Enmew, Fold, Frame, Grate, Hutch, Mew, Pen, PRISON, Trave

**Cahoots** Hugger-mugger

**Cairn** Barp, Dog, Man, Mound, Raise

**Caisson** Bends

**Caitiff** Meanie

**Cajole(ry)** Beflum, Beguile, Blandish, Blarney, Carn(e)y, COAX, Jolly, Wheedle

**Cake** Agnus dei, Angel, Baba, Baklava, Banbury, Bannock, Barmbrack, Battenberg, Birthday, Brioche, Brownie, Buckwheat bun, Carcake, Chapat(t)i, Chillada, Chupati, Chupattie, Chupatty, Clot, Coburg, Croquette, Cruller, Crumpet, Dainty, Dundee, Eccles, Eclair, Farl(e), Flapjack, Frangipane, Frangipani, Fritter, Galette, Genoa, Gingerbread, Girdle, HARDEN, Hockey, Jannock, Jumbal, Jumbles, Koeksister, Lamington, Layer, Linseed, Macaroon, Madeleine, Madeira, Meringue, Mud, Muffin, Napoleon, Nut, Oatmeal, Pan, Panettone, Paratha, Parkin, Pat, Pavlova, Pikelet, PLASTER, Pomfret, Pone, Pontefract, Poor, Puff, Puftaloon(a), Puri, Ratafia, Rout, Rusk, Sachertorte, Sally Lunn, Savarin, Scone, Set, Simnel, Singing-hinny, Slab, Soul, Sponge, Sushi, Tablet, Tansy, Tipsy, Torte, Tortilla, Wafer, Waffle, Wonder

> **Cake** may indicate an anagram

**Cake-shaped** Placentiform

**Cakestand** Curate

**Cakewalk** Doddle

**Calaboose** Jail, Loghouse

**Calamitous, Calamity** Blow, Catastrophe, Dire, DISASTER, Distress, Fatal, Ill, Jane, Ruth, Storm, Tragic, Unlucky, Visitation, Woe

**Calcareous** Lithite

**Calcium** Ca, Quicklime, Whewellite

**Calculate, Calculation, Calculator** Abacus, Actuary, Compute(r), Cost, Design, Estimate, Extrapolate, Log, Quip(p)u, Rate, RECKON, Slide-rule, Sofar, Soroban, Tell

**Calculus** Cholelith, Integral, Lith, Science, Stone, Urolith

**Calendar** Agenda, Almanac, Diary, Fasti, Gregorian, Journal, Julian, Luach, Menology, Newgate, New Style, Sothic

**Calender(ing)** Dervish, Mangle, Swissing

**Calf** Ass, Bobby, Cf, Deacon, Dogie, Dogy, Freemartin, Leg, Poddy, Stirk, Sural, Tollie, Tolly, Veal, Vitular

**Caliban**  Moon-calf

**Calibrate, Calibre**  Bore, Capacity, Graduate, Mark, QUALITY, Text

**Californium**  Cf

**Caliph**  Abbasid(e), Vathek

**Call(ed), Calling, Call on, Call up**  Appeal, Arraign, Art, Azan, Bawl, Beck, Behote, Bevy, Bid, Business, Buzz, Chamade, Cite, Claim, Clang, Clarion, Cleep, Clepe, Conscript Convene, Convoke, Cooee, Cry, Curtain, Dial, Drift, Dub, Evoke, Gam, Go, Hallali, Haro, Heads, Hech, Hete, Hey, Hight, Ho, Hot(e), Hurra(h), Job, Local, Métier, Mobilise, Mot, Name, Nap, Need, Nempt, Nominate, Olé, Page, Phone, Post, Proo, Pruh, Rechate, Recheat, Retreat, Reveille, Ring, Roll, Route, Sa-sa, Sennet, SHOUT, Shut-out, Slam, Slander, Slogan, Soho, Sola, STD, Style, Subpoena, Summon(s), Tails, Tantivy, Telephone, Term, Toho, Trumpet, Visit, Vocation, Whoa-ho-ho, Yell, Yo, Yodel, Yodle, Yoicks

**Calla(s)**  Aroid, Lily, Maria

**Caller**  Fresh, Herring, Inspector, Muezzin, Rep, Traveller, VISITOR

**Callosity, Callous**  Bunion, Cold, Corn, Hard, Horny, Obtuse, Seg, Thylose, Tough, Unfeeling

**Callow**  Crude, Green, Immature, Jejune

**Calm**  Abate, Alegge, Allay, Allege, Appease, Ataraxy, Composed, Cool, Doldrums, Easy, Easy-osy, Eye, Flat, Halcyon, Loun(d), Lown(d), Lull, Mild, Millpond, Pacify, Peaceful, Philosophical, Placate, Placid, Quell, Quiet, Repose, Serene, Settle, Sleek, SOOTHE, Still, Subside, Tranquil(lise), Unturbid, Windless

**Calumniate, Calumny**  Aspersion, Backbite, Defame, Libel, Malign, Slander, Slur

**Calvary**  Golgotha

**Calvin(ist)**  Accusative, Genevan, Hopkins, Huguenot, Infralapsarian, Predestination, Sublapsarian

**Calydonian**  Boar

**Calypso**  Ogygia, Siren, SONG

**Cam**  Cog, River, Snail, Tappet

**Camaraderie**  Fellowship, Rapport

**Camber**  Slope

**Cambium**  Phellogen

**Cambodian**  Khmer (Rouge)

**Cambria**  Wales

**Cambridge**  Cantab, Squat

**Came**  Arrived

**Camel, Camel train**  Artiodactyla, Bactrian, Caisson, Colt, Dromedary, Kafila, Llama, Oont, Sopwith

**Cameo**  Anaglyph, Camaieu, Carving

**Camera** Chambers, Cine, Flash, Iconoscope, Kodak, Obscura, Orthicon, Pantoscope, Pinhole, Somascope

**Camouflage** Conceal, DISGUISE, Mark, Maskirovka, War-dress

> **Camouflaged** may indicate an anagram

**Camp(er)** Affectation, Banal, Belsen, Bivouac, Caerleon, Castral, Colditz, David, Depot, D(o)uar, Dumdum, Faction, Flaunt, Gulag, L(a)ager, Lashkar, Leaguer, Manyata, Oflag, Outlie, Side, Stagey, Stalag, Stative, Swagman, Tent, Theatrical

**Campaign(er)** Battle, Blitz, Canvass, Crusade, Drive, Field, Jihad, Mission, Promotion, Run, Satyagraha, Smear, Stint, Venture, Veteran, War, Warray, Warrey, Whistle-stop

**Campanula** Rampion

**Campeador** Chief, Cid

**Camp-follower** Lascar, Sutler

**Camphor** Menthol

**Campion** Knap-bottle, Lychnis, Silene

> **Camptown** may indicate de-

**Can** Able, Billy, Bog, Capable, Churn, Gaol, Gents, Is able, Jug, Karsy, Loo, May, Nick, Pail, Pot, Preserve, PRISON, Stir, Tin

**Canadian** Acadian, Canuck, Inuit, Quebeccer

**Canal** Alimentary, Ampul, Channel, Conduit, Duct, Ea, Foss(e), Groove, Gut, Kiel, Lode, Meatus, Midi, Navigation, Panama, Pipe, Pound, Scala, Semi-circular, Soo, Suez, Urethra, Waterway, Zanja

**Canal-boat** Barge, Fly-boat, Gondola, Vaporetto

**Canapé** Cate, Snack, Titbit

**Canary** Bird, Grass, Roller, Serin, Singer, Yellow

**Cancel** Abrogate, Adeem, Annul, Counteract, Countermand, Delete, Destroy, Erase, Kill, Negate, Nullify, Remit, Repeal, Rescind, Retrait, Revoke, Scrub, Void

**Cancer(ous)** Carcinoma, Crab, Curse, Tropic, Tumour, Wolf

**Candela** Cd

> **Candelabra** see CANDLE(STICK)

**Candid, Candour** Albedo, Blunt, Camera, Frank, Honesty, Open

**Candidate** Applicant, Aspirant, Contestant, Entrant, Nominee, Postulant

**Candied, Candy** Caramel, Glace, Snow, Succade, Sweet

**Candle(stick), Candelabra** Amandine, Bougie, C(i)erge, Dip, Fetch, Jesse, Lampadary, Light, Menorah, Pricket, Roman, Rushlight, Sconce, Serge, Slut, Sperm, Tace, Tallow, Taper, Torchère, Tricerion, Wax

**Candlefish** Eulachon, Oolakon, Oulachon, Oulakon, Ulic(h)an, Ulic(h)on, Ulikon

**Cane** Arrow, Baculine, Bamboo, Baste, Beat, Birk, Dari, Dhurra, Doura,

Dur(r)a, Ferula, Ferule, Goor, Gur, Jambee, Malacca, Narthex, Penang-lawyer, Pointer, Rat(t)an, Rod, Stick, Swish, Switch, Tickler, Vare, Wand, Whangee

**Canine** Dog, Eye-tooth

**Canker** Corrosion, Curse, Lesion, Ulcer

**Cannabis** Bhang, Boneset, Ganja, Ganny, Hash, Hemp, Henry, Louie, Pot

**Cannibal** Anthropophagus, Heathen, Long pig, Ogre, Thyestean

**Cannon** Amusette, Barrage, Basilisk, Bombard, Carronade, Collide, Criterion, Culverin, Drake, Gun, Howitzer, Kiss, Nursery, Saker, Stern-chaser, Zamboorak, Zomboruk, Zumbooru(c)k

**Cannot** Canna, Cant, Downa(e), Downay

**Canny** Careful, Frugal, Prudent, Scot, Shrewd, Slee, Sly, Thrifty, Wily, Wise

**Canoe(ist)** Bidarka, Bidarkee, Canader, Dugout, Kayak, Monoxylon, Montaria, Oomiack, Paddler, Pirogue, Rob Roy, Woodskin

**Canon** Austin, Chapter, Chasuble, Code, Isodorian, LAW, Line, Mathurin(e), Nocturn, Polyphony, Prebendary, Rota, Round, Rule, Square, Squier, Squire, Standard, Tenet, Unity

**Canopy** Awning, Baldachin, Baldaquin, Dais, He(a)rse, Majesty, Marquee, Marquise, Pavilion, State, Tabernacle, Tent, Tester

**Cant** Argot, Bevel, Heel, Incline, Jargon, Mummery, Patois, Patter, Rogue's Latin, Shelta, Slang, Slope, Tip

**Cantankerous** Cussed, Fire-eater, Ornery

**Cantata** Motet, Tobacco

**Canteen** Chuck-wagon, Mess, Naafi

**Canter** Amble, Hypocrite, Jog, Lope, Tit(t)up, Tripple

**Canto** Air, Fit(te), Fitt, Fytte, Melody, Verse

**Canton** Basle, District, Jura, Quarter, Uri, Vaud

**Cantred** Commot(e)

**Canvas** Awning, Burlap, Dra(b)bler, Lug-sail, Mainsail, Marquee, Oil-cloth, Paint, Raven's-duck, Reef, SAIL, Staysail, Stunsail, Tent, Trysail, Wigan

**Canvass(er)** Agent, Doorstep, Drum, Poll, Solicit

> **Canvasser** may indicate a painter, or a camper

**Canyon** Canada, Defile, Nal(l)a, Nallah

**Cap(ped)** Abacot, Amorce, Balaclava, Balmoral, Barret, Bendigo, Ber(r)et, Biggin, Biretta, Blakey, Blue, Bonnet-rouge, Bycoket, Calotte, Calpac(k), Calyptrate, Capeline, Caul, Chaco, Chape, Chapeau, Chaperon, Chapka, Chechia, Cheese-cutter, Cloth, Cockernony, Coif, Cope, Cowl, CROWN, Czapka, Deerstalker, Dunce's, Ferrule, Havelock, HAT, Iceberg, International, Juliet, Kalpak, Kepi, Kilmarnock, Kippa, Kiss-me (quick), Knee, Lid, Mob, Monmouth, Monteer, Montero, Mor(r)ion, Mortar-board,

Mutch, Outdo, Pagri, Patellar, Percussion, Perplex, Phrygian, Pileus, Puggaree, Quoif, Schapska, Shako, Square, Summit, SURPASS, Taj, Tam(o-shanter), Toe, Top, Toque, Toy, Trencher, Tuque, Yarmulka, Yarmulke, Zuchetto

**Capable, Capability** Able, Brown, Capacity, Competent, Deft, Effectual, Efficient, Qualified, Skilled, Susceptible

**Capacity** Aptitude, Cab, Competence, Content, Cor, Cubic, Endowment, Function, Limit, Log, Power, Qua, Receipt, Scope, Size, Tonnage, Valence, Volume

**Caparison** Trap(pings)

**Cape** Agulhas, Canaveral, Cloak, Cod, Domino, Dungeness, Faldetta, Fanon, Farewell, Fear, Fichu, Finisterre, Flattery, Hatteras, Head(land), Hoe, Hogh, Horn, Inverness, Lizard, Mant(e)let, Mantle, Matapan, Mo(z)zetta, Muleta, Ness, North, Palatine, Pelerine, Peninsula, Point, Poncho, Race, Ras, Roca, Ruana, Sable, Sandy, Scaw, Skaw, Sontag, Talma, Tippet, Trafalgar, Ushant, Waterproof, Wrath

**Cape Town** SA

**Caper(ing)** Antic, Boer, Capparis, Capriole, Cavort, Dance, Dido, Flisk, Frisk, Frolic, Gambado, Gambol, Harmala, Harmalin(e), Harmel, Harmin(e), Prance, Prank, Saltant, Scoup, Scowp, Skip, Tit(t)up

**Capet** Marie Antoinette

**Capital** Abidjan, Abiya, Ac(c)ra, Agana, A1, Albany, Amman, Ankara, Antioch, Apia, Assets, Athens, Baghdad, Bamako, Bangui, Banjul, Belgrade, Berlin, Bogota, Bonn, Boodle, Brasilia, Bravo, Brno, Brussels, Bucharest, Bully, Cairo, Canberra, Cap, Caracas, Chapiter, Chaptrel, Charleston, Colombo, Constantinople, Copenhagen, Dacca, Dakar, Darwin, Delhi, Djibouti, Doha, Doric, Douglas, Enugu, Euge, Excellent, Faro, Float, Floating, Funchal, Great, Hanoi, Harare, Havana, Helix, Helsinki, Hobart, Honolulu, Ibadan, Initial, Ipoh, Jos, Kabul, Kampala, Karachi, Katmandu, Kiel, Kiev, Kingston, Kinshasa, Lagos, Laos, Lassa, Leningrad, Lethal, Lhasa, Lima, Lisbon, Little Rock, London, Lulu, Lusaka, Madrid, Male, Metropolis, Montevideo, Moscow, Muscat, Nairobi, Nassau, Nicosia, Nineveh, Nuuk, Oslo, Ottawa, Palermo, Pand(a)emonium, Paris, Peking, Persepolis, Pretoria, Principal, Providence, Quito, Rabat, Rangoon, Reykjavik, Riga, Rio, Riyadh, Rome, Santiago, Seat, Seoul, Shanghai, Sofia, Splendid, Sport, Stock, Stockholm, Sucré, Super, Susa, Suva, Taipei, Tashkent, Tbilisi, Teh(e)ran, Thebes, Tirana, Topping, Trebizond, UC, Ufa, Upper case, Vaduz, Valladolid, Valletta, Vienna, Warsaw, Washington, Wellington, Windhoek, Xian, Yerevan

**Capitalist** Financier, Moneyer

> **Capitalist** may indicate one living in a capital

**Capitulate** Acquiesce, Comply, SURRENDER

**Capless** Barc

> **Capless** may indicate first letter missing

**Capone** Al, Scarface

> **Capriccioso** may indicate an anagram

**Caprice, Capricious** Arbitrary, Boutade, Capernoitie, Conceit, Desultory, Erratic, Fancy, Fitful, Humoresk, Humoresque, Irony, Mood, Perverse, Quirk, Vagary, Wayward, Whim(sy)

**Capsize** Overbalance, Purl, Tip, Upset, Whemmle, Whomble

> **Capsized** may indicate a word upside down

**Capstan** Sprocket, Windlass

**Capsule** Amp(o)ule, Cachet, Habitat, Ootheca, Orbiter, Pill, Spacecraft, Urn

**Captain** Ahab, Bligh, Bobadil, Brassbound, Capt, Chief, Cid, Commander, Cook, Copper, Cuttle, Flint, Group, Hornblower, Kettle, Kidd, Leader, Macheath, Master, Nemo, Old man, Patroon, Privateer, Skip(per), Standish, Subah(dar), Subedar, Swing, Trierarch

**Caption** Heading, Headline, Inscription, Masthead, Sub-title, Title

**Captious** Critical, Peevish

**Captivate(d), Captivating** Beguile, Bewitch, Charm, Enamour, Enthrall, Epris(e), Take, Winsome

**Captive, Captivity** Bonds, Duress, POW, Prisoner, Slave

**Capture** Abduct, Annex, Bag, Catch, Collar, Cop, Grab, Land, Net, Prize, Rush, Seize, Snabble, Snaffle, Snare, TAKE

**Capuchin** Cebus, Monkey, Sajou

**Car** Astra, Audi, Auto, Banger, Beetle, BL, Bomb, Brake, Buick, Bus, Cab(riolet), Cadillac, Catafalco, Catafalque, Chariot, Coach, Convertible, Cortina, Coupé, Crate, Daimler, Diner, Dodgem, Drophead, Elf, Estate, Fastback, Fiat, Flivver, Ford, Formula, Gondola, GT, Hardtop, Hatchback, Heap, Hearse, Hillman, Hot-rod, Jalopy, Lada, Lagonda, Lancia, Landaulet, Limo, Limousine, Merc(edes), MG, Mini, Morris, Nacelle, Notchback, Opel, Panda, Racer, Ragtop, Roadster, Roller, Rolls, RR, Runabout, Sedan, Sleeper, Subcompact, Sunbeam, Telpher, Tin Lizzie, Tonneau, Tourer, Tram, Turbo, Vehicle, VW

**Caravan** Caf(f)ila, Convoy, Fleet, Kafila, Safari, Trailer

**Caravanserai** Choltry, Choutry, Inn, Khan

**Caraway** Aj(o)wan, Carvy, Seed

**Car-back** Boot, Dick(e)y, Tonneau

**Carbamide** Urea

**Carbine** Gun, Musket

**Carbohydrate** Cellulose, Gycogen, Inulin, Ketose, Pectin, Pentosane, Saccharide, Starch, Sugar

**Carbolic** Orcin

**Carbon(ate)** Ankerite, Austerite, C, Charcoal, Coke, Dialogite, Diamond, Flimsy, Graphite, Lampblack, Natron, Scawtite, Spode, Spodium, Urao

**Carbon deficiency** Acapnia

**Carbuncle** Anthrax, Ruby

**Carcase, Carcass** Body, Cadaver, Carrion, Corpse, Cutter, Krang, Kreng, Morkin

**Card(s)** Ace, Baccarat, Basto, Bill, Birthday, Bower, Canasta, Cartes, Caution, Chicane, Club, Comb, Deck, Deuce, Diamond, Ecarté, Eccentric, Euchre, Flaught, GAME, Hand, Heart, Honour, Identity, Jack, Joker, King, Loo, Manille, Matador, Meishi, Mise, Mistigris, Mogul, Mournival, Ombre, Pack, Pasteboard, PC, Placard, Plastic, Queen, Quiz, Rippler, Rove, Scribble, Singleton, Soda, Solo, Spade, Strawboard, Swab, Swob, Talon, Tarok, Tarot, Tease(r), Tenace, Ticket, Tose, Toze, Trump, Valentine, Wag, Weirdie, Wild, Zener

**Card-player** Dealer, Pone

**Cardigan** Jacket, Wam(m)us, Wampus, Woolly

**Cardinal** Camerlingo, Chief, College, Eminence, Eminent, Grosbeak, Hat, HE, Hume, Legate, Manning, Newman, Number, Pivotal, Polar, Prelate, Radical, Red, Richelieu, Sin, Spellman, Virtue, Vital, Ximenes

**Care** Attention, Burden, Cark, Caution, Cerne, Cherish, CONCERN, Cosset, Grief, Heed, Intensive, Kaugh, Keep, Kiaugh, Mind, Pains, Reck(e), Reke, Retch, TEND, Tenty, Worry

**Career** Course, Hurtle, Life, Line, Run, Rush, Speed, Start, Tear, Vocation

> **Carefree** see CARELESS

**Careful(ly)** Canny, Chary, Discreet, Gentle, Hooly, Meticulous, Mindful, Pernickety, Prudent, Scrimp, Studious, Tentie, Tenty, Vigilant, Ware, Wary

**Careless** Casual, Cheery, Debonair, Easy, Free-minded, Gallio, Inadvertent, Insouciance, Lax, Lighthearted, Négligé, NEGLIGENT, Nonchalant, Oversight, Rash, Remiss, Resigned, Riley, Slapdash, Slaphappy, Slipshod, Sloven(ly), Slubber, Taupie, Tawpie, Unguarded, Untenty, Unwary

> **Carelessly** may indicate an anagram

**Caress** Bill, Coy, Embrace, Fondle, Kiss, Noursle, Nursle, Pet, Touch

**Caretaker** Concierge, Curator, Custodian, Guardian, Janitor, Sexton, Warden

**Careworn** Haggard, Lined, Tired, Weary

**Cargo** Burden, Fraught, Freight, Lading, Last, LOAD, Payload, Shipment

**Caribbean** Soca, Sokah, WI

**Caricature, Caricaturist** Ape, Beerbohm, Burlesque, Caron d'Ache, Cartoon, Cruikshank, Doyle, Farce, Gillray, Rowlandson, Skit, Spy, Travesty

**Carlin** Pug

**Carmelite** Barefoot

**Carmen** AA, BL, Chai, RAC

**Carnage** Butchery, Massacre, Slaughter

**Carnal** Bestial, Lewd, Sensual, Sexual, Worldly

**Carnation** Dianthus, Malmaison, Picotee, Pink

**Carnival** Fair, Festival, Fete, Moomba, Revelry

**Carnivore** Cacomistle, Cacomixl, Creodont, Fo(u)ssa, Glutton

**Carob** Algarroba, Locust

**Carol** Noel, Sing, Song, Wassail, Yodel

**Carousal, Carouse** Bend, Birl(e), Bouse, Bride-ale, Compotation, Drink, Mallemaroking, Mollie, Orge, Orgy, REVEL, Roist, Screed, Spree, Upsee, Upsey, Upsy, Wassail

**Carp(er)** Beef, Censure, Complain, Crab, Critic, Crucian, Crusian, Gibel, Goldfish, Id(e), Kvetch, Mirror, Mome, Nag, Nibble, Roach, Roundfish, Scold, Twitch

**Carpenter** Cabinet-maker, Carfindo, Chips, Fitter, Joiner, Joseph, Menuisier, Quince, Tenoner, Wright

> **Carpenter** may indicate an anagram

**Carpet** Axminster, Aubusson, Beetle, Berate, Bessarabian, Broadloom, Brussels, Castigate, Chide, Drugget, Durrie, Kali, Kelim, Khilim, Kidderminster, Kilim, Kirman, Lecture, Mat, Moquette, Rate, Reprimand, Rug, Runner, Shark, Turkey, Wig

**Carriage** Bandy, Barouche, Bearing, Berlin(e), Bier, Brit(sch)ka, Britska, Britzka, Brougham, Buckboard, Cab, Calash, Caleche, Cariole, Caroche, Carriole, Chaise, Charet, Chariot, Chassis, Chay, Clarence, Coach, Coch, Conveyance, Coupé, Curricle, Demeanour, Dennet, Deportment, Désobligeante, Diner, Dos-a-dos, Do-si-do, Drag, Dros(h)ky, Ekka, Equipage, Fiacre, Fly, Gig, Go-cart, Growler, Haulage, Herdic, Horseless, Hurly-hacket, Landau(let), Non-smoker, Norimon, Phaeton, Pick-a-back, Pochaise, Pochay, Poise, Port(age), Postchaise, Posture, Poyse, Pram, Pullman, Ratha, Remise, Rickshaw, Rockaway, Shay, Sled, Sleeper, Sociable, Spider, Stanhope, Sulky, Taxi, Tenue, Tilbury, Tim-whiskey, Tonga, Trap, Vetture, Victoria, Wagonette, Whirligig, Whisk(e)y

**Carrier** Airline, Arm, Baldric, Barkis, Barrow, Bomb-ketch, Caddy, Cadge, Camel, Coaster, Conveyor, Fomes, Frog, Grid, Hamper, Haversack, Hod, Janker, Jill, Nosebag, Noyade, Pigeon, Porter, Rucksack, Satchel, Schistosoma, Semantide, Sling, Stretcher, TRAY, Vector

**Carrion** Cadaver, Carcase, Carcass, Flesh, Ket, Stapelia

**Carrots** Seseli, Titian

**Carry(ing)** Bear, Chair, Convey, Ferry, Frogmarch, Hawk, Hent, Hump, Land, Pack, Pickaback, Sustain, Tote, TRANSPORT, Trant, With, Yank

**Carry on** Continue, Wage

**Carry out** Execute, Pursue

**Cart** Bandy, Barrow, Bogey, Buck, Chapel, Dog, Dolly, Dray, Furphy, Gambo, Gill, Governess, Gurney, Hackery, Jag, Jill, Lead, Mail, Rickshaw, Shandry, Trolley, Tumbrel, Tumbril, Wag(g)on, Wain, Whitechapel

**Cartel** Duopoly, Ring, Syndicate

**Carthaginian** Punic

**Carthorse** Shire

**Carthusian** Bruno

**Cartilage** Chondrus, Cricoid, Gristle, Lytta, Meniscus, Tendron, Tragus

**Cartload** Seam

**Cartographer** Chartist, Mercator, Speed

**Carton** Box, Case, Crate, Sydney, Tub

**Cartoon(ist)** Animated, Bairnsfather, Caricature, Comic, Disney, Drawn, Emmet, Fougasse, Fumetto, Garland, Leech, Low, Mel, Partridge, Popeye, Short, Spy, Strip, Tenniel, Tintin, Trog

**Cartridge** Blank, Bullet, Cartouche, Doppie, Shell

**Cart-track** Rut

**Cartwheel** Handspring

**Caruncle** Carnosity

**Carve(d), Carver, Carving** Alcimedon, Armchair, Bas relief, Cameo, Chisel, Crocket, Cut, Dismember, Doone, Enchase Entail, Entayle, Gibbons, Glyptic, Hew, Incise, Inscribe, Intaglio, Netsuke, Nick, Petroglyph, Scrimshaw, Sculp(t), Slice, Tondo, Truncheon, Whittle

**Caryatid** Column, Telamon

**Casanova** Leman

**Cascade** Cataract, Fall, Lin(n), Stream, Waterfall

**Cascara** Buckthorn, Rhamnus, Wahoo

**Case(s), Casing** Abessive, Ablative, Accusative, Action, Adessive, Allative, Altered, Aril, Assumpsit, Attaché, Beer, Bere, Blimp, Box, Brief, C, Ca, Cabinet, Calyx, Canister, Canterbury, Capsule, Cartouch(e), Cartridge, Chase, Chrysalis, Cocoon, Compact, Crate, Crust, Dative, Declension, Detinue, Dispatch, Dossier, Elytron, Enallage, Essive, Etui, Etwee, Example, Flan, Flapjack, Frame, Genitive, Grip, Hanaper, Hold-all, Housewife, Hull, Humidor, Husk, IN CASE, Indusium, Instance, Keister, Locative, Locket, Lorica, Manche, Matter, Nacelle, Nominative, Non-suit, Nutshell, Objective, Ochrea, Ocrea, Papeterie, Patient, Penner, Phylactery, Plight, Plummer-block, Pod, Port, Possessive, Prima facie, Quiver, Sabretache, Scabbard, Sheath(e), Situation, Six-pack, Sporran, Stead, Sted, Subjunctive, Suit, Tantalus, Tea-chest, Theca, Tichborne, Trunk, Valise, Vasculum, Vocative, Volva, Walise, Wardian

**Case-harden** Nitrode

**Casein** Curd

**Casement** Frame, Roger, Sash, Window

**Cash** Blunt, Bonus, Bounty, Change, Coin, Dot, Float, Imprest, Lolly, MONEY, Needful, Ochre, Pence, Ready, Realise, Rhino, Spondulicks, Stumpy, Tender, Tin, Wampum, Wherewithal

**Cashier**  Annul, Break, Depose, Disbar, Dismiss, Teller, Treasurer

**Cashmere**  Circassienne

**Cask(et)**  Armet, Barrel, Barrico, Bas(i)net, Box, Breaker, Butt, Cade, Casque, Cassette, Drum, Firkin, Galeate, Harness, Heaume, Hogshead, Keg, Octave, Pin, Pipe, Puncheon, Pyxis, Run(d)let, Salade, Sallet, Sarcophagus, Shrine, Solera, Tierce, Tun

**Cask-stand**  Stillion

**Cassava**  Tapioca, Yucca

**Casserole**  Diable, Pot, Salmi, Terrine

**Cassette**  Cartridge

**Cassia**  Cleanser, Senna

**Cassio**  Lieutenant

**Cassiterite**  Needle-tin, Tinstone

**Cassock**  Gown, Soutane

**Cast (off)**  Actors, Add, Appearance, Bung, Die, Discard, Ecdysis, Eject, Exuviae, Exuvial, Fling, Found, Fusil, Heave, Hob, Hue, Hurl, Ingo(w)es, Keb, Look, Lose, Mew, Molt, Mould, Plaster(stone), Players, Put, Reject, Shed, Shoot, Sling, Slive, Slough, Spoil, THROW, Toss, Tot, Warp, Ytost

> **Cast**  may indicate an anagram or a piece of a word missing

**Castanet**  Crotal(um), Knackers

**Castaway**  Adrift, Crusoe, Left, Outcast, Stranded

> **Cast by**  may indicate surrounded by

**Caste**  Class, Group, Harijan, Hova, Rank, Sect, Sudra, Varna

**Castigate**  Berate, Chastise, Criticise, Keelhaul, Lash, Punish

**Cast-iron**  Spiegeleisen

**Castle(d)**  Adamant, Arundel, Balmoral, Bamburgh, Bastille, Broch, C, Carbonek, Casbah, Chillon, Citadel, Corfe, Dangerous, Despair, Doubting, Dunsinane, Egremont, Elephant, Elsinore, Fastness, Fort, Fotheringhay, Glamis, Harlech, Kasba(h), Leeds, Malperdy, Man, More, Otranto, Perilous, Rackrent, Raglan, Rook, Schloss, Span, Stokesay, Stronghold, Tintagel, Windsor

**Castor-oil**  Ricinus

**Castrate(d)**  Cut, Doctor, Emasculate, Eunuch, Evirate, Geld, Glib, Mutilate, Spado, Spay, Swig

**Castro**  Fidel

**Casual**  Accidental, Adventitious, Airy, Blasé, Chance, Grass, Haphazard, Idle, Incidental, Informal, Lackadaisical, Odd(ment), Offhand, Orra, Random, Sporadic, Stray, Temp

**Casualty**  Caduac, Chance-medley, VICTIM

**Casuist**  Jesuit

**Cat**  Abyssinian, Alley, Angora, Asparagus, Baudrons, Binturong, Bobcat,

Cacomistle, Cacomixl, Caracal, Cheetah, Cheshire, Civet, Clowder, Cop, Cougar, Dandy, Dasyure, Delundung, Eyra, Feline, Felix, Foss(a), Foussa, Genet(te), Gib, Gossip, Grimalkin, Gus, Hipster, Hodge, Jaguar(ondi), Jaguarundi, Jazzer, Kilkenny, Kit, Lair, Linsang, Lynx, Maltese, Manul, Margay, Marmalade, Mehitabel, Mewer, Mog, Mouser, Musang, Nandine, Neuter, Nib, Ocelot, Ounce, Painter, Pard, Practical, Puma, Puss, Rasse, Rex, Rumpy, Scourge, Seal-point, Serval, Siamese, Sick, Spew, Spue, Swinger, Tabby, Tibert, Tiger, Tigon, Tigress, Tobermory, Tom, Tortoise-shell, Tybalt, Viverra, Weasel, Zibet(h)

**Catacomb** Cemetery, Crypt, Hypogeum, Vault

**Catalepsy** Catatony, Trance

**Catalogue** Dewey, Index, Inventory, List, Litany, Messier, Ragman, Ragment, Raisonné, Record, Register, Table, Tabulate

**Catalyst** AcceleratorAgent, Influence, Unicase

**Catamite** Ingle

**Catapult** Ballista, Launch, Mangonel, Perrier, Petrary, Propel, Shanghai, Sling, Stone-bow, Tormentum, Trebuchet, Wye, Y

**Cataract** Cascade, Film, Pearl, Torrent, Waterfall, Web and pin

**Catarrh** Coryza, Rheum

**Catastrophe** Calamity, DISASTER, Doom, Epitasis, Fiasco, Meltdown

**Cat-call** Boo, Mew, Miaow, Miaul, Razz, Wawl, Wrawl

**Catch(y), Caught** Air, Apprehend, Attract, Bag, Benet, Bone, C, Chape, Clasp, Cog, Collar, Contract, Cop, Corner, Ct, Deprehend, Detent, Dolly, Engage, Enmesh, Ensnare, Entoil, Entrap, Fang, Field, Fumble, Gaper, Get, Glee(some), Grasp, Had, Hank, Haud, Haul, Hold, Hook, Inmesh, Keddah, Keight, Kep(pit), Kheda, Kill, Land, Lapse, Lasso, Latch, Lime, Morse, Nab, Nail, Net, Nick, Nim, Nobble, Noose, Overhear, Overhcnt, Overtake, Parti, Pawl, Rap, Release, Rope, Rub, Sear, See(n), Seize, SNAG, Snap, Snare, Snig, SONG, Surprise, Swindle, Tack, Take, Trammel, Trap, Trawl, Trick, Troll, Twig, Understand, Wrestle

**Catchword** Motto, Shibboleth, Slogan, Tag

**Catechism** Carritch, Test

**Categorise, Category** CLASS, Genus, Label, Order, Taxon

**Cater(er)** Acatour, Cellarer, Feed, Manciple, PROVIDE, Serve, Steward, Supply, Victualler

**Caterpillar** Aweto, Cutworm, Eruciform, Geometer, Hop-dog, Hornworm, Larva, Looper, Osmeterium, Palmer, Tent, Web-worm, Woolly-bear

**Catfish** Hassar, Woof

**Cathartic** Turbeth

**Cathedral** Basilica, Chartres, Chester, Cologne, Dome, Duomo, Ely, Minster, Notre Dame, Rheims, Sens, Wells, Winchester

**Catherine** Braganza, Parr

**Catherine-wheel** Girandole

**Cathode** Electrode, Filament, Ray

**Catholic** Broad, Ecumenical, General, Irvingism, Jebusite, Latin, Liberal, Marian, Ostiary, Papalist, Papaprelatist, Papist, Redemptionist, Roman, Spike, Taig, Teague, Thomist, Tory, Tridentine, Universal, Wide

**Catkin** Amentum, Chat, Pussy-willow

**Cat-lover** Ailurophile

**Catmint** Nep, Nepeta

**Cato** Porcian, Uticensis

**Cats-eye** Chatoyant, Cymophane

**Catsmeat** Lights

**Catspaw** Pawn, Tool

**Cat's tail** Reed-mace, Typha

**Cat's whiskers** Vibrissa

**Cattle(pen)** Africander, Ankole, Aver, Ayrshire, Beefalo, Buffalo, Charol(l)ais, Chillingham, Dexter, Drove, Durham, Fee, Friesland, Galloway, Gaur, Gayal, Gyal, Herd, Hereford, Highland, Kine, Kraal, Ky(e), Kyloe, Lairage, Limousin, Longhorn, Luing, Neat, Nout, Nowt, Owsen, Oxen, Rabble, Redpoll, Rother, Shorthorn, Simment(h)al, Soum, Sowm, Steer, Stock, Store, Stot, Teeswater

**Cattle disease** Anthrax, Quarter-ill, Red-water, Rinderpest, Scrapie

**Cattle food** Fodder

**Cattleman** Cowboy, Herder, Maverick, Rancher, Stock-rider

**Catty** Kin, Spiteful

**Caucasian** Aryan, European, Melanochroi, Paleface, Semite, Shemite, White, Yezdi, Yezidee, Zezidee

**Caucus** Assembly, Gathering, Race

> **Caught** see CATCH

**Caul** Baby-hood, Kell, Membrane, Sillyhow

**Cauldron** Kettle, Pot

**Cauliflower** Curd, Ear, Floret

**Caulk** Fill, Pitch, Snooze

**Causation, Cause(d)** Actiology, Agent, Beget, Breed, Compel, Create, Crusade, Due, Effect, Efficient, Factor, Flag-day, Formal, Gar(re), Generate, Ideal, Induce, Lead, Lost, Make, Material, Motive, OCCASION, Parent, Provoke, Reason, Root, Sake, Source, Topic, Ultimate

**Caustic** Acid, Acrimonious, Alkaline, Burning, Erodent, Escharotic, Moxa, Pungent, Sarcastic, Scathing, Seare, Tart, Vitriol, Withering

**Cauterise** Brand, Burn, Disinfect, Inustion

**Caution, Cautious (person)** Achitophel, Admonish, Ahithophel, Alert, Amber, Awarn, Beware, Cagey, Care, Cave, Caveat, Chary, Circumspect, Cure, Deliberate, Discretion, Fabian, Gingerly, Guard(ed), Heedful, Leery,

Prudent, Rum, Skite, Vigilant, Ware, WARN, Wary

**Cavalcade** Pageant, Parade, Procession, Sowarree, Sowarry

**Cavalier** Brusque, Cicisbeo, Gallant, Lively, Malignant, Offhand, Peart, Rider, Royalist

**Cavalry(man)** Blues, Cornet, Cossack, Dragoon, Horse, Hussar, Ironsides, Lancers, Ressaldar, Risaldar, Rutter, Sabres, Sillidar, Spahi, Uhlan, Yeomanry

**Cave(rn), Cave-dwelling** Acherusia, Altamira, Antar, Antre, Beware, Cellar, Collapse, Corycian, Den, Domdaniel, Erebus, Fore, Grot(to), Hollow, Look-out, Lupercal, Mammoth, Nix, Pot-hole, Proteus, Sepulchre, Spel(a)ean, Speleology, Spelunker, Speos, Tassili, Vault, Ware, Weem

**Caveman** Adullam, Aladdin, Fingal, Neanderthal, Primitive, Troglodyte

**Caviare** Beluga, Roe, Sturgeon

**Cavil** Carp, Haggle, Quibble

**Cavity** Amygdale, Atrial, Chamber, Coelom(e), Concepticle, Concha, Crater, Crypt, Dent, Druse, Enteron, Follicle, Foss, Gap, Geode, Hold, Hole, Lacuna, Locule, Orbita, Mediastinum, Orifice, Pocket, Sinus, Tear, Vacuole, Vein, Vesicle, Vitta, Vomica, Vug, Well

**Cavort(ing)** Jag

**Cavy** Agouti, Capybara, Hograt, Paca

**Cease** Abate, Blin, Cut, Desist, Die, Disappear, Halt, Lin, Lose, Pass, Refrain, STOP

**Ceaseless** Eternal, Incessant

**Cecil** Rhodes

**Cedar(wood)** Arolla, Deodar, Toon

**Ceiling** Cupola, Dome, Laquearia, Limit, Plafond, Roof, Soffit

**Celebrate(d), Celebration, Celebrity** Beanfeast, Besung, Bigwig, Binge, Carnival, Emblazon, Encaenia, Fame, Feast, Fest, Festivity, Fete, Fiesta, Gala, Gaudeamus, Gaudy, Glorify, Hold, Holiday, Honour, Jamboree, Jubilee, Keep, Laud, Lion, Maffick, Mardi gras, Name, Noted, Nuptials, Observe, Occasion, Orgy, Praise, Rejoice, Renown, Repute, Revel, Saturnalia, Sing, Spree, Star, Sung, Triumph, Wassail, Wet

**Celerity** Dispatch, Haste, Speed, Velocity

**Celery** Alexanders, Smallage, Stick

**Celestial** Chinese, Divine, Ethereal, Heavenly, Uranic

**Celibate, Celibacy** Bachelor, Chaste, Paterin(e), Rappist, Rappite, Shakers, Single, Spinster

**Cell(s), Cellular** Akaryote, Aplanogamete, Aplanospore, Arthrospore, Athrocyte, Ascus, Battery, Bullpen, Cadre, Cathode, Censor, Chamber, Chromosome, Clark, Cnidoblast, Comb, Corpuscle, Crypt, Cubicle, Cybrid, Cyte, Cytoid, Diaxon, Dungeon, Embryo-sac, Endoderm, Endosarc, Erythrocyte, Eukaryon, Gad, Gamete, Gonidium, Group, Hela, Idioblast, Laura, Leucocyte, Linin, Microgamete, Morula, Myoblast, Neuron,

Neutron, Normoblast, Odontoblast, Organelle, Osteoblast, Pec, Peter, Plastid, PRISON, Retinula, Schwann, Sensor, Seredium, Spermatocyte, Spore, Sporule, Synergid, Tapetum, Unipolar, Vesicle, Zeta, Zoospore, Zygote

**Cellar** Basement, Bodega, Dunny, Vault, Vaut

**Cell division** Amitosis

**Cellist, Cello** Hermit, Prisoner

**Celluloid, Cellulose** Acetate, Cel

**Celt(ic)** Breton, Brython, Druid, Gadhel, Gael, Goidel, Kelt, Taffy, Welsh

**Cement** Araldite, Compo, Concrete, Fix, Glue, Grout, Lute, Maltha, Mastic, Mortar, Paste, Putty, STICK, Trass

**Cemetery** Aceldama, Boneyard, Catacomb, God's acre, Golgotha, Graveyard, Necropolis, Père Lachaise, Saqqara, Urnfield

**Censer** Cassolette, Navicula, Thurible

**Censor, Censorious, Censure** Admonition, Animadvert, Appeach, Ban, Banner, Blame, Blue-pencil, Bowdler, Braid, Cato, Comstockery, CONDEMN, Critical, Criticise, Damn, Dang, Decry, Edit, Excommunicate, Excoriate, Expurgate, Gag, Obloquy, Rap, Reprimand, Reproach, Reprobate, Reprove, Satirise, Slam, Slate, Suppress, Tax, Tirade, Traduce, Wig

**Census** Count, Poll

**Cent** Bean, Coin, Ct, Penny, Red

**Centaur** Ch(e)iron, Horseman, Nessus, Sagittary

**Centenary, Centennial** Anniversary, Colorado

**Centipede** Chilopoda, Earwig, Polypod, Scolopendra, Scutiger

**Central, Centre** Amid, Attendance, Axis, Cardinal, Chakra, Core, Deuteron, Deuton, Downtown, Epergne, Eye, Focus, Frontal, Heart, Hub, Inmost, Internal, Kernel, Main, Mid(st), Nave, Nucleus, Waist

**Central heating** Cen, CH

> **Centre** may indicate middle letters

**Centrepiece** Epergne

**Century** Age, C, Era, Magdeburg, Period, Ton

**Cephalopod** Ammonite, Calamary, Cuttle, Loligo, Nautilus, Octopus, Sepia, Squid

**Ceramic(s)** Arcanist, China, Earthen, Porcelain, Pottery, Tiles

**Cereal** Amelcorn, Barley, Blé, Bran, Buckwheat, Bulgar, Bulg(h)ur, Cassava, Corn, Emmer, Farina, Gnocchi, Grain, Granola, Maize, Mandioc(a), Mandiocca, Mani(h)oc, Manihot, Mealie, Millet, Muesli, Oats, Paddy, Popcorn, Rye(corn), Sago, Samp, Seed, Semolina, Spelt, Tapioca, Tef(f), Triticale, Wheat, Zea

**Cerebrate, Cerebration** Pore, Thought

**Ceremonial, Ceremony** Amrit, Barmitzvah, Chanoyu, Doseh, Durbar,

Formal, Heraldry, Investiture, Mummery, Observance, Pageantry, Parade, Pomp, Protocol, Rite, Ritual, Service, State, Usage

**Cerium** Ce

**Cert(ain), Certainty** Absolute, Actual, Assured, Bound, Cinch, Cocksure, Confident, Convinced, Decided, Exact, Fact, Fate, Inevitable, Monte, Nap, One, Positive, Poz, Precise, Sicker, Some, Snip, SURE, Sure-fire, Truth, Yes

**Certainly** Ay, Fegs, Forsooth, Indeed, Iwis, Jokol, OK, Oke, Pardi(e), Pardy, Perdie, Siccar, Sicker, SURE, Truly, Verily, Yea, Yes, Yokul, Ywis

**Certificate, Certified, Certify** Affirm, Attest, Bond, Chit, Cocket, Confirm, Credential, Debenture, Depose, Diploma, Docket, Document, Enseal, Guarantee, Licence, Lines, MOT, Paper, Patent, Proven, Scrip, Sworn, Testamur, Testimonial, U, Voucher

**Cesspit** Bog, Dungmere, Slurry

**Cetacean** Dolphin, Porpoise, Whale

**Ceylon(ese)** Serendip, Vedda(h)

**Chafe** Chunter, Fray, Fret, Harass, Irritate, RUB, Seethe, Worry

**Chaff(y)** Badinage, Banter, Bran, Chip, Dross, Hay, Husk, Rag, Raillery, Rally, Ramentum, Refuse, Roast, Rot, Tease, Twit

**Chaffer(ing)** Bandy, Bargain, Haggle, Higgle, Hucksterage, Traffic

**Chaffinch** Whitewing

**Chagrin** Envy, Mortify, Spite, Vexation

**Chain(ed)** Acre's-breadth, Albert, Anklet, Bind, Bond, Bracelet, Bucket, Cable, Catena, Daisy, Decca, Dynasty, Esses, Fanfarona, Fetter, Fob, Furlong, Gleipnir, Gunter's, Gyve, Markor, Mayor, Micella(r), Micelle, Noria, Pennine, Pitch, Range, Seal, SERIES, Shackle, Slang, Sprocket, String, Strobila, Team

**Chain-gang** Coffle

**Chair** Bench, Bergère, Bosun's, Carver, Curule, Estate, Gestatorial, Guerite, Jampan, Lounger, Pew, Preside, Rocker, SEAT, Sedan, Stool, Throne, Wainscot, Windsor

**Chair-back** Ladder, Splat

**Chairman** Convener, Emeritus, Mao, MC, Pr(a)eses, Prof, Sheraton, Speaker

**Chalaza** Albumen, Treadle, Treddle

**Chaldean** Babylonian, Ur

**Chalet** Cabana, Cot, Skio

**Chalk(y)** Calcareous, Cauk, Cawk, Crayon, Credit, Cretaceous, Senonian, Soapstone, Steatite, White(n), Whit(en)ing

**Challenge(r), Challenging** Acock, Assay, Call, Cartel, Champion, Contest, Dare, Defy, Gage, Gauntlet, Glove, Hazard, Hen(ner), Impugn, Oppugn, Provoke, Query, Question, Recuse, Sconce, Shuttle, Tackle, Tank, Threat, Vie, Whynot

**Chamber(s)** Camarilla, Camera, Casemate, Cell(a), Chanty, Cubicle, Dene-hole, Dolmen, Gazunder, Hall, Horrors, Hypogea, Jordan, Kiva, Lethal, Locule, Mattamore, Po, Pot, Privy, Roum, Serdab, Silo, Synod, Thalamus, Undercroft, Utricle

**Chamberlain** Camerlengo, Camerlingo, Censor

**Chameleon** Ethiopian, Lizard, Tarand

**Chamfer** Bevel, Groove

**Chamois** Ibex, Izard, Shammy

**Champ** Bite, Chafe, Chew, Chomp, Eat, Gnash, Gnaw, Morsure, Munch

**Champagne** Boy, Bubbly, Charlie, Fizz, Gigglewater, Pop, Sillery, Simkin, Simpkin, Stillery, Troyes, Widow

**Champion** Ace, Ali, Apostle, Belt, Campeador, Cid, Cock, Defend, Doucepere, Douzeper, Dymoke, Enoch, Espouse, Gladiator, Harry, HERO, Horse, Kemp, Kemper(yman), King, Knight, Maintain, Matchless, Neil, Paladin, Palmerin, Peerless, Perseus, Promachos, Protagonist, Roland, St Anthony, St David, St Denis, St George, St James, St Patrick, Spiffing, Spokesman, Star, Support, Tribune, Upholder, Victor, Wardog, WINNER

**Championship** Open, Title

**Chance, Chancy** Accident, Aleatory, Aunter, Bet, Break, Buckley's, Cast, Casual, Contingent, Dice, FATE, Fluke, Fortuity, Fortuitous, Fortune, GAMBLE, Game, Hap, Happenstance, Hobnob, Iffy, Light, Look-in, Lot, LOTTERY, Luck, Meet, Mercy, Occur, Opening, Opportunity, Posse, Potluck, Prospect, Random, Rise, Risk, Serendipity, Slant, Spec, Stake, Stochastic, Sweep, Toss-up, Treble, Turn, Tychism, Ventre, Venture

**Chancel** Adytum, Bema, Nave

**Chancellor** Bismarck, Dollfuss, Kohl, Logothete, Minister, More

**Chancery** Court, Hanaper

**Chandelier** Candlestick, Corona, Drop, Electrolier, Gasolier, Girandole, Lustre, Pendant

**Chaney** Lon

**Change(able), Changing** Adapt, Adjust, Agio, ALTER, Amendment, Attorn, Barter, Become, Bob-major, Cash, Catalysis, Chop, Commute, Convert, Coppers, Denature, Departure, Edit, Enallage, Exchange, Find, Flighty, Fluctuate, Float, Flux, Guard, Gybe, Innovate, Killcrop, Labile, Metabolic, Metabolise, Metamorphose, Metamorphosis, Mobile, Mutable, Mutanda, Mutation, Parallax, Peal, Perpeteia, Prophase, Protean, Recant, Rectify, Reform, Rejig, Rest, Revise, Sandhi, Scourse, Sd, Seesaw, Shift, Substitute, Swap, Swing, Switch, Tolsel, Tolsey, Tolzey, Transfer, Transition, Transmute, Transpose, Turn, Upheaval, U-turn, Variant, Variation, Vary, Veer, Vicissitude, Volatile, Volte-face, Wankle, Washers, Wheel

> **Change(d)** may indicate an anagram

**Changeling** Auf, Killcrop, Oaf, Turncoat

**Channel** Access, Aflaj, Aqueduct, Artery, Bed, Bristol, Canal, Chimb,

Chime, Chine, Chute, Conduit, Culvert, Cut, Ditch, Drain, Duct, Dyke, Ea, Euripus, Falaj, Flume, Foss, Funnel, Furrow, Gat, Geo, Gio, Glyph, Gully, Gut, Gutter, Head-race, Ingate, Katabothron, Katavothron, Lane, Leat, Leet, Limber, Major, Meatus, Medium, Minch, Moat, Narrows, Penstock, Qanat, Rebate, Rigol(l), Rivulet, Sea-gate, Sewer, Sinus, Sloot, Sluice, Sluit, Sny(e), Solent, Sound, Spillway, Sprue, Strait, Sow, Suez, Tideway, Trough, Ureter, Vallecula

**Chant** Anthem, Antiphon, Cantillate, Chaunt, Decantate, Euouae, Evovae, Gregorian, Haka, Hymn, Intone, Introit, Motet, Pennillion-singing, Psalm, Sing, Slogan, Te deum

**Chantilly** Cream, Lace

**Chaos** Abyss, Anarchy, Confusion, Disorder, Hun-tun, Jumble, Mess, Muss, Shambles, Snafu, Tohu bohu

> **Chaotic** may indicate an anagram

**Chap(s)** Bloke, Bo, Bod, Bor, Chafe, Cheek, Chilblain, Cleft, Cod, Codger, Cove, Crack, Customer, Dog, Fella, Fellow, Flews, Gent, Gink, Guy, Hack, Joll, Jowl, Kibe, Lad, MAN, Mouth, Mum, Ocker, Rent, Rime, Spray, Spreathe, Spreethe, Spreaze, Spreeze, Wang

> **Chaps** may indicate an anagram

**Chapel** Bethel, Bethesda, Cha(u)ntry, Ebenezer, Oratory, Parabema, Prothesis, Sacellum, Sistine

**Chaperon(e)** Beard, Cap, Duenna, Escort, Gooseberry, Griffin, Griffon, Gryphon

**Chaplain** CF, Padre, Priest, Skypilot, Slope

**Chaplet** Anadem, Coronet, Fillet, Garland, Wreath

**Chapter** Accidents, C, Canon, Cap, Capitular, Ch, Chap, Cr, Division, Episode, Lodge, Phase, Section, Sura(h)

**Char(woman)** Adust, Burn, Cleaner, Coal, Daily, Duster, Mop(p), Scorch, Sear, Singe, Smoulder, Toast, Togue, Torgoch

**Charabanc** Bus, Chara, Coach

**Character** Aesc, Alphabet, Ampersand, Ampussyand, Aura, Brand, Calibre, Case, Cipher, Clef, Cliff, Climate, Contour, Credit, Devanagari, Eta, Ethos, FEATURE, Fist, Grain, Grit, Hieroglyphic, Ideogram, Ideograph, Italic, Kanji, Kern, Kind, La(m)bda, Letter, Logogram, Make-up, Mark, Nagari, NATURE, Ogam, Pahlavi, Pantaloon, Part, Pehlevi, Person(a), Personage, PERSONALITY, Phonogram, Physiognomy, Psi, Reference, Repute, Rho, Role, Rune, Runic, Sampi, San, Self, Sonancy, Stamp, Symbol, Testimonial, Ton(e), Trait, Uncial, Vav, Vee, Waw, Wen, Yogh, Zeta

**Characteristic, Characterised** Attribute, Aura, Cast, Colour, Distinctive, Ethos, Feature, Hair, Hallmark, Has, Headmark, Idiomatic, Idiosyncrasy, Jizz, Lineament, Mien, Nature, Peculiar, Persona, Point, Property, Quality, Streak, Style, TRAIT, Typical, Vein

**Characterless** Anon, Inane, Wet

**Charade** Enigma, Pretence, Riddle

**Charcoal** Carbon, Coke, Fusain

**Charge(s), Charged, Charger** Accuse, Agist, Allege, Annulet, Arraign, Ascribe, Bear, Behest, Blame, Brassage, Brush, Buckshot, Care, Cathexis, Commission, Complaint, Cost, Count, Damage, Debit, Delate, Delf, Delph, Demurrage, Depth, Depute, Directive, Dittay, Due, Duty, Electron, Entrust, Expense, Fare, Fee, Fill, Freight, Gravamen, Hot, Hypothec, Impeach, Impute, Indict, Inescutcheon, Inform, Instinct, Ion, Isoelectric, Last, Lioncel(le) Lionel, Live, Load, Mandate, Mine, Mount, Obtest, Onrush, Onus, Ordinary, Orle, Overhead, Pervade, Positive, Premium, Prime, Q, Rack-rent, Rap, Rate, Rent, Report, Reprise, Roundel, Run, RUSH, Saddle, Service, Steed, Tariff, Tax, Tear, Terms, Tilt, TRAY, Tressure, Trickle, Trust, Upfill, Verdoy, Ward, Wharfage

**Chariot(eer)** Auriga, Automedon, Biga, Cart, Hur, Quadriga, Wagon, Wain

**Charisma** Oomph

**Charitable, Charity** Alms, Awmous, Benign, Caritas, Dole, Dorcas, Eleemosynary, Largesse, Leniency, Liberal, Lion, Love, Mercy, Openhanded, Pelican, Zakat

**Charlatan** Cheat, Crocus, Escroc, Faker, Imposter, Katerfelto, Mountebank, Poseur, Quack(salver), Saltimbanco

**Charlemagne** Carlovingian

**Charles, Charley, Charlie** Beard, Car, Champagne, Chan, Checkpoint, Elia, Lamb, (Old) Rowley, Pretender, Rug-gown, Sap, Tail-end, Watchman

**Charles de Gaulle** Airport

**Charlotte** Bronte, Russe, Yonge

**Charm(er), Charming** Abracadabra, Allure, Amulet, Appeal, Aroma, Attraction, Beguile, Bewitch, Captivate, Charisma, Circe, Comether, Cute, Cutie, Emerods, Enamour, Enchant, Engaging, ENTRANCE, Fascinate, Fay, Fetish, Grace, Greegree, Gri(s)gris, Houri, Juju, Mascot, Mojo, Obeah, Obi(a), Periapt, Porte-bonheur, Prince, Quaint, Quark, Ravish, Siren, Spellbind, Sweetness, Talisman, Telesm, Tiki, Trinket, Unction, Voodoo, Winsome

> **Charming** may indicate an anagram

**Chart** Abac, Card, Diagram, Graph, Isogram, List, MAP, Mappemond, Nomogram, Plot, Portolano, Ringelmann, Table, Timetable, Waggoner

**Charter** Book, Covenant, Hire, Lease, Novodamus, Rent

**Chary** Cagey, Careful, Cautious, Frugal, Shy, Wary

**Charybdis** Maelstrom, Whirlpool

**Chase(r), Chasing** Cannock, Chace, Chevy, Chivy, Ciseleur, Ciselure, Course, Cranborne, Decorate, Drink, Game, Harass, Hound, HUNT, Jumper, Oxo, Pursuit, Race, Scorse, Sic(k), Steeple, Sue, Suit

**Chasm** Abyss, Crevasse, Gap, Gorge, Fissure, Gulf, Schism

**Chaste, Chastity** Agnes, Attic, Celibate, Classic, Clean, Florimell, Ines,

Innocent, Modesty, Nessa, PURE, Vestal, Virginal, Virtue

**Chastise(ment)** Beat, Correct, Discipline, Disple, Lash, Rib-roast, Rollicking, Scold, Scourge, Spank, Strap, Whip

**Chat, Chatter(box)** Babble, Bavardage, Blab(ber), Blether, Campanero, Causerie, Chelp, Chinwag, Clack, Confab(ulate), Converse, Cosher, Coze, Crack, Dialogue, Froth, Gab(ble), Gas, Gossip, Gup, Hobnob, Jabber, Jargon, Jaw, Kilfud, Madge, Mag(pie), Natter, Patter, Pie, Pourparler, Prate, Prattle, Rabbit, Rabble, Rap, Rattle, Scuttlebutt, Shmoose, Talk, Talkee-talkee, Tattle, Twattle, Waffle, Windbag, Witter, Wongi, Yacketyyak, Yak, Yarn, Yatter, Yoking

**Chateau** Castle, Cru, Malmaison, Schloss

**Chateaubriand** René

**Chattel** Asset, Deodand

**Chaucer(ian)** Dan, OE

**Chauffeur** Cabby, Coachy, Driver, Sice, Syce

**Chauvinist** Alf, Bigot, Jingo, MCP, Partisan, Sexist

**Cheap** Bargain, Base, Chintzy, Knockdown, Low, Poor, Sacrifice, Shoddy, Stingy, Tatty, Tawdry, Ticky-tacky, Tinpot, Tinselly, Trivial, Vile

> **Cheap** may indicate a d- or p- start to a word

**Cheapside** Bow

**Cheat(ers), Cheating** Bam, Beguile, Bilk, Bite(r), Bob, Bonnet, Bullock, Bucket, Chiaus, Chicane(ry), Chisel, Chouse, Clip, Cod, Cog(ger), Colt, Con, Cozen, Crib, Cross, Cross-bite(r), Cuckold, Delude, Diddle, Dingo, Dish, Do, Doublecross, Duckshove, Dupe, Faitor, Fiddle, Finagle, Flam, Fob, Foister, Fox, Fraud, Gaff, Gip, Glasses, Gum, Gyp, Hoax, Hocus, Hoodwink, Hornswoggle, Horse, Intake, Jew, Jockey, Magsman, Mulct, Mump, Nick, Picaroon, Poop, Queer, Rib, Rig, Rogue, Rook, Scam, Screw, Short-change, Slur, Smouch, Snap, Stack, Stiff, Sting, Swindle, Thimble-rigging, Trepan, Trim, Two-time, Welsh, Wheedle

**Check** Arrest, Audit, Ba(u)lk, Bauk, Bill, Bridle, Collate, Compesce, Control, Count, Cramp, Curb, Dam, Damp, Detent, Dogs-tooth, Examine, Foil, Frustrate, Halt, Hamper, Hobble, Inhibit, Jerk, Jerque, Let, Limit, Mate, Monitor, Overhaul, Prevent, Rebuff, Rebuke, Rein, Repress, Reprime, Repulse, Reread, RESTRAIN, Revoke, Saccade, Screen, Service, Setback, Sit-upon, Sneap, Sneb, Snib, Snub, STEM, Stop, Stunt, Tab, Tally, Tartan, Tattersall, Test, Tick, Trash, Verify, Vet

**Checkers** Chinese, Piece

**Cheddar** Cheese, Gorge

**Cheek(y)** Alforja, Audacity, Buccal, Chap, Chutzpah, Crust, Flippant, Fresh, Gum, Jowl, Lip, Malapert, Malar, Masseter, Neck, Nerve, Noma, Pert, Presumption, Sass, Sauce, Sideburns, Wang, Yankie, Zygoma

**Cheep** Chirp, Chirrup, Peep

**Cheer(s), Cheerful, Cheering** Acclaim, Agrin, Applaud, Banzai, Barrack, Blithe, Bonnie, Bravo, Bright, Bronx, Buck, Buoy, Cadgy, Cherry,

Chin-chin, Chipper, COMFORT, Crouse, Debonair, Drink, Ease, Elate, Elevate, Enliven, Exhilarate, Festive, Genial, Gladden, Happy-go-lucky, Hearten, Hilarity, Hooch, Hoorah, Huzzah, Jovial, Kia-ora, Lightsome, Lively, Ovate, Peart, Praise, Prosit, Rah, Riant, Rivo, Root, Shout, Skoal, Slainte, Sonsie, Sunny, Ta, Tata, Tiger, Toodle-oo, Winsome

**Cheerless** Dismal, Drab, Drear, Gloomy, Glum

**Cheese, Cheesy** Amsterdam, Appenzell, Belpaese, Boursin, Brie, Caboc, Caerphilly, Camembert, Cantal, Casein, Caseous, Cheddar, Cheshire, Chessel, Cottage, Coulommiers, Curd, Derby, Dunlop, Edam, Emmental(er), Emmenthal(er), Ermite, Esrom, Ewe, Fet(a), Fynbo, Gloucester, Gouda, Grand Panjandrum, Gruyère, Huntsman, Ilchester, Islay, Jarlsberg, Junket, Kebbock, Kebbuck, Kenno, Killarney, Leicester, Limburger, Lymeswold, Mascarpone, Mousetrap, Mozzarella, Mu(e)nster, Mycella, Neuchatel, Orkney, Parmesan, Pecorino, Port Salut, Provolone, Quark, Raclette, Rarebit, Rennet, Ricotta, Romano, Roquefort, Samso, Sapsago, Skyr, Stilton, Stracchino, Tilsit, Tofu, Truckle, VIP, Wensleydale

**Cheesecake** Pin-up

**Cheese-scoop** Pale

**Chekhov** Anton

**Chemical** Acanthin, Acid, Acrolein, Alar, Aldehyde, Alkali, Alum, Amide, Carbide, Catalyst, Dopamine, Enkephalin(e), Fixer, Glutamine, Glycol, Harmin, Hecogenin, Hexylene, Histamine, Hypo, ICI, Natron, Nitre, Olein, Olefin, Oxide, Oxysalt, Pentene, Phenol, Pheromone, Potash, Potassa, Psoralen, Ptomaine, Reagent, Soman, Sulphide, Thio-salt

**Chemise** Cymar, Sark, Serk, Shift, Shirt, Simar(re), Smock, Symar

**Chemist(ry)** Alchemy, Alchymy, Analyst, Apothecary, Bunsen, Davy, Dispenser, Druggist, Drugstore, FCS, Inorganic, Lavoisier, Liebig, LSA, MPS, Nobel, Organic, Paracelsus, Pasteur, Pottingar, Proust, Prout, RIC, Sanger, Spageric, Spagiric, Spagyric, Spicer, Stinks

**Cheops** Khufu

**Cheque** Giro, Gregory, Stumer, Tab

**Chequer** Dice

**Cherish(ed)** Dear, Dote, Enshrine, Entertain, Esteem, Foment, Foster, Harbour, Nestle, Nurse, Pamper, Pet, Precious, Treasure

**Cheroot** Cigar, Manil(l)a

**Cherry (tree)** Amarelle, Bigaroon, Blackheart, Cerise, Gean, Kearton, Kermes, Kermesite, Marasca, Maraschino, May-duke, Maz(z)ard, Merry, Morel(lo), Red, Whiteheart

**Cherry-pie** Heliotrope

**Cherub** Angel, Putto, Seraph

**Chess, Chess player** Black, Blindfold, FIDE, Miranda, Patzer, Plank, Shogi, White

**Chessman** Bishop, Black, Castle, Horse, King, Knight, Pawn, Pin, Queen, Rook, White

**Chest(y)**  Ark, Bahut, Bosom, Box, Breast, Buist, Bunker, Bureau, Bust, Caisson, Case, Cassone, Chapel, Chiffonier, Coffer, Coffin, Coffret, Commode, Cub, Hope, Kist, Larnax, Locker, Lowboy, Ottoman, Pectoral, Pereion, Pleural, Safe, Scrine, Scryne, Shrine, Sternum, Tallboy, Thorax, Toolbox, Trunk, Wangun, Wanigan

**Chester**  Deva

**Chestnut**  Auburn, Badious, Chincapin, Chinkapin, Chinquapin, Cliché, Conker, Favel(l), Hoary, Marron, Russet, Saligot, Soare, Sorrel

**Chest protector**  ARMOUR, Bib

**Chevalier**  Bayard, Knight, Pretender

**Chevron**  Dancette, Stripe

**Chew**  Bite, Champ, Cud, Gnaw, Manducate, Masticate, Maul, Meditate, Moop, Mou(p), Munch, Ruminate, Siri(h), Spearmint

**Chiastolite**  Macle

**Chic**  Dapper, Elegant, In, Kick, Modish, Posh, Smart, Soigné, Stylish, Tonish, Trim

**Chicane(ry)**  Artifice, Deception, Fraud, Wile

**Chichester**  Yachtsman

**Chichi**  Precious

**Chick(en)**  Battery, Biddy, Broiler, Cheeper, Chittagong, Chuckie, Clutch, Coward, Cowherd, Eirack, Gutless, Hen, Howtowdie, Layer, Marengo, Minorca, Niderling, Poltroon, Poot, Poult, Pout, Roaster, Spatchcock, Squab, Supreme, Wyandotte, Yellow

**Chickenfeed**  Maize

**Chickenpox**  Varicella

**Chicory**  Endive, Witloof

**Chide**  Admonish, Berate, Objurgate, Rate, Rebuke, Reprove, Row, Scold, Tick off, Twit, Upbraid

**Chief(tain)**  Arch, Ardrigh, Boss, Caboceer, Cacique, Calif, Caliph, Capital, Capitan, Capitayn, Capo, Caradoc, Cazique, Ch, Chagan, Dat(t)o, Dominant, Emir, First, Foremost, Geronimo, Grand, Haggis, HEAD, Hereward, Kaid, King, Leader, MAIN, Mass, Mugwump, Nizam, Oba, Overlord, Pendragon, Premier, Primal, Prime, Principal, Rangatira, Ratoo, Ratu, Sachem, Sagamore, Sudder, Supreme, Tanist, Tank, Top

**Chiffonier**  Cabinet, Commode

**Chilblain**  Kibe

**Child(ish), Children**  Aerie, Alannah, Babe, Baby, Badger, Bairn, Bambino, Bantling, Boy, Brat, Brood, Butter-print, Ch, Changeling, Cherub, Chick, Chit, Collop, Cub, Dream, Elfin, Eyas, Foundling, Ge(i)t, Girl, Gyte, Heir, Hurchcon, Imp, Infant, Issue, It, Juvenile, Kid(die), Kiddy, Kinder, Lad, Limb, Litter, Minion, Minor, Mite, Nursling, Offspring, Papoose, Piccaninny, Pickin, Progeny, Puerile, Rip, Scion, Smout, Smowt, Sprog, Subteen, Ted, Toddle(r), Tot(tie), Totty, Trot, Urchin, Wean, Whelp,

Youth

**Childbearing** Parity, Puerperal

**Child-killer** Herod

**Childless** Atocous, Atokous, Barren, Sp

**Chill(er), Chilly** Bleak, COLD, Frappé, Freeze, Freon, Frigid, Frosty, Gelid, Ice, Iciness, Mimi, Oorie, Ourie, Owrie, Parky, Raw, Rigor

**Chime(s)** Bell, Cymar, Jingle, Peal, Semantron, Tink, TOLL

**Chimney (pot), Chimney corner** Can, Cow(l), Femerall, Flue, Funnel, Lug, Lum, Stack, Stalk, Tallboy, Tunnel

**Chimp** Ape, Jocko

**Chin, Chinwag** Chitchat, Genial, Jaw, Mentum

**China(man), Chinese** Ami, Boxer, Cantonese, Cathay, Celestial, Ch, Chelsea, Chow, Coalport, Cochin, Cock, Confucius, Crackle, Crockery, Delft, Derby, Dresden, Eggshell, Etrurian, Google, Googly, Goss, Hakka, Han, Hizen, Imari, Kanji, Kaolin, Kuo-yu, Limoges, Manchu, Mangi, Maoist, Mate, Meissen, Ming, Minton, Oppo, Pal, Pareoean, Pekingese, Pe-tsai, Porcelain, POTTERY, Rockingham, Seric, Sèvres, Shanghai, Sinic, Spode, Sun Yat-sen, Tai-ping, Taoist, Teng, Wal(l)y, Ware, Wedgwood, Worcester, Wu

**Chine** Chink, Chynd, Ridge

**Chink** Chinaman, Chop, Cleft, Clink, Cloff, Crack, Cranny, Crevice, Gap, Rent, Rift, Rima, Sinic

**Chintz** Kalamkari

**Chip(s)** Bo(a)st, Carpenter, Counter, Cut, Fish, Flake, Fragment, Hack, Knap, Nacho, Nick, Pin, Shaving, Silicon, Spale, Spall

> **Chip** may indicate an anagram

**Chipmunk** Gopher, Hackee, Suslik

**Chipper** Jaunty, Spry, Wedge

**Chiron** Centaur

**Chirp(y), Chirrup** Cheep, Cherup, Chirm, Chirr, Cicada, Peep, Pip, Pipe, Pitter, Trill, Tweet, Twitter

**Chisel(ler), Chisel-like** Bam, Boaster, Bolster, Bur, Burin, Cheat, Clip, Drove, Firmer, GOUGE, Mason, Scalpriform, Scauper, Scorper, Sculpt

**Chit** Girl, Note, Voucher

**Chivalry, Chivalrous** Brave, Bushido, Courtly, Gallant

**Chivvy** Badger, Harass, Pursue

**Chloride, Chlorine** Calomel

**Chocolate** Aero, Brown, Cacao, Carob, Cocoa, Dragee, Neapolitan, Pinole, Theobroma, Truffle

**Choice, Choose, Choosy, Chosen** Adopt, Anthology, Appoint, Aryan, Cull, Dainty, Decide, Druthers, Eclectic, Elect, Elite, Esnecy, Fine, Free will, Hobson's, Leet, Leve, Lief, List, Opt, Option, Or, Ossian, Peach,

Peculiar, PICK, Pick(ing), Plump, Precious, Predilect, Prefer, Proairesis, Rare, Recherché, SELECT, Superb, Try(e), Wale

**Choiceless** Beggar

**Choir, Choral, Chorister, Chorus** Antiphony, Antistrophe, Anvil, Burden, Dawn, Decani, Faburden, Fauxbourdon, Group, Hallelujah, Harmony, Hymeneal, Motet, Parabasis, REFRAIN, Singing, Strophe, Treble, Triad, UNISON

**Choir-master** Precentor

**Choke(r)** Block, Clog, Gag, Silence, Smoor, Smore, Smother, Stifle, Stop, Strangle(hold), Strangulate, THROTTLE

**Choky** Can, Prison

**Choliamb** Scazon

> **Choose** see CHOICE

**Chop(per), Choppy** Adze, Ax(e), Celt, Charge, Cheek, Chump, Cleave, Côtelette, Cuff, Cutlet, Dice, Fell(er), Flew, Hack, Helicopter, Hew, Karate, Lop, Mince, Rotaplane, Rough, Suey, Wang

**Chopin** Pantoufle, Shoe

**Chopstick(s)** Waribishi

**Chord** Arpeggio, Diameter, Harmony, Nerve, Triad

**Chore** Darg, Duty, Task

**Choreographer** Arranger, Ashton, Balanchine, Fokine, Massine

**Chosen** Korea

**Chough** Chewet

**Chowder** Bouillabaisse, Soup

**Christ** Jesus, Messiah, Saviour, X

**Christen(ing)** Baptise, Launch, Name-day

**Christian** Albigenses, Believer, Coptic, Dior, Donatist, Ebionite, Galilean, Giaour, Goy, Marrano, Moral, Mozarab, Mutineer, Nazarene, Pilgrim, Protestant, RC, Quartodeciman, Sabotier, SCM, Traditor, Uniat(e), Unitarian, Waldensian, Xian

**Christian Scientist** Eddy

**Christmas(time)** Dec, Island, Nativity, Noel, Yuletide

**Christopher** Kit, Robin, Sly, Wren

**Chromium** Cr

**Chromosome** Aneuploid, Genome, Id(ant), Karyotype, X, Y

**Chronicle(r)** Anglo-Saxon, Annal, Brut, Calendar, Diary, Froissart, Hall, History, Holinshed, Logographer, Paralipomena, Parian, RECORD, Register, Stow

**Chrysalis** Nymph, Pupa

**Chrysanthemum** Corn-marigold, Feverfew

**Chrysolite** Olivine, Peridot

**Chub** Cheven, Chevin, Fish

**Chuck (out)** Berry, Buzz, Chook(ie), Discard, Eject, Food, Grub, Pat, Pitch, Shy, Sling, Toss, Turf

**Chuckle** Chortle, Giggle, Gurgle

**Chukka** Polo

**Chum(my)** Buddy, Cobber, Cock, Companion, Mate, Pal, Sociable, Sodality

**Chump** Mug(gins), Noddle, Sap, Stupid

**Chunk(y)** Chubby, Gob, Piece, Slab, Squat, Wad

**Church** Abbey, Basilica, Bethel, Bethesda, Byzantine, CE, Ch, Chapel, Clergy, Coptic, Delubrum, EC, Episcopalian, Established, Faith, Fold, Kirk, Lateran, Minster, Prebendal, Rome, Shrine, Stave, Steeple, Temple

**Churchill** Tank, Winston

**Churchgoer, Churchwarden** Antiburgher, Baptist, Believer, Clay, Cleric, Clerk, Congregation, Deacon, Dom, Elder, Evangelist, Hatto, Invisible, Knox, Lector, Lutheran, Methodist, Militant, Moderator, MU, Newman, Once, Parson, PE, Pipe, Pontiff, Prebendary, Precentor, Prelate, Presbyterian, Priest, Protestant, Puritan, Rector, Sacristan, Sidesman, Sim, Simeonite, Swedenborgian, Tantivy, Triumphant, Unitarian, Visible, Wesleyan, Worshipper, Wren

**Churl(ish)** Attercop, Boor, Crabby, Curmudgeonly, Cynical, Ethercap, Ettercap, Gruff, Nabal, Peasant, Rustic, Serf, Surly

**Churn** Bubble, Kirn, Seethe

**Chute** Runway

**CIC** Shogun, Sirdar

**Cicada** Greengrocer, Locust, Tettix

**Cicatrix** Scar

**Cicely** Myrrh, Sweet

**Cicero** Cic, Tully

**Cid** Campeador, Chief, Hero

**Cider** Drink, Perry, Scrumpy

**Ci-devant** Ex

**Cigar(ette)** Beedi(e), Caporal, Cheroot, Claro, Concha, Corona, Dog-end, Durry, Fag, Gasper, Giggle(-stick), Havana, Joint, Locofoco, Long-nine, Maduro, Manilla, Panatella, Perfecto, Reefer, Regalia, Roach, Smoke, Snout, Splif(f), Stogie, Stog(e)y, Weed, Whiff

**Cinch** Belt, Certainty, Girth

**Cinchona** Kina, Quina

**Cinder(s)** Ash, Breeze, Clinker, Dander, Embers, Slag

**Cinderella** Drudge, Stepdaughter

**Cinema(s)** Biograph, Bioscope, Circuit, Drive-in, Films, Fleapit, Flicks,

Movies, Mutoscope, Nickelodeon, Odeon, Plaza, Theatre, Tivoli

**Cinnabar**  Vermilion

**Cinnamon**  Canella, Cassia(bark), Spice

**Cipher**  Chi-rho, Code, Cryptogram, Nihil, Nobody, NOTHING, Number, O, Steganogram, Zero

**Circle**  Almacantar, Almucantar, Annulet, Antarctic, Arctic, Co, Colure, Company, Compass, Corolla, Coterie, Cromlech, Cyclolith, Disc, Eccentric, Embail, Enclose, Epicyclic, Equant, Equator, Girdle, Gyre, Halo, Hoop, Horizon, Inner, Lap, Loop, Malebolge, Mandala, Meridian, O, Orbit, Peristalith, Rigol, RING, Rotate, Roundure, Set, Sphere, Stemme, Surround, Tinchel, Tropic, Umbel, Vicious, Volt, Wheel

**Circuit(ous)**  AND, Ambit, Autodyne, Diocese, Eyre, IC, Lap, Limiter, NAND, NOR, NOT, OR, Perimeter, Ring, Round, Scaler, Tour, Windlass

**Circular**  Annular, Folder, Leaflet, Mailshot, Orby, Spiral, Unending, Wheely

**Circulate, Circulation**  Astir, Bloodstream, Cyclosis, Flow, Gyre, Issue, Mix, Orbit, Pass, Publish, Revolve, Rotate, Scope, Spread, Stir, Troll, Utter

> **Circulating**  may indicate an anagram

**Circumcise(r)**  Bris, Brith, Milah, Mohel

**Circumference**  Boundary, Girth, Perimeter, Size

**Circumlocution**  Periphrasis, Tautology

**Circumnavigation**  Periplus

**Circumscribe**  Define, Demarcate, Enclose, Restrain

**Circumspect**  Chary, Guarded, Prudential, Wary

**Circumstance, Circumstantial**  Case, Detail, Event, Fact, Formal, INCIDENT, Precise

**Circumvent**  Bypass, Dish, Evade, Outflank, Outwit, Usurp

**Circus, Circus boy**  Arena, Big top, Eros, Harrier, Hippodrome, Marquee, Monty Python, Ring, Sanger, Slang

**Cistercian**  Trappist

**Cistern**  Sump, Tank, Tub, Vat

**Citadel**  Acropolis, Alhambra, Castle, Fort(ress), Keep, Kremlin

**Citation, Cite**  Adduce, Allegation, Mention, Name, Quote, Recall, Reference, Repeat, Sist, Summon

**Citizen(ship)**  Burgess, Burgher, Civism, Denizen, Ephebe, Franchise, Freeman, Kane, National, Oppidan, People, Quirites, Resident, Roman, Voter

**Citroen**  DS

**Citrus**  Acid, Cedrate, Lemon, Limc, Mandarin, Min(n)eola, Orange, Pomelo, Tangerine, Ugli

**City**  Agra, Athens, Atlantis, Burgh, Carthage, EC, Empire, Eternal, Gath, LA, Leonine, Megalopolis, Metropolis, Petra, Pompeii, Rhodes, Smoke,

Sparta, Town, Ur, Vatican, Weldstadt

**Civet**   Binturong, Cat, Fo(u)ssa, Genet(te), Herpestes, Linsang, Musang, Nandine, Paradoxine, Rasse, Suricate, Toddy-cat, Viverra, Zibet

**Civil(ian), Civilisation, Civilised, Civility**   Amenity, Christian, Citizen, Civ(vy), Comity, Courtesy, Culture, Maya, Municipal, Polite, Politesse, Secular, Temporal, Urbane

**Civil Service**   CS

**Clag(gy)**   Stickjaw

**Claim**   Appeal, Arrogate, Assert, Bag, Challenge, Charge, Darraign(e), Darrain(e), Darrayn, Demand, Deraign, Droit, Haro, Harrow, Lien, List, Maintain, Nochel, Plea, Pose, Posit, Postulate, Pretence, Pretend, Profess, Pulture, Purport, Puture, Revendicate, Right, Sue, Title

**Claimant**   Petitioner, Pretender, Prospector, Tichborne, Usurper

**Clairvoyance, Clairvoyancy**   ESP, Insight, Lucidity, Psiphenomena, Taisch, Taish

**Clam**   Bivalve, Cohog, Mollusc, Mya, Quahog, Tridacna, Venus

**Clamant**   Vociferous

**Clamber**   Climb, Grawl, Scramble, Spra(i)ckle, Sprauchle

**Clammy**   Algid, Damp, Dank, Moist, Sticky, Sweaty

**Clamour(ing), Clamorous**   Blatant, Brouhaha, Din, Hubbub, Hue, Outcry, Racket, Raird, Reird, Rout, Shout, Strepitant, Uproar, Utis, Vociferate

**Clamp**   Clinch, Fasten, Grip, Pinchcock, Potato-pit, Stirrup, Vice

**Clan(sman)**   Cameron, Clique, Gens, Gentile, Group, Horde, Kiltie, Kindred, Name, Sect, Sept, Society, Stuart, Tribe

**Clang(er), Clanging, Clank**   Belleter, Boob, Boo-boo, Clash, Gong, Jangle, Plangent, Ring

**Clap(per), Clapping**   Applaud, Blow, Castanet, Chop, Crotal, Dose, Jinglet, Peal, Thunder, Tonant

**Claptrap**   Bilge, Blah, Bombast, Bunkum, Eyewash, Hokum, Rot

**Claque(ur)**   Fans, Hat, Laudator, Sycophant

**Clara**   Bow, Butt

**Claret**   Blood, Loll-shraub, Loll-shrub, Vin

**Clarify, Clarifier**   Clear, Explain, Explicate, Finings, Purge, Refine, Render, Simplify

**Clarinet**   Reed

**Clarion**   Brassy, Clear, Trumpet

**Clary**   Orval, Sage

**Clash(ing)**   Bang, Clangour, Clank, Claver, Coincide, Collide, Conflict, Friction, Gossip, IMPACT, Jar, Loud, Missuit, Shock, Showdown, Strike, Swash

**Clasp(ing)**   Adpress, Agraffe, Barrette, Brooch, Button, Catch, Clip,

Embrace, Fibula, Grasp, Hasp, Hesp, Hook, Hug, Inarm, Link, Morse, Ochreate, Ouch, Tach(e), Unite

**Class(ify), Classification, Classy** Arrange, Assort, Bracket, Brand, Breed, Caste, CATEGORY, Cheder, Cl, Clan, Clerisy, Clinic, Course, Criminal, Division, Estate, Faction, Form, Genera, Genus, Gentry, GRADE, Group, Heder, Ilk, Keep-fit, Linnean, List, Mammal, Number, Order, Pigeon-hole, Race, Range, Rank, Rate, Rating, Remove, Salariat, Seminar, Shell, Siege, Sort, Steerage, Stratum, Syntax, Tribe, TYPE, U, Varna, World

**Classic(al), Classics, Classicist** Ageless, Ancient, Basic, Derby, Elzevir, Greek, Humane, Leger, Literature, Pliny, Purist, Roman, Standard, Traditional, Vintage

**Clatch** Blunk, Smear, Spoil

**Clatter** Bicker, Charivari, Clack, Din, Noise, Rattle

**Clause** Apodosis, Article, Condition, Escalator, Filioque, Member, Protasis, Proviso, Reddendum, Rider, Salvo, Sentence, Tenendum, Testatum

**Claw** Chela, Claut, Crab, Grapple, Griff(e), Hook, Nail, Nipper, Pounce, Scrab, Sere, Talent, TALON, Tear

**Clay** Allophane, Argil, Barbotine, B(e)auxite, Bentonite, Blaes, Blaise, Blaize, Bole, Calm, Cam, Caum, Cimolite, Charoset(h), Cloam, Clunch, Cob, Earth, Fango, Gault, Glei, Gley, Hardpan, Haroset(h), Illite, Kaolin, Laterite, Lithomarge, Loam, Lute, Marl, Mire, Mortal, Mud, Pipestone, Pise, Pottery, Pug, Saggar(d), Sagger, Seggar, Slip, Smectite, Thill, Till(ite), Varve, Warrant, Wax

**Clean(se), Cleansing, Cleaner** Absterge, Besom, Bream, Broom, Careen, Catharise, Catharsis, Chaste, Clear, Daily, Debride, Depurate, Deterge(nt), Dhobi, Dialysis, Douche, Dust(er), Eluant, Emunge, Enema, Erase, Evacuant, Evacuate, Expurgate, Fay, Fettle, Fey, Floss, Flush, Full, Grave, Gut, Heels, Hygienic, Innocent, Launder, Lave, Lustrum, Lye, Mundify, Net, Overhaul, Porge, Pure, Purgative, Purge, Ramrod, Rebite, Rub, Rump, Scaffie, Scavenge, Scour, Scrub, Shampoo, Soap, Soogee, Soogie, Soojey, Spotless, Squeegee, Sujee, Swab, Sweep, Vacuum, WASH, Whistle, Wipe

**Clear(ance), Clearly** Acquit, Aloof, Apparent, Bell, Berth, Bold, Brighten, Bus, Clarify, Crystal, Decode, Definite, Diaphanous, Distinct, Downright, Eidetic, Evident, Exculpate, Exonerate, Explicit, Fair, Gain, Headroom, Hyaline, Intelligible, Iron, Laund, Leap, Legible, Limpid, Lucid, Luculent, Manifest, Mop, Neat, Negotiate, Net(t), NOT CLEAR, Obvious, Ope(n), Palpable, Pellucid, Plain, Play, Pratique, Predy, Pure, Quit, Rack, Realise, Remble, Rid, Sheer, Shere, Slum, Sweep, Thro(ugh), Thwaite, Translucent, Transparent, Unblock, Vault, Vivid, Well, Windage

**Clearing** Assart, Glade, Opening

**Cleat** Bitt, Wedge

**Cleave, Cleavage, Cleft** Adhere, Bisulcate, Chine, Cling, Cloff, Cut, Divide, Division, Divorce(ment), Gap, Ghaut, Goose-grass, Pharynx, Rift,

Riva, Severance, Slack, Space, Spathose

**Clematis** Montana, Old man's beard

**Clemenceau** Tiger

**Clemency** Ahimsa, Grace, Lenience, Lenity, Mercy, Mildness, Quarter

**Cleopatra** Needle

**Clergy(man)** Abbé, Canon, Cantor, Cardinal, Chaplain, Cleric, Clerk, Cloth, Curate, Curé, Deacon, Dean, Ecclesiast(ic), Goliard, Incumbent, Josser, Levite, Ministry, Parson, Pastor, Pontifex, Pontiff, Preacher, Prebendary, Precentor, Prelate, Presenter, Priest, Rabbi, Rector, Red-hat, Reverend, Shepherd, Slope, Squarson, Theologian, Vartabed, Vicar

**Clergy-hater** Misoclere

**Clerical** Ecclesiastic, Ministerial, Notarial, Proctor, Scribal, Secretarial

**Clerk(s)** Actuary, Baboo, Babu, Basoche, Cleric, Cratchit, Cursitor, Limb, Penman, Penpusher, Poster, Protonotary, Recorder, Scribe, Secretariat, Vicar, Writer

**Clever(ness)** Able, Adroit, Astute, Brainy, Bright, Cute, Daedal(e), Deep-browed, Deft, Gleg, Ingenious, Sage(ness), Shrewd, Skilful, Smart(y), Subtle

**Clevis** Becket

**Cliché** Banality, Commonplace, Corn, Platitude, Saying, Tag

**Click(er)** Castanet, Catch, Forge, Pawl, Ratch(et), Succeed, Tchick

**Client** Customer, John, Patron, Trick

**Cliff(s)** Beachy Head, Bluff, Cleve, Crag, Craig, Escarp, Palisade, Precipice, Sca(u)r

**Cliffhanger** Samphire, Serial, Thriller

**Climate** Atmosphere, Attitude, Mood, Sun, Temperament, Temperature, Weather

**Climax** Apex, Apogee, Catastasis, Come, Crescendo, Crest, Crisis, End, Head, Heyday, Top, Zenith

**Climb(er)** Aristolochia, Ascend, Breast, Briony, Bryony, Clamber, Clematis, Clusia, Cowage, Cowhage, Cowitch, Crampon, Creeper, Dodder, Heart-pea, Hedera, Ivy, Kie-kie, Kudzu, Lawyer, Liana, Liane, MOUNT, Pareira, Rise, Scale, Scan, Scansores, Sclim, Shin, Sklim, Smilax, Social, Speel, Sty(e), Swarm, Timbo, Tuft-hunter, Udo, Up(hill), Uprun, Vine, Wistaria, With(y)wind, Zoom

**Clinch** Attach, Carriwitchet, Ensure, Fix, Quibble, Rivet, Secure, Settle

**Cling(er), Clinging** Adhere, Bur(r), Cherish, Embrace, Hold, Hug, Ring, Tendril

**Clinic** Dispensary, Hospital, Hospitium, Mayo

**Clink** Gingle, Jail, Jingle, Lock up, Prison, Stir, Ting, Tinkle

**Clinker** Ash, Slag

**Clip(ped), Clipper, Clipping** Barrette, Brash, Bulldog, Clasp, Crop-ear,

Crutch, Curt, Curtail, Cut, Cutty Sark, Dag, Dock, Dod, Excerpt, Fleece, Jumar, Krab, Pace, Pare, Prerupt, Prune, Scissel, Secateur, Shear, Ship, Shore, Shorn, Snip, Staccato, Tie-tack, Tinsnips, Topiarist, Trim

**Clippy** Cad, Conductor

**Clique** Cabal, Clan, Coterie, Faction, Gang, Ring, Set

**Clive** Arcot

**Cloak(room), Cloaks** Aba, Abaya, Abba, Abolla, Amice, Burnous, Capa, Cape, Capote, Caracalla, Cardinal, Cassock, Chasuble, Chimer(e), Chlamydes, Chlamys, Chuddah, Chuddar, Conceal, Cope, Cover, Disguise, Dissemble, Djellaba(h), Domino, Gabardine, Gaberdine, Gal(l)abea(h), Gal(l)abi(y)a(h), Gal(l)abi(y)eh, Gentlemen, Gents, Hall-robe, Heal, Hele, Himation, Hood, Inverness, Jelab, Jellaba, Kaross, Manteel, Mantle, MASK, Mousquetaire, Mozetta, Paenula, Paletot, Pallium, Paludamentum, Pelisse, Pilch, Poncho, Rail, Revestry, Rocklay, Rokelay, Roquelaure, Sagum, Sarafan, Scapular, SCREEN, Swathe, Talma, Toga, Vestiary, Vestry, Visite

**Clobber** Anoint, Dress, Garb, Habiliments, Lam, Tack

**Clock** Alarm, Analogue, Beetle, Blowball, Bundy, Carriage, Clepsydra, Floral, Grandfather, Grandmother, Hit, Knock, Meter, Repeater, Speedo, Strike, Timer, Wag at the wa'

**Clockmaker** Fromanteel, Graham, Harrison, Knibb, Mudge, Tompion

**Clockwise** Deasil, Deasiul, Deasoil, Deiseal, Deisheal

**Clockwork** Precision, Regular

**Clod** Clumsy, Divot, Glebe, Lump, Put(t), Scraw, Sod, Stupid, Turf

**Clog** Accloy, Ball, Block, Clam, Crowd, Dance, Fur, Galosh, Golosh, Hamper, Jam, Lump, Mire, Obstruct, Overshoe, Patten, Sabot

**Cloisonné** Shippo

**Cloister** Arcade, Confine, Cortile, Immure, Monastery, Mure, Refuge

**Cloots** Worricow

**Close(d), Closing, Closure** Airless, Atresia, Block, Boon, By, Clammy, Clench, Complete, Dense, END, Epilogue, Ewest, Finale, Gare, Grapple, Handy, Hard, Imminent, Inbye, Intent, Intimate, Lock, Lucken, Mean, Miserly, Muggy, Mure, Narre, Narrow, Near, Neist, Nie, Nigh, Niggardly, Nip and tuck, Obturate, Occlusion, Oppressive, Parochial, Precinct, Reserved, Reticent, Seal, Secret, Serre, Serried, Shet, Shut(ter), Shutdown, Silly, Slam, Snug, Stap, Stuffy, Sultry, Tailgate, Temenos, Tight, Uproll, Yard

**Close-cropped** Crewcut, Not-pated

**Close-fitting** Skintight, Slinky, Tight

**Closet** Cabinet, Confine, Cubicle, Cupboard, Locker, Safe, Wardrobe, WC, Zeta

**Close-up** Detail, Fill, Shut, Stop, Zoom

**Closing-time** Eleven, End

**Clot** Agglutinate, Ass, Clag, Clump, Coagulate, Congeal, Crassamentum, Cruor, Curdle, Dag, Embolism, Embolus, Gel, Globule, Gob, Gout, Grume, Incrassate, Incrust, Jell, Lapper, Lopper, LUMP, Mass, Splatch, Stupid, Thicken, Thrombosis, Thrombus

**Cloth** Abb, Alepine, Algerine, Alpaca, American, Armozeen, Armozine, Atlas, Baft, Balzarine, Barathea, Barège, Bar(r)acan, Batiste, Beaver, Bengaline, Bombasine, Bouclé, Broadcloth, Brocade, Budge, Burlap, Burrel, Byssus, Cabbage, Calamanco, Cambric, Camlet, Cameline, Cam(e)lot, Canvas, Carmelite, Cashmere, Challis, Chambray, Chamelot, Charmeuse, Chenille, Cheviot, Chiffon, Chintz, Ciclato(u)n, Cilice, Clergy, Cloot, Clout, Coburg, Corduroy, Corporal(e), Coteline, Coutil(le), Crash, Crepe (de chine), Cretonne, Cubica, Cypress, Cyprus, Damask, Delaine, Denim, Dimity, Doeskin, Domett, Dornick, Dossal, Dossel, Dowlas, Drab(bet), Drabette, Drap-de-berry, Draper, Dreadnought, Drill, Droguet, Drugget, Duchesse, Duck, Duffel, Duffle, Dungaree, Duvetyn(e), Eolienne, FABRIC, Faille, Fannel(l), Fanon, Far(r)andine, Fearnought, FELT, Fent, Ferrandine, Filoselle, Flannel, Foulard, Foulé, Frieze, Frocking, Frontal, Fustian, Galatea, Gambroon, Genappe, Georgette, Gingham, Gloria, Greige, Gremial, Grenadine, Grogram, Grosgrain, Hai(c)k, Haique, Hammercloth, Harn, Hessian, Hodden, Holland, Homespun, Hopsack, Humhum, Hyke, Jaconet, Jeanette, Kelt, Kente, Kersey(mere), K(h)anga, Khaddar, Khadi, Kikoi, Kincob, Kitenge, Lamé, Lampas, Lava-lava, Lawn, Levantine, Line, Linen, Linsey-woolsey, Llama, Lockram, Loden, Loin, Lung, Lustring, Madras, Mandylion, Marocain, MATERIAL, Medley, Melton, Merino, Mohair, Mockado, Moreen, Mull, Mungo, Nainsook, Nankeen, Nankin, Nap, Napery, Napje, Nappie, Ninon, Organdie, Organza, Orleans, Orlon, Osnaburg, Pall, Pane, Panel, Panne, Par(r)amatta, Penistone, Percal(in)e, Perse, Persienne, Pilch, Pina, Piqué, Plaid, Plush, Pongee, Priesthood, Prunella, Puke, Rag, Raiment, Raploch, Rat(t)een, Rattine, Raven(s)duck, Rep, Rodevore, Roll, Rund, Runner, Russel, Sacking, Sarsenet, Satara, Say, Scarlet, Schappe, Scrim, Seersucker, Sempiternum, Serge, Serviette, Shabrack, Shalli, Shalloon, Sheet, Shoddy, Sicilian, Sindon, Soneri, Stammel, Stupe, Sudarium, Sulu, Surat, Surge, Swansdown, Tabaret, Tab(b)inet, Tabby, Tamin(e), Tammy, Tarlatan, Tarpaulin, Tartan, Tattersall, Terry, TEXTILE, Tibet, Tissue, Toile, Toilinet(te), Towel, Tricot, Tussore, Tweed, Tweel, Twill, Velvet(een), Vernicle, Veronica, Vicuna, Voile, Wadma(a)l, Web, Whipcord, Wigan, Wincey(ette), Winsey, Wool, Zibeline

**Cloth-designing** Batik

**Clothe(s), Clothing, Clothed** Apparel, Array, Attire, Cape, Casuals, Choli, Cits, Clad, Clobber, Combinations, Coordinates, Costume, Cover, Dicht, Dight, Don, Drag, DRESS, Duds, Emboss, Endue, Finery, Frippery, Garb, Garments, Gear, Gere, Habit, Judogi, Jumps, Outfit, Pannicle, Raiment, Rami, Rigout, Robes, Samfoo, Samfu, Schmutter, Shroud, Slop, Swaddling, Swathe, Swothling, Tackle, Togs, Tweeds, Vestiary, Vestiture, Vestment, Wardrobe, Yclad, Ycled

**Cloud(iness), Cloudy** Cirrus, Coma, Cumulus, Dim, Dull, Fog, Goat's hair, Haze, Milky, Mist, Nephele, Nephelometer, Nepho-, Nimbus, Nubecula, Obscure, Oort, Overcast, Pall, Rack, Stain, Stratus, Thunderhead, Virga, Water-dog, Woolpack

**Cloudberry**  Mountain bramble

**Clough**  Gorge, Ravine

**Clout**  Belt, Cloth, Hit, Influence, Lap(pie), Lapje, Pull, Raddle

**Clove**  Chive, Eugenia, Rose-apple, Split

**Clover**  Alfalfa, Alsike, Berseem, Calvary, Cow-grass, Ladino, Medic(k), Melilot, Serradella, Serradilla, Shamrock, Souple, Suckling, Trefoil

**Clown(ish)**  Antic, August(e), Boor, Bor(r)el, Buffoon, Carl, Chough, Chuff, Coco, Clout-shoe, COMEDIAN, Comic, Costard, Daff, Feste, Gobbo, Goon, Gracioso, Grimaldi, Hob, Jack-pudding, Jester, Joey, Joker, Joskin, Leno, Merry Andrew, Mountebank, Nedda, Nervo, Peasant, Pickle-herring, Pierrot, Put, Rustic, Slouch, Thalian, Touchstone, Wag, Zany

**Cloy(ing)**  Choke, Clog, Glut, Pall, Satiate, Surfeit, Sweet

**Club(s), Club-like**  Adelphi, Airn, Almack's, Alpeen, Artel, Association, Athen(a)eum, Baffy, Band(y), Basto, Bat, Beefsteak, Blackjack, Blaster, Bludgeon, Boodles, Bourdon, Brassie, Brook's, Bulger, C, Card, Carlton, Caterpillar, Cavalry, Cleek, Clip-joint, Combine, Cosh, Cotton, Crockford's, Cudgel, Driver, Drones, Fascio, Garrick, Guild, Hampden, Hell-fire, Honky-tonk, Indian, Iron, Jacobin, Jigger, Jockey, Kierie, Kiri, Kitcat, Kiwanis, Knobkerrie, League, Leander, Lofter, Mace, Mallet, Mashie, Maul, Mell, Mere, Meri, Mess, Niblick, Night(stick), Nighterie, Nulla(-nulla), Oddfellows, Patu, Polt, Priest, Pudding, Putter, RAC, Reform, Ring, Rota, Rotary, Savage's, Shillelagh, Slate, Society, Sorosis, Spoon, Spot, Spurs, Strike, Trefoil, Truncheon, Trunnion, Union, Variety, Waddy, Wedge, White's, Wood

**Club-foot**  Kyllosis, Polt-foot, Talipes, Varus

**Clubman**  Member

**Club-rush**  Deer-hair, Scirpus, Sedge

**Cluck**  Dent

**Clue**  Across, Anagram, Ball, Charade, Clave, Dabs, Down, HINT, Inkling, Key, Lead, Light, Rebus, Signpost, Thread, Tip

**Clueless**  Ignorant

**Clump**  Cluster, Finial, Knot, Mass, Mot(te), Patch, Plump, Tread, Tuft, Tump, Tussock

> **Clumsily**  may indicate an anagram

**Clumsy**  Awkward, Bauchle, Bungling, Butterfingers, Cack-handed, Calf, Chuckle, Clodhopper, Cumbersome, Dutch, Galoot, Gauche, Ham(-fisted), Horse-godmother, Inapt, Inelegant, Lob, Loutish, Lubbard, Lubber, Lumpish, Maladroit, Mauther, Mawr, Mawther, Messy, Mor, Nerd, Nurd, Off-ox, Palooka, Rough, Schlemihl, S(c)hlemiel, Squab, Swab, Swob, Taupie, Tawpie, Ungain, Unwieldy

**Cluster** Assemble, Bunch, Clump, Collection, Constellate, Corymb, Gather, Knot, Oakleaf, Packet, Plump, Raceme, Sheaf, Sorus, Strap, Thyrse, Truss, Tuffe, Tuft, Umbel

**Clutch** Battery, Brood, Chickens, Cling, Eggs, Glaum, Grab, GRASP, Nest, Seize, Sitting, Squeeze

**Clutter** Confusion, Litter, Mess, Rummage

**Coach** Berlin, Bogie, Bus, Car, Chara, Crammer, Diligence, Dilly, Double-decker, Drag, Edifier, Fly, Gig, Hackney, Landau(let), Microbus, Phaeton, Pullman, Rattler, Repetiteur, Saloon, Shay, Sleeper, Stage, Surrey, Tally, Teach(er), Thoroughbrace, Train(er), Tutor, Voiture

**Coach-horse** Rove-beetle

**Coachman** Automedon, Bunene, Coachy, Dragsman, Jarvey, Jehu, John

**Coagulant, Coagulate** Clot, Congeal, Curds, Jell, Rennet, Run, Runnet, Set, Solidify

**Coal** Anthracite, Burgee, Cannel, Clinker, Coom, Crow, Culm, Eldin, Ember, Fusain, Jud, Knob, Lignite, Open-cast, Score, Slack, Vitrain, Wallsend

**Coalesce(d)** Amalgamate, Fuse, Merge, Sintery, Unite

**Coalition** Alliance, Bloc, Janata, Merger, Tie

**Coal-tar** Cresol, Indene

**Coal-tub** Corf, Dan, Scuttle

**Coarse(ness)** Base, Blowzy, Bran, Broad, Common, Crude, Dowlas, Earthy, Foul, Grobian, Gross, Haggery, Ham, Illbred, Indelicate, Plebeian, Rank, Rappee, Raunchy, Ribald, Rough, Rudas, Rude, Sackcloth, Slob, Vulgar

**Coast(al)** Barbary, Beach, Coromandel, Costa, Drift, Freewheel, Glide, Hard, Littoral, Longshore, Maritime, Orarian, Riviera, Seaboard, SHORE, Strand, Toboggan

**Coaster** Beermat, Drog(h)er, Mat, Ship

**Coastguard** Gobby

**Coastline** Watermark

**Coast-road** Corniche

**Coat(ing)** Ab(b)a, Abaya, Achkan, Anarak, Anodise, Anorak, Balmacaan, Barathea, Benjamin, Blazer, Buff, Chesterfield, Cladding, Claw-hammer, Clearcole, Cloak, Cover, Creosote, Crust(a), Cutaway, Duster, Enamel, Fleece, Fur, Gambeson, Glaze, Grego, Ground, Hair, Happi, Impasto, Jack(et), Jemmy, Jerkin, Joseph, Jump, Jupon, Lacquer, Lammie, Lammy, Layer, Loden, Mac, Mackinaw, Matinee, Metallise, Paint, Paletot, Palla, Parka, Parkee, Patinate, Pelage, Perfuse, Peridium, Petersham, Plate, Pos(h)teen, Primer, Primine, Raglan, Redingote, Resin, Resist, Seal, Sheepskin, Shellac, Sherardise, Sherwani, Silver, Skinwork, Spencer, Surtout, Swagger, Tabard, Taglioni, Tar, Teflon, Truss, Trusty, Tunic, Ulster(ette), Veneer, Warm, Wash, Windjammer, Wrap-rascal, Zamarra, Zamarro, Zinc

**Coat of arms** Crest, Hatchment

**Coat-tail** Flap

**Coax** Blandish, Blarney, Cajole, Carn(e)y, Cuittle, Flatter, Lure, Persuade, Wheedle, Whilly(wha), Whillywhaw

**Cob** Hazel, Horse

**Cobalt** Co, Zaffer, Zaffre

**Cobble(rs)** Cosier, Cozier, Mend, Patch, Rot, Snob, Soutar, Souter, Sowter, Stone, Sutor, Vamp

**Cobweb(by)** Arachnoid, Araneous, Gossamer, Snare, Trap

**Cocaine** Charlie, Coke, Freebase, Moonrock, Number, Ready-washSnow

**Coccid** Wax-insect

**Cock(y)** Alectryon, Capon, Chanticleer, Erect, Flip, Fowl, France, Fugie, Hay, Jaunty, Penis, Roadrunner, Robin, Rooster, Snook, Strut, Swaggering, Tilt, Valve, Vain, Vane

**Cock-a-hoop** Crowing, Elated

**Cockatoo** Bird, Corella, Galah, Major Mitchell, Parrot

**Cockboat** Cog

**Cockchafer** Humbuzz, Maybug

**Cocker** Blenheim, Cuiter, Spaniel

**Cockeyed** Agee, Askew, Skewwhiff

**Cockfight** Main

**Cockle** Bulge, Crease, Wrinkle

> **Cockle(s)** may indicate an anagram

**Cockney** 'Arriet, 'Arry, Bow, Londoner, Londonese

> **Cockney** may indicate a missing h

**Cockpit** Greenhouse

**Cockroach** Archy, Beetle

> **Cockscomb** see COXCOMB

**Cocktail** Aperitif, Bloody Mary, Bumbo, Crusta, Daiquiri, Drink, Egg-flip, Gimlet, Manhattan, Margarita, Martini, Mix, Molotov, Old-fashioned, Prawn, Rickey, Rusty nail, Sazerac, Screwdriver, Side-car, Stengah, Stinger, Twist, White-lady

**Cocoa** Criollo, Nib(s)

**Coconut** Coco-de-mer, Coir, Copra, Head

**Cocoon** Dupion, Swathe, Trehala

**Cod** Bag, Cape, Fish, Gade, Gadus, Haberdine, Keeling, Kid, Lob, Morrhua, Stockfish, Torsk, Tusk

**Coda** Epilogue, Rondo, Tail

**Coddle** Cosset, Molly, Pamper, Pet, Poach

**Code** Alphanumeric, Amalfitan, Bushido, Canon, Cipher, Clarendon,

Codex, Cryptogram, Disciplinary, Ethics, Fuero, Genetic, Hollerith, Iddy-umpty, Justinian, Morse, Napoleon, Omerta, Rulebook, Scytale, Signal, Talmud, Zip

**Codger** Buffer, Fellow

**Codicil** Addition, Label, PS

**Coerce, Coercion** Bully, Compel, Dragoon, Gherao, Pressure, Railroad, Restrain, Threaten

**Coffee, Coffee beans** Arabica, Brazil, Cappuccino, Demi-tasse, Espresso, Expresso, Gaelic, Gloria, Granules, Instant, Irish, Java, Mocha, Robusta, Tan, Triage

**Coffee-house** Lloyd's

**Coffer** Ark, Box, Casket, Cassone, Chest, Locker

**Coffin** Bier, Casket, Hearse, Kist, Larnax, Sarcophagus, Shell

**Cog** Mitre-wheel, Nog, Pinion

**Cogent** Compelling, Forceful, Good, Telling

**Cogitate** Deliberate, Mull, Muse, Ponder

**Cohabit** Bed, Indwell, Share

**Co-heir** Parcener

**Cohere(nt)** Agglutinate, Clear, Cleave, Cling, Logical, Stick

**Cohort** Colleague, Crony, Soldier

**Coif** Calotte, Cap, Hood

**Coiffure** Hairdo, Pompadour, Tête

**Coil(ed)** Bight, Curl, Fake, Fank, Furl, Hank, Helix, Mortal, Rouleau, Solenoid, Spiral, Spiraster, Spire, Toroid, Twine, Twirl, WIND, Wound, Wreath, Writhe

**Coin** Angel, Anna, Antoninianus, Aurar, Aureus, Asper, Balboa, Bar, Bawbee, Bean, Bekah, Belga, Bender, Bezant, Bob, Bod(d)le, Broad(piece), Brockage, Brown, Butut, Byzant, Canary, Cardecu(e), Carolus, Cash, Cedi, Centavo, Change, Chervonets, Chiao, Chon, Cob, Copeck, Conto, Copper, Crown, Crusado, D, Dam, Danace, Dandiprat, Dandyprat, Daric, Décime, Dinar, Doctor, Dodkin, Dollar, Double, Doubloon, Drachm(a), Ducat(oon), Dump, Dupondius, Duro, Eagle, Ecu, Escudo, Eyrir, Farthing, Fen, Filler, Florin, Flu, Forint, Franc, Gerah, Gourde, Groat, Groschen, Grosz, G(u)ilder, Guinea, Gulden, Haler, Han(d)sel, Heller, Imperial, Inti, Invent, Jack, Jacobus, Jane, Jitney, Joannes, Johannes, Jun, Kobang, Kobo, Kr, Kreu(t)zer, Krona, Krone, Lei, Leone, Lepton, Liard, Likuta, Lion, Livre, Louis, Maik, Maile, Make, Makuta, Mancus, Maravedi, Mark, Mawpus, Merk, Mil, Millieme, Milreis, Mina, Mint, Mite, Mohur, Moidore, Mopus, Moy, Naira, Napoleon, Neoterise, Ngultrum, Noble, Nummary, Obang, Obol, Ore, Pagoda, Paisa, Paolo, Para, Pataca, Patrick, Paul, Peni(e), Penni(a), Peseta, Peso, Piastre, Picayune, Pice, Piece, Piefort, Pistareen, Pistole(t), Plack, Plate, Pollard, Portague, Portcullis, Portigue, Proof, Pul(i), Pya, Quadrans, Quarter, Razoo, Real, Red, Rider, Rigmarie, Rock, Rose noble, Royal, Ruddock, Ryal,

Satang, Sceat(t), Scudo, Semis, Semuncia, Sen, Sequin, Sesterce, Sextans, Shand, Shekel, Shilling, Shiner, Sickle, Siglos, Skilling, Slip, Slog, Smelt, Sol, Soldo, Solidare, Solidus, Sovereign, Specie, Stamp, Stater, Stiver, Strike, Sucre, Talent, Tanner, Tester, Teston, Testoon, Testril, Tetradrachm, Thrimsa, Thrymsa, Tical, Tick(e)y, Toman, Turner, Unicorn, Unite, Unity, Xerafin, Xeraphim, Xu, Yellowboy, Yellowgirl, Yuan, Zack, Zecchino, Zwanziger, Zuz

**Coinage**   Currency, Invention, Nonce-word

**Coincide(nt), Coincidence**   Accident, Chance, Consilience, Fit, Fluke, Overlap, Rabat(to), Simultaneous, Synastry, Synchronise, Tally

**Coke**   Chark, Coal, Cocaine, Kola

**Col**   Pass, Poort, Saddle

**Cold**   Ague, Algid, Arctic, Austere, Biting, Bitter, Bleak, C, Catarrh, Cauld(rife), Chill(y), Coryza, Frem(d), Fremit, Frigid, Frost(y), Gelid, Glacial, Hiemal, Icy, Impersonal, Jeel, Nippy, Nirlit, Parky, Perishing, Polar, Psychro-, Remote, Rheumy, Rigor, Rume, Snap, Sour, Streamer, Taters, Weed, Wintry

**Coldstream**   Borderer, Guard

**Cole**   Colza, King, Nat, Porter

**Colic**   Batts, Bots, Botts, Gripe, Upset

**Collaborate, Collaborator, Collaboration**   Assist, Combine, COOPERATE, Quisling, Synergy, Vichy

**Collapse**   Cave, Conk, Crash, Crumble, Crumple, Debacle, Downfall, Fail(ure), Fold, Founder, Give, Inburst, Meltdown, Phut, Purler, Rot, Ruin, Scat(ter), Sink, Slump, Tumble, Wilt

> **Collapsing**   may indicate an anagram

**Collar(ed)**   Arrest, Astrakhan, Bertha, Berthe, Brecham, Capture, Carcanet, Chevesaile, Choker, Collet, Dog, Esses, Hame, Holderbat, Jampot, Karenni, Moran, Mousquetaire, Nab, Neckband, Necklet, Peter Pan, Piccadilly, Pikadell, Polo, Rabato, Rebater, Rebato, Revers, Ruff, Seize, Tackle, Tappet, Torque, Turndown, Vandyke, Whisk, Yoke

**Collation**   Comparison, Meal, Repast

**Colleague**   Associate, Bedfellow, Mate, Oppo, Partner

**Collect(ed), Collection, Collector**   Accrue, Agglomerate, Aggregate, Album, Alms, Amass, Amildar, Ana, Anthology, Assemble, Aumil, Budget, Bundle, Calm, Cap, Cete, Clowder, Compendium, Compile, Congeries, Covey, Cull, Dustman, Exordial, Florilegium, Gather, Glean, Glossary, Heap, Herd, Hive, Idant, Kitty, Levy, Magpie, Meal, Miscellany, Montem, Museum, Muster, Nide, Offertory, Omnibus, Omnium-gatherum, Paddling, Pile, Plate, Pod, Post, Prayer, Quest, Raise, Recheat, Sedge, Serene, Set, Shoe, Siege, Skein, Smytrie, Sord, Sottisier, Sounder, Spring, Stand, Tahsildar, Team, Troop, Watch, Whipround, Wisp

> **Collection**   may indicate an anagram

**Collecting-box**   Brod

**Collectorate** Taluk

**College(s)** Academy, Ampleforth, All Souls, Balliol, Brasenose, Caius, Campus, CAT, Cheltenham, Clare, Corpus, Downing, Electoral, Emmanuel, Eton, Exeter, Foundation, Girton, Hall, Jail, Keble, King's, Lancing, Linacre, Lincoln, LSE, Lycée, Lyceum, Madras(s)a(h), Madressah, Magdalen(e), Medresseh, Merton, Newnham, Nuffield, Oriel, Poly, Protonotariat, Queen's, Ruskin, St. Johns, Saliens, Selwyn, Seminary, Somerville, Sorbonne, Tech(nical), Theologate, Trinity, Tug, Up, Wadham, Winchester

**Collide, Collision** Afoul, Barge, Bird-strike, Bump, Cannon, Carom(bole), Clash, Dash, Foul, Head-on, Impact, Into, Kiss, Meet, Strike, Thwack

**Collie** Border, Dog, Kelpic, Kclpy, Sheepdog

**Collier** Geordie, Hoastman, Miner, Necklace, Patience, Ship

**Colloid** Gel, Lyophil(e)

**Collude, Collusive** Abet, Cahoots, Conspire, Deceive

**Colon** Aspinwall

**Colonel** Blimp, Bogey, Chinstrap, Col, Everard, Goldstick, Newcome, Nissen, Pride

**Colonial, Colonist** Ant, Antenatal, Boer, Creole, Emigré, Oecist, Oikist, Overseas, Pioneer, Polyp(e), Settler, Sicel(iot), Sikel(ian), Sikeliot, Swarm, Territorial

**Colonnade** File, Gallery, Porch, Portico, Stoa

**Colony** Aden, Dependency, Hongkong, Rookery, Settlement, Zambia

**Colophony** Rosin

**Colossal** ENORMOUS, Epochal, Gigantic, Huge, Vast

**Colosseum** Amphitheatre

**Colour(ed), Colouring** Alizarin(e), Anil, Anthocyan, An(n)atta, An(n)atto, Arnotto, Auburn, Bedye, Bice, Bistre, Blee, Blue, Blush, Buff, C, Cap, Cappagh-brown, Cardinal, Chica, Chrome, Complementary, Complexion, Crayon, Criant, Cyan, Day-glo, Distort, Dye, Ecru, Eosin, Filemot, Flag, Florid, Gamboge, Gouache, HUE, Isabel, Kalamkari, Lake, Leer, Local, Lovat, Lutein, Magenta, Maroon, Mauve, Metif, Nankeen, Ochre, Orange, Orpiment, Palette, Pastel, Philamot, Philomot, Pied, Pigment, Pochoir, Polychrome, Primary, Prism, Puke, Reddle, Reseda, Riot, Roucou, Rouge, Ruddle, Sepia, Shade, Sienna, Solferino, Spectrum, Taupe, Tincture, Tinge, Tint, Titian, Tone, Umber, Umbrage, Uvea

> **Coloured** may indicate an anagram

**Colour blindness** Daltonism, Dichromism, Protanopic, Tritanopia

**Colourful** Abloom, Brave, Flamboyant, Iridescent, Opalescent, Vivid

**Colourless** Albino, Bleak, Drab, Dull, Hyalite, Pallid, Pallor, Wan, White

**Colt** Cade, Foal, Gun, Sta(i)g, Teenager

**Columbine** Aquilegia

**Column(s), Column foot** Anta, Atlantes, Commentary, Cylinder, Decastyle, Diastyle, Doric, Editorial, Eustyle, Fifth, File, Gossip, Impost, Lat, Monolith, Nelson's, Newel, Obelisk, Peristyle, Persian, Pilaster, PILLAR, Rouleau, Row, Spina, Spinal, Spine, Stylobate, Systyle, Tabulate, Telamone, Third, Tige, Tore, Torus, Trajan's

**Columnist** Advertiser, Caryatid, Newsman, Stylite, Telamon, Writer

**Coma** Apoplexy, Sleep, Torpor, Trance

**Comb(er), Combed, Combing** Alveolate, Beehive, Breaker, Card, Copple, Crest, Curry, Hackle, Heckle, Kaim, Kame, Kangha, Kemb, Noils, Rake, Red(d), Ripple(r), Search, Smooth, Teasel, Toaze, Tose, Toze, Trawl, Wave

**Combat(ant), Combative** Argument, BATTLE, Competitor, Conflict, Contest, Dispute, Duel, FIGHT, Gladiator, Joust, Jujitsu, Just, Karate, Kendo, List, Mêlée, Militant, Oppose, Protagonist, Spear-running, Unarmed, War

**Combination, Combine(d)** Accrete, Alligate, Ally, Amalgam, Associate, Axis, Bloc, Cartel, Cleave, Clique, Coalesce, Coalition, Concoction, Conflated, Conglomerate, Consortium, Crasis, Fuse, Group, Harvester, Join, Junta, Kartell, League, Meld, Merge(r), Mingle, Mixture, Perm(utation), Piece, Pool, Quill, Ring, Splice, Synthesis, Terrace, Trona, Unite, Wed

**Comb-like** Ctenoid, Pecten

**Combustible** Ardent, Fiery, Inflammable, Phlogistic, Phlogiston

> **Combustible** may indicate an anagram

**Come, Coming back, Coming out** Advent, Anear, Anon, Appear, Approach, Ar(r), Arise, Arrive, Attend, Debouch, Derive, Future, Happen, Iceman, Issue, Orgasm, Parousia, Pass, Pop, Respond, Via

**Comeback** Bounce, Echo, Homer, Quip, Rally, Rearise, Rebound, Recovery, Repartee, Reply, Retort, Retour, Return, Reversion, Riposte

**Comedian** Benny, Buffoon, Chaplin, CLOWN, Comic, Durante, Emery, Goon, Groucho, Joker, Karno, Leno, Robey, Scream, Tate, Tati, Wag, Wise

**Comedo** Blackhead

**Comedown** Avale, Bathetic, Bathos, Disappointment, Drop, Letdown, Shower

**Comedy** Com, Drama, Farce, Keystone, Knockabout, Lazzo, Millamant, Situation, Slapstick, Thalia, Travesty

**Comely** Beseen, Bonny, Fair, Goodly, Graceful, Jolly, Pleasing, Pretty, Proper

**Comestible(s)** Cate, Eats, Fare

**Comet** Geminid, Halley's, Meteor, Xiphias

**Come through** Weather

**Comfort(er), Comforting** Amenity, Analeptic, Balm, Bildad, Calm, Cheer, Cherish, Consolation, Console, Creature, Crumb, Dummy, Ease,

Eliphaz, Featherbed, Reassure, Relief, Relieve, Scarf, Solace, Soothe, Succour, Zophar

**Comfortable, Comfy** Bein, Canny, Cose, Cosh, Cosy, Couthie, Couthy, Cushy, Easy, Heeled, Relaxed, Rug, Snug, Tosh, Trig, Warm, Well

**Comic(al)** Beano, Buff, Buffo(on), Bumpkin, Buster, Chaplin, Clown, COMEDIAN, Dandy, Droll, Eagle, Fields, FUNNY, Hardy, Horror, Jester, Laurel, Leno, Mag, Manga, Quizzical, Robey, Strip, Tati, Trial, Zany

**Command(ing), Commandeer, Commandment(s)** Behest, Bid, Charge, Coerce, Control, Decalogue, Direction, Dominate, Edict, Fiat, Fighter, Firman, Hest, Imperious, Instruction, Jussive, Mandate, Mitzvah, ORDER, Precept, Press, Requisition, Rule, Seize, Ukase, Warn, Warrant, Will, Wish, Writ

**Commander** Ag(h)a, Bey, Bloke, Blucher, Boss, Brennus, Brig, Caliph, Centurion, Cid, Decurion, Emir, Emperor, Hipparch, Imperator, Killadar, Leader, Manager, Marshal, Master, Meer, Moore, Officer, Overlord, Pendragon, Raglan, Seraskier, Shogun, Sirdar, Taxiarch, Trierarch, Vaivode, Voivode, Waivode, Warlord

**Commando** Chindit(s), Fedayee(n), Raider, SAS

**Commemorate, Commemoration** Encaenia, Epitaph, Eulogy, Keep, Memorial, Monument, Plaque

**Commence** Begin, Initiate, Open, Start

**Commend(ation)** Belaud, Bestow, Encomium, Entrust, Laud, Panegyric, PRAISE, Roose, Tribute

**Commensal** Epizoon, Messmate

**Commensurate** Adequate, Enough, Equivalent, Relevant

**Comment(ary), Commentator** Analyst, Animadvert, Annotate, Comm, Critic, Descant, Discuss, Editorial, Essay, Explain, Exposition, Footnote, Gemara, Gloss(ographer), Hakam, Margin, Midrashim, Note, Par, Postil, Remark, Scholiast

**Commerce, Commercial** Ad, Barter, Cabotage, Jingle, Marketable, Mercantile, Mercenary, Merchant, Trade, Traffic

**Commercial traveller** Drummer, Rep

**Commiserate, Commiseration** Compassion, Pity, Sympathise

**Commission(er), Commissioned** Brevet, Brokerage, Charge, Delegation, Depute, ECE, Engage, Envoy, Errand, Factor, Husbandage, Job, Kickback, Magistrate, Mandate, Office(r), Official, Ombudsman, Order, Perpetration, Place, Poundage, Rake-off, Roskill, Task, Trust

**Commit(ment)** Consign, Contract, Decision, Dedication, Delegate, Do, Engage, Entrust, Enure, Perpetrate, Pledge

**Committee** Board, Body, Commission, Council, Group, Joint, Junta, Politburo, Presidium, Select, Standing, Steering, Syndicate, Table, Watch

**Commodious** Ample, Roomy, Spacious

**Commodity** Article, Item, Staple, Ware

**Common(s), Commoner, Commonly** Average, Cad, Conventional, Diet, Dirt, Ealing, Eatables, Enclosure, Epicene, Everyday, Familiar, Fare, Folk, General, Green, House, Law, Lay, Low, Mark, MP, Mutual, Naff, Non-U, Normal, People, Pleb, Prevalent, Prole, Public, Related, Rife, Roturier, Ryfe, Scran, Sense, Shared, Stray, Tie, Trite, Tritical, Tuft, Tye, Use, USUAL, Vile, Vul(gar), Vulgo, Vulgus, Wimbledon

**Commonplace** Banal, Copybook, Hackneyed, Homely, Humdrum, Ordinary, Philistine, Plain, Platitude, Prosaic, Quotidian, Trite

**Commonsense** Gumption, Nous, Wit

**Commotion** Bluster, Bustle, Carfuffle, Clatter, Curfuffle, Do, Dust, Ferment, Fraise, Fuss, Hell, Pother, Racket, Rort, Steer(y), Stir, Storm, Stushie, Tirrivee, Tirrivie, To-do, Toss, Tumult, Turmoil, Upheaval, Uproar, Wroth

**Communal, Commune** Agapemone, Collective, Com, Meditate, Mir, Phalanstery, Public, Talk, Township

**Communicate, Communication** Ampex, Announce, Baud, Boyau, Cable, Conversation, Cybernetic, E-mail, Impart, Inform, Intelsat, Message, Note, Prestel, Reach, Road, Signal, Telepathy, Telex, Telstar, Transmit

**Communion** Creed, Fellowship, Host, Housel

**Communiqué** Announcement, Statement

**Communism, Communist** Aspheterism, Bolshevist, Com, Comecon, Cominform, Comintern, Commo, Comsomol, Essene, Fourier, Komsomol, Leninite, Maoist, Perfectionist, Pinko, Politburo, Red, Soviet, Tanky, Titoist

**Community** Alterne, Body, Clachan, Coenobitism, Coenobium, Colony, EEC, Frat(e)ry, Kahal, Kibbutz, Neighbourhood, People, Phyle, Public, Pueblo, Shtetl, Society, Street, Tribe, Ujamaa, Zupa

**Commute(r)** Change, Convert, Reduce, Straphanger, Travel

**Como** Lake, Perry

**Compact** Agreement, Cement, Concise, Conglobe, Covenant, Covin, Coyne, Dense, Entente, Fast, Firm, Flapjack, Hard, Knit, League, Match, Pledge, Solid, Terse, Tight, Treaty, Well-knit

**Companion(able)** Achates, Associate, Attender, Barnacle, Bedfellow, Bud(dy), Butty, CH, China, Comate, Comrade, Contubernal, Crony, Cupman, Duenna, Ephesian, Escort, Felibre, FELLOW, Fere, Handbook, Mate, Pal, Pard, Thane, Thegn, Vade-mecum

**Company, Companies** Actors, Artel, Ass, Assembly, Band, Bank, Battalion, Bevy, BUSINESS, Cahoot, Cartel, Cast, Cavalcade, CIA, Circle, Club, Co, Conger, Consort, Cordwainers, Core, Corporation, Corps, Coy, Crew, Crowd, East India, Faction, Financer, FIRM, Flock, Gang, Garrison, Ging, Guild, Haberdashers, Heap, Hudson's Bay, ICI, Inc, Intercourse, Jingbang, Joint-stock, Limited, Livery, Maniple, Order, Organisation, Plc, Rep(ertory), SA, Set, Siege, Sort, Syndicate, Team, Thiasus, Troop, Troupe, Twa, Two(some), White

**Compare(d), Comparison** Analogy, Beside, Bracket, Collate, Contrast,

Correspond, Cp, Equate, Liken, Match, Odious, Parallel, Relation, Simile, Weigh

**Compartment** Bay, Booth, Box, Carriage, Cell, Chamber, Cubicle, Locellate, Loculament, Loculus, Partition, Pigeonhole, Pocket, Room, Severy, Stall, Till

**Compass** Ambit, Area, Bounds, Gamut, Goniometer, Gyro, Infold, Needle, Orbit, Pelorus, Perimeter, RANGE, Reach, Rhumb, Room, Scale, Sweep, Tessitura

**Compassion(ate)** Clemency, Mercy, Pity, Samaritan, Sympathy

**Compatible** Consistent, Harmonious

**Compatriot** National

**Compel(led), Compulsion, Compulsory** Addiction, Coact, Coerce, Command, Constrain, Dragoon, Enforce, Extort, Fain, FORCE, Gar, Make, Mandatory, Strongarm, Oblige, Tyrannise

**Compendium** Breviate

**Compensate, Compensation** Amend(s), Balance, Boot, Comp, Counterbalance, Counterpoise, Damages, Guerdon, Offset, Payment, Recoup, Redress, Reparation, Reprisal, Restore, Retaliation, Salvage, Satisfaction, Solatium, X-factor

**Compère** Emcee, Host, MC, Presenter

**Compete** Contend, Emulate, Enter, Match, Outvie, Play, Rival, Vie

**Competence, Competent** Ability, Able, Adequate, Can, Capacity, Dab, Fit, Responsible, Worthy

**Competition, Competitor** Agonist, Bee, Biathlon, Contest, Cup, Drive, Entrant, Event, Field, Gymkhana, Match, Opponent, Pentathlon, Player, Race, Rally, Repechage, Rival(ise), Tenson, Test, Tiger, Tournament, Tourney, Wap(p)enshaw

**Compile(r), Compilation** Anthology, Arrange, Collect, Edit, Prepare, Zadkiel

**Complacent** Babbitt, Fatuous, Joco, Pleasant, Smug

**Complain(t)** Adenoids, Affection, Affliction, Alas, Alastrim, Alopecia, Anaemia, Barrack, Beef, Bellyache, Bitch, Bleat, Carp, Charge, Chorea, Colic, Crab, Cramp, Criticise, Diatribe, Disorder, Dropsy, Epidemic, Ergot, Girn, Groan, Grouch, Grouse, Growl, Grudge, Grumble, Harangue, Hives, Hypochondria, ILLNESS, Jeremiad, Kvetch, Lupus, Malady, Mange, Mean(e), Mein, Mene, Moan, Morphew, Mumps, Murmur, Nag, Natter, Neuralgia, Pertussis, Plica, Protest, Pyelitis, Querimony, Rail, Rickets, Sapego, Sciatica, Scold, Sigh, Silicosis, Squawk, Staggers, Thrush, Tic, Tinea, Upset, Whimper, Whine, Whinge

**Complaisant** Agreeable, Flexible, Suave, Supple

**Complement** Amount, Balance, Finish, Gang, Lot, Reciprocate

**Complete(ly)** Absolute, Accomplish, All, Arrant, Clean, Congenital, Consummate, Crown, Do, End, Entire, Finalise, Finish, Fulfil, Full, Hollow, Incept, Integral, In toto, Out, Perfect, Quite, Sheer, Thorough,

Total, Unequivocal, Whole (hog)

**Complex(ity)** Abstruse, Compound, Difficult, Electra, Hard, Inferiority, Intricate, Intrince, Involute, Knot, Manifold, Mixed, Multinucleate, Nest, Network, Obsession, Paranoid, Syndrome, Web

**Complexion** Aspect, Blee, Hue, Temper, Tint, View

**Compliant, Comply** Agree, Assent, Conform, Obey, Observe, Sequacious, Surrender

**Complicate(d), Complication** Bewilder, Complex, Deep, Elaborate, Embroil, Implex, Intricate, Involve, Node, Nodus, Perplex, Rigmarole, Tangle, Tirlie-wirlie

> **Complicated** may indicate an anagram

**Compliment(s)** Baisemain, Congratulate, Flatter, Flummery, Praise, Soap, Tribute

**Component** Constituent, Contact, CRT, Element, Factor, Ingredient, PART

**Compose(d), Composure** Aplomb, Arrange, Calm, Consist, Cool, CREATE, Improvise, Indite, Lull, Placid, Poise, Produce, Reconcile, Sangfroid, Sedate, Serenity, Settle, Soothe, Tranquil

**Composer** Adam, Alaleona, Albeniz, Albinoni, Alfven, Allegri, Arne, Arnold, Azione, Bach, Bacharach, Balfe, Bantock, Barber, Bartok, Bax, Beethoven, Berg, Berlin, Bernstein, Bliss, Boito, Borodin, Boyce, Brahms, Brian, Bridge, Broughton, Bruckner, Busoni, Buxtehude, Byrd, Cage, Chabrier, Chaminade, Cherubini, Chopin, Coates, Copland, Corelli, Couperin, Crumb, Debussy, Delibes, Delius, Dima, Donizetti, Dukas, Elgar, Falla, Faure, Field, Finzi, Flotow, Franck, German, Gesualdo, Glass, Glière, Glinka, Gluck, Gounod, Grainger, Granados, Grieg, Handel, Harty, Haydn, Hindemith, Holst, Hummel, Ibert, Inventor, Ireland, Ives, Kern, Kreutzer, Lalo, Lasso, Lassus, Lehar, Ligeti, Liszt, Lully, Mahler, Maker, Marcello, Martinu, Massenet, Maxwell Davies, Mendelssohn, Messager, Monteverdi, Mozart, Musician, Mussorgsky, Nielsen, Novello, Offenbach, Orff, Palestrina, Parry, Ponchielli, Poulenc, Prokofiev, Prout, Puccini, Purcell, Purnell, Quilter, Raff, Rameau, Rawsthorne, Ravel, Reger, Respighi, Rodgers, Romberg, Rossi, Rossini, Roussel, Rubbra, Saint Saëns, Salieri, Satie, Scarlatti, Schnittke, Schubert, Schumann, Scriabin, Serialist, Shostakovich, Smetana, Sousa, Stainer, Stockhausen, Strauss, Stravinsky, Sullivan, Suppe, Tallis, Tartini, Taverner, Tchaikovsky, Tosti, Triadist, Varese, Verdi, Vivaldi, Wagner, Warlock, Watts, Weber, Weill, Williamson, Wolf, Wolf Ferrari, Writer, Youmans

> **Composing** may indicate an anagram

**Composite** Aster, Costmary, Foalfoot, Gerbera, Groundsel, Hybrid, Integral, Motley, Rag(weed), Synthesized, Thistle

**Composition, Compositor** Aleatory, Azione, Beaumontage, Beaumontague, Cob, Creation, Dite, Essay, Etude, Exaration, Fantasia, Ingredient, Inditement, Loam, Met, Montage, Morceau, Nonet(te), Opus, Oratorio, Pastiche, Piece, Poem, Printer, Quartette, Raga, Rhapsody, Ship,

Sing, Smoot, Sonata, Sonatina, Structure, Synthesis, Terracotta, Texture, Toccata, Treatise, Typesetter

**Compost** Dressing, Fertilizer, Vraic

**Compound** Acetal, Acetone, Acridin(e), Alum, Amalgam, Ammonia, Anhydride, Arginine, Arsine, Bahuvrihi, Baryta, Blend, Caliche, Carbide, Cellulose, Cetane, Chela, Chrome, Composite, Constitute, Coprosterol, Cortisone, C(o)umarin, Cyanide, Cyanogen, Diamine, Diazo, Diene, Dimer, Diode, Dioxide, Dvandva, Enol, Epimer, Erbia, Ester, Farnesol, Flavone, Formaldehyde, Glycol, Halide, Haloid, Halon, Hexene, Hydrate, Imide, Imine, Impsonite, Indican, Indoxyl, Isologue, Isomer, Ketone, Lithia, Massicot, Menthol, Metamer, Mix, Multiply, Niello, Nitrite, Olein, Oxime, Potin, Protein, Purine, Pyran, Pyracole, Pyrone, Qinghaosu, Quercetus, Quinone, Relagar, Retcnc, Rock-alum, Rotcnonc, Sarin, Scsquioxide, Skatole, Steroid, Stilbene, Sulphide, Tabun, Tartar, Tatpurusha, Taurine, Terpene, Thiol, Thiourea, Thymol, Trimer, Tritide, Trona, Type, Uridine, Wolfram, Zirconia

> **Compound(ed)** may indicate an anagram

**Comprehend, Comprehensive** All-in, Catch-all, Catholic, Compass, Contain, Fathom, Follow, General, Global, Grasp, Include, Indepth, Ken, Large, Omnibus, Perceive, School, Sweeping, Thoroughgoing, UNDERSTAND, Wide

**Compress(ed)** Astrict, Bale, Coarctate, Contract, Solidify, Squeeze, Stupe

**Comprise** Contain, Embody, Embrace, Include

**Compromise** Avoision, Brule, Commit, Concession, Endanger, Involve, Settlement, Time-server

> **Compulsion** see COMPEL

**Compunction** Hesitation, Regret, Remorse, Scruple, Sorrow

**Computation, Computer (language), Computer user** Ada, Algol, Apple, ASCII, Basic, C, Calculate, Calculus, Cast(er), COBOL, Counter, Earom, Eniac, Estimate, Figure, Fortran, Hacker, HAL, Holmes, ICL, Laptop, Mainframe, Measure, Micro, OCCAM, Pascal, Patch, Pixel, Program, PROM, RAM, Realtime, Reckoner, ROM, SNOBOL, Spreadsheet, Sprite, Tally, Wysiwyg

**Comrade** Achates, Ally, Buddy, Butty, China, Fellow, Friend, Kamerad, Mate, Pal, Pard, Tovarich, Tovaris(c)h

**Con(man)** Against, Anti, Bunco, Dupe, Hornswoggle, Jacob, Learn, Peruse, Read, Scam, Scan, Steer, Sucker, Swindle, Tweedler

**Concave** Dished

**Conceal(ment), Concealed** Blanket, Closet, Clothe, Cover, Doggo, Feal, Heal, Heel, Hele, HIDE, Latent, Occult, Misprision, Palm, Perdu(e), Recondite, Screen, Scriene, Secrete, Shroud, Stash, Subreption, Ulterior, Wrap

**Concede** Acknowledge, Admit, Allow, Compromise, Confess, Forfeit, Owe, Own

**Conceit(ed)** Bumptious, Caprice, Carriwitchet, Concetto, Crank, Crotchet, Device, Dicty, Egomania, Fancy, Fop, Fume, Hauteur, Idea, Notion, Podsnappery, Prig, Princock, Princox, Puppyism, Quiblin, Side, Snotty, Vainglory, Wind

**Conceive, Conceivable** Beget, Create, Credible, Imagine, Possible

**Concentrate(d), Concentration** Aim, Bunch, Centre, Collect, Condense, Dephlegmate, Distil, Elliptical, Essence, Extract, Focus, Intense, Listen, Major, Mantra, Mass, Potted, Rivet, Samadhi, Titre

**Concept(ion)** Brain, Hent, Ideal, Ideation, Image, Myth, Notion

**Concern(ing)** About, After, Ail, Altruism, Anent, As to, Business, Care, Company, Disturb, Intéressé, Interest, Into, Lookout, MATTER, Melt, Misease, Over, Pidgin, Pigeon, Re, Reck, Regard, Reke, Respect, Retch, Solicitude, Touch, Trouble

> **Concerned** may indicate an anagram

**Concert (place)** Agreement, Benefit, Charivari, Cooperation, Device, Gig, Hootananny, Hootenanny, Hootnannie, Odeon, Pop, Prom(enade), Recital, Singsong, Smoker, Symphony, Together, Wit

**Concertina** Pleat, Squeezebox, Squiffer

**Concerto** Emperor, Grosso

**Concession** Carta, Charter, Compromise, Favour, Franchise, Munich, Ou, Privilege, Sop

**Conch** Shell, Strombus

**Conchie** CO

**Conciliate** Allay, Calm, Disarm, Ease, Mollify, Placate, Reconcile

**Concise** Compact, Curt, Laconic, Short, Succinct, Terse, Tight

**Conclave** Assembly, Caucus, Confab, Meeting

**Conclude(d), Conclusion, Conclusive** Achieve, A fortiori, Afterword, Amen, Binding, Clinch, Close, Complete, Dead, Decide, Deduce, END, Envoi, Explicit, Fine, Finis, FINISH, Gather, Illation, Infer, Limit, Omega, Peroration, Point, Postlude, Resolve, Settle, Summary, Upshot, Uptie

**Conclusive** Cogent, Convincing, Estoppel, Final

**Concoct(ion)** Brew, Compound, Creation, Plan, Trump

**Concord** Consonance, Harmony, Peace, Plane, Sympathy, Treaty, Unity

**Concorde** SST

**Concourse** Assembly, Confluence, Esplanade, Throng

**Concrete, Concretion** Actual, Aggregate, Beton, Bezoar, Cake, Calculus, Clot, Dogger, Gunite, Hard, Mass, Minkstone, No-fines, Positive, Reify, Siporex, Solid, Tangible

**Concubine** Apple-squire, Campaspe, Harem, Hetaria, Madam, Mistress, Odalisk

**Concur** Accord, Agree, Coincide, Comply, CONSENT, Gree

**Concuss(ion)** Clash, Shock, Stun

**Condemn** Blame, Blast, Cast, Censor, Censure, Convict, Damn, Decry, Denounce, Doom, Judge, Kest, Obelise, Proscribe, Sentence, Upbraid

**Condense(r), Condensation** Abbreviate, Abridge, Capacitator, Compress, Contract, Distil, Encapsulate, Epitomise, Liebig, Précis, Rectifier, Reduce, Shorten, Shrink, Summarise

**Condescend** Deign, Patronise, Stoop, Vouchsafe

**Condiment** Cayenne, Chutney, Flavour, Kava, Relish, Sauce, Tracklement, Turmeric, Vinegar

**Condition(al)** Fettle, Going, Hood, If, IN GOOD CONDITION, Kelter, Kilter, Nick, Order, Pass, Plight, Pliskie, Point, Position, Predicament, Prepare, Prerequisite, Protasis, Proviso, Repair, Rider, Ropes, Sis, Standing, State, Sted, Stipulation, String, Term, Trim, Unless

**Condom** Cap, Gumboot, Rubber, Safe, Sheath

**Condone** Absolve, Excuse, Forgive, Overlook

**Conduct(or), Conductress** Accompany, Anode, Arm, Arrester, Bearing, Behaviour, Bulow, Bus-bar, Cad, Chobdar, Clippie, Coil, Demean(our), Deportment, Drive, Editor, Electrode, Escort, Fetch, Ignitron, Karajan, Kempe, Klemperer, Lead, Maestro, Microchip, Nerve, Outer, Parts, Photodiode, PILOT, Previn, Prosecute, Psychopomp, Rattle, Safe, Sargent, Scudaller, Scudler, Skudler, Solicit, Solti, Thermistor, Toscanini, Transact, USHER, Varactor, Varistor, Wire, Wood

> **Conducting** may indicate an '-ic' ending

**Conduit** Aqueduct, Canal, Carrier, Duct, Main, Panstock, Pipe, Tube

**Cone, Conical** Cappie, Fir, Moxa, Pastille, Peeoy, Pineal, Pingo, Pioy(e), Puy, Pyramid, Spire, Taper, Tee

**Coney** Daman, Doe, Hyrax

**Confection** Candy, Caramel, Chocolate, Concoction, Conserve, Ice, Kiss, Noisette, Nougat, Quiddery, Sweet

**Confederal, Confederate, Confederation** Accessory, Alliance, Ally, Association, Body, Bund, Bunkosteerer, Cover, League, Partner, Union

**Confer(ence)** Bestow, Cf, Colloquy, Council, Diet, Do, Dub, Fest, Forum, Grant, Huddle, Imparlance, Indaba, Lambeth, Meeting, Negotiate, Palaver, Parley, Pawaw, Pear, Potsdam, Pourparler, Powwow, Pugwash, Quadrant, Seminar, Summit, Symposium, Synod, TALK, Vouchsafe, Yalta

**Confess(or), Confession** Acknowledge, Admit, Agnise, Avowal, Concede, Declare, Disclose, Edward, Own, Recant, Shrift, Shriver, Sing, Whittle

**Confide(nce), Confident(ial), Confidant** Aplomb, Aside, Assertive, Assured, Bedpost, Belief, Cocksure, Cred, Crouse, Entre nous, Entrust, Faith, Gatepost, Hardy, Hope, Hush-hush, Intimate, Morale, Pack, Private, Privy, Sanguine, Secret, Sub rosa, Sure, Tell, Trust, Unbosom, Under the rose

**Confine(d), Confines, Confinement** Ambit, Bail, Bale, Cage, CB, Chain, Constrain, Cramp, Crib, Detain, Emmew, Enclose, Endemic,

Enmew, Gate, Immanacle, Immew, Immure, Impound, IMPRISON, Intern, Local, March, Mail, Mew, Mure, Narrow, Pen, Pent, Pinion, Poky, Restrict, Rules, Tether, Thirl, Trammel

**Confirm(ed), Confirmation** Addict, Assure, Attest, Bear, Certify, Chrisom, Christen, Chronic, Clinch, Corroborate, Endorse, Obsign, OK, Ratify, Sacrament, Sanction, Seal, Strengthen, Tie, Validate, Vouch

**Confiscate** Deprive, Dispossess, Distrain, Escheat, Impound, Seize, Sequestrate

**Conflagration** Blaze, Holocaust, Inferno, Wildfire

**Conflict** Agon, Armageddon, Battle, Camp, Clash, Contend, Contravene, Controversy, Feud, Fray, Jar, Lists, Mêlée, Muss, Oppose, Rift, Strife, STRUGGLE, Tergiversate, War

**Conform(ity)** Adjust, Comply, Consistence, Correspond, Normalise, Obey, Observe, Suit, Yield

**Confound(ed)** Abash, Amaze, Astound, Awhape, Baffle, Bewilder, Blamed, Blasted, Blest, Bumbaze, Contradict, Darn, Drat, Dumbfound, Elude, Floor, Jigger, Mate, Murrain, Nonplus, Perishing, Perplex, Rabbit, Spif(f)licate, Stump, Throw

> **Confound** may indicate an anagram

**Confrère** Ally

**Confront(ation)** Appose, Beard, Breast, Eyeball, Face, Meet, Nose, Oppose, Showdown, Tackle

**Confuse(d), Confusion** Addle, Anarchy, Astonishment, Babel, Baffle, Bedevil, Befog, Bemuse, Bewilder, Bustle, Chaos, Cloud, Clutter, Complicate, Debacle, Didder, Disconcert, Disorient, Distract, Dither, Dizzy, Dudder, Egarement, Embrangle, Embroglio, Embroil, Farrago, Flap, Flurry, Fluster, Fog, Fox, Fuddle, Galley-west, Hash, Havoc, Huddle, Hugger-mugger, Imbrangle, Imbroglio, IN CONFUSION, Litter, Lost, Lurry, Maelstrom, Mayhem, Maze, Melange, Mess, Mingle, Mish-mash, Mixtie-maxtie, Mizzle, Moider, Moither, MUDDLE, Overset, Pellmell, Perplex, Pi(e), Ravel, Rout, Snafu, Spin, Stump, Stupefy, Synchysis, Tangle, Throw, Topsy-turvy, Welter, Whemmle, Whomble, Whummle, Woozy

> **Confuse(d)** may indicate an anagram

**Confute** Confound, Contradict, Deny, Disprove, Infringe, Redargue, Refel

**Congeal** Coagulate, Freeze, Gel, Gunge, Set, Solidify

**Congenial** Agreeable, Amiable, Compatible, Connate, Happy, Kindred, Simpatico

**Congenital** Inborn, Innate, Inveterate

**Congest(ed), Congestion** Cram, Crowd, Engorge, Impact, Jam, Logjam, Turgid

**Conglomerate, Conglomeration** Aggregate, Gather, Heap, Mass

**Congratulate, Congratulation** Applaud, Felicitate, Laud, Preen, Salute

**Congregation(alist)** Assembly, Barnabite, Body, Brownist, Community, Conclave, Ecclesia, Flock, Gathering, Host, Laity, Oratory, Propaganda, Synagogue

**Congress(man)** Assembly, Conclave, Council, Eisteddfod, Intercourse, Legislature, Rally, Senator, Solon, Synod

**Conifer(ous)** Araucaria, Cedar, Cypress, Cyrus, Evergreen, Larch, Picea, Pine, Spruce, Taiga, Thuja, Yew

**Conjecture** Fancy, Guess, Speculate, Surmise, View

**Conjoin** Alligate, Ally, Connect, Knit

**Conjugate, Conjugation** Couple, Join, Nuptial, Synopsis, Typto

**Conjunction** Alligation, Ampersand, And, Combination, Consort, Synod, Together, Union

**Conjure, Conjuror** Angekkok, Charm, Contrive, Heypass, Heypresto, Hocus-pocus, Imagine, Invoke, Mage, Magic, Palmer, Prestidigitator, Thaumaturgus

**Connect(ed), Connection, Connector** Accolade, Adaptor, Affinity, Agnate, And, Associate, Attach, Band, Bind, Bridge, Bridle, Cable, Clientele, Coherent, Colligate, Conjugate, Couple, Dovetail, Drawbar, Fishplate, IN CONNECTION WITH, Join, Kinship, Liaison, Lifeline, Link, Marry, Merge, On, Pons, Rapport, Relate, Relative, Shuttle, Splice, Tendon, Through, Tie, Union, Yoke, Zygon

**Connecticut** Ct

**Connive, Connivance** Abet, Cahoots, Collude, Condone, Conspire, Plot

**Connoisseur** Aesthete, Cognoscente, Epicure, Expert, Fancier, Gourmet, Judge, Oenophil

**Connotate, Connotation** Imply, Infer, Intent, Meaning

**Conquer(or), Conquest** Beat, Conquistador, Crush, Debel, Genghis Khan, MASTER, Moor, Norman, Ostrogoth, Overcome, Overpower, Pizarro, Subjugate, Tame, Tamerlane, Vanquish, Victor

**Conquistador** Cortes, Cortez

**Conscience, Conscientious** Casuistic, Heart, Inwit, Morals, Pang, Remorse, Scruple(s), Sense, Superego, Syneidesis, Synteresis, Thorough

**Conscious(ness)** Awake, Aware, Limen, Sensible, Sentient

**Conscript(ion)** Blood-tax, Choco, Commandeer, Draft(ee), Impress, Landsturm, Levy, RECRUIT, Register

**Consecrate, Consecration** Bless, Hallow, Noint, Oint, Sacring, Sanctify, Venerate

**Consecutive** Sequential, Successive

**Consensus** Agreement, Harmony, Unanimity

**Consent** Accord, Affo(o)rd, Agree, Approbate, Comply, Concur, Grant, Permit, Volens, Yield

**Consequent, Consequence** Aftermath, Consectaneous, Effect, End, Importance, Issue, Moment, Outcome, Ramification, Repercussion,

RESULT, Sequel

**Conservative** Blue, C, Cautious, Diehard, Disraeli, Fabian, Hard-hat, Hunker, Right, Square, Thrifty, Tory, Unionist, Verkamp(te)

**Conservatory** Hothouse, Orangery, Solarium

**Conserve, Conservation(ist)** Comfiture, Husband(ry), Jam, Maintain, Maintenance, Protect, NT, Save

**Consider(able), Consideration** Animadvert, Avizandum, By-end, Case, Cogitate, Contemplate, Count, Courtesy, Debate, Deem, Deliberate, Entertain, Envisage, Fair, Feel, Heed, Importance, Inasmuch, Judge, Many, Meditate, Muse, Pay, Perpend, Poise, Ponder, Rate, Reckon, Reflect, Regard, Respect, See, Several, Solicitous, Song, Steem, Study, Think, Tidy, Ween, Weigh

**Consign(ment)** Allot, Award, Batch, Bequeath, Delegate, Deliver, Entrust, Lading, Ship, Transfer

**Consist(ent), Consistency** Coherent, Comprise, Enduring, Liaison, Rely, Steady

**Consolation, Console** Ancon, Appease, Balm, Comfort, Relief, Solace

**Consolidate** Coalesce, Combine, Compact, Gel, Merge, Unify

**Consommé** Julienne, Soup

**Consonant(s)** Affricate, Agma, Agreeing, Explosive, Harmonious, Labial, Lenis, Media, Plosive, Tenuis, Velar

**Consort** Ally, Associate, Maik, Mate, Moop, Moup, Partner, Spouse

**Consortium** Combine, Ring

**Conspicuous** Arresting, Blatant, Clear, Eminent, Glaring, Kenspeckle, Landmark, Manifest, Patent, Salient, Signal, Striking

**Conspiracy, Conspirator, Conspire** Cabal, Casca, Catiline, Cato St, Cinna, Collaborate, Colleague, Collogue, Collude, Complot, Connive, Coven, Covin, Guy, Intrigue, Oates, Omerta, PLOT, Ring, Scheme

**Constable** Beck, Catchpole, Cop, Dogberry, Dull, Elbow, Harman(-beck), Officer, Painter, Pointsman, Special, Thirdborough, Tipstaff, Verges

**Constancy, Constant** Abiding, Chronic, Coefficient, Devotion, Faith, G, H, Honesty, Hubble's, K, Lambert, Leal(ty), Loyal, Often, Parameter, PERPETUAL, Planck, Pole star, Resolute, Sad, Staunch, Steadfast, Steady, True, Unfailing, Uniform, Usual

**Constellation** Andromeda, Antlia, Aries, Corvus, Crater, Cynosure, Galaxy, Hercules, Lacerta, Leo, Mensa, Pegasus, PLANET, Sagitta, STAR

**Consternation** Alarm, Dismay, Doodah, Fear, Horror

**Constipated, Constipation** Astrict, Block, Costive, Stegnotic, Stenosis

**Constituency, Constituent** Borough, Component, Element, Part, Seat, Voter

> **Constituents** may indicate an anagram

**Constitute, Constitution(al)** Appoint, Charter, Compose, Comprise, Congenital, Creature, Establishment, Form, Fuero, Health, Physique,

Policy, Polity, Seat, State, Upmake, Walk

**Constrain(ed), Constraint** Bind, Bondage, Coerce, Confine, Coop, Curb, Duress(e), Hard, Oblige, Pressure, Repress, Stenosis

**Constrict(ed), Constriction** Choke, Contract, Cramp, Hour-glass, Impede, Limit, Squeeze, Stegnosis, Stenosis, Thlipsis

**Construct(ion), Constructor, Constructive** Build, Compile, Engineer, Erect, Fashion, Form, Frame, Make, Seabee, Tectonic

**Construe** Deduce, Explain, Expound, Infer

**Consul** Ambassador, Attaché, Horse, Praetor

**Consult(ant)** Confer, Deliberate, Discuss, Imparl, Peritus, See

**Consume(r), Consumption, Consumptive** Burn, Caterpillar, Decay, Devour, Diner, Eat, Engross, Exhaust, Expend, Feed, Glutton, Hectic, Mainline, Scoff, Spend, Swallow, TB, Use, Waste, Wear

**Consummate, Consummation** Keystone, Seal

**Contact** Abut, Adpress, Contingence, Liaise, Liaison, Meet, TOUCH

**Contagious, Contagion** Infection, Noxious, Poison, Taint, Variola, Viral

**Contain(er)** Amphora, Ampulla, Bass, Bin, Box, Cachepot, Can, Canakin, Canikin, Canister, Cannikin, Cantharus, Capsule, Carboy, Carry, Carton, Case, Cask, Cassette, Chase, Chest, Churn, Coffer, Comprise, Crate, Crater, Cup, Dracone, Dredger, Enclose, Encompass, Enseam, Esky, HOLD, House, Include, Jerrican, Jerrycan, Kirbeh, Leaguer, Lekythos, Olpe, Pithos, Pottle, Repository, Restrain, Saggar, Scyphus, Skin, Skip, Stamnos, Tank, Tub, Tun, Urn, Vessel

**Contaminate(d)** Corrupt, Defile, Flyblown, Infect, Soil, Stain, Tarnish

**Contemplate, Contemplation** Consider, Ecce, Envisage, Hesychasm, Meditate, Muse, Ponder, Reflect, Spell, Study, Think, Watch

**Contemporary** AD, Coetaneous, Current, Equal, Fellow, Modern, Present, Verism

**Contempt(ible), Contemptuous** Aha, Bah, BEF, Crud, Crumb, Cynical, Derision, Dog-bolt, Fig, Ignominious, Low, Mean, Measly, Misprision, Paltry, Pish, Pshaw, Razoo, Scarab, SCORN, Shabby, Sneeze, Sniff, Snot, Soldier, Sorry, Toad, Weed, Wretched

**Contend(er)** Candidate, Claim, Compete, Cope, Debate, Dispute, Fight, Grapple, Oppose, Stickle, STRIVE, Struggle, Submit, VIE, Wrestle

**Content** Apaid, Apay, Appay, Blissful, Happy, Inside, Please, Satisfy, Volume

> **Content** may indicate a hidden word

**Contention, Contentious** Argument, Case, Cantankerous, Combat, Competitive, Perverse, Polemical, Rivalry, Strife, Struggle, Sturt

**Contest(ant)** Agon, Battle, Bout, Challenge, Competition, Decathlon, Defend, Duel(lo), Entrant, Examinee, Fronde, Kriegspiel, Lampadephoria, Match, Olympiad, Pentathlon, Pingle, Prizer, Race, Set-to, Skirmish, Slugfest, Strife, Struggle, Tenson, Tournament, Vie, War, With

**Continent(al)** Abstinent, Asia, Atlantis, Austere, Chaste, Euro, Gallic, Gondwanaland, Lemuria, Mainland, Moderate, Pang(a)ea, Shelf, Teetotal, Temperate, Walloon

**Contingency, Contingent** Accident, Arm, Casual, Chance, Conditional, Dependent, Event, Fluke, Group, Prospect

**Continual(ly), Continuous** Adjoining, Away, Chronic, Connected, Endlong, Eternal, Ever, Frequent, Incessant, On(going)

**Continue, Continuation, Continuing, Continuity** Abye, Duration, Dure, During, Enduring, Enjamb(e)ment, Hold, Keep, Last, Link, Onward, Persevere, Persist, Proceed, Prolong, Resume, Sequence, Survive, Sustain, Tenor

> **Continuously** may indicate previous words to be linked

**Contort** Deform, Gnarl, Twist, Warp, Wry

**Contour** Curve, Graph, Isobase, Isocheim, Isochime, Isogeothermal, Line, Profile, Silhouette, Streamline, Tournure

**Contraband** Hot, Illicit, Prohibited, Smuggled

**Contraceptive** Cap, Pill, Prophylactic, Loop, Sheath

**Contract(ion), Contractor** Abbreviate, Abridge, Agreement, Appalto, Astringency, Bargain, Biceps, Bottomry, Bridge, Builder, Catch, Charter, Condense, Constringe, Contrahent, Cramp, Crasis, Curtail, Debt, Dwindle, Engage, Entrepreneur, Escrow, Gainsay, Guarantee, Hand-promise, Hire, Incur, Indenture, Jerk, Ketubah, Knit, Lease, Make, Narrow, Party, Promise, Pucker, Purse, Restriction, Shrink, Shrivel, Sign, Slam, Spasm, Specialty, Steelbow, Stenosis, Supplier, Systole, Tetanise, Tetanus, Tic, Tighten, Treaty, Triceps, Wrinkle

**Contradict(ion), Contradictory** Antilogy, Antimony, Contrary, Counter, Dementi, Deny, Disaffirm, Disprove, Dissent, GAINSAY, Negate, Oxymoron, Paradox, Sot, Traverse

**Contrarily, Contrary** Adverse, A rebours, Arsy-versy, But, Captious, Converse, Counter, Hostile, Inverse, Mary, Opposite, Ornery, Perverse, Rebuttal, Retrograde, Wayward, Withershins

**Contrast** Chiaroscuro, Clash, Compare, Differ, Foil, Relief

**Contravene** Infringe, Oppose, Thwart, Violate

**Contribute, Contribution** Abet, Add, Assist, Conduce, Donate, Furnish, Go, Help, Input, Mite, Offering, Share, Sub, Subscribe

> **Contributing to** may indicate a hidden word

**Contrite, Contrition** Penance, Penitent, Remorse, Repentant, Rue, SORRY

**Contrivance** Art, Contraption, Deckle, Device, Engine, Finesse, Gadget, Gin, Invention, Plot

**Contrive(r)** Chicaner, Cook, Devise, Engineer, Hatch, Intrigue, Machinate, Manage, Manoeuvre, Plan, Procure, Scheme, Secure, Stage, Weave

**Control(ler), Controllable** Ada, Bridle, Chair, Check, Corner, Corset,

Dirigible, Dirigism(e), Dominion, Fet(ch), Finger, Gerent, Govern, Gubernation, Have, Heck, Helm, Joystick, Knee-swell, Lead, Lever, MANAGE, Martinet, Mastery, Mouse, Nipple, Pilot, Police, Possess, Power, Preside, Regulate, Regulo, Rein, Remote, Repress, Restrain, Ride, Rule, Run, School, Servo, Snail, Steer, Stop, Stranglehold, Subject, Subjugate, Supervise, Sway, Thermostat, Tiller, Valve, Weld, Wield

**Controversial, Controversy** Argument, Contention, Debate, Dispute, Eristic(al), Furore, Hot potato, Polemic(al)

**Conundrum** Acrostic, Egma, Puzzle, Riddle

**Convalesce(nt), Convalescence** Anastatic, Mend, Rally, Recover, Recuperate, Rest-cure

> **Convene** see CONVOKE

**Convenience, Convenient** Eft, Expedient, Facility, Gain, Gents, HANDY, Hend, Lav, Leisure, Near, Opportune, Pat, Privy, Suitable, Toilet, Use, Well

**Convent** Cloister, Fratry, Friary, Nunnery, Port-royal, Priory, Retreat

**Convention(al)** Accepted, Babbitt, Blackwood, Bourgeois, Caucus, Conclave, CUSTOMARY, Diet, Done, Formal, Geneva, Iconic, Meeting, More, Nomic, Orthodox, Pompier, Starchy, Stereotyped, Stock, Synod, Uptight, Usage

**Converge** Approach, Focus, Meet

**Conversation(alist), Converse, Conversant** Abreast, Board, Buck, Cackle, Chat, Colloquy, Commune, Deipnosophist, Dialogue, Discourse, Eutrapelia, Eutrapely, Hobnob, Natter, Opposite, Palaver, Parley, Rap, Rhubarb, Shop, Socialise, TALK, Transpose, Wongi, Word

**Conversion, Converter, Convert(ible)** Adapt, Alter, Assimilate, Azotobacter, Catechumen, Change, Commute, Disciple, Encash, Exchange, Expropriate, Gummosis, Hodja, Kho(d)ja, Liquid, Marrano, Neophyte, Noviciate, Novitiate, Persuade, Proselyte, Put, Ragtop, Realise, Rebirth, Recycle, Souper, Tablet, Transmute, Try

> **Conversion, Converted** may indicate an anagram

**Convex (surface)** Arched, Bowed, Camber, Curved, Extrados, Gibbous, Nowy

**Convey(ance)** Assign, BS, Carousel, Carry, Charter, Coach, Conduct, Cycle, Deed, Eloi(g)n, Enfeoffment, Grant, Guide, Lease, Litter, Lorry, Re-lease, Sac and soc, Tip, Title deed, Tote, Transfer, Transit, Transmit, Transport, Vehicle

**Convict(ion)** Attaint, Belief, Bushranger, Certitude, Cockatoo, Cogence, Crawler, Credo, Creed, Criminal, Demon, Dogma, Faith, Felon, Forçat, Lag, Magwitch, PERSUASION, Plerophory, Ring, Trusty, Vehemence

**Convince(d), Convincing** Assure, Cogent, Persuade, Satisfy, Sold

**Convivial(ity)** Bowl, Festive, Gay, Genial, Jovial, Social

**Convoke** Assemble, Call, Convene, Summon

**Convolute(d), Convolution** Coiled, Gyrus, Spiral, Twisty, Writhen

**Convoy**  Caravan, Column, Conduct, Escort, Pilot, Train, Wagon-train

**Convulsion(s), Convulsive**  Agitate, Clonic, Commotion, Disturb, DT, Eclampsia, FIT, Galvanic, Paroxysm, Spasm, Throe, Tic

**Cook(s), Cooker, Cooking**  Aga, Babbler, Bake, Beeton, Benghazi, Bouche, Broil, Chef, Coddle, Concoct, Cuisine, Devil, Do, Doctor, Dumple, Edit, Fake, Falsify, Fiddle, Forge, Fry, Fudge, Greasy, Haybox, Poach, Prepare, Pressure, Ring, Roast, Roger, Spit, Steam, Stew, Tandoori, Tire

> **Cook**  may indicate an anagram

**Cool(er), Coolness**  Aloof, Aplomb, Calm, Can, Collected, Composed, Cryostat, Defervescence, Dispassionate, Distant, Esky, Fan, Frappé, Fridge, Frigid, Frosty, Gaol, Goglet, Ice(box), Jail, Jug, Keel, Phlegm, Prison, Quad, Quod, Refresh, Sangfroid, Serene, Skeigh, Stir, Temperate, Thou(sand), Unruffled

**Coop**  Cage, Cavie, Confine, Gaol, Hutch, Mew, Pen, Rip

**Cooper**  Gary, Henry, Tubman

**Cooperate, Cooperative**  Collaborate, Combine, Conspire, Contribute, Coop, Liaise, Together

**Coordinate(d), Coordination**  Abscissa, Abscisse, Agile, Arrange, Ensemble, Harmony, Nabla, Orchestrate, Ordonnance, Peer, Y

**Coot**  Stupid, Sultan

**Cop(s)**  Bag, Bull, Catch, Dick, Keystone, Peeler, Peon, POLICEMAN

**Copal**  Dammar, Resin

**Cope**  Chlamys, Deal, Face, Handle, MANAGE, Mantle, Meet, Pallium, Poncho

**Coping (stone)**  Balustrade, Capstone, Skew

**Copious**  Abundant, Affluent, Ample, Fecund, Fluent, Fruitful, Fulsome, Plentiful, Profuse

**Copper**  As, Atacamite, Bluebottle, Bobby, Bornite, Busy, Cash, Cent, Chessylite, COIN, Cu, D, Dam, Double, Erinite, Flatfoot, Lota(h), Malachite, Mountain-blue, Ormolu, Pence, Penny, Pfennig, Pie, Pig, Plack, Policeman, Red, Rosser, Rozzer, S, Sen(s), Slop, Special, Traybit, Venus, Washer

**Copulate**  Intercourse, Line, Mate, Roger

**Copy(ing), Copier, Copyist**  Aemule, Ape, Apograph, Autotype, Calk, Calque, Carbon, Clerk, Clone, Crib, Cyclostyle, Ditto, Echo, Echopraxia, Ectype, Edition, Eidograph, Emulate, Engross, Estreat, Example, Facsimile, Fax, Flimsy, IMITATE, Issue, Manifold, Manuscript, Match, Me-tooer, Mimic, Mirror, MS, Parrot, Photostat, Replica, Repro, Reproduce, Roneo (tdmk), Script, Scrivener, Sedulous, Simulate, Spit, Tenor, Tenure, Trace, Transcribe, Transume, Vidimus, Xerox (tdmk)

**Copyright**  C

**Coquette**  Agacerie, Flirt, Rosina, Tease, Vamp

**Coracle**  Currach, Curragh

**Coral (reef)**  Alcyonaria, Aldabra, Atoll, Laccadives, Madrepore, Millepore, Pink, Reef, Sea-pen, Zoothome

**Cord, Cord-like**  Band, Bind, Boondoggle, Cat-gut, Chenille, Creance, Drawstring, Flex, Fourragere, Funicle, Heddle, Laniard, Lanyard, Ligature, Line, Moreen, Myelon, Ocnus, Quipo, Quipu, Rep(s), Restiform, Rip, Rope, Service, STRING, Tendon, Tie, Twine, Umbilical

**Cordial**  Anise(ed), Anisette, Benedictine, Cassis, Drink, Gracious, Hearty, Hippocras, Kind, Oporice, Orangeade, Persico(t), Pleasant, Ratafia, Rosa-solis, Roso(g)lio, Shrub, Tar-water, Warm

**Cordon**  Picket, Ring, Surround

**Corduroy**  Rep(p)

**Cordyline**  Ti-tree

**Core**  Barysphere, Campana, Centre, Essence, Filament, Heart, Hub, Nife, Plerome, Quintessence

**Co-religionist**  Brother

**Corinthian(s)**  Casuals, Caulis, Epistolaters

**Cork(ed), Corker**  Balsa, Bouché, Bung, Float(er), Humdinger, Oner, Phellem, Phellogen, Plug, Seal, Shive, Stopper, Suber(ate)

**Corkscrew**  Bore, Opening, Spiral

**Cormorant**  Scart(h), Skart(h)

**Corn(y)**  Bajr(a), Banal, Blé, Cereal, Cob, Emmer, Epha, Gait, Graddan, Grain, Grist, Icker, Mabela, Maize, Mealie, Muid, Nubbin, Pickle, Pinole, Posho, Rabi, Shock, Straw, Thrave, Trite, Zea

**Corncrake**  Landrail

**Cornel**  Dogberry, Tree

**Corner**  Amen, Angle, Bend, Cantle, Canton, Cranny, Dangerous, Elbow, Entrap, Hole, Lug, Monopoly, NE, Niche, Nook, NW, Predicament, SE, Speaker's, SW, Tack, Tree

**Cornerstone**  Coi(g)n, Encoignure, Skew-corbel, Skew-put, Skew-table

**Cornet**  Cone, Horn

**Cornice**  Surbase

**Cornstalks**  Strammel, Straw, Strummel, Stubble

**Cornucopia**  Amalthea, Horn

**Cornwall**  SW

**Corollary**  Conclusion, Dogma, Porism, Rider, Theory, Truism

**Corona**  Aureole, Cigar, Larmier, Nimbus, Wreath

**Corporal**  Bardolph, Bodily, Bombardier, Lance-pesade, Lance-prisade, Lance-prisado, Lance-speisade, NCO, Nym, Pall, Trim

**Corporation**  Belly, Body, Commune, Company, Conglomerate, Guild, Kite, Kyte, Paunch, Stomach, Swag-belly, Tum, Wame, Wem

**Corps** Body, Crew, RAC, REME, Unit

**Corpse** Blob, Body, Cadaver, Carcass, Carrion, Goner, Like, Mort, Relic, Remains, Stiff, Zombi(e)

**Corpulence, Corpulent** Adipose, Fat, Obese, Stout, Tubby

**Corpuscle** Cell, Microcyte, Neutrophil, Phagocyte

**Correct(ing), Correction, Corrector** Accurate, Alexander, Align, Amend, Bodkin, Castigate, Chasten, Chastise, Check, Diorthortic, Emend, Exact, Fair, Grammatical, Legit, Preterition, Proper, Punish, Rebuke, Rectify, Redress, Reprove, Revise, Right(en), Scold, Sumpsimus, Trew, True, U

> **Corrected** may indicate an anagram

**Correspond(ence), Corresponding** Accord, Agree, Analogy, Assonance, Coincident, Communicate, Equate, Eye-rhyme, Fit, Identical, Match, On all fours, One to one, Relate, Symmetry, Tally, Veridical, Write

**Corridor** Aisle, Gallery, Lobby, Passage

**Corroborate** Confirm, Support, Verify

**Corrode(d), Corrosion, Corrosive** Acid, Burn, Canker, Decay, Eat, Erode, Etch, Fret, Gnaw, Hydrazine, Mordant, ROT, Rubiginous, Rust, Waste

**Corrupt(er), Corrupting, Corruption** Adulterate, Bribable, Canker, Debauch, Debosh, Decadent, Defile, Depravity, Dissolute, Emancipate, Embrace(o)r, Embrasor, Etch, Fester, Gangrene, Graft(er), Immoral, Impure, Jobbery, Leprosy, Nefarious, Obelus, Payola, Perverse, Pollute, Power, Ret(t), Rigged, Rot, Seduce, Sepsis, Septic, Spoil, Suborn, Tammany, Twist, Venal, Vice, Vitiate

**Corsage** Buttonhole, Pompadour, Posy, Spray

**Corsair** Barbary, Picaroon, Pirate, Privateer, Robber, Rover

**Corset, Corslet** Belt, Bodice, Busk, Girdle, Lorica, Roll-on, Stays, Thorax, Waspie

**Corsican** Napoleon

**Cortege** Parade, Retinue, Train

**Cortisone** Hecogenin

**Corundum** Emery, Sapphire

**Corvo** Rolfe

**Cosh** Sap

**Cosmetic** Beautifier, Blusher, Eyeliner, Foundation, Fucus, Lipstick, Lotion, Maquillage, Mascara, Paint, Powder, Reface, Rouge, Talcum

> **Cosmic** see COSMOS

**Cosmonaut** Gagarin, Spaceman

**Cosmopolitan** International, Urban

**Cosmos, Cosmic** Globe, Heaven, Infinite, Nature, Universe, World

**Cossack** Hetman, Mazeppa, Russian, Tartar, Zaporogian

**Cosset** Caress, Coddle, Fondle, Pamper

**Cost(ly)** Bomb, Carriage, Charge, Damage, Earth, Escuage, Estimate, Exes, EXPENSE, Hire, Outlay, Overhead, Precious, Price, Quotation, Rate, Sacrifice, Sumptuous, Toll, Upkeep, Usurious

**Costermonger** Barrow-boy, Kerb-merchant, Pearly

**Costume** Apparel, Attire, Cossie, Dress, Ensemble, Get-up, Gi(e), Guise, Livery, Maillot, Nebris, Polonaise, Rig, Surcoat, Tanga, Uniform

**Cosy** Cosh, Intime, Snug

**Coterie** Cell, Cenacle, Circle, Clan, Clique, Club, Ring, Set, Society

**Cottage(r)** Bach, Bordar, Bothie, Bothy, Box, Bungalow, Cabin, Chalet, Cot, Hut, Lodge, Mailer

**Cotton** Agree, AL, Alabama, Balbriggan, Batiste, Batting, Calico, Ceiba, Chino, Chintz, Collodion, Coutil(le), Denim, Dho(o)ti, Dimity, Ducks, Galatea, Gossypine, Gossypium, Humhum, Jaconet, Lawn, Lea, Lille, Lint, Lisle, Manchester, Marcella, Nainsook, Nankeen, Nankin, Pongee, Sea-island, Silesian, Surat, T-cloth, Thread, Twig

**Cotton soil** Regar, Regur

**Cotyledon** Seed-leaf

**Couch** Bed, Davenport, Daybed, DIVAN, Express, Grass, Lurk, Palanquin, Palkee, Palki, Sedan, Settee, Sofa, Triclinium, Word

**Coué** Auto-suggestion

**Cougar** Cat, Painter

**Cough(ing)** Bark, Croup, Hack, Hawk, Hem, Hoast, Kink, Pertussis, Phthisis, Rale, Tisick, Tussis, Ugh

**Could** Couth

**Council (meeting), Councillor, Counsel(lor)** Achitophel, Admonish, Admonitor, Advice, Advocate, Ahithophel, Anziani, Aread, Assembly, Attorney, Aulic, Ayuntamiento, Board, Body, Boule, Cabinet, Casemate, Committee, Cr, Dergue, Devil, Dietine, Divan, Douma, Duma, Egeria, Exhort, Greenbag, Indaba, Induna, Jirga, Junta, Kabele, Kebele, Kite, Landst(h)ing, Lateran, Leader, Mentor, Nestor, Nicaean, Panchayat, Paraclete, Parish, Powwow, Privy, Rede, Reichsrat, Sanhedrim, Sanhedrin, Shura, Sobranje, Sobranye, Soviet, Syndicate, Synedrion, Synod, Thing, Trent, Tridentine, Trullan, Whitley, Witan, Witenagemot

**Count(ess), Counted, Counter, Count on** Abacus, Add, Anti, Bar, Buck, Buffet, Calculate, Census, Chip, Compute, Coost, Desk, Dracula, Dump, Earl, Enumerate, Fish, Geiger, Graf(in), Grave, Itemise, Jet(t)on, Margrave, Matter, Merel(l), Meril, Number, Obviate, Olivia, Oppose, Palatine, Palsgrave, Presume, Rebut, RECKON, Refute, Rejoinder, Rely, Retaliate, Retort, Rhinegrave, Score, Statistician, Stop, Sum, Table, Tally, Tell, Tiddleywink, Ugolino, Weigh, Zeppelin

**Countenance** Approve, Endorse, Face, Favour, Mug, Sanction, Support, Visage

**Counteract(ing)** Ant-, Antidote, Cancel, Correct, Frustrate, Talion

**Counterbalance** Offset, Undo, Weigh

**Counter-charge** Recrimination

**Counterclockwise** L(a)evorotatory

**Counterfeit(er)** Belie, Bogus, Brum, Coiner, Duffer, Dummy, Fantasm, Flash, Forge, Imitant, Phantasm, Phoney, Pinchbeck, Postiche, Pseudo, Queer, Rap, Sham, Schlenter, Shan(d), Simulate, Slang, Slip, Smasher, Snide, Spurious, Stumer

**Counterglow** Gegenschein

**Countermand** Abrogate, Annul, Cancel, Override, Rescind, Retract, Revoke

**Counterpart** Copy, Double, Obverse, Oppo, Parallel, Similar, Spit(ting), Twin

**Counterpoint** Descant

**Countersign** Endorse, Password

**Countless** Infinite, Umpteen, Untold

**Country** Annam, Bangladesh, Boondocks, Bucolic, Champaign, Clime, Colchis, Edom, Enchorial, Karoo, Karroo, LAND, Lea, Lee, Mongolia, Nation, Parish, Paysage, People, Province, Realm, Region, Republic, Rural, Satellite, Soil, State, Tundra, Weald, Yemen

**Country girl** Amaryllis

**Country house** Hall, Manor, Quinta

**Countryman** Arcadian, Bacon, Boor, Hick, Hillbilly, Hodge, National, Native, Peasant, Un, Yokel

**County** Antrim, Armagh, Avon, Beds, Cavan, Champagne, Clare, Cleveland, Co, Comital, Cork, Cornwall, District, Donegal, Dorset, Down, Durham, Fife, Flint, Gwent, Herts, Hunts, Kesteven, Kildare, Leitrim, Loamshire, Louth, Mayo, Midlothian, NI, Norfolk, Notts, Offaly, Omagh, Palatine, Parish, Powys, Roscommon, Ross, Seat, Shire, Suffolk, Sy, Tipperary, Tyrone, Waterford, Wicklow, Wilts, Worcs

**Coup** Blow, Deal, KO, Move, Putsch, Scoop, Stroke

**Coupé** Cabriolet, Landaulet

**Couple(r), Coupling** Ally, Band, Brace, Bracket, Duet, Duo, Dyad, Gemini, Geminy, JOIN, Marry, Mate, Meng(e), Ment, Ming, Pair, Pr, Relate, Shackle, Tie, Tirasse, Tway, Union, Universal, Wed, Yoke

**Couple of ducks** Spectacles

**Coupon(s)** Ration, Ticket, Voucher

**Courage(ous)** Bottle, Bravado, Bravery, Bulldog, Dutch, Fortitude, Gallantry, Game, Gimp, Grit, Guts, Heart, Heroism, Lion-heart, Macho, Mettle, Moxie, Nerve, Pluck, Rum, Spirit, Spunk, Stalwart, Steel, Valiant, Valour, Wight

**Courgette** Zucchini

**Courier** Estafette, Guide, Harbinger, Herald, MESSENGER, Postillion

**Course(s)** Afters, Aim, Aintree, Antipasto, Appetiser, Arroyo, Ascot, Atlantic, Bearing, Beat, Canal, Career, Chantilly, Chase, Circuit, Consommé, Crash, Current, Curriculum, Cursus, Dessert, Diadrom, Dish, Dromic, Entrée, Fish, Food, Going, Goodwood, Greats, Heat, Isodomon, Lane, Lap, Layer, Leat, Leet, Line, Lingfield, Links, Longchamp, Meal, Meat, Mess, Newbury, Newmarket, Nulla, OF COURSE, Orbit, Period, Policy, PPE, Procedure, Process, Programme, Progress, Race, Raik, Refresher, Regimen, Rhumb, Ride, Ring, Rink, Rota, Route, Routine, Run, Rut, Sandown, Sandwich, Semester, Series, Soup, Starter, Stearage, Steerage, Step(s), Stratum, Streak, Stretch, Syllabus, Tack, Tanride, Tenor, Trade, Troon, Way

**Court(ier)** Address, Arches, Areopagus, Atrium, Attention, Audience, Audiencia, Aula, Banc, Bar, Basecourt, Bench, Boondock, Caravanserai, Cassation, Centre, Chancery, Consistory, CS, Ct, Curia, Curtilage, Cutcher(r)y, Dicastery, Diplock, Durbar, En tout cas, Evora, Eyre, Fehm(gericht), Fehmgerichte, Forensic, Forest, Forum, Garth, Guildenstern, Halimot(e), Hof, Hustings, Hypaethron, Invite, Jack, Kachahri, Kacheri, Kangaroo, King, Knave, Leet, Lobby, Marshalsea, Old Bailey, Parvis, Patio, Peristyle, Philander, Piepowder, Praetorium, Presbytery, Quad, Queen, Retinue, Royal, Sanhedrim, Sanhedrin, See, Spoon, Sue, Swanimote, Sweetheart, Thane, Thegn, Tribunal, Vehm, Vehmgericht(e), Vestibulum, Ward, Woo, Wow, Yard

**Courteous, Courtesy** Affable, Agrement, Bow, Comity, Etiquette, Genteel, Gracious, Hend, Polite, Refined, Urbanity

**Courtesan** Aspasia, Bona-roba, Delilah, Demi-monde, Demi-rep, Geisha, Hetaera, Lais, Lampadion, Lorette, Madam, Phryne, Plover, Pornocracy, Prostitute, Stallion, Thais

**Courtly** Chivalrous, Cringing, Dignified, Flattering, Refined

**Court-martial** Drumhead

**Courtyard** Area, Cortile, Patio, Quad

**Cousin(s)** Bette, Cater, Coz, German, Kin, Kissing, Robin, Skater

**Couturier** Dior, Dressmaker

**Cove** Abraham's, Arm, Bay, Bight, Buffer, Creek, Cure, Gink, Grot, Guy, Hithe, Hythe, Inlet, Lulworth, Nook

**Covenant(er)** Abrahamic, Alliance, Bond, Contract, Hillmen, Pledge, Warranty, Whiggamore

**Cover(ing)** A l'abri, Antimacassar, Apron, Aril, Attire, Awning, Barb, Bark, Bedspread, Bestrew, Bind, Blanket, Bodice, Brood, Camouflage, Canopy, Cap, Caparison, Casing, Casque, Caul, Ceil, Ciborium, Cladding, Clapboard, Cleithral, Clithral, Coat, Cocoon, Coleorhiza, Conceal, Cope, Copyright, Counterpane, Cour, Covert, Cowl, Curtain, Deck, Dome, Drape(t), Dripstone, Dust-sheet, Duvet, Encase, Enguard, Enshroud, Envelop(e), Exoderm(is), Exoskeleton, Face, Fanfare, Fielder, Flashing, Fother, Front, Gaiter, Gambado, Grolier, Hap, Hat, Hatch, Havelock, Heal, Heel, Hejab, Hele, Hell, Helmet, Hood, Immerse, Incase, Insulate, Insurance, Insure, Jacket, Lag, Lay, Leep, Lid, Manche, Mantle, Numnah,

Obscure, On, Operculum, Orillion, Orlop, Overlay, Palampore, Palempore, Pall, Pand, Parcel, Pasties, Patch, Pelmet, Periderm, Plaster, Plate, Pleura, Point, Pseudonym, Quilt, Radome, Regolith, Robe, Roof, Rug, Sally, Screen, Serviette, Setting, Sheath, Sheet, Shell, Shelter, Shield, Shroud, Shuck, Skin, Smokescreen, Span, Spat, Stifle, Swathe, Tarpaulin, Tectorial, Tegmen, Tegument, Tester, Thatch, Thimble, Tick(ing), Tilt, Top, Trench, Trip, Twill, Twilt, Umbrella, Upholster, Valance, Veil, Vele, Veneer, Vest, Visor, Whitewash, Wrap, Yapp

**Covert** Clandestine, Copse, Privy, SECRET, Shy, Sidelong, Tectrix, Ulterior

**Covet(ed), Covetous** Avaricious, Crave, Desiderata, Desire, Eager, Envy, Greedy, Hanker, Yearn

**Cow** Adaw, Alderney, Amate, Appal, Awe, Bovine, Browbeat, Charolais, Colly, Crummy, Danton, Daunt, Dexter, Dsomo, Dun, Galloway, Gally, Goujal, Guernsey, Hawkey, Hawkie, Heifer, Intimidate, Jersey, Kouprey, Kyloe, Mart, Mog(gie), Moggy, Mooly, Muley, Mulley, Overawe, Redpoll, Rother(-beast), Scare, Subact, Teeswater, Threaten, Unnerve, Vaccine, Zebu, Z(h)o

**Coward(ly)** Bessus, Chicken, Cocoa, Craven, Cuthbert, Dastard, Dingo, Dunghill, Fugie, Funk, Gutless, Hen, Hilding, Meacock, Niddering, Nidderling, Nidering, Niderling, Niding, Nithing, Noel, Poltroon, Pusillanimous, Recreant, Scaramouch, Sganarelle, Slag, Viliaco, Viliago, Villagio, Villiago, Yellow

**Cowboy, Cowgirl** Buckaroo, Gaucho, Inexpert, Io, Leger, Llanero, Puncher, Ranchero, Ritter, Roper, Vaquero, Waddy, Wrangler

**Cow-catcher** Fender, Reata

**Cower** Croodle, Crouch, Fawn, Quail, Skulk, Wince

**Cowl** Bonnet, Capuchin, Granny, Hood, Kilmarnock

**Cowshed, Cowstall** Byre, Crib, Shippen, Shippon, Stable, Stall, Staw

**Cowslip** Culver-key, Pa(i)gle

**Cox** Steerer

**Coxcomb** Crest, Dandy, Dude, Fop, Jackanapes, Popinjay, Yellow-rattle

**Coy** Arch, Coquettish, Laithfu', Mim, Shamefast, SHY, Skeigh, Skittish

**Coyote** SD

**CPRS** Think tank

**Crab(by)** Apple, Attercop, Cancer, Cantankerous, Capernoity, Cock, Daddy, Decapoda, Diogenes, Ethercap, Ettercap, Fiddler, Grouch, Horseman, Horseshoe, Limulus, Nebula, Ochidore, Pagurian, Partan, Perverse, Podite, Roast, Saucepan-fish, Scrawl, Sidle, Xiphosura, Zoea

> **Crab** may indicate an anagram

**Crab-apple** Scrog-bush, Scrog-buss

**Crab-eater** Urva

**Crabs-eye** Abrus

**Crack(ed), Cracker(s), Cracking** Admirable, Bananas, Biscuit, Bonbon, Break, Chap, Chasm, Chat, Chink, Chip, Chop, Cleave, Cleft, Cloff, Confab, Cranny, Craqueture, Craze, Crepitate, Crevasse, Crevice, Crispbread, Dawn, Decode, Doom, Dunt, Elite, Fatiscent, Fent, First-rate, Fisgig, Fissure, Fizgig, Flaw, Flip-flop, Fracture, Go, Graham, Grike, Gryke, Gully, Hairline, Hit, Jibe, Liar, Little-endian, Moulin, Oner, Pore, Praise, Quip, Rap, Report, Rhagades, Rictus, Rift, Rille, Rima, Rime, Rimous, Rive, Seam, Snap, Solve, Split, Squib, Sulcus, Top, Try, Waterloo

**Crackerjack** Ace, Nailer, Trump

**Crackle, Crackling** Craze, Crepitation, Crepitus, Crinkle, Decrepitate, Glaze, Skin

**Crackpot** Nutter

**Cracksman** Burglar, Peterman, Raffles

**Cradle** Bassinet, Berceau, Cat's, Cot, Crib, Cunabula, Hammock, Knife, Nestle, Rocker

**Craft(y)** Arch, Art, Aviette, Barbola, Boat, Cautel, Cunning, Disingenuous, Finesse, Fly, Guile, Ice-breaker, Insidious, Kontiki, Mister, Mystery, Oomiack, Reynard, Saic, Shallop, Ship, Shuttle, SKILL, Slee, Sleeveen, Slim, Sly, Slyboots, State, Subdolous, Subtil(e), Subtle, Suttle, Umiak, Versute, VESSEL, Wile, Workmanship

**Craftsman** AB, Artificer, Artisan, Artist, Cutler, Ebonist, Finisher, Gondolier, Guild, Hand, Joiner, Mason, Mechanic, Morris, Opificer, Wright

**Crag(gy)** Eyrie, Height, Heuch, Heugh, Krantz, Noup

**Cram(mer)** Bag, Candle-waster, Cluster, Craig, Fill, Gavage, Neck, Pang, Prime, Rugged, Scar(p), Spur, Stap, Stodge, Stow, Swat, Tuck

**Cramp(ed)** Confine, Constrict, Crick, Hamper, Myalgia, Pinch, Poky, Restrict, Rigor, Squeeze, Stunt, Tetany

**Crane** Brolga, Davit, Demoiselle, Derrick, Gantry, Herd, Heron, Hooper, Ichabod, Luffing-jib, Rail, Sarus, Sedge, Siege, Stretch, Whooper, Winch

**Crane-fly** Leatherjacket, Tipulidae

**Crank(y)** Eccentric, Grouch, Handle, Lever, Mot, Perverse, Whim, Wince, Winch, Wind

**Crash** Bingle, Collapse, Dush, Fail, Fall, Fragor, Intrude, Linen, Nosedive, Prang, Rack, Ram, Rote, Smash, Topple

> **Crashes** may indicate an anagram

**Crass** Coarse, Crude, Rough, Rude

**Crate** Biplane, Box, Case, Ceroon, Crib, Hamper, Sero(o)n, Tube

**Crater** Bailly, Caldera, Cavity, Hollow, Hole, Maar

**Cravat** Ascot, Neckatee, Neck-cloth, Oerlay, Overlay, Scarf, Soubise, Steenkirk, Tie

**Crave, Craving** Appetite, Aspire, Beg, Beseech, Covet, Desire, Entreat, Hanker, Hunger, Itch, Libido, Long, Lust, Methomania, Orexis, Pica, Thirst, Yearn, Yen

**Craven** Abject, Coward, Dastard, Recreant

**Crawl(er)** All fours, Clamber, Creep, Cringe, Drag, Grovel, Lag, Lickspittle, Pub, Reptile, Scramble, Skulk, Snail, Swim, Sycophant, Tantony, Trail, Trudgen, Yes-man

**Crayfish** Yabbie, Yabby

**Crayon** Chalk, Colour, Conté, Pastel, Pencil

**Craze, Crazy** Absurd, Ape, Barmy, Bats, Batty, Berserk, Bonkers, Break, Crack(ers), Crackpot, Cult, Daffy, Dement, Derange, Distraught, Doiled, Doilt, Dotty, Fad, Flaw, Folie, Frantic, Furious, Furore, Gaga, Geld, Gyte, Haywire, Loco, Loony, Lunatic, Madden, Maenad(ic), Mania, Manic, Mattoid, Meshug(g)a, Nuts, Porangi, Potty, Psycho(path), Rage, Rave, Scatty, Screwball, Skivie, Stunt, Unhinge, Wet, W(h)acky, Whim, Wowf, Zany

**Creak(y)** Cry, Grate, Grind, Rheumatic, Scraich, Scraigh, Scroop, Seam, Squeak

**Cream(y)** Best, Elite, Lanolin, Lotion, Mousse, Off-white, Ointment, Opal, Paragon, Pick, Ream, Rich, Sillabub, Skim, Syllabub

**Crease** Crumple, FOLD, Lirk, Pitch, Pleat, Popping, Ridge, Ruck(le), Wrinkle

**Create, Creation** Build, Compose, Engender, Establish, Fabricate, Forgetive, Form, Found, Generate, Genesis, Ideate, INVENT, Oratorio, Originate, Produce, Shape, Universe

**Creator** Ahura Mazda, Author, Demiurge, God, Inventor, Maker, Ormazd, Ormuzd

**Creature** Animal, Ankole, Basilisk, Beast, Being, Chevrotain, Cratur, Critter, Crittur, Man, Sphinx, Whiskey, Wight

**Credence, Credential(s)** Certificate, Document, Papers, Qualifications, Shelf, Testimonial

**Credibility** Street

**Credible, Credit(or)** Ascribe, Attribute, Belief, Byline, Esteem, Honour, Kite, Kudos, LC, Lender, Mense, Probable, Reliable, Renown, Strap, Tally, Tick, Title, Trust, Weight

**Credulous** Charlie, Gullible, Simple, Trusting

**Creed** Athanasian, Belief, Doctrine, Faith, Ism, Nicene, Outworn, Sect, Tenet

**Creek** Bay, Breaches, Cove, Estuary, Fleet, Geo, Indian, Inlet, Pow, Vae, Voe, Wick

**Creel** Basket, Hask, Scull, Skull

**Creep(er), Creeps** Ai, Ampelopsis, Cleavers. Crawl, Grew, Grovel, Grue, Herpetic, Inch, Insect, Ivy, Nerd, Nuthatch, Reptant, Sarmentous, Sittine, Skulk, Slink, Snake, Sobole(s), Tropaeolum, Truckle, Vine, Virginia, Willies

**Creeping Jenny** Moneywort

**Cremate, Cremation, Crematorium**  Burn, Char, Ghaut, Incinerate, Pyre, Sati, Suttee

**Creole**  Gullah, Papiamento

**Crepe**  Blini, Blintz(e), Pancake

**Crescent**  Barchan(e), Bark(h)an, Lune(tte), Lunulate, Lunule, Meniscus, Moon, Sickle, Waxing

**Cress**  Cardamine

**Crest(ed)**  Acme, Chine, Cimier, Cockscomb, Comb, Copple, Crista, Height, Kirimon, Knap, Mon, Peak, Pinnacle, Plume, Ridge, Summit, Tappit, Tee, TOP

**Cretaceous**  Chalky, Senonian

**Crevasse**  Bergschrund, Chasm, Gorge, Rimaye

**Crew**  Company, Core, Eight, Equipage, Four, Lot, Manners, Men, Oars, Sailors, Salts, Team, Teme, Torpid

**Crew-cut**  Not(t)

**Crib**  Cheat, Cot, Cratch, Filch, Horse, KEY, Manger, Pony, Purloin, Putz, Shack, Stall, Steal, Trot

**Crick**  Cramp, Kink, Spasm

**Cricket(er)**  Balm, Bat, Botham, Bowler, Bradman, Cicada, Dry-bob, Grasshopper, Grig, Hopper, Katydid, Keeper, Knott, Leg, Longstop, March, May, Mid-on, Muggleton, Nightwatchman, Opener, Packer, Point, Slip, Stridulate, Tate, Test, Tettix, Warner, XI(gent)

**Crier**  Bellman, Herald, Muezzin, Niobe

**Crime**  Attentat, Barratry, Chantage, Chaud-mellé, Fact, Felony, Fraud, Graft, Heist, Iniquity, Mayhem, Misdeed, OFFENCE, Ovicide, Peccadillo, Pilferage, Rap, Rape, Rebellion, SIN, Tort, Transgression, Treason, Wrong

**Criminal**  Bent, Con, Counterfeiter, Crack-rope, CROOK, Culpable, Culprit, Escroc, Felon, Flagitious, Gangster, Heavy, Heinous, Hoodlum, Jailbird, Ladrone, Lag, Larcener, Maf(f)ia, Malefactor, Mobster, Ndrangheta, Nefast, Outlaw, Racketeer, Recidivist, Rustler, Villain, Wicked

> **Criminal**  may indicate an anagram

**Crimp**  Pleat

**Crimson**  Carmine, Modena, Red, Scarlet

**Cringe, Cringing**  Cower, Creep, Crouch, Fawn, Grovel, Shrink, Sneaksby, Truckle

**Crinkle, Crinkly**  Rugate, Rugose

**Crinoline**  Farthingale, Hoop

**Cripple(d)**  Damage, Disable, Game, Hamstring, Handicap, Injure, LAME, Lameter, Lamiter, Maim, Paralyse, Polio, Scotch

**Crisis**  Acme, Crunch, Drama, Emergency, Fit, Flap, Head, Mid-life, Panic, Pass, Shake-out, Solution, Test

**Crisp**  Brisk, Clear, Crimp, Crunchy, Fresh, Sharp, Short, Terse

**Crispin**  Sutor(ial)

**Criss-cross**  Alternate, Interchange, Vein

**Criterion**  Benchmark, Gauge, Measure, Precedent, Proof, Rule, Shibboleth, STANDARD, Test, Touchstone

**Critic(al), Criticism, Criticize**  Acute, Agate, Animadversion, Archer, Aristarch, Armchair, Arnold, Attack, Bagehot, Barrack, Bellettrist, Blame, Boileau, Carp, Castigate, Cavil, Censor(ious), CENSURE, Climacteric, Comment, Condemn, Connoisseur, Crab, Criticaster, CRUCIAL, Crunch, Dangle, Decisive, Denounce, Desperate, Diatribe, Dutch uncle, Etain, Exacting, Feuilleton, Flak, Flay, Gosse, Important, Impugn, Inge, Judge, Knock(er), Masora(h), Mas(s)orete, Mordacious, Nag, Nasute, Nibble, Nice, Niggle, Pan, Pater, Puff, Rap, Rebuke, Review(er), Roast, Ruskin, Scalp, Scarify, Scathe, Scorn, Serious, Shaw, Slag, Slam, Slate, Sneer, Snipe, Stick, Stricture, Strop, Tense, Touch and go, Ultracrepidate, Urgent, Vet, Vituperation, Zoilism

**Croak**  Creak, Crow, Die, Grumble, Gutturalise

**Croatian**  Cravates, Serb

**Crochet**  Lace, Weave

**Crock**  Crate, Jar, Mug, Pig, Pitcher, Pot, Potshard, Potshare, Potsherd, Stean(e)

**Crockery**  Ceramics, China, Dishes, Earthenware, Oddment, Ware

> **Crocks**  may indicate an anagram

**Crocodile**  Cayman, File, Garial, Gavial, Gharial, Line, Mugger, River-dragon, Sebek, Teleosaur(ian)

**Crocus**  Saffron

**Croesus**  Lydia

**Cromwell(ian)**  Ironside, Noll, Oliver, Protector, Richard

**Crone**  Beldam(e), Ewe, Hag, Mawkin, Ribibe, Rudas, Sibyl, Sybil, Trot, Trout, WITCH

**Crony**  Anile, Chum, Intimate, Mate, Pal

**Crook(ed)**  Adunc, Ajee, Awry, Bad, Bend, Bow, Cam, Camsho(ch), Camsheugh, Criminal, Cromb, Crome, Crosier, Crump, Curve, Fraud, Heister, Hook, Indirect, Kam(me), Kebbie, Lituus, Malpractitioner, Shyster, Sick, Skew(whiff), Slick(er), Staff, Swindler, Thraward, Thrawart, Thrawn, Twister, Yeggman

> **Crooked**  may indicate an anagram

**Croon(er), Crooning**  Bing, Lament, Lull, Monody, Murmur, Sing

**Crop(s), Cropped**  Basset, Browse, Clip, Craw, Cut, Distress, Dock, Emblements, Epilate, Eton, Foison, Harvest, Hog, Ingluvies, Kharif, Milo, Not(t), Plant, Poll, Rod, Shingle, Stow, Top, Truncate

**Cropper**  Downfall, Header, Purler

**Croquette**  Kromesky, Rissole

**Cross(ing), Crossbred** Angry, Ankh, Ansate, Basta(a)rd, Beefalo, Boton(n)e, Burden, Calvary, Capital, Cattalo, Celtic, Channel, Chi, Chiasm(a), Cleche, Clover-leaf, Compital, Constantine, Crosslet, Crotchety, Crucifix, Crux, Decussate, Demi-wolf, Dihybrid, Dso(mo), Dzobo, Eleanor, Encolpion, Fiery, Fitché, Fleury, Foil, Footbridge, Ford, Frabbit, Fractious, Frampold, Franzy, Funnel, Fylfot, George, Greek, Humette, Hybrid, Ill, Imp, Indignant, Interbreed, Intersect, Intervein, Iracund, Irate, Jomo, Jumart, Ladino, Latin, Level, Liger, Lorraine, Lurcher, Maltese, Mameluco, Mix, Moline, Mongrel, Mule, Narky, Nattery, Node, Nuisance, Ordinary, Overpass, Overthwart, Papal, Patonce, Patriarchal, Patté, Pectoral, Pelican, Plumcot, Plus, Pommé, Potence, Potent, Quadrate, Ratty, Red, Rood, Rouen, Rouge, Rubicon, Ruthwell, Sain, St Andrew's, Saltier, Saltire, Satyr, Shirty, Sign, Snappy, Southern, Strid, Swastika, Tangelo, Tau, Ten, Testy, Thwart, Tigon, Timcs, Transit, Transom, Transverse, Traverse, Tree, Urdé, Weeping, Whippet, Wry, X, Yakow, Zambo, Zebra(ss), Zebrinny, Zebrula, Zebrule Z(h)o, Zobu

> **Cross** may indicate an anagram

**Cross-bearer** Crucifer

**Cross-bill** Metagnathous

**Cross-bow** Arbalest, Bal(l)ista

**Cross-country** Langlauf, Overland

**Cross-dressing** Eonism

**Cross-examine** Grill, Interrogate, Question, Targe

**Cross-fertilisation** Allogamy, Heterosis, Xenogamy

**Cross-grained** Ill-haired, Mashlam, Mashlim, Mas(h)lin, Mashlock, Mashlum, Stubborn

**Crosspiece, Cross-bar, Cross-timber** Bar, Cancelli, Footrail, Inter-tie, Lierne, Phillipsite, Putlock, Putlog, Serif, Seriph, Stempel, Stemple, Stull, Swingle-tree, Toggle, Transom, Whiffle-tree, Whipple-tree, Yoke

**Crossroads** Carfax, Carfox, Compital, Soap

**Crossword** Cryptic, Grid, Puzzle, Quickie

**Crotchet(y)** Eccentric, Fad, Fancy, Grouch, Kink, Toy

**Crouch** Bend, Cringe, Falcade, Fancy, Ruck, Set, Squat

**Croup** Cough, Kink, Rump

**Crow** Boast, Brag, Carrion, Chewet, Chough, Corbie, Corvus, Crake, Currawong, Daw, Gorcrow, Hooded, Huia, Jackdaw, Jim(my), Murder, Raven, Rook, Skite, Squawk, Swagger, Vaunt

**Crowbar** Gavelock, James, Jemmy, Lever

**Crowd(ed)** Abound, Army, Bike, Boodle, Bumper, Bunch, Byke, Caboodle, Clutter, Concourse, Crush, Crwth, Dedans, Drove, Fill, Galere, Gate, Gathering, Herd, Horde, HOST, Huddle, Jam, Lot, Mob, Mong, Pack, Pang, Press, Rabble, Raft, Ram, Ratpack, Ring, Ruck, Scrooge, Scrouge, Scrowdge, Serr(é), Shoal, Shove, Slew, Slue, Squeeze, Stuff, Swarm, Swell, Three, Throng, Trinity, Varletry

**Crowfoot** Gilcup

**Crown** Acme, Bays, Blockade, Bull, Camp, Cap, Capernoity, Cidaris, Civic, Coma, Corona, Cr, Diadem, Ecu, Engarland, Enthrone, Fillet, Gloria, Head, Instal, Iron, Ivy, Krantz, Laurel, Monarch, Mural, Naval, Nole, Noll, Noul(e), Nowl, Olive, Ore, Ovation, Pate, Pschent, Sconce, Taj, Tiara, TOP, Triple, Triumphal, Trophy, Vallary, Vertex

**Crucial** Acute, Critical, Essential, Key, Pivotal, Watershed

**Crucible** Cruset, Melting-pot, Vessel

**Crucifix, Crucify** Cross, Mortify, Rood, Torment, Torture

**Crude** Bald, Brute, Earthy, Halfbaked, Primitive, Raw, Rough, Tutty, Uncouth, Vulgar, Yahoo

**Cruel** Barbarous, Brutal, Dastardly, De Sade, Draconian, Fell, Hard, Heartless, Immane, Inhuman, Machiavellian, Neronic, Pitiless, Raw, Sadist(ic), Stern, Tormentor, Vicious

> **Cruel** may indicate an anagram

**Cruet** Ampulla, Condiments, Decanter

**Cruise(r)** Busk, Cabin, Nuke, Prowl, Sail, Ship, Tom, Travel, Trip, Voyager

**Crumb(le), Crumbly, Crumbs** Coo, Decay, Disintegrate, Ee, Fragment, Friable, Law, Leavings, Moulder, Mull, Murl, Nesh, Nirl, Ort, Ped, Rot

**Crumpet** Dish, Girl, Muffin, Nooky, Pash, Pikelet

**Crumple** Collapse, Crunkle, Crush, Scrunch, Wrinkle

**Crunch(y)** Chew, Craunch, Crisp, Gnash, Grind, Munch, Occlude, Scranch

**Crusade(r)** Campaign, Pilgrim, Tancred

**Crush(ed), Crusher** Acis, Anaconda, Annihilate, Bow, Champ, Conquer, Cranch, Crunch, Grind, Hug, Jam, Knapper, Mash, Molar, Oppress, Overcome, Overwhelm, Pash, Policeman, Pound, Press, Pulp, Quash, Ruin, Schwarmerei, Scotch, Scrum, Smash, Squabash, Squash, Squeeze, Squelch, Squish, Stamp, Steam-roll, Stove, Suppress, Trample

**Crust(y)** Argol, Beeswing, Cake, Coating, Coffin, Cover, Crabby, Craton, Fur, Heel, Horst, Kissing, Kraton, Osteocolla, Pie, Reh, Rind, Rine, Sal, Salband, Scab, Shell, Sial, Sima, Sinter, Surly, Tartar, Teachie, Tetchy

**Crustacea(n)** Barnacle, Branchiopoda, Camaron, Cirripede, Cirripid, Copepod, Crab, Crayfish, Cyprid, Cypris, Decapoda, Entomostraca, Foot-jaw, Gribble, Krill, Lobster, Macrura, Maron, Nauplius, Ostracoda, Pagurian, Phylliopod, Prawn, Sand-hopper, Scampi, Scampo, Slater, Squilla, Stomatopod

**Crux** Essence, Nub

**Cry(ing)** Aha, Alalagmus, Alew, Banzai, Bark, Bawl, Bell, Blat, Bleat, Bleb, Blub(ber), Boo, Bray, Bump, Caramba, Cheer, Chevy, Chirm, Chivy, Clang, Crake, Croak, Crow, Dire, Euoi, Eureka, Evoe, Exclaim, Fall, Gardyloo, Gowl, Greet, Halloo, Harambee, Haro, Harrow, Havoc, Heigh, Hemitrope, Herald, Hinny, Hoo, Hout(s)-tout(s), Howl, Humph, Io, Low, Mewl, Miaou, Miau(l), Miserere, Mourn, Night-shriek, O(c)hone, Olé, Ow,

Pugh, Rivo, Scape, Scream, Screech, Sell, Sese(y), Sessa, SHOUT, Shriek, Slogan, Snivel, Snotter, Sob, Soho, Sola, Squall, Squawk, Tantivy, Umph, Vagitus, Vivat, Wail, Watchword, Waul, Wawl, Weep, Wheeple, Whimper, Whine, Whinny, Whoa, Whoop, Winge, Wolf, Yammer, Yelp, Yikker, Yippee, Yoick, Yoop, Yowl

**Crypt(ic)** Catacomb, Cavern, Chamber, Grotto, Hidden, Obscure, Occult, Secret, Sepulchre, Short, Steganographic, Tomb, Unclear, Undercroft, Vault

**Cryptogam** Acotyledon, Acrogen, Fern(-ally), Moss, Pteridophyte

**Crystal(s), Crystal-gazer, Crystalline, Crystallise** Allotriomorphic, Axinite, Baccara(t), Beryl, Clear, Copperas, Coumarin, Cumarin, Dendrite, Druse, Enantiomorph, Erionite, Geode, Glass, Hemihedron, Hemitrope, Ice-stone, Macle, Macro-axis, Melamine, Nicol, Pellucid, Piezo, Pinacoid, Pinakoid, Prism, Pseudomorph, Purin(e), Quartz, R(h)aphide, R(h)aphis, Rhinestone, Rubicelle, Scryer, Shoot, Skryer, Snowflake, Spar, Spicule, Table, Trichite, Trilling, Xanthene

**Cub** Baby, Kit, Novice, Pup, Whelp

**Cube, Cubic** Cu, Die, Nosean, Rubik's, Serac, Smalto, Solid, Stere

**Cubicle** Alcove, Booth, Stall

**Cuckold** Actaeon, Cornute, Horner, Lenocinium, Wittol

**Cuckoo** Ament, Ani, April fool, Bird, Gouk, Gowk, Insane, Koel, MAD, Mental, Piet-my-vrou, Stupid

> **Cuckoo** may indicate an anagram

**Cuckoopint** Arum

**Cucumber** Choko, Colocynth, Coloquintida, Dill, Elaterium, Gherkin, Pickle, Sea-slug, Wolly

**Cuddle** Canoodle, Caress, Embrace, Fondle, Hug, Nooky, Smooch, Smuggle, Snuggle

**Cudgel** Alpeen, Ballow, Bludgeon, Brain, Club, Cosh, Drub, Fustigate, Plant, Shillelagh, Souple, Stick, Tan, Towel, Truncheon

**Cue** Cannonade, Catchword, Feed, Hint, Mace, PROMPT, Reminder, Rod, Sign, Signal, Wink

**Cuff** Box, Buffet, Clout, Iron, Strike, Swat

**Cuirass** Armour, Corselet, Lorica

**Cuisine** Cookery, Food, Menu

**Cul-de-sac** Blind, Dead-end, Impasse, Loke

**Cull** Gather, Pick, Select, Thin, Weed

**Culminate, Culmination** Apogean, Apogee, Climax, Conclusion, End

**Cult** Cabiri, Cargo, Creed, Rastafarian, Sect, Shinto, Worship

**Cultivate(d), Cultivation** Arty, Civilise, Dig, Dress, Genteel, Grow, Hoe, Improve, Labour, Pursue, Raise, Refine, Sative, Sophisticated, Tame, Tasteful, Till, Tilth

**Culture(d)** Agar, Art(y), Brahmin, Capsian, Civil(isation), Ethnic,

Experiment, Explant, Gel, Grecian, Hallstatt, Kultur(kreis), Learning, Mousterian, Polish, Refinement, Strepyan

**Cumbersome** Clumsy, Heavy, Lumbering, UNWIELDY

**Cunctator** Dilatory

**Cuneiform** Wedge(d)

**Cunning** Arch, Art, Craft(y), Deceit, Deep, Down, Finesse, Foxy, Leery, Machiavellian, Quaint, Skill, Slee(kit), Sleight, Sly(boots), Smart, Subtle, Vulpine, Wile

**Cup(s), Cupped** Aecidium, America's, Beaker, Calcutta, Calix, Cantharus, Chalice, Cotyle, Cruse, Cupule, Cyathus, Cylix, Demitasse, Deoch-an-doruis, Deuch-an-doris, Dish, Doch-an-dorach, Dop, Final, Fingan, Finjan, Glenoid, Goblet, Hanap, Horn, Kylix, Loving, Merry, Mug, Noggin, Pannikin, Plate, Pot, Procoelus, Quaich, Quaigh, Rhyton, Rider, Sangrado, Scyphus, Stirrup, Tantalus, Tass(ie), Tastevin, Tazza, Tea-dish, Tig, Tot, TROPHY, Tyg, Volva

**Cup-bearer** Ganymede, Hebe

**Cupboard** Almery, Almirah, A(u)mbry, Beauf(f)et, Cabinet, Closet, Credenza, Dresser, Locker, Press

**Cup-holder** Hanaper, Hebe, Plinth, Saucer, Zarf, Zurf

**Cupid** Amoretto, Amorino, Archer, Blind, Cherub, Dan, Eros, Love, Putto

**Cupola** Belfry, Dome, Tholos

**Cur** Dog, Messan, Mongrel, Mutt, Scab, Scoundrel, Wretch, Yap

**Curare, Curari** Ourali, Wourali

**Curassow** Crax

**Curate** Minister, Nathaniel, Padré, Priest

**Curb** Bit, Brake, Bridle, Check, Clamp, Coaming, Dam, Edge, Puteal, Rein, Restrain, Rim

**Curd(s)** Cheese, Junket, Lapper(ed)-milk, Skyr, Tofu

**Curdle** Congeal, Clot, Earn, Erne, Lopper, Run, Set, Sour, TURN, Whig, Yearn

**Cure(d), Curative** Amend, Antidote, Antirachitic, Bloater, Cold turkey, Dry-salt, Euphrasy, Ginseng, Hobday, Heal, Jerk, Kipper, Medicinal, Nostrum, Panacea, Park-leaves, PRESERVE, Recover, Recower, Reest, Remede, Remedy, Restore, Salt, Salve, Serum, Smoke, TREATMENT, Tutsan

> **Cure** may indicate an anagram

**Curfew** Gate, Prohibit, Proscribe

**Curie** Ci

**Curio, Curiosity, Curious** Agog, Bibelot, Freak, Meddlesome, Odd, Peculiar, Prurience, Rarity, Rum, STRANGE

> **Curious(ly)** may indicate an anagram

**Curium** Cm

**Curl(er), Curling** Cirrus, Coil, Crimp, Crinkle, Crisp, Crocket, Earlock, Friz(z), Frizzle, Heart-breaker, Hog, Inwick, Loop, Love-lock, Outwick, Perm, Repenter, Ringlet, Roll, Roulette, Shaving, Spiral, Twiddle, TWIST, Wave, Wind

**Curlew** Bird, Whaup, Whimbrel

**Curmudgeon** Boor, Churl, Grouch, Route, Runt

**Currant** Berry, Raisin, Rizard, Rizzar(t), Rizzer

**Currency** Cash, Circulation, Coinage, Finance, Franc, Monetary, MONEY, Qintar, Rupiah

> **Currency** may indicate a river

**Current** Abroad, AC, Amperage, Amp(ere), DC, Draught, Drift, Dynamo, Ebbtide, Electric, El Nino, Euripus, Existent, Flow, Foucault, Going, I, Immediate, Inst, Kuroshio, Labrador, Millrace, Modern, Now, Ongoing, Present, Prevalent, Race, Rapid, Rife, Roost, Running, Stream, Thames, Thermal, Tide, Topical, Torrent, Underset, Undertow

**Curriculum** Cursal, Programme

**Curry** Brush, Comb, Cuittle, Fawn, Groom, Ingratiate, Spice, Tan, Vindaloo

**Curse** Abuse, Anathema, Ban, Bane, Beshrew, BLASPHEME, Blast, Chide, Dam(me), Damn, Dee, Drat, Excommunicate, Execrate, Heck, Hex, Imprecate, Jinx, Malison, Maranatha, Mau(l)gré, Mockers, Moz(z), Mozzle, Oath, Pize, Plague, Rant, Scourge, Spell, Upbraid, Weary, Winze, Wo(e)

**Cursive** Run

**Cursorily, Cursory** Lax, Obiter, Passing, Sketchy

**Curt** Abrupt, Blunt, Laconic, Offhand, Short, Snappy

**Curtail(ment)** Apocope, Crop, Cut, Reduce, Shorten

**Curtain(s), Curtain-rod** Arras, Bamboo, Canopy, Caudle, Cloth, Demise, Drape, Drop, Dropscene, Hanging, Iron, Louvre, Net, Portière, Purdah, Screen, Scrim, Tab, Tringle, Valance, Vitrage

**Curtsey** Bob, Bow, Dip, Dop

**Curve(d), Curvy, Curvature, Curvaceous** Aduncate, Apophyge, Arc, Arch, Archivolt, Axoid, Bend, Bow, Camber, Cardioid, Catacaustic, Catenary, Caustic, Cissoid, Conchoid, Diacaustic, Epinastic, Ess, Extrados, Felloe, Felly, Hance, Helix, Hodograph, Hyperbola, Isochor, Laffer, Limacon, Liquidus, Lituus, Lordosis, Nowy, Ogee, Parabola, Rhumb, Roach, Rotundate, Scoliosis, Sinuate, Spiric, Tautochrone, Tie, Tractrix, Twist, Undulose, Witch

**Cushion** Allege, Bolster, Buffer, Hassock, PAD, Pillow, Pouffe, Soften, Squab, Upholster, Whoopee

**Cusp** Horn, Tine, Spinode

**Custard (apple)** Flam(m), Flan, Flaune, Flawn, Flummery, Pa(w)paw, Zabaglione

**Custodian, Custody** Care, Claviger, Guard, Hold, Janitor, Keeping, Sacrist, Steward, Trust, Ward

**Custom(ary), Customs** Agriology, Coast-waiters, Consuetude, Conventional, Couvade, De règle, Douane, Familiar, Fashion, HABIT, Lore, Manner, Montem, Mores, Nomic, Octroi, Ordinary, Practice, Relic, Rite, Routine, Rule, Sororate, Sunna, Tax, Thew, Tidesman, Tradition, Unwritten, Usance, Used, Usual, Won, Wont, Woon, Zollverein

**Customer** Client, Cove, Patron, Prospect, Shillaber, Shopper, Smooth, Trade, Trick

**Cut(ter), Cutting** Abate, Abjoint, Abridge, Abscission, Abscond, Acute, Adze, Aftermath, Amputate, Apocope, Axe, Bang, Bisect, Bit, Bowdlerise, Boycott, Brilliant, Broach, Caique, Canal, Cantle, Caper, Carve, Castrate, Caustic, Censor, Chap, Chisel, Chop, Chynd, Circumscribe, Clinker-built, Clip, Colter, Commission, Concise, Coulter, Coupé, Crew, Crop, Curtail, Dice, Discide, Disengage, Dissect, Division, Divorce, Dock, Dod, Edge, Edit, Emarginate, Engrave, Entail, Entayle, Epitomise, Eschew, Estrepe, Excise, Exscind, Exsect, Exude, Fashion, Fell, Fillet, Flench, Flense, Flinch, Form, Froe, Frow, Garb, Gash, Grate, Graven, Gride, Gryde, Hack, Handsaw, Hew(er), Ignore, Incision, Incisor, Indent, Intersect, Joint, Junk, Kerf, Kern, Kirn, Lacerate, Lance, Leat, Lesion, Lin, Lop, Math, Microtome, Mortice, Mortise, Mow, Nache, Nick, Not, Notch, Nott, Occlude, Omit, Open, Operate, Osteotome, Oxyacetylene, Pare, Pink, Plant, Pliers, Pone, Precisive, Proin, Race, Rake off, Rase, Razor, Reap, Rebate, Reduction, Resect, Retrench, Ripsaw, Roach, Rout, Saddle, Sarcastic, Saw(n), Scathing, Scion, Scission, Scissor, Score, Sculpt, Scye, Scythe, Secant, Sect, Sever, Sey, Share (out), Shave, Shear, Shingle, Ship, Shorn, Shred, Shun, Sickle, Sirloin, Skip, Slane, Slash, Slice, Slip, Slit, Sloop, Sned, Snee, Snick, Snip, Snub, Spade, Spin, Spud, Steak, Stencil, Stereotomy, Stir, Stramacon, Stramazon, Style, Surgeon, Tart, Tenotomy, Tomial, Tomium, Tonsure, Trash, Trench, Trenchant, Trepan, Trim, Truant, Truncate, Urchin, Whang, Whittle, Winey

> **Cut** may indicate an anagram

> **Cutback** may indicate a reversed word

**Cute** Ankle, Pert, Pretty

**Cut in** Interpose, Interrupt

**Cut off** Enisle, Inisle, Insulate, Intercept, ISOLATE, Lop, Prune

**Cut-throat** Razor, Ruinous

**Cuticle** Eponychium, Skin

**Cutlass** Machete, Sword

**Cutlery** Canteen, Flatware, Fork, Knife, Spoon, Tableware

**Cuttlebone, Cuttlefish** Octopus, Pen, Polyp(e)s, Polypus, Sea-sleeve, Sepia, Sepiost(aire), Sepium, Squid

**Cyanide** Acrylonitrile, Nitrile

**Cycad** Coontie, Coonty

**Cyclamen** Sow-bread

**Cycle, Cyclist** Arthurian, Bike, Cal(l)ippic, Carnot, Circadian, Daisy, Eon,

Era, Frequency, Indiction, Metonic, Orb, Pedal, Period, Repulp, Ride, Roadster, Rota, Round, Samsara, Saros, Scorch, Series, Sothic, Spin, Trike, Wheeler

**Cyclone** Storm, Tornado, Typhoon, Willywilly

**Cyclops** Arges, Arimasp(i), Brontes, Polyphemus, Steropes

**Cylinder, Cylindrical** Clave, Drum, Pipe, Roll, Steal, Stele, Terete, Torose, Tube

**Cymbal(s)** Hi-hat, Zel

**Cynic(al)** Crab, Diogenes, Doubter, Hard-boiled, Menippus, Pessimist, Sardonic, Sceptic, Timon

**Cynosure** Centre, Focus

**Cynthia** Artemis

**Cypress** Retinospora, Tree

**Cypriot** Enosis, Eoka

**Cyst** Atheroma, Bag, Blister, Chalazion, Hydatid, Ranula, Sac, Wen

**Czechoslovakia** CZ, Sudetenland

# Dd

**D**  Daughter, Delta, Died, Edh, Eth, Penny

**Dab(s)**  Bit, Daub, Fish, Flounder, Pat, Print, Ringer, Smear, Spot, Stupe, Whorl

**Dabble(r)**  Dally, Dilettante, Plouter, Plowter, Potter, Smatter, Splash, Stipple, Trifle

**Dachshund**  Teckel

**Dactyl**  Anapaest

**Dad(dy)**  Blow, Dev(v)el, Father, Generator, Hit, Male, Pa(pa), Pater, Polt, Pop, Sugar, Thump

**Daddy-longlegs**  Crane-fly, Jennyspinner, Leather-jacket, Spinning-jenny, Tipula

**Daffodil**  Asphodel, Jonquil, Lent-lily, Narcissus

**Daft**  Absurd, Crazy, Potty, Ridiculous, Silly, Simple, Stupid

**Dag**  Jag, Pierce, Pistol, Prick, Stab, Tag, Wool

**Dagger(s)**  An(e)lace, Ataghan, Baselard, Bayonet, Bodkin, Crease, Creese, Da(h), Diesis, Dirk, Dudgeon, Han(d)jar, Hanger, Jambiyah, Katar, Kindjahl, Kirpan, Kreese, Kris, Lath, Misericord(e), Obelisk, Obelus, Poi(g)nado, Poniard, Puncheon, Skean, Skene(-occle), Stiletto, Whiniard, Whinyard, W(h)inger, Yatag(h)an

**Dahlia**  Cosmea

**Daily**  Adays, Char, Diurnal, Domestic, Guardian, Help, Journal, Mail, Mirror, Paper, Quotidian, Rag, Regular, Scotsman, Sun, Tabloid

**Dainty**  Cate(s), Delicacy, Elegant, Entremesse, Entremets, Exquisite, Junket, Lickerish, Liquorish, Mignon(ne), MORSEL, Neat, Nice, Particular, Petite, Sunket, Twee

**Dairy**  Creamery, Loan, Parlour

**Dairymaid**  Dey, Patience

**Dais**  Estate, Platform, Podium, Pulpit, Stage

**Daisy**  Bell, Felicia, Gowan, Michaelmas, Ox-eye, Shasta

**Dale**  Dell, Dene, Dingle, Glen, Vale, Valley

**Dally**  Coquet(te), Dawdle, Finger, Flirt, Play, Spoon, Sport, Toy, Trifle, Wait

**Dam**  An(n)icut, Aswan, Bar, Barrage, Barrier, Block, Boulder, Bund, Cauld, Check, Hoover, Kariba, Kielder, Ma, Mater, Obstacle, Obstruct, Pen, STEM, Sudd, Weir

**Damage(d), Damages**  Bane, Bruise, Buckle, Cost, Cripple, Detriment, Devastate, Devastavit, Estrepe, Fault, Flea-bite, Harm, Havoc, Hit, Hole,

Hurt, Impair, Injury, Loss, Mar, Mayhem, Nobble, Prang, Price, Retree, Sabotage, Scaith, Scath(e), Scotch, Scratch, Skaith, SPOIL, Tangle, Toll, Violate, Wing, Wound

**Dambuster** Ondatra

**Dame** Crone, Dowager, Gammer, Lady, Matron, Nature, Naunt, Partlet, Peacherino, Sis, Title(d), Trot, Woman

**Damn(ed), Damnation** Attack, Blame, Condemn, Curse, Cuss, Darn, Dee, Execrate, Faust, Hell, Hoot, Malgre, Perdition, Predoom, Sink, Swear, Very

**Damp(ness)** Aslake, Check, Clam(my), Dank, Dewy, Humid, Moist, Muggy, Raw, Rheumy, Roric, Soggy, Unaired, WET

**Damper** Barrier, Check, Dashpot, Killjoy, Mute

**Damsel** Girl, Lass, Maiden, Wench

**Damson** Plumdamas

**Dan** Box, Cupid, Leno, Scuttle, Tribe

**Dance(r), Dancing** Allemande, Alma(in), Antistrophe, Apache, Baladine(e), Ball, Ballabile, Ballant, Ballerina, Ballet, Barn, Bayadère, Beguine, Bergamask, Bergomask, Bolero, Boogie, Bossanova, Boston, Bou(r)ée, Bran(s)le, Brantle, Brawl, Caballero, Cachucha, Cake-walk, Canary, Can-can, Cantico(y), Caper, Capoeira, Capuera, Carioca, Carmagnole, Carol, Cha-cha(-cha), Chaconne, Charleston, Cinque-pace, Clog, Comprimario, Coranto, Corroboree, Corybant, Coryphee, Cotill(i)on, Courant(e), Cracovienne, Csardas, Dervish, Disco, Dolin, Do-si-do, Dump, Ecossaise, Egg-dance, Eightsome, Fading, Fado, Fandango, Farandole, Farruca, Figurante, Flamenco, Fling, Flip-flop, Floral, Foot, Forlana, Foug, Foxtrot, Furlana, Furry, Galliard, Galop, Gallopade, Gavotte, German, Gig, Giga, Gigolo, Gigue, Glide, Go-go, Gopak, Habanera, Haka, Halling, Hay, Hay-de-guise, Hay-de-guy(es), Haymaker, Hetaera, Hetaira, Hey, Hey-de-guise, Hey-de-guy(es), Heythrop, Hoe-down, Hoofer, Hop, Hora(h), Hornpipe, Hula(-hula), Hustle, Irish-jig, Jack-in-the-green, Jitterbug, Jive, Joncanoe, Jota, Juba, Juke, Junkanoo, Kantikoy, Kathak(ali), Kazatzka, Kick-up, Knees-up, Kolo, Labanotation, Lambada, Lancers, Landler, Lavolt(a), Leap, Limbo, Loup, Loure, Macaber, Macabre, Maenad, Malaguena, Mambo, Marinera, Masurka, Maxixe, Mazurka, Measure, Merengue, Minuet, Mooch, Moresco, Morrice, Morris, Moshing, Murciana, Na(t)ch, Nautch-girl, Nureyev, Nijinsky, Oberek, Orchesis, Palais glide, Partner, Pas (de deux), Paso doble, Paspy, Passacaglia, Passamezzo, Passepied, Passy-measure, Passemeasure, Pastourelle, Pavan(e), Pavlova, Pericon, Petipa, Petronella, Pierette, Planxty, Polacca, Polka, Polo, Polonaise, Poussette, Pyrrhic, Quadrille, Redowa, Reel, Ridotto, Rigadoon, Robotics, Romaika, Ronggeng, Roundle, Rug-cutting, Routine, St Vitus, Salome, Salsa, Saltarello, Saltatorious, Samba, Saraband, Sardana, Sashaya, Schottische, Seguidilla, Shag, Shimmy(-shake), Shuffle, Siciliano, Sicilienne, Sink(e)-a-pace, Skank, Soft-shoe, Spring, Step, Stomp, Strathspey, Strut, Taglioni, Tanagra, Tango, Tap, Tarantella, Terpsichore, Tordion, Tread, Trenchmore, Trenise, Trip(pant), Tripudium, Trophe,

Trucking, Twist, Valeta, Valse, Variation, Varsovienne, Veleta, Vogueing, Volta, Waltz, Zapateado, Ziganka

**Dance movement**  Chassé, Entrechat, Glissade, Jeté, Lassu, Pantalon, Pirouette, Poule, Poussette, Routine, Step

**Dance tune**  Toy

> **Dancing**  may indicate an anagram

**Dancing party**  Ball, Ridotto

**Dandelion**  Kok-sagyz, Piss-a-bed, Scorzonera, Taraxacum

**Dander**  Anger, Gee, Passion, Saunter, Temper

**Dandle**  Dance, Doodle, Fondle, Pet

**Dandruff**  Furfur, Scurf

**Dandy**  Adonis, Beau, Blood, Boulevardier, Buck(een), Cat, Coxcomb, Dapper, DUDE, Exquisite, Fantastico, Fop, Gem, Jay, Jessamy, Johnny, Kiddy, Knut, Lair, Macaroni, Masher, Modist, Monarcho, Muscadin, Nash, Nut, Posh, Smart, Spiff, Swell, Ted, U, Yankee-doodle

**Dane(s)**  Clemence, Dansker, Ogier, Ostman

**Danger(ous)**  Apperil, Crisis, Dic(e)y, Dire, Emprise, Fear, Hairy, Hazard, Hearie, Hot, Insecure, Jeopardy, Menace, Mine, Nettle, Nocuous, Parlous, PERIL, Pitfall, Risk, Serious, Severe, Tight, Trap

**Dangle**  A(i)glet, Aiguillette, Critic, Flourish, Hang, Loll, Swing

**Daniel**  Dan, Defoe, Deronda, Lion-tamer, Portia, Quilp

**Dank**  Clammy, Damp, Humid, Moist, Wet, Wormy

**Daphne**  Agalloch, Agila, Eaglewood, Lace-bark, Laura, Laurel, Mezereon

**Dapper**  Dressy, Natty, Neat, Smart, Spiff, Spruce, Sprush, Spry, TRIM

**Darbies**  Cuffs, Irons, Snaps

**Dare, Daring**  Bold, Brave, Challenge, Courage, Da(u)nton, Defy, Durst, Emprise, Face, Gallant, Hazard, Hen, Prowess, Racy, Taunt, Venture

**Dark(en), Darkie, Darkness**  Aphelia, Aphotic, Apophis, Black, Blind, Cimmerean, Cloud, Depth, Dim, Dingy, Dirk(e), Dusky, Eclipse, Erebus, Evil, Gloom, Glum, Inumbrate, Mare, Maria, Melanous, Mulatto, Murk(y), Negro, Night, Obfuscate, Obscure, Pall, Phaeic, Pit-mirk, Rooky, Sable, Sad, Secret, Shuttered, Sinister, Solein, Sombre, Sphacelate, Sullen, Swarthy, Tar, Tenebrose, Unfair, Unlit, Yellowboy, Yellowgirl

**Darling**  Acushla, Alannah, Asthore, Beloved, Charlie, Cher, Chéri(e), Chick-a-biddy, Chick-a-diddle, Chuck-a-diddle, Dear, Dilling, Do(a)ting-piece, Duck(s), Favourite, Grace, Honey, Idol, Jarta, Jo(e), Mavourneen, Mavournin, Minikin, Minion, Oarswoman, Own, Peat, Pet, Poppet, Precious, Sugar, Sweetheart, Yarta, Yarto

**Darn**  Begorra, Blow, Doggone, Hang, Mend, Repair

**Dart(er)**  Abaris, Arrow, Banderilla, Dace, Dash, Deadener, Dodge, Fleat, Flit, Harpoon, Javelin, Launch, Leap, Scoot, Skrim, Speck, Strike, Thrust, Wheech

**Dash(ed), Dashing** Backhander, Bally, Blade, Blight, Buck, Charge, Collide, Cut, Dad, Dah, Dapper, Daud, Debonair, Ding, Elan, Fa(s)cia, Fly, Go-ahead, Hang, HURRY, Hustle, Hyphen, Impetuous, Jabble, Jaw, Jigger, Lace, Minus, Natty, Nip, Panache, Rash, Rule, Rush, Run, Sally, Scamp(er), Scart, Scoot, Scrattle, Scurry, Scuttle, Shatter, Showy, Soupçon, Souse, Spang, Speed, Splash, Sprint, Strack, Streak, Stroke, STYLE, Throw, Touch, Viretot

**Dashwood** Hell-fire club

**Dastard(ly)** Base, Coward, Craven, Nid(d)erling, Poltroon

**Data** Evidence, Facts, Fiche, File, Gen, Info, Input, Material, Matrix, News

**Date(d), Dates, Dating** AD, Age, Almanac, Appointment, Blind, Boyfriend, Calendar, Carbon, Court, Deadline, Engagement, Epoch, Equinox, Era, Escort, Exergue, Girlfriend, Ides, Meet, Outmoded, OUT OF DATE, Passé, Past, See, TRYST, Ult(imo)

**Daub** Begrime, Blob, Dab, Gaum, Mess, Moil, Noint, Plaister, Plaster, SMEAR, Smudge, Splodge, Teer, Wattle

**Daughter (in law)** Child, D, Elect, Girl, Jephthah's, Niece, Offspring

**Daunt** Adaw, Amate, Awe, Deter, Dishearten, Intimidate, Overawe, Quail, Stun, Stupefy, Subdue

**Dauphin** Delphin

**David** Dai, Psalmist

**Davit** Crane, Derrick, Hoist

**Davy** Crockett, Jones

**Daw** Bird, Magpie, Margery

**Dawdle(r)** Dally, Draggle, Drawl, Idle, LOITER, Potter, Shirk, Slowcoach, Troke, Truck

**Dawn** Aurora, Cockcrow, Daw, Daybreak, Dayspring, Eoan, Eos, Light, Morrow, Occur, Prime, Start, Sunrise

**Day(s)** Anzac, Armistice, Banian, Calends, Calpa, D, Date, Distaff, Ember, Fasti, Feria, Fri, Groundling, Hogmanay, Hundred, Ides, Independence, Intercalary, Kalends, Kalpa, Lady, Lammas, Laetare, Lay, Mardi, Midsummer, Mon, Morrow, Nones, Nychthemeron, Oak-apple, Octave, Poppy, Present, Primrose, Quarter, Robin, Rock, Rogation, Rood, Salad, Sat, Shick-shack, Solstice, Sun, Tag, Thurs, Time, Tues, Utas, VE, Wed

**Daybreak** Cockcrow

**Daydream(er)** Brown study, Fancy, Imagine, Mitty, Muse, Reverie

**Daylight** Dawn, Space, Sun

**Daze(d)** Amaze, Bemuse, Confuse, Dwaal, Muddle, Muzzy, Reeling, STUN, Stupefy, Stupor, Trance

**Dazzle(d), Dazzling** Bewilder, Blend, Blind, Eclipse, Foudroyant, Glare, Outshine, Radiance, Resplendent, Splendour, Yblent

**Deacon** Cleric, Doctor, Minister

**Deactivate** Unarm

**Dead(en)** Abrupt, Accurate, Alamort, Asgard, Asleep, Blunt, Bung, Cert, Cold, Complete, D, Deceased, Defunct, Doggo, Expired, Extinct, Gone(r), Inert, Infarct, Late, Lifeless, Muffle, Mute, Napoo, Numb, Obsolete, Obtund, Ringer, She'ol, Smother, True, Utter, Waned

**Dead end, Deadlock** Dilemma, Impasse, Logjam, Stalemate, Stoppage

**Dead-leaf colour** Filemot, Philamot, Philomot

**Deadline** Date, Epitaph, Limit

**Deadly** Baleful, Dull, Fell, Funest, Internecine, LETHAL, Malign, Mortal, Pestilent, Unerring, Venomous

**Deadly Nightshade** Dwale, Belladonna

**Deadpan** Expressionless

**Dead reckoning** Dr

**Dead tree** Rampick, Rampike

**Deaf(en), Deafness** Adder, Asonia, Deave, Deeve, Dunny, Heedless, Paracusis, Surd(ity)

**Deal(er), Dealings** Agent, Allot(ment), Arbitrageur, Brinjarry, Broker, Business, Chandler, Chapman, Commerce, Cope, Cover, Croupier, Dispense, Distributor, Do, Dole, Eggler, Exchange, Fripper, Goulash, Hand(le), Help, Inflict, Insider, Jobber, Lashing, Let, Manage, Mercer, Merchant, Mickle, Monger, Mort, Negotiate, Operator, Package, Pine, Raft, Sale, Serve, Spicer, Tape, Timber, TRADE, Traffic, Treat, Truck, Wheeler, Wield, Yardie

**Dean** Acheson, Arabin, Colet, Decani, Doyen, Forest, Head, Inge, Nellie, Provost, RD, Rural, Rusk, Slade, Spooner, Swift, Vale

**Dear(er), Dearest, Dear me** Ay, Bach, Beloved, Cher(e), Cherie, Chuckie, Darling, Duck(s), Expensive, High, Leve, Lief, Lieve, Loor, Love, Machree, Mouse, My, Pet, Pigsney, Pigsnic, Pigsny, Steep, Sweet, Toots(ie), Up

**Dearth** Famine, Lack, Paucity, Scantity, Scarcity, SHORTAGE

**Deaspiration** Psilosis

**Death(ly)** Bane, Bargaist, Barg(h)est, Black, Curtains, Demise, Dormition, End, Eschatology, Euthanasia, Exit, Extinction, Gangrene, Hallal, Jordan, Lethee, Leveller, Mors, Napoo, Necrosis, Nemesis, Night, Obit, Quietus, Reaper, Sati, Sergeant, Small-back, Strae, Sudden, Suttee, Terminal, Thanatism, Thanatopsis, Thanatos

**Death-flood** Styx

**Deathless(ness)** Athanasy, Eternal, Eterne, Immortal, Struldberg, Timeless, Undying

**Debacle** Cataclysm, Collapse, Disaster, Fiasco

**Debar** Deny, Exclude, Forbid, PREVENT, Prohibit

**Debase(d)** Adulterate, Bemean, Corrupt, Demean, Depreciate, Dialectician, Dirty, Grotesque, Hedge, Lower, Pervert, Traduce, Vitiate

**Debate(r)** Argue, Combat, Contention, Contest, Deliberate, Discept,

Discuss(ion), DISPUTE, Moot, Reason, Teach-in, Wrangle

**Debauch(ee), Debauchery** Corrupt, Defile, Degenerate Dissipate, Heliogabalus, Libertine, Orgy, Profligate, Rake-hell, Riot, Roist, Royst, Seduce, Spree, Stuprate, Wet

**Debenture** Bond, Security

**Debilitate(d), Debility** Asthenia, Atonic, Feeble, Languid, Weak

**Debit** Charge, Debt

**Debonair** Cavalier, Gay, Gracious, Jaunty

**Debris** Bahada, Bajada, Detritus, Eluvium, Moraine, Moslings, Refuse, RUBBLE, Ruins, Waste

> **Debris** may indicate an anagram

**Debt(or)** Alsatia, Arrears, Arrestee, Dr, Due, Insolvent, IOU, Liability, Moratoria, Obligation, Score, Tie

**Debt-collector** Bailiff, Remembrancer

**Debut** Launch, Opening

**Debutante** Bud, Deb

**Decade** Rosary, Ten

**Decadence, Decadent** Babylonian, Decaying, Degeneration, Dissolute, Effete, Fin-de-siècle

**Decamp** Abscond, Absquatulate, Bolt, Bunk, Depart, Flee, Guy, Levant, Mizzle, Slide, Slope, Vamoose

**Decant** Pour, Unload

**Decapitate, Decapitation** Aphesis, BEHEAD, Guillotine

> **Decapitated** may indicate first letter removed

**Decay(ed), Decaying** Appair, Blet, Canker, Caries, Crumble, Decadent, Declension, Decline, Decrepit, Doat, Doddard, Doddered, Dote, Dricksie, Druxy, Fail, Forfair, Impair, Pair(e), Ret, Rot, Sap-rot, Seedy, Sepsis, Spoil, Tabes

**Decease** Death, Demise, Die

**Deceit(ful), Deceive(r)** Abuse, Artifice, Bamboozle, Barrat, Befool, Bitten, Blind, Bluff, Braide, CHEAT, Chicane, Chouse, Cozen, Cuckold, Defraud, Delude, Diddle, Dissemble, Dupe, False(r), Fiddle, Flam, Fox, Fraud, Gag, Glose, Guile, Gull, Hoax, Hoodwink, Hornswoggle, Humbug, Hype, Imposition, Invention, Kid, Malengine, Mata Hari, Mislead, Phenakism, Poop, Poupe, Pretence, Punic, Rig, Ruse, Sell, Sham, Sinon, Spruce, Stratagem, Swindle, Swizzle, Tregetour, Trick, Trump, Two-time, Wile

**Decency, Decent** Chaste, Decorum, Fitting, Honest, Kind, Modest, Seemly, Sporting

**Decentralise** Disperse

**Deception, Deceptive** Artifice, Catchpenny, Cheat, DECEIT, Disguise, Dupe, Eyewash, Fallacious, False, Flam, Gag, Gammon, Guile, Have-on,

Hocus-pocus, Hokey-pokey, Hum, Hunt-the-gowks, Ignes-fatui, Ignis-fatuus, Illusion, Lie, Ruse, Sell, Specious, TRICK, Trompe l'oeil, Two-timing

**Decide(d), Decider** Addeem, Ballot, Barrage, Cast, Clinch, Conclude, DECISION, Deem, Definite, Determine, Distinct, Firm, Fix, Jump-off, Mediate, Opt, Parti, Pronounced, Rescript, RESOLVE, Rule, Run-off, See, Settle, Tiebreaker, Try

**Decimal** Mantissa

**Decimate** Destroy, Lessen, Weaken

**Decipher** Decode, Decrypt, Discover, Interpret

> **Decipher(ed)** may indicate an 'o' removed

**Decision** Arbitrium, Arrêt, Crossroads, Crunch, Decree, Fetwa, Judg(e)ment, Placit(um), Referendum, Resolve, Ruling, Sentence, Verdict

**Decisive** Climactic, Clincher, Critical, Crux, Definite, Final, Pivotal

**Deck** Adorn, Array, Attrap, Cards, Clad, Daiker, Daub, Decorate, Dizen, Embellish, Equip, Focsle, Garland, Hang, Orlop, Pack, Platform, Poop, Prim

**Declaim, Declare, Declaration, Decree** Affidavit, Affirm, Air, Allege, Announce, Assert, Asseverate, Aver, Avow, Balfour, Bann(s), Breda, Dictum, Doom, Edict, Enact, Fatwa, Fiat, Firman, Grace, Harangue, Hatti-sherif, Insist, Irade, Law, Mandate, Manifesto, Mecklenburg, Meld, Mou(th), Novella, Nullity, Orate, Ordain, Order, Ordinance, Parlando, Pontificate, Proclaim, Profess, Pronounce, Protest, Psephism, Publish, Rant, Recite, Resolve, Rescript, Rights, Rule, Ruling, SC, Sed, Senecan, Speak, Spout, State, Testimony, Testify, UDI, Unilateral, Vie, Vouch, Word

> **Declaring** may indicate a word beginning 'Im'

**Decline, Declining** Age, Comedown, Decadent, Degringoler, Deny, Descend, Deteriorate, Devall, Die, Dip, Dissent, Downtrend, Droop, Dwindle, Ebb, Fade, Fall, Flag, Forbear, Paracme, Quail, Recede, Recession, Refuse, Retrogression, Rot, Rust, Sag, Senile, Set, Sink, Slump, Stoop, Wane, Welke, WILT, Withdraw, Wither

**Decoct(ion)** Apozem, Cook, Devise, Ptisan, Tisane

**Decolleté** Low, Neckline

**Decompose, Decomposition** Biodegradable, Crumble, Decay, Disintegrate, Hydrolysis, Mor, Rot, Wither

**Decompression** Bends

**Decor** Background, Scenery

**Decorate(d), Decoration, Decorative** Adorn, Angelica, Aogai, Attrap, Award, Baroque, Braid, Brooch, Champlevé, Centrepiece, Chambranle, Chinoiserie, Cloissoné, Cul-de-lampe, Dentelle, Diamante, Dragée, Epergne, Etch, Fancy, Festoon, Filigree, Frieze, Frill, Frog, Garniture, Gaud, Goffer, Gradino, Guilloche, Historiated, Ice, Illuminate, Impearl, Inlay, Intarsia, Intarsio, Interior, Linen-fold, MC, Medal(lion), Oath, OBE, Order, ORNAMENT, Orphrey, Ovolo, Paint, Paper, Parament, Prink, Purfle, Rangoli, Rich, Rosemaling, Ruche, Scallop, Scrimshander, Set-off,

Skeuomorph, Spangle, Storiated, Tailpiece, Tattoo, TD, Titivate, Tool, Topiary, Trim, Wallpaper

**Decorous, Decorum** Becoming, Demure, Etiquette, Fitness, Prim, PROPER, Propriety, Seemlihe(a)d, SEEMLY, Staid

**Decoy** Allure, Bait, Bonnet, Button, Call-bird, Coach, Crimp, Entice, Lure, Piper, Roper, Ruse, Stale, Stalking-horse, Stool-pigeon, Tole, Toll, Trap, Trepan

**Decrease** Decrew, Diminish, Dwindle, Iron, Lessen, Press, Reduce, Subside, Wane, Wanze

> **Decree** see DECLAIM

**Decrepit** Dilapidated, Doddery, Failing, Feeble, Frail, Tumbledown, Warby, Weak

**Decry** Condemn, Crab, Denounce, Derogate, Detract, Downgrade

**Dedicate(d), Dedication** Corban, Devote, Endoss, Hallow, Inscribe, Oblate, Pious, Sacred, Votive

**Deduce, Deduction, Deductive** A priori, Assume, Conclude, Corollary, Derive, Discount, Gather, Illation, Infer(ence), Rebate, Recoup, Stoppage, Surmise, Syllogism

**Deed(s)** Achievement, Act(ion), Atweel, Charta, Charter, Escrol(l), Escrow, Exploit, Fact(um), Indeed, Indenture, Manoeuvre, Muniments, Starr, TITLE

**Deem** Consider, Opine, Ordain, Proclaim, Think

**Deep(en), Deeply** Bass(o), Brine, Briny, Enhance, Excavate, Grum, Gulf, Hadal, Intense, Low, Mindanao, Mysterious, OCEAN, Profound, Re-enter, Rich, Sea, Upsee, Ups(e)y

**Deep-rooted** Inveterate

**Deer(-like)** Axis, Bambi, Barasing(h)a, Brocket, Buck, Cariacou, Carjacou, Cervine, Chevrotain, Chital, Doe, Elaphine, Elk, Hart, Moose, Mouse, Muntjac, Muntjak, Pricket, Pudu, Rein, Roe, Rusa, Sambar, Sambur, Sika, Sorel(l), Spade, Spay(d), Spitter, Spottie, Stag(gard), Tragule, Wapiti

**Deer-hunter** Tinchel

**Deface** Disfigure, Spoil

> **Defaced** may indicate first letter missing

**Defame, Defamation** Abase, Blacken, Calumny, Cloud, Denigrate, Detract, Dishonour, Libel, Mud, Slander, Smear, Stigmatise, Traduce, Vilify

**Default(er)** Absentee, Bilk, Dando, Delinquent, Flit, Levant, Neglect, Omission, Waddle, Welsh

**Defeat(ed), Defeatist** Beat, Best, Caning, Capot, Codille, Conquer, Counteract, Debel, Defeasance, Demolish, Discomfit, Dish, Ditch, Fatalist, Floor, Foil, Foyle, Hammer, Hiding, Lick, Loss, Lurch, Master, Mate, Negative, Out, OVERCOME, Overthrow, Reverse, Rout, Rubicon, Scupper, Set, Sisera, Stump, Thrash, Thwart, Tonk, Trounce, Vanquish, War, Waterloo, Whap, Whip, Whitewash, Worst

**Defecate** Horse, Shit

**Defect(ion), Defective, Defector** Abandon, Amateur, Apostasy, Bug, Faulty, Flaw, FORSAKE, Hamartia, Manky, Mote, Natural, Psellism, Renegade, Renegate, Ridgel, Ridgil, Rig, Rogue, Runagate, Shortcoming, Terrace, Treason, Trick, Want, Weakness

**Defence, Defend(er)** Abat(t)is, Alibi, Antibody, Antidote, Antihistamine, Apologia, Back, Bailey, Barbican, Barmkin, Barricade, Bastion, Battery, Battlement, Bulwark, Calt(h)rop, Catenaccio, CD, Champion, Curtain, Demibastion, Ditch, Embrasure, Herisson, Hold, J(i)u-jitsu, Justify, Kaim, Keeper, Maintain, Martello Tower, Miniment, Moat, Muniment, Palisade, Parapet, Rampart, Redan, Redoubt, Resist, Ringwall, SHELTER, Shield, Stonewall, Support, Tenail(le), Testudo, Tower, Trench, Trou-de-loup, Uphold, Vindicate, Wall, Warran(t)

**Defenceless** Helpless, Inerm, Naked, Vulnerable

**Defendant** Accused, Apologist, Respondent, Richard Roe

**Defer(ence), Deferential** Bow, Delay, Dutiful, Homage, Morigerous, Obeisant, Pace, Polite, Postpone, Procrastinate, Protocol, Respect, Submit, Suspend, Waive, Yield

**Defiance, Defiant, Defy** Acock, Bold, Brave, Dare, Daring, Disregard, Outbrave, Outdare, Recusant, Stubborn, Unruly

**Deficiency, Deficient** Absence, Acapnia, Anaemia, Beriberi, Defect, Inadequate, Incomplete, Kwashiorkor, Lack, Osteomalacia, Scarcity, Shortage, Spanaemia, Want

> **Deficient** may indicate an anagram

**Deficit** Anaplerotic, Arrears, Defective, Ischemia, Loss, Poor, Shortfall

**Defile(ment)** Abuse, Barranca, Barranco, Besmear, Col, Conspurcation, Desecrate, Dishonour, Donga, Enseam, FOUL, Gate, Gorge, Gully, Inquinate, Inseem, Kloof, Pass, Pollute, Poort, Ravine, Roncesvalles, Smear, Spoil, SULLY

**Define(d), Definition, Definitive** Decide, Demarcate, Determine, Diorism, Distinct, Explain, Fix, Limit, Set, Tangible, Term

**Definite(ly)** Classic, Clear, Emphatic, Firm, Hard, Positive, Precise, Specific, Sure, Yes

**Deflate** Burst, Collapse, Flatten, Lower, Prick

**Deflect(or)** Avert, Bend, Detour, Diverge, Divert, Glance, Otter, Paravane, Refract, Snick, Swerve, Throw, Trochotron, Veer

**Deform(ed), Deformity** Anamorphosis, Blemish, Crooked, Disfigure, Distort, Gammy, Mishapt, Mutilate, Polt-foot, Stenosed, Talipes, Valgus, Warp

> **Deformed** may indicate an anagram

**Defraud** Bilk, Cheat, Cozen, Gyp, Mulct, Sting, Swindle, Trick

**Defray** Bear, Cover, Meet

**Defrost** Thaw

**Defunct** Deceased, Extinct, Obsolete

> **Defy** see DEFIANCE

**Degenerate, Degeneration** Acorn-shell, Ascidian, Atrophy, Balanus, Cirrhipedea, Cirrhipedia, Cirrhipod(a), Cirripedea, Cirripedia, Decadent, Deprave, Descend, Deteriorate, Fatty, Kaliyuga, Pejorate, Pervert, Rakehell, Relapse, Retrogress, Salp, Tunicate

**Degrade, Degradation** Abase, Cheapen, Culvertage, Debase, Demote, Diminish, Disennoble, Humble, Imbase, Lessen, Lower, SHAME, Waterloo

**Degree(s)** Aegrotat, As, Azimuthal, BA, Baccalaureate, BCom, BD, D, Desmond, Doctoral, Extent, Firman, First, German, Gradation, Grade, Grece, Gree(s), Greece, Gre(e)se, Grice, Griece, Grize, IN A HIGH DEGREE, Lambeth, Latitude, Letters, Level, MA, Measure, Nuance, Peg, PhD, Pin, Poll, Rate, Remove, Second, Stage, Status, Step, Third, Water

**Dehiscence** Suture

**Dehydrate** Exsiccate

**Deification, Deify** Apotheosis

**Deign** Condescend, Stoop

**Deity** Avatar, Demogorgon, Faun, Divine, GOD(DESS), Idolise, Immortalise, Numen, Pan, Satyr

**Dejected, Dejection** Abase, Abattu, Alamort, Amort, Chap-fallen, Crab, Crestfallen, Despondent, Dismay, Dispirited, Downcast, Gloomy, Hangdog, Humble, Melancholy

**Delay(ed)** Ambage, Avizandum, Check, Cunctator, Defer, Detention, Fabian, Filibuster, For(e)slow, Forsloe, Frist, Hesitate, Hinder, Hold up, Impede, Laches, Lag, Late, Laten, Let, Linger, Mora(torium), Obstruct, Procrastinate, Prolong, Prorogue, Remanet, Reprieve, Retard, Sloth, STALL, Stand-over, Stay, Wait

**Delectable** Delicious, Luscious, Tasty

**Delegate, Delegation** Agent, Amphictyon, Appoint, Assign, Decentralise, Depute, Mission, Nuncio, Representative, Transfer, Vicarial

**Delete** Cancel, Erase, Expunge, Purge, Rase, Scratch, Scrub

**Deliberate(ly)** Adagio, Consider, Debate, Intentional, Meditate, Moderate, Prepensely, Ponder, Studied, Voulu, Witting

**Delicacy, Delicate** Airy-fairy, Beccafico, Canape, Cate, Caviare, Dainty, Difficult, Discreet, Ectomorph, Ethereal, Flimsy, Fine, Finesse, Fragile, FRAIL, Gossamer, Guga, Hothouse, Inconie, Incony, Kickshaw, Kidglove, Light, Morbidezza, Nesh, Nicety, Oyster, Sensitive, Soft, Subtle(ty), Tender, Ticklish, Tidbit, Titbit, Truffle

**Delicious** Ambrosia, Delectable, Exquisite, Fragrant, Gorgeous, Lekker, Scrummy, Tasty, Toothsome

**Delight(ed), Delightful** Bliss, Chuff, Delice, Dreamy, Enamour, Enrapture, Exuberant, Felicity, Fetching, Frabjous, Gas, Glad, Glee, Gratify, Joy, Overjoy, Please, Pleasure, RAPTURE, Regale, Scrummy, Super, Taking, Turkish, Whee, Whoopee

**Delineate**  Draft, Sketch, Trace

**Delinquent**  Bodgie, Criminal, Halbstarker, Negligent, Offender, Ted

**Delirious, Delirium**  Deranged, DT, Frenetic, Frenzy, Insanity, Mania, Phrenetic, Wild

**Deliver(ance), Deliverer, Delivery**  Accouchement, Birth, Bowl, Caesarean, Convey, Escape, Give, Liberate, Orate, Over, Pronounce, Redeem, Release, Relieve, Render, Rendition, RESCUE, Rid, Round(sman), Salvation, Save, Sell, Speak, Tice, Transfer, Underarm, Underhand, Utter, Wide, Yorker

**Dell**  Dale, Dargle, Dene, Dimble, Dingle, Dingly, Glen, Valley

**Delphic**  Pythian

**Delta**  D, Triangle

**Delude, Delusion**  Bilk, Cheat, Deceive, Fallacy, Fool, Hoax, MISLEAD, Trick

**Deluge**  Avalanche, Flood, Ogygian, Saturate, Submerge, SWAMP

**De luxe**  Extra, Plush, Special

**Delve**  Burrow, Dig, Excavate, Exhume, Explore, Probe, Search

**Demagogue**  Agitator, Leader, Mobsman, Speaker, Tribune

**Demand(ing)**  Call, Claim, Cry, Dun, Exact, Exigent, Final, Hest, INSIST, Market, Need, Order, Postulate, Pressure, Request, Rush, Sale, Stern, Summon, Ultimatum, Want

**Demean**  Comport, Debase, Degrade, Lower, Maltreat

**Demeanour**  Air, Bearing, Conduct, Expression, Front, Mien, Port

**Demented**  Crazy, Hysterical, Insane, Mad

**Demi-god**  Aitu, Daemon, Garuda, Hero

**Demi-mondaine**  Cocotte, LOOSE WOMAN, Prostitute

**Demise**  Death, Decease, Finish

**Demo**  March, Parade, Protest, Rally, Sit-in

**Democracy, Democrat**  D, Locofoco, Montagnard, Popular, Republic, Tammany

**Demoiselle**  Damselfish

**Demolish, Demolition**  Devastate, Devour, Floor, Level, Rack, RAZE, Smash, Wreck

> **Demon**  see DEVIL

**Demoness**  Lilith

**Demonstrate, Demonstration, Demonstrator**  Agitate, Barrack, Display, Endeictic, Explain, Evince, Maffick, Manifest, March, Morcha, Portray, Protest, Prove, Provo, SHOW, Sit-in

**Demoralize**  Bewilder, Corrupt, Destroy, Shatter, Unman, Weaken

**Demote, Demotion**  Comedown, Degrade, Embace, Embase, Reduce, Relegate, Stellenbosch

**Demur** Hesitate, Jib, Object

**Demure** Coy, Mim, Modest, Prenzie, Primsie, Sedate, Shy

**Den** Dive, Domdaniel, Hide-away, Hell, Home, Lair, Lie, Room, Shebeen, Study, Sty, Wurley

> **Denial** see DENY

**Denigrate** Besmirch, Blacken, Defame, Tar

**Denim** Jeans

**Denizen** Diehard, Inhabitant, Resident

**Denomination** Category, Cult, Sect, Variety

**Denote** Import, Indicate, Mean, Signify

**Denouement** Climax, Coda, Exposure, Outcome

**Denounce, Denunciation** Ban, Commination, Condemn, Criticise, Decry, Diatribe, Proclaim, Proscribe, Stigmatise, Upbraid

**Denry** Card

**Density** Compact, Firm, Opaque, Solid, Spissitude, Tesla, Thick, Woofy

**Dent** Batter, Dancette, Depress, Dimple, Dint, Nock, V

**Dental, Dentist** DDS, Extractor, Kindhart, LDS, Odontic, Periodontic, Toothy

**Dentures** Plate, Wallies

**Deny, Denial, Denier** Abnegate, Antinomian, Aspheterism, Bar, Contradict, Démenti, Disavow, Disenfranchise, Disown, Forswear, GAINSAY, Nay, Negate, Nick, Protest, Refuse, Renague, Renay, Reneg(e), Renegue, Reney, Renig, Renounce, Reny, Repudiate, Withhold

**Deoxidise** Outgas, Reduce

**Depart(ed), Departure** Abscond, Absquatulate, Bunk, D, Dead, Decession, Defunct, Die, Digress, Divergence, Exit, Exodus, Flight, GO, Leave, Lucky, Remue, Vade

**Department** Allier, Angers, Arrondissement, Arta, Aude, Branch, Bureau, Cantal, Cher, Commissariat, Deme, Division, Eure, Faculty, FO, Gironde, Greencloth, Hanaper, Loire, Lot, Ministry, Nome, Nomos, Office, Oise, Orne, Province, Region, Sanjak, Savoie, Secretariat(e), Section, Somme, Sphere, Treasury, Tuscany, Var, Vienne, Yonne

**Depend(ant), Dependency, Dependent** Addicted, Child, Client, Colony, Conditional, Contingent, Count, Dangle, Fief, Hang, Hinge, Icicle, Lean, Minion, Pensioner, Relier, Rely, Retainer, Subject, Trust, Turn on, Vassal

**Dependable** Reliable, Reliant, Secure, Solid, Sound, Staunch, Sure, TRUSTWORTHY

**Depict** Delineate, Display, Draw, Limn, Paint, Portray, Represent

**Depilate, Depilatory** Grain, Rusma, Slate

**Deplete** Diminish, Drain, Exhaust, Reduce

**Deplorable, Deplore** Base, Bemoan, Chronic, Complain, Dolorous,

Grieve, Lament, Mourn, Piteous, Rue

**Deploy(ment)**   Extend, Herse, Unfold, Use

> **Deploy(ment)**   may indicate an anagram

**Deport(ment)**   Address, Air, Banish, BEARING, Carriage, Demeanour, Mien, Renvoi, Renvoy

**Depose, Deposition**   Affirm, Banish, Dethrone, Displace, Dispossess, Overthrow, Pieta, Testify

**Deposit**   Alluvial, Alluvium, Arcus, Bank, Bergmehl, Calc-sinter, Calc-tuff, Caliche, Cave-earth, Coral, Crag, Delta, Depone, Diluvium, File, Firn, Fur, Gyttja, Kieselguhr, Land, Lay, Lodge(ment), Loess, Löss, Measure, Natron, Park, Placer, Plank, Plaque, Repose, Residuum, Saburra, SEDIMENT, Silt, Sinter, Sludge, Stockwork, Stratum, Surety, Tartar, Terramara, Terramare, Tophus

**Depot**   Barracoon, Base, Depository, Station, Terminus, Treasure-city, Warehouse

**Depraved, Depravity**   Bestial, Cachexia, Cachexy, CORRUPT, Dissolute, Evil, Immoral, Low, Rotten, Turpitude, Ugly, Vice, Vicious, Vile

**Deprecate**   Censure, Deplore, Expostulate, Reproach

**Depreciate**   Abase, Belittle, Derogate, Detract, Discount

**Depredate, Depredation**   Pillage, Plunder, Rob

**Depress(ed), Depressing, Depression**   Accablé, Alamort, Alveolus, Amort, Attrist, Blight, Blues, Cafard, Canada, Canyon, Chill, Col, Combe, Couch, Crab, Crush, Cyclone, Dampen, Deject, Despair, Dell, Dene, Dent, DIMPLE, Dip, Dispirit, Dolina, Doline, Drear, Drere, Dumpish, Exanimate, Flatten, Fonticulus, Foss(ula), Fossa, Fovea, Frog, Ghilgai, Gilgai, Gilgie, Glen, Gloom, Graben, Ha-ha, Hammer, Hilar, Hilum, Hollow, Howe, Hyp, Kick(-up), Lacuna, Leaden, Low(ness), Moping, Neck, Pit, Prostrate, Recession, Re-entrant, Sad, Saddle, Salt-cellar, Salt-pan, Sink, Sinus, Slot, SLUMP, Swag, Swale, Trough, Vale, Valley

**Deprive(d), Deprivation**   Bereft, Deny, Disfrock, Disseise, Disseize, Have-not, Hunger, Reduce, Remove, Withhold

**Depth**   F, Fathom, Gravity, Intensity, Isobath, Pit, Profundity

**Deputise, Deputy**   Act, Agent, Aide, Assistant, Commissary, Delegate, Legate, Lieutenant, Locum, Loot, Proxy, Represent, Standby, Sub, Substitute, Surrogate, Vice, Viceregent, Vidame

**Derange(d)**   Craze, Détraqué, Disturb, Insane, Manic, Troppo, Unhinge, Unsettle

**Derby**   Eponym, Hat, Kentucky, Kiplingcotes, Race

**Deride, Derision, Derisive**   Contempt, Gup, Guy, Hoot, Jeer, Mock, Raspberry, RIDICULE, Sardonic, Scoff, Scorn, Snifty, Yah

**Derive, Derivation, Derivative**   Ancestry, Deduce, Descend, Extract, Get, Of, Offshoot, Origin, Pedigree, Secondary

> **Dermatitis**   see SKIN DISEASE

**Derogate, Derogatory** Belittle, Decry, Defamatory, Demeaning, Detract, Discredit, Personal, Snide

**Deronda** Daniel

**Derrick** Crane, Davit, Hoist, Jib, Spar

**Dervish** Calender, Doseh, Mawlawi, Mevlevi, Revolver, Santon, Whirling

**Descant** Comment, Discourse, Faburden, Melody, Song

**Descartes** René

**Descend(ant), Descent** Ancestry, Avail, Avale, Bathos, Blood, Chute, Cion, Decline, Degenerate, Derive, Dismount, Dive, Drop, Epigon(e), Extraction, Heir, Heraclid, LINEAGE, Offspring, Pedigree, Prone, Rappel, Scarp, Scion, Seed, Shelve, Sien(t), Sink, Stock, Vest, Volplane

**Describe, Description** Blurb, Define, Delineate, Depict, Epithet, Narrate, Outline, Paint, Portray, Recount, Relate, Report, Sea-letter, Sketch, Specification, Term, Trace

> **Describing** may indicate 'around'

**Descry** Behold, Discern, Get, Notice, Perceive

**Desecrate, Desecration** Abuse, Defile, Dishallow, Profane, Sacrilege, Unhallow

> **Desecrated** may indicate an anagram

**Desert(s), Deserted, Deserter** Abandon, Apostasy, Arabian, Arid, Arunta, Atacama, AWOL, Barren, Bug, Bunk, Come-uppance, D, Defect, Desolate, Dissident, Due, Empty, Eremic, Fail, Foresay, Forhoo, Forhow, Forlorn, Forsake, Forsay, Frondeur, Gila, Gobi, Heterodox, Kalahari, Merit, Mojave, Nafud, Namib, Negev, Nubia, Ogaden, Pindan, Rat, Refusenik, Reg, RENEGADE, Reward, Run, Sahara, Sahel, Sands, Secede, Simpson, Sinai, Sonoran, Sturt, Syrian, Tergiversate, Thar, Turncoat, Ust(y)urt, Void, Wadi, Waste, Worthiness

**Deserve(d)** Condign, Earn, MERIT, Worthy

**Desiccate(d)** Dry, Sere

**Design(er)** Adam, Aim, Architect, Batik, Cartoon, Castrametation, Create, Damascene, Decor, Depict, Devise, Draft, End, Engine(r), Engineer, Erté, Etch, Fashion, Former, Hitech, Iconic, Intend(ment), Intent(ion), Logo, Marquetry, Mean, Morris, Mosaic, Motif, PLAN, Plot, Propose, Quant, Ruse, Schema, Scheme, Seal, Sheraton, Sketch, Tatow, Tattoo, Tatu, Think, Tooling, Vignette, Watermark

**Designate** Earmark, Style, Title

**Desirable, Desire, Desirous** Ambition, Appetite, Aspire, Avid, Best, Cama, Conation, Covet, Crave, Cupidity, Epithymetic, Fancy, Gasp, Hanker, Hunger, Itch, Kama(deva), Le(t)ch, Libido, Long, Lust, Mania, Owlcar, Reck, Request, Residence, Salt, Streetcar, Thirst, Velleity, Vote, Want, Whim, Will, Wish, Yearn, Yen

**Desist** Abandon, Cease, Curb, Quit, Stop

**Desk** Ambo, Bureau, Carrel(l), Cheveret, Desse, Davenport, Devonport,

E(s)critoire, Lectern, Lettern, Prie-dieu, Pulpit, Roll-top, Vargueno

**Desolate** Bare, Barren, Devastate, Disconsolate, Forlorn, Gaunt, Gousty, Waste, Woebegone

**Despair, Desperate** Acharne, Despond, Dire, Extreme, Frantic, Giant, Gloom, Hairless, Headlong, Reckless, Unhopeful, Urgent, Wanhope

> **Despatch** see DISPATCH

**Desperado** Bandit, Bravo, Ruffian, Terrorist

**Despicable** Abject, Base, Caitiff, Cheap, Churl, Contemptible, Heinous, Ignoble, Ignominious, Mean, Shabby, Wretched

**Despise** Condemn, Contemn, Forhow, Hate, Ignore, Scorn, Spurn, Vilify, Vilipend

**Despite** For, Malgré, Notwithstanding, Pace, Though, Venom

**Despoil** Mar, Ravage, Vandalise

**Despondent** Dejected, Downcast, Forlorn, Gloomy, Sad

**Despot(ism)** Autarchy, Autocrat, Caesar, Darius, Dictator, Napoleon, Nero, Satrap, Stratocrat, Tsar, Tyrant, Tzar

**Dessert** Afters, Bombe, Coupe, Fool, Kissel, Mousse, Parfait, Pashka, Pavlova, Pudding, Tiramisu, Trifle, Vacherin

**Destination, Destine** Design, End, Fate, Foredoom, Goal, Home, Intend, Joss, Port, Purpose, Weird

**Destiny** Doom, FATE, Karma, Kismet, Lot, Moira

**Destitute** Bankrupt, Bare, Broke, Devoid, Helpless, Indigent, Needy, Poor, Sterile

**Destroy(er)** Annihilate, Antineutrino, Antineutron, Antiparticle, Apollyon, Blight, D, Deface, Delete, Demolish, Denature, Destruct, Dissolve, Efface, End, Eradicate, Erase, Estrepe, Exterminate, Extirpate, Flivver, Fordo, Harry, KILL, Murder, Perish, Ravage, Raze, Ruin, Saboteur, Slash, Smash, Spiflicate, Stew-can, Stonker, Subvert, Undo, Uproot, Vandal, Vitiate, Wreck, Zap

**Destruction, Destructive** Adverse, Bane, Can, Collapse, Devastation, Doom, Downfall, End, Grave, Havoc, Holocaust, Kali, Lethal, Loss, Pernicious, Rack, Ragnarok, Ravage, Sabotage, Stroy, Wrack

**Desultory** Aimless, Cursory, Fitful, Idle

**Detach(ed), Detachment** Abstract, Alienate, Aloof, Body, Clinical, Cut, Detail, Isolate, Loose, Outlying, Outpost, Separate, Sever, Staccato, Stoic, Unfasten, Unhinge

**Detached work** Ravelin

**Detail(s), Detailed** Dock, Elaborate, Embroider, Expatiate, Explicit, Expound, Instance, ITEM, Minutiae, Nicety, Particular(ise), Point, Recite, Relate, Respect, Send

> **Detailed** may indicate last letter missing

**Detain, Detention** Arrest, Buttonhole, Collar, Custody, Delay, Detinue,

Gate, Glasshouse, Hinder, Intern, Keep, Retard, Stay, WITHHOLD

**Detect(ive), Detector**  Agent, Arsène, Asdic, Bloodhound, Brown, Bucket, Busy, Catch, Chan, CID, Cuff, Dick, Discover, Divine, Doodlebug, Dupin, Espy, Eye, Fed, Find, Flambeau, Fortune, French, Geigercounter, Geophone, Gumshoe, Hanaud, Hercule, Holmes, Interpol, Investigator, Jack, Lecoq, Lupin, Maigret, Nose, PI, Pinkerton, Plant, Poirot, Private eye, Prodnose, Radar, Reagent, Rumble, Scent, Scerne, Sense, Sensor, Shadow, Shamus, Sherlock, SLEUTH, Sonar, Spot, Tabaret, Take, Tec, Thorndyke, Toff, Trace, Trent, Vance, Wimsey, Yard

**Detent**  Pawl, Trigger

**Deter**  Block, Check, Daunt, Dehort, Delay, Prevent, Restrain

**Detergent**  Cleaner, Solvent, Syndet, Tepol, Whitener

**Deteriorate, Deterioration**  Decadence, Degenerate, Rust, Worsen

> **Deterioration**  may indicate an anagram

**Determination, Determine(d)**  Arbitrament, Ascertain, Assign, Assoil, Bent, Condition, Dead-set, DECIDE, Define, Dogged, Drive, Fix, Govern, Grit(ty), Hell-bent, Influence, Intent, Judgement, Law, Out, Purpose, RESOLUTE, Resolve, Rigwiddie, Rigwoodie, Set, Settle, Shape, Stalwart, Weigh

> **Determination**  may indicate 'last letter'

**Detest(able)**  Abhor, Despise, Execrable, Execrate, Hate, Loathsome, Pestful, Vile

**Detonate, Detonator**  Blast, Explode, Fire, Fuse, Fuze, Ignite, Kindle, Plunger, Primer, Saucisse, Saucisson, Tetryl

**Detour**  Bypass, Deviate, Divert

**Detract**  Belittle, Decry, Diminish, Discount, Disparage

**Detriment(al)**  Adverse, Damage, Harm, Injury, Loss, Mischief

**Deuce**  Dickens, Old Harry, Twoer

**Deuteron**  Diplon

**Devalue**  Debase, Reduce, Undermine

**Devastate**  Demolish, Destroy, Overwhelm, Ravage, Sack, Waste

**Develop(er), Development**  Advance, Amidol, Aplasia, Breed, Build, Educe, Elaborate, Enlarge, Epigenetic, Evolve, Expand, Expatriate, Fulminant, Gestate, Grow, Hatch, Hydroquinone, Hypo, Imago, Improve, Larva, Mature, Metamorphose, Metol, Oidium, Pathogeny, Pullulate, Pupa, Pyro, Ribbon, Ripe(n), Shape, Soup, Sprawl

> **Develop**  may indicate an anagram

**Deviant, Deviate, Deviation**  Aberrance, Abnormal, Anomaly, Brisure, Deflect, Depart, Digress, Diverge, Divert, Error, Kurtosis, Pervert, Quartile, Sheer, Solecism, Sport, Stray, Swerve, TURN, Veer, Wander, Wend

**Device**  Appliance, Artifice, Audio, Baton-sinister, Bearing, Bug, Bungee, Charge, Comparator, Compass, Dodge, Dongle, Elevon, Emblem, Engine, Episemon, Excelsior, Expedient, Frame, Fuse, Gadget, Geophone,

Gimmick, Gizmo, Gobo, Gubbins, Imprese, Instrument, LED, Logo, Machine, Metronome, Mnemonic, Modern, Monogram, Orle, Pattern, Petar(d), Plan, Prism, Ratchet, Relay, Resonator, Rest, Selsyn, Sensor, Servo, Solenoid, Sonde, Sprag, STRATAGEM, Subterfuge, Synchro, Tactic, Tokamak, Trademark, Trick, Widget

**Devil(ish)** Abaddon, Afree, Afrit, Amaimon, Apollyon, Asmodeus, Atua, Auld Hornie, Azazel, Barbason, Beelzebub, Belial, Buckra, Clootie, Cloots, Dasyure, Davy Jones, Deev, Deil, Demogorgon, Demon, Deuce, Devling, Diable, Diabolic, Dickens, Div, Drudge, Eblis, Familiar, Fend, Fiend, Ghoul, Goodman, Goodyear, Grill, Hangie, Hornie, Iblis, Imp, Incubus, Infernal, Lamia, Legion, Lilith, Lori, Lucifer, Mahoun(d), Manta, Mara, Mazikeen, Mephistopheles, Nick, Old Bendy, Old Nick, Old One, Old Pandemonium, Old Poker, Old Roger, Old Split-foot, Old Toast, Ragamuffin, Rahu, Ralph, Satan, Sathanas, Satyr, Scour, Scratch, Screwtape, Season, Setebos, Shaitan, Shedeem, Sorra, Succubine, Succubus, Tailard, Tasmanian, Tempter, Titivil, Tutivillus, Wicked, Wirricow, Worricow, Worrycow, Zernebock

**Devious** Braide, Cunning, Deep, Erroneous, Implex, Indirect, Scheming, Shifty, Subtle, Tortuous, Tricky

**Devise(d)** Arrange, Contrive, Decoct, Hit-on, Imagine, Invenit, Invent, Plot

**Devitrified** Ambitty

**Devoid** Barren, Destitute, Empty, Vacant, Wanting

**Devolve** Occur, Result, Transmit

**Devote(e), Devotion(al), Devoted** Addiction, Angelus, Attached, Bhakti, Consecrate, Corban, Dedicate, Employ, Fan, Fervid, Fiend, Holy, Hound, Loyalty, Novena, Ophism, Passion, Pious, Religioso, S(h)akta, Solemn, True, Zealous

**Devour** Consume, Eat, Engorge, Engulf, Manducate, Moth-eat, Scarf, Scoff, SWALLOW

> **Devour** may indicate one word inside another

**Devout** Holy, Pious, Reverent, Sant, Sincere

**Dew(y)** Bloom, Moist, Mountain, Roral, Roric, Rorid, Roscid, Serene, Tranter

**Dexterity, Dexterous** Adept, Adroit, Aptitude, Cleverness, Craft, HANDY, Knack, Shrewd, Sleight, Slick

**Diabolic** Cruel, DEVILISH, Infernal

**Diadem** Coronet, Fillet, Garland, Tiara

**Diagnose, Diagnosis** Findings, Identify, Scan

**Diagonal** Bias, Cater(-corner), Counter, Oblique, Slant, Solidus, Twill

**Diagram** Chart, Drawing, Figure, Graph, Grid, Map, Plan, Plat, Schema, Venn

**Dial(ling)** Face, Mug, Phiz, Phone, STD, Visage

**Dialect** Accent, Aeolic, Alemannic, Burr, Doric, Eolic, Erse, Geechee,

Geordie, Idiom, Jargon, Joual, Koine, Lallans, Landsmaal, Lingo, Norman, Norn, Parsee, Patois, Prakrit, Scouse, Taal, Talkee-talkee, Tongue, Tshi, Yenglish, Yinglish

**Dialogue** Colloquy, Conversation, Critias, Discussion, Exchange, Lazzo, Speech, Talk, Upspeak

**Diameter** Breadth, Calibre, Gauge, Width

**Diamond(s)** Adamant, Boart, Brilliant, Carbonado, Cullinan, D, DE, Delaware, Eustace, Florentine, Hope, Ice, Jim, Koh-i-noor, Lasque, Lattice, Lozenge, Paragon, Pick, Pitch, Pitt, Rhinestone, Rhomb, Rock, Rose-cut, Rosser, Rough, Sancy, Solitaire, Sparklers, Suit

**Diana** Artemis, Di

**Diapason** Ottava

**Diaphanous** Clear, Sheer, Translucent

**Diaphoretic** Sweater

**Diaphragm** Cap, Mid-riff

**Diaresis** Trema

> **Diarist** see DIARY

**Diarrhoea** Lientery, Runs, Trots

**Diary, Diarist** Chronicle, Dale, Day-book, Evelyn, Hickey, Journal, Kilvert, Log, Nobody, Pepys, Pooter, Record

**Diatribe** Harangue, Invective, Philippic, Tirade

**Dice(y)** Aleatory, Astragals, Bale, Bones, Chop, Craps, Cube, Dodgy, Fulham, Fullams, Fullans, Gourd(s), Highman, Shoot, Snake-eyes, Tallmen

**Dichotomy** Split

**Dick(y), Dickey** Clever, Deadeye, Front, Moby, OED, Policeman, Rumble, Shaky, Shirt, Tec, Tonneau, Tucker, Unstable, Wankle, Weak, Whittington

> **Dick** may indicate a dictionary

**Dickens** Boz, Deuce, Devil, Mephistopheles

**Dicker** Bargain, Barter, Haggle, Trade

> **Dicky** may indicate an anagram

**Dictate, Dictator(ial)** Amin, Autocrat, Caesar, Castro, Cham, Command, Czar, Decree, Despot, Duce, Franco, Fu(e)hrer, Gauleiter, Hitler, Impose, Lenin, Ordain, Peremptory, Peron, Salazar, Shogun, Stalin, Tell, Tito, Tsar, Tyrant, Tzar

**Diction** Language, Speech, Style

**Dictionary** Alveary, Calepin, Chambers, Etymologicon, Fowler, Gazetteer, Glossary, Gradus, Hobson-Jobson, Johnson's, Idioticon, Larousse, Lexicon, Lexis, OED, Onomasticon, Thesaurus, Webster, Wordbook

**Did** Began, Couth, Fec(it), Gan

**Didactic** Sermonical

**Diddle** Cheat, Con, Hoax

**Dido** Antic, Caper, Elissa

**Die(d), Dying** Ache, Choke, Crater, Croak, Cube, D, Decadent, Desire, End, Evanish, Exit, Expire, Fade, Fail, Forfair, Fulham, Fulhan, Fullam, Go, Highman, Hop, Long, Morendo, Moribund, Ob(iit), Orb, Pass, Perdendosi, Perish, Peter, Snuff, Solidum, Sphacelation, Stamp, Sterve, Succumb, Suffer, Swage, Swelt, Tine, Wane

**Diehard** Blimp, Fanatic, Intransigent, Standpatter, Zealot

**Diet(er)** Assembly, Bant(ing), Council, Dail, Eat, Fare, Landtag, Lent, Parliament, Reduce, Regimen, Slim, Solid, Sprat, Staple, Strict, Tynwald, Worms

**Dietetics** Sit(i)ology

**Differ(ence), Different(ly)** Allo, Barney, Change, Contrast, Diesis, Disagree, Discord, Disparate, Dispute, Dissent, Distinct, Diverge, Else, Nuance, Other, Othergates, Otherguess, Otherness, Otherwise, Separate, Tiff, Unlike, Variform, Various, Vary

**Differential** Taxeme

**Difficult(y)** Ado, Aporia, Arduous, Augean, Bolshie, Bother, Catch, Corner, Dysphagia, Formidable, Gordian, HARD, Hassle, Hazard, Hiccup, Hobble, Hole, Ill, Kink, Knot, Lurch, Net, Nodus, Obstacle, Pig, Plight, Quandary, Recalcitrant, Rough, Rub, Scrape, Scrub, Setaceous, Snag, Soup, Steep, Stick, Stiff, Strait, Stubborn, Trial, Une(a)th

**Diffident** Bashful, Modest, Reserved, Shy

**Diffuse, Diffusion** Disperse, Disseminate, Endosmosis, Exude, Osmosis, Pervade, Radiate, Spread

**Dig(ger), Digging, Digs, Dig up** Antipodean, Australian, Beadle, Bed(e)ral, Billet, Bot, Burrow, Costean, Delve, Enjoy, Excavate, Flea-bag, Fossorial, Gibe, Gird, Graip, Grub, Howk, Jab, Kip, Lair, Like, Lodgings, Mine, Navvy, Nervy, Nudge, Pad, Pioneer, Probe, Prod, Raddleman, Resurrect, Root, Ruddleman, Sap, See, Spade, Spit, Spud, Star-nose, Taunt, Tonnell, Trench, Tunnel, Undermine, Unearth

**Digest(ible), Digestion, Digestive** Abridgement, Absorb, Abstract, Aperçu, Assimilate, Codify, Concoct, Endue, Epitome, Eupepsia, Eupepsy, Gastric, Indew, Indue, Light, Pandect, Pem(m)ican, Peptic, Précis, Salt-cat, SUMMARY

**Digit** Byte, Finger, Hallux, Number, Prehallux, Thumb, Toe

**Dignified, Dignify** August, Elevate, Exalt, Handsome, Honour, Lordly, Majestic, Manly, Proud, Stately

**Dignitary** Dean, Name, Personage, Provost, VIP

**Dignity** Aplomb, Bearing, Cathedra, Face, Glory, Maestoso, Majesty, Nobility, Presence, Scarf

**Digress(ion)** Deviate, Diverge, Ecbole, Episode, Excurse, Maunder, Veer, Wander

**Dike** Bank, Channel, Cludgie, Dam, Ditch, DYKE, Embank(ment),

Estacade, Levee, Wall

**Dilapidate(d), Dilapidation** Decrepit, Desolate, Eroded, Ruined, Tumbledown

**Dilate(d), Dilation, Dilatation** Amplify, Develop, Diastole, Ecstasis, Enlarge, Expand, Increase, Sinus, Tent, Varix

**Dilatory** Protracting, Slow, Sluggish, Tardy

**Dilemma** Choice, Cleft, Dulcarnon, Fix, Horn, Predicament, Quandary

**Dilettante** Aesthete, Amateur, Butterfly, Dabbler, Playboy

**Diligence, Diligent** Active, Application, Assiduous, Coach, Eident, Industry, Sedulous, Studious

**Dill** Anise, Pickle

**Dilute, Dilution** Adulterate, Diluent, Lavage, Simpson, Thin, Water, Weaken

**Dim(ness), Dimwit** Becloud, Blear, Blur, Caligo, Clueless, Dense, Eclipse, Fade, Faint, Feint, Indistinct, Mist, Ninny, Obscure, Overcast, Owl, Shadow

**Dimension** Area, Breadth, Extent, Height, Length, Measure, Size, Volume, Width

**Diminish(ed), Diminuendo, Diminution, Diminutive** Abatement, Assuage, Baby, Contract, Cot(t)ise, Deactivate, Decrease, Détente, Detract, Disparage, Dwarf, Dwindle, Erode, Fourth, Hypocorism(a), Lessen, Lilliputian, Minify, Minus, Mitigate, Petite, Pigmy, Scarp, Small, Toy, Trangle, Wane, Whittle

**Dimple** Dent, Depression, Hollow

**Din** Babel, Charivary, Chirm, Commotion, Deen, Discord, Gunga, Hubbub, NOISE, Rackct, Raird, Randan, Reel, Reird, Uproar, Utis

**Dine, Dining** Aristology, Eat, Feast, Sup

**Dingbat** Doodad

**Dinghy** Shallop, Ship, Skiff

**Dingo** Warrigal

**Dingy** Dark, Dirty, Drear, Dun, Fusc(ous), Grimy, Isabel(la), Isabelline, Lurid, Oorie, Ourie, Owrie, Shabby, Smoky

**Dining-room** Cafeteria, Cenacle, Frater, Hall, Refectory, Restaurant, Triclinium

**Dinner** Banquet, Collation, Feast, Hall, Kail, Kale, Meal, Prandial, Repast

**Dinosaur** Allosaurus, Brachiosaurus, Brontosaurus, Diplodocus, Hadrosaur, Iguanodon, Megalosaur, Prehistoric, Sauropod, Theropod, Triceratops

**Dint** Brunt, Dent, Depression, Force, Means, Power

**Diocese** Bishopric, District, Eparchate, See

**Diogenes** Cynic

**Dioxide** Cassiterite, Needle-tin

**Dip(per)** Baptise, Basin, Bathe, Bob, Brantub, Dabble, Dap, Dean, Dib, Dop, Duck, Dunk, Foveola, Geosyncline, Intinction, Ladle, Ouzel, Paddle, Rinse, Rollercoaster, Salute, Star, Submerge, Tzatziki, Ursa

**Diphthong** Synaeresis

**Diploma** Charter, Parchment, Qualification, Scroll, Sheepskin

**Diplomacy, Diplomat(ic)** Alternat, Ambassador, Attaché, CD, Consul, DA, Dean, Doyen, El(t)chi, Envoy, Fanariot, Gunboat, Legation, Lei(d)ger, Phanariot, Suave, TACT

> **Dippy** may indicate a bather

**Dipsomania** Oenomania

**Dire** Dreadful, Fatal, Fell, Hateful, Ominous, Urgent

**Direct(ly), Director** Administer, Advert, Aim, Airt, Auteur, Board, Boss, Cann, Channel, Charge, Command, Compere, Con(n), Conduct, Control, Cox, Dead, Due, Enjoin, Explicit, Forthright, Frontal, Guide, Helm, Hitchcock, Immediate, Impresario, Instruct, Kappelmeister, Manager, Navigate, Outright, Pilot, Play, Pointblank, Ready, Refer, Regisseur, Rudder, Signpost, Stear, STEER, Straight, Teach, Tell, Vector

**Direction** Aim, Airt, Astern, Bearings, Course, E, End-on, Guidance, Guide, Heading, Keblah, L, Line, N, Orders, Passim, R, Route, Rubric, S, Sanction, Send, Sense, Side, Slap, Tenor, Thataway, Trend, W, Way

**Direction-finder** Asdic, Compass, Decca, Quadrant, Radar, Sextant, Sonar

**Directory** Crockford, Debrett, Kelly, List, Red book, Register

**Dirge** Ballant, Coronach, Dirige, Epicedium, Knell, Monody, Requiem, Song, Threnody

**Dirigible** Airship, Balloon, Blimp, Zeppelin

**Dirk** Dagger, Skean, Whinger, Whiniard, Whinyard

**Dirt(y)** Begrime, Bemoil, Chatty, Clag, Clarty, Colly, Coom, Crock, Crud, Dung, Dust, Earth, Filth, Foul, Gore, Grime, Grufted, Grungy, Impure, Manky, Moit, Mote, Muck, Obscene, Ordure, Pay, Sculdudd(e)ry, Scuzzy, Skulduddery, Smirch, Smut(ch), Sordor, Squalid, Soil, Stain, Trash, Unclean, Yucky, Yukky

**Dis** Hades, Hell

**Disable, Disability** Cripple, Lame, Maim, Paralyse, Scotch, Wreck

**Disadvantage** Detriment, Drawback, Handicap, Mischief, Out, Penalise, Penalty, Supercherie, Upstage

**Disagree(ing), Disagreeable, Disagreement** Argue, Clash, Conflict, Contest, Debate, Differ, Discrepant, Dispute, Dissent, Dissonant, Evil, Friction, Pace, Rift

**Disappear(ing)** Cook, Evanesce, Evanish, Evaporate, Fade, Kook, Latescent, Melt, Occult, Pass, Skedaddle, Slope, VANISH

**Disappoint(ed), Disappointment** Anticlimax, Chagrin, Delude, Disgruntle, Frustrate, Lemon, Letdown, Regret, Sell, Sick, Suck-in, Sucks, Swiz(zle), Thwart

**Disapproval, Disapprove** Animadvert, Boo, Catcall, Censure, Deplore, Deprecate, Frown, Hiss, Napoo, Object, Raspberry, Reject, Reproach, Squint, Umph, Veto, Whiss

**Disarm(ament), Disarming** Bluff, Defuse, Demobilise, Nuclear, Winsome

**Disarrange** Disturb, Muddle, Ruffle, Tousle, Unsettle

**Disarray** Disorder, Mess, Rifle, Tash, Undress

**Disaster, Disastrous** Adversity, Bale, Calamity, Cataclysm(ic), Catastrophe, Debacle, Dire, Doom, Evil, Fatal, Fiasco, Flop, Impostor, Mishap, Rout, Ruin, Titanic, Tragedy

**Disavow** Abjure, Deny, Disclaim, Recant, Retract

**Disbelief, Disbelieve(r)** Acosmism, Anythingarian, Atheism, Incredulity, Mistrust, Nothingarianism, Occamist, Phew, Question, Sceptic

**Disburse** Distribute, Expend, Outlay, Spend

**Disc** Compact, Counter, EP, Epiphragm, Frisbee, Harrow, LP, Mono, O, Paten, Patin, Plate, Rayleigh, Record, Rowel, Slug, Stereo, Stylopodium, Token, Whorl, Wink

**Discard(ed)** Abandon, Crib, Dele, Jettison, Kill, Leave, Obsolete, Off, Offload, Oust, REJECT, Scrap, Shuck

**Discern(ing), Discernment** Acumen, Acute, Descry, Discrimination, Flair, Insight, Perceive, Percipient, Perspicacity, Realise, Sapient, Scry, See, Skry, TASTE, Tell, Wate

**Discharge** Acquit, Arc, Assoil, Blennorrhoea, Cashier, Catamenia, Catarrh, Dejecta, Demob, Disembogue, Disgorge, Dismiss, Dump, Efflux, Egest, Embogue, Emission, Emit, Evacuate, Execute, Expulsion, Exude, Fire, Flower, Flux, Frass, Free, Gleet, Lava, Lay off, Leak, Lochia, Loose, Mute, Offload, Otorrhoea, Oust, Ozaena, Pay, Perform, Planuria, Purulence, Pus, Pyorrhoea, Quietus, Rheum, Rhinorrhoeal, Sack, Salvo, Sanies, Secretion, Shrive, Snarler, Spark, Teem, Unload, Vent, Void

**Disciple** Adherent, Apostle, Catechumen, Follower, John, Judas, Luke, Mark, Matthew, Peter, Simon, Son, Student, Votary

**Discipline, Disciplinarian** Apollonian, Ascesis, Chasten, Chastise, Correct, Despot, Drill, Exercise, Inure, Martinet, Mathesis, Punish, Regulate, Science, Spartan, Stickler, Train, Tutor

**Disclaim(er)** Deny, Disown, No(t)chel, Renounce, REPUDIATE

**Disclose, Disclosure** Apocalypse, Confess, Divulge, Expose, Impart, Leak, Manifest, Propale, PUBLISH, Report, Reveal, Spill, Tell, Unheal, Unhele, Unveil

**Discolour, Discolo(u)ration** Bruise, Dyschroa, Ecchymosis, Livor, Stain, Streak, Tarnish, Tinge, Weather

**Discomfit(ure)** Abash, Confuse, Disconcert, Disturb, Frustrate, Lurch

**Discomfort** Ache, Angst, Heartburn, Pain, Unease

**Disconcert** Confuse, Disturb, Embarrass, Faze, Feeze, Flurry, Nonplus,

Phase, Pheese, Pheeze, Phese, RATTLE, Shatter, Throw, Upset

> **Disconcert(ed)** may indicate an anagram

**Disconnect(ed)** Asynartete, Detach, Disjointed, Sever, Uncouple, Undo, Unplug

**Disconsolate** Desolate, Doleful, Downcast, GLOOMY

**Discontent(ed)** Disquiet, Dissatisfied, Humph, Repined, Sour, Umph

**Discontinue** Abandon, Desist, Drop, Prorogue, Stop, Terminate

**Discord(ant)** Absonant, Conflict, Din, Dispute, Eris, Faction, Hoarse, Jangle, Jar, Raucous, Strife

> **Discord(ant)** may indicate an anagram

**Discount** Agio, Deduct, Disregard, Forfaiting, Invalidate, REBATE

**Discountenance** Disfavour, Efface, Embarrass

**Discourage(ment)** Caution, Chill, Dampen, Dash, Daunt, Demoralise, Deter, Dishearten, Disincentive, Dismay, Dissuade, Enervate, Frustrate, Opposition, Stifle

**Discourse** Address, Argument, Conversation, Descant, Diatribe, Dissertate, Eulogy, Expound, Homily, Lecture, Orate, Preach, Relate, Rigmarole, Sermon

**Discourteous, Discourtesy** Impolite, Insult, Rude, Slight, Uncivil

**Discover(er), Discovery** Amundsen, Ascertain, Betray, Breakthrough, Columbus, Cook, Descry, Detect, Discern, Discure, Eureka, FIND, Heureka, Learn, Locate, Manifest, Moresby, Protege, Rumble, Serendip, Spy, Tasman, Trace, Unearth, Unhale, Unveil

> **Discovered in** may indicate an anagram or a hidden word

**Discredit** Debunk, Decry, Disgrace, Explode, Infamy, Scandal

**Discreet, Discretion** Cautious, Circumspect, Freedom, Option, Polite, Politic, Prudence, Prudent, Trait, Wise

**Discrepancy** Difference, Lack, Shortfall, Variance

**Discrete** Distinct, Separate, Unrelated

**Discriminate, Discriminating, Discrimination** Diacritic, Differentiate, Discern, Distinguish, Invidious, Nasute, Racism, Secerne, Select, Sexism, Subtle, Taste

**Discuss(ing), Discussion** Air, Canvass, Commune, Debate, Dialectic, Dialogue, Dicker, Examine, Handle, Hob and nob, Moot, Over, Palaver, Parley, Rap, Re, Symposium, Tapis, Treatment

**Disdain(ful)** Belittle, Coy, Deride, Despise, Geck, Puh, Sassy, SCORN, Sniffy, Spurn, Supercilious

**Disease(d)** Acromegaly, Affection, Aids, Ailment, Alastrim, Anbury, Ascites, Babesiasis, Bagassosis, Beri-beri, Blight, Blotch, Boba, Brand, Bright's, Bunt, Canker, CD, Cholera, Chorea, Clap, Conk, Contagion, Crewels, Cruels, Cynanche, Dandy-fever, Dartre, Dengue, Diabetes, Diphtheria, Distemper, Dourine, Ebola, Edema, Elephantiasis, Endemic,

English, Epidemic, Ergot, Erysipelas, Farcin, Favus, Fever, Finger and toe, Flu, Frounce, Gaucher's, Glaucoma, Gout, Ilaw, Iatrogenic, Icterus, Ideopathy, Impaludism, Impetigo, Income, Infection, Jaundice, Kuru, Kwashiorkor, Lathyrism, Legionnaire's, Leprosy, Leuc(h)aemia, Leukaemia, Limber-neck, Lues, Lupus, Lurgi, Lurgy, Lyme, Maidism, Malady, Malaria, Marburg, Meazel, Mesel, Mildew, Minamata, Moniliasis, Moor-ill, Morbus, MS, Murrain, Myiasis, Myx(o)edema, Newcastle, Nosology, Oedema, Pandemic, Pathogen, Pebrine, Pellagra, Pellagrin, Phthisis, Phytosis, Pinta, Polio, Porrigo, Pox, Progeria, Purples, Rabid, Rachitis, Rickets, Rose-rash, Rosette, Rot, Sapego, Scabies, Scourge, Scrofula, Serpigo, Shingles, Sickness, Siderosis, Silicosis, Sprue, Suppeago, Surra, Syphilis, TB, Tetanus, Tetters, Trichophytosis, Tular(a)emia, Typhoid, Typhus, Ulitis, Urosis, Variola, VD, Wilson's, Wog, Yaws, Zoonosis, Zymosis

> **Diseased**  may indicate an anagram

**Disembark**  Alight, Detrain, Land

**Disembarrass**  Extricate, Rid, Unthread

**Disembowel**  Exenterate, Eviscerate, Gralloch, Gut

**Disenchant**  Disabuse, Dismay, Embitter

**Disencumber**  Free, Rid, Unburden

**Disengage(d), Disengagement**  Clear, Divorce, Liberate, Loosen, Release, Untie

**Disentangle**  Debarrass, Extricate, Red(d), Solve, Unravel, Unsnarl

**Disestablishmentarian**  Cosmist

**Disfigure(d)**  Agrise, Camsho, Deface, Deform, Mutilate, Scar, Spoil, Tash, Ugly

> **Disfigured**  may indicate an anagram

**Disgorge**  Discharge, Spew, Spill, Vent, Void

**Disgrace**  Atimy, Attaint, Baffle, Blot, Contumely, Degrade, Discredit, Dishonour, Dog-house, Ignominy, Indignity, Infamy, Obloquy, Opprobrium, Scandal, Shame, Shend, Slur, Soil, Stain, Stigma, Yshend

**Disgraceful**  Ignoble, Infamous, Mean, Notorious, Shameful, Turpitude

> **Disgruntled**  may indicate an anagram

**Disguise(d)**  Alias, Blessing, Camouflage, Cloak, Colour, Conceal, Cover, Covert, Dissemble, Hide, Hood, Incog(nito), Mantle, Mask, Masquerade, Obscure, Peruke, Pretence, Pseudonym, Travesty, Veil, Vele, Veneer, Visagiste, Vizard

> **Disguised**  may indicate an anagram

**Disgust(ing)**  Ad nauseam, Aversion, Aw, Bah, Cloy, Discomfort, Execrable, Faugh, Fie, Foh, Irk, Loathsome, Manky, Nauseous, Noisome, Obscene, Odium, Oughly, Ouglie, Pah, Pho(h), Repel, Repugnant, REVOLT, Revulsion, Scomfish, Scumfish, Scunner, SICKEN, Squalid, Ugsome, Yech

**Dish(es)** Allot, Apollo, Ashet, Basin, Belle, Bowl, Brandade, Brose, Charger, Chop suey, Cocotte, Comport, Compote, Compotier, Coolamon, Couscous(ou), Crowdie, Crumble, Curry, Cuscus, Custard, Cutie, Cuvette, Dariole, Dent, Dog's-body, Dole, Dolma, Enchilada, Entrée, Entremets, Epergne, Fajitas, Fal-a-fel, Fel-a-fel, Fool, Fricassee, Friture, Gadogado, Galantine, Gomer, Grail, Guacamole, Haggis, Halloumi, Howtowdie, Jambalaya, Kasha, Kickshaw, Kitchen, Kofta, Korma, Kouskous, Laggen, Laggin, Lanx, Luggie, Manicotti, Maror, Mazarine, Mess, Mous(s)aka, Mousse, Muesli, Padella, Paella, Pakora, Pan, Panada, Pannikin, Paten, Patera, Patin(e), Petri, Pilau, Pilow, Plate, Platter, Poi, Porridge, Porringer, Pot-roast, Quesadilla, Quiche, Raclette, Ragout, Raita, Ramekin, Ramen, Ramequin, Rarebit, Receptacle, Regale, Reistafel, Rijst(t)afel, Salmagundi, Salmi(s), Saltimbocca, Sangraal, Sangreal, Sangrail, Sashimi, Satay, Saucer, Scallop, Serve, Service, Sillabub, Smasher, Soss, Soufflé, Souvlaki(a), Sowans, Sowens, Spitchcock, Squarial, Stroganoff, Subgum, Succotash, Sukiyaki, Sushi, Syllabub, Tamal(e), Taramasalata, Tempura, Teriyaki, Terrine, Timbale, Tostada, Tsamba, Tzatziki, White-pot, Yakitori

**Dishabille** Disarray, Négligé, Undress

**Dishearten** Appal, Core(r), Cow, Daunt, Depress, Discourage, Dispirit

**Dishevel(led)** Blowsy, Blowzy, Mess, Rumpled, Touse, Tumble, Uncombed, Unkempt, Windswept

**Dishonest(y)** Bent, Crooked, Cross, False, Fraud, Graft, Hooky, Hot, Knavery, Malpractice, Shonky, Stink, Twister, Underhand

**Dishonour** Defile, Disgrace, Disparage, Ignominy, Seduce, SHAME, Violate, Wrong

**Disillusion** Disenchant, Sour

**Disinclined** Loth, Off, Reluctant

**Disinfect(ant)** Acriflavin(e), Carbolic, Cineol(e), Cleanse, Eucalyptole, Fumigate, Lysol, Phenol, Purify, Terebene

**Disingenuous** Insincere, Oblique, Two-faced

**Disinherit** Deprive, Dispossess

**Disintegrate, Disintegration** Break, Collapse, Crumble, Decay, Erode, Fragment, Lyse, Lysis, Rd, Rutherford

**Disinter** Exhume, Unearth

**Disinterested** Apathetic, Impartial, Incurious, Mugwump, Unbiased

**Disjointed** Incoherent, Rambling

> **Disk** see DISC

**Dislike(d)** Allergy, Animosity, Animus, Antipathy, Aversion, Derry, Disesteem, Displeasure, Distaste, Lump, Mind, Scunner, Warling

**Dislocate** Break, Displace, Luxate

**Dislodge** Displace, Expel, Oust, Rear, Tuft, Unship, Uproot

**Disloyal(ty)** False, Treason, Unfaithful

**Dismal** Black, Dark, Dowie, Drack, Dreary, Funereal, GLOOMY, Grey,

## Dismantle(d)

Morne, Obital, Sombre, Sullen, Trist(e), Wae

**Dismantle(d)** Divest, Sheer-hulk, Strip, Unrig

**Dismast** Unstep

**Dismay** Amate, Appal, Confound, Consternation, Coo, Daunt, Horrify, Qualms

**Dismiss(al)** Annul, Ax, Boot, Bowl(er), Cancel, Cashier, Catch, Chuck, Congé, Daff, Discard, Discharge, Expulsion, Fire, Mitten, Och, Prorogue, Push, Reform, Remove, Road, Sack, Scout, Send, Shoo, Spit, Stump, Via, York

**Dismount** Alight

**Disobedience, Disobedient, Disobey** Contumacy, Defy, Insubordination, Rebel, Wayward

**Disorder(ed)** Ague, Ailment, Asthma, Ataxia, Catatonia, Chaos, Confuse, Defuse, Derange, Deray, Dishevel, Entropy, Farrago, Hypallage, Mess, Mistemper, MUDDLE, Muss(y), Neurosis, Oncus, Onkus, Pandemonium, Psychosis, Rile, Tousle, Unhinge, Upset

> **Disorder(ed)** may indicate an anagram

**Disorderly** Irregular, Slovenly, Unruly

**Disown** Deny, Disclaim, Disinherit, Renounce, Repudiate, Unget

**Disparage, Disparaging** Abuse, Belittle, Decry, Defame, Denigrate, Depreciate, Detract, Discredit, Lessen, SLANDER, Slur, Snide

**Dispassionate** Calm, Clinical, Composed, Cool, Impartial, Serene

**Dispatch** Bowl, Celerity, Consign, Destroy, Dismiss, Expede, Expedite, Express, Gazette, Kibosh, Kill, Missive, Post, Pronto, Remit, Report, SEND, Ship, Slaughter, Slay

**Dispel** Disperse, Scatter

**Dispensation, Dispense(r), Dispense with** Absolve, Administer, Apothecary, Automat, Ax(e), Cashpoint, Chemist, Container, Distribute, Dose, Dropper, Exempt, Handout, Scrap

**Dispersable, Disperse, Dispersion** Diaspora, Diffuse, Disband, Dissolve, Lyophil(e), Scail, Scale, SCATTER, Skail, Strew

**Dispirit(ed)** Dampen, Dash, Daunt, Discourage, Dishearten, Exorcism, Listless, Sackless

**Displace(ment), Displaced** Depose, Disturb, Ectopia, Ectopy, Luxate, Move, Proptosis, Ptosis, Reffo, Stir, Unsettle, Uproot, Valgus

**Display, Display ground** Air, Array, Blaze, Blazon, Brandish, Depict, Eclat, Epideictic, Etalage, Evidence, Evince, Exhibition, Exposition, Express, Exude, Fireworks, Flaunt, Float, Gondola, Lek, Manifest, Mount, Muster, Ostentation, Outlay, Overdress, Pageant, Parade, Paraf(f)le, Pomp, Pyrotechnics, Rodeo, Scene, SHOW, Sight, Spectacle, Splash, Splurge, Sport, Spree, State, Stunt, Tableau, Tattoo, Tournament, Up, Vaunt, Wear

**Displease, Displeasure** Anger, Irritate, Provoke, Umbrage

**Disport** Amuse, Divert, Play

**Dispose(d), Disposal**  Arrange, Bestow, Cast, Despatch, Lay(-out), Prone, Sale, Sell, Service, Settle, Stagger

**Disposition**  Affectation, Attitude, Bent, Bias, Humour, Inclination, Kidney, Lie, Nature, Talent, Temper(ament), Trim

> **Disposed, Disposition**  may indicate an anagram

**Dispossess(ed)**  Abate, Attaint, Bereft, Depose, Deprive, Evict, Oust

**Disproportion(ate)**  Asymmetric, Extreme, Imbalance, Unequal

**Disprove**  Debunk, Discredit, Negate, Redargue, Refel, Refute

**Dispute(d), Disputant**  Argue, Barney, Brangle, Case, Chaffer, Chorizont(ist), Contend, Contest, Controversy, Debate, Deny, Discept, Discuss, Eristic, Fray, Haggle, Kilfud-yoking, Militate, Ob and soller, Odds, Oppugn, Plea, Polemic, Pro-and-con, QUESTION, Resist, Rag, Spar, Stickle, Threap(it), Threep(it), Tiff, Tissue, Wrangle

**Disqualify**  Debar, Reject, Unfit

**Disquiet(ed)**  Agitate, Discombobulate, Discomboberate, DISTURB, Pain, Perturb(ation), Solicit, Turmoil, Uneasy, Unnerve, Vex

**Disraeli**  Dizzy, Tancred

**Disregard(ed)**  Contempt, Disfavour, Flout, Forget, Ignore, Overlook, Oversee, Pass, Pretermit, Slight, Spare, Violate, Waive

**Disrepair**  Dilapidation, Ruin

**Disreputable, Disrepute**  Base, Disgrace, Louche, Low, Raffish, Ragamuffin, Rip, Seamy, Shameful

**Disrepect(ful)**  Contempt, Discourtesy, Impiety, Impolite, Slight, Uncivil

**Disrupt(ion)**  Breach, Cataclasm, Disorder, Distract, Hamper, Interrupt, Jetlag, Perturb, Quonk, Screw

> **Disruption**  may indicate an anagram

**Dissatisfaction**  Displeasure, Distaste, Humph, Umph

**Dissemble(r)**  Conceal, Feign, Fox, Hypocrite, Impostor

**Dissension, Dissent(er), Dissenting**  Contend, Differ, Disagree, Discord, Dissident, Faction, Heretic, Jain, Lollard, Noes, Non-CE, Non-con(formist), Pantile, Protest, Raskolnik, Recusant, STRIFE, Vary

**Dissertation**  Essay, Excursus, Lecture, Thesis, Treatise

> **Dissident**  see DESERTER

**Dissimilar**  Different, Diverse, Unlike

**Dissipate(d)**  Debauch, Diffuse, Disperse, Dissolute, Gay, Revel, Scatter, Shatter, Squander, Waste

> **Dissipated**  may indicate an anagram

**Dissociate**  Separate, Sever, Withdraw

**Dissolute**  Degenerate, Hell, Lax, Licentious, Loose, Rakish, Rip, Roué

> **Dissolute**  may indicate an anagram

**Dissolution**  Dismissal, Divorce, End, Separation

**Dissolve** Digest, Disband, Liquesce, Melt, Terminate, Thaw

**Dissonance** Wolf

**Dissuade** Dehort, Deter, Discourage

**Distaff** Clotho, Female, Lady, Rock, Stick

**Distance** Absciss(a), Afield, Breadth, Coss, Eloi(g)n, Foot, Height, Kos(s), Latitude, League, Length, Mileage, Parasang, Parsec, Range, Reserve, Rod, Span, Stade, Way, Yojan

**Distant** Aloof, Far, Frosty, Long, Remote, Tele-

**Distaste(ful)** Repugnant, Ropy, Scunner, Unpalatable, Unpleasant

**Distemper** Ailment, Hard-pad, Paint, Tempera

**Distend(ed), Distension** Bloat, Dilate, Emphysema, Expand, Inflate, STRETCH, Swell, Varicose

**Distil(late), Distillation, Distiller, Distilling** Alcohol, Alembic, Anthracine, Azeotrope, Brew, Condense, Drip, Pelican, Pyrene, Rosin, Turps, Vapour

> **Distillation** may indicate an anagram

**Distinct(ive)** Apparent, Characteristic, Clear, Evident, Individual, Peculiar, Plain, Separate, Several, Signal, SPECIAL, Stylistic, Vivid

**Distinction** Blue, Cachet, Credit, Diacritic, Difference, Dignity, Diorism, Disparity, Division, Eclat, Eminence, Honour, Mark, Note, Nuance, OM, Prominence, Rank, Renown, Style, Title

**Distinguish(ed), Distinguishing** Classify, Demarcate, Denote, Diacritic, Different(iate), Discern, Discriminate, Divide, Mark, Notable, Perceive, Prominent, Signal, Stamp

**Distort(ed), Distortion** Bend, Colour, Contort, Deface, Deform, Dent, Helium speech, Jaundiced, Mangle, Misshapen, Pervert, Rubato, Thraw, Twist, WARP, Wring, Wry

> **Distort(ed)** may indicate an anagram

**Distract(ed)** Absent, Agitate, Amuse, Bewilder, Divert, Éperdu, Forhaile, Frenetic, Lost, Madden, Mental, Perplex, Upstage

> **Distract(ed)** may indicate an anagram

**Distrain(t)** Na(a)m, Poind, Sequestrate, Stress

**Distraught** Deranged, Elfish, Elvan, Frantic, Mad, Troubled

**Distress(ed), Distressing** Afflict, Ail, Alack, Anger, Anguish, Antique, Distraint, Dolour, Exigence, Extremity, Grieve, Harass, Harrow, Hurt, Ill, IN DISTRESS, Irk, Misease, Misfortune, Need, Oppress, Pain, Poignant, Prey, Sad, Shorn, Sore, SOS, Straits, TROUBLE, Une(a)th

**Distribute(d), Distribution** Allocate, Allot, Busbar, Carve, Colportage, Deal, Deliver(y), Deploy, Dish, Dispense, Dispose, Issue, Lie, Lot, Mete, Out, Pattern, Serve, Share

> **Distributed** may indicate an anagram

**District** Alsatia, Amhara, Arcadia, Area, Bail(l)iwick, Banat, Barrio, Belt,

Canton, Cantred, Community, Diocese, End, Exurb, Gau, Ghetto, Hundred, Lathe, Liberty, Locality, Loin, Manor, NEIGHBOURHOOD, Oblast, Pachalic, Pale, Parish(en), Paroch, Pashalik, Patch, Province, Quarter, Quartier, Rape, REGION, Riding, Ruhr, Sanjak, Sheading, Soc, Soke(n), Stannary, Suburb, Sucken, Taluk, Tender, Venue, Vicinage, Walk, Wapentake, Way, Zila, Zillah, Zone

**Distrust** Caution, Doubt, Suspect

**Disturb(ance)** Aerate, Affray, Agitate, Atmospherics, Betoss, Brabble, Brainstorm, Brash, Brawl, Derange, Desecrate, Disquiet, Dust, Feeze, Fray, Fret, Harass, Hoopla, Incommode, Infest, Interrupt, Jee, Kick-up, Muss, Outbreak, Prabble, Ripple, Romage, Rouse, Ruckus, Ruction, Ruffle, Rumpus, Shake, Shindy, Stashie, Static, Steer, Stir, Sturt, Tremor, Trouble, Unquiet, Unrest, Unsettle, Uproot, UPSET, Vex

> **Disturb(ed)** may indicate an anagram

**Disunite** Alienate, Dissever, Divide, Divorce, Split

**Disuse** Abandon, Abeyance, Desuetude, Discard

**Ditch** Barathron, Barathrum, Channel, Cunette, Delf, Delph, Dike, Discard, Donga, Drainage, Drop, Dyke, Euripus, Foss(e), Graft, Grip, Gully, Haw-haw, Jettison, Khor, Level, Lode, Moat, Na(l)la(h), Nulla(h), Rean, Reen, Rhine, Sea, Sheuch, Sheugh, Sike, Sloot, Sluit, Spruit, Stank, Syke, Trench

**Dither** Agitato, Bother, Faff, Hesitate, Twitter

**Dittany** Gas-plant

**Ditty, Ditties** Air, Arietta, Canzonet, Departmental, Lay, Song

**Diva** Patti, Singer

**Divan** Compilement, Congress, Couch, Council, Settee, Sofa

**Dive(s), Diving** Duck, Header, Honkytonk, Jack-knife, Joint, Ken, Nitery, Plummet, Plunge, Plutocrat, Sound, Submerge, Urinant

**Diver(s)** Didapper, Duck, Embergoose, Flop, Gainer, Grebe, Guillemot, Loom, Loon, Lungie, Many, Merganser, Pearl, Pike, Plong(e), Pochard, Poker, Puffin, Scuba, Snake-bird, Speakeasy, Sundry, Urinator, Various, Zoom

**Diverge** Branch, Deviate, Spread, Swerve, Veer

**Divers** Some

**Diverse, Diversify** Alter, Dapple, Different, Interlard, Manifold, Motley, Multifarious, Separate, Variegate, Various, Vary

**Diversion, Divert(ing)** Amuse, Avocation, Beguile, Deflect, Disport, Dissuade, Distract, Game, Hare, Hobby, Interlude, Pastime, Pleasure, Ramp, Refract, Reroute, Ruse, Shunt, Sideshow, Sidetrack, Sport, Stratagem, Sway, Switch, Upstage, Yaw

> **Diverting** may indicate an anagram

**Divest** Denude, Rid, Strip, Undeck, Undress

**Divide(d)** Band, Bipartite, Bisect, Cantle, Cleft, Commot(e), Counter-pale,

Cut, Deal, Demerge, Estrange, Fork, Parcel, Part, Polarise, Rend, Rift, Separate, Sever, Share, SPLIT, Sunder, Watershed, Zone

**Dividend** Bonus, Interim, Into, Share

**Divine, Divinity** Acoemeti, Atman, Avatar, Beatific, Clergyman, Conjecture, Curate, DD, Deduce, Deity, Douse, Dowse, Ecclesiastic, Forecast, Foretell, Fuller, GOD, GODDESS, Guess, Hariolate, Heavenly, Holy, Immortal, Inge, Isiac, Mantic, Olympian, Pontiff, Predestinate, Predict, Presage, Priest, RE, RI, Rector, Rimmon, Scry, Sense, Seraphic, Spae, Supernal, Theologise, Theology, Triune

**Diviner, Divination** Augury, Auspices, Axinomancy, Belomancy, Botanomancy, Capnomancy, Cartomancy, Ceromancy, Chiromancy, Cleromancy, Coscinomancy, Crithomancy, Crystallomancy, Doodlebug, Dowser, Empyromancy, Geomancy, Gyromancy Hariolation, Haruspex, Hepatoscopy, Hieromancy, Hieroscopy, I Ching, Intuition, Magic, Myomancy, Oneiromancy, Palmistry, Pyromancy, Rhabdomancy, Scapulimancy, Sciomancy, Seer, Sibyl, Sortes, Sortilege, Spae(man), Spodomancy, Taghairm, Tais(c)h, Tripudiary, Xylomancy

**Divisible, Division** Amitosis, Arrondissement, Bajocian, Banat(e), Bannet, Bar, Branch, Caesura, Canton, Cantred, Cantref, Caste, Category, Chapter, Classification, Cleft, Cloison, Clove, Comitatus, Commune, Compartment, Corps, County, Crevasse, Curia, Department, Dichotomy, Disagreement, Disunity, Duan, Eyalet, Fissile, Fork, Grisons, Guberniya, Gulf, Gulph, Hedge, Hide, Hundred, Isogloss, Keuper, Kimeridgian, Lathe, Leet, Legion, Lindsey, List, Lobe, M(e)iosis, Mitosis, Mofussil, Nome, Pargana, Part, Partition, Passus, Pergunnah, Phratry, Phyle, Phylum, Pipe, Pitaka, Platoon, Presidency, Quotition, Rape, Region, Riding, Sanjak, Schism, Section, Sector, Segment, Semeion, Sept(ate), Sever, Share, Sheading, Shire, Stage, Subheading, Tahsil, Taxis, Tepal, Thanet, Trio, Troop, Tuath, Unit, Volost, Wapentake, Ward

**Divisor** Aliquant, Aliquot

**Divorce(d)** Diffarreation, Dissolve, Disunion, Div, Get(t), Part, Separate, Sequester, SUNDER, Talak, Talaq

**Divot** Clod, Sod, Turf

**Divulge** Confess, Disclose, Expose, Publish, Reveal, Split, Tell, Unveil, Utter

**Dizziness, Dizzy** Beaconsfield, Ben, Capricious, Dinic, Disraeli, Giddy, Giglot, Mirligoes, Swimming, VERTIGO

**DNA** Gene

**Do(es), Doing** Accomplish, Achieve, Act, Anent, Beano, Char, Cheat, Chisel, Cod, Con, Cozen, Deed, Dich, Dish, Div, Doth, Dupe, Enact, Execute, Gull, Handiwork, Mill, Perform, Same, Serve, Settle, Shindig, Spif(f)licate, Ut

> **Do** may indicate an anagram

**Do away** Abolish, Banish, Demolish, Kill

**Docile** Agreeable, Amenable, Biddable, Dutiful, Facile, Meek, Submissive,

Yielding

**Dock(er), Docked, Docks** Abridge, Barber, Basin, Bistort, Bob, Camber, Canaigre, Clip, Curta(i)l, Cut, Deduct, De-tail, Grapetree, Knotweed, Lop, Marina, Moor, Off-end, Patience, Pen, Pier, Quay, Rhubarb, Rumex, Rump, Seagull, Shorten, Snakeweed, Sorrel, Sourock, Tilbury, Wharf, Yard

**Docket** Invoice, Label, Tag

**Dockyard** Arsenal, Rosyth

**Doctor(s)** Allopath, Arnold, Asclepiad, Barefoot, Bleeder, BMA, Bones, Breeze, Bright, Brighton, Brown, Castrate, Chapitalize, Clinician, Cook, Cure(r), Dale, Diagnose, Dr, Dryasdust, Erasmus, Fake, Falsify, Faustus, Feldsher, Fell, Finlay, Foster, Galen, Geropiga, GP, Healer, Houseman, Imhotep, Intern, Jekyll, Jenner, Johnson, Kildare, Lace, Leach, Leech, Load, Locum, Luke, Manette, MB, MD, Medicate, Medico, Middleton, Mindererus, Minister, Misrepresent, MO, MOH, Molla(h), Mulla(h), Neuter, No, Ollamh, Ollav, Paean, Pangloss, Paracelsus, Pedro, Physician, Pill(s), Quack, RAMC, Registrar, Resident, Rig, Salk, Sangrado, Sawbones, Shaman, Slop, Stum, Surgeon, Syn, Syntax, Thorne, Treat, Vet, Watson, Who

> **Doctor(ed)** may indicate an anagram

**Doctrine** Adoptianism, Adoptionism, Apollinarian, Archology, Averr(h)oism, Bonism, Cab(b)ala, Calvanism, Chiliasm, Creed, Credo, Ditheletism, Docetism, Dogma, Esotery, Fideism, Gnosticism, Gospel, Infralapsinarianism, Islam, Ism, Jansenism, Krypsis, Lore, Malthusian, Metempsychosis, Molinism, Monergism, Monism, Monroe, Pragmatism, Sharia, Sheria, Shibboleth, Strong meat, Sublapsarianism, Subpanation, Teleology, TENET, Theory, Theravada, Thomism, Tutiorism, Whiteboyism

**Document(s)** Bumph, Carta, Certificate, Charter, Contract, Conveyance, Covenant, Daftar, Deed, Diploma, Dossier, Form, Mandamus, Papers, Ragman, Ragment, Roll, Roul(e), Screed, Writ

**Dod** Pet, Poll

**Dodder(y)** Shake, Stagger, Strangleweed, Totter, Tremble

**Dodge(r)** Avoid, Column, Artful, Elude, Evade, Evasion, Jink, Jouk, Racket, Ruse, Shirk, Sidestep, Skip, Slalom, Slinter, Tip, Trick, Twist, Urchin, Weave, Welsh, Wheeze, Wire, Wrinkle

**Doe(s)** Deer, Faun, Hind

**Doff** Avail(e), Avale, Remove, Rouse, Shed, Tip

**Dog(s)** Aardwolf, Aberdeen, Affenpinscher, Afghan, Airedale, Alans, Alsatian, Andiron, Apsos, Bandog, Barker, Basenji, Beagle, Blanch, Boerbul, Boots, Borzoi, Bowwow, Bouvier, Boxer, Brach(et), Brak, Bratchet, Briard, Caesar, Cairn, Canes, Canidae, Canine, Cerberus, Chenet, Chihuahua, Cocker, Collie, Cur, Dachshund, Dalmatian, Dandie Dinmont, Dane, Dangle, Dhole, Dingo, Elkhound, Feet, Fido, Gelert, Goorie, Griffon, Harlequin, Harrier, Haunt, Heel, Hound, Huntaway, Husky, Hyena, Iron, Jackal, Katmir, Kelpie, Kennel, Kennet, Ketmir, Komondor, Kratim, Kuri, Kurre, Labrador, Laika, Lassie, Lhasa apso, Lorel, Luath, Lurcher,

Malamute, Malemute, Maremma, Mastiff, Mauthe, Messan, Mongrel, Montmorency, Mutt, Newfoundland, Oath, Orthrus, Papillon, Peke, Pekinese, Pembroke, Pinscher, Pluto, Pointer, Pom(eranian), Pooch, Poodle, Pug, Puli, Pursue, Queue, Rab, Rach(e), Ranger, Reynard, Rottweiler, Rover, Saluki, Samoyed(e), Sapling, Schipperke, Schnauzer, Sealyham, Setter, Shadow, Shaggy, Shar-Pei, Sheltie, Shih tzu, Shin-barker, Shock, Shough, Showghe, Sirius, Sothic, Spitz, Spoor, Springer, Stag, Stalk, Starter, Tag, Tail, Talbot, Teckel, Tike, Toby, Tosa, Touser, Towser, Trail, Tray, Trendle-tail, Trindle-tail, Tripehound, Trundle-tail, Turnspit, Tyke, Vizsla, Volpino, Warragal, Warrigal, Weimaraner, Whelp, Whippet, Wishtonwish, Wolf, Yap(per), Yapster, Zorro

**Dog-bane** Apocynum

**Doge** Dandolo

**Dogfish** Huss

**Dogged** Determined, Die-hard, Dour, Stubborn, Sullen

**Doggerel** Crambo, Jingle, Laisse, Rat-rhyme

**Dog letter** R

**Dogma(tic)** Assertive, Belief, Conviction, Creed, Doctrinal, Opinionative, Ideology, Peremptory, Pontifical, Positive, TENET

**Do-gooder** Piarist, Reformer, Salvationist, Samaritan, Scout

**Dog's body** Bottle-washer, Skivvy

**Dog star** Lassie, Sirius, Sothic

**Do it** Dich

**Dolce** Stop, Sweet

**Dole** Alms, Batta, B(u)roo, Give, Grief, Maundy, Payment, Pittance, Ration, SHARE, Tichborne, Vail, Vales

**Doll(y)** Common, Crumpet, Dress, Golliwog, Kachina, Kewpie, Maiden, Marionette, Mommet, Mummet, Ookpik, Ornament, Parton, Poppet, Puppet, Sis(ter), Sitter, Toy, Tearsheet, Trolley, Varden, Washboard

**Dollar(s)** Balboa, Boliviano, Buck, Cob, Euro, Fin, Greenback, Peso, Piastre, S, Sawbuck, Scrip, Smacker, Spin, Wheel

**Dollop** Glob, Helping, Share

> **Dolly** may indicate an anagram

**Dolly-bird** Dish

**Dolour** Grief, Pain, Sorrow

**Dolphin** Arion, Beluga, Cetacean, Coryphene, Delphinus, Grampus, Lampuka, Lampuki, Meer-swine, Porpess(e), Sea-pig

**Dolt** Ass, Blockhead, Clodhopper, Noodle, Oaf, Owl, STUPID

**Domain** Bourne, Emirate, Empire, Estate, Manor, Rain, Realm, Region, Reign

**Dome** Cap, Cupola, Dagoba, Head, Imperial, Rotunda, Stupa, Tee, Tholos, Tholus, Tope, Vault

**Domestic** Char, Cleaner, Dom, Esne, Familiar, Home-keeping, Homely, House, Humanise, Interior, Internal, Intestine, Maid, Menial, SERVANT, Tame, Woman

**Domicile** Abode, Dwelling, Hearth, Home, Ménage

**Dominate, Dominance, Dominant** Ascendancy, Baasskap, Bethrall, Clou, Coerce, Control, Henpeck, Maisterdome, O(v)ergang, Overshadow, Power, Preponderant, Rule, Soh, SUBDUE, Tower

**Domineer** Boss, Henpeck, Lord, Swagger, Tyrannize

**Dominican** Jacobite, Monk, OP, Savonarola, WD

**Dominie** Maister, Master, Pastor, Sampson, Schoolmaster

**Dominion** Dom, Empire, Khanate, NZ, Realm, Reame, Reign, RULE, Supremacy, Sway, Territory

**Domino(es)** Card, Fats, Mask, Matador

**Don** Academic, Address, Assume, Caballero, Endue, Fellow, Garb, Giovanni, Indew, Juan, Lecturer, Prof, Quixote, Reader, Senor, Spaniard, Tutor, Wear

**Dona(h)** Duckie, Love

**Donate, Donation** Bestow, Contribution, Gift, Give, Present, Wakf, Waqf

**Done** Achieved, Complete, Crisp, Ended, Executed, Had, Over, Spitcher, Tired, Weary

**Donjon** Dungeon, Keep

**Donkey** Ass, Burro, Cardophagus, Cuddie, Cuddy, Dapple, Dick(e)y, Eeyore, Genet(te), Kulan, Modestine, Moke, Mule, Neddy, Onager, Stupid, Years

**Donor** Benefactor, Bestower

**Doo** Dove

**Doodle(r)** Scribble, Yankee

**Doodlebug** Antlion, Larva, V1

**Doom(ed)** Condemned, Date, Destine, Destiny, FATE, Fay, Fey, Fie, Goner, Lot, Predestine, Preordain, Ragnarok, Ruined, Sentence, Weird

**Doone** Carver, Lorna

**Door(way)** Aperture, Entry, Exit, Haik, Hake, Hatch, Heck, Ingress, Lintel, Portal, Postern, Rory, Vomitory, Wickct, Yett

**Doorkeeper, Doorman** Bouncer, Commissionaire, Guardian, Janitor, Ostiary, Porter, Tiler, Tyler, Usher

**Doorpost** Architrave, Dern, Durn, Jamb, Yate, Yett

**Dope** Acid, Amulet, Bang, Crack, DRUG, Gen, Info, Narcotic, Nobble, Rutin, Sedate, Soup, Tea

**Dorcas** Gazelle, Needle

**Dorian, Doric** Metope, Mutule

**Doris** Day, Lessing, Mollusc

**Dormant**  Abed, Comatose, Hibernating, Inactive, Inert, Joist, Latent, SLEEPING, Torpescent

**Dormitory**  Barrack, Dorter, Dortour, Hall, Hostel, Quarters

**Dormouse**  Loir

**Dorothy**  Bag, Dot, Sayers

**Dorsal**  Back, Neural, Notal

**Dory**  Fish, John

**Dose**  Administer, Cascara, Draught, Drug, MEASURE, Physic, Potion, Powder

**Doss (house)**  Dharmsala, Dharmshala, Kip, Padding-ken

**Dossier**  File, Record

**Dot(s), Dotted, Dotty**  Absurd, Bullet, Criblé, Dit, Dower, Leader, Lentiginose, Micro, Occult, Or, Particle, POINT, Polka, Precise, Punctuate, Punctu(l)ate, Schwa, Seme(e), Speck, Spot, Stigme, Stipple, Stud, Tap, Tittle, Trema, Umlaut

**Dote, Dotage, Doting, Dotard**  Adore, Anile, Anility, Dobbie, Idolise, Imbecile, Pet, Prize, Senile, Tendre, Twichild

**Double(s)**  Amphibious, Ancipital, Bi-, Bifold, Binate, Counterpart, Crease, Dimeric, Doppel-ganger, Dual, Duo, Duple(x), Duplicate, Equivocal, Fetch, Fold, Foursome, Geminate, Gimp, Image, Ingeminate, Ka, Loop, Martingale, Pair, Parlay, Polyseme, Reflex, Replica, Ringer, Run, Similitude, Spit, Trot, Turnback, Twae, TWIN, Two(fold)

**Double-barrelled**  Tautonym

**Double-cross**  Two-time

**Double-entendre**  Polyseme, Polysemy

**Doublet**  Pourpoint, TT

**Doubt(ful), Doubter**  Ambiguous, Aporia, Askance, But, Debatable, Distrust, Dubiety, Dubitate, Hesitate, Hum, Iffy, Mistrust, NO DOUBT, Precarious, Qualm, Query, QUESTION, Rack, Scepsis, Sceptic, Scruple, Shady, Shy, Sic, Skepsis, Sus, Suspect, Suss, Thomas, Thos, Umph, Uncertain, Unsure, Waver

**Doubtless**  Probably, Sure, Truly

**Douceur**  Bonus, Sop, Sweetener

**Douche**  Gush, Rinse, Shower, Wash

**Dough(y)**  Boodle, Cake, Cash, Duff, Knish, Loot, Magma, Masa, Money, Paste, Pop(p)adum, Ready, Sad, Spondulicks

**Doughboy**  Dumpling, Soldier

**Doughnut**  Cruller, Olycook, Olykoek, Sinker

**Doughty**  Brave, Intrepid, Resolute, Stalwart, Valiant

**Dour**  Glum, Hard, Mirthless, Morose, Reest, Reist, Sullen, Taciturn

**Douse**  Dip, Drench, Extinguish, Snuff, Splash

**Dove** Collared, Columbine, Culver, Cushat, Dog, Ice-bird, Pacifist, PIGEON, Rock, Stock, Turtle

**Dove-cot(e)** Columbarium, Columbary, Louver, Louvre, Lover

**Dovetail** Fit, Lewis(son), Mortise, Tally, Tenon

**Dowager** Elder, Widow

**Dowdy** Frumpish, Shabby, Sloppy, Slovenly

**Dowel** Peg, Pin

**Down(y)** A bas, Abattu, Alow, Amort, Below, Blue, Cast, Chapfallen, Comous, Cottony, Crouch, Dejected, Dowl(e), Drink, Epsom, Feather, Fledge, Flue, Floccus, Fluff, Fly, Fuzz, Goonhilly, Ground, Hair, Hill, Humble, Humiliate, Lanugo, Losing, Low, Lower, Nap, Oose, Ooze, Pappus, Pennae, Pile, Plumage, Quash, Repress, Sebum, Thesis, Thistle, Tomentum, Wretched

**Downcast** Abject, Chapfallen, Despondent, Disconsolate, Dumpish, Hopeless, Melancholy, Woebegone

**Downfall, Downpour** Cataract, Collapse, Deluge, Fate, Flood, Hail, Onding, Overthrow, Rain, Ruin, Thunder-plump, Torrent, Undoing

**Downright** Absolute, Arrant, Bluff, Candid, Clear, Complete, Flat, Plumb, Pure, Rank, Sheer, Stark, Utter

**Downstairs** Below

**Dowry** Dot, Dower, Lobola, Lobolo, Portion, Settlement, Tocher

**Dowse(r), Dowsing** Divine, Enew, Fireman, Rhabdomancy, Water-witch

**Doxology** Gloria, Glory

**Doxy** Harlot, Loose woman, Wench

**Doyen** Dean, Senior

**Doze** Ca(u)lk, Dove(r), Nap, Nod, Semi-coma, Sleep, Slip, Slumber

**Dozen(s)** Thr(e)ave, Twal, Twelve

**Dr** Debtor, Doctor, Dram

**Drab** Cloth, Dell, Dingy, Dull, Dun, Isabel(line), Lifeless, Livor, Prosaic, Pussel, Quaker-colour, Rig, Road, Slattern, Subfusc, Tart, Trull, Wanton, Whore

**Drabble** Bemoil, Draggle

**Dracula** Bat, Count, Vampire

**Draft** Cheque, Draw, Ebauche, Minute, MS, Outline, Plan, Press, Rough, Scheme, Scroll, SKETCH

**Drag** Car, Drail, Dredge, Drogue, Elicit, Eonism, Epicene, Extort, Hale, Harl, HAUL, Keelhaul, La Rue, Lug, Puff, Pull, Rash, Sag, Schlep, Shoe, Skidpan, Sled, Snig, Sweep, Toke, Tote, Trail, Train, Travail, Travois, Trawl, Treck, Trek, Tump

**Draggle** Drail, Lag, Straggle

**Dragon** Basilisk, Bellemère, Chaperon(e), Chindit, Draco, Drake, Fire-drake, Gargouille, Komodo, Kung-kung, Ladon, Lindworm, Opinicus,

Python, Rouge, Wantley, Wivern, Worm, Wyvern

**Dragonfly** Demoiselle, Nymph, Odonata

**Dragon's teeth** Cadmus, Spartae, Sparti

**Dragoon** Coerce, Force, Press, Trooper

**Drain(age), Draining** Buzz, Catchment, Channel, Cloaca, Cundy, Delf, Delph, Dewater, Ditch, Dry, Ea(u), EMPTY, Emulge(nt), Exhaust, Fleet, Grating, Grip, Gully, Gutter, Kotabothron, Ketavothron, Lade, Leach, Limber, Lose, Milk, Pump, Rack, Sap, Scupper, Seton, Sew(er), Sheuch, Sheugh, Sink, Silver, Siver, Sluice, Sluse, Soakaway, Sough, Stank, Sump, Sure, Syver, Tile, Trench, Trocar, Ureter, U-trap

**Dram** Drink, Drop, Nipperkin, Portion, Snifter, Tickler, Tiff, Tot, Wet

**Drama(tic), Drama school** Auto, Catastasis, Charade, Comedy, Farce, Kabuki, Kathakali, Legit, Mask, Masque, Mime, Moralities, No, Nogaku, Noh, Piece, Play, RADA, Scenic, Sensational, Singspiel, Stagy, Striking, Tetralogy, Theatric, Thespian, Tragedy, Unities, Wild

**Dramatist** Aristophanes, Beaumarchais, Calderon, Congreve, Corneille, Coward, Drinkwater, Euripides, Fletcher, Goldoni, Ibsen, Ionesco, Kyd, Lyly, Massinger, Menander, Middleton, Molière, Odets, O'Neill, Osborne, Otway, Pinero, Pirandello, Plautus, PLAYWRIGHT, Racine, Rostand, Seneca, Schiller, Shadwell, Strindberg, Terence, Udall, Vanbrugh, Webster, Wilde, Wilder, Will

**Dram-shop** Bar, Boozingken, Bousingken

**Drape** Adorn, Coverlet, Coverlid, Curtain, Festoon, Fold, Hang, Swathe, Valance, Veil, Vest

**Draper** Gilpin, Hosier, Mercer, Ruth

**Drastic** Dire, Extreme, Harsh, SEVERE, Violent

**Drat** Bother, Dang, Darn

**Draught(s), Draughtsman** Aloetic, Breeze, Dam, Design, Drench, Drink, Fish, Gulp, Gust, Haal, Hippocrene, King, Men, Nightcap, Outline, Plan, Potation, Potion, Pull, Quaff, Sketch, Slug, Swig, Tracer, Veronal, Waucht, Waught, Williewaught

> **Draught** may refer to fishing

**Draught-board** Dam-board, Dambrod

**Dravidian** Tamil

**Draw(er), Drawn, Drawers, Draw off** Adduct, Attract, Crayon, Dead-heat, Delineate, Derivation, Describe, Doodle, Dr, Draft, Drag, Dress, Educe, Entice, Equalise, Extract, Fetch, Gather, Gaunt, Glorybox, Gut, Haggard, Hale, Halve, Haul, Induce, Indue, Inhale, Limn, Longbow, Lottery, Pantalet(te)s, Panty, Protract, Pull, Rack, Raffle, Remark, Scent, Sesquipedalion, Shottle, Shuttle, Siphon, Sketch, Slub, Stalemate, Snig, Spin, Stumps, Sweepstake, Syphon, Tap, Taut, Tenniel, Tie, Toke, Tole, Tombola, Tose, Tow(age), Toze, Trice, Troll, Tug, Unsheathe, Uplift

> **Draw** may indicate something to smoke

**Drawback**  Catch, Ebb, Impediment, OBSTACLE, Rebate, Retraction, Shrink, Snag

**Drawbridge**  Bascule, Pontlevis

**Drawing**  Cartoon, Charcoal, Crayon, Dentistry, Elevation, Freehand, Fusain, Graphics, Monotint, Pastel, Profile, Seductive, Sepia, Study, Traction

**Drawl**  Dra(u)nt, Haw, Slur, Twang

> **Drawn**  may indicate an anagram

**Drawn up**  Atrip, Drafted

**Dray**  Cart, Lorry, Wagon

**Dread**  Angst, Anxiety, Awe, Fear, HORROR, Redoubt

**Dreadful**  Awful, Chronic, Dearn, Dire, Formidable, Ghastly, Horrendous, Penny, Sorry, Terrible

**Dream(er), Dreamy, Dream state**  Alchera, Alcheringa, Aspire, Desire, Drowsy, Dwa(u)m, Fantasy, Idealise, Imagine, Languor, Mare, Mirth, Moon, Morpheus, Muse, Nightmare, On(e)iric, Pensive, Pipe, REVERIE, Rêveur, Romantic, Stargazer, Surreal, Sweven, Trance, Trauma, Vague, Vision

**Dreary**  Bleak, Desolate, Dismal, Doleful, Dreich, Dull, Gloom, Gray, Grey, Oorie, Ourie, Owrie, Sad

**Dredger**  Caster

**Dregs**  Draff, Dunder, F(a)eces, Fecula, Gr(e)aves, Grounds, Lees, Legge, Mother, Mud, Riffraff, Scaff, Sediment, Silt, Snuff, Ullage

**Dreikanter**  Ventifact

**Drench**  Dowse, Soak, Souse, Steep, Submerge

**Dress(ed), Dressing**  Accoutre, Adorn, Align, Array, Attire, Attrap, Bandage, Bedizen, Bloomer, Boast, Bodice, Brilliantine, Busk, Charpie, Cheongsam, Chimer, Cimar, Clad, CLOTHING, Cocktail, Comb, Compost, Compress, Corsage, Corset, Costume, Curry, Cymar, Dight, Dirndl, Dizen, Doll, Dolly Varden, Dolman, Don, Dub, Elastoplast (tdmk), Endue, Enrobe, Evening, Farthingale, Fatigue, Fertiliser, Fig, Frock, Garb, Garnish, Girt, Gown, Graith, HABIT, Ihram, Jaconet, Ketchup, Lint, Lounger, Mayonnaise, Merveilleuse, Mob, Mother Hubbard, Mufti, Mulch, Muu-muu, Oil, Patch, Peplos, Plaster, Pledget, Plumage, Polonaise, Pomade, Poultice, Prank, Preen, Prepare, Rag, Raiment, Ray, Rehearsal, Rig, Robe, Rybat, Sack, Samfo, Sartorial, Sauce, Scutch, Shift, Shirt, Shirtwaister, Simar(re), Sterile, Stole, Stupe, Subfusc, Subfusk, Suit, Symar, Tasar, Taw, Tenue, Tew, Tiff, Tire, Tog, Toilet, Tonic, Treat, Trick, Trim, Tunic, Tusser, Tussore, Tuxedo, Uniform, Vest, Wear, Wig, Yclad, Ycled

**Dressage**  Manège, Passade, Passage, Pesade, Piaffe

> **Dressed up, Dressing**  may indicate an anagram

**Dresser**  Adze, Almery, Bureau, Chest, Couturier, Deuddarn, Dior, Lair,

Lowboy, Sideboard, Tridarn

**Dressing-gown**  Bathrobe, Negligee, Peignoir

**Dressing-room**  Apodyterium, Vestry

**Dressmaker**  Costumier, Dorcas, Modiste, Seamstress, Tailor

**Drew**  Steeld, Stelled

**Dribble**  Drip, Drivel, Drop, Slaver, Slop, Trickle

**Dried fish**  Bum(m)alo, Bummaloti, Haberdine, Speld(r)in(g), Stockfish

> **Dried fruit**  see DRY FRUIT

**Drift(er)**  Cruise, Current, Digress, Float, Heap, Impulse, Maunder, Plankton, Purport, Rorke, Slide, TENOR, Waft, Wander

**Drill**  Auger, Bore, Burr, Educate, Exercise, Form, Jerks, Monkey, PE, Pierce, PT, Ridge, Seeder, Sow, Square-bashing, Teach, Train, Twill, Wildcat

**Drink(er), Drunk(enness)**  AA, Absinth(e), Absorb, Aguardiente, Akvavit, Ale(berry), Alkie, Alky, Ambrosia, Amoroso, Amrita, Anisette, Aperitif, Apozem, Applejack, Aquavit, Aqua-vitae, Arrack, Assai, Asti, Ava, Ayahuasco, Bacardi (tdmk), Bacchian, Badminton, Benedictine, Beverage, Bev(v)y, Bezzle, Bib(ite), Binge, Bingo, Birl(e), Bishop, Blackstone, Blind, Blitzed, Bloat, Blotto, Bock, Boiler-maker, Bombo, Boose, Booze, Borachio, Bordeaux, Bosky, Bottled, Bouse, Bracer, Bub, Bull, Bumbo, Bumper, Burton, Busera, Calvados, Campari (tdmk), Carafe, Carousal, Cassis, Cat-lap, Caudle, Cauker, Cha, Chablis, Champagne, Champers, Charneco, Chartreuse (tdmk), Chaser, Chasse, Chianti, Chocolate, Cider(kin), Cobbler, Coca-cola (tdmk), Cocoa, Coke, Cooler, Cooper, Copus, Cordial, Corked, Crapulous, Crush, Cup, Curaçao, Curaçoa, Cut, Da(i)quiri, Demitasse, D(e)och-an-dor(u)is, Dipsomaniac, Doch-an-dorach, Doctor, Dog's nose, Dop, Doris, Double, Drain, Draught, Drop, Dubonnet (tdmk), Ebriose, Elixir, Entire, Enzian, Eye-opener, Fap, Febrifuge, Finger, Flip, Fou, Fuddle-cap, Fuddled, Geropiga, Gimlet, Gin(sling), Gingerade, Glogg, Grappa, Grenadine, Grog, Guarana, Half and-half, Haoma, High, Highball, Hippocras, Hogan, Hogshead, Hom(a), Honkers, Hooch, Hophead, Humpty-dumpty, Imbibe, Indulge, Inhaust, Irrigate, It, Italian, Ivresse, Jag, Jar, Joram, Jorum, Julep, Kalied, Kava, Kefir, Keltie, Kelty, Kephir, Kir, Kirsch, Kola, Koumiss, Kumiss, Kümmel, Kvass, Lambswool, Lassi, Lap, Legless, Lemonade, Lethean, Lit, Loaded, Lord, Lower, Lush(y), Mâcon, Maggoty, Mahogany, Malmsey, Manhattan, Maotai, Maraschino, Marcobrunner, Maudlin, Mead, Meath, Medoc, Merry, Metheglin, Methomania, Methysis, Mickey, Milkshake, Mineral, Mobbie, Mobby, Morat, Mortal, Mug, Mulse, Mum, Nappy, Neck, Nectar, Negus, Nepenthe, Niersteiner, Nightcap, Nipa, Nipperkin, Nobbler, Nog(gin), Obarni, Obfuscated, Oenomel, Oiled, Old-fashioned, One, Oolong, Oppignorate, Orgeat, Oulong, Overshot, Paid, Paint, Particular, Pastis, Pepsi (tdmk), Pernod (tdmk), Perry, Persico(t), Philter, Philtre, Pickled, Pick-me-up, Pie-eyed, Pils(e)ner, Pint(a), Pisshead, Plonk(o), Plotty, Polly, Pombe, Pop, Port, Posset, Potion, Primed, Pulque, Punch, Purl, Quaff, Ragmaker, Rakee, Raki, Ratafia, Refresher, Resinate, Reviver,

Rickey, Riesling, Rolling, Rosiner, Roso(g)lio, Rotgut, Rotten, Rum(my), Rye, Sack, Sake, Saki, Salo(o)p, Sangaree, Sangria, Sarsa(parilla), Sarza, Sauternes, Schnapps, Screech, Screwdriver, Screwed, Scrumpy, Sea, Shandy(gaff), Sherbet, Sherris, Sherry, Shicker, Short, Shrub, Silenus, Sip(ple), Skink, Skinned, Skokiaan, Slake, Slewed, Sling, Slivovica, Sloshed, Slug, Slurp, Smile(r), Snifter, Snort, Snowball, Soak, Soapolallie, Soda, Soma, Sour, Soused, Sponge, Spongy, Spritzer, Spunge, Squash, Squiffy, Stengah, Stewed, Stimulant, Stingo, Stinko, Stoned, Stotious, Stout, Strega, Strunt, Sundowner, Sup, Sura, Swacked, Swallow, Swig, Swill, Switchel, Swizzle, Tank, Tape, Tass, Tea, Temulence, Tent, Tequil(l)a, Tiddley, Tiff, Tift, Tight, Tio Pepe (tdmk), Tipple, Tipsy, Toddy, Tom Collins, Tom and Jerry, Tonic, Tope, Toss, Tossicated, Tost, Tot, Usual, Vermouth, Vin, Vodka, Warag, Wash, Wassail, Wat, Wauch, Waught, Wet, Williewaught, Winebag, Wino, Witblits, Yaqona, Yill, Zonked, Zythum

**Drink store**   Cellar

**Drip**   Bore, Dribble, Drop, Gutter, Leak, Seep, Stillicide, Trickle, Wimp

**Dripstone**   Larmier

**Drive(r), Drive out**   AA, Actuate, Ambition, Banish, Ca', Cabby, Campaign, Charioteer, Chauffeur, Coachee, Coact, Crew, Crowd, Dislodge, Dr, Drover, Drum, Eject, Emboss, Energy, Enew, Enforce, Engine, Expatriate, Faze, Feeze, Ferret, Fire, Firk, Fuel, Gadsman, Goad, Hack, Hammer, Haste, Heard, Herd, Hoosh, Hoy, Hunt, Hurl, Impel, Impetus, Impinge, Impulse, Jarvey, Jehu, Jockey, Juggernaut, Lash, Libido, Lunge, Mahout, Make, Mall, Miz(z)en, Motor, Offensive, Overland, Peg, Penetrate, Piston, Power, Propel, Put, RAC, Rack, Ram, Rebut, Ride, Road, Run, Scorch, Screw, Scud, Shepherd, Shoo, Spank, Spin, Spur, Start, Stroke, Sumpter-horse, Sweep, Task-master, Teamster, Tee, Thrust, Toad, Tool, Trot, Truckie, Tup, Urge, Urgence, Wagoner, Whist, Wreak

**Drivel**   Blether(skate), Drool, Humbug, Nonsense, Pap, Rot, Salivate, Slaver

**Driving club**   AA, Iron, RAC

**Drizzle**   Drow, Haze, Mist, Mizzle, Roke, Serein, Skiffle, Smir(r), Smur, Spit

**Droll**   Bizarre, Comic, Funny, Jocular, Queer, Waggish

**Drone**   Bee, Buzz, Dog-bee, Doodle, Dor(r), Drant, Draunt, Hanger-on, Hum, Idler, Parasite, Thrum, Windbag

**Drool**   Drivel, Gibber, Salivate, Slaver

**Droop(ing)**   Cernuous, Decline, Flag, Languish, Lill, Limp, Lob, Loll, Lop, Nutate, Oorie, Ourie, Owrie, Ptosis, SAG, Slink, Slouch, Welk(e), Wilt, Wither

**Drop(s), Dropping**   Acid, Apraxia, Bag, Bead, Blob, Cadence, Calve, Cascade, Cast, Chocolate, Dap, Descent, Dink, Drappie, Drib(let), Ebb, Escarp(ment), Fall, Floor, Fumet, Gallows, Globule, Gout(te), Guano, Gutta, Instil, Land, Modicum, Muff, Mute, Omit, Pilot, Plummet, Plump, Plunge, Precepit, Precipice, Prince Rupert's, Rain, Scat, Shed, Sip, Skat,

Stilliform, Tass, Taste, Tear

**Drop-out** Hippie, Hippy

**Drop-shot** Dink

**Dropsy** Anasarca, Ascites, Edema, Oedema

**Dross** Chaff, Dregs, Scoria, Scorious, Scum, Sinter, Slack, Slag, Waste

**Drought** Dearth, Drouth, Lack, Thirst

**Drove(r)** Band, Crowd, Flock, Herd, Masses, Overlander, Puncher

**Drown(ing)** Drook, Drouk, Engulf, Inundate, Noyade, Overcome, Sorrows, Submerge

**Drowse, Drowsiness, Drowsy** Blet, Comatose, Doze, Lethargic, Nap, Narcolepsy, Nod, Snooze

**Drub** Anoint, Thrash

**Drudge(ry)** Devil, Dogsbody, Fag, Grind, Hack, Jackal, Plod, Scrub, Slave, Snake, Sweat, Thraldom, Toil, Trauchle, Treadmill

**Drug(ged)** Acid, Adam, Aloes, Alpha-blocker, Aminobutene, Amphetamine, Amulet, Analeptic, Angel-dust, Antagonist, Anthelmint(h)ic, Antrycide, Atabrin, Atebrin, Atracurium, Bang, Banthine, Barbitone, Base, Benny, Beta-blocker, Benzedrine, Bhang, Biguanide, Blow, Bomber, Boo, Botanic, Bute, Candy, Cascara, Charas, Charlie, Churrus, Cilofibrate, Codeine, Curare, Curarine, Dagga, Dapsone, Deserpidine, Diazepam, Dope, Downer, Dragée, Ecbolic, Ecstasy, Electuary, Eucaine, Eve, Fantasy, Ganja, Gonadotropin, Goofball, Grass, Guarana, Hashish, Hemp, Henbane, Heroin, High, Hocus, Hop, Hyoscine, Hypnone, Ibuprofen, Ice, Indapamide, Insulin, Intal, Inulin, Ipratropopium, Iprindole, Isoniazid(e), Isoxsuprine, Jaborandi, Laudanum, Line, Load, LSD, Medicine, Mepacrine, Mersalyl, Mescalin, Methadon(e), Metopon, Miltown (tdmk), Morphia, Mummy, Naloxone, Narcotic, Nepenthe, Nikethamide, Nobble, Novocaine, Opiate, Opium, Paludrine (tdmk), Paregoric, Patulin, Peyote, Pharmacopoeia, Pituri, Poison, Practolol, Prednisone, Psilocybin, Q, Quina, Quinine, Quinquina, Reserpine, Roborant, Rutin, Salep, Salo(o)p, Scopolia, Seconal (tdmk), Sedate, Selegiline, Serevent (tdmk), Sida, Snort, Snowball, Soma, Speed, Spike, Steroid, Stimulant, Stramonium, Stupefy, Substance, Sudorific, Sulpha(nilamide), Suramin, Synergist, Tamoxifen, Taxol, Tea, Tetronal, Thalidomide, Thiazide, Totaquine, Tous-les-mois, Trional, Truth, Upper, Valium, Veronal (tdmk), Vinblastine, Vincristine, Weed, Zerumbet

**Druid** Gorsedd

**Drum(mer), Drumbeat** Arête, Atabal, Barrel, Bodhran, Bongo, Carousel, Chamade, Dash-wheel, Dr, Drub, Ear, Flam, Kettle, Lambeg, Mridamgam, Mridang(a), Mridangam, Myringa, Naker, Pan, Percussion, Rappel, Rataplan, Reel, Rep, Ridge, Rigger, Roll, Ruff, Ruffle, Salesman, Snare, Tabla, Tabour, Tabret, Tambourine, Tam-tam, Tap, Tattoo, Thrum, Timp(ano), Tom-tom, Touk, Traps, Traveller, Tuck, Tymbal, Tympanist, Tympano, Whim, Work

**Drum-belly** Hoven

**Drumstick**  Attorney, Leg, Rute

> **Drunk(ard)**  see DRINK

> **Drunken**  may indicate an anagram

**Dry(ing), Drier**  Air, Anhydrous, Arefaction, Arefy, Arid, Blot, Bone, Brut, Corpse, Crine, Dehydrate, Desiccate, Drain, Dull, Evaporate, Firlot, Fork, Harmattan, Hi(r)stie, Humidor, Jejune, Jerk, Khor, Kiln, Oast, PARCH, Reast, Reist, Rizzar, Rizzer, Rizzor, Scorch, Sear, Sec(co), Sere, Shrivel, Siccative, Sober, Sponge, Steme, Ted, Thirsty, Thristy, Toasted, Torrefy, Towel, Tribble, Trocken, TT, Watertight, Welt, Wilt, Win(n), Wipe, Wither, Wizened, Xeransis, Xerasia, Xero(sis), Xerostomia

**Dryad**  Nymph

**Dry fruit**  Achene, Akene, Currant, Mebos, Prune, Raisin, Samara, Silicula, Siliqua, Silique, Sultana

**Dry mouth**  Xerostoma

**DT's**  Dingbats, Hallucinations, Zooscopic

**Dual**  Double, Twin, Twofold

**Dub**  Array, CALL, Entitle, Hete, Knight, Name

**Dubious**  Doubtful, Equivocal, Fishy, Fly-by-night, Hesitant, Iffy, Improbable, Questionable, Scepsis, Sceptical, Sesey, Sessa, SHADY, Suspect, Unlikely

> **Dubious**  may indicate an anagram

**Duce**  Leader, Musso(lini)

**Duchess**  Anastasia, Malfi, Peeress, Titled

**Duchy**  Brabart, Cornwall, Dukedom, Omnium, Realm, Swabia, Westphalian

**Duck(ed)**  Amphibian, Avoid, Aylesbury, Bald-pate, Bargander, Bergander, Blob, Bob, Bufflehead, Bum(m)alo, Canard, Canvasback, COUPLE OF DUCKS, Dearie, Dip, Dodge, Dodo, Douse, Drook, Drouk, Dunk(er), Eider, Enew, Escape, Evade, Flapper, Gadwall, Garganey, Garrot, Golden eye, Goosander, Hareld, Harlequin, Heads, Herald, Immerse, Jook, Jouk, Mallard, Mandarin, Muscovy, Nil, O, Oldsquaw, Paddling, Palmated, Pekin, Pintail, Plunge, Pochard, Poker, Runner, Rush, Scaup, Scoter, Sheld(d)uck, Shieldrake, Shoveller, Shun, Smeath, Smee(th), Smew, Sord, Spatula, Teal, Team, Tunker, Widgeon, Wigeon, Zero

**Duckbill**  Ornithorhynchus, Platypus

**Duckwalk**  Waddle

**Duckweed**  Lemna

**Ducky**  Sweet, Twee

**Duct**  Channel, Conduit, Epididymus, Fistula, Gland, Lachrymal, Pipe, Tear, Tube, Ureter

**Dud**  Bouncer, Failure, Flop, Shan(d), Stumer

**Dude**  Cat, Coxcomb, Dandy, Fop, Lair, Macaroni, Popinjay

**Dudgeon** Anger, Hilt, Huff, Pique

**Due(s)** Adequate, Arrearage, Claim, Debt, Deserts, Forinsec, Geld, Heriot, Just, Lot, Mature, Owing, Reddendo, Rent, Right, SUITABLE, Thereanent, Tribute, Worthy

**Duel(list)** Mensur, Monomachy, Principal, Tilt

**Duenna** Chaperone, Dragon

**Duff** Bungle, Dough, Nelly, NG, Plum, Pudding, Rustle

**Duffer** Bungler, Rabbit, Useless

**Dug** Ploughed, Teat, Udder

**Dugong** Halicore, Sea-cow, Sea-pig, Sirenian

**Dug-out** Abri, Canoe, Pirogue, Shelter, Trench, Trough

**Duke(dom)** Alva, Clarence, D, Ellington, Fist, Iron, Milan, Orsino, Peer, Prospero, Rohan, Wellington

**Dulcimer** Cembalo, Citole, Cymbalo, Santir, Sant(o)ur

**Dull(ard), Dullness** Banal, Besot, Bland, Blear, Blunt, Boeotian, Cloudy, Dense, Dim, Dinge, Dingy, Doldrums, Dowf, Dowie, Drab, Drear, Dry, Dunce, Fozy, Grey, Heavy, Hebetate, Insipid, Lacklustre, Lifeless, Log(y), Mat(t), Matte, Monotonous, Mull, Obtuse, Opacity, Opiate, Ordinary, Overcast, Owlish, Pall, Pedestrian, Perstringe, Prosaic, Prose, Prosy, Rebate, Slow, Sopite, Staid, Stodger, Stodgy, Stolid, Stuffy, Stultify, STUPID, Sunless, Tame, Tarnish, Tedious, Toneless, Treadmill, Tubby, Vapid, Wooden, Zoid

**Dumb(ness)** Alalia, Aphonic, Crambo, Hobbididance, Inarticulate, Mute, Stupid

**Dumbfound(ed)** Amaze, Astound, Flabbergast, Stun, Stupefy, Stupent

**Dumb ox** Aquinas

**Dummy** Comforter, Copy, Effigy, Fathead, Flathead, Mock-up, Model, Pacifier, Table, Waxwork

**Dump(s)** Abandon, Blue, Dispirited, Doldrums, Empty, Jettison, Junk, Shoot, Tip, Unlade, Unload

**Dumpling** Dough(boy), Gnocchi, Knish, Kreplach, Norfolk, Quenelle, Suet, Won ton

**Dumpy** Pudgy, Squat

**Dun** Annoy, Cow, Importune, Pester, SUE, Tan

**Duncan** Isadora

**Dunce** Analphabet, Booby, Dolt, Donkey, Dullard, Fathead, Schmo, Schmuck, Schnook, Stupid

**Dune** Bar, Barchan(e), Bark(h)an, Erg, Sandbank, Seif

**Dung(hill)** Argol, Chip, Coprolite, Droppings, Fewmet, Fumet, Guano, Hing, Manure, Midden, Mixen, Mute, Ordure, Puer, Pure, Scat, Scumber, Shard, Sharn, Skat, Skummer, Sombrerite, Sombrero, Spraint, Stercoraceous, Tath

**Dungarees**  Overalls

**Dungeon**  Bastille, Cell, Confine, Donjon, Durance, Oubliette, Souterrain

**Dunk**  Immerse, Sop, Steep

**Dunnock**  Accentor

**Duo**  Couple, Pair, Twosome

**Dupe**  Catspaw, Chiaus, Chouse, Cony, Cully, Delude, Geck, Gull, Hoax, Hoodwink, Mug, Pawn, Pigeon, Plover, Sucker, Swindle, TRICK, Victim

**Duplex**  Twofold

**Duplicate**  Clone, Copy, Double, Facsimile, Match, Replica, Roneo, Spare

**Durable**  Enduring, Eternal, Eterne, Hardy, Permanent, Stout, Tough

**Duralumin**  Y-alloy

**Duration**  Extent, Period, Span

**Duress**  Coercion, Pressure, Restraint

**Durham**  Palatine

**During**  Amid, For, In, Throughout, While, Whilst

**Dusk(y)**  Dark, Dewfall, Dun, Eve, Gloaming, Gloom, Owl-light, Phaeic, Twilight

**Dust(y)**  Ash, Bo(a)rt, Calima, Clean, Coom, Derris, Devil, Earth, Fuss, Khaki, Lemel, Limail, Pollen, Pother, Pouder, Poudre, Powder, Pozz(u)olana, Pudder, Rouge, Seed, Shaitan, Stour, Wipe

> **Dusted**  may indicate an anagram

**Duster**  Cloth, Talcum, Torchon

**Dustman**  Garbo

**Dust measure**  Konimeter, Koniscope

**Dutch(man), Dutchwoman**  Batavian, Boor, Courage, D(u), Elm, Erasmus, Frow, Mynheer, Patron, Sooterkin, Taal, Wife

**Dutiful, Duty**  Ahimsa, Average, Blench, Bond, Charge, Customs, Debt, Devoir, Docile, Drow, Due, Duplicand, End, Excise, Fatigue, Function, Homage, Imposition, Impost, Incumbent, Lastage, Likin, Mission, Mistery, Mystery, Obedient, Obligation, Office, Onus, Pia, Point, Pious, Prisage, Rota, Shift, Stint, Tariff, TASK, Tax, Toll, Trow, Watch, Zabeta

**Dwarf(ism)**  Achondroplasia, Agate, Alberich, Andvari, Ateleiosis, Bashful, Belittle, Bes, Black, Bonsai, Doc, Dopey, Droich, Drow, Durgan, Elf, Gnome, Grumpy, Happy, Homuncle, Hop o' my thumb, Knurl, Laurin, Little man, Man(n)ikin, MIDGET, Mime, Minim, Nanism, Nectabanus, Ni(e)belung, Nurl, Overshadow, Pacolet, Pigmy, Pygmy, Regin, Ront, Rumpelstiltskin, Runt, Skrimp, Sleepy, Sneezy, STUNT, Titch, Tokoloshe, Tom Thumb, Toy, Troll, Trow

**Dwell(er), Dwelling**  Abide, Be, Bungalow, Cabin, Cell, Cot(tage), Descant, Discourse, Domicile, Harp, Heteroscian, House, Hut, Laura, Lavra, Live, Lodge, Mansion, Messuage, Palafitte, Pueblo, Reside, Roof, Tenement, Tepee, Won(ing)

**Dwindle**   Decline, Diminish, Fade, Lessen, Peter, Shrink, Wane

**Dye(ing)**   Alkanet, Anil, Archil, Bat(t)ik, Camwood, Carthamine, Catechin, Chay(a), Chica, Choy, Cinnabar, Cobalt, Cochineal, Colour, Corkir, Crocein, Crotal, Crottle, Cudbear, Embrue, Engrain, Envermeil, Eosin, Flavin(e), Fuchsine, Fustic, Fustoc, Gambi(e)r, Grain, Henna, Hue, Ikat, Imbrue, Imbue, Indican, Indigo, Induline, Ingrain, Kalamkari, Kamala, Kohl, Korkir, Madder, Magenta, Mauveine, Myrobalan, Nigrosine, Orchella, Orchil, Para-red, PIGMENT, Primuline, Purpura, Resorcinol, Rhodamine, Safranin, Shaya, STAIN, Stone-rag, Stone-raw, Sumach, Tartrazine, Tinct, Tint, Tropaelin, Turnsole, Valonia, Wald, Weld, Woad, Woald, Wold

**Dyke**   Aboideau, Aboiteau, Devil's, DIKE, Offa's

**Dynamic**   Energetic, Forceful, Potent

**Dynamite**   Blast, Explode, Gelignite, TNT, Trotyl

**Dynamo**   Alternator, Armature

**Dynasty**   Angevin, Bourbon, Carolingian, Chin(g), Era, Habsburg, Han, Hapsburg, Honan, Household, Hyksos, Khan, Manchu, Ming, Pahlavi, Qajar, Qin(g), Rameses, Romanov, Rule, Saga, Sassanid, Seleucid, Seljuk, Shang, Sung, Tai-ping, Tang, Tudor, Wei, Yuan

**Dyslexia**   Strephosymbolia

**Dyspeptic**   Cacogastric

**Dysprosium**   Dy

# Ee

**E**  Boat, East, Echo, Energy, English, Spain

**Each**  All, Apiece, Ea, EVERY, Ilka, Per, Severally

**Eager**  Agog, Ardent, Avid, Bore, Earnest, Enthusiastic, Fain, Fervent, Frack, Gung-ho, Hot, Intent, KEEN, Race, Raring, Rath(e), Ready, Roost, Sharp-set, Spoiling, Thirsty, Toey, Wishing, Yare

**Eagle**  Al(l)erion, Aquila, Bateleur, Berghaan, Bird, Erne, Ethon, Gier, Harpy, Hawk, Lettern, Ossifrage

**Ear(drum)**  Ant(i)helix, Attention, Audience, Auricle, Cauliflower, Dionysius, Dolichotus, Hearing, Icker, Jenkins, Listen, Locusta, Lug, Myringa, Nubbin, Otic, Paramastoid, Pavilion, Prootic, Spike, Tragus

**Earl(dom)**  Belted, Mar, Peer, Sandwich

**Earlier, Early**  Above, Ahead, Alsoon, AM, Antelucan, Auld, Betimes, Cockcrow, Daybreak, Ere-now, Ex, Or, Precocious, Prehistoric, Premature, Previous, Prevernal, Primeval, Prior, Rath(e), Rath(e)ripe, Rear, Rudimentary, Soon, Timely

> **Early**  may indicate belonging to an earl

**Early man**  Eoanthropus

> **Early stages of**  may indicate first one or two letters of the word(s) following

**Earmark**  Allocate, Bag, Book, Characteristic, RESERVE, Tag, Target

**Earn(er)**  Achieve, Breadwinner, Deserve, Gain, Make, Merit, Win

**Earnest**  Ardent, Arles(-penny), Deposit, Fervent, Imprest, Intent, Promise, Serious, Zealous

**Earring**  Drop, Hoop, Keeper, Pendant, Sleeper, Snap, Stud

**Earshot**  Hail, Hearing

**Earth(y)**  Antichthon, Art, Capricorn, Clay, Cloam, Cologne, Dirt, Drey, Dust, Eard, Edaphic, Epigene, Foxhole, Friable, Fuller's, Gaea, Gaia, Gault, Ge, Globe, Ground, Horst, Kadi, Lair, Lemnian, Loam, Malm, Mankind, Mantle, Mools, Mould, Mouls, Papa, Pise, Planet, Racy, Seat, Sett, Sod, SOIL, Taurus, Telluric, Tellus, Terra, Terrain, Terramara, Terrene, Topsoil, Virgo, Ye(a)rd, Yird

**Earth-bound**  Chthonian

**Earthenware**  Biscuit, Ceramic, Crock(ery), Delf(t), Della-robbia, Delph, Faience, Figuline, Maiolica, Majolica, Pig, Pot, Raku, Terracotta

**Earthquake**  Seism, Shake, Shock, Temblor

**Earth's surface**  Sal, Sial

**Earthworks**  Agger, Bank, Gazon, Parados, Rampart, Remblai

**Earthworm** Annelid, Bait, Night-crawler

**Ear trouble** Conchitis, Deafness, Myringitis, Otalgia, Otalgy, Paracusis

**Ease, Easing** Alleviate, Clover, Comfort, Content, Deregulate, Détente, Facility, Mitigate, Peace, Quiet, Relieve, Reposal, Repose, Soothe

**East(erly), Eastward** Anglia, Asia, Chevet, E, Eassel, Eassil, Eothen, Eurus, Levant, Orient, Ost, Sunrise

**Easter** Festival, Island, Pace, Pasch, Pasque

**Eastern(er), Eastern language** Asian, Kolarian, Oriental, Virginian

**East European** Lettic, Slovene

**Easy, Easily** ABC, Cakewalk, Carefree, Cinch, Cushy, Doddle, Eath(e), Ethe, Facile, Free, Gift, Glib, Jammy, Lax, Midshipman, Natural, Picnic, Pie, Pushover, Simple, Sitter, Snotty, Soft, Tolerant, Walk-over, Well, Yare

> **Easy** may indicate an anagram

**Easygoing** Carefree, Lax, Pococurante

**Eat(able), Eater, Eating** Bibite, Bite, Bolt, Chop, Consume, Corrode, Edible, Edite, Endew, Endue, Erode, Esculent, Etch, Fare, Feast, FEED, Fret, Gnaw, Go, Gobble, Graze, Grub, Hog, Mandicate, Munch, Nosh, Refect, Scoff, Stuff, Sup, Swallow, Syssitia, Take, Taste, Trencherman, Whale

**Eavesdrop(per)** Cowan, Earwig, Icicle, Listen, Overhear, Snoop, Stillicide, Tap

**Ebb** Abate, Decline, Recede, Sink, WANE

**Ebony** Black, Cocus-wood, Coromandel, Hebenon

**Ebullient** Brash, Effervescent, Fervid

**Eccentric(ity)** Abnormal, Cam, Card, Character, Crank, Curious, Dag, Deviant, Dingbat, E, Farouche, Fey, Fie, Freak, Gonzo, Iffish, Irregular, Kinky, Odd(ball), Offbeat, Original, Outré, PECULIAR, Phantasime, Queer, Quirky, Quiz, Rake, Raky, Recondite, Rum, Screwball, Wacky, Way-out, Weird(o)

> **Eccentric** may indicate an anagram

**Ecclesiastic** Abbé, Clergyman, Clerical, Secular, Theologian

**Echelon** Formation

**Echinoderm** Asteroidea, Crinoid, Sea-egg, Sea-urchin, Starfish

**Echo** Angel, Answer, Ditto, E, Imitate, Iterate, Rebound, Repeat, Resonant, RESOUND, Respeak, Reverberate, Ring, Rote

**Eclat** Flourish, Glory, Prestige, Renown

**Eclectic** Babist, Broad, Complex, Liberal

**Eclipse** Annular, Block, Cloud, Deliquium, Hide, Obscure, Outmatch, Outweigh, Overshadow, Penumbra, Transcend

**Eclogue** Bucolic, Idyll, Pastoral

**Economise** Budget, Conserve, Eke, Entrench, Husband, Intrench, Pinch, Retrench, Scrimp, Skimp, STINT

**Economist** Angell, Bentham, Chrematist, Cole, Friedman, Keynes, Malthus, Marginalist, Mill, Pareto, Physiocrat, Ricardo

**Economy, Economic(al), Economics** Agronomy, Careful, Cliometrics, Conversation, Frugal, Neat, Parsimony, Retrenchment, Shoestring, Thrift

**Ecstasy, Ecstatic** Bliss, Delight, E, Exultant, Joy, Lyrical, Rapture, Sent, Trance

**Ecumenical** Catholic, Lateran

**Eddy** Backset, Gurge, Maelstrom, Nelson, Pirl, Swelchie, Swirl, Vortex, Weel, Well, Whirlpool, Wiel

**Eden** Bliss, Fall, Heaven, Paradise, PM, Utopia

**Edentate** Sloth, Xenarthra

**Edge** Advantage, Arris, Border, Brim, Brink, Brittle, Brown, Burr, Deckle, End, Flange, Flounce, Frill, Fringe, Gunnel, Gunwale, Hem, Hone, Inch, Kerb, Leech, Limb(ate), Lip, List, Lute, Marge(nt), Margin, Orle, Parapet, Periphery, Picot, Pikadell, Piping, Rand, Rim, Rund, Rymme, Selvage, Selvedge, Sidle, Skirt, Strand, Verge

**Edible** Esculent, Nutritive

**Edict** Ban, Bull, Decree, Decretal, Fatwa, Interim, Irade, Nantes, Notice, Pragmatic, Proclamation, Rescript, Ukase

**Edifice** Booth, Building, Structure

**Edify** Instruct, Teach

**Edinburgh** Auld Reekie

**Edit(or), Editorial** Article, City, Cut, Emend, Dele, Garble, Leader, Prepare, Recense, Redact, Revise, Seaman

> **Edited** may indicate an anagram

**Edition** Aldine, Ed, Hexapla(r), Issue, Number, Omnibus, Version

**Edmond, Edmund** Burke, Gosse, Ironside(s), Rostand, Spenser

**Educate(d)** Baboo, Babu, Enlighten, Evolué, Informed, Instruct, Learned, Noursle, Nousell, Nousle, Nurture, Nuzzle, Scholarly, School, TEACH, Train

**Education(alist)** Adult, B.Ed, Classical, Didactics, Heurism, Learning, Montessori, Paedotrophy, Pedagogue, Pestalozzi, Piarist, Primary, Teacher, Upbringing

**Educe** Elicit, Evoke, Extract, Infer

**Edward** Confessor, Ed, Elder, Lear, Martyr, Ned, Ted

**Eel** Conger, Elver, Grig, Gulper, Gunnel, Lant, Launce, Leptocephalus, Moray, Murray, Murr(e)y, Snig, Spitchcock, Tuna

**Eerie** Spooky, Uncanny, Unked, Weird

**Efface** Cancel, Delete, Dislimn, ERASE, Expunge, Obliterate

**Effect(s), Effective, Effectual** Achieve, Acting, Auger, Bags, Belongings, Bit, Causal, Competent, Consequence, Coriolis, Doppler,

Enact, End, Estate, Fungibles, Gear, Hall, Home, Impact, Implement(al), Impression, Neat, Nisi, Operant, Outcome, Perficient, Potent, Promulgate, Raman, Repercussion, RESULT, Sovereign, Spin-off, Striking, Tableau, Telling, Upshot, Valid, Viable, Virtual, Win, Work, Zeeman

**Effeminate**   Camp, Carpet-knight, Carpet-monger, Cissy, Dildo, Epicene, Female, Milksop, Panty-waist, Prissy, Punce, Sissy, Tender, Unman

**Effervescence, Effervescent**   Bubbling, Ebullient, Fizz, Petillant, Soda

> **Effervescent**   may indicate an anagram

**Effete**   Camp

**Efficacious**   Effective, Operative, Potent

**Efficiency, Efficient**   Able, Capable, Competent, Ergonomics, Smart, Streamlined, Strong

**Effigy**   Figure, Guy, Idol, Image, Statua, Statue

**Efflorescence**   Bloom, Blossom, Reh

**Effluence, Effluent, Effluvia**   Air, Aura, Billabong, Discharge, Fume, Gas, Halitus, Miasma, Odour, Outflow, Outrush

**Effort**   Achievement, Attempt, Best, Conatus, Drive, Essay, Exertion, Fit, Herculean, Labour, Molimen, Nisus, Rally, Spurt, Stab, Strain, Struggle, TRY, Work, Yo

**Effrontery**   Audacity, Brass, Cheek, Neck, Nerve, Temerity

**Effulgent**   Bright, Radiant, Shining

**Effuse, Effusion**   Emanate, Exuberant, Exude, Gush, Lyric, Ode, Outburst, Prattle, Sanies, Screed, Spill

**Eg**   As, Example

**Egest**   Eliminate, Evacuate, Excrete, Void

**Egg(s)**   Abet, Berry, Bomb, Caviar(e), Chalaza, Clutch, Cockney, Collop, Easter, Edge, Fabergé, Fetus, Flyblow, Foetus, Glair(e), Goad, Goog, Graine, Hoy, Incite, Instigate, Layings, Mine, Nit, Oocyte, Oophoron, Ova, Ovum, Prairie oyster, Press, Raun, Roe, Seed, Spat, Spawn, Spur(ne), Tar(re), Treadle, Urge

**Egghead**   Don, Highbrow, Intellectual, Mensa, Pedant

**Egg-plant**   Aubergine, Brinjal

**Egg-producer**   Gametophyte, Hen, Ovipositor

**Egg-shaped**   Obovate, Oval, Ovate

**Egg-white**   Albumen, Glair

**Ego(ism)**   Conceit, I, Narcissism, Not-I, Pride, Self, Solipsism, Vanity

**Egocentric**   Solipsistic

**Egregious**   Eminent, Flagrant, Glaring, Shocking

**Egypt(ian), Egyptologist**   Arab, Cairene, Carter, Cheops, Chephren, Copt(ic), ET, Gippo, Goshen, Gyppo, Imhetop, Nasser, Nefertiti, Nilote, Nitrian, Osiris, Rameses, Syene, UAR, Wafd, Wog

**Eiderdown** Bedspread, Duvet, Quilt

**Eight(h), Eighth day** Acht, Byte, Crew, Nundine, Octal, Octastrophic, Octave, Octet, Ogdoad, Ure

**Eighteen** Majority

**Einsteinium** Es

**Either** Also, Both, O(u)ther, Such

**Ejaculate** Blurt, Discharge, Emit, Exclaim

**Eject** Bounce, Disgorge, Dismiss, Emit, Erupt, Expel, Oust, Propel, Spew, Spit

**Eke** Augment, Eche, Enlarge, Husband, Supplement

**Elaborate** Detail, Develop, Enlarge, Evolve, Florid, Improve, Intricate, Ornate, Stretch

**Elan** Dash, Drive, FLAIR, Gusto, Lotus, Spirit, Vigour

**Elapse** Glide, Intervene, Pass

**Elastic(ity)** Adaptable, Buoyant, Dopplerite, Elater, Flexible, Give, Resilient, Rubber, Springy, Stretchy, Tone

**Elate(d), Elation** Cheer, Euphoric, Exalt, Exhilarate, Gladden, Hault, Ruff(e)

**Elbow, Elbow tip** Akimbo, Ancon, Angle, Bender, Hustle, Joint, Jostle, Justle, Kimbo, Noop, Nudge, Olecranon

**Elder(ly), Eldest** Ancestor, Ancient, Bourtree, Chief, Classis, Eigne, Guru, OAP, Presbyter, SENIOR, Sire, Susanna, Wallwort

**Eldorado** Ophir

**Eleanor(a)** Bron, Duse, Nora(h)

**Elect(ed), Election, Electoral** Choice, Choose, Chosen, Eatanswill, Elite, Gerrymander, Hustings, In, Israelite, Opt, Pick, PR, Psephology, Rectorial, Return, Select

**Electrical discharge** Corposant, Ion, Zwitterion

**Electrical instrument** Battery, Charger, Galvaniser, Mains, Rheostat

**Electrical unit** Amp(ere), Coulomb, Farad, Kilowatt, Ohm, Volt, Watt

**Electric eye** Pec

**Electrician** Gaffer, Lineman, Ohm, Siemens, Sparks

**Electricity** Galvanism, HT, Juice, Power, Static

**Electrify** Astonish, Galvanise, Startle, Thrill

**Electrode** Anode, Element

**Electrolyte** Ampholyte

**Electro-magnet(ic)** Abampere, Oersted, Solenoid, Weber

**Electronic, Electronic device** FET, Linac, Martenot

**Elegance, Elegant** Artistic, Bijou, Chic, Classy, Debonair, Finesse, Gainly, Galant, Grace, Jimp, Luxurious, Polished, Ritzy, SMART, Soigné(e), Tall, Urbane

**Elegy**  Dirge, Lament, Poem

**Element(s), Elementary**  Abcee, Abecedarian, Absey, Actinide, Actinium (Ac), Air, Alabamine, Alloy, Aluminium (Al), Americium (Am), Antimony (Sb), Argon (Ar), Arsenic (As), Astatine (At), Atom, Barium (Ba), Berkelium (Bk), Beryllium (Be), Bismuth (Bi), Boron (B), Brimstone, Bromine (Br), Cadmium (Cd), Caesium (Cs), Calcium (Ca), Californium (Cf), Carbon (C), Cerium (Ce), Cesium, Chlorine (Cl), Chromium (Cr), Cobalt (Co), Columbium, COMPONENT, Copper (Cu), Curium (Cm), Detail, Didymium, Dyprosium (D), Earth, Einsteinium (Es), Erbium (Er), ESSENCE, Europium (Eu), Factor, Feature, Fermium (Fm), Fire, Fluorine (F), Francium (Fr), Gadolinium (Gd), Gallium (Ga), Germanium (Ge), Gold (Au), Hafnium (Hf), Hahnium (Hn), Halogen, Helium (He), Holmium (Ho), Hydrogen (H), Illinium, Inchoate, Indium (In), Iodine (I), Iridium (Ir), Iron (Fe), Isotope, Krypton (Kr), Lanthanide, Lanthanum (La), Lawrencium (Lr), Lead (Pb), Lithium (Li), Lutetium (Lu), Magnesium (Mg), Manganese (Mn), Mendelevium (Md), Mercury (Hg), Metalloid, Milieu, Molybdenum (Mo), Neodymium (Nd), Neon (Ne), Neptunium (Np), Nickel (Ni), Niobium (Nb), Niton, Nitrogen (N), Nobelium (No), Osmium (Os), Oxygen (O), Palladium (Pd), Phitonium, Phlogiston, Phosphorus (P), Platinum (Pt), Plutonium (Pu), Polonium (Po), Potassium (K), Praseodymium (Pr), Primary, Principle, Promethium (Pm), Protactinium (Pa), Radium (Ra), Radon (Rn), Rare Earth, Rhenium (Re), Rhodium (Rh), Rubidium (Rb), Rudimental, Ruthenium (Ru), Rutherfordium, Samarium (Sm), Scandium (Sc), Selenium (Se), Silicon (Si), Silver (Ag), Simple, Sodium (Na), Strontium (Sr), Sulphur (S), Tantalum (Ta), Technetium (Tc), Tellurium (Te), Terbium (Tb), Terra, Thallium (Tl), Thorium (Th), Thulium (Tm), Tin (Sn), Titanium (Ti), Trace, Tungsten (W), Uranium (U), Vanadium (V), Virginium, Water, Weather, Wolfram, Xenon (Xe), Ylem, Ytterbium (Yb), Yttrium (Y), Zinc (Zn), Zirconium (Zr)

**Elephant**  Babar, Hathi, Jumbo, Kheda, Mammoth, Mastodon, Oliphant, Pachyderm, Rogue, Subungulata, Trumpeter, Tusker, White

**Elephant-headed**  Ganesa

**Elephant's ears**  Begonia

**Elevate, Elevation, Elevator**  Agger, Attitude, Cheer, El, Eminence, Ennoble, Heighten, Hoist, Jack, Lift, Machan, Montic(u)le, Monticulus, Promote, RAISE, Random, Ridge, Steeve, Up(lift), Upraise

**Eleven**  Elf, Legs, Side, Team, XI

**Elf, Elves**  Alfar, Chiricaune, Fairy, Goblin, Imp, Ouph, Pigwiggen, Pixie, Ribhus

**Elicit**  Evoke, Extract, Toase, Toaze, Tose, Toze

**Eligible**  Available, Catch, Fit, Nubile, Parti, Qualified, Worthy

**Eliminate, Elimination**  Cull, Delete, Discard, Exclude, Execute, Heat, Omit, Purge, Separate, Void

**Elision**  Syncope

**Elite**  Best, Choice, Crack, CREAM, Elect, Flower, Ton, U, Zaibatsu

**Elixir**  Amrita, Arcanum, Bufo, Cordial, Daffy, Essence, Medicine, Panacea, Quintessence, Tinct

**Elizabeth**  Bess(ie), Gloriana, Oriano

**Elk**  Deer, Moose

**Elkoshite**  Nahum

**Ellipse, Elliptic**  Conic, Oblong, Oval

**Elm**  Slippery

**Elmer**  Gantry

**Elongate**  Extend, Lengthen, Protract, Stretch

**Elope**  Abscond, Decamp

**Eloquence, Eloquent**  Articulate, Demosthenic, Facundity, Fluent, Honey-tongued, Oracy, Rhetoric, Vocal

**Elsewhere**  Absent, Alibi, Aliunde

**Elucidate**  Explain, Expose

**Elude, Elusive**  Avoid, Dodge, Escape, EVADE, Evasive, Foil, Intangible, Jink, Slippy

> **Elves**  see ELF

**Em**  Mut(ton), Pica

**Emaciated, Emaciation**  Atrophy, Erasmus, Gaunt, Haggard, Lean, Skinny, Sweeny, Tabid, Thin, Wasted

**Emanate, Emanation**  Arise, Aura, Discharge, Exude, Issue, Miasma, Radiate, Spring

**Emancipate, Emancipation**  Deliver, Forisfamiliate, Free, LIBERATE, Manumission, Uhuru

**Emasculate**  Castrate, Debilitate, Evirate, Geld

**Embalm**  Anoint, Mummify, Preserve

**Embankment**  Bund, Causeway, Dam, Dyke, Earthwork, Levee, Mattress, Mound, Rampart, Remblai, Staith(e)

**Embargo**  BAN, Blockade, Edict, Restraint

**Embark**  Begin, Board, Enter, Inship, Launch, Sail

**Embarrass(ed), Embarrassment**  Abash, Ablush, Cheap, Disconcert, Gêne, Mess, Pose, Predicament, Shame, Sheepish, Squirming, Straitened, Upset

> **Embarrassed**  may indicate an anagram

**Embassy**  Consulate, Embassade, Legation, Mission

**Embed(ded)**  Fix, Immerse, Inlaid, Set

**Embellish(ed), Embellishment**  Adorn, Beautify, Deck, Decorate, Dress, Embroider, Enrich, Garnish, Garniture, ORNAMENT, Ornate, Rel(l)ish

**Ember(s)**  Ash, Cinder, Clinker, Gleed

**Embezzle**  Defalcate, Peculate, Purloin, STEAL

**Embitter(ed)**  Acerbate, Aggravate, Enfested, Rankle, Sour

**Emblem(atic)**  Badge, Bear, Colophon, Daffodil, Ichthys, Impresa, Insignia, Kikumon, Leek, Lis, Maple leaf, Oak, Rose, Roundel, Shamrock, Sign, Spear-thistle, SYMBOL, Tau-cross, Thistle, Token, Totem(ic), Triskelion, Wheel

**Embody, Embodied, Embodiment**  Epitome, Fuse, Incarnation, Incorporate, Quintessence

**Embolism**  Clot

**Emboss(ed)**  Adorn, Chase, Cloqué, Engrave, Pounce, Raise, Toreutic

**Embrace(d)**  Abrazo, Accolade, Arm, Canoodle, Clasp, Clinch, Clip, Coll, Complect, Comprise, Cuddle, Embosom, Encircle, Enclasp, Enclose, Enfold, Enlacement, Envelop, Espouse, Grab, Halse, Haulst, Hause, Hesp, Hug, Imbrast, Inarm, Inclip, Include, Kiss, Lasso, Neck, Press, Stemme, Twine, Welcome, Wrap

> **Embraces, Embracing**  may indicate a hidden word

**Embrocate, Embrocation**  Anoint, Arnica, Liniment

**Embroider(y)**  Arrasene, Battalia-pie, Braid, Brede, Couching, Embellish, Exaggerate, Handiwork, Lace(t), Mola, Needlepoint, Needlework, Ornament, Orphrey, Orris, Purl, Sampler, Sew, Smocking, Stitch, Stumpwork, Tambour, Tent, Wrap

**Embroideress**  Mimi

**Embroil**  Confuse, Entangle, Involve, Trouble

**Embryo(nic)**  Blastula, Epicotyl, Fo(e)tus, Gastrula, Germ, Mesoblast, Nepionic, Origin, Undeveloped

**Emend**  Adjust, Alter, Edit, Reform

**Emerald**  Beryl, Gem, Green, Smaragd

**Emerge(ncy), Emerging**  Anadyomene, Craunch, Crise, Crisis, Crunch, Eclose, Emanate, Enation, Erupt, Exigency, Issue, Loom, Need, Outcrop, Pinch, Spring, Stand-by, Strait, Surface

> **Emerge from**  may indicate an anagram or a hidden word

**Emerson**  Waldo

**Emetic**  Apomorphine, Cacoon, Epicac, Evacuant, Ipecacuanha, Puke, Stavesacre

**Emigrant, Emigration**  Chozrim, Colonist, Italiot, Jordim, Settler, Yordim

**Emile**  Zola

**Emily**  Ellis

**Eminence, Eminent**  Alp, Altitude, Cardinal, Distinguished, Grand, Height, Hill, Inselberg, Lion, Lofty, Noble, NOTABLE, Palatine, Prominence, Renown, Repute, Stature, Tor, Trochanter, VIP

**Emissary**  Agent, Envoy, Legate, Marco Polo

**Emit**  Discharge, Emanate, Give, Issue, Utter

**Emmer**  Amelcorn, Wheat

**Emollient**  Paregoric

**Emolument**  Income, Perk, Remuneration, Salary, Stipend, Tip, Wages

**Emotion(al)**  Anger, Anoesis, Chord, Ecstasy, Excitable, Feeling, Hysteria, Joy, Limbic, Passion, Reins, Sensitive, Sentiment, Spirit, Transport, Weepy

**Empathy**  Identifying, Rapport, Sympathy

**Emperor**  Agramant(e), Akbar, Antoninus, Augustus, Babur, Barbarossa, Caligula, Caracalla, Charlemagne, Claudius, Commodus, Concerto, Constantine, Diocletes, Domitian, Ferdinand, Gaius, Gratian, Hadrian, Hirohito, Imp, Inca, Jimmu, Justinian, Kaiser, Keasar, King, Maximilian, Mikado, Ming, Mogul, Montezuma, Mpret, Napoleon, Nero, Nerva, Otho, Otto, Penguin, Purple, Pu-yi, Rex, Rosco, Ruler, Sovereign, Sultan, Tenno, Tiberius, Titus, Trajan, Tsar, Valens, Valerian, Vespasian, Vitellius

**Emphasize, Emphatic**  Accent, Bold, Dramatise, Forcible, Forzando, Hendiadys, Italic, Marcato, Positive, Sforzando, STRESS, Underscore, Vehement

**Empire**  Assyria, Byzantine, Chain, Domain, Empery, Georgia, Kingdom, NY, Ottoman, Realm, Roman

**Emplacement**  Battery, Platform

**Employ(ment)**  Business, Calling, Engage, Hire, Occupy, Pay, Practice, Pursuit, Shiftwork, Trade, Use, Using, Utilise, Vocation

**Employee(s)**  Factotum, Hand, Help, Payroll, Personnel, Servant, Staff, Walla(h), Worker

**Employer**  Baas, Boss, Master, Padrone, User

> **Employs**  may indicate an anagram

**Emporium**  Bazaar, Shop, Store

**Empower**  Authorise, Enable, Entitle, Permit

**Empress**  Eugenie, Josephine, Messalina, Queen, Sultana, Tsarina

**Empty**  Addle, Bare, Barren, Blank, Buzz, Claptrap, Clear, Deplete, Devoid, Drain, Exhaust, Expel, Futile, Gut, Inane, Jejune, Lade, Lave, Null, Phrasy, Pump, Teem, Toom, Unoccupied, Unpeople, Vacant, Vacate, Vain, Viduous, VOID

> **Empty**  may indicate an 'o' in the word or an anagram

**Emulate**  Ape, Copy, Envy, Equal, Imitate, Match

**Emulsion**  Pseudosolution

**Enable**  Authorise, Empower, Potentiate, Qualify, Sanction

**Enact**  Adopt, Effect, Ordain, Personate, Portray

**Enamel(led), Enamel work**  Aumail, Champlevé, Cloisonné, Della-robbia, Dentine, Fabergé, Ganion, Lacquer, Polish, Schwarzlot, Shippo, Smalto

**Encampment**  Bivouac, Douar, Dowar, Duar, Laager, Laer, Settlement

**Encase(ment)**  Box, Crate, Emboîtement, Encapsulate, Enclose

**Enchant(ed), Enchantment** Captivate, Charm, Delight, Gramary(e), Incantation, Magic, Necromancy, Rapt, Sorcery, Spellbind, Thrill

**Enchanter, Enchantress** Archimage, Archimago, Armida, Comus, Circe, Fairy, Lorelei, Magician, Medea, Mermaid, Prospero, Reim-kennar, Sorcerer, Vivien, Witch

**Encircle(d)** Enclose, Encompass, Entrold, Gird, Introld, Orbit, Ring, SURROUND

**Enclave** ENCLOSURE, Pocket

**Enclose(d), Enclosure** Beset, Boma, Box, Cage, Carol, Carrel, Case, Common, Compound, Corral, Court, Embowel, Embower, Enceinte, Encircle, Enclave, Enshrine, Fence, Fold, Forecourt, Garth, Haggard, Haw, Hem, Hope, Impound, In, Incapsulate, Insert, Lairage, Pale, Peel, Pele, Pen(t), Pightle, Pin, Plenum, Rail, Recluse, Ree(d), Ring, Saddling, Seal, Sekos, Sept, Seraglio, Serail, Several, Stell, Stockade, Sty, SURROUND, Tine, Wrap

**Encomium** Eulogy, Praise, Sanction, Tribute

**Encompass** Bathe, Begird, Beset, Environ, Include, Surround

**Encore** Again, Ancora, Bis, Ditto, Do, Iterum, Leitmotiv, Recall, Repeat

**Encounter** Battle, Brush, Combat, Contend, Cope, Face, Incur, Interview, MEET, One-one, Rencontre, Skirmish

**Encourage(ment), Encouraging** Abet, Acco(u)rage, Animate, Boost, Brighten, Cheer, Cohortative, Comfort, Commend, Egg, Elate, Embolden, Empatron, Exhort, Fortify, Foster, Fuel, Gee, Hearten, Heigh, Help, Hope, Hortatory, Incite, Inspirit, Pat, Patronise, Porceleusmatic, Prod, Push, Reassure, Root, Support, Upcheer, Uplift, Urge, Wean, Yo

**Encroach(ment)** Impinge, Infringe, Intrude, Invade, Overlap, Overstep, Poach, Purpresture, Trespass

**Encumber, Encumbrance** Burden, Charge, Clog, Deadwood, Dependent, HANDICAP, Impede, Load, Obstruct, Saddle

**Encyclopaedic** Comprehensive, Diderot, Extensive, Universal, Vast

**End(ing)** Abolish, Abut, Aim, Ambition, Amen, Anus, Arse, Bourn(e), Butt, Cease, Climax, Close, Closure, Cloture, Coda, Conclude, Crust, Curtain, Death, Desinence, Destroy, Determine, Dissolve, Domino, Effect, Envoi, Envoy, Epilogue, Exigent, Expire, Extremity, Fatal, Fattrels, Final(e), Fine, Finis, FINISH, Finite, Grave, Heel, Ish, Izzard, Izzet, Kill, Kybosh, Last, Loose, Nirvana, Peter, Point, Purpose, Remnant, Rescind, Result, Roach, Scotch, Shank, Slaughter, Sopite, Stub, Supernaculum, Surcease, Swansong, Tail, Telesis, Telic, Telos, Term, Terminal, Terminate, Terminus, Thrum, Tip, Toe, Ultimate, Up, Upshot, Z

**Endanger** Hazard, Imperil, Risk

**Endear(ing), Endearment** Adorable, Affection, Asthore, Caress, Enamour, Ingratiate, Jarta, Mavourneen, Peat

**Endeavour** Aim, Effort, Enterprise, Strive, Struggle, Try, Venture

**Endemic** Local, Prevalent

**Endless** Continuous, Ecaudate, Eternal, Eterne, Infinite, Perpetual, Undated

> **Endlessly** may indicate a last letter missing

**End of the world** Ragnarok

**Endorse(ment)** Adopt, Affirm, Allonge, Approve, Assurance, Back, Okay, Oke, Sanction, Second, Sign, SUPPORT, Underwrite, Visa

**Endow(ment)** Assign, Bequeath, Bestow, Bless, Cha(u)ntry, Dot, Enrich, Foundation, Gift, Leave, State, Vest

**Endure(d), Endurance, Enduring** Abought, Aby(e), Bear, Brook, Dree, Have, Hold, LAST, Livelong, Lump, Patience, Perseverance, Pluck, Ride, Stamina, Stand, Stay, Stout, Support, Sustain, Tether, Thole, Tolerance, Undergo, Wear

**Endymion** Bluebell

**Enema** Catharsis, Clyster, Purge

**Enemy** Antagonist, Boer, Devil, Fifth column, Foe(n), Fone, Opponent, Time

**Energetic, Energise, Energy** Active, Amp, Animation, Arduous, Chi, Dash, Drive, Dynamic, Dynamo, E, Entropy, EV, Force, Gism, Go, Hartree, Input, Instress, Jism, Jissom, Joule, Kinetic, Libido, Magnon, Orgone, Pep, Phonon, Potency, POWER, Quantum, Rad, Rydberg, Solar, Steam, Trans-uranic, Vigour, Vim, Zing, Zip

**Enfold** Clasp, Envelop, Stemme, Swathe, Wrap

**Enforce(ment)** Administer, Coerce, Control, Exact, Implement

**Eng** Agma

**Engage(d), Engagement, Engaging** Absorb, Accept, Appointment, At, Attach, Bespoken, Betrothal, Bind, Book, Busy, Contract, Date, Embark, Employ, Engross, Enlist, Enmesh, Enter, Gear, Gig, Hire, Hold, Interest, Interlock, Lock, Mesh, Met, Occupy, Pledge, Promise, Prosecute, Reserve, Skirmish, Sponsal, Sponsion, Spousal, Sprocket, Trip, Wage, Winsome

> **Engagement** may indicate a battle

**Engender** Beget, Breed, Cause, Occasion, Produce

**Engine** Athodyd, Booster, Bricole, Catapult, Diesel, Donkey, Dynamo, Four, Gin, Lean-burn, Locomotive, Machine, Mangonel, MOTOR, Nacelle, Onager, Outboard, Petard, Petrary, Petter, Rocket, Scorpion, Scramjet, Stirling, Terebra, Testudo, Traction, Trompe, Turbine, Turbo-prop, Two-handed, Two-stroke, Vernier, Wankel, Warwolf, Winch

**Engineer(s)** AEU, Arrange, CE, Greaser, Manoeuvre, Mastermind, Mime, Operator, Organise, Otto, Planner, RE, Rig, Sapper, Scheme, Smeaton, Stage, Stephenson, Telford, Wangle, Wankel, Watt, Whitworth

**England** Albany, Albion, Blighty, Demi-paradise, Merrie

**English(man)** Anglican, Anglice, Baboo, Babu, Basic, Brit, Choom, E, Eng, Jackeroo, Kipper, Limey, Mister, New Speak, Pidgin, Pom(my), Pommie, Pongo, Pork-pudding, Qui-hi, Qui-hye, Rock, Rooinek, Sassenach, Saxon, Shopkeeper, Side

**Engorge**  Devour, Glut, Swallow

**Engraft**  Inset

**Engrave(r), Engraving**  Aquatint, Blake, Carve, Chase, Cut, Die-sinker, Dry-point, Durer, Enchase, Eng, Etch, Hogarth, Impress, Inciser, Inscribe, Insculp, Intagliate, Inter, Mezzotint, Niello, Photoglyphic, Plate, Scalp, Scrimshander, Scrimshandy, Scrimshaw, Stillet, Stipple, Stylet, Turn, Xylographer

**Engross(ed)**  Absorb, Engage, Enwrap, Immerse, Monopolise, OCCUPY, Preoccupy, Rapt, Sink, Writ large

**Enhance**  Augment, Elevate, Embellish, Exalt, Heighten, Intensify

**Enigma(tic)**  Charade, Conundrum, Dilemma, Giaconda, Mystery, Oracle, Poser, Problem, PUZZLE, Quandary, Question, Rebus, Riddle, Secret, Teaser

**Enjoin**  Command, Direct, Impose, Prohibit, Require

**Enjoy(able), Enjoyment**  Apolaustic, Appreciate, Ball, Brook, Delictation, Fruition, Glee, Groove, Gusto, Like, Possess, Relish, Ripping, Savour, Wallow

**Enlarge(ment), Enlarger**  Accrue, Add, Aneurism, Aneurysm, Augment, Blow-up, Diagraph, Dilate, Expand, Expatiate, Increase, MAGNIFY, Ream, Swell, Telescope, Varicosity

**Enlighten(ment)**  Awareness, Dewali, Divali, Edify, Educate, Explain, Illumine, Instruct, Satori

**Enlist**  Attest, Conscript, Draft, Engage, Enrol, Join, Levy, Prest, Recruit, Volunteer

**Enliven(ed)**  Animate, Arouse, Brighten, Cheer, Comfort, Exhilarate, Ginger, Invigorate, Merry, Pep, Refresh, Warm

**Enmity**  Animosity, Aversion, Hatred, Malice, Rancour, Spite

**Ennoble**  Dub, Elevate, Exalt, Honour, Raise

**Ennui**  Boredom, Tedium

**Enormous**  Colossal, Exorbitant, Googol, Huge, IMMENSE, Jumbo, Mammoth, Mega, Vast

**Enough**  Adequate, AMPLE, Basta, Enow, Fill, Geyan, Pax, Plenty, Qs, Sate, Satis, Suffice, Sufficient, Via

**Enounce**  Affirm, Declare, State

**Enquire, Enquiry**  Ask, Check, Eh, Inquire, Organon, Request, Scan, See, Trial

**Enrage(d)**  Emboss, Enfelon, Imboss, INCENSE, Inflame, Infuriate, Livid, Madden, Wild

**Enrapture(d)**  Enchant, Ravish, Sent, Transport

**Enrich**  Adorn, Endow, Enhance, Fortify, Fructify

**Enrol(ment)**  Empanel, Enlist, Enter, JOIN, List, Muster, Register

**Ensconce(d)**  Establish, Settle, Shelter, Snug

**Ensemble** Band, Orchestra, Outfit, Set, Tout, Whole

**Enshrine** Cherish, Sanctity

**Ensign** Ancient, Badge, Banner, Duster, FLAG, Gonfalon, Officer, Pennon

**Enslave(ment)** Addiction, Bondage, Captivate, Chain, Enthral, Thrall, Yoke

**Ensue** Follow, Result, Succeed, Transpire

**Entail** Involve, Necessitate, Require

**Entangle(ment)** Ball, Elf, Embroil, Encumber, Ensnarl, Fankle, Implicate, KNOT, Mat, Ravel, Retiarius, Trammel

**Enter** Admit, Board, Broach, Come, Enrol, Infiltrate, Ingo, Insert, Invade, Lodge, Log, Penetrate, Record, Run, Submit, Table

**Enterprise, Enterprising** Adventure, Aunter, Dash, Emprise, Goey, Go-getter, Gumption, Industry, Plan, Push, Spirit, Stunt, Venture

**Entertain(er), Entertaining, Entertainment** Accourt, Acrobat, Afterpiece, Amphitryon, Amuse, Balladeer, Beguile, Busk, Cater, Cheer, Chout, Circus, Comedian, Conjure, Consider, Cottabus, Cuddy, Diseuse, Divert, Divertissement, Fete, Foy, Gaff, Gala, Gaudy, Harbour, Have, Hospitality, Host(ess), Interest, Interlude, Lauder, Light, Minstrel, Olio, Panto, Pap, Piece, Pierrot, Raree-show, Regale, Review, Revue, Rodeo, Serenade, Showbiz, Table, Tamasha, Tattoo, Treat, Vaudeville, Wattle

**Enthral(l)** Charm, Enchant, Enslave, Spellbind

**Enthuse, Enthusiasm, Enthusiast(ic)** Ardour, Buff, Bug, Cat, Crusader, Demon, Devotee, Ebullience, Estro, Fandom, Fiend, Fire, Flame, Freak, Furor(e), Gung-ho, Gusto, Hearty, Into, Keen, Lyrical, Mad, Mania, Nympholept, Oomph, Outpour, Overboard, Passion, Raring, Rave, Rhapsodise, Schwarmerei, Spirit, Verve, Warmth, Whole-hearted, Zealot, Zest

**Entice** Allure, Angle, Cajole, Decoy, Lure, Persuade, TEMPT, Tole, Toll

**Entire(ly), Entirety** Absolute, All, Clean, Complete, Inly, Intact, Integral, In toto, Lot, Thorough, Total, WHOLE

**Entitle(ment)** Empower, Enable, Legitim, Name, Right

**Entity** Being, Body, Existence, Holon, Tensor, Thing

**Entomologist** Fabré

**Entrail(s)** Bowels, Chawdron, Giblets, Gralloch. Guts, Ha(r)slet, Humbles, Lights, Numbles, Offal, Quarry, Tripe, Umbles, Viscera

**Entrance(d), Entrant, Entry** Access, Adit, Anteroom, Arch, Atrium, Avernus, Bewitch, Charm, Contestant, Door, Dromos, Entry, Eye, Fascinate, Foyer, Gate, Hypnotise, Ingress, Inlet, Introitus, Jawhole, Mesmerise, Narthex, Porch, Portal, Porte-cochère, Postern, Ravish, Record, Registration, Stem, Spellbound, Stoa, Stoma, Stulm, Torii

**Entreat(y)** Appeal, Ask, Beg, Beseech, Flagitate, IMPLORE, Orison, Petition, Plead, Pray, Prevail, Prig, Rogation, Solicit, Sue

**Entrée** Access, Dish, Entry, Ingate

**Entrench(ment)**  Coupure, Encroach, Fortify, Trespass

**Entrepreneur**  Businessman, Executor, Impresario

**Entrust**  Confide, Delegate, Give

> **Entry**  see ENTRANCE

**Entwine**  Impleach, Lace, Twist, Weave

**Enumerate, Enumeration**  Catalogue, Count, Detail, Fansi, List, Tell

**Enunciate**  Articulate, Declare, Deliver, Proclaim

**Envelop(e)**  Arachnoid, Chorion, Cuma, Corona, Cover(ing), Enclose, Invest, Involucre, Muffle, Mulready, Perianth, Sachet, Serosa, Smother, Surround, Swathe

**Environment, Environmental(ist)**  Ambience, Ecofreak, Econut, Green, Habitat, Milieu, Realo, Setting, Sphere, Surroundings

**Envisage**  Contemplate, Imagine, Suppose

**Envoi**  Farewell, RIP

**Envoy**  Agent, Diplomat, Elchee, El(t)chi, Hermes, Legate, Plenipotentiary

**Envy**  Begrudge, Covet, Jealousy

**Enzyme**  Allosteric, Amylase, Asparaginase, Bromel(a)in, Casease, Cathepsin, Cytase, Diastase, Erepsin, Inulase, Invertase, Isomerase, Kinase, Lactase, Ligase, Lipase, Lyase, Maltase, Oxidase, Papain, Pectase, Pepsin(e), Plasmin, Protease, Ptyalin, Ren(n)in, Saccharase, Thrombin, Trypsin, Urease, Urokinase, Zymase

**Epaminondas**  Theban

**Ephemera(l)**  Brief, Day, Drake, Fungous, Mayfly, Passing, Transitory, Trappings

**Epic**  Aeneid, Ben Hur, Beowulf, Calliope, Colossal, Dunciad, Edda, Epopee, Gilgamesh, Heroic, Homeric, Iliad, Kalevala, Lusiad(s), Nibelungenlied, Odyssey, Ramayana, Rhapsody, Saga

**Epicene**  Hermaphrodite

**Epicure(an)**  Apicius, Apolaustic, Connoisseur, Friand, Gastrosopher, Glutton, GOURMAND, Gourmet, Hedonist

**Epidemic**  Pandemic, Plague, Prevalent

**Epigram**  Adage, Mot, Proverb

**Epigraph**  Citation, Inscription, RIP

**Epilepsy, Epileptic**  Clonic, Eclampsia, Fit, Grand mal, Petit mal, Turn

**Epilogue**  Appendix, Coda, Postscript

**Epiphenomenon**  ESP

**Epiphyte**  Air-plant

**Episcopalian**  PE

**Episode**  Chapter, Incident, Page, Scene

**Epistle**  Lesson, Letter, Missive

**Epitaph**  Ci-git, Inscription, RIP

**Epithet**  Adj(ective), Antonomasia, Apathaton, Byword, Curse, Expletive, Panomphaean, TERM, Title

**Epitome, Epitomise**  Abridge, Abstract, Digest, Image, Model, Summary

**Epoch**  Age, Era, Period

**Epsom salts**  Kieserite

**Equable, Equably**  Calm, Just, Pari passu, Smooth, Tranquil

**Equal(ly), Equality**  Ana, As, Balanced, Compeer, Egal(ity), Emulate, Equinox, Equity, Even, For, Identical, Identity, Is, Iso-, Level, Match, Mate, Owelty, Par, Pari passu, PEER, Peregal, Pheer(e), Rise, Rival, SO, Square, Upsides, Wyoming, Ylike

**Equanimity**  Aplomb, Balance, Poise, Serenity

**Equate, Equation**  Balance, Reduce, Relate, Simultaneous

**Equator(ial)**  Line, Tropical

**Equerry**  Courtier, Officer, Page

**Equilibrium**  Balance, Composure, Isostasy, Poise

**Equip(age), Equipment**  Accoutrement, Adorn, Aguise, Aguize, Apparatus, Apparel, Appliance, Array, Attire, Carriage, Deck, Dight, Expertise, FURNISH, Gear, Gere, Get-up, Graith, Kit, Material, Muniments, Outfit, Retinue, Rig, Sonar, Stock, Stuff, Tackle, Turn-out

**Equity**  Actors, Equality, Justice, Law, Union

**Equivalent**  Correspondent, Equal, Equipollent, Same, Tantamount

**Equivocal**  Ambiguous, Dubious, Evasive, Fishy, Oracular, Vague

**Equivocate**  Flannel, Lie, Palter, Prevaricate, Quibble, Tergiversate, Weasel

**Er**  Um

**Era**  Age, Decade, Dynasty, Epoch, Hegira, Hej(i)ra, Hijra, Lias, Period

**Eradicate, Erase**  Abolish, Delete, Demolish, Destroy, Efface, Expunge, Extirp, Obliterate, Purge, Root, Scratch, Stamp-out, Uproot

**Erasmus**  Humanist

**Erbium**  Er

**Erect(ing), Erection**  Attolent, Build, Construct(ion), Elevate, Perpendicular, Priapism, Prick, Rear, Tentigo, Upright, Vertical

**Ergo**  Argal, Hence, Therefore

**Erica**  Heather, Ling

**Ermine**  Fur, Miniver, Stoat

**Ernie**  Bondsman

**Erode, Erosion**  Denude, Destroy, Deteriorate, Etch, Fret, Wash, Wear, Yardang

**Eros, Erotic**  Amatory, Amorino, Amorous, Aphrodisiac, Carnal, Cupid, Philtre, Prurient, Salacious

**Err(or)**  Anachronism, Blooper, Blunder, Boner, Clanger, Comedy, EE, Fault, Glaring, Human, Jeofail, Lapse, Lapsus, Literal, Mesprise, Mesprize,

Misgo, Misprint, Misprise, Misprize, MISTAKE, Mumpsimus, Out, Rove, Sin, Slip, Solecism, Stray, Trip, Typo, Wander

**Errand** Chore, Commission, Message, Mission, Sleeveless, Task

**Errand-boy** Cad, Galopin, Page

**Erratic** Unstable

**Erroneous** False, Inaccurate, Mistaken, Non-sequitur

**Ersatz** Artificial, Synthetic

**Erudite, Erudition** Academic, Didactic, Learned, Savant, Scholar, Wisdom

**Erupt(ion), Erupture** Belch, Brash, Burst, Ecthyma, Eject, Emit, Emphlysis, Exanthem(a), Exanthemata, EXPLODE, Fumarole, Hornito, Lichen, Mal(l)ander, Mallender, Morphew, Outbreak, Papilla, Pompholyx, Pustule, Rash, Scissure

**Escalate, Escalator** Accrescence, Expand, Granary, Grow, Lift, Travolator

**Escape(e), Escapade** Abscond, Atride, Avoid, Bolt, Caper, Eject, Elope, Elude, Elusion, Evade, Exit, Flee, Flight, Frolic, Hole, Houdini, Lam, Leakage, Loop(-hole), Meuse, Mews, Muse, Outlet, Prank, Refuge, Runaway, Scapa, Scarper, Shave, Slip, Vent, Wilding, Wriggle

**Escapement** Foliot

**Eschew** Abandon, Avoid, Forego, Ignore, SHUN

**Escort** Accompany, Attend, Bodyguard, Chaperone, Comitatus, Conduct, Convoy, Cortege, Corvette, Date, Entourage, Frigate, Gallant, Gigolo, Guide, Lead, Outrider, Protector, Retinue, See, Squire, Take, Usher, Walker

**Escutcheon** Crest, Shield

**Eskimo** Aleut, Husky, In(n)uit, Inukitut, Thule, Yupik

**Esoteric** Abstruse, Acroamatic, Inner, Mystic, Occult, Orphic, Private, Rarefied, Recondite, Secret

**Especial(ly)** Chiefly, Esp, Outstanding, Particular

**Espionage** Spying, Surveillance

**Esplanade** Promenade, Walk

**Esprit** Insight, Spirit, Understanding, Wit

**Esquire** Armiger(o), Esq, Gent

**Essay** Article, Attempt, Causerie, Dabble, Endeavour, Go, Paper, Stab, Theme, Thesis, Treatise, Try

**Essayist** Addison, Bacon, Columnist, Elia, Ellis, Emerson, Hazlett, Holmes, Hunt, Huxley, Lamb, Locke, Montaigne, Pater, Prolusion, Ruskin, Scribe, WRITER

**Essence** Alma, Attar, Being, Core, Element, Entia, Esse, Extract, Fizzen, Flavouring, Foison, Gist, Heart, Hom(e)ousian, Inbeing, Inscape, Kernel, Marrow, Mirbane, Myrbane, Nub, Nutshell, Ottar, Otto, Perfume, Per-se, Pith, Quiddity, Ratafia, Soul, Ylang-ylang

**Essential(ly)** Basic, Central, Crucial, Entia, Fundamental, Imperative, Inherent, Integral, Intrinsic, Key, Linch-pin, Material, Must, Necessary, Per-se, Prana, Prerequisite, Radical, Requisite, Vital, Whatness

**Establish(ed)** Anchor, Ascertain, Base, Build, Create, Enact, Endemic, Ensconce, Fix, FOUND, Haft, Instal(l), Instate, Institute, Pitch, Pre-set, Prove, Raise, Root(ed), Set, Stable, Standing, Trad, Trite, Valorise, Verify

**Establishment** Building, Business, CE, Church, Co, Concern, Engrain, Evince, Hacienda, Institution, Lodge, Salon, School, Seat, System

**Estate** Allod(ium), Alod, Assets, Commons, Demesne, Domain, Dowry, Fazenda, Fee-simple, Fee-tail, Feu, General, Hacienda, Hagh, Haugh, Having, Hay, Land-living, Latifundium, Legitim, Manor, Messuage, Odal, Personality, Plantation, Press, PROPERTY, Runrig, Situation, Spiritual, Standing, Temporal, Udal

**Esteem(ed), Estimable** Account, Admiration, Appreciation, Count, Have, Honour, Los, Precious, Price, Pride, Prize, Rate, REGARD, Respect, Store, Value, Venerate, Wonder, Worthy

**Ester** Olein, Phthalate, Urethan(e)

> **Estimable** see ESTEEM

**Estimate, Estimation** Appraise, Assess, Calculate, Carat, Conceit, Esteem, Extrapolation, Forecast, Gauge, Guess, Opinion, Quotation, Rate, Rating, Reckon, Regard, Sight, Value, Weigh

**Estrange** Alienate, Disunite, Wean

**Estuary** Bay, Creek, Delta, Firth, Gironde, Humber, Inlet, Mouth, Ostial, Para

**Esurient** Arid, Insatiable

**Etc(etera)** Et al(ia), So on

**Etch(ing)** Aquafortis, Aquatint(a), Bite, ENGRAVE, Incise, Inscribe

**Eternal, Eternity** Ageless, Endless, Eviternal, Ewigkeit, Forever, Immortal, Infinity, Never-ending, Perdurable, Perpetual, Tarnal, Timeless

**Ether** Atmosphere, Ch'i, Gas, Sky, Yang, Yin

**Ethereal** Airy, Delicate, Fragile, Heavenly, Nymph

**Ethic(al), Ethics** Deontics, Marcionite, Moral, Principles

**Ethiopia(n)** African, Amharic, Asmara, Cushitic, Geez, Kabele, Kebele

**Ethnic** Racial

**Etiquette** Code, Conduct, MANNERS, Propriety, Protocol, Ps and Qs, Punctilio

**Etna** Empedocles, Vessel, Volcano

**Etonian** Oppidan, Victim

**Etymologist** Isodore

**Eucalyptus** Bloodwood, Coolabah, Gum-tree, Ironbark, Marri, Morrell, Sallee, Stingybark, Tewart, Tooart, Tuart, Wandoo

**Eucharist** Communion, Housel, Mass, Supper, Viaticum

**Eugene**  Aram, Onegin

**Eulogy**  Encomium, Panegyric, Praise

**Euphausia**  Krill, Shrimp

**Euphemism**  Fib, Gosh, Gracious, Heck, Hypocorism

**Euphoria, Euphoric**  Cock-a-hoop, Elation, High, Jubilation, Rapture

**Euphrasia**  Eyebright

**Eurasian**  Chee-chee, Chi-chi

**European**  Balt, Catalan, Community, Croat, E, Faringee, Faringhi, Feringhee, Fleming, Hungarian, Hunky, Japhetic, Lapp, Lithuanian, Polack, Ruthene, Ruthenian, Serb, Slovene, Topi-Wallah, Vlach

**Europium**  Eu

**Eustace**  Diamonds

**Evacuate, Evacuation**  Excrete, Expel, Getter, Planuria, Planury, Scramble, Vent, Void, Withdraw

**Evade, Evasion, Evasive**  Ambages, Avoid, Coy, Dodge, Duck, Elude, Escape, Fence, Hedge, Loophole, Prevaricate, Quibble, Quillet, Scrimshank, Shifty, Shirk, Shuffling, Sidestep, Skive, Skrimshank, Stall, Subterfuge, Waive

**Evaluate, Evaluation**  Appraise, Assess, Estimate, Gauge, Rate, Review, Waid(e), Weigh

**Evanescent**  Cursory, Fleeting, Fugacious

**Evangelical, Evangelist**  Converter, Crusader, Fisher, Gospeller, John, Luke, Marist, Mark, Matthew, Moody, Morisonian, Peculiar, Preacher, Stundist, Wild

**Evaporate, Evaporation**  Condense, Dehydrate, Desorb, Exhale, Steam, Steme, Ullage, Vaporise

**Evelyn**  Diarist, Hope

**Eve(n), Evening**  Albe(e), Albeit, All, Average, Balanced, Clean, Drawn, Dusk, Een, Ene, Equable, Equal, Fair, Flush, Iron, Level, Meet, Nightfall, Par, Plain, Plane, Plateau, Quits, Rib, Smooth, Subfusc, Subfusk, Sunset, Tib(b)s, Toss-up, Twilight, Vesperal, Vespertinal, Vigil, Yester, Yet

**Evening flight**  Ro(a)ding

**Evensong**  Vespers

**Event**  Case, Circumstance, Discus, Episode, Fest, Happening, Heat, Incident, Leg, Occasion, Occurrence, Ongoing, Outcome, Result

**Even-toed**  Artiodactyl

**Eventual(ly), Eventuality**  Case, Contingent, Finally, Future, In time, Nd

**Ever**  Always, Ay(e), Constantly, Eternal, Eviternity

**Everglade**  Vlei

**Evergreen**  Abies, Ageless, Arbutus, Cembra, Cypress, Gaultheria, Ivy, Myrtle, Periwinkle, Pinaster, Privet, Washington, Winterberry

**Everlasting** Cat's ear, Enduring, Eternal, Immortal, Immortelle, Recurrent, Tarnal

**Every(one), Everything** All, Complete, Each, Sum, The works, Tout, Universal, Varsal

**Everyday** Informal, Mundane, Natural, Ordinary, Plain

**Everywhere** Omnipresent, Passim, Rife, Throughout, Ubiquity

**Evict** Disnest, Eject, Expel, Oust

**Evidence, Evident** Adminicle, Apparent, Argument, Axiomatic, Circumstantial, Clear, Confessed, Distinct, Document, Flagrant, Indicate, Internal, Manifest, Obvious, Overt, PATENT, Plain, Proof, Record, Sign, Testimony, Understandable

**Evil** Ahriman, Alastor, Amiss, Badmash, Bale, Beelzebub, Budmash, Corrupt, Depraved, Eale, Guilty, Harm, Hydra, Ill, Iniquity, Malefic, Mischief, Necessary, Night, Perfidious, Shrewd, Sin, SINISTER, Turpitude, Vice, Wicked

**Evil eye** Jettatura

**Evince** Disclose, Exhibit, Indicate, MANIFEST, Show

**Eviscerate(d)** Debilitate, Disembowel, Drawn, Gralloch

**Evoke** Arouse, Awaken, Elicit, Move, Stir

**Evolution** Countermarch, Development, Growth, Holism, Moner(on), Turning

> **Evolution** may indicate an anagram

**Ewe** Crone, Gimmer, Sheep, Teg, Theave

**Ex** Former, Late, Quondam, Ten

**Exacerbate** Aggravate, Embitter, Exasperate, Irritate, Needle

**Exact(ing), Exactitude, Exactly** Accurate, Authentic, Careful, Dead, Definite, Due, Elicit, Estreat, Even, Exigent, Extort, Fine, Formal, It, Jump, Literal, Mathematical, Meticulous, Nice(ty), Pat, PRECISE, Require, Spang, Specific, Spot-on, Strict, T

**Exaction** Blackmail, Extortion, Impost, Montem, Sorelion, Tax

**Exaggerate(d), Exaggeration** Amplify, Boast, Camp, Colour, Distend, Dramatise, EMBROIDER, Goliathise, Hyperbole, Inflate, Magnify, Munch(h)ausen, Overdo, Overdraw, Overpaint, Overstate, Romance, Stretch, Tall

**Exalt(ed), Exaltation** Attitudes, Deify, Elation, Enhance, Ennoble, Erect, Extol, Glorify, High, Jubilance, Larks, PRAISE, Rapture, Ruff(e), Sublime, Supernal, Throne

**Exam(ine), Examinee, Examiner, Examination** Agrégé, A-level, Analyse, Analyst, Appose, Audit, Auscultation, Autopsy, Biopsy, Case, Check-up, Cognosce, Comb, CSE, Docimasy, Entrance, Expiscate, Explore, GCE, GCSE, Grade(s), Greats, Gulf, Haruspex, Hearing, Inspect, Inter, Interrogate, Jerque, Jury, Little-go, Local, Mark, Matriculation, Medical, Moderator, Mods, Mug, O-level, Once-over, Oral, Ordalian,

# Example

Ordeal, Overhaul, Palpate, Paper, Peruse, Post-mortem, Prelim, Probe, Pry, Pump, QUESTION, Quiz, Ransack, Recce, Reconnaissance, Responsions, Review, Sayer, Scan, Scrutator, Scrutinise, Search, Seek, Sift, Sit, Smalls, Sus(s), Test, Trial, Tripos, Try, Vet, Viva

**Example** Apotheosis, Assay-piece, Byword, Epitome, FOR EXAMPLE, Foretaste, Illustration, Instance, Lead, Model, Paradigm, Paragon, PATTERN, Praxis, Precedent, Prototype, Shining, Specimen, Standard, Type

**Exasperate, Exasperation** Anger, Irk, Irritate, Nettle, Provoke

**Excavate, Excavation, Excavator** Armadillo, Burrow, Catacomb, Crater, Delf, Delph, DIG, Dike, Ditch, Dredge, Drive, Gaulter, Hollow, Mine, Pichiciago, Pioneer, Pioner, Pyoner, Quarry, Shaft, Sondage, Stope, Well

**Exceed, Exceeding(ly)** Amain, Outdo, Overstep, Surpass, Transcend, Very

**Excel** Beat, Dominate, Outbrag, Outdo, Outtop, Overdo, Overtop, Ring, SHINE, Transcend, War

**Excellence, Excellency, Excellent** A1, Admirable, A-per-se, Assay-piece, Beaut, Blinder, Bravo, Boffo, Boss, Bully, Capital, Champion, Cheese, Choice, Class(y), Copacetic, Copasetic, Copesettic, Corking, Crack, Crucial, Daisy, Def, Dic(k)ty, Dilly, Elegant, Exemplary, Fab, Fantastic, Great, Grit, HE, High, Humdinger, Inimitable, Jake, Jammy, Lummy, Matchless, Mean, Merit, Noble, Paragon, Prime, Rad, Rare, Rattling, Ripping, Say-piece, Spiffing, Super-duper, Superior, Supreme, Tip-top, Top-hole, Topping, Virtue, Wal(l)y, Wicked, Worth

**Except(ion)** Bar, But, Else, Exc, Nobbut, Omit, Save, Unless

**Exceptional** Abnormal, Anomaly, Especial, Extraordinary, Rare, Singular, Special, Uncommon

**Excerpt** Extract, Passage, Scrap

**Excess(ive), Excessively** All-fired, Basinful, Exorbitant, Extortionate, Extravagant, Flood, Fulsome, Glut, Hard, Inordinate, LAVISH, Nimiety, OD, Old, OTT, Outrage, Over, Overcome, Overdose, Overmuch, Owercome, Plethora, Preponderance, Salt, Satiety, Spate, Spilth, Steep, Superabundant, Superfluity, Surfeit, Surplus, Ultra, Undue, Unequal, Woundily

**Exchange** Baltic, Bandy, Barter, Bourse, Cambist, Catallactic, Change, Chop, Commute, Contango, Convert, Cope, Enallage, Excambion, Inosculate, Interplay, MARKET, Mart, Paraphrase, Rally, Recourse, Rialto, Royal, Scorse, Scourse, Stock, Swap, Switch, Swop, Tolsel, Tolsey, Tolzey, TRADE, Traffic, Trophallaxis, Truck

**Excise(man), Excise district** Ablate, Crop, Expunge, Gauger, Resect, Ride, Tax

**Excite(d), Excitable, Excitement, Exciting** Aerate, Agog, Amove, Animate, Aphrodisiac, Arouse, Athrill, Awaken, Brouhaha, Combustible, Commotion, Electrify, Emove, Enthuse, Erethism, Feisty, Fever, Fire, Flap,

Frantic, Frenzy, Frisson, Furore, Fuss, Galvanise, Gas, Headiness, Heat, Hectic, Het, Hey-go-mad, Hilarity, Hobson-Jobson, Hoopla, Hothead, Hysterical, Impel, Incite, Inflame, Intoxicate, Kick, Kindle, Metastable, Must, Neurotic, Orgasm, Panic, Passion, Pride, Provoke, Racy, Rile, ROUSE, Ruff, Rut, Send, Spin, Spur, Startle, Stimulate, Stir(e), Suscitate, Tetany, Tew, Thrill, Trickle, Twitter, Upraise, Waken, Yerk

**Excite(d)** may indicate an anagram

**Exclaim, Exclamation** Ahem, Blurt, Crikey, Criv(v)ens, Ejaculate, Epiphonema, Eureka, Good-now, Haith, Heigh-ho, Hem, Hosanna, Pling, Protest, Pshaw, Sasa, Sese(y), Sessa, Walker, Whau, Yippee, Zounds

**Exclude, Exclusion** Ban, Bar, Block, Debar, Disbar, Eliminate, Except, Omit, Ostracise, Outbar, Outwith

**Exclusive** Closed-shop, Complete, Debarment, Elect, Monopoly, Particular, Pure, Rare, Scoop, Select, Single, Sole

**Excommunicate** Curse

**Excoriate** Flay, Slam

**Excrement** Dirt, Dung, Faeces, Frass, Meconium, Ordure, Refuse, Puer, Pure, Sir-reverence, Shit(e), Turd, Waste

**Excrescence** Aril, Carnosity, Caruncle, Enate, Gall, Growth, Knob, Lump, Pimple, Spavin(e), Strophiole, Talpa, Twitter(-bone), Wart

**Excruciate, Excruciating** Agonising, Rack, Torment, Torture

**Exculpate** Acquit, Clear, Forgive

**Excursion** Cruise, Dart, Digression, Jaunt, Outing, Road, Sally, Sashay, Sortie, Tour, Trip

**Excusable, Excuse** Absolve, Alibi, Amnesty, Condone, Essoin, Essoyne, Exempt, Exonerate, Forgive, Occasion, Out, Overlook, Palliate, PARDON, Pretext, Release, Salvo, Venial, Viable, Whitewash

**Execrate** Abhor, Ban, Boo, Curse

**Execute(d), Executioner, Executive, Executor** Abhorson, Accomplish, Administrate, Behead, Carnifex, Discharge, Exor, Finish, Gan, Gar(r)otte, Gin, Guardian, Hang, Implement, Ketch, Kill, Koko, Management, Official, Perform, Pierrepoint, Politburo, Scamp, Top, Trustee

**Exemplar(y)** Byword, Laudable, Model, Paragon, St, Warning

**Exemplify** Cite, Epitomise, Illustrate, Instantiate, Satisfy

**Exempt(ion)** Dispensation, Exclude, Exeem, Fainites, Fains, Free, Immune, Impunity, Indemnity, Overslaugh, Quarter, Spare, Vains

**Exercise(s)** Aerobics, Air, Antic, Callanetics, Cal(l)isthenics, Cloze, Constitutional, Drill, Employ, Enure, Eurhythmics, Exert, Gradus, Inure, Isometrics, Kata, Lesson, Limber, Medau, Op, PE, Ply, Practice, Practise, PT, Push-up, Qigong, Shintaido, Solfeggi(o), Thema, Thesis, Train, Use, Wield, Work, Xyst(us), Yomp

> **Exercise(d)** may indicate an anagram

**Exert(ion)** Conatus, EFFORT, Exercise, Labour, Operate, Strain, Strive,

Struggle, Trouble, Wield

**Ex-European**  Japhetic

**Exhalation, Exhale**  Breath, Fume, Miasma, Reek, Vapour, Transpire

**Exhaust(ed), Exhausting, Exhaustion, Exhaustive**  All-in, Beaten, Bugger(ed), Burn, Bushed, Consume, Deadbeat, Debility, Deplete, Detailed, Do, Done, Drain, Effete, Empty, End, Fatigue, Forfeuchen, Forfoughen, Forfoughten, Forjaskit, Forjeskit, Forswink, Frazzle, Gruelling, Inanition, Jet-stream, Jiggered, Mate, Milk, Out, Poop, Rag, Rundown, Shot, Spend, Spent, Stonkered, Tire, Use, Wabbit, Wappend, Warby, Wasted, Waygone, WEARY, Wind, Worn, Zonked

**Exhibit(ion), Exhibitioner**  Circus, Demo, Demonstrate, Demy, Diorama, Discover, Display, Evince, Expo, Expose, Fair, Hang, Indicate, MANIFEST, Olympia, Pageant, Panopticon, Parade, Present, Retrospective, Salon, Scene, Show(piece)

**Exhilarate(d)**  Bubble, Cheer, Elate, Enliven

**Exhort(ation)**  Admonish, Allocution, Caution, Counsel, Incite, Lecture, Para(e)nesis, Persuade, Urge

**Exhume**  Delve, Disinter, Resurrect, Unearth

**Exigency, Exigent**  Emergency, Pressing, Taxing, Urgent, Vital

**Exile**  Babylon, Banish, Deport, Emigré, Expatriate, Exul, Galut(h), Ostracise, Outlaw, Relegate, Wretch

**Exist(ence), Existing**  Be(ing), Dwell, Enhypostasia, Esse, Extant, Identity, Life, Live, Perseity, Substantial

**Existentialist**  Camus, Sartre

**Exit**  Door, Egress, Gate, Leave, Outlet

**Exodus**  Book, Departure, Flight, Hegira, Hejira

**Ex-official**  Outler

**Exonerate(d)**  Absolve, Acquit, Clear, Excuse, Exempt, Shriven

**Exorbitant**  Excessive, Expensive, Steep, Tall, Undue

**Exorcise, Exorcist**  Benet, Lay

**Exordium**  Opening, Preface, Prelude

**Exotic**  Alien, Ethnic, Foreign, Strange, Outlandish

**Expand, Expanse, Expansion**  Amplify, Boom, Develop, Dilate, Distend, Ectasis, Elaborate, ENLARGE, Escalate, Grow, Increase, Magnify, Ocean, Spread, Stretch, Swell, Wax, Wire-draw

**Expatiate**  Amplify, Descant, Dwell, Enlarge, Perorate

**Expatriate**  Banish, Colonial, Emigrate, Exile, Outcast

**Expect(ation), Expected, Expecting**  Agog, Anticipate, Ask, Due, Foresee, Gravid, Hope, Lippen, Look, Natural, Par, Pregnant, Presume, Prospect, Require, SUPPOSE, Tendance, Thought, Usual, Ween

**Expectorate**  Expel, Hawk, Spit

**Expedient**  Advisable, Artifice, Contrivance, Fend, Make-do, Makeshift,

Measure, Politic, Resort, Resource, Shift, Stopgap, Suitable, Wise

**Expedite, Expedition**  Advance, Alacrity, Anabasis, Celerity, Crusade, Dispatch, Excursion, Fastness, Field trip, Hasten, Hurry, Kon-tiki, Pilgrimage, Post-haste, Safari, Speed, Trek, Trip, Voyage

**Expel**  Amove, Egest, Evacuate, Evict, Exile, Exorcize, Hoof, Oust, Out(cast), Void

**Expend(iture)**  Budget, Consume, Cost, Dues, Gavel, Mise, Occupy, Oncost, Outgo(ing), Outlay, Poll, Squander, Tithe, Toll, Use, Waste

**Expendable**  Cannon-fodder

**Expense(s)**  Charge, Cost, Exes, Fee, Outgoing, Outlay, Overhead, Price, Sumptuary

**Expensive**  Chargeful, Costly, Dear, Executive, Salt, Steep, Valuable

**Experience(d)**  Accomplished, A posteriori, Assay, Blasé, Discovery, Empiric, Encounter, Expert, FEEL, Felt, Freak-out, Gust, Know, Learn, Live, Mature, Meet, Pass, Plumb, Seasoned, See, Senior, Sense, Sensory, Stager, Stand, Taste, Transference, Trial, Trip, Try, Undergo, Versed

**Experiment(al)**  Attempt, Avant-garde, Essay, Peirastic, Sample, Taste, Tentative, TRIAL, Try, Venture

**Expert(ise)**  Accomplished, Ace, Adept, Adroit, Arch, Authority, Buff, Cognoscente, Connoisseur, Crack, Dab(ster), Dan, Deft, Don, Egghead, Fundi, Gun, Hotshot, Know-how, Maestro, Masterly, Mavin, Nark, Oner, Oneyer, Oneyre, Peritus, Practised, Pro, Proficient, Pundit, Ringer, Savvy, Science, Skill(y), Sly, Specialist, Technique, Technocrat, Ulema, Used, Whiz

**Expiate, Expiation, Expiatory**  Amends, Atone, Penance, Piacular

**Expire(d), Expiry**  Blow, Collapse, Croak, DIE, End, Exhale, Invalid, Ish, Lapse, Neese, Pant, Sneeze, Terminate

**Explain**  Account, Aread, Arede, Arreede, Conster, Construe, Decline, Define, Describe, Elucidate, Expose, Expound, Gloss, Gloze, Justify, Salve, Solve, Upknit

**Explanation, Explanatory**  Apology, Exegesis, Exegetic, Farse, Gloss, Gloze, Key, Note, Preface, Reading, Rigmarole, Solution, Theory

**Expletive**  Arrah, Darn, Exclamation, Oath, Ruddy, Sapperment

**Explicit**  Clear, Definite, Express, Frank, Outspoken, PRECISE, Specific

**Explode**  Backfire, Burst, Crump, Detonate, Erupt, EXPLOSION, Pop, Snake

**Exploit(er)**  Adventure, Deed, Develop, Escapade, Gest, Harness, Ill-use, Impose, Kulak, Manoeuvre, Milk, Mission, Ramp, Stunt, Sweat, Use

**Explore(r), Exploration**  Amerigo, Baffin, Balboa, Bandeirante, Banks, Bering, Boone, Burton, Cabot, Cartier, Chart, Columbus, Cook, Da Gama, Dampier, Darwin, Discover, Dredge, Eric, Eriksson, Examine, Feel, Frobisher, Fuchs, Investigate, Livingstone, Magellan, Map, Marco Polo, Nansen, Navigator, Peary, Pioneer, Probe, Przewalski, Rale(i)gh, Research, Rhodes, Ross, Scott, Scout, Search, Shackleton, Spaceship, Speke, Stanley,

Tasman, Vancouver, Vasco da Gama, Vespucci

**Explosion, Explosive** Agene, Amatol, Ammonal, ANFO, Antimatter, Aquafortis, Backfire, Bang, Blast, Cap, Cheddite, Chug, Cordite, Crump, Dualin, Euchloric, Euchlorine, Firedamp, Fulminant, Gasohol, Gelatine, Gelignite, Grenade, Guncotton, Gunpowder, HE, Iracund, Jelly, Lyddite, Megaton, Melinite, Mine, Nitroglycerine, Outburst, Paravane, Petar(d), Petre, Pluff, Population, Ptarmic, Pustular, Report, Roburite, SAM, Semtex, Sneeze, Soup, Tetryl, Thunderflash, Tonite, TNT, Trotyl, Volcanic, Warhead, Xyloidin(e)

> **Explosive** may indicate an anagram

**Exponent** Advocate, Example, Index, Interpreter, Logarithm

**Export** Despatch, Ship

**Expose(d), Exposure** Air, Anagogic, Bare, Blot, Debag, Debunk, Denude, Desert, Disclose, Endanger, En prisé, Exhibit, Flashing, Moon, Nude, Object, Open, Out, Over, Reveal, Snapshot, Streak, Strip, Subject, Unmask

**Exposition** Aperçu

**Expostulate, Expostulation** Argue, Arrah, Protest, Remonstrate

**Expound(ers)** Discourse, Discuss, Explain, Open, Prelict, Red, Scribe, Ulema

**Express(ed), Expression** Air, APT, Aspect, Breathe, Cliché, Concetto, Couch, Countenance, Declare, Denote, Epithet, Explicit, Face, Fargo, Gup, Hang-dog, Idiom, Locution, Manifest, Metonym, Mien, Neologism, Non-stop, Orient, Phrase, Pleonasm, Pony, Pronto, Quep, Register, Show, Soulful, SPEAK, State, Strain, Succus, Term, Token, Tone, Utterance, Vent, VOICE

**Expressionless** Blank, Deadpan, Inscrutable, Vacant, Wooden

**Expressman** Fargo

**Expropriate** Dispossess, Pirate, Seize

**Expulsion** Discharge, Eccrisis, Ejection, Eviction, Exile, Sacking, Synaeresis

**Expunge** Cancel, Delete, Erase, Obliterate

**Expurgate** Bowdlerize, Castrate, Censor, Purge

**Exquisite** Beautiful, Choice, Fine, Intense, Macaroni, Pink, Princox, Refined, Soigné(e), Too-too

**Ex-serviceman** Vet

**Extemporise** Ad lib, Improvise, Pong

**Extend(ed), Extension** Aspread, Augment, Draw, Eke, Elapse, Elongate, Enlarge, Escalate, Expand, Grow, Increase, Long, Offer, Overbite, Overlap, Porrect, Proffer, Prolong, Propagate, Protract, Span, Spread, Steso, STRETCH, Widen

**Extensive, Extent** Ambit, Area, Capacious, Compass, Comprehensive, Distance, Large, Length, Limit, MAGNITUDE, Panoramic, Range, Reach,

Scale, Size, Spacious, Sweeping, Wide

**Extenuate** Diminish, Lessen, Mitigate, Palliate

**Exterior** Aspect, Crust, Derm, Facade, Outer, OUTSIDE, Shell, Surface

**Exterminate** Abolish, Annihilate, Destroy, Uproot

**External** Exoteric, Exterior, Extraneous, Foreign, Outer

**Extinct(ion)** Bygone, Dead, Death, Defunct, Obsolete, Rasure

**Extinguish** Douse, Dout, Dowse, Extirpate, Obscure, Quell, Quench, Slake, Snuff, Stifle, Suppress

**Extirpate** Erase, Excise, Obliterate, Root, Uproot

**Extol** Commend, Enhance, Eulogise, Exalt, Laud, Puff

**Extort(ion), Extortioner** Barathrum, Blackmail, Bleed, Chantage, Chout, Churn, Compel, Exact, Force, Rachman, Rack, Racketeer, Ransom, Screw, Shank, Squeeze, Sweat, Urge, Vampire, Wrest, Wring

**Extra** Accessory, Additament, Addition(al), Additive, And, Annexe, Attachment, Bonus, By(e), Debauchery, Encore, Etcetera, Gash, Lagniappe, Leg bye, Make-weight, More, Nimiety, Odd, Optional, Out, Over, Perk, Plus, Plusage, Reserve, Ripieno, SPARE, Spilth, Staffage, Sundry, Super, Supernumerary, Surplus, Trop, Undue, Walking-gentleman, Walking-lady, Wide, Woundy

**Extract(ion), Extractor** Bleed, Breeding, Catechu, Clip, Corkscrew, Decoction, Descent, Distil, Draw, Educe, Elicit, Emulsin, Enucleate, Essence, Estreat, Excerpt, Extort, Gist, Gobbet, Insulin, Kino, Milk, Parentage, Passage, Pericope, Piece, Pry, Pyrene, Smelt, Suck, Summary, Tap, Trie, Try, Vanilla, Winkle, Worm, Wring, Yohimbine

**Extradition** Renvoi

**Extraneous** Foreign, Irrelevant, Outlying, Spurious

**Extraordinary** Amazing, By-ordinar, Case, Curious, Humdinger, Important, Rare, Singular, Startling, Strange, Unusual

**Extravagant, Extravaganza** Excessive, Fancy, Feerie, Heroic, Hyperbole, Lavish, Luxury, Outré, Prodigal, Profuse, Rampant, Reckless, Splash, Splurge, Squander, Waste

**Extreme(ly), Extremist** Acute, Die-hard, Drastic, Edge, Exceptional, Farthermost, Gross, INTENSE, Jacobin, Mondo, Opposite, Parlous, Radical, Root and branch, Steep, Thule, Too, Tremendous, Ultima thule, Ultimate, Ultra, Utmost, VERY, Wing

> **Extreme** may indicate a first or last letter

**Extremity** Bourn(e), Crisis, Digit, Ending, Finger(-tip), Limb, Limit, Pole, Tip, Toe, Utterance

**Extricate** Liberate, Loose, Rescue, Untangle

**Extrinsic** External, Irrelevant, Outward

**Extrovert** Outgoing

**Extrude** Debar, Eject, Project

**Exuberance, Exuberant** Brio, Copious, Ebullient, Effusive, Gusto, Hearty, Lavish, Mad, Profuse, Streamered

**Exudation, Exude** Ectoplasm, Emit, Guttate, Ooze, Secrete, Still, Sweat, Ulmin, Weep

**Exult(ant)** Crow, Elated, GLOAT, Glorify, Jubilant, Rejoice, Whoop

**Eye(s), Eye-ball** Cringle, Ee, Eine, Emmetropia, Evil, Glim, Glom, Goggles, Iris, Jack, Keek, Klieg, Lamp, Lens, Mincepie, Naked, OBSERVE, Ocellar, Ogle, Ommateum, Optic, Orb, Pedicel, Peeper, PI, Pigsn(e)y, Pigsnie, Pupil, Regard, Retina, Sclera, Sight, Spy, Storm-centre, Tec, Watch, Water-pump, Winker

**Eyebright** Euphrasy

**Eyebrow** Bree, Brent-hill, Glib, Penthouse, Superciliary

**Eyeglass** Loupe

**Eyelash** Cilium

**Eyelet** Cringle, Hole

**Eyelid** Canthus, Ectropion, Haw, Palpebral

**Eye-rod** Rhabdom

**Eye-shadow** Kohl

**Eyesore** Blot, Disfigurement, Sty(e)

**Eye-stalk** Ommatophore

**Eye trouble** Astigmatism, Cataract, Ceratitis, Coloboma, Diplopia, Entropion, Glaucoma, Hemi(an)op(s)ia, Iritis, Keratitis, Leucoma, Lippitude, Micropsia, Nebula, Nyctalopia, Nystagmus, Ommateum, Presbyopia, Retinitis, Scotomata, Shiner, Strabismus, Synechia, Teichopsia, Thylose, Thylosis, Trachoma, Tylosis, Wall-eye, Xeroma

**Eye-wash** Collyrium

**Eyrie** Nest

**Ezra** Pound

# Ff

**F**  Fahrenheit, Fellow, Feminine, Fluorine, Following, Force, Foxtrot

**Fab**  Super

**Fabian, Fabius**  Dilatory, Washington

**Fable(s)**  Aesop, Allegory, Apologue, Exemplum, Fiction, Hitopadesa, La Fontaine, Legend, Marchen, Milesian, Myth, Panchatantra, Parable, Romance, Tale

**Fabric**  Alepine, Armure, Arrasene, Baft, Balbriggan, Barathea, Barège, Bayadère, Beige, Bengaline, Binca, Brocade, Brocatel(le), Broche, Calamanco, Celanese, Challis, Chambray, Chenille, Chiffon, Chintz, Ciré, CLOTH, Coutil(le), Crepoline, Cretonne, Cubica, Dhurrie, Droguet, Drugget, Duroy, Durrie, Duvetin, Eolienne, Faconné, Faille, Felt, Florentine, Foulard, Framework, Gloria, Grenadine, Gunny, Harden, Harn, Herden, Holland, Hopsack, Hurden, Ikat, Khadder, Khadi, Kincob, Knit, Leather-cloth, Leno, Levantine, Marcella, MATERIAL, Merino, Mongo(e), Moquette, Moreen, Mungo, Ninon, Orleans, Orlon, Paisley, Par(r)amatta, Pique, Plush, Print, Rabanna, Raschel, Ratine, Ratteen, Russel, Sagathy, Samite, Schappe, Scrim, Shalloon, Shantung, Sicilienne, Silesia, Stockinet, Swanskin, Tabaret, Tammy, Tapestry, Tartan, Terry, Textile, Tiffany, Tissue, Tweed, Twill, Union, Wadmal, Webbing, Whipcord, Wigan, Wire-gauze, Woolsey, Worsted, Zanella, Zibel(l)ine

**Fabricate, Fabrication**  Artefact, Concoct, Construct, Contrive, Cook, Fake, Figment, Forge, INVENT, Lie, Porky, Trump

**Fabulous, Fabulous beast**  Apocryphal, Chichevache, Chimera, Cockatrice, Fictitious, Fung, Gear, Griffin, Hippogriff, Hippogryph, Huma, Incredible, Jabberwock(y), Kylin, Legendary, Magic, Manticora, Manticore, Merman, Monoceros, Mythical, Opinicus, Orc, Phoenix, Roc, Romantic, Simorg, Simurg(h), Sphinx, Tarand, Tragelaph, Unicorn, Wivern, Wyvern, Yale

**Facade**  Front(age), Frontal, Mask, Pretence

**Face, Facing**  Abide, Affront, Ashlar, Ashler, Aspect, Audacity, Brave, Brazen, Caboched, Caboshed, Cheek, Chiv(v)y, Coal, Countenance, Culet, Dalle, Dare, Dartle, Deadpan, Dial, Eek, Elevation, Encounter, Favour, Features, Fineer, Fortune, FRONT, Girn, Gonium, Groof, Grouf, Grufe, Gurn, Jib, Kisser, Lining, Look, Meet, Metope, Moe, Mug, Mush, Opposite, Outward, Pan, Paper tiger, Phisnomy, Phiz(og), Physiognomy, Poker, Puss, Revet, Roughcast, Rud, Rybat, Side, Snoot, Socle, Stucco, Veneer, Vis(age), Visnomy, Zocco(lo)

**Face-ache**  Noli-me-tangere

**Face-lift**  Rhytidectomy

**Face-saving**  Redeeming, Salvo

**Facet(ed)**  Angle, Aspect, Bezel, Culet, Face, Polyhedron

**Facetious**  Frivolous, Jocular, Waggish, Witty

**Facile**  Able, Adept, Complaisant, Ductile, Easy, Fluent

**Facilitate, Facility**  Amenity, Assist, Benefit, Capability, EASE, Expedite, Gift, Knack, Skill

**Facsimile**  Copy, Replica, Repro

**Fact(ual)**  Actual, Case, Correct, Data, Datum, Detail, Literal, Mainor, Nay, Really, Truism, Truth, Yes

**Faction**  Bloc, Cabal, Caucus, Clique, Contingent, Junto, Schism, Sect

**Factor**  Agent, Aliquot, Cause, Co-efficient, COMPONENT, Element, Representative, Steward

**Factory**  Cannery, Hacienda, Maquiladora, Mill, Plant, Refinery, Works, Workshop

**Factotum**  Circar, Handyman, Servant, Sircar, Sirkar

**Faculty**  Aptitude, Arts, Capacity, Department, Ear, Ease, Knack, Power, School, Sense, Speech, TALENT, Teachers, Wits

**Fad(dish)**  Crank, Craze, Cult, Fashion, Foible, Ismy, Thing, Vogue, Whim

**Fade(d), Fading**  Blanch, Die, Diminuendo, Dinge, Elapsion, Etiolate, Evanescent, Fall, Filemot, Lessen, Mancando, Pale, Passé, Perdendo(si), Peter, Smorzando, Smorzato, Vade, Vanish, Wallow, Wilt, Wither

**Faeces**  Dung, Scybalum, Skatole, Stools

**Fag**  Chore, Cigarette, Drag, Drudge, Gasper, Homosexual, Menial, Quean, Reefer, Snout, Tire, Toil, Weary

**Fag-end**  Ash, Lag, Stub

**Fag(g)ot(s)**  Bavin, Bundle, Firewood, Homosexual, Kid, Knitch, Twigs

**Fail(ing), Failure**  Anile, Blemish, Blow, Bomb, COLLAPSE, Conk, Crash, Cropper, Decline, Default, Defect, Demerit, Die, Dud, Fault, Feal, Fiasco, Flivver, Flop, Flunk, Fold, Founder, Frost, Lapse, Lose, Manqué, Mis-, Miscarry, Miss, Muff, Nerd, No-no, Omit, Pip, Plough, Pluck, Refer, Refusal, Short(coming), Smash, Spin, Stumer, Turkey, Vice, Wash-out, Weakness, Wipeout

**Fain**  Lief

**Faineant**  Gallio

**Faint(ness)**  Black-out, Conk, Dim, Dizzy, Dwalm, Fade, Lassitude, Pale, Stanck, Swarf, Swarve, Swelt, Swerf, Swerve, Swoon, Syncope, Unclear, Wan

**Faint-heart**  Coward, Craven, Timid, Wet

**Fair**  A(e)fald, Aefauld, Afawld, Barnet, Bartholomew, Bazaar, Beauteous, Belle, Blond, Bon(n)ie, Bonny, Brigg, Decent, Donnybrook, Equal, Equitable, Exhibition, Fine, Funfair, Gaff, Gey, Goose, Hiring, Honest, Hopping, Isle, JUST, Kermess, Kermis, Kirmess, Market, Mart, Mediocre, Mop, Nundinal, Objective, Paddington, Passable, Play, Pro rata, Rosamond, Sabrina, Square, Statute, Straight, Tavistock, Tidy, Tolerable, Tow-headed,

Trade, Tryst, Unbias(s)ed, Wake, Widdicombe

**Fair-buttocked**  Callipygean

**Fairing**  Ornament, Spat

**Fairly**  Clearly, Evenly, Moderately, Properly, Quite, Ratherish

**Fairway**  Dog-leg, Pretty

**Fairy**  Banshee, Befana, Cobweb, Dobbie, Dobby, Elf(in), Fay, Gloriana, Hob, Hop o' my thumb, Leprechaun, Lilian, Mab, Morgan le Fay, Morgane(tta), Moth, Nis, Peri, Pigwidgin, Pigwiggen, Pisky, Pixie, Pouf, Puck, Punce, Sandman, Spirit, Sprite, Sugar-plum, Tink(erbell), Titania, Urchin-shows

**Faith(ful)**  Accurate, Achates, Belief, Constant, Creed, Devoted, Doctrine, Faix, Fay, Feal, Fegs, Haith, Implicit, Islam, Lay, Loyal, Plerophory, Puritanism, Quaker, Religion, Solifidian, Staunch, Strict, Troth, TRUE(ness), True-blue, Trust

**Faithless**  Disloyal, False, Hollow, Perfidious

**Fake(r), Faking**  Bodgie, Bogus, Copy, Counterfeit, Duffer, Ersatz, False, Fold, Fraud, Fudge, Imitation, Imposter, Impostor, Paste, Phoney, Pretend, Sham, Spurious, Trucage, Truquage, Unreal

**Falcon**  Gentle, Hawk, Hobby, Kestrel, Lanner(et), Merlin, Nyas, Peregrine, Saker, Sakeret, Sparrow-hawk, Stallion, Staniel, Stannel, Stanyel, Tassel-gentle, Tassell-gent, Tercel-gentle

**Falklander**  Kelper

**Fall(s), Fallen, Falling**  Abate, Accrue, Arches, Astart, Autumn, Cadence, Cascade, Cataract, Chute, Collapse, Crash, Cropper, Declension, Decrease, Degenerate, Descent, Dip, Douse, Dowse, DROP, Ebb, Firn, Flop, Flump, Free, Grabble, Gutser, Gutzer, Horseshoe, Idaho, Incidence, Lag, Landslide, Lapse, Niagara, Oct(ober), Owen, Perish, Plonk, Plummet, Plump, Plunge, Prolapse, Purl(er), Rain, Relapse, Ruin, Sheet, Sin, Sleet, Snow, Spill, Tailor, Topple, Trip, Tumble, Victoria, Voluntary, Wipeout

**Fallacious, Fallacy**  Elench(us), Error, Idolum, Illogical, Illusion, Pathetic, Sophism, Unsound

**Fallible**  Human, Imperfect

> **Falling**  may indicate an anagram or a word backwards

**Fallow**  Barren, Lea, Tan, Uncared, Uncultivated, Untilled

**False, Falsify**  Adulterate, Bastard, Bogus, Braide, Canard, Cavil, Charlatan, Cook, Deceitful, Disloyal, Dissemble, Fake, Feigned, Fiddle, Forge, Illusory, Knave, Lying, Mock, Perjury, Pinchbeck, Postiche, Pretence, Pseudo, Roorback, Sham, Specious, Spoof, Spurious, Treacherous, Two-faced, Untrue

**False notions**  Idola

**Falter**  Hesitate, Limp, Totter, Waver

**Fame, Famous**  Bruit, Eminent, Glitterati, Gloire, Glory, History, Humour, Kudos, Noted, Prestige, Renown, Repute, Rumour, Spur,

Stardom, Word

**Familiar(ise), Familiarity** Accustom, Acquaint, Assuefaction, Auld, Chummy, Comrade, Conversant, Crony, Dear, Easy, Free, Friend, Habitual, Homely, Homey, Incubus, Intimate, Known, Liberty, Maty, Old, Privy, Python, Used, Versed

**Family** Ancestry, Bairn-team, Blood, Breed, Clan, Class, Cognate, Descent, Dynasty, House(hold), Issue, Kin, Kind, Line, Name, Nuclear, Orange, People, Phratry, Progeny, Quiverful, Race, Sept, Sib(b), Sibship, Stem, Stirps, Strain, Taffy, Talbot, Tribe

**Famish(ed)** Esurient, Hungry, Ravenous, Starving

> **Famished** may indicate an 'o' in the middle of a word

**Fan(s), Fan-like** Alligator, Admirer, Aficionado, Arouse, Blow, Cat, Claque, Colmar, Cone, Cool, Cuscus, Devotee, Diadrom, Enthusiast, Extractor, Fiend, Flabellum, Following, Groupie, Khuskhus, Outspread, Partisan, Punka(h), Rhipidate, Ringsider, Sail, Spread, Supporter, Tifosi, Ventilate, Votary, Voteen, Washingtonia, Wing, Winnow, Zealot, Zelant

> **Fan** may indicate an anagram

**Fanatic(al)** Bigot, Devotee, Energumen, Enthusiastic, Extremist, Fiend, Frenetic, Glutton, Mad, Nut, Partisan, Phrenetic, Picard, Rabid, Santon, Ultra, Wowser, Zealot

**Fancy** Caprice, Chim(a)era, Conceit, Concetto, Crotchet, Daydream, Dream, Dudish, Elaborate, Fangle, Fantasy, Fit, Flam, Frothy, Guess, Hallo, Idea(te), Idolon, IMAGINE, Inclination, Lacy, Liking, Maya, Mind, My, Nap, Notion, Ornamental, Ornate, Picture, Predilection, Rococo, Thought, Vagary, Ween, Whigmaleerie, Whigmaleery, Whim(sy)

> **Fancy** may indicate an anagram

**Fane** Banner, Pronaos

**Fanfare** Flourish, Sennet, Show, Tantara, Trump, Tucket

**Fang** Tooth, Tusk

**Fanny** Adams, Bottom, Gas-lit, Price

**Fantastic, Fantasy** Absurd, Antic, Bizarre, Caprice, Chimera, Cockaigne, Cockayne, Fab, Fanciful, Grotesque, Hallucination, Kickshaw(s), Lucio, Myth, Outré, Queer, Unreal, WHIM, Wild

**Far** Apogean, Away, Distal, Distant, Outlying, Remote

**Farce(ur)** Burletta, Charade, Comedy, Exode, Feydeau, Lazzo, Mime, Mockery, Pantomime, Rex, Sham

**Fare** Charge, Cheer, Commons, Do, Eat, FOOD, Go, Passage, Passenger, Rate, Table, Traveller

**Farewell** Adieu, Aloha, Apopemptic, Bye, Cheerio, Departure, GOODBYE, Leave, Prosper, Sayonara, So long, Vale, Valediction

**Far-fetched** Fanciful, Improbable, Recherché

**Farm(ing)** Agronomy, Arable, Bowery, Croft, Cultivate, Dairy, Deep-litter, Emmerdale, Estancia, Grange, Hacienda, Homestead, Husbandry, Kolkhoz,

Land, Location, Mains, Mas, Orley, Pen, Poultry, Ranch, Rent, Sovkhoz, Station, Stead, Sted(d), Sted(d)e, Steed, Till, Toun, Town, Wick

**Farmer** Boer, Campesino, Carl, Cockatoo, Cocky, Crofter, Estanciero, Gebur, George, Giles, Hick, Macdonald, Metayer, NFU, Peasant, Ryot, Share-cropper, Squatter, Tiller, Yeoman, Zeminda(r)

**Farmhand** Cadet, Cotter, Ditcher, Hand, He(a)rdsman, Hind, Ploughman, Rouseabout, Roustabout

**Farmhouse** Grange

**Farmyard** Barton, Villatic

**Farouche** Awkward, Shy, Sullen

**Farrago** Hotch-potch, Jumble, Medley, Mélange

**Farrier** Marshal, Smith

**Farrow** Litter, Mia, Sow

**Farthing** F, Fadge, Har(r)ington, Mite, Q, Quadragesimal, Rag

**Fascia** Band, Fillet, Platband

**Fascinate, Fascinating** Allure, Attract, Bewitch, CHARM, Dare, Enchant, Engross, Enthral(l), Fetching, Inthral, Intrigue, Kill, Rivet, Siren, Witch

**Fascist** Blackshirt, Blue shirt, Dictator, Falange, Falangist, Lictor, Nazi, Neo-nazi, Rexist, Sinarchist, Sinarquist

**Fashion(able), Fashioned** Aguise, A la (mode), Bristol, Build, Chic, Construct, Convention, Corinthian, Craze, Create, Cult, Custom, Cut, Deign, Elegant, Entail, Fad, Feat, Feign, Form, Genteel, Go, Hew, Hip, In, Invent, Look, MAKE, Manière, Manners, Mode, Mould, Newgate, Pink, Preppy, Rage, Rate, Sc, Shape, Smart, Smith, Snazzy, Stile, Stylar, Style, Swish, Tailor, Ton, TREND(Y), Turn, Twig, Vogue, Way, Wear, Work, Wrought

**Fast** Abstain, Apace, Ashura, Breakneck, Citigrade, Clem, Daring, Elaphine, Express, Fizzer, Fleet, Immobile, Lent, Lightning, Loyal, Maigre, Meteoric, Moharram, Muharram, Muharrem, Pac(e)y, Pronto, Quick, Raffish, Raking, Ramadan, Rash, Spanking, Speedy, Stretta, Stretto, Stuck, Tachyon, Thick, Yom Kippur

**Fast and loose** Fickle, Pick-the-garter, Strap-game

**Fasten(er), Fastening** Anchor, Attach, Bar, Bind, Bolt, Buckle, Button, Chain, Clamp, Clasp, Clinch, Dead-eye, Diamond-hitch, Espagnolette, Frog, Hasp, Hesp, Hook, Lace, Latch, Lock, Moor, Morse, Nail, Netsuke, Padlock, Parral, Pectoral, Pin, Preen, Reeve, Rivet, Rope, Rove, Seal, SECURE, Shut, Spar, Sprig, Staple, Tach(e), Tag, Tassel, Tether, Tintack, Toggle, Velcro, Wedge, Zip

**Fastidious** Chary, Critical, Dainty, Fussy, Nice, Particular, Squeamish

**Fat(s), Fatten, Fatty** Adipic, Adipocere, Aldermanly, Aliphatic, Arcus, Bard, Batten, Battle, Blubber, Butter, Cellulite, Chubbed, Chubby, Corpulent, Creesh, Degras, Dika-oil, Dosh, Embonpoint, Enarm, Endomorph, Flab, Fozy, Fubsy, Galam-butter, Grease, Keech, Lanolin,

Lard, Lipoma, Margarine, Marge, Obese, Oil, OS, Palmitin, Pinguid, Plump, Poddy, Podgy, Portly, Pursy, Rich, Rolypoly, Rotund, Saginate, Saim, Schmal(t)z, Seam(e), Sebacic, Sebum, Shortening, Soil, Spe(c)k, Squab, Stearic, Suet, Tallow, Tin, Tomalley, Tub, Vanaspati, Waller

**Fatal(ism), Fate(ful), Fated** Apnoea, Atropos, Chance, Clotho, Deadly, Death, Decuma, Destiny, Doom, End, Fay, Fell, Joss, Karma, Kismet, Lachesis, Lethal, Lot, Meant, Moira, Mortal, Nemesis, Norn(a), Parca, Pernicious, Predestination, Portion, Skuld, Urd, Verdande, Weird

**Father(ly)** Abba, Abuna, Adopt, Bapu, Begetter, Brown, Curé, Dad, Engender, Fr, Generator, Genitor, Getter, Governor, Male, Pa, Padre, Papa, Parent, Pater(nal), Patriarch, Père, Pop(pa), Popper, Priest, Rev, Sire, Stud, Thames, Tiber

**Father-lasher** Sea-scorpion

**Fathom** Depth, Delve, F, Plumb, Understand

**Fatigue** Exhaust, Fag, Jade, Overdo, Tire, Weariness, Weary

**Fatuous** Gaga, Idiotic, Silly, Stupid

**Faucet** Cock, Spigot, Tap

**Fault(y)** Bad, Beam, Blame(worthy), Blunder, Bug, Cacology, Carp, Culpable, Defect, Demerit, ERROR, Failing, Flaw, Literal, Frailty, Gall, Glitch, Henpeck, Massif, MISTAKE, Nibble, Niggle, Nit-pick, Out, Outcrop, Rate, Reprehend, Rift, Short, Trap, Vice

**Faultless** Impeccable, Perfect

**Fauvist** Matisse

**Faux pas** Blunder, Boner, Gaffe, Leglen-girth, Solecism

**Favour(able), Favoured, Favourite** Advance, Advantage(ous), Aggrace, Agraste, Alder-liefest, Approval, Back, Befriend, Behalf, Benign, Bless, Boon, Bribe, Cert, Chosen, Cockade, Curry, Darling, Fancy, Favodian, Grace, Gratify, Graste, Gree, Hackle, Hot, In, Indulge, Kickback, Minion, Odour, Particular, Peat, Persona grata, Pet, Pettle, Popular, PREFER, Promising, Propitious, Resemble, Rib(b)and, Roseate, Rose-knot, Rosette, Smile, Token

**Fawn(ing)** Adulate, Beige, Blandish, Crawl, Creep, Cringe, Deer, Ecru, Flatter, Fleech, Grovel, Kowtow, Obsequious, Servile, Smarm, Smoo(d)ge, Sycophant, Tasar, Toady, Truckle, Tussah, Tusseh, Tusser, Tussore

**Fay** Fairy, Korrigan, Peri

**FBI** G-men

**Fear** Apprehension, Awe, Crap, Dismay, Doubt, Drad, Dread, Foreboding, FOR FEAR, Fright, Funk, Hang-up, Horror, PHOBIA, Redoubt, Revere, Terror, Trepidation

**Fearful** Afraid, Cowardly, Dire, Nervous, Pavid, Rad, Redoubtable, Timorous, Windy

**Fearless** Bold, Brave, Courageous, Gallant, Impavid, Intrepid

**Fearsome** Dire, Formidable

**Feasible** Goer, Likely, On, Possible, Practical, Probable, Viable

**Feast** Adonia, Agape, Assumption, Banquet, Barmecide, Beano, Belshazzar's, Blow-out, Candlemas, Carousal, Celebration, Dine, Double, Eat, Epiphany, Epulation, Festival, Fleshpots, Fool's, Gaudeamus, Gaudy, Hallowmas, Hockey, Hogmanay, Id-al-Adha, Id-al-Fitr, Isodia, Junket, Kai-kai, Lady Day, Lammas, Luau, Martinmas, Michaelmas, Movable, Noel, Passover, Pentecost, Pig, Potlatch, Purim, Regale, Revel, Roodmas, Seder, Shindig, Spread, Succoth, Sukkot(h), Tabernacles, Wayzgoose, Yule, Zagmuk

**Feast-day** Mass

**Feat** Achievement, Deed, Effort, Exploit, Gambado, Stunt, Trick

**Feather(ed), Feathers** Alula, Barbicel, Boa, Braccate, Crissum, Down, Duster, Filoplume, Fledged, Fletch, Gemmule, Hackle, Harl, Hatchel, Herl, Lure, Macaroni, Ostrich, Pen(na), Pinna, Pith, Plumage, Plume, Plumule, Pteryla, Ptilosis, QUILL, Rectrix, Remex, Remiges, Saddle-hackle, Scapus, Standard, Stipa, Tectrix, Tertial, Vibrissa

**Feather-worker** Plumassier

**Feature(s)** Article, Aspect, Attribute, Brow, Character, Chin, Depict, Eye, Face, Figure, Hallmark, Highlight, Item, Lineament, Nose, Nucleus, Phiz(og), Physiognomy, Spandrel, Star, Temple, Trait

**Featureless** Flat

**Febrifuge** Atabrin, Atebrin, Mepacrine, Quina

**February** Fill-dyke

**Fecund(ity)** Fertile, Fruitful, Prolific, Uberty

**Federal, Federation** Alliance, Bund, Commonwealth, League, Statal, Union

**Fee** Charge, Dues, Duty, Faldage, Fine, Hire, Honorarium, Mortuary, Mouter, Multure, Obvention, Pay, Premium, Refresher, Retainer, Sub, Tribute

**Feeble** Characterless, Daidling, Debile, Droob, Effete, Flaccid, Footling, Fragile, Geld, Ineffective, Infirm, Pale, Puny, Sickly, Slender, Tailor, Tame, Tootle, Wallydrag, Wallydraigle, Washy, Wastrel, Weak, Weed, Wersh, Wet, Wimpish, Worn

**Feed(er), Feeding** Battle, Browse, Cater, Cibation, Clover, Dine, EAT, Fatten, Fire, Fodder, Food, Gavage, Graze, Hay, Lunch, Meal, Nourish, Paid, Pecten, Provender, Refect, Repast, Sate, Soil, Stoke, Stooge, Stover, Sustain, Tire, Wean

**Feel, Feeling(s)** Aesthesia, Atmosphere, Compassion, Darshan, EMOTION, Empathy, Empfindung, Euphoria, EXPERIENCE, Finger, Frisk, Grope, Handle, Heart, Hunch, Intuit, Knock, Know, Palp, Passion, Pity, Premonition, Probe, Realise, Sensate, Sensation, SENSE, Sensitive, Sentiment, Spirit, Touch, Turn, Vibes

**Feeler** Antenna, Exploratory, Overture, Palp, Sensillum, Tentacle

> **Feet** see FOOT

**Feign** Act, Affect, Colour, Fake, Malinger, Mime, Mock, PRETEND, Sham, Simulate

**Feint** Deke, Disguise, Dodge, Faint, Fake, Spoof, Trick

**Fel(d)spar** Adularia, Albite, Gneiss, Hyalophane, Moonstone, Petuntse, Petuntze, Sun-stone

**Felicity** Bliss, Happiness, Joy, Relevance

> **Feline** see CAT

**Fell** Axe, Chop, Cruel, Deadly, Dire, Dread, Fierce, Hew, Hide, Hill, Inhuman, Knock-down, KO, Lit, Moor, Pelt, Poleaxe, Ruthless, Sca, Shap, Skittle

**Fellow(ship)** Academic, Associate, Bawcock, Birkie, Bo, Bro, Buffer, Carlot, Cat, Chal, Chap, Chi, China, Cock, Cod(ger), Collaborator, Co-mate, Communion, Companion, Comrade, Confrère, Cove, Cully, Cuss, Dandy, Dean, Dog, Don, Dude, Equal, F, Fogey, Fop, Gadgie, Gadje, Gaudgie, Gauje, Gink, Guy, Joker, Josser, Lad, Like, M, Mall, Man, Mate, Member, Mister, Mun, Partner, Peer, Professor, Rival, Sister, Sociate, Sodality, Swab, Twin, Waghalter, Wallah

**Felon(y)** Bandit, Convict, Crime, Gangster, Offence, Villain

**Felt** Bat(t), Drugget, Knew, Met, Numdah, Numnah, Pannose, Roofing, Sensed, Tactile, Underlay, Velour

**Female (bodies), Feminine, Feminist** Bint, Bit, Dame, Distaff, Doe, F, Filly, Girl, Hen, Her, Kermes, Lady, Libber, Pen, Petticoated, Sakti, Shakti, She, Sheila, Shidder, Soft, Spindle, Thelytoky, WOMAN, Yin

> **Female, Feminine** may indicate an -ess ending

**Fen** Bog, Carr, Ea, Jiao, Marsh, Morass

**Fence(r), Fencing** Bar, Barrier, Enclose, Epee, Fraise, Haha, Hay, Hedge, Hurdle, Iaido, Imbrocate, Kendo, Link, Mensur, Netting, Obstacle, Oxer, Pale, Paling, Palisade, Pen, Picket, Rail, Rasper, Receiver, Reset, Scrimure, Seconde, Sept(um), Singlestick, Stramac, Stramazon, Swordplay, Trellis, Virginia, Wattle, Wear, Weir, Wire

**Fencing position** Carte, Passado, Quart(e)

**Fend(er)** Buffer, Bumper, Curb, Parry, Provide, Resist, Ward, Wing

**Fennel** Finoc(c)hio, Finnochio, Herb, Love-in-a-mist, Ragged lady

**Fent** Offcut, Remnant, Slit

**Feral** Brutal, Fierce, Savage, Wild

**Ferdinand** Archduke, Bull

**Ferment(ation)** Barm, Enzym(e), Leaven, Mowburn, Protease, Ptyalin, Seethe, Trypsin, Turn, Working, Ye(a)st, Zyme, Zymosis, Zymurgy

**Fermium** Fm

**Fern** Acrogenous, Adder's-tongue, Adiantum, Archegonial, Aspidium, Asplenium, Azolla, Barometz, Bracken, Brake, Ceterach, Cyathea, Cycad, Dicksonia, Filicales, Filices, Hart's-tongue, Isoetes, Marsilia, Moonwort, Mulewort, Nardoo, Ophioglossum, Osmunda, Pepperwort, Polypod, Ponga,

Pteris, Schizaea, Staghorn, Tara, Woodsia

**Ferocious** Brutal, Cruel, Fell, Predatory, Rambunctious

**Ferret** Fesnyng, Gill, Hob, Jill, Nose, Polecat, Ribbon, Rootle, Snoop, Trace

**Ferry(man)** Charon, Convey, Hovercraft, Passage, Plier, Roll-on, RORO, Sealink, Shuttle, Traject, Tranect

**Fertile, Fertility (symbol)** Battle, Fat, Fecund, Fruitful, Linga, Productive, Prolific, Rhiannon, Rich, Uberous

**Fertilise(r), Fertilisation** Ammonia, Bee, Bone-ash, Bone-earth, Bone-meal, Caliche, Compost, Guano, Heterosis, Humogen, Humus, Kainite, Manure, Nitrate, Nitre, Pearl-ash, Phosphate, Pollen, Potash, Self, Sharn, Stamen

**Fervent, Fervid, Fervour** Ardent, Burning, Earnest, Heat, Hwyl, Intense, Keen, Passionate, White-hot, Zeal, Zeloso

**Fester** Putrefy, Rankle, Rot, Suppurate

**Festival, Festive, Festivity** Adonia, Ale, Ambarvalia, Anniversary, Anthesteria, Bairam, Bayreuth, Beano, Beltane, Candlemas, Carnival, Celebration, Cerealia, Chanuk(k)ah, Childermas, Church-ale, Commemoration, Convivial, Corroboree, Crouchmas, Dewali, Dionysia, Divali, Diwali, Doseh, Druid, Easter, Eisteddfod, Encaenia, Epiphany, FAIR, Feast, Feis, Fete, Fiesta, Gaff, GALA, Gaudy, Gregory, Hanukkah, Harvest, Hock-tide, Holi, Holiday, Holy-ale, Id-al-fitr, Kermess, Kermiss, Kirmess, Lammas, Lemural, Lemuria, Lupercalia, Mela, Merry-night, Michaelmas, Mod, Noel, Palilia, Panathenaean, Panegyry, Pasch, Passover, Pentecost, Pesa(c)h, Play, Pongal, Potlach, Puja, Purim, Quirinalia, Revel, Rosh Hashanah, Samhain, Saturnalia, Semi-double, Shrove(tide), Terminalia, Tet, Thargelia, Thesmophoria, Tide, Up-Helly-Aa, Utas, Vinalia, Visitation, Vulcanalia, Wake, Yomtov, Yule(tide)

**Festoon** Deck, Decorate, Garland, Swag, Wreathe

**Fetch(ing)** Attract, Bring, Charming, Fet(t), Get, Realise

**Fete** Bazaar, Champetre, Entertain, FESTIVITY, Gala, Honour, Tattoo

**Fetish** Charm, Compulsion, Idol, Ju-ju, Obeah, Obi(a), Talisman, Totem, Voodoo

**Fetter** Basil, Bilboes, Chain, Gyve, Hamshackle, Hopple, Iron, Leg-iron, Manacle, Shackle

**Fettle** Arrange, Condition, Frig, Potter, Repair

**Feud** Affray, Clash, Feoff, Fief, Quarrel, Strife, VENDETTA

**Feudal (service)** Arriage, Auld-farrant, Forinsec, Old

**Fever(ish)** Ague, Blackwater, Calenture, Dengue, Enteric, Ferment, Frenetic, Hectic, Hyperpyretic, Intense, Kala-azar, Lassa, Malaria, Passion, Pyretic, Pyrexia, Quartan, Tap, Tertian, Trench, Typhoid, Typhus, Undulant, Verruga, Vomito, Whot, Yellow(jack)

**Few(er)** Handful, Infrequent, LESS, Limited, Scarce, Some, Wheen

**Fey** Clairvoyant, Eccentric, Elfin, Weird

**Fez** Tarboosh, Tarboush, Tarbush

**Fiancé(e)** Betrothed, Intended, Promised

**Fiasco** Bomb, Debacle, Disaster, Failure, Flask, Flop, Lash-up, Wash-out

**Fiat** Command, Decree, Edict, Order, Ukase

**Fib** Gag, LIE, Prevaricate, Story, Taradiddle

**Fibre, Fibrous** Abaca, Acrilan (tdmk), Acrylic, Aramid, Arghan, Backbone, Bass, Bast, Buaze, Bwazi, Cantala, Coir, Constitution, Courtelle, Cuscus, Dralon, Filament, Filasse, Flax, Hair, Hemp, Herl, Hypha, Istle, Ixtle, Jute, Kapok, Kenaf, Kevlar, Kittul, Monomode, Mungo, Myotube, Noil(s), Oakum, Piassaba, Piassava, Pita, Polyarch, Pons, Pulu, Raffia, Ramee, Rami, Rhea, Roughage, Sida, Silk, Sisal, Sleave, Spandex, Staple, Strand, Strick, Sunn-hemp, Tampico, Toquilla, Tow, Viver, Watap, Whisker

**Fibula** Bone, Brooch, Perone

**Fickle(ness)** Capricious, Change, False, Inconstant, Light, Mutable, Protean, Shifty, Varying, Volatile

**Fiction(al), Fictitious** Bogus, Fable, Fabrication, Pap, Phoney, Romance, STORY

**Fiddle(r), Fiddling** Amati, Bow, Calling-crab, Cello, Cheat, Crab, Cremona, Croud, Crouth, Crowd, Crwth, Fidget, Fix, Ground, Gu(e), Kit, Nero, Peculate, Petty, Potter, Racket, Rebec(k), Rig, Rote, Sarangi, Saw, Sawah, Scam, Scrape, Spiel, Strad, TAMPER, Tinker, Trifle, Tweedle(-dee), Twiddle, Viola, VIOLIN, Wangle

**Fidelity** Accuracy, Faith, Fealty, Loyalty, Troth

**Fidget(y)** Fantad, Fanteeg, Fantigue, Fantod, Fike, Fuss, Fyke, Jimjams, Jittery, Niggle, Trifle, Twiddle, Twitch, Uneasy

**Fief** Benefice, Fee

**Field(er), Fields(man)** Aalu, Aaru, Abroad, Aceldama, Aerodrome, Area, Arena, Arish, Arpent, Arrish, Campestral, Campestrian, Catch, Champ(s), Close, Cover, Domain, Elysian, Entry, Fid, Forte, Fylde, Glebe, Grid(iron), Gully, Hop-yard, Land, Lare, Lay, Lea(-rig), Ley, Line, Longstop, Magnetic, Mead(ow), Mid-off, Mine, Oil, Padang, Paddock, Parrock, Pasture, Pitch, Point, Province, Runners, Salting, Sawah, Scarecrow, Scope, Scout, Slip, Shamba, Sphere, Stage, Tract, World

> **Field** may indicate cricket

**Field marshal** Allenby, Bulow, French, Haig, Ironside, Kesselring, Kitchener, Montgomery, Roberts, Robertson, Rommel, Slim, Wavell

**Fieldwork** Lunette, Ravelin, Redan, Redoubt

**Fiend** Barbason, Demon, DEVIL, Enthusiast, Flibbertigibbet, Frateretto, Hobbididance, Mahu, Modo, Obidicut, Smulkin, Succubus

**Fierce(ly)** Billyo, Breem, Breme, Cruel, Draconic, Dragon, Grim, Ogreish, Rampant, Renfierst, SAVAGE, Severe, Tigrish, Violent, Wild, Wood, Wud

**Fiery** Ardent, Argand, Aries, Dry, Fervent, Hot, Igneous, Leo, Mettlesome, Phlogiston, Sagittarius, Salamander, Zealous

**Fiesta**  Festival, Fete, Gala, Holiday

**Fife**  Piffero

**Fifth**  Column, Diapente, Hemiol(i)a, Quint, Sesquialtera

**Fifty**  Demi-c, Jubilee, L

**Fig**  Bania, Benjamin-tree, Caprifig, Fico, Figo, Footra, Fouter, Foutra, Foutre, Sycamore, Sycomore, Syncomium, Trifle

**Fight(er), Fighting**  Affray, Agonistics, Alpino, Altercate, Barney, BATTLE, Bicker, Bout, Box, Brave, Brawl, Bruiser, Bundeswehr, Bush-whack, Campaign, Chaud-mellé, Chindit, Combat, Conflict, Contest, Crusader, Cuirassier, Defender, Dog, Donnybrook, Duel, Fecht, Fence, Flyting, Fray, Freedom, Free-for-all, Gladiator, Grap(p)le, Gurkha, Hurricane, Lapith, Marine, Med(d)le, Medley, Mêlée, Mercenary, MIG, Mill, Mujahed(d)in, Mujahidin, Naumachy, Partisan, Pellmell, PLO, Prawle, Press, Pugilist, Pugnacity, Rammy, Repugn, Resist, Ruck, Rumble, Savate, Sciamachy, Scrap, Shine, Skiamachy, Skirmish, Slam, Spar, Spitfire, Squabble, Stoush, Strife, Struggle, Sumo, Swordsman, Tar, Thersites, Tuilyie, Tuilzie, Tussle, Umbrella, War(-dog), War-horse, War-man, Warrior, Wraxle, Wrestle, Zero

**Figment**  Delusion, Fiction, Invention

**Figure(s), Figurine**  Arabic, Aumail, Bas-relief, Body, Build, Canephorus, Caryatid, Cast, Cinque, Cipher, Cone, Cube, Cypher, Decahedron, Digit, Ecorché, Effigy, Eight, Ellipse, Enneagon, Enneahedron, Epanadiplosis, FORM, Fusil, Girth, Gnomon, Graph, Heptagon, Hexagon, Icon, Idol, Ikon, Image, Insect, Intaglio, Integer, Lay, Magot, Motif, Nonagon, Number, Numeral, Octagon, Orant, Outline, Parallelogram, Pentacle, Pentalpha, Poussette, Prism, Puppet, Pyramid, Reckon, See, SHAPE, Sheela-na-gig, Simplex, Statistics, Statue(tte), Tanagra, Telamon, Tetragon, Torus, Triangle, Trihedron, Triskele, Triskelion, Ushabti, Waxwork

**Figure of speech**  Allegory, Analogy, Antimask, Antimasque, Antimetabole, Antithesis, Asyndeton, Catachresis, Chiasmus, Diallage, Ellipsis, Euphemism, Hypallage, Irony, Litotes, Meiosis, Metalepsis, Metaphor, Metonymy, Oxymoron, Paral(e)ipsis, Simile, Syllepsis, Synecdoche, Tmesis, Trope, Zeugma

**Figure study**  Arithmetic, Mathematics, Numeration

**Figure-weaver**  Draw-boy

**Filament**  Barbule, Byssus, Fibre, Fimbria, Floss, Gossamer, Hair, Hypha, Mycor(r)hiza, Paraphysis, Protonema, THREAD

**Filch**  Appropriate, Drib, Pilfer, Pinch, Purloin, Smouch, STEAL

**File, Filing(s)**  Abrade, Archive, Box, Clyfaker, Coffle, Croc(odile), Disc, Disk, Dossier, Enter, Generation, Index, Indian, Line, Pigeon-hole, Pollute, Quannet, Rank, Rasp, Rat-tail, Riffler, Row, Scalprum, String, Swarf

**Filial generation**  F1

**Filibuster**  Freebooter, Hinder, Obstruct, Run on, Stonewall

**Filigree**  Delicate, Fretwork, Sheer

**Filipino** Moro

**Fill(er), Filling** Anaplerosis, Balaam, Beaumontag(u)e, Beaumontique, Billow, Bloat, Brick-nog, Brim, Bump, Centre, Charge, Cram, Gather, Gorge, Imbue, Impregnate, Inlay, Mastic, Occupy, Pabulous, Packing, Plug, Repletive, Salpicon, Sate, Satisfy, Shim, Stock, Stopping, STUFF, Teem, Ullage

**Fillet(s)** Anadem, Annulet, Band, Bandeau, Bandelet, Bone, Cloisonné, Fret, Grenadine, Headband, Infula, Label, List(el), Moulding, Reglet, Regula, Ribbon, Slice, Snood, Sphendone, Striga, Taeniate, Tape, Teniate, Tournedos, Vitta

**Fillip** Boost, Kick, Snap, Stimulus

**Filly** Colt, Foal, She

**Film(s), Filmy** Acetate, Amnion, Biopic, Caul, Cel, Cine, Cliffhanger, Clip, Deepie, Dew, Diorama, Dust, Epic, ET, Exposure, Fiche, Flick, Footage, Gigi, Gossamer, Hammer, Haze, Horror, Kell, Lacquer, Layer, Loid, Mask, Membrane, Mist, Montage, Newsreel, Oater, Panchromatic, Patina, Pellicle, Photo, Plaque, Prequel, Psycho, Quickie, Reel, Release, Rush, Scale, Scent-scale, Screen, Scum, Short, Shot, Skin, Slick, Trailer, Ultrafiche, Varnish, Video, Web, Weepie, Weepy, Weft, Western

**Film star** Extra, Vedette

**Filter** Clarify, Leach, Percolate, Perk, Seep, Sieve, SIFT, Strain

**Filth(y)** Addle, Augean, Bilge, Colluvies, Crock, Crud, Defile, Dirt, Dung, Foul, Grime, Lucre, Muck, Obscene, Pythogenic, Refuse, Slime, Smut(ch), Soil, Squalor, Stercoral

**Fin** Ctene, Dollars, Fluke, Pectoral, Pinna, Rib, Skeg, Ventral

**Final(e), Finalise** Absolute, Closing, Coda, Conclusive, Decider, End, Eventual, Extreme, Last, Net(t), Peremptory, Sew up, Ultimate, Utter

**Finance, Financial, Financier** Ad crumenan, Angel, Back, Banian, Banker, Bankroll, Banyan, Cambism, Chrematistic, Exchequer, Fiscal, Monetary, Revenue, Sponsor, Subsidise, Treasurer, Underwrite

**Finch** Bird, Brambling, Bunting, Canary, Charm, Chewink, Crossbill, Fringillid, Linnet, Peter, Serin, Siskin, Spink, Twite

**Find(ing)** Ascertain, Detect, Discover(y), Get, Hit, Inquest, LOCATE, Meet, Provide, Rumble, Trace, Trouvaille, Verdict

**Fine, Fine words** Amende, Amerce, Amerciament, Arts, Assess, Beau(t), Boshta, Boshter, Brave, Braw, Champion, Dainty, Dandy, Dick, End, Eriach, Eric(k), Estreat, F, Fair, Famous, Forfeit, Good(ly), Gossamer, Gradely, Grand, Grassum, Hair, Handsome, Heriot, Hunkydory, Immense, Impalpable, Inconie, Incony, Infangthief, Issue, Log, Merchet, Mooi, Mulct, Nifty, Niminy-piminy, Noble, OK, Oke, Outfangthief, PENALTY, Precise, Pure, Relief, Sconce, Sheer, Sicker, Slender, Spanking, Subtle, Summery, Super, Tax, Ticket(t)y-boo, Tiptop, Topping, Unlaw, Waly, Wally, Wer(e)gild

**Fine-collector** Cheater

**Finery** Braws, Fallal, Frills, Frippery, Gaudery, Ornament, Trinket, Wally

**Finesse** Artifice, Artistry, Delicacy, Skill, Strategy

**Fine-weather** All-hallond, All-hallow(e)n, All-hollown

**Finger** Dactyl, Digit, Fork, Handle, Index, Medius, Name, Pinky, Pointer, Prepollex, Pusher, Shop, Talaunt, Talon

**Finger-hole** Lill, Ring

**Fingerprint** Dabs, Dactylogram, Loop, Whorl

**Fingerstall** Hutkin

**Finial** Bunch, Knob, Ornament, Tee

**Finicky** Fastidious, Fussy, Particular, Precise

**Finis, Finish(ed), Finishing touch** Arch, Close, Coating, Coda, Complete, CONCLUDE, Crown, Die, Dish, Do, Dope, Dress, END, Epiphenomena, Exact, Full, Kibosh, Lacquer, Neat, Outgo, Outwork, Perfect, Photo, Refine, Ripe, Round, Settle, Shot, Spitcher, Surface, Terminate, Through, Up (tie)

**Finite** Bounded, Limited

**Finn(ish)** Esth, Huck(leberry), Mickey, Suomic, Udmurt, Votyak

**Fiord** Bay, Hardanger, Inlet

**Fir** Abies, Larch

**Fire(side)** Accend, Agni, Animate, Arson, Arouse, Atar, Axe, Bake, Bale, Barbecue, Barrage, Beacon, Behram, Blaze, Boot, Brand, Brazier, Burn, Chassé, Corposant, Delope, Discharge, Dismiss, Elan, Element, Embolden, Ena, Energy, Enfilade, Flak, Flame, Furnace, Gun, Hearth, Hob, Ignite, Inferno, Ingle, Inspire, Kentish, Kiln, Kindle, Launch, Light, Lowe, Pop, Prime, Pull, Sack, St Anthony's, St Elmo's, Scorch, Shoot, Smudge, Spark, Spunk, Stoke, Stove, Strafe, Tracer, Wisp, Zeal

> **Firearm** see GUN

**Fireback** Reredos

**Fireball** Bolide

**Fire-break** Epaulement

**Fire-dog** Andiron

**Fire-extinguisher** Hell-bender, Salamander

**Firefly** Glow-worm, Luciferin, Pyrophorus

**Fire-guard** Fender

**Fireman** Abednego, Brigade, Deputy, Prometheus, Stoker

**Fire-opal** Girasol

**Fireplace** Chimney, Grate, Hearth, Hob, Ingle, Loop-hole, Range

**Fireplug** H, Hydrant

**Fireproof** Abednego, Asbestos, Incombustible, Inflammable, Meshach, Shadrach, Uralite

**Firewalker** Salamander

**Firewood** Billet, Faggot, Knitch, Tinder

**Firework(s)** Banger, Bengali-light, Cracker, Devil, Fisgig, Fizgig, Fountain, Gerbe, Girandole, Maroon, Pastille, Peeoy, Petard, Pinwheel, Pioy(e), Pyrotechnics, Realgar, Rocket, Sparkler, Squib, Tantrum, Throwdown, Tourbill(i)on, Volcano, Wheel, Whizzbang

**Fire-worshipper** Parsee

**Firing** Baking, Fusillade, Mitten, Salvo

**Firm** Agency, Binding, Business, Collected, Compact, Company, Concern, Concrete, Constant, Crisp, Decided, Determined, Duro, Faithful, Fast, Fixed, Hard, Inc, Oaky. Obdurate, Obstinate, RESOLUTE, Sclerotal, Secure, Set, Siccar, Sicker, SOLID, Stable, Stalwart, Staunch, Ste(a)dfast, Steady, Steeve, Stern, Stieve, Stiff, Sturdy, Tight, Well-knit

**Firmament** Canopy, Empyrean, Heaven, Sky

**First** Ab initio, Alpha, Arch, Archetype, Best, Chief, Earliest, E(a)rst, Foremost, Former, Front, Head, I, Ideal, Imprimis, Initial, 1st, Led, Maiden, No 1, One, Opener, Or, Original, Pioneer, Pole, Premier, Primal, Prime, Primo, Principal, Prototype, Rudimentary, Senior, Starters, Top, Victor, Yama

**First born** Ariki, Eigne, Eldest, Heir, Major, Senior

**First class, First rate** A1, Crack, Prime, Supreme, Tiptop, Top(notch)

**First day** Calends

**First fruits** Annat, Arles, Primitiae, Windfalls

**First man** Adam, Premier, President, Yama

**First offender** Eve, Probationer

> **First rate** see FIRST CLASS

**First woman** Embla, Eve, Pandora, Premier

**Firth** Estuary, Inlet, Moray

**Fish(ing)** Ablet, Ai, Albacore, Alevin, Ale-wife, Allice, Allis, Amberjack, Anabas, Anableps, Anchovy, Angel, Angle, Angler, Apode, Arapaima, Aster(o)id, Atherine, Ayu, Azurine, Ballan(-wrasse), Bar, Barbel, Barracoota, Barracouta, Barracuda, Barramunda, Bass(e), Belone, Beluga, Bergylt, Bib, Big-eye, Bitterling, Blay, Bleak, Blenny, Bley, Bloater, Blueback, Bluecap, Bob, Bombay duck, Bonito, Bottlehead, Bounce, Bowfin, Braise, Braize, Brassie, Bream, Brill, Brisling, Brit, Bullhead, Bullhorn, Bully, Bumalo, Burbot, But(t), Cabezon(e), Callop, Capelin, Caplin, Capon, Caranx, Caribe, Carp, Cascadura, Cast, Cat, Catch, Cavalla, Cavally, Ceratodus, Cero, Ceviche, Chad, Chaetodon, Char(r), Characin, Chavender, Cheven, Chimaera, Chondrostei, Chowder, Chub, Chum, Cichlid, Cisco, Clupea, Clupeidae, Cobia, Cockabully, Cockle, Cod(fish), Coho(e), Coley, Comber, Conger, Conner, Copepod, Coregonus, Corkwing, Coryphene, Cottus, Cow, Cran, Crappie, Cray, Creel, Crucian, Crusian, Cudden, Cuddin, Cunner, Cuddy, Cusk, Cuttle, Cyprinid, Dab, Dace, Danio, Dare, Dart, Dentex, Dib, Diodon, Dipnoi, Discus, Doctor, Dog(fish), Dolly Varden, Dorad(o), Doras, Doree, Dorse, Dory, Dragonet,

Dredge, Drumfish, Dry-fly, Eagle-ray, Eel(-pout), Elasmobranch, Elops, Elver, Episcate, Escallop, Escolar, Etheostoma, Eulachon, Father-lasher, Findram, Fingerling, Finnac(k), Finnan, Finnock, Flathead, Flounder, Fluke, Flutemouth, Fly, Fogash, Four-eyes, Fry, Fumado, Gade, Gadoid, Gadus, Ganoidei, Gar(fish), Garvie, Garvock, Gaspereau, Ged, Geelbek, Gefilte, Gibel, Gilgie, Gillaroo, Gilthead, Gobiidae, Goby, Goldeye, Goldsinny, Golomynka, Goramy, Gourami, Graining, Grayling, Grenadier, Groper, Grouper, Growler, Grunion, Grunt, Guddle, Gudgeon, Gulper, Gump, Gunnel, Gurami, Gurnard, Gurnet, Gwiniad, Gwyniad, Haberdine, Hackbolt, Haddock, Hagdown, Hag(fish), Hair-tail, Hake, Halibut, Halieutics, Harl, Hassar, Haul, Herling, Herring, Heterosomata, Hirling, Histiophorus, Hoki, Holostei, Homelyn, Hornbeak, Hornpout, Hottentot, Houting, Huso, Huss, Ichthyornis, Ichthys, Id(e), Inconnu, Jack, Jerker, Jilgie, Kabeljou(w), Kahawai, Keeling, Kelt, Keta, Kingclip, Kipper, Labrus, Lampern, Lamprey, Lampuki, Lance, Lant, Launce, Lax, Ledger, Ling, Loach, Lob(ster), Louvar, Luce, Luderick, Lump(fish), Lumpsucker, Lyomeri, Lythe, Mackerel, Mahi-mahi, Mahseer, Mahsir, Maid, Maise, Maize, Manatee, Manta, Marlin, Maskal(l)onge, Maskanonge, Masus, Maskinonge, Maze, Meagre, Mease, Medacca, Medaka, Medusa, Megrim, Menhaden, Menominee, Merling, Mess, Milkfish, Miller's thumb, Milter, Minnow, Moki, Molly, Moon-eye, Morgay, Mort, Morwong, Mossbunker, Mouthbrooder, Mudskipper, Mullet, Mulloway, Mur(a)ena, Murre, Murry, Muskellunge, Nannygai, Nennigai, Nerite, Nerka, Net, Nine-eyes, Nurse-hound, Oarfish, Old-wife, Oolakan, Opah, Orfe, Osseter, Oulachon, Oulakan, Oulicon, Overnet, Oxyrhynchus, Oyster, Pad(d)le, Paidle, Pakoko, Panchax, Pandora, Par(r), Peal, Peel, Pegasus, Perai, Perca, Pholas, Pickerel, Pike, Pilchard, Piper, Pirai, Piranha, Pirarucu, Piraya, Piscine, Plaice, Platy, Plectognathi, Pod(ley), Pogge, Pollack, Pollan, Pomfret, Pompano, Pope, Porbeagle, Porgie, Pout, Powan, Prawn, Rainbow-trout, Rasbora, Raun, Rawn, Ray, Remora, Rig(g), Roach, Robalo, Rock-cook, Rockling, Roe, Roker, Roncador, Rorqual, Roughy, Roussette, Rudd, Ruff(e), Saibling, Saith(e), Salmon, Samlet, Sander, Sar, Sardel(le), Sardine, Sargo, Sargus, Sashimi, Sauger, Saurel, Saury, Scad, Scalare, Scallop, Scampi, Scar, Scat, Schnapper, Scopelidae, Scorpaena, Scrod, Sculpin, Scup(paug), Sea-bass, Sea-bat, Sea-cock, Sea-dace, Sea-devil, Sea-lemon, Sea-owl, Sea-pike, Sea-robin, Sea-star, Sea-sturgeon, Sea-wife, Seeder, Seer, Seir, Selachion, Serran(us), Serrasalmo, Sewen, Sewin, Shad, Shanny, Shark, Sheat(h), Shiner, Shoal, Shovelnose, Shubunkin, Sild, Sillock, Siluridae, Skate, Skegger, Skelly, Skipjack, Slip, Slope, Smear-dab, Smelt, Snake-eel, Snapper, Snig, Sniggle, Snoek, Snook, Sock-eye, Sole, Solen, Spar(o)id, Sparling, Speck, Spin, Spot, Sprat, Sprod, Squeteague, Star, Steenbras, Stenlock, Sterlet, Stickleback, Stingaree, Sting-ray, Stockfish, Sturgeon, Sucker, Surgeon, Surmullet, Tai, Tarakihi, Tarpon, Tarwhine, Tautog, Teleost(ome), Tench, Teraglin, Terokihi, Tetra, Thornback, Threadfin, Tiddler, Tilapia, Tile-fish, Titling, Titarakura, Tittlebat, Toadfish, Toguc, Toitoi, Top(e), Torgoch, Torpedo, Torsk, Trachinus, Trawl, Trevally, Troll, Tropical, Trot, Trout, Trygon, Tub, Tuna, Tunny, Tusk, Twaite, Ulic(h)on, Ulikon, Umber, Vendace, Vendis, Wahoo, Wall-eye, Weever, Whale, Whiff, Whiting, Whitling, Wide-gab, Wirra,

Witch, Wolffish, Woof, Wrasse, Wreckfish, Yabbie, Yabby, Zander, Zingel

**Fish-basket**  Creel, Hask, Kipe

**Fish disease**  Argulus

**Fisher(man)**  Ahab, Andrew, Angler, Black cat, Caper, High-liner, Pedro, Peter, Piscator, Rodster, Sharesman, Walton

**Fish-hawk**  Osprey

**Fishing-ground**  Haaf

**Fishing-line**  G(u)imp, Gymp, Paternoster

**Fishpond**  Ocean, Stew, Vivarium

**Fishseller**  Fishwife, Molly Malone, Ripp(i)er

**Fishy**  Botargo, Suspicious, Vacant

**Fissure**  Chasm, Cleft, Crack, Crevasse, Crevice, Gap, Grike, Gryke, Lode, Sand-crack, Scam, Vallecula, Vein, Zygon

**Fist**  Clench, Dukes, Hand, Join-hand, Neaf(fe), Neif, Neive, Nief, Nieve, Pud, Punch, Thump

**Fit(ting), Fitness**  Able, Access, Adapt, Ague, Appointment, Appropriate, Apropos, Apt, Babbitt, Bout, Canto, Cataleptic, Cataplexy, Concinnous, Condign, Conniption, Convulsion, Culver-tail, Decent, Decorous, Dove-tail, Due, Eligible, Ensconce, Equip, Exies, Expedient, Fay, Fiddle, Furniment, Furnishing, Fytte, Gee, Germane, Habile, Hale, Hang, Health, Huff, In-form, Just, Lune, Mate, Meet, Mood, Paroxysm, Passus, Pertinent, Prepared, PROPER, Queme, Ready, Rig, Rind, Ripe, Rynd, Seemly, Seizure, Set, Sit, Sort, Sound, Spasm, Spell, Start, Suit(able), Syncope, Tantrum, Throe, To prepon, Turn, Up to, Well, Worthy, Wrath

> **Fit(ting)** may indicate a 't'

**Fitful**  Intermittent

**Fitment**  Adaptor, Unit

**Fitzgerald**  Edward, Ella, Scott

**Five(s)**  Cinque, Pallone, Pedro, Pentad, Quintet, Sextan, Towns, V

**Five years**  Lustre, Lustrum

**Fix(ed), Fixer**  Affeer, Anchor, Appoint, Appraise, ARRANGE, Assess, Assign, Attach, Bind, Cement, Clamp, Clew, Constant, Corking-pin, Decide, Destine, Destinate, Determine, Do, Embed, Empight, Engrain, Establish, Fast, Firm, Fit, Freeze, Hold, Immutable, Impaction, Imprint, Ingrain, Jag, Jam, Nail, Name, Narcotic, Nobble, Orientate, Peg, Persistent, Pin, Point, Repair, Resolute, Rig, Rigid, Rivet, Rove, Rut, Scrape, Screw, Seat, Seize, Set, Settle, Ship, Shoo, Skewer, Splice, Staple, Static, Stell, Step, Stew, Tie, Weld

**Fixture**  Attachment, Event, Match, Permanence

**Fizz(ed), Fizzy**  Effervesce, Gas, Hiss, Pop, Sherbet, Sod, Soda

**Fizzle**  Failure, Flop, Hiss, Washout

**Flabbergast**  Amaze, Astound, Floor

**Flabby**  Flaccid, Lank, Lax, Limp, Pendulous, Saggy

**Flaccid**  Flabby, Limp, Soft

**Flag(gy)**  Acorus, Ancient, Banderol, Banner, Blackjack, Blue Peter, Bunting, Burgee, Calamus, Colour(s) Dan(n)ebrog, Decline, Droop, Duster, Ensign, Fail, Falter, Fane, Fanion, Gladdon, Gonfalon, Guidon, Hoist, Irideal, Iris, Jack, Jade, Kerbstone, Languish, Lis, Old Glory, Orris, Pave(ment), Pavilion, Pencel, Pennant, Pennon, Pensel, Pensil, Peter, Pin, Rag, Sag, Sedge, Semaphore, Sink, Slab(stone), Slack, Standard, Streamer, Tricolour, Union Jack, Vane, Waif, Whift, Wilt, Wither

**Flagday**  Tagday

**Flagellate**  Beat, Mastigophora, Scourge, Trypanosome, Whip

**Flagon**  Bottle, Carafe, Jug, Stoop, Stoup, Vessel

**Flagpole**  Pin, Staff

**Flagrant**  Egregious, Glaring, Heinous, Patent, Wanton

**Flagship**  Admiral, Victory

**Flail**  Beat, Drub, Swingle, Threshel

**Flair**  Art, Bent, Elan, Gift, Knack, Panache, Style, TALENT

**Flak**  AA, Attack, Criticism

**Flake**  Chip, Flame, Flaught, Flaw, Fragment, Peel, Scale, Smut, Snow

**Flam**  Impose

**Flamboyant**  Baroque, Brilliant, Florid, Garish, Grandiose, Ornate, Ostentatious

**Flame, Flaming**  Ardent, Blaze, Fire, Flake, Flambé, Flammule, Glow, Kindle, Leman, Lover, Lowe, Sweetheart

**Flan**  Pastry, Quiche, Tart

**Flanders**  Mare, Moll

**Flange**  Border, Collar, Lip, Rim

**Flank(s)**  Accompany, Anta, Flange, Flitch, Ilia, Loin, Side, Spur

**Flannel**  Blather, Cloth, Soft-soap, Waffle, Zephyr

**Flap(ped), Flapper, Flapping**  Aileron, Alar, Alarm(ist), Aventail(e), Bate, Beat, Bird, Bobbysoxer, Chit, Dither, Elevon, Epiglottis, Fipple, Flacker, Flaff, Flag, Flaught, Flutter, Fly, Fuss, Giglet, Giglot, Hover, IN A FLAP, Labium, Labrum, Lapel, Loma, Lug, Panic, Tab, Tag, Tiswas, To-do, Tongue, Volucrine, Wave, Whisk

**Flare (up)**  Bell, Flame, Flanch, Flaunch, Godet, Magnesium, Scene, Signal, Spread, Spunk, Ver(e)y, Widen

**Flash(y), Flasher**  Cursor, Fire-flag, Flare, Flaught, Fulgid, Fulgural, Garish, Gaudy, Glaik, Gleam, Glisten, Green ray, Instant, Jay, Lairy, Levin, Lightning, Loud, Magnesium, Meretricious, Mo, Photopsy, Raffish, Ribbon, Roary, Sequin, Showy, Sluice, Snazzy, Spark, Streak, Strobe, Swank(e)y, Tick, Tigrish, Trice, Vivid, Wire

**> Flashing**  may indicate an anagram

**Flask** Ampulla, Aryballos, Bottle, Canteen, Carafe, Cucurbit, Dewar, Fiasco, Flacket, Lekythos, Matrass, Mick(e)(y), Retort, Thermos, Vacuum, Vial

**Flat(s), Flatten(ed), Flattener** Apartment, Bald, Banal, Beat, Blow-out, Callow, Complanate, Compress, Condominium, Corymb(ose), Coulisse, Dead, Demolish, Dress, Dull, Even, Floor, Flue, Fool, Guyot, Haugh, Homaloid, Horizontal, Insipid, Ironed, Jacent, Key, KO, Llano, Level, Lifeless, Marsh, Monotonous, Nitwit, Oblate, Pad, Pancake, Pedestrian, Penthouse, Pentice, Plain, Plane, Planish, Plat, Plateau, Prone, Prostrate, Recumbent, Scenery, Spread-edged, Squash, Tableland, Tabular, Tame, Tasteless, Tenement, True, Vapid

**Flat-chested** Cithara

**Flat-faced** Socle

**Flat-foot(ed)** Policeman, Splay

**Flat-nosed** Camus

**Flatter(ing), Flatterer, Flattery** Adulate, Beslaver, Blandish, Blarney, Butter, Cajole, Candied, Carn(e)y, Claw(back), Complimentary, Earwiggy, Fawn, Fillibrush, Flannel, Flannen, Fleech, Flummery, Gloze, Gnathonic(al), Honey, Imitation, Moody, Palp, Phrase, Sawder, Soap, Smarm, Snow-job, Spaniel, Stroke, Sugar, Sycophant, Taffy, Toady, Treacle, Unction, Wheedle

**Flatulence** Belch, Colic, Borborygmus, Burp, Carminative, Gas, Wind

**Flaunt** Brandish, Flourish, Gibe, Parade, Skyre, Strout, Strut, Wave

**Flavour(ed), Flavouring** Absinth(e), Alecost, Angostura, Aniseed, Bold, Borage, Clove, Coriander, Essence, Flor, Garni, Marinate, Mint, Orgeat, Quark, Race, Ratafia, Relish, Sair, Sassafras, Tack, Tang, Tarragon, TASTE, Tincture, Twang, Vanilla

**Flaw** Blemish, Brack, Bug, Chip, Crack, Defect, Fallacy, FAULT, Hamartia, Kink, Spot, Taint, Tear, Thief

**Flax(en)** Aleseed, Blonde, Codilla, Harden, Hards, Herden, Herl, Hurden, Line, Lint, Linum, Mill-mountain, Poi, Tow

**Flay** Excoriate, Fleece, Scourge, Skin, Strip, Uncase, Whip

**Flea** Aphaniptera, Chigger, Chigoe, Chigre, Daphnid, Hopper, Itch-mite, Pulex

**Fleabite** Denier

**Fleck** Dash, Freak, Spot, Streak

**Fledgling** Aerie, Eyas, Sorage

**Flee** Abscond, Bolt, Decamp, Escape, Eschew, Fly, Loup, Run, Scram

**Fleece** Bleed, Coat, Despoil, Lambskin, Pash(i)m, Pashmina, Plot, Pluck, Rifte, Ring, Rob, Rook, Shave, Shear, Sheepskin, Skin, SWINDLE, Toison

**Fleer** Ogle

**Fleet(ing)** Armada, Brief, Camilla, Ephemeral, Fast, Flit, Flota, Flotilla, Fugacious, Hasty, Hollow, Lightfoot, Navy, Passing, Prison, Spry, Street,

Transient, Velocipede

**Flesh(y)** Beefy, Body, Carneous, Carrion, Corporeal, Corpulent, Creatic, Digastric, Hypersarcoma, Joint, Meat, Muscle, Sarcous, Tissue

**Flesh-eating** Cannibalism, Carnassial, Creophagus, Omophagic

**Fleshless** Dry, Maigre, Pem(m)ican

**Flex(ible), Flexibility** Adaptable, Bend(y), Elastic, Limber, Lissom(e), Lithe, Pliant, RESILIENT, Tensile, Tonus, Wieldy, Willing, Wiry

> **Flexible, Flexuous** may indicate an anagram

**Flick(er), Flicks** Bioscope, Cinema, Fillip, Film, Flip, Flirt, Flutter, Glimmer, Gutter, Movie, Movy, Snap, Switch, Talkie, Twinkle, Waver

**Flickertail** ND

**Flier** Airman, Alcock, Amy, Aviator, Blimp, Brown, Crow, Daedalus, Erk, Fur, George, Gotha, Handout, Icarus, Pilot, RAF, Scotsman, Spec, Speedy

> **Flier** may indicate a bird

**Flight(y)** Backfisch, Birdbrain, Bolt, Bubble-headed, Capricious, Dart, Departure, Escalier, Escape, Exaltation, Exodus, Fast, Fickle, Flaught, Flibbertigibbet, Flip, Flock, Fugue, Giddy, Grese, Grise, Guy, Hegira, Hejira, Hejra, Hellicat, Hijra, Lam, Pair, Redeye, Ro(a)ding, Rode, Rout, Sortie, Stairs, STAMPEDE, Steps, Swarm, Tower, Trap, Vol(age), Volatile, Volley, Whisky-frisky, Wing

**Flightless** Kakapo, Rhea

> **Flighty** may indicate an anagram

**Flimsy** Finespun, Gimcrack, Gossamer, Jimcrack, Sleazy, Sleezy, Tenuous, Thin, Weak, Wispy

**Flinch** Blench, Cringe, Funk, Quail, Recoil, Shrink, Start, Wince

**Fling** Dance, Flounce, Highland, Hurl, Pitch, Shy, Slat, Slug, Slump, Spree, Throw, TOSS

**Flint** Chert, Firestone, Granite, Hag-stone, Hornstone, Pirate, Rock, Silex, Microlith, Mischmetal, Silica, Stone

**Flip(pant), Flipping** Airy, Bally, Brash, Cocky, Flick, Frivolous, Impudent, Jerk, Nog, Pert, Purl, Sassy, Saucy, Toss, Turn

**Flipper(s)** Fin-toed

**Flirt(ing)** Bill, Carve, Chippy, Coquet(te), Dalliance, Footsie, Gallivant, Heart-breaker, Mash, Neck, Philander(er), Rig, Toy, Trifle, Vamp, Wow

**Flit** Dart, Decamp, Flicker, Flutter, Scoot

**Float(er), Floating** Balsa, Bob, Buoy, Caisson, Carley, Drift, Fleet, Levitate, Lifebuoy, Milk, Neuston, Oropesa, Outrigger, Planula, Pontoon, Pram, Quill, Raft, Ride, Sail, Skim, Sponson, Trimmer, Vacillate, Waft, Waggler

**Floating garden** Chinampa

**Flock** Assemble, Bevy, Charm, Chirm, Company, Drove, Flight, Fold, Forgather, Gaggle, Gather, Herd, Mob, Rally, Sedge, Spring, Trip, Tuft,

Vulgar, Wing, Wisp, Wool

**Flog(ger), Flogging**  Beat, Birch, Breech, Cane, Cat, Exert, Flay, Hide, Knout, Lace, Lambast, Larrup, Lash, Lather, Orbilius, Rope's end, Scourge, Sell, Strap, Tat, THRASH, Thwack, Tout, Vapulate, Whip

**Flood**  Bore, Cataclysm, Deluge, Deucalion, Diluvium, Dump, Eger, Freshet, Gush, Inundate, Irrigate, Noachic, Overflow, Overwhelm, Pour, Rage, Spate, Speat, Swamp, Tide, TORRENT, Undam

**Floodgate**  St(a)unch

**Floodlight**  Blonde

**Floor(ing)**  Area, Astound, Baffle, Deck, Dev(v)el, Down, Entresol, Etage, Fell, Flatten, Flight, Gravel, Kayo, KO, Parquet, Planch, Platform, Screed, Stage, Story, Stump, Tessella, Tessera, Thill

**Flop**  Collapse, Dud, Failure, Fosbury, Lollop, Mare's-nest, Misgo, Phut, Plump, Purler, Washout, Whap, Whitewash

**Flora**  Benthos, Biota, Cybele, Flowers

**Florid**  Coloratura, Cultism, Flamboyant, Fresh, Gongorism, High, Red, Rococo, Rubicund, Ruddy, Taffeta

**Florida**  Fa

**Floss(y)**  Flashy, Florence, Ornate, Silk

**Flotilla**  Armada, Escadrille

**Flotsam**  Detritus, Driftwood, Flotage, Waveson

**Flounce**  Falbala, Frill, Furbelow, Huff, Prance, Ruffle, Sashay, Toss

**Flounder**  Fluke, Slosh, Struggle, Stumble, Tolter, Toss, Wallow

**Flour**  Couscous(ou), Farina, Graham, Gram, Kouskous, Meal, Middlings, Pinole, Powder, Red-dog

**Flourish(ed), Flourishing**  Blague, Bless, Bloom, Blossom, Boast, Brandish, Bravura, Burgeon, Cadenza, Epiphonema, Fanfare, Fiorita, Fl, Flare, Grow, Kicking, Mort, Palmy, Paraph, Prosper, Scroll, Swash, Thrive, Tucket, Veronica, Vigorous, Wave, Welfare

**Flout**  Disdain, Insult, Malign, Mock, Profane, Scorn, Scout

**Flow(ing)**  Abound, Cantabile, Current, Cursive, Cusec, Distil, Ebb, Emanate, Estrang(h)elo, Fleet, Fluent, Flush, Flux, Gush, Liquid, Loose-bodied, Nappe, Onrush, Ooze, Popple, Pour, Purl, Rail(e), Rayle, Rill, Rin, Run, Scapa, Seamless, Spate, Stream, Teem, Torrent

**Flower (part), Flowering, Flower bed**  Abutilon, Aconite, Adonis, Agave, Alyssum, Amaranth, Arabis, Argemone, Arum, Asphodel, Aster, Astilbe, Bald-money, Bel(l)amoure, Best, Bloom, Bloosme, Blossom, Bluebell, Boutonniere, Brook, Bugle, Bugloss, Bur-marigold, Buttercup, Buttonhole, Camas(s), Camash, Campion, Carolina, Columbine, Coronation, Corymb, Crants, Cyclamen, Cyme, Daffodil, Dahlia, Daisy, Develop, Edelweiss, Elite, Enemy, Floscule, Freesia, Fumaria, Gentian, Gessamine, Gillyflower, Gillyvor, Gilt-cup, Glacier, Glory-pea, Godetia, Gold, Gollan(d), Gool, Gowland, Gule, Heliotrope, Hellebore, Henbit,

Hepatica, Hibiscus, Hosta, Immortelle, Ipomoea, Irid, Iris, Jessamine, Kikumon, Knot, Kok-sagyz, Larkspur, Lily, Loose-strife, Madder, Magnolia, Maguey, Marigold, Meadow-sweet, Melampode, Melilot, Myosotis, None-so-pretty, Nosegay, Oleander, Onagra, Orchid, Padma, Paeony, Parterre, Pentstemon, Petunia, Phlox, Pink, Plant, Poinsettia, Poppy, Pre-vernal, Prime, Protea, Quamash, Rampion, RIVER, Rose, Rudbeckia, Safety, Santonica, Saxifrage, Scilla, Sesame, Silene, Smilax, Spadix, Spray, Stalked, Stapelia, Stream, Strobilus, Tansy, Toran(a), Tradescantia, Tuberose, Tulip, Turnsole, Umbel, Valerian, Verbena, Vernal, Wreath

> **Flower** may indicate a river

**Flower arrangement** Ikebana

**Flowery** Anthemia, Damassin, Orchideous, ORNATE, Pseudocarp, Verbose

**Flu** Grippe

**Fluctuate(r), Fluctuation** Ambivalence, Balance, Seiche, Trimmer, Unsteady, Vacillate, Vary, Waver

**Flue** Chimney, Duct, Funnel, Pipe, Tewel, Uptake, Vent

**Fluent** Eloquent, Facile, Flowing, Glib, Liquid, Verbose, Voluble

**Fluff(y)** Bungle, Dowl(e), Down, Dust, Feathery, Flocculent, Floss, Flue, Fug, Fuzz, Girl, Lint, Noil, Oose, Ooze

**Fluid** Broo, Chyle, Cisterna, Condy's, Enema, Fl, Humour, Juice, LIQUID, Lymph, Mucus, Oedema, Plasma, Sap, Serum, Shifting, Synovia, Vitreum, Vril, Water

> **Fluid** may indicate an anagram

**Fluke** Accident, Anchor, Chance, Fan, Flounder, Ga(u)nch, Grapnel, Killock, Redia, Scratch

**Flummox** Baffle, Bamboozle, Floor

**Flunk** Fail

**Flunkey** Chasseur, Clawback, Haiduck, Heyduck, Jeames, Lackey, Servant, Toady

**Fluorescence** Bloom, Epipolism, Glow

**Fluorine** F

**Flurry** Bustle, Fluster, Haste, Hoo-ha, Shower

**Flush(ed)** Affluent, Beat, Even, Ferret, Florid, Flow, Gild, Hectic, Level, Red, Rolling, Rose, Royal, Rud, Scour, Sluice, Spaniel, Start, Thrill, Tierce, Vigour, Wash

**Fluster** Befuddle, Confuse, Disconcert, Flap, Rattle, Shake

**Flute (player)** Bellows-maker, Channel, Crimp, Fife, Flageolet, Glass, Glyph, Groove, Marsyas, Ocarina, Piccolo, Pipe, Poogye(e), Quena, Shakuhachi, Sulcus, Thisbe, Tibia, Toot, Whistle

**Flutter** Bat, Bet, Fan, Fibrillate, Flaffer, Flichter, Flicker, Fly, GAMBLE, Hover, Palpitate, Play, Pulse, Sensation, Twitter, Waft, Winnow

**Flux**  D, Flow, Fusion, Maxwell, Melt, Tesla, Weber

**Fly(ing), Flies**  Abscond, Agaric, Alder, Alert, Astute, Aviation, Awake, A-wing, Baker, Bedstead, Bluebottle, Bolt, Bot, Breese, Breeze, Brize, Brommer, Cab, Caddis, Carriage, Cecidomyia, Cleg, Cock-a-bondy, CUNNING, Decamp, Diptera, Doctor, Dragon, Drake, Drosophila, Dutchman, Escape, Fiacre, Flee, Flit, Fox, Frit, Glide, Glossina, Gnat, Grannom, Greenbottle, Greenhead, Hackle, Hedge-hop, Hessian, Homoptera, Hop, Hurtle, Ichneumon, Jenny-spinner, Jock Scott, Lace-wing, Laputan, Mosquito, Motuca, Musca, Mutuca, Nymph, Opening, Ox-warble, Palmer, Para, Pilot, Pium, Rapid, Saucer, Sciaridae, Scotsman, Scud, Sedge, Simulium, Smart, Soar, Spanish, Speed, Syrphidae, Tabanid, Tachina, Thrips, Tipula, Tsetse, Volatic, Volitate, Watchet, Wide-awake, Wing, Yogic, Zebub, Zimb, Zipper

**Fly-catcher**  Attercop, Cobweb, Darlingtonia, Dionaea, King-bird, Phoebe, Spider, Tanrec

**Flying-fox**  Fruit-bat, Kalong

**Flying saucer**  UFO

**Fly-killer**  Chowri, Chowry, DDT, Swat

**Foam**  Barm, Bubble, Froth, Lather, Mousse, Ream, Scum, Seethe, Spindrift, Spume, Sud(s), Surf, Yeast, Yest

**Fob**  Chain, Defer, Fub, Pocket, Slang

**Focal, Focus**  Centre, Converge, Fix, Hinge, Hub, Pinpoint, Point, Spotlight, Train

**Fodder**  Alfalfa, Browsing, Cannon, Clover, Eatage, Ensilage, Foon, Forage, Gama-grass, Grama, Hay, Lucerne, Oats, Pasture, Rye-grass, Sainfoin, Silage, Stover

**Foe**  Contender, ENEMY, Opponent, Rival

**Foetus**  Embryo

**Fog**  Brume, Cloud, Damp, Fret, Haar, Miasm(a), Mist, Murk, Obscure, Pea-soup, Roke, Sea-fret, Sea-haar, Smog, Smoke, Soup, Thick, Vapour

**Fogg**  Phileas, Solicitor

**Foible**  Failing, Flaw, Quirk, Weakness

**Foil(ed)**  Ba(u)lk, Chaff, Cross, Dupe, Epée, Frustrate, Lametta, Offset, Paillon, Pip, Scotch, Silver, Stooge, Stump, Thwart, Touché

**Foist**  Fob, Insert, Suborn, Wish

**Fold(ed), Folder, Folding**  Anticline, Bend, Binder, Close, Collapse, Corrugate, Cote, Crash, Crease, Crimp, Crinkle, Crunkle, Diapir, Diptych, Double, Epiploon, Fake, File, Fr(a)enum, Frill, Furl, Gather, Jack-knife, Lap(p)et, Lapel, Lirk, Mesentery, Obvolute, Octuple, Omentum, Pen, Pintuck, PLEAT, Plica, Ply, Pran(c)k, Prancke, Ptyxis, Ruck(le), Ruga, Sheep-pen, Syncline, Triptych, Tuck, Wrap

**Foliage**  Coma, Finial, Frond, Greenery, Leafage

**Folio(s)**  Ff, File, Percy

**Folk(sy)** Beaker, Homespun, Kin, People, Public

**Follow(er), Following** After, Agree, Anthony, Attend(ant), Believer, Clientele, Consequence, Copy, Dangle, Disciple, Dog, Echo, Ensew, Ensue, Entourage, Epigon(e), Equipage, F, Fan, Groupie, Henchman, Hunt, Man, Muggletonian, Myrmidon, Neist, Next, Obey, Pan, Post, Pursue, Rake, Road, Run, Satellite, School, Secundum, Segue, Sequel, Seriation, Shadow, Sheep, Sidekick, Stag, Stalk, Stear, Steer, Subsequent, Succeed, Sue, Suivez, Supervene, Tag, Tail, Tantony, Trace, Track, Trail, Train, Use, Vocation

> **Follower** 'a follower' may indicate B

**Folly** Antic, Bêtise, Idiocy, Imprudence, Lunacy, Mistake, Moria, Vanity

**Foment(ation)** Arouse, Brew, Embrocation, Excite, Poultice, Stupe

**Fond(ness)** Ardour, Dote, Keen, Loving, Partial, Tender, Tendre

**Fondant** Ice, Sweet

**Fondle** Canoodle, Caress, Dandle, Grope, Hug, Nurse, Pet, Snuggle

**Font** Bénitier, Delubrum, Source

**Food** Aliment, Ambrosia, Bakemeat, Batten, Battill, Battle, Bellytimber, Board, Bord, Broth, Browse, Bully, Burger, Cate, Cheer, Cheese, Chop, Chow, Chuck, Collation, Comestible, Commons, Course, Curd, Deutoplasm, DISH, Dodger, Dog's body, Dunderfunk, Eats, Esculents, Eutrophy, Falafel, Fare, Felafel, Fodder, Forage, Fuel, Grub, Kai, Keep, Long-pig, Manna, Mato(o)ke, Meat, Nardoo, Nosebag, Nosh, Nourriture, Pabulum, Pannage, Pap, Pasta, Peck, Pemmican, Provender, Provision, Sambal, Sap, Scaff, Scoff, Sizings, Snack, Soil, Staple, Sushi, Table, Tack, Tamale, Taro, Tempura, Tuck(er), Viand, Victuals, Vivers, Waffle

**Food-plant** Laser, Silphium

**Foodstore** Delicatessen, Grocery, Larder, Pantry, Silo

**Fool(hardy), Foolish(ness)** Air-head, April, Assot, Berk, BL, Bob, Brash, Buffoon, Cake, Capocchia, Chump, Clot, Clown, Coxcomb, Cully, Dagonet, Daw, Delude, Dummy, Dunce, Empty, Feste, Flannel, Folly, Fon, Fond, Gaby, Gaga, Galah, Git, Glaikit, Goat, Gobbo, Goon, Goose, Gooseberry, Groserts, Gubbins, Gull, Highland, Idiotic, Imbecile, Inane, Ineptitude, Jest, Joke, Kid, Lark, Mamba, Mislead, Mome, Moron, Muggins, Niaiserie, Nignog, Ni(n)compoop, Ninny, Nong, Omadhaun, Patch, Poop, Poupe, Rash, Sawney, Scogan, Scoggin, Senseless, Shallow, Snipe, Soft, Sot, Spoony, STUPID, Tom (noddy), Trifle, Unwitty, Vice, Wantwit, Yorick, Zany

**Foolproof** Fail-safe

**Foot(ing), Footwork, Feet** Amphibrach, Anap(a)est, Antibacchius, Antispast, Bacchius, Ball, Base, Choliamb, Choree, Choriamb, Cretic, Dactyl, Dance, Dochmii, Dochmius, Epitrite, Hephthemimer, Hoof, Hoppus, Iamb(us), Infantry, Molossus, Pad, Paean, Paeon, Paw, Pay, Pedate, Plates, Podium, Procleusmatic, Pyrrhic, Roothold, Scazon, Semeia, Spondee, Standing, Tarsus, Terms, Tootsie, Tootsy, Tread, Tribrach, Trotter, Verse

**Football(er)** Back, Barbarian, Ba'spiel, Camp, Centre, FIFA, Goalie, Keeper, Kicker, Libero, Lock, Pele, Pigskin, RU, Rugby, Rugger, Rules, Safety, Soccer, Sport, Striker, Sweeper, Wing

**Foot-fault** Bunion, Corn, Hammer-toe, Verruca

**Foothold** Lodgement, Purchase, Stirrup

**Footloose** Peripatetic

**Footman** Attendant, Flunkey, Lackey, Pedestrian, Pompey, Yellowplush

**Footnote** Addendum, PS

**Footpad** Land-rat, Mugger, Robber

**Footprint** Ichnite, Ichnolite, Pad, Prick, Pug, Seal, Slot, Trace, Track, Vestige

**Footrest** Coaster, Hassock, Stirrup, Stool, Tramp

**Footsore** Blister, Bunion, Corn, Surbate, Surbet, Weary, Wire-heel

**Footwashing** Maundy, Nipter

**Footwear** Gumboot, Shoe, Slipper, Sock, Spats, Stocking

**Fop(pish)** Apery, Beau, Buck, Cat, Coxcomb, Dandy, Dude, Exquisite, Fantastico, Finical, La-di-da, Macaroni, Monarcho, Muscadin, Popinjay, Toff

**For** Ayes, Because, Concerning, Cos, Pro, Since, To

**Forage** Alfalfa, Fodder, Graze, Greenfeed, Lucern(e), Pickeer, Prog, Raid, Rummage, Search

**Foray** Attack, Creach, Creagh, Raid, Sortie

**Forbear(ance), Forbearing** Abstain, Clement, Endure, Indulgent, Lenience, Lineage, Longanimity, Mercy, Pardon, Parent, Patient, Quarter, REFRAIN, Suffer, Tolerant, Withhold

**Forbid(den), Forbidding** Ban, Bar, Denied, Dour, Enjoin, For(e)speak, Gaunt, Grim, Hostile, Loury, NL, Prohibit, Stern, Taboo, Tabu, Tapu, Tref(a), Veto

**Force(d), Forceful, Forces, Forcible** Activist, Agency, Army, Bathmism, Bind, Birr, Bludgeon, Body, Brigade, Brunt, Bulldoze, Cadre, Cascade, Centrifugal, Chi, Coerce, Cogency, Commando, Compel, Constrain, Cram, Detachment, Dint, Domineer, Downflow, Dragoon, Drive, Duress(e), Dynamic, Dyne, E, Emphatic, Energetic, Erdgeist, Erg, Expeditionary, Extort, Extrude, F, Farci, Fire brigade, Frogmarch, G, Gilbert, Gism, Gouge, Hale, Hurricane, Impetus, Impress, Instress, Intense, Irgun, Irrupt, Jism, Kinetic, Labour, Legion, Lorentz, Magnus, Make, Mana, Manpower, Militia, Moment, Muscle, Navy, Newton, Oblige, Od, Odyl(e), OGPU, Orgone, Personnel, Phrenism, Pigs, Pion, Pithy, Police, Posse, Potent, Poundal, Prana, Press(gang), Prise, Pull, Put, Qi, Railroad, Regular, Require, Restem, Route, Rush, SAS, Sforzando, Snorting, Spetsnaz, Steam(roller), Strained, STRESS, Subject, Telergy, Thrust, Torque, Troops, Vehement, Vigorous, Violence, Vim, Vis, Vital, Vively, Vril, Wrench, Wrest, Wring, Zap

> **Force(d)** may indicate an anagram

**Forced labour** Begar

**Forceps** Crow(s)bill, Pedicellaria, Pincers, Tenaculum, Vulsella

**Ford** Anglia, Car, Crossing, Escort, Strid, Tin Lizzy, Wade

**Forearm** Radius, Ulna

> **Forebear** see FORBEAR

**Foreboding** Anxiety, Augury, Cloudage, Croak, Feeling, Freet, OMEN, Ominous, Presage, Presentiment, Sinister, Zoomantic

**Forecast(er)** Augury, Auspice, Divine, Extrapolation, Horoscope, Metcast, Perm, Precurse, Predict, Presage, Prognosis, Prognosticate, Prophesy, Rainbird, Soothsay, Spae, Tip

**Foreclose** Bar, Block, Obstruct, Preclude

**Forefather(s)** Ancestor, Elder, Forebear, Parent, Rude

**Forefront** Van

**Forehead** Brow, Front(let), Glabella(r), Temple

**Foreign(er)** Alien, Arab, Auslander, Barbarian, Easterling, Eleanor, Exotic, External, Extraneous, Extrinsic, Forane, Forinsecal, Forren, Fraim, Fremit, Gaijin, German, Gringo, Metic, Moit, Mote, Outside, Oversea, Peregrine, Remote, STRANGE, Stranger, Taipan, Tramontane, Uitlander, Unfamiliar

**Foreman** Boss, Bosun, Gaffer, Ganger, Manager, Overseer, Steward, Superintendent

**Foremost** First, Front, Leading, Prime, Primary, Supreme, Van

> **Foremost** may indicate first letters of words following

**Forenoon** Undern

**Forepart** Cutwater, Front

**Forerunner** Augury, Harbinger, Herald, Messenger, Omen, Pioneer, Trailer, Vaunt-courier

**Foresee** Anticipate, Divine, Preview, Prophesy, Scry

**Foreshadow** Adumbrate, Bode, Forebode, Hint, Portend, Prefigure, Presage, Type

**Foreshow** Betoken, Bode, Signify

**Foresight** Ganesa, Prescience, Prophecy, Prospect, Providence, Prudence, Taish, Vision

**Forest** Arden, Ashdown, Bush, Caatinga, Charnwood, Chase, Dean, Epping, Gapo, Glade, Greenwood, Igapo, Jungle, Monte, Nandi, Nemoral, New, Savernake, Selva, Sherwood, Taiga, Urman, WOOD

**Forestall** Anticipate, Obviate, Pip, Prevent, Queer

**Forester** Foster, Lumberjack, Verderer, Walker, Woodman, Woodward

**Forestry** Woodcraft

**Foretaste** Antepast, Antipasto, Appetiser, Pregustation, Prelibation,

Sample, Trailer

**Foretell, Forewarn** Augur, Bode, Caution, Divine, Forecast, Portend, Predict, Premonish, Presage, Prognosticate, Prophecy, Soothsay, Spae

**Forethought** Anticipation, Caution, Prometheus, Provision, Prudence

**Forever** Always, Ay(e), Eternal, Evermore, Keeps

> **Forewarn** see FORETELL

**Foreword** Introduction, Preamble, Preface, Proem, Prologue

**For example** Eg, Say, Vg, ZB

**For fear** Lest

**Forfeit** Deodand, Fine, Forgo, PENALTY, Relinquish, Sconce

**Forge(d), Forger(y)** Blacksmith, Copy, Counterfeit, Dud, Fabricate, Fashion, Foundry, Hammer, Heater, Horseshoe, Ireland, Lauder, Mint, Paper-hanger, Pigott, Progress, Smith(y), Spurious, Stiff, Stithy, Stumer, Trucage, Truquage, Utter, Vermeer, Vulcan

**Forget(ful), Forget-me-not** Amnesia, Dry, Fluff, Lethe, Myosotis, Neglect, Oblivious, Omit, Overlook

**Forgive(ness), Forgiving** Absolution, Amnesty, Clement, Condone, Merciful, Overlook, Pardon, Placable, Remission, Remittal

**Forgo(ne)** Abstain, Expected, Refrain, Renounce, Waive

**Forgotten** Bygone, Missed, Sad

**Forjeskit** Overscutched

**Fork(ed)** Bifurcate, Branch, Caudine, Cleft, Crotch, Forficate, Fourchette, Grain, Graip, Morton's, Osmeterium, Prong, Runcible, Tine, Toaster, Tormentor, Trident, Trifid, Tuner, Y

**Forlorn(ness)** Abject, Aidless, Desolate, Destitute, Drearisome, Miserable, Nightingale, Sad

**Form(s)** Alumni, Bench, Bumf, Cast, Ceremonial, Class, Constitute, Coupon, Create, Document, Experience, Fashion, Feature, Fig, FIGURE, Formula, Game, Gestalt, Hare, Image, Mode, Mood, Mould, Order, Originate, OUT OF FORM, Protocol, Questionnaire, Redia, Remove, Rite, Ritual, Schedule, Shape, Shell, Stage, Stamp, State, Structure, Style, Symmetry, Version

**Formal** Conventional, Dry, Exact, Fit, Official, Pedantic, Precise, Prim, Routine, Set, Starched, Stiff, Stodgy, Tails

**Formality** Ceremony, Ice, Protocol, Punctilio, Starch

**Formation** Battalion, Configuration, Diapyesis, Echelon, Eocene, Fours, Growth, Line, Manufacture, Origin, Pattern, Phalanx, Prophase, Riss, Wedge

**Former(ly)** Auld, Before, Ci-devant, Earlier, Ere-now, Erst(while), Ex, Late, Maker, Once, Past, Previous, Prior, Pristine, Quondam, Sometime, Then, Umquhile, Whilom

**Formidable** Alarming, Armipotent, Battleaxe, Fearful, Forbidding, Powerful, Shrewd, Stoor, Stour, Stowre, Sture

**Formless** Amorphous, Invertebrate, Shapeless

> **Form of, Forming** may indicate an anagram

**Formosan** Tai

**Formula(te)** Define, Devise, Doctrine, Equation, Frame, Invent, Lurry, Paternoster, Protocol, Prescription, RECIPE, Rite, Ritual

**Forsake** Abandon, Desert, Quit, Renounce

**Forsooth** Certes, Certy, Even, Marry

**Forswear** Abandon, Abjure, Disavow, Renounce, Reny

**Forsyte** Fleur, Saga

**Fort(ification), Fortress** Acropolis, Alamo, Alhambra, Balclutha, Bastille, Bastion, Battlement, Bawn, Blockhouse, Bonnet, Burg, Casbah, Castellated, Castle, Citadel, Contravallation, Crémaillère, Deva, Dun, Edinburgh, Enceinte, Epaule, Fastness, Fortalice, Fortilage, Fortlet, Ft, Gabionade, Garrison, Haven, Hedgehog, Kaim, Kame, Kasba(h), Keep, La(a)ger, Malakoff, Martello tower, Masada, Merlon, Moineau, Orillion, Pa(h), Peel, Pele, Pentagon, Place, Rampart, Rath, Redoubt, Reduit, Sconce, Stronghold, Sumter, Terreplein, Tower

**Forte** F, Specialty, Strength

**Forth** Away, From, Hence, Out

**Forthright** Candid, Direct, Frank, Prompt

**Forthwith** Anon, Directly, Eft(soons), Immediately

**Fortify** Arm, Augment, Brace, Casemate, Embattle, Lace, Munify, Steel, STRENGTHEN

**Fortitude** Endurance, Grit, Mettle, Patience, Pluck, STAMINA

**Fortunate** Auspicious, Blessed, Blest, Happy, LUCKY, Providential

**Fortune (teller), Fortune-telling** Auspicious, Bumby, Chaldee, Cha(u)nce, Destiny, Dukkeripen, Fame, Fate, Felicity, Genethliac, Geomancy, Hap, Luck, Mint, Motser, Motza, Oracle, Palmist, Peripety, Pile, Prescience, Sibyl, Soothsayer, Sortilege, Spaewife, Success, Taroc, Tarok, Tarot, Tyche, Wealth, Windfall

**Forty, Forties** Capot, F, Hungry, Kemple, Roaring

**Forty-ninth** Parallel

**Forum** Arena, Assembly, Debate, Platform, Tribunal

**Forward(s)** Accede, Advanced, Ahead, Along, Arch, Assertive, Bright, Early, Flanker, Forrad, Forrit, Forth, Fresh, Future, Hasten, Hooker, Immodest, Impudent, Lock, Malapert, On(wards), Pack, Pert, Petulant, Precocious, PROGRESS, Promote, Prop, Readdress, Redirect, Scrum, Send, Stem, To(ward), Van, Wing

**Fossil(ise)** Amber, Ammonite, Baculite, Belemnite, Blastoid(ea), Calamite, Conodont, Cordaites, Enerinite, Eohippus, Eozoon, Eurypterus, Exuviae, Fogy, Goniatite, Graptolite, Ichnite, Ichthyodurolite, Ichthyolite, Lingulella, Mosasauros, Nummulite, Olenus, Osteolepis, Ostracoderm, Petrifaction, Phytolite, Plesiosaur, Pliohippus, Pterygotus, Pythonomorph,

Relics, Reliquiae, Remanié, Sigillaria, Sinanthropus, Snakestone, Stigmaria, Trilobite, Uintatherium, Wood-opal, Zoolite

**Foster (child, mother)** Adopt, Cherish, Da(u)lt, Develop, Feed, Fornent, Further, Harbour, Metapelet, Metaplot, Nourish, Nourse(l), Noursle, Nousell, Nurse, Nurture, Nuzzle, REAR

**Foul** Base, Beray, Besmirch, Besmutch, Bungle, DEFILE, Dreggy, Drevill, Enseam, Evil, Feculent, Gross, Hassle, Hing, Mephitic, Mud, Noisome, Olid, Osmeterium, Putid, Putrid, RANK, Reekie, Rotten, Sewage, Soiled, Stagnant, Stain, Unclean, Unfair, Vile, Violation, Virose

> **Foul** may indicate an anagram

**Found (in)** Among, Base, Bed, Bottom, Build, Cast, Emong, Endow, ESTABLISH, Eureka, Institute, Introduce, Met, Plant, Recovered, Start, Table

**Foundation(s)** Base, Bedrock, Cribwork, Establishment, Footing, Girdle, Grillage, Ground, Hard-core, Institution, Matrix, Pile, Rockefeller, Scholarship, Stays, Substrata, Substructure, Underlie, Underlinen

> **Foundations** may indicate last letters

**Founder** Author, Crumple, Fail, Inventor, Iron-master, Miscarry, Oecist, Oekist, Patriarch, Perish, Settle, Sink, Stumble

**Fount** Source, Springlet

**Fountain** Acadine, Aganippe, Castalian, Cause, Conduit, Fons, Gerbe, Head, Hippocrene, Jet, Pant, Pirene, Salmacis, Scuttlebutt, Soda, Spring, Trevi, Youth

**Fountain basin** Laver

**Four(some)** Cater, Georges, Horsemen, IV, Mess, Quartet, Reel, Tessara, Tessera, Tetrad, Tiddy, Warp

**Fourpence** Groat

**Fourteenth** Bastille, Valentine

**Fourth** Deltaic, Estate, Forpet, Forpit, July, Quartet, Quaternary, Sesquitertia, Tritone

**Fowl** Barnyard, Biddy, Boiler, Brahma, Brissle-cock, Burrow-duck, Chicken, Chittagong, Cob, Cock, Coot, Duck, Ember, Gallinaceous, Gallinule, Game, Hamburg(h), HEN, Houdan, Kora, Leghorn, Moorhen, Partridge, Pheasant, Pintado, Poultry, Quail, Rooster, Rumkin, Solan, Spatchcock, Spitchcock, Sussex, Teal, Turkey, Wyandotte

**Fox(y)** Alopecoid, Baffle, Charley, Charlie, Corsac, Cunning, Desert, Fennec, Fool, Friend, Kit, Lowrie(-tod), Outwit, Pug, Puzzle, Reynard, Rommel, Russel, Skulk, SLY (boots), Tod, Uffa, Uneatable, Vixen, Zerda, Zoril(le), Zorro

**Foxglove** Digitalis, Witches-thimble

**Foxhole** Earth

**Foyer** Hall, Lobby

**Fracas** Brawl, Dispute, Mêlée, Prawle, Riot, Rumpus, Shindig, Uproar

**Fraction** Ligroin, Mantissa, Part, Scrap, Some

**Fracture** Break, Crack, Fissure, Greenstick, Impacted, Rupture, Split

**Fragile** Brittle, Crisp, Delicate, Frail, Nesh, Slender, Weak

**Fragment(s)** Atom, Bit, Blaud, Brash, Breccia, Brockram, Cantlet, Clastic, Crumb, Flinder, Fritter, Frust, Lapilli, Morceau, Morsel, Ort, PARTICLE, Piece, Rubble, Scrap, Segment, Shard, Shatter, Sheave, Shrapnel, Skerrick, Sliver, Smithereens, Smithers, Snatch, Splinter

> **Fragment of** may indicate a hidden word

**Fragrance, Fragrant** Aromatic, Attar, Bouquet, Conima, Odour, Olent, PERFUME, Pot-pourri, Redolent, SCENT, Sent, Spicy, Suaveolent

**Frail** Brittle, Delicate, Feeble, Flimsy, FRAGILE, Puny, Slight, Slimsy, Weak

**Framboesia** Morula, Yaws

**Frame(work)** Adjust, Angle, Bail, Bayle, Body, Build, Cadre, Cadge, Cage, Casement, Cent(e)ring, Centreing, Chase, Chassis, Compages, Companion, Cratch, Deckel, Deckle, Entablature, Fabric, Fiddley, Flake, Form, Frisket, Gantry, Gate, Grid-iron, Heck, Horse, Hull, Mood, Mount, Mullion, Muntin(g), Newsreel, Pannier, Parameter, Partner, Passe-partout, Pergola, Pillory, Plant, Plot, Rack, Redact, Retable, Rim, Sash, Scaffold, Scuncheon, Sect(ion), Set, Setting, Skeleton, Spring-box, Stanchion, Stillage, Stocks, Stroma, STRUCTURE, Surround, Tambour, Tent(er), Tepee, Trave, Trellis, Tress, Trestle, Tribble, Victimize, Wattle, Way, Yoke, Zimmer

**Framley** Parsonage

**Franc** Fr, Leu, Lev, Lew

**France** Anatole, Marianne, RF, Thibault

**Franchise** Charter, Contract, Liberty, Right, Suffrage, Vote, Warrant

**Franciscan** Observant, Scotist, Tertiaries

**Francium** Fr

**Franck** Cesar

**Frank** Blunt, CANDID, Direct, Easy, Free, Honest, Ingenuous, Man-to-man, Natural, Open, Outspoken, Postage, Postmark, Salian, Sincere, Stamp, Straight, Sty

**Frankincense** Laser, Olibanum, Thus

**Frans, Franz** Hals, Lehar

**Frantic** Deranged, Frenzied, Hectic, Mad, Overwrought, Phrenetic, Rabid, Violent

> **Frantic** may indicate an anagram

**Frappé** Iced

**Fraternlse, Fraternity** Affiliate, Brotherhood, Consort, Elk, Fellowship, Lodge, Mingle, Moose, Order

**Fratricide** Cain

**Fraud** Barratry, Bobol, Bubble, Charlatan, Cheat, Chisel, Collusion, Covin, Deceit, Diddle, Do, Fineer, Gyp, Humbug, IMPOSTOR, Imposture, Jiggery-pokery, Peculator, Piltdown, Pious, Pseud(o), Rip-off, Roguery, Rort, Scam, South Sea Bubble, Stellionate, Supercherie, Swindle, Swiz(zle), Tartuffe, Trick

**Fraught** Perilous

**Fray(ed)** Bagarre, Brawl, Contest, Feaze, Frazzle, Fret, Fridge, Ravel, Scrimmage

**Freak** Cantrip, Caprice, Chimera, Deviant, Geek, Sport, Teras, Whim, Whimsy

**Freckle** Ephelis, Fern(i)ticle, Fern(i)tickle, Heatspot, Lentigines, Lentigo, Spot, Sunspot

**Frederick** Barbarossa, Carno, Great

**Free(d), Freely** Assoil, Buckshee, Candid, Canny, Church, Cuffo, Dead-head, Devoid, Disburden, Disburthen, Disengage, Eleutherian, Emancipate, Enlarge, Excuse, Exeem, Exeme, Exempt, Exonerate, Extricate, Familiar, Footloose, Frank, French, Gratis, House, Idle, Immune, Independent, Kick, Large, Lavish, Lax, Leisure, Let, Liberate, Loose, Manumit, Open, Quit(e), Range, Ransom, Redeem, RELEASE, Relieve, Rescue, Reskew, Rick, Rid, Sciolto, Solute, Stald, Stall, Trade, Unlock, Unmew, Unsnarl, Untie, Vacant, Verse, Voluntary

> **Free** may indicate an anagram

**Freebooter** Cateran, Corsair, Franklin, Marauder, Pad, Pindaree, Pindari, Pirate, Rapparee, Snapha(u)nce, Snaphaunch, Thief, Viking

**Freedom** Abandon, Autonomy, Breadth, Carte blanche, Eleutherian, Exemption, Fear, Four, Immunity, Latitude, Liberty, Licence, Play, Releasement, Speech, Uhuru, UNITA, Want, Worship

**Free gift** Bonus, Charism, Perk

**Freehold(er)** Franklin, Seisin, Udal(ler), Yeoman

**Freelance** Eclectic, Independent, Mercenary

**Freeloader** Sponge

> **Freely** may indicate an anagram

**Freeman** Burgess, Ceorl, Churl, Franklin, Liveryman, Thegn, Thete, Villein

**Freemason(ry), Freemason's son** Craft, Lewis, Lodge, Moose, Templar

**Free-range** Eggs, Outler

**Free State** Orange

**Freethinker** Agnostic, Bradlaugh, Cynic, Libertine, Sceptic

**Free-trade(r)** Cobdenism, Wright

**Free-wheel** Coast

**Freeze(r), Freezing** Alcarrazo, Benumb, Congeal, Cool, Cryogenic,

Freon, Frost, Harden, Ice, Nip, Numb, Paralyse, Riss, Soften

**Freight**  Cargo, Carriage, Fraught, Goods, Load

**French(man), Frenchwoman**  Breton, Crapaud, Frog, Gallic(e), Gaston, Gaul, Gombo, Grisette, Huguenot, Joual, M, Mamselle, Marianne, Midi, Mounseer, Neo-Latin, Norman, René, Rhemish, Savoyard

**Frenetic**  Deranged, Frantic, Overwrought

**Frenzied, Frenzy**  Amok, Berserk, Corybantic, Deliration, Delirium, Demoniac, Enrage, Enrapt, Euhoe, Euoi, Evoe, Fit, Fury, Hectic, Hysteric, Lune, Maenad, Mania, Must, Oestrus, Phrenetic, Rage

**Frequency, Frequent(er), Frequently**  Attend, Audio, Channel, Constant, Familiar, FR, Fresnel, Habitué, Haunt, Hertz, Incidence, Megahertz, Often, Pulsatance, Recurrent, Thick

**Fresco**  Sinopia, Tempera

**Fresh(en)**  Aurorean, Brash, Caller, Chilly, Crisp, Dewy, Entire, Forward, Green, Hot, Lively, Maiden, New, Novel, Quick, Rebite, Recent, Roral, Roric, Rorid, Smart, Span-new, Sweet, Tangy, Uncured, Vernal, Virent

**Freshman**  Bajan, Bejan(t), Fresher, Pennal, Recruit, Student

**Fret(ful)**  Chafe, Filigree, Fray, Grate, Grecque, Haze, Impatient, Irritate, Ornament, Peevish, Repine, Rile, Ripple, Roil, Rub, Tetchy, Tracery, Worry

**Friable**  Crisp, Crumbling, Powdery

**Friar**  Augustinian, Austin, Bacon, Barefoot, Black, Brother, Bungay, Capuchin, Carmelite, Cordelier, Crutched, Curtal, Dervish, Dominican, Fra(ter), Franciscan, Laurence, Limiter, Lymiter, Minim, Minorite, MONK, Observantine, Recollect, Recollet, Rush, Tuck

**Friction**  Attrition, Conflict, Dissent, Drag, Rift, Rub, Stridulation, Tribology, Tripsis, Wear, Xerotripsis

**Friday**  Black, Good, Man, Savage

**Fridge**  Esky, Freezer, Icebox, Rub

**Fried cake**  Croquette, Cruller

**Friend(ly)**  Achates, Affable, Ally, Alter ego, Ami(cable), Amigo, Approachable, Belamy, Boet(ie), Bosom, Bud(dy), Buster, Butty, China, Chum, Cobber, Cohort, Companion, Confidant, Comrade, Cordial, Couthie, Crony, Damon, Downhome, Edwin, Familiar, Feare, Feathered, Feer, Fere, Fiere, Ingle, Intimate, Inward, Kith, Marrow, Mate, Mentor, Outgoing, Paisano, Pal, Paranymph, Penn, Pheere, Privado, Quaker, Sociable, Societal, Sport, Tonga, Tosh, Wack(er), Well-wisher, Wus(s)

**Friendliness, Friendship**  Amity, Bonhomie, Camaraderie, Contesseration, Entente, Sodality

**Frieze**  Dado, Metope

**Fright(en), Frightened, Frightful**  Afear, Affear(e), Agrise, Agrize, Agryze, Alarm, Aroint, Aroynt, Ashake, Chilling, Cow, Daunt, Deter, Eek, Eerie, Faceache, Fear(some), Flay, Fleg, Fleme, Fley, Flush, Gallow, Gally, Ghast, Gliff, Glift, Grim, Grisly, Hairy, Horrid, Horrific, Intimidate,

Ordeal, Panic, Scar, SCARE, Scarre, Scaur, Schrecklich, Sight, Skear, Skeer, Skrik, Startle, Terrible, Terrify, Terror, Tirrit, Unco, Windy

**Frigid** Bleak, Cold, Dry, Frosty, Ice, Indifferent, Serac, Stiff

**Frill** Armilla, Furbelow, Jabot, Ornament, Papillote, Ruche, Ruff(le), Tucker, Valance

> **Frilly** may indicate an anagram

**Fringe(d)** Bang, Border, Bullion, Ciliated, Ciliolate, Edge, Fimbria, Frisette, Laciniate, Loma, Macramé, Macrami, Pelmet, Peripheral, Robin, Run, Thrum, Toupee, Toupit, Valance, Verge, Zizith

**Frisk(y)** Caper, Cavort, Curvet, Fisk, Flimp, Frolic, Gambol, Search, Skip, Wanton

**Fritillary** Snake's-head

**Fritter** Batter, Beignet, Dribble, Dwindle, Fragment, Squander, Waste

**Frivolous** Butterfly, Empty(-headed), Featherbrain, Flighty, Frothy, Futile, Giddy, Idle, Light, Skittish, Trivial

**Frizz(le), Frizzly** Afro, Crape, Crimp, Crinkle, Curly, Fry, Fuzz, Hiss

**Frock** Dress, Gown, Ordain, Robe, Smock

**Frog** Anoura, Anura, Batrachia(n), Braid, Frenchman, Frush, Goliath, Hyla, Mounseer, Nic, Paddock, Peeper, Platanna, Puttock, Rana, Ranidae, Xenopus

**Frogman** Diver

**Frogmouth** Mo(re)poke, Podargus

**Frog spawn** Redd, Tadpole

**Frolic(some)** Bender, Bust(er), Cabriole, Caper, Disport, Escapade, FRISK(Y), Fun, Galravage, Galravitch, Gambol, Gammock, Gil(l)ravage, Jink, Kittenish, Lark, Play, Prank, Rag, Rand, Rig, Romp, Scamper, Skylark, Splore, Sport, Spree, Tittup

**From** A, Against, Ex, For, Frae, Off, Thrae

**Frond** Fern, Leaf, Tendril

**Front(al), Frontman** Antependium, Anterior, Bow, Brass, Brow, Dead, Dickey, Dicky, Facade, Face, Fore(head), Groof, Grouf, Head, Metope, National, Newscaster, Paravant, Plastron, Popular, Pose, Pro, Prom, Prow, Sector, Sinciput, Tabula, Van, Vaward

**Frontier(sman)** Afghan, Barrier, Border, Boundary, Checkpoint, Limit, List, March, North-west, Pathan

**Front page** P1

**Front-ranker** Pawn

**Frost(ing), Frosty** Alcorza, Chill, Cranreuch, Cryo-, Freon, Frigid, Frore(n), Frorne, Glacé, Hore, Ice, Icing, Jack, Mat, Rime, White

**Froth(y)** Barm, Bubble, Foam, Frogspit, Gas, Head, Lather, Off-scum, Ream, Saponin, Scum, Seethe, Shallow, Spoom, Spoon, Spume, Sud, Yeasty, Yest

**Frown** Glower, Lour, Lower, Scowl

**Frozen** Froren, Gelid, Glacé, Graupel, Ice-bound

**Fructification, Fructify** Aecidium, Basidium, Fertilise, Flower, Fruit

**Frugal** Meagre, Parsimonious, Prudent, Scant, Skimpy, Spare, Spartan, Thrifty

**Fruit(ing), Fruit tree, Fruity** Abricock, Achene, Acinus, Ackee, Akee, Akene, Algarroba, Allocarpy, Anana(s), Anona, Apothecium, Apple(-john), Apricock, Apricot, Assai, Aubergine, Autocarp, Avocado, abaco, Bacciform, Bael, Banana, Bergamot, Berry, Bito, Blimbing, Boysenberry, Bread, Bullace, Calabash, Canteloup(e), Carica, Caryopsis, Cedrate, Chayote, Cherimoya, Cherimoyer, Cherry, Chocho, Citron, Citrus, Clementine, Clingstone, Coccus, Compot(e), Confect, Crab-nut, Cremocarp, Crop, Custard-apple, Date, Dessert, Dewberry, Drupe, Durian, Durion, Eater, Elderberry, Emblic, Encarpus, Etaerio, Feijoa, Fig, Follicle, Fritter, Gage, Gean, Geebung, Genipap, Goosegog, Gourd, Granadilla, Grenadilla, Guava, Haanepoot, Harvest, Haw, Hedgehog, Hep, Hip, Hop, Issue, Jaffa, Jargonelle, Kaki, Kalumpit, Key, Leechee, Lime, Li(t)chee, Litchi, Lotus, Lychee, Mammee, Mango(steen), Manjack, Marionberry, Medlar, Mirabelle, Morello, Mulberry, Myrobalan, Nancy, Nar(r)as, Naseberry, Nectarine, Neli(e)s, Nut, Olive, Orchard, Ortanique, Pampelmoose, Pampelmouse, Passion, Pa(w)paw, Pepino, Pepo, Persimmon, Pick-cheese, Pimento, Pinguin, Plantain, Plumdamas, Pomegranate, Pome(lo), Pompelmoose, Pompelmouse, Poof, Poperin, Poppering, Product, Pruine, Prune, Punicaceae, Pupunha, Quince, Raisin, Rambutan, Rath(e)ripe, Regma(ta), Rennet, Replum, Result, Return, Rich, Rowan, Ruddock, Russet, Samara, Sapota, Saskatoon, Satsuma, Sebesten, Seed, Service-berry, Shaddock, Sloe, Sorosis, Sour-sop, Squash, Star-apple, Stoneless, Succade, Syconium, Syncarp, Tamarind, Tangelo, Tayberry, Tomato, Ugli, Valve, Victorine, Wampee, Whort, Winesap, Xylocarp, Yield, Youngberry

**Fruitful(ness)** Ephraim, Fat, Fecund, Feracious, Fertile, Productive, Prolific, Uberty, Worthwhile

**Fruitless** Bare, Futile, Sisyphean, Sterile, Useless, Vain

**Frump(ish)** Dowdy, Judy, Shabby, Unkempt

**Frustrate** Baffle, Ba(u)lk, Blight, Bugger, Check, Confound, Dash, Discomfit, Dish, Foil, Outwit, Scotch, Thwart

**Fry, Fried** Blot, Brit, Fricassee, Frizzle, Sauté, Spawn, Whippersnapper, Whitebait

**Fuddle(d)** Drunk, Fluster, Fuzzle, Maudlin, Ta(i)vert, Tosticated, Woozy

> **Fuddle(d)** may indicate an anagram

**Fudge** Doctor, Dodge, Drivel, Evade, Fiddlesticks, Nonsense, Rot

**Fuel** Anthracite, Argol, Astatki, Avgas, Briquet, Bunker, Butane, Candle-coal, Cannel, Coal, Coke, Derv, Diesel, Eilding, Eldin(g), Faggot, Fire(wood), Gasohol, Gasoline, Hydrazine, Hydyne, Kerosene, Kerosine, Kindling, Knitch, Lignite, Napalm, Naphtha, Paraffin, Peat, Propellant,

Stoke, Triptane, Yealdon

**Fug** Frowst

**Fugitive** Absconder, Ephemeral, Escapee, Fleeting, Lot, Outlaw, Refugee, Runaway, Runner

**Fugue** Ricercar(e), Ricercata

**Fulcrum** Key-pin, Pivot

**Fulfil(ment)** Accomplish, Complete, Fruition, Honour, Meet, Pass, Realise, SATISFY

**Fulgent** Bright, Shining

**Full(ness), Fully** Abrim, Ample, Bouffant, Capacity, Chock-a-block, Complete, Copious, Embonpoint, Entire, Fat, Fed, Frontal, German, High, Mill, Plein, Plenary, Plenitude, Pleroma, Plethora, Replete, Rich, Sated, Satiated, Thorough, Toss, Ullage, Up, Wau(l)k, Wholly

**Full-faced** Caboched, Caboshed

**Full-throated** Goitred

**Fulminate, Fulmination** Detonate, Explode, Levin, Lightning, Rail, Renounce, Thunder

**Fumarole** Mofette

**Fumble** Blunder, Faff, Grope, Misfield, Muff

**Fume(s)** Bluster, Gas, Halitus, Nidor, Rage, Reech, Reek, Settle, Smoke, Stum, Vapours

**Fumigate** Disinfect, Smoke

**Fun(ny), Funny bone** Antic, Boat, Buffo, Caper, Clownery, Comedy, Comic(al), Delight, Droll, Frolic, Gammock, Giocoso, Gig, Glaik, Guy, Hilarity, Humerus, Humorous, Jest, Jouisance, Jouysaunce, Lark, Pleasure, Rag, Rich, Rummy, Scream, Skylark, Sport, Weird(o), Yell

**Funambulist** Blondin, Equilibrist, Tight-rope

**Function(al)** Act, Antilog, Arccos, Arcsine, Arctan, Ceremony, Cosec, Cotangent, Coth, Dynamic, Job, Logarithm, OPERATE, Periodic, Quantical, Role, Service, Sine, Tan(h), Tick, Use, WORK

**Functionless** Otiose

**Fund(s)** Bank, Barrel, Capital, Consolidated, Emendals, Endow, Fisc, Fisk, Jackpot, Kitty, Prebend, Stock, Treasury

**Fundamental** Basic(s), Bedrock, Cardinal, Essence, Grass-roots, Nitty-gritty, Prime, Principle, Radical, Rudimentary, Ultimate

**Fund-holder** Rentier

**Funeral, Funereal** Charnel, Cortege, Dismal, Exequy, Feral, Obit, Obsequy, Sad-coloured, Solemn, Tangi

**Fungicide** Captan, Thiram, Zineb

**Fungoid, Fungus** Agaric, Aminata, Ambrosia, Apothecium, Asci(us), Asomycete, Basidium, Black, Boletus, Bunt, Candida, Chantarelle, Chanterelle, Cladosporum, Craterellus, Death-cap, Death-cup,

Discomycetes, Earth-star, Empusa, Ergot, Eumycetes, Fuss-ball, Fuzz-ball, Gall, Gibberella, Hypersarcoma, Hypha, Ink-cap, Ithyphallus, Jew's ear, Lichen, Merulius, Mildew, Monilia, Morel, Mould, Mucor(ales), Mushroom, Mycelium, Mycetes, Mycology, Oak-leather, Oidium, Pest, Peziza, Phallus, Pileum, Puccinia, Puffball, Pythium, Rhizopus, Rhytisma, Russula, Saccharomyces, Saprolegnia, Sariodes, Scab, Shoestring, Smut, Spunk, Stinkhorn, Tarspot, Thalline, Toadstool, Tremella, Trichophyton, Truffle, Tuckahoe, Uredine, Ustilago, Yeast, Zygospore

**Fungus-eater**  Mycophagist

**Funicular**  Cable-car

**Funk(y)**  Dodge, Dread, Fear, Scared, Stylish

**Funnel**  Chimney, Choana, Flue, Hopper, Stack, Tun-dish

**Fur**  Astrakhan, Beaver(skin), Boa, Broadtail, Budge, Calabre, Caracul, Castor, Chinchilla, Ermelin, Ermine, Fitchew, Flix, Flue, Galyac, Galyak, Genet, Kolinsky, Krimmer, Minever, Miniver, Mink, Mouton, Musquash, Ocelot, Otter, Pashm, Pean, Pekan, Sable, Sea-otter, Stole, Tippet, Vair(e), Victorine, Zorino

**Furbish**  Polish, Renovate, Spruce, Vamp

**Furl**  Fold, Roll, Stow, Wrap

**Furlough**  Congé, Leave

**Furnace**  Athanor, Bloomery, Calcar, Cockle, Cupola, Devil, Forge, Glory-hole, Kiln, Lime-kiln, Oast, Oon, Oven, Producer, Scaldino

**Furnish(ing)**  Appoint, Array, Deck, Decorate, Endow, Endue, Equip, Feed, Fledge, Gird, Lend, Produce, Provision, Stock, Supply, Tabaret, Upholster

**Furniture**  Chattels, Chippendale, Encoignure, Escritoire, Hepplewhite, Insight, Lumber, Sheraton, Sticks, Stoutherie, Tire, Unit, Whatnot

**Furore**  Brouhaha, Commotion, Outburst, Storm, Uproar

**Furrier**  Trapper

**Furrow(ed)**  Crease, Furr, Groove, Gutter, Plough, Pucker, Rill(e), Rugose, Rut, Stria, Vallecula, Wrinkle

**Fur-seal**  Seecatch(ie)

**Further(more), Furthest**  Additional, Advance, Again, Aid, Also, Besides, Deeper, Else, Extra, Extend, Extreme, Fresh, Infra, Longer, Mo(e), Mow, Other, Promote, Serve, Speed, Then

**Furtive(ly)**  Clandestine, Cunning, Secret, Sly, Sneaky, Stealthy, Stowlins, Stownlins

**Fury, Furies, Furious**  Acharné, Agitato, Alecto, ANGER, Apoplexy, Atropos, Avenger, Eriny(e)s, Eumenides, Exasperation, Frantic, Frenzied, Furor, Incensed, IRE, Livid, Maenad, Megaera, Rabid, Rage, Savage, Tisiphone, Virago, Wrath, Yond

**Furze**  Gorse, Whin

**Fuse, Fusion**  Anchylosis, Ankylosis, Blend, Coalesce, Conflate,

Endosmosis, Flow, Flux, Match, Merge, Merit, Portfire, Rigelation, Run, Slow-match, Syngamy, Unite

**Fuselage** Body, Monocoque, Structure

**Fuss(y)** Ado, Agitation, Ballyho, Bother, Br(o)uhaha, Bustle, Carfuffle, Chichi, Coil, Commotion, Complain, Cosset, Create, Cu(r)fuffle, Faff, Fantad, Fantod, Fiddle-faddle, Finical, Finikin, Hairsplitter, Niggle, Overnice, Palaver, Particular, Perjink, Pother, Precise, Prejink, Primp, Prissy, Racket, Rout, Song, Spoffish, Spoffy, Spruce, Stashie, STIR, Stishie, Stooshie, Stushie, Tamasha, To-do, Tracasserie

**Fustian** Bombast, Gas, Pompous, Rant

**Futile** Feckless, Idle, Inept, No-go, Nugatory, Null, Otiose, Sleeveless, Stultified, Trivial, VAIN

**Future, Futurist** Coming, Demain, Hence, Horoscope, Later, Offing, Ovist, Prospect, To-be, Tomorrow

**Fuzz(y)** Crepe, Fluff, Foggy, Lint, Pig, Policeman

# Gg

**G** George, Golf, Gravity

**Gab(ble), Gabbler** Chatter, Dovercourt, Jabber, Pie, Prattle, Talkative, Yabber

**Gable** Clark, Pediment

**Gabriel** Angel, Walter

**Gad(about), Gadzooks** Gallivant, Lud, Rover, Sbuddikins, Sdeath, Traipse, Trape(s), Viretot

**Gadfly** Breese, Breeze, Brize

**Gadget** Appliance, Artifice, Device, Dingbat, Dingus, Doodad, Doodah, Gismo, Gizmo, Gubbins, Hickey, Jimjam, Notion, Possum, Utility, Widget

**Gadolinium** Gd

**Gadzooks** Odsbobs

**Gaekwar** Baroda

**Gael(ic)** Celt, Erse, Goidel, Teague

**Gaff(e), Gaffer** Bloomer, Error, Floater, Foreman, Gamble, Game, Solecism, Spar, Throat, Trysail, Yokel

**Gag** Brank, Choke, Estoppel, Joke, Pong, Prank, Silence(r), Smother, Wheeze

**Gage** Challenge, Pawn, Pledge, Plum

> **Gaiety** see GAY

**Gain(s)** Acquire, Appreciate, Attain, Bunce, Carry, Catch, Chevisance, Clean-up, Derive, Earn, GET, Gravy, Land, Lucre, Obtain, Plus, Profit, Rake-off, Reap, Thrift, Velvet, Win, Windfall, Winnings

**Gainsay** Contradict, Deny

**Gait** Bearing, Canter, Pace, Rack, Trot

**Gaiter(s)** Cootikin, Cu(i)tikin, Gambado, Hogger, Legging(s), Spat(s), Spattee, Spatterdash, Vamp

**Gala** Banquet, Festival

**Galaxy** Heaven, Milky Way, Seyfert, Stars

**Galbanum** Ferula

**Gale** Backfielder, Peal, Ripsnorter, Snorter, Squall, Storm, Tempest, Winder

**Gall** Bedeguar, Bitterness, Canker, Ellagic, Enrage, Fell, Irritate, Mad-apple, Maugre, Maulgre, Oaknut, Sage-apple, Sandiver, SAUCE, Tacahout

**Gallant(ry)** Amorist, Beau, Blade, Buck, Cavalier, Chevalier, Cicisbeo, Courtliness, Lover, Prow, Romeo, Sigisbeo, Spark, Valiance

**Galleon**  Galloon, Ghostly, Ship

**Gallery**  Alure, Amphitheatre, Arcade, Belvedere, Brattice, Bretasche, Bretesse, Brettice, Brow, Catacomb, Celestials, Cupola, Dedans, Gods, Hayward, Hermitage, Jube, Loft, Loggia, Louvre, Machicolation, National, Pawn, Pinacotheca, Pinakothek, Pitti, Prado, Rogue's, Serpentine, Tate, Terrace, Triforium, Uffizi, Veranda(h), Whispering, Whitechapel

**Galley**  Bireme, Bucentaur, Caboose, Drake, Galliot, Kitchen, Lymphad, Pentaconter, Proof

**Gallimaufry**  Macedoine, Mishmash, Stew

**Gallium**  Ga

**Gallon(s)**  Bushel, Congius, Cran, Hin

**Gallop(er)**  Aide, Canter, Career, Lope, Trot, Wallop

**Gallows**  Bough, Drop, Dule-tree, Forks, Gibbet, Nub, Nubbing-cheat, Patibulary, Tree, Tyburn, Widow, Woodie

**Gallows-bird**  Crack-halter, Crack-hemp, Crack-rope

**Gall-stone**  Cholelith

**Galore**  Abundance, A gogo, Plenty

**Galosh**  Overshoe, Rubber

**Galvanise**  Ginger, Rouse, Zinc

**Gam**  Pod

**Gambit**  Manoeuvre, Ploy, Stratagem

**Gamble(r), Gambling place**  Adventure, Back, Bet, Casino, Chance, Dice(-play), Flutter, Gaff, Hold, Jeff, Martingale, Mise, Partingale, Plunge, Policy, Punter, Raffle, Reno, Risk, Roulette, Spec, Speculate, Speculator, Sweep(stake), Throw(ster), Tombola, Tontine, Two-up, WAGER

**Gambol**  Frisk, Frolic

**Game(s)**  All-fours, Angel-beast, Baccarat, Badminton, Bagatelle, Barley-brake, Base, Ba'spiel, Basset, Bezique, Billiards, Bingo, Black-cock, Black-jack, Boston, Bouillotte, Boule, Bowls, Braemar, Brag, Bull, Bumble-puppy, Bumpball, Camogue, Canfield, Cards, Cas(s)ino, Catch-the-ten, Charade, Chemmy, Chess, Cinch, Clumps, Codille, Consequences, Coon-can, Crambo, Crap(s), Cribbage, Croquet, Curling, Darts, Decider, Diabolo, Dibs, Doubles, Dumb Crambo, Duplicate, Ecarté, Eo, Euchre, Fa-fi, Fantan, Faro, Fillipeen, Fives, Football, Forfeits, Foursome, Frame, Gallant, Gammon, Gerrymander, Gleek, Go, Gobang, Goff, Golf, Gomoku, Goose, Grab, Gutsy, Halma, Handicap, Handy-dandy, Hangman, Hob, Hockey, Hoopla, Hopscotch, House, Hurley, Hurling, In-and-In, Intrepid, I-spy, Isthmian, Jackstones, Jackstraws, Jai Alai, Jeu, Jingo-ring, Jukskei, Kabaddi, Keno, Kill, Kitcat, Klondike, Klondyke, Knurr-spell, Korfball, Laik, LAME, Lansquenet, Lanterloo, Leapfrog, Level-coil, Loo, Loto, Lottery, Lotto, Ludo, Lurch, Mahjong(g), Main, Marbles, Matador, Match, Matrimony, Maw, Merel(l), Meril, Mistigris, Monopoly, Monte, Mor(r)a, Muggins, Mumchance, Nap, Nemean, Netball, Newmarket, Nim, Ninepins, Noddy, Novum, Octopush, Old Maid,

Olympic, Omber, Ombre, On, One-and-thirty, Pachinko, Pachisi, Pallone, Palm, Pam, Parcheesi, Parlour, Pastance, Patience, PE, Peekaboo, Pelota, Penneech, Penneeck, Penuchle, Petanque, Pharaoh, Phillipina, Phillipine, Philopoena, Pinochle, Pit, Pitch and toss, Plafond, Play, Poker, Polo, Pool, Pope Joan, Postman's knock, Preference, Primero, Put(t), Pythian, Quadrille, Quoits, Rackets, Raffle, Reversi(s), Ring-taw, Rolypoly, Roque, Roulette, Rounders, Rubber, Ruff, Rummy, Sancho-pedro, Scat, Scrabble, Shinny, Shinty, Shogi, Shovelboard, Shuffleboard, Singles, Skat, Skittles, Slam, Slapjack, Snap, Snip-snap-snorum, Snooker, Soccer, Socker, Softball, Solitaire, Solo, Span-farthing, Speculation, Sphairee, Spillikins, Spoof, Sport, Squail, Square, Stoolball, Swy, Tablanette, Tag, Tarot, Taws, Tchoukball, Teetotum, Tip-and-run, Tipcat, Tray-trip, Tred(r)ille, Tric(k)-trac(k), Troll-madam, Troll-my-dame(s), Trou-madame, Trugo, Uckers, Verquere, Vie, Vigoro, Vingt(-et)-un, Vint, Volley-ball, Whisk, Whist, Willing

**Game, Game birds** Bag, Fowl, Grouse, Guan, Hare, Meat, Partridge, Pheasant, Quail, QUARRY, Rype(r), Woodcock

**Gamekeeper** Velveteen, Venerer, Warrener

**Gaming place** Bucket-shop, Casino, Saloon, Table

**Gammerstang** Taupie, Tawpie

**Gammon** Bilge, Tosh

**Gamut** Compass, Range

**Gander** Airport, Look-see

**Gandhi** Mahatma

**Gang** Band(itti), Bing, Coffle, Core, Crew, Crue, Elk, Go, Horde, Mob, Nest, Outfit, Pack, Press, Push, Tribulation, Troop, Yardie

**Gangrene** Canker, Phaged(a)ena, Sphacelate

**Gangster** Bandit, Capone, Crook, Hatchet-man, Highbinder, Hood, Ochlocrat, Yakuza

**Gangway** Brow, Catwalk, Road

**Gannet** Booby, Guga, Solan(d)

**Gantry** Elmer

**Ganymede** Cupper

**Gaol(er)** see JAIL(ER)

**Gap** Breach, Chasm, Chink, Day, Diastema, Embrasure, F-hole, Flaw, Fontanel(le), Hair-space, Hiatus, Hole, Interlude, Lacunae, Loophole, M(e)use, Mews, Muset, Musit, Opening, Ostiole, Pass, Rest, Shard, Sherd, Slap, SPACE, Street

**Gape(r), Gaping** Comber, Dehisce, Fatiscent, Gant, Ga(u)p, Gerne, Hiant, Mya, Rictal, Rictus, Ringent, Stare, Yawn, Yawp

**Garage** Carport, Hangar, Lock-up

**Garb** Apparel, Costume, Gear, Gere, Guise, Ihram, Invest, Leotard, Raiment, Toilet

**Garbage**  Bunkum, Junk, Refuse, Rubbish, Trash

**Garble**  Edit, Jumble, Muddle

> **Garble**  may indicate an anagram

**Garden(ing), Gardens**  Area, Babylon(ian), Chinampa, Colegarth, Covent, Cremorne, Dig, Eden, Erf, Floriculture, Garth, Gethsemane, Hanging, Hoe, Kew, Knot, Lyceum, Monastery, NJ, Olitory, Paradise, Pleasance, Plot, Ranelegh, Rockery, Roji, Rosary, Rosery, Tilth, Topiary, Tuileries, Vauxhall, Welwyn, Yard

**Gardener**  Adam, Capability Brown, Mali, Mallee, Mary

**Gargantuan**  Enormous, Huge, Pantagruel, Vast

**Gargle**  Gargarism, Mouthwash

**Gargoyle**  Waterspout

**Garish**  Criant, Flashy, Gaudy, Glitzy, Jazzy, Painty, Roary, Rorie, Rory

**Garland**  Anadem, Anthology, Chaplet, Coronal, Crants, Festoon, Lei, Stemma, Torana, Wreath

**Garlic**  Clove, Rams(on), Rocambole

**Garment**  Aba(ya), Alb, Barrow, Blouse, Blouson, Bodice, Bolero, B(o)ub(o)u, B(o)urk(h)a, Burnous, Burqa, Caftan, Chador, Chasuble, Chimer, Cilice, Cimar, Cote-hardie, Cotta, Dalmatic, Dashiki, Dirndl, Djibbah, Doublet, Exomion, Exomis, Fanon, Gambeson, Habit, Himation, Ihram, Izar, Jeistiecor, Jibbah, Jubbah, Kaftan, Kanzu, Kaross, K(h)anga, Lingerie, Mandilion, Mandylion, Mantle, Negligee, Partlet, Pelerine, Pelisse, Pilch, Rail, Ramee, Rami(e), Rompers, Sanbenito, Sari, Sarong, Scapular, Singlet, Slop, Step-in, Stola, Stole, Surcoat, Surplice, Togs, Tunic(le), Unitard, Vestment, Vesture, Weed, Zephyr

**Garnet**  Alabandine, Almandine, Carbuncle, Demantoid, Essonite, Grossular(ite), Melanite, Pyrope, Rhodolite, Spessartite, Uvarovite

**Garnish**  Adorn, Attach, Crouton, Decorate, Gremolata, Lard, Sippet, Staffage

**Garret**  Attic, Loft, Sol(l)ar, Sol(l)er

**Garrison**  Fort, Man, Presidial

**Garrulity, Garrulous**  Babbling, Gas, Gushy, Windbag

**Garter**  Crewel, G(r)amash, Gramosh, Nicky-tam

**Gary**  Glitter, Player

**Gas(sy)**  Acetylene, Afterdamp, Air, Ammonia, Argon, Arsine, Blather, Blether, Butane, BZ, Calor, Chat, Chlorine, CN, Coal-oil, Crypton, CS, Emanation, Ethane, Ethene, Ether(ion), Ethine, Ethylene, Firedamp, Gabnash, H, Halitus, He, Helium, Hot-air, Hydrogen, Inert, Jaw, Ketene, Kr(ypton), Laughing, Lurgi, Mace, Methane, Mofette, Ne, Neon, Nitrogen, Noble, Nox, O, Olefin(e), Orotund, Oxyacetylene, Oxygen, Petrol, Phosgene, Plasma, Prate, Propane, Propylene, Propene, Protostar, Radon, RN, Sarin, Silane, Solfatara, Stibine, Tabun, TALK, Tear, Therm, Thoron, V-agent, Vapour, Waffle, Whitedamp, WIND, Xenon

**Gasbag** Blimp, Envelope, Prattler

**Gas-mask** Inhaler

**Gascon(ade)** Boast, Braggart, Skite

**Gash** Incise, Rift, Score, Scotch, SLASH

**Gasp(ing)** Anhelation, Apn(o)ea, Chink, Exhale, Kink, Oh, Pant, Puff, Sob

**Gast(e)ropod** Cowrie, Cowry, Dorididae, Euthyneura, Fusus, Limpet, Mollusc, Murex, Nerita, Nerite, Ormer, Periwinkle, Purpura, Sea-ear, Sea-hare, Slug, Snail, Spindle-shell, Stromb, Turbo, Whelk

**Gate(way)** Alley, Brandenburg, Caisson, Crowd, Decuman, Entry, Erpingham, Golden, Lych, Menin, Nor, Portal, Postern, Propylaeum, Propylon, Pylon, Toran(a), Traitor's, Turnstile, Wicket, Yate, Yet(t)

**Gatecrash(er)** Interloper, Intrude, Ligger, Sorn, Unasked

**Gatepost** Sconcheon, Scontion, Scuncheon

> **Gateshead** may indicate 'g'

**Gather(ed), Gathering** Amass, Assemble, Bee, Cluster, Collate, COLLECT, Concourse, Conglomerate, Congregate, Corroboree, Crop, Crowd, Cull, Eve, Function, Gabfest, Galaxy, Glean, Glomerate, Harvest, Hootenanny, Hui, In, Infer, Jamboree, Kommers, Lirk, Pleat, Plica, Plissé, Pucker, Raft, Rake, Reef, Reunion, Ruche, Shindig, Shir(r), Shoal, Shovel, Take, Tuck, Vindemiate, Vintage, Wappensc(h)aw

**Gauche** Awkward, Clumsy, Farouche, Graceless

**Gaudy** Criant, Fantoosh, Flash, Garish, Glitz(y), Tinsel

**Gauge** Alidad(e), Anemometer, ASSESS, Calibre, Denier, Etalon, Estimate, Evaluate, Judge, Manometer, Measure, Meter, Ombrometer, Oncometer, Rate, Scantle, Size, Tape, Tonometer, Tram, Tread

**Gauguin** Paul

**Gaunt** Haggard, Lancaster, Lean, Randletree, Ranneltree, Rannletree, Rantletree, Rawbone, THIN

**Gauntlet** Gantlope

**Gauss** G

**Gautama** Buddha

**Gauze, Gauzy** Gossamer, Muslin, Sheer, Tiffany

**Gawky** Clumsy, Cow, Gammerstang

**Gay, Gaiety** Blithe, Bonny, Boon, Buxom, Camp, Canty, Daffing, Debonair, Festal, Frolic, Gallant, Gladsome, Glee, Gordon, Grisette, Inverted, Jolly, Lightsome, May, Merry, Nitid, Rackety, Riant, Rorty, Tit(t)upy, Volatile

**Gaze** Moon, Pore, Stare

**Gazelle** Ariel, Gerenuk, Goa, Mhorr, Mohr

**Gazette** London, Paper

**Gear** Attire, Bags, Clobber, Derailleur, Differential, Duds, Fab, Finery, Harness, Kit, Lay-shaft, Mesh, Neutral, Overdrive, Ratio, Rig, Rudder, Sun and planet, TACKLE, Trim, Worm-wheel

**Gecko** Tokay

**Gee** Horse, Hump, My, Reist, Sulk, Tout, Towt, Urge

**Geiger-counter** Scintillator

**Geisha** Maiko

**Gelatine, Gelatinous** Calipash, Collagen, Glutinous, Isinglass, Tunicin

**Geld(ing)** Castrate, Lib, Neuter, Spado

**Geller** Uri

**Gem** Agate, Asteria, Baguette, Boule, Brilliant, Briolette, Cachalong, Cairngorm, Carnelian, Cornelian, Diamond, Emerald, ID, Idaho, Iolite, Jacinth, Jasper, Jaspis, JEWEL, Ligure, Marquise, Moonstone, Pearl, Peridot(e), Prase, Pyrope, Rhinestone, Rhodolite, Ruby, Sapphire, Sard, Scarab, Scarabaeoid, Smaragd, Sparkler, Starstone, Stone, Tiger's eye, Tourmaline, Turquoise

**Gemination, Gemini** Diplogenesis, Twins

**Gen** Info

**Gendarme** Flic

**Gender** Form, Sex

**Gene(tics)** Allele, Allelomorph, Codon, Creation, Exon, Factor, Intron, Lysenkoism, Mendel, Michurinism, Muton, Operon

**Genealogist, Genealogy** Armory, Heraldry, Line, Pedigree, Seannachie, Seannachy, Sennachie

**General** Agamemnon, Agricola, Agrippa, Alcibiades, Allenby, Antigonus, Ataman, Booth, Broad, Boulanger, C in C, Common, Communal, Conde, Crassus, Current, Custer, De Wet, Diadochi, Eclectic, Ecumenical, Election, Franco, Gamelin, Gen, GOC, Gordon, Grant, Hadrian, Hannibal, Holofernes, Ike, Inspector, Joshua, Kitchener, Lee, Leslie, Macarthur, Main, Marian, Marshall, Montcalm, Napier, Napoleon, Omnify, Overall, Overhead, Patton, Pershing, Prevailing, Pompey, Raglan, Regulus, Rife, Rommel, Scipio, Sherman, Shrapnel, Stilwell, Strategist, Tom Thumb, Turenne, UNIVERSAL, Vague, Wide

**Generate, Generation, Generator** Abiogenetic, Age, Beget, Breeder, Charger, Create, Dynamo, Epigon, Father, Fuel-cell, House, Kipp, Magneto, Olds, Sire, Spawn, Stallion, Yield

**Generosity, Generous** Bounty, Charitable, Free-handed, Handsome, Kind, Largess(e), LAVISH, Liberal, Magnanimous, Munificent, Noble (minded), Open, Sporting

> **Genetic** see GENE

**Geneva** Gin, Hollands

**Genial(ity)** Amiable, Benign, Bluff, Bonhomie, Human, Mellow

**Genie** Mazikeen, Shedeem

**Genipap** Lana

**Genital(s)** Ballocks, Bollocks, Bol(l)ix, Box, Cunt, Fanny, Muff, Privates, Pudendum, Quim, Secrets, Tail, Twat, Vagina, Vulva, Yoni

**Genius** Agathodaimon, Daemon, Engine, Flash, Ka, Numen, Prodigy

**Genteel** Conish, Polite, Proper, Refined

**Gentian** Felwort, Violet

**Gentile** Aryan, Ethnic, Goy, Shi(c)ksa

**Gentle** Amenable, Amenage, Clement, Gradual, Grub, Light, Maggot, Mansuete, Mild, Tame, Tender

**Gentleman, Gentlemen** Amateur, Baboo, Babu, Caballero, Cavalier, Duni(e)wassal, Dunniewassal, Esquire, Gemman, Gemmen, Knight, Messrs, Milord, Mister, Mr, Nob, Proteus, Ritter, Runner, Rye, Sahib, Senor, Signor, Sir, Sirra(h), Smuggler, Squire, Sri, Stalko, Stir(rah), Tea, Toff, Von, Yeoman

**Gentry** County, Quality, Squir(e)age

**Gents** Bog, John, Lav, Loo

**Genuflexion** Bend, Curts(e)y, Kowtow, Salaam

**Genuine** Authentic, Bona-fide, Dinkum, Echt, Frank, Heartfelt, Intrinsic, Kosher, Legit(imate), Nain, Pucka, Pukka, Pure, REAL, Right, Simon Pure, Sincere, Square, Sterling, True, Veritable

**Genus** Class, -Ia, Mustela

**Geode** Druse

**Geographer, Geography** Chorography, Mercator, Pausanias, Strabo

**Geometer, Geometrician, Geometry** Conics, Euclid(ean), Moth, Topologist

**George(s)** Autopilot, Borrow, Eliot, Farmer, Lloyd, Orwell, Pilot, Sand

**Georgia(n)** Ga, Hanover, Iberian

**Geraint** Knight

**Geranium** Dove's foot, Stork's bill

**Gerbil** Jird

**Germ** Bacteria, Bug, Klebsiella, Seed, Spirilla, Strep, Virus, Zyme

**German(y)** Al(e)main(e), Alemannic, Angle, Bavarian, Blood-brother, Boche, Frank, Fritz, Goth, Hans, Herr, Hessian, Hun, Jerry, Jute, Kaiser, Kraut, Landgrave, Palsgrave, Pruce, Prussian, Salic, Saxon, Tedesco, Teuton(ic)

**Germane** Apt, PERTINENT, Relevant

**Germanium** Ge

**Germ-free** Aseptic

**Germinate** Grow, Sprout

**Gesticulate, Gesticulation, Gesture(s)** Ameslan, Beck(on), Ch(e)ironomy, Fico, Gest(e), Mime, Motion, Mudra, Salute, SIGN, Signal, Snook, Token

**Get, Get by, Get On** Acquire, Advance, Annoy, Attain, Become, Brat, Bring, Capture, Cop, Cope, Derive, Fet(ch), Fette, Gain, Gee, Learn, Make, Manage, Milk, Noy, OBTAIN, Procure, Progress, Reach, Realise, Rile, Roil, Secure, Sire, Twig, Understand, Win

**Getaway** Escape, Vamoose

> **Getting** may indicate an anagram

**Getting better** Convalescing, Improving, Lysis

**Get-up** Tog(s)

**Geum** Avens

**Gewgaw** Bagatelle, Bauble, Doit, Tat, Trifle

**Geyser** Soffioni, Therm

**Ghanaian** Ashanti, Fantee, Fanti, Tshi, Twi

**Ghastly** Gash, Grim, Hideous, Lurid, Macabre, Pallid, Welladay, White

**Ghetto** Barrio, Slum

**Ghost(ly)** Acheri, Apparition, Caddy, Chthonic, Duppy, Eerie, Eery, Fantasm, Fetch, Gytrash, Hint, Jumbie, Jumby, Larva(e), Lemur, Malmag, No'canny, Pepper's, Phantasm(agoria), Phantom, Revenant, Sampford, Shade, Shadow, Spectre, SPIRIT, Spook, Trace, Truepenny, Umbra, Vision, Waff, Wraith

**Ghoul** Fiend

**GI** Joe, Yankee

**Giant(ess)** Alcyoneus, Alifanfaron, Anak, Antaeus, Archiloro, Ascapart, Balan, Balor, Bellerus, Blunderbore, Bran, Briareus, Brobdingnagian, Cacus, Colbrand, Colbronde, Colossus, Coltys, Cormoran, Cottus, Cyclop(e)s, Despair, Enceladus, Ephialtes, Eten, Ettin, Ferragus, Gabbara, Galligantus, Gargantua, Géant, Gefion, Geirred, Gigantic, Gog, Goliath, Grim, Harapha, Hrungnir, Hymir, Idris, Jotun(n), Jumbo, Krasir, Lestrigon, Leviathan, Magog, Mammoth, Mimir, Monster, Oak, Og, Ogre, Otus, Pallas, Pantagruel, Patagonian, Polyphemus, Pope, Rounceval, Skrymir, Slaygood, Talos, Talus, Thrym, Titan, Tityus, Tregeagle, Triton, Troll, Tryphoeus, Typhon, Urizen, Utgard, Ymir, Yowie

**Gibberish** Claptrap, Greek

**Gibbet** Gallows, Patibulary, Potence, Ravenstone, Tree

**Gibbon(s)** Hoolock, Hylobate, Orlando, Siamang, Stanley, Wou-wou, Wow-wow

**Gibe** Barb, Brocard, Chaff, Fleer, Glike, Jeer, Jibe, Shy, Slant

**Gibraltar** Calpe

**Giddy (girl)** Dizzy, Fisgig, Fishgig, Fizgig, Giglot, Glaikit, Glaky, Haverel, Hellicat, Hoity-toity, Jillet, Light, Sturdy, Turn, Volage(ous), Wheel, Woozy

**Gift(s), Gifted** Ability, Alms, Aptitude, Bef(f)ana, Bequest, Blessing, Blest, Bonbon, Bonsel(l)a, Boon, Bounty, Charism(a), Congiary, Corban, Cumshaw, Dash, Deodate, DONATION, Etrenne, Fairing, Flair, Foy,

Freebie, Gab, Garnish, Godsend, Grant, Han(d)sel, Hogmanay, Knack, Lagniappe, Largesse, Legacy, Manna, Ne'erday, Nuzzer, Offering, Parting, Potlatch, PRESENT, Presentation, Prezzie, Propine, Sop, Talent, Tongues, Windfall

**Gig**  Cart, Dennet, Moze, Whisk(e)y

**Gigantic**  Atlantean, Briarean, Colossal, HUGE, Immense, Mammoth, Rounceval, Titan

**Giggle**  Cackle, Ha, Keckle, Simper, Snigger, Tehee, Titter

**Gigolo**  Gallant, Ladykiller, Pimp

**Gilbert**  Bab, Gb, White, WS

**Gild(ed), Gilding**  Checklaton, Embellish, Enhance, Inaurate, Ormolu, S(c)hecklaton, Vermeil

**Gill(s)**  Beard, Branchia, Jill, Spiracle

**Gillman's**  Aqualung

**Gilpin**  Draper, John, Renowned

**Gilt**  Sow

**Gimcrack**  Gewgaw, Tawdry, Trangam

**Gimmick**  Doodad, Doodah, Hype, Ploy, Ruse, Stunt

**Gin**  Bathtub, Geneva, Hollands, Juniper, Lubra, Max, Noose, Old Tom, Ruin, Schiedam, Schnapp(s), Snare, Springe, Toil, Trap, Trepan, Twankay

**Ginger**  Activist, Amomum, Asarum, Cassumunar, Costus, Curcuma, Galanga(l), Galengale, Galingale, Nut, Pachak, Pep, Pop, Putchock, Putchuk, Race, Rase, Red(head), Spice, Turmeric, Zedoary, Zingiber

**Gingerbread**  D(o)um-palm, Parkin, Parliament-cake

> **Gipsy**  see GYPSY

**Giraffe**  Camelopard, Okapi

**Gird**  Accinge, Belt, Equip, Quip

**Girder**  Beam, Binder, I-beam, Loincloth, Spar

**Girdle**  Baldric, Center, Cestus, Chastity, Cincture, Cingulum, Corset, Enzone, Hippolyte, Hoop, Mitre, Sash, Surround, Zona, Zone

**Girl(s)**  Backfisch, Bimbo, Bint, Bird, Bit, Bobby-dazzler, Bohemian, Broad, Burd, Charlie, Chit, Chorus, Coed, Colleen, Crumpet, Cummer, Cutey, Cutie, Dam(o)sel, Deb, Dell, Demoiselle, Dish, Doll, Filly, Fisgig, Fizgig, Flapper, Fluff, Fraulein, Gaiety, Gal, Gammerstang, Geisha, Gibson, Gill(et), Gouge, Grisette, Hen, Hoiden, Hoyden, Hussy, Italian, Kimmer, Kinchinmort, Lass(ock), Lorette, Maid(en), Mauther, Mawr, Mawther, May, Miss(y), Moppet, Mor, Mousmé, Mousmee, Mystery, Nautch, Number, Nymphet, Peach, Petticoat, Piece, Pigeon, Popsy, Puss, Quean, Queyn, Quin(i)e, Randy, Senorita, Sheila, Shi(c)ksa, Sis(s), Smock, Taupie, Tawpie, Tit, Trull, Wench, Wimp

> **Girl**  may indicate a female name

**Girl friend**  Chérie, Confidante, Date, Flame, Hinny, Leman, Moll, Peat

**Girth**  Cinch, Compass, Size, Surcingle

**Gist**  Essence, Kernel, NUB, Pith, Substance

**Give, Give up, Giving**  Abandon, Accord, Administer, Award, Bend, Bestow, Buckle, Cede, Confiscate, Dative, Dispense, Dole, DONATE, Duck, Elasticity, Enable, Forswear, Gie, Impart, Jack, Largition, Render, Sacrifice, Sag, Spring, Stop, Tip, Vacate, Yeve

**Give-away**  Freebie, Gift-horse

**Given**  If

**Give out**  Bestow, Dispense, Exude, Peter

**Give over**  Cease, Lin

**Glacial, Glaciation**  Gunz, Mindel, Riss, Wurm

**Glacier**  Aletsch, Crevasse, Drumline, Iceberg, Ice-cap, Moraine, Riss, Serac

**Glad(ly), Gladden**  Cheer, Fain, HAPPY, Lief, Willing

**Glade**  La(u)nd

**Gladiator**  Retiarius, Spartacus

**Glamour(ise), Glamorous**  Charm, Glitter(ati), Glitz, Halo, It, Prestige, SA, Spell

**Glamour girl**  Cheesecake, Odalisk, Odalisque, Pin-up

**Glance**  Amoret, Argentite, Blink, Browse, Draw, Eld, Eliad, Eye-beam, Galena, Glimpse, Illiad, Inwick, Oeillade, Peek, PEEP, Ray, Redruthite, Ricochet, Snick, Squint, Vision

**Gland**  Adenoid, Adrenal, Bartholin, Conarium, Crypt, Eccrine, Endocrine, Epiphysis, Goitre, Liver, Lymph, Ovary, Paranephros, Parotid, Parotis, Pineal, Pope's eye, Prostate, Tarsel, Testicle, Thymus, Thyroid, Tonsil

**Glanders**  Farcy

**Glandular (trouble)**  Adenitis

**Glare, Glaring**  Astare, Blare, Dazzle, Flagrant, Garish, Gleam, Glower, Holophotal, Lour, Low(e), Vivid, Whally

**Glass(es), Glassware, Glassy**  Amen, Ampul(la), Aneroid, Avanturine, Aventurine, Baccara(t), Barometer, Brimmer, Bumper, Calcedonio, Chevalier, Cloche, Copita, Coupe, Crookes, Crystal, Cullet, Eden, Euphon, Favrile, Flute, Frigger, Frit, Glare, Goblet, Humpen, Hyaline, Jar, Jena, Lalique, Latticinio, Lens, Loupe, Lozen(ge), Magma, Metal, Mica, Middy, Millefiori, Mirror, Monocle, Mousseline, Murr(h)ine, Obsidian, Pane, Parison, Paste, Pebble, Peeper, Pele, Perlite, Pitchstone, Pon(e)y, Prunt, Psyche, Pyrex, Quarrel-pane, Quarry, Roemer, Rummer, Schmelz, Schooner, Seam, Silex, Sleever, Smalt(o), Snifter, Stein, Stone, Strass, Tachilite, Tachylite, Tektite, Telescope, Tiffany, Tumbler, Venetian, Vita, Vitrail, Vitreous, Vitro-di-trina, Waterford

**Glasses**  Bifocals, Goggles, Horn-rims, Lorgnette, Pince-nez, Specs

**Glass-gall**  Sandiver

**Glass-house**  Conservatory, Orangery

**Glassite**  Sandemania

**Glass-maker**  Annealer, Blower, Glazier, Pontie, Pontil, Ponty, Puntee, Punty

**Glaze(d), Glazing**  Ciré, Coat, Film, Flambé, Frit, Glost, Ice, Majolica, Sancai, Slip, Tammy, Velatura

**Gleam(ing)**  Blink, Glitter, Gloss, Light, Ray, Relucent, Sheen, Shimmer, SHINE

**Glean(er)**  Gather, Harvest, Lease, Stibbler

**Glee**  Joy, Mirth, Song

**Glen**  Affric, Ghyll, Gill, Rushy, Vale

**Glib**  Flip, Slick, Smooth

**Glide (away), Glider**  Aquaplane, Coast, Elapse, Float, Illapse, Lapse, Luge, Microlight, Portamento, Sail, Scrieve, Skate, Ski, Skim, Sleek, Slide, Slip, Swim, Volplane

**Glimmer**  Gleam, Glent, Glint, Glow, Inkling, Stime, Styme, Twinkle, Wink

**Glimpse**  Aperçu, Flash, Glance, Glisk, Stime, Styme, Waff

**Glint**  Flash, Shimmer, SPARKLE, Trace, Twinkle

**Glisten(ing)**  Ganoid, Glint, Sheen, Shimmer, SHINE, Sparkle

**Glitter(ing)**  Clinquant, Gemmeous, Paillon, Sequin, Spang(le), Sparkle, Tinsel

**Gloat(ing)**  Crow, Drool, Enjoy, Exult, Schadenfreude

**Globe, Globule**  Ball, Bead, Drop, Earth, Orb, Shot, Sphear, Sphere

**Globulin**  Legumin, Protein

**Gloom(y)**  Benight, Blues, Cheerless, Cimmerian, Cloud, Crepuscular, Damp, Dark, DESPAIR, Dingy, Disconsolate, Dismal, Dool(e), Drab, Drear, Drumly, Dump(s), Funereal, Glum, Louring, Mirk, Misery, Mopish, Morose, Murk, Obscurity, Overcast, Sad, Saturnine, Sepulchral, Solein, SOMBRE, Stygian

**Glorification, Glorify**  Aggrandise, Apotheosis, Avatar, Bless, EXALT, Halo, Laud, Lionise, Praise, Radiance

**Glorious, Gloria, Glory**  Chorale, Grand, Halo, Hosanna, Ichabod, Kudos, Lustre, Magnificent, Nimbus, Strut, Sublime, Twelfth

**Glory-pea**  Kaka-beak, Kaka-bill, Kowhai

**Gloss(y)**  Enamel, Gild, Glacé, Japan, Lustre, Patina, POLISH, Postillate, Sheen, Sleek, Slick, Slide, Slur, Veneer, Whitewash

**Glossary**  Catalogue, Clavis, Index, K'thibh

**Glove**  Cestus, Dannock, Gage, Gauntlet, Mitten

**Glow(ing)**  Aflame, Ashine, Aura, Bloom, Burn, Calescence, Candent, Candescence, Flush, Gegenschein, Gleam, Incandescence, Leam, Leme, Lustre, Phosphorescence, Radiant, Reflet, Rushlight, Shine, WARMTH

**Glucin(i)um**  Gl

**Glucose, Glucoside**  Dextrose, Indican, Saponin, Solanine

**Glue(y)**  Araldite, Cement, Colloidal, Gelatin(e), Ichthyocolla, Isinglass, Paste, Propolis, Size, Spetch

**Glum**  Dour, Lugubrious, Moody, Morose, Ron, Sombre

**Glut**  Choke, Gorge, Sate, Satiate, Saturate, Surfeit

**Gluten, Glutinous**  Goo, Seiten, Sticky, Tar, Viscid, Zymome

**Glutton(ous), Gluttony**  Bellygod, Carcajou, Cormorant, Edacity, Gannet, Gourmand, Gutsy, Lurcher, Pig, Ratel, Scoffer, Sin, Trimalchio, Wolverine

**Glyceride, Glycerine**  Ester, Olein

**Gnarl**  Knot, Knur, Nob

**Gnash(ing)**  Bruxism, Champ, Grate

**Gnat**  Culex, Culicidae, Midge, Mosquito

**Gnaw(ing)**  Corrode, Erode, Fret, Rodent

**Gnome**  Adage, Bank-man, Chad, Cobalt, Financier, Kobold, Motto, Proverb, Saw, Sprite

**Gnostic**  Archontic, Cainite, Mand(a)ean, Ophite, Sabian, Tsabian, Zabian

**Gnu**  Wildebeest

**Go, Going (after, for, off, on, up, etc)**  Advance, Afoot, Anabasis, Animation, Assail, Attempt, Bash, Bing, Brio, Clamber, Continuance, Depart, Die, Do, Energy, Fare, Gae, Gang, Gee, Green, Hamba, Hark, Hence, Hie, Imshi, Imshy, Ish, LEAVE, March, Match, Off, Path, Pep, Perpetual, Ply, Quit, Raik, Repair, Resort, Resume, Run, Scram, Segue, Shoo, Skedaddle, Snick-up, Sour, Spank, Stab, Success, Transitory, Trine, Try, Turn, Vam(o)ose, Verve, Via, Viable, Wend, Work, Yead, Yede, Yeed, Zing, Zip

**Goad**  Ankus, Brod, Incite, NEEDLE, Prod, Spur, Stimulate, Stimulus, Taunt

**Goal**  Ambition, Bourn(e), Dool, Dream, Dule, End, Grail, Hail, Home, Horme, Hunk, Limit, Mission, Score, Target

**Goat(-like)**  Amalthea, Angora, Antelope, Antilope, Billy, Bok, Buck, Caprine, Gate, Goral, Hircine, Ibex, Izard, Kid, Libido, Markhor, Nanny, Saanen, Sassaby, Serow, Serpent-eater, Steenbok, Steinbock, Tahr, Takin, Tehr, Thar

**Goatsucker**  Fern-owl, Nightjar

**Gob**  Clot, Mouth, Yap

**Gobble**  Bolt, Devour, Gorge, Gulp, Wolf

**Gobelin**  Tapestry

**Go-between**  Broker, Factor, Link, Mediate, Middleman, Pandarus, Pander, Shuttle

**Goblet**  Chalice, Hanap

**Goblin**  Bargaist, Barg(h)est, Bodach, Bogey, Bogle, Bogy, Bucca, Croquemitaine, Empusa, Erl-king, Genie, Gnome, Gremlin, Knocker,

Lutin, Nis(se), Phooka, Phynnodderree, Pooka, Pouke, Puca, Pug, Red-cowl, Shellycoat, SPRITE, Troll, Trow

**Goby** Dragonet

**God(s)** Abba, Achelous, Adonai, Adrammelech, Aeolus, Aesculapius, Aesir, Agni, Aitu, All-father, Alpheus, Amen-ra, Ammon, Amon-ra, Amun, An(u), Anubis, Apis, Apollo, Ares, As, Asclepius, Ashtar, Asshur, Asur, Aten, Atum, Avatar, Baal, Bacchus, Balder, Bel, Bes, Boreas, Brag, Brahma, Cabiri, Cama, Chemos(h), Comus, Cupid, D, Dagon, Daikoku, Delian, Demogorgon, Deva, Dieu, Dionysus, Dis, Divine, Donar, Elegabalus, Elohim, Eros, Fabulinus, Faunus, Frey(r), Gad, Gallery, Ganes(h)a, Garuda, Geb, Gracious, Haoma, Hashem, Helios, Hermes, Horus, Hughie, Hymen, Hyperion, Hypnos, Indra, Jagganath, Janus, Jehovah, Joss, Juggernaut, Jupiter, Kama, Kami, Karttikaya, Krishna, Kronos, Lar, Liber, Lir, Lludd, Llyr, Loki, Lug(h), Mahadeva, Maker, Mammon, Marduk, Mars, Mercury, Mexitl, Mextli, Mimir, Mithra(s), Moloch, Momus, Morpheus, Mors, Mot, Mulciber, Mumbo-jumbo, Nebo, Neptune, Nereus, Nisroch, Numen, Oannes, Oceanus, Od(d), Odin, Orcus, Ormazd, Ormuzd, Osiris, Pales, Pan, Panisc, Panisk, Pantheon, Penates, Picus, Pluto, Plutus, Poseidon, Priapus, Promachos, Prometheus, Proteus, Ptah, Quirinus, Ra, Rama, Rameses, Re, Rimmon, Rudra, Sarapis, Saturn, Satyr, Serapis, Set, Setebos, Shamash, Silenus, Silvanus, Siva, Sol, Soma, Somnus, Surya, Tammuz, Terminus, Teshup, Thamiz, Thammuz, Thor, Thoth, Tiu, Tiw, Trimurti, Triton, Tum, Tyr, Unknown, Uranus, Vanir, Varuna, Vertumnus, Vishnu, Vulcan, Wahiguru, Woden, Yahve, Yahwe(h), Zagreus, Zernebock, Zeus, Zombie

**God-bearing** Deiparous

**Goddess(es)** Amphitrite, Aphrodite, Artemis, Aruru, Ashnan, Ashtaroth, Ashtoreth, Astarte, Ate, Athene, Aurora, Bastet, Bellona, Ceres, Cloacina, Cotytto, Cybcle, Cynthia, Cyrene, Demeter, Dian(a), Dione, Divine, Durga, Eastre, Eos, Eris, Flora, Frey(j)a, Frigga, Gaea, Gaia, Ge, Grace, Graeae, Graiae, Hathor, Hecate, Hel, Hera, Hertha, Hestia, Horae, Houri, Hulda(r), Hyaeia, Idalia, Idun(a), Irene, Iris, Ishtar, Isis, Juno, Kali, Kotys, Kotytto, Lakshmi, Leda, Leto, Libitina, Lucina, Luna, Maat, Maut, Minerva, Mnemosyne, Muse, Mut, Nemesis, Nike, Norn, Nox, Nyx, Ops, Pales, Pallas, Parcae, Pele, Phoebe, Pomona, Proserpina, Proserpine, Rhea, Sabrina, Satyra, Selene, Semele, Strenia, Tanit, Tellus, Tethys, Thea, Themis, Thetis, Tyche, Valkyrie, Venus, Vesta, Walkyrie

**Godfather, Godmother** Capo, Cummer, Gossip, Kimmer, Rama, Sponsor, Woden

**Godless** Agnostic, Atheistic, Atheous, Impious, Profane

**Godly** Deist, Devout, Holy, Pious

**Godown** Hong

**God-willing** DV

**Go-getter** Arriviste, Hustler

**Goggle** Stare

**Going wrong** Aglee, Agley, Misfiring

> **Going wrong** may indicate an anagram

**Goitre** Struma

**Gold(en)** Age, Amber, Apple, Ass, Au, Auriferous, Bough, Bull, Bullion, California, Doubloon, Dutch, Eagle, Emerods, Filigree, Fleece, Fool's, Gate, Handshake, Hind, Horde, Horn, Ingot, Leaf, Lingot, Moidore, Muck, Nugget, Oaker, Obang, Ochre, Ophir, Or, Oreide, Ormolu, Oroide, Pistole, Placer, Pyrites, Red, Reef, Silence, Sol, Standard, Stubborn, Talmi, Tolosa, Treasury, Yellow

**Gold-digger** Forty-niner, Prospector

**Goldfield** Rand

**Goldfinch** Charm, Chirm

**Goldsmith** Cellini, Fabergé, Oliver

**Golf ball** Gutta, Repaint

**Golfer** Alliss, Braid, Faldo, Hogan, Pivoter, Roundsman, Seve, Teer, Trevino, Wolstenholme

**Golly** Crumbs, Gosh

**Gondolier** Bargee

**Gone** Ago, Defunct, Napoo, Out, Past, Ygo(e), Yod

> **Gone off** may indicate an anagram

**Gone west** Had it

**Gong** Bell, DSO, Medal, Tam-tam, VC

**Goo** Gleet, Gunge, Poise, Ulmin

**Good(ness), Goody-goody** Agathodaimon, Bad, Bein, Benefit, Bonzer, Bosker, Blesses, Bounty, Brod, Budgeree, Canny, Castor, Coo, Cool, Dab, Dow, Enid, Estimable, First-class, Gear, Gosh, Guid, Lois, Lor, Nobility, NO GOOD, Pi, Plum, Proper, Purler, Rectitude, Riddance, Right, Salutary, Samaritan, Sanctity, St, Suitable, Tollol, Topping, Valid, Virtue, Virtuous, Weal, Welfare, Whacko, Wholesome

**Goodbye** Addio, Adieu, Adios, Aloha, Apopemptic, Arrivederci, Cheerio, Ciao, Congé, Farewell, Hooray, Sayonara, Tata, Toodle-oo, Vale

**Good evening** Den

**Goodfellow** Brick, Puck, Robin, Samaritan, Worthy

**Good for nothing** Bum, Donnat, Donnot, Dud, Idler, Layabout, Lorel, Lorrell, Losel, Napoo, Sca(l)lawag, Scallywag, Shot-clog, Useless, Vaurien, Waff, Waster, Wastrel

**Good Friday** Parasceve

**Good-looking** Bon(n)ie, Bonny, Bonwie, Comely, Fair, Handsome, Personable, Pretty, Wally

**Good-nature(d)** Amiable, Bonhomie, Kind

**Good news** Evangel

**Good number**  Thr(e)ave

**Good order**  Eutaxy, Shipshape

**Goods**  Bona, Cargo, Durables, Flotsam, Freight, Futures, Gear, Insight, Ironware, Lay-away, Line, Property, Sparterie, Truck, Wares

**Goodwill**  Amity, Bonhom(m)ie, Favour, Gree

**Goon**  Secombe, Sellers

**Goose**  Anserine, Barnacle, Brent, Canada, Daftie, Ember, Gander, Gannet, Goose, Greylag, Grope, Idiot, Nene, Roger, Silly, Simpleton, Skein, Solan, Strasbourg, Stubble, Team, Wav(e)y, Wawa

**Gooseberry**  Cape, Chaperon(e), Detrop, Fool, Gog, Groser(t), Groset, Grossart

**Gooseflesh**  Horripilation

**Goosefoot**  Allgood, Amarantaceae, Beet, Blite, Fat-hen, Mercury, Orache, Saltbush

**Gooseherd**  Quill-driver

**Gopher**  Camass-rat, Minnesota

**Gordian**  Knot

**Gordon**  Chinese, Flash, Rioter

**Gore**  Blood, Cloy, Gair, Horn

**Gorge(s)**  Barranca, Barranco, Canyon, Chasm, Cheddar, Cleft, Couloir, Cram, Defile, Donga, Flume, Gap, Ghyll, Glut, Gulch, Khor, Kloof, Lin(n), Nala, Nalla(h), Nulla(h), Overeat, Pass, Ravine, Staw, STUFF, Tums, Valley, Yosemite

**Gorgeous**  Grand, Splendid, Superb

**Gorgon**  Euryale, Medusa, Ogress, Stheno

> **Gorilla**  see MONKEY

**Gorse**  Broom, Furze, Gosse, Ulex, Whin

**Gosh**  Begad, Begorra, Blimey, Cor, Gadzooks, Gee, Gum, Lor, My, Odsbobs, Odso

**Gospel(ler)**  Creed, Evangel, Fact, John, Kerygma, Luke, Mark, Matthew, Nicodemus, Synoptic, Waldensian

**Gossamer(y)**  Araneous, Byssoid, Cobwebby, Gauzy

**Gossip**  Ana(s), Aunt, Backbite, Cackle, Causerie, Chat, Chin, Chitchat, Clash, Claver, Clish-clash, Clishmaclaver, Confab, Coze, Crack, Cummer, Dirt, Flibbertigibbet, Gab(nash), Gas, Gup, Hen, Maundrel, Nashgab, Natter, Noise, On dit, Personalist, Prattle, Quidnunc, Rumour, Scandal(monger), Schmooze, Scuttlebutt, Shmoose, Shmooze, Tabby(cat), Talk(er), Tattle, Tibby, Tittle(-tattle), Twattle, Yatter, Yenta

**Got**  Gat, Obtained

**Goth(ic)**  Alaric, Moesia

**Gothamite**  Abderian, New Yorker

**Gouge** Chisel, Groove, Scoop

**Gourd** Calabash, Courgette, Guiro, Loofa, Melon, Pumpkin, Squash, Zucchini

**Gourmand, Gourmet** Apicius, EPICURE, Gastronome, Gastrosopher, Table, Ventripotent

**Gout** Chiragra, Hamarthritis, Podagra, Taste, Tophus

**Govern(or), Government** Adelantado, Administer, Ag(h)a, Amban, Amman, Amtman, Autocrat, Autonomy, Bahram, Ban, Beg, Beglerbeg, Bey, Bridler, Bureaucracy, Burgrave, Cabinet, Caretaker, Castellan, Catapan, Cham, Circar, Coalition, Command, Commonweal, Constable, Constitution, Cybernetic, Darogha, Dey, Diarchy, Dinarchy, Dominate, Duarchy, Duumvirate, Dyarchy, Dynast, Earl, Empery, Eparch, Escapement, Ethnarch Exarch, G, Gerontocracy, Gov, Grieve, Gubernator, Hague, Hakim, Harmost, HE, Helm, Hospodar, Ins, Inspector, Junta, Kaimakam, Kalistocracy, Khalifate, Khan, Kremlin, Majlis, Monarchy, Mudir, Nabob, Naik, Nomarch, Nomocracy, Oireachtas, Optic, Pa, Pacha, Padishah, Pasha, Père, Pentarch, Petticoat, Placemen, Plutocracy, Podesta, Porte, Power, Proconsul, Proveditor, Provedor(e), Providor, Quirinal, Raj, Realpolitik, Rection, Rector, Rectrix, Regency, Regime(n), Reign, Rein, Ride, RULE, Satrap, Senate, Serkali, Signoria, Sircar, Sirkar, Stad(t)holder, Statecraft, Steer, Subadar, Sway, Timocracy, Tuchun, Vali, Viceregal, Wali, Warden, Wealsman, Whitehall, Witan

**Governess** Duenna, Eyre, Fraulein, Griffin, Mademoiselle, Vicereine

**Government revenue** Jaghir(e), Jagir

**Gown** Banian, Banyan, Geneva, Green, Hubbard, Manteau, Manto, Mantua, Peignoir, Robe, Slammakin, Slammerkin, Slop, Stola, Wrap(per)

**Grab** Annexe, Bag, Clutch, Cly, Collar, Grapnel, Hold, Holt, Rap, Seize, SNATCH, Swipe

**Gracchi** Jewels

**Grace(s), Graceful** Aglaia, Anna, Beauty, Become, Benediction, Bethankit, Blessing, Charis(ma), Charites, Charity, Darling, Dr, Elegance, Euphrosyne, Fluent, Gainly, Genteel, Genty, Mense, Mercy, Molinism, Mordent, Omnium, Ornament, Pralltriller, Sacrament, Streamlined, Style, Thalia, WG

**Gracious** Benign, By George, Charismatic, Generous, Good, Handsome, Hend, Merciful, Polite

**Gradation** Cline, Degree, Nuance, Stage

**Grade, Gradient** Analyse, Angle, Class(ify), Dan, Degree, Echelon, Gon, Hierarchy, Inclination, Kyu, Lapse, Measure, Order, Rank, Score, Seed, Slope, Status

**Gradual** Gentle, Grail, Inchmeal, Slow

**Graduate, Graduation** Alumnus, BA, Bachelor, Calibrate, Incept, Laureateship, Licentiate, LlB, MA, Master, Nuance, Optime, Ovate

**Graffiti** Bomb, Doodle, Tag

**Graft** Anaplasty, Autoplasty, Boodle, Bribery, Bud, Dub, Enarch, Enrace, Imp, Implant, Inarch, Inoculate, Payola, Racket, Scion, Shoot, Slip, Transplant, Ympe

**Grail** Chalice, Cup, Sangraal, Sangrail, Sangreal

**Grain(y)** Bajra, Bajree, Bajri, Bear, Bere, Boll, Bran, Cereal, Corn, Couscous, Crop, Curn, Cuscus, Gr, Graddan, Granule, Grumose, Intine, Kaoliang, Malt, Mashlam, Mashlin, Mashloch, Mashlum, Maslin, Mealie, Millet, Milo, Minim, Mongcorn, Oats, Pinole, Pollen, Popcorn, Rabi, Raggee, Ragi, Raggy, Rhy, Rye, Sand, Scruple, Seed, Semsem, Tola, Touch, Wheat, Wholemeal

**Gram** Chich, Chick-pea, Teen, Tene

**Grammar(ian)** Accidence, Donat, Donet, Gr, Linguistics, Paradigm, Primer, Priscianist, Scholiast, Syntax

**Grampus** Orc, Whale

**Granary** Barn, Girnal, Silo

**Grand** Canyon, Epical, Flugel, G, Gorgeous, Guignol, Hotel, Imposing, La(h)-di-da(h), Lordly, Magnificent, Majestic, Palatial, Piano(forte), Pompous, Regal, Splendid, Stately, Stoor, Stour, Stowre, Sture, Sublime, Swell, Tour

**Grandchild** Niece, Oe, Oy(e)

**Grandee** Adelantado, Don, Magnifico

**Grandfather** Ancient, Avital, Clock, Goodsire, Gramps, Gutcher, Oldster, Old-timer, Oupa

**Grandmother** Gran(nie), Granny, Moses, Nan(a), Ouma

**Grandparent(al)** Aval, Avital

**Grand Prix** Race(-cup)

**Grandsire** Peal

**Grange** Moated

**Granite** Aberdeen, Chinastone, Greisen, Luxul(l)ianite, Luxulyanite, NH, Pegmatite, Protogine

**Grannie** Forebear, Knot, Nan(a)

**Grant(ed)** Accord, Aid, Award, Bestow, Beteem(e), Bursary, Carta, Cary, Charta, Charter, Concession, CONFER, Cy, Datum, Exhibition, Feoff, Lend, Let, Munich, Patent, President, Send, Sop, Subsidy, Teene, Vouchsafe, Yeven, Yield

**Granulate** Kern, Pound

**Grape(s)** Botros, Botryoid, Cabernet, Catawba, Chardonnay, Delaware, Gamay, Haanepoot, Hamburg(h), Hanepoot, Honeypot, Hyacinth, Malmsey, Malvasia, Malvoisie, Muscadel, Muscadine, Muscat(el), Pinot, Rape, Sauvignon, Scuppernong, Semillon, Scrcial, Shiraz, Sour, Staphyline, Sultana, Sweet-water, Sylvaner, Syrah, Uva, Verdelho, Vino, Wineberry, Zinfandel

**Grapefruit** Pampelmoose, Pomelo, Pompelmouse, Pompelo, Pumple-nose,

Ugli

**Grapeshot** Mitraille

**Grape-sugar** Glucose

**Grapevine** Hearsay

**Graph(ic)** Chart, Contour, Diagram, Ogive, Picturesque, Profile, Table, Vivid

**Graphite** Kish, Plumbago

**Grapple** Clinch, Struggle, Wrestle

**Grasp(ing)** Apprehend, Catch, Clat, Claut, CLUTCH, Compass, Comprehend, Fathom, Get, Grab, Grapple, Greedy, Grip(e), Hent, Hug, Prehensile, Raptorial, Realise, Rumble, Sense, Snap, Snatch, Twig, Uptak(e)

**Grass(land), Grass roots, Grassy** Agrostology, Alang, Alfa(lfa), Avena, Bamboo, Barley, Bennet, Bent, Blade, Brome-grass, Bromus, Buffalo, Canary, Cane, Canna, Cat's tail, Citronella, Cleavers, Clivers, Clover, Cochlearia, Cocksfoot, Cogon, Cortaderia, Couch, Culm, Cuscus, Dari, Darnel, Dhura, Diss, Divot, Dogstail, Doob, Doura, Dura, Durra, Eddish, Elephant, Esparto, Feather, Fescue, Fiorin, Flinders, Fog, Foggage, Foxtail, Gama-grass, Ganja, Glume, Glumella, Grama, Green(sward), Halfa, Hassock, Hay, INFORM, Jawar(i), Jowar(i), Kangaroo, Kans, Khuskhus, Kikuyu, Knoll, Knot, Lalang, Laund, Lawn, Locusta, Lolium, Lop, Lucern(e), Marram, Marrum, Matweed, Mead, Melic, Millet, Milo, Moor, Nark, Oat, Oryza, Palet, Pamir, Pampas, Panic, Paspalum, Pasturage, Peach, Pennisetum, Persicaria, Phleum, Plume, Poa, Pot, Puszta, Quick, Quitch, Ramee, Rami(e), Reed, Redtop, Rice, Rips, Roosa, Rough, Rumble(r), Rusa, Sacaton, Savannah, Scraw, Scutch, Sea-reed, Sedge, Sesame, Shop, Sinsemilla, Sisal, Sneak(er), Snitch, Snout, Sorghum, Sour-gourd, Sourveld, Spinifex, Split, Squeal, Squitch, Squirrel-tail, Stag, Star(r), Stipa, Stool-pigeon, Storm, Sward, Swath(e), Tath, Tea, Tef(f), Tell, Teosinte, Timothy, Toetoe, Toitoi, Triticale, Tuffet, Turf, Tussac, Tussock, Twitch, Veld(t), Vetiver, Whangee, Whitlow, Windlestraw, Yorkshire fog, Zizania, Zoysia

**Grasshopper** Cicada, Cricket, Grig, Katydid, Tettix, Weta

**Grate(r), Grating** Abrade, Burr, Cancelli, Chirk, FRET, Grid, Guichet, Hack, Hearth, Heck, Hoarse, Ingle, Jar, Portcullis, Rasp, Risp, Rub, Ruling, Scrannel, SCRAPE, Scrat, Shred, Siver, Strident, Syver

**Grateful** Beholden, Cinders, Indebted, Obliged

**Gratification, Gratify** Aggrate, Indulge, Kick, Oblige, Pleasure, Regale, Reward

**Gratitude** God 'a mercy, Ta, Thanks

**Gratuitous, Gratuity** Baksheesh, Beer-money, Bonus, Bounty, Cumshaw, Free, Gratis, Tip

**Grave(yard)** Accent, Arlington, Bass, Bier, Burial, Charnel, Chase, Darga, Demure, Dust, God's acre, Heinous, Important, Ingroove, Kistvaen, Kurgan, Mound, Pit, Sad, Saturnine, Serious, Sober, Sombre, Speos, Staid, Stern, Tomb, Watery

**Grave-digger**  Bederal, Fossor, Sexton

**Gravel(ly)**  Calculus, Chesil, Chisel, Eskar, Esker, Glareous, Grail(e), Grit, Hoggin(g), Murram, Nonplus, Pingo, Shingle

**Gravity**  Barycentric, G, Geotaxis, Geotropism, Magnitude, Weight

**Gravy**  Baster, Browning, Coin

**Gravy-boat**  Argyle, Argyll

> **Gray**  see GREY

**Grayling**  Umber

**Graze, Grazing**  Abrade, Agist, Bark, Brush, Crop, Feed, Herdwick, Leasow(e), Pasture, Scrape, Scrawn, Shieling

**Grease, Greasy**  Bribe, Creesh, Dope, Dubbing, Elaeolite, Enseam, Glit, Lard, Seam(e), Smarm, Suint, Unctuous

**Great(est)**  Ali, Astronomical, Bully, Extreme, Gay, Gey, Gran(d), Grit, Gt, Guns, Important, Lion, Macro, Main, Major, Mickle, Mochell, Much, Muchel(l), OS, Stoor, Stour, Sture, Super, Swingeing, Tall, Titan(ic), Tremendous, Unco, Utmost, Vast, Zenith

**Great deal**  Mort

**Grebe**  Cargoose

**Grecian**  Bend, Nose

**Greed(y)**  Avarice, Avid, Bulimia, Bulimy, Cupidity, Edacious, Esurient, Gannet, Gare, Mercenary, Pleonexia, Rapacity, Selfish, Solan, Voracity, Wolfish

**Greek(s)**  Achaean, Achaian, Achilles, Aeolic, Agamemnon, Ajax, Aonian, Arcadia, Archimedes, Argive, Aristides, Athenian, Attic, Cadmean, Cleruch, Corinthian, Cretan, Delphian, Diomedes, Dorian, Doric, Eoka, Eolic, Epaminondas, Ephebe, Epirus, Euclid, Evzone, Gr, Helladic, Hellene, Hellenic, Homer, Hoplite, Ionian, Isocrates, Italiot(e), Javan, Katharevousa, Klepht, Koine, Leonidas, Locrian, Lucian, Macedonia, Momus, Nestor, Nike, Orestes, Paestum, Patroclus, Pelasgic, Pelopid, Perseus, Phanariot, Pythagoras, Romaic, Samiot, Seminole, Spartacus, Spartan, Strabo, Sybarite, Tean, Teian, Theban, Thersites, Theseus, Typto, Uniat, Xenophon, Zorba

**Green(ery)**  Biliverdin, Callow, Celadon, Cerulein, Chard, Chlorophyll, Cole, Collard, Common, Copper, Corbeau, Dioptase, Eco-, Emerald, Emerande, Envious, Erin, Foliage, Fundie, Fundy, Gaudy, Glaucous, Go, Goddess, Gretna, Gull, Immature, Inexpert, Kendal, Kensal, Lawn, Leafage, Lime, Lincoln, Mead, Moulding, Naive, New, Nile, Oasis, Olive, Pea, Peridot, Porraceous, Raw, Realo, Reseda, Rink, Sage, Scheele's, Sludge, Smaragdine, Sward, Teal, Tender, Turacoverdin, Tyro, Unfledged, Uninitiated, Unripe, Uranite, Verdant, Verdigris, Verdure, Vert, Virent, Virid

**Greenheart**  Bebeern

**Greenhorn**  Baby, Dupe, Putt, Rookie, Sucker

**Greenhouse**  Conservatory, Orangery, Phytotron

**Greens** Broccoli, Cabbage, Calabrese, Cash, Money, Sprout, Vegetable(s)

**Greet(ing)** Abrazo, Accost, Arvo, Banzai, Benedicite, Blubber, Chimo, Ciao, Hail, Hallo, Halse, Handshake, Heil, Hello, Herald, Hi, High five, Hongi, How, Jambo, Kiss, Namaskar, Namaste, Respects, Salaam, Salute, Salve, Sd, Shalom, Sorry, Wave, WELCOME, Wotcher

**Gregarious** Social

**Gregorian** Chant, NS

> **Gremlin** see GOBLIN

**Grenade** Bomb, Egg, Pineapple

**Greta** Garbo

**Grey, Gray** Age, Agnes, Argent, Ashen Ashy, Beige, Bloncket, Cinereous, Dorian, Drab, Glaucous, Gloomy, Gridelin, Griesie, Gries(l)y, Grise, Grisy, Grizzled, Gunmetal, Gy, Hoary, Hore, Inn, Leaden, Liard, Lucia, Lyart, Slaty, Taupe

**Greyfriars** Bunter, Magnet

**Greyhound** Grew, Longtail, Saluki, Sapling, Whippet

**Grey matter** Cinerea

**Grid(dle), Gridiron** Bar, Barbecue, Brandreth, Grate, Graticule, Grating, Network, Reseau, Tava(h), Tawa, Windscale

**Gride** Creak, Grate

**Grief, Grievance, Grievous** Axe, Bitter, Complaint, Cry, Dear(e), Deere, Distress, Dole, Dolour, Gram(e), Gravamen, Heartbreak, Hone, Illy, Io, MISERY, Monody, O(c)hone, Pain, Pathetic, Plaint, Sorrow, Teen, Tene, Tragic, Wayment, Wrong

**Griffin** Gripe, Grype, Novice, Pony

**Grill(ing), Grille** Brander, Broil, Carbonado, Crisp, Devil, Gridiron, Inquisition, Interrogate, Kebab, Pump, Question, Rack, Reja, Yakimona

**Grim** Dire, Dour, Gaunt, Glum, Gurly, Hard, Stern

> **Grim** may indicate an anagram

**Grimace** Face, Girn, Moe, Mop, Moue, Mouth, Mow, Murgeon, Pout

**Grime(s)** Colly, Dirt, Peter, Soil, Sweep

**Grin** Girn, Risus, Simper, Smirk

**Grind(ing), Grinder** Bray, Bruxism, Chew, Crunch, CRUSH, Droil, Gnash, Grate, Graunch, Grit, Kern, Kibble, Levigate, Mano, Mill, Mince, Molar, Pulverise, Slog, Triturate

**Grip(ping)** Bite, Clamp, Clip, Clutch, Craple, Embrace, Enthral, Get, Grapple, GRASP, Haft, Hairpin, Hend, Hold, Hug, Kirby, Obsess, Pincer, Pinion, Prehensile, Purchase, Raven, Rhine, Sipe, Strain, Streigne, Valise, Vice, Walise, Wrestle

**Gripe(s)** Complain, Ditch, Grasp, Griffin, Ileus, Pain, Tormina

**Grist** Burden

**Gristle, Gristly** Cartilage, Chondroid, Lytta

**Grit(ty)**  Blinding, Clench, Gnash, Granular, Grate, Guts, Pluck, Resolution, Sabulose, Sand, Shingle, Swarf

**Grizzle(d)**  Grey

**Groan(er)**  Bewail, Bing, Moan

**Grocer**  Grasshopper, Jorrocks, Pepperer

**Groggy**  Dazed, Shaky

**Groin**  Gnarr, Inguinal, Lisk

**Groom**  Coistrel, Coistril, Curry, Fettler, Ostler, Palfrenier, Paranymph, Preen, S(a)ice, Smarten, Strapper, Syce, Tiger, Tracer, Train

> **Groom**  may indicate an anagram

**Groove(d), Groovy**  Bezel, Canal, Cannelure, Chamfer, Channel, Chase, Clevis, Coulisse, Croze, Exarate, Fissure, Flute, Fuller, Furr, Furrow, Glyph, Gouge, Kerf, Keyway, Oche, Pod, Rabbet, Raggle, Rebate, Rif(f)le, Rigol(l), RUT, Scrobe, Sipe, Slot, Sulcus, Track, Trough, Vallecula

**Grope**  Feel, Fumble, Grabble, Ripe

**Gross**  All-up, Coarse, Complete, Crass, Dense, Earthy, Flagrant, Frankish, Gr, Material, Obese, Outsize, Overweight, Rank, Ribald, Rough, Stupid, Whole

> **Gross**  may indicate an anagram

**Grotesque**  Antic, Bizarre, Fantastic, Fright, Gargoyle, Magot, Outlandish, Rabelaisian, Rococo

**Grotto**  Cave, Lupercal

**Ground(s)**  Arena, Astroturf, Basis, Bottom, Campus, Cause, Common, Criterion, Crushed, Deck, Dregs, Eard, Earth, Epig(a)eal, Epig(a)ean, Epig(a)eous, Footing, Grated, Grist, Lees, Leeway, Lek, Lords, Marl, Mealed, Occasion, Parade, Pitch, Plot, Policy, Proving, Quad, REASON, Ring, Sediment, Slade, Soil, Solum, Stadium, Terra, Terrain, Tract, Turf, Udal, Venue, Yard, Yird

> **Ground**  may indicate an anagram

**Groundbait**  Chum

**Ground-crew**  Erk

**Ground-rent**  Crevasse

**Groundsheet**  Hutchie

**Group**  Band, Batch, Beatles, Bee, Bevy, Bloc(k), Blood, Bloomsbury, Body, Bracket, Caboodle, Cadre, Caucus, Cave, Cell, Chain, Chordata, Circle, Clade, Class(is), Clique, Cluster, Cohort, Colony, Combo, Commune, Community, Contingent, Coterie, Crew, Deme, Denomination, Detail, Ensemble, Faction, Fascio, Galère, Genus, Globe, Guild, Heading, Hexad, House, Kit, Knot, League, Marshal, Order, Outfit, Oxford, Pack(et), Panel, Phalange, Phratry, Phylum, Pocket, Pool, Push, Raceme, Racemose, Ring, Rush, School, Sector, Seminar, Series, Set, Several, Sex, Shower, Society, Sort, Sorus, Splinter, Stream, String, Sub-order, Syndicate, Tales, Taxon, Tetrad, Tithing, T-Rex, Tribe, Trio, TU, Unit, Zupa

**Grouse** Bleat, Capercaillie, Capercailzie, Covey, Gorcock, Growl, Grumble, Hazel-hen, Heath-hen, Jeremiad, Moan, Moorcock, Moorfowl, Moor-pout, Muir-poot, Muir-pout, Natter, Peeve, Pintail, Prairie-hen, Ptarmigan, Resent, Rype(r), Snarl, Twelfth, Wheenge, W(h)inge

**Grove** Academy, Arboretum, Copse, Glade, Hurst, Lyceum, Nemoral, Silva, Tope

**Grovel** Crawl, Creep, Fawn, Kowtow

**Grow(ing), Grow out, Growth** Accrete, Accrue, Aggrandisement, Angioma, Arborescence, Auxesis, Bedeguar, Boom, Braird, Burgeon, Car(b)uncle, Condyloma, Crescendo, Crop, Culture, Cyst, Ectopia, Edema, Ellagic, Enate, Enchondroma, Enlarge, Epinasty, Epitaxy, Excrescence, Expansion, Flourish, Flush, Gain, Gall, Germinate, Goitre, Hepatocele, Hummie, Increase, Knur(r), Lipoma, Mushroom, Nur(r), Oedema, Oncology, Osselet, Polyp, Proleg, Rampant, Scirrhus, Septal, Spavin, SPROUT, Tariff, Thrive, Tyloses, Vegetable, Wart, Wax, Wox

> **Grow(n)** may indicate an anagram

**Growl(ing)** Fremescent, Gnar, Groin, Grr, Gurl, Roar(e), Roin, Royne, Snar(l)

**Grown up** Adult, Mature, Risen

**Grub** Assart, Bardy, Caddis, Caterpillar, Cheer, Chow, Chrysalis, Dig, Eats, Fare, FOOD, Gentle, Groo-groo, Gru-gru, Larva, Leatherjacket, Mawk, Mess, Nosh, Palmerworm, Peck, Pupa, Root(le), Rout, Rowt, Sap, Slave, Stub, Wireworm, Witchetty, Worm

**Grudge, Grudging** Chip, Derry, Envy, Grutch, Resent, Score, Sparse, Spite, Spleen

**Gruel** Brochan, Bross, Loblolly, Skilligalee, Skilligolee, Skilly

**Gruesome** Ghastly, Grooly, Horror, Macaberesque, Macabre, MORBID, Sick

**Gruff** Hoarse, Surly

**Grumble** Beef, Bellyache, Bitch, Bleat, Chunter, Croak, Gripe, Grizzle, Groin, Growl, Moan, Murmur, Mutter, Nark, Natter, Repine, Rumble, Yammer

**Grumpy** Attercop, Bearish, Cross, Ettercap, Grouchy, Moody, Surly

**Grunt** Groin, Grumph, Humph, Oink, Pigfish, Ugh, Wheugh

**Guanoco** Llama

**Guarantee** Assure, Avouch, Certify, Ensure, Gage, Hallmark, Insure, Mainprise, Money-back, Pignerate, Pignorate, PLEDGE, Plight, Seal, Secure, Sponsion, Surety, VOUCH(safe), Warrandice, Warrant(y)

**Guard(ed), Guards** Acolouthos, Beefeaters, Blues, Bostangi, Bouncer, Cabiri, Cage, Cerberus, Chaperon(e), Chary, Cheesemongers, Cherry-pickers, Coldstream, Cordon, Curator, Custodian, Custos, Diehards, Dragoons, Duenna, Equerry, Escort, Eunuch, Excubant, Fence, Fender, Grenadiers, Greys, INS, Jailer, Keep, Lancers, Lilywhites, Look out, Mort-safe, Nutcrackers, Out-rider, Out-sentry, Pad, Patrol, Picket,

Praetorian, PROTECT, Quillon, Rail, Secure, Sentinel, Sentry, Shield, SS, Strelitz, Streltzi, Swiss, Tapadera, Tapadero, Tile, Toecap, Vamplate, Vigilante, Visor, Wage, Wait(e), Ward, Wary, Watch (and ward), Wear, Weir, Yeoman

**Guardian** Altair, Argus, Curator, Custodian, Custos, Dragon, Gemini, Granthi, Janus, Julius, Miminger, Templar, Tutelar(y), Warder, Watchdog, Xerxes

**Gudgeon** Fish, Pin, Trunnion

**Guenon** Grivet, Vervet

**Guerilla** Bushwhacker, Chetnik, Gook, Komitaji, Maquis, Mujaheddin, Partisan, Tupamaro, Urban, Zapata

**Guess** Aread, Arede, Arreede, Divine, Estimate, Harp, Imagine, Infer, Level, Mor(r)a, Mull, Shot, Speculate, Suppose, Surmise, Theorise

**Guessing game** Handy-dandy, Mor(r)a, Quiz

**Guest(s)** Caller, Company, Parasite, PG, Symbion(t), Symphile, Synoecete, Visitant, VISITOR, Xenial

**Guesthouse** Xenodochium

**Guff** Bosh, Gas

**Guianian** S(a)ouari

**Guidance, Guide(line)** Advice, Antibarbus, Auspice, Baedeker, Bradshaw, Cicerone, Clue, Concordance, Conduct, Counsel, Courier, Curb, Director(y), Dragoman, Drive, ESCORT, Gillie, Helm, Index, Inertial, Inspire, Itinerary, Jig, Key, Lad, Landmark, Lead, Mark, Map, Model, Nose, Pelorus, Pilot, Postil(l)ion, Principle, Range, Ranger, Reference, Rein, Rudder, Sabot, Sherpa, Shikaree, Shikari, Sign, Sixer, Stear, Steer, Stire, Template, Templet, Tiller, Train, Travelogue, Voyageur, Weise, Weize, Wise

**Guild** Artel, Basoche, Company, Gyeld, Hanse, League, Society, Tong, Union

**Guile** Art, Cunning, Deceit, Dole, Malengine

**Guillotine** Closure, Louisiette, Maiden, Marianne

**Guilt(y)** Blame, Cognovit, Nocent, Peccavi, Remorse, Wicked

**Guinea(s)** Geordie, Gns, Job, Ls, Meg, Spade

**Guinea-fowl** Pintado

**Guinea-pig** Agoute, Agouti, Cavie, Cavy

**Guinea-worm** Dracunculus

**Guise** Form, Manner, Shape

**Guitar** Axe(man), Cithern, Cittern, Dobro, Gittern, Lute, Samisen, Sancho, Sanko, Sitar, Shamisen, Ukulele

**Gulf** Aden, Bay, Chasm, Darien, Fonseca, Lepanto, Maw, Mexico, Persian

**Gull(s)** Bonxie, Cheat, Cob(b), Cod, Cozen, Dupe, Fool, Geck, Hoodwink, Laridae, Larus, Maw, Mew, Pickmaw, Pigeon, Queer, Rook, Sea-cob,

Sea-mew, Sell, Simp, Skua, Sucker, Tern, Tystie, Xema

**Gullet** Crop, Enterate, Maw, Throat, Weasand-pipe

**Gullible** Green, Naive, Sucker

**Gulliver** Lemuel

**Gully** Couloir, Donga, Geo, Gio, Goe, Grough, Gulch, Pit, Ravine, Sloot, Sluit, Wadi

**Gulp** Bolt, Draught, Gollop, Quaff, Sob, SWALLOW, Swipe, Wolf

**Gum (tree)** Acacia, Acajou, Agar, Algin, Angico, Arabic, Arabin, Arar, Arctic, Asafoetida, Balata, Balm, Bandoline, Bdellium, Benjamin, Benzoin, Bloodwood, Boot, Cerasin, Chicle, Chuddy, Chutty, Coolabah, Courbaril, Dragon's-blood, Ee-by, Eucalyptus, Frankincense, Galbanum, Gamboge, Gingival, GLUE, Goat's-thorn, Gosh, Guar, Ironbark, Karri, Lac, Lentisk, Mastic(h), Mucilage, Myrrh, Olibanum, Opopanax, Oshac, Sagapenum, Sarcocolla, Size, Sleep, Sterculia, Stringybark, Tacamahac, Tupelo

**Gumbo** Okra

**Gumboil** Parulis

**Gumption** Spirit

**Gun(fire), Guns** Amusette, Archibald, Archie, Arquebus, Barker, Bazooka, Big Bertha, Biscayan, Bofors, Bombard, Breech(-loader), Bren, Broadside, Brown Bess, Bulldog, Bundook, Caliver, Cannonade, Carbine, Carronade, Chokebore, Coehorn, Colt, Dag, Derringer, Escopette, Falcon(et), Flintlock, Fowler, Garand, Gat(ling), Gingal(l), HA, Hackbut, Harquebus, Heater, Howitzer, Jezail, Jingal, Kalashnikov, Lewis, Long Tom, Luger, Machine, Martini-Henry, Matchlock, Mauser, Maxim, Metal, Minnie, Minute, Mitrailleuse, Morris Meg, Mortar, Musket(oon), Muzzle-loader, Noonday, Oerlikon, Ordnance, Paderero, Paterero, Ped(e)rero, Pelican, Perrier, Petronal, Piece, Pistol(et), Pompom, Quaker, Repeater, Rod, Roscoe, Saker, Sarbacane, Shooter, Siege, Spearmint, Spray, Sten, Sterculia, Sterling, Stern-cannon, Stern-chaser, Tea, Tier, Tupelo, Uzi

**Gunman** Assassin, Bandit, Earp, Greaser, Pistoleer, Sniper, Starter

**Gunner, Gunner's assistant** Arquebusier, Arsenal, Artillerist, Cannoneer, Cannonier, Culverineer, Gr, Matross, RA

**Gunpowder** Charcoal, Saucisse, Saucisson

**Gunwale** Gunnel, Portland, Portlast, Portoise

**Gurgle** Clunk, Gollar, Guggle, Ruckle, Squelch

**Gurnard** Tubfish

**Guru** Teacher

**Gush(ing)** Blether, Effusive, FLOOD, Flow, Jet, Outpour, Rail, Scaturient, Spirt, Spout, Spurt

**Gusset** Godet, Gore, Insert, Inset, Mitre

**Gust** Blast, Blore, Flaught, Flaw, Flurry, Puff, Sar, Waff

**Gusto** Elan, Relish, Verve, Zest

**Gut(s), Gutty**  Archenteron, Bowel(s), Chitterlings, Duodenum, Draw, Enteral, Enteron, Entrails, Gill, Ileum, Insides, Kyle, Mesenteron, Omental, Omentum, Remake, Sack, Sand, Snell, Stamina, Staying-power, Strip, Thairm, Tripe, Viscera

**Gutta-percha**  Jelutong, Pontianac, Pontianak

**Gutter(ing)**  Channel, Conduit, Cullis, Grip, Kennel, Rhone, Rigol(l), Roan, Rone, Spout, Strand, Sweal, Sweel

**Guttersnipe**  Arab, Gamin, Thief

**Guy**  Backstay, Bo, Burgess, Clewline, Decamp, Deride, Effigy, Fall, Fawkes, Fellow, Gink, Josh, Mannering, Parody, Rib, Rope, Scarecrow, Stay, Tease, Vang, Wise

**Gwyn**  Nell

**Gymnasium, Gymnast(ic)**  Acrobat, Akhara, Arena, Lyceum, Palaestra, PE, PT, Sokol, Tumbler

**Gymnosophist**  Yogi

**Gypsum**  Alabaster, Gesso, Plaster, Satin-stone, Selenite

**Gypsy**  Bohemian, Cagot, Caird, Caqueux, Chal, Chi, Collibert, Esmeralda, Faw, Gipsen, Gitano, Hayraddin, Lavengro, Rom(any), Rye, Scholar, Tinker, Tsigane, Vagabond, Wanderer, Zigan, Zigeuner, Zincala, Zincalo, Zingaro

**Gyrate**  Revolve, Rotate, SPIN, Twirl

# Hh

**H** Ache, Aitch, Aspirate, Height, Hospital, Hotel, Hydrant, Hydrogen

**Haberdasher(y)** Clothier, Ferret, Hosier, Notions

**Habit(ual), Habituate, Habitué** Accustom, Addiction, Apparel, Assuefaction, Assuetude, Bent, Cacoethes, Chronic, Coat, Consuetude, Custom, Diathesis, Dress, Ephod, Frequenter, Inure, Inveterate, Motley, Mufti, Nature, Outfit, Practice, Raiment, Regular, Robe, Rochet, Routine, Scapular, Schema, Season, Set, Soutane, Suit, Surplice, Toge, Trait, Tway, Usual, Way, Won, Wont, Xerotes

**Habitat** Environment, Haunt, Home, Locality, Station

**Hack** Chip, Chop, Cough, Cut, Drudge, Garble, Gash, Ghost, Hag, Hash, Hedge-writer, Heel, Hew, Horse, Mangle, Mutilate, Nag, Notch, Pad, Penny-a-liner, Pot-boiler, Rosinante, Spurn, Tadpole, Taper, Tussis, Unseam

**Hackle(s)** Comb, Rough

**Hackneyed** Banal, Cab, Cliché, Corny, Percoct, Stale, Threadbare, Tired, Trite

**Had to** Moten, Must, Obliged

**Haddock** Findram, Finnan, Fish, Speldin(g), Speldrin(g), Whitefish

**Hades** Dis, Hell, Orcus, Pit, Tartarus

**Haematite** Oligist

**Haemorrhoid** Pile

**Hafnium** Hf

**Hag(-like)** Anile, Beldame, Besom, Crone, Harpy, Harridan, Hex, Nickneven, Occasion, Rudas, Runnion, Trot, Underwood, Witch

**Haggard** Drawn, GAUNT, Pale, Rider

**Haggis** Kishke

**Haggle** Argue, Badger, BARGAIN, Barter, Chaffer, Dicker, Horse-trade, Niffer, Palter

**Ha-ha** Dike, Sunk-fence

**Hahnium** Hn

**Hail(er)** Acclaim, Ahoy, Ave, Bull-horn, Cheer, Fusillade, Greet, Hi, Ho, Salue, Salute, Shower, Signal, Skoal, Skol, Sola, Stentor, Storm

**Hair(like), Hairy, Hair condition/cut/style** Afro, Ainu, Alopecia, Bang, Barnet, Beard, Bingle, Bob, Braid, Brede, Bristle, Brutus, Bun, Butch, Cadogan, Capillary, Catogan, Chignon, Cilia, Coat, Cockernony, Coiffure, Comal, Cornrow, Corymbus, Cowlick, Crinal, Cronet, Crop, Cue, DA, Dangerous, Dreadlocks, Elf locks, Esau, Feather, Fetlock, Filament,

Floccus, Fringe, Fur, Glib(s), Heard, Heer(i)e, Hispid, Hog, Indumentum, Kemp, Kesh, Lanugo, List, Lock, Madarosis, Mane, Mohican, Mop, Not(t), Pageboy, Pappus, Pele(s), Pelt, Perm(anent), Pigtail, Pika, Pilus, Plait, Plica, Pompadour, Pouf(fe), Queue, Quiff, Radicle, Rat-tail, Rhizoid, Roach, Scopate, Shag, Shingle, Shock, Sideburns, Snell, Strammel, Strigose, Strummel, Switch, Tête, Thatch, Tomentose, Tonsure, Topknot, Tragus, Tress, Trichoid, Trichome, Trim, Vibrissi, Villi, Villus, Wig, Wisp, WOOL, Xerasia

**Hair-cream, Hair-oil**  Conditioner, Pomade

**Hairdresser**  Barber, Coiffeur, Comb, Friseur, Marcel, Salon, Stylist, Trichologist

**Hairless**  Bald, Callow, Glabrate, Glabrous, Irate

**Hairnet**  Kell, Snood

**Hairpiece**  Merkin, Toupee, Wig

**Hairpin**  Bodkin, Slide, U, U-turn

**Hair-shirt**  Ab(b)a, Cilice

**Haiti**  RH

**Hal**  Prince

**Halberd**  Spontoon

**Halcyon**  Calm, Kingfisher, Mild

**Hale(r)**  Drag, Healthy, Koruna, Robust, Well

**Half, Halved**  Bifid, Demi, Dimidiate, Divide, Hemi, Moiety, Semi, Share, Split, Stand-off, Term

**Half-a-dozen**  Six, VI

**Half-asleep, Half-conscious**  Dove, Dozy

**Half-baked**  Mediocre, Samel

**Half-breed, Half-caste**  Bastard, Baster, Creole, Eurasian, Mameluco, Mestee, Mestiza, Mestizo, Metif, Métis(se), Mongrel, Mulatto, Mustee, Octaroon, Quadroon, Quarteroon, Quintero, Quintroon, Sambo, Zambo

**Half-guinea**  Smelt

**Half-hour**  Bell

**Half-pence, Half-penny**  Mag, Maik, Mail(e), Make, Obolus, Patrick, Rap, Wood's

**Half-turn**  Caracol(e), Demivolt

**Half-wit**  Changeling, Mome, Simpleton, STUPID

**Hall**  Apadana, Atrium, Auditorium, Aula, Basilica, Casino, Chamber, Citadel, Concourse, Corridor, Domdaniel, Dome, Dotheboys, Ex(h)edra, Foyer, Gallen, Liberty, Lobby, Locksley, Megaron, Odeon, Palais, Passage, Rathaus, Salle, Saloon, Tammany, Tara, Tolsel, Valhalla, Vestibule, Wildfell

**Hallmark**  Brand, Logo, Seal, Stamp

> **Hallo**  see HELLO

**Hallucinate, Hallucination** Autoscopy, Fantasy, Illusion, Image, Mirage

**Halo** Antheolion, Areola, Aura, Corona, Gloria, Gloriole, Mandorla, Nimbus, Rim, Vesica

**Halogen** Iodine

**Halt(er)** Arrest, Block, Brake, Bridle, Cavesson, Cease, Game, Hackamore, Hilch, Lame(d), Limp, Noose, Prorogue, Rope, Standstill, STOP, Toho, Tyburn-tippet, Whoa

**Ham(s)** Amateur, Barnstormer, Gammon, Haunch, Hock, Hoke, Hough, Hunker, Jambon, Jay, Nates, Overact, Overplay, Parma, Prat, Prosciutto, Tiro, York

**Hamfisted** Maladroit, Unheppen

**Hamite** Berber, Nilot(e)

**Hamlet** Aldea, Auburn, Cigar, Dane, Dorp, Hero, Kraal, Stead, Thorp(e), Vill(age), Wick

**Hammer(ed), Hammerhead** Beetle, Bully, Celt, Claw, Excudit, Flatten, Fuller, Gavel, Incuse, Knap, Madge, Mall(et), Malleate, Martel, Maul, Mjol(l)nir, Oliver, Pane, Pean, Peen, Pene, Plessor, Plexor, Repoussé, Sheep's-foot, Shingle, Sledge, Strike, Umbre, Wippen

> **Hammered** may indicate an anagram

**Hammerthrower** Thor

**Hammock** Cott

> **Hammy** may indicate an anagram

**Hamper** Basket, Ceroon, Cramp, Cumber, Delay, Encumber, Entrammel, Handicap, Hobble, Obstruct, Pad, Pannier, Ped, Pinch, Restrict, Rub, Sero(o)n, Shackle, Tangle, Trammel, Tuck

**Hamster** Cricetus

**Hamstring** Cramp, Hock, Hox, Lame, Popliteal, Thwart

**Hand(s), Hand down, Hand-like, Handwriting** Assist(ance), Bananas, Bequeath, Calligraphy, Chicane, Chirography, Claque, Clutch, Copperplate, Crew, Cursive, Daddle, Deal, Deliver, Devolve, Dukes, Dummy, Famble, Fin, Fist, Flipper, Flush, Help, Hond, Impart, Israel, Italian, Jambone, Jamboree, Kana, L, Man, Manual, Manus, Medieval, Mitt(en), Nes(h)ki, Operative, Pad, Palm(atifid), Pass, Paw, Podium, Post, Pud, R, Rein (arm), Script, Signature, Span, Straight, Text, Tiger, Widow, Worker, Yarborough

**Handbag** Caba(s), Grip, Purse, Reticule, Valise

**Handbook** Baedeker, Guide, Manual, Vade-mecum

**Handcuff(s)** Bracelet, Darbies, Irons, Manacle, Mittens, Nippers, Snaps

**Handful** Few, Gowpen, Grip, Problem, Pugil, Rip(p), V

**Handicap** Bisque, Burden, Ebor, Encumber, Hamper, Impede, Impost, Lincolnshire, OBSTACLE, Off, Restrict, Welter-race

**Handkerchief, Hanky** Bandan(n)a, Belcher, Billy, Clout, Fogle, Foulard,

Madam, Madras, Monteith, Muckender, Nose-rag, Orarium, Romal, Rumal, Sudary, Tissue, Wipe(r)

**Handle(d)** Ansate, Bail, Bale, Brake, Broomstick, Cope, Deal, Doorknob, Dudgeon, Ear, Finger, Forename, Gaum, Gorm, Grip, Haft, Helve, Hilt, Hold, Knob, Knub, Lug, MANAGE, Manipulate, Manubrium, Maul, Name, Nib, Palp, Paw, Process, Rounce, Shaft, Snath, Snead, Sneath, Sned, Staff, Staghorn, Stale, Steal(e), Steel, Steil, Stele, Stock, Tiller, Title, To-name, Touch, Treat, Use, Wield, Withe

**Handmaid(en)** Iras, Manicurist, Valkyrie

**Hand-out** Alms, Charity, Dole, Gift, Release, Sample

**Hand-signal** Beck(on), Point, Wave

**Handsome** Adonis, Apollo, Bonny, Brave, Comely, Featuous, Gracious, Liberal

**Handspring** Cartwheel

**Hand-warmer** Muff, Pome

**Hand-washer** Pilate

**Handy(man)** Accessible, Close, Convenient, Deft, Dext(e)rous, Digit, Factotum, Jack, Near, Nigh, Palmate, Palmist, Ready, Skilful, Spartan, Useful

**Hang, Hanger, Hanging(s)** Append, Arras, Chick, Chik, Dangle, Darn, Depend, Dewitt, Dossal, Dossel, Dosser, Drape, Droop, Gobelin, Hinge, Hoove, Hove(r), Kilt, Lobed, Loll, Lop, Lynch, Mooch, Noose, Nub, Pend(ant), Sag, Scenery, Scrag, Sit, Sling, Suspend, Suspercollate, Swing, Tapestry, Tapet, Tapis

**Hanger-on** Bur, Lackey, Leech, Limpet, Liripoop, Parasite, Satellite, Sycophant, Toady

**Hangman, Hangmen** Bull, Calcraft, Dennis, Derrick, Gregory, Ketch, Marwood, Nubbing-cove, Pierrepoint

**Hangnail** Agnail

**Hangover** Canopy, Cornice, Crapulence, Drape, DT, Head, Hot coppers, Katzenjammer, Mistletoe, Tester

**Hank** Bobbin, Coil, Fake, Skein

**Hanker** Desire, Envy, Hunger, Itch, Long, Yearn

**Hannibal** Punic

**Hansard** Minutes

**Haphazard** Casual, Chance, Promiscuous, RANDOM, Slapdash

**Happen(ing), Happen to** Afoot, Befall, Befortune, Betide, Come, Event(uate), Fall-out, OCCUR, Pan, Pass, Prove, Tide, Transpire, Worth

**Happiness, Happy** Ave, Beatific, Beatitude, Blessed, Bliss, Bonny, Carefree, Cheery, Dwarf, Ecstatic, Elated, Eud(a)emony, Felicity, Fortunate, Glad(some), Gleeful, Golden, Goshen, Halcyon, Hedonism, Jovial, Joy, Larry, Merry, Rapture, Sandboy, Seal, Seel, Sele, Serene, Sunny, Tipsy, Trigger, Warrior

**Hara-kiri** Eventration, Seppuku, Suicide

**Harangue** Declaim, Diatribe, Lecture, Oration, Perorate, Philippic, Sermon, Speech, Spruik, Tirade

**Harass(ed)** Afflict, Annoy, Badger, Bait, Beleaguer, Bother, Chivvy, Distract, Gall, Grill, Grind, Grounden, Hassle, Haze, Heckle, Hector, Hound, Irritate, Persecute, Pester, Plague, Press, Thwart, Trash, Vex

**Harbinger** Herald, Omen, Precursor, Usher

**Harbour** Anchorage, Basin, Brest, Cherish, Dock, Entertain, Herd, Marina, Mulberry, Pearl, PLA, Port, Reset, SHELTER

**Hard(en), Hardness** Abstruse, Adamant(ine), Adularia, Bony, Brinell, Brittle, Cake, Callous, Caramel, Chitin, Cornute, Crusty, Difficult, Draconian, Ebonite, Endure, Enure, Firm, Flint(y), Geal, Granite, Gruelling, H, Hellish, HH, Horny, Inure, Iron(y), Knotty, Liparite, Lithoid, Metallic, Metally, Moh, Nails, Obdurate, Obdure, Osseous, Ossify, Permafrost, Picrite, Raw, Ruthless, Schist, Scleral, Set, Severe, Solid, Sore, Steel(y), Steep, Stereo, Stern, Stoic, Stony, Teak, Temper, Tough

**Hard-core** Riprap, Scalpins

**Harding** Warden

**Hardly** Borderline, Ill, Just, Scarcely, Uneath(es), Unnethes

**Hard-pressed** Strait, Taxed

**Hardship** Affliiction, Grief, Mill, Mishap, Penance, Privation, Rigour, Trial, Trouble

**Hardware** Gear, Ironmongery

**Hardy** Brave, Dour, Durable, Manful, Oliver, Ollie, Rugged, Spartan, Sturdy, Thomas

**Hare** Baud(rons), Bawd, Doe, Dolicholis, Down, Electric, Husk, Lam, Leporine, Malkin, Mara, Ochotona, Pika, Puss, Scut, Wat

**Hare-brained** Giddy, Madcap, Scatty

**Harem** Gynaeceum, Gynoecium, Seraglio, Serai(l), Zenana

**Hark(en)** Ear, Hear, List(en)

**Harlequin** Chequered, Columbine, Pantaloon

**Harlot** Blue gown, Drab, Hussy, Loose, Paramour, Plover, Pusle, Pussel, Quail, Rahab, Slut, Strumpet, Whore

**Harm(ed), Harmful** Aggrieve, Bane, Deleterious, Evil, Hurt, Inimical, Injury, Malignant, Maltreat. Mischief, Noxious, Pernicious, Sinister, Spoil, Wroken, Wrong

**Harmless** Benign, Canny, Drudge, Informidable, Innocent, Innocuous, Inoffensive

**Harmonica** Harpoon

**Harmonious, Harmonise, Harmony** Agree(ment), Alan, Atone, Attune, Balanced, Blend, Chord, Concent, Concert, Concinnity, Concord, Congruous, Consort, Correspondence, Counterpoint, Descant, Diapason, Diatessaron, Euphony, Eur(h)ythmy, Faburden, Jibe, Melody, Musical,

Symmetry, Sympathy, Thorough-bass, Tune, Unanimity, Unison

**Harmotome** Cross-stone

**Harness(maker)** Breeching, Bridle, Cinch, Equipage, Frenum, Gear, Girth, Hitch, Lorimer, Loriner, Pad-tree, Partnership, Tack(le), Trace, Yoke

**Harp(sichord)** Aeolian, Clairschach, Clarsach, Clavier, Drone, Dwell, Lyre, Nebel, Trigon, Virginal, Zither

**Harpagon** Miser

**Harpoon(er)** Bart, Fis(h)gig, Fizgig, Grain, Iron, Peg, Spear, Specktioneer, Tow-iron, Trident

**Harpy** Eagle

**Harridan** Hag, Harpy, Shrew, Xantippe, Zantippe, Zentippe

**Harriet** Hetty, Martineau

**Harrow** Alas, Appal, Brake, Disc, Frighten, Herse, Plough, Rake, Rend, Shock

**Harry** Aggravate, Badger, Champion, Chase, Chivvy, Coppernose, Dragoon, Flash, Fret, Hal, Harass, Hector, Herry, Houdini, Hound, Lauder, Lime, Maraud, Molest, Nag, Pester, Plague, Rag, Reave, Reive, Rieve, Rile, Tate, Tchick, Torment

> **Harry** may indicate an anagram

**Harsh(ness)** Acerbic, Austere, Barbaric, Brassy, Cruel, Desolate, Discordant, Draconian, Grating, Gravelly, Grim, Gruff, Hard, Inclement, Raucle, Raucous, Raw, Rigour, Rude, Scabrid, SEVERE, Sharp, Spartan, Stark, Stern, Stoor, Stour, Stowre, Strict, Strident

**Hart** Deer, Spade, Spay, Spay(a)d, Venison

**Hartebeest** Kaama

**Harum-scarum** Bayard, Chaotic, Madcap, Rantipole

**Harvest(er), Harvest home** Combine, Crop, Cull, Fruit, GATHER, Hairst, Hawkey, Hay(sel), Hockey, Horkey, In(ning), Kirn, Lease, Nutting, Pick, Produce, Rabi, Random, Reap, Shock, Spatlese, Tattie-howking, Thresh, Vendage

**Has** Habet, Hath, 's, Owns

**Has-been** Effete, Ex, Outmoded

**Hash** Bungle, Discuss, Garble, Garboil, Hachis, Lobscouse, Mince, Pi(e), Ragout

> **Hashed** may indicate an anagram

**Hasn't** Hant, Nas

**Hassle** Aggro, Bother

**Hassock** Kneeler, Pouf(fe), Stool, Tuffet

**Haste(n), Hastening, Hastily, Hasty** Cursory, Despatch, Express, Festinately, Fly, Hare, Headlong, Hie, Hotfoot, HURRY, Impetuous, Race, Ramstam, Rash, Rush, Scuttle, Speed, Spur, Stringendo, Subitaneous, Sudden, Tear, Tilt

**Hastings**  Banda, Bustles, Senlac, Warren

**Hat**  Ascot, Balibuntal, Balmoral, Basher, Beanie, Beany, Bearskin, Beaver, Beret, Billycock, Biretta, Boater, Bowler, Boxer, Brass, Breton, Busby, Cap, Cartwheel, Castor, Chapeau, Cheese-cutter, Chimneypot, Claque, Cloche, Cockle-hat, Curch, Deerstalker, Derby, Dunstable, Fedora, Fez, Fore-and-after, Gibus, Glengarry, Hattock, Headdress, Head-rig, Hennin, Homburg, Kamelaukion, Leghorn, Lid, Lum, Mitre, Mob-cap, Mushroom, Nab, Opera, Pagri, Panama, Petasus, Pill-box, Plateau, Poke(-bonnet), Pork-pie, Puggaree, Ramil(l)ies, Runcible, Shako, Shovel, Slouch, Snood, Sola(-helmet), Sola-topi, Sombrero, Souwester, Steeple-crown, Stetson, Stovepipe, Straw, Sundown, Tam(o'shanter), Tarboosh, Tarb(o)ush, Terai, Tile, Titfer, Toorie, Topee, Topi, Topper, Toque, Tricorn(e), Trilby, Turban, Tyrolean, Ugly, Wide-awake

**Hat-band**  Weeper

**Hatch(ment), Hatching**  Achievement, Breed, Brood, Cleck, Clutch, Concoct, Cover, Devise, Eclosion, Emerge, Incubate, Set, Trap-door

**Hatchet(-shaped)**  Axe, Bill, Chopper, Cleaver, Dolabriform, Tomahawk

> **Hatching**  may indicate an anagram

**Hatchway (surround)**  Fiddley, Porthole, Scuttle

**Hate(ful), Hatred**  Abhor, Abominable, Abominate, Aversion, Bugbear, Detest, Enmity, Haterent, Loathe, Misogyny, Odium, Phobia, Spite, Ug(h)

**Hat-plant**  S(h)ola

**Hatty**  Etta

**Haughty**  Aristocratic, Arrogant, Bashaw, Disdainful, High, Hogen-mogen, Hyc, Lofty, Orgillous, Orgulous, PROUD, Scornful, Sdeignful, Sniffy, Upstage

**Haul**  Bag, Bouse, Bowse, Brail, Carry, Cart, Catch, Drag, Heave, Hove, Loot, Plunder, Pull, Rug, Sally, Snig, Touse, Touze, Tow(se), Towze, Trice, Winch, Yank

**Haunch**  Hance, Hip, Huckle, Hunkers, Quarter

**Haunt**  Catchy, Den, Dive, Frequent, Ghost, Hang-out, Houf(f), Howf(f), Infest, Obsess, Resort, Spot, Spright

**Hauteur**  Bashawism, Height, Morgue, Vanity

**Have, Having**  Bear, Ha(e), Han, Hoax, Hold, Of, OWN, Possess, Sell

**Haven**  Asylum, Harbour, Hithe, Hythe, Oasis, Port, Retreat

**Haver(s)**  Blether, Clanjamfray, Dither, Gibber, Nigel

**Havoc**  Desolation, Devastation, Hell, Ravage, Waste

> **Havoc**  may indicate an anagram

**Haw**  Hip, Sloe

**Hawaiian**  Kanaka

**Hawk(er)**  Accipitrine, Auceps, Badger, Bastard, Buzzard, Cadger, Camelot, Caracara, Cast, Cheapjack, Eagle, Elanet, Eyas, Falcon,

Gerfalcon, Goshawk, Haggard, Harrier, Hobby, Keelie, Kestrel, Kite, Lammergeier, Lanner(et), Merlin, Molla(h), Monger, Moolah, Mullah, Musket, Nyas, Osprey, Ossifrage, Pearlie, Pearly, Pedlar, Peddle, Peregrine, Sacre(t), Sell, Soar(e), Sorage, Sore(-eagle), Sparrow, Spiv, Staniel, Sutler, Tallyman, Tarsal, Tarsel(l), Tassel, Tercel(et), Tiersel, Trant(er)

**Hawkeye** IA, Iowa

**Hawk-keeper** Austringer, Ostreger

**Hawser** Line, Rope

**Hawthorn** Albespine, Abespyne, May(flower), Quickset

**Hay, Hey** Antic, Cock, Contra-dance, Fodder, Goaf, Hi, Kemple, Math, Mow, Pleach, Stack, Straw, Windrow

**Haymaker** Blow, Slog

**Hayseed** Chaw-bacon, Hodge, Rustic

**Hazard(ous)** Bunker, Chance, Danger, Dare, Die, Dye, Game, Imperil, In-off, Jeopardy, Main, Nice, Peril, Play, Queasy, RISK, Stake, Venture, Wage

**Haze, Hazy** Blear, Cloud, Filmy, Fog, MIST, Mock, Muzzy, Nebulous, Smog, Tease

> **Haze** may indicate an anagram

**Hazel(wort)** Amenta, Asarabacca, Catkin, Cob, Corylus, Filbert

**HC** Encomia, Encomium

**He, HE** A, Helium, Tag, TNT

**Head(s), Heading, Headman, Heady** Aim, Apex, Ard-ri(gh), Beachy, Bean, Behead, Bill, Block, Bonce, Boss, Brain, Bregma, Brow, But(t), Caboceer, Cape, Capitani, Capitulum, Capo, Captain, Caption, Caput, Caudillo, Chaton, Chief, Coarb, Coconut, Coma, Commander, Conk, Cop, Costard, Crest, Crisis, Crown, Crumpet, Director, Dome, Each, Ear, Exarch, Figure, Froth, Herm(a), Hoe, Hogh, Jowl, Knob, Knowledge-box, Lead(er), Lid, Loaf, Loave, Loo, Lore, Malik, Manager, Mayor, Maz(z)ard, Melik, Mocuddum, Mokaddam, Mull, Muqaddam, Nab, Nana, Napper, Nappy, Ness, Nob, Noddle, Noggin, Noll, Noup, Nowl, Nut, Obverse, Occiput, Onion, Pash, Pate, Pater(familias), Patriarch, Point, Poll, Pow, Prefect, President, Principal, Promontory, Provost, Ras, Ream, Rubric, Sarpanch, Scalp, Scaup, Scaw, Scholarch, Sconce, Sinciput, Skaw, Skull, Source, Spume, Squeers, Starosta, Superior, Tanadar, Tete, Thanadar, Title, Toilet, Top, Topic, Twopenny, Vaivode, Voivode, Yorick, Zupan

> **Head** may indicate the first letter of a word

**Headache** Hangover, Megrim, Migraine, Neuralgia, Scotodinia, Splitter

**Headband** Fillet, Garland, Infula, Sphendone

**Headdress, Head cover** Balaclava, Bandeau, Bas(i)net, Bonnet, Burnous(e), Calotte, Caul, Chaplet, Circlet, Comb, Cor(o)net, Cowl, Coxcomb, Crownet, Curch, Doek, Dopatta, Dupatta, Fascinator, Fontange, Hat(tock), Helm(et), Juliet cap, Kaffiyeh, Kuffiyeh, Kufiah, Kufiya(h), Kell, Kerchief, Mantilla, Modius, Nubia, Periwig, Pill-box, Porringer,

Romal, Ship-tire, Silly-how, Stephane, Tarbush, Tiara, Tower, Tulban, Turban, Wig, Wimple

**Header** Bonder, Dive, Fall

**Headhunter** Naga

**Headland** Bill, Cape, Head-rig, Hoe, Hogh, Naze, Ness, Noup, Promontory, Ras, Ross, Scaw, Skaw

**Headless** Acephalous

**Headlight** Beam, Dip, Halo

**Headline** Banner, Caption, Frown, Scare-head, Screamer, Streamer, Title

**Headlock** Chancery

**Headlong** Precipitate, Ramstam, Reckless, Steep, Sudden, Tantivy, Tearaway

> **Headman** see HEAD

**Headmaster** Principal, Squeers

**Headphone(s)** Cans, Earpiece, Walkman

**Headquarters** Base, Command, Depot, Guildhall, Pentagon, SHAPE, Station

**Headstrong** Obstinate, Rash, Stubborn, Unruly, Wayward

**Head-to-tail** Tête-bêche

**Headway** Advancement, Headroom, Progress

**Head-word** Lemma

**Heal(ing)** Aesculapian, Balsam, Chiropractic, Cicatrise, Cleanse, Cure, Esculapian, G(u)arish, Hele, Hippocratise, Knit, Mend, Olosis, Osteopathy, Restore, Sain, Salve, Sanitory, Therapeutic

**Healer** Asa, Doctor, Homeopath, Naturopath, Osteopath, Shaman, Time

**Health(y)** Bracing, Chin-chin, Doer, Fit, Flourishing, Gesundheit, Hail, Hale, Hartie-hale, Heart, Kia-ora, Lustique, Lusty, Pink, Prosit, Robust, Salubrious, Sane, Slainte, Sound, Toast, Vigour, Well, WHO, Wholesome

**Heap(ed)** Acervate, Agglomerate, Amass, Bing, Bulk, Car, Clamp, Cock, Concervate, Congeries, Cumulus, Drift, Hog, Jalopy, Lot, Pile, Rick(le), Ruck, Scrap, Stash, Tass, Toorie, Up-piled

**Hear(ing)** Acoustic, Attend, Audience, Audile, Clairaudience, Dirdum, Ear, Harken, List(en), Oyer, Oyez

> **Hear(say)** may indicate a word sounding like one given

**Hearsay** Account, Gossip, Report, Rumour, Surmise

**Hearse** Bier, Catafalco, Catafalque

**Heart(en), Hearty, Heart-shaped** AB, Auricle, Beater, Bluff, Bosom, Cant, Cardiac, Centre, Cheer, Cockles, Columella, Cordate, Cordial, Core, Crossed, Courage, Daddock, Embolden, Essence, Gist, H, Hale, Herz, Inmost, Jarta, Kernel, Lepid, Mesial, Mid(st), Nucleus, Obcordate, Purple, Robust, Sacred, Sailor, Seafarer, Seaman, Staunch, Tar, Ticker, Yarta, Yarto

**Heart-break** Crève-coeur, Grief, Sorrow

**Heartfelt** Deep, Genuine, Real, Sincere

**Hearth** Cupel, Fireside, Home, Ingle

**Heartless** Callous, Cored, Cruel, Three-suited

**Heart's ease** Pansy

**Heat(ed), Heater, Heating** Anneal, Ardour, Barrage, Beath, Brazier, Califont, Caloric, Calorifier, Central, Chafe, Dudgeon, Eccaleobion, Element, Eliminator, Endothermic, Enthalpy, Etna, Excite, Exothermic, Ferment, Fever, Fire, Fluster, Fug, Furnace, Het, Hibachi, Hypocaust, Immersion, J, Kindle, Lust, Moxibustion, Normalise, Oestrus, Prelim, Radiator, Rankine, Repechage, Rut, Salt, Scald, Sinter, Sizzle, Specific, Spice, Stew, Storage, Stove, Teend, Tind, Tine, Tynd(e), Warmth

**Heath** Bearberry, Bent, Briar, Brier, Egdon, Epacrid, Erica, Lande, Manoao, Manzanita, Moor, Muir, Stead, Ted

**Heathen** Ethnic, Gentile, Infidel, Litholatrous, Pagan, Pa(i)nim, Paynim, Philistine, Primitive, Profane

**Heather** Broom, Calluna, Epacrid, Erica, Ling, Sprig

> **Heating** may indicate an anagram

**Heave(d)** Cast, Fling, Heeze, Hoist, Hump, Hurl, Popple, Retch, Shy, Sigh, Vomit

> **Heave** may indicate 'discard'

**Heaven(s), Heavenly** Aloft, Ama, Asgard, Bliss, Celestial, Divine, Ecstasy, Elysian, Elysium, Empyrean, Ethereal, Fiddler's Green, Firmament, Hereafter, Himmel, Holy, Leal, Lift, Mackerel, Olympus, Paradise, Pole, Seventh, Shangri-la, Sion, Sky, Supernal, Svarga, Swarga, Swerga, Tur-na-n'og, Uranian, Welkin, Zion

**Heavy(weight), Heavily** Ali, Dutch, Endomorph, Grave, Hefty, Last, Leaden, Onerous, Osmium, Pesante, Ponderous, Sad, Scelerate, Stout, Upsee, Ups(e)y, Weighty, Wicked

**Hebe** Barmaid

**Hebrew** Aramaic, Eli, Heb, Jesse, Levi, Mishnayoth, Yid

**Hebridean** Harris

**Heckle** Badger, Gibe, Harass, Needle

**Hectic** Ding-dong, Feverish, Frenetic

**Hector** Badger, Bluster, Browbeat, Bully, HARASS, Nag

**Hedge, Hedging** Box, Bullfinch, Enclosure, Haw, Hay, Meuse, Mews, Muse, Pleach, Privet, Quickset, Raddle, Sepiment, Shield, Stonewall, Thicket

**Hedgehog** Gymnure, Hérisson, Tenrec, Tiggywinkle, Urchin

**Hedge-parson** Bucklebeggar, Patercove

**Hedge-sparrow** Accentor

**Hedonist** Cyreniac, Epicurean, Playboy

**Heed(ed), Heedful**  Attend, Listen, MIND, Notice, Observe, Rear, Reck, Regard(ant), Respect, Rought, Tent

**Heedless**  Careless, Rash, Scapegrace, Scatterbrain

**Heel**  Cad, Calcaneum, Cant, Careen, Cuban, Dogbolt, Foot, List, Louse, Rogue, Seel, Stiletto, Tilt, Wedge

**Heel-tap**  Snuff

**Hefty**  Brawny, Heavy, Weighty

**Heifer**  Io, Quey, Stirk

**Height(en), Heights**  Abraham, Altitude, Cairngorm, Ceiling, Dimension, Elevation, Embroider, Eminence, Enhance, Golan, H, Hill, Level, Peak, Stature, Stud, Sum, SUMMIT, Tor

**Heinous**  Abominable, Atrocious, Flagrant

**Heir**  Alienee, Claimant, Coparcener, Dauphin, Devisee, Eigne, Institute, Intitule, Legatee, Parcener, Scion, Sprig, Tanist

**Heirless**  Escheat, Intestate

**Held**  Captive, Hostage, Sostenuto

> **Held by**  may indicate a hidden word

**Helen**  Nell(y)

**Helicopter, Heliport**  Airstop, Chopper, Egg-beater, Hover, Rotodyne, Whirlybird

**Helios**  Hyperion

**Helium**  He

**Hell(ish)**  Abaddon, Ades, Amenthes, Annw(yf)n, Avernus, Below, Chthonic, Dis, Erebus, Furnace, Gehenna, Hades, Heck, Inferno, Malebolge, Naraka, Orcus, Perditious, Pit, Sheol, Stygian, Tartar(ean), Tartarus, Tophet, Torment

**Hellbender**  Menopome, Mud-puppy

**Hellebore**  Itchweed, Setterwort

**Hellespont**  Dardanelles

**Hello, Hallo, Hullo**  Aloha, Chin-chin, Ciao, Hi, Ho(a), Howdy

**Helm(sman)**  Cox, Pilot, Steer, Tiller, Timon(eer)

**Helmet**  Armet, Balaclava, Basinet, Beaver, Burganet, Burgonet, Cask, Casque, Comb, Crash, Galea, Heaume, Knapscal, Knapscull, Knapskull, Mor(r)ion, Nasal, Pickelhaube, Pith, Pot, Salade, Sal(l)et, Shako, Topee, Topi

**Helot**  Esne, Slave

**Help(er), Helping, Helpful**  Abet, Adjuvant, Advantage, Aid(ance), Aidant, Aide, Alleviate, Ally, ASSIST, Avail, Back, Benefit, Befriend, Bestead, Boon, Char(woman), Coadjutor, Daily, Dollop, Dose, Forward, Further(some), Go, Hand, Hint, Instrumental, Mayday, Obliging, Order, Patronage, Ration, Recourse, Servant, Serve, Slice, SOS, Stead, Subserve, Subvention, Succour, Taste

**Helpless(ness)** Adynamia, Anomie, Feeble, Impotent, Paralytic, Useless

**Hem** Border, Fringe, Hoop, List

**He-man** Adonis, Hunk, Jock, Macho

**Hemisphere, Hemispherical** Magdeburg, Rose-cut

**Hemlock** Conia, Cowbane, Insane root, Tsuga

**Hemp** Abaca, Choke-weed, Codilla, Dagga, Fimble, Ganja, K(a)if, Kef, Manilla, Moorva, Murva, Pita, Sida, Sunn, Tat, Tow

**Hen** Ancona, Andalusian, Australorp, Biddy, Buff Orpington, Chock, Cochin, Eirack, Fowl, Houdan, Langshan, Layer, Leghorn, Partlet, Pertelote, Poulard, Pullet, Ree(ve), Sitter, Sultan, Tappit, Welsummer, Wyandotte

**Hence** Apage, Avaunt, Ergo, Go, Hinc, So, Therefore, Thus

**Henchman** Attendant, Follower, Satellite

**Hen-house** Battery, Eggery

**Hen-pecked** Spineless, Woman-tired

**Henna** Camphire

**Hennery** Run

**Henry** Eighth, H, Hal, Hy, James, Navigator, O

**Hep** Bacca, Berry, Hip

**Hepatic** Scale-moss

**Hepatitis** Favism, Jaundice

**Herald(ic), Heraldry** Abatement, Argent, Armory, Azure, Bars, Bend, Bloody Hand, Bluemantle, Bordure, Caboched, Chevron, Chief, Cicerone, Cinquefoil, Clarenc(i)eux, Compony, Couchant, Counter-passant, Coue, Couped, Coward, Crier, Difference, Displayed, Dormant, Endorse, Erased, Fecial, Fess(e), Fetial, File, Forerunner, Gardant, Garter, Golp(e), Gules, Hauriant, Hermes, Issuant, Lodged, Lyon, Martlet, Messenger, Mullet, Naiant, Nascent, Norroy, Opinicus, Or, Ordinary, Pale, Pallet, Passant, Pile, Portcullis, Precursor, Proclaim, Purpure, Pursuivant, Quartering, Rampant, Red Hand, Regardant, Roundel, Roundle, Sable, Salient, Sea lion, Sejant, Statant, Stentor, Trangle, Tressure, Trippant, Urinant, Usher, Verdoy, Vert, Vol(ant)

**Herb(s)** Aconite, Aristolochia, Avens, Basil, Bay, Bennet, Bergamot, Borage, Chervil, C(h)ive, Cilanto, Comfrey, Coriander, Costmary, Cum(m)in, Dill, Dittany, Eruca, Exacum, Eyebright, Fennel, Ferula, Feverfew, Fireweed, Fluellin, Forb, Garlic, Garnish, Gentian, Germander, Good-King-Henry, Gunnera, Hyssop, Inula, Knapweed, Laserpicium, Laserwort, Lovage, Mandrake, Marjoram, Maror, Medic, Mint, Moly, Mustard, Oca, Oleraceous, Oregano, Origan(e), Ornithogalum, Parsley, Pia, Plantain, Purpie, Purslane, Rest-harrow, Rodgersia, Rosemary, Rue, Sage, Savory, Senna, Sesame, Sorrel, Southernwood, Spearmint, Staragen, Tacca, Tansy, Tarragon, Thyme, Tormentil, Typha, Valerian, Vervain, Weed, Wort, Yarrow, Yerba

**Herbert**  Alan, AP(H), Lom, Spencer

**Herbivore**  Sauropod

**Hercules**  Alcides, Huge, Rustam, Rustem

**Herd(er), Herdsman**  Band, Corral, Drive, Drover, Flock, Gang, Pod, Raggle-taggle, Round-up, Shepherd, Tinchel, Vaquero

**Here**  Adsum, Hi, Hic, Hither, Local, Now, Present

**Hereditary, Heredity**  Ancestry, Blood, Breeding, Codon, Genetics, Id(ant), Idioplasm, Mendelism

> **Herein**  may indicate a hidden word

**Here is laid**  HS

**Heresiarch**  Nestor

**Heresy, Heretic**  Agnoitae, Albigensian, Apostasy, Arian, Bogomil, Bugger, Docete, Dulcinist, Eudoxian, Giaour, Heterodoxy, Lollard, Montanism, Nonconformist, Origen, Patarin(e), Phrygian, Racovian, Rebel, Unitarian

**Heritage**  Birthright, Due, Ottilie

**Hermaphrodite**  Androgenous, Gynandromorph, Monochinous, Monoecious

**Hermes (rod)**  Caduceus, Mercury

**Hermetic**  Alchemist, Sealed

**Hermit(age)**  Anchorite, Ascetic, Ashram(a), Austin, Cell, Cloister, Crab, Eremite, Grandmontine, Marabout, Monk, Museum, Nitrian, Peter, Recluse, Retreat, Robber-crab, Sannyasi, Soldier-crab, Solitary

**Hernia**  Enterocele, Rupture

**Hero(ic)**  Achilles, Agamemnon, Aitu, Ajax, Alcides, Amadis, Bellerophon, Beowulf, Brave, Champ(ion), Cid, Couplet, Crockett, Cuchulain, Cyrano, Demigod, Epic, Eponym, Eric, Faust, Fingal, Finn, Garibaldi, God, Goody, Great, Hector, Heracles, Hercules, Hiawatha, Howleglass, Ideal, Idol, Jason, Kami, Leonidas, Lion, Lochinvar, Lothair, Marmion, Meleager, Nestor, Noble, Oliver, Owl(e)glass, Ow(l)spiegle, Paladin, Parsifal, Pericles, Perseus, Priestess, Principal, Resolute, Revere, Rinaldo, Roderick, Roderego, Roland, Rustem, Rustum, Saladin, Sheik, Siegfried, Sigurd, Tam o'Shanter, Tancred, Tell, Theseus, Triptolemus, Tristan, Trist(r)am, Ulysses, Valiant, Vercingetorix, Volsung

**Herod**  Agrippa

**Heroin**  Dogfood, Doojie, Dynamite, Gumball, H, Harry, Henry, Horse, Jack, Junk, Scag, Skag, Smack, Snow, Sugar

**Heroine**  Andromeda, Candida, Darling, Hedda, Imogen, Isolde, Juliet, Mimi, Nana, Norma, Pamela, Star, Tess, Una

**Heron(s)**  Ardea, Bird, Bittern, Butter-bump, Egret, Handsaw, Kotuko, Screamer, Sedge, Siege, Squacco

**Herpes**  Dartre, Shingles

**Herring** Bismarck, Bloater, Brisling, Brit, Buckling, Caller, Cisco, Clupea, Kipper, Maise, Maize, Ma(a)tjes, Mattie, Maze, Mease, Menhaden, Red, Rollmop, Sea-stick, Shotten, Sild, Silt

**Herringbone** Sloping

**Hesitate, Hesitation** Balance, Boggle, Delay, Demur, Dicker, Dither, Doubtful, Falter, Haver, Haw, Mammer, PAUSE, Qualm, Scruple, Shillyshally, Shrink, Stagger, Stammer, Swither, Tarrow, Um, Ur, Vacillate, Waver

**Hesperus** Vesper

**Hessian** Burlap, Hireling

**Heterodoxy** Heresy

**Heterogeneous** Diverse, Motley

**Hew** Ax, Chop, Cut, Hack, Sever

**Hex** Jinx, Voodoo

> **Hey** see HAY

**Heyday** Prime

**Hi** Cooee, Hello

**Hiatus** Caesura, Gap, Hernia, Interregnum, Lacuna, Lull

**Hibernate** Estivate, Sleep, Winter

**Hibernian** Irish

**Hibiscus** Okra, Roselle, Rozelle

**Hiccup** Glitch, Singultus, Snag, Spasm, Yex

**Hick** Jake, Podunk, Rube, Yokel

**Hickory** Jackson, Pecan, Shagbark

**Hidden** Buried, Covert, De(a)rn, Doggo, Hooded, Latent, Obscure, Occult, Pentimento, Recondite, Screened, Shuttered, Sly, Ulterior, Veiled, Wrapped

> **Hidden** may indicate a concealed word

**Hide, Hiding** Abscond, Befog, Bield(y), Box-calf, Burrow, Cache, Camouflage, Ceroon, Coat, CONCEAL, Cordwain, Couch, Cour, Crop, Curtain, Doggo, Earth, Eclipse, Encave, Ensconce, Envelop, Epidermis, Fell, Flaught, Flay, Harbour, Heal, Heel, Hele, Hell, Incave, Inter, Kip, Lair, Leather, Mask, Nebris, OBSCURE, Parfleche, Pell, Pelt, Plank, Plant, Robe, Screen, Secrete, Shadow, Shellac(k), Skin, Spetch, Stash, Strap-oil, Tappice, Thrashing, Trove, Veil, Wallop, Wrap

**Hideous(ness)** Deform(ed), Enormity, Gash, Grotesque, Horrible, Odious, Ugly, Ugsome

**Hierarchic, Hierarchy** Byzantine, Elite, Theocracy

**Hieroglyph** Cipher, Pictogram

**Higgledy-piggledy** Mixtie-maxtie

**High(er), Highly** Alt(a), Altissimo, Apogee, Atop, Brent, Climax, Drugged, E-la, Elation, Elevated, Eminent, Exalted, Excelsior, Frequency,

Gamy, Haut(e), Intoxicated, Lofty, Orthian, Prime, Ripe, School, Senior, Sent, Shrill, So, Steep, Stoned, Strong, Superior, Swollen, Tall, Tension, Top-lofty, Topmost, Treble, Up(per), Very, Wired

> **High** may indicate an anagram

**High and mighty** Haughty, Hogen-mogen

**Highball** Drink, Lob, Loft

**Highbrow** Brain, Egghead, Intelligentsia

**High-class** Best, Superior, U

**High-crowned** Copataine

**Highest** Best, Climax, Mostwhat, Supreme

**Highest note** E-la

**High-flown** Bombastic, Euphuism

**Highland(er)** Blue-bonnet, Blue-cap, Cameron, Cat(h)eran, Down, Dun(n)iewassal, Duniwassal, Gael, Kiltie, Nainsel(l), Plaid(man), Redshank, Riff, Scot, Seaforth, Teuchter

**Highlight** Feature, Focus, Heighten, Stress

> **High-pitched** see HIGH

**High tension** HT

**Highway** Autobahn, Autopista, Autostrada, Flyover, Freeway, Motorway, Overpass, Pass, Thoroughfare, Tightrope

**Highwayman, Highway robber(y)** Bandit, Bandolero, Duval, Footpad, Fraternity, Gilderoy, Jack Sheppard, Land-pirate, Land-rat, Latrocinium, MacHeath, Motorist, Rank-rider, Scamp, Skyjacker, Toby, Turpin, Twitcher, Wheel

**Hijack(er)** Abduct, Pirate

**Hike(r)** Backpack, Rambler, Ramp, Traipse, Tramp, Trape(s), Upraise

**Hilarious, Hilarity** Hysterical, Jollity, Mirth

**Hilary** Term

**Hill(ock), Hills, Hillside** Areopagus, Aventine, Barrow, Beacon, Ben, Bent, Beverly, Bluff, Brae, Butte, Caelian, Calvan, Capitol(ine), Cheviots, Cleve, Cone, Coteau, Crest, Djebel, Drumlin, Dun(e), Esquiline, Fell, Golgotha, Gradient, Grampians, Hammock, Height, Highgate, Horst, How, Hummock, Incline, Inselberg, Jebel, Kip(p), Knap, Knoll, Knot, Kop(je), Koppie, Lavender, Law, Low, Ludgate, Mamelon, Man, Mendip, Mesa, Monadnock, Monticule, Morro, Mound, Nab, Palatine, Pennines, Pike, Pnyx, Quantocks, Quirinal, Rand, Range, Sion, Stoss, Tara, Tel(l), Toft, Toot, Tump, Viminal, Wrekin, Zion

**Hillbilly** Yap

**Hill-dweller** Ant

**Hillman** Areopagite, Nepalese

**Hilltop** Crest, Knoll, Nab

**Hilt** Haft, Handle, Hasp, Shaft

**Him(self)** He, Ipse, Un

**Himalaya(n)** Nepali, Tibetan

**Hind(most)** Back, Deer, Lag, Rear

**Hinder, Hindrance** Back, Bar, Block, Check, Counteract, Cumber, Debar, DELAY, Deter, Estop, Hamper, Harass, Impeach, Impede, Obstacle, Overslaugh, Posterior, Rear, Rein, Remora, Rump, Shackle, Slow, Stop, Stunt, Taigle, Trammel

**Hindquarters** Backside, Crupper, Haunches

**Hindu** Arya Samaj, Babu, Bania(n), Banyan, Brahman, Brahmin, Gentoo, Harijan, Jaina, Kshatriya, Maharishi, Rama, Sad(d)hu, Sankhya, Shaiva, Sheik(h), Sudra, Swami, Trimurti, Urdu, Vais(h)ya, Varna, Vedanta

**Hinge** Cardinal, Cross-garnet, Garnet, Gemel, Gimmer, Joint, Knee, Pivot

> **Hinge(s)** may indicate a word reversal

**Hingeless** Ecardinate

**Hinny** Ass, Donkey, Joe

**Hint** Allude, Clew, Clue, Cue, Element, Gleam, Hunch, Inkle, Inkling, Innuendo, Insinuate, Intimate, Key, Mint, Nuance, Office, Overtone, Pointer, Scintilla, Shadow, Soupçon, SUGGEST, Tang, Tip, Touch, Trace, Trick, Wind, Wink, Wisp, Word, Wrinkle

> **Hint** may indicate a first letter

**Hip(pie), Hippy** Cafard, Cheer, Coxa(l), Drop-out, Huck(le), Informed, Ischium, Sciatic

**Hippopotamus** Behemoth, River-horse, Sea-cow

**Hire(d), Hiring** Affreightment, Charter, Engage, Fee, Freightage, Lease, Merc(enary), Rent, Ticca, Wage

**Hirsute** Hairy, Pilose, Shaggy

> **His** may indicate greetings

**Hiss** Boo, Goose, Hish, Sibilant, Siffle, Sizzle, Swish

**Historian** Acton, Adams, Antiquary, Archivist, Arrian, Asellio, Bede, Biographer, Bryant, Buckle, Camden, Carlyle, Centuriator, Chronicler, Etain, Froude, Gibbon, Gildas, Green, Herodotus, Knickerbocker, Livy, Macaulay, Oman, Pliny, Ponsonby, Renan, Roper, Sallust, Strachey, Suetonius, Tacitus, Thiers, Thucydides, Toynbee, Trevelyan, Wells, Xenophon

**History** Account, Annal, Bunk, Chronicle, Clio, Epoch(a), Ere-now, Ever, Legend, Natural, Ontogency, Past, Record

**Histrionic** Operatic, Theatrical

**Hit** Bang, Bash, Baste, Bat, Belt, Blip, Blow, Bludgeon, Bonk, Bunt, Clobber, Clock, Clout, Collide, Cuff, Dot, Flail, Flip, Foul, Fourpenny-one, Get, Hay, Home( thrust), Impact, Knock, Lam, Mug, Pepper, Prang, Score, Six, Skier, Sky, Slam, Slap, Slosh, Smash(eroo), Smit(e), Sock, Spank, Stoush, Stricken, Strike, Strook, Struck, SUCCESS, Swat, Switch, Thwack, Tip, Tonk, Touché, Venewe, Venue, Wallop, Wing, Ythundered, Zap

**Hitch** Catch, Contretemps, Edge, Espouse, Hike, Hirsle, Hoi(c)k, Hotch, Jerk, Lorry-hop, Rub, Sheepshank, Sheet bend, Shrug, Snag, Technical, Thumb

**Hitherto** Before, Yet

**Hittite** Uriah

**Hive** Skep, Spread, Swarm

**Hoar(y)** Ashen(-grey), Canescent, Froren, Frost, Gaudy-day, Grizzled, Rime

**Hoard(ing)** Accumulate, Amass, Bill, Cache, Eke, Heap, Hoord, Husband, Hutch, Muck(er), Plant, Pose, Save, Sciurine, Snudge, Squirrel, Stash, Stock, Store, Treasure

**Hoarse** Croupy, Grating, Gruff, Husky, Raucous, Roar(er), Roopit, Roopy, Throaty

**Hoax** Bam, Canard, Cod, Do, Doff, Fub, Fun, Gag, Gammon, Gull, Hum, Huntie-gowk, Kid, Leg-pull, Piltdown, Sell, Skit, Spoof, String, Stuff, TRICK

**Hobble, Hobbling** Game, Hamshackle, Hilch, Hitch, Lame, Limp, Pastern, Picket, Spancel, Stagger, Tether

**Hobby** Falcon, Interest, Pastance, PASTIME, Predator, Pursuit, Recreation, Scrimshaw

**Hobby-horse** Dada, Obsession

**Hobgoblin** Bog(e)y, Puck

**Hobnail** Clinker, Tacket

**Hobnob** Chat, Mingle

**Hobo** Bum, TRAMP, Vagrant

**Hock** Cambrel, Dip, Gambrel, Gambril, Gammon, Ham, Heel, Hough, Hypothecate, Pawn, Pledge, Rhenish, Wine

**Hockey** Hurling, Shinny, Shinty

**Hod** Carrier, Tray

**Hodge** Peasant, Rustic, Yokel

**Hoe** Claut, Grub, Jembe, Nab, Pecker, Rake, Scuffle, Weed

**Hog** Babiroussa, Babirussa, Boar, Glutton, Guttle, Peccary, Pig, Porker, Shoat, Shott

**Hogmanay** Ne'erday

**Hog-rat** Hutia

**Hogshead** Butt, Cask, Muid

**Hogwash** Nonsense, Swill, Twaddle

**Hoi-polloi** Prole(tariat), Rabble

**Hoist** Boom, Crane, Davit, Derrick, Gin, Heft, Jack, Lewis, Lift, Raise, Sheerlegs, Sheers, Sway, Teagle, Trice, Whip-and-derry, Wince, Winch, Windas, Windlass

**Hold(er), Holding, Hold back, up, etc** Anchor, Believe, Canister, Cease, Cement, Cinch, Clamp, Clasp, Cling, Clutch, Contain, Cotland, Delay, Detain, Display, Dog, Embrace, Engross, Er, Fast, Fief, Fistful, Frog, Garter, GRASP, Grip, Grovet, Hammerlock, Handle, Haud, Have, Headlock, Heft, Heist, Hinder, Hitch, Ho(a), Hoy, Impedance, Impede, Impediment, Impound, Intern, Keep, Lease, Maintain, Nelson, Own, Proffer, Rack, Reluct, Reserve, Rivet, Rob, Rundale, Runrig, Save, Scissors, Shelve, Shore, Sleeve, Sostenuto, Stand, Suplex, Suspend, Tenancy, Tenement, Tenure, Toft, Tripod, Zarf

**Hole(y)** Agloo, Aglu, Antrum, Aubrey, Cave, Cavity, Cenote, Coalsack, Crater, Cubby, Dell, Den, Dreamhole, Dugout, Earth, Ethmoid, Eye(let), Foramen, Gap, Geat, Gnamma, Gutta, Hideout, Lenticel, Loop, Loup, Lumina, Maar, Mortise, Moulin, Nineteenth, Oillet, OPENING, Orifex, Orifice, Perforate, Pierce, Pigeon, Pit, Pore, Port, Pot, Punctum, Rowport, Sallyport, Scupper, Scuttle, Scye, Slot, Spiraculum, Stead, Stop, Stove, Tear, Thirl, Trema, Vent, Voided, Wookey

**Holiday(s)** Benjo, Break, Ferial, Festa, Fete, Fiesta, Furlough, Gala, Half(term), Laik, Leasure, Leave, Leisure, Long, Outing, Packaged, Pink-eye, Playtime, Repose, Rest, Roman, Seaside, Shabuoth, Shavuot, Sunday, VAC(ATION), Villegiatura, Wakes, Whitsun

**Holinshed** Chronicler

**Holland(s)** Genevese, Gin, Hogen-mogen, Netherlands, NL

**Hollow** Acetabulum, Alveary, Antar, Antre, Antrum, Armpit, Boss, Bowl, Cave(rn), Cavity, Chasm, Cirque, Cleché, Comb(e), Concave, Coomb, Corrie, Cup(mark), Cwm, Deaf, Dean, Dell, Delve, Den(e), Dent, Dimple, Dingle, Dip, Dolina, Doline, Empty, Gilgai, Glenoid, Gnamma-hole, Grot(to), Hole, How, Incavo, Insincere, Keck(sy), Kex, Khud, Lip-deep, Mortise, Namma-hole, Niche, Orbita, Pan, Rut, Scoop, Sinus, Slade, Sleepy, Slot, Slough, Socket, Swirc, Trematic, Trough, Vlei, Vola

**Holly** Aquifoliaceae, Eryngo, Ilex, Mate

**Hollyhock** Althaea

**Hollywood** Bowl

**Holm** Isle

**Holmes** Sherlock, Wendell

**Holmium** Ho

**Hologram, Holograph** Laser, MS

**Holothurian** Trepang

**Holster** Sheath

**Holy(man), Holiness** Adytum, Alliance, Blessed, DIVINE, Godly, Grail, Halidom, Helga, Hery, Khalif, Loch, Mountain, Orders, Pious, Sacred, Sacrosanct, Sad(d)hu, Saintly, Sanctitude, Sannayasi(n), Santon, Sekos, Sepulchre, Shrine, Starets, Staretz, SV, War

**Holy books, Holy writing** Adigranth, Atharvaveda, Bible, Gemara, Granth, Koran, NT, OT, Pia, Purana, Rigveda, SCRIPTURE, Shaster,

Shastra, Smriti, Sura(h), Writ

**Holy building, Holy place** Chapel, Church, Kaaba, Penetralia, Synagogue, Temenos, Temple

**Holy water** Amrit

**Homage** Bow, Cense, Honour, Kneel, Manred, Obeisance, Tribute, Vail

**Home** Abode, Base, Blighty, Cheshire, Clinic, Domal, Domicile, Earth, Fireside, Gaff, Goal, Habitat, Heame, Hearth, Heme, Hospice, House, Libken, Montacute, Nest, Pad, Plas Newydd, Remand, Stately, Villa

**Homecoming** Nostos

**Home counties** SE

**Homer(ic)** Comatose, Cor, Nod, Pigeon, Somnolent

**Home-rule** Parnellism, Swaraj

**Homespun** Plain, Raploch, Russet, Simple

**Homestead** Ranch, Toft

**Homework** Prep

**Homicide** Killing, Manslaughter

**Homily** Lecture, Pi, Postil, Prone, Sermon

> **Homing** may indicate coming back

**Hominid** Oreopitheous

**Homosexual(ity)** Bardash, Bender, Camp, Cat, Dike, Dyke, Fag(g)ot, Fairy, Fruit, Gay, Ginger, Invert, Lesbian, Poof(tah), Poofter, Poove, Pouf(fe), Poufter, Puff, Quean, Queer, Quiff, Tonk, Tribade, Uranism, Urning, Woofter

**Hone** Grind, SHARPEN, Whet

**Honest(y)** Afauld, Afawld, Candour, Clean, Genuine, Injun, Jake, Legitimate, Lunaria, Lunary, Penny, Probity, Righteous, Round, Sincere, Square, Straight, TRUE(penny), Upright

**Honey** Comb, Flattery, Hybla, Hymettus, Mel, Nectar, Oenomel, Peach, Popsy-wopsy, Sis, Sugar, Sweetheart, Sweetie

**Honeycombed** Cellular, Favose, Waxwork

**Honey-eater** Bear, Blue-eye

**Honeypot** Haanepoot

**Honeysuckle** Abelia, Anthemion, Caprifole, Lonicera, Woodbind, Woodbine

**Honorary, Honour(able), Honours, Honorific** Accolade, Ace, Blue, CBE, Commemorate, Credit, Dan, Elate, Emeritus, ESTEEM, Ethic, Face-card, Fame, Fete, Greats, Glory, Homage, Insignia, Invest, King, Knave, Knight, Laudation, Laurels, MBE, Mention, OBE, Pundonor, Queen, Repute, Respect, Revere, Reward, Ten, Titular, Tripos, Venerate, Worship

**Honourable companion** CH

**Honourless** Yarborough

**Hooch** Moonshine

**Hood(ed)** Almuce, Amant, Amice, Amowt, Apache, Balaclava, Bashlyk, Biggin, Blindfold, Calash, Calèche, Calyptra, Capeline, Capuccio, Capuche, Chaperon(e), Coif, Cope, Cowl, Cucullate(d), Gangster, Jacobin, Liripipe, Liripoop, Mantle, Mazarine, Robin, Rowdy, Trot-cosey, Trot-cozy

**Hoodlum** Gangster, Roughneck, Thug

**Hoodwink(ed)** Blear, Bluff, Cheat, DECEIVE, Gull, Nose-led, Seel

**Hoof(ed)** Artiodactyla, Cloot, Coffin, Frog, Trotter, Ungula

**Hoohah** Humdudgeon

**Hook(ed), Hooker** Addict, Adunc, Barb(icel), Becket, Butcher's, Cantdog, Catch, Chape, Claw, Cleek, Clip, Corvus, Crampon, Cromb, Crome, Crook, Crotchet, Cup, Drail, Fish, Gaff, Grapnel, Hamate, Hamose, Heel, Hitch, Inveigle, Kype, Meat, Pot, Prostitute, Snell, Sniggle, Tala(u)nt, Tenaculum, Tenter, Tie, Trip, Uncus, Wanton

**Hookah** Chillum, Hubble-bubble, Pipe

**Hooligan** Apache, Desperado, Drool, Hobbledehoy, Keelie, Larrikin, Lout, Ned, Rough(neck), Ruffian, Skollie, Skolly, Tearaway, Tough, Tsotsi

**Hoop** Bail, Band, Circle, Farthingale, Gird, Girr, Hula, O, RING, Tire, Trochus

**Hooray** Whoopee, Yippee

**Hoot(er)** Deride, Honk, Madge, Nose, Owl, Screech-owl, Siren, Ululate

**Hoover** Dam

**Hop(per)** An(o)ura, Bin, Cuscus, Dance, Flight, Jeté, Jump, Kangaroo, Leap, Lilt, Opium, Pogo, Saltate, Scotch, Skip, Tremié, Vine

**Hope(ful)** Anticipate, Aspirant, Contender, Daydream, Desire, Dream, Esperance, Evelyn, Expectancy, Forlorn, Gleam, Pipe-dream, Promising, Rosy, Sanguine, Trust, Wish

**Hopeless(ness), Hopeless quest** Anomie, Anomy, Black, Despair, Forlorn, Goner, Perdu, Pessimist

**Horace** Flaccus, Ode, Satirist

**Horatio** Nelson

**Horatius** Cocles

**Horde** Many, Mass, Swarm

**Horizon** Scope, Sea-line, Skyline

**Horizontal** Flat, Level, Prone, Supine

**Hormone** Adrenalin, Androsterone, Autacoid, Auxin, Cortisone, Ecdysone, Estrogen, Florigen, Gastrin, Gibberellin, Glucagon, Insulin, Kinin, Oestrogen, Oxytocin, Progesterone, Prolactin, Relaxin, Secretin, Secretion, Steroid, Stilboestrol, Testosterone, Vasopressin

**Horn(y)** Advancer, Amalthea, Antenna(e), Basset, Brass, Bez, Bugle, Cape, Ceratoid, Cor, Cornet, Cornopean, Cornu(a), Cornucopia, Cromorna,

Cromorne, Cusp, Dilemma, Flugel-horn, Frog, Gore, Hooter, HORNBLOWER, Ivory, Keratin, Klaxon, Lur, Morsing, Mot, Oliphant, Plenty, Pryse, Shofar, Spongin, Trey, Trez, Trumpet, Waldhorn

**Hornblower** Brain, Horatio, Peel, Triton, Trumpeter

**Hornbook** Battledoor, Battledore

**Horned (sheep)** Cabrié, Cabrit, Cornute, Hamate, Lunate, Mouflon, Muflon

**Hornless** Doddy, Humbel, Humlie, Hummel, Mooly, Mul(l)ey, Poley, Polled

**Hornpipe** Matelote

**Horoscope** Future, Prophecy, Star-map

**Horrible, Horror** Aw(e)some, Dire, Dread(ful), Execrable, Ghastly, Grisly, Gruesome, Hideous, Odious, Shock, Terror, Ugh

**Horrid, Horrific, Horrify(ing)** Dire, Dismay, Dreadful, Frightful, Ghastly, Gothic, Grim, Grisly, H, Loathy, Odious, Spiteful, Ugly

**Hors d'oeuvres** Antipasto, Canapé, Hummus, Mez(z)e, Pâté, Smorgasbord, Zak(o)uski

**Horse** Airer, Ambler, Appaloosa, Aquiline, Arab, Arion, Arkle, Ass, Aver, Bangtail, Barb, Bathorse, Bay, Bayard, Bevis, Bidet, Black Bess, Bloodstock, Boerperd, Borer, Breaker, Bronco, Brumby, Bucephalus, Buckjumper, Caballine, Calico, Canuck, Caple, Capul, Cavalry, Cayuse, Cert, Charger, Chaser, Clavileno, Clay-bank, Clipper, Clydesdale, Coacher, Cob, Cocktail, Colt, Cooser, Copenhagen, Courser, Crib, Cu(i)sser, Curtal, Cut, Daisy-cutter, Destrier, Dobbin, Doer, Draught, Drier, Dun, Eclipse, Entire, Equine, Eventer, Filly, Foal, Galloway, Ganger, Garran, Garron, Gee, Genet, Gennet, GG, Gringolet, H, Hackney, Hambletonian, Heroin, High, Hobbler, Hobby, Houyhnhnm, Hunter, Hyperion, Incitatus, Jade, Jennet, Kanuck, Keffel, Knight, Kochlani, Kt, Lampos, Liberty, Lipizzaner, Mare, Marengo, Marocco, Morel, Morgan, Morocco, Mudder, Mustang, Nag, Neddy, Outsider, Pacer, Pad, Pad-nag, Palfrey, Pegasus, Percheron, Piebald, Pinto, Plater, Pliohippus, Plug, Pony, Poster, Pot, Prad, Przewalski(s), Punch, Quagga, Randem, Remuda, Ride, Rip, Roan, Roarer, Rocking, Rogue, Rosinante, Rouncy, Rozinante, Runner, Saddler, Schimmel, Screw, Seian, Sense, Sheltie, Shire, Shoo-in, Skewbald, Sleipnir, Sorel(l), Sorrel, Span, Spanker, Springer, Stallion, Starter, Stayer, Steed, Stibbler, String, Stud, Stumer, Summer, Sumpter, Svadilfari, Swallow, Swinger, Tacky, Tak(h)i, Tandem, Tarpan, Tit, Tracer, Trestle, Trojan, Troop, Trot(ter), Vanner, Waler, Warmblood, Warragal, Warragle, Warragul, Warrigal, Wheeler, Whistler, Wooden, Xanthos, Xanthus, Yarraman, Yaud

**Horseback** Croup

**Horse-box** Stable, Stall

**Horse-chestnut** Aesculus, Conker

**Horse collar** Brecham, Hame

**Horse-dealer** Coper

**Horse-disease**  Curb, Dourine, Equinia, Eweneck, Farcy, Fives, Frush, Glanders, Gourdy, Malander, Nagana, Quitter, Quittor, Sallenders, Scratches, Seedy-toe, Strangles, Surra, Sweeny, Thrush, Vives, Wire-heel, Yellows

**Horse-lover**  Philip

**Horseman**  Ataman, Caballero, Cavalry, Centaur, Conquest, Cossack, Cowboy, Death, Dragman, Famine, Farrier, Hussar, Knight, Lancer, Nessus, Ostler, Parthian, Picador, Pricker, Quadrille, Revere, RIDER, Slaughter, Spahi, Stradiot

**Horsemanship**  Manège

**Horseplay**  Caper, Polo, Rag, Rant, Romp

**Horsepower**  Hp, Ps

**Horseradish**  Ben, Moringa

**Horseshoe(-shaped)**  Hippocrepian, Lunette, Plate

**Horsetail**  Equisetum

**Horse thief**  Blanco, Rustler

**Horticulturist**  Grower, RHS

**Hose**  Chausses, Fishnet, Galligaskins, Gaskins, Netherstock(ing), Nylons, Sock, Stockings, Tights, Tube

**Hospitable, Hospitality**  Convivial, Entertainment, Euxine, Lucullan, Philoxenia, Social, Xenial

**Hospital**  Ambulance, Asylum, Barts, Bedlam, Clinic, Cottage, ENT, Guys, H, Home, Hospice, Imaret, Lazaretto, Leprosery, Lock, Nosocomial, Pest-house, San, Scutari, Sick bay, Spital, Spittle, UCH

**Host(ess)**  Amphitryon, Army, Barmecide, Chatelaine, Crowd, Emcee, Entertainer, Hirsel, Hotelier, Innkeeper, Laban, Landlady, Landlord, Legion, Lion-hunter, Lot, Mass, Mavin, MC, Publican, Swarm, Taverner, Throng, Trimalchio

**Hostage**  Pawn, Pledge, POW

**Hostel**  Dorm, Entry, Inn, YHA

**Hostile, Hostility**  Adverse, Aggressive, Alien, Animus, Diatribe, Feud, Hating, Ill, Inimical, Inveterate, War

**Hot (tempered)**  Ardent, Breem, Breme, Cajun, Calid, Candent, Fervid, Feverish, Fuggy, Gospeller, Incandescent, Irascible, Lewd, Mustard, Pepper, Piping, Potato, Randy, Roaster, Scorcher, Sizzling, Spicy, Stewy, Stolen, Sweltry, Tabasco, Thermidor, Torrid, Toustie, Tropical

**Hotchpotch**  Farrago, Mish-mash, Powsowdy, Welter

**Hotel**  Bo(a)tel, Flophouse, Gasthaus, Gasthof, H, Hilton, Hydro, Inn, Motel, Ritz, Savoy, Tavern

**Hothead(ed)**  Impetuous, Rash, Spitfire, Volcano

**Hot-house**  Conservatory, Nursery, Orangery, Vinery

**Hot plate**  Salamander

**Hot rod** Dragster

**Hotspur** Harry, Hothead, Rantipole

**Hottentot** Griqua, Khoikhoi, Strandloper

**Hot water** Soup, Therm

**Hound(s)** Afghan, Basset, Beagle, Brach, Cad, Canine, Cry, DOG, Entry, Harass, Harrier, Hen-harrier, Javel, Kennet, Lyam, Lym(e), Mute, Pack, Pursue, Rache, Ranter, Reporter, Saluki, Talbot, True

**Hound's bane** Palay

**Hour** H, Hr, Complin(e), Elder's, Orthros, Prime, Rush, Sext, Terce, Tide, Time, Vespers, Witching, Zero

**House(s), Household(er)** Althing, Astrology, Audience, Auditorium, B, Bach, Bastide, Beth, Biggin, Bingo, Block, Bondage, Bourbon, Brownstone, Bundestag, Casa, Chalet, Chamber, Chapter, Chateau, Clapboard, Clearing, Commons, Convent, Cote, Crib, Custom, Dacha, Dail, Demain, Demesne, Domal, Domicile, Door, Dwelling, Dynasty, Entertain, Establishment, Este, Firm, Garage, Habitat, Hacienda, Hanover, Harbour, Heartbreak, Hearth, HK, Ho, Home, Igloo, Inn, Insula, Ken, Keys, Knesset, Lagthing, Lancaster, Lords, Lot(t)o, Mansion, Mas, Meinie, Meiny, Ménage, Messuage, Montagne, Odelst(h)ing, Orange, Osborne, Pad, Pent, Plantagenet, Prefab, Quinta, Ratepayer, Residence, Rough, Satis, Scala, Schloss, Seat, Semi, Shanty, Sign, Somerset, Stable, Stuart, Tavern, Terrace, Theatre, Tombola, Trinity, Tudor, Usher, Vicarage, Villa, Wendy, Whare, Windsor, York, Zero

**House-boat** Wanigan

**House-builder** Jack

**House-keeper** Chatelaine, Matron, Publican

**House-leek** Sengreen

**Housemaid's knee** Bursa

**Houseman** Betty, Doctor, Intern, Peer

**Housewarming** Infare

**Housewife** Etui, Needlecase

**Housework** Chore, Diy

**Housing** Case, Shabrack, Shelter

**Hova** Malagash

**Hove** Plim, Swell

**Hovel** Cru(i)ve, Den, Pigsty, Shanty

**Hover** Hang, Lurk, Poise

**How** Hill, Hollow

**Howdyedo** Hallo, Pass

**However** As, But, Leastwise, Sed, Still, Though, Yet

**Howitzer** Gun

**Howl(er)** Banshee, Bawl, Bay, Bloop, Clanger, Hue, Mycetes, Ululate, Wow, Yawl, Yowl

**Hoy** Bilander, Ship

**HQ** Centre, Headquarters, SHAPE

**Hub** Boss, Centre, Focus, Hob, Nave, Pivot, Tee

**Hubbub** Charivari, Chirm, Coil, Din, Level-coil, Racket, Row, Stir

**Hubris** Pride

**Huckster** Hawker, Kidd(i)er, Pedlar

**Huddle** Cringe, Gather, Hunch, Shrink

**Hue** Colour, Dye, Outcry, Proscription, Steven, Tincture, Tinge

**Huff** Dudgeon, Hector, Pant, Pet, Pique, Strunt, Umbrage, Vex

**Hug** Cuddle, EMBRACE, Squeeze

**Huge (number)** Astronomical, Brobdingnag, Colossal, Enorm(ous), Gargantuan, Giant, GIGANTIC, Gillion, Ginormous, Humongous, Humungous, Immane, Immense, Leviathan, Lulu, Milliard, Octillion, Socking, Titanian, Tremendous

**Hugo** Victor

**Huguenot** Canisard

**Hulk** Lout, Ruin, Shale, Shell, Ship

**Hull** Bottom, Framework, Husk, Monocoque, Pod, Sheal, Sheel, Shell, Shiel, Shill

**Hullabaloo** Raz(z)mataz(z), Razzamatazz

> **Hullo** see HELLO

**Hum(ming)** Bombilate, Bombinate, Bum, Chirm, Drone, Lilt, Moan, Murmur, Nos(e)y, Pong, Sowf(f), Sowth, Stink, Stir, Zing

**Human(e), Humanist, Humanity** Bang, Colet, Earthling, Erasmus, Kindness, Mandom, Merciful, Mortal, Philanthropic, Species, Sympathy

**Humble** Abate, Abash, Afflict, Baseborn, Degrade, Demean, Demiss(ly), Lower, Lowly, Mean, MEEK, Modest, Obscure, Rude, Small, Truckle

**Humbug** Blarney, Blague, Claptrap, Con, Delude, Flam, Flummery, Fraud, Fudge, Gaff, Gammon, Gas, Guff, Gum, Hoax, Hoodwink, Hookey-walker, Kibosh, Liar, Maw-worm, Nonsense, Shenanigan, Wind

**Humdinger** Lulu

**Humdrum** Banal, Bourgeois, Monotonous, Mundane, Ordinary, Prosaic, Tedious

**Humid** Clammy, Damp, Dank, Muggy, Steam

**Humiliate, Humiliation, Humility** Abase, Abash, Baseness, Degrade, Disbench, Fast, Mortify, Put-down, SHAME, Skeleton, Take-down

**Humming-bird** Colibri, Hermit, Rainbow, Sappho, Sylph, Thornbill, Topaz, Trochilus

**Hummock** Tump

**Humorist** Cartoonist, Comedian, Jester, Leacock, Lear, Punster, Twain, Wodehouse

**Humour** Aqueous, Bile, Caprice, Cardinal, Chaff, Coax, Cocker, Coddle, Cosher, Cuiter, Cuittle, Daut, Dawt, Dry, Fun, Gallows, Ichor, Indulge, Juice, Kidney, Levity, Light, MOOD, Observe, Pamper, Phlegm, Ribaldry, Serum, Temper, Trim, Vitreum, Wetness, Whim, Wit

**Humourless** Dry, Po(-faced)

**Hump(ed)** Boy, Bulge, Dorts, Gibbose, Gibbous, Hog, Huff, Hummock, Hunch, Pip, Ramp, Tussock

> **Humpback** see HUNCHBACK

**Humphrey** Bogart

**Humus** Compost, Leafmould, Moder, Mor, Mull

**Hun** Alaric, Atli, Attila, Fritz, German

**Hunch, Hunchback** Camel, Chum, Crookback, Intuition, Kyphosis, Premonition, Quasimodo, Roundback, Urchin

**Hundred(s)** Burnham, C, Cantred, Cantref, Cent, Century, Chiltern, Commot, Desborough, Host, IN A HUNDRED, Northstead, Shire, Stoke, Ton, Wapentake

**Hundred and fifty** CL, Y

**Hundredweight** Centner, Quintal

**Hung** Displayed, Executed, Framed, High

**Hungarian** Bohunk, Csardas, Magyar, Szekely, Ugric, Vogul

**Hunger, Hungry** Appestat, Appetite, Bulimia, Bulimy, Clem, CRAVE, Desire, Edacity, Empty, Esurient, Famine, Famish, Fast, Hunter, Pant, Peckish, Rapacious, Raven, Ravin, Sharp-set, Unfed, Yaup

> **Hungry** may indicate an 'o' in another word

**Hunk(s)** Chunk, Dry-fist, Miser(ly), Slab

**Hunt(er), Hunting, Huntress, Huntsman** Actaeon, Atalanta, Battue, Beagle, Bellman, Calydon, Chace, Chase(r), Chasseur, Chevy, Crockett, Cynegetic, Dog, Drag, Esau, Ferret, Free-shot, Gun, Herne, Hound, Jager, Leigh, Montero, Nimrod, Orion, Peel, Poot, Pout, Predator, Pursue, Quest, Quorn, Rabbit, Rach(e), Ran, Rancel, Ranzel, Ride, Rummage, Run, Scorse, SEARCH, Seek, Shikar(ee), Shikari, Slipper, Stalk, Sticker, Terrier, Thimble, Tinchel, Tower, Trail, Trap, Venatic, Venator, Venerer, Venery, Watch, Whip, Yager

**Hunting-call** Rechate, Recheat, Tally-ho, View-halloo

**Hunting-ground** Forestation, Walk

**Hurdle(r)** Barrier, Doll, Fence, Flake, Gate, Hemery, Raddle, Sticks, Wattle

**Hurdy (gurdy)** Barrel-organ, Hainch, Haunch, Vielle

**Hurl(ing)** Camogie, Cast, Dash, FLING, Heave, Put(t), Throw, TOSS

**Hurly-burly** Furore, Noise

**Hurrah** Cheers, Huzza, Io

**Hurricane** Baguio, Tornade, Tornado, Typhoon, WIND

**Hurry** Belt, Bustle, Chivvy, Dart, Dash, Drive, Festinate, Fisk, Frisk, Gad, Giddap, Giddup, Hare, Haste, Hie, Hightail, Mosey, Post-haste, Press, Push, Race, RUSH, Scamper, Scoot, Scramble. Scur(ry), Scutter, Scuttle, Skelter, Skurry, Speed, Streak, Tear

**Hurt(ful)** Abuse, Ache, Ake, Bruise, Damage, De(a)re, Disservice, Harrow, Hit, INJURE, Lesion, Maim, Nocent, Nocuous, Noxious, Noyous, Pain, Pang, Scaith

**Hurtle** Rush, Spin, Streak, Streek

**Husband(ly)** Add, Baron, Darby, Ear, Eche, Economy, Eke, Ere, farm, Georgic, Goodman, Groom, H, Hubby, Ideal, Man, Mate, Partner, Retrench, Save, Scrape, Scrimp, Spouse, Squirrel, STORE, Tillage

**Hush(-hush)** Bestill, Gag, Sh, Silent, St, Tace, Wheesh(t), Whisht

**Husk(y)** Acerose, Bran, Eskimo, Hoarse, Hull, Malemute, Seed, Sheal, Shuck

**Hussar** Cherry-picker, Cherubim

**Hussite** Calixtin(e)

**Hussy** Besom, Hen, Loose, Minx, Vamp

**Hustle(r)** Frogmarch, Jostle, Pro, Push, Railroad, Shoulder, Shove

**Hut** Banda, Booth, Bothie, Bothy, Cabin, Chalet, Choltry, Gunyah, Hogan, Humpy, Igloo, Mia-mia, Nissen, Pondok(kie), Quonset, Rancho, Rondavel, Shack, Shanty, Sheal(ing), Shebang, Shed, Shiel(ing), Skeo, Skio, Succah, Sukkah, Tilt, Wan(n)igan, Wi(c)kiup, Wigwam, Wil(t)ja, Wurley

**Hutch** Buddle, Crate, Pen

**Hybrid** Bigener, Catalo, Centaur, Chamois, Citrange, Cross, Dso, Funnel, Geep, Interbred, Jomo, Jumart, Lurcher, Mermaid, Merman, Metis, Mongrel, Mule, Mutation, Percolin, Ringed, Tangelo, Tiglon, Tigon, Ugli, Zho(mo)

> **Hybrid** may indicate an anagram

**Hydra** Polyp

**Hydrant** Fireplug, H

**Hydrocarbon** Acetylene, Aldrin, Alkane, Alkene, Alkyne, Amylene, Arene, Asphaltite, Benzene, Butadiene, Butane, Butene, Camphene, Cetane, Decane, Diphenyl, Ethane, Halon, Hatchettite, Heptane, Hexane, Hexyl, Indene, Ligroin, Mesitylene, Naphtha, Nonane, Olefine, Pentane, Pentene, Phene, Picene, Propane, Pyrene, Retene, Squalene, Stilbene, Styrene, Terpene, Toluene, Triptane, Wax

**Hydrogen** Deut(er)on, Diplon, Ethene, H, Protium, Tritium

**Hydrophobic** Rabid

**Hydroponic** Soil

**Hydrozoa** Campanularia

**Hyena** Strand-wolf, Tiger-wolf

**Hygiene, Hygienic** Aseptic, Sanitary, Sepsis

**Hymn** Anthem, Canticle, Carol, Cathisma, Choral(e), Coronach, Dithyramb, Doxology, Hallel, Introit(us), Lay, Magnificat, Mantra, Marseillaise, Nunc dimittus, Ode, P(a)ean, Psalm, Recessional, Sanctus, Sequence, Stabat mater, Sticheron, Tantum ergo, Te deum, Trisagion, Troparion

**Hymnographer, Hymnologist** Faber, Heber, Moody, Neale, Parry, Sankey, Watts

**Hyperbole, Hyperbolic** Auxesis, Exaggeration, Sech

**Hypercritical** Captious

**Hyperion** Titan

**Hypersensitive** Allergic, Idiosyncratic

**Hyphen** Dash

**Hypnosis, Hypnotise, Hypnotic, Hypnotism** Braidism, Chloral, Codeine, Entrance, Magnetic, Mesmerism, Svengali

**Hypochondria(c)** Hyp, Nosophobia, Phrenesiac

**Hypocrisy, Hypocrite, Hypocritical** Archimago, Bigot, Byends, Cant, Carper, Chadband, Deceit, Dissembler, Heep, Holy Willie, Humbug, Mucker, Nitouche, Pecksniff, Pharisaic, Pharisee, Sepulchre, Tartuf(f)e

**Hypothetical** Gluon, Graviton

**Hyrax** Cony, Daman, Dassie, Klipdas

**Hysteria, Hysteric(al)** Conniption, Delirium, Frenzy, Meemie, Mother

# Ii

**I** A, Ch, Cham, Che, Dotted, Ego, Ich, Indeed, India, Iodine, Italy, J, Je

**Ian** Scot

**Ibex** Izard

**Ibis** Waldrapp

**Ice(d), Ice cream, Icing, Icy** Alcorza, Arctic, Berg, Cassata, Cone, Cool, Cornet, Coupe, Cream, Crystal, Diamonds, Floe, Frappé, Frazil, Freeze, Frigid, Frore, Frosting, Frosty, Gelato, Gelid, Gems, Glacé, Glacial, Glacier, Glare, Granita, Graupel, Growler, Hailstone, Hok(e)y-pok(e)y, Hommock, Hummock, Lolly, Macallum, Marzipan, Pingo, Polar, Rime, Rink, Serac, Sconce, Sherbet, Slider, Sorbet, Spumone, Spumoni, Sugar, Topping, Tortoni, Tutti-frutti, Verglas, Virga, Wafer, Wintry

**Ice-axe** Piolet

**Ice-berg** Calf, Floe, Growler

**Ice-box** Cooler, Freezer, Fridge, Frig, Yakhdan

> **Ice-cream** see ICE

**Iceland** IS

**Ice-skating** Choctaw, Figure, Glide

**Icicle** Tangle

**Icon** Idol, Image, Sprite

**Icterus** Jaundice

**Id(e)** Ego, Fish, Orfe

**Idea** Archetype, Brainwave, Clou, Clue, Conceit, Concept, Fancy, Germ, Hunch, Idolum, Image, Inkling, Inspiration, Interpretation, Light, NOTION, Obsession, Plan, Plank, Rationale, Recept, Theory, Thought

**Ideal(ise)** Abstract, A1, Dream, Eden, Goal, Halo, Hero, Model, Monist, Nirvana, Notional, Paragon, Pattern, PERFECT, Siddhi, Sidha, Sublimate, Utopian, Vision

**Idealist(ic)** More, Perfectionist, Quixotic, Visionary

**Identical** Alike, Clone, Congruent, Equal, Menechmian, Same, Selfsame, Very

**Identification, Identify** Bertillonage, Credentials, Diagnosis, Discern, Document, Dog-tag, Empathy, Finger(print), ID, Label, Mark, Password, Place, Recognise, Spot, Swan-hopping, Swan-upping, Verify

**Identikit** E-fit

**Identity** Appearance, Credentials, Espy, Likeness, Oneness, Self

**Idiom** Americanism, Argot, Britishism, Cant, Expression, Idioticon, Jargon,

Language, Parlance, Syri(a)cism, Syrism

**Idiosyncrasy** Foible, Mannerism, Nature, Quirk, Way

**Idiot(ic), Idiocy** Congenital, Fool, Imbecile, Inane, Moron, Natural, Nerk, Nidget, Oaf, Ouph(e), STUPID, Tony, Twit, Zany

**Idle(ness), Idler** Bludger, Bum, Bumble, Bummle, Cockaigne, Dally, Donnat, Donnot, Do-nothingism, Drone, Fainéant, Flaneur, Flim-flam, Footle, Frivolous, Groundless, Hawm, Inaction, Indolent, Inert, Laesie, Lallygag, Layabout, Laze, Lazy, Lead-swinger, Lie, Light, Limer, Loaf, Lollop, Lollygag, Lotophagus, Lounge, Lusk, Mike, Mollusc, Mooch, Mouch, Otiose, Otium, Patagonian, Piddle, Ride, Sloth, Spiv, Stalko, Stock-still, Stooge, Stroam, Tarry, Transcendental, Trock, Troke, Truant, Truck, Unbusy, Vain, Waste

**Idol(ise)** Adore, Adulate, Baal(im), Baphomet, Bel, Crush, Fetich(e), Fetish, God, Hero, Icon, Image, Joss, Lion, Mammet, Manito, Maumet, Mawmet, Molech, Moloch, Mommet, Mumbo-jumbo, Swami, Teraphim, Termagant, Vision, Wood, Worship

**Idyll(ic)** Arcady, Eclogue, Pastoral, Peneian

**Ie** Sc

**If, If it** All-be, An('t), Condition, Gif, Gin, In case, Pot, Provided, Sobeit, Whether

**Igloo** Snowden

**Ignis-fatuus** Elf-fire, Fire-dragon, Fire-drake, Friar's lanthorn, Wildfire

**Ignite, Ignition** Coil, Flare, Kindle, Lightning, Spark, Starter

**Ignoble** Base, Inferior, Mean, Vile

**Ignominious, Ignominy** Base, Dishonour, Fiasco, Infamous, Scandal, SHAME

**Ignorance, Ignorant** Analphabet, Artless, Darkness, Green, Illiterate, Inerudite, Ingram, Ingrum, Inscient, Lewd, Misken, Nescience, Night, Unaware, Unread, Untold, Unversed, Unwist

**Ignore** Ba(u)lk, Blink, Bypass, Connive, Cut, Discount, Disregard, Neglect, Omit, Overlook, Override, Pass, Rump, Snub

**Igor** Prince

**I know** Iwis, Ywis

**Ill** Adverse, All-overish, Bad, Bilious, Cronk, Evil, Income, Poorly, Queer, Sea-sick, SICK, Unwell, Valetudinarian, Wog, Wrong

> **Ill** may indicate an anagram

**Ill-balanced** Lop-sided

**Ill-bred** Churlish, Plebeian, Uncouth, Unmannerly

> **Ill-composed** may indicate an anagram

**Ill-defined** Diagnosis, Hazy, Unclear, Vague

**Ill-dressed** Frumpish

**Illegal, Illicit** Adulterine, Black, Breach, Bootleg, Furtive, Shonky,

Unlawful

**Illegitimate** Bastard, Come-o'-will, Fitz, Irregular, Lucky-piece, Mamzer, Momzer, Natural, Scarp, Spurious, Unlineal

**Ill-favoured** Offensive, Lean, Thin, Ugly

**Ill-feeling, Ill-humour** Bile, Curt, Dudgeon, Glum, Hate, Miff, Peevish, Pique

**Illiberal** Insular

> **Illicit** see ILLEGAL

**Illiterate** Ignoramus, Unlettered, Unread

**Ill-looking** Peaky, Poorly

**Ill-luck** Ambs-ace, Ames-ace, Deuce-ace, Misfortune

**Ill-natured** Attercop, Crabby, Ethercap, Ettercap, Huffy, Stingy, Sullen, Ugly, Unkind

**Illness** Aids, Ailment, Attack, Brucellosis, Complaint, Croup, Diabetes, Disease, DS, Dwalm, Dwaum, Dyscrasia, Eclampsia, Grippe, Malady, Scarletina, Sickness, Toxaemia, Weed, Weid

**Ill-nourished** Emaciated

**Ill-smelling** F(o)etid, High, Hing, Miasmic, Stinking

> **Ill-tempered** see ILL-NATURED

**Ill-timed** Inopportune, Unseasonable

**Illuminate(d), Illumination** Brighten, Clarify, Cul-de-lampe, Decorate, Enlighten, Floodlit, Lamplight, Langley, Light, Limn, Miniate, Nernst, Pixel, Radiate, Rushlight

**Illusion, Illusory** Air, Apparition, Barmecide, Deception, Fallacy, Fancy, Fantasy, Hallucination, Ignis-fatuus, Mare's-nest, Maya, Mirage, Optical, Phantom, Specious, Will o'the wisp

**Illustrate, Illustration, Illustrator** Case, Collotype, Demonstrate, Drawing, Eg, Exemplify, Explain, Figure, Frontispiece, Grangerize, Graphic, Instance, Instantiate, Limner, Plate, Show, Sidelight, Show, Spotlight, Tenniel, Vignette

**Illustrious** Bright, Celebrated, Famous, Legendary, Renowned

**Ill-will** Animosity, Enmity, Grudge, Hostility, Malice, Spite

**I'm** I'se

**Image** Blip, Discus, Effigy, Eidolon, Eikon, Enantiomorph, Graven, Hologram, Icon, Idol, Joss, Likeness, Matte, Paranthelium, Pentimento, Phantasmagoria, Picture, Poetic, Recept, Simulacrum, Spectrum, Stereotype, Symbol, Teraph(im), Tiki, Totem, Xoanon

**Imaginary, Imaginative, Imagine(d)** Assume, Believe, Conceive, Conjure, Esemplasy, Faery, Faine, Fancy, Feign, Fictional, Fictitious, Fictor, Figment, Figure, Ideate, Invent, Oz, Picture, Poetical, Prefigure, Recapture, Straw, SUPPOSE, Surmise, Think, Whangam

**Imbecile** Anile, Fool, Idiot, STUPID

> **Imbecile** may indicate an anagram

**Imbibe** Absorb, Drink, Lap, Quaff, Suck, Swallow

**Imbricate** Overlie

**Imbroglio** Complication, Maze

**Imbrue, Imbue** Colour, Infuse, Indoctrinate, Inoculate, Permeate, Soak, Steep

**Imitate, Imitation, Imitator** Act, Ape, Copy(cat), Counterfeit, Dud, Echo, Emulate, Epigon(e), Ersatz, Fake, False, Marinist, Me-too, Mime, Mimic(ry), Monkey, Parody, Parrot, Paste, Pastiche, Pinchbeck, Potichomania, Sham, Simulate, Stumer, Travesty

**Immaculate** Conception, Flawless, Lily-white, Perfect, Spotless, Virgin

**Immaterial** Insignificant, Spiritual, Trifling

**Immature, Immaturity** Callow, Crude, Embryo, Ergate(s), Green, Larval, Neotenic, Puberal, Puberulent, Pupa, Raw, Unripe, Young

> **Immature** may indicate a word incompleted

**Immediate(ly)** Alsoon, At once, Direct, Eftsoons, Ekdum, First-time, Forthwith, Imminent, Instantaneous, Instanter, NOW, Present, Pronto, Short-term, Slapbang, Straight, Sudden, Then

**Immense** Brobdingnag, Cosmic, Enormous, GIGANTIC, Huge, Vast

**Immerse** Baptise, Demerge, Demerse, Drench, Emplonge, Enew, Engage, Plunge, Soak, Steep

**Immigrant, Immigration** Aliyah, Carpet-bagger, Chalutz, Greener, Illegal, Incomer, Issei, Metric, Nisei, Olim, Pilgrim, Pommy, Redemption(er), Sanei, Sansei, Settler, Wetback

**Imminent** Approaching, Close, Immediate, Pending

**Immobility, Immobilize** Cataplexy, Catatonia, Hog-tie, Inertia, Rigidity, Tether

**Immoderate** Excessive, Extreme, Inordinate, Lavish, Undue

**Immodest** Brash, Brazen, Forward, Unchaste

**Immolation** Sacrifice, Sati, Suttee

**Immoral** Corrupt, Dissolute, Evil, Wanton

**Immortal(ity)** Agelong, Amarant(h), Amritattva, Athanasy, DIVINE, Enoch, Eternal, Famous, Godlike, Memory, Sin, Struldbrug, Undying

**Immovable** Fast, Firm, Obdurate, Rigid, Stable, Stubborn

**Immune, Immunise(r)** Free, Inoculate, Klendusic, Properdin, Serum, Vaccine

**Immure** Confine, Encloister, Imprison

**Imp(ish)** Devilet, Elf, Flibbertigibbet, Gamin(e), Hobgoblin, Limb, Lincoln, Litherly, Nickum, Nis(se), Puck, Rascal, Sprite

**Impact** Bearing, Bump, Clash, Collision, Feeze, Impinge, Jar, Jolt, Pack, Percuss, Pow, Souse, Wham

**Impair(ed), Impairment** Cripple, Damage, Disease, Enfeeble, HARM, Injure, Lame, Odd, Paralogia, Stale

**Impale** Ga(u)nch, Skewer, Spike, Transfix

**Impart** Bestow, Convey, Divulge, Impute, Infect, Shed, Tell

**Impartial** Candid, Detached, Equitable, Fair, Just, Neutral, Unbiased

**Impassable, Impasse** Deadlock, Dilemma, Invious, Jam, Snooker, Stalemate, Zugzwang

**Impassioned** Emotional, Fervid, Fiery

**Impassive** Apathetic, Deadpan, Stoical, Stolid

**Impatience, Impatient** Chafing, Chut, Dysphoria, Fretful, Irritable, Peevish, Petulant, Tilly-fally, Till(e)y-vall(e)y, Tut

**Impeach** Accuse, Challenge, Charge, Indict

**Impeccable** Faultless, Novice

**Impecunious** Penniless, Poor, Short

**Impedance, Impede, Impediment** Burr, Clog, Dam, Encumber, Halt, Handicap, HINDER, Let, Log, Obstacle, Obstruct, Rub, Shackle, Snag, Stammer, Trammel, Veto, Z

**Impel(led)** Actuate, Coerce, Drave, Drive, Drove, Goad, Inspire, URGE

**Impend(ing)** Imminent, Looming, Toward

**Impenetrable** Adamantine, Air-tight, Dense, Hard, Impervious, Proof

**Imperative** Dire, Need-be, Pressing, Vital

**Imperceptible** Invisible, Latent, Subtle

**Imperfect(ion)** Aplasia, Aplastic, Blotch, Defect, Deficient, Faculty, Kink, Lame, Poor, Rough, Second

**Imperial(ist), Imperious** Beard, Commanding, Haughty, Majestic, Masterful, Mint, Peremptory, Regal, Rhodes, Royal, Tuft

**Imperil** Endanger, Risk

**Imperishable** Eternal, Immortal, Indestructible

**Impermeable** Athermanous, Proof, Resistant

**Impersonal** Abstract, Cold, Detached, Inhuman

**Impersonate, Impersonating** Amphitryon, Ape, As, Imitate, Mimic, Pose

**Impertinence, Impertinent** Crust, Flippant, Fresh, Impudent, Irrelevant, Rude, Sass, Sauce

**Imperturbable** Cool, Placid, Stoic, Tranquil

**Impervious** Callous, Hardened, Obdurate, Proof, Tight

**Impetuous, Impetuosity** Birr, Brash, Bullheaded, Elan, HASTY, Heady, Hothead, Impulsive, Rash, Tearaway, Vehement, Violent

**Impetus** Birr, Drift, Incentive, Momentum, Propulsion, Slancio

**Impious** Blasphemous, Godless, Irreverent, Unholy

**Implant(ation)** AID, Embed, Graft, Instil, Sow

**Implement** Agent, Celt, Eolith, Flail, Fork, Fulfil, Hacksaw, Muller, Pin, Rest, Ripple, Spatula, Squeegee, TOOL, Utensil

**Implicate, Implication** Accuse, Concern, Embroil, Incriminate, Innuendo, INVOLVE, Overtone

**Implore** Beg, Beseech, Crave, ENTREAT, Obsecrate, Petition, Plead, Pray

**Imply, Implied** Hint, Insinuate, Involve, Signify, SUGGEST, Tacit

**Impolite** Ill-bred, Rude, Uncivil

**Import** Convey, Denote, Drift, Mean, Sense, Signify, Spell

**Importance, Important** Big, Calibre, Cardinal, Central, Cheese, Cob, Core, Critical, Crucial, Eminent, Epochal, Grave, Gravitas, Greatness, Heavy, High-muck-a-muck, Huzoor, Key, Magnitude, Main, Major, Material, Matters, Mighty, Milestone, Moment(ous), Nabob, Nib, Note, Pivotal, Pot, Salient, Seminal, Serious, Special, Status, Stress, Urgent, VIP, Weight

**Importune, Importunate** Beg, Coax, Flagitate, Press(ing), Prig, Solicit, Urgent

**Impose, Imposing, Imposition** Assess, August, Charge, Diktat, Dread, Enjoin, Fine, Flam, Foist, Fraud, Grand(iose), Hidage, Homeric, Hum, Impot, Inflict, Kid, Levy, Lumber, Majestic, Obtrude, Pensum, Pole, Scot, Sublime, Whillywhaw

**Impossible** Hopeless, Insoluble, No-no, Unacceptable

**Impost** Excise, Levy, Tax, Toll

**Imposter, Impostor** Bunyup, Charlatan, Disaster, Faitor, FAKE, Fraud, Idol, Pretender, Sham, Triumph, Warbeck

**Impotent** Barren, Helpless, Spado, Sterile, Weak

**Impound(er)** Appropriate, Bond, Confiscate, Intern, Pen, Pinder

**Impoverish** Bankrupt, Beggar, Exhaust, Straiten

**Impractical** Absurd, Idealist, Other-worldly, Useless

**Imprecation** Oath, Pize

**Imprecise** Approximate, Inaccurate, Loose, Nebulous, Rough

**Impregnate** Conceive, Imbue, Inseminate, Milt, Permeate

**Impresario** Maestro, Manager, Producer, Showman

**Impress(ive), Impression(able)** Astonish, Awe, Blur, Blurb, Brand, Cliché, Conscript, Crimp, Dent, Dramatic, Edition, Effect, Engram(ma), Engrave, Enstamp, Epic, Feel(ing), Fingerprint, Frank, Gas, Grab, Grandiose, Homeric, Imprint, Incuse, Knock, Let, Liebermann, Niello, Noble, Note, Palimpsest, Plastic, Plate, Pliable, Powerful, Prent, Press(gang), Print, Proof, Recruit, Repute, Responsive, Rotund, Seal, Seize, Sense, Shanghai, Slay, Smite, Soft, Spectacular, Stamp, Stereotype, Strike, Susceptible, Sway, Tableau, Touch, Watermark, Weal, Weighty

**Impression(ist)** Lumin(ar)ist, Manet, Monet, Morisot, Renoir

**Imprint** Edition, Engrave, Etch, Stamp

**Imprison(ment)** Cape, Confine, Constrain, Custody, Durance, Incarcerate, Intern, Jail, Quad, Quod, Time

**Improbable** Dubious, Unlikely

**Impromptu** Extempore, Improvised, Spontaneous, Sudden, Unrehearsed

**Improper, Impropriety** Abnormal, Blue, False, Indecent, Indecorum, Outré, Prurient, Solecism, Undue, Unmeet, Unseemly

> **Improperly** may indicate an anagram

**Improve(ment), Improving** Advance, Ameliorate, Beet, Benefit, Bete, Break, Buck, Chasten, Détente, Didactic, Ease, Edify, Embellish, Emend, Enhance, Enrich, Eugenic, Meliorate, Mend, Promote, Rally, Refine, Reform, Resipiscence, Retouch, Surpass, Tatt, Upturn

**Improvise(d), Improvisation** Adlib, Break, Devise, Extemporise, Knock-up, Lash-up, Noodle, Ride, Scratch, Sudden

**Imprudent** Foolhardy, Foolish, Impetuous, Impolitic, Indiscreet, Rash, Reckless, Unwary

**Impudence, Impudent** Audacious, Backchat, Bold, Brash, Brazen, Brassy, Cheeky, Cool, Crust, Forward, Gall, Impertinent, Insolent, Jackanapes, Lip, Neck, NERVE, Pert, Sass(y), Sauce, Saucy, Yankie

**Impugn** Censure, Defame, Impeach, Malign

**Impulse, Impulsive** Compelling, Conatus, Dictate, Drive, Headlong, Horme, Ideopraxist, Impetus, Instigation, INSTINCT, Madcap, Nisus, Premotion, Send, Signal, Snap, Spontaneous, Tendency, Thrust, Tic, Urge, Whim

**Impure, Impurity** Adulterated, Donor, Faints, Feints, Indecent, Lees, Lewd, Regulus, Scum, Unclean

**Imputation, Impute** Ascribe, Attribute, Charge, Scandal, Slander, Slur

**In** A, Amid, Chic, Home, Hostel, I', Inn, Intil, Occupying, Pop(ular), Trendy, Within

**Inability** Anosmia, Aphagia, Aphasia

**Inaccessible** Abaton, Impervious, Remote, Unattainable

**Inaccurate** Erroneous, Faulty, Imprecise, Inexact, Out, Rough, Slipshod

**Inactive, Inactivity** Acedia, Cabbage, Comatose, Dead, Dormant, Idle, Inert, Moratorium, Passive, Sluggish, Torpid

**In addition** Else, Further, Moreover, Plus, Too

**Inadequate** Feeble, Inapt, Inferior, Pathetic, Poor, Ropy, Thin

**Inadvertent(ly)** Accidental, Careless, Chance, Unwitting

> **In a flap** may indicate an anagram

**In a high degree** So

**In a hundred** Percent

**Inane** Empty, Foolish, Imbecile, Silly, Vacant

**Inanimate** Abiotic

**Inappropriate** Amiss, Infelicitous, Unapt, Undue, Unsuitable, Untoward

**Inapt** Maladroit, Unsuitable

**Inarticulate(ness)** Indistinct, Mumbling, Psellism

**Inartistic** Artless, Crude

**Inattentive** Deaf, Distrait, Heedless, Slack, Unheeding

**Inaudible** Silent, Superhet

**Inaugurate** Han(d)sel, Initiate, Install, Introduce

**Inauspicious** Adverse, Ominous, Sinister

> **In a whirl** may indicate an anagram

> **In a word** may indicate two clue words linked to form one

**Inborn, Inbred** Inherent, Innate, Native, Selfed, Sib

**Incalculable** Endless, Unpredictable, Untold

**Incandescent** Alight, Bright, Brilliant, Excited

**Incantation** Charm, Magic, Mantra, Spell

**Incapable** Can't, Powerless, Unable, Useless

**Incarnation** Advent, Avatar, Embodiment, Fleshing, Krishna, Rama

**In case** Lest, So

**Incautious** Foolhardy, Rash, Reckless, Unwary

**Incendiary** Arsonist, Combustible, Firebug, Fire-lighter

**Incense(d), Incenser** Anger, Aroma, Elemi, Enfelon, Enrage, Homage, Hot, INFLAME, Onycha, Outrage, Pastil(le), Provoke, Thurible, Thus, Vex, Wrathful

**Incentive** Carrot, Fillip, Impetus, Motive, Premium, Spur, Stimulus

**Incessant** Constant, Endless

**Inch** Ait, Edge, Isle, Sidle, Uncial

**Inchoate** Formless, Immature, Incipient

**Incident(al)** Affair, Baur, Bawr, Chance, Circumstance, Episode, Event, Negligible, Occasion, Page, Scene

**Incinerate** Burn, Combust, Cremate

**Incipient** Beginning, Germinal, Inchoate

**Incise, Incision, Incisive** Cut, Engrave, Incavo, Mordant, Scribe, Slit, Surgical, Trenchant

**Incite(ment)** Egg, Fillip, Hortative, Hoy, Inflame, Instigate, Kindle, Motivate, Prod, Prompt, Provoke, Put, Rouse, Sa sa, Set, Sic(k), Sool, SPUR, Tar, Urge

**Incline(d), Inclination** Acclivity, Angle, Aslope, Atilt, Bank, Batter, Bent, Bias, Bow, Clinamen, Dip, Disposed, Drift, Enclitic, GRADIENT, Hade, Heel, Hill, Kant, Kip, Lean, Liking, List, Minded, Nod, Partial, Peck, Penchant, Prone, Propensity, Rake, Ramp, Ready, Rollway, Set, Shelve,

Slant, SLOPE, Steep, Steeve, Stomach, Supine, Tend, Tilt, Tip, Trend, Upgrade, Verge, Will

**Include(d)** Add, Bracket, Compass, Comprise, Connotate, Contain, Cover, Embody, Embrace, Enclose, Involve, Subsume, Therein

**Incognito** Anonymous, Disguised, Faceless, Secret, Unnamed

**Incoherent** Confused, Disconnected, Disjointed, Rambling, Spluttering

**Income** Annuity, Dividend, Earned, Entry, Living, Penny-rent, Prebend, Primitiae, Proceeds, Rent, Returns, Revenue, Salary, Stipend, Unearned, Wages

**Incommunicado** Isolated, Silent

**Incomparable** Supreme, Unequalled, Unmatched

**Incompatible** Contradictory, Inconsistent, Mismatched, Unsuited

**Incompetent** Bungler, Helpless, Inefficient, Inept, Palooka, Unable, Unfit

**Incomplete** Catalectic, Deficient, Inchoate, Lacking, Partial, Pendent, Rough, Unfinished

**Incomprehensible** Hard, Unbelievable

**Inconceivable** Impossible, Incredible

> **In confusion** may indicate an anagram

**Incongruous** Absurd, Discordant, Irish, Ironic

**In connection with** Re

**Inconsiderable** Light, Slight

**Inconsiderate** Petty, Roughshod, Thoughtless, Unkind

**Inconsistent** Alien, Contradictory, Oxymoronic, Paradoxical, Unequal

**Inconsolable** Heartbroken, Niobe

**Inconstant** Chameleon, Desultory, Fickle, Light, VARIABLE

**Inconvenience, inconvenient** Awkward, Bother, Fleabite, TROUBLE, Untoward

**Incorporate(d)** Absorb, Embody, Inc, Integrate, Join, Merge

**Incorporeal** Aery, Airy, Spiritual

**Incorrect** False, Improper, Naughty

**Incorrigible** Hopeless, Obstinate

**Incorruptible** Honest, Immortal, Pure, Robespierre, Sea-green

**Increase, Increasing** Accelerate, Accrue, Add, Aggrandise, Amplify, Appreciate, Augment, Auxetic, Bulge, Crescendo, Crescent, Deepen, Dilate, Double, Ech(e), Eech, Eik, Eke, Enhance, Enlarge, EXPAND, Explosion, Greaten, GROW, Heighten, Ich, Increment, Interbreed, Jack, Magnify, Mount, Multiply, Plus, Proliferate, Propagate, Regrate, Rise, Snowball, Swell, Up, Wax

**Incredible** Amazing, Extraordinary, Fantastic, Steep, Tall

**Incredulity, Incredulous** Distrust, Infidel, Suspicion, Unbelief

**Increment** Accrual, Augment, Growth, Increase

**Incriminate**  Accuse, Implicate

**Incubate, Incubator**  Develop, Eccaleobion, Hatch

**Incubus**  Demon, Load, Nightmare

**Inculcate**  Infuse

**Incumbent**  Lying, Obligatory, Occupier, Official

**Incur**  Assume, Earn, Involve

**Incursion**  Foray, Inroad, Invasion, Razzia

**Indecent**  Bare, Free, Immoral, Improper, Lewd, Obscene, Scurril(e), Sotadic, Unproper

**Indecision, Indecisive**  Demur, Dithery, Doubt, Hamlet, Hung jury, Suspense, Swither

**Indeclinable**  Aptote

**Indecorous**  Graceless, Immodest, Outré, Unbecoming

**Indeed**  Atweel, Ay, Da, Een, Even, Faith, Haith, Insooth, La, Marry, Verily, Yea

**Indefensible**  Implausible, Inexcusable, Vincible

**Indefinite(ly)**  A, An, Any, Evermore, Hazy, Some, Undecided, Vague

**Indelible**  Fast, Permanent

**Indelicate**  Broad, Coarse, Improper, Vulgar, Warm

**Indemnify, Indemnification, Indemnity**  Assythement, Compensation, Insurance

**Indent(ed), Indentation**  Apprentice, Contract, Crenellate, Dancetty, Dimple, Impress, Niche, Notch, Order, Subentire

**Independence, Independent**  Autocephalous, Autogenous, Autonomy, Crossbencher, Detached, Extraneous, Free(dom), Free-lance, I, Liberty, Mugwump, Perseity, Separate, Separatist, Swaraj, Udal, Uhuru

**Indescribable**  Incredible, Ineffable

**Indestructible**  Enduring, Impenetrable

**Indeterminate**  Borderline, Formless, Incalculable, Open-ended, Unknown

**Index**  Alidad(e), Catalogue, Dial, Dow Jones, Exponent, Finger, Fist, Footsie, Forefinger, Gazetteer, Kwic, Nikkei, REGISTER, Table

**India**  Bharat

**Indiaman**  Clive

**Indian**  Ab(e)naki, Adivasi, Algonki(a)n, Algonqui(a)n, Apache, Arapaho, Araucanian, Arawak, Ayah, Aymara, Aztec, Baboo, Babu, Bharat(i), Blackfoot, Brave, Canarese, Cayuga, Cherokee, Cheyenne, Chibcha, Chinook, Choctaw, Comanche, Copperskin, Cree(k), Crow, Dard, Dravidian, File, Geronimo, Gond(wana), Guarani, Gujarati, Haida, Harijan, Hiawatha, Hindu, Hopi, Huron, Inca, Ink, Iroquois, Jain, Jat, Jemadar, Kanarese, Khalsa, Kisan, Kolarian, Kshatriyas, Kwakiuth, Mahratta, mam, Manhattan, Manitou, Maratha, Maya, Mazhbi, Micmac, Mofussil, Mogul, Mohawk, Mohegan, Mohican, Mugwump, Munda, Munshi, Muskogean,

Nagari, Nair, Narraganset, Natchez, Nation, Navaho, Navajo, Nayar, Ocean, Oglala, Ojibwa(y), Oneida, Oriya, Osage, Pali, Papoose, Parsee, Parsi, Pawnee, Pequot, Peshwa, Piro, Plains, Pocahontas, Pontiac, Prakrit, Pueblo, Punjabi, Quapaw, Quechua, Quichua, Redskin, Sachem, Sagamore, Salish, Sannup, Sanskrit, Scalper, Seminole, Seneca(n), Sepoy, Serrano, Shawnee, Shoshone, Shri, Sikh, Siwash, Sowar, Squaw, Summer, Suquamish, Swadeshi, Taino, Tamil, Tapuyan, Telegu, Telugu, Toltec, Tottee, Tribe, Tupi, Tuscan, Ute, Vakeel, Vakil, Yuman, Zuni

**Indicate, Indication, Indicative** Adumbrate, Allude, Argue, Cite, Cursor, DENOTE, Design, Desine, Dial, Endeixis, Evidence, Evince, Gnomon, Manifest, Mean, Mood, Notation, Point, Portend, Proof, Ray, Register, Representative, Reveal, SIGN, Signify, Specify, Symptom, Tip, Token, Trace, Trait

**Indictment** Accusation, Caption, Charge, Dittay, Reproach

**Indifference, Indifferent** Adiaphoron, Aloof, Apathetic, Apathy, Blasé, Blithe, Callous, Cold, Cool(th), Dead, Detached, Disdain, Incurious, Insouciant, Mediocre, Neutral, Nonchalant, Perfunctory, Phlegm, Pococurante, So-so, Stoical, Supine, Tepid

**Indigence, Indigent** Need, Penury, Poverty, Want

**Indigenous** Endemic, Native

> **Indi-gent** may indicate Baboo or Babu

**Indigestion** Apepsia, Apepsy, Dyspepsia, Heartburn

**Indignant, Indignation** Anger, Annoyed, Incensed, Irate, Resentful, Wrathful

**Indignity** Outrage

**Indigo** Anil, Blue, Indole, Isatin(e)

**Indirect** Back-handed, By(c), Devious, Implicit, Mediate, Oblique, Remote, Roundabout, Sidelong, Zig-zag

**Indiscreet, Indiscretion** Folly, Gaffe, Imprudence, Indelicate, Rash

**Indiscriminate** Haphazard, Random, Sweeping

**Indispensable** Basic, Essential, King-pin, Necessary, Vital

**Indispose(d), Indisposition** Adverse, Disincline, Ill, Incapacitate, Sick, Unwell

**Indistinct** Ambiguous, Bleary, Blur, Bumble, Bummle, Faint, Fuzzy, Hazy, Pale, VAGUE

> **In distress** may indicate an anagram

**Indite** Compose, Pen, Write

**Indium** In

**Individual(ity)** Being, Discrete, Haecceity, Gemma, Identity, Ka, Man, Particular, Person, Poll, Respective, Separate, Single, Solo, Special, Unit

**Indoctrinate** Brainwash, Discipline, Instruct

**Indolence, Indolent** Inactive, Languid, Lazy, Sloth, Sluggish, Supine

**Indomitable** Brave, Dauntless, Invincible

**Indonesia(n)** Batavian, Nesiot, RI

**Indoor(s)** Within

**Indubitably** Certainly, Certes, Manifestly, Surely

**Induce** Bribe, Cause, Coax, Encourage, Get, Inveigle, Lead, Motivate, PERSUADE, Prevail, Suborn, Tempt

**Induct(ion), Inductance** Epagoge, Henry, Inaugurate, Initiate, Install, L, Logic, Prelude

**Indulge(nce), Indulgent** Absolution, Drink, Favour, Gratify, Humour, Luxuriate, Oblige, Pamper, Pander, Pardon, Pet, Please, SATISFY, Splurge, Spoil, Spoonfeed, Tolerant, Venery

**Industrial, Industrious, Industry** Appliance, Business, Busy, Cottage, Deedy, Diligence, Eident, Energetic, Labour, Ocnus, Operose, Ruhr, Technical

> **Inebriate** see INTOXICATE

**Inedible** Inesculent, Noisome, Rotten

**Ineffective, Ineffectual** Clumsy, Deadhead, Drippy, Dud, Empty, Fainéant, Futile, Idle, Ill, Impotent, Neutralised, Sterile, USELESS, Void, Weak, Wet

**Inefficient** Clumsy, Incompetent, Lame, Shiftless, Slack

**Inelegant** Awkward, Stiff, Turgid, Unneat

**Ineligible** Unqualified

**Inept** Absurd, Farouche, Schlimazel, Unskilled, Wet

**Inequality** Anomaly, Disparity, Injustice, Odds

**Inert(ia)** Comatose, Dead, Dull, Inactive, Leaden, Mollusc, Neon, Potato, Sluggish, Stagnant, Stagnation, Thowless, Torpid

**Inestimable** Incalculable, Invaluable, Priceless

**Inevitable, Inevitably** Automatic, Certain, Fateful, Inexorable, Needs, Perforce, TINA

**Inexact(itude)** Cretism, Incorrect, Terminological, Wrong

**Inexorable** Relentless

**Inexpedient** Impolitic, Imprudent, Unwise

**Inexpensive** Bargain, Cheap

**Inexperience(d), Inexpert** Amateur, Callow, Colt, Crude, GREEN, Ham, Ingénue, Raw, Rookie, Rude, Unconversant, Unseasoned, Unseen, Youthful

**Inexplicable** Magical, Mysterious, Paranormal, Unaccountable

**Infallible** Foolproof, Right, Unerring

**Infamous, Infamy** Base, Ignominious, Notorious, Opprobrium, Shameful, Villainy

**Infant** Babe, Baby, Innocent, Lamb, Minor

**Infantry(man)** Buff, Foot, Jaeger, Phalanx, Pultan, Pulto(o)n, Pultun,

SOLDIER, Tercio, Turco

> **Infantry** may refer to babies

**Infatuate(d), Infatuation** Assot, Besot, Crush, Enamoured, Engou(e)ment, Entêté, Fanatic, Foolish, OBSESSION, Rave, Turn

**Infect(ed), Infecting, Infection, Infectious** Angina, Anthrax, Catching, Catchy, Contaminate, Corrupt, Diseased, Fester, Fomes, Gonorrhoea, Listeria, NSU, Orf, Overrun, Poison, POLLUTE, Py(a)emia, Roup, Salmonella, Septic, Shingles, Smit(tle), Taint, Virulent, Zymosis

**Infeftment** Sasine, Seisin

**Infer(ence)** Conclude, Deduce, Divine, Extrapolate, Generalise, Guess, Illation, Imply, Judge, Surmise

> **Infer** may indicate 'fer' around another word

**Inferior** Base, Cheap-jack, Dog, Gimcrack, Grody, Grub-street, Indifferent, Infra, Less, Lo-fi, Lower, Minor, Naff, Nether, One-horse, Ornery, Paravail, Rop(e)y, Schlock, Second, Shoddy, Subjacent, Subordinate, Surat, Tinpot, Trashy, Under(man), Underneath, Understrapper, Waste, Worse

**Infernal** Demogorgon, Diabolic, Hellish, Unholy

**Infest(ed), Infestation** Acrawl, Beset, Blight, Dog, Overrun, Phthiriasis, PLAGUE, Stylopised, Swarm, Torment

**Infidel** Atheist, Caffre, Giaour, Heathen, Heretic, Kafir, Pagan, Paynim, Saracen

**Infield** Intown

**Infiltrate** Encroach, Enter, Instil, Intrude, Pervade

**Infinite, Infinity** Cosmic, Endless, Eternal, N

**Infirm** Decrepit, Doddery, Feeble, Lame, Shaky

> **Infirm** may indicate 'co' around another word

**Inflame(d), Inflammable, Inflammation** Acne, Adenitis, Afire, Ancome, Anger, Angina, AROUSE, Bloodshot, Bubonic, Catarrh, Coryza, Croup, Enamoured, Enchafe, Enfire, Enkindle, Enteritis, Felon, Fever, Fibrosis, Fire, Garget, Ignatis, Ignite, Incense, Infection, Intertrigo, Ire, Iritis, Keratitis, Metritis, Myelitis, Napalm, Naphtha, Noma, Orchitis, Otitis, Paronychia, Phlebitis, Phlegmasia, Phlegmon, Phlogistic, Phrenitis, Pleurisy, Prurigo, Pyelitis, RED, Salpingitis, Sinusitis, Splenitis, Spondylitis, Stimulate, Strumitis, Sty(e), Swelling, Sycosis, Thoroughpin, Thrush, Touchwood, Tylosis, Typhlitis, Ulitis, Whitlow

**Inflate(d), Inflation** Aerate, Aggrandise, Bloat, Dilate, Distend, Distent, Increase, Pneumatic, Pump, Remonetise, Spiral, Swell

**Inflexible, Inflexibility** Adamant(ine), Byzantine, Iron, Obstinate, Resolute, Rigid, Rigour, Set, Stubborn

**Inflict(ion)** Deal, Force, Give, Impose, Trouble, Visit, Wreak

**Inflorescence** Bostryx, Catkin, Ci(n)cinnus, Drepanium, Panicle, Pleiochasium, Raceme, Umbel

**Inflow** Affluence, Influx

**Influence, Influential** Act, Affect, Backstairs, Charm, Clout, Credit, Determine, Drag, Earwig, Eminence grise, Factor, Force, Govern, Hold, Impress, Incubus, Inspire, Interfere, Lead, Leverage, Lobby, Mastery, Militate, Mogul, Octopus, Operation, Power, Pressure, Prestige, PULL, Push, Rust, Say, Seminal, Star, Star-blasting, Stimulus, Sway, Telegony, Will, Work, Wull

**Influenza** Flu, Grippe, Wog

**Inform(ation), Informed, Informer** Acquaint, Advise, Agitprop, Apprise, Aware, Beagle, Burst, Canary, Contact, Datum, Delate, Dob(ber), Dope, Education, Facts, Fink, Fisgig, Fiz(z)gig, Gen, Grapevine, Grass, Griff, Gunsel, Hep, Input, Inside, Instruct, Light, Lowdown, Media, Moiser, Nark, Nepit, Nit, Nose, Occasion, Peach, Pem(m)ican, Poop, Prime, Propaganda, Rat, Read-out, Rheme, Rumble, Shelf, Shop, Sidelight, Sing, Sneak, Snitch, Squeak, Squeal, Stag, Sycophant, Tell, Tidings, Up, Whistle-blower

**Informal** Casual, Intimate, Irregular, Outgoing, Unofficial

**Infra** Under

**Infrequent** Casual, Occasional, Rare, Scant, Seldom, Sparse

**Infringe** Contravene, Violate

**Infuriate** Anger, Bemad, Bepester, Enrage, Exasperate, Incense, Madden, Pester, Provoke

**Infuse, Infusion** Brew, Distill, Gallise, Instil, Mash, Saloop, Saturate, Steep, Tea, Tisane, Uva-ursi

**Ingenious, Ingenuity** Adept, Adroit, Art, Clever, Cunning, Cute, Inventive, Neat, Resourceful, Smart, Subtle, Wit

**Ingenuous** Artless, Candid, Innocent, Naive, Open

**Ingest** Eat, Endue, Incept, Indue, Swallow

**In good condition** Fit, Shipshape, Taut, Trim

**Ingot** Bar, Bullion, Lingot, Sycee

**Ingrain** Fix, Impregnate, Train

**Ingrate** Thankless, Viper

**Ingratiate, Ingratiating** Butter, Flatter, Smarm

**Ingredient(s)** Additive, Admixture, Basis, Content, Element, Factor

**Ingrowing, Ingrowth** Onychocryptosis, T(h)ylosis

**Inhabit(ants)** Affect, Children, Denizen, Dweller, Inholder, Inmate, Live, Native, Occupant, People, Resident

**Inhale, Inhalation** Aspirate, Breath(e), Gas, Inspire, Sniff, Take

**Inharmonious** Patchy

**Inherent** Characteristic, Essential, Immanent, Inbred, Innate, Native

**Inherit(ance), Inheritor** Accede, Birthright, Borough-English, Gene, Genom, Legacy, Meek, Mendelism, Patrimony, Reversion, Succeed, Tichborne

**Inhibit(ing)** Chalone, Chalonic, Deter, Forbid, Restrain, Suppress

**Inhuman** Barbarous, Brutal, Merciless

**Inimical** Adverse, Harmful, Hostile

**Iniquity** Evil, Offence, Sin, Vice

**Initial** Acronym, First, Letter, Monogram, Paraph, Prelim(inary), Primary, Rubric

> **Initially** may indicate first letters

**Initiate(d), Initiation, Initiative** Begin, Bejesuit, Blood, Bora, Bring, Ceremony, Debut, Eater, Enterprise, Epopt, Esoteric, Gumption, Induct, Instigate, Instruct, LAUNCH, Nous, START

**Inject(or), Injection** Enema, Implant, Innerve, Instil, Introduce, Jab, Mainline, Reheat, Serum, Shoot, Syringe

**Injunction** Command, Embargo, Mandate, Swear, Writ

**Injure(d), Injury, Injustice** ABH, Abuse, Aggrieve, Bale, Bled, Contrecoup, Damage, De(a)re, Forslack, GBH, Harm, HURT, Ill-turn, Impair, Iniquity, Lesion, Malign, Mar, Mayhem, Mistreat, Mutilate, Noxal, Nuisance, Oppression, Outrage, Packet, Paire, Prejudice, Rifle, Scath(e), Scotch, Sprain, Teen(e), Tene, Trauma, Umbrage, Wound, Wrong

> **Injury** see AFTER INJURY

**Ink(y)** Atramental, Black, Bray, Cyan, Indian, Sepia, Stained

**Inkling** Clue, Glimpse, Hint, Idea

**Inkpot** Standish

**Inland** Interior, Up

**Inlay, Inlaid** Buhl, Emblemata, Empaestic, Enamel, Enchase, Incrust, Intarsia, Intarsio, Koftgari, Marquetrie, Marquetry, Pietra-dura, Piqué, Set, Tarsia, Veneer

**Inlet** Arm, Bay, Cove, Creek, Entry, Fiord, Firth, Fjord, Fleet, Gusset, Wash

> **Inlet** may indicate 'let' around annther word

**Inmate** Intern(e), Lodger, Patient, Prisoner, Resident

**Inn(keeper)** Albergo, Alehouse, Auberge, Barnard's, Boniface, Caravanserai, Gray's, Halfway-house, Host, Hostelry, House, Hotel, Imaret, In, Khan, Ladin(ity), Law, Licensee, Lincoln's, Lodging, Luckie, Lucky, Padrone, Parador, Patron, Posada, Posthouse, Publican, Roadhouse, Ryokan, Serai, Tabard, Tavern(er)

> **Inn** may refer to the law

**Innards** Entrails, Gizzard, Guts, Harigals, Harslet, Haslet, Rein, Viscera

**Innate** Congenital, Essential, Natural, Inborn, Instinctive

**Inner** Bencher, Esoteric, Internal, Lining, Private

**Innings** Chance, Turn

> **Innkeeper** see INN

**Innocent** Absolved, Arcadian, Babe, Cherub, Childlike, Clean, Doddypoll,

Dodipoll, Dove, Encyclical, Green, Idyllic, Ingenue, Lamb, Lily-white, Maiden, Naive, Opsimath, PURE, Sackless, Seely, Simple, St, White

**Innocuous** Harmless, Innocent

**Innovation, Innovator** Alteration, Newell, Novelty, Pioneer

**Inn-sign** Bush

**Innumerable** Countless, Infinite, N

**Inoculate, Inoculation** Engraft, Immunise, Jab, Protect, Vaccine

**Inoperative** Futile, Nugatory, Silent, Void

**Inopportune** Inconvenient, Untimely

**Inordinate** Excessive, Irregular, Undue

> **Inordinately** may indicate an anagram

**In place of** For, Qua, Vice, With

**Inquest** Debriefing, Hearing, Inquiry, Investigation

**Inquire, Inquiring, Inquiry** Ask, Demand, Investigation, Maieutic, Nose, Organon, Probe, Query, Question, See, Speer, Speir

**Inquisition, Inquisitive** Curious, Interrogation, Meddlesome, Nosy, Prying, Rubberneck, Snooper, Stickybeak

> **In revolt, In revolution** may indicate an anagram

**Inroad(s)** Breach, Encroachment, Honeycomb, Invasion

**Insane, Insanity** Absurd, Batty, Crazy, Deranged, Loco, Lune, Mad, Manic, Mattoid, Paranoia, Pellagra, Psycho, Schizo, Yarra

**Insatiable** Greedy, Ravenous, Voracious

**Insatiate child** Killcrop

**Inscribe(d), Inscription** Chisel, Colophon, Dedicate, Emblazon, Engrave, Enter, Epigraph, Epitaph, Exergue, Graffiti, Lapidary, Legend, Lettering, Writ

**Inscrutable** Deadpan, Esoteric, Mysterious, Sphinx

**Insect(s)** Acarid, Ametabola, Ant, Aphis, Bee, Bluebottle, Breeze, Bug, Buzzard, Chigger, Chigoe, Chironomic, Cicada, Cicala, Cimex, Circutio, Coccidae, Cochineal, Cockroach, Coleoptera, Collembola, Crane-fly, Creepy-crawly, Cricket, Daddy-long-legs, Day-fly, Dragonfly, Emmet, Entomic, Ephemeron, Fan-cricket, Fen-cricket, Firebrat, Flea, Froghopper, Gadfly, Gnat, Gogga, Grayfly, Greenbottle, Hemiptera, Hexapod, Hive-bee, Homoptera, Hornet, Horntail, Humbuzz, Instar, Itchmite, Katydid, Lacewing, Ladybird, Leaf-cutter, Leatherjacket, Lice, Louse, Mallophaga, Mantid, Mantis, Mayfly, Mealybug, Mecoptera, Metabola, Midge, Millepede, Mite, Mosquito, Moth, Myriapod, Nymph, Odonata, Oestrus, Oniscus, Ox-bot, Phasmid, Plum, Psocoptera, Psylla, Puss-moth, Pyralis, Rearhorse, Rhipidoptera, Rhipiptera, Ruby-tail, Scarab(ee), Silverfish, Spectre, Spider, Springtail, Staphylinidae, Stonefly, Strepsiptera, Stylops, Tabanidae, Termite, Thousand-legs, Thrips, Thysanoptera, Tick, Tiger-beetle, Tiger-moth, Trichoptera, Wasp, Waterbug, Weevil, Wog, Zebub, Zimb

**Insecticide**  Chromene, DDT, Derris, Flycatcher, Gammexane (tdmk), Lindane (tdmk), Malathion, Naphthalene, Rotenone, Spray, Zineb

**Insectivore**  Agouta, Desman, Donaea, Drosera, Hedgehog, Jacamar, Nepenthaceae, Tanrec, Tenrec(idae), Zalambdodont

**Insecure**  Infirm, LOOSE, Precarious, Shaky, Unsafe, Unstable, Vulnerable

**Insensitive**  Blunt, Callous, Dead, Log, Numb, Obtuse, Tactless

**Inseparable**  One, United

**Insert(ion), Inset**  Empiecement, Enchase, Enter, Entry, Foist, Fudge, Godet, Gore, Graft, Gusset, Immit, Imp, Implant, Inject, Inlay, Input, Interpolate, Interpose, Introduce, Intromit, Mitre, Pin, Sandwich

**Inside(r)**  Content, Core, Entrails, Gaol, Heart, Indoors, Interior, Internal, Interne, Inward, Inwith, Mole, Tum, WITHIN

**Insidious**  Artful, Crafty, Sly

**Insight**  Acumen, Anagoge, Aperçu, Hunch, Inkling, Intuition, PERCEPTION, Tais(c)h

**Insignia**  Armour, Arms, Badger, Charge, Chevron, Mark, Regalia, Ribbon, Roundel

**Insignificant (person)**  Fico, Flea-bite, Fractional, Gnat, Miniscule, Nobody, Nominal, One-eyed, Petit, Petty, Pipsqueak, Quat, Scoot, Scout, Scrub, Shrimp, Slight, Squit, Trifling, Trivial, Two-bit, Unimportant, Whippersnapper

**Insincere**  Affected, Artificial, Cant, Double, Empty, Faithless, False, Glib, Hollow, Shallow

**Insinuate, Insinuating, Insinuation**  Allude, Hint, Imply, Innuendo, Intimate, Sleek, Sneck-draw

**Insipid**  Banal, Blah, Flat, Insulse, Jejune, Lash, Tame, Tasteless, Vapid, Weak

**Insist(ent)**  Assert, Demand, Dogmatic, Exact, STIPULATE, Stress, Threap, Threep, Urge

**Insolence, Insolent**  Audacity, Cheek, Contumely, Effrontery, Gum, Hubris, Hybris, Impudence, Lip, Rude, Snash, Stroppy

**Insoluble**  Cerasin, Hard, Irresolvable, Mysterious

**Insolvent**  Bankrupt, Broke, Destitute, Penniless

**Insomnia**  Sleeplessness, Wakefulness

**Insouciant**  Carefree, Careless, Cavalier

**Inspect(ion), Inspector**  Alnage(r), Auditor, Comb, Conner, Examine, Government, Investigator, Jerque, Keeker, Muster, Once-over, Peep, Perlustrate, Proveditor, Recce, Review, Scrutinise, Survey, Test, Vet

**Inspiration, Inspire(d), Inspiring**  Actuate, Afflatus, Aerate, Aganippe, Animate, Brainstorm, Brainwave, Breath(e), Castalian, Elate, Exalt, Flash, Draw, Fire, Hearten, Hunch, Idea, Illuminate, Impulse, Induce, Move, Muse, Pegasus, Prompt, Prophetic, Satori, Sniff(le), Stimulus, Taghairm, Theopneust(y), Uplift, Vatic

**Install(ation)** Enchase, Enthrone, Inaugurate, Induction, Invest, Put (in)

**Instalment** Episode, Fascicle, Heft, Livraison, Never-never, Part, Serial, Tranche

**Instance, Instant** As, Case, Chronon, Example, Flash, Jiffy, Moment, Present, Say, Shake, Spur, Tick, Trice, Twinkling, Urgent

**Instead (of)** Deputy, For, Lieu, Locum, Vice

**Instigate** Arouse, Foment, Impel, Incite, Prompt, Spur

**Instil(l)** Implant, Inculcate, Infuse, Teach

**Instinct(ive)** Automatic, Flair, Id, Impulse, Innate, Intuition, Nature, Nose, Talent, Tendency, Visceral

**Institute, Institution** Academy, Activate, Bank, Bring, Charity, College, Erect, Found(ation), I, Inaugurate, MORI, Orphanage, Raise, Redbrick, Retraict, Retrait(e), Retreat, Smithsonian, Start, University

**Instruct(ed), Instruction, Instructor** Advice, Brief, Catechism, Clinic, Coach, Course, Didactic, Direct(ive), Document, Edify, Educate, Ground(ing), Inform, Manual, Mystagogue, Mystagogus, Notify, Order, Percept, Recipe, Rubric, Swami, TEACH, Train, Tutorial, Up

**Instrument(al)** Ablative, Act, Aethrioscope, Agent, Alidade, Almacantar, Almucantar, Alphonsin, Altazimuth, Anemometer, Astrolabe, Atmometer, Aux(an)ometer, Barnacle, Barometer, Baryscope, Bolometer, Brake, Broach, Cadrans, Caltrop, Clam, Colposcope, Crows-bill, Cryophorus, Curette, Dip-circle, Dividers, Ecraseur, Eriometer, Etalon, Fan, Fleam, Float, Forceps, Fork, Gadge, Groma, Helpful, Hodometer, Keraunograph, Konimeter, Megascope, Meter, Metronome, Microphone, MUSICAL INSTRUMENT, Myringoscope, Nocturnal, Odometer, Organ(ic), Otoscope, Oximeter, Pelican, Pilliwinks, Pinniewinkle, Pinnywinkle, Probang, Prog, Protractor, Rasp(atory), RESPONSIBLE, Rote, Scythe, Sextant, Spatula, Stethoscope, Strickle, Strigil, Strobe, Syringe, Tachometer, Telescope, Tellurian, Tellurion, Tenaculum, Theodolite, TOOL, Tram(mel), Trephine, Trocar, UTENSIL, Waywiser, Wecht, Zenith-sector

**Insubordinate** Faction, Mutinous, Rebel, Refractory

**Insubstantial** Airy, Brief, Frothy, Illusory, Jackstraw, Slight, Ye(a)sty

**Insufficient** Inadequate, Poor, Scant, Shortfall

**Insular** Isolated, Moated, Narrow, Xenophobe

**Insulate, Insulation, Insulator** Biotite, Dielectric, Lagging, Mica, Non-conductor, Padding, Pugging, Tog

**Insult(ing)** Abuse, Affront, Aspersion, Barb, Contumely, Cut, Dyslogistic, Embarrass, Facer, Fig, Mud, Offend, Skit, Slight, Slur, Snub, Trauma, Verbal

**Insurance, Insure(r)** Abandonee, Cover, Guarantee, Hedge, Indemnity, Policy, Security, Underwrite

**Insurgent, Insurrection** Mutiny, Outbreak, Rebel, Revolt, Sedition

**Intact** Complete, Entire, Inviolate, Unused, Whole

**Intaglio** Diaglyph

**Intake** Absorption, Entry, Fuel

**Integer, Integral** Component, Entire, Inbuilt, Needful, Number, Organic, Unitary

**Integrate(d)** Amalgamate, Assimilate, Combine, Fuse, Harmonious, Mainstream, Merge

**Integrity** Honesty, Principle, Rectitude, Strength, Uprightness, Whole

**Integument** Coat, Sheath, Skin, Velum

**Intellect(ual)** Academic, Aptitude, Brain, Cerebral, Dianoetic, Egghead, Far-out, Genius, Intelligent, -ist, Mental(ity), Mind, Noesis, Noetic, Noology, Nous, Profound, Reason

**Intelligence, Intelligent** Advice, Brains, Bright, CIA, Discerning, Dope, Eggmass, Info, Ingenious, Knowledgeable, MI, Mossad, News, Rational, Sense, Shrewd, Tidings, Wit

**Intemperance** Acrasia, Crapulent, Excess, Gluttony, Immoderation

**Intend(ed), Intending** Allot, Contemplate, Design, Destine, Ettle, Fiancé(e), Going, MEAN, Meditate, Propose

**Intense, Intensify, Intensity** Acute, Aggravate, Ardent, Depth, Earnest, Enhance, Emotional, Escalate, Estro, Excess, Extreme, Fervent, Keen, Might, Profound, Redouble, Sharpen, Vehement, Vivid

**Intent, Intention(al)** A dessein, Animus, Deliberate, Dole, Earnest, Hellbent, Manifesto, Purpose, Rapt, Resolute, Set, Studious, Systematic, Thought, Witting

**Inter** Bury, Entomb

**Intercalation** Embolism

**Intercede, Intercession** Mediate, Negotiate, Plead, Prayer

**Intercept** Absciss(a), Abscisse, Check, Meet

**Interchange(d)** Altercation, Alternate, Clover-leaf, Mutual, Permute, Reciprocate, Substitute

**Intercourse** Ball, Bang, Bed, Boff, Bonk, Coition, Coitus, Commerce, Commixture, Congress, Converse, Copulation, Enjoy, Fluff, Greens, Jass, Jazz, Jump, Laying, Make, Naughty, Nookie, Nooky, Poontang, Pussy, Ride, Rim, Roger, Root, Rumpy(-pumpy), Screw, Shaft, Shag, Shtup, Stuff, Swive, Tail, Trade

**Interdict** Ban, Forbid, Prohibit, Taboo

**Interest(ed), Interesting** Amusive, Behalf, Benefit, Clou, Concern, Coupon, Dividend, Engage, Engross, Hot, Import, Income, Int(o), Intrigue, Line, Part, Partisan, Percentage, Readable, Respect, Revenue, Scene, Share, Side, Spice, Stake, Topical, Usage, Usance, Usure, Usury, Warm

**Interfere(r), Interference** Busybody, Clutter, Disrupt, Hamper, Hinder, Intrude, Mar, MEDDLE, Molest, Pry, Shash, Static, Tamper

**Interferometer** Etalon

**Intergrowth** Perthite

**Interim**  Break, Meanwhile, Temporary

**Interior**  Backblocks, Cyclorama, Domestic, Innards, Innate, Inner, Inside, Plain, Up-country, Vitals

**Interject(ion)**  Ahem, Begorra(h), Haith, Hoo-oo, Interpolate, Lumme, Nation, Sese(y), Sessa, 'Sheart, 'Slid, Tarnation, Tush

**Interlace**  Mingle, Weave, Wreathe

**Interlock**  Dovetail, Knit, Tangle

**Interlocutor**  Elihu, MC, Questioner

**Interloper**  Gate-crasher, Intruder, Trespasser

**Interlude**  Antimask, Antimasque, Entr'acte, Interruption, Kyogen, Lunch-hour, Meantime, Pause, Verset

**Intermediary, Intermediate**  Agent, Comprador(e), Go-between, Instar, Mean, Medial, Mesne, Mezzanine, Middleman

**Interminable**  Endless, Infinite

**Intermission**  Apyrexia, Break, Interval, Pause, Recess

**Intermittent**  Broken, Fitful, Periodic, Random, Spasmic, Spasmodic

**Intern(e)**  Confine, Doctor, Impound, Restrict, Trainee

**Internal**  Domestic, Inner, Inward, Within

**International**  Cap, Cosmopolitan, UN, Universal

**Interpolate**  Insert, Interrupt

**Interpose**  Interject, Intervene, Spatchcock, Stickle

**Interpret(er)**  Conster, Construe, Decipher, Decode, Dobhash, Dragoman, Exegete, Explain, Exponent, Expositor, Expound, Hermeneutist, Latiner, Lingster, Moonshee, Moonshi, Oneirocritic, Origenist, Prophet, Read, Rede, Render, Represent, Spokesman, TRANSLATE, Truchman, Ulema

**Interpretation**  Anagoge, Anagogy, Construction, Exegesis, Exegete, Gematria, Gloss(ary), Gospel, Halacha(h), Halakah, Hermeneutics, Portray, Reading, Rendition, Targum, Translation

**Interrogate, Interrogation**  Catechism, Enquire, Examine, Grill, Pump, QUESTION, Quiz

**Interrupt(ion), Interrupter**  Ahem, Blip, Break, Butt, Chip in, Disturb, Entr'acte, Heckle, Hiatus, Interfere, Intrusion, Overtalk, Portage, Rheotome, Stop, Suspend

**Intersect(ion)**  Carfax, Chiasm(a), Cross, Cut, Decussate, Divide, Groin, Metacentre, Orthocentre

**Intersperse**  Dot, Interpose, Scatter, Sprinkle

**Interstice**  Areole, Interlude, Pore, Space

**Intertwine**  Braid, Impleach, Knit, Lace, Plait, Splice, Twist, Writhe

**Interval**  Between, Break, Breather, Comma, Diapente, Diastaltic, Diatesseron, Diesis, Distance, Ditone, Duodecimo, Entr'acte, Fifth, Gap, Half-time, Hiatus, Hourly, Interim, Interlude, Lucid, Lull, Meantime, Meantone, Meanwhile, Microtone, Ninth, Octave, Ottava, Pycnon, Respite,

Rest, Schisma, Semitone, Sixth, Space, Spell, Tritone, Wait

**Intervene** Arbitrate, Interfere, Interrupt, Mediate, Mesne, Up

**Interview** Audience, Audition, Conference, Examine, Hearing, Oral, See, Vox pop

**Interweave, Interwoven** Entwine, Interlace, Monogram, Plait, Plash, Pleach, Raddle, Wreathed

**Intestate** Heirless, Unwilling

**Intestine(s)** Bowel, Duodenum, Entrails, Guts, Harigals, Innards, Omenta, Splanchnic, Thairm, Viscera

**Intimacy, Intimate(ly)** Achates, Bosom, Connote, Familiar, Friend, Inmost, Innuendo, Intrigue, Nearness, Opine, Pack, Private, Signal, Special, Thick, Throng, Warm, Well

**Intimation** Clue, Hint, Implication, Inkling, Si quis

**Intimidate, Intimidating** Browbeat, Bulldoze, Bully, Cow, Daunt, Dragon, Hector, Psych, Threaten, Tyrannise, Unnerve

**Into** Intil, Within

**Intolerable, Intolerant** Allergic, Bigotry, Excessive, Illiberal, Impossible, Ombrophobe

**Intone, Intonation** Cadence

**In touch** Au fait

**Intoxicant, Intoxicate(d), Intoxicating** Alcoholic, Benj, Coca, Corn, Disguise, Fuddle, Ganja, Heady, HIGH, Hocus, Inebriate, Merry, Mescal, Peyote, Rumbullion, Slewed, Soma, Sozzle, Spirituous, Temulent

**Intractable** Disobedient, Kittle, Mulish, Obdurate, Perverse, Surly, Unruly, Wilful

**Intransigent** Adamant, Inflexible, Rigid, Uncompromising

**Intransitive** Neuter, Objectless

**Intrepid** Aweless, Bold, Brave, Doughty, Firm, RESOLUTE, Valiant

**Intricate** Complex, Daedal(ian), Daedale, Dedal, Gordian, Intrince, Involute, Knotty, Tirlie-wirlie, Tricky, Vitruvian

**Intrigue(r), Intriguing** Affaire, Artifice, Brigue, Cabal, Camarilla, Cloak and dagger, Collogue, Fascinate, Hotbed, Ignatian, Jesuit, Jobbery, Liaison, Machinate, Plot, Politic, Rat, SCHEME, Strategy, Trinketer

**Intrinsic(ally)** Basically, Genuine, Inherent, Innate, Per se

> **Intrinsically** may indicate something within a word

**Introduce, Introduction, Introductory** Acquaint, Anacrusis, Curtain-raiser, Enseam, Exordial, Foreword, Immit, Import, Induct, Initiate, Inject, Insert, Instil(l), Introit, Isagogic, Opening, Plant, Preamble, Preface, Preliminary, Prelude, Prelusory, Preparatory, Present, Proem, Prolegomena, Prolegomenon, Prologue, Proponent, Start, Usher

> **Introduction** may indicate a first letter

**Introspective** Musing, Reflex, Ruminant

> **In trouble** may indicate an anagram

**Introvert(ed)** Cerebrotonic, Ingrow, In-toed, Reserved, Shy

**Intrude(r), Intrusion, Intrusive** Abate, Aggress, Annoy, Bother, ENCROACH, Gatecrash, Interloper, Invade, Meddle, Nosey, Porlocking, Presume, Raid, Sorn, Trespass

**Intuition** ESP, Hunch, Insight, Instinct, Inwit, Noumenon, Telepathy, Theosophy

> **In two words** may indicate a word to be split

**Inundate, Inundation** Flood, Overflow, Overwhelm, Submerge, Swamp

**Inure** Acclimatise, Accustom, Harden, Season, Steel

**Invade(r), Invasion** Angle, Attack, Attila, Dane, Descent, Encroach, Hacker, Hengist, Horsa, Infest, Inroad, Jute, Lombard, Martian, Norman, Norsemen, Ostrogoth, Overrun, Permeate, Raid, Trespass, Vandal

**Invalid(ate)** Bad, Bogus, Bunbury, Cancel, Chronic, Clinic, Erroneous, Expired, False, Inauthentic, Inform, Inoperative, Irritate, Lapsed, Nugatory, Null, Refute, Shut-in, Terminate, Vitiate, Void

**Invaluable** Essential, Excellent, Precious, Useful

**Invariable, Invariably** Always, Constant, Habitual, Perpetual, Steady, Uniform

**Invective** Abuse, Billingsgate, Diatribe, Philippic, Reproach, Ribaldry, Tirade

**Inveigh** Declaim, Denounce, Protest, Rail

**Invent(ion), Inventive** Adroit, Brainchild, Chimera, Coin, Contrive, CREATE, Daedal, Design, Device, Fabricate, Fain, Feign, Figment, Imaginary, Improvise, Mint, Originate, Patent, Resourceful, Wit

**Inventor** Arkwright, Author, Baird, Bell, Boys, Bramah, Celsius, Coiner, Creator, Edison, Engineer, Geiger, Hansom, Marconi, Minié, Mint-master, Morse, Nernst, Nobel, Patentee, Savery, Tesla, Torricelli, Tull, Watt, Wheatstone

**Inventory** Account, Index, Itemise, List, Register, Steelbow, Stock

**Inversion, Invert** Anastrophe, Antimetabole, Antimetathesis, Capsize, Chiasmus, Entropion, Entropium, Opposite, Overset, Reverse, Turn, Upset

**Invertebrate** Annelida, Arthropod, Crinoid, Mollusc, Poriferan, Spineless, Trochelminth, Worm

**Invest(or), Investment** Agamemnon, Ambient, Bate, Beleaguer, Besiege, Bet, Blockade, Blue-chip, Capitalist, Dignify, Embark, Empanoply, Enclothe, Endow, Enrobe, Flutter, Gilt, Girt, Holding, Infeft, Install, On, Pannicle, Panniculus, Parlay, Place, Portfolio, Put, Ring, Robe, Share, Siege, Sink, Spec, Stake, Stock, Surround, Trust, Venture

> **Invest** may indicate one word surrounding another

**Investigate, Investigator, Investigation** Canvass, Case, CID, Delve, Examine, Explore, Fed, Inquest, Inquirendo, Inquisition, Nose, Organon, Organum, Probe, Pry, Quester, Rapporteur, Research, Scan, Scrutinise,

Search, Sleuth, Snoop, Study, Suss, Tec, Test, Track, Try, Zetetic

**Investiture**  Award, Inauguration

**Inveterate**  Chronic, Engrained, Habitual, Hardened

**Invidious**  Harmful, Hostile, Malign

**Invigorate, Invigorating, Invigoration**  Brace, Cheer, Elixir, Energise, Enliven, Fortify, Insinew, Pep, Refresh, Renew, Stimulate, Tonic, Vital

**Invincible**  Almighty, Brave, Stalwart, Valiant

**Inviolable**  Sacred, Sacrosanct

**Invisible**  Hidden, Imageless, Infra-red, Secret, Tusche, Unseen

**Invite, Invitation**  Ask, Attract, Bid, Call, Card, Overture, REQUEST, Solicit, Summons, Tempt

**Invocation, Invoke**  Appeal, Call, Conjure, Entreat, Epiclesis, Solicit

**Invoice**  Account, Bill, Itemise, Manifest, Pro forma

**Involuntary**  Automatic, Instinctive, Unwitting

**Involve(d), Involvement**  Commitment, Complicate, Concern, Embroil, Engage, Entail, Envelop, Imbroglio, Immerse, IMPLICATE, Include, Intricate, Meet, Necessitate, Tangle

> **Involved**  may indicate an anagram

**Inward(s)**  Afferent, Homefelt, Mental, Private, Varus, Within

**Iodine**  I, Kelp

**Ion**  Anion, Isomer, Zwitterion

**Ionian**  Iastic

**Iota**  Atom, Jot, Subscript, Whit

**IOU**  Cedula, Market, PN, Vowels

**IOW**  Vectis

**Iranian**  Babist, Kurd, Mede, Parsee

**Irascible**  Choleric, Fiery, Peevish, Snappy, Tetchy, Toustie

**Irate**  Angry, Cross, Infuriated, Wrathful

**Ire**  Anger, Cholera, Fury, Rage, Wrath

**Ireland**  Composer, Deirdre, Gaeltacht, Hibernia, Innisfail, Irena, IRL, Iverna

**Iridescence, Iridescent**  Opaline, Reflet, Shimmering, Shot, Water-gall

**Iridium**  Ir

**Iris**  Areola, Eye, Flag, Fleur-de-lis, Gladden, Lily, Lis, Orris, Rainbow, Sedge, Seg, Sunbow

**Irish(man)**  Bark, Boy, Bog-trotter, Celt(ic), Clan-na-gael, Defender, Eamon(n), Eirann, Erse, Fenian, Gaeltacht, Goidel, Greek, Keltic, Kern(e), Mick(e)(y), Milesian, Mulligan, Ogamic, Orange(man), Ostmen, Paddy(-whack), Partholon, Pat(rick), Rapparee, Redshank, Rory, Sean, Shoneen, Teague, Temper, Ultonian, Whiteboy, Wildgeese

**Irk(some)** Annoy, Bother, Irritate, Tedious

**Iron(s), Ironwork(s)** Airn, Carron, Cautery, Chains, Chalybeate, Crimp, Derringer, Dogs, Fe, Fetter, Fiddley, Flip-dog, Golfclub, Goose, Grappling, Grim, GUN, Gyve, Kamacite, Marcasite, Mars, Mashie, Mashy, Pig, PRESS, Pro-metal, Rabble, Rod, Smoother, Soldering, Spiegeleisen, Steam, Stirrup, Strong, Taggers, Terne, Waffle, Wedge

**Iron age** Latene, Villanovan

**Ironic, Irony** Antiphrasis, Asteism, Meiosis, Metal, Ridicule, Sarcasm, Satire, Trope, Wry

**Ironside** Edmund

**Ironwood** Pyengadu

> **Ironwork(s)** see IRON

**Irrational** Absurd, Brute, Foolish, Illogical, Surd, Wild

**Irrefutable** Evident, Positive, Undeniable

**Irregular(ity)** Abnormal, Alloiostrophus, Anomaly, Aperiodic, A salti, Asymmetric, Bashi-bazouk, Blotchy, Crazy, Erratic, Flawed, Formless, Guerilla, Heteroclitic, Incondite, Inordinate, Occasional, Orthotone, Para-military, Partisan, Patchy, Random, Scalene, Sebundy, Scrawl, Sharawadgi, Sharawaggi, Snatchy, Solecism, Sporadic, TA, Uneven, Variable, Zigzag

> **Irregular** may indicate an anagram

**Irrelevant** Digression, Gratuitous, Immaterial, Inept

**Irreligious** Heathen, Impious, Pagan, Profane

**Irremedial** Hopeless, Incurable, Laches

**Irreproachable** Blameless, Spotless, Stainless

**Irresistible** Almighty, Endearing, Inevitable, Mesmeric

**Irresolute, Irresolution** Aboulia, Doubtful, Hesitant, Timid, Unsure

**Irresponsible** Capricious, Feckless, Strawen, Wanton, Wildcat

**Irreverent** Disrespectful, Impious, Profane

**Irrigate, Irrigation** Canalise, Douche, Enema, Flood, Get, Water

**Irritable, Irritability, Irritant, Irritate(d), Irritation** Acerbate, Annoy, Bug, Chafe, Chauff, Crabby, Crusty, Dod, Dyspeptic, Edgy, Enchafe, Erethism, Ewk, Exasperate, Fantod, Feverish, Fleabite, Frabbit, Gall, Get, Goad, Grate, Intertrigo, Irk, Itch, Livery, Needle, Nettle, Niggly, Peevish, Pesky, Pet, Petulance, Pinprick, Pique, Provoke, Rag'd, Ragde, Rankle, Rattle, Ratty, Rile, Roil, Rub, Ruffle, Savin(e), Scratchy, Snappy, Sting, Tease, Techy, Testy, Tetchy, Tickle, Touchy, Uptight, VEX, Yuke

> **Irritated** may indicate an anagram

**Irving** Actor, Berlin

**Is** Est, Ist

**Isaiah** Is

**Isinglass** Carlock, Mica, Sturgeon

**Islam(ic)** Crescent, Sheriat, Shia(h)

**Islander** Chian, Cretan, D(a)yak, Filipino, Kanaka, Laputan, Maltese, Native, Nesiot, Orcadian, Rhodian, Samiot, Sican, Singalese

**Isle(t), Island** Achill, Ait, Aland, Aldabra, Alderney, Aleutian, Amager, Andaman, Anglesey, Anguilla, Antigua, Antilles, Archipelagos, Arran, Ar(r)u, Aruba, Ascension, Atlantis, Atoll, Attu, Avalon, Azores, Baffin, Balearic, Bali, Banaba, Barataria, Barbados, Barbuda, Barra, Benbecula, Bermoothes, Bermuda, Bikini, Billiton, Blefuscu, Borneo, Bute, Calf, Canaries, Canvey, Capri, Cassiterides, Cay, Cayman, Celebes, Ceylon, Char, Chios, Christmas, Cocos, Coney, Coral, Corfu, Corregidor, Cos, Crannog, Crete, Cuba, Curacao, Cyclades, Cyprus, Cythera, Delos, Devil's, Disko, Diu, Dodecanese, Dogs, Dominica, Easter, Eigg, Elba, Elephanta, Ellesmere, Ellice, Ellis, Emerald, Erin, Eriskay, Euboea, Eyot, Falklands, Farne, Faroe, Fiji, Fortunate, Foulness, Friendly, Frisian, Fuerteventura, Fyn, Galapagos, Gilbert, Glub(b)dubdrib, Grenada, Guadalcanal, Guam, Guernsey, Haiti, Hawaii, Hebrides, Herm, Hokkaido, Holm, Holy, Honshu, Hormuz, Hova, Hoy, I, Ibiza, Inch, Indies, Innisfree, Insula, Iona, Is, Ischia, Islay, Isola, Ithaca, Jamaica, Java, Jersey, Jolo, Jura, Key, Kyushu, Ladrones, Laputa, Leeward, Lemnos, Lesbos, Lewis, Lindisfarne, Lipari, Luggnagg, Lundy, Luzon, Madagascar, Madura, Majorca, Maldives, Mallorca, Malta, Man, Manhattan, Marianas, Marquesa, Martinique, May, Melanesia, Melos, Micronesia, Midway, Minorca, Moluccas, Mona, Muck, Mull, Nantucket, Nauru, Naxos, Negros, Newfoundland, Norfolk, Oahu, Oceania, Ogygia, Okinawa, Orcades, Orkneys, Ormuz, Palawan, Paphos, Patmos, Pescadores, Pharos, Philippines, Pitcairn, Polynesia, Rathlin, Refuge, Reil's, Reunion, Rhode(s), Rockall, Rum, Runnymede, St Helena, St Lucia, Salamis, Samar, Samoa, Samos, Samothrace, Sardinia, Saria, Sark, Scilly, Sheppey, Shetlands, Shikoku, Sicily, Skerry, Skye, Socotra, Solomon, Spice, Sporades, Staffa, Staten, Sumatra, Sunda, Surtsey, Tahiti, Tasmania, Tenedos, Thanet, Thule, Timor, Tiree, Tobago, Tonga, Tortuga, Tresco, TT, Tuvalu, Uist, Unst, Upolu, Ushant, Wake, Wight, Yap, Yell, Zante, Zealand, Zetland

**Isn't** Aint, Nis, Nys

**Isolate(d)** Ancress, Backwater, Cut off, Enisle, Incommunicado, Inisle, Lone, Maroon, Pocket, Quarantine, Sea-girt, Seclude, Secret, Segregate, Separate, Solitary, Stray

**Isomer** Carvacrol

**Isosceles** Triangle

**Isotope** Actinon, Muonium, Protium, Thoron

**Israel(i)** IL, Meir, Sabra

**Issue(s)** Come, Crux, Debouch, Denouement, Derive, Disclose, Edition, Effluence, EMANATE, Emerge, Emit, Exit, Exodus, Family, Feduciary, Flotation, Gush, Ish, Litter, Number, Offspring, Outflow, Part, Proof, Publish, Result, Sally, Seed, Son, Spawn, Spring, Stream, Subject, Topic, Turn, Utter

**Isthmus**  Darien, Kra, Neck, Panama

**It**  A, Chic, Hep, Id, Italian, SA, 't, Vermouth

**Italian, Italy**  Alpini, Ausonia, Bolognese, Calibrian, Chian, Dago, Este, Etnean, Etrurian, Etruscan, Eyeti(e), Eytie, Florentine, Genoese, Ghibelline, Guelf, Guelph, Hesperia, It, Latin, Lombard, Medici, Oscan, Paduan, Patarin(e), Roman, Sabine, Samnite, Sicel, Sikel, Sienese, Signor(i), Spag, Tuscan, Umbrian, Venetian, Vermouth, Volscian, Wop

**Itch**  Acariasis, Annoy, Cacoethes, Euk, Ewk, Hanker, Photopsy, Prickle, Prurience, Prurigo, Psora, Scabies, Scrapie, Tickle, URGE, Yeuk, Youk, Yuck, Yuke

**Item(ise)**  Also, Article, Bulletin, Detail, Entry, Flash, List, Number, Piece, Point, Spot, Too

**Iterate**  Repeat

**Itinerant, Itinerary**  Ambulant, Didakai, Didakei, Did(d)icoy, Gipsy, Gypsy, Journey, Log, Pedlar, Peripatetic, Pie-powder, Roadman, Roamer, Romany, Rootless, Route, Stroller, Traveller

**Itself**  Per se

**Ivan**  Russian, Terrible

**Ivory (tower)**  Bone, Dentine, Distant, Eburnean, Impractical, Key, Solitude, Teeth, Tusk

**Ivy**  Angelica-tree, Aralia, Bush, Cat's-foot, Creeper, Evergreen, Gill, Hedera, Helix, Panax, Udo

# Jj

**J** Curve, Juliet, Pen

**Jab(ber)** Chatter, Foin, Gabble, Immunologist, Inject, Jaw, Nudge, Poke, Prattle, Prod, Proke, Punch, Puncture, Sook, Sputter, Stab, Venepuncture, Yak

**Jack(s)** AB, Apple, Artocarpus, Ass, Ball, Boot, Bower, Bowl(s), Boy, Card, Cheap, Deckhand, Dibs(tones), Flag, Frost, Hoist, Honour, Hopper, Horner, Idle, J, Jock, Ketch, Kitty, Knave, London, Mark, Matlow, Mistress, Nob, Noddy, Point, Pot, Pur, Rabbit, Raise, Ripper, Robinson, Russell, Sailor, Salt, Shaun, Sprat, Steeple, Sticker, Straw, Tar, Tec, Tradesman, Turnspit, Union, Wood

**Jackal** Anubis, Dieb, Hack, Stooge

**Jackass** Aliboron, Goburra, Kookaburra, Stupid

**Jackdaw** Bird, Chough, Daw, Kae, Raven, Rheims, Thief

**Jacket** Acton, Anorak, Baju, Bania(n), Banyan, Basque, Blouson, Bolero, Brigandine, Bumfreezer, Cagoul(e), Camisole, Can, Cardigan, Carmagnole, Casing, COAT, Dolman, Donkey, Dust-cover, Dustwrapper, Gambeson, Grego, Ha(c)queton, Jerkin, Jupon, Kagool, Matinee, Monkey, Norfolk, Parka, Pierrot, Polka, Potato, Reefer, Sayon, Simar(re), Sleeve, Spencer, Strait, Tabard, Tunic, Tux(edo), Tweed, Vareuse, Waistcoat, Wam(m)us, Wampus, Windbreaker, Windcheater, Zouave

**Jackknife** Dive, Fold, Jockteleg, Pike

**Jackpot** Cornucopia, Kitty, Pool

**Jackson** Stonewall

**Jackstraw** Spil(l)ikin

**Jacobite** Non-compounder, Non-juror

**Jacquard** Matelasse

**Ja(c)ques** Melancholy, Tati

**Jade(d)** Axe-stone, Bidet, Cloy, Crock, Disjaskit, Exhaust, Fatigue, Hack, Hag, Horse, Hussy, Limmer, Minx, Nag, Nephrite, Rosinante, Sate, Slut, Stale, Tired, Weary, Yu(-stone)

**Jag(ged)** Barbed, Cart, Drinking, Erose, Gimp, Injection, Ragde, Ragged, Snag, Spree, Spur, Tooth

**Jaguar** Car, Caracal, Cat, E-type, Ounce, Tiger

**Jail(er)** Adam, Alcaide, Alcatraz, Bedford, Bin, Bridewell, Can, Clink, Commit, Cooler, Gaol, Hoosegow, Imprison, Incarcerate, Keeper, Kitty, Lockup, Marshalsea, Newgate, Nick, Pen, Pokey, PRISON, Screw, Shop, Strangeways, Turnkey, Warder

**Jailbird** Con, Lag, Lifer, Trusty

**Jakarta** Batavia

**Jake** Honest, Hunkydory, Rube

**Jalopy** Banger, Buggy, Car, Crate, Heap, Shandry(dan), Stock-car

**Jam** Block, Choke, Clog, Crush, Dilemma, Gridlock, Hold-up, Lock, PREDICAMENT, Preserve, Press, Quince, Seize, Snarl-up, Spot, Stick, Tailback, Traffic, Vice, Vise, Wedge

**Jamaica(n)** Rasta(farian), Rastaman, Yardie

**Jamb** Doorpost, Durn, Sconcheon, Scontion, Scuncheon, Upright

**James** Agee, Bond, Bothwell, Henry, Jacobite, Jemmy, Jesse, Jim, Joyce, Screw, Seamus, Seumas, Watt

**Jane** Austen, Calamity, Eyre, Seymour, Shore, Sian

**Jangle** Clank, Clapperclaw, Clash, Rattle, Wrangle

**Janitor** Servitor, Tiler

**Jankers** KP

**Janus** Two-faced

**Japan(ese), Japanese drama** Ainu, Daimio, Eta, Geisha, Genro, Gloss, Haiku, Hondo, Honshu, Issei, Kabuki, Kami, Kana, Kirimon, Lacquer, Mandarin, Mikado, Mousmé, Mousmee, Nippon, No(h), Resin, Sansei, Satsuma, Shinto, Shogun, Togo, Tycoon, Yamato

**Jape** Jeer, Joke, Prank

**Jar** Albarello, Amphora, Canopus, Churr, Clash, Crock, Cruet, Din, Dolium, Enrough, Gallipot, Grate, Greybeard, Gride, Grind, Gryde, JOLT, Kalpis, Kang, Kilner, Leyden, Olla, Pithos, Pot(iche), Rasp, Shelta, Shock, Stamnos, Start, Stean, Steen, Stein, Tankard, Tinaja, Turn, Vessel, Water-monkey

**Jargon** Argot, Baragouin, Beach-la-mar, Buzzword, Cant, Chinook, Gobbledegook, Gobbledygook, Kennick, Lingo, Lingua franca, Newspeak, Parlance, Patois, Patter, Shelta, SLANG, Vernacular

**Jasmine** Frangipani, Jessamy

**Jasper** Basanite, Bloodstone

**Jaundice(d)** Cynical, Icterus, Prejudiced, Sallow, Yellow

**Jaunt** Journey, Outing, Sally, Stroll, Swan, Trip

**Jaunty** Airy, Akimbo, Chipper, Debonair, Perky, Rakish

> **Jaunty** may indicate an anagram

**Javelin** Dart, Gavelock, Harpoon, Jereed, Jerid, Pile, Pilum, Spear

**Jaw(s), Jawbone** Blab, Chaft, Chap, Chat, Chaw, Cheek, Chin, Entry, Gnathite, Jobe, Lantern, Mandible, Maxilla, Muzzle, Natter, Pi, Premaxillary, Prognathous, Ramus, Shark, Wapper-jaw, Ya(c)kety-Ya(c)k

**Jay** Bird, J, Sirgang, Whisky-jack, Whisky-john

**Jazz(er), Jazzman** Barber, Bebop, Blues, Boogie, Bop, Cat, Dixieland, Enliven, Gig, Gutbucket, Hipster, Jive, Mainstream, Ragtime, Riff, Skiffle, Stomp, Swinger, Trad

**Jealous(y)** Envious, Green(-eyed), Grudging, Zelotypia

**Jean(s)** Chino, Denim, Levis (tdmk), Pants, Trousers, Wranglers (tdmk)

**Jeer(ing)** Ballyrag, Barrack, Birl, Boo, Burl, Digs, Fleer, Flout, Gird, Hoot, Jape, Jibe, MOCK, Rail, Razz, Ridicule, Scoff, Sneer, Taunt, Twit

**Jeeves** Valet

**Jehovah** God, Lord, Yahve(h), Yahwe(h)

**Jehu** Charioteer, Driver

**Jejune** Arid, Barren, Dry, Insipid, Juvenile

**Jelly** Acaleph(a), Acalephe, Agar(-agar), Aspic, Brawn, Calf's foot, Chaudfroid, Cow-heel, EXPLOSIVE, Flummery, Gel, Isinglass, Jam, Kanten, Macedoine, Medusa, Mould, Napalm, Neat's foot, Quiddany, Royal, Shape, Tunicin

> **Jelly** may indicate an anagram

**Jellyfish** Acaleph(a), Acalephe, Aurelia, Blubber, Cnidaria, Discomedusae, Discophora, Hydromedusa, Medusa, Mesogloea, Planoblast, Quarl, Scyphistoma, Sea-blubber, Sea-nettle

**Jemmy** Betty, Crowbar, Lever

**Jenkins** Ear, Roy, Up

**Jenny** Ass, Lind, Mule, Spinner, Spinster, Wren

**Jeopardise, Jeopardy** Danger, Expose, Hazard, Peril, Risk

**Jeremiad** Lament, Tragedy, Woe

**Jeremy** Fisher, Jerry

**Jerk(ily), Jerks** Aerobics, A salti, Bob, Braid, Diddle, Ebrillade, Flirt, Flounce, Gym(nastics), Hike, Hitch, Hoi(c)k, Jut, Kant, PE, Peck, Physical, Saccade, Shove, Spasm, Surge, Tic, Toss(en), Tweak, TWITCH, Wrench, Yank

**Jerkin** Jacket

**Jerome** Kern, Vulgate

**Jerry, Jerry-built** Boche, Flimsy, Fritz, Hun, Kraut, Mouse, Po(t)

**Jersey(s)** Cow, Frock, Gansey, Guernsey, Kine, Lily, Maillot, Polo, Roll-neck, Singlet, SWEATER, Zephyr

**Jerusalem** Ariel, Hierosolymitan, Zion

**Jess(e)** James, Strap

**Jest(er)** Badinage, Barm, Baur, Bawr, Bourd(er), Buffoon, Clown, Cod, Comic, Droll, Goliard, Jape, Joker, Josh, Miller, Motley, Patch, Quip, Raillery, Ribaldry, Rigoletto, Scogan, Scoggin, Sport, Toy, Trinculo, Wag, Wit, Yorick

**Jesuit** Bollandist, Ignatius, Loyola, SJ

**Jesus** Christ, Emmanuel, IHS, Immanuel, INRI, Jabers, Lord

**Jet** Airbus, Aircraft, Black, Burner, Chirt, Douche, Fountain, Geat, Harrier, Plane, Pump, Soffione, Spirt, Spout, Spray, Spurt, Squirt, Stream, Turbine,

Turbo, Vapour

**Jettison** Discard, Dump, Flotsam, Jetsam, Lagan, Ligan

**Jetty** Mole, Pier, Wharf

**Jew(ish), Jews** Ashkenazi, Chas(s)id, Diaspora, Essene, Falasha, Grecian, Has(s)id, Hebrew, Kahal, Karaite, Kike, Levite, Lubavitch, Maccabee, Marrano, Pharisee, Sabra, Sadducee, Semite, Sephardim, Sheeny, Shemite, Shtetl, Smouch, Smous(e), Tobit, Wandering, Yid(dish), Zealot

**Jewel(lery)** Agate, Almandine, Beryl, Brilliant, Chrysoprase, Cloisonné, Cornelian, Costume, Diamond, Ear-drop, Emerald, Ewe-lamb, Ferron(n)ière, Garnet, GEM, Gracchi, Jade, Lherzolite, Marcasite, Navette, Olivine, Opal, Paste, Pavé, Pearl, Pendant, Peridot, Rivière, Rubin(e), Ruby, Sapphire, Sard, Scarab, Smaragd, Solitaire, Stone, Sunburst, Tom, Topaz, Torc, Treasure

**Jezebel** Harlot, Loose, Whore

**Jib** Ba(u)lk, Boggle, DEMUR, Face, Foresail, Genoa, Milk, Reest, Reist, Stay-sail

**Jibe** Bob, Correspond, Fling, JEER, Mock, Sarcasm, Slant, Taunt

**Jiffy** Mo, Pronto, Twinkling

**Jig(gle)** Bob, Bounce, Dance, Fling, Frisk, Jog, Juggle

**Jigger(ed)** Beat, Chigoe, Jolley, Ruin

**Jilt** Discard, Reject, Shed, Throw-over

**Jim(my)** Diamond, Dismal, Jas, Lucky, Pee, Piddle, Riddle

**Jingle(r)** Clerihew, Clink, Ditty, Doggerel, Rhyme, Tambourine, Tinkle

**Jingo(ism)** Odzooks, Patriot, War-rant

**Jinn(i)** Afreet, Eblis, Genie, Marid, Spirit

**Jinx** Curse, Hex, Jonah, Kibosh, Spoil, Whammy

**Jitter(s), Jittery** Coggly, DT, Fidgets, Funk, Jumpy, Nervous, Willies

> **Jitter(s)** may indicate an anagram

**Jo** Sweetheart

**Job** Appointment, Berth, Career, Chore, Comforter, Crib, Darg, Errand, Gig, Metier, Oratorio, Patient, Pensum, Plum, Post, Problem, Put-up, Sinecure, Spot, Steady, TASK, Ticket, Trotter, Undertaking, Work

> **Job** may indicate the biblical character

**Jock** DJ, Mac, Scot

**Jockey** Carr, Cheat, Diddle, Jostle, Lester, Manoeuvre, Rider, Steve, Swindle, Trick, Winter

> **Jockey** may indicate an anagram

**Jocose, Jocular, Jocund** Cheerful, Debonair, Facetious, Jesting, Lepid, Scurril(e), Waggish

**Joe(y), Joseph** Addison, Dogsbody, GI, Kangaroo, Pal, Roo, Sloppy, Stalin, Surface, Trey

**Jog(gle), Jog-trot** Arouse, Dunch, Dunsh, Heich-how, Heigh-ho, Hod, Jiggle, Jolt, Jostle, Mosey, Nudge, Prompt, Ranke, Remind, Run, Shake, Shog, Tickle, Trot, Whig

**John(ny)** Ajax, Augustus, Barleycorn, Bog, Bright, Brown, Bull, Cloaca, Collins, Doree, Dory, Elton, Evan, Gaunt, Gents, Gilpin, Groats, Halifax, Ivan, Lackland, Lav, Little, Loo, Peel, Prester, Stage-door, WC

**Johnson** Cham, Doctor, Idler

**Join(er)** Abut, Accede, Accompany, Add, Ally, And, Annex, Associate, Attach, Butt-end, Cement, Cleave, Combine, Conflate, Conjugate, Connect, COUPLE, Dovetail, Engraft, Enlist, Enrol, Enter, Fuse, Glue, Graft, Hasp, Hitch, Hyphen, Include, Jugate, Knit, Link, Marry, Meet, Menuisier, Merge, Mix, Mortar, Mortise, Oop, Oup, Piece, Rebate, Rivet, Scarf, Seam, Siamize, Snug, Solder, Splice, Squirrel, Tenon, Unite, Wed, Weld, Yoke

**Joint(ed)** Ancon, Ankle, Arthrosis, Articular, Ball and socket, Bar, Baron, Cardan, Carpus, Chine, Co, Commissure, Cuit, Cut, Dive, Dovetail, Elbow, Enarthrosis, Entrecôte, Gimmal, Gimmer, Ginglymus, Hainch, Haunch, Heel, Hinge, Hip, Hough, Huck, J, Joggle, Jolly, Junction, Knee, Knuckle, Lith, Loin, Marijuana, Meat, Mitre, Mortise, Mouse (buttuck), Mouse-piece, Mutton, Mutual, Phalange, Popliteal, Psoas, Rack, Raphe, Reducer, Reefer, Rhaphe, Roast, Saddle, Scarf, Schindylesis, Seam, Shoulder, Silverside, Sirloin, Splice, Spliff, Stifle, Symphysis, Tarsus, T-bone, Tenon, Together, Topside, Trochanter, Undercut, Universal, Vertebra, Weld, Wrist

**Joist** Bar, Beam, Dormant, Rib, Sleeper, Solive

**Joke(r)** Banter, Bar, Booby-trap, Chaff, Chestnut, CLOWN, Cod, Comic, Crack, Farceur, Farceuse, Fool, Fun, Gab, Gag, Glike, Guy, Have-on, Hazer, Hum, Humorist, Jape, Jest, Jig, Lark, Legpull, Merryman, Mistigris, One-liner, Pleasantry, Practical, Prank(ster), Pun, Pundigrion, Quip, Sally, Scherzo, Sick, Skylark, Sottisier, Squib, Wag, Wheeze, Wisecrack, Wild, Wit

**Jollity, Jolly** 'Arryish, Bally, Convivial, Cordial, Do, Festive, Galoot, Gaucie, Gaucy, Gawcy, Gawsy, Gay, Hilarious, Jocose, Jovial, Marine, Mirth, Rag, RM, Roger, Sandboy, Tar, Very

**Jolt** Bump, Jar, Jig-a-jig, Jostle, Jounce, Shake, Shog, Start

**Jonah** Hoodoo, Jinx

**Jones** Davy, Emperor, Inigo

**Jordan** Pot, Urinal

**Joris** Horseman

> **Joseph** see JOE

**Josh** Chaff, Kid, Rib, Tease

**Josiah** Stamp, Wedgewood

**Joss** Incense, Luck, Stick

**Jostle** Barge, Compete, Elbow, Hustle, Push, Shoulder, SHOVE

**Jot, Jotting(s)** Ace, Iota, Memo, Mite, Note, Tittle, Whit

**Journal** Daily, Daybook, Diary, Ephemeris, Gazette, Hansard, Lancet, Log, Noctuary, Organ, Paper, Pictorial, Punch, Rag, Record, TES, TLS

**Journalism, Journalist** Columnist, Contributor, Diarist, Diurnalist, Ed, Fleet St, (GA)Sala, Hack, Inkslinger, Lobby, Northcliffe, NUJ, Pepys, Press(man), Reporter, Reviewer, Scribe, Stead, Stringer, WRITER

**Journey** Circuit, Cruise, Errand, Expedition, Eyre, Hadj, Jaunce, Jaunse, Jaunt, Odyssey, Passage, Periegesis, Ply, Raik, Rake, Run, Sentimental, Tour, Travel, Trek

**Journeyman** Artisan, Commuter, Craftsman, Sterne, Yeoman

**Joust** Tilt, Tournament, Tourney

**Jove** Egad, Gad, Igad, Jupiter, Thunderer

**Jovial** Bacchic, Festive, Genial, Jolly

**Jowl** Cheek, Chops, Jaw

**Joy(ful), Joyous** Blithe, DELIGHT, Dream, Ecstasy, Elation, Exulting, Fain, Felicity, Festal, Frabjous, Glad, Glee, Gloat, Hah, Jubilant, Nirvana, Rapture, Schadenfreude, Sele, Transport, Treat

**JP** Beak

**Jubilant, Jubilation, Jubilee** Celebration, Cock-a-hoop, Ecstatic, Elated, Holiday, Joy, Triumphant

**Judaism** Semitism

**Judas** Traitor, Tree

**Judder** Shake, Vibrate

**Jude** Obscure

**Judge(ment), Judges** Addoom, Adjudicator, Agonothetes, Alacus, Alcalde, Arbiter, Areopagite, Aret(t), Arrêt, Assess, Assize, Auto-da-fé, Avizandum, Brehon, Cadi, Calculate, Censure, Centumvirus, Connoisseur, Consider, Coroner, Court, Critic(ise), Daniel, Daysman, Deborah, Decern(e), Decide, Decision, Deem(ster), Dicast, Differential, Dikast, Discern(ment), Ephor, Estimate, Evaluate, Gauge, Gesse, Gideon, Good-sense, Guess, Hakim, Hearing, Hold, Honour, J, Jeffreys, Jephthah, Justice, Lud, Lynch, Minos, Mufti, Nonsuit, Opine, Opinion, Outfangthief, Paris, Podesta, Puisne, Puny, Reckon(ing), Recorder, Ref(eree), Regard, Rhadamanthus, Ruler, Scan, See, Sentence, Sentiment, Shallow, Sheriff, Solomon, Sound, Suppose, Syndic, Think, Trior, Try, Umpire, Verdict, Wig, Wisdom, Worship

**Judicious** Critical, Discreet, Politic, Rational, Sage, Sensible, Shrewd, Sound

**Judo** Dojo

**Jug** Amphora, Bellarmine, Bird, Blackjack, Bombard, Can, Cooler, Cream, Crock, Enghalskrug, Ewer, Gaol, Gotch, Greybeard, Growler, Malling, Olpe, Pitcher, Pound, Pourer, Pourie, PRISON, Quad, Quod, Shop, Stir, Toby, Urceolus

**Juggle(r)** Conjuror, Cook, Fake

**Juice, Juicy** Bacca, Cassareep, Cassaripe, Cremor, Current, Fluid, Fruity, Ichor, Laser, Latex, Lush, Oil, Rare, Sap, Soma, Spanish, Succulent, Succ(o)us, Thridace, Vril, Zest

**Juju** Charm, Fetish

**Jujube** Lotus, Padma, Sweet

**Jukebox** Nickelodeon

**Julian** Apostate

**Jumble** Chaos, Conglomeration, Farrago, Huddle, Jabble, Lumber, Mass, Medley, Mingle-mangle, Mish-mash, Mixter-maxter, Mixtie-maxtie, Mixture, Mix(t)y-max(t)y, Pastiche, Ragbag, Scramble, Shuffle, Wuzzle

> **Jumbled** may indicate an anagram

**Jumbo** Aircraft, Elephant, Jet, Large-scale, Mammoth, OS

**Jump(er), Jumping, Jumpy** Assemble, Batterie, Boome, Caper, Cicada, Cicata, Cricket, Croupade, Desultory, Entrechat, Euro, Flea, Gazump, Halma, Hurdle, Impala, Itchy, Joey, Kangaroo, Knight, Lammie, Lammy, Leap(frog), Lep, Lope, Lutz, Nervous, Nervy, Parachute, Pounce, Prance, Prank, Quersprung, Salchow, Saltigrade, Scissors, Scoup, Scowp, Skipjack, SPRING, Start, Sweater, Trampoline, Vault

**Jumping-jack** Pantine

**Junction** Abutment, Bregma, Carfax, Clover-leaf, Connection, Crewe, Crossroads, Intersection, Joint, Josephson, Knitting, Meeting, Point, Raphe, Spaghetti, Suture, T, Union

**Juneberry** Saskatoon, Shadbush

**Jungle** Blackboard, Boondocks, Bush, Forest, Shola, Tangle

**Junior** Cadet, Cion, Dogsbody, Name-son, Petty, Puisne, Scion, Sub(ordinate), Underling, Understrapper, Younger

**Juniper** Red-cedar, Savin(e)

**Junk** Bric-a-brac, Jettison, Litter, Lorcha, Lumber, Refuse, Ship, Tatt, Trash

> **Junk** may indicate an anagram

**Junker** Prussian

**Junket(ing)** Beano, Creel, Custard, Feast, Picnic, Rennet, Spree

**Junta** Cabal, Council

**Jupiter** Jove, Newspaper

**Jurassic** Lias, Rhaetic

**Jurisdiction** Authority, Bailiewick, Domain, Province, Soke(n)

**Juror, Jury** Assize, Dicast, Inquest, Judges, Mickleton, Pais, Panel, Bail, Tales, Tribunal, Venire

**Just(ice)** Alcalde, All, Aristides, Astraea, Balanced, Cupar, Equity, Fair, Honest, Impartial, J, Jasper, Jeddart, Jethart, Jurat, Mere, Nemesis, Newly, Nice, Only, Piso, Poetic, Provost, Recent, Right(ful), Rightness, Shallow, Silenoe, Themis, Tilt, Upright

**Justifiable, Justification, Justify** Apology, Autotelic, Avenge, Aver,

Avowry, Clear, Darraign(e), Darrain(e), Darrayn, Defend, Deraign, Excusable, Explain, Grounds, Rationale, Vindicate, Warrant

**Just so** Exactly, Sic, Stories

**Jut** Beetle, Bulge, Overhang, Project, Protrude, Sail

**Jute** Burlap, Corchorus, Gunny, Hengist, Hessian, Horsa, Urena

**Juvenile** Childish, Teenage(r), Yonkers, Young, Younkers

# Kk

**K** Kelvin, Kilo, King, Kirkpatrick

**K2** Dapsang, Godwin Austen

**Kaffir** Shares, Xosa

**Kail, Kale** Cabbage, Cole, Ninepins

**Kaiser** Doorn

**Kaleidoscope** Dappled, Motley, Myrioscope, Various

**Kangaroo** Beltong, Boomer, Bounder, Cus-cus, Diprotodont, Euro, Forester, Joey, Macropodidae, Nototherium, Old man, Potoroo, Steamer, Troop, Wallaby, Wallaroo

**Karate** Kung Fu, Wushu

**Karma** Destiny, Fate, Predestination

**Kate** Greenaway, Shrew

**Kebab** Cevapcici, Satay, Sate, Shashli(c)k

**Keel** Bottom, Carina, Centreboard, Faint, List, Overturn, Skeg(g)

**Keen(ness), Keener** Acid, Acute, Agog, Argute, Astute, Athirst, Avid, Aygre, Bemoan, Bewail, Breem, Breme, Coronach, Dash, Devotee, Dirge, Eager, Elegy, Enthusiastic, Fanatical, Fell, Greet, Hone, Howl, Lament, Mourn, Mustard, Mute, Narrow, Ochone, Ohone, Perceant, Persant, Raring, Red-hot, Rhapsodic, Sharp, Shrewd, Shrill, Snell, Thirsting, Thrillant, Trenchant, Ululate, Wail, Whet, Zeal(ous)

**Keep(er), Keeping** Ames, Armature, Austringer, Castellan, Castle, Celebrate, Chatelain(e), Citadel, Conceal, Conserve, Curator, Custodian, Custody, Detain, Fort, Gaoler, Goalie, Guardian, Have, Hoard, HOLD, Maintain, Nab, Net, Observe, Ostreger, Pickle, Preserve, Retain, Stet, Stock, Store, Stow, Support, Sustain, Tower, Withhold

**Keep back** Detain, Recoup, Reserve, Retard, Stave

**Keepsake** Memento

**Keep under** Cow, Subdue, Submerge

**Keg** Barrel, Cask, Tub, Tun, Vat

**Kelly('s)** Eye, Gene

**Kelvin** K

**Ken** Eyeshot, Know(ledge), Range

**Kennel(s)** Guard, Home, House, Shelter

**Kent** Lathe, SE

**Kentuckian, Kentucky** Chicken, Corn-cracker, Derby, KY

**Kenya(n)** Masai

**Kerala**  Nair, Nayar

**Kerb**  Edge, Gutter, Roadside

**Kerchief**  Babushka, Bandan(n)a, Headcloth, Romal, Scarf

**Kernel**  Copra, Core, Grain, Nucleus, Praline, Prawlin

**Kestrel**  Bird, Hawk, Keelie, Stallion, Staniel, Stannel, Stanyel, Windhover

**Ket**  Carrion, Wool

**Ketch**  Jack

**Ketchup**  Relish, Sauce, Tomato

**Kettle**  Boiler, Cauldron, Dixie, Dixy, Drum, Fanny, Pot, Turpin

**Key(hole)**  A, Allen, Ash, B, Basic, C, Cay, Central, Chip, Cipher, Clavis, Clew, Clink, Clue, Crib, D, Digital, Dital, E, Essential, F, Flat, Fruit, G, Holm, Ignition, Important, Inch, Index, Instrumental, Islet, Ivory, Kaie, King-pin, Latch, Legend, Linchpin, Locker, Main, Major, Minor, Note, Octachord, Opener, Oustiti, Outsiders, Passe-partout, Pivot, Pony, Reef, Signature, Skeleton, Spanner, Spline, Stimulate, Tab, Table, Tonal, Vital, Wedge, Yale

**Keyboard**  Console, Digitorium, DVORAK, Manual, Martenot, Piano(la), Qwerty, Spinet

**Keyholder**  Occupant, Resident, Tenant, Warder

**Key man**  Islander, Kingpin

**Keynote**  Line, Mese, Theme, Tonic

**Keystone**  Cops, Crux, PA, Pennsylvania, Quoin, Sagitta, Voussoir

**Keyword**  Kwic, Sesame

**Khan**  Aga, Chagan, Cham, Serai, Shere

**Kick(ing)**  Boot, Buzz, Corner, Dribble, Drop, Fling, Garryowen, Hack, Hoof, Lash, Pause, Pile, Punt, Recoil, Savate, Sixpence, Spur, Spurn, Tanner, Thrill, Toe, Vigour, Wince, Yerk, Zip

**Kid**  Arab, Befool, Billy, Cheverel, Chevrette, Child, Chit, Con, Delude, Goat, Hoax, Hocus, Hoodwink, Hum, Joke, Leather, Misguide, Nipper, Offspring, Pretend, Rib, Spoof, Suede, Sundance, TEASE, Tot, Trick

**Kidnap**  Abduct, Hijack, Plagium, Snatch, Spirit, Steal

**Kidney(-shaped)**  Character, Mettle, Nature, Reins, Renal, Reniform, Sort

**Kill(er), Killing**  Assassin, Battue, Behead, Biocidal, Boojum, Butcher, Carnage, Carnifex, Chance-medley, Comical, Croak, Crucify, Cull, Despatch, Destroy, Execute, Exterminate, For(e)do, Frag, Garotte, Germicide, Gun, Homicide, Ice, K, Knacker, Lynch, Misadventure, Mortify, Murder, Napoo, Ninja, NK, Orc(a), -phage, Pip, Predator, Quell, Quietus, Regrate, Sacrifice, Shochet, Slaughter, Slay(er), Slew, Smite, Snuff, Stifle, Stonker, Swat, Tailor, Thagi, Thug(gee), Toreador, Veto, Zap

**Killjoy**  Crab, Puritan, Sourpuss, Spoilsport

**Kiln**  Oast, Oven

**Kilometre**  Km, Verst

**Kilt** Drape, Filabeg, Fil(l)ibeg, Fustanella, Phil(l)abeg, Phil(l)ibeg, Plaid, Tartan

**Kin(sman)** Ally, Family, Kith, Like, Nearest, Relation, Sib(b), Sybbe

**Kind(ly)** Akin, Amiable, Benefic, Benevolent, Benign, Boon, Breed, Brood, Brotherly, Category, Class, Clement, Considerate, Favourable, Gender, Generic, Generous, Genre, Gentle, Genus, Good, Humane, Ilk, Kidney, Kin, Lenient, Manner, Modal, Nature, Sisterly, SORT, Species, Strain, Strene, Trine, Type, Understanding, Variety, Ylke

**Kindle** Accend, Fire, Ignite, Incense, Incite, Inflame, LIGHT, Litter, Lunt, Stimulate, Teend, Tind, Tine, Tynd(e)

**Kindness** Aloha, Benevolence, Clemency, Favour, Humanity

**Kindred** Allied, Blood, Like, Related

**King(s), Kingly** Acestes, Aegeus, Agag, Agamemnon, Agis, Ahab, Ahasuerus, Alexander, Alfred, Alonso, Amasis, Apple, Ard-ri(gh), Arthur, Asa, Athelstan, Attila, Balak, Belshazzar, Bretwalda, Brut(e), Brutus, Busiris, Butcher, Canute, Caractacus, Caradoc, Ceyx, Cheops, Clovis, Cobra, Cole, Conchobar, Cophetua, Cotton, Creon, Croesus, Cunobelin, Cymbeline, Cyrus, Darius, David, Duncan, Edwin, Egbert, Elidure, Endymion, English, ER, Ethelbert, Evander, Evil, Fahd, Farouk, Frederick, Florestan, GR, Gyges, Hardicanute, Harold, Herod, Highness, Hiram, Hyksos, Idris, Inca, Ine, Ixion, Jereboam, Jonathan, Kong, Lalus, Leonidas, Lionheart, Lir, Lludd, Log, Louis, Lucomo, Lud, Ludwig, Majesty, Memnon, Menelaus, Midas, Milesian, Minos, Monarch, Mpret, Nebuchadnezzar, Negus, Nestor, Ninus, Nudd, Numa, Oberon, Odysseus, Oedipus, Offa, Og, Ogyges, Ozymandias, Pearly, Penda, Penguin, Peishwa(h), Peshwa, Pharaoh, Philip, Priam, Ptolemy, Pygmalion, R, Ransom, Ras Tafari, Re, Rehoboam, Reigner, Rex, Rhesus, Rial, Roi, Royalet, Rufus, Ruler, Ryal, Sailor, Saul, Sennacherib, Seven, Shah, Shilling, Solomon, Sovereign, Stephen, Stork, Tantalus, Tarquin, Tigranes, Uther (Pendragon), Vortigern, Wenceslas, Xerxes, Zedekiah, Zog

**Kingdom, Kingship** Animal, Aragon, Barataria, Bohemia, Brunel, Dominion, Elam, Fife, Jordan, Lydia, Mercia, Mineral, Navarre, Nepal, Noricum, Parthia, Realm, Reign, Royalty, Sphere, Throne, Tonga, Vegetable, Wessex, World

**Kingfisher** Alcyone, Halcyon

**Kingmaker** Neville, Warwick

**King-of-arms** Clarenc(i)eux, Garter, Lyon, Norroy (and Ulster)

**King's evil** Crewels, Cruels, Scrofula

**King's son** Dauphin, Delphin, P, Prince

**Kink(y)** Bent, Buckle, Crapy, Enmeshed, Flaw, Knurl, Null, Nurl, Odd, Perm, Perverted, Quirk, Twist, Wavy

> **Kink(y)** may indicate an anagram

**Kinkajou** Potto

**Kip, Kipper** Cure, Dosser, Doze, Limey, Nap, Sleeper, Smoke

**Kipling** Beetle

> **Kipper** see KIP

**Kirkpatrick** K

**Kismet** Destiny, Fate, Karma, Predestination

**Kiss(er), Kissing** Buss, Caress, Contrecoup, Lip, Neck, Osculate, Pax(-board), Pax-brede, Peck, Pet, Plonker, Pree, Salue, Salute, Smacker, Smooch, Smouch, Snog, Spoon, Thimble, X, Yap

**Kit** Christopher, Housewife, Layette, Marlowe, OUTFIT, Rig, Set, Slops, Sportswear, Tackle, Uniform

**Kitchen** Caboose, Cookhouse, Cuisine, Galley, Scullery

**Kite** Belly, Bird, Chil, Crate, Dragon, Elanet, Forktail, Gled(e), Hawk, Milvus, Paunch, Puttock, Rokkaku

**Kitten(ish)** Cute, Kindle, Sexy

**Kittiwake** Bird, Gull, Hacklet, Haglet

**Kitty** Ante, Cat, Fisher, Float, Fund, Jackpot, Pool, Tronc

**Kiwi** Apteryx, NZ, Ratitae

**Knack** Art, Flair, Forte, Gift, Hang, Instinct, TALENT, Trick

**Knacker** Castanet, Exhaust

**Knapsack** Musette

**Knapweed** Matfelon

**Knave(ry)** Bower, Boy, Card, Coistril, Coystril, Custrel, Dog, Drole, Fripon, Jack(-a-napes), Jock, Loon, Makar, Maker, Nob, Pam, Pur, Rapscallion, RASCAL, Recreant, Ropery, Scoundrel, Taroc, Tarot, Tom, Treachery, Varlet, Villain

**Knead** Conch, Malax(ate), Massage, Mould, Pug, Pummel, Work

**Knee (pan)** Genu, Hock, Housemaid's, Lap, Patella, Poleyn, Propliteal, Punch, Rotula

**Kneel(er)** Defer, Genuflect, Hassock, Kowtow, Truckle

**Knell** Bell, Curfew, Dirge, Peal, Ring, Toll

**Knicker(bocker), Knickers** Bloomers, Culottes, Directoire, Irving, Panties, Plus-fours, Shorts, Trousers

**Knick-knack** Bagatelle, Bibelot, Bric-a-brac, Gewgaw, Pretty(-pretty), Quip, Smytrie, Toy, Trangam, Trifle, Victoriana

**Knife** Anelace, Barong, Bistoury, Blade, Bolo, Bolster, Bowie, Carver, Catling, Chakra, Clasp, Cradle, Cuttle, Cutto(e), Da(h), Dagger, Flick, Gull(e)y, Jockteleg, Kard, Kukri, Lance(t), Machete, Matchet, Panga, Scalpel, Shiv, Simi, Slash, Snee, Snickersnee, Spade, Stab, Stanley, Tranchet

**Knight** Accolon, Alphagus, Artegal, Banneret, Bayard, Bedivere, Bliant, Bors, Britomart, Caballero, Calidore, Cambel, Caradoc, Carpet, Cavalier, Chevalier, Crusader, Douceper, Douzeper, Dub, Errant, Galahad, Gallant, Gareth, Garter, Gawain, Guyon, Hospitaller, Kay, KB, KBE, KG,

La(u)ncelot, Lionel, Lochinvar, Lohengrin, Maecenas, Malta, Medjidie, Melius, Modred, N, Noble, Orlando, Paladin, Palmerin, Parsifal, Perceforest, Perceval, Percival, Pharamond, Pinel, Ritter, Samurai, Sir, Tannhauser, Templar, Teutonic, Trencher, Tristan, Tristram

**Knit(ting)** Contract, Crochet, Entwine, Interlock, K, Mesh, Porosis, Purl, Seam, Set, Stockinet, Weave, Wrinkle

**Knob(by)** Berry, Boll, Boss, Botoné, Bottony, Bur(r), Cam, Caput, Croche, Handle, Hill, Inion, Knur(r), Noop, Pellet, Pommel, Protuberance, Pulvinar, Snib, Snub, Snuff, Stud, Torose, Tuber, Tuner

**Knobless** Enodal

**Knock (down, off, out)** Bang, Beaut, Biff, Blow, Bump, Ca(a), Chap, Clash, Clour, Collide, Con, Criticise, Daud, Dawd, Degrade, Denigrate, Deride, Dev(v)el, Ding, Dinnyhauser, Etherise, Eyeful, Floor, Grace-stroke, HIT, Innings, KO, Lowse, Lowsit, Mickey Finn, Pan, Pink, Quietus, Rap, Rat-tat, Skittle, Spat, Steal, Stop, Strike, Tap, Thump, Wow

**Knock-kneed** Valgus

**Knot(ted), Knotty** Baff, Bend, Bow, Burl, Bur(r), Carrick-bend, Cat's paw, Clinch, Cluster, Crochet, Entangle, GNARL, Gordian, Granny, Herculean, Hitch, Knag, Knap, Knar, Knur(r), Macramé, Macrami, Mouse, Nirl, Node, Nowed, Nur(r), Picot, Problem, Reef, Rosette, Sheepshank, Sleave, Spurr(e)y, Tangle, Tat, Tie, Tubercle, Turk's head, Windsor

**Know(how), Knowing, Knowledge(able), Known** Acquaintance, Aware, Cognition, Comprehend, Epistemics, Expertise, Famous, Fly, Gnostic, Have, Hep, Info, Insight, Intentional, Intuition, Jnana, Ken, Kith, Kydst, Lare, Light, Lore, Mindful, Omniscience, On, Pansophy, Party, RECOGNISE, Sapient, Savvy, Science, Scilicet, Shrewd, Smattering, Understand(ing), Up, Versed, Wat(e), Weet(e), Wise, Wist, Wit, Wot

**Know-all** Arrogant, Besserwisser, Bumptious, Cognoscenti, Pansophist, Polymath, Wiseacre

**Knuckle** Apply, Fist, Joint, Ossein, Submit

**Koko** List

**Kop** Spion

**Koran** Scripture, Sura(h)

**Korean** ROK

**Kosher** Approved, Genuine, Legitimate, Real

**Kremlin** Fortress

**Kri** Masora

**Krypton** Kr

**Kudos** Credit, Glory, Praise

**Kyanite** Disthene

# LI

**L** Latitude, League, Learner, Left, Length, Liberal, Lima, Litre, Long, Luxembourg, Pound

**La** Indeed, My

**Label** Band, Brand, Docket, File, Mark, Sticker, Tab, Tag, Tally, Ticket, Trace

**Labiate** Catmint, Hoarhound, Horehound

**Labour(er), Laboured, Laborious** Arduous, Begar, Birth, Carl, Casual, Chirl, Chore, Coolie, Corvée, Cottager, Cottar, Dataller, Dwell, Gandy-dancer, Gibeonite, Grecian, Grind, Hercules, Ida, Job, Journeyman, Kanaka, Katorga, Leaden, Manpower, Moil, Navvy, Operose, Pain, Peon, Pioneer, Prole, Redneck, Roll, Roustabout, Sisyphean, Slave, Stint, Strive, Sudra, Sweated, Task, TOIL(some), Toss, Travail, Uphill, Vineyard, WORK(er), Workmen

**Labrador** Retriever, Tea

**Labyrinth** Daedalus, Maze, Mizmaze, Web

> **Labyrinthine** may indicate an anagram

**Lac** Lacquer, Lakh, Resin, Shellac, Tomans

**Lace, Lacy** Alençon, Babiche, Beat, Brussels, Chantilly, Colbertine, Dash, Dentelle, Duchesse, Filet, Galloon, Guipure, Honiton, Inweave, Jabot, Lash, Macramé, Malines, Mechlin, Mignonette, Mode, Net, Orris, Pearlin, Picot, Point, Reseau, Reticella, Ricrac, Rosaline, Shoe-tie, Spike, Tat(ting), Thrash, Torchon, Trim, Trol(le)y, Valenciennes, Weave, Welt, Window-bar

**Lacerate(d)** Ganch, Gash, Gaunch, Rent, Rip, Slash, Tear

**Lachrymose** Maudlin, Niobe, Tearful, Water-standing, WEEPY

**Lack(ing), Lacks** Absence, Aplasia, Dearth, Famine, Ha'n't, Minus, NEED, Poverty, Shortfall, Shy, Void, Want

**Lack of confidence** Doubt, Scepsis

**Lackadaisical** Languid, Listless, Torpid

**Lackaday** Haro

**Lackey** Boots, Flunkey, Moth, Page, Satellite, Skip-kennel

**Lacklustre** Dull, Insipid, Matt

**Laconic** Blunt, Close-mouthed, Curt, Spartan, Succinct, Terse

**Lacquer** Coromandel, Enamel, Japan, Shellac, VARNISH

**Lad** Boy(o), Bucko, Callan(t), Chield, Geit, Gyte, Knight, Loonie, Nipper, Shaver, Stableman, Tad, Whipper-snapper

**Ladder(y)** Companion, Etrier, Jacob's, Pompier, Potence, Rope, Run, Scalado, Scalar, Stie, Sty, Trap

**Ladle**  Bail, Dipper, Scoop

**Lady**  Baroness, Bevy, Bountiful, Burd, Dame, Dark, Don(n)a, Duenna, Female, Frau, Frow, Gemma, Godiva, Hen, Luck, Khanum, Maam, Madam(e), Memsahib, Nicotine, Peeress, Senora, Signora, Windermere

> **Lady**  may indicate an '-ess' ending

**Ladybird**  Cushcow, Hen, Vedalia

> **Ladybird**  may indicate a female of a bird family

**Ladykiller**  Bluebeard, Wolf

**Lady of the lake**  Vivian

**Lady's fingers**  Gumbo, Okra

**Lady's maid**  Abigail

**Lag**  Dawdle, Delay, Drag, Flag, Hysteresis, Inmate, Jailbird, Leng, LINGER, Loiter, Prisoner, Retard, Tortoise, Trail

**Lager**  Pils(e)ner

**Lagoon**  Haff, Pool, Salina, Saline

> **Laic, Laid**  see LAY

**Lair**  Couch, Den, Earth, Haunt, Hideaway, Kennel, Lodge

**Lake**  Albert, Aral Sea, Atlin, Avernus, Axolotl, Baikal, Bala, Balaton, Balkhash, Bangweulu, Basin, Bayou, Bled, Buttermere, Carmine, Chad, Champlain, Chott, Clearwater, Como, Constance, Corrib, Cowal, Crimson, Ennerdale, Erie, Erne, Everglade, Ewe, Eyre, Garda, Geneva, Huron, Ilmen, Innisfree, Kariba, Killarney, Koko Nor, L, Lacustrine, Ladoga, Lagoon, Lagune, Leven, LOCH, Lough, Lucerne, Lugano, Madder, Manitoba, Mead, Mere, Michigan, Miveru, Naumachia, Naumachy, No, Nyanza, Nyasa, Nyos, Onega, Oneida, Ontario, Ox-bow, Playa, Poets, Pool, Red, Regillus, Reservoir, Scafell, Serpentine, Shott, Sirbonian, Superior, Tana, Tanganyika, Tarn, Thun, Titicaca, Toronto, Torrens, Trasimene, Tsana, Turkana, Ullswater, Van, Vanern, Veronica, Victoria, Vlei, Wastwater, Windermere, Winnebago, Winnipeg

**Lake-dwelling**  Crannog

**Lakeland**  Cumbria

**Lam**  Flee, Scram

**Lamb(skin)**  Baa, Barometz, Budge, Cade, Caracul, Cosset, Ean(ling), Elia, Innocent, Keb, Larry, Noisette, Paschal, Persian, Shearling, Target, Yean(ling)

**Lambent**  Flickering, Glowing, Licking

**Lambert**  Constant

**Lame**  Accloy, Cripple, Crock, Game, Gammy, Gimp(y), Halt, Hamstring, Hirple, Hors de combat, Maim, Main, Spavined, Stringhalt, Weak

**Lament(able), Lamentation, Lamenter**  Bemoan, Bewail, Beweep, Complain, Croon, Cry, Dirge, Dumka, Elegy, Funest, Jeremiad, Jeremiah, Keen, Meane, Mein, Mene, Moon, Mourn, Ochone, Paltry, Piteous, Plain,

Repine, Sorry, Threne, Threnody, Ululate, WAIL, Welladay, Wel(l)away, Yammer

**Lamia** Deadnettle

**Lamina(te)** Film, Flake, Folium, Formica, Lamella, Layer, Plate, Scale, Table

**Lamp(s)** Aldis, Arc, Argand, Bowat, Bowet, Buat, Cru(i)sie, Crusy, Davy, Eye, Eyne, Geordie, Lantern, Lucigen, Nernst, Padella, Scamper, Signal, Stride, Tilley, Veilleuse, Xenon

**Lamplighter** Leerie, Spill

**Lampoon** Caricature, Parody, Pasquil, Pasquin(ade), Satire, Squib

**Lamprey** Lampern

**Lancaster** Burt, Osbert

**Lance** Dart, Harpoon, Morne, Pesade, Pike, Prisade, Prisado, Rejon, Spear, Speisade, Thermic

**Lancelet** Amphious

**Lancer** Bengal, Picador, Uhlan

**Land(ed)** Acreage, Alight, Alluvion, Arpent, Bag, Beach, Bigha, Bovate, Carucate, Cavel, Country, Demain, Demesne, Disbark, Disembark, Ditch, Doab, Dock, Earth, Edom, Estate, Fallow, Farren, Fee, Feod, Feoff, Feud, Fief, Freeboard, Gair, Glebe, Ground, Hide, Holm, Horst, Innings, Isthmus, Kingdom, Laurasia, Lea, Leal, Ley, Light, Machair, Maidan, Manor, Métairie, Morgen, Mortmain, Nation, Nod, No man's, Odal, Onshore, Oxgang, Oxgate, Panhandle, Pasture, Peninsula, Plot, Ploughgate, Polder, Pr(a)edial, Promised, Property, Purlieu, Realty, Reservation, Roman candle, Rundale, Savanna(h), Settle, Spit, Swidden, Taluk, Terra(e), Terrain, Territory, Thwaite, Tie, Tye, Udal, Unship, Ure, Veld(t), Wainage, Yird

**Landing** Halfpace, Pancake, Solar

**Landing Craft** LEM, Module

**Landing-stair** Gha(u)t

**Landing system** Autoflare

**Landlock** Embay

**Landlord, Land owner** Balt, Boniface, Copyholder, Franklin, Herself, Host, Innkeeper, Junker, Laird, Lessor, Letter, Patron, Proprietor, Publican, Rachman, Rentier, Squire, Thane, Zamindar(i), Zemindar

**Landmark** Meith

**Landmass** Laurasia

**Land right** Emphyteusis

**Landscape** Paysage, Picture, Saikei, Scene

**Landslide** Eboulement, Scree

**Land-tenure** Frankalmoign, Raiyatwari, Ryotwari

**Lane** Boreen, Corridor, Drury, Fetter, Gut, Loan, Lois, Loke, Mincing, Passage, Petticoat, Pudding, Sea-road, Twitten, Twitting, Vennel, Wynd

**Langerhans** Islets, Insulin

**Language(s)** Akkadian, Algonkian, Algonquian, Amharic, Arabic, Aramaic, Argot, Aryan, Austric, Bantu, Basque, Basutu, Bat, Bengali, Billingsgate, Bulgaric, Cajum, Cant, Carib, Catalan, Centum, Chinook, Circassian, Cobol, Coptic, Dardic, Dialect, Doric, Dravidian, Esperanto, Erse, Eteocretan, Euskarian, Fanagalo, Fantee, Fanti, Franglais, Frisian, Geez, Giz, Gujarat(h)i, Gujerat(h)i, Hausa, Hebrew, Hindi, Hindustani, Hittite, Hottentot, Humanities, Ibo, Idiolect, Idiom, Ido, Igbo, Interglossa, Interlingua, Janlish, Japlish, Jargon, Kannada, Kolarian, Kolne, Kuo-yu, Ladin(o), Lallans, Landsmaal, Latin, Lingo, Macaroni, Malay, Malayala(a)m, Manchu, Mandarin, Mon-Khmer, Motu, Munda, Na-Dene, Nahuatl, Neo, Newspeak, Norse, Novial, Oriya, Oscan, Pahari, Pakhti, Pali, Papiamento, Parlance, Pashto, Pashtu, P-Celt, Philology, Pidgin, Platt-deutsch, Prakrit, Prose, Pushto(o), Pushtu, Rhetoric, Romance, Romans(c)h, Romany, Roumansch, Rumansch, Rumonsch, Samoyed, Sanscrit, Sanskrit, Satem, Sea-speak, Semitic, Serbo-croat, Shan, Shelta, Sin(g)halese, Sinhala, Sociolect, Sotho, SPEECH, Strine, Sumerian, Suomi, Swahili, Taal, Taino, Tamil, Telegraphese, Telugu, Tessaraglot, Tigrinya, Tlingit, Tocharian, Tokharian, Tokharish, TONGUE, Tshi, Tupi, Turanian, Turki, Twi, Ugrian, Urdu, Vedic, Vernacular, Vocabulary, Volapuk, Walloon, Wolof, Words, X(h)osa, Yakut, Yiddish

**Languid, Languish** Die, Divine, Droop, Feeble, Flagging, Listless, Lukewarm, Lydia, Melancholy, Quail, Torpid, Wilt

**Languor** Lassitude

**Lanky** Beanpole, Gangly, Gawky, Spindleshanks, Windlestraw

**Lantern** Aristotle's, Bowat, Bowet, Buat, Bull's eye, Chinese, Dark(e)y, Epidiascope, Episcope, Glim, Magic, Sconce, Stereopticon

**Lanthanum** La

**Laodicean** Lukewarm

**Lap** Gremial, Leg, Lick, Lip, Luxury, Override, Sypher

**Lapdog** Messan

**Lapel** Revers

**Laplander, Lapp** Saam(e), Sabme, Sabmi, Sami

**Lapse** Drop, Error, Expire, Fa', Fall, Nod, Sliding, Trip

**Larch** Hackmatack, Tamarack

**Lard** Enarm, Saim, Seam(e)

**Larder** Buttery, Pantry, Spence, Springhouse

**Large** Big, Boomer, Buster, Colossus, Commodious, Decuman, Enormous, Epical, Gargantuan, GIGANTIC, Ginormous, Great, Grit, Gross, Hefty, Helluva, Huge, Hulking, Lunker, Massive, Rounceval, Rouncival, Skookum, Slew, Slue, Sollicker, Spanking, Stout, Swingeing, Tidy, Titanic, Vast, Whopping

**Large number** Fermi, Giga, Gillion, Googol, Jillion, Nation, Nonillion, Raft, Sea, Slew, Slue, Zillion

**Largess**  Alms, Charity, Frumentation

**Lariat**  Lasso, Reata, Riata

**Lark**  Adventure, Aunter, Caper, Dido, Dunstable, Exaltation, Fool, Giggle, Guy, Laverock, Mud, Pipit, Prank

**Larkspur**  Stavesacre

**Larva**  Axolotl, Bot(t), Caddice, Caddis, Cercaria, Doodlebug, Grub, Hellgram(m)ite, Hydatid, Indusium, Maggot, Measle, Nauplius, Ox-bot, Planula, Porina, Redia, Shade, Trochosphere, Veliger, Witchetty

**Laryngitis**  Croup, Hives

**Lascar**  Seacunny, Tindal

**Lascivious(ness)**  Crude, Goaty, Horny, Lewd, Lubric, Paphian, Satyric, Sotadic, Tentigo

**Lash(ed), Lashings**  Cat, Cilium, Firk, Flagellum, Frap, Gammon, Knout, Mastigophora, Oodles, Oup, Quirt, Riem, Rope's end, Scourge, Secure, Sjambok, Stripe, Swinge, Tether, Thong, Trice, Whang, WHIP

**Lass(ie)**  Damsel, Maid, Quean, Queyn, Quin(i)e

**Lassitude**  Accidie, Acedie, Languor, Lethargy

**Lasso**  Lariat, Reata, Rope

**Last(ing)**  Abide, Aftermost, AT LAST, Boot-tree, Bottom, Chronic, Dernier, Dure, Endurance, Endure, Extend, Extreme, FINAL, Hinder, Latest, Linger, Live, Model, Outstay, Permanent, Perpetuate, Persist, Spin, Stable, Stay, Supper, Survive, Thiller, Thule, Tree, Trump, Ult(imate), Utmost, Weight, Whipper-in, Z

**Last drop**  Supernaculum

**Last syllable**  Ultima

**Last word(s)**  Amen, Envoi, Ultimatum, Zythum

**Latch**  Bar, Clicket, Clink, Espagnolette, Lock, Sneck

**Late(r), Latest**  After(wards), Afterthought, Behindhand, Chit-chat, Dead, Ex, Former, Gen, Lag, Lamented, New(s), Overdue, Recent, Sine, Slow, Stop-press, Syne, Tardive, Tardy, Trendy, Umquhile

**Late-learner**  Opsimath

**Latent**  Concealed, Delitescent, Dormant, Potential

**Lateral**  Askant, Edgeways, Sideways

**Latex**  Antiar, Gutta-percha, Ule

**Lath**  Lag

**Lathe**  Capstan, Mandrel, Mandril

**Lather**  Flap, Foam, Froth, Sapples, Suds, Tan

**Latin(ist)**  Criollo, Dago, Erasmus, Eyeti, Humanity, Italiot, L, Neapolitan, Romanic, Romish, Scattermouch, Spic, Wop

**Latitude**  Breadth, Horse, L, Liberty, Licence, Meridian, Parallel, Play, Roaring forties, Scope, Tropic, Width

**Latrine** Ablutions, Bog, Cloaca, Furphy, Loo, Privy, Rear

**Latter** Last, Previous

**Latter-day** Recent, Saints, Young

**Lattice** Clathrate, Espalier, Grille, Treillage, Trellis

**Lattice-leaf** Ouvirandra

**Latvian** Lett

**Laud(er)** Commend, Eulogist, Extol, Harry, Praise

**Lauderdale** Caballer

**Laugh(ing), Laughable, Laughter** Cachinnate, Cackle, Chortle, Chuckle, Cod, Deride, Derision, Democritus, Fit, Fou rire, Gelastic, Giggle, Guffaw, Ha, He-he, Ho-ho, Homeric, Hoot, Hout, Irrision, Lauch, Leuch, Levity, MIRTH, Mock, Peal, Present, Riancy, Riant, Rich, Rident, Ridicule, Risus, Scream, Snigger, Snirt(le), Snort, Tehee, Titter, Yo(c)k

**Laughing-stock** Outspeckle, Sport

**Launcelot** Gobbo

**Launch(ing)** Begin, Catapult, Chuck, Float, Hurl, Initiate, Lift-off, Pioneer, Presentation, Release, Unstock, Upsend, VTO

**Launder, Laundry** Clean, Steamie, Tramp, Transfer, Wash

**Laurel(s)** Aucuba, Bay, Camphor, Daphne, Kalmia, Kudos, Pichurim, Sassafras, Stan

**Laurence** Sterne

**Lava** Aa, Bomb, Coulee, Dacite, Lahar, Lapilli, Magma, Nuée ardente, Pahoehoe, Palagonite, Pitchstone, Pumice, Scoria, Tephra, Toadstone

**Lavatory** Ajax, Can, Carsey, Carzey, Cludgie, Convenience, Cottage, Dike, Dunnakin, Dunny, Dyke, Elsan, Facilities, Furphey, Gents, Jane, John, Khazi, Ladies, Lat(rine), Loo, Necessary, Office, Reredorter, Shouse, Thunderbox, Toot, Tout, Urinal, Washroom, WC

**Lave** Lip, Wash

**Lavender** Aspic, Spike

**Lavengro** Borrow

**Laver** Moabite, Ore-weed

**Lavish** Copious, Excessive, Exuberant, Flush, Free, Generous, Lucullan, Lush, Prodigal, Sumptuous, Wanton, Waste

**Law** Abingdon, Act, Agrarian, Anti-trust, Ass, Avogadro's, Barratry, BILL, Bode's, Bonar, Boyle's, Brehon, Brocard, Byelaw, Cain, Canon, Capitulary, Chancery, Code, Constitution, Cupar, Cy pres, Dead-letter, Decree, Decretals, Deodand, Dharma, Dictate, Digest, Din, Edict, Enact, Fuzz, Gresham's, Grimm's, Halifax, Irade, Jura, Jure, Jus, Kain, Kepler's, Lay, Lien, Lor(d), Losh, Lydford, Lynch, Mishna(h), Mishnic, Mosaic, Ordinance, Pandect, Plebescite, Principle, Rubric, Rule, Salic, Salique, Shariah, Sheria(t), Snell's, STATUTE, Table, Talmud, Tenet, Thorah, Torah, Tort, Tradition, Ulema, Unwritten, Use, Verner's, Vigilante

**Lawlessness** Anarchy, Anomie, Anomy, Antimonian, Piratical

**Lawmaker, Lawman, Lawyer** Alfaqui, Attorney, AV, Barrister, Bencher, BL, Bluebottle, Bramble, Coke, Counsel, DA, Defence, Draco, Fiscal, Greenbag, Grotius, Hammurabi, Jurist, Legist, Mooktar, Moses, MP, Mufti, Mukhtar, Notary, Penang, Pettifoggers, Rabbi, Shirra, Shyster, Silk, Solicitor, Spenlow, Talmudist, Templar, Thesmothete, WS

**Lawn** Grass, Green, Linen, Sward, Turf

**Lawrence** DH, Ross, TE, Shaw

**Lawrencium** Lr

**Lawsuit** Case, Cause, Plea, Trover

> **Lawyer(s), Lawman** see LAWMAKER

**Lax(ity)** Freedom, Inexact, Laissez-aller, Latitude, Loose, Remiss, SLACK, Wide

> **Lax** may indicate an anagram

**Laxative** Aperitive, Cascara, Cathartic, Eccoprotic, Elaterin, Elaterium, Gregory (powder), PURGE, Saline, Taraxacum

**Lay(ing), Layman, Laic, Laid** Air, Aria, Ballad, Bed, Bet, Blow, Chant, Ditty, Drop, Earthly, Egg, Embed, Fit, Impose, Lied, Lodge, Man, Minstrel, Oat, Ode, Oviparous, Oviposit, Parabolanus, Secular, Set, Sirvente, SONG, Sypher, Tertiary, Tribal, Wager, Warp

**Layabout** Loafer, Lotophagus

**Layer(s)** Ancona, Appleton, Battery, Cake, Coating, Crust, Ectoplasm, Ectosarc, Epiblast, Epilimnion, Film, Flake, Ganoin, Heaviside, HEN, Kerf, Lamella, Lamina, Lap, Leghorn, Lie, Media, Miocene, Ozone, Pan, Paviour, Ply, Retina, Scale, Skin, Sliver, Spathic, Stratum, Tabular, Tapetum, Tier, Tremie, Varve, Vein, Velamen

**Lay-off** Dismiss, Hedge

**Lay-out** Ante, Design, Fell, Map, Mise, Pattern, Spend, Straucht, Straught, Streak, Streek, Stretch

**Laze, Laziness, Lazy** Bed-presser, Hallian, Hallion, Hallyon, Indolent, Inert, Lackadaisical, Languid, Layabout, Lie-abed, Lither, Loaf, Lusk, Oblomovism, Resty, Sloth, Slouch, Slug (a-bed), Susan, Sweer, Sweir

> **Lazily** may indicate an anagram

**Lea** Grass, Meadow

**Leaching** Lixivial, Ooze

**Lead(er), Leading, Leadership** Ag(h)a, Anglesite, Article, Atabeg, Atabek, Ayatollah, Bluey, Cade, Calif, Caliph, Capitano, Capo, Captain, Castro, Caudillo, Causal, Centre, Ceruse, Cheer, Chieftain, Chiliarch, Chin, Choragus, Choregus, CO, Condottiere, Conduct, Coryphaeus, Demagogue, Dictator, Duce, Dux, Editorial, Escort, Ethnarch, Figure-head, Fugleman, Fu(e)hrer, Gaffer, Guide(r), Halter, Hand, Headman, Headmost, Headnote, Hegemony, Hero, Hetman, Honcho, Idi, Imam, Imaum, Jason, Kame, King, Ksar, Leam, Litharge, Livid, Lost, Lyam, Mahatma, Mahdi, Main, Marshal,

Massicot, Masticot, Mayor, Nanak, No 1, Nomarch, Nose, Omrah, Pacemaker, Padishah, Pb, Pilot, Pioneer, Plumb, Plummet, PM, Precentor, Premier(e), President, Rebecca, Role, Ruler, Sachem, Saturn, Scuddaler, Scudler, Sharif, Sixer, Skipper, Skudler, Soul, Spearhead, Staple, Star, Sultan, Taoiseach, Tribune, Tsaddik, Tsaddiq, Tzaddik, Up, Usher, Vaivode, Van(guard), Va(u)nt, Vaunt-courier, Voivode, Vozhd, Waivode, Whitechapel, Wulfenite, Zaddik, Zia

> **Lead(s), Leaders** may indicate first letters of words

**Leaden** Flat, Plumbeous, Saturnine

**Lead-glance** Galena

**Leading to** Pre

**Leaf(y), Leaves** Acanthus, Acrospire, Amphigastrium, Amplexicaul, Betel, Blade, Bract, Carpel, Cataphyll, Cladode, Consent, Corolla, Cotyledon, Duff, Fig, Finial, Foil, Foliage, Foliar, Folio(se), Folium, Frond, Holiday, Jugum, Needle, Nervate, Out, P, Pad, Page, Phyllome, Qat, Repair, Riffle, Rosula, Secede, Siri(h), Skip, Spathe, Stipule, Tea, TTL, Valve, Vert, Withdraw

**Leafhopper** Thrip

**Leafless** Ebracteate, Scape

**Leaflet** At(t)ap, Bill, Bracteole, Circular, Foliolose, Handbill, Pinna, Pinnula, Prophyll, Stipel, TRACT

**League** Alliance, Band, Bund, Entente, Federation, Gueux, Guild, Hanse(atic), Holy, Ivy, Land, Parasang, Primrose, Redheaded, Union, Zollverein, Zupa

**Leak(y)** Bilge, Drip, Escape, Gizzen, Holed, Holey, Ooze, Porous, Seepage, Sype, Trickle, Wee, Weep

**Leamington** Spa

**Lean(ing)** Abut, Barren, Batter, Bend, Careen, Carneous, Carnose, Griskin, Heel, INCLINE, Lie, Lig(ge), Propend, Rake, Rely, Rest, Scraggy, Scrawny, Skinny, Spare, Stoop, Taste, Tend, Tilt, Tip, Walty

**Leander** Abydos

**Lean-to** Skillion

**Leap(ing), Leapt** Assemblé, Bound, Brise, Cabriole, Caper, Capriole, Cavort, Clear, Croupade, Curvet, Echappé, Entrechat, Fishdive, Frisk, Gambol, Jeté, Jump, Loup, Luppen, Over, Pronk, Sally, Somersa(u)lt, Somerset, SPRING, Transilient, Vault, Volte

**Leap year** Bissextile, Penteteric

**Lear** Edward, King, Nonsense

**Learn(ed), Learner** Beginner, Blue, Bluestocking, Chela, Con, Discover, Doctor, Don, Erudite, Gather, Get, Glean, Hear, Kond, L, Lear(e), Leir, Lere, Literate, Literati, Literato, Lucubrate, Master, Memorise, Mirza, NOVICE, Pandit, Pundit, Pupil, Rookie, Savant, Scan, Scholar, See, Starter, Student, STUDY, Tiro, Trainee, Tutee, Tyro, Wise

**Learning** Culture, Discipline, Erudition, Insight, Lore, Opsimathy, Rep, Wit

**Lease** Charter, Farm, Feu, Hire, Let, RENT, Set(t), Tack

**Leash** Lead, Lyam, Lym(e), Slip, Three, Trash, Triplet

**Least** Minimum

**Leather** Bouilli, Bouilly, Box-calf, Buff, Cabretta, Calf, Capeskin, Chamois, Checklaton, Cheverel, Cordovan, Cordwain, Corium, Cuir(-bouilli), Deacon, Deerskin, Diphthera, Dogskin, Durant, Hide, Kid, Kip(-skin), Lamp, Levant, Marocain, Maroquin, Mocha, Morocco, Nap(p)a, Oxhide, Rand, Riem(pie), Roan, Russia, Saffian, Shagreen, Shammy, Shecklaton, Skiver, Split, Strap, Suede, Tan, Upper, Wallop, Yuft

**Leatherneck** Marine, RM

**Leave(r), Leavings** Abandon, Abiturient, Abscond, Absit, Acquittal, Bequeath, Blessing, Bug, Congé, Congee, Decamp, Depart, Desert, Devisal, Devise, Ditch, Exeat, Exit, Exodus, Forego, Forgo, Forsake, French, Furlough, Garlandage, GO, Inspan, Ish, Legate, Licence, Maroon, Omit, Orts, Pace, Park, Part, PERMISSION, Permit, QUIT, Residue, Resign, Sabbatical, Scram, Vacate, Vade, Vamo(o)se

**Leaven** Barm, Ferment, Yeast

**Lebanese** Druse

**Lecher(ous), Lechery** Gate, Goaty, Libertine, Lickerish, Lustful, Profligate, Rake, Roué, Salaciousness, Satirisk, Satyr, Silen, Wolf

**Lectern** Ambo, Desk, Eagle, Oratory

**Lecture(r), Lectures** Address, Aristotelean, Creed, Curtain, Dissert(ator), Don, Homily, Hulsean, Jaw, Jobe, L, Lector, Prelect, Prone, Rate, Read(er), Rede, Reith, SERMON, Talk, Teacher, Wigging

**Ledge** Altar, Berm, Channel, Fillet, Scarcement, Settle, SHELF

**Ledger** Book, Register

**Lee(s)** Dregs, Dunder, Heeltaps, Sediment, Shelter, Ullage

**Leech** Bleeder, Parasite, Rhynchobdellida

**Leek** Allium, Fouat, Fouet, Porraceous

**Leer** Eliad, Fleer, Oeillade, Ogle

**Leeway** Drift

**Left(-handed), Left-hander, Left-winger** Balance, Bolshy, Corrie-fisted, L, Larboard, Links, Lorn, Near, Over, Pink, Port, Rad, Red, Relic, Residuum, Resigned, Sinister, Soc(ialist), Southpaw, Thin, Titoism, Trot, Verso, Vo, Went, West, Yet

**Left-over** End, Oddment, Remanet, REMNANT, Waste

**Leg(s), Leggings, Leggy, Leg-wear** Antigropelo(e)s, Breeches, Cabriole, Chaparajos, Chaparejos, Chaps, Crural, Dib, Drumstick, Gaiter, Galligaskins, Gam(b), Gamash, Gambado, Garter, Gigot, Gramash, Gramosh, Haunch, Jamb, Limb, Member, Myriapod, On(side), Peg, Peraeopod, Periopod, Pestle, Pin, Podite, Proleg, Puttees, Pylon, Relay,

Section, Shanks, Shaps, Shin, Spats, Spatterdash, Spindleshanks, Stage, Stump, Thigh, Tights

**Legacy**   Bequest, Dowry, Entail, Heirloom

**Legal(ism), Legally, Legitimate**   Bencher, Forensic, Halacha(h), Halakah, Lawful, Licit, Nomism, Scienter

**Legal book**   Halacha(h), Halaka, Talmud

**Leg-armour**   Cootikin, Cu(i)tikin, Jamb(e), Pad

**Legate**   Ambassador, Consul, Emissary, Envoy, Nuncio

**Legend**   Arthurian, Caption, Edda, Fable, Motto, Myth, Saga, Story

> **Legend**   may indicate leg-end, (e.g. foot, talus)

**Leger**   Swindler

**Leghorn**   Livorno

**Legible**   Clear, Lucid, Plain

**Legion(ary), Legionnaire**   Alauda, Army, Cohort, Countless, Deserter, Foreign, Geste, Honour, HOST, Many, Throng

**Legislate, Legislator, Legislature**   Assemblyman, Decemvir, Decree, MP, Nomothete, Oireachtas, Persian, Solon

**Legless**   Amelia, Blotto, Caecilia, Psyche

**Leg-pull**   Chaff, Joke, Rise, Rot

**Legume**   Bean, Guar, Lentil, Pea, Pod, Pulse

**Leibniz**   Monadism

**Leigh**   Amyas

**Leisure(ly)**   Adagio, Ease, Liberty, Moderato, Otium, Respite, Rest, Vacation

**Lemon**   Answer, Citron, Citrus, Smear-dab, Sole, Yellow

**Lemur**   Angwantibo, Aye-aye, Babacoote, Bush-baby, Colugo, Galago, Half-ape, Indri(s), Loris, Macaco, Malmag, MONKEY, Mongoose, Potto, Sifaka, Tana, Tarsier

**Lend**   Advance, Prest, Vaunce

**Length(y), Lengthen(ing), Lengthwise**   Arsheen, Arshin(e), Aune, Braccio, Cable, Chain, Cubit, Distance, Eke, Ell, ELONGATE, Endways, Epenthetic, Expand, Extensive, Ley, Piece, Prolix, Prolong, Protract, Reach, Remen, Rod, Rope, Slow, Span, Stadium, Toise, Vara, Verbose

**Lenient**   Clement, Exurable, Lax, Mild, Permissive, Tolerant

**Lens**   Anastigmat, Contact, Cornea, Diopter, Dioptre, Eye, Fish-eye, Lentil, Optic, Pantoscope, Stanhope, Telephoto, Zoom

**Lent**   Careme, Fast, Laetare, Out, Term

**Lentil(s)**   D(h)al, Dholl, Ervalenta, Lens, Phacoid, Pulse, Revalenta

**Leonora**   Overture

**Leopard**   Leap, Libbard, Ounce, Panther, Pard, Spots

**Leopold**   Bloom

**Leper, Leprosy** Lazar, Leontiasis, Lionism, Meazel, Mesel, Outcast, Pariah

**Lepidopterist** Aurelian, Moth-er, Pendleton, Treacler

**Leprechaun** Elf, Gremlin, Imp

**Lesbian** Crunchie, Diesel, Dike, Dyke, Lipstick, Sapphist, Tribade

**Lesion** Cut, Gash, Scar, Sore

**Less(en), Lesser** Abate, Alaiment, Bate, Contract, Decline, Deplete, Derogate, Dilute, DWINDLE, Extenuate, Fewer, Junior, Littler, Minus, Reduce, Under

**Lesson** Example, Lear(e), Lection, Leir, Lere, Moral, Object, Period, Sermon, Tutorial

**Let (go, out), Letting** Allow, Charter, Conacre, Divulge, Enable, Entitle, Hire, Impediment, Indulge, Lease, Litten, Loot(en), Luit(en), Lutten, Obstacle, Obstruct, PERMIT, Rent, Sett, Unhand, Warrant

**Let down** Abseil, Betray, Lower, Sell, Vail

**Lethal** Deadly, Fatal, Fell, Mortal

**Lethargic, Lethargy** Accidie, Apathy, Coma, Drowsy, Inertia, Passive, Sleepy, Sluggish, Stupor, Supine, Torpid

**Letter(s)** Ache, Aesc, Airgraph, Aleph, Alif, Alpha, A(y)in, Bayer, Beta, Beth, Breve, Caph, Capital, Capon, Casket, Cheth, Chi, Collins, Consonant, Cue, Cuneiform, Daleth, Delta, Digraph, Edh, Ef(f), Emma, Encyclical, Ep(isemon), Epistle, Epsilon, Eta, Eth, Favour, Fraktur, Gamma, Gimel, Grapheme, Heth, Initial, Iota, Izzard, Kaph, Kappa, Koppa, Kufic, Labda, Lambda, Landlord, Lessee, Lessor, Literal, Mail, Majuscule, Memo, Miniscule, Minuscule, Missive, Monogram, Mu, Note, Nu, Qoph, Og(h)am, Omega, Omicron, Pahlavi, Paston, Pastoral, Patent, Pehlevi, Phi, Pi, Postbag, Psi, Resh, Rho, Rom, Runestave, Sad(h)e, Samekh, Samian, Sampi, San, Screed, Screwtape, Script, Shin, Siglum, Sigma, Sign, Sin, Sort, Swash, Tau, Tav, Taw, Teth, Theta, Thorn, Toc, Tsade, Typo, Uncial, Upsilon, Vau, Vav, Versal, Vowel, Waw, Xi, Yod(h), Yogh, Ypsilon, Zayin, Zed, Zeta

**Lettering** Cufic, Kufic

**Lettuce** Chicon, Corn-salad, Cos, Romaine, Salad, Thridace

**Leucoma** Albugo

**Levant(ine)** Coptic, Go, Israelite, Jew, Ottamite, Ottomite

**Levee** Bank, Dyke, Embankment, Party

**Level(ler)** A, Abney, Aclinic, Aim, Degree, Echelon, Equal, EVEN, Extent, Flat, Flush, Grade, O, Par, Plat(eau), Race, Rase, Raze, Savanna, SQUARE, Stratum, Strew, Strickle, Tier

**Lever(age)** Backfall, Crowbar, Dues, Handspike, Jemmy, Key, Landsturm, Peav(e)y, Pry, Purchase, Treadle, Trigger

**Leviathan** Whale

**Levitate** Float, Hover, Rise

**Levity** Flippancy, Glee, Humour, Jollity

**Levy** Impose, Imposition, Leave, Octroi, Raise, Scutage, Talliate, Tax, Tithe

**Lewd** Bawdy, Blue, Impure, Obscene, Prurient, Silen(us), Unclean

**Lewis** Carroll, Tenon

**Lexicographer, Lexicon** Compiler, Drudge, Etymologist, Fowler, Grove, Johnsonian, Larousse, Liddell, OED, Thesaurus, Vocabulist, Webster, Words-man

**Liability, Liable** Apt, Debt, Incur, Limited, Open, Prone, Subject, Susceptible

**Liaison** Affair, Contact, Link

**Liana** Guarana

**Libel(lous)** Defamatory, Malign, Slander, Sully, Vilify

**Liberal** Abundant, Adullamites, Ample, Besant, Bounteous, Bountiful, Bright, Broad, Free(hander), GENEROUS, Giver, Grimond, Grey, Handsome, Indulgent, L, Largesse, Lavish, Octobrist, Open, PROFUSE, Rad(ical), Samuelite, Simonite, Steel, Tolerant, Trivium, Verlig, Whig

**Liberate, Liberator** Bolivar, Deliver, Emancipate, FREE, Inkatha, Messiah, Release, Save, Sucre, Unfetter

**Liberian** Kroo, Kru

**Libertarian, Libertine** Chartered, Corinthian, Debauchee, Laxist, Lecher, Lothario, Lovelace, Rake, Rip, Roué, Wencher, Wolf

**Liberty** Bail, Discretion, Franchise, Freedom, Hall, Mill, Sauce

**Library** BL, Bodleian, Cottonian, Harleian, Laurentian, Lending, Mazarin, Radcliffe, Reference, Tauchnitz

**Librettist** Gilbert, Lyricist

> **Lice** see LOUSE

**Licence, License** Abandon, Allow, Authorisation, Carnet, Dispensation, Enable, Exequatur, Fling, Free(dom), Gale, Imprimatur, Indult, LATITUDE, Let, Passport, PERMIT, Poetic, Pratique, Rope, Slang

**Licentious** Artistic, Corinthian, Hot, Immoral, Large, Lax, Loose, Prurient, Ribald, Sensual, Wanton

**Lichen** Apothecia, Archil, Corkir, Crotal, Crottle, Epiphyte, Epiphytic, Graphis, Korkir, Lecanora, Orchel, Orchil(la), Orcine, Orseille, Parella, Parelle, Roccella, Stone-rag, Stone-raw, Tree-moss, Usnea

**Lick(ing)** Bat, Beat, Lambent, Lap, Slake, Speed, Whip

**Licorice** Nail, Sugarallie

**Lid** Cover, Hat, Maximum, Opercula

**Liddell** Alice

**Lido** Beach, Pool

**Lie(s), Liar, Lying** Abed, Accubation, Accumbent, Ananias, Bam, Bare-faced, Bask, Billy, Bounce(r), Braide, Cau(l)ker, Cellier, Clipe, Clype, Contour, Couchant, Cracker, Cram(mer), Cretism, Cumbent, Deception,

Decumbent, Direct, Doggo, Fable, False(r), Falsehood, Falsify, Fib, Figment, Flam, Gag, Incumbent, Invention, Kip, Lair, Leasing, Lee(ar), Lig(ge), Lurk, Obreption, Oner, Perjury, Plumper, Porky, Prone, Prostrate, Pseudologia, Recline, Recumbent, Repent, Ride, Romance(r), Sham, Sleep, Strapper, Stretcher, Supine, Tale, Tappice, Tar(r)adiddle, Thumper, Tissue, Try, Untruth, Whid, White, Whopper, Yanker

**Lien**  Mortgage, Title

**Lieu**  Locus, Place

**Lieutenant**  Flag, No 1, Loot, Lt, Sub(altern)

**Life**  Age, Animation, Being, Biog(raphy), Brio, Clerihew, Esse, Existence, Heart, Plasma, Span, Spirit, Subsistence, Time, Vita

**Life-blood**  Essence, Lethee

**Lifeboat**  Ark

**Life-cell**  Energid

**Life-cycle**  Redia

**Lifeguard**  Cheesemonger

**Lifeless(ness)**  Abiosis, Algidity, Amort, Azoic, Barren, DEAD, Dull, Flat, Inanimate, Inert, Log, Mineral, Possum, Sterile, Stonen, Wooden

**Lifelike**  Breathing, Speaking

**Lifeline**  Umbilicus

**Life-rent**  Usufruct

**Life-saver**  Preserver, Raft

**Lift(ed), Lifter**  Arsis, Bone, Camel, Cly, Copy, Crane, Davit, Elate, Elevator, Enhance, Filch, Heave, Heeze, Heezie, Heft, Heist, Hitch, Hoise, Hoist, Hove, Jack, Leaven, Lefte, Lever, Lewis, Nab, Nap, Paternoster, Pilfer, Pulley, RAISE, Ride, Scoop, Sky, Snatch, Steal, T-bar, Thumb, Up, Winch

**Ligament**  Fr(a)enum, Tendon, Urachus

**Ligature**  Aesc, Bandage, Bind

**Light(en), Lighting, Lights**  Aerate, Airy, Albedo, Alow, Ale, Ancient, Arc, Aurora, Batswing, Beacon, Beam, Bengal, Bezel, Bleach, Bude, Bulb, Candle, Cannel, Casement, Chiaroscuro, Cierge, Clue, Day, Dewali, Diwali, Dream-hole, Drummond, Earth-shine, Eddystone, Electrolier, Ethereal, Fall, Fan, Fantastic, Fastnet, Fidibus, Fire, Flambeau, Flame, Flare, Flicker, Flippant, Flit(t), Flood, Frothy, Fuffy, Gleam, Glim(mer), Glow, Gossamer, Guiding, Gurney, Haggis, Head, Ignite, Illum(in)e, Irradiate, Kindle, Kleig, Klieg, Lamp, Land, Lantern, Lanthorn, Laser, Leerie, Leggiero, Lime, Link, Loadstar, Lobuli, Lodestar, Lozen, Lucigen, Luminaire, Luminescence, Luminous, Lustre, Lux, Match, Mercurial, Merry-dancers, Mithra(s), Moon, Naphtha, Neon, Nit, Northern, Od(yl), Optics, Pale, Pane, Phosphene, Phosphorence, Phot, Pilot, Portable, Producer-gas, Relume, Rocket, Rush, Satori, Sea-dog, Search, Shy, Spot, Spry, Strip, Strobe, Subtle, Sun, Suttle, Svelte, Tail, Taper, Taps, Tind, Tine, Torch, Torchère, Traffic, Unchaste, Unoppressive, UV, Ver(e)y,

Vesta, Windock, Window, Winnock, Zodiacal

> **Light** may indicate an anagram

**Lighter** Barge, Birlinn, Casco, Gas-poker, Keel, Linstock, Lunt, Match, Pontoon, Pra(a)m, Spill, Taper

**Lighthouse** Beacon, Eddystone, Fanal, Fastnet, Phare, Pharos, Signal

**Lightless** Aphotic, Dark, Obscure, Unlit

**Lightness** Buoyancy, Galant, Levity, Pallor

**Lightning** Catequil, Eclair, Enfouldered, Forked, Fulmination, Levin, Thunderbolt, Wildfire

**Lightship** Nore

**Lightweight** Oz, Trivial

**Lignite** Jet, Surtarbrand, Surturbrand

**Like(ness), Liking** As, Broo, Care, Corpse, Dig, Duplicate, Effigy, Eg, Egal, Enjoy, Equal, Fancy, Fellow, Lich, Parallel, Peas, Penchant, Please, Semblant, Shine, Similar, Simile, Sort, Speaking, Tiki

**Likely** Apt, Fair, On, Plausible, Possible, Probable, Probit, Prone

**Likewise** Also, Do, Eke, Item, So, Too

**Lilac** Laylock, Mauve, Pipe-tree, Syringa

**Lilliputian** Minute

**Lilt** Swing

**Lily** Agapanthus, Aloe, Amaryllis, Annunciation, Arum, Asphodel, Aspidistra, Calla, Camas(h), Camass, Candock, Colchicum, Colocasia, Convallaria, Crinum, Dale, Elaine, Fritillary, Haemanthus, Herb-paris, Kniphofia, Laguna, Lote, Lotus, Madonna, Mariposa, Martagon, Moorva, Nelumbo, Nenuphar, Nerine, Nuphar, Padma, Phormium, Quamash, Richardia, Sarsa, Sego, Smilax, Solomon's scal, Tiger, Trillium, Tritoma, Victoria, Yucca

**Lily-maid** Elaine

**Limb** Arm, Bough, Branch, Crural, Hindleg, Imp, Leg, Leg-end, Member, Ramus, Scion, Shin, Spald, Spall, Spaul(d)

**Limbless** Amelia

**Limbo** Bardo, Isolation

**Lime** Bass(wood), Beton, Calc, Lind(en), Teil, Tilia, Trap, Viscum, Whitewash

**Limerick** Doggerel, Twiner, Verse

**Limestone** Calp, Clint, Coquina, Cornbrash, Karst, Kentish rag, Kunkar, Kunkur, Oolite, Pisolite, Rottenstone, Scaglia, Travertine

**Limey** Rooinek

**Limit(ation), Limited, Limiting** Ambit, Bind, Border, Borné, Bound, Bourn(e), Brink, Cap, Ceiling, Climax, Compass, Confine, Deadline, Define, Demark, Determine, Earshot, Edge, End, Entail, Esoteric, EXTENT, Extreme, Finite, Frontier, Gate, Goal, Gole, Impound, Induciae,

Insular, Limes, Lynchet, March, Meare, Mete, Nth, Outedge, Pale, Parameter, Perimeter, Periphery, Predetermine, Qualify, Range, Ration, Reservation, Restrict, Rim, Roof, Sky, Stint, String, Sumptuary, Tail(lie), Tailye, Tailzie, Term(inus), Tether, Threshold, Thule, Tie, Tropic, Utmost, Utter, Verge

> **Limit**  may indicate 'surrounding'

**Limousine**  Daimler, Rolls, Zil

**Limner**  RA

**Limp**  Claudication, Dot, Droopy, Flabby, Flaccid, Flimsy, Floppy, Hilch, Hirple, Hitch, Hobble, Hop, Lifeless, Tangle

**Limpet**  Patella, Streptoneura

**Limpid**  Clear, Lucid, Pure

**Linch**  Terrace

**Lincoln(shire)**  Abe, Poacher

**Linden**  Baucis, Lime, Tilia

**Line(d), Lines, Lining**  Abreast, Agate, Agonic, Allan, Anacreontic, ANCESTRY, Angle, Apothem, Arew, Assembly, Asymptote, Axis, Babbitt, Baulk, Bluebell, Bombast, Boundary, BR, Brail, Branch, Bread, Bush, Canal, Carolingian, Casing, Ceil, Ceriph, Chord, Ciel, Coffle, Column, Contour, Cord(on), Course, Crease, Crowsfoot, Curve, Cushion, Dancette, Datum, Descent, Diagonal, Diameter, Distaff, Dotted, Doublure, Dress, Dynasty, Earing, Encase, Equator, Faint, Fall(s), Feint, Fess(e), Fettle, File, Flex, Fraunhofer, Frontier, Furr(ow), Geodesic, Gimp, Giron, Graph, Gridiron, Gymp, Gyron, Hachure, Hatching, Hawser, Hindenburg, Hockey, Hogscore, House, Impot, Incase, Intima, Isallobar, Isobar, Isobront, Isocryme, Isogloss, Isogonal, Isohyet, Isothere, Isotherm, Knittle, L, Lane, Lap, Lariat, Leash, Ley, Ling, LMS, Load, Lye, Macron, Maginot, Mark, Mason-Dixon, Median, Meridian, Monorail, Nidation, Noose, Norsel, Northern, Oche, Octastichon, Ode, Og(h)am, Onedin, Ordinate, Painter, Parallel, Parameter, Party, Paternoster, Path, Pencil, Poetastery, Phalanx, Picket, Plimsoll, Police, Profession, Queue, Race, Radius, Rail, Rank, Raster, Ratlin(e), Ratling, Rattlin, Ray, Retinue, Rhumb, Ripcord, Rope, Route, Row, Rugose, Rugous, Rule, Ry, Secant, Serif, Seriph, Siding, Siegfried, Sield, Snood, SR, Stance, Stanza, Stean, Steen, Stein, Stem, Stich(os), Stock, Streak, Striate, String, Subtense, Swifter, Syzygy, Tangent, Teagle, Thread, Throwaway, Trade, Transoceanic, Tropic, Trunk, Tudor, Variety, Verse, Vinculum, Virgule, Wad, Wallace's, Widow, Wire, Wrinkle, Zollner

**Lineage**  Ancestry, Descent, Extraction, Pedigree

**Linen**  Amice, Amis, Byssus, Cambric, Crash, Damask, Dornick, Dowlas, Ecru, Harn, Huckaback, Inkle, Lawn, Lint, Lockram, Moygashel, Napery, Percale, Seersucker, Sendal, Silesia, Toile

**Liner**  Artist, RMS, Ship, Steamer, Steen

**Linesman**  Parodist, POET, Touch-judge

**Linger** Dawdle, Dwell, Hang, Hove(r), Lag, LOITER, Straggle, Tarry, Tie

**Lingerie** Bra, Drawers, Undies

**Lingo** Cant, Jargon, Speech

**Linguistic** Glottic, Philological

**Liniment** Balm, Carron-oil, Embrocation, Opodeldoc, Salve

**Link(ing), Links** Associate, Between, Bond, Bridge, Chain, Cleek, Concatenation, Copula, Couple, Desmid, Ess, Flambeau, Interface, Internet, Karabiner, Liaise, Machair, Nexus, Pons, Preposition, Relate, Tead(e), TIE, Torch, Unite, Yoke

**Linkman** Lamplighter, Mediator

**Linnet** Finch, Twite

**Lint** Charpie

**Lintel** Summer, Transom

**Lion(ess)** Androcles, Chindit, Elsa, Glitterati, Hero, Leo, Nemean, Opinicus, Personage, Pride, Simba

**Lionel** Trilling

**Lion-tamer** Dan(iel)

**Lip(py), Lips** Cheek, Fipple, Flews, Helmet, Jib, Labellum, Labiate, Labret, Labrum, Ligula, Muffle, RIM, Rubies, Sauce, Slack-jaw

**Liquefy** Dissolve, Fuse, Melt

**Liqueur, Liquor** Ale, Amaretto, Anisette, Bree, Brew, Broo, Broth, Calvados, Chartreuse, Chassé, Chicha, Cointreau, Creature, Crème, Curaçao, Elixir, Enzian, Feni, Fenny, Fustian, Geropiga, Hogan, Hogen(-mogen), Hooch, Kaoliang, Kirschwasser, Kummel, Lager, Lap, Malt, Maraschino, Mastic, Metheglin, Mirabelle, Mobbie, Mobby, Noyau, Oedema, Ooze, Ouzo, Pastis, Persico, Pousse-café, Prunelle, Rakee, Raki, Ratafia, Rotgut, Rum, Samshoo, Schnapps, Shypoo, Skink, Stingo, Stock, Stout, Strega, Strunt, Stuff, Supermaculum, Tape, Tiff, Wine, Witblits, Wort

**Liquid(ate), Liquidity, Liquids, Liquefaction** Amortise, Annihilate, Apprize, Azeotrope, Bittern, Cacodyl, Cash, Clyster, Eluate, Erase, Fluid, Jaw, Lewisite, Lye, Massacre, Mess, Minim, Mouillé, Picamar, Ptisan, Serum, Solution, Solvent, Terebene, Thixotropy, Ullage, Whey

**Liquorice** Jequirity, Pontefract-cake, Sugar-ally

**Lis** Iris, Lily

**Lisa** Mona

**Lisp(er)** Ephraimite, Sibilance

**Lissom(e)** Agile, Lithe, Nimble

**Listing, List(s)** Active, Agenda, Antibarbarus, Atilt, Barocco, Barrace, Bead roll, Canon, Cant, Catalog(ue), Categorise, Catelog, Civil, Class, Entry, Enumerate, Glossary, Hark, Hearken, Heel, Index, Inventory, Itemise, Lean, Leet, Notitia, Panel, Register, Roll, Roon, Roster, Rota, Rund, Schedule, Slate, Slope, Strip, Table, Tariff, Ticket, Tilt, Tip, Waybill

> **List** may indicate 'listen'

**Listen(er)** Attend, Auditor, Ear, Eavesdropper, Gobemouche, Hark, HEED, Lithe, Lug, Monitor, Oyez

> **Listen to** may indicate a word sounding like another

**Listless(ness)** Abulia, Accidie, Acedia, Apathetic, Dawney, Indolent, Lackadaisical, Languor, Mooning, Mope, Mopus, Sloth, Torpor, Waff

**Lit** Alight, Landed

> **Lit** may indicate an anagram

**Literal(ly), Literal sense** Etymon, Misprint, Simply, Verbatim

**Literary** Academic, Bas bleu, Booksie, Erudite, Lettered

**Literary girls** Althea, Jenny, Maud, Pippa

**Literature** Belles lettres, Corpus, Fiction, Page, Picaresque, Prose

**Lithe** Flexible, Limber, Pliant, Souple, SUPPLE, Svelte, Willowy

**Lithium** Li

**Litigant** Barrator, John-a-Nokes, John-a-Stiles, John Doe, Party, Richard Roe, Suer, Suitor

**Litmus** Indicator, Lacmus

**Litre** L

**Litter** Bed, Brancard, Brood, Cacolet, Cubs, Debris, Doolie, Farrow, Jampan, Kago, Kajawah, Kindle, Mahmal, Nest, Norimon, Palankeen, Palanquin, Palkee, Palki, Pup, REFUSE, Scrap, Sedan, Stretcher, Team

**Little** Bagatelle, Billee, Brief, Chota, Curn, Dorrit, Drib, Drop, Fewtrils, Insect, Iota, John, Jot, Leet, Lilliputian, Limited, Lite, Lyte, Mini, Miniscule, Minuscule, MINUTE, Morceau, Nell, Paltry, Paucity, Petite, Pink, Scant, Shade, Shoestring, Shred, Shrimp, Slight, SMALL, Smattering, Smidge(o)n, Smidgin, Some, Soupçon, Spot, Tad, Tich, Tine, Titch, Touch, Tyne, Vestige, Wee, Weedy, Whit, Women

**Liturgical, Liturgy** Doxology, Rite, Versicle

**Live(d), Liveliness, Lively, Lives** Active, Allegro, Animated, Animation, A.v, Awake, Be, Breezy, Brio, Brisk, Cant(y), Capriccio, Cheery, Chipper, Chirpy, Cohabit, Crouse, Durante vita, DWELL, Ebullient, Entrain, Exist, Frisky, Galliard, Giocoso, Grig, Hang-out, Hard, Is, Jazz, Kedge, Lad, Lead, Mercurial, Merry, Pacey, Peart, Pep, Piert, Quicksilver, Racy, Reside, Saut, Scherzo, Skittish, Spiritoso, Sprack, Spry, Vibrant, Vivace, Vivo, VOLATILE, Zoe

**Livelihood** Bread, Crust

**Liver(ish)** Hepar, Hepatic(al), Porta, Puce, Resident, Tomalley

**Liverpool, Liverpudlian** Scouse

**Liverwort** Gemma-cup, Hepatica, Riccia

**Livery(man)** Ermine, Flunkeydom, Goldsmith, Skinner, Tiger, Uniform

**Livid** Blae, Bruised, FURIOUS, Pale

**Living** Advowson, Benefice, Biont, Canonry, Glebe, Lodging, Quick, Resident, Simony, Symbiotic, Vicarage, Vital

**Livingstone** Doctor, Ken

**Liza, Lizzie** Bess, Betty, Flivver, Hexam, Tin

**Lizard** Abas, Agama, Amphisboena, Anguis, Anole, Basilisk, Blindworm, Brontosaurus, Chameleon, Chuckwalla, Dinosaur, Draco, Eft, Evet, Galliwasp, Gecko(ne), Gila, Goanna, Guana, Hatteria, Hellbender, Iguana, Komodo, Lacerta, Leguan, Lounge, Menopome, Moloch, Monitor, Newt, Perentie, Perenty, Reptile, Sauria, Scincoid, Seps, Skink, Slow-worm, Stellio(n), Tegu(exin), Tokay, Tuatara, Tuatera, Varan, Worral, Worrel

**Llama** Alpaca, Alpaco, Guanaco, Paco, Vicuna

**Load(ed), Loader** Accommodation, Ballast, Burden, Cargo, Charge, Cobblers, Dope, Drunk, Fardel, Fother, Freight, Full, Gestant, Heap, Input, Jag, Lade, Lard, Last, Onus, Pack, Pay, Prime, Rich, Seam, Shipment, Some, Surcharge, TIGHT, Tod, Weight, Wharfinger

**Loaf(er)** Baguette, Baton, Bloomer, Bludge, Brick, Bum, Bu(r)ster, Cad, Cob, Coburg, Cottage, Hawm, Idle, LAZE, Lusk, Manchet, Miche, Mouch, Pan(h)agia, Roll, Roti, Slosh, Tin, Vantage, Yob

**Loam** Clay, Loess, Loss, Malm

**Loan** Advance, Benevolence, Bottomry, Imprest, Lane, Mutuum, Out, Prest, Respondentia, Sub

**Loathe, Loathing, Loathsome** Abhor(rent), Abominate, Detest, Hate, Nauseate, Ug(h)

**Lob** Loft, Sky, Underarm

**Lobby** Demo, Entry, Foyer, Hall, Press, Urge

**Lobe(d)** Fluke, Lacinia, Lap, Palmate, Runcinate, Uvula, Vermis

**Lobster** Cock, Crawfish, Crayfish, Crustacean, Decapoda, Langouste, Pot, Scampo, Tomalley

**Local(ity)** Area, Endemic, Home, Inn, Landlord, Native, Nearby, Neighbourhood, Number, Parochial, Pub, Regional, Tavern, Topical, Vicinal

> **Local** may indicate a dialect word

**Locale** Scene, Site

**Locate** Connect, Find, Fix, Lay, Pinpoint, Plant, Site, Spot

**Location** Address, Milieu, Place, Site, Situation, Sofar, Ubiety, Zone

**Loch, Lough** Ashie, Awe, Earn, Eil, Erne, Etive, Fine, Gare, Garten, Holy, Hourn, Katrine, LAKE, Larne, Leven, Lomond, Long, Moidart, Morar, More, Neagh, Ness, Ryan, Tay, Torridon

**Lock(er), Locks, Lock up** Bar, Bolt, Chubb, Clinch, Combination, Cowlick, Curlicue, Davy Jones, Deadbolt, Fastener, Foretop, Haffet, Haffit, Hasp, Intern, Key, Latch, Lazaretto, Quiff, Ragbolt, Ringlet, Sasse, SECURE, Sluice, Snap, Strand, Tag, Talon, Tress, Tuft, Villus, Ward, Wrestle, Yale

**Locket**  Lucy

**Lockjaw**  Tetanus, Trismus

**Locksmith**  Garret-master, Hairdresser

**Locomotive**  Banker, Bogie, Bul(l)gine, Engine, Mobile, Rocket, Steamer, Train

**Locum**  Deputy, Relief

**Locus**  Centrode, Lemniscate, Place, Spot

**Locust**  Carob, Cicada, Hopper, Robinia, Voetganger

**Lode**  Lodge, Reef, Vein

**Lodestone**  Magnes, Magnet

**Lodge(r)**  Billet, Board(er), Box, Cosher, Deposit, Dig, Doss, Freemason, Guest, Harbour, Host, Inmate, Masonic, Lie, Parasite, PG, Quarter, Rancho, Room(er), Stay, Storehouse, Stow, Tenant, Tepee, Wigwam

**Lodging(s)**  B and B, Chummage, Dharms(h)ala, Digs, Ferm, Grange, Grove, Hostel, Inquiline, Kip, Minshuku, Pad, Pension, Pied-à-terre, Quarters, Resiant, Rooms, Singleen, YHA

**Loft(iness), Lofty**  Aerial, Airy, Arrogant, Attic, Celsitude, Garret, Grand, Haymow, High, Jube, Lordly, Noble, Rarefied, Rood, Roost, Tallat, Tallet, Tallot

**Log**  Billet, Black box, Cabin, Chock, Diarise, Diary, Mantissa, Nap(i)erian, Neper, RECORD, Stock

**Logarithm**  Nap(i)erian, Natural

**Logic(al)**  Alethic, Dialectic(s), Organon, Ramism, Rational(e), Reason, Sorites

**Loin(s)**  Flank, Inguinal, Lungie, Lunyie, Reins

**Loincloth**  Dhoti, Lungi, Waist-cloth

**Loiter(ing)**  Dally, Dare, Dawdle, Dilatory, Dilly-dally, Idle, Lag, Lallygag, Leng, Lime, LINGER, Mooch, Mouch, Potter, Saunter, Suss, Tarry

**Lola**  Dolores

**Loll**  Lounge, Sprawl

**Lollipop**  Lulibub

**Lolly**  Money, Sweetmeat

**London(er)**  'Arry, Cockaigne, Co(c)kayne, East-ender, Flat-cap, Jack, Smoke, Town, Troynovant, Wen

**London pride**  None-so-pretty

**Lone(r), Lonely**  Remote, Rogue, Secluded, Sole, Solitary, Unked, Unket, Unkid

**Long(er), Longing**  Ache, Aitch, Ake, Appetent, Aspire, Brame, Covet, Desire, Die, Earn, Erne, Far, Greed, Green, Grein, HANKER, Huey, Hunger, Island, Itch, L, Lanky, Large, Lengthy, Longa, Lust, Macron, More, NO LONGER, Nostalgia, Option, Pant, Parsec, PINE, Prolix, Side, Sigh, Tall, Thirst, Weary, Wish, Yearn, Yen

**Long-eared**  Spicate

**Longitude**  Meridian

**Long-lashed**  Mastigophora(n)

**Long live**  Banzai, Viva, Zindabad

**Longshoreman**  Hobbler, Hoveller, Wharfinger

**Long-suffering**  Job, Patient, Stoical

**Long-tailed**  Macrural

**Long-winded**  Prolix

**Loo**  Ajax, Bog, Can, Chapel, Game, Gents, Jakes, John, Privy, Toilet

**Look**  Air, Aspect, Belgard, Behold, Bonne-mine, Busk, Butcher's, Clock, Crane, Daggers, Decko, Dekko, Ecce, Ecco, Expression, Eye, Face, Facies, Gander, Gawp, Gaze, Geek, Glance, Gledge, Glimpse, Goggle, Grin, Hallo, Hangdog, Hey, Inspect, La, Lo, Mien, New, Ogle, Peek, Peep, Prospect, Ray, Recce, Refer, REGARD, Scan, Scrutinise, Search, See, Seek, Shade, Shufti, Shufty, Spy, Squint, Squiz, Toot, V, Vista

**Look-out (man)**  Cockatoo, Crow's nest, Huer, Mirador, Sangar, Sentry, Sungar, Toot(er), Watch

> **Look silly**  may indicate an anagram

**Loom**  Beamer, Emerge, Impend, Jacquard, Lathe, Menace, Picker, Temple, Threaten, Tower

**Loon**  Diver

**Loop(ed), Loophole, Loopy**  Becket, Bight, Billabong, Bouclé, Chink, Coil, Eyelet, Eyesplice, Fake, Frog, Grom(m)et, Grummet, Hank, Kink, Knop, Lasket, Lug, Noose, Oillet, Parral, Parrel, Pearl(-edge), Picot, Staple, Terry, Twist

**Loos**  Anita

**Loose(n), Loose woman**  Absolve, Abstrict, Afloat, Anonyma, Baggage, Bail, Besom, Cocotte, Demi-mondaine, Demirep, Dissolute, Dissolve, Draggletail, Dratchell, Drazel, Emit, Flirt-gill, Floosie, Floozie, Floozy, Floppy, Franion, Free, Gangling, Gay, Hussy, Insecure, Jade, Jezebel, Lax, Mob, Mort, Pinnace, Profligate, Quail, Ramp, RELAX, Sandy, Slag, Streel, Tart, Tramp, Trull, Unhasp, Unhitch, Unlace, Unpin, Unreined, Unscrew, Untie, Vague, Wappend, Whore

**Loot**  Boodle, Booty, Creach, Cragh, Foray, Haul, Peel, Pluck, PLUNDER, Ransack, Rape, Reave, Rieve, Rob, Sack, Smug, Spoils, Spoliate, Swag, Treasure

**Lop**  Behead, Clop, Curtail, Detruncate, Droop, Shroud, Sned, Trash

**Lorgnette**  Starers

**Loquacious**  Chatty, Gabby, Rambling

**Lord(s), Lordship**  Adonai, Arrogant, Boss, Byron, Domineer, Dominical, Duc, Earl, Elgin, Gad, God, Haw-haw, Herr, Imperious, Jim, Justice, Kami, Kitchener, Landgrave, Ld, Liege, Losh, Lud, Misrule, Mynheer, Naik, Omrah, Ordinary, Ormazd, Ormuzd, Seigneur, Seignior, Shaftesbury, Sire,

Spiritual, Taverner, Temporal, Tuan, Ullin

**Lords and ladies** Wake-robin

**Lore** Cab(b)ala, Edda, Lair, Lare, Upanished

**Lorelei** Siren

**Lorry** Artic(ulated), Camion, Drag, Juggernaut, Rig, Low-loader, Tipper, TRUCK, Wagon

**Lose(r)** Also-ran, Decrease, Drop, Elude, Forfeit, Leese, Misère, Mislay, Misplace, Nowhere, Tank, Throw, Tine(r), Tyne, Underdog, Waste, Weeper

**Loss** Anosmia, Aphesis, Aphonia, Apraxia, Attainder, Cost, Decrease, Detriment, Disadvantage, Elision, Outage, Pentimento, Perdition, Privation, Psilosis, Tine, Tinsel, Toll, Traik, Tyne, Ullage, Wastage, Will, Wull

**Loss of memory** Amnesia, Black-out, Fugue

**Lost** Astray, Boohai, Chord, Foredamned, Forfeited, Forgotten, Forlorn, Gone, Lore, Lorn, Missing, Perdu, Perished, Preoccupied, Tine, Tint, Tribes, Tyne(d), Unredeemed, Wasted

> **Lost** may indicate an anagram, or an obselete word

**Lot(s)** Abundant, Amount, Aret(t), Badly, Batch, Boatload, Caboodle, Cavel, Chance, Deal, Dole, Doom, Due, FATE, Fortune, Hantle, Hap, Heaps, Horde, Host, Item, Kevel, Kismet, Lashings, Legion, Luck, Manifold, Many, Mass, Mob, Moira, Mony, Mort, Myriad, Oceans, Omnibus, Oodles, Pack, Parcel, Plenitude, Plenty, Portion, Power, Raft, Scads, Set, Sight, Slather, Slew, Slue, Sortilege, Stack, Sum, Tons, Vole, Wagonload, Weird

**Loth** Averse, Sweer(t), Sweir(t)

**Lothario** Rake, Libertine, Womaniser

**Lotion** After-shave, Calamine, Unguent, Wash

**Lottery, Lotto** Bingo, Cavel, Draw, Gamble, Pakapoo, Pools, Raffle, Sweepstake, Tombola

**Lotus (eater), Lotus land** Asana, Djerba, Lotophagus

**Loud(ness), Loudly** Bel, Big, Booming, Decibel, F, FF, Flashy, Forte, Fracas, Garish, Gaudy, Hammerklavier, High, Lumpkin, Noisy, Raucous, Roarie, Siren, Sone, Stentor(ian), Strident, Tarty, Vociferous, Vulgar

**Loudspeaker** Action, Boanerges, Hailer, Megaphone, Stentor, Tannoy, Tweeter, Woofer

> **Lough** see LOCH

**Louis** Baker, Roi

**Louisianian** Cajun

**Lounge** Da(c)ker, Daiker, Hawm, Idle, Laze, Lizard, Loll, Lollop, Parlour, Slouch

**Louse (up), Lousy, Lice** Acrawl, Argulus, Bolix, Bollocks, Chat, Cootie, Crab, Crummy, Isopod(a), Nit, Oniscus, Pedicular, Psocoptera, Psylla, Slater, Snot, Sowbug, Vermin

**Lout** Clod(hopper), Coof, Cuif, Hallian, Hallion, Hallyon, Hick, Hobbledehoy, Hooligan, Hoon, Jack, Jake, Keelie, Lob(lolly), Loord, Lubber, Lumpkin, Oaf, Oik, Rube, Swad, Tout, Yahoo, Yob(bo)

**Love(r)** Abelard, Adore, Adulator, Affection, Aloha, Amant, Amateur, Amoroso, Amour, Antony, Ardour, Aucassin, Beau, Blob, Calf, Care, Casanova, Cicisbeo, Concubine, Coquet, Court, Cupboard, Cupid, Dote, Doxy, Duck(s), Ducky, Eloise, Eloper, Enamorado, Eros, Fan, Flame, Frauendienst, Goose-egg, Idolise, Inamorata, Inamorato, Isolde, Jo, Lad, Leman, Like, Lochinvar, Loe, Loo, Nihility, Nil, Nothing, Nought, O, Pairs, Paramour, Pash, Passion, Philander, Platonic, Protestant, Psychodelic, Revere, Romance, Romeo, Spooner, Stale, Storge, Suitor, Swain, Thisbe, Troilus, Turtle(-dove), Valentine, Venus, Virtu, Zeal, Zero

**Love-apple** Tomato, Wolf's-peach

**Love-child** Come-by-chance

**Love-in-a-mist** Nigella

**Lovely** Adorable, Belle, Dishy, Dreamy

**Love-making** INTERCOURSE, Sex, Snog

**Love-sick** Smit(ten), Strephon

**Loving** Amorous, Fond, Tender

**Low(est), Low-cut, Lower(ing)** Abase, Abate, Abysmal, Amort, Area, Avail(e), Avale, B, Base(-born), Bass(o), Beneath, Cartoonist, Church, Condescend, Contralto, Cow, Croon, Crude, Darken, Debase, Décolleté, Degrade, Demean, Demit, Demote, Depress, Devalue, Dim, Dip, Dispirited, Doldrums, Drop, Embase, Flat, Foot, Frown, Glare, Guernsey, Gurly, Hedge, Humble, Ignoble, Imbase, Inferior, Jersey, Laigh, Lallan, Law, Mass, Mean, Moo, Mopus, Morose, Nadir, Net, Nether, Nett, Ostinato, Paravail, Plebeianise, Profound, Prole, Relegate, Ribald, Rock-bottom, Sad, Scoundrel, Scowl, Short, Soft, Stoop, Sudra, Undermost, Vail, Vulgar, Weak, Wretched

> **Lower** may refer to cattle

**Lowbrow** Philistine

**Lowdown** Gen, Info

**Lowland(er)** Carse, Gallovidian, Glen, Laigh, Lallans, Merse, Plain, Polder, Sassenach

**Lowlying** Epigeous, Inferior

**Low woman, Low person** Boor, Bunter, Cad, Caitiff

**Loyal(ty)** Adherence, Allegiant, Brick, Dependable, Faithful, Fast, Fidelity, Gungho, Leal, Patriotic, Stalwart, Staunch, TRUE, Trusty

**Loyalist** Paisley, Patriot, Tory

**Lozenge** Cachou, Fusil, Jujube, Mascle, Pastille, Pill, Rhomb, Rustre, Tablet, Troche

**LSD** Acid, Money

**Lubber(ly), Lubbers** Booby, Clod, Clumsy, Gawky, Hulk, Looby, Oaf,

Slowback, Swab, Swads

**Lubricant, Lubricate**  Carap-oil, Coolant, Derv, Grease, Oil, Unguent

**Luce**  Ged

**Lucerne**  Alfalfa, Medick, Nonsuch

**Lucia**  Mimi

**Lucid**  Bright, Clear, Perspicuous, Sane

**Lucifer**  Devil, Match, Proud

**Luck(y)**  Amulet, Auspicious, Bonanza, Break, Caduac, Cess, Chance, Charmed, Chaunce, Daikoku, Dip, Fate, Fluke, FORTUNE, Godsend, Hap, Heather, Hit, Jam(my), Joss, Lot, Mascot, Mozzle, Pudding-bag, Seal, Seel, Sele, Serendipity, Sess, Sonsie, Sonsy, Star(s), Streak, Success, Talisman, Tinny, Turn-up, Windfall

**Luckless**  Hapless, Wight

**Lucre**  Money, Pelf, Tin

**Lucy**  Locket

**Lud**  Gad

**Luddite**  Saboteur, Wrecker

**Ludicrous**  Bathos, Farcical, Inane, Laughable, Risible

**Luff**  Derrick

**Lug**  Ear, Sea-worm, Tote, Tow

**Luggage**  Bags, Cases, Dunnage, Kit, Petara, Traps, Trunk

**Luggage-carrier**  Grid

**Lugubrious**  Dismal, Drear

**Luke-warm**  Laodicean, Lew, Tepid

**Lull**  Calm, Respite, Rock, Soothe, Sopite

**Lulu**  Stunner

**Lumber**  Clump, Galumph, Jumble, Pawn, Raffle, Saddle, Scamble, Timber

**Lumberjack**  Feller, Logger

**Luminance, Luminous**  Aglow, Arc, Glow, Ignis-fatuus, L, Light, Nit, Phosphorescent, Wildfire, Will o' the wisp

**Lumme**  Coo, Lor

**Lump(y)**  Aggregate, Bubo, Bud, Bulge, Bur(r), Caruncle, Chuck, Clat, Claut, Clod, Clot, Cob, Combine, Da(u)d, Dallop, Dollop, Enhydros, Epulis, Flocculate, Ganglion, Geode, Gnarl, Gob(bet), Goiter, Goitre, Grape, Hunch, Hunk, Inium, Knarl, Knob, Knub, Knur(r), Knurl, Lob, Lunch, Malleolus, Mote, Mott, Myxoma, Neuroma, Nibble, Nirl, Node, Nodule, Nodulus, Nugget, Nurl, Nur(r), Osteophyte, Plook, Plouk, Quinsy, Raguly, Sarcoma, Scybalum, Sitfast, Slub, Strophiole, Tragus, Tuber(cle), Wart, Wodge

**Lumpsucker**  Sea-owl

**Lunacy, Lunatic**  Dementia, Demonomania, Folly, Insanity, Mad(ness),

Psychosis

> **Lunatic**   may indicate an anagram

**Lunch(time)**   Dejeune, Déjeuner, l, L, Nacket, Nuncheon, Piece, Pm, Tiffin

**Lung(s)**   Bellows, Lights, Pulmo, Soul

**Lunge**   Breenge, Breinge, Dive, Stab, Thrust, Venue

**Lungfish**   Dipnoi(an)

**Lupin**   Arsene

**Lurch**   Reel, Stoit, Stumble, Swee

**Lure**   Bait, Bribe, Carrot, Decoy, Entice, Horn, Inveigle, Roper, Spinner, Stale, Temptation, Tice, Tole, Toll, Train, Trepan

**Lurid**   Gruesome, Purple

**Lurk(ing)**   Dare, Latitant, Skulk, Slink, Snoke, Snook, Snowk

**Luscious**   Succulent

**Lush**   Drunk, Fertile, Green, Juicy, Lydian, Sot, Tosspot

**Lust(ful), Lusty**   Cama, Concupiscence, Corflambo, Desire, Eros, Frack, Greed, Kama, Lech(ery), Lewd, Obidicut, Randy, Rank, Raunchy, Salacious, Venereous

**Lustre, Lustrous**   Census, Galena, Gaum, Gilt, Gloss, Gorm, Inaurate, Lead-glance, Pentad, Schiller, SHEEN, Water

**Lute, Lutist**   Amphion, Chitarrone, Dichord, Orpharion, Theorbo, Vielle

**Lutetium**   Lu

**Lutheran**   Adiaphorist, Calixtin(e), Pietist

**Lux**   Lx

**Luxemburg**   L

**Luxuriant, Luxuriate, Luxurious, Luxury (lover)**   Bask, Clover, Cockaigne, Cockayne, Copious, Deluxe, Dolce vita, Extravagant, Lavish, Lucullan, Lush, Ornate, Pie, Plush, Posh, RICH, Ritzy, Sumptuous, Sybarite, Wallow

**Lycanthropist**   Werewolf

**Lydia**   Languish

> **Lying**   see LIE

**Lymph**   Chyle

**Lynch**   Dewitt, Hang

**Lynx**   Bobcat, Caracal, Rooicat

**Lyre**   Cithern, Harp, Psaltery, Testudo

**Lyric(al), Lyricist, Lyrist**   Cavalier, Dit(t), Epode, Gilbert, Melic, Ode, Orphean, Paean, Pean, Poem, Rhapsodic, Song

# Mm

**M** Married, Member, Metre, Mike, Mile, Thousand

**Mac** Mino, Scot, Waterproof

**Macabre** Grotesque, Sick

**Macaroni** Beau, Blood, Cat, Dandy, Exquisite, Fop, Jack-a-dandy, Pasta, Petitmaitre

**Macaroon** Biscuit, Signal

**Macaulay** Layman

**Mace** Club, Nutmeg, Sceptre, Spice

**Mace-bearer** Beadle, Bedel

**Macedonian** Philip

**Machine(ry)** Apparat(us), Appliance, Automaton, Calender, DEVICE, Engine, Fax, Gin, Heck, Instrument, Lathe, Loom, Moulinet, Mule, Plant, Press, Robot, Slot, Throstle

**Mackerel** Albacore, Brack, Dory, Fish, Scad, Scumber, Sky, Trevally

**Mackintosh** Mac, Mino, Oilskin, Slicker, Waterproof

**Macropus** Euro, Wallaroo

**Mad(den), Madman, Madness** Angry, Balmy, Bananas, Barking, Barmy, Bedlam, Bonkers, Crackpot, Crazy, Cuckoo, Delirious, Dement, Distract, Enrage, Fey, Folie, Frantic, Frenetic(al), Furioso, Fury, Gelt, Gyte, Harpic, Hatter, Idiotic, Insane, Insanie, Insanity, Into, Irritate, Kook, Loco, Lunatic, Lycanthropy, Mania, Mental, Meshug(g)a, Midsummer, Mullah, Rabid, Raving, Redwood, Redwud, Scatty, Touched, Unhinged, Wood, Wowf, Wrath, Wud, Xenomania, Yond, Zany

> **Mad(den)** may indicate an anagram

**Madagascan** Aye-aye, Hova

**Madam(e)** Baggage, Lady, Proprietress

**Madcap** Impulsive, Tearaway

**Madder** Alizari, Chay(a), Gardenia, Genipap, Rose, Rubia, Shaya

**Made (it)** Built, Did, Fec(it), Ff, Gart, Invented

**Madge** Pie

> **Madly** may indicate an anagram

**Madonna** Lady, Lily, Mary, Pietà, Virgin

**Madrigal** Ballet, Fala, Song

**Maelstrom** Voraginous, Vortex, Whirlpool

**Maestro** Artist

**Mafia** Camorra, Godfather, Mob, Ndrangheta

**Mag** Mail

**Magazine** Arsenal, Clip, Colliers, Cornhill, Cosmopolitan, Economist, Field, Girlie, Glossy, Granta, Lady, Lancet, Listener, Magnet, Organ, Periodical, Pictorial, Playboy, Punch, She, Slick, Spectator, Store, Strand, Tatler, Vogue, Warehouse, Weekly, Yoof

**Magdalene** St. Mary

**Maggie** Rita

**Maggot** Bot, Gentle, Grub, Larva, Mawk, Whim, Worm

**Magi** Balthazar, Gaspar, Melchior

**Magic(al), Magician** Archimage, Art, Baetyl, Charm, Conjury, Diablerie, Diablery, Enchanting, Faust, Genie, Goetic, Goety, Gramary(e), Grimoire, Hermetic, Houdini, Illusionist, Math, Medea, Merlin, Mojo, Moly, Morgan le Fay, Myal, Pawaw, Powwow, Prospero, Reim-kenner, Rhombus, Sorcery, Spell, Speller, Supernatural, Talisman, Thaumaturgics, Theurgy, Voodoo, Wizard, Zendik

**Magistracy, Magistrate** Aedile, Amman, Amtman, Archon, Avoyer, Bailie, Bailiff, Bailli(e), Burgess, Burgomaster, Cadi, Censor, Consul, Corregidor, Demiurge, Doge(ate), Edile, Effendi, Ephor, Finer, Foud, JP, Judiciary, Jurat, Kotwal, Landamman(n), Landdrost, Maire, Mayor, Mittimus, Podesta, Portreeve, Pr(a)efect, Prior, Proconsul, Propraetor, Provost, Qadi, Quaestor, Recorder, Reeve, Shereef, Sherif, Stipendiary, Syndic, Tribune, Worship

**Magnanimity, Magnanimous** Big, Charitable, GENEROUS, Largeness, Lofty, Noble

**Magnate** Baron, Bigwig, Industrialist, Mogul, Tycoon, VIP

**Magnesia, Magnesium** Mg, Periclase

**Magnet(ic), Magnetism** Attraction, Charisma, Gauss, Horseshoe, It, Loadstone, Lodestone, Maxwell, Od, Oersted, Polar, Pole, Pull, Solenoid, Terrella, Tesla, Tole

**Magnificence, Magnificent** Gorgeous, Grandeur, Imperial, Laurentian, Lordly, Noble, Pride, Regal, Royal, Splendid, State, Superb

**Magnifier, Magnify(ing)** Binocle, ENLARGE, Exaggerate, Increase, Loupe, Microscope, Teinoscope, Telescope

**Magniloquent** Bombastic, Orotund

**Magnitude** Abundance, Extent, Muchness, Size

**Magnolia** Beaver-tree, Champac, Champak, Mississippi, Sweet bay, Umbrella-tree, Yulan

**Magpie** Bird, Chatterer, Madge, Margaret, Outer, Pica, Piet, Pyat, Pyet, Pyot

**Magus** Artist

**Magyar** Hungarian, Szekler, Ugrian, Ugric

**Mahogany** Acajou, Carapa, Cedrela, Wood

**Mahommedan** Dervish, Shiah

**Maid(en)** Abigail, Aia, Amah, Biddy, Bonibell, Bonne, Bonnibell, Chamber, Chloe, Damosel, Dell, Dey, First, Girl, Guillotine, Ignis-fatuus, Imago, Inaugural, Io, Iras, Lorelei, M, Marian, May, Miss, Nymph, Opening, Over, Pucelle, Rhine, Skivvy, Soubrette, Suivante, Thestylis, Tweeny, Valkyrie, Virgin, Wench

**Maidenhair** Fern, Ginkgo

**Mail** ARMOUR, Byrnie, Chain, Da(w)k, Habergeon, Helm, Letter, Panoply, Post, Send, Tuille(tte)

**Mailboat** Packet

**Maim** Cripple, Impair, Lame, Mayhem, Mutilate, Vuln

**Main(s)** Brine, Briny, CENTRAL, Chief, Conduit, Essential, Foremost, Generally, Grid, Gross, Head, KEY, Lead(ing), Palmany, Predominant, Prime, SEA, Sheer, Spanish, Staple

**Mainland** Continent, Pomona

**Mainstay** Backbone, Bastion, Pillar, Support

**Maintain, Maintenance** Alimony, Allege, Ap(p)anage, Argue, Assert, Aver, Avow, Claim, Contend, Continue, Defend, Escot, Insist, Preserve, Run, Sustain, Upbear, Uphold, Upkeep

**Maize** Corn, Hominy, Indian, Mealie, Samp, Silk, Stamp, Zea

**Majestic, Majesty** August, Britannic, Dignity, Eagle, Grandeur, Imperial, Maestoso, Olympian, Regal, SM, Sovereign, Stately, Sublime, Tuanku

**Major (domo)** Drum, IMPORTANT, PM, Seneschal, Senior, Sergeant, Trumpet

**Majority** Age, Body, Eighteen, Latchkey, Most

**Make(r), Make do, Making** Amass, Brand, Coerce, Coin, Compel, Compulse, Concoct, Creant, Create, Devise, Earn, Execute, Fabricate, Fashion, Fet(t), Forge, Form, Gar(re), God, Halfpenny, Mail(e), Manage, Prepare, Production, Reach, Render, Shape, Temporise, Wright

> **Make** may indicate an anagram

**Make believe** Fantasy, Fictitious, Pretend, Pseudo

**Make good** Abet, Compensate, Remedy, Succeed, Ulling

**Make hay** Ted

**Make off** Bolt, Leg it, Mosey, Run, Scarper

**Makeshift** Bandaid, Crude, Cutcha, Expedient, Kacha, Kutcha, Pis-aller, Rude, Stopgap, Timenoguy

**Make up** Ad lib, Compose, Constitution, Cosmetics, Gaud, Gawd, Gene, Identikit, Kohl, Liner, Lipstick, Maquillage, Mascara, Paint, Powder, Reconcile, Rouge, Slap, Tidivate, Titivate

**Maladroit** Awkward, Clumsy, Graceless, Inelegant

**Malady** Disease, Illness

**Malagas(e)y** Hova, RM

**Malapropism** Slipslop

**Malaria** Ague, Tap

**Malawi** Nyasa

**Malay(an), Malaysian** Austronesian, Datuk, Dyak, Madurese, Moro, Sakai, Tokay

**Male** Arrhenotoky, Buck, Bull, Dog, Ephebe, Ephebus, Gent, Macho, Mansize, Masculine, Ram, Rogue, Spear(side), Stag, Stamened, Telamon, Tom

**Malediction** Curse, Cuss, Oath, Slander

**Malefactor** Criminal, Felon, Villain

**Malevolent, Malevolence** Evil, Fell, Malign

**Malfunction** Glitch

**Mali** RMM

**Malice, Malicious** Bitchy, Catty, Cruel, Despiteous, Envy, Malevolent, Malign, Schadenfreude, Serpent, Snide, Spite, Spleen, Venom

**Malign(ant), Malignity** Asperse, Baleful, Defame, Denigrate, Gall, Harm, Hatred, Libel, Sinister, Slander, Spiteful, Swarthy, Toxin, Vicious, Vilify, Viperous, Virulent

**Malinger(er)** Dodge, Leadswinger, Scrimshank, Shirk, Skrimshank, Truant

**Mallard** Duck, Sord

**Malleable** Clay, Ductile, Pliable

> **Malleable** may indicate an anagram

**Mallet** Beetle, Club, Hammer, Mace, Maul

**Mallow** Abutilon

**Malpractice(s)** Sculduggery, Skulduggery

**Malt** Grains, Grist, Wort

**Maltese (cross)** Falcon, GC

**Maltreat** Abuse, Harm, Maul, Mishandle, Misuse

**Mammal** Animal, Charronia, Eutheria, Glires, Grison, Guanaco, Hydrax, Indri, Lagomorph, Numbat, Peccany, Pekan, Primate, Rhytina, Solenodon, Taguan, Takin, Tayra, Tenrec, Tylopod, Whale

**Mammon** Money, Riches, Wealth

**Mammoth** Epic, Gigantic, Huge, Jumbo, Mastodon, Whopping

**Man(kind)** Ask(r), Betty, Bimanal, Biped, Bloke, Bo, Boy, Cad, Cairn, Calf, Cat, Chal, Chap, Cob, Cockey, Cro-Magnon, Crew, Cuffin, Cully, Dog, Don, Draught, Fellow, Friday, G, Gent, Guy, He, Heidelberg, Hombre, Hominid, Homme, Homo, IOM, Isle, Jack, John(nie), Lollipop, M, Male, Microcosm, Mister, Mon, Mi, Mun, Neanderthal, Oreopithecus, Pawn, Peking, Person, Piece, Pin, Piltdown, Raff, Rook, Servant, Servitor, Ship, Sodor, Staff, Stag, Straw, Thursday, Twelfth, Tyke, Type, Valet, Vir, Wight

**Manacle** Fetter, Handcuff, Iron, Shackle

**Manage(r), Manageable, Management, Managing** Administer, Amildar, Attain, Aumil, Behave, Boss, Chief, Conduct, Contrive, Control, Cope, Direct, Docile, Executive, Fare, Find, Govern, Handle, Honcho, IC, Impresario, Intendant, MacReady, Manipulate, Manoeuvre, Proctor, Procurator, Regisseur, Rig, RUN, Scrape, Shift, Steward, Succeed, Suit, Superintend, Tawie, Tractable, Treatment, Trustee, Wangle, Wield(y), Yare

**Manatee** Lamantum, Mermaid, Sea-ape

**Manchu** Fu

**Mandarin** Bureaucrat, Chinaman, Kuo-Yu, Nodding, Satsuma, Yamen

**Mandate** Authority, Decree, Fiat, Order

**Mandrel** Triblet

**Mane(d), Manes** Crest, Encolure, Jubate, Larva(e), Shades

**Manege** Horseplay, Train

**Manganese** Mn, Synadelphite, Wadd

**Manger** Cratch, Crib, Hack, Stall

**Mangle** Agrise, Distort, Garble, Hack, Wring(er)

> **Mangle** may indicate an anagram

**Mango** Dika

**Manhandle** Frogmarch, Maul, Rough

**Manhater** Misanthrope

**Manhattan** Bowery

**Mania** Craze, Frenzy, Passion, Rage

**Manichaean** Albi

**Manifest(ation), Manifestly** Attest, Evident, Evince, Exhibit, Feat, List, Marked, Mode, Notably, Obvious, Open, Show

**Manifesto** Plank, Platform, Policy, Pronunciamento

**Manifold** Many, Multiple

**Manila** Abaca, Cheroot

**Maniple** Fannel, Fanon

**Manipulate, Manipulator** Chiropractor, Control, Cook, Fashion, Gerrymander, Handle, Jerrymander, Juggle, Osteopath, Ply, Rig, Use, Wangle, WIELD

> **Manipulate** may indicate an anagram

**Manna** Alhagi, Food, Trehala

**Manner(ism), Mannerly, Manners** Accent, A la, Appearance, Attitude, Bedside, Behaved, Behaviour, Breeding, Conduct, Crew, Custom, Deportment, Ethos, Etiquette, Farand, Farrand, Farrant, Habit, How, Mien, Mode, Morality, Mores, Of, Ostent, Panache, P's & Q's, Rate, Sort, Style, Thew(s), Thewe(s), Trick, Upsee, Upsey, Upsy, Urbanity, Way, Wise

**Manoeuvre** Campaign, Castle, Engineer, Exercise, Fork, Gambit, Hot-dog,

Jink(s), Jockey, Manipulate, Op(eration), Pesade, Ploy, Ruse, Skewer, Use, Wile, Zigzag

> **Manoeuvre** may indicate an anagram

**Man-of-war** Armada, Destroyer, Ironclad

**Manor (house)** Area, Demain, Demesne, Estate, Hall, Vill(a)

**Mansion** Seat

**Mantle** Authority, Burnous(e), Capote, Caracalla, Dolman, Elijah, Gas, Pall, Pallium, Paludament, Pelisse, Rochet, Sima, Toga, Tunic, Veil

**Mantuan** Maro, Virgil

**Manual** Bradshaw, Cambist, Console, Enchiridion, Guide, Hand, Handbook, How-to, Portolan(o)

**Manufacture** Fabricate, Make, Produce

**Manure** Compost, Dung, Fertiliser, Guano, Hen-pen, Lime, Muck, Sha(i)rn, Tath

**Manuscript** Codex, Folio, Hand, Holograph, Longhand, MS, Opisthograph, Palimpsest, Papyrus, Parchment, Script, Scroll, Scrowl(e)

**Manx(man)** Cat, IOM, Kelly, Kelt

> **Manx** may indicate a last letter missing

**Many** C, CD, Countless, D, Hantle, Herd, Horde, Host, L, Lot, M, Manifold, Multi(tude), Myriad, Scad, Sight, Tons, Umpteen

> **Many** may indicate the use of a Roman numeral letter

**Maori (house)** Hauhau, Wahine, Whare

**Map** Atlas, Card, Cartogram, Chart, Face, Inset, Key, OS, Plan, Plot, Relief, Sea-card, Sea-chart

**Maple** Acer, Mazer, Sycamore, Syrup

**Map-maker** Cartographer, OS, Speed

**Maquis** Underground

**Mar** Blight, Denature, Impair, Soil, Spoil

**Marabout** Sofi, Sufi

**Marathon** Huge, Race

**Marauder** Attacker, Bandit, Pillager, Pirate, Predator, Prowler

**Marble(s)** Aeginetan, Agate, All(e)y, Arch, Arundelian, Bonce, Bool, Bonduc, Boondoggle, Bowl, Cipollino, Commoney, Dump, Elgin, Humite, Hymettus, Knicker, Marl, Marmoreal, Mottle, Nero-antico, Nickar, Nicker, Onychite, Paragon, Parian, Pavonazzo, Phigalian, Plonker, Plunker, Purbeck, Rance, Ring-taw, Sanity, Scagliola, Spangcockle, Taw, Xanthian

**Marcel** Proust

**March** Abut, Adjoin, Advance, Anabasis, Border(er), Borderland, Defile, Demo, Etape, File, Footslog, Fringe, Galumph, Go, Goosestep, Ides, Lide, Limes, Meare, Music, PARADE, Progress, Protest, Step, Strunt, Strut, Tromp, Yomp

**Marco** Il Milione, Polo

**Mare** Dam, Flanders, Horse, M, Shank's, Yaud

**Margaret** Anjou, Meg, Peg, Rita

**Margarine** Oleo

**Marge, Margin(al)** Annotate, Border, Brim, Brink, Curb, Edge, Lean, Limit, Littoral, Neck, Nose, Peristome, Rand, Repand, RIM, Sideline, Term

**Marginal note** Apostil(le), K'ri

**Margosa** Melia, Nim

**Marianne** France

**Marie** Dressler, Tempest

**Marigold** Calendula, Kingcup, Tagetes

**Marijuana** Alfalfa, Dagga, Gage, Ganja, Grass, Greens, Gungeon, Ha-ha, Hay, Herb, Kaif, Jive, Kef, Kif, Pot, Roach, Rope, Sinsemilla, Splay, Spliff, Tea

**Marine (creature)** Bootie, Bootneck, Ctenophora, Cunjevoi, Enteropneusta, Flustra, Galoot, Harumfrodite, Hemichorda, Jolly, Leatherneck, Lobster, Mercantile, Mere-swine, Mistress Roper, Oceanic, Physalia, Sea-soldier, Thalassian, Ultra

**Mariner** AB, MN, RM, Sailor, Salt, Seafarer, Tar

**Marionette(s)** Fantoccini, Puppet

**Marjoram** Amaracus

**Mark(ed)** Accent, Antony, Apostrophe, Badge, Bethumb, Blaze, Blot, Brand, Bruise, Bull, Butt, Cachet, Caract, Caret, Cedilla, Chequer, Cicatrix, Clout, Colon, Comma, Coronis, Crease, Dash, Denote, Dent, Diaeresis, Dieresis, Distinction, DM, Ensign, Enstamp, Exclamation, Feer, Gospel, Hacek, Hash, Hatch, Heed, Hyphen, Impress(ion), Indicium, Ink, Inscribe, Insignia, Lentigo, Line, Ling, Logo, M, Macron, MB, Merk, NB, Notal, Note, Notice, Obelisk, Observe, Oche, Paraph, Period, Pilcrow, Pit, Point, Popinjay, Presa, Record, Roundel, Scar, Score, Sigil, Sign, Smit, Smut, Speck, Splodge, Splotch, Stain, Stencil, Stigma(ta), Sucker, Symbol, Target, Tatow, Tattoo, Tee, Theta, Tick, Tika, Tittle, Token, Track, Trout, Twain, Umlaut, Ure, Victim, Watch, Weal, Welt

**Marker** Flag, Ink, Scorer

**Market (day), Market place** Agora, Alcaiceria, Baltic, Bazaar, Billingsgate, Borgo, Change, EC, Emporium, Errand, Exchange, Fair, Forum, Kerb, Mart, Mercat, Nundine, Outlet, Piazza, Sale, Shop, Sook, Souk, Stance, Staple, Test, Trade, Tron, Tryst, Vent

**Marksman** Sharpshooter, Shot, Sniper, Tell

**Marlborough** Blenheim

**Marlene** Lilli

**Marmalade** Cat, Preserve, Squish

**Marmoset** Jacchus, Mico, Midas, Monkey, Wistiti

**Marmot** Bobac, Bobak, Dassie, Hyrax, Rodent, Woodchuck

**Maroon** Brown, Enisle, Firework, Inisle, Isolate, Strand

**Marquee** Pavilion, Tent, Top

**Marquess, Marquis** Granby, Lorne, Sade

**Marquetry** Boul(le), Buhl

**Marriage** ALLIANCE, Bed, Beenah, Bigamy, Bridal, Coemption, Confarreation, Conjugal, Connubial, Endogamy, Espousal, Exogamy, Gandharva, Genial, Hymeneal, Jugal, Knot, Levirate, Match, Mating, Matrimony, Morganatic, Nuptial, Pantagamy, Punalua, Shidduch, Tie, UNION, Wedding, Wedlock

**Marriageable** Marrow, Nubile, Parti

**Marrow** Courgette, Friend, Gist, Medulla, Myeloid, Pith, Pumpkin, Squash

**Marry, Married** Ally, Amate, Buckle, Cleek(it), Confarreate, Couple, Espouse, Forsooth, Hitch, Join, Knit, M, Mate, Matron, Memsahib, Pair, Pardie, Quotha, Splice, Tie, Troggs, Troth, Unite, W, Wed, Wive

**Mars** Areography, Ares, Red (planet)

**Marsh(y)** Bayou, Bog, Chott, Corcass, Emys, Everglade, Fen, Hackney, Maremma, Merse, Mire, Morass, Ngaio, Paludal, Pontine, Quagmire, Romney, Salina, Shott, Slade, Slough, Sog, Spew, Spue, Swale, Swamp, Taiga, Terai, Vlei, Wetlands

**Marshal** Arrange, Array, Commander, Earp, Foch, MacMahon, Muster, Neil, Ney, Order, Pétain, Shepherd, Usher

**Marshmallow** Althaea

**Marsupial** Bandicoot, Bilby, Cus-cus, Dasyure, Dibbler, Didelphia, Diprotodont, Dunnart, Kangaroo, Koala, Metatheria, Notoryctes, Nototherium, Numbat, Opossum, Petaurist, Phalanger, Possum, Potoroo, Quokka, Quoll, Roo, Theria, Thylacine, Tuan, Wallaby, Wambenger, Wombat, Yapo(c)k

**Marten** Mustela, Pekan, Sable

**Martha** Vineyard

**Martial (arts)** Bellicose, Budo, Capoeira, Capuera, Dojo, Iai-do, Judo, Ju-jitsu, Karate, Kung Fu, Militant, Ninjutsu, Warlike, Wushu

**Martin** Bird, Luther, Swallow

**Martinet** Captious, Ramrod, Stickler

**Martini** Cocktail, Henry

**Martyr(dom), Martyrs** Alban, Colosseum, Donatist, Justin, Latimer, MM, Persecute, Sebastian, Stephen, Suffer, Tolpuddle, Wishart

**Marvel(lous)** Bully, Fab, Marl, Miracle, Mirific, Phenomenon, Superb, Terrific, Wonder

**Marx(ism), Marxist** Aspheterism, Chico, Groucho, Gummo, Harpo, Karl, Tanky, Zeppo

**Mary** Bloody, Celeste, Madonna, Moll, Morison, Tum(my), Virgin

**Marylebone** Station

**Masculine** He, M, Macho, Male, Manly, Virile

**Maser** Laser

**Mash(er)** Beau, Beetle, Brew, Lady-killer, Pap, Pestle, Pound, Squash

**Mask** Camouflage, Cloak, Cokuloris, Disguise, Dissemble, Domino, Mascaron, Matte, Persona, Screen, Semblance, Stalking-horse, Template, Visor, Vizard

**Mason(ry)** Ashlar, Ashler, Brother, Builder, Cowan, Emplecton, Isodoma, Isodomon, Lodge, Moellon, Opus, Perry, Random, Squinch

**Masque(rade), Masquerader** Comus, Domino, Guisard, Mum, Pose, Pretend

**Mass(es)** Agnus dei, Aggregate, Anniversary, Banket, Bezoar, Bike, Body, Bulk, Cake, Clot, Conglomeration, Crith, Crowd, Demos, Density, Flake, Flysch, Great, Herd, Horde, Hulk, Jud, Kermesse, Kermis, Kilo(gram), Kirmess, M, Majority, Missa, Mop, Nest, Phalanx, Pile, Plumb, Populace, Raft, Requiem, Ruck, Salamon, Salmon, Scrum, Serac, Service, Shock, Sicilian, Size, Slub, Slug, Stack, Stroma, Te Igitur, Tektite, Trental, Vesper, Volume, Wad, Weight, Welter

**Massacre** Amritsar, Blood-bath, Butcher, Carnage, Glencoe, Havock, Manchester, Peterloo, Pogrom, Scullabogue, Scupper, September, Sicilian vespers, Slaughter, Slay

**Massage, Masseur** Chafer, Effleurage, KNEAD, Malax, Palp, Petrissage, Rolf(ing), Rubber, Shampoo, Tapotement, Tripsis

**Massive** Big, Bull, Colossal, Huge, Monumental, Strong, Titan

**Mast** Acorn, Jury, Mizzen, Pannage, Pole, Racahout, Spar

**Master** Baas, Beat, Boss, Buddha, Bwana, Careers, Checkmate, Conquer, Control, Dan, Dominate, Dominie, Employer, Enslave, Exarch, Expert, Herr, Learn, Lord, MA, Maestro, Mas(s), Massa, Mes(s), Ollamh, Ollav, Oner, Oppress, Original, Overcome, Overpower, Overseer, Pedant, Rabboni, Seigneur, Seignior, Sir(e), Skipper, SUBDUE, Superate, Swami, Tame, Thakin, Towkay, Tuan, Usher, Vanquish, Virtuoso

**Mastermind** Brain, Conceive, Direct

**Masterpiece** Creation

**Master-stroke** Coup, Triumph

**Masthead** Banner, Flag, M, Truck

**Masturbate, Masturbation** Abuse, Frig, Gratify, Onanism, Wank

**Mat(ted), Matting** Bast, Dojo, Doily, Doyley, Felt, Inlace, Pad, Rug, TANGLE, Tat(ami), Tatty, Taut, Tawt, Tomentose, Welcome, Zarf

**Matador** Card, Espada, Ordonez, Theseus, Torero

**Match(ed)** Agree, Alliance, Amate, Balance, Besort, Bonspiel, Bout, Carousel, Compare, Congreve, Contest, Cope, Correspond, Counterpane, Engagement, Equal(ise), Equate, Even, Fellow, Fit, Fixture, Friendly, Fusee, Fuzee, Game, Go, International, Light, Locofoco, Lucifer, Main,

Meet, Mouse, Needle, Pair(s), Paragon, Parti, Pit, Promethean, Reproduce, Rival, Roland, Rubber, Safety, Slanging, Spunk, Striker, Suit, TALLY, Team, Test, Tie, Twin, Union, Vesta, Vesuvian, Wedding

**Matchbox label (collecting)** Phillumeny

**Match girl** Bride

**Match-holder** Lin(t)stock

**Matchless** Non(e)such, Orinda

**Matchmaker** Blackfoot, Broker, Pairer, Promoter, Shadchan

**Mate, Mating** Achates, Adam, Bedfellow, Bo, Breed, Buffer, Buddy, Butty, Chess, China, Cobber, Comrade, Consort, Crony, Eve, Feare, Feer, Fellow, Fere, Fiere, Fool's, Husband, Maik, Make, Marrow, Marry, Match, Mister, Oldster, Oppo, PAIR, Pal, Paragon, Partner, Pheer(e), Pirrauru, Serve, Sex, Skaines, SPOUSE, Tea, Wack, Wife, Wus(s)

**Material** Agalmatolite, Aggregate, Apt, Armure, Batiste, Blastema, Bole, Byssus, Calamanco, Cambric, Canvas, Cellulose, Cermet, Charmeuse, Chiffon, Ciré, CLOTH, Coburg, Copy, Corporeal, Crash, Cretonne, Data, Dimity, Earthy, FABRIC, Factual, Fuel, Gaberdine, Genappe, Germane, Hessian, Homespun, Hylic, Illusion, Jeanette, Lamé, Lawn, Marocain, Metal, Oilskin, Pertinent, Physical, Pina-cloth, Polyester, Positive, Relevant, Russel, Soneri, Stockingette, Stuff, Substance, Tangible, Tape, Tarpaulin, Textile, Thingy, Toile, Twill, Winceyette, Wool, Worcester

**Materialise** Appear, Apport, Click, Reify

**Materialist(ic)** Banausian, Hylist, Hyloist, Philistine, Somatist

**Mathematician** Apollonius, Archimedes, Boole, Cocker, Descartes, Diophantos, Euclid, Euler, Fermat, Fourier, Gunter, Laplace, Leibniz, Lie, Mercator, Napier, Newton, Optime, Pascal, Poisson, Ptolemy, Pythagoras, Riemann, Torricelli, Wrangler

**Mathematics, Maths** Algebra, Arithmetic, Arsmetrick, Geometry, Logarithms, Mechanics, Numbers, Trig

**Matilda** Liar, Swag, Untruthful, Waltzing

**Matinee** Coat, Idol, Show

**Mating** Pangamy

**Matins** Nocturn

**Matricide** Orestes

**Matrimony** Bed, Conjugal, Marriage, Sponsal, Wedlock

**Matrix** Array, Jacobian, Mould, Pattern, Uterus

**Matron** Dame, Hausfrau, Lucretia, Nurse, Warden

**Matt(e)** Dense, Dingy, Dull

**Matter** Alluvium, Bioblast, Biogen, Body, Concern, Consequence, Empyema, Go, Gear, Gluon, Grcy, Hyle, Impost(h)ume, Issue, Mass, Material, Molecule, Phlegm, Pith, Point, Positron, Protoplasm, Pulp, Pus, Reck, Reke, Scum, Shebang, Signify, Subject, SUBSTANCE, Topic, Tousle, Touzle, Ylem

**Matthew** Arnold

**Mattress** Bed(ding), Biscuit, Futon, Lilo, Pallet, Palliasse, Tick

**Mature, Maturity** Adult, Age, Blossom, Bold, Develop, Mellow, Metaplasis, Ripe(n), Seasoned, Upgrow(n)

**Maudlin** Fuddled, Mawkish, Sentimental, Sloppy, Too-too

**Maul** Hammer, Manhandle, Paw, Rough

**Maundy** Money, Nipter, Thursday

**Mauretanian** Moor

**Mausoleum** Mole, Sepulchre, Taj Mahal, Tomb

**Mauve** Lilac, Mallow

**Maverick** Misfit, Nonconformist, Rogue

**Mavis** Throstle

**Maw** Crop, Gorge, Gull(et), Oesophagus

**Maxim** Adage, Apophthegm, Byword, Gnome, Gorki, Gun, Hiram, Moral, Motto, Proverb, Restaurateur, RULE, Saw, Saying, Sentence, Sentiment, Watchword

**Maximum** Full, Highest, Most, Peak

**May** Blossom, Can, Hawthorn, Merry, Might, Month, Mote, Quickthorn, Whitethorn

**Maybe** Happen, Mebbe, Peradventure, Percase, Perchance, Perhaps, Possibly

> **May become** may indicate an anagram

**May day** Beltane, SOS

**Mayfair** W1

**Mayfly** Ephemera, Ephemeroptera, Green-drake, Sedge

**Mayhem** Chaos, Crime, Damage

**Mayonnaise** Aioli

**Mayor** Casterbridge, Porteeve, Provost, Whittington

**Maze** Labyrinth, Meander, Warren

**MC** Compere, Host

**MD** Doctor, Healer

**Me** I, Mi

**Mead(ow)** Grass, Haugh, Inch, Lea(se), Ley, Meath(e), Metheglin, PASTURE, Runnymede, Saeter, Salting

**Meadowsweet** Dropwort

**Meagre** Bare, Exiguous, Measly, Paltry, Pittance, Scant, Scrannel, Scranny, Skimpy, Skinny, Stingy, Thin

**Meal** Breakfast, Brunch, Buffet, Cassava, Cereal, Chota-hazri, Collation, Cornflour, Cribble, Dinner, Farina, Flour, Food, Grits, Grout, Lock, Lunch, Mandioc, Mandioc(c)a, Mani(h)oc, Melder, Meltith, Mess, Mush, No-cake,

Nuncheon, Piece, Plate, Polenta, Porridge, Prandial, Rac(c)about, Refection, Repast, Revalenta, Salep, Scambling, Scoff, Seder, Snack, Spread, Supper, Tea, Tiffin, Tightener, Undern

**Meal-ticket** LV

**Mean, Meaning, Meant** Aim, Average, Base, Betoken, Caitiff, Denotate, Denote, Dirty, Drift, Essence, Ettle, Feck, Footy, Foul, Gist, Hang, Humble, Hunks, Ignoble, Illiberal, Imply, Import, Inferior, Intend, Intermediate, Low, Mang(e)y, Marrow, Medium, Mesquin, Method, Mid, Miserly, Narrow, Near, Nothing, One-horse, Organ, Ornery, Paltry, Petty, Pinch-penny, Pith, Point, Purport, PURPOSE, Ratfink, Revenue, Roinish, Roynish, Scall, Scrub, Scurvy, Semanteme, Sense, Shabby, Signify, Slight, Small, Sneaky, Snot, Sordid, Sparing, Spell, Stingy, Stink(ard), Stinty, Substance, Symbol, Thin, Two-bit, Value, Whoreson

**Meander** Fret, Stray, Wander, Weave, Wind

**Meaningless** Ducdame, Empty, Hollow, Nonny, Rumbelow

**Means** Agency, Dint, Income, Media, Mode, Resources, Staple, Substance, Ways, Wherewithal

**Meantime, Meanwhile** Among, Emong, Greenwich, Interim

**Measles** Morbilli, Rubella, Rubeola

**Measure(d), Measuring, Measurement** Acre, Amphimacer, Anemometer, Anker, Ardeb, Are, Arpent, Arshin(e), As, Astrolabe, Aune, Barleycorn, Barrel, Barren, Barye, Bath, Beegha, Bekah, Bel, Bigha, Boll, Bovate, Breadth, Burette, Bushel, By(e)law, Cab, Calibre, Cal(l)iper, Caneh, Carat, Carucate, Cathetometer, Centimetre, Chain, Chalder, Chaldron, Ch(o)enix, Chopin, Clove, Comb(e), Coomb, Cor, Cord, Coss, Coulomb, Cran, Crannock, Crore, Cryometer, Cubage, Cubit, Cumec, Cusec, Cyathus, DANCE, Decalitre, Decastere, Decibel, Demarche, Denier, Depth, Dessiatine, Dessyatine, Desyatin, Diameter, DIMENSION, Distance, Dose, Dram, Drastic, Ell, Em, En, Entropy, Epha(h), Erg, Etalon, Fat, Fathom, Fermi, Firkin, Firlot, Fistmeal, Fistmele, Foot, Furlong, Ga(u)ge, Gallon, Gavotte, Geodesy, Gill, Grain, Groma, Hanap, Hemina, Height, Hide, Hin, Hogshead, Homer, Inch, Intoximeter, Jigger, Joule, Kaneh, Kilerg, Kilometre, Koss, Lambert, Last, Lay, Lea, League(r), Lento, Ley, Liang, Ligne, Limit, Line, Lippie, Lippy, Log, Loure, Lug, Lysimeter, Manometer, Maze, Mease, Mekometer, Mete(r), Metre, Mil, Mile, Millimetre, Modius, Mott, Mu, Muid, Mutchkin, Nail, Nephelometer, Nipperkin, Odometer, Of, Omer, Opisometer, Optic, Oxgang, Oximeter, Pace, Parasang, Parsec, Pascal, Peck, Perch, Pint, Plumb, Pole, Pood, Potometer, Pottle, Puncheon, Quart(er), Quickstep, Radius, Ream, Riddle, Rod, Romer, Rood, Rope, Ruler, Run(d)let, Sazhen, Scale, Share, Shot, SIZE, Sleever, Sound, Span, Spondee, Stade, Stadia, Standard, Statute, Step, Steradian, Stere(ometer), Strike, Survey, Tape(-line), Tappet-hen, Tesla, Tierce, Titration, Toise, Token, Tot, Unit, Vara, Verst, Virgate, Volt, Warp, Waywiser, Wey, Winchester, Yard, Yojan(a)

**Meat(s)** Aitchbone, Bacon, Bard, Beef, Biltong, Brawn, Burger, Cabob, Carbonado, Carrion, Chop, Collop, Croquette, Cut, Edgebone, Escalope,

Essence, Flesh, Flitch, Force, Galantine, Gigot, Gobbet, Gosht, Griskin, Ham, Haslet, Joint, Junk, Kabab, Kabob, Kebab, Kebob, Lamb, Mutton, Noisette, Offal, Olive, Pastrami, Pith, Pork, Rillettes, Roast, Saddle, Salary, Scran, Scrapple, Sey, Spam, Steak, Tenderloin, Tongue, Veal, Venison, Vifda, Virgate, Vivda

**Meat extract** Brawn, Gravy, Juice, Stock

**Meatball(s)** Cecils, Croquette, Faggot, Falafel, Felafel, Fricadel, Kofta, Kromesky, Quenelle, Rissole

**Meatless** Banian, Lent, Maigre, Vegetarian

**Mecca** Centre, Kaaba, Keblah, Kiblah, Qibla

**Mechanic** Apron-man, Artificer, Artisan, Banausic, Engineer, Fitter, Fundi, Hand, Journeyman, Operative, Technician

**Mechanical, Mechanism** Action, Apparatus, Auto, Gimmal, Instrument, Machinery, Movement, Organical, Servo, Works

**Medal(lion)** Award, Bar, Bronze, Decoration, Dickin, DSM, GC, George, Gold, Gong, Gorget, MM, Putty, Roundel, Silver, Touchpiece, VC, Vernicle

**Meddle(r), Meddlesome** Busybody, Dabble, Finger, Hen-hussy, INTERFERE, Marplot, Mell, Monkey, Officious, Potter, Pragmatic, Pry, Snooper, Tamper, Tinker

**Media** PR

**Mediate, Mediator** ACAS, Arbitrate, Interpose, Intervene, Liaison, Referee, Thirdsman

**Medical, Medicament, Medication, Medicine (chest)** Allopathy, Anodyne, Antacid, Antibiotic, Antidote, Antisepsis, Antiseptic, Arnica, Asafetida, Bismuth, Brunonian, Buchu, Bucku, Calumba, Carminative, Charm, Chrysarobin, Cubeb, Curative, Diapente, Diascordium, Diatessaron, Dose, Drops, DRUG, Electuary, Elixir, Emmenagogue, Empirics, Enema, Epulotic, Excipient, Fall-trank, Forensic, Galen, Herb, Iatric(al), Imhotep, Inro, Iodine, Ipecac(uanha), Iron, Laxative, Menthol, Mishmi, Mixture, Muti, Nephritic, Nervine, Nostrum, Oporice, Panacea, Paregoric, Pharmacy, Physic, Pill, Placebo, Polychrest, Potion, Poultice, Preparation, Quinine, Relaxative, REMEDY, Salve, Sanative, Senna, Specific, Syrup, Tabasheer, Tabashir, Tablet, Tar-water, Tetracycline, Tisane, Tonic, Trade, Treatment, Valerian, Veronal

**Medicine man** Koradji

**Medick** Snail

**Medieval** Archaic, Feudal, Gothic, Med, Old, Trecento

**Mediocre** Fair, Indifferent, Middling, Ordinary, So-So

**Meditate, Meditation, Meditator** Brood, Chew, Cogitate, Gymnosophy, Hesychast, Muse, Ponder, Reflect, Reverie, Revery, Ruminate, Transcendental, Weigh

**Mediterranean** Levant, Midi

**Medium** Agency, Average, Clairvoyant, Element, Ether, Even, Home, Magilp, Mean, Megilp, Midway, Milieu, Oils, Organ, Ouija, Press, Radio,

Spiritist, Spiritualist, Television, Telly, TV, Vehicle

**Medley**  Charivari, Collection, Gallimaufry, Jumble, Melange, Mix, Pastiche, Patchwork, Pi(e), Pot-pourri, Quodlibet, Ragbag, Salad, Salmagundi, Series

> **Medley**  may indicate an anagram

**Meek**  Docile, Griselda, Humble, Milquetoast, Patient, Tame

**Meerschaum**  Sepiolite

**Meet(ing), Meeting place**  Abide, Abutment, AGM, Appointment, Apropos, Assemble, Assembly, Assignation, Audience, Baraza, Caucus, Chautauqua, Clash, Concourse, Concur, Confluence, Confrontation, Congress, Connivance, Contact, Conterminous, Convene, Convent(icle), Convention, Converge, Conversazione, Correspond, Defray, Demo, Encounter, Ends, Face, Find, Fit, For(e)gather, Forum, Fulfil, Gemot, Giron, Gorsedd, Guild, Gyeld, Gymkhana, Gyron, Howf(f), Hunt, Hustings, Indaba, Interface, Interview, Join, Junction, Marae, Moot, Occur, Oppose, Pay, Pow-wow, Prosper, Quorum, Races, Rally, Rencontre, Rendezvous, Reunion, Satisfy, Seance, See, Session, Sit, Social, Suitable, Summit, Symposium, Synastry, Synaxis, Synod, Tackle, Tryst, Venue, Vestry, Wapinshaw, Wardmote, Workshop

**Megapode**  Mound-bird, Talegalla

**Megalithic**  Stonehenge

**Megaphone**  Bull-horn

**Meiosis**  Understatement

**Melancholy**  Allicholy, Allycholly, Atrabilious, Cafard, Despond(ency), Dreary, Dump(s), Gloom, Heart-sore, Hipped, Hump, Hyp, Hypochondria, Pensieroso, Pensive, Saturn, Sombre, Spleen, Splenetic, Triste

**Melanesian**  Kanak

**Mêlée**  Brawl, Commotion, Fracas, Rally, Salmagundi, Scrum

**Melia**  Margosa, Neem, Nim

**Mellow**  Genial, Mature, Ripe, Smooth

**Melodrama(tic)**  Bathos, Histrionic, Sensation, Transpontine

**Melody, Melodious**  Air, Arioso, Cantilena, Cantus, Conductus, Counterpoint, Descant, Dulcet, Euphonic, Fading, Musical, Orphean, Plainsong, Ranz-des-vaches, Strain, Theme, Tunable, TUNE(FUL)

**Melon(like)**  Cantaloup(e), Cas(s)aba, Gourd, Mango, Nar(r)as, Ogen, Pepo, Spanspek

**Melt(ed), Melting**  Ablate, Colliquate, DISSOLVE, Eutectic, Eutexia, Flux, Found, Fuse, Fusil(e), Liquescent, Liquid, Run, Syntexis, Thaw

**Member**  Adherent, Arm, Branch, Bro(ther), Chin, Confrère, Cornice, Crossbeam, Crypto, Direction, Felibre, Forearm, Gremial, Insider, Leg, Limb, Longeron, M, MBE, Montant, MP, Organ, Part, Rood-beam, Soroptomist, Stringer, Strut, Syndic, Toe

**Membrane, Membranous**  Amnion, Caul, Chorion, Cornea, Decidua,

Exine, Extine, Film, Haw, Hymen, Indusium, Intima, Intine, Meninx, Patagium, Pericarp, Periton(a)eum, Pleura, Putamen, Rim, Scarious, Schneiderian, Sclera, Serosa, Tela, Tissue, Tonoplast, Trophoblast, Velum, Web

**Memento, Memoir**  Keepsake, Locket, Relic, Souvenir, Token, Trophy

**Memo(randum)**  Bordereau, Cahier, Chit, IOU, Jot, Jurat, Minute, Note, REMINDER

**Memorial**  Cenotaph, Cromlech, Ebenezer, Gravestone, Marker, Monument, Obelisk, Plaque, Relic, Statue, Tomb, Trophy

**Memorise, Memory**  Con, Engram(ma), Get, Learn, Memoriter, Mind, Mneme, Mnemonic, Mnemosyne, Recall, REMEMBER, Ro(a)te, ROM, Samskara, Souvenir, Sovenance

**Men(folk)**  Chaps, Chess, Cuffins, Male, Mortals, OR, Race, Troops

**Menace, Menacing**  Danger, Endanger, Foreboding, Minatory, Peril, Pest, Threat(en)

**Menagerie**  Ark, Circus, Zoo

**Mend**  Beet, Bete, Bushel, Cobble, Correct, Darn, Fix, Heal, Improved, Patch, Piece, Recover, Remedy, REPAIR, Set, Sew, Solder

**Mendelevium**  Md

**Mendicant**  Beggar, Franciscan, Servite

**Menial**  Drug, Drudge, Eta, Fag, Flunkey, Lowly, Scullion, Servile, Toady, Underling

**Meninx**  (D)jerba

**Mental (condition)**  Alienism, Eject, Insane, Noetic, Psychic

**Mention(ed)**  Bename, Benempt, Broach, Bynempt, Citation, Hint, Name, Notice, Quote, Refer, Speech, State, Suggest, Touch

**Menu**  Card, Carte, Fare, List

**Mercantile**  Commercial, Trade

**Mercator**  Cartographer

**Mercenary**  Arnaout, Condottiore, Freelance, Greedy, Hack, Hessian, Hireling, Landsknecht, Legionnaire, Pindaree, Pindari, Rutter, Sordid, Spoilsman, Venal, Wildgeese

**Merchandise**  Cargo, Goods, Line, Produce, Ware(s)

**Merchant(man)**  Abudah, Antonio, Broker, Bun(n)ia, Burgher, Chandler, Chap, Crare, Crayer, Dealer, Factor, Flota, Hoastman, Importer, Magnate, Marcantant, Mercer, Monger, Négociant, Retailer, Shipper, Stapler, Trader, Vintner, Wholesaler

**Mercia**  Offa

**Merciful, Mercy**  Amnesty, Charity, Clement, Compassionate, Grace, Humane, Kind, Kyrie, Lenient, Miserere, Misericord(e), Pacable, Pity, Quarter, Ruth, Sparing

**Merciless**  Cruel, Hard, Pitiless

**Mercurial, Mercuric sulphide, Mercury** Azoth, Cyllenius, Herald, Hermes, Hg, Messenger, Quicksilver, Red-man, Spurge, Volatile

**Mere(ly)** Allenarly, Bare, Common, Lake, Pond, Pool, Pure, Sheer, Tarn, Very

**Merge(r)** Amalgamate, Blend, Coalesce, Consolidate, Die, Fusion, Meld, Melt, Mingle, Unite

**Meridian** Noonday

**Merit(ed)** CL, Condign, Deserve, Due, Earn, Found, Rate, Virtue, Worth(iness)

**Mermaid** Dugong, Halicore, Merrow, Siren, Tavern, Undine

**Merry** Andrew, Bonny, Boon, Cherry, Chirpy, Crank, Gay, Gean, Gleesome, Greek, Jocose, Jocular, Jocund, Jolly, Joyous, Lively, On, Page, Riant, Sportive, Sunny, Wassail

**Merry-go-round** Carousel, Whirligig

**Merry-making** Carnival, Festivity, Gaiety, Gaud, Gawd, Revel

**Merrythought** Clavicle, Collarbone, Wishbone

**Mesh** Chain, Entangle, Net, Reseau

**Mess(y)** Bedraggled, Boss, Botch, Canteen, Caudle, Chaos, Clutter, Failure, Farrago, Fiasco, Garboil, Glop, Gunk, Gun-room, Hash, Horlicks, Hotch-potch, Louse, Mash, Meal, Mismanage, Mix, Muck, Muff, Muss, Mux, Pi(e), Plight, Pollute, Pottage, Shambles, Shemozzle, Sight, Slaister, Smudge, Snafu, Soss, Sty, Sully, Untidy

**Message** Aerogram, Bull, Bulletin, Cable, Despatch, Dispatch, Errand, Missive, News, Note, Radiogram, Rumour, Signal, SOS, Telegram, Telephone, Telex, Tidings, Wire, WORD

**Messenger** Angel, Apostle, Azrael, Caddie, Caddy, Chaprassi, Chuprassy, Courier, Culver, Despatch-rider, Emissary, Envoy, Gaga, Gillie Whitefoot, Hatta, Herald, Hermes, Iris, Ladas, Mercury, Nuncio, Peon, Post, Runner, Send, Shellycoat, Valkyrie

**Messiah** Christ, Emmanuel, Mahdi, Saviour

**Met** Weather

**Metal(lic)** Ag, Aglet, Aiglet, Aiguillette, Al, Aluminium, Babbitt, Billon, Brassy, Britannia, Cadmium, Chrome, Cobalt, Copper, Dysprosium, Er(bium), Foil, Gallium, Germanium, Gib, Ingot, Invar, Iridium, Iron, Jangling, Manganese, Mineral, Muntz, Nickel, Ore, Osmium, Platinum, Prince's, Regulus, Rhenium, Rhutenium, Samarium, Sm, Sn, Sodium, Sprue, Steel, Strontium, Taggers, Terbic, Terbium, Terne, Thallium, Thorium, Tin, Tole, Tutania, Tutenag, Wolfram, Zinc

**Metal-worker** Founder, Smith, Spurrier, Tubal Cain

> **Metamorphosing** may indicate an anagram

**Metaphor** Conceit, Figure, Image, Symbol, Trope, Tropical

**Mete** Inflict

**Meteor(ite)** Aerolite, Bolide, Comet, Drake, Fireball, Leonid, Perseid,

Siderite, Star(dust)

**Meter** Alidad(e)

**Methedrine** Speed

**Method(ical)** Art, Line, Manner, Mode, Modus, Neat, Orderly, Painstaking, Ploy, Process, Stanislavski, SYSTEM, Tactics, Technique, Way

**Methodism, Methodist** Jumper, Methody, Primitive, Ranter, Scientism, Southcottian, Swaddler, Wesley

**Methuselah** Bottle, Macrobiote

**Meticulous** Careful, EXACT, Finicky, Minute, Precise, Punctilious

**Metier** Line, Trade, Vocation

**Metre** Alexandrine, Amphibrach, Anapaest, Antispast, Arsis, Cadence, Choliamb, Choree, Choriamb, Galliambic, Iambic, M, Rhythm, Scazon, Spondee, Trochee

**Metric (system)** MKS

**Metroland** Subtopia

**Metropolitan** Eparch

**Mettle** Bravery, Courage, Ginger, Guts, PLUCK, Pride, Smeddum, Spirit, Spunk

**Mew** Caterwaul, Miaou, Miaow, Pen, Purr, Seagull, Waul, Wrawl

**Mews** Meuse, Muse(t), Musit, Stables

**Mexican** Aztec, Chicano, Chichibec, Diaz, Greaser, Hairless, Maya, Mixtec, Montezuma, Otomi, Spic, Spik, Toltec, Zapotec

**Mezzo-soprano** Tessa

**Mica** Biotite, Daze, Fuchsite, Glimmer, Lepidomelane, Muscovite, Paragonite, Phlogopite, Rubellan, Talc, Verdite

**Mick(ey)** Greek, Mouse

**Micro** Mu

**Microbe** Germ, Organism

**Microphone** Bug, Mike

**Microscope** Electron, Lens

**Mid** Amongst

**Midas** Goldfinger, Tamarin

**Midday** Meridian, N, Noon

**Middle** Active, Centre, Core, Crown, Enteron, Eye, Girth, Heart, Loins, Median, Meridian, Meseraic, Mesial, Meso, Midriff, Moderate, Noon, Passive, Tum, Twixt, Wa(i)st

**Middle-cambrian** Menevian

**Middle class** Bourgeois, Hova

**Middle Eastern** Arab, Iraqi, Omani

**Middleman** Broker, Camparador, Diaphragm, Intermediary, Jobber, Median, Navel, Regrater, Regrator

**Middlesex** Hermaphrodite

**Midget** Dwarf, Pygmy, Homunculus, Shrimp

**Midianite** Prowler

**Midlands** Mercia

**Midnight** G, O am

**Midriff** Phrenic, Skirt, Waist

**Midshipman** Brass-bounder, Easy, Middy, Oldster, Reefer, Snottie, Snotty

**Midwife** Howdie, Howdy, Lucina, Mab, Obstetric

**Mien** Air, Bearing, Demean, Manner

**Might(iness), Mighty** Force, Main, Mote, Nibs, Potence, POWER, Prowess, Puissant, Should, Strength

**Mignon(ette)** Dyer's rocket, Fillet, Reseda, Weld

**Migraine** Megrim, Scotodinia, Teichopsia

**Migrant** Externe, Gastarbeiter, Lemming, Traveller

**Migrate, Migration, Migratory** Colonise, Diapedesis, Diaspora, Drift, Exodus, Fleet, Run, Tre(c)k

**Mikado** Kami

**Mike** Bug, Stentorphone

**Milanese** Patarine

**Mild(ly)** Balmy, Benign, Bland, Clement, Euphemism, Genial, Gentle, Lenient, Litotes, Mansuete, Meek, MODERATE, Pacific, Patient, Sarcenet, Sars(e)net, Temperate

**Mildew** Fungus, Mould, Oidium

**Mile(s)** Coverdale, Li, Nautical, Royal, Soldier, Standish

**Milesian** Teague

**Milestone** Milliary, MS

**Milfoil** Yarrow

**Militant** Activist, Aggressive, Hostile, Ireton, Martial

**Military** Commando, Mameluke, Martial, Presidio

**Militia** Fyrd, Guard, Haganah, Minuteman, Reserve, Yeomanry

**Milk(er), Milky** Beestings, Bland, Bleed, Bonny-clabber, Bristol, Casein, Colostrum, Crud, Curd, Exploit, Galactic, Jib, K(o)umiss, Lactation, Lacteal, Latex, Madzoon, Magnesia, Matzoon, Mess, Pinta, Sap, Shedder, Stroke, Suckle, UHT, Whig, Yaourt, Yogh(o)urt

**Milking-pail** Leglan, Leglen, Leglin

**Milking-machine** Tapper

**Milkless** Agalactic, Dry, Eild

**Milkmaid, Milkman** Chalker, Dey, Emulge, Kefir, Kephir, Radha,

Rounder, Roundsman, Skimmed

**Milksop** Coward, Meacock, Namby-pamby, Nance, Pance, Weakling

**Milk-vetch** Loco

**Milkweed** Asclepias

**Milkwort** Senega

**Mill(ing), Mills** Aswarm, Barker's, Grinder, Hayley, Knurl, Melder, Molar, Nurl, Press, Quern, Reave, Rob, Satanic, Smock, Surge, Thou, Works

**Miller** Dusty, Glen, Grinder, Jester, Joe, Molendinar

**Millet** Bajra, Bajree, Bajrii, Couscous, Dari, Doura, Dur(r)a, Grain, Negro-corn, Ragee, Ragi, Whisk

**Millionaire** Carnegie, Rockefeller, Rothschild, Vanderbilt

**Millions, Millionth** Crore, Femto, Muckle

**Millipede** Songololo

**Mim** Perjink

**Mime, Mimic** Ape, Copycat, Farce, Imitate, Impersonate, Mummer, Sturnine

**Mimosa** Cacoon, Saman

**Mince** Cecils, Chop, Dice, Grate, Grind, Prance, Rice

**Mind(er)** Beware, Brain, Genius, Handler, HEED, Herd, Id, Intellect, Noology, Noosphere, Psyche, Resent, Sensorium, Tend, Thinker, Wit

**Mine** Acoustic, Bomb, Bonanza, Burrow, Camouflet, Claymore, Colliery, Dane-hole, Dig(gings), Egg, Eldorado, Excavate, Explosive, Fougade, Fougasse, Gallery, Gob, Golconda, Gopher, Grass, Nostromo, Open-cast, Ophir, Pit, Placer, Prospect, Sap, Set(t), Show, Stannary, Stope, Strike, Undercut, Wheal, Win, Workings

**Mine-deflector** Otter, Paravane

**Mine-owner** Operator

**Miner, Mine-worker, Mine-working** Butty-gang, Collier, Cutter, Digger, Geordie, NUM, Oncost, Pitman, Shot-firer, Stall, UDM

**Mineral** Adularia, Alabandine, Alabandite, Alabaster, Albite, Alexandrite, Amphibole, Anatase, Andesine, Anhydrite, Antimony, Apatite, Apophyllite, Aragonite, Arfvedsonite, Arsenopyrite, Asbestos, Atacamite, Augite, Autunite, Axinite, Babingtonite, Baddeleyite, Balas, Blende, Boracite, Borax, Brookite, Brucite, Calamine, Calcite, Calomel, Carnelian, Carnotite, Catseye, Cheralite, Chert, Chromite, Chrysolite, Cinnabar, Cleveite, Clinochlore, Coccolite, Columbate, Columbite, Cordierite, Corundum, Covellite, Crocidolite, Dendrachate, Diallage, Diamond, Diaspore, Disthene, Dolomite, Dolomitic, Dyscrasite, Dysodil(e), Dysodyle, Elaeolite, Emery, Endomorph, Enhydrite, Enstatite, Epidote, Epsomite, Erinite, Euclase, Eucrite, Euxenite, Fayalite, Feldspar, Feldspathoid, Felspar, Fibrolite, Flinkite, Flint, Fluor(ite), Franklinite, Galinite, Garnet, Garnierite, Germanite, Glance, Glauconite, Gmelinite, Go(e)thite, Greenockite, Goethite, Gummite, Gypsum, Halloysite, Hauyne,

Hornblende, Ice spar, Idocrase, Illite, Ilmenite, Indicolite, Indigolite, Iodyrite, Jamesonite, Jargon, Jargoon, Jarosite, Josephinite, Kainite, Kermesite, Kernite, Kyanite, Laurdalite, Lazurite, Leucite, Lewisite, Lithia, Margarite, Massicot, Meerschaum, Melilite, Mellite, Mica, Microlite, Microlith, Mimetite, Mispickel, Monazite, Moonstone, Nacrite, Nepheline, Niccolite, Nitre, Nosean, Noselite, Olivenite, Olivine, Orpiment, Orthoclase, Ottrelite, Parnasite, Pennine, Peridot, Perimorph, Perovskite, Petuntse, Phenacite, Piedmontite, Pinite, Pleonaste, Polianite, Powellite, Prase, Prehnite, Proustite, Pyrite(s), Pyroxene, Quartz, Realgar, Redruthite, Resalgar, Rock-salt, Rosaker, Rutile, Samarskite, Sanidine, Saponite, Sard, Scapolite, Scheelite, Schorl, Scolecite, Serpentine, Siderite, Silica, Sillimanite, Skutterudite, Smectite, Smithsonite, Sodalite, Spar, Sperrylite, Sphalerite, Sphene, Spinel, Stannite, Stibnite, Stilbite, Sylvanite, Taconite, Talc, Tantalite, Tennantite, Thaumasite, Thorite, Thulite, Titanite, Topaz, Tourmaline, Tremolite, Tripoli, Troilite, Troostite, Turgite, Ulexite, Umber, Uranium, Variscite, Vermiculite, Vulpinite, Wavellite, Willemite, Witherite, Wolframite, Wollastonite, Wulfenite, Zaratite, Zeolite, Zinkenite, Zircon, Zoisite, Zorgite

**Mineral water** Apollinaris, Tonic

**Minesweeper** Oropesa, Unity

**Mingle** Blend, Consort, Mell, MIX, Participate, Unite

**Mini** Car, Skirt, Teen(s)y

**Miniature, Miniaturist** Cosway, Microcosm, Midget

**Minimum (range)** Bare, Fewest, Least, Neap, Shoestring, Stime, Styme

> **Minimum of** may indicate the first letter

**Minion** Flunkey, Lackey, Pet, Subordinate, Vassal

**Minister** Ambassador, Attend, Buckle-beggar, Chancellor, Chaplain, Cleric, Coarb, Commissar, Deacon, Dewan, Diplomat, Divine, D(i)wan, Mas(s)john, Mes(s)john, Nurse, Officiant, Padre, Parson, Peshwa, Preacher, Presbyter, Predikant, Rector, Secretary, Seraskier, SERVE, Tend, Visier, Vizier, Wazir, Wizier

**Ministry** Defence, Department, Dept, DoE, MOD, MOT, Orders, Service

**Mink** Kolinsky, Vison

**Minnow** Penk, Pink

**Minor(ity)** Child, Infant, Junior, Less, Minutia, Nonage, Petty, Pupillage, Slight, Trivial, Ward

**Minotaur** Bull-headed

**Minstrel** Allan-a-dale, Bard, Blondel, Bones, Busker, Cantabank, Christy, Cornerman, Gleeman, Hamfatter, Jongleur, Minnesinger, Nigger, Pierrot, Scop, Singer, Taillefer

**Mint** Aim, Catnip, Coin, Ettle, Fortune, Herb, Humbug, Monetise, Nep, New, Penny-royal, Polo, Stamp, Strike, Unused, Utter

**Minute(s)** Acta, Alto, Detailed, Diatom, Entry, Infinitesimal, Little, Micron, Mo, Mu, Nano-, Resume, Small, Teeny, Tine, Tiny, Tyne, Wee

**Minx** Hellion

**Miracle** Cana, Marvel, Merel(l), Meril, Morris, Mystery, Phenomenon, Thaumaturgic, Theurgy, Wonder

**Mirage** Fata morgana, Illusion, Northern lights

**Mire** Bog, Glaur, Lair(y), Lerna, Lerne, Marsh, Mud, Quag, Sludge, Soil

**Mirky** Dark, Dirk(e)

**Mirror(ed)** Alasnam, Busybody, Cambuscan, Catoptric, Cheval, Coelostat, Conde, Enantiomorph, Glass, Image, Imitate, Lao, Merlin, Pierglass, Psyche, REFLECT, Reynard, Siderostat, Sign, Specular, Speculum, Stone, Vulcan

**Mirror-image** Perversion

**Mirth(ful)** Cheer, Dream, Festive, Hilarity, Joy, Laughter, Spleen

> **Misalliance** may indicate an anagram

**Misanthrope** Cynic, Timon

**Misapplication** Catachresis, Misuse

**Misappropriate** Asport, Purloin, Steal

**Miscarry** Abort, Backfire, Fail, Slink

**Miscegenation** Allocarpy

**Miscellaneous, Miscellany** Assortment, Collectanea, Diverse, Misc, Olio, Omnium-gatherum, Raft, Ragbag, Sundry, Various

**Mischief(-maker), Mischievous** Ate, Bale, Bane, Cantrip, Cloots, Devilment, Diablerie, Disservice, Gremlin, Harm, Hellion, Hob, Imp, Injury, Malicho, Mallecho, Nickum, Owl-spiegle, Pickle, Prank, Puckish, Rascal, Scapegrace, Shenanigans, Spriteful, Wag, Wicked

**Misconception** Delusion, Idol(on), Idolum, Misunderstanding

**Misdeed** Offence, Trespass, Wrong

> **Misdelivered** may indicate an anagram

**Misdemeanour** Peccadillo, Tort

**Miser(ly)** Carl, Cheapskate, Cheese-parer, Close, Curmudgeon, Gare, Grasping, Harpagon, Hunks, Marner, Niggard, Nipcheese, Nipfarthing, Pennyfather, Pinch-commons, Puckfist, Runt, Scrape-good, Scrape-penny, Scrimping, Screw, Scrooge, Skinflint, Snudge, Storer, Tightwad, Timon

**Miserable, Misery** Abject, Bale, Cat-lap, Distress, Dole, Forlorn, Gloom, Grief, Hell, Joyless, Lousy, Sorry, Triste, UNHAPPY, Woe(begone), Wretched

**Misfire** Dud

**Misfit** Drop-out, Loner, Maverick

**Misfortune** Accident, Affliction, Bale, Calamity, Curse, Disaster, Distress, Dole, Ill, Reverse, Wroath

**Misgiving(s)** Anxiety, Doubt, Dubiety, Qualms, Scruples

**Misguide(d)** Impolitic

> **Misguided**  may indicate an anagram

**Mishandle**  Abuse

**Mishap**  Accident, Contretemps, Misaunter, Misfortune, Wroath

**Mishit, Misstroke**  Crab, Edge, Fluff, Muff, Sclaff, Shank, Slice, Top

**Mislay**  Leese, Lose

**Mislead(ing)**  Blind, Cover-up, Deceive, Delude, Dupe, Equivocate, Fallacious, False, Gag

> **Misled**  may indicate an anagram

**Mismanage**  Blunder, Bungle, Muddle

**Mismatch**  Kludge

**Misplace(ment)**  Ectopia

**Misplay**  Fluff, Whitechapel

**Misprint**  Error, Literal, Slip, Typo

**Misrepresent(ation)**  Belie, Calumny, Caricature, Colour, Distort, Falsify, Garble, Lie, Slander, Traduce

**Miss(ing)**  Abord, Avoid, Colleen, Dodge, Drib, Err(or), Fail, Forego, Gal, GIRL, Kumari, Lack, Lass, Link, Lose, Maiden, Mile, Muff(et), Neglect, Negligence, Otis, Overlook, Skip, Spinster, Wanting

> **Miss**  may refer to Missouri

**Missal**  Breviary, Te igitur, Triodion

**Misshapen**  Crooked, Deformed, Dysmelia, Gnarled

**Missile**  Air-to-air, Ammo, Anti-ballistic, Arrow, Atlas, Ball, Bolas, Bomb, Boomerang, Brickbat, Bullet, Cruise, Dart, Doodlebug, Dum-dum, Exocet, Flechette, Grenade, Harpoon, Kiley, Kyley, Kylie, Minuteman, MIRV, Missive, Patriot, Pellet, Pershing, Polaris, Quarrel, Rocket, SAM, Scud, Shell, Shot, Side-winder, Snowball, Spear, Styx, Thor, Titan, Torpedo, Tracer, Trident

**Mission(ary)**  Aidan, Alamo, Antioch, Apostle, Assignment, Bethel, Caravan, Charge, Delegation, Embassage, Embassy, Errand, Evangelist, Iona, Legation, Livingstone, LMS, Message, Op, Quest, Reclaimer, Task, Vocation, Xavier

**Missis, Missus**  Maam, Mrs, Wife

**Missive**  Letter, Message, Note

**Missouri**  Mo

> **Misstroke**  see MISHIT

**Mist(y)**  Blur, Brume, Cloud, Dew, Drow, Fog, Haar, Haze, Hoar, Miasma, Moch, Nebular, Niflheim, Rack, Roke, Sfumato, Smir(r), Smog, Smur, Vapour

**Mistake(n)**  Bish, Bloomer, Blooper, Blunder, Boner, Booboo, Boss, Botch, Clanger, Confound, Deluded, Erratum, Error, Fault, Floater, Flub, Fluff, Gaffe, Goof, Howler, Incorrect, Lapse, Malapropism, Miss, Muff, Nod,

Oversight, Plonker, Pratfall, SLIP, Solecism, Stumer, Trip

> **Mistake(n)** may indicate an anagram

**Mister** Babu, Mr, Sahib, Senor, Shri, Sir, Sri

**Mistletoe** Album, Missel, Parasite, Viscum

**Mistreat** Abuse, Attrite, Violate

**Mistress** Amie, Aspasia, Canary-bird, Chatelaine, Concubine, Courtesan, Demimondaine, Devi, Doxy, Goodwife, Herself, Hussif, Inamorata, Instructress, Lady, Leman, Maintenon, Montespan, Mrs, Natural, Paramour, Stepney, Teacher, Wardrobe, Wife

**Mistrust** Doubt, Gaingiving, Suspect

**Misunderstand(ing)** Disagreement, Discord, Mistake

**Misuse** Abuse, Malappropriate, Maltreat, Perversion, Torment

**Mite** Acaridian, Acarus, Bit, Child, Lepton, Little, Speck, Tyroglyphid, Varroa, Widow's

**Mitigate, Mitigating** Abate, Allay, Allieve, Ameliorate, Extenuating, Lenitive, Lessen, Palliate, Quell, Relief, Relieve

**Mitosis** Anaphase

**Mitre** Hat, Tiar(a)

**Mitt(en)** Fist, Glove, Hand, Paw

**Mix(ed), Mixture, Mix-up** Alloy, Amalgam, Assortment, Attemper, Balderdash, Bigener, Bland, Blend, Blunge, Brew, Card, Caudle, Cocktail, Co-meddle, Compo, Compound, Conglomerate, Consort, Cross, Disperse, Drammock, Embroil, Emulsion, Farrago, Garble, Grill, Griqua, Hobnob, Hotchpotch, Hybrid, Imbroglio, Intermingle, Jumble, Lace, Lard, Linctus, Load, Macedoine, Meddle, Medley, Melange, Mell, Meng(e), Ment, Mess, Ming(le), Miscellaneous, Miscellany, Mishmash, Mong, Motley, Muddle, Muss(e), Neapolitan, Olio, Olla, Pi(e), Potin, Pousowdie, Powsowdy, Salad, Scramble, Stew, Stir, Through-other, Yblent

> **Mixed** may indicate an anagram

**Mizzle** Scapa, Scarper

**Mnemonic** Quipo, Quipu, Reminder

**Moab(ite)** Balak, Ruth, Wash-pot

**Moan(ing)** Beef, Bleat, Groan, Keen, LAMENT, Meane, Plangent, Sough, Wail, W(h)inge

**Moat** Dike, Ditch, Fuss

**Mob(ster)** Assail, Canaille, Crew, Crowd, Gang, Herd, Hoi-polloi, Hoodlum, Ochlocrat, Press, Rabble, Raft, Rout, Scar-face

**Mobile, Mobilise** Donna, Fluid, Movable, Plastic, Rally, Thin, Vagile

**Mob-rule** Ochlocracy

**Mocassin** Larrigan, Shoe, Snake

**Mock(ery), Mocking** Ape, Banter, Chaff, Chyack, Cynical, Deride, Derisory, Dor, Ersatz, False, Farce, Fleer, Flout, Gab, Geck, Guy, Imitation,

Irony, JEER, Jibe, Lampoon, Mimic, Narquois, Paste, Pillorise, Rail(lery), Ridicule, Sardonic, Satirise, Scout, Sham, Simulate, Slag, Travesty

**Mocking-bird** Mimus, Sage-thrasher

**Mode** Aeolian, Convention, Dorian, Fashion, Form, Iastic, Lydian, Manner, Phrygian, Rate, Step, Style, Ton

**Model(ler)** Archetype, Bozzeto, Cast, Copy, Diorama, Doll, Dummy, Ecorché, Effigy, Epitome, Example, Exemplar, Fictor, Figure, Figurine, Icon, Image, Instar, Jig, Last, Layman, Manakin, Mannequin, Maquette, Mock-up, MOULD, Norm, Original, Orrery, Parade, Paragon, Pattern, Pilot, Pose(r), Posture-maker, Prototype, Replica, Sedulous, Sitter, Specimen, Standard, T, Template, Templet, Terrella, Toy, Trilby, Twiggy, Type, Typify

> **Model(s)** may indicate an anagram

**Modem** Subset

**Moderate(ly), Moderation** Abate, Allay, Alleviate, Average, Centre, Continent, Diminish, Discretion, Ease, Girondist, Ho, Lessen, Measure, Medium, Menshevik, Mezzo, Middling, Mild, Mitigate, Politique, Reason(able), Slake, So-so, Temper(ate), Tolerant, Tone, Via media

**Modern(ise)** AD, Aggiornamento, Contemporary, Fresh, Latter(-day), Neonomian, Neoterical, NEW, Progressive, Recent, Swinger, Update

**Modest(y)** Aidos, Blaise, Chaste, Decent, Demure, Humble, Ladylike, Maidenly, Mussorgsky, Prudish, Pudency, Pure, Reserved, Shame, Shy, Unpretending, Verecund

**Modifiable, Modify** Alter, Backpedal, Change, Enhance, H, Leaven, Plastic, Qualify, Retrofit, Scumble, Soup, Temper, Vary

**Modulation, Module, Modulus** Accent, Cadence, Inflexion, Lem, Mitigate, Tune, Unit, Vary, Young

**Mogul** Bigwig, Magnate, Padishah, Plutocrat, Taipan, VIP

**Mohair** Moire

**Mohammed, Mohammedan (era)** Hegira, Hejira, Hejra, Hijra, Islamite, Mahdi, Mahoun(d), Moslem, Muezzin, Mussulman, Prophet, Said, Shiite

**Moist(en), Moisture** Bedew, Damp, Dank, De(a)w, Humect, Latch, Love-in-a-mist, Madefy, Nigella, Sponge, Wet

> **Moither** may indicate an anagram

**Molar** Grinder, Tooth, Wang

**Molasses** Sorghum, Treacle

**Mole(hill)** Breakwater, Fen-cricket, Jetty, Miner, Mo(u)diewart, Moudi(e)wart, Mouldiwarp, Naeve, Notoryctes, Orology, Pier, Sea-wall, Spot, Spy, Star-nose, Talpa, Want(hill), Warp

**Molecule** Atom, Buckyball, Closed chain, Dimer, DNA, Fullerene, Hapten, Iota, Ligand, Quark, Semantide, Trimer

**Molendinar** Mill

**Molest(er)** Annoy, Bother, Harass, Nonce, Scour

**Moll(y)** Bloom, Bonnie, Cutpurse, Flanders, Girl, Maguire, Malone, May, Sissy

**Mollify** Appease, Fob, Mease, Mitigate, Pacify, Relax, Soften, Temper

**Mollusc(s)** Amphineura, Argonaut, Clam, Cockle, Conch, Cone-shell, Cowrie, Cowry, Cuttle(fish), Doris, Gaper, Gast(e)ropod, Limpet, Malacology, Murex, Mussels, Mya, Nautilus, Neopilina, Octopod, Octopus, Paper-sailor, Pecten, Pelican's-foot, Pholas, Piddock, Pinna, Quahaug, Quahog, Saxicava, Scallop, Scaphopoda, Sea-hare, Sea-lemon, Sea-slug, Sepia, Shipworm, Slug, Snail, Solen, Spoot, Squid, Tectibranch, Tellin, Teredo, Toheroa, Triton, Trochus, Turbo, Unio, Veliger, Vitrina, Wentletrap, Winkle

**Mollycoddle** Indulge, Pamper

**Moloch** Thorn-devil

**Molten** Dissolved, Fusil, Melted

**Molybdenum** Mo

**Moment(s), Momentous** Bit, Flash, Import, Instant, Jiffy, MINUTE, Mo, Nonce, Pun(c)to, Sands, Sec, Shake, Stound, Stownd, Tick, Time, Trice, Twinkling, Weighty, Wink

**Momentum** Impetus, L, Speed, Thrust

**Mona(s)** I, IOM

**Monaco** Grimaldi

**Monarch(y)** Autocrat, Crown, Emperor, HM, Karling, King, Potentate, Queen, Raine, Reign, Ruler, Tsar

**Monastery** Abbey, Abthane, Chartreuse, Cloister, Community, Hospice, Lamaserai, Lamasery, Laura, Priory, Vihara, Wat

**Monastic** Abthane, Celibate, Holy, Monkish, Oblate, Secluded

**Monday** Collop, Meal, Oatmeal, Plough, Whit

**Mondrian** Piet

**Monetary, Money** Ackers, Agora, Agorot, Akkas, Alfalfa, Allowance, Annat, Ante, As, Assignat, Baht, Balboa, Ban, Banco, Bani, Batta, Belga, Billon, Birr, Blunt, Bob, Bolivar, Boliviano, Boodle, Brass, Bread, Buck, Bunce, Butat, Capital, Cash, Cedi, Cent, Change, Chiao, Chink, Chon, COIN, Cole, Collateral, Colon, Conscience, Conto, Cordoba, Couter, Crap, Crore, Crusado, Cruzeiro, Currency, D, Dalasi, Dam, Danger, Daric, Deaner, Denarius, Denier, Derham, Deutschmark, Dib, Didrachma, Dime, Dinar, Dinero, Dingbat, Dirham, Dirhem, DM, Doit, Dollar, Dong, Dosh, Drachma, Ducat, Dump(s), Duro, Dust, Ekuele, Elepwele, Emalangeni, Escudo, Fat, Fee, Fen, Fil(s), Fin, Fiver, Float, Florin, Forint, Franc, Fund, Gelt, Gilt, Gold, Gourde, Grant, Gravy, Greens, Groschen, Guarani, Guilder, Haler, Hao, Hoot, Hush, Ingots, Inti, Investment, Jack, Jiao, Kale, Kina, Kip, Koruna, Kreutzer, Krona, Kroner, Kwacha, Kyat, L, Legem pone, Lei, Lek, Lempira, Leone, Leu, Lev(a), Lew, Liard, Lilangeni, Lira, Lolly, Loot, Loti, Lucre, Lwei, Lyart, M, Mammon, Mancus, Maneh, Maravedi, Mark, Markka, Mazuma, Means, Merk, Metical, Mil, Mill,

Mina, Mint, Mna, Mongo, Moola(h), Naira, Needful, Nest-egg, Ngultrum, Note, Numismatic, Nummary, Oaker, Ochre, Offertory, Oof, Ore, P, Packet, Para, Pataca, Peag, Peanuts, Pec, Pelf, Pengo, Penni, Penny, Peseta, Pesewa, Peso, Pin, Plum, Posh, Pound, Prize, Profit, Pul(a), Puli, Punt, Purse, Qintar, Quetzal, Quid(s), Rand, Rd, Ready, Rebate, Red, Reis, Renminbi, Resources, Revenue, Rhino, Riel, Ringgit, Ri(y)al, Rouble, Rowdy, Ruble, Rufiyaa, Rupee, Rupiah, Salt(s), Satang, Schilling, Shilling, Scrip, Sestertia, Shekel, Shin-plaster, Ship, Siller, Silver, Soap, Sou, Specie, Spondulicks, Spur, Stake, Sterling, Stiver, Stotinka, Sucre, Sugar, Sum, Sycee, Tael, Taka, Takings, Talent, Tambala, Thaler, Tin, Toea, Tranche, Tugrik, Vatu, Vellon, Vliaticum, Wad, Wakiki, Wealth, Won, Wonga, Wrath, Wroth, Yen, Yuan, Zaire, Zimbi, Zloty

**Money-box** Penny-pig

**Moneylender** Gombeen, Shylock, Usurer

**Moneymaking** Profitable, Quaestuary

**Mongol(ian)** Calmuck, Kalmuck, Lapp, Mogul, Samoyed, Shan, Tatar, Tungus(ic), Ural-altaic

**Mongoose** Ichneumon, Mangouste, Suricate, Urva

**Mongrel** Bitser, Cross(bred), DOG, Hybrid, Kuri, Lurcher, Underbred

**Monitor** Detect, Goanna, Iguana, Lizard, Observe, Prefect, Record, Track, Warship, Worral, Worrel

**Monk(s)** Abbey-lubber, Abbot, Acoemeti, Archimandrite, Arhat, Asser, Augustinian, Austin, Basilian, Beghard, Bernardine, Benedictine, Bethlehemite, Brother, Caloyer, Carthusian, Celestine, Cellarist, Cenobite, Cistercian, Cluniac, Coenobite, Cowl, Culdee, Dan, Dervish, Dominican, Feuillant, Fraticelli, Friar, General, Hegumen, Hermit, Ignorantine, Jacobin, Jacobite, Lama, Mechitharist, Mekhitarist, Mendel, Norbertine, Obedientiary, Oblate, Olivetan, Order, Pelagian, Prior, Rakehell, Rasputin, Recluse, Recollect, Roshi, Sangha, Savonarola, Silverback, Sub-prior, Talapoin, Theatine, Thelemite, Thelonius, Tironensian, Trappist, Votary

**Monkey** Anger, Ape, Baboon, Bandar, Capuchin, Catar(r)hine, Cebidae, Cebus, Chacma, Coaita, Colobus, Cynomolgus, Diana, Douc, Douroucouli, Drill, Durukuli, Entellus, Gelada, Gibbon, Grease, Grison, Grivet, Guenon, Guereza, Hanuman, Hoolock, Howler, Hylobates, Indri, Jackey, Jocko, Kippage, Langur, Lemur, Macaque, Magot, Mandrill, Mangabey, Marmoset, Meerkat, Mico, Midas, Mona, Mycetes, Nala, Nasalis, Ouakari, Ouistiti, Phalanger, Powder, Pug, Ram, Rhesus, Sago(u)in, Saguin, Sai(miri), Sajou, Saki, Sapajou, Siamang, Silen(us), Silverback, Simian, Simpai, Talapoin, Tamarin, Tamper, Tee-tee, Titi, Toque, Trip-hammer, Tup, Uakari, Vervet, Wanderoo, Wistiti, Wou-wou, Wow-wow, Wrath, Zati

**Monkey-nut** Earth-pea

**Monkey-puzzle** Araucaria, Bunya-bunya

**Monkshood** Aconite

**Monocle** Eye-glass, Gig-lamp, Quiz(zing-glass)

**Monocot(yledon)** Araceae, Endogen, Tradescantia

**Monodon**  Narwhal

**Monogram, Monograph**  Chi-rho, Study, Treatise, Tug(h)ra

**Monopolise, Monoply**  Appalto, Bloc, Cartel, Corner, Engross, Octroi, Régie, Trust

**Monotonous, Monotony**  Boring, Dull, FLAT, Grey, Humdrum, Sing-song, Tedious

**Monsoon**  Hurricane, Typhoon, WIND

> **Monsoon**  may indicate weekend (Mon soon)

**Monster, Monstrous**  Alecto, Asmodeus, Bandersnatch, Bunyip, Caliban, Cerberus, Chichevache, Chim(a)era, Cockatrice, Colossal, Cyclops, Dabbat, Deform, Dinoceras, Dismayd, Div, Dragon, Echidna, Enormous, Erebus, Erinys, Erl-king, Eten, Ettin, Evil-one, Fiend, Fire-drake, Frankenstein, Freak, Geryon, Ghost, Giant, Gorgon, Green-eyed, Grendel, Harpy, Hippocampus, Hippogriff, Huge, Hydra, Jabberwock, Kraken, Lamia, Leviathan, Lilith, Mastodon, Medusa, Minotaur, Misbegotten, Moloch, Mylodont, Nessie, Nicker, Nightmare, Orc, Ogre, Ogr(e)ish, Opinicus, Outrageous, Pongo, Sarsquatch, Satyral, Scylla, Shadow, Simorg, Simurg(h), Siren, Skull, Snark, Spectre, Sphinx, Spook, Stegodon, Stegosaur, Succubus, Taniwha, Teras, Teratoid, Triceratops, Troll, Typhoeus, Typhon, Unnatural, Vampire, Vast, Wasserman, Wendego, Wendigo, Wer(e)wolf, Wyvern, Xiphopagus, Yowie, Ziffius

**Month(ly)**  Ab, Abib, Adar, Brumaire, Cheshvan, Chislev, Elul, Floreal, Frimaire, Fructidor, Germinal, Hes(h)van, Iy(y)ar, Jumada, Kisleu, Kislev, Lide, Lunar, Messidor, Mo, Moharram, Moon, Muharram, Nisan, Nivose, October, Periodical, Pluviose, Prairial, Rabi, Rajab, Ramadan, Safar, Saphar, S(h)ebat, Shawwal, Sivan, Tammuz, Tebeth, Thermidor, Tisri, Veadar, Vendemiaire, Ventose

**Monument**  Arch, Archive, Cenotaph, Column, Cromlech, Dolmen, Henge, Megalith, Memorial, Menhir, Pantheon, Pyramid, Stele(ne), Stone, Stonehenge, Stupa, Talayot, Tombstone, Trilith, Urn

**Mood(y)**  Active, Anger, Atmosphere, Attitude, Dudgeon, Enallage, Fit, Glum, Grammar, Humour, Hump, Imperative, Optative, Passive, Peat, Pet, Revivalist, Sankey, Spleen, Temper, Tid, Tone, Tune, Vein, Vinegar, Whim

**Moon(light), Moony**  Aah, Alignak, Aningan, Apogee, Artemis, Astarte, Callisto, Cheese, Cynthia, Diana, Epact, Eye, Flit, Full, Ganymede, Gibbous, Glimmer, Harvest, Hecate, Inconstant, Lucina, Luna(r), Mani, Mascon, McFarlane's Buat, Month, Mope, Paraselene, Phoebe, Raker, Satellite, Selene, Set, Shot, Sickle, Sideline, Silvery, Sonata, Stargaze, Stone, Syzygy, Thoth, Titan, Wander

**Moonraker**  Astrogeologist, Gothamite

**Moor(ing), Moorish**  Berth, Dock, Fen, Heath, Iago, Ilkley, Moroccan, Mudejar, Palustrine, Roadstead, Ryepeck, Saracen, Tether, TIE, Wold

**Mop(ping)**  Dwile, Flibbertigibbet, Girn, Glib, Shag, Squeegee, Squilgee, Swab, Swob, Thatch, WIPE

**Mope**  Brood, Peak, Sulk

**Moral(ity), Morals** Apologue, Ethic(al), Ethos, Everyman, Fable, Integrity, Puritanic, Sittlichkeit, Tag, Upright, Virtuous, Well-thewed

**Morale** Ego, Mood, Spirit, Zeal

**Moralise** Preach

**Moralist** Prig, Prude, Puritan, Whitecap

**Morass** Bog, Fen, Flow, Marsh, Moss, Quagmire, Slough

**Morbid(ity)** Anasarca, Ascites, Cachaemia, Dropsy, Ectopia, Ghoul(ish), Gruesome, Pathological, Plethora, Prurient, Sick, Sombre

**Mordant** Biting, Caustic, Critic(al), Sarcastic, Tooth

**More** Additional, Else, Extra, Increase, Less, Mae, Merrier, Mo(e), NO MORE, Over, Piu, Plus, Stump, Utopia

**Moreover** Also, Besides, Eft, Either, Further, Too, Yet

**Morgan** Buccaneer, Pirate

**Moribund** Dying, Stagnant, Withered

**Mormon** Danite, Utah, Young

**Morning** Ack-emma, Am, Antemeridian, Dawn, Early, Matin, Morrow

**Morning-glory** Bindweed, Ipomoea, Turbith, Turpeth

**Morning-star** Morgenstern, Phosphor(us), Threshel, Venus

**Moroccan, Morocco** Agadir, Leather, MA, Mo(o)r, Riff, Tangerine, Venus

**Moron** Fool, Idiot, Schmuck, STUPID

**Morose** Acid, Boody, Churlish, Cynical, Gloomy, Glum, Grum, Moody, Sullen, Surly

**Morris** Car, Dance, Merel(l), Meril

**Morrow** Future

**Morse** Code, Iddy-umpty, Walrus

**Morsel** Bit, Bite, Bouche, Canape, Crumb, Dainty, Morceau, Ort, Scrap, Sippet, Sop, Tidbit, Titbit

**Mortal(ity)** Averr(h)oism, Being, Deathly, FATAL, Grave, Human, Lethal, Yama

**Mortar, Mortar-board** Bowl, Cannon, Cement, Co(e)horn, Coeho(o)rn, Compo, Grout, Hawk, Minnie, Parget, Plaster, Screed, Square, Squid, Toc emma, Trench(er)

**Mortgage(e)** Bond, Debt, Dip, Encumbrance, Hypothecator, Pledge, Wadset(t)

**Mortification, Mortified, Mortify** Abash, Chagrin, Crucify, Crush, Gangrene, Humble, Humiliate, Infarct, Necrose, Penance, Sick, Wormwood

**Mosaic** Buhl, Inlay, Intarsia, Musive, Screen, Terrazzo, Tessella, Tessera

**Moscow** Dynamo

**Moses** Grandma

> **Moslem** see MUSLIM

**Mosque** El Asqa, Masjid

**Mosquito** Aedes, Anopheles, Culex, Culicine, Gnat, Parasite, Stegomyia

**Moss(y)** Acrogen, Agate, Bryology, Fog, Fontinalis, Hag(g), Hypnum, Lecanoram, Lichen, Litmus, Lycopod, Marsh, Musci, Muscoid, Parella, Polytrichum, Reindeer, Selaginella, Sphagnum, Staghorn, Usnea, Wolf's claw

**Most** Largest, Major, Maxi(mum), Optimum

**Mot** Quip, Saying

**Mote** Atom, Particle, Speck

**Moth(s)** Abraxas, Arch, Arctiidae, Bobowler, Bombycid, Bugong, Burnet, Clearwing, Clothes, Dart-moth, Death's head, Eggar, Egger, Emperor, Geometer, Geometrid, Imago, Io, Lackey, Luna, Lymantriidae, Noctua, Noctuid, Notodonta, Nun, Oak-egger, Owlet, Puss, Pyralidae, Sallow-kitten, Saturnia, Silkworm, Sphingid, Tinea, Tineidae, Tortrix, Tussock, Unicorn, Veneer, Wainscot, Y-moth, Zygaena

**Mothball(s)** Abeyance, Camphor, Naphtha, Preserver

**Mother** Bearer, Church, Cognate, Cosset, Courage, Dam(e), Dregs, Ean, Earth, Eve, Generatrix, Genetrix, Goose, Hubbard, Lees, Ma, Machree, Mam(a), Mamma, Mater, Minnie, Mom, Mum, Nature, Nourish, Parity, Pourer, Reverend, Shipton, Superior, Wit

> **Mother** may indicate a lepidopterist (moth-er)

**Motherless** Adam, Orphan

**Motif** Design, Gist, Idée, Theme

**Motion** Gesture, Impulse, Kinetic, Move, Offer, Perpetual, Proposal, Rider, Spasm

**Motionless** Doggo, Frozen, Immobile, Quiescent, Stagnant, Still

**Motive, Motivate** Actuate, Cause, Ideal, Intention, Mobile, Object, PURPOSE, Spur, Ulterior

**Motley** Jaspé, Medley, Piebald, Pied

**Motor(boat)** Auto, Car, Dynamo, Engine, Jato, Outboard, Scooter, Thruster, Turbine

**Motor-cycle** Moped, Pipsqueak, Scramble

**Motorist(s)** AA, Driver, RAC

**Motorman** Austin, Benz, Ford, Morris

**Motor race** Rally, Scramble, TT

**Motorway** Autobahn, Autopista, Autoput, Autoroute, Autostrada, M(1)

**Mottle(d)** Brindled, Chiné, Jaspé, Marbled, Marly, Mirly, Pinto, Poikilitic, Tabby

**Motto** Device, Epigraph, Gnome, Impresa, Imprese, Impress(e), Legend, Maxim, Posy, Saw

**Mou(e)** Grimace, Mim

**Mould(ed), Moulding, Mouldy** Architrave, Astragal, Archivolt,

Baguette, Balection, Beading, Bend, Bolection, Briquet(te), Cabling, Casement, Cast(ing), Cavetto, Chessel, Chill, Comice, Coving, Cyma, Dariole, Die, Doucine, Dripstone, Echinus, Egg and dart, Flong, FORM, Fungose, Fungus, Fusarol(e), Fust, Gadroon, Hood-mould, Hore, Humus, Matrix, Mildew, Model, Mool, Moulage, Mucid, Must, Nebule, Ogee, Ovolo, Palmette, Papier-mâché, Plasm(a), Plastic, Plat, Prototype, Prunt, Reglet, Rot, Rust, Sandbox, Scotia, Shape, Smut, Soil, Storiated, Stringcourse, Surbase, Tailor, Talon, Template, Templet, Torus, Trochilus, Vinew

**Moult** Cast, Mew, Shed

**Mound** Agger, Bank, Barp, Barrow, Berm, Cone, Dun, Embankment, Heap, Hog, Mogul, Monticule, Mote, Motte, Orb, Pile, Pingo, Pome, Rampart, Rampire, Tel(l), Teocalli, Teopan, Tuffet, Tumulus

**Mound-bird** Megapode

**Mount(ed), Mounting, Mountain (peak)** Abora, Aconcagua, Alai, Aldan, Alp, Altai, Am(h)ara, Anadyr, Andes, Annapurna, Aorangi, Apennines, Arafat, Ararat, Athos, Atlas, Averno, Back, Badon, Balkan, Barp, Ben, Ben Nevis, Berg, Bernina, Blanc, Blue, Board, Breast, Butter, Cairngorm, Calvary, Cambrian, Cantabrian, Cariboo, Carmel, Carpathian, Cascade, Catskills, Caucasian, Chain, Charger, CLIMB, Clinkers, Colt, Cook, Corbett, Cordillera, Dapsang, Delectable, Dew, Display, Djebel, Dolomites, Dragon, Egmont, Eiger, Elbrus, Ellis, Erymanthus, Etna, Everest, Fairweather, Frame, Fuji, Ghats, Godwin Austen, Great Gable, Guyot, Harz, Hekla, Helicon, Helvellyn, Hermon, Highlands, Himalayas, Hinge, Hoggar, Hoosac, Horeb, Horse, Horselberg, Hoss, Hymettus, Ida, Idris, Inselberg, Jebel, Jungfrau, Jura, K2, Kaf, Kan(g)chenjunga, Karakoram, Kilimanjaro, Laurentian, Lhotse, Marmolada, Massif, Matterhorn, McKinley, Meru, Montserrat, Monture, Mt, Munro, Nebo, Nunatak, Oeta, Olympus, Orography, Orology, Ortles, Ossa, Ozark, Palomar, Pamirs, Parnassus, Passe-partout, Pelion, Pennines, Pentelikon, Pike, Pilatus, Pile, Pin, Pisgah, Pownie, Pyrenees, Quad, Rainier, Ride, Rigi, Robson, Rocky, Rushmore, Rydal, Saddlehorse, Salmon, Scafell, Scalado, Scale, Scopus, Set, Sinai, Skiddaw, Snowdon, Snowy, Soar, Sorata, Stage, STEED, Strideways, Sudeten, Table, Tatra, Tel, Tier, Tor, Turret, Urals, Venusberg, Vernon, Volcano, Vosges, Zagros

**Mountain-building** Orogenesis

**Mountaineer(ing)** Abseil, Alpinist, Arnaut, Climber, Hunt, Smythe, Upleader

**Mountebank** Antic(ke), Baladin(e), Charlatan, Jongleur, Quack, Saltimbanco

**Mourn(er), Mournful, Mourning** Adonia, Black, Dirge, Dole, Elegiac, Grieve, Grone, Hatchment, Keen, Lament, Ovel, Saulie, Shivah, Shloshim, Sorrow, Threnetic, Threnodial, Weeds, Weep, Willow

**Mouse(like), Mousy** Black eye, Dun(nart), Flitter, Icon, Muridae, Murine, Rodent, Shiner, Shrew, Vermin, Waltzer

**Moustache** Charley, Charlie, Excrement, Walrus, Zapata

**Mouth(piece)** Aboral, Bazoo, Brag, Buccal, Cakehole, Chapper, Check, Crater, Debouchure, Delta, Embouchure, Estuary, Gab, Gam, Gills, Gob, Gum, Kisser, Labret, Lawyer, Lip, Maw, Neb, Orifex, Orifice, Oscule, Ostium, Port, Speaker, Spokesman, Spout, Stoma, Swazzle, Swozzle, Teat, Trap, Uvula

**Mouthful** Bite, Gob, Morceau, Morsel, Sip, Sup, Taste

**Mouthless** Astomatous

**Mouth-organ** Harmonica, Harp, Palp, Sang

**Move(r), Movable, Moving** Act, Actuate, Affect, Andante, Astir, Budge, Carry, Chattel, Coast, Counter-measure, Coup, Decant, Démarche, Displace, Disturb, Ease, Edge, Flit, Fluctuate, Forge, Gambit, Gee, Go, Haulier, Hustle, Inch, Instigate, Jee, Jink, Kedge, Kinetic, Link, Mill, Mobile, Mosey, Motivate, Opening, Pan, Poignant, Proceed, Prompt, Propel, Qui(t)ch, Rearrange, Remuage, Retrocede, Roll, Rouse, Roust, Scoot, Scuttle, Sell, Shift, Shoo, Shunt, Sidle, Skelp, Slide, Soulful, Spank, Steal, Steer, Step, Stir, Styre, Tactic, Tack, Taxi, Translate, Troll, Trundle, Turn, Unstep, Up, Vacillate, Vagile, Wag, Whirry, Whish, Whisk, Wuther, Yank, Zoom, Zwischenzug

**Movement** Action, Advection, Aerotaxis, Allegro, Allemande, Almain, Andantino, Antic, Bandwagon, Brownian, Cadence, Cell, Chartism, Chemonasty, Course, Crusade, Dadaism, Diaspora, Diastole, Eurhythmics, Fianchetto, Fris(ka), Gesture, Groundswell, Indraught, Inkatha, Intermezzo, Jhala, Jor, Keplarian, Kin(a)esthetic, Kinesis, Kinetic, Larghetto, Largo, Lassu, Ligne, Manoeuvre, Operation, Orchesis, Oxford, Parallax, Pase, Pedesis, Piaffer, Play, Poule, Progress, Rondo, Romantic, Scherzo, Stir(e), Swadeshi, Tachism, Taxis, Tide, Trend, Trenise, Wheel

**Movie** Bioscope, Cine(ma), Film, Flick

**Mow(er), Mowing** Aftermath, Cut, Grimace, Math, Rowan, Rowen, Scytheman, Shear, Sickle, Tass, Trim

**MP** Backbencher, Commoner, Gendarme, Member, Provost, Redcap, Snowdrop, Stannator, Statist, TD

**Mrs Copperfield** Agnes, Dora

**Mrs Siddons** Tragic muse

**Much** Abundant, Far, Glut, Great, Lots, Mickle, Scad, Sore, Viel

**Mucilage** Gum, MUCUS, Putty, Resin

**Muck (up), Mucky** Bungle, Dirt, Dung, Island, Leep, Manure, Midden, Mire, Rot, Soil, Spoil, Stercoral

**Mucker** Fall, Pal, Purler

**Mucus** Phlegm, Snivel, Snot, Sputum

**Mud(dy)** Adobe, Clabber, Clart, Clay, Cutcha, Dirt, Dubs, Fango, Glaur, Gutter, Kacha, Lahar, Lairy, Limous, MIRE, Moya, Ooze, Peloid, Pise, Riley, Roily, Salse, Slab, Slake, Sleech, Slime, Slob, Slough, Sludge, Slur(ry), Slush, Turbid

**Muddle** Befog, Bemuse, Botch, Cock up, Confuse, Disorder, Embrangle,

Fluster, Mash, Mêlée, Mess, Mix, Mull, Pickle, Stupefy, Tangle

> **Muddled** may indicate an anagram

**Mudfish** Lepidosiren

**Mudguard** Wing

**Mudlark** Ragamuffin, Urchin

**Muff** Boob, Botch, Bungle, Drop

**Muffin** Bun, Mule, Popover

**Muffle(d), Muffler** Damp, Envelop, Hollow, Mob(b)le, Mute, Scarf, Silencer, Sourdine, Stifle

**Mug(ger), Muggy** Assault, Attack, Bash, Beaker, Bock, Can, Club, Con, Croc(odile), Cup, Dial, Dupe, Enghalskrug, Face, Fool, Footpad, Gob, Humid, Idiot, Learn, Mou, Noggin, Pan, Pot, Puss, Rob, Roll, Sandbag, Sap, Sconce, Simpleton, Stein, Sucker, Swot, Tankard, Tax, Thug(gee), Tinnie, Tinny, Toby, Trap, Ugly, Visage, Yap

**Mulatto** Griff(e)

**Mulberry** Artocarpus, Breadfruit, Contrayerva, Cow-tree, Jack, Morat, Morus, Murrey, Overlord, Sycamine

**Mulch** Compost

**Mule** Ass, Bab(o)uche, Donkey, Funnel, Hybrid, Mocassin, Moccasin, Moyl(e), Muffin, Muil, Shoe, Slipper, Sumpter

**Muleteer** Arriero

**Mull** Brood, Chew, Kintyre, Ponder, Promontory, Study

**Mullein** Aaron's rod

**Mullet** Goatfish

**Mullion** Monial

**Multi-coloured** Scroddled

**Multiform** Allotropic, Diverse, Manifold

**Multiple, Multiplied, Multiplier, Multiply** Augment, Breed, Double, INCREASE, Modulus, Product, Proliferate, Propagate, Severalfold

**Multi-purpose** Polychrest

**Multitude** Army, Crowd, Hirsel, Horde, Host, Legion, Populace, Sight, Throng, Zillion

**Mum(my)** Boutonné, Corpse, Egyptian, Mamma, Mute, Quiet, Sh, Silent, Tacit, Whisht, Wordless

**Mumble** Grumble, Moop, Moup, Mouth, Mump, Mutter, Royne, Slur

**Mumbo-jumbo** Hocus pocus, Mammet, Maumet, Mawmet, Mommet

**Mummer** Actor, Mime, Scuddaler, Scudler, Skudler

**Mumps** Parotitis

**Munch** Champ, Chew, Chomp, Scranch

**Mundane** Banal, Common, Earthly, Ordinary, Prosaic, Secular, Trite, Workaday, Worldly

**Munificent** Bounteous, Generous, Liberal, Profuse

**Munition(s)** Arms, Artillery, Ordnance

**Munro** Saki

**Mural(s)** Fresco, Graffiti

**Murder(er), Murderess** Aram, Assassin, Bluebeard, Bravo, Burke, Butcher, Butler, Cain, Cathedral, Crackhalter, Crippen, Cutthroat, Do in, Eliminate, Fratricide, Genocide, Hare, Homicide, KILL, Liquidate, Locusta, Massacre, Matricide, Modo, Parricide, Patricide, Poison, Red, Regicide, Ritz, Slaughter, Slay, Strangle(r), Thagi, Throttle, Thug(gee), Whodun(n)it

**Murk(y)** Black, Dirk(e), Gloom, Obscure, Rookish, Stygian

**Murmur(ing)** Brool, Bur(r), Burble, Coo, Croodle, Croon, Grudge, Hum, MUTTER, Repine, Rhubarb, Rumble, Rumour, Souffle, Sowf(f), Sowth, Sturnoid, Undertone, Whisper

**Murphy** Chat, Potato, Pratie, Spud, Tater

**Muscle, Muscular** Athletic, Attollens, Beef(y), Biceps, Bowr, Brawn, Buccinator, Clout, Corrugator, Creature, Cremaster, Elevator, Erecter, Erector, Evertor, Extensor, Gastrocnemius, Glut(a)eus, Iliacus, Kreatine, Lat, Laxator, Levator, Masseter, Mesomorph, Might, Motor, Mouse, Occlusor, Omohyoid, Perforans, Peroneus, Platysma, POWER, Protractor, Psoas, Quadratus, Quadriceps, Rectus, Retractor, Rotator, Sarcolemma, Sarcous, Sartorius, Scalene, Scalenus, Serratus, Sinew, Soleus, Sphincter, Splenial, Supinator, Tendon, Tensor, Teres, Thew, Trapezius, Triceps

**Muscovite** Mica

**Muse(s), Muse's home, Musing** Aglaia, Aonia(n), Attic, Calliope, Clio, Cogitate, Consider, Erato, Euphrosyne, Euterpe, Helicon, Inspiration, IX, Melpomene, Nine, Nonet, Pensée, Pierides, Poly(hy)mnia, Ponder, REFLECT, Ruminate, Study, Teian, Terpsichore, Thalia, Tragic, Urania, Wonder

**Museum** Ashmolean, BM, Fitzwilliam, Gallery, Hermitage, Louvre, Parnassus, Prado, Repository, Smithsonian, Tate, VA, V and A

**Mush** Cree, Goo, Mess, Porridge, Puree, Schmaltz, Slop

**Mushroom** Agaric, Blewits, Burgeon, Cep, Champignon, Enoki, Expand, Fungus, Hypha(l), Ink-cap, Morel, Scotch bonnet, Shiitake, Spread, Start-up, Upstart

**Music (pen)** Air, Ala(a)p, Alapa, Allegro, Allemande, Anacrustic, Andante, Antiphony, AOR, Bagatelle, Ballade, Bebop, Berceuse, Bhangra, Boogie-woogie, Cadenza, Canon, Cantata, Ceilidh, Chamber, Chant, Chopsticks, Chorale, Cliff, Coloratura, Concerto, Disco, Divertimento, Dixieland, Dream, Duet, Enigma, Entracte, Euterpe, Facade, Fanfare, Fantasia, Flamenco, Folk, Fugato, Fugue, Funk(y), Gagaku, Galant, Garage, Gat, Gothic, Honky-tonk, Humoresque, Incidental, Introit, Jazz, Jhala, Jor, Kwela, Largo, Lollipop, Lydian, Madrigal, Mantra, March, Mbaqanga, Melody, Morceau, Motown, Neume, Nocturne, Nonet, Note, Obbligato, Opus, Oratorio, Orphean, Partita, Passacaglia, Pastorale,

Pecking, Piece, Plainsong, Polyhymnia, Polyphony, Pralltriller, Prelude, Prom, Psalmody, Pycnon, Quartet, Quintet, Rag, Raga, Ragtime, Rai, Rastrum, Redowa, Requiem, Rhapsody, Rhythm, Ricercar(e), Riff, Rock, Rockabilly, Rocksteady, Romanza, Rondeau, Rondino, Rondo, Rosalia, Roulade, Salsa, Scherzo, Score, Seguidilla, Septimole, Serenade, Serenata, Setting, Sextet, Ska, Skiffle, Soca, Sonata, Soukous, Soul, Spiritual, Staff, Strain, Suite, Swing, Symphony, Tala, Techno, Thema, Thrash, Toccata, Toccatella, Toccatina, Trad, Trio, Truth, Tune, Voluntary, Warehouse, Zouk, Zydeco

**Musical** Arcadian, Azione, Brigadoon, Cats, Euphonic, Evergreen, Evita, Gigi, Grease, Hair, Harmonious, Kabuki, Kismet, Lyric, Mame, Melodic, Oliver, Opera, Operetta, Orphean, Revue

**Musical box** Juke-box, Polyphon(e)

**Musical chairs** Level-coil

**Musical instrument** Accordion, Alpenhorn, Angklung, Archlute, Aulos, Autoharp, Axe, Bagpipe, Balalaika, Bandoneon, Bandore, Bandura, Banjo, Baryton(e), Baryulele, Bassoon, Bazooka, Bombardon, Bouzouki, Calliope, Canorous, Celesta, Celeste, Cello, Cembalo, Chalumeau, Charango, Chikara, Chitarrone, Chordophone, Cimbalom, Cithara, Citole, Cittern, Clairschach, Clarinet, Clarion, Clarsach, Clave(cin), Clavicembalo, Clavichord, Clavier, Cobza, Console, Contrabasso(on), Contrafagotto, Cor anglais, Corn, Cornemuse, Cornet(t), Cornetto, Corno, Cornpipe, Cromorna, Cromorne, Cr(o)wd, Crumhorn, Crwth, Cymbal, Decachord, Dichord, Didgeridoo, Drum, Dulcian, Dulcimer, Euphon(ium), Fagotto, Fife, Flageolet, Flugelhorn, Flute, Flutina, French horn, Gamelan, Gittern, Glockenspiel, Gong, Gu(e), Guarneri, Guimbard, Guiro, Guitar, Gusla, Gusle, Gusli, Harmonica, Harmonium, Harp, Harpsichord, Hautboy, Heckelphone, Helicon, Horn, Humstrum, Hurdy-gurdy, Idiophone, Jew's harp, Kalimba, Kanoon, Kantele, Kazoo, Kettledrum, Kithara, Klavier, Kora, Koto, Krummhorn, Langsp(i)el, Lute, Lyra-viol, Lyre, Mandola, Mandolin(e), Manzello, Maraca, Marimba, Martenot, Mbira, Melodeon, Melodica, Metallophone, Mirliton, Monochord, Moog, Naker, Nebel, Oboe, Ophicleide, Orchestrion, Orpharion, Orpheoreon, Organ, Ottavino, Oud, Pandora, Pandore, Pandura, Panharmonicon, Pantaleon, Pastorale, Penny-whistle, Phonofiddle, Phorminx, Physharmonica, Piano, Piccolo, Polyphon(e), Poogy(e), Posaune, Psaltery, Quena, Racket(t), Rate, Rebec(k), Recorder, Reed, Ribibe, Rote, Sackbut, Sambuca, Samisen, Sancho, Sang, Sanko, Sansa, Santir, Santour, Santur, Sarangi, Sarod, Sarrusophone, Saxhorn, Saxophone, Saz, Seraphine, Serpent, Shakuhachi, Shalm(e), Shawm, Sitar, Sittar, Slughorn(e), Snare-drum, Sousaphone, Spinet(te), Squeeze-box, Sticcado, Sticcato, Stock and horn, Stradivarius, Straduarius, Surbahar, Symphonium, Tabla, Tabor, Tambour(ine), Tamb(o)ura, Tamburin, Tenoroon, Theorbo, Tibia, Timbrel, Triangle, Trigon, Tromba-marina, Trombone, Trompette, Trumpet, Trump-marine, Tuba, Tympany, Veena, Vibraphone, Vielle, Vihuela, Vina, Viol(a), Violin(cello), Virginal, Vocalion, Xylophone, Xylorimba, Zambomba, Zampogna, Zanze, Zel, Zeze, Zinke, Zither, Zuf(f)olo

**Musician, Musicologist** Accompanist, Arion, Arist, Brain, Chanter, Combo, COMPOSER, Conductor, Crowder, Ensemble, Flautist, Gate, Grove, Guslar, Handel, Joplin, Mahler, Menuhin, Minstrel, Muso, Orphean, Pianist, Rapper, Reed(s)man, Rubinstein, Sideman, Spohr, String, Tortelier, Violinist

**Music-hall** Alhambra, Disco, Empire, Odeon

**Musk** Mimulus, Must

**Musket** Brown Bess, Caliver, Carabine, Eyas, Flintlock, Fusil, Hawk, Nyas, Queen's-arm, Weapon

**Musketeer** Aramis, Athos, D'Artagnan, Fusilier, Ja(e)gar, Porthos, Rifleman, Sam

**Muslim (ritual), Moslem** Ali, Berber, Caliph, Dato, Dervish, Fatimid, Ghazi, Hadji, Hafiz, Hajji, Iranian, Islamic, Ismaili, Karmathian, Khotbah, Khotbeh, Khutbah, Moor, Moro, Mufti, Mus(s)ulman, Nawab, Paynim, Pomak, Said, Saracen, Say(y)id, Senussi, Shafiite, Shia(h), Shiite, Sofi, Sonnite, Sufi, Sulu, Sunna, Sunni(te), Turk, Wahabee, Wahabi(te)

**Muslin** Cloth, Coteline, Gurrah, Jamdani, Leno, Mousseline, Mull, Nainsook, Organdie, Tarlatan, Tiffany

**Musquash** Ondatra

**Mussel** Bivalve, Clabby-doo, Clam, Clappy-doo, Mytilus, Niggerhead, Unio

**Mussorgsky** Modest

**Must(y)** Amok, Essential, Foughty, Froughy, Frowy, Fust, Man, Maun(na), Mote, Mould, Mucid, Mun, Need(s)-be, Shall, Should, Stum, Wine

**Mustard** Charlock, Cress, Erysimum, Praiseach, Runch, Sauce-alone, Senvy

**Mustard plaster** Sinapism

**Muster** Assemble, Call up, Mass, Raise, Rally, Really, Recruit, Round-up, Wappenshaw

**Mutation** Change, Sport, Transform

> **Mutation** may indicate an anagram

**Mute(d)** Deaden, Dumb, Noiseless, Silent, Sordino, Sordo, Sourdine, Stifle

**Mutilate(d), Mutilation** Castrate, Concise, Deface, Dismember, Distort, Garble, Hamble, Injure, Maim, Mangle, Mayhem, Riglin

> **Mutilate(d)** may indicate an anagram

**Mutineer, Mutiny** Bounty, Caine, Curragh, Insurrection, Nore, Pandy, REVOLT, Rising

**Mutter(ing)** Chunter, Mumble, Mump, Murmur, Mussitate, Rhubarb, Roin, Royne, Rumble, Whittie-whattie

**Mutton** Ewes, Fanny Adams, Gigot, Macon, Saddle, Sheep, Theave

**Mutual (aid)** Common, Log-roll, Reciprocal, Symbiosis

**Muzzle** Decorticate, Gag, Jaw, Mouth, Restrain, Snout

**My**  Coo, Gemini, Golly, Odso, Oh, Our, Tush

**Mynah**  Stare, Starling

**Mynheer**  Stadholder

**Myopia, Myopic**  Hidebound, Mouse-sight, Narrow, Short-sighted, Thick-eyed

**Myriad**  Host, Zillion

**Myristic**  Nutmeg

**Myrrh**  Stacte

**Myrtle**  Callistemon, Eucalyptus, Gale, Jambolana

**Mysterious, Mystery**  Abdabs, Abdals, Arcane, Arcanum, Acroamatic, Cabbala, Craft, Cryptic, Dark, Eleusinian, Enigma, Esoteric, Grocer, Incarnation, Miracle, Occult, Original sin, Orphic, Riddle, SECRET, Telestic, Trinity, UFO, Uncanny

> **Mysterious(ly)**  may indicate an anagram

**Mystic (word)**  Abraxas, Agnostic, Cab(e)iri, Epopt, Fakir, Mahatma, Occultist, Rasputin, Secret, Sofi, Sufi, Swami, Theosophy

**Mystify**  Baffle, Bewilder, Metagrabolise, Metagrobolise, Puzzle

**Myth(ology), Mythical (beast)**  Allegory, Euhemerism, Fable, Fantasy, Fictitious, Folklore, Garuda, Geryon, Griffin, Impundulu, Legend, Lore, Otnit, Pantheon, Speewah, Sphinx, Unicorn, Yale

# Nn

**N** Name, Nitrogen, Noon, North, November

**Nab** Arrest, Capture, Collar, Grab, Seize

**Nabob** Deputy, Nawab, Wealthy

**Nadir** Bottom, Depths, Dregs, Minimum

**Nag(ging)** Badger, Bidet, Callet, Cap, Captious, Complain, Fret, Fuss, Harangue, Henpeck, Horse, Jade, Keffel, Pester, Plague, Rosinante, Rouncy, SCOLD, Tit, Yaff

**Nail(ed)** Brad, Brod, Catch, Fasten, Hob, Keratin, Onyx, Pin, Rivet, Sisera, Sparable, Spick, Spike, Sprig, Staple, Stud, Tack(et), Talon, Tenterhook, Thumb, Tingle, Toe

**Naive(té)** Artless, Green, Guileless, Ingenuous, Innocence, Open, Simpliste, Simplistic

**Naked** Adamical, Artless, Bare, Blunt, Buff, Clear, Cuerpo, Defenceless, Encuerpo, Exposed, Gymno-, Nuddy, Nude, Querpo, Raw, Scud, Simple, Stark(ers), Uncovered

**Namby-pamby** Sissy, Weak

**Name(d)** Agnomen, Alias, Appellation, Appoint, Baptise, Behight, Call, Celebrity, Cite, Cleep, Clepe, Designate, Dinges, Dingus, Dub, Epithet, Eponym, Handle, Hete, Hight, Hypocorism, Identify, Identity, Label, Marque, Mention, Moni(c)ker, N, Nom, Nomen(clature), Noun, Onomastic, Pennant, Personage, Pseudonym, Quote, Red(d), Repute, Scilicet, Sign, Signature, Sir, Specify, Substantive, Tag, Teknonymy, Term, TITLE, Titular, Titule

**Name-dropper** Eponym

**Nameless** Anon, Unchrisom

**Namely** Ie, Scilicet, To-wit, Videlicet, Viz

**Namesake** Homonym

**Name unknown** Anon, A N Other, NU

**Nancy** Coddle, Effeminate, Milksop

**Nanny** Ayah, Foster, Goat, Nurse

**Naos** Cell(a)

**Nap(py)** Bonaparte, Diaper, Doze, Drowse, Frieze(d), Fuzz, Kip, Moze, Oose, Ooze, Oozy, Put(t), Shag, Siesta, SLEEP, Snooze, Tease, Teasel, Teaze, Tuft

**Nape** Nucha, Scrag, Scruff, Scuft

**Napier** Logarithm

**Napkin** Cloth, Diaper, Doyly, Muckender, Serviette

**Napoleon** Badinguet, Bonaparte, Boustrapa, Cognac, Coin, Corporal Violet, Corsican, December, Little Corporal, Nantz, Nap, Pig, Rantipole

**Napper** Bonce, Shearman

**Narcissus** Egocentric, Jonquil

**Narcotic** Ava, B(h)ang, Benj, Charas, Churrus, Coca, Codeine, Datura, Dope, DRUG, Heroin, Hop, Mandrake, Marijuana, Meconium, Morphia, Opiate, Pituri, Sedative, Tea, Trional

**Nark** Grass, Inform, Irritate, Nose, Roil, Squealer, Stag

**Narrate, Narration, Narrative, Narrator** Allegory, Anecdote, Cantata, Describe, Diegesis, Fable, History, Plot, Raconteur, Recite, Recount, Saga, Scheherazade, Story, Tell

**Narrow(ing), Narrow-minded** Alf, Bigoted, Cramp, Hidebound, Insular, Kyle, Limited, Meagre, Nary, One-idead, Parochial, Phimosis, Scant, Shrink, Slender, Slit, Specialise, Squeak, Stenosed, Strait, Suburban, Verkramp, Waist

**Narwhal** Monodon

**Nasal** Adenoidal, Twang

**Nash** Beau

**Nashville** Bath

**Nastiness, Nasty** Disagreeable, Drevill, Filth, Fink, Ghastly, Lemon, Lo(a)th, Malign(ant), Noxious, Obscene, Odious, Offensive, Vile

**Nat(haniel)** Hawthorne, Winkle

**Natal** Inborn, Native, Patrial

**Natant** Afloat, Swimming

**Nation, National(ist)** Anthem, Baathist, Casement, Country, Cuban, Debt, Eta, Federal, Folk, Grand, Indian, Jingoist, Land, Mexican, Patriot, PEOPLE, Race, Risorgimento, Scottish, Subject, Swadeshi, Wafd, Zionist

**Native(s)** Abo(rigin), Aborigine, African, Annamese, Arab, Ascian, Australian, Aztec, Basuto, Belonging, Bengali, Boy, Cairene, Carib, Chaldeen, Citizen, Colchester, Conch, Creole, Criollo, Dyak, Edo, Enchorial, Fleming, Genuine, Habitual, Inborn, Indigenous, Indigene, Inhabitant, Intuitive, Kaffir, Libyan, Local, Malay, Maori, Moroccan, Norwegian, Oyster, Polack, Portuguese, Son, Spaniard, Te(i)an, Thai, Tibetan, Uzbeg, Uzbek, Whitstable, Yugoslav

**Nativity** Birth, Jataka, Putz

**Natron** Urao

**Natter** Chat, Gossip, Jack, Prate

**Natty** Bumppo, Chic, Dapper, Leatherstocking, Smart, Spruce

**Natural** Ass, Genuine, Homely, Idiot, Illegitimate, Inborn, Ingenerate, Inherent, Innate, Moron, Native, Nidget, Nitwit, Nude, Ordinary, Organic, Prat, Real, Simpleton

**Naturalist** Buffon, Darwin, Wallace, White

**Nature** Adam, Character, Disposition, Esse(nce), Ethos, Mould, Quintessence, Second, SN, Temperament

**Naught** Cypher, Failure, Nil, Nothing, Zero

**Naughty** Bad, Girly, Improper, Light, Marietta, Rascal, Remiss, Spright, Sprite, Wayward

**Nausea, Nauseous** Disgust, Fulsome, Malaise, Sickness, Squeamish, Wamble

**Nave** Aisle, Apse, Centre, Hub, Nef

**Navel** Nave, Omphalos, Umbilicus

**Navigate, Navigator** Bougainville, Cabot, Cartier, Control, Da Gama, Dias, Direct, Franklin, Frobisher, Gilbert, Henry, Hudson, Keel, Magellan, Navvy, Pilot, Sail, Star-read, STEER, Tasman, Traverse, Vespucci

**Navigation (aid, system)** Asdic, Decca, Dectra, Fido, Gee, Loran, Navarho, Portolan(o), Portulan, Radar, Satnav, Shoran, Tacan, Teleran, Vor

**Navy, Naval** AB, Armada, Blue, Fleet, Maritime, N, Red, RN, Wren

**Nawab** Huzoor, Nabob, Viceroy

**Nazi** Gauleiter, Hess, Hitler, Jackboot, SS, Stormtrooper, Wer(e)wolf

**NCO** Bombardier, Corp(oral), Havildar, Noncom, SM, Sergeant

**Neanderthal** Mousterian

**Neap** Low, Tide

**Neapolitan** Ice

**Near(est), Nearby, Nearly, Nearness** About, Adjacent, All-but, Almost, Approach, Approximate, By, Close, Degree, Even, Ewest, Forby, Gain, Handy, Hither, Imminent, Inby(e), Mean, Miserly, Neist, Next, Nie, Niggardly, Nigh, Outby, Propinquity, Proximity, Stingy, To, Warm

**Neat(ly)** Bandbox, Cattle, Clever, Dainty, Dapper, Deft, Dink(y), Doddy, Donsie, Elegant, Feat(e)ous, Featuous, Gayal, Genty, Gyal, Intact, Jemmy, Jimpy, Ninepence, Ox(en), Pretty, Rother, Shipshape, Short, Smug, Snod, Spruce, Straight, TIDY, Trig, Trim, Unwatered

**Neb** Beak, Bill, Nose, Snout

**Nebulous** Aeriform, Celestial, Cloudy, Hazy, Obscure, Shadowy, Vague

**Necessary, Necessarily** Bog, Cash, ESSENTIAL, Estovers, Important, Intrinsic, Money, Needful, Ought, Perforce, Requisite, Vital

**Necessitate, Necessity** Ananke, Compel, Constrain, Emergency, Entail, Exigent, Fate, Indigence, Must, Need, Oblige, Perforce, Require, Requisite

**Neck(ed)** Bottle, Brass, Cervical, Cervix, Channel, Col, Crag, Craig, Crop, Embrace, Gall, Gorgerin, Halse, Hawse, Inarm, Inclip, Isthmus, Kiss, Mash, Nape, Pet, Rubber, Scrag, Scruff, Smooch, Snog, Strait, Swire, Theorbo, Torticullus, Trachelate, Vee

> **Necking** may indicate one word around another

**Necklace** Anodyne, Brisingamen, Chain, Choker, Collar, Corals, Lava(l)lière, Mangalsutra, Pearls, Rope, Sautoir, String, Torc, Torque

**Neckline** Boat, Collar, Plunging, Turtle, Vee

**Neckwear** Ascot, Barcelona, Boa, Bow, Collar, Cravat, Fur, Steenkirk, Stock, Tie

**Necromancer** Goetic, Magician, Ormandine, Osmand, Witch, Wizard

**Necrosis** Infarct, Sphacelus

**Nectar** Ambrosia, Amrita, Honey, Mead

**Ned(dy)** Donkey, Kelly, Ludd

**Need(ed), Needy** Call, Demand, Desiderata, Egence, Egency, Exigency, Gap, Impecunious, Indigent, LACK, Mister, Pressing, Require, Want

**Needle** Acerose, Acicular, Aciform, Between, Bodkin, Goad, Hype, Icicle, Inoculate, Leucotome, Miff, Monolith, Neeld, Neele, Obelisk, Pinnacle, Pointer, Prick, R(h)aphis, Sew, Sharp, Spike, Spine, Stylus, Tattoo, Tease, Thorn

**Needlewoman** Cleopatra

**Needlework** Baste, Crewel, Embroidery, Mola, Sampler, Tapestry, Tattoo

**Neer-do-well** Badmash, Budmash, Bum, Good-for-nothing, Shiftless, Skellum, Wastrel

**Negation, Negative** Anion, Apophatic, Cathode, Denial, Enantiosis, Ne, No, Non, Nope, Nullify, Photograph, Refusal, Resinous, Unresponsive, Veto, Yin

**Neglect(ed), Neglectful, Negligence, Negligent** Careless, Casual, Cinderella, Cuff, Default, Dereliction, Disregard, Disuse, Failure, Forget, Forlorn, Heedless, Laches, Misprision, Omission, Oversight, Pass, REMISS, Shirk, Slight, Slipshod, Undone

> **Neglected** may indicate an anagram

**Negligee** Déshabillé, Manteau, Mob, Nightgown, Peignoir, Robe

**Negotiate, Negotiator** Arrange, Bargain, Clear, Confer, Deal, Diplomat, Intermediary, Liaise, Manoeuvre, Mediator, Parley, Trade, Transact, Treat(y), Weather

**Negro** Black, Buck, Creole, Cuffee, Cuffy, Ebon(y), Ethiop, Gullah, Hausa, Hottentot, Jim Crow, Kikuyu, Luba, Mestee, Moke, Moor, Mustee, Nilote, Nyanja, Pondo, Quashee, Quashie, Sambo, Snowball, Spade, Susu, Thick-lips, TIV, Tonga, Tswana, Uncle Tom, Watu(t)si, Zambo, Zulu

**Negus** Emperor, Rumfruction, Selassie

**Nehru** Pandit

**Neigh** Bray, Hinny, Nicker, Whicker, Whinny

**Neighbour(ly), Neighbouring** Abut(ter), Alongside, Amicable, Border, But, Friendly, Nearby, Next-door

**Neighbourhood** Area, Community, District, Environs, Locality, Precinct, Vicinage, Vicinity

**Neither** Nor

**Nell(ie), Nelly** Bly, Dean, Trent

**Nelson**  Columnist, Eddy, Horatio

**Nemesis**  Alastor, Avenger, Deserts, Downfall, Fate, Retribution, Revenge

**Neodymium**  Nd

**Neon**  Ne

**Nepalese**  Gurkha

**Neper**  N

**Nephrite**  Yu

**Nepotism**  Kin, Partisan, Patronage

**Neptune**  God, Planet, Poseidon

**Neptunium**  Np

**Nereid**  Cymodoce, Nymph, Panope

**Nerve(s), Nervous (centre), Nervure, Nervy**  Abdabs, Abducens, Afferent, Appestat, Axon, Bottle, Bouton, Chord, Chutzpah, Collywobbles, Column, Courage, Cyton, Edgy, Electrotonus, Gall, Ganglion, Grit, Guts, High, Hyp, Impudence, Jitters, Jittery, Mid-rib, Motor, Myelon, Neck, Nidus, Optic, Pavid, Rad, Radial, Restless, Sangfroid, Sciatic, Shaky, Spunk, Steel, Tense, Toey, Trembler, Tremulous, Twitchy, Vagus, Vapours, Windy, Yips

**Nervous disease**  Chorea, Epilepsy, Neuritis

> **Nervously**  may indicate an anagram

**Ness**  Cape, Headland, Ras

**Nessus**  Centaur

**Nest**  Aerie, Aery, Ayrie, Bink, Brood, Cabinet, Cage, Clutch, Dray, Drey, Eyrie, Eyry, Nid, Nide, Nidify, Nidus, Sett, Wurley

**Nestle**  Burrow, Cose, Cuddle, Nuzzle, Snug(gle)

**Nestor**  Counsellor, Kea, Sage

**Net(ting), Nets**  Bunt, Catch, Caul, Clear, Crinoline, Drift, Earn, Eel-set, Enmesh, Filet, Final, Fish, Flew, Flue, Fyke, Hammock, Lace, Land, Leap, Linin, Malines, MESH, Purse-seine, Rete, Retiary, Sagene, Screen, Sean, Seine, Snood, Toil, Trammel, Trap, Trawl, Tulle, Web

**Netball**  Let

**Nether**  Below, Inferior, Infernal, Lower, Under

**Nettle(rash)**  Anger, Annoy, Day, Dead, Hives, Irritate, Labiate, Nark, Pellitory, Pique, Ramee, Rami, Ramie, Rile, Ruffle, Sting, Urtica(ceae), Urticaria

**Network**  Anastomosis, BR, Cobweb, GRID, Lattice, Linin, Maze, Old boys', Plexus, Reseau, Reticle, System, Tela, Web

**Neuralgia, Neuritis**  Migraine, Sciatica, Tic

**Neuter**  Castrate, Gib, Impartial, Neutral, Sexless, Spay

**Neutral(ise)**  Alkalify, Buffer zone, Counteract, Grey, Impartial, Schwa, Sheva, Shiva, Unbiased

**Never(more)** Nary, Nathemo(re), No more, Nowise, St Tibb's Eve

**Nevertheless** Algate, Anyhow, But, However, Still, Yet

> **New** may indicate an anagram

**New(s), News agency** Bulletin, Copy, Coranto, Dope, Euphobia, Evangel, Flash, Forest, Fresh, Fudge, Gen, Green, Griff, Info, Innovation, Intelligence, Item, Latest, Modern, Mint, N, Novel, Oils, Original, PA, Paragraph, Pastures, Propaganda, Pristine, Recent, Report, Reuter, Scoop, Span, Tass, Tidings, Ultramodern, Unco, Word

**New boy** Gyte

**Newcomer** Dog, Freshman, Griffin, Immigrant, Jackaroo, Jackeroo, Jillaroo, Novice, Parvenu, Pilgrim, Settler, Tenderfoot, Upstart

**Newfoundland** Dog, Nana

**Newgate** Calendar

**Newly wed** Benedick, Benedict, Bride, Groom, Honeymooner, Neogamist

**Newman** Cardinal, Noggs

**Newsman, News-reader** Announcer, Editor, Journalist, Press, Reporter, Sub, Sysop

**Newsmonger, News-vendor** Butcher, Gossip, Quidnunc

**Newspaper** Blat(t), Broadsheet, Courier, Daily, Express, Fanzine, Gazette, Guardian, Herald, Journal, Jupiter, Le Monde, Mercury, National, Organ, Patent inside, Patent outside, Post, Press, Print, Rag, Sheet, Squeak, Sun, Tabloid

**Newsreel** Actualities

**Newt(s)** Ask(er), Eft, Evet, Swift, Triton, Urodela

**Newton** N

**New world** USA

**New year** Hogmanay, Neer-day, Tet

**New York(er)** Big apple, Gotham, Knickerbocker

**New Zealand(ers)** Aotearoa, Enzed, Kiwis, Maori, Pakeha, Pig Island, Shagroon

**Next** Adjacent, Adjoining, After, Alongside, Beside, Following, Immediate, Later, Nearest, Neist, Proximate, Sine, Subsequent, Syne

**Nib** J, Pen, Point, Tip

**Nibble** Bite, Brouse, Browse, Crop, Eat, Gnaw, Knap(ple), Moop, Moup, Munch, Nag, Nosh, Peck, Pick, Snack

**Nice(ty)** Accurate, Amene, Appealing, Dainty, Fastidious, Fine, Finical, Genteel, Lepid, Ninepence, Pat, Pleasant, Precise, Quaint, Rare, Refined, Subtil(e), Subtle, Sweet, T

**Niche** Alcove, Almery, Ambry, Apse, Aumbry, Awmrie, Awmry, Cranny, Fenestella, Mihrab, Recess, Slot

**Nicholas** Santa

**Nick(ed)** Appropriate, Arrest, Bin, Can, Chip, Cly, Colin, Cut, Denay, Dent, Deny, Erose, Groove, Hoosegow, Kitty, Knock, Nab, Nap, Nim, Nock, Notch, Pinch, Pook, Pouk, Prison, Scratch, STEAL, Thieve

**Nickel (silver)** Coin, Ni, Packfong, Paktong, Zaratite

**Nicker** Bonduc, Neigh, Whinny

**Nickname** Alias, Byword, Cognomen, So(u)briquet, To-name

**Nicotine** Tobacco, Weed

**Nifty** Smart, Stylish

**Nigeria(n)** Efik, Ibo, Igbo, WAN, Yoruba

**Niggard(ly)** Illiberal, Mean, Miser, Near-gaun, Nippy, Nirlit, Parsimonious, Scrunt, Tightwad

**Niggle** Carp, Gripe, Nag, Trifle

**Night(s), Nightfall** Acronychal, Arabian, Darkmans, Nacht, Nicka-nan, Nutcrack, Nyx, Twelfth, Twilight, Walpurgis

**Night-blindness** Day-sight, Nyctalopia

**Night-cap** Biggin, Cocoa, Nip, Pirnie, Sundowner

**Night-dew** Serein, Serene

**Nightingale** Bulbul, Florence, Jugger, Lind, Philomel, Scutari, Swedish, Watch

**Nightjar** Evejar, Fern-owl, Goatsucker, Poorwill

**Night-light** Moonbeam

**Nightmare** Cacod(a)emon, Ephialtes, Incubus, Oneirodynia, Phantasmagoria

**Nightshade** Belladonna, Bittersweet, Circaea, Dwale, Henbane, Morel, Solanum

**Nightwatchman** Charley, Charlie, Rug-gown

**Nightwork** Lucubrate

**Nihilist** Anarchist, Red, Sceptic

**Nil** Nothing, Nought, Zero

**Nimble** Active, AGILE, Alert, Deft, Deliver, Fleet, Light, Lissom, Lithe, Quiver, Springe, Spry, Supple, Swack, Wan(d)le, Wannel, Wight, Ya(u)ld

**Nimbus** Aura, Aureole, Cloud, Gloriole, Halo

**Nimrod** Hunter

**Nincompoop** Ass, Imbecile, Ninny, Stupid

**Nine** Ennead, Muses, Nonary, Nonet, Novenary, Pins, Sancho, Skittles, Tailors, Worthies

**Nine hundred** Sampi

**Nineteen(th)** Bar, Decennoval

**Ninety** N

**Ninevite** Assyrian

**Ninny (hammer)** Fool, Goose, Idiot, Stupid, Tony

**Ninon** Nan

**Niobium** Nb

**Nip(per)** Bite, Check, Chela, Chill, Claw, Dram, Gook, Jap, Lad, Lop, Nep, Nirl, Peck, Pincers, Pinch, Pook, Scotch, Sneap, Susan, Taste, Tot, Tweak, Urchin, Vice, Vise

**Nipa** At(t)ap, Palm

**Nipple** Dug, Mastoid, Pap, Teat

**Nis** Brownie, Goblin, Kobold, Sprite

**Nitre** Saltpetre

**Nitric, Nitrogen** Azote, Azotic, Gas, N

**Nitroglycerine** Glonoin

**Nitwit** Ass, Flat, Fool, Simpleton, STUPID

**No** Aikona, Denial, Na(e), Negative, Nix, Nope, Nyet, O

**Noah** Arkite, Beery, Utnapishtim

**Nob(by)** Grandee, Parage, Prince, Swell, Toff

**Nobble** Dope, Hilch, Injure, Interfere

> **Nobbled** may indicate an anagram

**Nobelium** No

**Noble(man)** Adeline, Aristocrat, Atheling, Baronet, Bart, Bt, Childe, Count, County, Daimio, Dom, Don, Doucepere, Douzeper(s), Duc, Duke, Earl, Eorl, Fine, Gent, Glorious, Graf, Grandee, Great, Heroic, Hidalgo, Highborn, Jarl, Junker, King, Landgrave, Lord, Manly, Marquis, Palatine, Patrician, Peer, Rank, Stately, Thane, Thegn, Titled, Toiseach, Toisech, Vicomte

**Nobody** Gnatling, Jack-straw, Nemo, None, Nonentity, Nyaff, Pooter, Quat, Scoot, Shlep

**Nocturnal (creature)** Bat, Galago, Moth, Night, Owl

**Nod(ding)** Agree, Assent, Beck(on), Bob, Browse, Catnap, Cernuous, Doze, Mandarin, Nutant, Somnolent

**Node, Nodular, Nodule** Boss, Enhydros, Geode, Knot, Lump, Pea-iron, Swelling, Thorn

**No doubt** Iwis, Ywis

**Noel** Christmas, Coward, Yule

**Nog(gin)** Ale, Cup, DRINK, Peg

**No good** Dud, NG, Ropy

**Noise, Noisy** Babel, Bedlam, Blare, Blip, Bobbery, Boing, Boink, Bruit, Cangle, Charm, Clamant, Clamour, Clangour, Clash, Clatter, Clitter, Clutter, Coil, Deen, Din, Dirdum, Euphonia, Euphony, F, Fuss, Hewgh, Hubbub, Hue, Hum, Loud, Obstreperous, Ping, Plangent, Quonk, Racket, Report, Roar, Robustious, Rort, Rowdedow, Row(dow-dow),

Rowdy(dow)(dy), Scream, Screech, Shindig, Shindy, Shreek, Shreik, Shriech, Shriek, Sone, Sonorous, Sound, Strepent, Strepitation, Strepitoso, Tumult, UPROAR, VIP, Vociferous, Zoom

**Noisome** Fetid, Invidious, Noxious, Offensive, Rank

**No longer** Ex, Past

**Nomad** Bedawin, Bed(o)uin, Bedu, Berber, Chal, Edom(ite), Gypsy, Kurd, Rom, Rover, Saracen, Strayer, Tsigane, Tsigany, Tuareg, Vagabond, Vagrant, Zigan

**Noman** Ta(r)tar

**Nome** Province

**Nominal** Formal, Onomastic, Titular, Trifling

**Nominate, Nomination** Appoint, Baptism, Designate, Elect, Present, PROPOSE, Slate, Term

**Nomogram** Abac

**No more** Gone, Napoo

**Nomothete** Enactor, Legislator

**Non-attender** Absentee, Recusant

**Non-believer** Atheist, Cynic, Infidel, Sceptic

**Nonchalance, Nonchalant** Blasé, Casual, Cool, Debonair, Jaunty

**Noncommittal** Trimmer

**Non-conformist, Non-conformity** Beatnik, Bohemian, Chapel, Deviant, Dissent(er), Dissident, Ebenezer, Heresiarch, Maverick, Odd-ball, Pantile, Patarine, Rebel, Recusant, Renegade, Renegate, Sectarian, Wesleyan

**Nondescript** Dull, Insipid, Nyaff

**None** Nary, Nil, Nought, Zero

**Nonentity** Cipher, Nebbich, Nebbish(er), Nebish, Nobody, Pipsqueak, Quat

**Non-essential** Adiaphoron, Extrinsic

**Nonesuch** Model, Nonpareil, Paradigm, Paragon, Rarity

> **Nonetheless** may indicate an 'o' to be omitted

**Non-gypsy** Gajo, Gorgio

**Non-Jewish** Goy, Shicksa

**Non-juror** Usager

**Nonpareil** Nonesuch, Pearl, Peerless, Type, Unequal, Unique

**Nonplus(sed)** Baffle, Bewilder, Blank, Perplex, Stump

**Non-professional** Amateur, Laic

**Non-radiative** Auger

**Non-resident** Outlier

**Non-runner** Scratched, Solid

**Nonsense** Absurdity, Amphigon, Amphigory, Balderdash, Baloney, Bilge, Blah, Blarney, Blat(her), Blether, Boloney, Borak, Borax, Bosh, Bull,

Bunkum, Claptrap, Cobblers, Cock, Cod, Codswallop, Crap, Drivel, Eyewash, Faddle, Fandangle, Fiddlededee, Fiddlesticks, Flapdoodle, Flim-flam, Folderol, Footling, Fudge, Gaff, Galimatias, Gammon, Get away, Gibberish, Guff, Gum, Haver, Hogwash, Hooey, Horsefeathers, Humbug, Kibosh, Malarkey, Moonshine, Piffle, Pshaw, Pulp, Rats, Rhubarb, Rigmarole, Rot, Rubbish, Scat, Squit, Tom(foolery), Tommy-rot, Tosh, Tripe, Twaddle, Unreason, Waffle

**Non-sequitur**  Anacoluthia, Irrelevant

**Non-stick**  Tusche

**Non-violence**  Ahimsa, Pacificism, Satyagraha

**Non-white**  Coloured, Yolk

**Noodle(s)**  Crispy, Daw, Fool, Head, Lokshen, Moony, Pasta, Sammy, Simpleton

**Nook**  Alcove, Angle, Corner, Cranny, Niche, Recess, Rookery

**Noon**  Am end, M, Midday, Narrowdale

**No one**  Nemo, None

**Noose**  Fank, Halter, Lanyard, Loop, Rope, Snare

> **Nor**  see NOT

**Nordic**  Icelander, Scandinavian

**Norm**  Canon, Criterion, Rule, Standard

**Normal**  Average, Natural, Norm, Ordinary, Par, Perpendicular, Regular, Standard, Usual

**Normal eyes**  Emmetropia

**Norman**  French, Rufus

**North(ern), Northerner**  Arctic, Cispontine, Copperhead, Eskimo, Hyperborean, N, Norland, Runic, Septentrion, Up

**Northwestern**  Aeolis

**Norway, Norwegian**  Bokmal, Fortinbras, Landsma(a)l, N, Nordic, Nynorsk, Rollo

**Nose, Nosy**  A(d)jutage, Beak, Bergerac, Boko, Bouquet, Conk, Cromwell, Curious, Desman, Fink, Gnomon, Grass, Hooter, Index, Informer, Meddle, Muzzle, Nark, Neb, Nozzle, Nuzzle, Proboscis, Prying, Roman, Schnozzle, Shove, Smelly, Sneb, Sniff, Snoot, Snout, Snub, Squeal, Stag, Stickybeak, Toffee

**Noseband**  Barnacle, Cavesson, Musrol

**Nose-bleed**  Epistaxis

**Nosh**  Eat, Food, Nibble, Snack

**Nostalgia**  Longing, Yearning

**Nostril(s)**  Blowhole, Cere, Choana, Nare

**Nostrum**  Elixir, Medicine, Remede, Remedy

**Not, Nor**  Dis-, Na(e), Ne, Neither, Never, No, Pas, Polled, Taint

**Notable, Notability** Conspicuous, Distinguished, Eminent, Especial, Landmark, Large, Memorable, Signal, Striking, Unco, VIP, Worthy

**Not allowed** NL

> **Not allowed** may indicate a word to be omitted

**Notation** Benesh, Entry, Memo, Romic

**Not clear** Blocked, NL, Obscure, Opaque, Pearl

**Notch(ed)** Crena(l), Crenel, Cut, Dent, Erode, Erose, Gap, Gimp, Indent, Jag, Kerf, Nick, Nock, Raffle, Sinus, Snick, Vandyke

**Note(s)** A, Accidental, Adversaria, Agogic, Apostil(le), Apparatus, Appoggiatura, Arpeggio, B, Bill(et), Bradbury, Breve, C, Cedula, Chit(ty), Cob, Comment, Conceit, Continental, Crotchet, D, Dig, Dominant, E, E-la, F, Fa(h), Fiver, Flat, G, Gamut, Gloss(ary), Grace, Greenback, IOU, Item(ise), Jot(tings), Jug(-jug), Key, Kudos, La, Lichanos, Line, Log, Long, Longa, Marginalia, Masora(h), Me, Melisma, Memo(randum), Mese, Mi, Minim, Minute, Natural, NB, Nete, Neum(e), Oblong, Observe, Octave, Oncer, Parhypate, Pound, Proslambanomenos, Protocol, PS, Quaver, Rag-money, Re, Record, Remark, Renown, Scholion, Scholium, Semibreve, Semitone, Sextolet, Sharp, Shinplaster, Si, Sol, Stem, Submediant, Te, Ten(ner), Third, Tonic, Treasure, Treble, Ut, Variorum, Wad, Warison

**Note-case** Pochette, Purse, Wallet

> **Notes** may indicate the use of letters A-G

**Noteworthy** Eminent, Extraordinary, Memorable, Particular, Signal, Special

**Nothing, Nought** Cipher, Devoid, Emptiness, FA, Gratis, Nada, Naught, Nihil, Niks-nie, Nil, Nix(-nie), Noumenon, Nowt, O, Rap, Rien, Void, Zero, Zilch, Zip(po)

**Notice(able)** Ad(vertisement), Advice, Affiche, Apprise, Attention, Avis(o), Banns, Bill, Blurb, Caveat, Circular, Cognisance, Crit, D, Descry, Discern, Dismissal, Gaum, Get, Gorm, HEED, Intimation, Marked, Mention, NB, No(t)chel, Obit, Observe, Oyez, Placard, Plaque, Playbill, Poster, Press, REMARK, See, Si quis, Spot, Sticker, Tent, Whip

**Notify** Acquaint, Advise, Apprise, Awarn, Inform, TELL

**Notion** Conceit, CONCEPT, Crotchet, Fancy, Hunch, Idea, Idolum, Inkling, Opinion, Reverie, Whim

**Notoriety, Notorious** Arrant, Byword, Crying, Esclandre, Fame, Flagrant, Infamous, Infamy, Proverbial, Reclame, RENOWN, Repute

**No trump** Laical, Lay, NT

**Notwithstanding** Although, Despite, Even, However, Nath(e)less, Natheless(e), Naythles, Nevertheless, Spite

> **Nought** see NOTHING

**Noughts and crosses** Tick-tack-toe

**Noun** Aptote, Gerund, N

**Nourish(ing), Nourishment** Aliment, Cherish, Cultivate, Feed, Meat, Nurse, Nurture, Nutrient, Promote, Trophic

**Nous** Intellect, Intelligence, Reason

**Nova Scotia(n)** Acadia, Blue-nose

**Novel(ty)** Bildungsroman, Book, Change, Different, Dime, Emma, Fad, Fiction, Fresh, Gimmick, Gothic, Innovation, Ivanhoe, Kenilworth, Kidnapped, Kim, Middlemarch, NEW(fangled), Original, Pamela, Paperback, Pendennis, Persuasion, Picaresque, Pot-boiler, Primeur, Rebecca, Romance, Whodun(n)it, Yellowback

> **Novel** may indicate an anagram

**Novelist** Ainsworth, Amis, APH, Author, Ayres, Balzac, Bellow, Blackmore, Boccaccio, Caine, Cervantes, Chekhov, Chesterton, Deeping, Drabble, Dreiser, Dumas, Du Maurier, Durrell, Fielding, Fitzgerald, Flaubert, Forster, Galsworthy, Gide, Greene, Hardy, Hesse, James, Joyce, Lawrence, Lewis, Linklater, London, Lytton, Mann, Mannin, Mason, Maupassant, Meredith, Moravia, Morgan, Naipaul, Onions, Ouida, Paton, Priestley, Proust, Reade, Richardson, Rousseau, Sand, Scott, Shute, Snow, Stendhal, Synge, Trollope, Wells, Wodehouse, Woolf, WRITER

**Novice** Acolyte, Apprentice, Beginner, Chela, Colt, Cub, Greenhorn, Griffin, Kyu, L, Learner, Neophyte, Postulant, Prentice, Rookie, Tenderfoot, Tyro(ne), Unweaned

**Now(adays)** AD, Alate, Anymore, Current, Here, Immediate, Instanter, Nonce, Nunc, Present, Pro tem, This

**Nowhere** Limbo

**Nowt** Cattle, Cows, Ky(e), Neat, Nothing

**Noxious** Harmful, Offensive, Poisonous, Venomous

**Nozzle** A(d)jutage, Nose, Rose, Spout, Syringe, Tewel, Tuyere, Tweer, Twier, Twire, Twyer(e)

**Nuance** Gradation, Nicety, Overtone, Shade

**Nub** Crux, Gist, Knob, Lump, Point

**Nubile** Marriageable, Parti

**Nuclear, Nucleus** Cadre, Centre, Core, Crux, Hub, Isomer, Kernel, Linin, Mushroom, Nuke, Pith, Prokaryon, Triton

> **Nucleus** may indicate the heart of a word

**Nude, Nudism, Nudist, Nudity** Adamite, Altogether, Aphylly, Bare, Buff, Eve, Exposed, Gymnosophy, NAKED, Scud, Stark, Undress

**Nudge** Dunch, Dunsh, Elbow, Jostle, Poke, Prod

**Nudibranch** Sea-slug

**Nugget** Chunk, Cob, Gold, Lump

**Nuisance** Bore, Bot, Bugbear, Drag, Mischief, Pest, Plague, Terror

**Null(ification), Nullify** Abate, Cancel, Defeasance, Destroy, Diriment, Disarm, Invalid(ate), Negate, Recant, Terminate, Undo, Veto, Void

**Numb(ness)** Asleep, Blunt, Dead(en), Stun, Stupor

**Number(s)** Abundant, Air, Algorithm, Amiable, Anaesthetic, Antilog, Apocalyptic, Apostrophus, Army, Atomic, Avogadro's, Babylonian, Calculate, Cardinal, Cocaine, Concrete, Constant, Count, Cyclic, Decillion, Deficient, Deficit, Diapason, Digit, Drove, E, Epidural, Ether, Feck, Frost(bite), Gas, Googol, Hemlock, Host, Isospin, Lac, Lakh, Legion(s), Local, Mach, Magazine, Milliard, Minuend, Mort, Muckle, Multiple, Multiplex, Myriadth, Nasik, No(s), Nonillion, Nth, Num, Octillion, Opiate, Opus, Ordinal, OT, Paginate, Par, Peck, Perfect, Pile, Pin, Plural, Quorum, Radix, Raft, Reckon, Repunit, Reynold's, Scads, Sight, Slew, Slue, Some, Strength, Tale, Tell, Totient, Totitive, Troop, Umpteen, Umpty, Urethane, Verse

> **Number** may indicate a drug

**Numeral(s)** Arabic, Chapter, Figure, Ghubar, Gobar, Integer, Number

**Numerous** Divers, Galore, Legion, Lots, Many, Myriad

**Numskull** Blockhead, Booby, Dunce, Stupid

**Nun** Beguine, Clare, Cluniac, Conceptionist, Dame, Minoress, Pigeon, Religeuse, Sister, Top, Vestal, Vowess, Zelator, Zelatrice, Zelatriks

> **Nun** a biblical character, father of Joshua

**Nuptial (chamber)** Bridal, Marital, Marriage, Thalamus

**Nurse(ry)** Aia, Alice, Amah, Ayah, Bonne, Caledonia, Care(r), Cavell, Cherish, Deborah, Flo(rence), Foster, Gamp, Glumdalclitch, Mammy, Mother, Minister, Mrs Gamp, Nan(n)a, Nanny, Nightingale, Nourice, Parabolanus, Probationer, Seminary, SEN, Sister, Suckle, Tend, VAD, Wet

**Nursery(man)** Crèche, Conservatory, Garden, Hothouse, Rhyme, Seedsman, Slope

> **Nursing** may indicate one word within another

**Nurture** Cultivate, Educate, Feed, Foster, Suckle, Tend

**Nut(s), Nutcase, Nutshell, Nut tree, Nutty** Acajou, Acorn, Amygdalus, Anacardium, Aphorism, Arachis, Areca, Arnut, Babassu, Barcelona, Barmy, Bats, Beech-mast, Bertholletia, Betel, Briefly, Butterfly, Butternut, Cashew, Cola, Coquilla, Core, Cranium, Cuckoo, Filberd, Filbert, Gelt, Gilbert, Gland, Glans, Hazel, Head, Hickory, Illipe, Kernel, Kola, Lunatic, Macadamia, Manic, Mast, Mockernut, Noodle, Nucule, Para, Pate, Pecan, Philippina, Philippine, Philopoena, Pili, Pistachio, Praline, Prawlin, Rhus, Sapucaia, Sassafras, Shell, Skull, Slack, Sleeve, Zany, Zealot

> **Nut** Egyptian god, father of Osiris

> **Nutcase, Nutshell** see NUT

**Nutmeg** Connecticut, CT, Mace

**Nutrient, Nutriment, Nutrition** Food, Ingesta, Protein, Sustenance, Trace element, Trophic

> **Nuts** may indicate an anagram

**Nuzzle** Snoozle

**Nymph(et)**  Aegina, Aegle, Amalthea, Arethusa, Callisto, Calypso, Camenae, Clytie, Constant, Cymodoce, Daphne, Doris, Dryad, Echo, Egeria, Eurydice, Galatea, Hamadryad, Hesperides, Houri, Hyades, Ida, Insect, Larva, Liberty, Lolita, Maelid, Maia, Maiden, Mermaid, Naiad, Nereid, Oceanid, Oenone, Oread, Pupa, Rusalka, Sabrina, Scylla, Siren, Sylph, Syrinx, Tessa, Tethys, Thetis

# Oo

**O** Blob, Duck, Nought, Omega, Omicron, Oscar, Oxygen, Spangle, Tan, Zero

**Oaf** Auf, Changeling, Dolt, Fool, Ocker, Stupid

**Oak** Cerris, Dumbarton, Durmast, Flittern, Fumed, Gabriel, Holm, Ilex, Philemon, Quercus, Roble, TREE

**Oakley** Annie

**Oar(s), Oarsmen** Blade, Ctene, Eight, Leander, Organ, Paddle, Propel, Rower, Scull, Spoon, Sweep

**Oasis** Buraimi, Haven, Refuge, Spring

**Oat(meal), Oats** Ait, Athole brose, Brome-grass, Fodder, Grain, Grits, Groats, Gruel, Haver, Loblolly, Pilcorn, Pipe, Porridge, Quaker

**Oatcake** Bannock, Clapbread, Farle, Flapjack, Jannock

**Oath** Begorrah, Curse, Dang, Demme, Doggone, Drat, Egad, Expletive, God-so, Halidom, Hippocratic, Igad, Imprecation, Lumme, Lummy, Oons, Promise, Sacrament, Sal(a)mon, Sapperment, Sdeath, Sfoot, Sheart, Strewth, Tarnation, Tennis-court, Voir dire, Vow, Zbud

**Obdurate** Adamant, Cruel, Hard, Intransigent, Stony, Stubborn

**Obedient, Obey** Comply, Dutiful, Follow, Hear, Mindful, Obsequious, Observe, Obtemper, Perform, Pliant, Servant, Yielding

**Obeisance** BOW, Salaam

**Obelisk, Obelus** Column, Dagger, Monument, Needle, Pillar

**Oberon** King, Merle

**Object(s), Objector, Objective(ness)** Aim, Ambition, Argue, Article, Bar, Case, Cavil, Challenge, Clinical, Complain, Conchy, Conscientious, Demur, End, GOAL, Her, Him, Impersonal, Indifferent, Intention, It, Item, Jib, Loathe, Mind, Moral, Niggle, Non-ego, Oppose, Outness, Point, Protest, Recuse, Refuse, Resist, Subject, Sublime, Target, Thing, Unbiased, Ultimate, Virtu

> **Object** may indicate a grammatical variant

**Objection(able)** Ah, Beef, Cavil, Challenge, Complaint, Cow, Exception, Fuss, Improper, Obnoxious, Offensive, Question, Scruple, Tut

**Objectless** Intransitive

**Oblate, Oblation** Gift, Monk, Offering, Sacrifice

**Oblige, Obliging, Obligation, Obligatory** Accommodate, Affable, Behold, Binding, Burden, Charge, Compel, Complaisant, Compliant, Contract, Corvée, Debt, Duty, Easy, Encumbent, Force, Gratify, Impel, Incumbent, IOU, Mandatory, Necessitate, Promise, Sonties, Tie, Wattle

**Oblique(ly)** Askance, Askew, Asklent, Athwart, Awry, Cross, Diagonal, Perverse, Separatrix, Skew, Slanting, Solidus, Squint, Virgule

> **Oblique** may indicate an anagram

**Obliterate(d)** Annul, Blot, Dele(te), Efface, Expunge, Exterminate, Rase, Rast, Raze, Wipe

**Oblivion, Oblivious** Forgetful, Lethe, Limbo, Nirvana, Obscurity

**Oblong** Rectangular

**Obnoxious** Foul, Horrid, Offensive, Pestilent, Repugnant, Septic

**Obscene** Bawdy, Blue, Fescennine, Gross, Indecent, Lewd, Paw(paw), Porn(o), Salacious, Vulgar

**Obscure, Obscurity** Abstruse, Anheires, Becloud, Befog, Blend, Cloud, Conceal, Cover, Darken, Deep, Dim, Disguise, Eclipse, Envelop, Filmy, Fog, Hermetic, Hide, Mantle, Mist, Murk, Nebular, Nebecula, Obfuscate, Opaque, Oracular, Overcloud, Overshade, Overshadow, Recondite, Tenebrific, Unclear, VAGUE, Veil, Vele, Wrap

> **Obscure(d)** may indicate an anagram

**Obsequious** Bootlicker, Fawn, Fulsome, Grovelling, Menial, Parasitic, Pig, Servile, Slimy, Sycophantic, Tantony, Toady

**Observance, Observant, Observation** Adherence, Alert, Attention, Comment, Custom, Empirical, Espial, Eyeful, Holy, Honour, Lectisternium, NOTICE, Recce, Remark, Right, Rite, Ritual, Vising

**Observatory** Atalaya, Lookout, Tower

**Observe(d), Observer** Behold, Bystander, Celebrate, Espy, Eye, Heed, Keep, Mark, NB, Note, Notice, Onlooker, Optic, Regard(er), Remark, Rite, Scry, See, Sight, Spectator, Spial, Spot, Spy, Study, Twig, Witness

**Obsess(ed), Obsession** Besot, Craze, Dominate, Fetish, Fixation, Hang-up, Haunt, Hobbyhorse, Hooked, Idée fixe, Infatuation, Mania, Monomania, Preoccupy, Thing

**Obsolete, Obsolescent** Abandoned, Antique, Archaic, Dated, Dead, Defunct, Disused, Extinct, Obs, Outdated, Outworn

**Obstacle** Barrage, Barrier, Boyg, Chicane, Dam, Drag, Drawback, Handicap, Hindrance, Hitch, Hurdle, Node, Remora, Rock, Snag, Stymie

**Obstetrics** Gynaecology, Midwifery, Tocology, Tokology

**Obstinacy, Obstinate** Asinine, Bullish, Contumacious, Cussed, Dour, Froward, Headstrong, Inflexible, Intransigent, Mule, Persistent, Perverse, Pervicacious, Pig-headed, Recalcitrant, Refractory, Restive, Resty, Self-will, Stiff(-necked), Stubborn, Wilful

**Obstreperous** Noisy, Unruly

**Obstruct(ion)** Bar, Block, Bottleneck, Clog, Crab, Cumber, Dam, Fil(l)ibuster, Hamper, Hedge, Hinder, Hurdle, Ileus, Impede, Let, Obstacle, Snooker, Stap, Stonewall, Stop, Stymie, Sudd, Thwart, Trammel, Trump

**Obtain** Achieve, Acquire, Exist, Gain, Get, Land, Pan, Prevail, Procure, Realise, Secure, Succeed, Win, Wangle

**Obtrude, Obtrusive** Expel, Impose, Loud, Prominent, Push, Sorn, Thrust

**Obtuse** Blunt, Dense, Dull, Stupid, Thick

**Obverse** Complement, Face, Front, Head

**Obviate** Forestall, Preclude, Prevent

**Obvious** Apparent, Axiom, Blatant, Brobdingnag, Clear, Distinct, Evident, Flagrant, Frank, Kenspeck(le), Manifest, Marked, Open(ness), Overt, Palpable, Patent, Pikestaff, Plain, Salient, Transparent, Truism, Visible

**Occasion** Call, Cause, Ceremony, Encheason, Event, Fete, Field day, Nonce, OPPORTUNITY, Reason, Ride, Tide, Time

**Occasional(ly)** Casual, Chance, Daimen, Irregular, Orra, Periodic, Sometimes, Sporadic

**Occident(al)** West, Western(er)

**Occlude, Occlusion** Absorb, Clog, Coronary, Embolism, Obstruct

**Occult(ist)** Angekkok, Arcane, Art, Esoteric, I-ching, Magic, Mysterious

**Occupant, Occupation, Occupy(ing)** Absorb, Activity, Avocation, Business, Busy, Denizen, Embusy, Engage, Engross, Hold, In, Incumbent, Indwell, Inhabitant, Inmate, Involve, Line, Metier, Profession, Pursuit, Resident, Runrig, Squat, Stay, Tenancy, Tenant, Tenure, Thrift, Trade, Upon, Use

**Occur(rence)** Arise, Be, Betide, Betime, Case, Event, Fall, Happen, Incident, Instance, Outcrop, Pass, Phenomenon

**Ocean(ic)** Abundance, Antarctic, Arctic, Atlantic, Blue, Deep, Herring-pond, Indian, Pacific, Pelagic, Sea(way), Waves

**Och aye** Troggs

**Ochre** Keel, Ruddle, Sienna

**Octave** Diapason, Eight, Ottava, Utas

**Octopus** Cephalopod, Polyp, Poulp(e), Scuttle, Squid

**Octoroon** Mestee, Mestizo, Mustee

**Od** Energy, Force

**Odd (person), Oddity** Anomaly, Bizarre, Card, Cure, Curio, Droll, Eccentric, Erratic, Impair, Imparity, Offbeat, Orra, Outré, Parity, Peculiar, Queer, Quiz, Random, Rare, Remote, Rum, Screwball, Singular, STRANGE, Uneven, Unusual, Whims(e)y

> **Odd(s)** may indicate an anagram, or the odd letters in words

**Odd job man** Joey, Orraman, Rouster, Smoot

**Odds** Bits, Chance, Handicap, Line, Price, SP, Tails, Variance

**Ode** Awdl, Dit, Epicede, Epicedium, Epinicion, Epinikion, Genethliacon, Horatian, Hymn, Lyric, Monody, Paeon, Pindaric, Poem, Sapphic, Song, Stasimon, Threnody, Verse

**Odin** One-eyed, Woden

**Odium, Odious** Comparison, Disestimation, Disgrace, Foul, Hatred, Heinous, Invidious, Repugnant, Stigma

**Odorous, Odour** Air, BO, Flavour, Hum, Opopanax, Perfume, Quality, Redolence, Sanctity, Scent, Smell

**Odyssey** Epic, Journey, Wandering

**Oedipus** Complex, Parricide

**Oeillade** Glance, Leer, Ogle, Wink

**Oestrogen, Oestrus** Frenzy, Heat, Must, Rut, Stilb(o)estrol

**Of (me)** About, Among, Aus, By, De, From, My, Re

> **Of** may indicate an anagram

**Of course** Certainly, Natch, Yes

**Off** Absent, Agee, Ajee, Away, Discount, Distance, Far, From, High, Licence, Odd, Reasty, Reesty, Relache

> **Off** may indicate an anagram

**Offal** Cagmag, Carrion, Chitterling, Entrails, Gralloch, Gurry, Ha(r)slet, Heart, Innards, Kidney, Lights, Liver

**Off-beat** Zoppo

**Off-colour** Pale, Seedy, Wan

> **Off-colour** may indicate an anagram

**Offence** Attack, Crime, Delict, Distaste, Fault, Huff, Hurt, Lapse, Miff, Misprision, Outrage, Peccadillo, Pip, Pique, Piracy, Regrate, Sedition, SIN, Trespass, Umbrage

**Offend(ed), Offender** Affront, Anger, Annoy, Bridles, Culprit, Disoblige, Displease, Distaste, Hip, Huff, Hurt, Hyp, Infringe, Inveigh, Miffy, Miscreant, Nettle, Nonce, Nuisance, Provoke, Sin(ner), Stray, Violate, Wrongdoer

**Offensive** Affront, Aggressive, Alien, Attack, Bombardment, Campaign, Cruel, Embracery, Foul, Hedgehog, Hedgepig, Indelicate, Miasmic, Nasty, Noisome, Obnoxious, Obscene, Peccant, Personal, Push, Putrid, Rank, Repugnant, RUDE, Scandalous, Scurrilous, Sortie, Storm, Ugly, Unbecoming

**Offer(ing)** Alms, Altarage, Anaphora, Bid, Bode, Corban, Dolly, Epanophora, Extend, Gift, Hold, Inferiae, Oblation, Overture, Peddle, Present, PROPOSAL, Propose, Propound, Sacrifice, Shewbread, Shore, S(h)raddha, Submit, Stand, Tender, Volunteer, Votive

**Offhand** Airy, Banana, Brusque, Casual, Cavalier, Curt, Extempore, Impromptu, Indifferent

**Office(s)** Agency, Bedelship, Branch, Broo, Bureau, Buroo, Chair, Complin(e), Daftar, Dataria, Dead-letter, Evensong, Function, Holy, Job, Lats, Mayoralty, Ministry, Missa, Mudiria, Mutessarifat, Mistery, Mystery, Nocturn, Nones, Place, Plum, Portfolio, Position, Post, Prime, Provosty, Registry, Rite, See, Seraskierate, Sinecure, Situation, Tenebrae, Terce, Tierce, Tribunate, Vespers, Yamen

**Officer(s)** Acater, Adjutant, Admiral, Ag(h)a, Agistor, Aide, Apparitor, Beatty, Bimbashi, Blimp, Bombardier, Bos(u)n, Brass-hat, Brigadier,

Capt(ain), Catchpole, Catchpoll, Cater, Centurion, Chamberlain, Chancellor, CIGS, Colonel, Commander, Commodore, Constable, Cop(per), Cornet, Coroner, Counter-round, Cursitor, Datary, Decurion, Ensign, Equerry, Exciseman, Exon, Filacer, Filazer, Flying, Gallant, Gen(eral), GOC, Group, Gunner, Hayward, Hetman, Ima(u)m, Intendant, Jamadar, Janty, Jauntie, Jaunty, Jemadar, Jemidar, Jonty, Jurat, Lictor, Lt, Marshal, Mate, NCO, Oxon, PO, Posse, Provost, Purser, Pursuivant, Remembrancer, Samurai, Sbirro, Schout, Second mate, Sexton, Sewer, Sheriff, Skipper, SL, Speaker, Striper, Sub(altern), Tahsildar, Tindal, Tipstaff, Treasurer, Tribune, Usher, Varlet, Warden, Wardroom, Warrant

**Official(s), Officious** Agent, Amban, Amtman, Atabeg, Atabek, Attaché, Authorised, Beadle, Bossy, Bureaucrat, Catchpole, Censor, Chinovnik, Claviger, Commissar, Consul, Ealdorman, Ephor, Equerry, Executive, FORMAL, Hayward, Jobsworth, Keeper, Landdrost, Lictor, Mandarin, Marplot, Marshal, Mayor, MC, Meddlesome, Mirza, Mueddin, Nazir, Notary, Ombudsman, Polemarch, Poohbah, Postmaster, Pragmatic, Proctor, Procurator, Prog, Proveditor, Staff, Steward, Suffete, Syndic, Valid, Veep, Whiffler

**Off-putting** Dehortative, Discouraging, Manana, Procrastination, Repellent

**Offset** Balance, Cancel, Compensate, Counter(act), Counterbalance

**Offshoot** Bough, Branch, Limb, Lye, Member, Outgrowth, Plant, Scion, Sien, Swarm

**Offspring** Boy, Chick, Children, Daughter, Descendant, Family, Fry, Get, Girl, Heir, Product, Seed, Sient, Son, Spawn

**Offstage** Wings

**Often** Frequent, Habitual, Repeated

> **Often** may indicate 'of ten'

**Ogee** Cyma, Moulding, Talon

**Ogle** Eliad, Eye, Glance, Leer, Oeillade

**Ogre(ss)** Baba yaga, Boyg, Brute, Eten, Etten, Fiend, Giant, Monster, Orc

**Ohio** Buckeye

**Oil(y), Oil producer** Aj(o)wan, Aleuritis, Anoint, Apiezon, Argan, Attar, Balm, Beech-mast, Benne, Benni, Bergamot, BP, Bribe, Brilliantine, Cajeput, Cajuput, Camphire, Camphor, Carapa, Carron, Castor, Chaulmoogra, Chaulmugra, Cohune, Colza, Copra, Cotton-seed, Creasote, Creosote, Croton, Cruse, Diesel, Dittany, Elaeis, Essence, Eucalyptus, Eugenol, Fixed, Fusel, Gingelli, Gingelly, Gingili, Golomynka, Guttiferae, Jojoba, Kerosene, Kerosine, Lavender, Linseed, Lipid, Lubricant, Lumbang, Macassar, Magilp, Megilp, Midnight, Mirbane, Moringa, Myrbane, Myrrhol, Naphtha, Neat's-foot, Neem, Neroli, Nim, Oint, Oiticica, Olea, Olive, Ottar, Otto, Paraffin, Parathion, Picamar, Pomade, Poon, Pristane, Pulza, Pyrrole, Ramtil, Rape, Retinol, Ricinus, Safrole, Sassafras, Savin, Sleek, Slick, Slum, Smalmy, Smarmy, Smeary, Sperm, Spikenard, Star-anise, Sunflower, Tallow, Tolu, Train, Tung, Turpentine, Ulyie, Ulzie, Unction, Wintergreen, Yolk

**Oilcake**  Poonac

**Oilcan**  Pourie

**Oilcloth**  American, Lino

**Oilman**  Driller, Prospector, Rigger, Texan

**Oil painting**  Master, Titian

**Ointment**  Balm, Basilicon, Boracic, Boric, Cerate, Cream, Nard, Pomade, Pomatum, Salve, Spikenard, Unguent

**OK**  Agree(d), Approve, Authorise, Clearance, Copacetic, Copesettic, Hunky-dory, Initial, Right(o), Sanction, Sound, U, Vet

**Old(er)**  Ae(t), Aged, Aine(e), Ancient, Antique, Auld, Bean, Decrepit, Dutch, Fogram, Former, Gaffer, Geriatric, Glory, Gray, Grey, Hills, Hoary, Methusaleh, Moore, Nestor, Nick, O, OAP, Obsolete, Off, One-time, Outworn, Palae-, Passé, Primeval, Rugose, Sen(escent), Senile, Senior, Stale, Trite, Venerable, Veteran, Victorian(a)

**Old boy, Old girl**  Alumnae, Alumnus, OB

**Old days**  Once, Past, Yore

**Old English**  OE

**Old-fashioned**  Aging, Ancient, Antediluvian, Arch(aic), Arriere, Bygone, Corn(y), Dated, Dowdy, Medieval, No tech, Obsolete, Ogygian, Passé, Primeval, Quaint, Retro, Rinky-dink, Shot, Square, Steam, Traditional, Uncool, Worm-eaten

**Old maid**  Biddy, Spinster

**Old man, Old woman**  Anile, Aunty, Burd, Cailleach, Faggot, Fantad, Fantod, Fogey, Fussy, Gammer, Geezer, Grannam, Greybeard, Husband, Kangaroo, Luckie, Lucky, Methuselah, Mzee, OAP, Oom, Presbyte, Trout, Wife, Wrinkly

**Old-timer**  Hourglass, Sundial, Veteran

**Olid**  Fetid, Foul, High, Rancid, Rank

**Olio**  Hash, Medley, Mess, Potpourri, Stew

**Olive (grove), Olivine**  Drupe, Dunite, Gethsemane, Olea(ster), Peridot

**Oliver**  Cromwell, Goldsmith, Hardy, Noll, Protector, Twist

**Olympian, Olympus**  Asgard, Athlete, Celestial, Elis, Pantheon, Quadrennium, Zeus

**Omelette**  Crepe, Foo yong, Foo yung, Fu yung, Pancake

**Omen**  Abodement, Absit, Augury, Auspice, Foreboding, Forewarning, Freet, Freit, Portent, Presage, Prodrome, Sign, Token, Warning

**Omentum**  Caul, Epiploon

**Ominous**  Alarming, Baleful, Bodeful, Dour, Forbidding, Grim, Oracular, Sinister, Threatening

**Omission, Omit**  Apocope, Apospory, Apostrophe, Caret, Disregard, Drop, Elide, Ellipse, Ellipsis, Failure, Miss, Neglect, Nonfeasance, Oversight, Paral(e)ipomenon, Senza, Skip

**Omnibus**   Anthology, Coach, Collection

**Omniscient**   Encyclopedia

**Omnivorous**   Pantophagous

**On (it)**   Agreed, An, An't, At, Atop, By, Game, Leg, O', Of, Over, Pon, Re, Tipsy, Up(on)

> **On**   may indicate an anagram

> **On board**   may indicate chess, draughts, or 'SS' around another word

**Once(r)**   Ance, AT ONCE, Bradbury, Earst, Erst(while), Ever, Ex, Fore, Former, Jadis, Oner, Onst, Secular, Sole, Sometime, Whilom

**One(self)**   A, Ace, Ae, Alike, An(e), Any, Body, Ego, Ein, Individual, Integer, Me, Monad, Per se, Single(ton), Singular, Solo, Tane, Un, United, Unit(y), Yin, You

**One-act-er**   Playlet

**One-eared**   Monaural

**One-eyed**   Arimasp(ian), Cyclops

**One-man band**   Moke

**One o'clock**   1 am, NNE

**One-rayed**   Monact

**Onerous**   Arduous, Exacting, Tedious, Weighty

**Onion(s)**   Bengi, Bonce, Bulb, Chibol, Chive, Cibol, Cive, Eschalot, Head, Ingan, Leek, Moly, Ramp, Rocambole, Ropes, Scallion, Shal(l)ot, Sybo(e), Sybow

**Onlooker**   Bystander, Kibitzer, Rubberneck, Spectator, Witness

**Only**   Allenarly, Anerly, But, Except, Just, Merely, Nobbut, Seul, Singly, Sole

**Onset**   Affret, Attack, Beginning, Charge, Dash, Rush, START, Thrust

**Onslaught**   Attack, Dead-set, Onset, Raid, Spreagh, Storm

**On time**   Pat, Prompt, Punctual

**Onus**   Burden, Charge, DUTY, Responsibility

**Onward**   Advance, Ahead, Away, Forth, Forward, Progress

**Oodles**   Heaps, Lashings, Lots, Slather

**Oolite**   Roestone

**Oomph**   Energy, It, SA, Verve

**Ooze**   Drip, Exhale, Exude, Gleet, Mud, Percolate, Pteropod(a), Seep, Sew, Sipe, Slob, Slime, Spew, Spue, Sweat, Sype, Transude

**Opal(escent)**   Cymophanous, Gem, Girasol, Hyalite, Hydrophane, Potch

**Opaque, Opacity**   Dense, Dull, Leucoma, Obscure, Obtuse, Onycha, Thick

**Open(er), Opening**   Adit, Ajar, Antithesis, Anus, Apert(ure), Apparent, Apse, Bald, Bare, Bole, Breach, Break, Broach, Buttonhole, Candid, Cavity, Champaign, Chasm, Circumscissile, Clear, Crevasse, Dehisce,

Deploy, Dispark, Door, Dup, Embrasure, Eyelet, Fair, Fenestra, Fissure, Fistula, Flue, Fontanel(le), Foramen, Frank, Free, Gambit, Gap, Gaping, Gat, Gate, Give, Glasnost, Guichet, Hatch, Hiatus, HOLE, Inaugural, Intro, Key, Lacy, Lead, Loid, Loophole, Loose, Manhole, Meatus, Micropyle, Mofette, Mouth, Oillet, Ostiole, Ostium, Overture, Patent, Peephole, Pert, Pervious, Pick(lock), Placket, Pore, Port(age), Porthole, Preliminary, Premiere, Prise, Pro-am, Public, Pylorus, Receptive, Rent, Riva, Room, Scye, Sesame, Sicilian, Sincere, Slit, Spirant, Start, Stenopaic, Storna, Thereout, Trapdoor, Trema, Trou, Truthful, Unbar, Uncork, Undo, Unhasp, Unlatch, Unscrew, Untie, Vent, Vulnerable

**Open air** Alfresco, Sub divo, Sub jove

**Opera** Aida, Ariadne, Bouffe, Burletta, Comic, Ernani, Fidelio, Glyndebourne, Grand, Hansel and Gretel, Idomineo, Iolanthe, Lohengrin, Lulu, Met, Musical, Norma, Oberon, Onegin, Orfeo, Otello, Parsifal, Patience, Pinafore, Ruddigore, Savoy, Scala, Singspiel, Soap, Tell, The Met, Tosca, Turandot, Work, Zarzuela

**Opera-glasses** Jumelle

**Opera-lover** Wagnerite

**Opera-singer** Baritone, Bass, Contralto, Diva, Savoyard, Soprano

**Operate, Operation, Operative** Act(ion), Activate, Actuate, Agent, Artisan, Attuition, Campaign, Caesarean, Conduct, Current, Detective, Exercise, Function, Hobday, Keystroke, Mechanic, Overlord, Practice, Run, Sortie, Strabotomy, Ure, Valid, Work

**Operator** Agent, Conductor, Dealer, Manipulator, Sparks, Surgeon

**Opiate, Opium** Dope, Drug, Hop, Laudanum, Meconin, Narcotic, Religion, Soporific, Thebaine

**Opinion, Opinionative** Attitude, Belief, Bet, Consensus, Cri, Dictum, Dogma, Doxy, Entêté, Esteem, Feeling, Guess, Judgement, Mind, Say, Sense, Sentence, Sentiment, Tenet, Utterance, View, Voice, Vox pop

**Opossum** Lie, Marmose, Phalanger, Tarsipes, Yapo(c)k

**Oppidan** Cit, Townsman, Urban

**Opponent(s)** Adversary, Antagonist, Anti, E-N, Enemy, E-S, Foe, Gainsayer, N-E, N-W, S-E, S-W, W-N, W-S

**Opportune, Opportunist, Opportunity** Appropriate, Apropos, Break, CHANCE, Day, Facility, Favourable, Go-go, Occasion, Opening, Pat, Room, Seal, Seel, Sele, Snatcher, Tide, Timely, Timous, Window

**Oppose(d), Opposing, Opposite, Opposition** Against, Agin, Anti, Antipathy, Antipodes, Antiscian, Antithesis, Antithetic, Antonym, Argue, At, Averse, Battle, Black, Breast, Combat, Confront, Contradict, Contrary, Converse, Counter, Diametric, E contrario, Face, Foreanent, Fornen(s)t, Hinder, Hostile, Impugn, Inimical, Inverse, Militate, Noes, Object, Polar, Reaction, Repugn, Resist, Reverse, Rival, Shadow, Subtend, Teeth, Thereagainst, Thwart, Traverse, Toto caelo, V, Versus, Vis-a-vis, Withstand

**Oppress(ive)** Bind, Burden, Crush, Despotic, Incubus, Onerous, Overpower, Persecute, Ride, Sultry, Tyrannise

**Opprobrium**  Disgrace, Envy, Odium, Scandal

**Oppugn**  Attack, Criticise

**Opt, Option(al)**  Alternative, CHOICE, Choose, Elect, Fine, Menu, Pick, Plump, Select, Voluntary, Votive, Wale

**Optical**  Lens, Prism, Reticle, Visual

**Optimism, Optimist(ic)**  Chiliast, Expectant, Hopeful, Morale, Pangloss, Polyanna, Rosy, Sanguine, Upbeat, Utopiast

**Opulent**  Abundant, Affluent, Moneyed, Rich, Wealthy

**Opus**  Piece, Study, Work

**Or**  Au, Either, Ere, Gold, Ossia, Otherwise, Sol

**Oracle(s), Oracular**  Delphi, Dodonian, Mirror, Prophet, Pythian, Sage, Seer, Sibyl(line), Thummim, Urim, Vatic

**Oral**  Acroamatic, Sonant, Spoken, Verbal, Viva, Vocal

**Orange**  An(n)atta, Annatto, Arnotto, Aurora, Bergamot, Bigarade, Chica, Clockwork, Croceate, Flame, Flamingo, Jaffa, Kamala, Kamela, Kamila, Karaka, Mandarin, Naartje, Nacarat, Nartjie, Navel, Pig, Roucou, Ruta, Satsuma, Seville, Shaddock, Tangerine, Tenné, Ugli

**Orang-utan**  Ape, Monkey, Satyr

**Orate, Oration**  Address, Eloge, Elogium, Elogy, Eulogy, Harangue, Panegyric, Speech

**Oratorio, Orator(y)**  Boanerges, Brompton, Brougham, Cantata, Cicero, Creation, Demosthenes, Diction, Elijah, Hwyl, Isocrates, Morin, Nestor, Prevaricator, Proseucha, Proseuche, Rhetor, Spellbinder, Stump, Tub-thumper, Windbag, Yarra-banker

**Orb**  Ball, Eyeball, Firmament, Globe, Mound, Sphere

**Orbit**  Circuit, Eccentric, Ellipse, Path, Revolution

**Orcadian**  Hoy

**Orchard**  Arbour, Grove, Holt

**Orchestra(te), Orchestration**  Ensemble, Gamelan, Hallé, LSO, Ripieno, Score, Symphony

**Orchid**  Arethusa, Calanthe, Calypso, Cattleya, Cymbidium, Disa, Epidendrum, Lady's slipper, Oncidium, Salep, Snakemouth, Twayblade, Vanda, Vanilla

**Ord**  Beginning, Point

**Ordain**  Arrange, Command, Decree, Destine, Enact, Induct, Japan

**Ordeal**  Corsned, Disaster, Preeve, Test, TRIAL

**Order(ed), Orderly, Orders**  Acoemeti, Adjust, Alphabetical, Apollonian, Apple-pie, Arrange, Array, Attendant, Attic, Avast, Bade, Bath, Batman, Battalia, Bed, Behest, Benedictine, Bespoke, Bid, Book, Canon, Category, Caveat, CB, Chaprassi, Charter, Cheque, Chuprassy, Class, Command(ment), Committal, Composite, Corinthian, Cosmos, Decorum, Decree, Demand, Diktat, Direct(ion), Directive, Dispone, Dominican,

Doric, DSO, Edict, Enjoin, Establishment, Eutaxy, Feldsher, Fiat, Firman, Form(ation), Franciscan, Fraternity, Garter, Ginkgo, Habeas corpus, Heast(e), Hecht, Hest, Holy, Indent, Injunction, Ionic, Irade, Kilter, Kosmos, Language, Mandate, Marshal, Masonic, Medjidie, Merit, Methodical, Monastic, Monitor, Neatness, Nunnery, OBE, Official, OM, Orange, Ord, Ordain, Organic, Postal, Precedence, Premonstrant, Prescribe, Pyragyrite, Rank, Règle, Regular, Right, Rule, Ruly, Series, Settle, Shipshape, Standing, State, Subpoena, Supersedere, System, Tabulate, Taxis, Tell, Thistle, Tidy, Trim, Tuscan, Ukase, Uniformity

> **Ordering**   may indicate an anagram

**Ordinal**   Book, Number, Sequence

**Ordinance**   Byelaw, Decree, Edict, Law, Rite, Statute

**Ordinary**   Average, Banal, Canton, Comely, Common (or garden), Commonplace, Cot(t)ise, Everyday, Fess(e), Flanch, Flange, Hackneyed, Mediocre, Mundane, NORMAL, OR, Plain, Prosy, Pub, Saltier, Saltire, Simple, Tressure, Trivial, Usual, Workaday, Your

**Ordnance**   Artillery, Cannon, Guns, Supply

**Ordure**   Cess, Dung, Fertiliser, Manure

**Ore**   Alga, Babingtonite, Bornite, Calaverite, Coffinite, Coin, Copper, Element, Glance, Haematite, Hedyphane, Ilmenite, Ironstone, Limonite, Mat, Melaconite, Mineral, Niobite, Oligist, Phacolite, Proustite, Pyragyrite, Schlich, Seaweed, Slug, Smaltite, Stephanite, Stilpnosiderite, Stream-tin, Tenorite, Tetrahedrite, Tin, Wad(d)

**Organ(ic), Organs**   Anlage, Apollonicon, Archegonium, Barrel, Calliope, Console, Ctene, Cort's, Ear, Echo, Feeler, Fin, Gill, Glairin, Gonad, Hapteron, Harmonium, Isomere, Kidney, Lien, Liver, Means, Media, Medulla, Melodion, Ministry, Nasal, Natural, Nectary, Newspaper, Oogonia, Palp, Part, Pipe, Pulmones, Pyrophon, Receptor, Recit, Regal, Sang, Saprobe, Spleen, Stamen, Stratocyst, Tentacle, Thymus, Tongue, Tonsil, Viscera, Viscus, Voice, Wurlitzer

**Organise(d), Organisation, Organiser**   Activate, Anatomy, ARRANGE, Association, Brigade, Caucus, Collect, Company, Design, Embody, Fascio, Firm, Impresario, Machine, Mafia, Marshal, Orchestrate, Outfit, Rally, Regiment, Run, Stage, Steward, System, Tidy, UN

> **Organise(d)**   may indicate an anagram

**Organism**   Aerobe, Being, Biont, Biotic, Cell, Ecad, Entity, Euglena, Germ, Halobiont, Halophile, Infusoria, Moneron, Nekton, Neuston, Pathogen, Plankton, Protist, Saprobe, Streptococcus, Symbiont, Torula, Volvox

**Organ-stop**   Bourdon, Clarabella, Diapason, Gamba, Nasard, Principal, Quint, Salicet

**Organ-tuner**   Reed-knife

**Orgy**   Bacchanalia(n), Binge, Carousal, Dionysian, Feast, Revel, Saturnalia, Spree, Wassail

**Orient(al)** Adjust, Annamite, Chinoiserie, Dawn, Dayak, E, East(ern), Fu Manchu, Hindu, Levant, Malay, Mongolian, Shan, Sunrise, Tatar, Thai, Turk(o)man

**Orifice** Aperture, Gap, Hole, Nare, Opening, Pore, Spiracle, Trema, Vent

**Origen's work** Tetrapla

**Origin(al), Originate, Originating** Abo, Adam, Arise, Beginning, Birth, Come, Cradle, Creation, Derive, Elemental, Emanate, Epicentre, Extraction, Etymon, First, Focus, Found, Genesis, Genetical, Grow, Hatch, Incunabula, Innovate, Invent, Master, Mother, Nascence, Natality, New, Novel, Ord, Primal, Primary, Primigenial, Primordial, Pristine, Prototype, Rise, Root, Seminal, Source, Spring, Start, Ur, Zoism

**Oriole** Firebird, Hangbird

**Orison** Blessing, Prayer

**Ormer** Abalone, Haliotis

**Ornament(al), Ornamentation** Acroter(ia), Adorn, Anaglyph, Antefix, Anthemion, Aplustre, Arabesque, Ball-flower, Barbola, Baroque, Barrette, Bead, Bedeck, Billet, Bracelet, Breloque, Broider, Bugle, Bulla, Cartouche, Chase, Clock, Cockade, Crocket, Curin, Decorate, Decoration, Diglyph, Dog's-tooth, Doodad, Embellish, Emblema, Enrich, Epaulet(te), Epergne, Fallal, Figurine, Filagree, Filigrain, Filigree, Fleuret, Fleuron, Florid, Fret, Frill, Furnish, Gadroon, Gaud, Guilloche, Heitiki, Illustrate, Inlay, Knotwork, Lambrequin, Leglet, Mense, Moresque, Motif, Nail-head, Netsuke, Nicknackery, Niello, Okimono, Ovolo, Palmette, Parure, Paua, Pawa, Pectoral, Pendant, Picot, Pipe, Pompom, Pompo(o)n, Pounce, Pralltriller, Prunt, Purfle, Rel(l)ish, Rocaille, Rococo, Tassel, Tettix, Tiki, Tool, Torque, Torsade, Tracery, Trappings, Trimming, Trinket, Triquetra, Wally, Water-leaf, Whigmaleerie, Whigmaleery

**Ornate** Baroque, Churrigueresque, Dressy, Elaborate, Fancy, Florid, Flowery

**Ornithologist** Audubon, Birdman

**Orotund** Bombastic, Grandiose, Pompous, Rhetorical, Sonant

**Orphan** Foundling, Ward

**Orpiment** Arsenic, Zarnich

**Orpington** Buff, Hen

**Ort** Bit, Crumb, Morsel, Remnant

**Orthodox** Cocker, Conventional, Hardshell, Proper, Sound, Standard

**Orthorhombic** Enstatite

**Ortolan** Bird, Bunting, Rail

**Oscar** Award, O, Wilde

**Oscillate** Fluctuate, Librate, Rock, Seiche, Squeg, Swing, Vibrate, Waver

**Osier** Reed, Sallow, Willow

**Osmium** Os

**Osprey** Ossifrage, Pandion

**Osseous** Bony, Hard, Skeletal, Spiny

**Ostensibly** Apparent, External, Seeming

**Ostentation, Ostentatious** Display, Dog, Eclat, Epideictical, Extravagant, Flamboyant, Flash(y), Flaunt, Florid, Flourish, Garish, Gaudy, Parade, Pomp, Pretence, SHOW(y), Side, Splash, Swank, Tacky

**Ostracise, Ostracism** Banish, Blackball, Boycott, Cut, Exclude, Exile, Potsherd, Snub, Taboo

**Ostrich** Em(e)u, Estrich, Estridge, Nandoo, Nandu, Ratite, Rhea, Struthio(nes)

**Othello** Moor, Morisco

**Other(wise), Others** Additional, Aka, Alia, Alias, Allo-, Besides, Different, Distinct, Else, Et al, Etc, Excluding, Former, Further, Rest

**Other things** Alia

> **Otherwise** may indicate an anagram

**Otiose** Idle, Indolent, Ineffective, Lazy, Superfluous

**Otis** Bustard

**Otter** Edal, Tarka

**Otto** Attar, Chypre, Mahratta

**Ottoman** Porte, Turk

**Oubliette** Dungeon, Pit, Prison

**Ouch** Brooch, Ornament, Ow

**Ought** All, Should

**Ouida** Ramee

**Ounce** Cat, Liang, Oz, Panther, Tael, Uncial

**Our(selves)** Us, We

**Oust** Depose, Dislodge, Eject, Evict, Expel, Fire, Supplant, Unnest

**Out** Absent, Aglee, Agley, Aus, Begone, Bowl, Dated, Exposed, External, Forth, Haro, Harrow, Hors, Oust, Skittle, Stump, Uit, Unfashionable, Up, York

> **Out** may indicate an anagram

**Out and out** Absolute, Arrant, Sheer, Stark, Teetotal, Thorough, Totally, Utter

**Outback** Bundu

**Outbreak** Epidemic, Eruption, Explosion, Plague, Putsch, Rash

**Outburst** Access, Blurt, Boutade, Evoe, Explosion, Fit, Flaw, Fusillade, Gush, Gust, Passion, Storm, Tantrum, Tumult, Volley

**Outcast** Cagot, Discard, Exile, Exul, Ishmael, Leper, Mesel, Pariah, Rogue

**Outcome** Aftermath, Consequence, Dénouement, Effect, Emergence, End, Event, RESULT, Sequel, Upshot

**Outcrop** Basset, Blossom, Crag, Inlier, Mesa, Spur

**Outcry** Bray, CLAMOUR, Howl, Hue, Protest, Racket, Steven, Uproar, Utas

**Outdated** Archaic, Dinosaur, Effete, Obsolete, Outmoded, Passé, Square

**Outdo** Beat, Cap, Picnic, Surpass, Top, Trump, Worst

**Outdoor(s)** Alfresco, External, Garden, Plein-air

**Outer** External, Extrogenous, Magpie, Top

**Outfit** Ensemble, Equipage, Fitout, Furnish, Habit, Kit, Rig, Samfoo, Samfu, Suit, Team, Trousseau

**Outflow** Anticyclone, Discharge, Effluence, Eruption, Surge

**Outgoing** Egression, Exiting, Extrovert, Open, Retiring

**Outgrowth** Ala(te), Aril, Bud, Enation, Epiphenomenon, Offshoot, Root-hair, Sequel, Trichome

**Outhouse** Lean to, Privy, Shed, Skilling, Skipper, Stable

**Outing** Excursion, Jaunt, Junket, Picnic, Spin, Spree, Treat, Trip, Wayzgoose

**Outlandish** Barbarous, Bizarre, Exotic, Foreign, Peregrine, Rum

**Outlaw** Attaint, Badman, Ban, Bandit(ti), Banish, Exile, Fugitive, Hereward, Horn, Proscribe, Rob Roy, Ronin

**Outlay** Cost, Expense, Mise

**Outlet** Egress, Estuary, Exit, Femerell, Market, Opening, Outfall, Sluice, Socket, Tuyere, Tweer, Twier, Twire, Twyer(e), Vent

**Outline** Adumbration, Aperçu, Configuration, Contorno, Contour, Delineate, Digest, DRAFT, Footprint, Layout, Note, Perimeter, Plan, Profile, Scenario, Schematic, Shape, Silhouette, Skeletal, Skeleton, Sketch, Summary, Syllabus, Synopsis, T(h)alweg, Trace

**Outlook** Casement, Perspective, Prospect, View, Vista

**Outmoded** Wasm

> **Out of** may indicate an anagram

**Out of date** Corny, Obs, Passé, Scrap, Square, Worn

**Out of form** Amorphous, Awry

**Out of order** Fritz

**Out of sorts** Cachectic, Nohow, Peevish, Poorly

> **Out of sorts** may indicate an anagram

**Out of tune** Discordant, Flat, Scordato, Scordatura

**Outpost** Colony, Picquet

**Outpour(ing)** Effuse, Flood, Flow, Gush, Libation, Stream, Torrent

**Output** Data, Get, Produce, Production, Turnout, Yield

> **Output** may indicate an anagram

**Outrage(ous)** Affront, Atrocity, Desecrate, Disgust, Enormity, Flagrant, Insult, OTT, Sacrilege, Scandal, Ungodly, Violate

> **Outrageously** may indicate an anagram

**Outright** Clean, Complete, Entire, Utter

**Outset** Beginning, Start

**Outshine** Eclipse, Excel, Overshadow, Surpass

**Outside** Ab extra, Crust, Exterior, External, Front, Furth, Hors, Periphery, Rim, Rind, Rine, Surface

**Outsider** Alien, Bounder, Cad, Extern, Extremist, Foreigner, Incomer, Oustiti, Pariah, Stranger, Stumer, Unseeded, Upstart

**Outsize** Capacious, Giant, Gigantic, Huge, OS

**Outskirts** Edge, Fringe, Periphery, Purlieu

**Outspoken** Bluff, Blunt, Broad, Candid, Explicit, Forthright, Frank, Plain, Rabelaisian, Round, Vocal

**Outstanding** Ace, Billowing, Bulge, Chief, Eminent, Especial, First, Fugleman, Highlight, Impasto, Jut, Lulu, Marked, Oner, Owing, Paragon, Prince, Prize, Prominent, Promontory, Prosilient, Proud, Relief, Relievo, Salient, Signal, Squarrose, Star, Strout, Superb, Unpaid, Unsettled

**Outstrip** Best, Cap, Cote, Distance, Exceed, Overtake

**Outward** Efferent, External, Extern(e), Extrinsic, Extrorse, Postliminary, Superficial

**Outwit** Baffle, Best, Circumvent, Dish, Euchre, Fox, Over-reach, THWART, Trick

**Outwork** Demilune, Jetty, Moon, Tenail(le), Tenaillon

**Outworn** Decrepit, Obsolete, Used

**Oval** Cartouche, Ellipse, Henge, Navette, Ooidal

**Ovary** Oophoron

**Ovation** Applause, Cheer

**Oven(-like)** Aga, Calcar, Cul-de-four, Furnace, Haybox, Hornito, Kiln, Lear, Leer, Lehr, Microwave, Muffle, Oast, Oon, Stove

**Over** Above, Across, Again, Atop, C, Clear, Done, Finished, Hexad, Of, On, Ort, Owre, Sopra, Spare, Superior, Surplus, Uber, Yon

**Overact** Burlesque, Emote, Ham, Hell, Hoke

**Overall(s)** Denims, Dungarees, Dust-coat, Fatigues, Smicket, Smock

**Overbearing** Arrogant, Dogmatic, Domineering, Imperious, Insolent, Lordly

**Overbid** Gazump

**Overcast** Cloudy, Lowering, Sew, Sombre

**Overcharge** Clip, Extort, Fleece, Gyp, OC, Rack-rent, Rook, Rush, Soak, Sting

**Overcoat** Benjamin, Dolman, Grego, Inverness, Joseph, Paletot, Pos(h)teen, Raglan, Redingote, Spencer, Tabard, Ulster, Warm, Wrap-rascal

**Overcome** Beat, Bested, Conquer, Convince, Defeat, Kill, Master, Mither,

Prevail, Quell, Speechless, Subjugate, Surmount, Vanquish, Win

**Overcrowd**  Congest, Jam, Pack

**Overdo(ne)**  Exceed, Ham, OTT, Percoct, Tire

**Overdraft**  Red

> **Overdrawn**  may indicate 'red' outside another word

**Overdress(ing)**  Dudism, Flossy, Overall

**Overdue**  Belated, Excessive, Late

**Overeat(ing)**  Gorge, Hypertrophy, Satiate

**Overemphasize**  Rub in, Stress

**Overfeed**  Gorge, Sate, Stuff

**Overflow**  Lip, Nappe, Redound, Spillage, Surfeit, Teem

**Overfull**  Brimming, Hept

**Overgrow(n)**  Ivy'd, Jungle, Ramp(ant), Rhinophyma

**Overhang**  Beetle, Bulge, JUT, Project

**Overhaul**  Bump, Catch, Overtake, Recondition, Revision, Service, Strip

**Overhead(s)**  Above, Aloft, Ceiling, Cost, Hair(s), Headgear, Oncost, Rafter, Upkeep, Zenith

**Overhear**  Catch, Eavesdrop, Tap

**Overjoy**  Elate, Thrill

**Overland**  Portage

**Overlap(ping)**  Correspond, Equitant, Imbricate, Incubous, Tace, Tasse

**Overlay**  Ceil, Smother, Stucco, Superimpose, Veneer

**Overlearned**  Pedantic

**Overload**  Burden, Plaster, Strain, Surcharge, Tax

**Overlook**  Condone, Disregard, Excuse, Forget, Miss, Superintend

**Overlord**  Excess, Invasion

**Overlying**  Incumbent, Jessant, Pressing

**Overmuch**  Excessive, Surplus, Too, Undue

**Overpower(ing)**  Crush, Evince, Mighty, Onerous, Oppress, Overwhelm, Subdue, Surmount

**Overpraise**  Adulate

**Over-refined**  Dainty, Nice, Pernickety, Precious

**Overrule**  Abrogate, Disallow, Veto

**Overrun**  Exceed, Extra, Infest, Inundate, Invade, Swarm, Teem

**Overseas**  Abroad, Outremer

**Oversee(r)**  Baas, Boss, Captain, Care, Deputy, Direct, Eyebrow, Foreman, Handle, Induna, Periscope, Supercargo, Survey(or)

**Oversentimental**  Byronic, Slushy

**Overshadow**  Cloud, Dominate, Eclipse, Obscure

**Overshoe** Arctic, Galosh, Sandal

**Oversight** Blunder, Care, Error, Gaffe, Lapse, Neglect, Parablepsis

**Overstate(ment)** Embroider, Exaggerate, Hyperbole

**Overstrained** Epitonic

**Overt** Manifest, Patent, Plain, Public

**Overtake** Catch, For(e)hent, Lap, Overget, Overhaul, PASS, Supersede

**Overthrow** Dash, Defeat, Demolish, Depose, Down, Ruin, Smite, Stonker, Subvert, Supplant, Vanquish, Whemmle, Whommle, Whummle, Worst

**Overture** Advance, Carnival, Egmont, Hebrides, Leonora, Offer, OPENING, Prelude, Propose, Toccata, Toccatella, Toccatina

**Overturn(ing)** Catastrophe, Quash, Reverse, Tip, Topple, Up(set), Whemmle

**Overvalue** Exaggerate, Salt

**Overweening** Bashaw, Cocky, Excessive, Imperious, Presumptuous

**Overwhelm(ed)** Accablé, Assail, CRUSH, Inundate, KO, Overcome, Scupper, Smother, Submerge, Swamp

**Overwork(ed)** Fag, Hackneyed, Ornament, Slog, Stale, Supererogation, Tax, Tire, Toil

**Overwrought** Frantic, Hysterical, Ore-rested, Ornate

**Ovid** Naso

**Ovum** Egg, Oosphere, Seed

**Owe(d), Owing** Attribute, Due, OD

**Owen** Glendower

**Owl(s)** Barn, Blinker, Boobook, Bunter, Elegant, Glimmergowk, Hooter, Jenny, Longhorn, Madge, Moper, Mopoke, Mopus, Ogle, Ruru, Scops, Snowy, Strich, Striges, Strigiformes

**Own(er), Ownership** Admit, Domain, Have, Hold, Mortmain, Nain, Possess, Proper, Proprietor, Recognise, Use

**Ox(en)** Anoa, Aurochs, Aquinas, Banteng, Banting, Bison, Bonas(s)us, Buffalo, Bugle, Bullock, Cat(t)alo, Fee, Gaur, Gayal, Gyal, Mart, Musk, Neat, Ovibos, Rother, Sapi-utan, S(e)ladang, Steare, Steer, Taurus, Ure, Urus, Yak, Zebu

**Oxford (group)** Buchmanism, OU, Shoe

**Oxhead** Aleph

**Oxidation, Oxide** Alumina, Anatase, Erbium, Eremacausis, Gothite, Holmia, Lithia, Magnesia, Nitrous, Samarskite, Strontia, Zaffer, Zaffre

> **Oxtail** may indicate 'x'

**Oxygen (and lack of)** Anoxia, Lox, Loxygen, O

**Oyer** Hearing, Trial

**Oyster (bed), Oyster-eater** Avicula, Bivalve, Cul(t)ch, Kentish, Lay, Mollusc, Native, Ostrea, Ostreophage, Pandore, Plant, Prairie, Scalp,

Scaup, Seedling, Spat, Spondyl

**Oyster-catcher**  Sea-pie

**Oyster-plant**  Gromwell, Salsify

**Oz**  Amos, Australia

**Ozone**  Air, Atmosphere

# Pp

**P** Papa, Parking, Penny, Piano, Prince

**PA** Aide

**Pabulum** Aliment, Cheer, Food, Fuel, Nourishment

**Pace** Canter, Clip, Cracking, Gait, Lope, Measure, Pari passu, RATE, Spank, Speed, Stroll, Tempo, Tread, Trot

**Pachyderm** Armadillo, Elephant, Hippo, Mastodon, Rhino

**Pacific, Pacify** Appease, Conciliate, Dove, Ease, Lull, Mild, Moderate, Ocean, Placid, Quiet, Serene, Sooth, Subdue, Sweeten, Tranquil

**Pacifist** CO, Conciliator, D(o)ukhobor

**Pack(age), Packed, Packing** Bale, Box, Bundle, Cards, Compress, Congest, Cram, Crate, Crowd, Cry, Deck, Dense, Dunnage, Embox, Entity, Fardel, Floe, Gasket, Gaskin, Hamper, Hunt, Jam, Kennel, Knapsack, Load, Matilda, Pair, PARCEL, Pikau, Rout, Set, Shiralee, Stow, Suits, Tamp, Tread, Troop, Truss, Wad, Wrap

**Packet** Boat, Bundle, Liner, Mailboat, Parcel, Roll, Sachet, Steamboat

**Pack-horse** Sumpter

**Packman** Chapman, Hawker, Hiker, Pedlar, Tinker

**Pact** Agreement, Alliance, Bargain, Bilateral, Cartel, Contract, Covenant, Locarno, TREATY

**Pad(ding)** Bombast, Bustle, Compress, Cushion, Dossil, Enswathe, Expand, Falsies, Hassock, Horse, Leg-guard, Lily, Nag, Numnah, Paw, Ped, Pillow, Pledget, Pouf(fe), Protract, Pulvillus, Stuff, Sunk, Tablet, Thief, Tournure, Tympan, Velour(s), Velure, Wad, Wase

**Paddington** Bear, Station

**Paddle (-foot)** Canoe, Dabble, Oar, Pinniped, Seal, Side-wheel, Spank, Splash, Wade

**Paddock** Field, Frog, Meadow, Park

**Paddy** Fury, Ire, Irishman, Mick, Pat(rick), Pet, Rag, Rage, Tantrum, Temper, Wax

**Padre** Chaplain, Cleric, Father, Monk, Priest

**Paean** Hymn, Ode, Praise, Psalm

**Pagan** Atheist, Gentile, Gentoo, Heathen, Idolater, Infidel, Odinist, Saracen

**Page(s), Pageboy** Bellboy, Bellhop, Bleep, Boy, Buttons, Flyleaf, Folio, Gate-fold, Groom, Haircut, Leaf, Messenger, Moth, P, PP, Ream, Recto, Ro, Servant, Sheet, Side, Squire, Tiger, Varlet, Verso

**Pageant** Cavalcade, Pomp, Spectacle, Tattoo, Triumph

**Pagoda** Temple

**Pah**   Pish, Tush, Umph

> **Paid**   see PAY

**Pail**   Bucket, Kettle, Leglan, Leglen, Leglin, Piggin

**Pain(ful), Pains**   Ache, Aggrieve, Agony, Ake, Angina, Anguish, Arthralgia, Bad, Bitter, Bore, Bot(t), Bother, Cramp, Crick, Distress, Dole, Doleur, Dolour, Dysury, Excruciating, Gip, Grief, Gripe, Gyp, Harrow, Heartburn, HURT, Ill, Kink, Laborious, Mal, Migraine, Misery, Mulligrubs, Myalgia, Neuralgia, Pang, Persuant, Pest, Prick, Pungent, Rack, Raw, Sair, Smart, Sore, Sorrow, Sten(d), Sting, Stitch, Strangury, Stung, Teen(e), Tene, Throe, Torment, Tormina, Torture, Twinge, Wrench, Wring

> **Pain**   may indicate bread (French)

**Painkiller**   Aminobutene, Analgesic, Bute, Cocaine, Enkephalin, Meperidine, Metopon, Morphine, Pethidine

**Painlessness**   Analgesia

**Painstaking**   Assiduous, Careful, Diligent, Elaborate, Exacting, Sedulous, Studious, Thorough

**Paint(ed), Painting**   Abstract, Acrylic, Alla prima, Aquarelle, Art autre, Art deco, Art nouveau, Artificial, Barbizon, Bice, Blottesque, Camaieu, Canvas, Cellulose, Chiaroscuro, Coat, Colour, Cubism, Dadaism, Daub, Decorate, Depict, Distemper, Eggshell, Emulsion, Enamel, Encaustic, Fard, Fauvism, Finery, Flemish, Fresco, Fucus, Genre, Gild, Gouache, Grease, Grisaille, Impasto, Limn, Magilp, Megilp, Miniate, Miniature, Nihonga, Oaker, Ochre, Oil, Oleo(graph), Op art, Orphism, Paysage, Pict, Picture, Pigment, Pinxit, Pointillism(e), Portray, Post-Impressionism, Predella, Primitive, Quadratura, Raddle, Rosemaling, Scumble, Secco, Sfumato, Sien(n)ese, Stencil, Stipple, Tablature, Tachism(e), Tall-oil, Tanka, Tempera, Thangka, Tondo, Ukiyo-e, Umber, Vanitas

**Painted woman**   Courtesan, Harlot, Pict, Tart

**Painter**   Alma-Tadema, Apelles, Appel, Arp, ARTIST, Barbizon, Bellini, Bosch, Botticelli, Braque, Burne-Jones, Canaletto, Carpaccio, Cézanne, Cimabue, Claude, Collier, Colourist, Constable, Corot, Cox, Crome, Cubist, Dadd, Dali, Da Vinci, Deccie, Decorator, Dégas, Delacroix, Die Brucke, Donatello, Durer, Eastlake, El Greco, Ensor, Ernst, Etty, Fauve, Fragonard, Gainsborough, Gauguin, Gilder, Giotto, Goya, Greuze, Guardi, Hals, Haydon, Headfast, Hoare, Hobbema, Hogarth, Holbein, Hooch, Hoppner, Ingres, John, Klee, Kneller, Landseer, Lely, Le Nain, Limner, Lippi, Lotto, Matisse, Michelangelo, Millais, Millet, Miniaturist, Moor, Munch, Murillo, Nattier, Opie, Orpen, Picasso, Plein-airist, Primitive, Prudhon, RA, Raddle, Raeburn, Raphael, Redon, Rembrandt, Renoir, Reynolds, Rivera, Romney, Rousseau, Rubens, Sargent, Seurat, Sickert, Sien(n)ese, Signorelli, Spencer, Steen, Steer, Sternfast, Stubbs, Tiepolo, Tissot, Titian, Turner, Utrillo, Van Dyke, Van Eyck, Van Gogh, Velasquez, Vermeer, Veronese, Watteau, Watts, Whistler, Zeuxian, Zoffany

**Pair**   Brace, Couple(t), Duad, Duo, Dyad(ic), Fellows, Jugate, Link, Match,

Mate, Ocrea, Pigeon, Pr, Span, Tandem, Thummim, Twa(e), Tway, Two, Urim, Yoke

**Paisley** Orange, Shawl

**Pal** Ally, Amigo, Bud(dy), China, Chum, Comrade, Crony, Cully, Mate

**Palace** Alhambra, Basilica, Blenheim, Buckingham, Court, Crystal, Edo, Elysee, Escorial, Escurial, Fontainebleau, Holyrood, Istana, Lambeth, Lateran, Louvre, Mansion, Nonsuch, Palatine, Pitti, Quirinal, Sans Souci, Schloss, Seraglio, Serail, Shushan, Topkapi, Trianon, Tuileries, Valhalla, Vatican, Versailles

**Paladin** Champion, Charlemagne, Defender, Douzeper, Fièrabras, Ganelon, KNIGHT, Ogier, Oliver, Orlando, Rinaldo, Roland

**Palanquin** Doolie, Litter, Palkee, Palki, Sedan

**Palatable, Palate** Dainty, Relish, Roof, Sapid, Savoury, Taste, Toothsome, Uranic, Uraniscus, Velum

**Palatine** Officer

**Palatial** Ornate, Splendid

**Palaver** Chatter, Debate, Parley, Powwow, TALK

**Pale, Paling** Ashen, Blanch, Bleach, Cere, Dim, Etiolate(d), Fade, FAINT, Fence, Haggard, Insipid, Lily (white), Livid, Mealy, Ox-fence, Pastel, Peelie-wally, Picket, Sallow, Shilpit, Stang, Verge, Wan, White

**Paleography** Diplomatics

**Paleolithic** Acheulean, Acheulian, Chellean, Strepyan

**Palestine, Palestinian** Amorite, Gadarene, Israel, Pal, PLO, Samaria

**Palette** Board, Cokuloris

**Palindrome** Sotadic

**Palisade** Barrier, Fence, Fraise, Stacket, Stockade

**Pall** Bore, Cloy, Damper, Glut, Mantle, Satiate, Shroud

**Palladium** Defence, Pd, Safeguard

**Pallas** Athene

**Pallet** Bed, Cot, Couch, Mattress, Tick

**Palliate, Palliative** Alleviate, Ease, Extenuate, Lessen, Mitigate, Reduce, Sedative

**Pallid** Anaemic, Ashen, Insipid, Pale, Wan, Waxy

**Palm** Accolade, Areca, Assai, Atap, Babassu, Buriti, Bussu, Calamus, Carnauba, Carna(h)uba, Chamaerops, Chiqui-chiqui, Coco, Cohune, Conceal, Coquito, Corozo, Corypha, Date (tree), Elaeis, Euterpe, Fob, Foist, Gomuti, Gomuto, Groo-groo, Gru-gru, Hand, Ita, Itching, Jippi-Jappa, Jipyapa, Jupati, Kittul, Laurels, Loof, Looves, Macaw, Macoya, Moriche, Nikau, Nipa, Palmyra, Paxiuba, Pupunha, Raffia, Raphia, Rat(t)an, Sabal, Sago, Talipat, Talipot, Thenar, Toddy, Triumph, Troelie, Troolie, Trooly, Trophy, Vola, Washingtonia, Zatia

**Palmer** Lilli, Pilgrim

**Palmerston** Pam

**Palmistry** Ch(e)irognomy

**Palm-leaf** Frond

**Palpable** Evident, Gross, Manifest, Patent, Plain

**Palpitate** Flutter, Pulsate, Throb, Twitter, Vibrate

**Palsy** Paralysis, Shakes

**Paltry** Bald, Cheap, Mean, Measly, Peanuts, Pelting, Petty, Poor, Puny, Scalled, Sorry, Tin(-pot), Tinny, Trashy, Trifling, Two-bit, Vile, Waff, Whiffet

**Pamper(ed)** Cocker, Coddle, Cosher, Cosset, Cuiter, Feather-bed, Gratify, High-fed, INDULGE, Mollycoddle, Pet, Spoon-fed

**Pamphlet** Brochure, Catalogue, Leaflet, Notice, Sheet, Tract

**Pan** Agree, Auld Hornie, Bainmarie, Basin, Betel(-pepper), Braincase, Chafer, Dent, Dial, Goat-god, Goblet, God, Ice-floe, Ladle, Nature-god, Pancheon, Panchion, Patella, Patina, Peter, Poacher, Prospect, Roast, Search, Skillet, Slate, Spider, Vessel, Wo(c)k, Work

**Panacea** All-heal, Azoth, Catholicon, Cure(-all), Elixir, Ginseng, Remedy, Tutsan

**Panache** Bravura, Crest, Flair, Paz(z)azz, Piz(z)azz, Plume, Pzazz, Show, Talent

**Pancake** Blin(i), Blintz(e), Crêpe, Flam(m), Flapjack, Flaune, Flawn, Fraise, Fritter, Froise, Pikelet, Poppadum, Slapjack, Suzette, Taco, Tortilla, Waffle

**Panda** Bear-cat, Chi-chi, Chitwah

**Pandarus** Go-between

**Pandemonium** Inferno

**Pander** Indulge, Pimp, Procurer, Toady

**Pane** Glass, Light, Panel, Quarrel, Quarry, Sheet

**Panegyric** Eulogy, Laudation, Praise, Tribute

**Panel(ling)** Board, Cartouche, Dashboard, Fa(s)cia, Gore, Inset, Jury, Mandorla, Orb, Screen, Skreen, Stile, Tablet, Valance, Volet, Wainscot

**Pang** Achage, Ache, Qualm, Spasm, Stab, Twinge, Wrench

**Pangolin** Ant-eater, Manis

**Panhandle** W. Virginia

**Panic** Alar(u)m, Amaze, Consternation, Fear, Flap, Fright, Funk, Guinea-grass, Millet, Raggee, Raggy, Ragi, SCARE, Stampede, Stampedo, Stew, Tailspin, TERROR

**Panicle** Thyrse

**Panjandrum** Bashaw

**Pannier** Basket, Cacolet, Corbeil, Dosser, Skip, Whisket

**Panoply** Armour, Array, Pomp

**Panorama** Range, Scenery, Veduta, View, Vista

**Pansy** Gay, Heart's-ease, Kiss-me, Nance, Powder-puff, Queer, Viola

**Pant(s)** Bags, Breeches, Drawers, Flaff, Gasp, Long johns, Pech, Pegh, Puff, Slacks, Throb, Trews, Trousers, Wheeze, Yearn

**Pantaloon** Columbine, Dupe, Pants

**Pantheism** Idolatry, Immanency

**Panther** Bagheera, Cat, Cougar, Jaguar, Leopard, Pink

**Panties** Briefs, Knickers, Scanties, Step-ins, Undies

**Pantomime** Charade, Cheironomy, Dumb-show, Farce, Galanty, Play

**Pantry** Buttery, Closet, Larder, Spence, Stillroom

**Pap** Dug, Mush, Nipple, Teat, Udder

**Papal, Papist** Catholic, Clementine, Concordat, Guelf, Guelph, Pontifical, RC, Roman, Vatican

**Paper(s)** Allonge, Atlas, Baryta, Bond, Broadsheet, Broadside, Bromide, Bumf, Bumph, Cartridge, Chad, Chiyogami, Colombier, Confetti, Cream-laid, Cream-wove, Crepe, Crown, Cutch, Daily, Decorate, Demy, Document, Dossier, Elephant, Emery, Emperor, Essay, Exam, File, Final, Folio, Foolscap, Galley, Gem, Guardian, Hieratica, India, Jesus, Journal, Kent cap, Kraft, Kutch, Laud, Litmus, Manilla, Mirror, News(print), Note, Onion-skin, Page, Papillote, Papyrus. Parchment, Pickwick, Post, Pot(t), Pravda, Press, Print, Quarto, Quire, Rag, Ramee, Rami(e), Ream, Retree, Rhea, Rice, Royal, Saxe, Scent, Scotsman, Sheaf, Sheet, Sugar, Tabloid, Tap(p)a, TES, Thesis, Tiger, Tissue, Torchon, Treatise, Vellum, Voucher, Web, Whatman, Willesden, Wove

**Paperback** Limp(back)

**Papier-mâché** Flong

**Par** Average, Equate, Equivalent, NORMAL, Scratch

**Parable** Allegory, Fable, Proverb

**Parabola** Arc, Curve, Hyperbola

**Parachute, Parachutist** Aigrette, Drogue, Float, Jump, Para, Red Devil, Silk, Skyman, Thistledown

**Parade (ground)** Air, Arcade, Cavalcade, Display, Flaunt, Gala, Identity, Maidan, March-past, Pageantry, Pomp, Promenade, Show

**Paradise** Arcadia, Avalon, Bliss, Eden, Elysium, Garden, Heaven, Lost, Malaguetta, Nirvana, Park, Regained, Shangri-la, Svarga, Swarga, Swerga, UTOPIA

**Paradox(ical)** Absurdity, Contradiction, Dilemma, Gilbertian, Olber's, Puzzle, Zeno's

**Paraffin** Kerosene, Kerosine, Ozocerite, Ozokerite, Photogen(e), Propane

**Paragon** Model, Non(e)such, Pattern, Pearl, Phoenix, Rose

**Paragraph (mark)** Balaam, Note, Passage, Piece, Pilcrow

**Parakeet** Parrot, Popinjay, Rosella

**Parallel**  Analog, Collimate, Corresponding, Equal, Even, Like

**Parallelogram**  Rhomb

**Paralysis, Paralyse**  Apoplexy, Cataplexy, Cramp, Halt, Monoplegia, Numbness, Paraplegia, Paresis, Polio, Scram, Shock, Shut, Stun

**Paramount**  Chief, Dominant, Greatest, Overall, Premier, SUPREME, Topless, Utmost

**Paramour**  Franion, Gallant, Leman, Lover, Mistress, Thais

**Paranormal**  ESP, Spiritual, Telekinesis

**Parapet (space)**  Bartisan, Bartizan, Battlement, Brisure, Bulwark, Crenel, Flèche, Merlon, Rampart, Redan, Surtout, Terreplein, Top, Wall

**Paraphernalia**  Belongings, Equipment, Gear, Trappings

**Parasite, Parasitic**  Ascarid, Biogenous, Bladder-worm, Bonamia, Bot, Coccus, Conk, Copepod, Dodder, Entophyte, Entozoon, Epiphyte, Epizoon, Filarium, Flea, Gregarinida, Hair-eel, Ichneumon, Isopod, Kade, Ked, Lackey, Lamprey, Leech, Licktrencher, Louse, Macdonald, Mallophagous, Mistletoe, Nematode, Nit, Orobanche, Puccinia, Rhipidoptera, Scrounger, Shark, Smut-fungus, Sponge(r), Strepsiptera, Strongyle, Strongyloid, Stylops, Sucker, Symphile, Tapeworm, Tick, Toady, Trencher-friend, Trencher-knight, Trichina, Tryp(anosoma), Vampire, Viscum

**Parasol**  Awning, Brolly, En tout cas, Sunshade, Umbrella

**Parcel**  Allot, Aret, Bale, Bundle, Holding, Lot, Package, Packet, Sort, Wrap

**Parch(ed)**  Arid, Bake, Dry, Graddan, Roast, Scorched, Sere, Thirsty, Torrid

**Parchment**  Diploma, Forel, Mezuzah, Papyrus, Pell, Pergameneous, Roll, Roule, Scroll, Sheepskin, Vellum

**Pard**  Leopard, Pal, Partner

**Pardon(able)**  Absolve, Amnesty, Assoil, Clear, Condone, Eh, Excuse, FORGIVE, Grace, Mercy, Release, Remission, Remit, Reprieve, Venial, What

**Pare**  Flaught, Flay, Peel, Shave, Skive, Sliver, Strip, Whittle

**Parent(al)**  Ancestral, Father, Forebear, Genitor, Maternal, Mother, Paternal, Storge

**Parenthesis**  Aside, Brackets, Innuendo

**Pariah**  Ishmael, Leper, Outcast, Pi(e)dog, Pyedog

**Paris(ian), Parisienne**  Abductor, Athene, Elle, Gai, Gay, Grisette, Lutetian, Maillotin, Midinette, Trojan

**Parish**  District, Flock, Kirkto(w)n, Parochin(e), Parischan(e), Parishen, Peculiar, Province, Title

**Parity**  Smithsonian

**Park(ing)**  Battery, Common, Enclosure, Everglades, Garage, Green, Grounds, Hyde, Lung, Mansfield, Mungo, Osterley, P, Phoenix, Pitch, Prater, Preserve, Rec, Sanctuary, Sandown, Serengeti, Snowdonia, Stop, Yellowstone, Yosemite

**Parker** Dorothy, Nos(e)y

**Parkleaves** Tutsan

**Parley** Confer, Discourse, Palaver, Speak, Tret

**Parliament** Addled, Althing, Barebones, Black, Boule, Bundestag, Commons, Congress, Cortes, Council, Cross-bench, Dail, Diet, D(o)uma, Drunken, Eduskunta, Folketing, House, Knesset, Lack-learning, Lagt(h)ing, Landst(h)ing, Lawless, Legislature, Lok Sabha, Long, Lords, Majlis, Merciless, Mongrel, Odelsting, Rajya Sabha, Reichstag, Riksdag, Rump, Sanhedrin, Seanad, Sejm, Short, St Stephens, States-general, Stirthing, Stormont, Stort(h)ing, Thing, Tynwald, Unlearned, Useless, Volkskammer, Westminster

**Parliamentarian** Cabinet, Fairfax, Ireton, Leveller, Member, MP, Roundhead

**Parlour** Lounge, Salon, Snug

**Parnassus** Museum, Verse

**Parody** Burlesque, Lampoon, Mock, Satire, Skit, Spoof, Travesty

**Parole** Pledge, Promise, Trust, Word

**Paronychia** Agnail, Felon, Whitlow

**Paroxysm** Fit, Rapture, Spasm, Throe

**Parricide** Cenci

**Parrot** Amazon, Cockatoo, Conure, Copy, Flint, Green leek, Imitate, Kaka(po), Kea, Lory, Macaw, Mimic, Nestor, Parakeet, Paroquet, Poll(y), Popinjay, Quarrion, Repeat, Rosella, Rote, Stri(n)gops, T(o)uraco

**Parrot-bill** Glory-pea

**Parry** Block, Counter, Defend, Dodge, Forestall, Riposte, Sixte, Tac-au-tac, Thwart, Ward

**Parsimonious, Parsimony** Cheese-paring, Mean, Narrow, Near(ness), Niggardly, Stingy, Tight

**Parsley** Apiol, Kecks, Kex

**Parsnip** Buttered, Buttery, Dill, Masterwort, Sium, Skirret

**Parson** Clergyman, Cleric, Minister, Non-juror, Pastor, Priest, Rector, Rev, Sky-pilot, Soul-curer, Yorick

**Part(ing)** Aliquot, Antimere, Area, Aught, Bulk, Bye, Cameo, Character, Component, Constituent, Crack, Cue, Dislink, Diverge, Dole, Element, Episode, Escapement, Farewell, Fascicle, Fork, Fraction, Goodbye, Half, Instalment, Lathe, Lead, Leave, Leg, Lill, Lilt, Lines, Member, Parcel, PIECE, Portion, Pt, Quota, Rape, Ratio, Rive, Role, Scena, Scene, Secondo, Section, Sector, Segment, Separate, Sever, Shade, Share, Shed, Sleave, Sle(i)ded, SOME, Spare, Split, Stator, Sunder, Tithe, Unit, Vaunt, Wrench

**Partake** Eat, Participate, Share

**Parthogenesis** Thelytoky

**Partial(ity), Partially** Biased, Ex-parte, Fan, Favour, Halflins, Incomplete, One-sided, Predilection, Slightly, Unequal, Weakness

**Participate** Engage, Join, Partake, Share

**Particle(s)** Anion, Antineutron, Antiproton, Atom, Baryon, Bit, Boson, Curn, Deuteron, Effluvium, Fermion, Fragment, Gluon, Grain, Graviton, Hadron, Hyperon, Ion, Jot, Kaon, Lepton, Meson, Mite, Molecule, Muon, Neutrino, Neutron, Positron, Proton, Quark, Smithereen, Speck, Subatom, Tachyon, Tardyon, Thermion, Virion, Whit, WIMP

**Parti-coloured** Fancy, Motley, Piebald, Pied, Variegated

**Particular** Choosy, Dainty, DETAIL, Endemic, Especial, Essential, Express, Fiky, Fog, Fussy, Item, Itself, London fog, Nice, Niffy-naffy, Pea-souper, Peculiar, Point, Prim, Proper, RESPECT, Special, Specific, Stickler, Stripe

**Partisan** Adherent, Axe, Biased, Carlist, Champion, Devotee, Factional, Fan, Irregular, Partial, Provo, Sider, Spear, Supporter, Yorkist

**Partition** Abjoint, Bail, Barrier, Bretasche, Bulkhead, Cloison, Diaphragm, Dissepiment, Division, Hallan, Parpane, Parpen(d), Parpent, Parpoint, Perpend, Perpent, Replum, SCREEN, Scriene, Septum, Tabula, Wall, With

**Partlet** Hen, Overlaid

**Partner(ship)** Accomplice, Ally, Associate, Cahoot(s), Coachfellow, Colleague, Comrade, Consort, Dutch, Escort, E-W, Firm, Gigolo, Mate, N-S, Pal, Pard, Sparring, Spouse, Stand, Symbiosis

> **Part of** may indicate a hidden word

**Partridge** Bird, Chuka, Chuker, Chik(h)or, Covey, Quail, Tinamou, Ynambu

**Party** Alliance, Apparat, Assembly, At-home, Band, Bash, Beano, Bee, Bloc, Body, Bottle, Bunfight, Bust, Camp, Carousal, Caucus, Celebration, Clambake, Commando, Communist, Conservative, Contingent, Cookie-shine, Coterie, Cult, Democratic, Detail, Ding, Discotheque, Do, Drum, Faction, Falange, Fest, Fine Gael, Green, Guelf, Guelph, Hen, High heels, Hoedown, Hooley, Hoot(a)nannie, Hoot(a)nanny, Hootenannie, Hootenanny, Hurricane, Irredentist, Junket, Junto, Kettledrum, Knees-up, Kuomintang, L, Labour, Lib, Liberal, Low heels, Neck-tie, Octobrist, Opposition, Person, Plaid, Rave, Reception, Revel, Republican, Ridotto, Rocking, Rout, SDP, Sect, Set, Shindig, Shine, Shivoo, Shower, Side, Smoker, SNP, Soc(ialist), Social, Soiree, Spree, Squad(rone), Stag, Symposium, Thrash, Tory, Treat, Ultramontane, Unionist, Whig, Wingding

**Party-piece** Solo

**Parvenu** Arriviste, Upstart

**Pascal** Blaise, Pressure

**Pash** Crush, Devotion

**Pasha** Achmed, Emir, Ismet

**Pass(ed), Passing, Pass on, Past** Ago, Agon, Approve, Arise, Before, Behind, Beyond, Botte, Brenner, Brief, By, Bygone, Chal(l)an, Chine, Chit(ty), Clear, Col, Cote, Cursory, Defile, Delate, Demise, Diadron, Die, Disappear, Double, Elapse, End, Ensue, Ephemeral, Exceed, Exeat, Foist,

Forby, Forgone, Former, Gap, Gate, Gha(u)t, Glide, Go, Gulch, Halse,
Hand, Happen, Hause, Impart, Impermanent, In transit, Jark, Khyber,
Kloof, Lap, Lead, Mesmerism, Migrate, Nek, Notch, Nutmeg, Nye, Occur,
Oer, OK, Omit, Overhaul, Overshoot, Overslaugh, Overtake, Pa, Palm,
Participle, Perish, Permeate, Permit, Poll, Poort, Preterit(e), Proceed,
Propagate, Pun(c)to, Qualify, Reach, Refer, Relay, Retroactive, Retrospect,
Roncesvalles, St Bernard, Sanitation, Scissors, Serve, Shipka, Simplon,
Since, Skim, Skip, Skirt, Slap, Sling, Spend, State, Thermopylae, Through,
Ticket, Tip, Transient, Transilient, Transitory, Transmit, Travel, Triptyque,
Troop, Veronica, Vet, Visa, Visé, Wayleave, While, Wrynose, Yesterday,
Yesteryear, Ygoe

**Passable** Adequate, Fair, Navigable, Tolerable

**Passage** Adit, Aisle, Alley(way), Alure, Arcade, Archway, Arterial,
Atresia, Cadenza, Caponier(e) Career, Channel, Citation, Clause, Close,
Coda, Corridor, Creep, Crossing, Crush, Cundy, Deambulatory, Defile,
Drift, Duct, Eel-fare, Episode, Excerpt, Extract, Fare, Fat, Fistula, Flat,
Flight, Flue, Gallery, Gangway, Gap, Gat, Gate, Ginnel, Gut, Hall, Head,
Inlet, Kyle, Lane, Lapse, Larynx, Loan, Lobby, Locus, Meatus, Melisma,
Movement, Northeast, Northwest, Para(graph), Path, Pend, Pericope,
Phrase, Pore, Portion, Prelude, Prose, Ride, Rite, Ritornell(o), Route,
Sailing, Slap, Slype, Sprue, Strait, Stretta, Stretto, Subway, Thirl,
Thoroughfare, Tour, Trachea, Trance, Transe, Transit(ion), Travel, Tunnel,
Undercast, Unseen, Ureter, Voyage, Way

> **Passage of arms** may indicate 'sleeve'

**Passé** Dated, Ex, Obsolete

**Passenger** Cad, Commuter, Fare, Pillion, Steerage, Traveller, Voyager,
Wayfarer

**Passion(ate)** Anger, Appetite, Ardour, Fervour, Fire, Frampold, Fury,
Gust, Heat, Hot, Hunger, Ileac, Iliac, Intense, Ire, Irish, Kama, Love, Lust,
Mania, Obsession, Oestrus, Rage, Stormy, Torrid, Violent, Warm, Wax,
Wrath, Yen

**Passion-fruit** Water-lemon

**Passive (stage)** Apathetic, Dormant, Inert, Patient, Pupa, Supine, Yielding

**Pass out** Faint, Graduate, Swoon

**Passover** Agadah, Haggada, Omer, Pesach

**Passport** Access, Clearance, Congé(e), Key, Nansen, Navicert, Visa

**Password** Code, Countersign, Nayword, Parole, Sesame, Shibboleth,
Tessera, Watchword

**Pasta** Cannelloni, Conchiglie, Durum, Fedelini, Fettuc(c)ine, Fusilli,
Lasagna, Lasagne, Linguini, Manicotti, Macaroni, Noodles, Ravioli,
Rigatoni, Spaghetti, Tagliarini, Tagliatelle, Tortellini, Vermicelli, Ziti

**Paste, Pasty** Ashen, Batter, Beat, Botargo, Boulc, Bridic, Ccrate, Clobber,
Cornish, Dough, Fake, Filler, Glue, Knish, Magma, Marzipan, Miso, Pale,
Pallid, Pâté, Patty, Pearl-essence, Pie, Poonac, Punch, Rhinestone, Slip,
Slurry, Spread, Strass, Tahina, Tahini, Tapenade, Wan

**Pastern**  Hobble, Knee, Tether

**Pastiche**  Cento, Collage, Medley, Patchwork, Potpourri

**Pastille**  Jujube, Lozenge

**Pastime**  Diversion, Game, Hobby, Recreation, Seesaw, Sport

**Past master**  Champion, Expert, Historian, Pro

**Past midnight**  1 am

**Pastor(al)**  Arcadia, Bucolic, Curé, Eclogue, Endymion, Idyl(l), Minister, Priest, Rector, Rural, Shepherd, Simple

**Pastry**  Apfelstrudel, Baclava, Baklava, Calzone, Croustade, Cruller, Crust, Danish, Dariole, Dough, Eclair, Feuilleté, Filo, Flan, Gougere, Pie, Phyllo, Pirog, Piroshki, Pirozhki, Profiterole, Puff, Quiche, Rug(g)elach, Samosa, Strudel, Tart, Vol-au-vent

**Pasture**  Alp, Eadish, Eddish, Feed, Fell, Fodder, Grassland, Graze, Herbage, Kar(r)oo, Lair, Lare, Lea, Lease, Leasow(e), Leaze, Ley, Machair, Mead(ow), Pannage, Potrero, Raik, Rake, Soum, Sowm, Tie, Transhume, Tye

**Pat**  Apt, Bog-trotter, Butter, Dab, Glib, Lump, Print, Prompt, Rap, Slap, Tap

**Patch(y)**  Bed, Bit, Cabbage, Clout, Cobble, Cooper, Court plaster, Cover, Friar, Fudge, MEND, Mosaic, Pasty, Piebald, Piece, Plaster, Pot, Solder, Tingle, Tinker, Vamp

**Patchwork**  Cento, Miscellany, Mosaic

**Pate**  Crown, Paste, Rillettes, Terrine

**Patent(ed)**  Breveté, Copyright, Evident, Licence, License, Obvious, Overt, Plain, Rolls

**Pater**  Father, Walter

**Paterfamilias**  Coarb, Master

**Path(way)**  Aisle, Allée, Alley, Arc, Boreen, Borstal(l), Bridle, Causeway, Causey, Course, Gate, Ginnel, Lane, Ley, Locus, Orbit, Pad, Parabola, Primrose, Route, Runway, Sidewalk, Spurway, Stie, Sty(e), Track, Trail, Trod, WAY

**Pathan**  Pakhto, Pakhtu, Pashto, Pashtu, Pushto(o), Pushtu

**Pathetic**  Forlorn, Piteous, Poignant, Sad, Touching

**Pathfinder**  Compass, Explorer, Guide, Pioneer, Scout

**Pathological**  Diseased, Morbid, Septic

**Pathos**  Bathos, Pity, Sadness, Sob-stuff

**Patience**  Calm, Endurance, Forbearance, Fortitude, Monument, Solitaire, Stoicism, Virtue

**Patient**  Calm, Case, Clinic, Forbearing, Grisel(da), Grisilda, Invalid, Job, Passive, Subject

**Patois**  Argot, Cant, Dialect, Jargon, Lingo, Scouse

**Patriarch**  Aaron, Abuna, Catholicos, Elder, Isaac, Levi, Maron, Methuselah, Nestor, Noah, Pope, Simeon, Venerable

**Patrician** Aristocrat, Noble, Senator

**Patrick** Mick, Paddy, Pat, Spens

**Patrimony** Ancestry, Estate, Heritage

**Patriot(ic), Patriotism** Cavour, Chauvinist, DAR, Emmet, Flamingant, Garibaldi, Hereward, Jingoism, Loyalist, Maquis, Nationalist, Tell

**Patrol** Armilla, Guard, Picket, Piquet, Prowl-car, Scout, Sentinel

**Patron(age), Patronise(d), Patronising** Advowson, Aegis, Auspices, Benefactor, Business, Champion, Client, Customer, Donator, Egis, Fautor, Maecenas, Nepotic, Protégé, Provider, Shopper, SPONSOR

**Patsy** Hendren, Scapegoat, Stooge

**Patter** Backchat, Cant, Jargon, Lingo, Mag, Rap, S(c)htick, Schtik, Spiel

**Pattern(ed)** Argyle, Blueprint, Check, Clock, Design, Diaper, Dog's tooth, Draft, Epitome, Example, Exemplar, Format, Gestalt, Herringbone, Intarsia, Matel(l)asse, Matrix, Meander, MODEL, Mosaic, Norm, Paisley, Paradigm, Paragon, Pinstripe, Plan, Precedent, Prototype, Stencil, Syndrome, Tangram, Template, Tessella, Tessera, Tracery, Tread, Type, Willow

**Patty** Bouché, Pie

**Paul** Jones, Oom, Pry, Revere, Robeson, S, St

**Pauline** Day-boy, Perils

**Paunch** Belly, Corporation, Gut, Kite, Kyte, Pod, Rumen, Tripe, Tum

**Pauper** Bankrupt, Beggar, Have-not, Mendicant, Penniless

**Pause** Break, Breather, Caesura, Cesura, Comma, Desist, Er, Fermata, Hesitate, Interval, Limma, Lull, RESPITE, Rest, Selah, Stop

**Pavement, Paving** Causeway, Clint, Path, Roadside, Set(t), Sidewalk, Trottoir

**Pavilion** Gazebo, Kiosk, Marquee, Tent

**Paw** Maul, Mitt, Pad, Pat, Pud, Pug

**Pawky** Dry, Humorous, Shrewd, Sly

**Pawn(shop)** Agent, Betel, Chessman, Counter, Derby, Dip, Gage, Gallery, Hock, Hostage, Leaving-shop, Lumber, Mont-de-piété, Monti di pieta, Pan, Peacock, Piece, Pignerate, Pignorate, Pledge, Pop, Siri, Spout, Tiddleywink, Tool, Wadset, Weed

**Pawnbroker, Pawnee** Hockshop, Lumber, Moneylender, Nunky, Uncle, Usurer

**Pax** Peace, Truce

**Pay(master), Payment, Paid, Pay out** Advertise, Annat, Annuity, Ante, Arles, Basic, Batta, Blench, Bonus, Buckshee, Bukshi, Cashier, Cens, Commute, Compensate, Consideration, Damage, Defray, Disburse, Discharge, Dividend, Dub, Emolument, Endow, Escot, Farm, Fee, Finance, Foot, Fork out, Fund, Gale, Gate, Give, Grassum, Grave, Han(d)sel, Hire, Hoot(oo), HP, Imburse, Meet, Metayage, Mise, Modus, Overtime, Pension, Pittance, Pony, Prebendal, Premium, Primage, Pro, Pro forma, Purser,

Quit(-rent), Ransom, Refund, Remuneration, Rent, Requite, Respects, Royalty, Salary, Satisfaction, Scot, Screw, Scutage, Settle, Shell, Sink, Sold(e), Soul-scat, Soul-scot, SPEND, Square, Stipend, Stump, Sub, Subscribe, Table, Tar, Tender, Token, Tommy, Treasure, Treat, Tribute, Truck, Usance, Veer, Wage, Wardcorn

**Pea** Carling, Chickling, D(h)al, Dholl, Garbanzo, Legume, Mangetout, Marrowfat, Pulse, Rounceval

**Peace(ful), Peace-keeper, Peace organisation, Peace symbol** Ahimsa, Calm, Frith, Halcyon, Interceder, Irenic(on), Lee, Lull, Nirvana, Olive, Pacific, Pax, Quiet, Repose, Rest, Salem, Serene, Sh, Shalom, Siesta, Still, Tranquil, Truce, UN

**Peacemaker** ACAS, Arbitrator, Conciliator, Mediator, Trouble-shooter

**Peach** Blab, Cling, Dish, Dob, Freestone, Inform, Malakatoone, Melocoto(o)n, Nectarine, Oner, Quandang, Shop, Sneak, Split, Squeak, Stunner, Tattle, Tell, Victorine

**Peachum** Polly

**Peacock** Coxcomb, Dandy, Fop, Junonian, Muster, Paiock(e), Pajock(e), Payock(e), Pavo(ne), Pawn, Pown, Sashay

**Peak(y)** Acme, Alp, Apex, Ben, Comble, Crag, Crest, Darien, Drawn, Eiger, Gable, Matterhorn, Mons, MOUNTAIN, Nib, Optimum, Pale, Pin, Pinnacle, Rainier, Sallow, Snowdon, Spire, Top, Tor, Zenith

**Peal** Carillon, Chime, Clap, Toll, Triple

**Peanut(e)** Arnut, Chickenfeed, Goober, Groundnut, Monkey-nut

**Pear** Aguacate, Alligator, Anchovy, Avocado, Bergamot, Beurré, Blanquet, Catherine, Carmelite, Colmar, Conference, Cuisse-madame, Jargonelle, Nelis, Perry, Poperin, Poppering, Poprin, Pyrus, Queez-maddam, Seckel, Warden, William

**Pearl(s), Pearly** Barocco, Barock, Baroque, Gem, Jewel, Margaric, Nacrous, Olivet, Orient, Prize, Rope, String, Unio(n)

**Pear-shaped** Obconic, Pyriform

**Peasant** Bonhomme, Boor, Bumpkin, Chouan, Churl, Clodhopper, Contadino, Cottar, Cott(i)er, Fellah(s), Fellahin, Hick, Jungli, Kern(e), Kisan, Kulak, M(o)ujik, Muzhik, Raiyat, Rustic, Ryot, Swain, Tyrolean, Whiteboy, Yokel

**Peat** Moss-litter, Sod, Turbary, Turf, Yarfa, Yarpha

**Pebble(s), Pebbly** Banket, Calculus, Cobblestone, Dreikanter, Gallet, Gooley, Gravel, Psephism, Pumie, Pumy, Scree, Shingle

**Peccadillo** Mischief, Misdemeanour, Offence

**Peck** Bill, Bushel, Dab, Forpet, Forpit, Gregory, Kiss, Lip, Lippie, Nibble, Tap

**Pecksniff** Charity

**Peculiar(ity)** Appropriate, Characteristic, Distinct, Eccentric, Especial, Exclusive, Funny, Idiosyncratic, Kink, Kooky, Odd, Own, Proper, Queer,

Quirk, SPECIAL, Specific, Strange, Unusual

> **Peculiar**   may indicate an anagram

**Pedagogue**   Academic, B.Ed, Teacher

**Pedal**   Bike, Cycle, Lever, P, Rat-trap, Treadle, Treddle

**Pedal-coupler**   Tirasse

**Pedant(ic)**   Dogmatic, Intellectual, Lucubrate, Pedagogue, Pompous, Precisian, Quibbler, Scholastic, Sesquipedalian

**Peddle, Pedlar**   Bodger, Boxwallah, Chapman, Cheapjack, Colporteur, Drummer, Duffer, Hawk, Huckster, Jagger, Packman, Pedder, Pether, Sell, Smouch, Smouse(r), Sutler, Tink(er), Yagger

> **Peddling**   may indicate an anagram

**Pedestal**   Acroter(ion), Dado, Pillar, Support

**Pedestrian**   Banal, Commonplace, Dull, Hike, Itinerant, Trite, Mundane, Walker

**Pedigree(s)**   Ancestry, Blood, Breeding, Descent, Lineage, Phylogeny, Stirp, Stemma(ta), Thoroughbred

**Pediment**   Fronton

**Peduncle**   Scape, Stalk

**Peek**   Eye, Glance, Glimpse, Peep

**Peel(er)**   Bark, Bobby, Candied, Decorticate, Flype, Pare, PC, Rind, Rine, Scale, Shell, Skin, STRIP, Tirr, Zest

> **Peeled**   may indicate outside letter(s) to be removed from a word

**Peep(er)**   Cheep, Cook, Glance, Gledge, Keek, Kook, Lamp, Nose, Peek, Pink, Pry, Squeak, Squint, Spy, Stime, Styme, Voyeur

**Peer(age), Peers**   Archduke, Aristocrat, Backwoodsman, Baron(et), Burke, Coeval, Daimio, Doucepere, Douzeper(s), Duke, Earl, Egal, Elevation, Equal, Gynt, Lord, Noble, Paladin, Peregal, Pink, Rank, Scry, Squint, Stime, Styme, Toot, Tweer, Twire

**Peerless**   Matchless, Nonpareil, Supreme

**Peevish(ness)**   Capernoited, Captious, Crabby, Cross, Doddy, Frabbit, Frampal, Frampold, Franzy, Fretful, Lienal, Moody, Nattered, Petulant, Pindling, Protervity, Shirty, Sour, Teachie, Te(t)chy, Testy

**Peewit**   Lapwing, Peewee

**Peg**   Cheville, Cleat, Cotter-pin, Die, Fix, Freeze, Knag, Leg, Margaret, Nail, Nog, Pin, Piton, Snort, Spigot, Spile, Stengah, Stinger, Support, Tap, Tee, Thole, Thowel, Tot, Woffington

**Pegboard**   Solitaire

**Pelagic**   Deep-sea, Marine, Oceanic

**Pelf**   Lucre, Mammon, Money, Notes, Riches

**Pelican**   Alcatras, Bird, Crossing, Golden Hind, LA, Louisiana, Steganopode

**Pellagra** Maidism

**Pellet** Bolus, Buckshot, Bullet, Pill, Prill, Slug

**Pelt** Assail, Clod, Fleece, Fur, Hail, Hide, Hie, Lam, Pepper, Random, Shower, Skin, Squail, Stone

**Peltast** Soldier, Targeteer

**Pen** Ballpoint, Bic (tdmk), Biro, Cage, Calamus, Confine, Coop, Corral, Crawl, Cru(i)ve, Cub, Enclosure, Fank, Farm, Fold, Hen, Hoosegow, J, JAIL, Keddah, Kraal, Lair, Mew, Mure, Piggery, Pound, Quill, Ree, Reed, Ring, Scribe, Stell, Stie, Stir, Sty(e), Stylet, Stylo, Stylus, Swan, Tank, Write

> **Pen** may indicate a writer

**Penal(ize)** Cost, Fine, Gate, Handicap, Huff, Punitive, Servitude

**Penalty** Abye, Amende, Cost, Eric, Fine, Forfeit, Han(d)sel, Pain, Price, Punishment, Sanction, Wide

**Penance** Atonement, Shrift

**Pence** D, P, Peter's

**Penchant** Predilection

**Pencil** Beam, Ca(l)m, Charcoal, Chinagraph, Crayon, Caum, Draft, Draw, Fusain, Keelivine, Keelyvine, Outline

**Pendant** Albert, Chandelier, Drop, Girandole, Laval(l)ière, Necklace, Poffle

**Pending** Imminent, Unresolved, Until

**Pendragon** Uther

**Pendulous, Pendulum** Dewlap, Metronome, Noddy, One-way, Swing, Wavering

**Penetrate, Penetration** Acumen, Acuminate, Bite, Bore, Cut, Enpierce, Enter, Imbue, Impale, Incisive, Indent, Indepth, Insight, Into, Lance, Permeate, Pierce, Probe, Sagacious, Touch, Thrust

**Penguin** Aeroplane, Anana, Auk, Emperor, Gentoo, Korora, Macaroni, Rock-hopper

**Peninsula** Alte, Antarctic, Arm, Balkan, Bataan, Cape, Chersonese, Crimea, Deccan, Eyre, Florida, Gaspé, Gower, Iberia, Istria, Kola, Kowloon, Labrador, Neck, Palmer, Peloponnese, Promontory, Scandanavia, Sinai, Spit, Spur, Wirral, Yorke, Yucatan

**Penis** Archie, Cor(e)y, Dick, Dildo(e), Dipstick, Dong, Ferret, Giggle(stick), Horn, Jack, John Thomas, Knob, Mojo, Pecker, Percy, Phallus, Pillicock, Pintle, Pizzle, Plonker, Prick, Rod, Roger, Shaft, Tonk, Tool, W(h)ang, Willie, Willy, Winkle, Yard, Zeppelin

**Penitent(iary)** Calaboose, Clink, Contrite, Gaol, Jail, Jug, Prison, Repenter, Stir

**Pennant, Pennon** Banner, Bunting, Fane, Flag, Guinon, Streamer

**Penniless** Bankrupt, Boracic, Broke, Bust, Poor, Skint, Strapped

**Penny** Bean, Cartwheel, Cent, Copper, D, Dreadful, P, Sen, Sou, Sterling, Stiver, Win(n), Wing

**Pension(er)** Allowance, Ann(at), Board, Chelsea, Cod, Cor(r)ody, Gratuity, Payment, Retire, Stipend

**Pensive** Dreamy, Moody, Musing, Thoughtful, Triste

**Pentateuch** T(h)orah

**Pentecost** Whit(sun)

**Penthouse** Cat, Lean-to, Roof

**Peon** Peasant, Serf, Slave, Ticca

**Peony** Moutan

**People** Body, Chosen, Commons, Demos, Ecology, Enchorial, Folk, Guild, Human, Kin, Land, Lapith, Lay, Man(kind), Men, Nair, Nation(s), Nayar, One, Personalities, Phalange, Populace, Public, Race, Settle, Society, Souls, Tribe

**Pep** Buck, Dash, Enliven, Gism, Go, Jism, Jissom, Stamina, Verve, Vim

**Pepper** All-spice, Ava, Capsicum, Cayenne, Chilli, Condiment, Cubeb, Devil, Dittander, Dittany, Jalapeno, Kava, Malaguetta, Matico, Pelt, Pim(i)ento, Piper, Riddle, Spice, Sprinkle, Tabasco

**Per** By, Each, Through

**Perambulate, Perambulator** Buggy, Expatiate, Pedestrian, Pram, Stroller, Wagon, Walker

**Perceive** Apprehend, Descry, Discern, Divine, Feel, Intuit, Notice, Observe, Remark, SEE, Sense

**Percentage** Agio, Commission, Contango, Cut, Proportion, Royalty, Share, Vigorish

**Perception, Perceptive** Acumen, Albert, Anschauung, Clairvoyance, Clear-eyed, Cryptaesthetic, ESP, Insight, Intelligence, Intuition, Pan(a)esthesia, Sensitive, Sentience, Shrewd, Tact, Taste

**Perch** Alight, Anabis, Bass, Comber, Eyrie, Fish, Fogash, Gaper, Lug, Perca, Pole, Roost, Ruff(e), Seat, Serranid, SIT

**Percolate, Percolation** Filter, Infiltrate, Leach, Ooze, Osmosis, Permeate, Seep, Soak, Strain

**Percussion (cap)** Amorce, Idiophone, Impact, Knee, Knock, Thump

**Perdition** Ades, Hades

**Peremptory** Absolute, Decisive, Haughty, Imperative, Imperious

**Perennial** Continual, Enduring, Flower, Livelong, Perpetual, Recurrent

**Perfect, Perfection(ist)** Absolute, Accomplish, Accurate, Acme, Bloom, Complete, Consummation, Dead, Develop, Finish, Flawless, Fulfil, Full, Holy, Ideal(ist), Intact, It, Mint, Par, Paragon, Past, Peace, Pedant, Practice, Pure, Refine, Soma, Sound, Spot-on, Stainless, Sublime, Thorough, Unblemished, Unqualified, Utopian, Utter, Whole, Witeless

**Perfidy** Betrayal, Falsehood, Treachery, Treason

**Perforate(d), Perforation, Perforator** Cribrate, Cribrose, Drill, Eyelet, Hole, PIERCE, Prick, Punch, Puncture, Riddle, Trephine, Trocar

**Perforce** Necessarily, Needs

**Perform(ed), Performer, Performing** Achieve, Act(or), Artist(e), Basoche, Busk, Do, Enact, Entertainer, Execute, Exert, Exhibit, Fulfil, Function, Geek, Hand, Implement, Make, Moke, On, Player, Recite, Render, Ripieno, Throw, Virtuoso

**Performance** Accomplishment, Achievement, Act, Bravura, Broadcast, Deed, Demonstration, Discharge, Entracte, Execution, Gas, Gig, Hierurgy, Matinee, Operation, Perpetration, Recital, Rendering, Rendition, Rigmarole, Scene, Show, Solo, Stunt, Turn

**Perfume (box)** Aroma, Attar, Cassolette, Civet, Cologne, Fragrance, Frangipani, Incense, Ionone, Lavender, Linalool, Myrrh, Opopanax, Orris, Patchouli, Patchouly, Pomander, Potpourri, Redolence, SCENT, Terpineol

**Perfunctory** Apathetic, Careless, Cursory, Indifferent

**Perhaps** A(i)blins, Haply, Happen, May(be), Peradventure, Percase, Perchance, Possibly, Relative, Say, Yibbles

> **Perhaps** may indicate an anagram

**Perigee** Apsis, Epigeum

**Peril** DANGER, Hazard, Jeopardy, Risk, Threat

**Perimeter** Boundary, Circuit, Circumference, Limits

**Period** AD, Age, Aurignacian, Azilian, Chukka, Chukker, Curse, Cycle, Day, Dot, DURATION, Eocene, Epoch, Floruit, Full-stop, Kalpa, Lesson, Limit, Mesolithic, Miocene, Neolithic, Olde-worlde, Oligocene, Paleolithic, Phoenix, Pleistocene, Pliocene, Rent, Season, Session, Span, Spell, Stage, Stop, Term, Trecento, Triassic, Trimester, Usance

**Periodic(al)** Catamenia, Comic, Digest, Economist, Etesian, Journal, Liassic, Listener, Mag, New Yorker, Organ, Paper, Phase, Publication, Punch, Rambler, Regency, Review, Solutrean, Solutian, Spectator, Strand, Stretch, Tatler, Tract

**Peripatetic** Gadabout, Itinerant, Promenader, Travelling

**Periphery** Ambit, Bounds, Fringe, Outskirts, Surface

**Periscope** Eye(-stalk)

**Perish(able), Perished, Perishing** Brittle, DIE, End, Ephemeral, Expire, Fade, Forfair, Fungibles, Icy, Tine, Tint, Transitory, Tyne, Vanish

**Periwinkle** Apocynum, Blue, Myrtle

**Perjure(d)** Forswear, Lie, Mansworn

**Perk(s), Perky** Brighten, Chipper, Freshen, Jaunty, LV, Perquisite

**Perm(anent)** Abiding, Durable, Eternal, Everlasting, Fixed, Full-time, LASTING, Marcel, Stable, Standing, Stative, Wave

**Permeate** Infiltrate, Leaven, Osmosis, Penetrate, Pervade, Seep

**Permission** Congé(e), Copyright, Latitude, Leave, Liberty, Licence, Lief,

Ok(e), Pace, Placet, Power, Pratique, Privilege, Sanction, Way-leave

**Permit** Allow, Authorise, Carnet, Chop, Congé, Enable, Grant, Lacet, Leave, Legal, Let, Licence, License, Nihil obstat, Pass, Placet, Sanction, Stamp-note, Suffer, Triptyque, Visa, Way-leave

**Pernicious** Evil, Harmful, Lethal, Noisome, Pestilent, Wicked

**Pernickety** Fikish, Niggly

**Peroration** Pirlicue, Purlicue

**Peroxide** Bleach, Blonde, Colcothar

**Perpendicular** Aplomb, Apothem, Atrip, Cathetus, Erect, Normal, Plumb, Sheer, Sine, UPRIGHT, Vertical

**Perpetrate** Commit, Effect, Execute

**Perpetual** Constant, Eternal, Incessant, Sempiternal

**Perplex(ed), Perplexity** Anan, Baffle, Bamboozle, Beset, Bewilder, Bother, Buffalo, Cap, Confound, Confuse, Feague, Floor, Flummox, Knotty, Mystify, Nonplus, Out, Puzzle, Stump, Tickle, Tostication

**Perquisite** Ap(p)anage, Emolument, Extra, Gratuity, PERK, Tip

**Perrier** Stoner

**Perry** Mason

**Persecute, Persecution** Afflict, Annoy, Badger, Crucify, Dragon(n)ades, Harass, Haze, Intolerant, Oppress, Ride, Torture

**Persevere, Perseverance** Assiduity, Continue, Fortitude, Insist, Patience, Persist, Plug, Stamina, Steadfastness, Stick, Tenacity

**Persia(n)** Babee, Babi, Bahai, Cyrus, Iran(ian), Mazdean, Mede, Pahlavi, Parasang, Parsee, Pehlevi, Pushtu, Samanid, Sassanid, Sohrab, Xerxes, Zoroaster

**Persimmon** Kaki

**Persist(ence), Persistent** Adhere, Assiduity, Chronic, Continual, Diligent, Doggedness, Endure, Labour, Longeval, Persevere, Press, Sneaking, Stick, Tenacity, Urgent

**Person(s), Personal** Alter, Being, Bird, Bod(y), Chai, Chal, Chi, Cookie, Entity, Figure, Fish, Flesh, Head, Human, Individual, One, Own, Party, Private, Quidam, Selfhood, Soul, Specimen, Tales

**Personage, Personality** Anima, Celeb(rity), Character, Charisma, Dignitary, Ego, Grandee, Identity, Noble, Panjandrum, Presence, Seity, Sel, Self, Sell, Star, Tycoon

**Personified, Personification, Personify** Embody, Incarnate, Prosopop(o)eia, Represent

**Personnel** Employees, Hands, Liveware, Staff

**Perspective** Attitude, Distance, Proportion, View, Vista

**Perspicacious** Astute, Discerning, Keen, Shrewd

**Perspiration, Perspire** Forswatt, Glow, Hidrosis, Sudor, Suint, Sweat, Swelter

**Persuade(d), Persuasion, Persuasive** Cajole, Coax, Cogent, Conviction, Convince, Disarm, Eloquent, Faith, Feel, Geed, Get, Induce, Inveigle, Plausible, PREVAIL, Religion, Truckled, Wheedle

**Pert(ness)** Bold, Cocky, Dicacity, Flippant, Forward, Fresh, Impertinent, Insolent, Jackanapes, Minx, Saucy

**Pertain** Belong, Concern, Relate, Touch

**Pertinacious** Dogged, Obstinate, Persistent, Stickler, Stubborn

**Pertinent** Apropos, Apt, Fit, Germane, Relevant, Timely

**Perturb(ation)** Aerate, Confuse, Dismay, Disturb, Dither, State, Trouble, Upset, Worry

**Peru(vian)** Inca, PE, Quechua(n), Quichua(n)

**Peruse** Examine, Inspect, Read, Scan, STUDY

**Pervade, Pervasion, Pervasive(ness)** Diffuse, Drench, Immanence, Permeate, Saturate

**Perverse, Perversion, Perverted** Aberrant, Abnormal, Awry, Cam(stairy), Camsteary, Camsteerie, Cantankerous, CONTRARY, Corrupt, Cussed, Deviate, Distort, Donsie, False, Gee, Kam(me), Kinky, Licentious, Misuse, Paraphilia, Sadist, Stubborn, Thrawn, Traduce, Unnatural, Untoward, Uranism, Warp(ed), Wayward, Wilful, Wrest, Wry

> **Perverted** may indicate an anagram

**Pessimist(ic)** Alarmist, Cynic, Defeatist, Doubter, Fatalist, Jeremiah, Killjoy, Negative

**Pest(er)** Badger, Blight, Bot, BOTHER, Brat, Breese, Disagreeable, Dim, Fly, Harass, Irritate, Nag, Nudnik, Nuisance, Pize, Plague, Rotter, Scourge, Tease, Terror, Thysanoptera, Vermin, Weevil

**Pesticide** DDT, Derris, Mouser, Synergist, Warfarin

**Pestilence, Pestilent** Curse, Epidemic, Evil, Murrain, Noxious, Pernicious, Plague

**Pet** Aversion, Cade, Canoodle, Caress, Chou, Coax, Cosset, Dandle, Daut(ie), Dawt(ie), Dod, Dort, Ducky, Favourite, Fondle, Glumps, Huff, Hump, Ire, Jarta, Jo, Lallygag, Lapdog, Miff, Mouse, Neck, Pique, Rabbit, Smooch, Snog, Spat, Strunt, Sulk(s), Tantrum, Tiff, Tout, Towt, Umbrage, Yarta

**Petal** Ala, Keels, Labellum

**Petard** Firework, Squib

**Peter** Aumbry, Bell, Dwindle, Grimes, Pan, Quince, Quint, Rabbit, Safe, Simon, Simple, Wane, Weaken

**Petite** Dainty, Mignon, Small

**Petition(er)** Appeal, Beg, Boon, Crave, Entreaty, Orison, Plaintiff, Postulant, Prayer, Representation, Solicit, Sue, Suit(or), Suppli(c)ant, Vesper

**Pet-name** Hypocorisma, Nickname, So(u)briquet

**Petrel** Bird, Nelly, Prion

**Petrify(ing)** Frighten, Lapidescent, Niobe, Numb, Ossify, Scare, Terrify

**Petrol(eum)** Cetane, Diesel, Esso (tdmk), Fuel, Gas, Ligroin, Maz(o)ut, Octane, Olein, Rock-tar

**Petticoat** Balmoral, Basquine, Crinoline, Female, Filabeg, Fil(l)ibeg, Jupon, Kilt, Kirtle, Phil(l)abeg, Phil(l)ibeg, Placket, Sarong, Shift, Underskirt, Wylie-coat

**Pettifogger** Lawmonger

**Petty** Baubling, Bumbledom, Little, Mean, Minor, Narrow, Niggling, One-horse, Picayunish, Pimping, Shoestring, Small, Stingy, Tin, Trivial

**Petulance, Petulant** Fretful, Huff, Moody, Peevish, Perverse, Procacity, Sullen, Toutie

**Pew** Box, Chair, Seat, Stall

**Pewter** Trifle, Tutenag

**Phalanger** Cus-cus, Honey-mouse, Opossum, Petaurist, Possum, Tait, Tuan

**Phalanx** Cohort, Coterie, Legion

**Phallus** Linga(m), Penis, Priapus

**Phantasist, Phantasm** Apparition, Chimera, Spectre, Werewolf

**Phantom** Apparition, Bogey, Bugbear, Eidolon, Idol, Incubus, Maya, Shade, Spectre, Tut, Wraith

**Pharaoh** Amenhotep, Cheops, Egyptian, Rameses, Tut, Tyrant

**Pharisee** Formalist, Humbug, Hypocrite, Nicodemus

**Pharmacist** CHEMIST, Dispenser, MPS, Preparator

**Phase** Cycle, Form, Period, REM, Stage, State, Synchronise

**Pheasant** Argus, Bird, Mona(u)l, Nide, Nye, Tragopan

**Phenol** Orcine, Orcinol, Resorcin, Xylenol

**Phenomenon** Effect, Event, Marvel, Miracle, Mirage, Psi

**Phial** Bologna, Bottle, Flask

**Phil, Philip** Fluter, Macedonia, Pip

**Philander(er)** Flirt, Lothario, Playboy, Toyer, TRIFLE, Wolf, Womaniser

**Philanthropist, Philanthropy** Altruist, Benefactor, Charity, Coram, Donor, Nobel, Rockefeller, Samaritan, Shaftesbury, Tate, Wilberforce

**Philately** Timbromania

**Phileas** Fogg

> **Philip** see PHIL

**Philippic** Diatribe, Invective, Tirade

**Philippine** Bisayan, Igorot, Moro, Tagalog, Visayan

**Philistine, Philistinism** Artless, Ashdod, Barbarian, Foe, Gath, Gigman, Goliath, Goth, Lowbrow, Podsnappery, Vandal

**Philology**  Linguistics, Semantics, Speechcraft

**Philosopher, Philosophy**  Academist, Activism, Amiel, Anacharsis, Anaximander, Anaximenes, Antiochian, Antiochene, Antisthenes, Apemanthus, Apollonus, Aquinus, Aristippus, Aristotle, Atomist, Attitude, Aver, Averr(h)oism, Avicenna, Ayer, Bacon, Bentham, Bergson, Berkeley, Bosanquet, Callisthenes, Campanella, Cartesian, Chrysippus, Comte, Comtism, Confucius, Cracker-barrel, Croce, Cynic, Cyreniac, Deipnosophist, Democritus, Descartes, Diderot, Diogenes, Eclectic, Eleatic, Emerson, Empedocles, Engels, Epicurus, Erasmus, Erigena, Ethics, Euhemerus, Existentialism, Godwin, Gymnosophist, Harrison, Hegel, Herbart, Hobbes, Hobbism, Holist, Hume, I Ching, Ideology, Kant, Locke, Mach, Malthus, Marcuse, Marxism, Materialism, Megarian, Meng-tse, Menippus, Metaphysician, Mill, Monism, Montesquieu, Neoplatonism, Nietzsche, Nominalist, Occamist, Ockhamist, Old Moore, Opinion, Ortega, Pascal, Plato, Plotinus, Plutarch, Protagoras, Pyrrho, Pythagoras, Renan, Rosminian, Russell, Sage, Sankhya, Sartre, Schelling, Schoolman, Schopenhauer, Seneca, Sensist, Smith, Socrates, Sophist, Spencer, Spinoza, Stoic, Swedenborg, Taine, Taoism, Thales, Thomist, Ultraism, Vedanta, Whitehead, Xenophon, Yoga, Yogi, Zeno

**Philosophic(al)**  Rational, Resigned, Thoughtful, Tranquil

**Philtre**  Aphrodisiac, Charm, Drug, Hippomanes, Potion

**Phlegm(atic)**  Calm, Composed, Pituita(ry), Pituite, Stolid, Unperturbed, Unruffled

**Phloem**  Leptome

**Phobia**  Aversion, Dread, Fear, Thing

**Phoebe, Phoebus**  Apollo, Artemis, Day-star, Deaconess, Moon, Selene, Sol, Sun

**Phoenix**  Fum, Fung, Paragon, Self-begotten

**Phone**  Blower, Call, Cellular, Intercom, Ring

**Phonetic**  Oral, Palaeotype, Spoken, Symbol

> **Phonetically**  may indicate a word sounding like another

**Phon(e)y**  Bogus, Charlatan, Counterfeit, Fake, Impostor, Poseur, SHAM, Specious, Spurious

> **Phony**  may indicate an anagram

**Phosphate**  Monazite, Torbernite, Vivianite, Wavellite

**Phosphor(escent), Phosphorus**  Briming, Foxfire, Luminescent, P, Pyrosome, Sarin, Tabun

**Photo(copy), Photograph(ic), Photo finish**  Ambrotype, Angiogram, Calotype, Close-up, Daguerrotype, Diazo, Duplicate, Enprint, Exposure, Film, Kodak (tdmk), Microdot, Picture, Positive, Print, Resorcin, Shot, Snap, Still, Take, Talbotype, Tintype, Woodburytype, X-ray

**Photographer**  Cameraman, Paparazzo

**Phrase**  Buzzword, Cliché, Comma, Expression, Heroic, Laconism,

Leitmotiv, Phr, Riff, Slogan, Tag, Term

**Phrygian** Midas

**Phthisis** Decay, TB

**Phylactery** Amulet, Talisman, Tephillin

**Phyllopod** Brine-shrimp

**Physic(s)** Cryogenics, Culver's, Cure, Dose, Medicine, Purge, Remedy, Science

**Physical** Bodily, Carnal, Corporal, Material, Tangible

**Physician** Allopath, Doctor, Galen, Hakim, Harvey, Hippocrates, Leech, Linacre, Lister, Medico, Mesmer, Mindererus, Paean, Paracelsus, Practitioner, Quack, Therapist, Time

**Physicist** Ampere, Angstrom, Appleton, Archimedes, Avogadro, Becquerel, Curie, Debye, Einstein, Fermi, Gauss, Geiger, Giorgi, Heaviside, Henry, Lodge, Mach, Marconi, Newton, Ohm, Pauli, Picard, Planck, Popov, Reaumur, Rontgen, Scientist, Stark

**Physiognomist, Physiognomy** Face, Features, Lavater

**Physiologist** Pavlov

**Physiotherapist** Masseur

**Physique** Body, Build, Figure

**Pi, Pious** Devotional, Devout, Fraud, Gallio, Godly, Holy, Mid-Victorian, Sanctimonious, Savoury, Smug, Zaddik

**Pianist** Anda, Hambourg, Hess, Hofmann, Liszt, Pachmann, Padarewski, Vamper, Virtuoso

**Piano** Bechstein, Celesta, Celeste, Cottage, Flugel, Forte, Grand, Honkytonk, Keyboard, Overstrung, P, Softly, Steinway, Stride, Upright

**Piano-maker** Erard

**Picaroon** Brigand, Corsair, Pirate, Rogue

**Piccadilly** Whist

**Pick(er), Picking** Break, Choice, CHOOSE, Cream, Cull, Elite, Flower, Gather, Glean, Hack, Hopper, Mattock, Nap, Nibble, Oakum, Plectrum, Pluck, Plum, Select, Single, Sort, Steal, Strum, Wale

> **Picked** may indicate an anagram

**Picket** Demonstrate, Pale, Palisade, Protester, Stake, Tether, Tie

**Pickings** Harvest, Profits, Scrounging, Spoils

**Pickle(r)** Brine, Cabbage, Caper, Chutney, Corn, Cure, Dill, Eisel, Esile, Gherkin, Girkin, Jam, Marinade, Marinate, Mess, Mull, Olive, Onion, Peculate, Peregrine, Piccalilli, PLIGHT, Scrape, Souse, Vinegar, Wolly

**Picklock** Oustiti, Peterman

**Pick-me-up** Bracer, Drink, Restorer, Reviver, Tonic

**Pickpocket** Adept, Cly-faker, Cutpurse, Dip, Diver, File, Nipper, Wire

**Pick-up** Arrest, Light o'love, Truck, Ute

**Picnic** Alfresco, Clambake, Fun, Outing, Push-over, Spread, Wase-goose, Wayzgoose

**Picture(s)** Anaglyph, Arpillera, Art, Bambocciades, Canvas, Collage, Depict, Describe, Diptych, Drawing, Emblem, Epitome, Etching, Film, Flick, Fresco, Gouache, Graphic, Histogram, Icon, Identikit, Imagery, Inset, Kakemono, Landscape, Likeness, Montage, Motion, Movie, Movy, Myriorama, Oil, Photo, Pin-up, Plate, Portrait, Predella, Prent, Print, Retraitt, Retrate, Shot, Slide, Snapshot, Table(au), Talkie, Transfer, Transparency

**Picturesque** Idyllic, Scenic

**Pidgin** Creole, Fanagalo, Fanakolo

**Pie(s)** Anna, Battalia, Bridie, Chewet, Easy, Flan, Madge, Mess, Pandowdy, Pastry, Pasty, Patty, Pica, Piet, Pirog, Pizza, Pyat, Pyet, Pyot, Quiche, Shepherd's, Squab, Star(ry)-gazy, Tart, Turnover, Tyropitta, Vol-au-vent, Warden

> **Pie** may indicate an anagram

**Piebald** Calico, Dappled, Motley, Pied, Pinto, Skewbald

**Piece(s)** Add, Bit, Blot, Cameo, Cannon, Charm, CHESSMAN, Chip, Chunk, Coin, Component, Concerto, Crumb, Domino, End, Extract, Flitters, Fragment, Frust, Goring, Haet, Hait, Hunk, Item, Join, Mite, Morceau, Morsel, Nip, Off-cut, Ort, Part, Patch, Pawn, Peso, PORTION, Recital, Scliff, Scrap, Section, Shard, Sherd, Skliff, Slice, Sliver, Sou, Speck, Stub, Tait, Tate, Tile, Toccata, Wedge

**Pièce de resistance** Star-turn

**Piecemeal, Piecework** Gradually, Intermittent, Jigsaw, Serial, Tut

**Pie-crust** Coffin, Lid, Pastry

**Pied-à-terre** Nest, Pad

**Pieman** Shepherd

**Pier(s)** Anta, Groyne, Jetty, Jutty, Landing, Mole, Plowman, Quay, Slipway, Swiss roll, Wharf

**Pierce(d), Piercer, Piercing** Accloy, Awl, Dart, Drill, Endart, Gore, Gride, Gryde, Impale, Jag, Keen, Lance, Lancinate, Lobe, Move, Needle, Penetrate, Perforate, Pike, Poignant, Punch, Puncture, Shrill, Skewer, Slap, Sleeper, Spear, Spike, Spit, Stab, Steek, Stiletto, Sting, Thrill(ant)

**Piety** Devotion, Purity, Sanctity

**Piffle** Bilge, Codswallop, Hogwash, Tommy-rot, Twaddle

**Pig(s)** Anthony, Babirusa, Barrow, Bartholomew, Bessemer, Bland, Boar, Doll, Elt, Farrow, Gadarene, Gilt, Glutton, Grice, Grumphie, Gus, Ham, Hog, Ingot, Iron, Kentledge, Kintledge, Lacombe, Landrace, Lingot, Long, Peccary, Pork(er), Runt, Saddleback, Shoat, Shot(e), Shott, Slip, Snowball, Sounder, Sow, Squealer, Suidae, Tamworth, Tayassuid, Tithe, Toe, Yelt

**Pigeon** Archangel, Barb, Bird, Carrier, Culver, Dove, Fantail, Goura, Gull, Homer, Horseman, Jacobin, Kuku, Manumea, Nun, Owl, Passenger, Peristeronic, Pouter, Ringdove, Rock(er), Roller, Ront(e), Ruff, Runt,

Scandaroon, Solitaire, Spot, Squab, Squealer, Stock-dove, Stool, Talkee-talkee, Tippler, Tumbler, Turbit, Wonga-wonga, Zoozoo

**Pigeonhole** Classify, Compartment, File, Postpone, Shelve, Slot, Stereotype

**Pigeon-house** Columbary, Cote, Dovecot(e)

**Pig-food** Mast, Swill

**Pig-iron** Kentledge, Kintledge

**Pigment(ation)** Anthoclore, Anthocyan(in), Argyria, Bister, Bistre, Cappagh-brown, Carotene, Carotin, Chlorophyll, Chrome, Cobalt, Colour, Dye, Etiolin, Gamboge, Haem, Hem(e), Iodopsin, Lamp-black, Lithopone, Madder, Melanin, Naevus, Ochre, Orpiment, Paris-green, Phycoxanthin, Pterin, Quercetin, Realgar, Red lead, Retinene, Rhodopsin, Sepia, Sienna, Sinopia, Smalt, Tapetum, Terre-verte, Tincture, Umber, Verditer, Xanthopterin

**Pigtail** Braid, Cue, Plait, Queue

**Pi-jaw** Cant

**Pike** Assegai, Crag, Dory, Fogash, Garfish, Ged, Gisarme, Glaive, Hie, Holostei, Javelin, Lance, Luce, Partisan, Pickerel, Ravensbill, Scafell, Snoek, Spear, Spontoon, Vouge

> **Pilaster** see PILLAR

**Pile(d), Piles, Piling** Agger, Bing, Bomb, Camp-sheathing, Camp-shedding, Camp-sheeting, Camp-shot, Clamp, Cock, Column, Crowd, Deal, Down, Emerods, Farmers, Fortune, Hair, Heap, Hept, Historic, Hoard, Load, Lot, Marleys, Mass, Nap, Post, Pyre, Reactor, Ream(s), Rouleau, STACK, Starling, Stilt, Trichome, Wealth, Wodge

**Pile-driver** Tup

**Pilfer** Crib, Filch, Finger, Maraud, Miche, Nick, Peculate, Pinch, Plagiarise, Plunder, Purloin, Snitch, STEAL

**Pilgrim(age)** Aske, Childe Harold, Expedition, Hadj(i), Hajj(i), Loreto, Lourdes, Mecca, Palmer, Pardoner, Reeve, Scallop-shell, Shrine, Voyage

**Pill** Ball, Bolus, Capsule, Dex, Doll, Dose, Globule, Lob, Medicine, Peel, Pellet, Placebo, Protoplasmal, Spansule, Tablet, Troche, Trochisk, Upper

**Pillage** Booty, Devastate, Plunder, Ransack, Rapine, Ravage, Razzia, Robbery, Sack, Spoil

**Pillar(ed)** Anta, Apostle, Atlantes, Baluster, Balustrade, Boaz, Canton, Caryatides, Cippus, Columel, Column, Eustyle, Gendarme, Hercules, Herm, Impost, Jachin, Lat, Man, Monolith, Newel, Obelisk, Pedestal, Peristyle, Pier, Post, Respond, Stoop, Telamon, Trumeau

**Pillion** Cushion, Pad, Rear

**Pillory** Cang(ue), Cippus, Crucify, Jougs, Little-ease, Pelt, Satirise, Slam

**Pillow(case)** Bear, Beer, Bere, Bolster, Cod, Cushion, Headrest, Pad

**Pilot** Airman, Aviator, Captain, CONDUCT, Experimental, George, Govern, Guide, Hobbler, Lead, Lodesman, Palinure, Palinurus, Pitt, Prune,

Steer, Test, Tiphys, Trial, Usher

**Pimento** Allspice

**Pimp** Apple-squire, Bludger, Hoon, Mack, Pandarus, Pander, Ponce, Procurer, Solicit, Souteneur

**Pimpernel** Scarlet, Wincopipe, Wink-a-peep

**Pimple, Pimply** Gooseflesh, Grog-blossom, Horripilation, Papula, Plook, Plouk, Pustule, Quat, Rumblossom, Spot, Uredinial, Wen, Whelk

**Pin** Bayonet, Bolt, Brooch, Cotter, Dowel, Drift, Fasten, Fid, Fix, Gudgeon, Hob, Kevel, Needle, Nog, Peg, Pivot, Preen, Rivet, Rolling, Skewer, Skittle, Skiver, Spike, Spindle, Staple, Stump, Thole, Tre(e)nail, U-bolt, Woolder

**Pinafore** Apron, Brat, HMS, Overall, Pinny, Save-all, Tire

**Pince-nez** Nose-nippers

**Pincers** Chela, Claw, Forceps, Forfex, Nipper, Tweezers

**Pinch(ed)** Arrest, Bit, Bone, Chack, Constrict, Cramp, Crisis, Emergency, Gaunt, Misappropriate, Nab, Nick, Nim, Nip, Peculate, Peel, Pilfer, Pocket, Pook(it), Prig, Pugil, Raft, Rob, Scrimp, Scrounge, Skimp, Snabble, Snaffle, Sneak, Sneap, Sneeshing, Snuff, Squeeze, STEAL, Swipe, Tate, Tweak, Twinge

**Pine(s), Pining** Arolla, Bristlecone, Cembra, Cone, Conifer, Droop, Dwine, Earn, Erne, Fret, Hone, Huon, Jack, Kauri, Languish, Languor, Loblolly, Long, Monkey-puzzle, Picea, Pitch, Radiata, Tree, Urman, Waste, Yearn

**Pineapple** Anana, Bomb, Bromelia, Grenade, Pina, Poll, Sorosis, Tillandsia

**Ping** Knock, Whir(r)

**Pinguin** Anana(s)

**Pinion** Fetter, Penne, Pinnoed, Secure, Shackle, Wing

**Pink** Carolina, Castory, Colour, Coral, Dianthus, Emperce, Lake, Lychnis, Oyster, Peak, Perce, Pierce, Pounce, Rose(ate), Scallop, Shrimp, Spigelia, Spit, Stab, Tiny

**Pinnacle** Acme, Apex, Crest, Crown, Height, Summit

**Pinniped** Seal

**Pin-point** Focus, Identify, Isolate, Localise

**Pint** Jar, Log

**Pintail** Duck, Smeath, Smee(th)

**Pin-up** Cheesecake, Star

**Pioneer** Baird, Bandeirante, Blaze, Boone, Emigrant, Explore, Fargo, Fleming, Harbinger, Innovator, Lead, Marconi, Oecist, Pathfinder, Rochdale, Sandgroper, Spearhead, Settler, Trail-blazer, Trekker, Voortrekker, Wells

**> Pious** see PI

**Pip** Ace, Acinus, Blackball, Bleep, Hip, Hump, Phil, Pyrene, Seed

**Pipe, Piper, Pipeline, Piping** Antara, Aulos, Barrel, Blub, Bong, Broseley, Bubble, Call, Calumet, Cheep, Cherrywood, Chibouk, Chibouque, Chillum, Churchwarden, Clay, Conduit, Corncob, Crane, Cutty, Drain, Duct, Dudeen, Ell, Exhaust, Faucet, Fistula, Flue, Flute, Gage, Hod, Hogger, Hooka(h), Hose, Hubble-bubble, Kalian, Kelly, Mains, Manifold, Marsyas, Meerschaum, Mirliton, Montre, Narghile, Nargile(h), Narg(h)il(l)y, Oat(en), Oboe, Pepper, Pibroch, Piccolo, Pied, Pifferaro, Pitch, Poverty, Pule, Qanat, Quill, Ree(d), Rise, Sack-doudling, Sennit, Serpent, Shalm, Shawm, Shrike, Siphon, Skirl, Sluice, Squeak, Stack, Syrinx, Tibia, Tootle, Trachea, Tube, Tubule, Tweet, Uillean, Uptake, Weasand, Whistle

**Pipe-laying** Graft

**Pipit** Bird, Skylark, Titlark

**Pippin** Apple, Orange, Ribston

**Pipsqueak** Nobody

**Piquancy, Piquant** Pungent, Racy, Relish, Salt, Sharp, Spicy, Tangy

**Pique** Dod, Huff, Resentment

**Piracy, Pirate, Piratical** Algerine, Barbarossa, Blackbeard, Boarder, Bootleg, Brigand, Buccaneer, Buccanier, Cateran, Condottier, Conrad, Corsair, Crib, Dampier, Fil(l)ibuster, Flint, Hijack, Hook, Kidd, Lift, Loot, Picaroon, Plagiarise, Plunder, Rakish, Rover, Sallee-man, Sallee-rover, Sea-rat, Sea-robber, Silver, Smee, Steal, Teach, Viking, Water-rat, Water-thief

**Piranha** Caribe, Characinoid, Piraya

**Pistillate** Female

**Pistol** Automatic, Barker, Colt, Dag, Derringer, Gat, GUN, Petronel, Revolver, Rod, Shooter, Starter, Starting, Weapon

**Piston** Plunger, Ram

**Pit** Abyss, Alveolus, Antrum, Cesspool, Chasm, Cloaca, Crater, Den, Depth, Depression, Ensile, Fossa, Fovea, Foxhole, Hell, Hole, Hollow, Inferno, Khud, Match, MINE, Parterre, Pip, Play, Pock, Putamen, Pyrene, Ravine, Silo, Solar plexus, Stone, Sump, Trap, Trou-de-loup

**Pitch** Asphalt, Atilt, Attune, Bitumen, Concert, Crease, Diamond, Dive, Ela, Elect, Encamp, Erect, Establish, Fling, Fork, Ground, Key, Labour, Length, Level, Lurch, Maltha, Neume, Patter, Peck, Pin, Plong(e), Plunge, Pop, Resin, Rock, Ruff(e), Scend, Seel, Send, Shape, Sling, Spiel, Stoit, Tar, Tone, Tonemic, Tonus, Tune, Wicket

**Pitcher(-shaped)** Ascidium, Aryt(a)enoid, Bowler, Cruse, Ewer, Jug, Steen, Urceolus

**Pitchfork** Hurl, Toss

**Pitfall** Danger, Hazard, Trap

**Pith(y)** Ambatch, Aphorism, Apo(ph)thegm, Core, Essence, Gnomic, Hat-plant, Heart, Marrow, Medulla, Nucleus, Rag, Succinct, Terse

**Pithead** Broo, Brow, Minehead

**Pithless**  Thowless

**Pitiless**  Hard, Ruthless

**Piton**  Rurp

**Pitt**  Chatham

**Pity, Piteous**  Ah, Alack, Alas, Commiseration, COMPASSION, Mercy, Pathos, Rue, Ruth(ful), Shame, Sin, Sympathy

**Pivot(al)**  Ax(i)le, Central, Focal, Gooseneck, Gudgeon, Revolve, Rotate, Slue, SWIVEL, Turn, Wheel

**Pixie**  Brownie, Elf, Fairy, Gremlin, Sprite

**Pizza**  Calzone

**Placard**  Affiche, Bill, Playbill, Poster

**Place**  Aim, Allocate, Berth, Bro, Deploy, Deposit, Fix, Habitat, Hither, Identify, Impose, IN PLACE OF, Install, Job, Joint, Lay, Lieu, Locality, Locate, Locus, Pitch, Plat, Plaza, Point, Posit, POSITION, Put, Realm, Region, Scene, Second, Set, Site, Situate, Situation, Spot, Stead, Sted(e), Stedd(e), Town, Vendome

**Placid**  Cool, Easy, Easy-osy, Quiet, Tame, Tranquil

**Plagiarise, Plagiarist**  Copy, Crib, Lift, Pirate, Steal

**Plague (spot)**  Annoy, Bane, Bedevil, Boil, Bubonic, Burden, Curse, Dog, Dun, Goodyear, Harry, Infestation, Locusts, Lues, Murrain, Murren, Murrin, Murrion, Pest, Pox, Scourge, Tease, Token, Torture, Vex

**Plaid**  Maud, Roon, Tartan, Wales

**Plain(s)**  Abraham, Artless, Ascetic, Bald, Bare, Blatant, Broad, Campo, Candid, Carse, Clear, Cook, Downright, Dry, Evident, Explicit, Flat, Girondist, Homely, Homespun, Inornate, Kar(r)oo, Lande, Llano, Lombardy, Lowland, Maidan, Manifest, Marathon, Mare, Monochrome, Nullarbor, Obvious, Olympia, ORDINARY, Outspoken, Overt, Pampa(s), Paramo, Pikestaff, Prairie, Sabkha(h), Sabkhat, Sailing, Savanna(h), Secco, Sharon, Simple, Sodom, Spoken, Steppe, Tundra, Vega, Visible

**Plainsman**  Llanero

**Plainsong**  Ambrosian, Chant

**Plaint(ive)**  Complaint, Dirge, Lagrimoso, Lament, Melancholy, Sad, Whiny

**Plaintiff**  Doe, Impeacher, Litigant, Suer

**Plait**  Braid, Crimp, Frounce, Pigtail, Plica, Queue, Ruche, Sennit, Splice

**Plan(ned), Planner**  Aim, Angle, Architect, Blueprint, Chart, Complot, Contrive, Dart, Deliberate, Design, Desyne, Device, Devise, Diagram, Draft, Drawing, Elevation, Engineer, Format, Hang, Idea, Intent, Lay(out), Map, Marshall, Outline, Pattern, Plot, Ploy, Policy, Premeditate, Procedure, Programme, Project, Proposal, Scenario, Schedule, Scheme, Spec(ification), Stratagem, Strategy, System, Wheeze

**Plane**  Aero(dyne), Air, Aircraft, Airliner, Airship, Bandit, Boeing, Bomber, Bus, Camel, Canard, Chenar, Chinar, Comet, Concorde, Crate, Dakota,

Delta-wing, Facet, Fillister, Flat, Glider, Gotha, Hurricane, Icosohedra, Jet, Jumbo, Level, MIG, Mirage, Mosquito, Moth, Octagon, Platanus, Polygon, Router, Shackleton, Shave, Smooth, Spitfire, Spokeshave, STOL, Surface, Sycamore, Taube, Trainer, Tree, Trident, Viscount

**Plane figure** Endecagon, Hendecagon

**Planet(ary)** Alphonsine, Ariel, Asteroid, Body, Cabiri, Ceres, Constellation, Earth, Eros, Hyleg, Jupiter, Mars, Mercury, Moon, Neptune, Pluto, Psyche, Saturn, Sphere, Starry, Sun, Terrestrial, Uranus, Venus, Vista, Vulcan, World

**Plank** Board, Chess, Duckboard, Plonk, Sarking, Slab, Spirketing, Straik, Strake, Stringer, Wood

**Plankton** Seston

**Plant (part)** Acacia, Acanthus, Acorus, Adam's flannel, Adderwort, Agrimony, Ajowan, Ajwan, Alexanders, Alga, Alisma, Alkanet, All-good, Aloe, Alyssum, Andromeda, Angelica, Angiosperm, Anise, Annual, Anther, Arenaria, Arnica, Arrowroot, Artemisia, Asphodel, Aspidistra, Astralagus, Aubrietia, Bablah, Bald-money, Bears-breech, Bed, Betony, Biennial, Biota, Blite, Boree, Brinjal, Bristle-fern, Brooklime, Broom-rape, Buckbean, Bugle, Buplever, Burdock, Burnet, Butterbur, Cactus, Calla, Callitriche, Camomile, Canaigre, Canna, Cardoon, Carduus, Cassia, Catnep, Cat's ear, Centaury, Chervil, Chincherinchee, Clary, Clote, Cnicus, Colocasia, Coltsfoot, Cordaites, Coriander, Cosmos, Costmary, Cress, Croton, Dal, Dasheen, Datura, Deme, Derris, Diandria, Dielytra, Dittander, Dittany, Dodder, Dumbcane, Dusty-miller, Dyer's-broom, Earth-smoke, Ecad, Embed, Enrace, Epacridaceae, Ephedra, Erythrina, Establish, Euphorbia, Exogen, Eyebright, Factory, Fenugreek, Fern, Filaree, Fix, Fluellin, Fly-trap, Forb, Fouat, Fouet, Fraxinella, Freesia, Frogbit, Fumitory, Gemma, Gentian, Gerbera, Germander, Gesnaria, Glaux, Gnetales, Gnetum, Goat-sallow, Goats-thorn, Goat-willow, Goldilocks, Gorse, Groundsel, Growth, Guaco, Haemony, Hag-taper, Henbane, Henequen, Hepatica, Herb(arium), Herb-paris, Hibiscus, Horse-tail, Hosta, Hurtleberry, Hyssop, Icosandria, Insert, Instil, Inter, Inula, Ipomoea, Kali, Kex, Kudzu, Land, Lantana, Larkspur, Lathe, Lavender, Liver-wort, Loco, Lords and ladies, Lotus, Lousewort, Lucerne, Lurgi, Lychnis, Machinery, Madder, Mahonia, Maidenhair, Mallow, Mandrake, Mare's-tail, Medick, Mercury, Meu, Mimosa, Moneywort, Monstera, Moorva, More(l), Mullein, Murva, Musci, Nancy-pretty, Nard, Nemesia, Nerium, Nettle, Nigella, Nuphar, Nonsuch, Oleander, Opuntia, Orchis, Ornamental, Orpin(e), Oshac, Panax, Pareira, Parkleaves, Parsley-piert, Petunia, Phloem, Phytobenthos, Pia, Pimpernel, Plumbago, Portulaca, Protea, Psilotum, Ragwort, Ratsbane, Rattle, Reseda, Rest-harrow, Retama, Rhodora, Rhus, Rocambole, Roly-poly, Rue, Ruellia, Saffron, Salicornia, Salsola, Samphire, Sampire, Sanicle, Scammony, Scandix, Screwpine, Sedge, Sedum, Sego, Self-heal, Sere, Sesame, Set(wall), Shepherd's purse, Shrub, Silene, Silphium, Skirret, Smilax, Sola, Sole, Southernwood, Sow, Sparaxis, Spearmint, Spearwort, Spergula, Spignel, Spikenard, Spink, Spurge, Spurr(e)y, Squill, Stapela, Staragen, Starwort, Stone-crop,

Succulent, Sunn, Sweet-gale, Syringa, Tagetes, Tamarisk, Taro, Teasel, Tetra, Thallophyte, Thea, Thrift, Til, Tomatillo, Tormentil, Tree, Triffid, Tritoma, Tritonia, Tropophyte, Tulipa, Udo, Urd, Vanilla, Vine, Wait-a-bit, Water-soldier, Weld, Wincopipe, Works, Yam, Yarr(ow), Yellowroot, Zedoary

**Plantagenet** Angevin, Broom

**Plantain** Waybread

**Plantation** Arboretum, Bosket, Bosquet, Estate, Grove, Hacienda, Pen, Pinetum, Ranch, Tara, Vineyard

**Plant disease** Bunt, Club-root, Rosette

**Planted** In

**Planter** Dibber, Farmer, Settler, Trowel

**Plaque** Plateau, Scale

**Plaster(ed)** Bandage, Blotto, Cake, Cataplasm, Clam, Clatch, Compo, Daub, Diachylon, Diachylum, Drunk, Emplastrum, Fresco, Gesso, Grout, Gypsum, Intonaco, Leep, Lit, Mud, Oiled, Parge(t), Poultice, Render, Scratch-coat, Screed, Secco, Shellac, Sinapism, Smalm, Smarm, Smear, Sowsed, Staff, Stookie, Stucco, Teer

**Plastic** Bakelite, Ductile, Fictile, Fluon, Laminate, Loid, Lucite, Melamine, Pliant, Polyethylene, Polythene, PVC, Wet-look, Yielding

> **Plastic** may indicate an anagram

**Plate(d)** Ailette, Anode, Armadillo, Ashet, Baffle, Baleen, Brass, Chamfrain, Chape, Coat, Copper, Dasypus, Denture, Disc, Dish, Electro, Elytron, Elytrum, Enamel, Entoplastron, Fine, Fish, Foil, Gula, Illustration, L, Lame, Lamella, Lamina, Lanx, Mazarine, Nail, Nef, Ortho, Osteoderm, Paten, Patina, Patine, Pauldron, Peba, Plaque, Platter, Pleximeter, Poitrel, Prescutum, Print, Race, Riza, Rove, Salamander, Scale, Scute, Scutum, Seg, Sheffield, Shield, Silver, Slab, Soup, Spoiler, Stencil, Stereo(type), Sternite, Strake, Tablet, Tace, Tasse(l), Terne, Torsel, Trencher, Trophy, Tuill(ett)e, Tymp, Urostegite, Vassail, Vessail, Vessel, Web, Whirtle, Wortle

**Plateau** Altiplano, Fjeld, Highland, Horst, Kar(r)oo, Meseta, Paramo, Puna, Tableland

**Platform** Almemar, Barbette, Base, Bema, Bier, Catafalque, Crane, Dais, Deck, Dolly, Emplacement, Entablement, Estrade, Exedra, Exhedra, Foretop, Gantry, Gauntree, Gauntry, Hustings, Kang, Machan, Pallet, Perron, Plank, Podium, Predella, Programme, Pulpit, Raft, Rig, Rostrum, Round-top, Scaffold, Sponson, STAGE, Stand, Stoep, Tee, Thrall, Top, Tribune

**Platinum** Pt, Ruthenium, Sperrylite

**Platitude** Bromide, Cliché, Truism

**Platocephalus** Flat-headed

**Platonic, Platonist** Academician, Ideal, Spiritual

**Platoon** Company, Squad, Team

**Platter**   Dish, EP, Graal, Grail, Lanx, LP, Plate, Record, Salver, Trencher

**Platypus**   Duck-mole

**Plausible, Plausibility**   Cogent, Credible, Fair, Glib, Oil, Probable, Proball, Sleek, Smooth, Specious

**Play(ing)**   Accompany, Active, Amusement, Brand, Candida, Charm, Clearance, Crucible, Daff, Dandle, Drama, Echo, Endgame, Finesse, Frisk, Frolic, Fun, Gamble, Gambol, Game, Ghosts, Hamlet, Holiday, Inside, Interlude, Jam, Jest, Kinderspiel, Laik, Lake, Latitude, Lear, Licence, Macbeth, Mask, Masque, Melodrama, Miracle, Morality, Mousetrap, Mummers, Mysteries, Nurse, Passion, Perform, Personate, Portray, Pretend, Recreation, Represent, Riff, Rollick, Romp, Room, Rope, RUR, Saw, Sketch, Sport, Strain, Strum, Tolerance, Toy, Tragedy, Trifle, Tweedle, Twiddle, Two-hander, Vamp, Vent

> **Play**   may indicate an anagram

**Playback**   Echo, Repeat, Replay

**Player(s)**   Actor, Athlete, Back, Black, Brass, Bugler, Busker, Cast, CD, Colt, East, Equity, Fiddle, Gary, Half, Juke-box, Kest, Lutanist, Lutenist, Mid-on, Mime, Musician, Nero, North, Orpheus, Pagliacci, Participant, Pianola, Pitcher, Pone, Pro, Scratch, Secondo, Seed, Shortstop, Side, South, Stereo, Strolling, Super, Sweeper, Team, Thespian, Troubador, Troupe, Upright, Virtuosi, West, White, Wing

**Playfair**   Code

**Playfellow**   Actor, Chum, Companion

**Playful**   Arch, Coy, Frisky, Humorous, Ludic, Merry, Piacevole, Scherzo, Sportive

**Playgirl**   Actress, Electra

**Playground**   Close, Garden, Park, Theatre, Yard

**Playhouse**   Cinema, Theatre, Wendy

**Playsuit**   Rompers

**Playwright**   Aeschylus, Albee, Arden, Ayckbourn, Barrie, Barry, Beaumont, Beckett, Behan, Bellow, Bennett, Besier, Brecht, Chekhov, Congreve, Coward, Dekker, Delaney, DRAMATIST, Dramaturgist, Euripides, Fletcher, Gems, Genet, Goldoni, Gorky, Harwood, Hay, Ibsen, Jonson, Marlowe, Massinger, Menander, Molière, Mortimer, Odets, O'Neill, Orton, Osborne, Pinero, Pinter, Pirandello, Priestley, Rattigan, Scriptwriter, Shaw, Sheridan, Sherry, Simpson, Sophocles, Stoppard, Storey, Strindberg, Synge, Tate, Terence, Thespis, Travers, Vanbrugh, Wesker, Wilde

**Plea**   Appeal, Claim, Defence, Entreaty, Excuse, Exoration, Orison, Placitum, Prayer, Rebuttal, Rebutter, Rogation, Suit

**Plead(er)**   Answer, Argue, Beg, Entreat, IMPLORE, Intercede, Litigate, Moot, Vakeel, Vakil

**Please(d), Pleasant, Pleasing**   Aggrate, Agreeable, Alcina, Amene, Amuse, Arride, Bitte, Cheerful, Chuffed, Comely, Content, Cute, Delight,

Do, Euphonic, Fair, Fit, Flatter, Genial, Glad, Gratify, Jammy, Kindly, Lepid, List, Oblige, Prithee, Prythee, Satisfy, Suit, Tickle, Winsome

**Pleasure** Algolagnia, Comfort, Delice, Delight, Fun, Hedonism, Joy, Vanity, Will, Xanadu List

**Pleasure-garden, Pleasure-ground** Lung, Oasis, Park, Policy, Ranelagh, Tivoli

**Pleat** Accordion, Crimp, Fold, Frill, Goffer, Gusset, Plait, Pranck(e), Prank, Sunray

**Pleb(eian)** Common, Homely, Laic, Ordinary, Roturier

**Pledge** Affidavit, Arles, Band, Betroth, Bond, Borrow, Bottomry, Dedicate, Deposit, Earnest(-penny), Engage, Fine, Gage, Guarantee, Hypothecate, Hock, Impignorate, Mortgage, Oath, Pass, Pawn, Pignerate, Pignorate, Plight, Propine, Sacrament, Security, Stake, Troth, Undertake, Wad, Wed

**Plentiful, Plenty** Abounding, Abundance, Abundant, Ample, Bags, Copious, Copy, Excess, Foison, Fouth, Ful(l)ness, Fushion, Galore, Goshen, Lashings, Lots, Oodles, Pleroma, Profusion, Quantity, Riches, Rife, Routh, Rowth, Scouth, Scowth, Slue, Sonce, Sonse, Umpteen

**Plenum** Spaceless

**Pliable, Pliant** Amenable, Flexible, Limber, Limp, Lithe, Plastic, Supple, Swack, Swank

> **Pliers** see PLY

**Plight** Betrothal, Case, Misdight, Peril, Pickle, Pledge, State, Troth

**Plimsoll(s)** Dap, Gym-shoe, Line, Mutton-dummies, Tacky

**Plinth** Acroter, Base, Block, Stand

**Plod** Drudge, Traipse, Tramp, Trog, Trudge

**Plonk** Rotgut, Wine

**Plop** Drop, Fall, Plap, Plump

**Plot(s)** Allotment, Babington, Bed, Brew, Chart, Cliché, Conspiracy, Conspire, Covin, Covyne, Engineer, Erf, Erven, Graph, Gunpowder, Imbroglio, Intrigue, Locus, Lot, Machination, Map, Meal-tub, Pack, Patch, Plan, Plat, Rye-house, Scenario, SCHEME, Sect(ion), Shot, Site, Story, Taluk, Terf, Turf, Web

**Plotter** Artist, Cabal, Camarilla, Catesby, Conspirator, Engineer, Oates, Schemer

**Plough(man), Ploughed** Arable, Ard, Arval, Chamfer, Charles's wain, Ear, Earth-board, Ere, Fail, Fallow, Farmer, Feer, Gadsman, Great bear, Harrow, Lister, Middlebreaker, Piers, Pip, Push, Rafter, Rib, Rive, Scooter, Septentrion(e)s, Sow, Till(er), Triones

**Plough-cleaner** Pattle, Pettle

**Ploughshare** Sock

**Ploughwise** Boustrophedon

**Plover** Bud, Lapwing, Pretincole, Prostitute, Stand, Tewit

**Plowman** Piers

**Ploy** Manoeuvre, Stratagem, Strike, Tactic

**Pluck(ing), Plucky** Avulse, Bare, Carphology, Cock, Courage, Deplume, Epilate, Evulse, Gallus, Game, GRIT, Guts, Loot, Mettle, Pick, Pinch, Pip, Pizzicato, Plectron, Plectrum, Plot, Plunk, Pook(it), Pouk(it), Pull, Race, Snatch, Spin, Spirit, Summon, Tug, Twang, Tweak, Tweeze, Yank

**Plug** Ad, Block, Bung, Caulk, Chew, Dam, Dook, Dossil, Dottle, Fipple, Fother, Hype, Lam, Pessary, Prod, Promote, Publicity, Ram, Recommendation, Sparking, Spile, Spiling, Stop(per), Stopple, Tampion, Tap, Tompion, Tent, Wedge

**Plum** Bullace, Choice, Damson, Gage, Greengage, Kaki, Mammee-sapota, Maroon, Mirabelle, Mussel, Myrobalan, Naseberry, Persimmon, Proin(e), Pruin(e), Prune, Quetsch, Sapodilla, Sebesten

**Plumage, Plume** Aigrette, Crest, Egret, Feather, Hackle, Panache, Preen, Ptilosis, Quill

**Plumb(er)** Bullet, Dredge, Fathom, Lead(sman), Perpendicular, Plummet, Sheer, Sound, Test, True, Vertical

**Plumbago** Graphite

**Plummet** Dive, Drop, PLUNGE

**Plump(er)** Bold, Bonny, Buxom, Chubbed, Choose, Chubby, Embonpoint, Fat, Fleshy, Flop, Fubsy, Full, Lie, Opt, Plonk, Plop, Podgy, Portly, Roll-about, Rotund, Round, Soss, Souse, Squab, Stout, Swap, Swop

**Plunder(er)** Berob, Booty, Depredate, Despoil, Devastate, Escheat, Fleece, Forage, Gut, Harry, Haul, Hership, Loot, Maraud, Peel, Pill(age), Privateer, RANSACK, Rape, Rapparee, Ravine, Reave, Reif, Reive, Rob, Sack, Shave, Spoil(s), Spoliate, Sprechery, Spuilzie, Spuly(i)e, Spulzie, Swag

**Plunge** Demerge, Dive, Douse, Dowse, Duck, Encw, Immerge, Immerse, La(u)nch, Nose-dive, Plummet, Raker, Send, Sink, Souse, Swoop, Thrust

**Plural** Multiply, Pl

**Plus** Addition, And, Gain, More, Positive

**Plush(ed)** Die, Luxurious, Smart, Tint, Velour, Velvet

**Pluto(nic)** Abyssal, Dis, Hades, Pipeline, Underground

**Plutonium** Pu

**Ply, Plier(s)** Bend, Cab, Exercise, Exert, Gondoliers, Importune, Layer, Practise, Trade, Wield

> **Plying** may indicate an anagram

**PM** Afternoon, Attlee, Bute, Disraeli, Gladstone, Melbourne, Major, Peel, Pitt, Premier

**Poach** Cook, Encroach, Filch, Lag, Steal, Trespass

**Pochard** Duck, Scaup

**Pocket** Bag, Bin, Cavity, Gly, Cup, Enclave, Fob, Glom, Hideaway, Jenny, Misappropriate, Placket, Pot, Pouch, Purloin, Purse, Sac, Sky, Sling, Steal

**Pod(s)** Babul, Bean, Belly, Carob, Chilli, Dividivi, Lomentum, Neb-neb, Okra, Pipi, Pregnant, Siliqua, Tamarind, Vanilla

**Poem(s), Poetry** Aeneid, Alcaic, Anthology, Awdl, Ballad(e), Bestiary, Byliny, Caccia, Canzone, Cargoes, Cento, Choliamb, Choriamb, Cicada, Cinquain, Complaint, Decastich, Dit(t), Divan, Dizain, Doggerel, Duan, Dunciad, Eclogue, Elegy, Elene, Epic(ede), Epigram, Epilogue, Epode, Epopee, Epopoeia, Epos, Epyllion, Finlandia, Gauchesco, Georgic, Haikai, Haiku, Hexastich, Hull, Idyll, If, Iliad, Imagism, Lay, Limerick, London, Metre, Monostich, Nostos, Ode, Palinode, Paracrostic, Parnassus, Pastoral, Penill(ion), Poesy, Prelude, Prothalamion, Purana, Qasada, Quatrain, Quire, Rat-rhyme, Renga, Rhapsody, Rime, Rondeau, Rondel, Rubai(yat), Sestina, Sijo, Sirvante, Song, Sonnet, Stanza, Stornello, Tanka, Telestich, Temora, Triolet, Tristich, Verse, Versicle, Villanelle, Voluspa, Voluspe, Waka

**Poet(s)** Abse, Addison, AE, Aeschylus, Alcaeus, Anacreon, Archilochian, Aretino, Arion, Ariosto, Aristophanes, Arnold, Asclepiades, Auden, Austin, Bard(ling), Barham, Barnes, Baudelaire, Belleau, Belloc, Betjeman, Blair, Blake, Brecht, Bridges, Brooke, Browning, Bunthorne, Burns, Butler, Byron, Cadou, Caedmon, Campbell, Campion, Carew, Catullus, Cavalier, Chapman, Chatterton, Chaucer, Cinna, Clare, Clough, Coleridge, Collins, Corinna, Cory, Cowper, Crabbe, Cumberland, Cyclic, Dante, Davenant, De la Mare, Donne, Dowson, Drinkwater, Dunbar, Dyer, Elegist, Eliot, Emerson, Ennius, Ettrick, Euripides, Fitzgerald, Flaccus, Flecker, Frost, Gay, Georgian, Glycon, Goethe, Goldsmith, Gower, Graves, Gray, Griot, Gunn, Hamilton, Heine, Heredia, Herrick, Hesiod, Homer, Hood, Hopkins, Horace, Horne, Housman, Hughes, Hugo, Hulme, Hunt, Iambist, Iqbal, Juvenal, Keats, Keyes, Lake, Lamartine, Landor, Lang, Langland, Larkin, Laureate, Layman, Leopardi, Lewis, Logue, Longfellow, Lorca, Lovelace, Lowell, Lucan, Lucretius, Lyrist, Makar, Maker, Mallarmé, Marot, Martial, Marvell, Masefield, Meistersinger, Menander, Metaphysical, Metrist, Meyer, Minnesinger, Minstrel, Milton, Mistral, Moore, Morris, Motion, Nashe, Newbolt, Noyes, Odist, Omar, Orpheus, Ossian, Ovid, Owen, Petrarch, Pindar, PL, Plath, Pleiade, Poe, Poetaster, Pope, Pound, Prior, Propertius, Pushkin, Quasimodo, Racine, Rhymer, Rhymester, Rilke, Rishi, Ronsard, Rossetti, Rowe, Rumi, Russell, Rymer, Sachs, Sappho, Sassoon, Scald, Schiller, Scop, Seaman, Service, Shadwell, Shanks, Shelley, Shenstone, Sidney, Simonides, Sitwell, Sonneteer, Skald, Skelton, Smart, Sophocles, Southey, Spasmodic, Spender, Spenser, Statius, Stephens, Stevenson, Suckling, Swinburne, Tagore, Taliesin, Tannhauser, Tasso, Tate, Tennyson, Terence, Theocritus, Theon, Thespis, Thomas, Thompson, Thomson, Tragic, Traherne, Trench, Troubadour, Trouvère, Trouveur, Tyrtaeus, Verlaine, Virgil, Waller, Whitman, Whittier, Wordsworth, Yeats, Young

**Poetaster** Della-Cruscan

**Poetess** Ingelow, Orinda

**Poet laureate** PL

> **Poetry** see POEM

**Poignant** Acute, Biting, Keen, Pungent, Stirring, Touching

**Point(ed), Pointer, Points** Ace, Acro-, Aculeate, Antinode, Antler, Apex, Aphelion, Apogee, Appui, Apse, Apsis, Barb, Bisque, Calk, Cape, Cardinal, Centre, Clou, Clue, Colon, Comma, Cone, Conic, Corner, Crisis, Crux, Cultrate, Cusp, Cursor, Cuss, Decimal, Degree, Detail, Direct, Dot, E, Epanodos, Epee, Fastigiate, Feature, Fitch(e), Focal, Focus, Foreland, Fulcrum, Germane, Gist, Gnomon, Hastate, Head, Index, Indicate, Indicator, Ippon, Jester, Keblah, Kiblah, Kip(p), Knub, Lance, Lead, Limit, Lizard, Locate, Locus, Mark, Metacentre, Moot, Mucro, N, Nail, Nasion, Neb, Needle, Ness, Nib, Node, Nombril, Now, Nub, Obelion, Obelisk, Opinion, Ord, Particle, Peak, Perigee, Perihelion, Perilune, Pin, Pinnacle, Place, Prong, Prow, Punctilio, Punctual, Punctum, Ras, Rhumb, S, Scribe, Seg(h)ol, Shaft, Sheva, Show, Shy, Silly, Socket, Spearhead, Spicate, Spick, Spike, Spinode, Stage, Star, Stigme, Stiletto, Sting, Stipule, Sum, Tacnode, Taper, Tine, TIP, Tongue, Urde(e), Urdy, Use, Vane, Verge, Verse, W

**Pointless** Blunt, Curtana, Flat, Futile, Inane, Muticous, Otiose, Stupid, Vain

**Point of honour** Pundonor

**Poise** Aplomb, Balance, Composure, P, Serenity

**Poison(er), Poisoning, Poisonous** Abrin, Aconite, Antiar, Apocynum, Aqua-tofana, Arsenic, Aspic, Atropia, Atrupin(e), Bane, Barbasco, Belladonna, Borgia, Cacodyl, Calabar-bean, Cicuta, Coniine, Cowbane, Curare, Curari, Datura, Daturine, Digitalin, Dioxin, Echidnine, Embolism, Envenom, Ergotise, Gelsemin(in)e, Gila, Gossypol, Hebenon, Hebona, Hemlock, Henbane, Limberneck, Lindane, Lobeline, Malevolent, Mandragora, Miasma, Mineral, Monkshood, Muscarine, Neurine, Noxious, Ouabain, Ourali, Ourari, Paraquat, Phallin, Ptomaine, Raphania, Rot, Samnitis, Santonin, Saturnism, Saxitoxin, Stibium, Strophanthus, Strychnine, Surinam, Tanghin, Tetrodotoxin, Thebaine, Thorn-apple, Timbo, Toxic, Toxin, Tropine, Tutu, Upas, Urali, Uroshiol, Venin, Venom(ous), Veratrin(e), Viperous, Virous, Virulent, Wabain, Warfarin, Wolfbane, Woorali, Woorara, Wourali, Yohimbine

**Poke, Poky** Bonnet, Broddle, Garget, Itchweed, Jab, Meddle, Mock, Nousle, Nudge, Nuzzle, Ombu, Peg, Pick, Pote, Pouch, Powter, PRISON, PROD, Prog, Proke, Punch, Root(le), Rout, Rowt, Stab, Thrust

**Poker (work)** Curate, Game, Mistigris, Pyrography, Salamander, Stud(-horse), Tickler, Tine

**Poland** PL, Sarmatia

**Polar, Pole** Anode, Antarctic, Arctic, Boom, Caber, Copernicus, Cracovian, Extremity, Flagstaff, Janker, Kent, Lug, Mast, N, Nadir, Nib, North, Periscian, PO, Polack, Punt, Quant, Racovian, Ripeck, Rood, Ry(e)peck, S, Shaft, Slav, South, Spar, Sprit, Staff, Stang, Starosta, Stilt, Sting, Thyrsos, Thyrsus, Topmast, Totem, Zenith

> **Polar** may indicate with a pole

**Polecat** Ferret, Fitch, Foulmart, Foumart, Weasel

**Polemic(al)** Argument, Controversy, Debate, Eristic(al)

**Police(man)** Babylon, Bear, Beast, Blue, Bluebottle, Bobby, Bog(e)y, Bull, Busy, Carabiniere, Centenier, Cheka, CID, Constable, Cop(per), Cotwal, Crusher, Detective, Druzhinnik, Filth, Flatfoot, Flattie, Flic, Force, Fuzz, Garda, Gendarme, Gestapo, G-man, Guard, Gumshoe, Harmanbeck, Heat, Hermandad, Inspector, Interpol, Jamadar, Jemadar, Keystone, Kotwal, Limb, Met(ropolitan), Mountie, Mulligan, Nabman, Ochrana, Officer, OGPU, Ovra, Peeler, Peon, PO, Polizei, Posse (comitatus), Prefect, Redbreast, Redcap, Regulate, RIC, Robert, Rozzer, RUC, Sbirro, SC, Sepoy, Shamus, Slop, Smokey, Sowar(ry), Special, Stasi, Super, Sureté, Sweeney, T(h)anadar, The Law, Thirdborough, Trap, Wolly, Woodentop, Zaptiah, Zaptieh, Zomo

**Police car** Black Maria, Panda, Patrol, Prowl

**Police station** Lock-up, Tana, Tanna(h), Thana(h), Thanna(h)

**Policy** Assurance, Comprehensive, Course, Demesne, Endowment, Expedience, Insurance, Laisser-faire, Lend-lease, Line, Method, Platform, Practice, Programme, Scorched earth, Tack, Tactics, Ticket

**Polish(ed), Polisher** Beeswax, Black, Blacklead, Buff, Bull, Burnish, Complaisant, Edit, Elaborate, Elegant, Emery, Enamel, Finish, Furbish, Gentlemanly, Glass, Gloss, Heelball, Hone, Inland, Lap, Lustre, Perfect, Planish, Polite, Refinement, Refurbish, Rottenstone, Rub, Sand, Sejm, Sheen, Shellac, Shine, Slick, Urbane, Veneer, Wax

**Polite** Civil, Courteous, Genteel, Grandisonian, Suave, Urbane

**Politic(al), Politics** Apparat, Body, Civic, Diplomacy, Discreet, Expedient, Falange, Public, Statecraft, Tactful, Wise

**Politician(s)** Bright, Carpet-bagger, Catiline, Demo(crat), Diehard, Disraeli, Eden, Ins, Isolationist, Laski, Left, Legislator, Liberal, MEP, MP, Parnell, Polly, Rad, Rep, Senator, Socialist, Statesman, Statist, Tadpole, Taper, TD, Tory, Trotsky, Unionist, Whig

**Poll** Ballot, Bean, Canvass, Count, Cut, Dod, Election, Gallup, Head, Humlie, Hummel, MORI, Nestor, Not(t), Parrot, Pineapple, Pow, Scrutiny, Straw, Votes

> **Poll** may indicate a first letter

**Pollack** Fish, Lob, Lythe

**Pollard** Doddered

**Pollen, Pollinated** Anemophilous, Dust, Farina, Fertilised, Witch-meal, Xenia

**Pollenbrush** Scopa

**Pollex** Thumb

**Pollster** Psephologist

**Pollute, Pollution** Adulterate, Contaminate, Defile, Dirty, File, Foul, Infect, Miasma, Soil, Stain, Taint, Violate

**Polly** Flinders, Parrot, Peachum

**Polo**  Chukka, Marco, Mint, Navigator

**Polonium**  Po

**Poltergeist**  Apport, Ghost, Spirit, Trouble-house

**Poltroon**  Coward, Craven, Dastard, Scald, Scaramouch

**Polyandry**  Nair

**Polygraph**  Lie-detector

**Polymath**  Knowall, Toynbee

**Polymer**  Isotactic, Resin, Silicone

**Polymorphic**  Multiform, Proteus, Variform

**Polynesian**  Tahitian, Tongan

**Polyp(s)**  Alcyonaria, Sea-anemone, Tumour

**Polyphony**  Counterpoint

**Polyzoan**  Sea-mat

**Pom**  Choom

**Pomander**  Pounce(t)-box

**Pommel**  Beat, Knob, Pound, Pummel

**Pomp(ous)**  Big, Bombastic, Budge, Ceremonial, Display, Dogberry, Grandiose, Heavy, Highfalutin(g), High-flown, Hogen-mogen, Inflated, Orotund, Ostentatious, Pageantry, Parade, Pretentious, Solemn, Splendour, Starchy, State, Stilted, Turgid

**Pom-pom**  Ball, Tassel

**Ponce**  Pander, Solicit, Souteneur

**Pond(s)**  Dub, Hampstead, Pool, Puddle, Slough, Stank, Stew, Tank, Turlough, Vivarium, Viver

**Ponder(ous)**  Brood, Cogitate, Contemplate, Deliberate, Heavy, Laboured, Mull, Muse, Poise, Pore, Reflect, Ruminate, THINK, Volve, Weight, Wonder

**Poniard**  Bodkin, DAGGER, Dirk, Stiletto

**Pontifical**  Aaronic, Papal

**Pontoon**  Bridge, Caisson, Chess, Game, Vingt-et-un

**Pony**  Cayuse, Dartmoor, Exmoor, Garran, Gen(n)et, GG, Griffin, Griffon, Gryfon, Gryphon, Jennet, Mustang, New Forest, Pownie, Shanks', Sheltie, Tangun, Tat(too)

**Poodle**  Barbet, Swan

**Pooh**  Bah, Bear, Pugh, Winnie, Yah

**Pool**  Bank, Bethesda, Billabong, Cess, Collect, Combine, Dub, Dump, Flash, Flow, Jackpot, Kitty, Lido, Lin(n), Meer, Mere, Mickery, Milkvah, Milkveh, Natatorium, Pescina, Pescine, Plash, Plesh, POND, Reserve, Snooker, Stank, Sump, Tank, Tarn

**Poor(ly)**  Bad, Bare, Base, Breadline, Buckeen, Cronk, Destitute, Gritty, Hard-up, Hopeless, Humble, Hungry, Ill(-off), Indigent, Lean, Meagre,

Mean, Needy, Obolary, Pauper, Roinish, Roynish, Ropy, Sad, Scrub, Shabby, Sorry, Sub, Thin, Third-rate, Trashy, Undeserving, Unwell

> **Poor**   may indicate an anagram

**Poorhouse**   Union, Workhouse

**Pooter**   Nobody, Nonentity

**Pop (off), Popping**   Bang, Burst, Cloop, Crease, Die, Father, Fr, Gingerbeer, Hip-hop, Hock, Insert, Lumber, Mineral, Nip, Pater, Pawn, Pledge, Population, Punk, Sherbet, Soda, Weasel

> **Pop**   may indicate an anagram

**Pope(s)**   Adrian, Alexander, Atticus, Boniface, Clement, Dunciad, Eminence, Fish, Gregory, Hildebrand, Holiness, Innocent, Joan, Leo, Papa, Pius, Pontiff, Ruff(e), Schism, Theocrat, Tiara, Urban

**Pop-gun**   Bourtree-gun

**Popinjay**   Barbermonger, Coxcomb, Fop, Macaroni, Prig, Skipjack

**Poplar**   Abele, Aspen, Cottonwood, Lombardy

**Poppet**   Valve

**Poppy**   Argemone, Bloodroot, Chicolate, Diacodin, Eschscholtzia, Flanders, Opium, Ponceau, Puccoon, Rhoeadales, Shirley

**Poppycock**   Bosh, Nonsense, Rubbish

**Popular(ity)**   Common, Demotic, General, Hit, In, Laic, Lay, Mass, Plebeian, Prevalent, Public, Successful, Tipped, Vogue

**Population, Populace**   Census, Demography, Inhabitants, Mass, Mob, PEOPLE, Public, Universe

**Porcelain**   Arita, Bamboo, Belleek, Blanc-de-chine, Chelsea, China, Coalport, Dresden, Eggshell, Famille, Hard-paste, Hizen, Imari, Jasper, Lithophane, Minton, Parian, Sèvres, Spode, Sung

**Porch**   Galilee, Stoa, Stoep, Veranda(h)

**Porcupine**   Hedgehog, Urson

**Pore**   Browse, Hole, Lenticel, Muse, Ostium, Outlet, Ponder, Study

**Porgy**   Braise, Scup(paug)

**Pork**   Bacon, Boar, Brawn, Chap, Crackling, Flitch, Griskin, Ham, Spare-rib

**Porn(ography)**   Erotica, Hard, Rhyparography, Soft

**Porous**   Cellular, Permeable, Pumice, Sponge

**Porpoise**   Bucker, Dolphin, Mereswine, Pellach, Pellack, Pellock, Phocaena

**Porridge**   Berry, Brochan, Brose, Crowdie, Drammach, Drammock, Gaol, Grouts, Gruel, Hominy, Kasha, Oaten, Oatmeal, Polenta, Pottage, Praiseach, Sadza, Samp, Sentence, Skilly, Stirabout, Stretch, Sup(p)awn, Time, Ugali

**Porridge stick**   Thible, Thivel

**Port(s)**   Abadan, Abidjan, Abo, Acapulco, Acre, Aden, Agadir, Alexandria, Alicante, Amoy, Anchorage, Annapolis, Antibes, Antwerp, Apia, Aqaba,

Archangel, Arica, Augusta, Aulis, Ayr, Baku, Baltimore, Bari, Barranquilla, Basra, Beeswing, Benghazi, Bergen, Bootle, Bordeaux, Bratislava, Bremen, Brest, Brindisi, Bristol, Buffalo, Calais, Callao, Canton, Carry, Cartagena, Catania, Charleston, Cinque, Cobh, Cochin, Colon, Conakry, Cork, Danzig, Dartmouth, Deal, Dieppe, Dill(i), Dover, Dubai, Dubrovnik, Dunedin, Eilat, Elat, Ellesmere, Emden, Entrepot, Famagusta, Fishguard, Fleetwood, Flushing, Foochow, Funchal, Gallipoli, Gate, Gateshead, Geelong, Genoa, Geropiga, Goa, Gravesend, Greenock, Grimsby, Haifa, HARBOUR, Harfleur, Harwich, Havana, Haven, Hilo, Hithe, Hobart, Holyhead, Honolulu, Hue, Hull, Hythe, Icel, Iloilo, Inchon, Iquitos, Istanbul, Izmir, Kiel, Kinsale, Kobe, Kowloon, Larboard, Larne, Latakia, Launceston, Legaspi, Leith, Lima, Lobito, Lorient, Lulea, Malmo, Manner, Marsala, Messina, Mien, Mirmansk, Mobile, Mocha, Mombasa, Nagasaki, Nantes, Nassau, Newhaven, Oban, Odense, Odessa, Oran, Osaka, Ostend, Ostia, Padang, Palermo, Penzance, Perm, Pevensey, Piraeus, Plymouth, Pula, Puri, Queenstown, Rabat, Ragusa, Rangoon, Rapallo, Recife, Rimini, Rio, Rosario, Rostock, Rostov, Rotterdam, Runcorn, Rye, Said, Salermo, Salto, San Diego, Sandwich, Schiedam, Seattle, Seville, Shanghai, Sheerness, Sidon, Smyrna, Southampton, Split, Stavanger, Stettin, Stornaway, Suez, Surat, Swansea, Syracuse, Tacoma, Tampa, Tampico, Tangier, Taranto, Tarragona, Tawny, Treaty, Trieste, Trincomalee, Tripoli, Trondheim, Tunis, Turku, Tyre, Ushuaia, Venice, Vigo, Visby, Volgograd, Wick, Wine, Yalta, Yokohama

**Portend, Portent** Augur, Bode, Omen, Phenomenon, Presage, WARN(ING)

**Porter** Ale, Bearer, Bummaree, Caddie, Caddy, Cole, Concierge, Coolie, Doorman, Door-keeper, Dvornik, Entire, Ham(m)al, Hamaul, Janitor, October, Ostiary, Red-cap, Stout

**Portico** Colonnade, Decastyle, Distyle, Dodecastyle, Exedra, Loggia, Narthex, Parvis(e), Porch, Prostyle, Stoa, Veranda(h), Xystus

**Portion** Ann(at), Bit, Deal, Distribute, Dole, Dose, Dotation, Fragment, Helping, Heritage, Hunk, Jointure, Lot, Modicum, Ounce, PART, Piece, Ratio, Scantle, Section, Segment, Share, Size, Slice, Tait, Taste, Tate, Tittle, Wodge

**Portland** Bill, Cement, Stone,

**Portly** Ample, Corpulent, Gaucie, Gaucy, Gawcy, Gawsy, Stout

**Portmanteau** Bag, Combination, Holdall, Valise

**Portrait(ist)** Depiction, Drawing, Eikon, Icon, Ikon, Image, Kitcat, Lely, Likeness, Painting, Retraitt, Retrate, Sketch, Vignette

**Portray(al)** Caricature, Depict, Describe, Feature, Image, Limn, Paint, Render, Represent, SHOW

**Portsmouth** Pompey

**Portugal, Portuguese** Lusitania(n)

**Pose(r), Poseur** Aesthete, Affect(ation), Asana, Lotus, Masquerade, Model, Place, Posture, Pretend, Problem, Propound, Pseud, Sit, Stance

**Poseidon** Earthshaker

**Posh** Grand, Ornate, Ritzy, Swanky, Swish, U

**Position** Asana, Bearing(s), Foothold, Grade, Instal, Lay, Lie, Location, Locus, Lodg(e)ment, Office, Pass, Peak, Place, Plant, Point, Pole, Post, Seat, Set(ting), Site, Situ, Stance, Standing, Standpoint, Station, Status, Syzygy, Tagmeme, Thesis, Tierce, Viewpoint

**Positive, Positivist** Absolute, Anode, Assertive, Categorical, CERTAIN, Comte, Definite, Emphatic, Plus, Print, Sure, Thetic, Upbeat, Yang, Yes

**Posse** Band, Mob, Vigilantes

**Possess(ed), Possession, Possessive** Apostrophe, Asset, Aver, Bedevil, Belonging(s), Demonic, Driven, Energumen, Estate, Have, Haveour, Haviour, Heirloom, His, Hogging, Know, Lares (et) penates, Mad, Obsessed, Occupation, OWN, Sasine, Seisin, Sprechery, Usucap(t)ion, Worth

**Possible, Possibly** Able, Contingency, Feasible, Likely, Peradventure, Perchance, Perhaps, Posse, Potential, Viable, Will

> **Possibly** may indicate an anagram

**Possum** Cataplexy, Opossum

**Post** Affix, After, Assign, Bitt, Bollard, Dak, Dawk, Delivery, Emily, Flagpole, Hurter, Listening, Log, Mail, Mast, Newel, Pale, Paling, Parcel, Penny, Picket, Pile, Piling, Piquet, Placard, Place, Plant, Plum, Pole, Position, Presidio, Puncheon, Quintain, Quoin, Remit, RM, Seat, Send, Staff, Stake, Station, Stell, Studdle, Tom, Upright, Vacancy

**Postcard(s)** Deltiology

**Poster** Advertisement, Bill, Broadsheet, Placard, Sender

**Posterior** Behind, Bottom, Jacksie, Jacksy, Later, Lumbar, Pygal, Rear, Tail

**Post-free** Franco

**Postman, Postmaster, Postwoman** Carrier, Courier, Emily, Hill, Messenger, Nasby, Pat, Portionist, Sorter

**Postmark** Frank

**Post mortem** Autopsy, Enquiry

**Postpone(ment)** Adjourn, Contango, Defer, Delay, Frist, Moratorio, Mothball, Pigeon-hole, Prorogue, Reprieve, Shelve, Stay, Suspend, Withhold

**Postulant** Candidate, Novice

**Postulate** Assert, Assume, Claim, Propound

**Posture** Affectation, Asana, Attitude, Deportment, Pose, Site, Stance, Vorlage

**Posy** Bouquet, Buttonhole, Corsage, Nosegay, Tuzzi-muzzy

**Pot(s), Potty** Abridge, Aludel, Bankroll, Basil, Belly, Cannabis, Casserole, Ca(u)ldron, Ceramic, Chanty, Chatty, Crewe, Crock(ery), Crucible,

Cruse(t), Delf(t), Dixie, Ewer, Flesh, Gallipot, Gaze, Gazunder, Grass, Hash(ish), Helmet, Hemp, In off, Inurn, Jordan, Kettle, Kitty, Lota(h), Maiolica, Majolica, Marijuana, Marmite, Ming, Olla, Olpe, Pan, Pat, Pipkin, Pocket, Poot, Posnet, POTTERY, Pout, Prize, Samovar, Shoot, Skillet, Stomach, Tajine, Tea, Test, Trivet, Tureen, Urn, Vial, Ware, Wok

**Potash** Polverine, Sylvine, Sylvite

**Potassium** K, Kalium, Saleratus, Saltpetre

**Potation** Dram, Drink

**Potato(es)** Batata, Chat, Datura, Duchesse, Fluke, Hog, Hole, Jersey, Kumara, Murphy, Peel-and-eat, Pratie, Praty, Seed, Solanum, Stovies, Tatie, Tuber, Ware, Yam

**Pot-bearer** Trivet

**Pot-bellied** Kedge, Kedgy, Kidge, Paunchy, Portly, Stout

**Pot-boy** Basil, Ganymede, Scullion

**Potent(ate)** Dynamic, Emperor, Huzoor, Influential, Mogul, Nawab, Panjandrum, Powerful, Ruler, Squirearch, Sultan

**Potential** Capacity, Making(s), Manqué, Possible, Promise, Scope, Viable

> **Potentially** may indicate an anagram

**Pot-house** Shebeen, Tavern

**Potion** Dose, Draught, Drink, Dwale, Mixture, Philtre, Tincture

**Pot-pourri** Hotchpotch, Medley, Pasticcio, Salmi

**Pottage** Berry

**Potter** Cue, Dabbity, Dacker, Daidle, Daiker, Dibble, Dodder, Etruscan, Fettle, Fiddle, Gamesmanship, Idle, Mess, Minton, Muck, Niggle, One-upmanship, Plouter, Plowter, Spode, Thrower, Tiddle, Tink(er), Troke, Truck, Wcdgwood

> **Potter** may indicate a snooker-player

**Pottery** Bank, Celadon, Ceramet, Ceramic, China, Crock, Delf(t), Etruria, Faience, Gombroon, Jomon, Majolica, Ming, Raku, Scroddled, Sgraffito, Spode, Spongeware, Sung, Ware, Wedgwood, Wemyss, Wheldon

**Pouch** Bag, Bursa, Caecum, Marsupial, Poke, Purse, Sac, Scrip, Spleuchan, Sporran

**Poultice** Application, Cataplasm, Embrocation, Epithem(a), Lenient, Plaster

**Poultry** Dorking, Fowl, Gallinaceous, Poot, Pout, Welsummer

**Pounce** Claw, Jump, Lunge, Powder, Sere, Souse, Sprinkle, Swoop

**Pound(er)** As, Bar, Bash, Batter, Beat, Bombard, Bradbury, Bray, Broadpiece, Bruise, Contund, Coop, Drub, Embale, Enclosure, Ezra, Fold, Hammer, Hatter, Imagist, Intern, Jail, Kiddle, Kidel, Kin, Knevell, L, Lam, Lb, Lock, Mash, Nevel, Nicker, Oncer, One-er, Oner, Pale, Pen, Penfold, Pestle, Pin, Pindar, Pinfold, Powder, Pulverise, Pun, Quop, Rint, Smacker, Sov(ereign), Stamp, Strum, Thump, Tower, Weight

**Pour** Birl(e), Bucket, Cascade, Circumfuse, Decant, Diffuse, Flood, Flow, Jaw, Jirble, Libate, Rain, Seil, Shed, Sile, Skink, Spew, Stream, Teem, Vent, Weep, Well

**Pout** Blain, Brassy, Fish, Mope, Mou(e), Scowl, Sulk, Tout, Towt

**Poverty** Beggary, Dearth, Illth, Indigence, LACK, Need, Penury, Poortith, Want

**Powder(ed), Powdery** Amberite, Araroba, Ballistite, Boracic, Chalk, Cosmetic, Crocus, Culm, Dover's, Dust, Explosive, Floury, Gregory, Grind, Kohl, Levigate, Lupulin, Meal, Moust, Mu(i)st, Pounce, Pruinose, Pulver, Pulvil, Rachel, Rochelle, Saleratus, Seidlitz, Seme(e), Smeddum, Spode, Talc, Triturate

**Power(ful), Powers** Ability, Able, Aeon, Amandla, Arm, Attorney, Autarchy, Authority, Axis, Big, Chakra, Cham, Charisma, Clairvoyance, Clout, Cogency, Command, Corridor, Cube, Danger, Dioptre, Effective, Eminence, Empathy, Empery, Energy, Eon, Exponent, Facility, Flower, Force, High, Hildebrandic, Horse, Hp, Influence, Kilowatt, Log, Logarithm, Mana, Mastery, Might, Mogul, Motive, Muscle, Nature, Nth, Od-force, P, Panjandrum, Posse, Potency, Prepollence, Puissant, Punch, Regime, Siddhi, Sinew, Soup, Stamina, Steam, Strength, STRONG, Supreme, Suzerain, Teeth, Telling, Tyrone, Valency, Vigour, Vis, Volt, Vroom, Watt, Weight

**Powerless** Diriment, Downa-do, Hamstrung, Helpless, Impotent, Incapable, Unarmed, Weak

**Powwow** Confab, Conference, Council, Meeting

**Pox** Pize

**Practical** Active, Joker, Pragmatic, Realist(ic), Realpolitik, Sensible, Useful, Viable, Virtual

**Practice, Practise** Abuse, Custom, Do, Drill, Enure, Exercise, Habit, Ism, Keep, Knock-up, Operate, Order, Ply, Policy, Praxis, Prosecution, Pursuit, Rehearsal, Rehearse, Rite, Rut, Trade, Train, Trial, Ure, Usage, Use

**Pragmatic, Pragmatist** Ad hoc, Busy, Dogmatic, Humanist, Meddling, Officious, Realist

**Prairie** IL, Illinois, Llano, Plain, Savanna, Steppe, Tundra, Veldt

**Prairie dog** Whippoorwill, Wishtonwish

**Praise** Acclaim, Adulation, Alleluia, Allow, Applause, Belaud, Bless, Blurb, Bouquet, Butter, CL, Commend(ation), Dulia, Encomium, Envy, Eulogise, Eulogium, Eulogy, Exalt, Extol, Gloria, Glory, Herry, Hery(e), Hosanna, Incense, Laud, Lo(o)s, Panegyric, Rap, Roose, Tribute

**Pram** Carriage, Cart, Scow

**Prance** Brank, Canary, Caper, Cavort, Galumph, Gambol, Jaunce, Jaunse, Prank(le), Swagger, Tittup

**Prang** Accident, Crash, Smash, Whale

**Prank(s)** Attrap, Bedeck, Bedizen, Caper, Dido, Escapade, Frolic, Gaud, Jape, Lark, Mischief, Rag, Reak, Reik, Rex, Spoof, Trick, Vagary

**Praseodymium** Pr

**Prat** Bottom, STUPID PERSON

**Prate** Babble, Boast, Haver, Talk

**Prattle** Blat(her), Chatter, Gab(nash), Gas, Gossip, Gup, Lalage, Patter

**Prawn** Scampi, Shrimp

**Pray(ing)** Appeal, Beg, Beseech, ENTREAT, Intone, Invoke, Kneel, Mantis, Solicit, Wrestle

**Prayer (book)** Act, Amidah, Angelus, Ardas, Ave (Maria), Bead, Bede, Bene, Collect, Confiteor, Cry, Cursus, Daven, Deus det, Devotion, Embolism, Entreaty, Epiclesis, Grace, Hallan-shaker, Imam, Kaddish, Khotbah, Khotbeh, Khutbah, Kyrie, Lauds, Litany, Lychnapsia, Ma(c)hzor, Missal, Novena, Orant, Orarium, Orison, Our Father, Paternoster, Patter, Petition, Placebo, Plea, Proseucha, Proseuche, Puja, Requiem, Requiescat, Rogation, Secret, Shema, Siddur, Suffrage, Triduum, Yizkov

> **Prayer** may indicate one who begs

**Preach(er)** Ainger, Boanerges, Donne, Ecclesiastes, Exhort, Evangelist, Gospeller, Graham, Itinerant, Knox, Lecture, Mar-text, Minister, MORALISE, Patercove, Postillate, Predicant, Predicate, Predikant, Priest, Prophet, Pulpiteer, Rant, Spintext, Spurgeon, Teach

**Preamble** Introduction, Preface, Proem, Prologue

**Precarious** Dangerous, Perilous, Risky, Uncertain

**Precaution** Care, Guard, Fail-safe, In case, Safeguard

**Precede(nce)** Antedate, Forego, Forerun, Herald, Pas, Predate, Preface, Priority, Protocol

**Precept** Adage, Canon, Commandment, Maxim, Motto, Saw

**Precinct(s)** Ambit, Area, Banlieue, Close, Courtyard, District, Environs, Peribolos, Region, Temenos, Verge, Vihara

**Precious** Chichi, Costly, Dear, Ewe-lamb, La-di-da, Owre, Precise, Rare, Valuable

**Precipice** Bluff, Cliff, Crag, Krans, Kran(t)z, Sheer

**Precipitate, Precipitation, Precipitous** Abrupt, Accelerate, Cause, Deposit, Hailstone, Headlong, Impetuous, Launch, Lees, Pellmell, Pitchfork, Rash, Sca(u)r, Sheer, Shoot, Sleet, Snowflakc, Start, STEEP

**Precis** Abstract, Aperçu, Epitome, Résumé, Summary

**Precise(ly), Precisian, Precision** Absolute, Accurate, Dry, Exact, Explicit, Nice(ty), Particular, Perfect, Plumb, Prig, Prim, Punctilious, Spang, Specific, Starchy, Stringent, Tight, Very

**Preclude** Bar, Debar, Estop, Foreclose, Hinder, Impede, Prevent

**Precocious** Advanced, Bratpack, Forward, Premature

**Precursor** Forerunner, Harbinger

**Predator(y)** Eagle, Fox, Glede, Harpy-eagle, Jackal, Kestrel, Kite, Lycosa, Marauder, Predacious, Tanrec, Tenrec

**Pre-dawn** Antelucan

**Predecessor**  Ancestor, Forebear, Foregoer

**Predestined**  Doomed, Fated, Tramway

**Predicament**  Box, Dilemma, Embroglio, Hobble, Hole, Jam, Pass, Peril, Pickle, Plight, Quandary, Scrape, Spot

**Predict(or), Prediction**  Augur, Bet, Forecast, Foretell, Forsay, Nap, Portend, Presage, Prognosis, Prophesy, Soothsayer

**Predilection**  Fancy, Liking, Prejudice, Taste, Tendency

**Predisposition**  Aptitude, Inclination, Parti-pris, Tendency

**Predominate**  Abound, Govern, Overshadow, Prevail, Reign

**Pre-eminence, Pre-eminent**  Arch, Foremost, Palm, Paramount, Primacy, Supreme, Topnotch, Unique

**Pre-empt**  Enter

**Preen**  Perk, Primp, Prink, Prune

**Prefab(ricated)**  Quonset

**Preface**  Foreword, Herald, Intro, Preamble, Proem, Usher

**Prefect**  Prepositor

**Prefer(ence), Preferred**  Advance, Choose, Elect, Faard, Faurd, Favour, Incline, Lean, Predilect(ion), Prefard, Priority, Promote, Sooner, Stocks, Will

**Prefix**  Eka, Introduce, Name

**Pregnancy, Pregnant**  Big, Clucky, Cyesis, Enceinte, Fertile, Gestation, Gravid, Heavy, Knocked-up

**Prehistoric**  Ancient, Azilian, Brontosaurus, Cro-magnon, Eocene, Primeval, Primitive, Pteranodon, Pterodactyl(e), Pterosaur, Saurian, Sinanthropus, Titanosaurus

**Prejudice(d)**  Bias, Discrimination, Down, Impede, Injure, Insular, Intolerance, Partiality, Parti pris, Preoccupy, Racism

**Prelate**  Cardinal, Churchman, Exarch, Monsignor, Odo, Priest

**Preliminary**  Exploration, Heat, Initial, Introductory, Precursory, Previous, Prodrome, Prolusion, Rough, Title-sheet

**Prelude**  Entree, Forerunner, Overture, Proem(ial), Ritornell(e), Ritornello

**Premature**  Early, Precocious, Pre(e)mie, Premy, Previous, Untimely, Untimeous

**Premeditate**  Anticipate, Foresee, Plan

**Premier**  Chief, Leader, Main, PM, PRIME MINISTER, Tojo

**Premise(s)**  Assumption, Datum, Epicheirema, Ground, Inference, Lemma, Postulate, Property, Reason

**Premium**  Bond, Bonus, Discount, Grassum, Pm, Reward, Scarce

**Premonition**  Hunch, Omen, Presentiment, Prodromal, Warning

**Preoccupation, Preoccupied, Preoccupy**  Absorb, Abstracted, Distrait, Engross, Hang-up, Intent, Obsess, Thing

**Prepaid** Sae

**Prepare(d), Preparation** Address, Arrange, Attire, Boun, Bowne, Busk, Calver, Cock, Concoct, Cooper, Decoct, Did, Do, Dress, Edit, Game, Groom, Ground, Inspan, Lay, Legwork, Lotion, Measure, Parascene, Prime, Procinct, Provide, Psych, READY, Rehearsal, Ripe, Set, Stand-to, Train, Truss, Yare

> **Prepare(d)** may indicate an anagram

**Preponderance, Preponderant, Preponderate** Important, Majority, Outweigh, Paramount, Prevalence

**Preposition** Premise

**Prepossessing, Prepossession** Attractive, Fetching, Predilection, Winsome

**Preposterous** Absurd, Chimeric, Foolish, Grotesque, Unreasonable

> **Preposterous** may indicate a word reversed

**Pre-Raphaelite** Rossetti

**Prerequisite** Condition, Essential, Necessity, Sine qua non

**Prerogative** Faculty, Franchise, Liberty, Privilege, Right

**Presage** Abode, Foresight, Omen, Portend, Presentiment, Prophesy

**Presbyter(ian)** Blue, Cameronian, Covenanter, Elder, Knox, Moderator, Sacrarium, Whig(gamore)

**Prescient** Clairvoyant, Fly

**Prescribe** Appoint, Assign, Dictate, Enjoin, Impose, Ordain, Rule, Set

**Prescription** Cipher, Decree, Direction, Formula, Medicine, R, Rec, Receipt, Ritual, Specific

**Presence** Aspect, Bearing, Closeness, Company, Debut, Hereness, Shechinah, Shekinah, Spirit

**Present(ed), Presenter, Presently** Anon, Assists, Award, Bestow, Boon, Bounty, Box, Congiary, Coram, Current, Debut, Donate, Dotal, Douceur, Dower, Endew, Endow, Endue, Enow, Etrenne, Existent, Fairing, Feature, Front-man, Gie, GIFT, Give, Going, Gratuity, Hand, Here, Hodiernal, Introduce, Inst, Largess(e), Linkman, Mod, Nonce, Now, Nuzzer, Pr, Produce, Proffer, Pro-tem, Render, Show, Slice, Tip, Today, Xenium, Yeven

**Preserve(d), Preservative, Preserver** Bottle, Can, Chill, Corn, Creosote, Cure, Embalm, Formaldehyde, Freeze, Guard, Hair, Hesperides, Jam, Keep, kinin, Kipper, Konfyt, Kyanise, MAINTAIN, Marmalade, Mummify, Pectin, Peculiar, Piccalilli, Pickle, Pot, Powellise, Salt, Salve, Saut, Souse, Store, Stuff, Tanalized, Tar, Tin, Vinegar

**Preside(nt)** Abe, Adams, Banda, Carter, Chair, Childers, Cleveland, Coty, Dean, Director, Ford, Grant, Harding, Harrison, Hoover, Ike, Kennedy, Kruger, Lincoln, Madison, Moderator, Nixon, P, Peron, Polk, Pr(a)eses, Prexy, Roosevelt, Saadat, Speaker, Superintendent, Supervisor, Taft, Tito, Truman, Tyler

**Press(ed), Pressing, Pressure** Acute, Aldine, Armoire, Atmospheric, Bar, Bramah, Button, Cabinet, Clarendon, Coerce, Cram, Crease, Crimp, Critical, Crowd, Crush, Cupboard, Dragoon, Dun, Duress, Enslave, Exigent, Force, Fourth estate, Goad, Hasten, Head, Heat, Herd, Hie, Hug, Hustle, Important, Importune, Inarm, Iron, Isobar, Jam, Knead, Lie, Lobby, Mangle, Microbar, Mill, Minerva, Newspapers, Obligate, PA, Pascal, Persist, Ply, Psi, Pump, PUSH, Ram, Record, Recruit, Reporter, Ridge, Roll, Rounce, Rush, Samizdat, Screw, Scrooge, Scrouge, Scrowdge, Scrum, Serr(e), Sit, Speed, Spur, Squash, Squeeze, Straint, Stress, Tension, Thlipsis, Threap, Threep, Throng, Throttle, Torr, Tourniquet, URGE(NCE), Urgency, Vice, Waid(e), Wardrobe, Weight, Wring

**Press-gang** Force, Impress, Shanghai

**Pressman** Ed, Reporter, PRO, Twicer

**Prestidigitate(r)** Conjure, Juggle, Legerdemain, Magician, Palm

**Prestige, Prestigious** Cachet, Credit, Distinguished, Fame, Influence, Kudos, Notable, Status

**Presume, Presumably, Presumption, Presumptuous** Allege, Arrogant, Audacity, Believe, Bold, Brass, Cocksure, Cocky, Doubtless, EXPECT, Familiar, Gall, Impertinent, Insolent, Liberty, Outrecuidance, Pert, Probably, Suppose, Uppish, Whipper-snapper

**Pretence, Pretend(er), Pretext** Act, Affect(ation), Afflict, Assume, Blind, Bluff, Charade, Charlatan, Claim, Cover, Dissimulate, Excuse, Feign, Feint, Gondolier, Humbug, Impostor, Jactitation, Lambert Simnel, Malinger, Obreption, Parolles, Pose, Profess, Pseudo, Quack, Sham, Simulate, Stale, Stalking-horse, Subterfuge, Suppose, Warbeck

**Pretension, Pretentious** Bombast, Fustian, Gaudy, Grandiose, Kitsch, La-di-da, Orotund, Ostentatious, Overblown, Paraf(f)le, Pompous, Pseud(o), Sciolism, Showy, Snobbish, Tinhorn, Uppity

**Pretty** Becoming, Comely, Cute, Dish, Decorate, Elegant, Fair(ish), Fairway, Inconie, Incony, Moderately, Pass, Peach, Primp, Quite, Sweet, Twee, Winsome

**Prevail(ing)** Endure, Go, Induce, Persist, Persuade, Predominant, Preponderate, Reign, Triumph, Victor, Win

**Prevalent** Catholic, Common, Endemic, Epidemic, Obtaining, Rife, Widespread

**Prevaricate, Prevarication** Equivocate, Hedge, Lie, Runaround, Stall, Whittie-whattie

**Prevent(ive)** Avert, Bar, Debar, Deter, Embar, Estop, Foreclose, Help, Impound, Inhibit, Keep, Let, Obstruct, Obviate, Preclude, Prophylactic, Stop, Theriac

**Preview** Sneak, Trailer

**Previous(ly)** Afore, Already, Before, Earlier, Ere(-now), Fore, Former, Hitherto, Once, Prior

**Prey** Booty, Feed, Kill, Pelt, Plunder, Proul, Prowl, Quarry, Raven,

Ravin(e), Soyle, Spreagh, Victim

**Price(d), Price-raising** Appraise, Assess, Charge, Consequence, Contango, COST, Dearth, Due, Evens, Expense, Fee, Fiars, Hire, List, Packet, Quotation, Quote, Rate, Regrate, Song, Upset, Value, Vincent, Weregild, Wergeld, Wergild, Worth, Yardage

**Priceless** Killing, Unique

**Prick(ed), Prickle, Prickly** Acanaceous, Accloy, Argemone, Arrect, Bearded, Brakier, Bramble, Brog, Bunya, Cactus, Cloy, Cnicus, Echinate, Goad, Gore, Hedgehog, Hedgepig, Impel, Inject, Jab, Jook, Juk, Kali, Penis, Pierce, Prod, Puncture, Rubus, Ruellia, Smart, Spinate, Stab, Star-thistle, Stimulus, Sting, Tattoo, Tatu, Teasel, Thistle, Thorn, Tingle, Urge

**Prickly-pear** Opuntia, Tuna

**Pride** Bombast, Conceit, Elation, Glory, Hauteur, Hubris, Inordinate, Lions, London, Machismo, Plume, Preen, Purge, Vanity

**Priest(ess), Priests** Aaron, Abaris, Abbess, Abbot, Ananias, Annas, Bacchantes, Baptes, Becket, Bonze, Brahmin, Cardinal, Clergyman, Cleric, Corybant(es), Curé, Druid, Eli, Elisha, Flamen, Fr, Hero, Hieratic, Hierophant, Io, Jethro, Lama, Laocoon, Levite, Lucumo, Mage, Magus, Mambo, Marabout, Metropolitan, Missionary, Monsignor, Mufti, Oratorian, Padre, Papa, Pastor, Patercove, Patrico, Pawaw, Père, Pontifex, Pontiff, Pope, Powwow, Pr, Preacher, Prelate, Prior(ess), Pythia, Rabbi, Rebbe, Rev, Sacerdotal, Savonarola, Shaman, Shaveling, Tohunga, Vicar, Vivaldi, Zadok

**Prig** Dandy, Fop, Humbug, Nimmer, Pilfer, Prude, Puritan

**Prim** Demure, Mun, Neat, Old-maidish, Preceese, Precise, Proper, Starchy

**Primacy, Primate** Ape, Bandar, Bigfoot, Bishop, Cardinal, Ebor, Gibbon, Hanuman, Hominid, Jackanapes, King-kong, Loris, Macaque, Magot, Mammal, Orang, Pongid, Prosimian, Quadruman, Rhesus, Sifaka

**Prima donna** Diva, Patti, Star

**Prim(a)eval** Ancient, Prehistoric, Primitive

**Prime(r), Primary, Priming** Basic, Bloom, Cardinal, Charging, Chief, Choice, Claircolle, Clearcole, Clerecole, Donat, Donet, Election, Enarm, First, Flower, Heyday, Mature, Original, Peak, Radical, Remex, Supreme, Thirteen, Tip-top, Totient, Totitive, Valuable, Windac, Windas, Ylem

**Prime Minister** Asquith, Attlee, Baldwin, Begin, Bute, Canning, Chamberlain, Chatham, Dewan, Diwan, Eden, Grey, Home, North, Peel, Pitt, PM, Premier, Shastri, Tanaiste, Taoiseach, Thatcher, Walpole

**Primitive** Aborigine, Amoeba, Antediluvian, Arabic, Archaic, Barbaric, Caveman, Crude, Early, Evolué, Fundamental, Neanderthal, Neolithic, Old, Persian, Pro, Prothyl(e), Protyl(e), Radical, Rudimentary, Savage, Turkish, Uncivilised, Ur

**Primordial** Blastema, Fundamental, Original

**Primrose, Primula** League, Oenothera, Onagra, Ox-lip, Pa(i)gle,

Rosebery, Vicar, Yellow

**Prince(ly)** Ahmed, Albert, Amir, Amphitryon, Anchises, Atheling, Cadmus, Caliph, Chagan, Charming, Elector, Equerry, Eugene, Florizel, Fortinbras, Gaekwar, Guicowar, Hal, Highness, Hospodar, Huzoor, Igor, Inca, Infante, Khan, Ksar, Lavish, Lucumo, Margrave, Mirza, Nawab, Nizam, Noble, Otto, P, Pendragon, Porphyrogenite, Potentate, Rainier, Rajah, Rana, Ras, Rasselas, Ratoo, Ratu, Regal, RH, Rupert, Serene, Shereef, Sherif, Student, Tengku, Tsar(evich), Tunku, Upper Roger

**Princess** Andromache, Andromeda, Anne, Ariadne, Begum, Czarevna, Czarista, Danae, Di(ana), Electra, Electress, Eudocia, Europa, Hermione, Ida, Imogen, Infanta, Iseult, Isolde, Jezebel, Maharanee, Maharani, Procne, Rani, Regan, Tou Wan, Tsarevna, Tsarista, Turandot

**Principal** Arch, Capital, Central, CHIEF, Decuman, Especial, First, Foremost, Head, Leading, Main(stay), Major, Mass, Protagonist, Ringleader, Staple

**Principle(s), Principled** Animistic, Archimedes, Axiom, Basis, Brocard, Canon, Code, Criterion, Cy pres, Doctrine, Dogma, Element, Entelechy, Essential, Generale, Germ, Honourable, Key, Law, Logos, Ormazd, Ormuzd, Peter, Precept, Rationale, Reason, Rudiment, Rule, Sakti, Seed, Shakti, Spirit, Tenet, Theorem, Ticket, Yang

**Prink** Beautify, Bedeck, Dress

**Print(er), Printing** Baskerville, Batik, Bromide, Calotype, Caseman, Chromo, Collotype, Dab, Elzevir, Engrave, Etching, Font, Gravure, Gurmukhi, Impress, Incunabula, Italic, Letterpress, Lino-cut, Lithograph, Lower-case, Monotype, Offset, Oleo, Plate, Positive, Press, Publish, Report, Reproduction, Samizdat, Ship, Splash, Stamp, Stenochrome, Stonehand, Typesetter, Whorl, Zincograph

**Printing-press** Rounce

**Prior(ity)** Abbot, Afore, Antecedent, Earlier, Former, Hitherto, Monk, Overslaugh, Pre-, Precedence, Prefard, Preference, Previous, Privilege

> **Prise** see PRIZE

**Prism(s), Prismatic** Catadioptric, Iriscope, Periaktos, Spectrum, Teinoscope, Wollaston

**Prison** Alcatraz, Bagnio, Bastille, Bin, Bird, Bridewell, Brig, Brixton, Cage, Can, Cell, Chillon, Chok(e)y, Clink, Club, Cooler, Coop, Counter, Dartmoor, Dungeon, Durance, Fleet, Fotheringhay, gaol, Glass-house, Gulag, Hokey, Holloway, Hoos(e)gow, Hulk(s), JAIL, Jug, Kitty, Limbo, Lob's pound, Lock-up, Logs, Lumber, Marshalsea, Massymore, Maze, Newgate, Nick, Oflag, Panopticon, Pen, Pentonville, Pit, Poke(y), Pound, Quad, Quod, Roundhouse, Scrubs, Shop, Slammer, Spandau, Stalag, Stir, Strangeways, The Leads, Tolbooth, Tronk, Wandsworth

**Prisoner** Canary-bird, Captive, Collegian, Collegiate, Con(vict), Detainee, Detenu, Inmate, Internee, Lag, Lifer, Political, POW, Trustee, Trusty, Zek

**Pristine** Fresh, New, Original, Unspoiled

**Private(ly)** Aside, Atkins, Auricular, Buccaneer, Byroom, Clandestine,

Close, Confidential, Enisle(d), Esoteric, In camera, Individual, Inner, Intimate, Non-com, Own, Personal, Piou-piou, Poilu, Proprietary, Pte, Rank(er), Retired, Sanction, Sapper, Secret, Several, SOLDIER, Sub rosa, Tommy

**Privateer(s)** Buccaneer, Corsair, Freebooter, Marque(s), Pirate

**Privation** Hardship, Penury, Want

**Privilege(d)** Blest, Charter, Exempt, Favour, Franchise, Freedom, Indulgence, Liberty, Mozarab, Patent, Prerogative, Pryse, Regale, Regalia, Right, Sac

**Privy** Apprised, Can, Intimate, Jakes, John, Loo, Necessary, Reredorter, Secret, Sedge, Siege

**Prize(s)** Acquest, Apple, Assess, Award, Best, Booker, Bravie, Capture, Champion, Creach, Cup, Efforce, ESTEEM, Force, Grice, Honour, Jackpot, Jemmy, Lever, Lot, Money, Nobel, Palm, Pie, Plum, Plunder, Pot, Pulitzer, Purse, Ram, Reprisal, REWARD, Scalp, Ship, Spreaghery, Sprechery, Tern, Treasure, Trophy, Value

**Pro** Aye, Coach, For, Harlot, Moll, Paid, Yes

**Probable** Apparent, Belike, Likely, Possible

**Probation(er)** Novice, Novitiate, Test, Trainee, Trial

**Probe** Antenna, Bore, Delve, Dredge, Explore, Fathom, Feeler, Fossick, Inquire, Investigate, Pelican, Poke, Pump, SEARCH, Stylet, Tent, Thrust, Tracer

**Probity** Honour, Integrity, Justice

**Problem** Acrostic, Boyg, Crux, Dilemma, Egma, Enigma, Facer, Glitch, Hang-up, Headache, Hitch, Indaba, Knot(ty), Koan, Musive, Net, Nuisance, Obstacle, Poser, Quandary, Question, Re, Rebus, Riddle, Rider, Snag, Sorites, Sum, Teaser, Thing, Tickler, Yips

**Proboscis** Haustellum, Promuscis, Snout, Trunk

**Proceed(s), Proceeding, Procedure** Acta, Afoot, Continue, Course, Drill, Fand, Flow, Goes, Haul, Issue, Machinery, March, Mine, Modal, Move, On, Pass, Practice, Praxis, Process, Profit, Punctilio, Pursue, Put, Rake, Return, Rite, Routine, Sap, Steps, System, Take, Use, Yead(s), Yede, Yeed

**Process(ion)** Acromion, Action, Ala, Ambarvalia, Axon, Cortège, Demo, Handle, Method, Moharram, Motorcade, Muharram, Pageant, Parade, Pipeline, Pomp, Recycle, Series, Skimmington, Solvay, String, Train, Treat, Trial

**Proclaim, Proclamation** Announce, Annunciate, Ban, Blaze, Boast, Broadsheet, Cry, Edict, Enounce, Enunciate, Oyez, Preconise, Profess, Publish, Ring, Shout, Trumpet, Ukase

**Procrastinate, Procrastinating** Defer, Delay, Dilatory, Dilly-dally, Linger, Postpone, Shelve, Vacillate

**Procreate** Beget, Engender, Generate, Initiate

**Procrustean** Conformity

**Proctor**  Agent, Monitor, Prog, Proxy

**Procurator, Procure(r)**  Achieve, Aunt, Crimp, Earn, Get, Induce, Naunt, Obtain, Pander, Pilate, Pimp, Sort, Suborn

**Prod**  Egg, Goad, Jab, Job, Jog, Nudge, Poke, Pote

**Prodigal**  Costly, Lavish, Profligate, Wanton, Wasteful, Waster

**Prodigious, Prodigy**  Abnormal, Amazing, Huge, Immense, Monster, Monument, Mozart, Phenomenal, Portentous, Tremendous, Wonder, Wunderkind

**Produce(r)**  Afford, Cause, Create, Crop, Ean, Edit, Effect, Engender, Exhibit, Extend, Fruit, Generate, Get, Grow, Impresario, Issue, Kind, Make, Offspring, Output, Propage, Raise, Son, Stage, Supply, Teem, Throw, Yield

> **Produces**  may indicate an anagram

**Product(ion), Productive(ness), Productivity**  Actualities, Artefact, Ashtareth, Ashtaroth, Astarte, Bore, Coefficient, Drama, Fecund, Fertile, Fruit, Genesis, Harvest, Output, Result, Rich, Show, Speiss, Uberous, Uberty, Work, Yield

> **Production**  may indicate an anagram

**Proem**  Pre, Preface, Foreword, Overture

**Profane**  Coarse, Desecrate, Impious, Irreverent, Unholy, Violate

**Profess(ed), Professor**  Absent-minded, Academic, Adjoint, Admit, Asset, Challenger, Claim, Declare, Disney, Emeritus, Higgins, Ostensible, Own, Practise, Pundit, Regent, Regius, RP, STP

**Profession(al)**  Admission, Assurance, Business, Career, Creed, Expert, Métier, Pretence, Pursuit, Regular, Salaried, Skilled, Trade, Vocation, Yuppie

**Proffer**  Give, Present, Proposition, Tender

**Proficiency, Proficient**  Adept, Alert, Dan, Expert, Forte, Practised, Skill

**Profile**  Analysis, Contour, Half-face, Loral, Outline, Silhouette, Sketch, Statant, T(h)alweg, Vignette

**Profit(able), Profiteer, Profits**  Advantage, Asset, Avail, Benefit, Boot, Bunce, Cere, Clear, Divi(dend), Economic, Edge, Emoluments, Exploit, Fat, Gain, Graft, Gravy, Grist, Income, Increment, Issue, Leech, Lucrative, Melon, Mileage, Net, Pay(ing), Perk, Rake-off, Return, Reward, Royalty, Spoils, Use, Utile, Utility, Vail

**Profligate**  Corinthian, Corrupt, Degenerate, Dissolute, Extravagant, Libertine, Lorel, Losel(l), Oatmeal, Rakehell, Reprobate, Roué, Spend-all, Wastrel

**Profound**  Bottomless, Complete, Deep, Intense, Recondite

**Profuse, Profusion**  Abundant, Copious, Excess, Free, Galore, Lavish, Liberal, Lush, Quantity, Rank, Rich

**Progenitor, Progenitrix**  Ancestor, Ma, Predecessor, Sire, Stock

**Progeny**  Children, Descendants, Fruit, Issue, Offspring, Seed

**Prognosis**  Forecast, Prediction

**Prognosticate, Prognostication**  Augur, Foretell, Omen, Predict, Prophesy

**Program(ming) language, Programmer**  Ada, Algol, Basic, Cobol, Fortran, Linker, LISP, Logo, Pascal

**Programme**  Agenda, Broadcast, Card, Event, Prank, Playbill, Schedule, Scheme, Sked, Soap, Software, Spreadsheet, Syllabus, System, Telecast, Timetable

**Progress(ive), Progression**  ADVANCE, Afoot, Avant garde, Course, Fabian, Forge, Forward, Gain, Go, Growth, Headway, Incede, Liberal, Move, Onwards, Paraphonia, Pilgrim's, Prosper, Rack, Rake's, Reformer, Roll, Run, Sequence, Series, Step, Vaunce, Way, Yead, Yede, Yeed

**Prohibit(ion), Prohibitionist**  Ban, Block, Debar, Embargo, Estop, Forbid, Hinder, Index, Interdict, Prevent, Pussyfoot, Taboo, Tabu, Veto

**Project(ile), Projecting, Projection, Projector**  Aim, Ammo, Assignment, Astrut, Ball, Ballistic, Beetle, Bullet, Butt, Buttress, Cam, Cast, Catapult, Condyle, Console, Corbel, Crossette, Coving, Cutwater, Diascope, Discus, Eaves, Echinus, Elance, Enterprise, Episcope, Excrescence, Exsert, Extrapolate, Flange, Gair, Gore, Guess, Hangover, Hoe, Jut, Kern, Knob, Ledge, Lobe, Lug, Malleolus, Mitraille, Nab, Nose, Nunatak(er), Outcrop, Overhang, Oversail, PROTRUDE, Prouder, Raguly, Rocket, Sail, Salient, Scaw, Scheme, Screen, Shelf, Shrapnel, Skaw, Snag, Snout, Spline, Sponson, Spur, Squarrose, Tang, Tappet, Tenon, Throw, Toe, Tracer, Trippet, Trunnion, Tusk, Umbo, Undertaking, Villus, Vitascope

**Proletarian, Proletariat**  People, Plebeian, Popular

**Proliferate**  Expand, Increase, Multiply, Propagate, Snowball

**Prolific**  Abounding, Fecund, Fertile, Fruitful, Profuse, Teeming

**Prolix(ity)**  Lengthy, Prosaic, Rambling, Rigmarole, Verbose, Wire-draw, Wordy

**Prologue**  Introduce, Preface

**Prolong(ed)**  Extend, Lengthen, Protract, Sostenuto, Spin, Sustain

**Prom(enade)**  Cakewalk, Catwalk, Crush-room, Esplanade, Front, Mall, Parade, Paseo, Pier, Sea-front, Stroll, WALK

**Prometheus**  Fire

**Promethium**  Pm

**Prominence, Prominent**  Antitragus, Blatant, Bold, Condyle, Conspicuous, Egregious, Emphasis, Featured, Gonion, Important, Insistent, Manifest, Marked, Salient, Signal, Toot, Tragus

**Promiscuous, Promiscuity**  Casual, Free, Indiscriminate, Light, Motley, Pell-mell, Whoredom

**Promise, Promising**  Accept, Augur, Avoure, Behest, Behight, Behote, Bode, Coming, Covenant, Engagement, Foretaste, Guarantee, Hecht, Hest, Hight, IOU, Likely, Manifest, Parole, Pledge, Plight, Pollicitation,

Potential, Rosy, Sign, Sponsor, Swear, Tile, Undertake, Vow, Warranty, Word

**Promised land** Beulah, Canaan, Israel

**Promissory note** IOU, PN

**Promontory** Bill, Cliff, Foreland, Headland, Hoe, Hogh, Mull, Naze, Nose, Ness, Peak, Spit

**Promote(r), Promotion** Advance, ADVERTISE, Aggrandise, Aid, Assist, Boost, Campaign, Elevate, Encourage, Foster, Further, Help, Hype, Increase, Prefer, Provoke, Rear, Run, Sell, Sponsor, Stage, Step, Upgrade, Uplead, Uprate

**Prompt(er), Promptly, Promptness** Actuate, Alacrity, Autocue, Believe, Celerity, Chop-chop, Cue, Egg, Expeditious, Frack, Idiot-board, Immediate, Incite, Inspire, Instigate, Move, Punctual, Quick, Ready, Speed(y), Spur, Stimulate, Sudden, Tight, Tit(e), Titely, Tyte, Urgent

**Promulgate** Preach, Proclaim, Publish, Spread

**Prone** Apt, Groof, Grouf, Grovel, Liable, Lying, Prostrate, Recumbent, Subject

**Prong** Fang, Fork, Grain, Peg, Tine

**Pronghorn** Cabrie, Cabrit

**Pronounce(d), Pronouncement** Adjudicate, Affirm, Articulate, Assert, Conspicuous, Clear, Declare, Dictum, Enunciate, Fiat, Marked, Opinion, Palatalise, Recite, Utter, Vocal, Vote

**Pronunciation** Betacism, Cacoepy, Delivery, Diction, Etacism, Itacism, Orthology, Plateasm, Sound

**Proof** Apagoge, Argument, Bona fides, Evidence, Firm, Galley, Positive, Preif(e), Probate, Pull, Quality, Resistant, Revision, Secure, Strength, Test, Tight, Token, Trial, Validity

**Prop** Airscrew, Bolster, Buttress, Crutch, Dog-shore, Fulcrum, Leg, Loosehead, Misericord(e), Punch(eon), Rance, Rest, Shore, Sprag, Spur, Staff, Stay, Stempel, Stemple, Stilt, Stoop, Stoup, Stull, SUPPORT, Tighthead, Underpin

**Propaganda, Propagandist** Agitprop, Ballyhoo, Brainwashing, Chevalier, Doctrine, Promotion, Publicity

**Propagate, Propagator** Dispread, Generate, Graft, Hatch, Increase, Produce, Promulgate, Provine, Spread, Tan-bed

**Propel(ler)** Ca', Drive, Fin, Launch, Leg, Lox, MOVE, Oar, Project, Push, Rotor, Row, Screw, Throw

**Propensity** Aptness, Bent, Inclination, Penchant, Tendency

**Proper(ly)** Ain, Correct, Decent, Decorous, Due, En règle, Ethical, FIT, Genteel, Governessy, Kosher, Noun, Ought, Own, Pakka, Pathan, Prim, Pucka, Pukka, Puritanic, Seemly, Suitable, Tao, Trew, True, Well

**Property** Assets, Attribute, Aver, Belongings, Chattel, Chose, Contenement, Demesne, Dowry, Effects, Enclave, Escheat, Estate, Fee,

Flavour, Fonds, Goods, Hereditament, Living, Means, Peculium, Personal, Premises, Quale, Quality, Stock, Stolen, Theft, Trait, Usucapion, Usucaption

**Prophesy, Prophet(ess), Prophetic** Amos, Augur, Bab, Balaam, Calchas, Cassandra, Daniel, Divine, Deborah, Elias, Elijah, Elisha, Ezekiel, Ezra, Fatal, Fatidical, Forecast, Foretell, Germancer, Habakkuk, Haggai, Hosea, Is, Isa, Is(a)iah, Jeremiah, Joel, Jonah, Mahound, Malachi, Mantic, Micah, Mohammed, Mormon, Mopsus, Moses, Nahum, Obadiah, Ominous, Oracle, Portend, Predictor, Prognosticate, Pythoness, Seer, Sibyl, Tiresias, Vatic, Voluspa, Zwickau

**Prophylactic, Prophylaxis** Inoculation, Preventive, Serum, Vaccine, Variolation

**Propitiate** Appease, Atone, Pacify, Reconcile, Sop

**Propitious** Benign, Favourable, Lucky

**Proponent** Advocate, Backer, Partisan

**Proportion(ate)** Commensurable, Dimension, Portion, Pro rata, Quantity, Quota, Ratio, Reason, Regulate, Relation, Sine, Size, Soum, Sowm

**Proposal, Propose** Advance, Bid, Bill, Feeler, Irenicon, Mean, Motion, Move, Nominate, Offer, Overture, Plan, Pop, Propound, Recommend, Resolution, Scheme, Slate, SUGGEST, Tender, Woot, Would

**Proposition** Axiom, Corollary, Deal, Ergo, Hypothesis, Lemma, Overture, Pons asinorum, Porism, Premise, Premiss, Rider, Sorites, Spec, Superaltern, Theorem, Thesis

**Propound** Advocate, Purpose, State

**Proprietor, Propriety** Decorum, Etiquette, Grundy, Keeper, Master, Owner, Patron, Rectitude

**Prosaic** Common, Drab, Flat, Humdrum, Tedious, Workaday

**Proscenium** Forestage

**Proscribe** Exile, Outlaw

**Prose, Prosy** Haikai, Saga, Verbose, Writing

**Prosecute, Prosecutor** Allege, Avvogadore, Charge, Fiscal, Indict, Practise, Sue, Wage

**Proselytism** Indoctrination, Propagandism

**Prospect(or)** Explore, Fossick, Look-out, Mine, OUTLOOK, Panorama, Perspective, Pleases, Reefer, Scenery, Search, Sourdough, View, Vista, Visto

**Prosper(ity), Prosperous** Blessed, Blossom, Boom, Fair, Flourish, Mérimée, SUCCEED, Thee, Thrive, Up, Warison, Wealth, Welfare, Well-to-do

**Prostitute** Brass, Bulker, Catamite, Chippie, Cockatrice, Cocotte, Debase, Dell, Doxy, Harlot, Loose woman, Madam, Magdalen(e), Mutton, Plover, Pole-cat, Pro, Punk, Quail, Road, Stew, Trull, Venture, Whore

**Prostrate, Prostration** Collapse, Exhausted, Fell, Flat, Ko(w)tow, Laid, Obeisance, Overcome, Prone, Repent, Throw

**Protactinium** Pa

**Protean** Amoebic, Fusible, Variable

**Protect(ion), Protector** Aegis, Alexin, Arm, Asylum, Auspice, Bastion, Bestride, Bield, Buckler, Charm, Cloche, Coat, Cocoon, Coleor(r)hiza, Cover, Covert, Cromwell, Cushion, Danegeld, Defend, Degauss, Egis, Entrenchment, Escort, Estacade, Flank, Guard(ian), Gumshield, Hedge, House, Insure, Keckle, Keep, Kickback, Mac(k)intosh, Mail, Male, Mother, Noll, Nosey, Orillion, Overall, Parados, Patent, Patron, Preserve, Rabbit's foot, Safeguard, Sandbag, Save, Screen, Scug, Skug, Shadow, Shelter, SHIELD, Splasher, Starling, Tribute, Tutelar, Vaccine, Ward(ship), Warhead, Warrant, Wing

**Protégé** Pupil, Ward

**Protein** Abrin, Actin, Alanine, Albumen, Albumin, Aleurone, Amandine, Analogon, Antibody, Avidin, Bradykinin, Collagen, Conchiolin, Cytokine, Elastin, Fibr(a)in, Flagellin, Gelatin, Gliadin, Glob(ul)in, Gluten, Histone, Hordein, Incaparina, Interferon, Interleukin, Legumin, Leucin(e), Lysin, Meat, Myogen, Myosin, Opsin, Pepsin(e), Prion, Prolamin(e), Protamine, Renin, Sericin, Spongin, Soya, Tempeh, Transferrin, Tubulin, Vitellin, Zein

**Protest** Avouch, Clamour, Come, Demo, Demonstrate, Demur, Deprecate, Dharna, Dissent, Expostulate, Inveigh, Lock-out, March, Object, Outcry, Picket, Plea, Remonstrate, Sit-in, Squeak, Squeal

**Protestant** Anabaptist, Anglo, Calvin, Cranmer, Evangelic, Gospeller, Huguenot, Independent, Lady, Lutheran, Mennonite, Methodist, Moravian, Nonconformist, Oak-boy, Orangeman, Pentecostal, Prod, Puritan, Stundist, Swaddler

**Protocol** Agreement, Code, Convention

**Protoplasm(ic)** Cytode, Sarcode

**Prototype** Exemplar, Model, Original, Pattern

**Protozoa** Am(o)eba, Gregarine, Moner(a), Moneron, Radiolaria

**Protract(ed)** Delay, EXTEND, Lengthen, Livelong, Prolong

**Protrude, Protrusion** Bulge, Exsert, Jut, Pop, Pout, Project, Strout, Tel

**Protuberance, Protuberant** Apophysis, Bulge, Bump, Condyle, Gibbous, Hump, Knap, Knob, Malleolus, Node, Papillose, Spadix, Swelling, Tragus, Tuber, Venter

**Proud** Arrogant, Boaster, Conceited, Dic(k)ty, Elated, Flush, Haughty, Haut, Level, Lordly, Superb, Vain

**Prove** Argue, Ascertain, Assay, Attest, Authenticate, Aver, Confirm, Convince, Evince, Justify, SHOW, Substantiate, Test

**Proverb** Adage, Axiom, Byword, Gnome, Maxim, Paroemia, Saw

> **Proverbial** may refer to the biblical Proverbs

**Provide(d), Provident** Afford, Allow, Arrange, Cater, Compare, Conditional, Endow, Equip, Far-seeing, Fend, Find, Furnish, Generate, Give, If, Maintain, Proviso, Purvey, Serve, So, Sobeit, SUPPLY

**Province, Provincial(ism)** Alberta, Anjou, Antwerp, Area, District, Eritrea, Exclave, Forte, Gascony, Insular, Land, Manitoba, Maritime, Mofussil, Munster, Narrow, Nome, Normandy, Oblast, Palatinate, Pale, Patavinity, Picardy, Realm, Regional, R(h)aetia, Rural, Satrapy, Shoa, Sircar, Subah, Suburban, Territory, Tyrol, Ulster, Vilayet

**Provision(s)** Acates, Board, Fodder, Larder, Proggins, Scran, Skran, Stock, Supply, Suttle, Viands, Viaticum, Victuals

**Proviso, Provisional** Caution, Caveat, Clause, Condition, Interim, IRA, Reservation, Salvo, Temporary, Tentative

**Provocative, Provoke** Agacant, Alluring, Egg, Elicit, Exacerbate, Harass, Incense, Induce, Instigate, Irk, Irritate, Needle, Nettle, Occasion, Pique, Prompt, Spark, Stimulate, Tar, Tease, Vex

**Provost** Keeper, Marshal, Warden

**Prow** Bow, Fore, Nose, Prore, Stem

**Pro-war** Hawk

**Prowess** Ability, Bravery, Forte, Fortitude

**Prowl(er)** Hunt, Lurk, Mooch, Prole, Ramble, Roam, Rove, Snoke, Snook, Snowk, Tenebrio, Tom

**Proxime accessit** Next best

**Proximity** Handiness

**Proxy** Agent, Attorn, Deputy, PP, Regent, Sub, Surrogate, Vicar, Vice

**Prude(nce), Prudent, Prudery** Canny, Caution, Comstocker, Conservative, Discreet, Discretion, Foresight, Frugal, Grundyism, Metis, Politic, Prig, Prissy, Provident, Sage, Sensible, Sparing, Strait-laced, Strait-lacer, Thrifty, Victorian, Ware, Wary, Wise

**Prune(r)** Bill-hook, Dehorn, Lop, Plum, Proign, Proin(e), Reduce, Secateur, Sned, Thin, Trim

**Prunella** Hedge-sparrow, Self-heal

**Prurient** Avaricious, Itchy, Lewd, Obscene

**Prussia(n)** Blue, Junker, Pruce, Spruce

**Pry** Ferret, Force, Lever, Meddle, Nose, Peep, Question, Search, Snoop, Toot

**Psalm** Anthem, Cantate, Chorale, Hymn, Introit, Jubilate, Miserere, Neck-verse, Paean, Ps, Song, Tone, Tract, Venite

**Pseudo** Bogus, Mock, Sham, Spurious

**Pseudonym** Aka, Alias, Allonym, Anonym, Pen-name, Stage-name

**Pshaw** Chut, Pooh, Tilley-valley, Tilly-fally, Tilly-vally

**Psyche** Self, Soul, Spirit

**Psychiatrist, Psychologist** Adler, Alienist, Coué, Ellis, Freud, Jung, Reich, Shrink, Trick-cyclist

**Psychic** ESP, Lodge, Medium, Seer

**Psychology** Behaviourism, Gestalt

**Ptomaine** Neurine

**Pub** Bar, Boozer, Gin-palace, Houf(f), House, Howf(f), Inn, Joint, Local, Pothouse, Shanty, Tavern

**Puberty** Adolescence, Teens

**Pubescence** Tomentum

**Public** Apert, Bar, Civil, Common, Demos, General, Inn, Lay, Limelight, National, Open, Overt, Populace, State, World

**Publican** Ale-keeper, Bung, Host, Landlord, Licensee, Tapster, Taverner

**Publication** Announcement, Broadsheet, Edition, Issue, JOURNAL, Lady, Mag, Organ, Pictorial, Samizdat, Tabloid, Tatler, Tract, Tribune, Yearbook

**Publicist, Publicity** Ad(vert), Airing, Ballyhoo, Coverage, Flack, Leakage, Limelight, Plug, PRO, Promotion, Réclame, Spin-doctor, Splash

**Publish(ed), Publisher, Publicise** Air, Blaze, Disclose, Edit, Issue, Noise, OUP, Out, Plug, Post, Print(er), Proclaim, Propagate, Release, Run, Vent, Ventilate

**Puck** Disc, Elf, Lob, Sprite

**Pucker(ed)** Cockle, Contract, Gather, Plissé, Purse, Ruck, Shir(r), Wrinkle

**Pud** Fin, Paw

**Pudding** Afters, Blancmange, Cabinet, College, Custard, Dessert, Drisheen, Duff, Dumpling, Fritter, Haggis, Hasty, Nesselrode, Panada, Parfait, Pease, Popover, Roly-poly, Sowens, Sponge, Stickjaw, Stodge, Sundae, Tansy, Tapioca, Umbles, Yorkshire, Zabaglione

**Puddle** Collect, Dub, Flush, Pant, Plash, Plouter, Plowter, Pool, Sop

**Puff(ed), Puffer** Advertise, Blow, Blowfish, Blurb, Breath, Chuff, Chug, Drag, Encomist, Eulogy, Exsufflicate, Fag, Flatus, Fuff, Globe-fish, Grampus, Gust, Lunt, Pech, Pegh, Plug, Recommend, Skiff, Slogan, Steam, Swell, Toke, Waft, Whiff

**Puffin** Sea-parrot, Tammie Norie, Tam Noddy

**Pug(ilist)** Belcher, Boxer, Bruiser, Fancy, Fistic, Monkey

**Pugnacious** Aggressive, Belligerent, Combative

**Puke** Retch, Sick, Vomit

**Pukka** Authentic, Genuine, Real, True

**Pulchritude** Beauty, Cheese-cake, Grace

**Pull (up)** Adduce, Attraction, Crane, Drag, Draw, Force, Haul, Heave, Heeze, Hook, INFLUENCE, Lug, Mousle, Pluck, Rein, Rove, Rug, Sally, Sole, Soole, Sowl(e), Stop, Tit, Tow, Trice, Tug, Undertow, Yank

**Pulley** Block, Capstan, Idle, Swig, Trice, Trochlea, Truckle

**Pullulate** Teem

> **Pull up** see PULL

**Pulp** Cellulose, Chyme, Chymify, Crush, Kenaf, Marrow, Mash, Mush, Pap, Paste, Pomace, Pound, Rot, Rubbish, Squeeze, Squidge

**Pulpit(e)**  Ambo(nes), Lectern, Mimbar, Minbar, Pew, Rostrum, Tent, Tub, Wood

**Pulsate**  Beat, Palpitate, Quiver, Throb, Vibrate

**Pulse**  Beat, Calavance, Caravance, D(h)al, Dholl, Dicrotic, Gram, Ictus, Lentil, Pea, Rhythm, Sain(t)foin, Soy beans, Sphygmus, Systole, Throb

**Pulverise**  Calcine, Comminute, Contriturate, Demolish, Grind, POUND, Powder

**Puma**  Catamount, Cougar, Panther

**Pummel(ling)**  Beat, Drub, Fib, Nevel, Pound, Tapotement, Thump

> **Pummelled**  may indicate an anagram

**Pump**  Bellows, Bowser, Compressor, Drive, Elicit, Grease-gun, Grill, Heart, Hydropult, Inflate, Knee-swell, Piston, Question, Shoe, Suction

**Pumphandle**  Sweep

**Pumpkin**  Cashaw, Gourd, Quash

**Pun**  Calembour, Clinch, Equivoque, Paragram, Paronomasia, Quibble, Ram

**Punch(ed)**  Antic, Blow, Boff, Bolo, Box, Bradawl, Bumbo, Check, Chop, Dry-beat, Fib, Fid, Fist(ic), Glogg, Haymaker, Hit, Hook, Horse, Jab, Knobble, Knubble, KO, Lander, Mat, Nubble, One-er, Perforate, Pertuse, Plug, Poke, Polt, Pommel, Prod, Pummel, Rabbit, Rumbo, Slosh, Sock, Sting(o), Suffolk, Swop, Upper-cut, Wap, Wind, Zest

**Punctilious**  Exact, Formal, Nice, Particular, Picked, Precise, Prim, Stickler

**Punctual(ity)**  Politesse, Prompt, Regular

**Punctuate, Punctuation**  Bracket, Emphasize, Interrupt, Mark

**Puncture**  Centesis, Crible, Deflate, Drill, Flat, Hole, Lumbar, Perforate, Pierce, Prick

**Pundit**  Expert, Guru, Oracle, Sage, Savant, Swami, Teacher

**Pungency, Pungent**  Acid, Acrid, Acrolein, Alum, Ammonia, Bite, Bitter, Caustic, Hot, Mordant, Piquant, Poignant, Point, Racy, Spice, Sting, Tangy, Witty

**Punish(ed), Punishment**  Amerce, Attainder, Baffle, Bastinado, Beat, Birch, Cane, Cart, Castigate, Chasten, Chastise, Corporal, Detention, DISCIPLINE, Fine, Flog, Gantlope, Gate, Gauntlet, Gruel, Horsing, Imposition, Impot, Interdict, Jankers, Jougs, Keelhaul, Lambast(e), Lines, Log, Marmalise, Nemesis, Pack-drill, Pandy, Penalise, Penance, Penology, Picket, Pillory, Pine, Rap, Reprisal, Ruler, Scaffold, Scath, Scourge, Sentence, Smack, Smite, Spif(f)licate, Stocks, Strafe, Straff, Strap, Strappado, Talion, Toco, Toko, Treadmill, Trim, Tron, Trounce, Tumbrel, Tumbril, Visit, Whip, Ywrake, Ywroke

> **Punish**  may indicate an anagram

**Punk**  Inferior, Neer-do-well, Nobody, Worthless

**Punnet**  Basket, Trug

**Punt(ing)**  Antepost, Back, Bet, Gamble, Kent, Kick, Pound, Quant

**Puny** Frail, Inferior, Petty, Runtish, Scram, Shilpit, Sickly, Small, Weak

**Pup(py)** Cub, Whelp

**Pupa** Chrysalis, Nymph, Obtect

**Pupil** Abiturient, Apple, Apprentice, Boarder, Cadet, Catechumen, Disciple, Eyeball, Follower, Gyte, L, Prefect, Protégé(e), Scholar, Student, Ward

> **Pupil** may refer to an eye

**Puppet(eer)** Bunraku, Creature, Doll, Dummy, Faineant, Fantoccini, Guignol, Jack-a-lent, Judy, Marionette, Mawmet, Mommet, Motion(-man), Pawn, Pinocchio, Promotion, Punch(inello), Quisling

**Purchase** Bargain, Buy, Coff, Earn, Emption, Get, Grip, Halliard, Halyard, Hold, LEVERAGE, Louisiana, Parbuckle, Secure, Shop, Toehold

**Pure, Purity** Absolute, Candour, Chaste, Clean(ly), Cosher, Fine, Good, Holy, Innocent, Intemerate, Inviolate, Kosher, Lily, Lilywhite, Me(a)re, Net(t), Pristine, Sheer, Simon, Simple, Sincere, Snow-white, Stainless, True, Unalloyed, Vertue, Virgin, Virtue, White

**Puree** Coulis, Fool

**Purgative, Purge** Aloes, Aloetic, Araroba, Calomel, Cascara, Cassia, Castor-oil, Catharsis, Cholalogue, Croton, Delete, Diacatholicon, Diarrh(o)ea, Drastic, Elaterin, Eliminate, Eluant, Emetic, Enos (tdk), Erase, Evacuant, Exonerate, Expiate, Gleichschaltung, Hiera-picra, Ipomoea, Jalap, Laxative, Picra, Scour, Senna, Soil, Turbith, Turpeth, Wahoo

**Purification, Purifier, Purify(ing)** Absolve, Bowdlerise, Clay, Clean(se), Depurate, Dialysis, Distil, Edulcorate, Elution, Exalt, Expurgate, Filter, Fine, Gas-lime, Lustre, Lustrum, Refine, Retort, Samskara, Sanctify, Scrub, Try

**Puritan** Bluenose, Ireton, Ironsides, Pi, Prude, Prynne, Roundhead, Seeker, Traskite, Waldenses, Wowser, Zealot

**Purl(er)** Cropper, Eddy, Fall, Knit, Ripple, Stream

**Purloin** Abstract, Appropriate, Lift, Nab, Pilfer, Snaffle, Steal

**Purple** Amarantin, Aubergine, Chlamys, Corkir, Cudbear, Dubonnet, Eminence, Golp(e), Imperial, Indigo, Korkir, Lilac, Magenta, Mallow, Murrey, Orcein, Orcin(e), Orcinol, Pance, Pansy, Plum, Pompadour, Pontiff, Porporate, Proin(e), Puce, Puke, Punic, Rhodopsin, Tyrian, Violet

**Purport** Bear, Claim, Drift, Feck, Mean, Tenor

**Purpose** Advertent, Aim, Avail, Cautel, Design, Ettle, Goal, Here-to, INTENT, Mean(ing), Meant, Mint, Motive, Object, Plan, Point, REASON, Resolution, Resolve, Sake, Telic, Tenor, Use

**Purposeless** Dysteleology, Otiose

**Purr** Curr, Rumble

**Purse** Ad crumenam, Bag, Bung, Caba, Crease, Crumenal, Fisc, Fisk, Long Melford, Pocket, Prim, Prize, Pucker, Spleuchan, Sporran, Wallet, Whistle

> **Pursed** may indicate one word within another

**Pursue(r), Pursuit** Alecto, Business, Chase, Chivvy, Course, Dog, Follow, Hobby, Hot-trod, Hound, Hunt, Practice, Practise, Proceed, Prosecute, Quest, Scouring, Stalk

**Purvey(or)** Cater, Provide, Provisor, Sell, Supply

**Pus** Empyema, Matter, Purulence, Quitter, Quittor

**Push** Barge, Birr, Boost, Bunt, Detrude, Drive, Edge, Effort, Elbow, Fire, Horn, Hustle, Impulse, Jostle, Nose, Nudge, Obtrude, Plod, Ply, Press, Promote, Propel, Railroad, Ram, Sell, SHOVE, Subtrude, Thrust, Urge

**Pushover** Doddle, Soda

**Pusillanimous** Coward, Timid, Weak, Yellow

**Puss(y)** Amentum, CAT, Catkins, Face, Galore, Hare, Mouth, Rabbit, Septic

**Pussyfoot** Dry, Equivocate, Inch, Paw, Steal, TT

**Put (off; on; out; up)** Accommodate, Add, Bet, Cup, Daff, Defer, Dish, Do, Don, Douse, Implant, Impose, Incommode, Inn, Lade, Lodge, Lump, Oust, Pit, Place, Plonk, Set, Smore, Station, Stow

**Put away** Sheathe, Store, Stow

**Put down** Disparage, Floor, Humiliate, Land, Write

> **Put off** may indicate an anagram

**Putrefaction, Putrefy(ing), Putrid** Bitter, Corrupt, Decay, Fester, Olid, Rot, Sepsis, Septic

**Putt(ing)** Green, Hash, Sink, STUPID PERSON

**Putter** Chug, Club

**Put together** Assemble, Compile, Synthesize

**Puzzle(r)** Acrostic, Baffle, Bemuse, Bewilder, Confuse, Conundrum, Crossword, Crux, Egma, Elude, Enigma, Fox, Glaik, Gravel, Intrigue, Jigsaw, Kittle, Logogriph, Mind-bender, Monkey, Mystify, Nonplus, Perplex, Ponder, Pose(r), Rebus, Riddle, Sorites, Sphinx, Sticker, Stump, Tangram, Tickler

**Pygmy** Atomy, Dwarf, Negrito, Pyknic, Thumbling

**Pyramid** Cheops, Chephren, Frustum, Stack, Teocalli

**Pyre** Bale(-fire), Bonfire, Brasero, Darga, Gha(u)t

**Pyrenian** Basque

**Pyrites** Mispickel, Mundic

**Pyrotechnics** Arson, Fireworks

**Pyroxene** Aegirine, Aegirite, Diopside

**Pyrus** Service-tree

**Pythagoras** Samian

**Pythian (seat)** Delphic, Tripod

**Python** Anaconda, Kaa, SNAKE, Zombi(e)

# Qq

**Q**  Koppa, Quebec, Question

**QC**  Silk

**Qua**  As

**Quack**  Charlatan, Crocus, Dulcamara, Empiric, Fake, IMPOSTOR, Katerfelto, Mountebank, Pretender, Saltimbanco

**Quad(rangle)**  Close, Compluvium, Court, Horse, Pane

**Quadrille**  Dance, Lancers, Matador(e), Pantalon

**Quaff**  Carouse, Drink, Imbibe

**Quagmire**  Bog, Fen, Imbroglio, Marsh, Morass, Swamp, Wagmoire

**Quail**  Asteria, Bevy, Bird, Blench, Bob-white, Caille, Colin, Flinch, Harlot, Quake, Shrink, Tremble

**Quaint**  Naive, Odd, Picturesque, Strange, Twee

**Quake(r), Quaking**  Aminadab, Broad-brim, Dither, Dodder, Fox, Friend, Fry, Hicksite, Obadiah, Penn, Quail, Seism, Shake, Shiver, Trepid, TREMBLE, Tremor

**Qualification, Qualified, Qualify**  Able, Adapt, Capacitate, Caveat, Competent, Condition, Diplomatic, Entitle, Graduate, Habilitate, Meet, Pass, Proviso, Restrict, Temper, Versed

**Quality**  Aroma, Attribute, Body, Calibre, Cast, Essence, Fabric, Fame, Flavour, Grade, It, Property, Q, Quale, Reception, Sort, Standard, Stature, Substance, Thew, Thisness, Timbre, Virtu(e), Water, Worth

**Qualm**  Compunction, Misgiving, Scruple

**Quandary**  Dilemma, Fix, Predicament

**Quantity**  AMOUNT, Batch, Bundle, Deal, Dose, Feck, Fother, Hundredweight, Intake, Jag, Lot, Mass, Measure, Myriad, Nonillion, Number, Ocean(s), Operand, Parameter, Parcel, Peck, Plenty, Posology, Pottle, Qs, Qt, Quire, Quota, Quotient, Slather, Slew, Slue, Sum, Surd, Tret, Vector, Warp, Whips

**Quantum**  Graviton

**Quarantine**  Isolate

**Quarrel(some)**  Affray, Aggress, Altercate, Arrow, Barney, Bate, Bicker, Brattle, Brawl, Breach, Breeze, Broil, Brulyie, Brulzie, Cagmag, Cantankerous, Chide, Combative, Difference, Disagree, Dispute, Eristic, Estrangement, Exchange, Fracas, Fractious, Fratch(ety), Fray, Hassle, Issue, Jar, Outcast, Outfall, Pugnacious, Ragbolt, Row, Spat, Squabble, Tiff, Vendetta, Wap, Whid, Wrangle

**Quarry**  Game, Mine, Pit, Prey, Scabble, Scent, Victim

**Quarter(ing), Quarters** Airt, Barrio, Billet, Canton(ment), Casern(e), Chinatown, Clemency, Coshery, District, Dorm, E, Enclave, Fardel, Focsle, Forpet, Forpit, Fourth, Ghetto, Ham(s), Harbour, Haunch, Latin, Medina, MERCY, N, Note, Oda, Pity, Point, Principium, Quadrant, Region, S, Season, Sector, Tail, Trimester, W, Warp

**Quarter-day** LD

> **Quarterdeck** may indicate a suit of cards

**Quartet** Foursome, Mess, Tetrad

**Quartz** Agate, Amethyst, Buhrstone, Cacholong, Cairngorm, Citrine, Jasper, Morion, Onyx, Plasma, Prase, Rubasse, Silica, Tiger-eye, Tonalite

**Quash** Abrogate, Annul, Quell, Recant, Scotch, Subdue, Suppress, Terminate, Void

**Quaver** Shake, Trill, Vibrate, Warble

**Quay** Bund, Levee, Wharf

**Queasy** Delicate, Nauseous, Squeamish

**Queen(ly)** Adelaide, African, Alcestis, Alexandra, Anna, Anne, Artemesia, Atossa, Balkis, Bee, Begum, Bess, Boadicea, Brunhild(e), Camilla, Candace, Caroline, Cleopatra, Dido, Eleanor(a), Ellery, Ena, ER, Esther, Gertrude, Guinevere, Hecuba, Hermione, Hippolyta, Isabel, Jocasta, Leda, Maam, Mab, Maeve, Marie Antoinette, Mary, Maya, Medb, Mobled, Monarch, Nance, Nefertiti, Omphale, Pance, Pansy, Parr, Paunce, Pawnce, Penelope, Persephone, Phaedram, Prince, Prosperina, Qu, R, Ranee, Rani, Regal, Regina(l), Semiramis, Sheba, Sultana, Titania, Warrior

**Queen Anne** Mrs Morley

**Queer(ness)** Abnormal, Berdash, Bizarre, Crazy, Cure, Curious, Fey, Fie, Fifish, Gay, Nance, Nancy, ODD, Outlandish, Peculiar, Pervert, Poorly, Quaint, Rum, Uranism, Vert

**Quell** Alegge, Allay, Calm, Quiet, Repress, Subdue, Suppress

**Quench** Assuage, Cool, Extinguish, Satisfy, Slake, Slo(c)ken, Sta(u)nch, Yslake

**Query** Ask, Dispute, Doubt, Question

**Quest** Goal, Graal, Grail, Hunt, Pursuit, Venture

**Question(ing)** Ask, Bi-lateral, Catechise, Contest, Conundrum, Cross-examine, Debrief, Dispute, Doubt, Erotema, Eroteme, Erotesis, Examine, Grill, Heckle, Impeach, Impugn, Interpellation, Interrogate, Interview, Koan, Oppugn, Pop, Problem, Pump, Q, Qu, Quiz, Rapid-fire, Refute, Rhetorical, Riddle, Speer, Speir, Suspect, Teaser, Vexed, What

**Questionable** Ambiguous, Dubious, Fishy, Socratic

**Question-master** Interrogator, Torquemada, Ximenes

**Queue** Braid, Cercus, Crocodile, Cue, Dog, File, LINE, Pigtail, Plait, Plat, Tail(back), Track

**Quibble(r)** Balk, Carp, Carriwitchet, Casuist, Cavil, Chicaner, Dodge, Elenchus, Equivocate, Pettifoggery, Prevaricate, Quillet, Sophist

**Quiche** Flan, Tart

**Quick(er), Quickly, Quickness** Accelerate, Acumen, Adroit, Agile, Alive, Animate, Apace, Breakneck, Breathing, Brisk, Celerity, Chop-chop, Citigrade, Cito, Con moto, Core, Cuticle, Enliven, Existent, Express, Fastness, Gleg, Hasten, Hie, High-speed, Hotfoot, Impulsive, Jiffy, Keen, Lickety-split, Living, Mercurial, Mistress, Mosso, Nailbed, Piercing, Piu mosso, Post-haste, Prestissimo, Presto, Prompt, Pronto, Rapid, Rath(e), Schnell, Sharp, Skin, Smart, Snappy, Snort, Sodain(e), Soon, Spry, Sudden, Swift, Swith, Trice, Veloce, Vital, Vite

**Quicksand** Flow, Syrtis

**Quicksilver** Mercury

**Quid** Chaw, Chew, L, Nicker, Plug, Pound, Quo, Sov, Tertium, Tobacco

**Quid pro quo** Mutuum, Tit-for-tat

**Quiescence, Quiescent** Calm, Di(o)estrus, Inactive, Inert, Latent, Still

**Quiet(en), Quietly** Accoy, Allay, Appease, Barnacle, Calm, Compose, Conticent, Doggo, Ease, Easy, Encalm, Grave, Kail, Laconic, Loun(d), Low, Lown(d), Lull, Meek, Mp, Muffle, P, Pause, Peace, Piano, QT, Reserved, Sedate, Settle, Sh, Shtoom, Silence, Sitzkrieg, Sly, Sober, Sotto voce, Still, Stum(m), Tace, Tranquil, Whish, Whist

**Quill** Calamus, Feather, Float, Plectre, Plectron, Plectrum, Plume, Remex

**Quillwort** Isoetes

**Quilt(ing)** Comfort(er), Counterpane, Cover, Doona, Duvet, Eiderdown, Futon, Kantha, Trapunto

**Quince** Bael, Bel, Bhel, Japonica

**Quinine** China, Crown-bark, Kina, Quina, Tonic

**Quinsy** Angina, Cynanche, Garget, Squinancy

**Quintessence** Heart, Pith

**Quintet** Pentad, Trout

**Quip** Carriwitchet, Crack, Epigram, Gibe, Jest, Jibe, Joke, Taunt, Zinger

**Quirk** Concert, Foible, Idiosyncrasy, Irony, Kink, Twist

**Quisling** Collaborator, Traitor

**Quit(s)** Abandon, Absolve, Cease, Desert, Even(s), Go, Leave, Meet, Resign, STOP

**Quite** Actually, All, Ap(p)ay, Clean, Dead, Fairly, Fully, Precisely, Real, Right, Sheer, Very

**Quiver(ing)** Aspen, Quake, Shake, Sheath, Tremble, Tremolo, Tremor, Tremulate, Trepid, Vibrant, Vibrate

**Qui vive** Go-go

**Quixote, Quixotic** Don, Errant, Impractical

**Quiz** Bandalore, Catechism, Examine, Interrogate, I-spy, Mastermind, Oddity, Probe, Question, Smoke, Trail, Yo-yo

**Quizzical** Curious, Derisive, Odd, Queer, Socratic

**Quod** Can, Clink, Jail, Prison

**Quoit** Disc(us), Disk, Ring

**Quondam** Once, Sometime, Whilom

**Quorum** Minyan

**Quota** Proportion, Ration, Share

**Quotation, Quote(d)** Adduce, Citation, Cite, Co(a)te, Evens, Extract, Name, Price, Recite, Reference, Say, Tag, Verbatim

**Quoth** Co, Said

**Quotient** Kerma

# Rr

**R** Arithmetic, King, Queen, Reading, Recipe, Right, Romeo, Run, Writing

**Rabbit** Angora, Astrex, Brer, Buck, Bun(ny), Chat, Con(e)y, Cottontail, Daman, Dassie, Doe, Harp, Hyrax, Jack, Klipdas, Marmot, Muff, Novice, Oarlap, Patzer, Prate, Rex, Tapeti, Terricole, Waffle, Yatter

**Rabble** Canaille, Clamjamphrie, Clanjamfray, Colluvies, Crowd, Doggery, Herd, Hoi-polloi, Horde, Legge, Mob, Raffle, Rag-tag, Rascal, Riff-raff, Rout, Scaff-raff, Shower, Tag

**Rabelaisian** Pantagruel, Panurge

**Rabid, Rabies** Extreme, Frenzied, Hydrophobia, Lyssa, Mad, Raging, Virulent

**Raccoon** Coati, Panda, Procyon

**Race(course), Race meeting** Aintree, Ascot, Autocross, Breed, Broose, Brouze, Career, Caucus, Cesarewitch, Chase, Classic, Cone, Contest, Corso, Country, Course, Current, Cursus, Dash, Derby, Dogs, Doncaster, Dromos, Epsom, Event, Fastnet, Flat, Flow, Generation, Ginger, Goodwood, Grand prix, Handicap, Human(kind), Inca, Indy, Kermesse, Kind, Lampadedromy, Lampadephoria, Leat, Leet, Leger, Lick, Lignage, Line(age), Longchamps, Man, Marathon, Meets, Mile, NATIONAL, Newmarket, Nursery, Oaks, Obstacle, One-horse, Paceway, Palio, Plate, Pluck, Point-to-point, Pursuit, Rapids, Rat, Redcar, Regatta, Relay, Rill, Rod, Ronne, Roost, St Leger, Scramble, Scratch, Scud, Scurry, Seed, Shan, Slalom, Slipstream, Sloot, Sluit, Speedway, Sprint, Stakes, Steeplechase, Stem, Stirp(s), Stirpes, Stock, Strain, Streak, Strene, Sweepstake, Taste, Tear, Torpids, Towcester, Tribe, TT, Turf, Two-horse, Velodrome, Volsungs, Walk-over, Waterway, Whid, Wincanton

**Racehorse, Racer** Eclipse, Filly, Hare, Maiden, Plater, Red Rum, Steeplechaser, Trotter

**Raceme** Corymb

**Racial (area)** Apartheid, Colour, Ethnic, Ghetto, Quarter

**Rack** Bin, Cloud, Drier, Flake, Frame, Hake, Pulley, Stretcher, Torment, Torture

**Racket** BAT, Bassoon, Battledore, Brattle, Caterwaul, Chirm, Clamour, Crime, Deen, Din, Discord, FIDDLE, Gyp, Hubbub, Hustle, NOISE, Noisiness, Protection, Ramp, Rort, Stridor, Swindle, Tumult, Utis

**Racy** Ethnic, Piquant, Pungent, Ribald, Spicy, Spirited

**Rad** Rem

**Radar** Gee, Loran, Rebecca-eureka, Shoran

**Raddle** Hurdle, Ochre, Red

**Radial** Quadrant, Rotula, Spoke

**Radiance, Radiant** Actinic, Aglow, Aureola, Beamish, Brilliant, Glory, Glow, Happy, Lustre, Refulgent, Sheen

**Radiate, Radiating, Radiation, Radiator** Actinal, Air-colour, Beam, Effuse, Emanate, Fluorescence, Glow, Heater, Photon, Pulsar, Quasar, Rem(s), Rep, SHINE, Sievert, Spoke, Stellate, SU, Sun, Van Allen

**Radical** Allyl, Amyl, Aryl, Benzoyl, Bolshevist, Bolshie, Cetyl, Ester, Extreme, Fundamental, Gauchist, Glyceryl, Glycosol, Innate, Isopropyl, Leftist, Leveller, Ligand, Methyl, Montagnard, Nitryl, Oxonium, Parsnip, Phenyl, Pink, Propyl, Red, Revolutionary, Rhizocaul, Root, Rudiment, Trot(sky), Vinyl, Whig

**Radio(-active)** Boom-box, CB, Citizen's band, Crystal set, Emanation, Ether, Hot, Loudspeaker, Marconigraph, Receiver, Set, Simplex, Sound, Steam, Thorium, Tranny, Transmitter, Transponder, Uranite, Walkman, Wireless

**Radiogram** Cable, Telegram, Wire

**Radish** Charlock, Mooli, Runch

**Radium** Ra

**Radon** Rn

**Raffia** Rabanna

**Raffle** Draw, Lottery, Sweepstake

**Raft** Balsa, Catamaran, Float, Kontiki, Pontoon

**Rafter** Barge-couple, Beam, Chevron, Jack, Joist, Ridge, Spar, Timber

**Rag(ged), Rags** Bait, Bate, Clout, Coral, Deckle, Dud(s), Duddery, Duddie, Duster, Fent, Figleaf, Glad, Guyed, Haze, Kid, Lap(pie), Lapje, Mop, Paper, Remnant, Revel, Rivlins, Rot, Scold, Scrap, SHRED, Slate, Slut, Splore, Tat(t), Tatter(demalion), Tatty, TEASE, Tiger, Tongue, Uneven

> **Rag(ged)** may indicate an anagram

**Rage, Raging** ANGER, Ardour, Bait, Bate, Bayt, Explode, Fashion, Fierce, Fit, Fiz(z), Fume, Furibund, Furore, Fury, Gibber, Go, Ire, Mode, Paddy(-whack), Passion, Pelt, Pet, Rabid, Ramp, Rant, Snit, Storm, Tear, Temper, Utis, Wax, Wrath

**Raglan** Sleeve

**Ragout** Goulash, Haricot, Stew

**Rag-picker** Bunter

**Raid(er)** Assault, Attack, Bodrag, Bust, Camisado, Chappow, Commando, Do, For(r)ay, Imburst, Inroad, Inrush, Invade, Jameson, Maraud, March-treason, Mosstrooper, Pict, Pillage, Plunder, Ransel, Razzia, Reive, Sack, Scrump, Skrimp, Skrump, Smash-and-grab, Sortie, Spreagh, Storm, Viking

**Rail(er), Railing** Abuse, Amtrack, Arm, Aris, Balustrade, Ban, Banister, BAR, Barre, Barrier, Bird, Conductor, Coot, Corncrake, Criticise, Dado,

Fender, Flow, Gush, Insult, Inveigh, Metal, Notornis, Parclose, Post, Pulpit, Rag, Rate, Rave, Scold, Slate, Snash, Sneer, Sora, Soree, Spar, Taunt, Thersites, Train, Vituperation, Weka

**Raillery** Badinage, Banter, Chaff, Persiflage, Sport

**Railroad, Railway** Amtrak, BR, Bulldoze, Cog, Cremaillière, El, Funicular, GWR, Lines, LMS, LNER, Maglev, Metro, Monorail, Rack, Rly, Road, Ry, Scenic, SR, Switchback, Telpher-line, Track, Train, Tramline, Tramway, Tube, Underground

**Railwayman** Driver, Guard, NUR, Stephenson, Stoker

**Raiment** Apparel, Clothes, Garb, Ihram

**Rain(y)** Brash, Deluge, Drizzle, Hyad(e)s, Hyetal, Mizzle, Oncome, Onding, Onfall, Pelt, Pour, Precipitation, Right, Roke, Scat, Seil, Serein, Serene, Shell, Shower, Sile, Skiffle, Skit, Smir(r), Smur, Soft, Spat, Spet, Spit, Storm, Thunder-plump, Weep, Wet

**Rainbow(-maker)** Arc, Bifrost, Bruise, Iris, Spectroscope, Water-gall, Weather-gall

**Raincoat** Burberry, Gaberdine, Mac, Mino, Oils(kins), Waterproof

**Raingauge** Ombrometer, Udometer

**Rain-maker** Indra

**Raise(d), Raising** Advance, Aggrade, Attollent, Boost, Build, Cat, Coaming, Cock, Collect, Elate, ELEVATE, Emboss, Enhance, Ennoble, Escalate, Exalt, Fledge, Grow, Heave, Heft, High, Hike, Hoist, Increase, Jack, Key, Leaven, Lift, Mention, Overcall, Perk, Rear, Regrate, Repoussé, Revie, Rouse, Siege, Sky, Snarl, Upgrade

**Rake, Rakish** Casanova, Comb, Corinthian, Dapper, Dissolute, Enfilade, Jaunty, Lecher, Libertine, Lothario, Raff, Reprobate, Rip, Roué, Scan, Scour, Scowerer, Scratch, Strafe, Swash-buckler, Swinge-buckler

**Rale** Crepitus, Rattle

**Rally, Rallying-point** Autocross, Autopoint, Badinage, Banter, Demo, Gather, Jamboree, Meeting, Mobilise, Monte Carlo, Muster, Oriflamme, Persiflage, Recover, Rely, Rest, Risorgimento, Roast, Rouse, Scramble

**Ralph** Imp, Nader, Rackstraw

**Ram** Aries, Buck, Bunt, Butter, Crash, Drive, Hidder, Hydraulic, Mendes, Pun, Sheep, Stem, Tamp, Tup, Wether

**Ramble(r), Rambling** Aberrant, Digress, Incoherent, Liana, Liane, Rigmarole, Roam, Rose, Rove, Skamble, Skimble(-skamble), Sprawl, Stray, Vagabond, Wander

**Rameses** Pharaoh

**Ramp** Bank, Gradient, Incline, Slope

**Rampage** Fury, Spree, Storm

**Rampant** Lionel, Predominant, Profuse, Rearing, Rife

> **Rampant** may indicate an anagram or a reversed word

**Rampart** Abat(t)is, Brisure, Butt, Defence, Fortification, Parapet,

Terreplein, Vallum, Wall

**Ramrod** Gunstick

**Ramshackle** Decrepit, Rickety, Rickle

**Ranch** Bowery, Corral, Farm, Hacienda, Spread

**Rancid** Frowy, Reast(y), Reest(y), Sour, Turned

**Rancour** Hate, Malice, Resentment, Spite

**Rand** Border, R, Roon

**Random** Accidental, Arbitrary, AT RANDOM, Casual, Fitful, HAPHAZARD, Harvest, Sporadic, Stochastic

> **Random(ly)** may indicate an anagram

**Range(r), Rangy** Align, Ambit, Andes, Atlas, AZ, Ballpark, Bowshot, Carry, Cheviot, Compass, Course, Diapason, Dispace, Dolomites, Err, EXTENT, Flinders, Gamut, Glasgow, Helicon, Himalayas, Ken(ning), Ladakh, Leggy, Limit, Massif, MOUNT, Orbit, Oven, Palette, Point-blank, Purview, Rake, Reach, Register, Roam, Scale, Scope, Sc(o)ur, Selection, Sierra, Sloan, Spectrum, Sphere, Stove, Tape, Tessitura, Texas, Tier, Urals, Waldgrave, Woomera

**Rank(s)** Begum, Brevet, Caste, Category, Cense, Classify, Cornet, Degree, Dignity, Downright, Earldom, Estate, Etats, Grade, Graveolent, Gross, High, Majority, Olid, Place, Range, Rate, Rooty, Row, Sergeant, Seigniorage, Serried, Shoulder-strap, Sort, STATION, Status, Tier, TITLE, Titule, Utter

**Rankle** Chafe, Gall, Irritate, Nag

**Ransack** Pillage, Plunder, Rifle, Ripe, Rob, Rummage

**Ransom** Redeem, Release, Rescue

**Rant(er), Ranting** Bombast, Declaim, Fustian, Ham, Haranguc, Rail, Rodomontade, Scold, Spout, Spruik, Stump, Tub-thump

**Rap(ped)** Blame, Censure, Clour, Halfpenny, Knock, Ratatat, Shand, Strike, Swapt, Tack, Tap

**Rapacious** Accipitrine, Esurient, Exorbitant, Greedy, Harpy, Predatory, Ravenous, Ravine

**Rape** Abuse, Assault, Belinda, Cole-seed, Colza, Creach, Creagh, Deflower, Despoil, Hundred, Lock, Lucretia, Navew, Plunder, Stuprate, Thack, Violate

**Rapid(ity), Rapidly** Chute, Express, Fast, Meteoric, Mosso, Presto, Pronto, Riffle, Sault, Speedy, Stickle, Swift, Veloce

**Rapier** Sword, Tuck

**Rappel** Abseil

**Rapport** Accord, Affinity, Agreement, Harmony

**Rapprochement** Detente, Reconciliation

**Rapt** Riveted

**Raptor** Stooper

**Rapture, Rapturous** Bliss, DELIGHT, Ecstasy, Elation, Joy, Trance

**Rare, Rarity** Blue moon, Curio, Geason, Infrequent, Rear, Recherché, Scarce, Seld(om), Singular, UNCOMMON, Uncooked, Underdone, Unusual

**Rarefied** Thin

**Rascal(ly)** Arrant, Cad, Cullion, Cur, Devil, Gamin, Hallian, Hallion, Hallyon, KNAVE, Limner, Loon, Rogue, Scamp, Schelm, Skeesicks, Skellum, Skelm, Smaik, Spalpeen, Tinker, Toe-rag, Varlet, Varmint, Villain

**Rash(er)** Bacon, Brash, Collop, Daredevil, Eruption, Fast, Foolhardy, Harum-scarum, HASTY, Headlong, Hives, Impetigo, Impetuous, Imprudent, Impulsive, Lardo(o)n, Lichen, Madbrain, Madcap, Morphew, Outbreak, Overhasty, Purpura, Reckless, Roseola, Rubella, Sapego, Serpigo, Spots, Tetter, Thoughtless, Unheeding, Unthinking, Urticaria

**Rasp(er)** File, Grate, Odontophore, Risp, Rub, Scrape, Xyster

**Raspberry** Berate, Etaerio, Razz

**Rastafarian** Dread

**Rat(s), Ratty** Agouta, Bandicoot, Blackleg, Blackneb, Bug-out, Cur, Defect, Fink, Geomyoid, Heck, Hydromys, Informer, Poppycock, Potoroo, Pshaw, Pup(py), Rodent, Roland, Rot(ten), Scab, Shirty, Turncoat, Vole

**Rat-catcher** Cat, Ichneumon, Mongoose, Pied Piper

**Rate, Rating** Appreciate, Assess, Castigate, Cess, Classify, Count, Deserve, Erk, Estimate, Evaluate, Grade, Hearty, MPH, OS, Pace, Percentage, Rag, Red, Reproof, Rocket, Row, Sailor, Scold, SET, SPEED, Standing, TAM, Tax, Tempo, Upbraid, Value, Wig

**Rather** Degree, Instead, Lief, Liever, Loor, More, Pretty, Some(what), Sooner

**Ratify** Approve, Confirm, Pass, Sanction, Validate

**Ratio** Cosine, Fraction, Neper, Pi, Proportion, PE, Sin(e), Tensor

**Ration(s)** Allocate, Apportion, Compo, Dole, Etape, Iron, Quota, Restrict, Scran, Share, Size

**Rational** Dianoetic, Logical, Lucid, Sane, Sensible, Sine, Sober

**Rationale** Motive

**Rattle (box)** Chatter, Clack, Clank, Clap, Clatter, Clitter, Conductor, Crescelle, Crotalaria, Demoralise, Disconcert, Gas-bag, Jabber, Jangle, Jar, Maraca, Natter, Nonplus, Rale, Rap, Reel, Ruckle, Shake, Sistrum, Sunn, Tirl, Upset

**Raucous** Guttural, Hoarse, Loud, Strident

**Ravage** Depredation, Desecrate, Despoil, Havoc, Pillage, Prey, Ruin, Sack, Waste

**Rave, Raving** Enthuse, Praise, Redwood, Redwud, Storm, Ta(i)ver, Tear

**Ravel** Disentangle, Explain, Involve, Snarl, Tangle

**Raven(ous)** Black, Corbel, Corbie, Corvine, Croaker, Daw, Grip, Hugin, Munin

**Ravine** Arroyo, Barranca, Barranco, Canada, Chasm, Chine, Clough, Coulee, Couloir, Dip, Flume, Ghyll, Gorge, Grike, Gulch, Gully, Khor, Khud, Kloof, Lin(n), Nal(l)a, Nallah, Nulla(h), Pit

**Ravish** Constuprate, Debauch, Defile, Rape, Stuprate, Transport, Violate

**Raw** Brut, Chill, Coarse, Crude, Crudy, Damp, Fresh, Greenhorn, Natural, Recruit, Rude, Uncooked, Wersh

**Raw-boned** Gaunt, Lanky, Lean, Randle-tree

**Ray(ed)** Actinic, Alpha, Beam, Beta, Cathode, Diactine, Dun-cow, Electric, Fish, Gamma, Homelyn, Manta, Monactine, Polyact, R, Radius, Re, Roentgen, Roker, Rontgen, Sawfish, Sea-devil, Sea-eagle, Sephen, Shaft, Skate, Stick, Stingaree, Tetract, Thornback, Torpedo

**Rayon** Acetate, Faille, Viscose

**Raze** Annihilate, Bulldoze, Demolish, Destroy, Level

**Razorbill** Murre

**Razor-fish** Solen

**Razor-maker** Occam

**Razz** Raspberry

**RE** Sappers

**Re** About, Touching

**Reach** Ar(rive), Attain, Boak, Boke, Carry, Come, Get out, Hent, Hit, Key-bugle, Lode, Octave, Peak, Retch, Seize, Stretch, Touch, Win

**Reach-me-downs** Slop-clothing

**React(or), Reaction(ary)** Allergy, Answer, Backlash, Backwash, Behave, Blimp, Bourbon, Breeder, Bristle, Core, Dibasic, Falange, Furnace, Gut, Kickback, Neanderthal, Pile, Reciprocate, Recoil, Redox, Repercussion, Respond, Rigid, Sensitive, Spallation, Sprocket, Swing-back, Tokamak

> **Reactionary** may indicate reversed, or an anagram

**Read(ing)** Bearing, Browse, Decipher, Decode, Exegesis, Interpret, Learn, Lection, Lesson, Lu, Pericope, Peruse, Pore, Rad, Rennet-bag, Scan, See, Solve, STUDY, Vell, Ycond

**Reader** ABC, Alidad(e), Bookworm, Editor, Epistoler, Lector, Primer, Silas Wegg, Taster

**Readiest, Readiness, Ready** Alacrity, Alamain, Alert, Amber, Apt, Atrip, Available, Bound, Brass, Cash, Dough, Eager, Eftest, Fettle, Fit, Forward, Game, Go, Keyed, Lolly, Masterman, Money, Predy, Prepared, Present, Prest, Primed, Prompt, Reckoner, Ripe, Set, Soon, Spot, Turnkey, Usable, Willing, Yare

**Readjust** Mend, Regulate, Retrue

**Readymade** Bought, Precast, Prepared, Prêt-à-porter, Slops, Stock, Store

**Reagent** Reactor

**Real, Reality, Realities, Really** Actual, Bona-fide, Coin, Dinkum,

Dinky-di(e), Earnest, Echt, Ens, Entia, Entity, Essence, GENUINE, Honest, Indeed, McCoy, McKoy, Royal, Simon Pure, Sooth, Sterling, Substantial, Tennis, Thingliness, True, Verismo

**Realgar** Rosaker, Zarnec, Zarnich

**Realise, Realism** Achieve, Attain, Attuite, Cash, Embody, Encash, Fetch, Fulfil, Learn, Sell, Sense, Understand

> **Realities, Reality** see REAL

**Realm** Dominion, Field, Kingdom, Land, Region, Special(i)ty, UK

**Ream** Bore, Foam, Froth, Paper, Rime, Screed

**Reap(er)** Binder, Crop, Death, Earn, Gather, Glean, Harvest, Scythe, Solitary, Stibbler

**Reappear(ance)** Emersion, Materialise, Recrudesce

**Rear(ing)** Aft, Back(side), Baft, Behind, Bring-up, Bunt, Cabré, Derrière, Foster, Hind, Loo, Nousell, Nurture, Prat, RAISE, Serafile, Serrefile, Tonneau

**Rearrange(ment)** Adjust, Anagram, Ectopia

**Reason(ing)** A fortiori, Analytical, Apagoge, A priori, Argue, Argument, Basis, Call, Cause, Colour, Consideration, Deduce, Ground(s), Ijtihad, Inductive, Logic, Motive, Point, Pro, Proof, Purpose, Rationale, Sanity, Sense, Settler, Syllogism, Synthesis, Think, Why, Wit

**Reasonable** Fair, Intelligent, Logical, Moderate, Rational, Sensible

**Reave** Despoil, Reif, Rob, Spoil

**Rebate** Diminish, Lessen, Refund, Repayment

**Rebecca** Sharp

**Rebel(lion), Rebellious** Aginner, Apostate, Bolshy, Cade, Contra, Croppy, Danton, Diehard, Fifteen, Forty-five, Frondeur, Glendower, Hampden, Iconoclast, Insurgent, IRA, Jacobite, Jacquerie, Kick, Luddite, Mutine(er), Mutiny, Oates, Putsch, Resist, Revolt, Rise, Scofflaw, Sedition, Steelboy, Straw, Tai-ping, Ted, Titanism, Tyler, Venner, Warbeck, Whiteboy

> **Rebellious** may indicate a word reversed

**Rebirth** Palingenesis, Renaissance, Revival

**Rebound** Bounce, Cannon, Recoil, Ricochet

**Rebuff** Check, Cold-shoulder, Noser, Quelch, Repulse, Retort, Rubber, Sneb, Snib, Snub

**Rebuke** Berate, Check, Chide, Earful, Lecture, Neb, Objurgate, Rap, Rate, Razz, Reprove, Reprimand, Scold, Slap, Slate, Snub, Threap, Threep, Tick off, Trim, Tut, Upbraid, Wig

**Rebut** Refute, Repulse, Retreat

**Recalcitrant** Mulish, Obstinate, Unruly, Wilful

**Recall(ing)** Annul, Eidetic, Encore, Evocative, Reclaim, Recollect, Redolent, Remember, Remind, Reminisce, Repeal, Retrace, Revoke,

Withdraw

**Recant(ation)**  Disclaim, Palinode, Retract, Revoke

**Recap(itulate), Recapitulation**  Epanodos, Summarise

> **Recast**  may indicate an anagram

> **Recce**  see RECONNAISSANCE

**Recede**  Decline, Ebb, Lessen, Regress, Shrink, Withdraw

**Receipt(s)**  Acknowledge, Chit, Docket, Recipe, Revenue, Take, Voucher

**Receive(d), Receiver**  Accept, Accoil, Antenna, Assignee, Bailee, Dipole, Dish, Donee, Ear, Fence, Get, Grantee, Greet, Inherit, Pernancy, Phone, Pocket, Radio, Reset, Roger, Set, Take, Tap, Transistor

**Recent(ly)**  Alate, Current, Fresh, Hot, Late, Modern, New, Yesterday, Yestereve, Yesterweek

**Receptacle**  Ash-tray, Basket, Bin, Bowl, Box, Ciborium, Container, Cyst, Hell-box, Monstrance, Reliquary, Relique, Thalamus, Tore, Torus

**Reception, Receptive**  Accoil, At home, Bel-accoyle, Couchée, Court, Durbar, Greeting, Infare, Kursaal, Levée, Open, Ovation, Ruelle, Saloon, Sensory, Teleasthetic

**Recess(ion)**  Alcove, Antrum, Apse, Apsidal, Apsis, Bay, Bole, Bower, Break, Closet, Columbarium, Corrie, Cove, Croze, Dinette, Ebb, Embrasure, Exedra, Grotto, Hitch, Interval, Loculus, Mortise, NICHE, Nook, Outshot, Respite, Rest, Slump, Withdrawal

> **Recess**  may indicate 'reversed'

**Rechabite**  TT

**Réchauffé**  Hachis, Hash, Salmi

**Recidivist**  Relapser

> **Recidivist**  may indicate 'reversed'

**Recipe**  Dish, Formula, Prescription, R, Receipt

**Recipient**  Assignee, Beneficiary, Disponee, Grantee, Heir, Legatee, Receiver

**Reciprocal, Reciprocate**  Corresponding, Exchange, Inter(act), Mutual, Repay, Return

**Recital, Recitationist, Recite**  Declaim, Diseuse, Enumerate, Litany, Monologue, Parlando, Quote, Reading, Reel, Relate, Say, Sing, Tell

**Reckless(ness)**  Blindfold, Careless, Catiline, Desperado, Devil-may-care, Hasty, Headfirst, Headlong, Hell-bent, Madcap, Perdu(e), Ramstam, Rantipole, RASH, Slapdash, Temerity, Ton-up, Wanton

> **Reckless**  may indicate an anagram

**Reckon(ing)**  Assess, Calculate, Cast, Census, Computer, Consider, Count, Date, Estimate, Figure, Number, Rate, Settlement, Shot, Tab

**Reclaim(ed), Reclamation**  Assart, Empolder, Impolder, Innings, Novalia, Polder, Recover, Redeem, Restore, Swidden, Tame, Thwaite

**Recline** Lean, Lie, Lounge, Rest

**Recluse** Anchor(et), Anchorite, Eremite, Hermit, Solitaire

**Recognise(d), Recognition** Accept, Acknow(ledge), Anagnorisis, Appreciate, Ascetic, Exequatur, Identify, Isolated, Ken, KNOW, Onst, Own, Reward, Scent, Weet

**Recoil** Backlash, Bounce, Kick(back), Rebound, Redound, Resile, Reverberate, Shrink, Shy, Spring, Start

**Recollect(ion)** Anamnesis, Memory, Pelmanism, Recall, REMEMBER, Reminisce

> **Recollection** may indicate an anagram

**Recommend(ation)** Advise, Advocate, Counsel, Direct, Endorse, Nap, Promote, Rider, Suggest, Testimonial, Tip, Tout

**Recompense** Cognisance, Deodand, Deserts, Guerdon, Pay, Remunerate, Repayment, Restitution, Reward

**Reconcile(d)** Adapt, Adjust, Affrended, Atone, Harmonise, Henotic, Make up, Mend

**Recondite** Difficult, Esoteric, Mystic, Obscure, Occult, Profound

**Reconnaissance, Reconnoitre** Case, Investigate, Recce, Scout, Survey

**Reconstitute, Reconstitution** Diagenesis

**Reconstruction** Perestroika

**Record(er), Record company** Album, Ampex, Annal(ist), Archive, Archivist, Bench-mark, Black box, Book, Can, Chart, Chronicle, Clog-almanac, Coat(e), Daybook, Diary, Disc, Document, Dossier, Eloge, Elpee, EMI, Enter, Entry, EP, Estreat, Ever, Filater, File, Film, Flute, Form, Forty-five, Gram, Hansard, Hierogrammat, History, Journal, Ledger, List, Log, LP, Mark, Memento, Memo(randum), Memorial, Meter, Mind, Minute, Mono, Noctuary, Notate, Notch, Note, Odometer, Platter, Playback, Pressing, Quipo, Quipu, Quote, Regest, Register, Roll, Score(board), Seventy-eight, Single, Tally, Tape, Trace, Track, Transcript, VERA, Vid(eo), Vote, Wax, Wisden, Write

**Record-holder** Champion, Sleeve

**Record-player** DJ, Stereo

**Recount** Describe, Enumerate, NARRATE, Relate, Tell

**Recourse** Access, Resort

**Recover(y)** Amend, Clawback, Comeback, Convalescence, Cure, Lysis, Over, Perk, Rally, Reclaim, Redeem, Regain, Repaint, Replevin, Replevy, Rescue, Resile, RETRIEVE, Revanche, Salvage, Salve, Upswing

**Recreate, Recreation** Diversion, Hobby, Palingenesia, Pastime, Play, Revive, Sport

**Recriminate, Recrimination** Ruction

**Recruit(s)** Attestor, Bezonian, Choco, Conscript, Draft, Employ, Engage, Enlist, Enrol, Headhunt, Intake, Muster, Nignog, Rookie, Sprog, Volunteer, Wart, Yobbo

**Rectangle, Rectangular** Matrix, Oblong, Quad, Square

**Rectify** Adjust, Amend, Dephlegmate, Redress, Regulate, REMEDY, Right

**Recto** Ro

**Rectum** Tewel

**Recuperate** Convalesce, Rally, Recover

**Recur(rent), Recurring** Chronic, Quartan, Quintan, Repeated, Repetend, Return

> **Recurrent** may indicate 'reversed'

**Red(den), Redness** Alizarin, Angry, Archil, Ashamed, Auburn, Beet, Bilrubin, Blush, Bolshevik, Burgundy, C, Carmine, Castory, Cent, Cerise, Cherry, Chica, Choy-root, Cinnabar, Claret, Coccineous, Communist, Congo, Coquelicot, Coral, Corallin(e), Corkir, Cramesy, Cromosin, Cuprite, Cyanin, Damask, Debit, Duster, Embarrassed, Eosin, Eric, Erik, Erythema, Florid, Flush, Gory, Grog-blossom, Gu(les), Hat, Herring, Incardine, Inflamed, Infra, Inner, Intertrigo, Jacqueminot, Keel, Korkir, Lac-lake, Lake, Lateritious, Lefty, Lenin, Letter, Magenta, Maoist, Marxist, Menshevik, Miniate, Minium, Modena, Murrey, Neaten, Orchel, Orchilla-weed, Orseille, Plethoric, Ponceau, Pyrrhous, Raddle, Radical, Raw, Realgar, Rhodamine, Ridinghood, Roan, Rose, Rot, Rouge, Roy, Rubefy, Rubella, Rubric, Ruby, Ruddle, Rufescent, Russ(e), Russet, Russian, Rust(y), Rutilant, Sard, Setter, Solferino, Stammel, Tape, Tidy, Titian, Trot, Turacin, Tyrian, Vermeil, Vermilion, Vermily, Wine

> **Red** may indicate an anagram

**Redcoat** Rust, Soldier

**Redeem, Redemption** Liberate, Mathurin, Ransom, Retrieve, Salvation, Save

**Red-faced** Coaita, Florid, Flushed

**Red-head** Auburn, Carroty, Commissar, Mao, Rufus

**Red herring** Soldier

> **Rediscovered** may indicate an anagram

**Redolent** Aromatic, Fragrant, Reeking, Suggestive

**Redoubtable** Stalwart

**Redress** Amends, Offset, Recompense, Rectify, Remedy, Right

**Redshank** Gambet, Totanus

**Redskin** Indian, Tomato,

**Red spot** Tika

**Reduce(r), Reduction** Abatement, Allay, Alleviate, Attenuate, Beggar, Beneficiate, Clip, Condense, Contract, Cut, Damping, Debase, Decimate, Decrease, Demote, Deplete, Detract, Devalue, Diminish, Diminuendo, Discount, Downsize, Epitomise, Grind, Kinone, LESSEN, Markdown, Mitigate, Moderate, Pot, Put, Quinol, Rundown, Scant, Shade, Shorten, Slash, Strain, Taper, Telescope, Thin, Weaken

**Redundancy, Redundant** Frill, Needless, Pleonasm, Surplus

**Redwood** Amboyna, Mahogany, Sanders, Wellingtonia

**Reed** Arundinaceous, Calamus, Oboe, Papyrus, Pipe, Quill, Raupo, Rush, Sedge, Seg, Sley, Spear, Sudd, Syrinx, Thatch, Twill, Whistle

**Reef** Atoll, Bombora, Cay, Key, Knot, Motu, Sca(u)r, Skerry, Witwatersrand

**Reefer** Cigarette, Jacket, Joint

**Reek** Emit, Exude, Stink

**Reel** Bobbin, Dance, Eightsome, Hoolachan, Hoolican, Pirn, Spin, Spool, Stagger, Strathspey, Sway, Swift, Swim, Totter, Wheel, Whirl, Wintle

**Refectory** Frater

**Refer** Advert, Allude, Assign, Cite, Direct, Mention, Pertain, Relate, Renvoi, Renvoy, See, Submit

**Referee** Arbiter, Mediate, Ref, Umpire, Voucher, Whistler

**Reference** Allusion, Apropos, Character, Coat, Index, Innuendo, Mention, Passion, Quote, Regard, Renvoi, Respect, Retrospect, Testimonial

**Referendum** Mandate, Plebescite, Vox populi

**Refill** Replenish

**Refine(d), Refinement, Refiner** Alembicate, Attic, Catcracker, Couth, Cultivate, Culture, Distinction, Elegance, Exility, Genteel, Grace, Nice, Polish(ed), Polite, Pure, Rare(fy), Recherché, Sift, Smelt, Subtilise, Try, U, Urbane, Veneer

**Reflect(ing), Reflection, Reflector** Albedo, Blame, Catoptric, Cats-eye, Chew, Cogitate, CONSIDER, Echo, Glass, Glint, Image, Meditate, Mirror, Muse, Ponder, Ruminate, Spectacular, Speculum, Thought

**Reflex** Bent, Cancrizans, Re-entrant, Tic

**Reform(er)** Amend, Apostle, Beveridge, Bloomer, Calvin, Chartism, Correct, Enrage, Fry, Ghandi, Howard, Improve, Knox, Lollard, Luther, Mucker, New Deal, PR, Protestant, Proudhorn, Puritan, Rad(ical), Really, Recast, Reclaim, Rectify, Regenerate, Resipiscence, Ruskin, Savonarola, Syncretise, Transmute

> **Reform(ed)** may indicate an anagram

**Reformatory** Borstal, Magdalen(e)

**Refractive, Refractor(y)** Anaclastic, Firestone, Obstinate, Perverse, Prism, Recalcitrant, Refringe, Restive, Stubborn, Sullen, Wayward

**Refrain** Abstain, Alay, Avoid, Bob, Burden, Chorus, Desist, Epistrophe, Fa-la, Forebear, Hemistich, Repetend, Ritornello, Rumpti-iddity, Spare, Tag, Tirra-lirra, Tirra-lyra, Undersong, Wheel

**Refresh(er), Refreshment** Air, Bait, Be(a)vers, Cheer, Elevenses, Enliven, Food, Nap, New, Nourishment, Reflect, Refocillate, Renew, Repast, Restore, Revive, Seltzer, Shire, Slake, Water

**Refrigerator** Chill, Cooler, Esky, Freezer, Fridge, Ice-box, Reefer

**Refuge**  Asylum, Bolthole, Dive, Girth, Grith, Harbour, Haven, Hideaway, Hole, Holt, Home, Hospice, Oasis, Port, Reefer, Resort, Retreat, SHELTER, Soil

**Refugee**  DP, Escapist, Fugitive, Grenzganger, Huguenot

> **Refurbished**  may indicate an anagram

**Refusal, Refuse**  Attle, Bagasse, Ba(u)lk, Bilge, Bin, Black, Bovril, Bran, Brash, Breeze, Brock, Bull, Bunkum, Chaff, Clap-trap, Crane, Crap, Cul(t)ch, Debris, Decline, Denay, Deny, Disown, Draff, Drivel, Dross, Dunder, Dung, Fag-end, Fenks, Fiddlesticks, Finks, Flock, Frass, Garbage, Gob, Guff, Husk, Interdict, Junk, Knickknackery, Knub, Lay-stall, Leavings, Litter, Lumber, Marc, Megass(e), Midden, Mullock, Mush, Nay(-say), Nill, No, Nould, Nub, Offal, Off-scum, Orts, Pellet, Pigwash, Punk, Raffle, Rape(cake), Rat(s), Rebuff, Recrement, Recusance, Red(d), Redargue, Reest, Regret, Reneg(u)e, Renig, Rot, RUBBISH, Ruderal, Scaff, Scrap, Scree, Scum, Sewage, Shant, Sordes, Spurn, Sullage, Sweepings, Tinpot, Tip, Toom, Tosh, Trade, Trash, Tripe, Trock, Troke, Trumpery, Twaddle, Unsay, Utter, Wash, Waste, Wastrel

> **Re-fused**  may indicate an anagram

**Refutation, Refute**  Deny, Disprove, Elench(us), Rebut, Redargue, Refel

> **Regal**  see ROYAL

**Regalia**  Mound, Orb, Sceptre

**Regard(ing)**  As to, Attention, Care, Consider, ESTEEM, Eye, Gaum, Look, Observe, Odour, Pace, Rate, Re, Respect, Revere, Sake, Steem, Value

**Regardless**  Despite, Heedless, Notwithstanding, Rash, Uncaring, Willy-nilly

**Regatta**  Henley

**Regent**  Interrex, Ruler, Viceroy

**Regent's Park**  Zoo

**Reggae**  Ska

**Regicide**  Ireton, Macbeth

**Regime(n)**  Administration, Control, Diet(etics), Method

**Regiment**  Buffs, Colour(s), Discipline, Greys, Lifeguard, Monstrous, Nutcrackers, Organise, RA, RE, REME, Rifle, Royals, Tercio, Tertia

**Region**  Arctogaea, AREA, Belt, Bundu, Camargue, Climate, Clime, District, End, Hinterland, Hundred, Midi, Offing, Pargana, Part, Pergunnah, Province, Quart(er), Realm, Refugium, Ruthenia, Sector, Stannery, Subtopia, Tagma, Territory, Tract, Tundra, Umbria, Vaud, Weald, Zone

**Register(ing)**  Actuarial, Almanac, Annal, Cadastral, Cadastre, Calendar, Cartulary, Census, Check-in, Diptych, Enrol, Enter, Index, Indicate, Inscribe, Inventory, Ledger, List, Log, Matricula, Menology, Note, Notitia, Patent, Read, Record, Roll, Roule, Score, Soprano, Terrier, Voice

**Registrar**  Actuary, Greffier, Recorder

**Regress(ion)**  Backslide, Recidivism, Revert

**Regret(ful), Regrettable** Alack, Alas, Apologise, Deplore, Deprecate, Forthwink, Ichabod, Lackaday, Lament, Mourn, Otis, Pity, Remorse, Repentance, Repine, RUE, Ruth, Tragic

**Regular(ity), Regularly** Clockwork, Constant, Custom, Episodic, Even, Giusto, Goer, Habitué, Hourly, Insider, Methodic, Normal, Often, Orderly, Orthodox, Patron, Peloria, Periodic, Rhythmic, Routine, Set, Smooth, STANDARD, Stated, Steady, Strict, Symmetric, Uniform, Usual, Yearly

**Regulate, Regulator** Adjust, Control, Direct, Gibberellin, Governor, Guide, Order, Police, Snail, Stickle, Valve

**Regulation** Bye-law, Code, Correction, Curfew, Customary, Ordinance, Rule, Standard, Statute

**Regulus** Matte

**Rehearsal, Rehearse** Drill, Dry-run, Dummy-run, Practice, Practise, Preview, Recite, Repeat, Trial

**Reichenbach** Falls, Od

**Reign** Era, Govern, Prevail, Raine, Realm, RULE

**Reimburse(ment)** Indemnity, Redress, Repay

**Rein(s)** Check, Control, Curb, Lumbar, Restrain

**Reindeer** Caribou, Moss, Tarand

**Reinforce(ment)** Aid, Augment, Bolster, Boost, Brace, Buttress, Cleat, Line, Recruit, Reserve, STRENGTHEN, Support, Tetrapod

**Reinstate** Repone

**Reinvigorate** Recruit

**Reiterate(d)** Emphasize, Plug, Ostinato, REPEAT

**Reject(ion)** Abhor, Athetise, Blackball, Cast, Deny, Dice, Discard, Disclaim, Disdain, Flout, Frass, Jilt, Kest, Kill, Ostracise, Oust, Outcast, Pip, Plough, Rebuff, Recuse, Refuse, Reny, Repudiate, Repulse, Scout, Scrub, Spet, Spin, Spit, SPURN, Sputum, Veto

**Rejoice, Rejoicing** Celebrate, Exult, Festivity, Gaude, Glory, Joy, Maffick, Sing

**Rejoin(der), Rejoined** Answer, Counter, Relide, Reply, Response, Retort, Reunite

**Rejuvenation** Shunamitism

**Relapse** Deteriorate, Recidivism, Regress, Revert, Sink

**Relate(d), Relation(ship), Relative** Account, Affair, Affine, Affinity, Agnate, Akin, Allied, Appertain, Associate, Brer, Brisure, Cognate, Concern, Connection, Connexion, Coosen, Cousin, Coz, Deixis, Eme, Enate, German(e), Granny, Impart, Kin, Link, Mater, Material, Narrative, Pertain, Pi, Plutonic, Privity, PROPORTION, Rapport, Rapprochement, Ratio, Recite, Recount, Rede, Refer(ence), Relevant, Respect(s), Sib(b), Sibbe, Sibling, Sine, Sybbe, Tale, Tell, Who

**Relating to** Of

**Relax(ation), Relaxed** Abate, Atony, Calm, Chalone, Com(m)odo,

Detente, Diversion, Downbeat, Ease, Flaccid, LOOSEN, Mitigate, Peace, Relent, Relief, Remit, Rest, Slacken, Sleep, Toneless, Unbend, Unknit, Untie, Unwind

> **Relaxed** may indicate an anagram

**Relay(er)** Convey, Race, Shift, Tell, Telstar, Torch-race

> **Relay(ing)** may indicate an anagram

**Release** Announcement, Bail, Clear, Death, Deliver(y), Desorb, Discharge, Disclose, Disimprison, Disorb, Emancipate, Enfree, Excuse, Exeem, Exeme, Free, LIBERATE, Manumit, Moksa, Parole, Quietus, Ripcord, Tre corde, Unconfine, Undo, Unhand, Unloose, Unpen, Unshackle, Untie

**Relegate** Banish, Consign, Demote, Stellenbosch

**Relent** Bend, Mollify, Soften, Yield

**Relentless** Cruel, Hard, Pitiless, Rigorous, Stern

**Relevance, Relevant** Ad rem, Apposite, Apropos, Apt, Germane, Material, Pertinent, Point, Valid

> **Reliable, Reliance** see RELY

**Relic** Antique, Ark, Artefact, Fossil, Leftover, Memento, Neolith, Remains, Sangraal, Sangrail, Sangreal, Souvenir, Survival

**Relict** Survivor, Widow

**Relief, Relieve(d)** Aid, Air-lift, Allegeance, Alleviate, Alms, Anaglyph, Assistance, Assuage, Bas, Beet, Beste(a)d, Bete, Cameo, Cavo-relievo, Comfort, Cure, Détente, Ease(ment), Emboss, Emollient, Free, Grisaille, Let-up, Lighten, Palliate, Pog(e)y, Redress, Remedy, Replacement, Repoussé, Reprieve, RESCUE, Respite, Rid, Spell, Stiacciato, Succour, Tondo

**Religion, Religious (sect)** Bahai, Biblist, Bogomil, Camaldolite, Carthusian, Celestine, Christadelphian, Creed, Culdee, Devout, Doctrine, Druse, Druz(e), Faith, Gilbertine, Gueber, Guebre, Hadith, Hieratic, Ignorantine, Islam, Ismaili, Jain(a), Jewry, Lamaism, Loyola, Mahatma, Manichee, Mazdaism, Mazdeism, Missionary, Missioner, Mithraism, Mormonism, Nun, Opium, Pi, Piarist, Pietà, Sabian, Serious, Shaker, Shinto(ism), Sikhism, Sunna, Taoism, Theatine, Tsabian, Whore, Zabian, Zarathustric, Zealous, Zend-avesta, Zoroaster

**Religious book** Bible, Koran, Missal, NT, OT, Sefer, Tantra, Targum, T(h)orah

**Relinquish** Abdicate, Cede, Discard, Drop, Forlend, Waive(r), Yield

**Reliquary** Chef, Encolpion, Encolpium

**Relish** Botargo, Catsup, Chow-chow, Condiment, Enjoy, Flavour, Gout, Gust(o), Ketchup, Lap(-up), Lust, Opsonium, Palate, Sar, Sauce, Savour, Seasoning, Tang, Tooth, Worcester sauce, Zest

**Reluctant** Averse, Backward, Chary, Grudging, Laith, Loth, Nolition, Renitent, Shy, Unwilling

**Rely, Reliance, Reliant, Reliable** Addiction, Authentic, Bank,

Confidence, Constant, COUNT, Dependent, Found, Hope, Lean, Loyal, Presume, Pukka, Safe, Secure, Sound, Sponge, Stand-by, Staunch, Trusty

**Remain(der), Remaining, Remains** Abide, Ash(es), Balance, Bide, Continue, Corse, Dwell, Estate, Fag-end, Kreng, Last, Late, Lave, Left, Lie, Locorestive, Manet, Nose, Oddment, Other, Outstand, Relic(ts), Reliquae, Remnant, Residue, Rest, Ruins, Scraps, Stay, Stick, Stub, Surplus, Survive, Tag-end, Talon, Tarry, Wait

**Remark** Aside, Barb, Bromide, Comment(ary), Dig, Generalise, Mention, Noise, NOTE, Notice, Observe, Platitude, Reason, Sally, Shot, State

**Remarkable, Remarkably** Arresting, Beauty, Conspicuous, Egregious, Extraordinary, Legendary, Lulu, Mirable, Notendum, Noteworthy, Phenomenal, Rattling, SIGNAL, Singular, Some, Striking, Tall, Unco, Visible

**Remedial, Remedy** Aid, Antacid, Antibiotic, Antidote, Antiodontalgic, Arcanum, Arnica, Azoth, Calomel, Catholicon, Corrective, Cortisone, CURE, Drug, Elixir, Heal, Ipecac, Medicate, Medicine, Moxa, Nostrum, Panacea, Panpharmacon, Paregoric, Repair, Rectify, Redress, Salutory, Salve, Simillimum, Simple, Specific, Therapeutic, Tonga, Treatment, Tutsan

**Remember, Remembrance** Bethink, Commemorate, Con, Mention, Memorial, Memorise, Recall, Recollect, Remind, Reminisce, Retain, Rosemary, Souvenir

> **Remember** may indicate RE-member, viz. Sapper

**Remind(er)** Aftertaste, Aide-memoire, Bookmark, Evocatory, Evoke, Jog, Keepsake, Mark, Memo, Mnemonic, Mnemotechnic, Monition, Nudge, Phylactery, Prod, Prompt, Souvenir, Token

**Reminiscence(s), Reminiscent** Ana, Memory, Recall, Recollect, Remember, Retrospect

**Remiss** Careless, Derelict, Lax, Lazy, Negligent, Tardy

**Remission** Abatement, Acceptilation, Indulgence, Pardon, Pause

**Remit** Excuse, Forward, Pardon, Postpone

**Remnant** Butt, End, Fent, Left-over, Odd-come-short, Offcut, Relic, REMAINDER, Rump, Trace, Vestige

**Remonstrate** Argue, Complain, Expostulate, Protest, Reproach

**Remorse** Angst, Ayenbite, Compunction, Contrition, Had-i-wist, Pity, REGRET, Rue, Ruing, Ruth, Sorrow

**Remote** Aloof, Backwater, Backwood, Bundu, DISTANT, Insular, Irrelevant, Jericho, Long(inquity), Out(part), Scrub, Secluded, Slightest, Surrealistic, Unlikely, Withdrawn

**Remount(s)** Remuda

**Removal, Remove(d)** Abduct, Ablation, Abstract, Apocope, Asport, Banish, Blot, Dele(te), Depilate, Depose, Detach, Detract, Dislodge, Dispel, Doff, Efface, Eject, Eloi(g)n, Eradicate, Erase, Esloyne, Estrange, Evacuate, Evict, Exalt, Extirpate, Far, Flit, Huff, Remble, Razee, Rid, Scratch,

Sequester, Shift, Spirit, Sublate, Subtract, Supplant, Transfer, Transport, Unseat, Uproot

**Remuneration**  Pay, Return, Reward, Salary, Solde

**Remus**  Uncle

**Renaissance**  Awakening, Cinquecento, Revival

**Rend**  Cleave, Harrow, Lacerate, Rip, Rive, Rupture, Tear

**Render(ing)**  Construe, Deliver, Do, Gie, Give, Interpretation, Make, Melt, Pebble-dash, Plaster, Provide, Recite, Represent, Restore, Setting, Tallow, Try

**Rendezvous**  Date, Meeting, Philippi, Tryst, Venue

**Rendition**  Account, Delivery, Interpretation, Translation

**Rene**  Descartes

**Renegade, Renege**  Apostate, Default, Defector, Deserter, Rat(ton), Traitor, Turncoat

> **Renegade**  may indicate a word reversal

**Renew(al)**  Instauration, Palingenesis, Refresh, Replace, Resumption, Retrace, Revival

**Rennet**  Steep, Vell

**Renounce, Renunciation**  Abandon, Abdicate, Abjure, Abnegate, Disclaim, Disown, Foresake, Forego, For(e)say, Forfeit, Forisfamiliate, Forswear, Kenosis, Relinquish, Renay, Sacrifice

**Renovate**  Refurbish, Renew, Repair, Restore, Revamp

**Renown**  Fame, Glory, Kudos, Lustre, Notoriety, Prestige

**Rent**  Broken, Charge, Cornage, Crack, Cranny, Cuddeehih, Cuddy, Division, Fee, Fissure, Gale, Gavel, HIRE, Lease, Let, Mail, Occupy, Quit-rent, Rack, Rip, Rived, Riven, Slit, Split, Stallage, Tare, Tithe, Tore, Torn, Tythe

**Reorientate**  Rabat

**Repair(er), Reparation**  Amend(s), Anaplasty, Botch, Cobble, Damages, Darn, Doctor, Fettle, Fitter, Go, Haro, Harrow, MEND, Overhaul, Patch, Recompense, Redress, Refit, Reheel, Remedy, Renew, Resort, Restore, Stitch, Ulling, Vamp, Volery

**Repartee**  Backchat, Badinage, Banter, Rejoinder, Retort, Riposte, Wit

**Repast**  Bever, Collection, Food, Meal, Tea, Treat

**Repay**  Compensate, Quit, Refund, Retaliate, Reward

**Repeal**  Abrogate, Annul, Cancel, Rescind, Revoke

**Repeat, Repetition, Repetitive**  Again, Alliteration, Anadiplosis, Anaphora, Battology, Bis, Burden, Burp, Copy, Ditto(graphy), Duplicate, ECHO(ise), Echolalia, Encore, Epanalepsis, Epizuexis, Eruct, Facsimile, Harp, Image, Imitate, Ingeminate, Iterate, Iterum, Leit-motiv, Merism, Ostinato, Palillogy, Parrot, Playback, Polysyndeton, Recite(r), Redo, Reiterate, Renew, Rep, Rerun, Retail, Rondo, Rosalia, Rote, Same(y),

Screed, Segno, Symploce, Tautology, Thrum, Verbigerate

**Repel(lent)** Estrange, Harsh, Offensive, Rebarbative, Reject, Repulse, Revolt, Squalid, Ug(h), Ward

**Repent(ant)** Metanoia, Penitent, Regret, Rue

**Repercussion** Backlash, Backwash, Effect, Impact, Recoil

**Repertoire, Repertory** Company, Depot, Rep, Store

**Replace(ment), Replacing** Change, Deputise, For, Pre-empt, Raincheck, Refill, Restore, Substitute, Supersede, Supplant, Surrogate, Taxis

**Replay** Segno

**Replenish** Refill, Refresh, Revictual, Stock, Supply, Top

**Replete, Repletion** Awash, Full, Gorged, Plethora, Sated, Satiation

**Replica** Clone, Copy, Duplicate, Facsimile, Image, Spit

**Reply** Accept, Answer, Churlish, Duply, Rejoinder, Rescript, Response, Retort, Surrebut, Surrejoin

**Report(er)** Account, Announce, Bang, Bulletin, Bruit, Clap, Columnist, Comment, Correspondent, Cover, Crack, Crump, Cub, Debrief, Disclose, Dispatch, Explosion, Fame, Grapevine, Hansard, Hearsay, Jenkins, Journalist, Legman, Libel, News, Newshawk, Newshound, Noise, Pop, Pressman, Protocol, Relate, Relay, Repute, Return, Rumour, Sitrep, Sound(bite), State(ment), Stringer, Tale, TELL, Transcribe, Tripehound, Troop, Whang

> **Reported** may indicate the sound of a letter or word

**Repose** Ease, Kaif, Kef, Kif, Lie, Lig, Peace, Relax, REST, Serenity

**Repository** Ark, Cabinet, Container, Reservoir, Sepulchre, Vault

**Reprehend** Blame, Censure, Criticise, Rebuke, Warn

**Represent(ation), Representative** Agent, Ambassador, Anaconic, Caricature, Commercial, Cross-section, Delegate, Depict, Deputation, Describe, Display, Drawing, Effigy, Elchee, Eltchi, Emblem, Embody, Emissary, Example, Image, John Bull, Lobby, Map, Mouthpiece, MP, Personify, Portray, Rep, Resemble, Salesman, Senator, Spokesman, Stand-in, Steward, Symbolic, Tableau, Tiki, Typical, Vakeel, Vakil, Vehicle

> **Represented** may indicate an anagram

**Repress(ed)** Check, Curb, Pent, Quell, Sneap, Stifle, Subjugate, Withhold

**Reprieve** Delay, Postpone, Relief, Respite

**Reprimand** Bounce, Carpet, CENSURE, Chide, Earful, Jobe, Lace, Lecture, Rating, Rebuke, Reproof, Rocket, Slate, Strafe, Tick off, Wig

**Reprint** Copy, Paperback, Replica

**Reprisal** Retaliation, Revenge

**Reproach** Blame, Braid, Byword, Chide, Discredit, Gib, Odium, Opprobrium, Rebuke, Ronyon, Runnion, Scold, Shend, Sloan, Stigma, Taunt, Upbraid, Upcast

**Reprobate** Outcast, Rascal, Scallywag, Scamp

**Reprocess** Re-make

**Reproduce(r), Reproduction, Reproductive** Amphimixis, Clone, Copy, Counterfeit, Depict, Edition, Etch, Gamogenesis, Gemmate, Isospory, Megaspore, Meristematic, Mono, Multiply, Ozalid, Phon(e)y, Propagate, Refer, Replica, Roneo, Seminal, Simulate, Stereo

> **Reproduce** may indicate an anagram

**Reproof, Reprove** Admonish, Berate, Chide, Correction, Lecture, Rate, Rebuff, Rebuke, Scold, Sloan, Tut, Upbraid

**Reptile, Reptilian** Agamid, Alligarta, Alligator, Base, Basilisk, Caiman, Cayman, Creeper, Crocodile, Diapsid, Dicynodont, Dinosaur, Goanna, Herpetology, Lizard, Mamba, Pterodactyl, Sauroid, SNAKE, Squamata, Synapsid, Thecodont, Therapsid, Tortoise, Tuatara, Tuatera, Worm

**Republic** Andorra, Banana, Benin, Cameroon, Chile, Costa Rica, Djibouti, Ecuador, Egypt, Eire, Est(h)onia, Gabon, Guatemala, Guyana, Haiti, Iceland, Israel, Liberia, Lithuania, Malagasy, Malawi, Nicaragua, Niger, Panama, Peru, Philippines, R, San Marino, Serbia, Sinn Fein, Somali, State, Togo, Tunisia, Ukraine, Vanuatu, Weimar, Yemen

**Republican** Antimonarchist, Democrat, Fenian, Fianna Fail, Girondist, IRA, Iraqi, Leveller, Mugwump, Plato, Red, Sans-culotte, Sans-culottic, Sinn Fein, Whig

**Repudiate** Abjure, Deny, Discard, Disclaim, Disown, Ignore, Reject, Renounce, Repel

**Repugnance, Repugnant** Abhorrent, Alien, Disgust, Distaste, Fulsome, Horror, Loathing, Revulsion

**Repulse, Repulsive** Grooly, Lo(a)th, Rebut, Rebuff, Refel, Refuse, Repel, Repugnant, Slimy, Squalid, Ugly, Vile

**Reputable, Reputation, Repute(d)** Bubble, Dit, Estimate, Fame, Good, Izzat, Loos, Los, Name, Note, Notoriety, Odour, Opinion, Prestige, Putative, Regard, Renown, Said, Sar, STANDING, Stink, Trustworthy

**Request** Adjure, Appeal, Apply, Ask, Desire, Entreaty, Invite, Petition, Plea, Prayer, Solicit

**Require(d), Requirement** Charge, Crave, Desire, Enjoin, Exact, Expect, Incumbent, Lack, Necessity, Need

**Requisite, Requisition** Commandeer, Due, Embargo, Essential, Indent, Necessary, Needful, Order, Press

**Rescind** Abrogate, Annul, Recant, Remove, Repeal

**Rescue** Aid, Air-sea, Deliver, Free, Liberate, Ransom, Recover, Recower, Redeem, Regain, Relieve, Salvage, Salvation, SAVE

**Research(er)** Delve, Dig, Enquiry, Explore, Fieldwork, Investigate, Market, Pioneer, Sus(s)

**Resemblance, Resemble, Resembling** Affinity, Approach, Assonant, Likeness, -oid, Replica, Simulate

**Resent(ful), Resentment** Anger, Bridle, Choler, Cross, Dudgeon, Grudge, Indignation, Ire, Malign, Miff, Pique, Smart, Spite, Umbrage

**Reservation, Reserve(d), Reservist(s)** Aloof, Backlog, Bashful, Book, By, Caveat, Cold, Distant, Earmark, Engage, Ersatz, Except, Hold, Husband, Ice, Landwehr, Locum, Nest-egg, Proviso, Qualification, Reddendum, Rest, Restraint, Retain, Reticence, Salvo, Save, Scruple, Special, Stand-offishness, Stock(pile), TA(men), Uncommunicate, Understudy, Warren, Withhold

**Reservoir** Basin, Cistern, G(h)ilgai, Gilgie, Repository, Stock, Sump, Tank

**Reside(nce), Resident** Abode, Address, Amban, Commorant, Denizen, Dwell, Embassy, Establishment, Expatriate, Guest, Home, Indweller, Inholder, Inmate, Intern, Lei(d)ger, Lodger, Metic, Pad, Resiant, Settle, Sojourn, Stay, Tenant, Villager, Yamen

**Residual, Residue** Ash, Astatki, Calx, Caput, Chaff, Cinders, Crud, Draff, Dregs, Greaves, Leavings, Mazout, Mortuum, Remainder, Remanent, Remnant, Slag, Slurry, Snuff, Vinasse

**Resign(ed), Resignation** Abandon, Abdicate, Demit, Fatalism, Leave, QUIT, Reconcile, Stoic, Submit

**Resilience, Resilient** Bounce, Buoyant, Elastic, Flexible, Recoil

**Resin** Agila, Alkyd, Amber, Amine, Anime, Arar, Asafetida, Bakelite, Balsam, Benjamin, Benzoin, Bursera, Caranna, Carauna, Charas, Churrus, Colophony, Conima, Copal(ba), Coumarone, Courbaril, Dam(m)ar, Elemi, Epoxy, Frankincense, Galbanum, Gambi(e)r, Gamboge, Glyptal, Hing, Jalapin, Kino, Lac, Ladanum, Lignaloes, Mastic, Olibanum, Opopanax, Propolis, Roset, Rosin, Rosit, Rozet, Rozit, Sagapenum, Sandarac(h), Saran, Scammony, Shellac, Storax, Styrax, Takamaka, Taxin

**Resist** Bristle, Buck, Contest, Defy, Face, Fend, Gainstrive, Impede, Oppose, Redound, Reluct, Stand, WITHSTAND

**Resistance, Resistant, Resistor** Ceramal, Cermet, Coccidiostat, Drag, Element, Friction, Impediment, Klepht, Maquis, Maraging, Megohm, Microhm, Obstacle, Ohm, R, Renitent, Rheostat, Satyagraha, Stand, Stonde, Stubborn, Tough

**Resolute, Resolution** Analysis, Bold, Cast-iron, Courage, Decided, Decision, Determined, FIRM, Fortitude, Granite, Grim, Grit, Hardiness, Insist, Pertinacity, Promotion, Rede, Resolve, Stable, Stalwart, Staunch, Stout, Strength, Sturdy, Unbending, Valiant

**Resolve(d)** Analyse, Calculate, Decide, Declare, DETERMINE, Factorise, Fix, Hellbent, Intent, PURPOSE, Settle, Steadfast, Tenacity, Vow

> **Resolved** may indicate an anagram

**Resonance, Resonant** Electromer, Orotund, Ringing, Sonorous, Timbre, Vibrant

**Resort** Centre, Etaples, Expedient, Frame, Frequent, Haunt, Hove, Hydro, Invoke, Lair, Las Vegas, Morecambe, Nassau, Pau, Pis aller, Rapallo, Recourse, Repair, Riviera, Southend, Spa(w), Use

> **Resort(ing)** may indicate an anagram

**Resound(ing)** Echo, Plangent, Reboant, Reboation, Reverberate, Ring

**Resource(s), Resourceful** Assets, Beans, Bottom, Clever, Faculty, Funds, Gumption, Ingenious, Input, Means, Sharp, VERSATILE, Wealth

**Respect(ed), Respectable, Respectful** Admire, Aspect, Behalf, Consider, Decent, Deference, Devoir, Duty, Esteem, Gigman, Homage, HONOUR, Kempt, Latria, Obeisant, Officious, Pace, Particular, Proper, Reference, Regard, Relation, Reputable, Revere, Sir, U, Venerate, Wise

**Respirator, Respire** Blow, Breathe, Exhale, Gasmask, Inhale, Pant, Snorkel

**Respite** Break, Breather, Interval, Leisure, Pause, Reprieve, Rest, Stay, Truce

**Respond, Response, Responsive** Amenable, Answer, Antiphon, Echo, Feedback, Kyrie, Litany, Photonasty, React(ion), Reflex, Reply, Rheotaxis, Synapte, Tender, Thigmotropic, Tic, Warm

**Responsibility, Responsible** Answerable, Baby, Blame, Buck, Charge, Culpable, Dependable, Duty, Instrumental, Liable, Onus, Pigeon, Sane, Solid, Trust

**Rest (day)** Anchor, Alt, Avocation, Balance, Bed, Beulah, Break, Breather, Calm, Catnap, Cetera, Comma, Depend, Ease, Easel, Etc, Feutre, Fewter, Gite, Halt, Inaction, Lave, Lean, Lie, Light, Lodge, Loll, Lound, Lyte, Nap, Nooning, Others, Pause, Quiescence, Quiet, Relache, Relax, Rely, Remainder, Repose, Requiem, Respite, Sabbath, Siesta, SLEEP, Sloom, Slumber, Spell, Spider, Stopover, Support, Surplus, Y-level

**Re-start** Da capo

**Restaurant** Automat, Beanery, Bistro, Brasserie, Cabaret, Cafe, Canteen, Commissary, Diner, Eatery, Estaminet, Grill, Maxim's, Noshen, Slap-bang, Taverna, Trattoria

**Rest-home** Aggie, Hospice

**Resting-place** Bed, Couch, Dharmsala, Gite, Grave, Inn, Khan, Serai, She'ol, Stage

**Restitute, Restitution** Amends, Apocatastasis, Reparation, Restore, Return

**Restive, Restless(ness)** Chafing, Chorea, Fikish, Free-arm, Itchy, Toey, Unsettled

> **Restless** may indicate an anagram

**Restorative, Restore** Cure, Heal, Mend, Pick-me-up, Redeem, Redintegrate, Regenerate, Rehabilitate, Remedial, Renew, Repone, Restitute, Revamp, Revive, Stet

**Restrain(ed), Restraint** Ban, Bate, Bit, Bottle, Bridle, Cage, Chain, Chasten, CHECK, Cohibit, Compesce, Confinement, Contain, Control, Cramp, Curb, Decorum, Detent, Dry, Duress, Embargo, Enfetter, Freeze, Halt, Hamshackle, Handcuffs, Harness, Heft, Hinder, Hopple, Impound, Inhibit, Jess, Lid, Manacle, Measure, Mince, Moderation, Muzzle, Quiet, Rein, Restrict, Ritenuto, Shackle, Sober, Sobriety, Squeeze, Stay, Stent, Stint, Temper, Tether, Tie, Trash

**Restrict(ed), Restriction**  Band, Bar, Bind, Bit, Cage, Catch, Chain, Closet, Condition, Cord, Cramp, Curb, DORA, Fence, Fold, Gate, Ground, Guard, Hamper, Hidebound, Hobble, Intern, Kennel, Let, LIMIT, Lock, Mere, Narrow, Net, Nick, Pale, Parochial, Pen, Pier, Pin, Private, Proscribed, Regulate, Rein, Rope, Scant, Seal, Selected, Shackle, Snare, Squeeze, Stenopaic, Stint, Stop, Straiten, Tether, Tie

**Result(s)**  Aftermath, Ans(wer), Bring, Causal, Consequence, Effect, Emanate, End, Ensue, Entail, Event, Fruict, Fruits, Issue, Karmic, Lattermath, OUTCOME, Outturn, Pan, Proceeds, Sequel, Side-effect, Sum, Upshot, Wale

**Resume, Résumé**  Continue, Pirlicue, Purlicue, Summary

**Resurrection**  Rebirth, Revive

**Resuscitate(d)**  Quicken, Redivivus, Restore, Revive

**Retail(er)**  Chandler, Dealer, NARRATE, Sell, Shopkeeper, Tell

**Retain(er), Retains**  Contain, Deposit, Fee, Hold, Keep, Panter, Pantler, Reserve, Retinue, Servant

**Retaliate, Retaliation**  Avenge, Counter, Quit(e), Redress, Repay, Reprisal, Requite, Retort, Talion

**Retard(ed)**  Arrest, Brake, Encumber, Hinder, Slow

**Retch**  Boak, Bock, Boke, Gap, Heave, Keck, Reach, Vomit

**Reticence, Reticent**  Clam, Coy, Dark, Reserve, Restraint, Secretive, Shy, Taciturn

**Reticule, Reticulum**  Bag, Carryall, Dragnet, Lattice, Net

**Retinue**  Company, Cortège, Equipage, Following, Meiney, Meinie, Meiny, Sowarry, Suite

**Retire(d), Retirement, Retiring**  Abed, Aloof, Baccare, Backare, Backpedal, Blate, Bowler-hat, Cede, Coy, Ebb, Emeritus, Essene, Former, Lonely, Modest, Nun, Outgoing, Pension, Private, Quit, Recede, Recluse, Reserved, Resign, Retract, Retreat, Roost, Rusticate, Scratch, Shy, Superannuate, Unassertive, Withdraw

> **Retirement**  may indicate 'bed' around another word, or word reversed

**Retort**  Alembic, Comeback, Courteous, Quip, Repartee, REPLY, Retaliate, Riposte, Still

**Retract(ion)**  Disavow, Epanorthosis, Recall, Recant, Renounce, Revoke

**Retreat**  Abbey, Arbour, Ashram(a), Asylum, Backwater, Bower, Cell, Cloister, Convent, Crawfish, Dacha, Departure, Donjon, Hermitage, Hideaway, Hide-out, Hole, Ivory-tower, Lair, Lama(sery), Mew, Monastery, Nest, Neuk, Nook, Recede, Recoil, Recu(i)le, Redoubt, Reduit, Refuge, Retire, Retraite, Rout, Shelter, Skedaddle, Stronghold, Withdraw

**Retribution**  Come-uppance, Deserts, Nemesis, Revenge, Reward, Utu, Vengeance

**Retrieve(r), Retrieval**  Bird-dog, Field, Gundog, Labrador, Read-out, Recall, Recoup, Recover, Redeem, Rescue, Salvage

**Retrograde**  Backward, Decadent, Decline, Hindward, Rearward, Regrede

**Retrospect(ive)**  Contemplative, Hindsight, Regardant

**Return(s)**  Agen, Census, Comeback, Dividend, Elect, Er, Gain, Pay, Profit, Rebate, Recur, Redound, Regress, Reject, Render, Rent, Repay, Replace, Reply, Requital, Respond, Restore, Revenue, Reverse, Riposte, Takings, YIELD

**Rev**  Gun, Minister

**Reveal(ing), Revelation**  Advertise, Apocalyptic, Bare, Betray, Confess, Descry, Disclose, Discover, Discure, DIVULGE, Exhibit, Explain, Expose, Giveaway, Hierophantic, Impart, Indicate, Ingo, Leak, Manifest, Open, Satori, SHOW, Spill, Tell-tale, Unclose, Uncover, Unfold, Unheal, Unmask, Unveil

**Revel(ling), Revelry**  Ariot, Bacchanalia, Bend, Carnival, Carouse, Comus, Dionysian, Feast, Gloat, Glory, Joy, Merriment, Orgy, Rant, Rejoice, Riot, Rollicks, Rooster, Rout, Saturnalia, Splore, Upsee, Ups(e)y, Wallow, Wassail, Whoopee

**Reveller**  Bacchant, Birler, Guisard, Guiser, Maenad, Orgiast, Silenus

**Revenant**  Fetch, Ghost, Spectre

**Revenge(ful)**  Aftergame, Avenge, Commination, Goel, Grenville, Reprise, Requite, Retaliation, Revanche, Ultion, Vindictive

**Revenue**  Capital, Finance, Fisc(al), Fisk, Income, Inland, Jag(h)ir, Jaghire, Prebend, Rent, Taille, Tax, Turnover, Zamindar, Zemindar

**Reverberate**  Echo, Recoil, Reflect, Repercuss, Resound

**Revere(nce)**  Admire, Awe, Bostonian, Dread, Dulia, Esteem, Hallow, Hery, Homage, HONOUR, Hyperdulia, Latria, Obeisance, Paul, Respect, Venerate

**Reverie**  Dream(iness), Fantasy, Memento

**Revers**  Lap(p)el

**Reverse, Reversing, Reversion**  Antithesis, Antonym, Atavism, Back(slide), Change-over, Chiasmus, Counter(mand), Escheat, Exergue, Flip, Misfortune, OPPOSITE, Palindrome, Pile, Regress, Revoke, Rheotropic, Switchback, Tails, Throwback, Transit, Turn, Un-, Undo, U-turn, Verso, Volte-face

**Revert**  Annul, Backslide, Relapse, Resort, Return

**Review(er)**  Appeal, Censor, Critic, Critique, Editor, Footlights, Inspect, Magazine, March-past, Notice, Pan, Recapitulate, Repeat, Revise, Rundown, Spithead, Summary, Survey

> **Review**  may indicate an anagram, or a reversed word

**Revile**  Abuse, Execrate, Inveigh, Rail, Vilify

**Revise(r), Revision**  Alter, Amend, Correct, Diaskeuast, Edit, Peruse, Reappraise, Reassess, Recense, Reform, Rev, Update

> **Revise(d)**  may indicate an anagram

**Revival, Revive, Revivify, Reviving**  Araise, Enliven, Rally, Reanimate,

Reawake(n), Redintegrate, Refresh, Renaissance, Renascent, Renew, Renovate, Restore, Resurrect, Resuscitate, Risorgimento, Romantic, Rouse, Wake

**Revoke** Abrogate, Cancel, Negate, RECALL, Repeal, Rescind

**Revolt(ing), Revolution(ary)** Agitator, Agitprop, Anarchist, Apostasy, Appal, Bolshevik, Bolshevist, Boxer, Bulldog, Cade, Chartist, Che, Circle, Coup d'etat, Cycle, Danton, Dervish, Disgust, Emeute, Emmet, Enrage, Foul, Girondin, Girondist, Gyration, Inqilab, IN REVOLT, Insurgent, Insurrection, Intifada, Jacquerie, IRA, Jacobin, Komitaji, Lap, Lenin, Marat, Maypole, Mountain, Mutiny, Nihilist, Orbit, Outbreak, Putsch, Radical, REBEL(lion), Red, Reformation, Riot, Rise, Robespierre, Roll, Rotation, Round, Run, Sandinista, Sansculotte(rie), Sedition, Spartacus, Thermidor, Trot(sky), Twist, Up(rise), UPRISING, Villa, Whirl, Zapata

> **Revolutionary** may indicate 'reversed'

**Revolve(r)** Carrier, Catherine wheel, Centrifuge, Colt, Gat, Girandole, Grindstone, GUN, Gyrate, Iron, Klinostat, Lathe, Maelstrom, Pistol, Pivot, Roller, Rotate, Rotifer, Rotor, Roundabout, Run, Tone, Turn(stile), Turntable, Turret, Wheel, Whirl(igig), Whirlpool

**Revue** Follies

**Reward** Albricias, Bonus, Consideration, Desert, Emolument, Fee, Guerdon, Meed, Payment, Premium, Price, Prize, Profit, Recompense, Reguerdon, Remuneration, Requital, Requite, S, Shilling, Wage

**Reworking** Rifacimento

**Rex** Priam, R

**Reynolds** Joshua, PRA

**Rhapsodic, Rhapsody** Ecstasy, Epic, Music, Unconnected

**Rhea** Em(e)u, Nandoo, Nandu, Ostrich

**Rhenium** Re

**Rhesus** Bandar, Macaque, Monkey

**Rhetoric(al)** Anaphora, Aureate, Bombast, Eloquence, Enantiosis, Erotema, Eroteme, Erotesis, Hendiadys, Oratory, Peroration

**Rhino** Blunt, Bread, Cash, Lolly, Money, Tin

**Rhinoceros** Baluchitherium, Keitloa

**Rhodes, Rhodesia(n)** Cecil, Ridgeback, Scholar, Zimbabwe

**Rhodium** Rh

**Rhubarb** Pie-plant, Rhapontic, Rheum, Rot, Spat

**Rhyme(r), Rhyming** Assonance, Clerihew, Couplet, Crambo, Doggerel, Eye, Masculine, Measure, Nursery, Poetry, Perfect, Rondel, Runic, Slang, Tercet, Terza-rima, Thomas, VERSE, Virelay

**Rhythm(ic)** Agoge, Asynartete, Beat, Cadence, Circadian, In-step, Meter, Movement, Oompah, Rubato, Sdrucciola, Swing, Tala, Talea, TEMPO, Time, Voltinism,

**Rib(bed), Ribbing, Rib-joint** Chaff, Cod, Costa, Dutch, Eve, Futtock,

Groin, Intercostal, Lierne, Nervate, Nervular, Nervure, Ogive, Persiflage, Rally, Sub-costa, Tease, Tierceron, Tracery, Wife

**Ribald(ry)** Balderdash, Coarse, Scurrilous, Smut, Sotadic, Vulgar

**Ribbon** Band, Bow, Braid, Caddis, Caddyss, Cordon, Fattrels, Ferret, Fillet, Grosgrain, Hatband, Infula, Pad, Petersham, Radula, Rein, Soutache, Taenia, Tape, Teniate, Tie, Torsade

**Ribless** Ecostate

**Rice** Basmati, Elmer, Kedgeree, Patna, Pilaf, Pilau, Reis, Risotto, Sushi, Twigs

**Rich(es)** Abounding, Abundant, Affluent, Amusing, Bonanza, Comic, Copious, Croesus, Dives, Edmund, Edwin, Fat, Feast, Fertile, Flush, Fruity, Golconda, Heeled, Loaded, Lush, Luxurious, Mammon, Moneyed, Nabob, Oberous, OPULENT, Plenteous, Plush, Plutocrat, Rolling, Sumptuous, Toff, Vulgarian, WEALTHY, Well-heeled, Well-to-do

**Richard** Angevin, Burbage, Dick(y), Lionheart, Rick, Roe

**Rickshaw** Pedicab

**Richthofen** Red Baron

**Rick (burning)** Goaf, Sprain, Swingism, Wrench

**Rickets, Rickety** Dilapidated, Rachitis, Ramshackle, Shaky, Unsound

> **Rickety** may indicate an anagram

**Ricochet** Boomerang, Glance, Rebound

**Rid** Clear, Deliver, Ditch, Eliminate, Eradicate, Free, Obviate, Offload, Purge

**Riddle** Boulter, Charade, Colander, Dilemma, Enigma, Koan, Logogriph, Pepper, Perforate, Permeate, Puzzle, Screen, Searce, Search, Sieve, Sift, Siler, Sorites, Strain, Tems(e)

**Ride, Riding** Bareback, Bestride, Bruise, Canter, Coast, Cycle, District, Division, Drive, Equitation, Field, Hack, Harass, Mount, Pick-a-back, Rape, Revere's, Roadstead, Sit, Spin, Stang, Third, Trot, Weather, Welter, Wheelie

**Rider** Addendum, Adjunct, Appendage, Attachment, Cavalier, Charioteer, Condition, Corollary, Equestrian, Haggard, Horseman, Jockey, Lochinvar, Postillion, PS, Revere

**Ridge** Anthelix, Antihelix, Arete, As(ar), Balk, Bank, Baulk, Berm, Bur(r), Carina, Chine, Crease, Crista, Cuesta, Drill, Drum(lin), Dune, Esker, Fret, Hammock, Hoe, Hogback, Horst, Hummock, Keel, Knur(l), Ledge, Linch, Lynchet, Nek, Promontory, Ramp, Rand, Raphe, Razor-back, Reef, Rib, Rig, Rim, Sastruga, Screw-thread, Torus, Varix, Verumontanum, Vimy, Wale, Weal, Whelp, Windrow, Withers, Yardang, Zastruga

**Ridicule, Ridiculous** Absurd, Badinage, Bathos, Chaff, Deride, Derisory, Foolish, Gibe, Gird, Guy, Jibe, Josh, Laughable, Mimic, Mock, Paradox, Pasquin, Pillory, Pish, Pooh-pooh, Raillery, Rich, Roast, Satire, Scoff, Scout, Screwy, Sight, Silly, Skimmington, Taunt, Travesty

**Ridinghood** Nithsdale, Red

**Riding-master** RM

**Riding-school** Manège

**Rife** Abundant, Manifest, Numerous, Prevalent

**Riff-raff** Canaille, Hoi polloi, Mob, Populace, Rag-tag, Scaff, Scum, Trash

**Rifle** Bone, Bundook, Burgle, Carbine, Chassepot, Enfield, Express, Garand, GUN, Loot, Martini, Mauser, Minié, Pilfer, Ransack, Repeater, Rob, Winchester

**Rift** Altercation, Chasm, Crevasse, Fault, Fissure, Gap, Gulf, Split

**Rig(ging)** Accoutre, Attire, Bermuda, Equip, Feer, Gaff, Get-up, Gunter, Hoax, Manipulate, Martingale, Outfit, Panoply, Ratline, Ropes, Sport, Stack, Swindle, Tackle, Trull

> **Rigged** may indicate an anagram

**Right(en), Rightness, Rights** Accurate, Advowson, Angary, Appropriate, Appurtenance, Befit, Blue-pencil, Bote, Champart, Claim, Competence, Conjugal, Conservative, Copyhold, CORRECT, Coshery, Cure, Curtesy, Customer, Dexter, Direct, Doctor, Droit, Due, Easement, Emphyteusis, Equity, Esnecy, Estover, Ethical, Exactly, Faldage, Farren, Fascist, Feu, Fire-bote, Fitting, Franchise, Freedom, Germane, Gunter, Haybote, Infangthief, Interest, Junior, Jural, Jus, Leet, Legit, Lien, Maritage, Meet, Moral, Naam, Ninepence, Off, Offhand, Offside, Ortho-, Oughtness, Paine, Passant, Pat, Ploughbote, Pose, Postliminy, Prisage, Privilege, Proper, R, Rain, Reason, Rectify, Rectitude, Redress, Remainder, Repair, Rt, Sac, Sake, Side, Soc, Squatter's, Stillicide, Terce, Ticket, Title, Trivet, True, User, Usufruct, Venville, Vert, Warren

**Right-angle(d)** Orthogonal

**Righteous** Devout, Good, Just, Moral, Pharisee, Prig, Virtuous

**Right-hand** Dexter, E, Far, Recto, RH, Ro

**Right-winger** Falangist

**Rigid(ity)** Acierated, Catalepsy, Craton, Extreme, Fixed, Formal, Hidebound, Inflexible, Set, Starch(y), Stern, Stiff, Stretchless, Strict, Stringent, Tense

**Rigmarole** Nonsense, Palaver, Paraphernalia, Protocol, Riddlemeree, Screed

**Rigorous, Rigour** Accurate, Austere, Cruel, Exact, Firm, Hard, Inclement, Stern, Strait, Strict, Stringent

**Rile** Anger, Annoy, Harry, Irritate, NETTLE, Vex

> **Rile(y)** may indicate an anagram

**Rill** Purl

**Rim** Border, Chimb, Chime, Edge, Felloe, Felly, Flange, LIP, Margin, Strake, Verge

**Rime** Crust, Frost, Hoar, Rhyme, Rhythm

**Rind** Bark, Peel, Skin

**Ring(ed), Ringing** Angelus, Annulus, Anthelion, Arcus, Arena, Band, Bangle, Bell, Broch, Brogh, Call, Cartel, Cartouche, Change, Chime, Circinate, Circle, Circus, Clam, Clang, Clink, Coil, Collet, Cordon, Corral, Crawl, Cricoid, Cringle, Cycle, Cyclic, Dial, Dicyclic, Ding, Disc, Dohyo, Dong, Draupnir, Encircle, Encompass, Engagement, Enlace, Environ, Enzone, Eternity, Ferrule, Fisherman, Fistic(uffs), Gimmal, Gird(le), Girr, Gloriole, Groin, Grom(m)et, Grummet, Gyges, Gymmal, Gyre, Halo, Hob, HOOP, Hoop-la, Ideal, Inorb, Inner, Jougs, Jow, Karabiner, Kartell, Keeper, Knell, Knock-out, Kraal, Link, Loop, Luned, Lute, Magpie, Marquise, Nibelung, O, Orb, Outer, Pappus, Peal, Pele, Pen, Phone, Ping, Puteal, Quoit, Resonant, Resound, Round, Rundle, Runner, Signet, Sound, Spell, Stemma, Stemme, Surround, Swivel, Syndicate, Tang, Tattersall, Terret, Territ, Ting, Tink, Tinnitus, Tintinnabulate, Toll, Toplady, Tore, Torret, Torus, Travelling, Turret, Tweed, Varvel, Vervel, Wagnerian, Washer, Welkin, Withe, Woggle, Zero

**Ring-dance** Carol

**Ring-leader** Bell-wether, Fugleman, Instigator

**Ringlet** Curl(icue), Lock, Tendril, Tress

**Ringmaster** Wagner

**Ringworm** Serpigo, Tinea

**Rinse** Bathe, Cleanse, Douche, Sind, Sine, Swill, Synd, Syne, Tint, Wash

**Riot(er), Riotous(ly), Riots** Anarchy, Brawl, Clamour, Demo, Deray, Gordon, Hilarious, Hubbub, Luddite, Medley, Melee, Orgy, Pandemonium, Peterloo, Porteous, Profusion, Quorum, Rag, Rebecca, Rebel, Roister, Rout, Rowdy, Ruffianly, Swing, Tumult

> **Rioters, Riotous** may indicate an anagram

**Rip(ping)** Basket, Buller, Cur, Grand, Handful, Horse, Lacerate, Rent, Rep, Splendid, Tear, Tide, Topnotch, To-rend, Unseam

**Ripe** Auspicious, Full, Mature, Mellow, Ready

**Riposte** Repartee, Retaliate, Retort

**Ripple** Bradyseism, Fret, Purl, Undulation, Wave, Wrinkle

> **Rippling** may indicate an anagram

**Rise(r), Rising** Advance, Appreciate, Ascend, Assurgent, Bull, Butte, Cause, Eger, Elevation, Emeute, Eminence, Erect, Escalate, Hance, Hauriant, Haurient, Heave, Hill, Hummock, Hunt's up, Improve, Increase, Insurgent, Intumesce, Jibe, Knap, Knoll, Lark, Levee, Lift, Mutiny, Orient, Peripety, Putsch, Rear, REVOLT, Saleratus, Scarp, Soar, Stand, Stie, Sty, Surge, Tor, Tower, Transcend, Up, Upbrast, Upburst, Upgo, Uprest, Upsurge, Upswarm, Upturn, Well

**Risk(y)** Adventure, Calculated, Chance, Compromise, DANGER, Daring, Dice, Dicy, Emprise, Endanger, Fear, Gamble, Hairy, Hazard, Imperil, Liability, Peril, Precarious, Spec, Venture

**Risorgimento** Renaissance

**Risqué** Blue, Racy, Salty, Scabrous, Spicy

**Rissole(s)** Cecils, Croquette, Faggot, Quennelle

**Rite(s)** Asperges, Bora, Ceremony, Exequies, Initiation, Liturgy, Nagmaal, Obsequies, Powwow, Ritual, Sacrament, Superstition

**Ritual** Agadah, Ceremony, Chanoyu, Customary, Formality, Haggada, Lavabo, Liturgy, Rite, Seder, Social, Use

**Rival(ry)** Absolute, Acres, Aemule, Compete, Emulate, Envy, MATCH, Needle, Opponent, Touch, Vie

**River** Aar, Abana, Abus, Abzu, Acheron, Acis, Acton, Adige, Adur, Afton, Agate, Aire, Aisne, Alma, Aln, Alph, Amazon, Amur, Argun, Arno, Arun, Aruwimi, Arzina, Avoca, Avon, Axe, Ayr, Back, Billabong, Blackwater, Bug, Cam, Cherwell, Chindwin, Clyde, Cocytus, Congo, Crouch, Cydnus, Damodar, Danube, Darling, Dart, Dasht, Dee, Demerara, Derwent, Desna, Deva, Dnieper, Don, Doon, Douro, Dove, Dubglas, Duddon, Duero, Durance, Ea, Ebbw, Eblis, Ebro, Eden, Eder, Elbe, Ems, Esk, Esla, Estuary, Ettrick, Euphrates, Eure, Exe, Fal, Firth, Fleet, Flood, Flower, Fluvial, Forth, Ganges, Garonne, Gironde, Godavari, Gota, Granta, Han, Havel, Hodder, Hudson, Humber, Huon, Hwangho, Idle, Indre, Indus, Inn, Irrawaddy, Irwell, Isar, Iser, Isere, Isis, Itchen, Javari, Javary, Jordan, Juba, Jumna, Kenga, Kennet, Kill, Klondike, Krishna, Kwai, Lahn, Lech, Lee, Leno, Lethe, Liard, Limpopo, Loire, Lot, Lune, Maas, Mackenzie, Madeira, Maeander, Main, Marne, Medway, Mekong, Mersey, Meta, Meuse, Min(h)o, Mississippi, Missouri, Mole, Mosel(le), Mulla, Murray, Nar, Neckar, Negro, Nene, Neva, Nile, Nith, Ob, Oder, Ohio, Oise, Onega, Ord, Orinoco, Orontes, Orwell, Oxus, Pactolus, Pahang, Parana, Peace, Pearl, Pecos, Pharpar, Phlegethon, Piave, Pison, Plate, Po, Pochora, Potamic, Potomac, Pripet, Pruth, R, Rance, Red, Rhine, Rhone, Ribble, Riffle, Rio Grande, Riverain, Rother, Rubicon, Ruhr, Runner, Sabrina, Salween, Salzach, Sanders, San(tee), Seine, Senegal, Shannon, Snake, Soar, Somme, Spey, Spree, Staff, St Lawrence, Stour, Stream, Struma, Styx, Swale, Swanee, Taff, Tagus, Tamar, Tapti, Tarn, Tarsus, Tay, Tees, Teign, Teme, Terek, Test, Tet, Teviot, Thames, Tiber, Ticino, Tigris, Torridge, Toulouse, Trent, Tributary, Tweed, Tyburn, Tyne, Ural, Ure, Usk, Vaal, Vistula, Volga, Volta, Wabash, Waterway, Wear, Welland, Wensum, Weser, Wharfe, Wye, Xero, Yalu, Yangtse, Yaqui, Yare, Yarra, Yarrow, Yate, Yellow, Yuan, Yuen, Yukon, Zambesi

**River-bank, Riverside** Brim, Carse, Riparian

**River-bed** Thalweg

**River-mouth** Firth, Frith

**Rivet** Bolt, Clinch, Clink, Concentrate, Fasten, Fix, Stud, Transfix

**Rivulet** Beck, Brook, Burn, Gill, Rill, Runnel, Strand

**Roach** Fish, Red-eye

**Road(side)** A, A1, Anchorage, Arterial, Autobahn, Autostrada, Ave(nue), B, Burma, Carriageway, Causeway, Corniche, Course, Fairway, Freeway, Highway, Kerb, Lane, Loan, Loke, Mall, Metal, M1, Path, Pike, Rd, Ride,

ROUTE, Shoulder, Shunpike, Spurway, St(reet), Thoroughfare, Toby, Turning, Turnpike, Verge, Via, Way

**Road-keeper** Way-warden

**Road-maker** Drunkard, Macadam, Navigator, Telford, Wade

**Roam** Peregrinate, Rake, Ramble, Rove, Stray, Wander, Wheel

**Roan** Barbary, Bay, Horse, Leather, Schimmel

**Roar(ing)** Bawl, Bell(ow), Bluster, Boom, Boys, Cry, Forties, Laugh, Roin, Rote, Rout, Royne, Thunder, Tumult, Vroom, Zoom

**Roast** Barbecue, Bake, Baste, Birsle, Brent, Cabob, Cook, Crab, Grill, Kabob, Pan, Ridicule, Scathe, Scald, Slate, Tan

**Rob(bed), Robber(y)** Abduct, Bandalero, Bandit, Barabbas, Bereave, Blag, Brigand, Burgle, Bust, Cabbage, Cacus, Cateran, Clyde, Dacoit, Dakoit, Daylight, Depredation, Do, Drawlatch, Fake, Filch, Fleece, Flimp, Footpad, Gilderoy, Heist, Hership, Highwayman, Hold-up, Hustle, Ladrone, Larceny, Latrocincum, Latron, Mill, Mosstrooper, Pad, Pandoor, Pandour, Pinch, Piracy, Plunder, Procrustes, Rapine, Reave, Reive, Rifle, Roberdsman, Robertsman, Roll, Rover, Roy, Rubbet, Rustler, Sack, Sciron, Sinis, Skinner, Snaphaunch, STEAL, Sting, Swindle, Thief, Toby, Turn-over, Turpin

**Robe(s)** Alb, Amice, Amis, Attrap, Camis, Camus, Cassock, Chimer, Chrisom(-cloth), Christom, Dalmatic, Dolman, DRESS, Gown, Kanzu, Khalat, Khilat, Kill(a)ut, Kimono, Mantle, Parliament, Pedro, Peplos, Regalia, Sanbenuto, Soutane, Sticharion, Stola, Stole, Talar, Tire, Vestment, Yukata

**Robert** Bob(by), Bridges, Browning, Burns, Cop, Flic, Peel, Rab, Rob

**Robin** Adair, Bird, Cock, Day, Goodfellow, Hob, Hood, Puck(-hairy), Ragged, Redbreast, Round, Ruddock, Starveling, Wake

**Robot** Android, Automaton, Cyborg, Dalek, Golem, Puppet, RUR, Telechir

**Robust** Hale, Hardy, Healthy, Hearty, Iron, Sound, Stalwart, Stout, Strapping, Sturdy, Vigorous

**Roc** Bird, Ruc, Rukh

**Rock(er), Rocking, Rocks, Rocky** Aa, Adularia, Ages, Agglomerate, Ailsa Craig, Amygdaloid, Annabergite, Anticline, Aphanite, Aplite, Aquifer, Astound, Babingtonite, Basalt, Batholite, Bell, Bluestone, Boulder, Brash, Breccia, Brockram, Calc-tufa, Calc-tuff, Calpe, Chair, Chalk, Chert, Ciminite, Clastic, Cliff, Country, Cradle, Crag, Cuprite, Cyanean, Dacite, Dalradian, Diabasic, Diamond, Diorite, Dolerite, Dolomite, Dunite, Eclogite, Eddystone, Edinburgh, Eklogite, Elvan(ite), Epidiorite, Eucrite, Fastnet, Felsite, Firestone, Flaser, Flint, Flowstone, Fossil, Foundation, Gabbro, Gang(ue), Gem, Geode, Gib(raltar), Glass, Gneiss, Goslarite, Gossan, Gozzan, Granite, Greensand, Greywacke, Halleflinta, Hepatite, Hornfels, Hornstone, Hypersthenite, Idocrase, Ignimbrite, Inchcape, Inlier, Intrusion, Jow, Jura, Kimberlite, Kingle, Laccolite, Lamprophyre, Lava, Lias, Limburgite, Limestone, Lorelei, Magma, Marciano, Masada, Mesolite, Meteorite, Minette, Molasse,

Monchiquite, Monzonite, Moraine, Mortstone, Mudstone, Muglarite, Mylonite, Nappe, Natrolite, Needles, Norite, Noup, Novaculite, Neocomian, Nunatak(kr), Obsidian, Oolite, Ophites, Ottrelite, Outcrop, Palagonite, Pelite, Peperino, Peridot, Petuntse, Phillipsite, Phonolite, Phyllite, Pisolite, Pleonaste, Pluton(ic), Plymouth, Porphyry, Protogine, Psammite, Psephite, Pumice, Punk, Quake, Ragstone, Reef, Reggae, Regolith, Rhaetic, Rhyolite, Rip-rap, Rocaille, Roe-stone, Rognon, Rupestrian, Sarsen, Scablands, Scalp, Schalstein, Schist, Scorpion, Scree, Serpentine, SHAKE, Shale, Showd, Sill, Siltstone, Sima, Sinking, Sinter, Skerry, Sklate, Slate, Solid, S. Peter, Spilite, Stilbite, Stone, Stonebrash, Stonehenge, Stonen, Stromatolite, Stun, Sway, Swee, Swing, Syenite, Symplegades, Syntagmata, Syntagmatite, Taconite, Tachylyte, Tarpeian, Ted, Teeter, Tephra, Tephrite, Teschenite, Theralite, Thulite, Tinguaite, Toadstone, Tonalite, Tor, Totter, Touchstone, Trachyte, Trap(pean), Trass, Travertin(e), Tripoli, Troctolite, Tufa, Tuff, Unstable, Unsteady, Wacke, Wenlock, Whinstone, Whunstane, Xenolith, Zechstein, Zoic

**Rock-boring**  Pholas

**Rock-cress**  Arabis

**Rocket**  Arugula, Booster, Capsule, Carpet, Congreve, Drake, Engine, Flare, Jato, Onion, Posigrade, Reprimand, Reproof, Retro, SAM, Skylark, Soar, Stephenson, Tourbillion, Upshoot, V1, Warhead, Weld

**Rock-living**  Rupicoline, Saxatile, Saxicoline, Saxicolous

**Rock-pipit**  Sea-lark

> **Rocky**  may indicate an anagram

**Rococo**  Baroque, Fancy, Ornate, Quaint

**Rod(like)**  Aaron's, Bar, Caduceus, Came, Can, Cane, Cue, Cuisenaire, Dowser, Ellwand, Fasces, Firearm, Fisher, Gun, Handspike, Kame, Laver, Lug, Moses, Newel, Notochord, Perch, Pin, Pistol, Pitman, Pointer, Pole, Pontie, Pontil, Ponty, Probang, Puntee, Punty, Raddle, Rhabdoid, Rhabdus, Rood, Scollop, Spindle, Spit, Stadia, Stanchion, Staple, Stave, Stay-bolt, Stick, Strickle, Switch, Tringle, Twig, Verge, Virgate, Virgulate, Wand

**Rod-bearer**  Lictor

**Rodent**  Acouchy, Ag(o)uti, Bandicoot, Bangsring, Banxring, Beaver, Biscacha, Bizcacha, Bobac, Bobak, Boomer, Capybara, Cavy, Chickaree, Chincha, Chinchilla, Civet, Coypu, Cricetus, Dassie, Delundung, Dormouse, Gerbil, Glires, Glutton, Gnawer, Gopher, Ham(p)ster, Hog-rat, Hutia, Hyrax, Jerboa, Lemming, Marmot, Mouse, Mus, Musk-rat, Ochotona, Ondatra, Paca, Porcupine, Potoroo, Rat, Ratel, Ratton, Renegade, Runagate, Sewellel, Shrew, Spermophile, Springhaas, Squirrel, Taira, Tuco-tuco, Tucu-tuco, Vermin, Viscacha, Vole

**Roderick**  Random, Usher

**Rodomontade**  Bluster, Boast, Bombast, Brag, Gas

**Roe**  Caviare, Coral, Fry, Melt, Milt(z), Pea, Raun, Rawn

**Roger**  Ascham, Bacon, Jolly, OK, Rights

**Rogue, Roguish(ness)** Arch, Bounder, Charlatan, Chiseller, Drole, Dummerer, Elephant, Espiegle(rie), Ganef, Ganev, Ganof, Gonif, Gonof, Greek, Hempy, Herries, Imp, Knave, Latin, Limmer, Panurge, Picaroon, Rapparee, Riderhood, Savage, Schellum, Schelm, Skellum, Swindler, Varlet, Villain

**Roil** Agitate, Annoy, Churn, Provoke, Vex

**Roister(er)** Blister, Carouse, Ephesian, Revel, Scowrer, Swashbuckler, Swinge-buckler

**Role** Bit, Cameo, Capacity, Function, Metier, PART, Prima-donna

**Roll(er), Roll-call, Rolling, Rolls** Absence, Bagel, Bap, Beigel, Billow, Bolt, Brioche, Chamade, Comber, Convolv(ut)e, Croissant, Cylinder, Electoral, Enswathe, Even, Fardel, Fardle, Flatten, Furl, Go, Inker, Labour, List, Lurch, Makimono, Mangle, Mano, Matricula, Motmot, Moving, Notitia, Opulent, Paradiddle, Pipe, Platen, Ragman, Ra(p)scal(l)ion, Record, Reef, Register, Ren, Revolve, Rhotacism, Rob, Roster, Rota, Rotifer, Roulade, Rouleau, RR, Rub-a-dub, Rumble, Run, Schnecken, Spool, Sway, Swell, Swiss, Table, Taxi, Temple, Tent, Tommy, Trill, Trindle, Trundle, Volume, Volutation, Wad, Wallow, Wamble, Waul, Wave, Wawl, Web, Welter, Wince, Wrap

**Rollick(ing)** Frolic, Gambol, Romp, Sport

> **Rollicking** may indicate an anagram

**Roman** Agricola, Agrippa, Candle, Calpurnia, Catholic, Cato, Consul, CR, Crassus, Decemviri, Decurion, Empire, Flavian, Galba, Holiday, Italian, Jebusite, Latin, Maecenas, Papist, Patrician, PR, Raetic, RC, Retarius, Rhaetia, Road, Scipio, Sulla, Tarquin, Tiberius, Type, Uriconian

**Romance, Romantic** Affair, Amorous, Byronic, Casanova, Catalan, Dreamy, Fancy, Fantasise, Fib, Fiction, Gest(e), Gothic, Invention, Ladin(o), Languc d'oc(ian), Langue d'oil, Langue d'oui, Lie, Neo-Latin, Novelette, Poetic, Quixotic, R(o)uman, Tale

> **Romanian** see RO(U)MANIAN

**Romanov** Nicholas

**Romantic talk** Ladinity

> **Romany** see GYPSY

**Romeo** Casanova, Montagu, Swain

**Romp** Carouse, Fisgig, Fizgig, Frisk, Frolic, Hoyden, Rig, Sport, Spree

**Ron** Glum, Moody

**Rondo** Rota

**Rontgen** R

**Roo** Joey

**Roof (edge), Roofing** Ceil, Cl(c)ithral, Cover, Divot, Dome, Drip, Gambrel, Hardtop, Home, Leads, Mansard, Palate, Porte-cochère, Shingle, Tectiform, Teguila, Thatch, Thetch, Top, Uraniscus

**Roof-climber** Stegopholist

**Roofless** Hypaethral, Upaithric

**Rook** Bird, Castle, Cheat, Crow, Fleece, Fool, R, Swindle

**Rookie** Beginner, Colt, Greenhorn, Nignog, Novice, Recruit, Tyro

**Room(s), Roomy** Antechamber, Anteroom, Apadana, Apartment, Attic, Ben, Berth, Bibby, Boudoir, Bower, But, Cabin(et), Camarilla, Camera, Capacity, Casemate, CC, Ceiling, Cell, Cellar, Cenacle, Chamber, Chaumer, Closet, Commodious, Compartment, Conclave, Cubicle, Cuddy, Digs, Divan, Dojo, Durbar, Elbow, End, Ex(h)edra, Extension, Foyer, Garret, Genizah, Kursaal, Lab, Latitude, Laura, Lavra, Lebensraum, Leeway, Library, Lodge, Loft, Loo, Lounge, Margin, Misericord, Oda, Orderly, Oriel, Pad, Parlour, Parvis, Penetralia, Pentice, Pentise, Robing, Sanctum, Scope, Scriptorium, Shebang, Solar, SPACE, Spence, Strong, Studio, Study, Suite, Tap, Ullage, Ward, Zeta

**Roost(er)** Cock, Perch, Siskin, Sit

**Root(ing), Roots** Calumba, Cassava, Cheer, Costus, Delve, Deracinate, Derris, Dig, Eddo, Elacampane, Eradicate, Eringo, Eryngo, Etymic, Extirpate, Foundation, Gelseminine, Ginseng, Grass, Grout, Grub, Heritage, Hurrah, Irradicate, Licorice, Mandrake, Mangold, Mishmee, Mishmi, More, Myall, Orris, Pachak, Poke, Pry, Putchock, Putchuk, Radish, Radix, Repent, Rhizic, Rhizoid, Rhizome, Scorzonera, Senega, Setwall, Snuzzle, Stock, Tap, Taro, Tuber, Turbith, Turnip, Turpeth, Vetiver, Yam, Zedoary

**Rootless** Psilotum

**Rope** Abaca, Ba(u)lk, Bind, Bobstay, Brail, Breeching, Cable, Colt, Cord, Cringle, Downhaul, Earing, Fake, Forestay, Gantline, Grist, Guy, Halliard, Halser, Halter, Halyard, Hawser, Headfast, Inhaul, Jeff, Knittle, Ladder, Lanyard, Lasher, Line, Longe, Lunge, Marline, Messenger, Nettle, Noose, Oakum, Painter, Prolonge, Prusik, Rawhide, Riata, Roband, Robbin, Rode, Runner, Sally, Seal, Selvagee, Sennit, Sheet, Shroud, Sinnet, Span, Spun-yarn, Stay, Sternfast, Stirrup, String, Sugan, Swifter, Tether, Tie, Timenoguy, Tippet, Tow(line), Trace, Triatic, Vang, Wanty, Warp, Widdy

**Rosalind** Ganymede

**Rosary** Beads, Paternoster

**Rose(-red), Rosy** Albertine, Amelanchier, Aurorean, Avens, Blooming, Bourbon, Breare, Briar, Brier, Cabbage, Canker, Eglantine, Eglatère, England, Floribunda, Geum, Hybrid, Jacqueminot, Lal(age), Lancaster, Moss, Noisette, Opulus, Peace, Petra, Pink, Promising, Pyrus, Rambler, Red(dish), Remontant, Rhodo-, Snowball, Sprinkler, Standard, Tea, Tokyo, Tudor, Whitethorn, York

**Rose-apple** Jamboo, Jambu

**Rose-bay** Oleander

**Rosette** Buttonhole, Cockade, Favour, Patera

**Rosin** Colophony, Resin, Roset, Rosit, Rozet, Rozit

**Rosinante** Jade

**Roster** List, Register, Scroll, Table

**Rostrum** Ambo, Bema, Lectern, Pulpit

**Rot(ten), Rotting** Addle, Boo, Bosh, Bull, Caries, Carious, Corrode, Corrupt, Daddock, Decadent, DECAY, Decompose, Dotage, Eat, Erode, Fester, Foul, Kibosh, Nonsense, Poppycock, Poxy, Punk, Putrefy, Putrid, Rail, Rank, Rat, Ret, Rust, Septic, Sour, Squish, Twaddle

**Rotate(r)** Gyrate, Pivot, Rabat(te), Reamer, Revolve, Roll, Trundle, Turn, Wheel

**Rote** Heart, Memory, Recite, Routine

> **Rotten** see ROT

> **Rotten** may indicate an anagram

**Rotter** Cad, Knave, Swine

**Rotund** Chubby, Corpulent, Plump, Round, Stout

**Rotunda** Pantheon

**Roué** Debauchee, Decadent, Libertine, Profligate, Rake(-shame), Rip

**Rouge** Blush, Raddle, Redden, Reddle, Ruddy

**Rough(en), Roughly, Roughness** About, Approximate, Asper(ate), Burr, C, Ca, Choppy, Circa, Coarse, Craggy, Crude, Frampler, Grained, Gross, Gruff, Gurly, Gusty, Hard, Harsh, Hispid, Hoodlum, Hooligan, Impolite, Imprecise, Incondite, Inexact, Irregular, Jagged, Karst, Muricate, Push, Ragged, Ramgunshoch, Raspy, Raucle, Rip, Risp, Row, Rude, Rugged, Rusticate, Rusty, Scabrid, Sea, Shaggy, Sketchy, Some, Spray, Spreathe, Squarrose, Stab, Strong-arm, Swab, Tartar, Tearaway, Ted, Textured, Uncut, Violent

**Roughage** Ballast, Bran, Fodder

**Rough breathing** Asper, Rale, Wheeze

**Rough cast** Harl

> **Roughly** may indicate an anagram

**Ro(u)manian, Rumanian** R(o)uman, Vlach, Wal(l)achian

**Round** About, Ammo, Ball, Beat, Bombe, Bout, Cartridge, Catch, Circle, Complete, Cycle, Dome, Doorstep, Figure, Full, Global, Globate, Hand, Lap, Leg, O, Oblate, Orb, Orbicular, Ought, Peri-, Pirouette, Plump, Quarter-final, Rev, Ring, Robin, Roly-poly, Ronde, Rota, Rotund, Routine, Rundle, Salvo, Sandwich, Sellinger's, Semi-final, Skirt, Slice, Spherical, Spiral, Step, Table, Tour, Tubby, U-turn

> **Round** may indicate a word reversed

**Roundabout** Ambages, Approximately, Bypass, Carousel, Circuit, Circumambient, Circus, Devious, Eddy, INDIRECT, Peripheral, Rotary, Tortuous, Turntable, Whirligig

**Round building** Tholos, Tholus

**Round-mouth** Hag

**Round-up** Collate, Corner, Corral, Gather, Herd, Rodeo, Spiral

**Roup** Auction, Croak, Pip, Roop

**Rouse, Rousing** Abrade, Abraid, Abray, Amo(o)ve, Animate, Beat, Bestir, Emotive, Firk, Flush, Hearten, Heat, Innate, Kindle, Send, Stimulate, Suscitate, Unbed, Waken

**Rousseau** Emile

**Rout** Clamour, Debacle, Defeat, Drub, Fleme, Flight, Hubbub, Hurricane, Rabble, Retreat, Rhonchal, Snore, Thiasus, Upsee, Upsey, Upsy, Vanquish, Whoobub

**Route** Avenue, Causeway, Course, Direction, Itinerary, Line, Path, Road, Track, Via, Way

**Routine** Automatic, Drill, Everyday, Grind, Groove, Habitual, Pattern, Pipe-clay, Red tape, Rota, Rote, Round, Rut, S(c)htick, Schtik, Treadmill, Workaday

**Rove(r), Roving** Discursive, Enrange, Globetrotter, Marauder, Nomad, Proler, Prowl, Ralph, Range, ROAM, Slub(b), Stray, Vagabond, Varangarian, Viking, Wander

**Row(er)** Align, Altercation, Arew, Argue, Argument, Bank, Barney, Bedlam, Bobbery, Bow, Brattle, Cannery, Colonnade, Debate, Deen, Din, Dispute, Dust-up, Feud, Fireworks, Food, Hullabaloo, Line(-up), Noise, Oar, Paddle, Parade, Pull, Quarrel, Rammy, Range, Rank, Raunge, Rew, Rhubarb, Rotten, Ruction, Rumpus, Scene, Scull, Series, Set, Shindig, Shindy, Shine, Skid, Spat, Splore, Stern, Street, Stridor, Stroke, Sweep, Terrace, Tier, Tiff, Torpid, Wetbob, Wherryman

**Rowan** Ash, Quicken

**Rowdy** Hooligan, Loud, Noisy, Rorty, Rough, Ruffian, Scourer, Skinhead, Stroppy, Unruly

**Roy** Rob

**Royal(ty), Royalist** Academy, Angevin, Basilical, Bourbon, Emigré, Exchange, Fee, Hanoverian, Imperial, Imposing, Inca, Kingly, Majestic, Malignant, Palatine, Payment, Pharaoh, Plantagenet, Prince, Purple, Queenly, Regal, Regis, Regius, Regnal, Sail, Society

**Rub(bing), Rubber(y), Rub out** Abrade, Attrition, Balata, Buna, Buff, Bungie, Bungy, Bunje(e), Bunjie, Bunjy, Calk, Calque, Camelback, Caoutchouc, Chafe, Condom, Corrade, Corrode, Crepe, Cul(t)ch, Destroy, Dunlop (tdmk), Ebonite, Elastic, Elastomer, Embrocate, Emery, Erase, Factice, Fray, Fret, Friction, Fridge, Frottage, Fudge, Funtumia, Galoch, Goodyear (tdmk), Grate, Graze, Grind, Guayule, Grind, Hevea, Hule, India, Inunction, Irritate, Isoprene, Latex, Leather, Masseur, Negrohead, Neoprene, Obstacle, Para, Polish, Pontiac, Safe, Sandpaper, Scour, Scrub, Scuff, Seringa, Silastic, Sorbo, Stroke, Towel, Trace, Ule, Vulcanite, Wipe, Xerotripsis

> **Rubbed** may indicate an anagram

**Rubbish** Bull, Bunkum, Clap-trap, Drivel, Fiddlesticks, Phooey, REFUSE, Tinpot, Tip, Tosh, Twaddle

**Rubbish heap** Dump, Lay-stall, Sweepings

**Rubble**  Brash, Debris, Detritus, Moellon, Remains, Riprap

**Rubidium**  Rb

**Ruby**  Agate, Balas, Pigeon's blood, Port, Red

**Ruck**  Furrow, Scrum, Wrinkle

**Rucksack**  Backpack

**Ruction**  Ado, Fuss, Quarrel

**Rudder**  Budget, Helm, Steerer

**Ruddy**  Bally, Bloody, Florid, Flushy, Red, Roseate, Rubicund, Sanguine

**Rude**  Barbaric, Bestial, Bumpkin, Callow, Churlish, Coarse, Discourteous, Elemental, Green, Ill-bred, Impolite, Inficete, Ingram, Ingrum, Insolent, Ocker, Offensive, Peasant, Raw, Rough, Simple, Unbred, Uncomplimentary, Uncourtly, Unlettered, Unmannered, Vulgar

**Rudiment(ary), Rudiments**  ABC, Absey, Anlage, Beginning, Element, Embryo, Foundation, Germ(en), Inchoate, Vestige

**Rudolph**  Hess, Reindeer

**Rue(ful)**  Boulevard, Dittany, Harmala, Harmel, Mourn, Regret, Repent, Ruta, Sorry

**Ruff**  Collar, Crest, Fraise, Frill, Partlet, Pope, Ree, Trump

**Ruffian**  Apache, Bashi-bazouk, Brute, Bully, Cut-throat, Desperado, Highbinder, Hoodlum, Hooligan, Keelie, Larrikin, Lout, Miscreant, Mohock, Myrmidon, Phansigar, Plug-ugly, Raff, Rowdy, Sweater, Tearaway, Thug, Toe-ragger, Tumbler

**Ruffle(d)**  Bait, Dishevel, Flounce, Fluster, Fret, FRILL, Gather, Irritate, Jabot, Peplum, Rouse, Rumple, Ruche, Shirty, Tousle

> **Ruffle**  may indicate an anagram

**Rug**  Afghan, Carpet, Drugget, Ensi, Flokati, Gabbeh, Kelim, K(h)ilim, Mat, Maud, Numdah, Runner, Rya

**Rugby (player)**  Back, Fifteen, Forward, Harlequin, Lion, Pack, Quin, RU, Scrum, Sevens, Threequarter, Wing

**Rugged**  Craggy, Harsh, Knaggy, Rough, Strong

**Ruin(ed)**  Annihilate, Blast, Blight, Corrupt, Crash, Crock, Damn, Decay, Defeat, Demolish, Despoil, Destroy, Devastate, Disfigure, Dish, Dogs, Doom, Downfall, End, Fordo, Hamstring, Heap, Hell, Insolvent, Inure, Kaput(t), Kibosh, Loss, Mar, Overthrow, Petra, Pot, Puckerwood, Reck, Relic, Scotch, Scupper, Scuttle, Shatter, Sink, Smash, SPOIL, Stramash, Undo, Unmade, Ur, Violate, Whelm, Woe, Wrack

> **Ruined**  may indicate an anagram

**Rule(r), Rules, Ruling**  Abbasid, Algorithm, Align, Ameer, Amir, Ardri(gh), Arret, Article, Atabeg, Atabek, Autocrat, Bajayet, Bajazet, Ban, Bey, Bretwalda, Britannia, Burgrave, Caesar, Caliph, Canon, Catapan, Caudillo, Chagan, Cham, Cheops, Chogyal, Club-law, Code, Condominium, Control, Criterion, Czar, Decree, Dergue, Despot, Dewan, Dey, Dictator, Diwan, Doge, Dominion, Duce, Dynast, Emir, Emperor,

Empire, Exarch, Fatwa, Feint, Fetwa, Formula, Fuhrer, Gaekwar, Gaikwar, Gerent, Govern, Govern-all, Heptarch, Herod, Hierarch, Hyleg, Inca, Jackboot, K, Kabaka, Kaiser, Khan, Khedive, King, Law, Lesbian, Lex, Liner, Maharaja, Mameluke, Manchu, Matriarchy, Maxim, Mede, Meteyard, Method, Mikado, Ministrate, Mir, Mistress, Mogul, Monarchy, Motto, Mpret, Mudir, Nawab, Negus, Nizam, Norm(a), Ochlocratic, Oligarchy, Oppress, Ordinal, Padishah, Pasha, Pendragon, Pharaoh, Pie, Potentate, Precept, Prevail, Prince, Principle, Pye, Queen, Queensbury, R, Raine, Raj(ah), Rajpramukh, Rana, Realm, Rector, Regal, Regent, Regula, Reign, Rex, Ring, Rubric, Sachem, Sagamore, Saladin, Satrap, Scammozzi's, Shah, Sheik, Sherif, Shogun, Sirdar, Slide, Sophi, Sophy, Souldan, Sovereign, Squier, Squire, Stadtholder, Standard, Statocracy, Statute, Sultan, Sutra, Suzerain, Swaraj, Sway, Tamerlane, Tetrarch, Thearchy, Three, Thumb, Toparch, Tsar, T-square, Tycoon, Vali, Wali, Wield, Zamorin

**Rule-book**  Code, Pie, Pye

**Rum(mer)**  Bacardi, Demerara, Eerie, Eery, Glass, Grog, Island, Odd(er), Peculiar, Quaint, Queer, Strange, Tafia

**Rumanian**  see R(O)UMANIAN

**Rumble, Rumbling**  Borborygmus, Brool, Curmurring, Drum-roll, Groan, Growl, Guess, Mutter, Rumour, Thunder, Tonneau, Twig

**Ruminant, Ruminate**  Antelope, Cabrie, Camel, Cavicornia, Champ, Chew, Contemplate, Cow, Goat, Meditate, Merycism, Pecora

**Rummage**  Delve, Fish, Foray, Jumble, Ransack, Root, Search, Tot

**Rummy**  Canasta, Cooncan, Game, Gin, Queer

**Rumour**  Breeze, Bruit, Buzz, Canard, Cry, Fame, Furphy, GOSSIP, Grapevine, Hearsay, Kite, Noise, On-dit, Pig's-whisper, Report, Say-so, Smear, Talk, Unfounded, Vine, Voice. Whisper, Word

**Rump**  Arse, Bottom, Buttocks, Croup(e), Croupon, Crupper, Curpel, Derriere, Parliament, Podex, Pygal, Steak

**Rumple**  Corrugate, Crease, Mess, Tousle, Wrinkle

**Rumpus**  Commotion, Riot, Row, Ruction, Shindig, Shindy, Shine, Tirrivee, Uproar

**Run(ning), Run into, Runny**  Admin(ister), Arpeggio, Bolt, Break, Bye, Career, Chase, Coop, Corso, Course, Cresta, Current, Cursive, Cut, Dash, Decamp, Direct, Double, Drive, Escape, Extra, Fartlek, Flee, Flow, Fly, Follow, Gad, Gallop, Go, Hare, Haste(n), Hennery, Idle, Jog, Ladder, Lauf, Leg, Lienteric, Lope, Manage, Marathon, Melt, Mizzle, Molt, Neume, Now, On, On-line, Operate, Pace, Pelt, Ply, Pour, Purulent, R, Race, Renne, Rin, Romp, Roulade, Rounder, Ruck, Scapa, Scamper, Scarper, Schuss, Scud, Scutter, Scuttle, See, Sequence, Shoot, Single, Skedaddle, Skid, Slalom, Smuggle, Spew, Spread, Sprint, Sprue, Stampede, Straight, Streak, Taxi, Tear, Tenor, Trickle, Trill, Trot

**Runaway**  Drain, Easy, Escapee, Fugue, Fugitive, Refugee

**Run down**  Belie, Belittle, Calumniate, Denigrate, Derelict, Dilapidated,

Infame, Knock, Low, Obsolesce(nt), Poorly, Rack, Résumé, Scud, Tirade, Traduce

**Rune, Runic** Futhark, Futhorc, Futhork, Kri, Ogham, Thorn, Wen, Wyn(n)

**Rung** Crossbar, Roundel, Rundle, Tolled, Tread

**Runner(s)** Atalanta, Bean, Blade, Carpet, Coe, Courser, Deserter, Emu, Field, Geat, Gentleman, Harrier, Internuncio, Messenger, Miler, Mousetrap, Nurmi, Owler, Sarmentum, Shoot, Skate, Ski, Skid, Slide, Slipe, Smuggler, Stolon, Stream

> **Running, Runny** may indicate an anagram

**Runt** Dilling, Oobit, Oubit, Reckling, Scalawag, Scrog, Smallest, Titman, Woobut, Woubit

**Run through** Impale, Pierce, Rehearsal

**Runway** Airstrip, Drive, Slipway, Tarmac

**Run wild** Lamp, Rampage

**Rupee(s)** Lac, Lakh

**Rupert** Bear

**Rupture** Breach, Burst, Crack, Hernia, Rend, Rhexis, Rift, Split

**Rural** Agrarian, Agrestic, Bucolic, Boondocks, Country, Forane, Mofussil, Platteland, Praedial, Predial, Redneck, Rustic, Sticks

**Ruse** Artifice, Dodge, Engine, Hoax, Pawk, Stratagem, TRICK

**Rush(ed)** Accelerate, Barge, Bolt, Bustle, Career, Charge, Dart, Dash, Eriocaulon, Expedite, Faze, Feese, Feeze, Feze, Fly, Frail, Friar, Gad, Hare, Hasten, High-tail, HURRY, Hurtle, Jet, Juncus, Lance, Leap, Luzula, Moses, Palmiet, Pellmell, Phase, Pheese, Pheeze, Phese, Plunge, Precipitate, Railroad, Rampa(u)ge, Rash, Reed, Rip, Scamp(er), Scirpus, Scour, Scud, Sedge, Spate, Speed, Stampede, Star(r), Streak, Streck, Surge, Swoop, Tear, Thrash, Thresh, Tilt, Tule, Viretot, Zap, Zoom

**Rusk** Zwieback

**Russell** AE, Bertrand, Jack

**Russia(n), Russian headman, Russian villagers** Apparatchik, Ataman, Belorussian, Beria, Bolshevik, Boris, Boyar, Byelorussian, Circassian, Cossack, D(o)ukhobor, Esth, Igor, Ivan, Lett, Mari, Menshevik, Minimalist, Mir, Muscovy, Red, Romanov, Rus, Russ(niak), Ruthene, Serge, Slav, Stakhanovite, SU, Uzbeg, Uzbek, Zyrian

**Rust(y)** Aeci(di)um, Brown, Corrode, Cor(ro)sive, Erode, Etch, Iron-stick, Maderise, Oxidise, Rubiginous, Soare, Teleutospore, Uredine, Uredo, Verdigris

**Rust-fungus** Aecidiospore

**Rustic** Arcady, Bacon, Bor(r)el(l), Bucolic, Chawbacon, Churl, Clodhopper, Clown, Corydon, Damon, Doric, Forest, Georgic, Hayseed, Hick, Hillbilly, Hind, Hob, Hobbinoll, Hodge, Pastorale, Peasant, Pr(a)edial, Put(t), Rube, Rural, Strephon, Swain, Villager, Villatic, Yokel

> **Rustic** may indicate an anagram

**Rusticate**  Banish, Seclude

**Rustle(r), Rustling**  Abactor, Duff, Fissle, Frou-frou, Poach, Speagh(ery), Sprechery, Stead, Susurration, Swish, Thief, Whig

**Rust-proof**  Zinced

**Rut**  Channel, Furrow, Groove, Heat, Routine, Track

**Ruth**  Babe, Compassion, Mercy, Pity

**Ruthenium**  Ru

**Rutherfordium**  Rf

**Ruthless**  Brutal, Cruel, Fell, Hard

**Rye**  Gentleman, Grain, Grass, Spelt, Whisky

# Ss

**S** Ogee, Saint, Second, Sierra, Society, South, Square

**SA** It, Lure

**Sabbatarian** Wee Free

**Sabbath** Juma, Rest-day, Sunday, Witches

**Sabbatical** Leave

**Sabine** Horace, Women

**Sable** Black, Jet, Pean, Zibel(l)ine

**Sabotage, Saboteur** Destroy, Frame-breaker, Ratten, Spoil, Wrecker

**Sabre, Sabre rattler** Jingo, Sword, Tulwar

**Sabrina** Severn

**Sac** Amnion, Bag, Bladder, Bursa, Cyst, Pod, Vesica

**Sack(cloth), Sacking** Bag, Bed, Boot, Bounce, Budget, Burlap, Can, Cashier, Chasse, Congé, Congee, Dash, Depredate, Despoil, Discharge, Doss, Fire, Gunny, Havoc, Jute, Knap, Loot, Maraud, Mitten, Pillage, Plunder, Poke, Push, Reave, Road, Rob, Sanbenito, Sherris, Sherry, Vandalise

**> Sacks** may indicate an anagram

**Sacrament** Baptism, Confirmation, Eucharist, Extreme unction, Housel, Lord's supper, Matrimony, Nagmaal, Orders, Penance, Promise, Ritual, Unction, Viaticum

**Sacred, Sacred place** Adytum, Churinga, Hallowed, Heart, Holy, Nine, Padma, Pietà, Sacrosanct, Sanctum, Taboo

**Sacrifice** Alcestic, Cenote, Forego, Gambit, Hecatomb, Holocaust, Immolate, Iphigenia, Isaac, Lay down, Molech, Moloch, Oblation, OFFERING, Relinquish, Sati, Suovetaurilia, Supreme, Surrender, Suttee, Taurobolium, Tophet, Victim

**Sacrilege, Sacrilegious** Blaspheme, Impiety, Profane, Violation

**Sacristan, Sacristy** Diaconicon, Sceuophylax, Sexton

**Sad(den), Sadly, Sadness** Alas, Attrist, Blue, Dejected, Desolate, Disconsolate, Dismal, Doleful, Downcast, Drear, Dull, Heartache, Low, Mesto, Oh, Plangent, Sorry, Tear-jerker, Threnody, Tragic, Triste, Unhappy, Wan, Wo(e)begone

**Saddle (bag, girth, pad)** Alforja, Burden, Cantle, Cinch, Col, Crupper, Demipique, Numnah, Oppress, Panel, Pigskin, Pilch, Pillion, Seat, Sell(c), Shabrack, Tree

**Saddle-bow** Arson

**Saddler** Whittaw(er)

**Sadie** Thompson

**Sadistic** Cruel

> **Sadly** may indicate an anagram

**Safari** Expedition, Hunt

**Safe(ty)** Allright, Almery, Ambry, Delouse, GRAS, Harmless, Impunity, Inviolate, Peter, Reliable, Sanctuary, Secure, Sound, Strong-box, Sure, Worthy

**Safeguard** Bulwark, Caution, Ensure, Frithborh, Fuse, Hedge, Palladium, Protection, Register, Ward

**Saffron** Crocus, Yellow

**Sag** Decline, Dip, Droop, Hang, Lop, Slump, Swayback

**Saga** Chronicle, Edda, Epic, Icelandic, Laxdale, Legend, Odyssey, Volsunga

**Sagacity** Commonsense, Depth, Elephant, Judgement, Sapience, Wisdom

**Sage** Abaris, Aquinian, Bactrian, Bias, Carlyle, Cheronian, Chilo(n), Clary, Cleobulus, Counsellor, Greybeard, Hakam, Herb, Imhotep, Maharishi, Mahatma, Malmesbury, Manu, Orval, Pandit, Periander, Philosopher, Pittacus, Rishi, Salvia, Savant, Solon, Thales, Wiseacre

**Sage-brush** Nevada

**Sahib** Pukka

**Said** Co, Emir, Port, Quo(th), Related, Reputed, Spoken, Stated

> **Said** may indicate 'sounding like'

**Sail(s)** Bunt, Canvas, Circumnavigate, Coast, Cloth, Course, Cross-jack, Cruise, Fan, Genoa, Jib, Jut, Lateen, Leech, Luff, Lug, Moonraker, Muslin, Navigate, Peak, Ply, Rag, Reef, Rig, Ring-tail, Royal, Sheet, Spanker, Spencer, Spinnaker, Steer, Studding, Stun, Suit, Top(-gallant), Van, Vela, Wardrobe, Yard

**Sailor(s)** AB, Admiral, Anson, Argonaut, Blue-jacket, Boatswain, Bosun, Commodore, Crew, Deckhand, Drake, Evans, Galiongee, Gob, Grommet, Hat, Hearties, Helmsman, Hornblower, Jack, Janty, Jauntie, Jaunty, Jonty, Khalasi, Killick, Killock, Kroo(boy), Krooman, Kru(boy), Kruman, Lascar, Lt, Lubber, Mariner, Matelot, Matlo(w), Middy, MN, Nelson, Noah, Oceaner, OS, Popeye, Privateer, Rating, RN, Salt, Sea-dog, Sea-lord, Seaman, Serang, Shellback, Sin(d)bad, Stowaway, Tar, Tarp(aulin), Tarry-breeks, Tindal, Triton, Waister, Water-dog

**Saint(ly), Saints** Agatha, Agnes, Aidan, Alban, Alexis, Alvis, Ambrose, Andrew, Anselm, Anthony, Asaph, Audrey, Augustine, Barbara, Barnabas, Bartholomew, Basil, Bees, Benedict, Bernard, Boniface, Brandan, Brendan, Bridget, Catharine, Cecilia, Chad, Christopher, Clement, Columba(n), Crispian, Crispin(ian), Cuthbert, Cyr, David, Denis, Denys, Diego, Dominic, Dorothea, Dunstan, Dymphna, Elmo, Eloi, Elvis, Eulalie, Francis, Genevieve, George, Giles, Gertrude, Hallowed, Helena, Hilary, Hilda, Hugh, Ignatius, James, Jerome, John, Joseph, Jude, Kentigern, Kevin, Kilda, Latterday, Lawrence, Leger, Leonard, Linus, Loyola, Lucy, Luke, Malo, Margaret, Mark, Martha, Martin, Matthew, Michael, Monica,

Mungo, Nicholas, Ninian, Odyl, Olaf, Oswald, Pancras, Patrick, Patron, Paul(inus), Peter, Pillar, Quentin, Regulus, Ride, Roch, Ronan, Roque, Rosalie, Rule, S, Sebastian, Severus, Simeon, Simon, SS, St, Stanislaus, Stephen, Swithin, Templar, Teresa, Thecia, Theresa, Thomas, Tobias, Ursula, Valentine, Veronica, Vincent, Vitus, Walstan, Wilfred, William, Winifred

**St Anthony's Fire**  Ergotism, Erysipelas

**St Elmo's Fire**  Corposant

**St James**  Scallop-shell

**St John's bread**  Carob

**St Paul's**  Wren-ch

**Sake**  Account, Behalf, Cause, Drink

**Sal**  Volatile

**Salacious, Salacity**  Lewd, Lust, Obscene, Scabrous

**Salad**  Chicon, Cos, Cress, Cucumber, Days, Endive, Fennel, Finnochio, Finoc(c)hio, Guacamole, Lettuce, Lovage, Mesclum, Mesclun, Mixture, Niçoise, Radish, Rampion, Rocket, Rojak, Russian, Slaw, Tabbouleh, Tomato

> **Salad**  may indicate an anagram

**Salamander**  Axolotl, Ewt, Hellbender, Lizard, Menopome, Olm, Proteus, Spring-keeper

**Salami**  Peperoni

**Salary**  Emolument, Fee, Hire, Pay, Prebend, Screw, Stipend, WAGE

**Sale**  Auction, Cant, Clearance, Market, Outroop, Outrope, Raffle, Retail, Roup, Subhastation, Venal, Vendue, Vent

**Saleroom**  Pantechnicon

**Salesman**  Agent, Assistant, Broker, Buccaneer, Bummaree, Counterhand, Drummer, Huckster, Loman, Pedlar, Rep, Retailer, Tallyman, Tout, Traveller

**Salient**  Coign, Jut, Projection, Prominent, Spur

**Saliva**  Drool, Parotid, Ptyalism, Sial(oid), Slobber, Spit(tle), Sputum

**Sallow**  Adust, Pallid, Pasty, Sale, Sauch, Wan

**Sally**  Aunt, Charge, Dash, Escape, Excursion, Flight, Foray, Issue, Jest, Mot, Pleasantry, Quip, Sarah, Sortie, Witticism

**Salmagundi**  Mess

**Salmon**  Baggit, Blue-cap, Blueback, Boaz, Chinook, Chum, Cock, Coho(e), Dog, Grav(ad)lax, Grilse, Humpback, Kelt, Keta, Kipper, Kokanee, Lax, Ligger, Lox, Masu, Mort, Nerka, Oncorhynchus, Ouananiche, Par(r), Peal, Pink, Quinnat, Redfish, Samlet, Shedder, Skegger, Smelt, Smolt, Smout, Smowt, Sockeye, Sparling, Spirling, Sprod

**Salon, Saloon**  Barrel-house, Car, Hall, Honkytonk, Lounge, Pullman, Sedan, Shebang, Tavern

**Salt(s), Salty** Aluminate, Andalusite, Attic, Aurate, Bicarbonate, Bichromate, Borate, Borax, Brackish, Brine, Bromate, Bromide, Capr(o)ate, Caprylate, Carbamate, Carbonate, Cerusite, Chlorate, Citrate, Corn, Cure(d), Datolite, Dithionate, Enos, Epsom, Formate, Glauber, Halite, Ioduret, Lactate, Lake-basin, Lithate, Malate, Malonate, Manganate, Matelot, Mucate, Muriate, Nitrate, Oleate, Osm(i)ate, Oxalate, Palmitate, Perchlorate, Periodate, Phosphate, Phthalate, Piquancy, Plumbite, Powder, Propionate, Rating, Rochelle, Sailor, Salify, Saut, Sea-dog, Seasoned, Sebate, Selenate, Soap, Stannate, Stearate, Succinate, Tannate, Tartrate, Titanate, Uranin, Urao, Urate, Water-dog, Wit(ty), Xanthate

**Saltpetre** Caliche, Nitre

**Salt-water** Sea

**Salubrious** Healthy, Sanitary, Wholesome

**Salutary** Beneficial, Good, Wholesome

**Salutation, Salute** Address, Ave, Banzai, Bid, Cheer, Command, Curtsey, Embrace, Fly-past, Greet, Hail, Hallo, Halse, Homage, Honour, Jambo, Kiss, Present, Salvo, Toast, Tribute, Wassail

**Salvador** Dali

**Salvage** Dredge, Lagan, Ligan, Reclaim, Recover, Recycle, Rescue, Retrieve, Tot

**Salvation(ist)** Booth, Redemption, Rescue, Yeo

**Salve** Anele, Anoint, Assuage, Ave, Lanolin(e), Lotion, Ointment, Remedy, Saw, Tolu, Unguent

**Salver** Tray, Waiter

**Salvo** Fusillade, Salute, Volley

**Sam** Browne, Uncle, Weller

**Samara** Ash-key

**Samarium** Sm

**Same(ness)** Ae, Agnatic, Contemporaneous, Do, Egal, Equal, Ib(id), Ibidem, Id, Idem, Identical, Identity, Ilk, Iq, Like, One, Thick(y), Thilk, Uniform, Ylke

**Samovar** Urn

**Samoyed** Dog, Uralian, Uralic

**Sample** Browse, Example, Foretaste, Muster, Pattern, Pree, Scantling, Specimen, Swatch, Switch, TASTE, Transect, Try

**Samuel** Pepys, Smiles

**Samurai** Ronin

> **Sam Weller** indicates the use of 'v' for 'w'

**Sanctify** Consecrate, Purify, Saint

**Sanctimonious** Banbury, Devout, Pi, Righteous, Saintly

**Sanction** Allow, Appro, Approbate, Approof, Approve, Authorise, Bar, Countenance, Endorse, Imprimatur, Mandate, OK, Pass, Pragmatic, Ratify

**Sanctities, Sanctity** Halidom, Holiness, Hollidam, Sonties

**Sanctuary, Sanctum** Adytum, Asylum, By-room, Ch, Church, Firthsoken, Girth, Grith, Holy, Lair, Naos, Oracle, Penetralia, Preserve, Refuge, Sacellum, SHELTER, Shrine, Temple

**Sand(bank), Sands, Sandy** Alec, Alex, Areg, Arena(ceous), Arenose, As, Atoll, Barchan(e), Bark(h)an, Beach, Dene, Desert, Down, Dudevant, Dune, Dupin, Eremic, Erg, Esker, Gat, George, Ginger, Goodwin, Grain, Granulose, Hazard, Loess, Machair, Nore, Podsol, Podzol, Portlandian, Psammite, Ridge, Sabulous, Sawney, Seif, Shelf, Shoal, Shore, Tee, Time

**Sandal(s)** Alpargata, Calceamentum, Chappal, Espadrille, Flip-flop, Geta, Huarache, Patten, Pump, Talaria

**Sandalwood** Algum, Almug, Santal

**Sandarac** Arar

**Sander** Pike-perch

**Sandhurst** RMA

**Sand-loving** Ammophilous, Psammophil

**Sandpiper** Bird, Knot, Ree, Ruff, Sandpeep, Stint, Terek

**Sandstone** Arkose, Dogger, Fa(i)kes, Flysch, Grit, Hassock, Kingle, Red

**Sandstorm** Haboob, Tebbad

**Sandwich** Butty, Doorstep, Earl, Hamburger, Island, Roti, Round, Sarney, Sarnie, Smorbrod, Smorgasbord, Smorrebrod, Sub, Thumber, Twitcher

> **Sandwich(es)** may indicate a hidden word

**Sane, Sanity** Healthy, Judgement, Rational, Reason, Sensible

**Sangfroid** Aplomb, Cool, Poise

**Sanguine** Confident, Hopeful, Optimistic, Roseate, Ruddy

**Sanitary** Hygienic, Salubrious, Sterile

**Sanskrit** Purana, Ramayana, Sutra, Upanishad

**Santa Claus** Abonde

**Sap** Bleed, Cremor, Drain, Enervate, Entrench, Ichor, Juice, Laser, Latex, Lymph, Mine, Mug, Pulque, Ratten, Resin, Roset, Rosin, Rozet, Rozit, Secretion, Soma, Sura, Swot, Undermine, Weaken

**Sapid** Flavoursome, Savoury, Tasty

**Sapience, Sapient** Discernment, Sage, Wisdom

**Sapling** Ash-plant, Ground-ash, Plant, Tellar, Teller, Tiller, Youth

**Sapper(s)** Miner, RE

**Sappho** Lesbian

**Sapwood** Alburnum

**Sarah** Battle, Gamp, Sal

**Sarcasm, Sarcastic** Biting, Cutting, Cynical, Derision, Irony, Pungent, Sarky, Satire, Sharp

**Sardine** Fish, Sard

**Sardonic**  Cutting, Cynical, Ironical, Scornful

**Sargasso**  Ore, Sea(weed)

**Sark**  Chemist, CI, Shirt

**Sarong**  Sulu

**Sash**  Baldric(k), Band, Belt, Burdash, Cummerbund, Obi, Window

**Sassaby**  Tsessebe

**Sassenach**  English, Lowlander, Pock-pudding

**Satan**  Adversary, Apollyon, Arch-enemy, Cram, DEVIL, Eblis, Lucifer, Shaitan

**Satchel**  Bag, Scrip

**Sate(d), Satiate**  Glut, Replete, Sad, Surfeit

**Satellite**  Ariel, Astra, Attendant, Callisto, Comsat, Dione, Disciple, Early bird, Enceladus, Follower, Ganymede, Henchman, Hyperion, Iapetus, Intelsat, Io, Janus, Mimas, Moon, Nereid, Oberon, Orbiter, Phoebe, Rhea, Sputnik, Syncom, Telstar, Tethys, Tiros, Titan, Titania, Triton

> **Satin**  see SILK

**Satire, Satirical, Satirist**  Archilochus, Burlesque, Candide, Chaldee, Horace, Iambographer, Juvenal, Lampoon, Lucian, Menippean, Mockery, Pantagruel, Parody, Pasquil, Pasquin(ade), Pope, Raillery, Sarky, Sotadic, Spoof, Squib, Travesty

**Satisfaction, Satisfactory, Satisfy**  Agree, Ah, Ap(p)ay, Appease, Atone, Change, Compensation, CONTENT, Defrayment, Enough, Feed, Fill, Fulfil, Glut, Gratify, Indulge, Liking, Meet, OK, Palatable, Pay, Please, Propitiate, Qualify, Redress, Repay, Replete, Sate, Satiate, Serve, Settlement, Slake, Square, Suffice, Well

**Saturate(d)**  Drench, Glut, Imbue, Impregnate, Infuse, Permeate, SOAK, Sodden, Steep

**Saturn**  God, Kronos, Lead, Planet, Rocket

**Satyr**  Faun, Leshy, Lesiy, Libertine, Marsyas, Pan, Silen(us), Woodhouse, Woodwose

**Sauce, Saucy**  Arch, Allemanse, Baggage, Béarnaise, Bechamel, Caper, Catchup, Catsup, Chaudfroid, Cheek, Condiment, Cranberry, Cream, Custard, Dapper, Dip, Dressing, Enchilada, Espagnole, Fenberry, Fondue, Gall, Garum, Gravy, Hollandaise, Horseradish, HP, Impudence, Ketchup, Lip, Matelote, Mayonnaise, Mint, Mirepoix, Mole, Mornay, Mousseline, Nerve, Nuoc mam, Oxymal, Panada, Parsley, Peart, Pert, Pesto, Piri-piri, Ravigote, Relish, Remoulade, Rouille, Sabayon, Sal, Salpicon, Salsa, Sambal, Sass, Shoyu, Soja, Soubise, Soy, Soya, Sue, Supreme, Tabasco, Tamari, Tartar(e), Tomato, Tossy, Veloute, Worcester

**Sauceboat-shaped**  Scaphocephalate

**Saucepan**  Chafer, Skillet, Stockpot

**Saucer**  Ashtray, Discobolus, UFO

**Sauna**  Bath, Sudorific

**Saunter**  Amble, Dander, Lag, Promenade, Roam, Shool, Stroll

**Sausage(s)**  Andouillette, Banger, Bologna, Bratwurst, Cervelat, Cheerio, Chipolata, Chorizo, Drisheen, Frankfurter, Liverwurst, Mortadella, Pep(p)eroni, Polony, Salami, Saveloy, Snag(s), String, Wiener(wurst), Wurst, Zampone

**Sausage-shaped**  Allantoid

**Savage**  Ape, Barbarian, Boor, Brute, Cannibal, Cruel, Feral, Fierce, Grim, Gubbins, Immane, Inhuman, Maul, Sadistic, Truculent, Wild

**Savanna**  Plain, Sahel

**Savant**  Expert, Sage, Scholar

**Save, Saving(s)**  Bank, Bar, Besides, But, Capital, Conserve, Deposit, Economy, Except, Hain, Hoard, Husband, Layby, Keep, Nirlie, Nirly, Preserve, Reclaim, Redeem, Relieve, Reprieve, RESCUE, Reskew, Sa', Salt, Salvage, Scrape, Scrimp, Slate club, Spare, Unless

**Saviour**  Deliverer, Jesu(s), Messiah, Redeemer

**Savour(ed), Savoury**  Aigrette, Canapé, Essence, Fagot, Flavour, Olent, Ramekin, Relish, Resent, Sair, Sapid, Sar, Smack, Starter, Tang, TASTE

**Savoy**  Cabbage, Opera

**Saw**  Adage, Aphorism, Apothegm, Beheld, Cliché, Cross-cut, Cut, Fret, Gnome, Hack, Legend, Maxim, Met, Motto, Proverb, Ribbon, Rip, Saying, Serra, Slogan, Spied, Stadda, Trepan, Trephine, Whip, Witnessed

**Sawbones**  Surgeon

**Saxon**  Cedric, Hengist, Wend

**Say(ing)**  Adage, Agrapha, Aphorism, Apophthegm, Apostrophise, Articulate, Axiom, Beatitude, Bromide, Byword, Cant, Catchphrase, Cliché, Declare, Dict(um), Eg, Enunciate, Epigram, Express, Fadaise, Gnome, Impute, Logia, Logion, MAXIM, Mean, Mot, Mouth, Observe, Predicate, Pronounce, Proverb, Put, Quip, Recite, Rede, Relate, Remark, Report, Saine, Saw, Sc, SPEAK, Suppose, Utter, Voice, Word

> **Say**  may indicate a word sounding like another

**Scab(by)**  Blackleg, Crust, Eschar, Leggism, Leprose, Mangy, Rat, Scald, Scall, Sore

**Scabbard**  Frog, Pilcher, Sheath, Tsuba

**Scabies**  Itch, Psora

**Scabrous**  Harsh, Rough

**Scaffold(ing)**  Gallows, Gantry, Hoarding, Putlock, Putlog, Rig, Stage

**Scald**  Blanch, Burn, Leep, Ploat, Plot

**Scale, Scaly**  Analemma, Ascend, Balance, Beaufort, Bismar, Brix, Celsius, Centigrade, Ceterach, Chromatic, CLIMB, Desquamate, Diatonic, Flo, Escalade, Fahrenheit, Flake, Gamme, Gamut, Ganoid, Gauge, Gunter's, Kelvin, Ladder, Lamina, Layer, Lepid, Leprose, Libra, Ligule, Lodicule, Loricate, Major, Mercalli, Minor, Mohs, Octad, Palea, Palet, Patagium, Peel, Pentatonic, Pholidosis, Plate, Ramentum, RANGE,

Rankine, Reaumur, Richter, Scan, Scarious, Scincoid, Scurf, Scutellate, Shin, Skink, Sliding, Speel, Squama, Squame(lla), Tegula, Tonal, Tron(e), Tridymite, Vernier

**Scallop(ed)**  Bivalve, Clam, Coquille, Crenate, Escalop, Frill, Gimp, Mush, Vandyke

**Scallywag**  Rascal, Scamp, Skeesicks

**Scalp**  Cut, Scrape, Skin, Trophy

**Scalpel**  Bistoury, Knife

**Scamp**  Fripon, Imp, Limb. Lorel, Lorrell, Losel, Lozell, Neglect, RASCAL, Reprobate, Rip, Rogue, Scallywag, Skeesicks

**Scamper**  Gambol, Lamp, Run, Scurry, Skedaddle, Skelter

**Scan(ning), Scanner**  CAT, CT, Examine, OCR, Peruse, PET, Rake, Raster, Scrutinise, Survey, Vet

**Scandal(ous), Scandalise**  Belie, Canard, Disgrace, Gamy, Hearsay, Outrage, Shame, Slander, Stigma

**Scandinavian**  Dane, Finn, Laplander, Lapp, Nordic, Norseland, Runic, Swede, Varangian, Viking

**Scandium**  Sc

**Scant(y)**  Bare, Brief, Exiguous, Ihram, Jejune, Jimp, Poor, Short, Shy, Slender, Spare, Sparse, Stingy

**Scapegoat**  Butt, Fall-guy, Hazazel, Target, Victim

**Scapula**  Blade, Omoplate

**Scar(face)**  Al, Blemish, Cheloid, Cicatrix, Cliff, Craig, Hylum, Keloid, Mark, Stigma, Ulosis, Wipe

**Scarab**  Beetle, Gem

**Scarce(ly), Scarcity**  Barely, Dear, Dearth, Famine, Few, Hardly, Ill, Lack, Rare, Scanty, Seldom, Short, Uncommon, Want

**Scare(mongering), Scaring**  Alarmist, Amaze, Fleg, Fright, Gally, Hairy, Panic, Startle

**Scarecrow**  Bogle, Bugaboo, Dudder, Dudsman, Gallibagger, Gallibeggar, Gallicrow, Gallybagger, Gallybeggar, Gallycrow, Malkin, Potato-bogle, Ragman, S(h)ewel, Tattie-bogle

**Scarf**  Babushka, Belcher, Cataract, Comforter, Cravat, Curch, Doek, Dupatta, Fichu, Hai(c)k, Haique, Hyke, Madras, Mantilla, Muffettee, Muffler, Neckatee, Nightingale, Orarium, Pagri, Palatine, Rebozo, Sash, Screen, Stole, Tallith, Tippet, Trot-cosy, Trot-cozy

**Scarifier**  Scuffler

**Scarlet**  Crimson, Pimpernel, Ponceau, Red, Vermilion

**Scarper**  Bunk, Run, Shoo, Welsh

**Scat**  Aroint, Dropping

**Scathe, Scathing**  Mordant, Sarcastic, Savage, Severe, Vitriolic

**Scatter(ed), Scattering**  Bestrew, Broadcast, Diaspora, Disject, Dispel,

DISPERSE, Dissipate, Flurr, Litter, Rout, Scail, Skail, Sow, Sparge, Splutter, Sporadic, Spread, Sprinkle, Straw, Strew

**Scavenge(r)** Forage, Hunt, Hy(a)ena, Jackal, Rake, Ratton, Rotten, Sweeper, Totter

**Scenario** Outline, Plot, Script

**Scene(ry)** Arena, Boscage, Decor, Flat(s), Landscape, Locale, Prospect, Sight, Site, Sketch, Stage, Tableau, Tormenter, Tormentor, Venue, View

**Scent** Aroma, Attar, Chypre, Cologne, Essence, Fragrance, Frangipani, Fumet(te), Gale, Moschatel, Odour, Ottar, Otto, Perfume, Sachet, Smell, Spoor, Vent, Wind

**Scentless** Anosmia

**Sceptic(al)** Cynic, Doubter, Incredulous, Infidel, Jaundiced, Nihilistic, Pyrrho(nic), Sadducee

**Schedule** Agenda, Calendar, Itinerary, Programme, Register, Table, Timetable

**Scheme, Scheming** Concoct, Conspire, Crafty, Cunning, Dare, Darien, Decoct, Devisal, Diagram, Dodge, Draft, Gin, Intrigue, Machiavellian, Machinate, Manoeuvre, Nostrum, PLAN, Plot, Project, Purpose, Racket, Ruse, Stratagem, System, Table, Wangle, Wheeze

**Schism** Disunion, Division, Rent, Split

**Schizo** Catatonic

**Schmaltz** Goo, Slush

**Schmieder** S

**Schmuck** Gunsel

**Scholar** Abelard, Academic, Alumni, Atticus, BA, Bookman, Boursier, Catachumen, Clergy, Clerisy, Clerk, Commoner, Demy, Disciple, Erasmus, Erudite, Extern(e), Externat, Goliard, Graduate, Grecian, Littérateur, MA, Pauline, Plutarch, Polymath, Pupil, Rhodes, Sap, Savant, Schoolboy, Sizar, Soph, STUDENT, Tabardar, Taberdar, Taberder, Tom Brown

**Scholarship** Bursary, Education Erudition, Exhibition, Grant, Learning, Lore, Mass, Rhodes

**School** Academy, Ampleforth, Benenden, Bluecoat, Charm, Charterhouse, Chartreux, Chautauqua, Comprehensive, Conservative, Conservatory, Crammer, Dada, Downside, Driving, Educate, Essenes, Eton, Exercise, Fettes, Finishing, Flemish, Gam, Giggleswick, Gordonstoun, Group, Gymnasien, Gymnasium, Harrow, High, Hospital, Institute, Kailyard, Kant, Kindergarten, Lancing, Loretto, LSE, Lycée, Madrassah, Marlborough, Oundle, Palaestra, Parnassian, Pensionnat, Perse, Pod, Poly, Porpoises, Prep, Progymnasium, RADA, RAM, Ramean, Reformatory, Repton, Roedean, Rossall, Rydal, Sadducee, Scandalous, Scul, Scull(e), Sect, Seminary, Shoal, Slade, Stonyhurst, Stowe, Style, Teach, Tonbridge, TRAIN, Tutor, Wellington, Whales, Winchester, Yeshiva

**Schoolboy, Schoolgirl** Carthusian, Coed, Colleger, East, Etonian, Fag, Miss, Monitor, Oppidan, Petty, Stalky

**School-leaver** Abiturient

**Schoolmaam, Schoolman, Schoolmaster, Schoolmistress** Beak, Dominie, Duns, Holofernes, Miss, Occam, Orbilius, Pedagogue, Pedant, Sir, Squeers, Teacher, Ursuline

**Schooner** Glass, Hesperus, Prairie, Ship, Tern

**Science** Anatomy, Anthropology, Art, Atmology, Axiology, Biology, Botany, Chemistry, Dismal, Eth(n)ology, Geology, Noble, Nomology, Ology, Optics, Pedagogy, Physics, Skill, Tactics, Technology

**Scientist** Anatomist, Archimedes, Aston, Astronomer, Atomist, Boffin, BSc, Cavendish, Copernicus, Curie, Dalton, Davy, Einstein, Expert, Faraday, FRS, Galileo, Geodesist, Harvey, Heaviside, Kennelly, Lodge, Lovell, Newton, Oersted, Pascal, Piccard, Potamologist, Volta

**Scimitar** Acinaciform, Sword

**Scintillate** Dazzle, Emicate, Gleam, Glitter, SPARKLE

**Scion** Graft, Imp, Offspring, Sprig

**Scissors** Clippers, Criss-cross, Cutters, Forfex, Nail, Shears

**Scoff** Belittle, Boo, Chaff, Deride, Dor, Eat, Flout, Food, Gall, Gibe, Gird, Gobble, JEER, Mock, Rail, Rib, Ridicule, Scaff, Scorn, Sneer, Taunt

**Scold(ing)** Admonish, Berate, Callet, Catamaran, Chastise, Chide, Clapperclaw, Do, Flite, Flyte, Fuss, Jaw(bation), Jobation, Lecture, Nag, Objurgate, Philippic, Rant, Rate, REBUKE, Reprimand, Reprove, Revile, Rouse on, Sas(s)arara, Sis(s)erary, Slang, Slate, Termagant, Trimmer, Upbraid, Virago, Wig, Xant(h)ippe, Yaff, Yankie, Yap

**Sconce** Candlestick, Crown, Forfeit, Head, Ice, Nole

**Scoop** Bale, Dipper, Exclusive, Gouge, Grab, Hollow, Ladle, Lap, Pale, Shovel, Trowel

**Scope** Ambit, Domain, Extent, Freedom, Gamut, Ken, Latitude, Leeway, Purview, Range, Room, Rope, Scouth, Scowth, Size, Sphere

**Scorch(er)** Adust, Blister, Brasero, BURN, Char, Destroy, Frizzle, Fry, Parch, Scouther, Scowder, Scowther, Sear, Singe, Soar, Speed, Swale, Swayl, Sweal, Sweel, Torrefy, Torrid, Wither

**Score** Bill, Bye, Capot, Chase, Conversion, Count, Crena, Groove, Hail, Ingroove, Ippon, Law, Make, Music, Net, Notation, Notch, Partitur(a), Peg, Point, Record, Repique, Rit(t), Rouge, Run, Rut, Scotch, Scratch, Scribe, Scrive, Set, Single, Stria, String, Sum, Tablature, TALLY, Twenty, Waza-ari, Win

**Score-board, Score-sheet** Card, Telegraph

> **Scoring** may indicate an anagram

**Scorn(ful)** Arrogant, Contempt, Contumely, Deride, Despise, Disdain, Dislike, Flout, Geck, Haughty, Insult, Mock, Rebuff, Ridicule, Sarcastic, Sarky, Scout, Sdaine, Sdeigne, Sneer, Spurn, Wither

**Scorpion** Chelifer, Pedipalp(us), Vinegarroon

**Scot(sman), Scots(woman), Scottish** Angus, Antenati, Berean,

Bluecap, Caledonian, Celt, Clansman, Covenanter, Duni(e)wassal, Dunniewassal, Gael, Ian, Jock, Kelt, Kiltie, Knox, Laird, Lallan(s), Lot, Luckie, Lucky, Mac, Mon, Peght, Pict, Sandy, Sawn(e)y, Stuart, Teuchter, Torridonian

**Scotch(man)** Censor, Distiller, Glenlivet (tdmk), Notch, Score, Scratch, Thwart, Usquebaugh, Whisky

**Scot-free** Wreakless

**Scotland** Alban(y), Albion, Caledonia, Lallans, Lothian, NB, Norland, Scotia

**Scoundrel** Knave, Reprobate, Scab, Varlet, VILLAIN

**Scour** Beat, Depurate, Full, Holystone, Purge, Quarter, Scrub

> **Scour** may indicate an anagram

**Scourge** Bible-thumper, Cat, Discipline, Knout, Lash, Pest, PLAGUE, Scorpion, Whip, Wire

**Scout** Beaver, Colony, Disdain, Explorer, Flout, Guide, Outrider, Pickeer, Pioneer, Reconnoitre, Rover, Runner, Scoff, Scorn, Scourer, Scurrier, Scurriour, Spyal, Talent, Tenderfoot

**Scowl(ing)** Frown, Glower, Gnar, Lour, Lower, Sullen

**Scrabble** Paw

**Scrag(gy)** Bony, Dewitt, Ewe-necked, Neck, Scrawny

**Scram** Begone, Hence, Scat, Shoo

**Scramble** Addle, Clamber, Encode, Grubble, Hurry, Mêlée, Mix, Motocross, Muss(e), Scamble, Sprattle, Sprawl, Swerve

**Scrap(s), Scrappy** Abandon, Abrogate, BIT, Conflict, Discard, Dump, FIGHT, Fisticuffs, Fragment, Fray, Iota, Jot, Mêlée, Mellay, Morceau, Morsel, Odd, Off-cut, Ort, Ounce, Piece, Pig's-wash, Rag, Rase, Raze, Remnant, Scarmoge, Scissel, Scissil, Scrub, Set-to, Shard, Sherd, Shred, Skerrick, Skirmish, Snap, Snippet, Spall, Tait, Tate, Tatter, Titbit, Truculent, Whit

**Scrap book** Album, Grangerism

**Scrap box** Tidy

**Scrape(r)** Abrade, Agar, Bark, Clat, Claw, Comb, Curette, Escapade, Grate, Harl, Hoe, Hole, Jar, Kowtow, Lesion, Lute, Predicament, Racloir, Rake, Rasorial, Rasp, Rasure, Raze, Razure, Scalp, Scart, Scratch, Scroop, Scuff, Shave, Skimp, Strake, Strigil, Xyster

**Scraping noise** Curr, Scroop

**Scrap merchant** Didakai, Didakei, Diddicoi, Diddicoy, Didicoi, Didicoy, Gold-end-man, Totter

**Scratch(ed)** Cancel, Cla(u)t, Claw, Curry, Devil, Efface, Graze, Nick, Par, Periwig, Quit, Race, Rase, Rasp, Rast, Root, Satan, Scarify, Scart, Scrab(ble), Scram(b), Scrape, Scrattle, Scrawm, Scrub, Spag, Tease, Teaze, Wig

> **Scratch(ed)** may indicate an anagram

**Scrawl** Doodle, Scribble

**Scream(er)** Bellow, Cariama, Caterwaul, Comedian, Comic, Cry, Headline, Hern, Kamichi, Priceless, Scare-line, Screech, Seriema, Shriek, Skirl, Squall, Sutch, Yell

**Scree** Bahada, Bajada, Eluvium, Talus

**Screech(ing)** Cry, Screak, Screich, Screigh, Scriech, Scritch, Skreigh, Skriech, Skriegh, Ululant, Whoot

**Screed** Megillah, Ms, Tirade

**Screen** Abat-jour, Arras, Blind(age), Camouflage, Chancel, Chick, Cinerama, Cloak, Cornea, Cover, Cribble, Curtain, Eyelid, Festoon-blind, Glib, Gobo, Grille, Hallan, Hide, Hoarding, Iconostas(is), Jube, Lattice, Mantelet, Mask, Nonny, Obscure, Over-cover, Parclose, Partition, Pella, Purdah, Radar, Riddle, Sconce, SHADE, Shelter, Shield, Shoji, Show, Sift, Televise, Transenna, Traverse, Umbrella, Vet, Windbreak

**Screw** Adam, Dungeoner, Extort, Jailer, Jailor, Miser, Monkey-wrench, Niggard, Phillips, Prop(ellor), Salary, Skinflint, Spiral, Thumb(i)kins, Twist, Vice, Worm

**Scribble** Doodle, Pen, Scrawl

**Scribe** Clerk, Ezra, Mallam, Scrivener, Sopherim, Tabellion, Writer, WS

**Scrimmage** Bully, Maul, Mêlée, Rouge, Scrap, Skirmish, Struggle

**Script** Book, Gurmukhi, Hand, Italic, Jawi, Kana, Libretto, Linear A, Linear B, Lines, Lombardic, Nagari, Nastalik, Nastaliq, Ogam, Ronde, Scenario, Writing

**Scripture, Scriptural version** Agadah, Antilegomena, Avesta, Bible, Gemara, Gematria, Gospel, Granth, Haggada(h), Hermeneutics, Holy book, Holy writ, Koran, Lesson, Mishna(h), OT, Rig-veda, Tantra, Targum, Testament, Upanishad, Veda, Vedic, Verse, Vulgate

**Scrofula** Crewels, Cruel(l)s, King's evil, Struma

**Scroll(-work)** Cartouche, Dead sea, Mezuza(h), Makimono, Megillah, Parchment, Pell, Roll, Roul(e), Turbinate, Vitruvian, Volume, Volute

**Scrooge** Blagueur, Miser

**Scrounge(r)** Bludger, Borrow, Bot, Cadge, Forage, Layabout, Ligger

**Scrub(ber)** Cancel, Chaparral, Cleanse, Dele(te), Gar(r)igue, Loofa(h), Luffa, Masseur, Pro, Rub, Scour, Tart

> **Scrub** may indicate 'delete'

**Scruff(y)** Grubby, Nape, Raddled, Tatty, Untidy

**Scrum** Maul, Mob, Rouge, Ruck

**Scrummy, Scrumptious** Delectable, Delicious, Toothy, Yum-yum

**Scrunt** Carl

**Scruple(s), Scrupulous** Compunction, Doubt, Nicety, Precise, Punctilious, Qualm, Righteous, Stickle

**Scrutinise, Scrutiny** Check, Docimasy, Examine, Observe, Peruse, Pore,

Pry, SCAN, Study

**Scud** East, Scoot, Spindrift, Spoom, Spoon, Spray

**Scuff** Brush, Shuffle

**Scuffle** Brawl, Scarmage, Skirmish, Struggle, Tussle

> **Scuffle** may indicate an anagram

**Scull** Oar, Row

**Sculpt(ure)** Aeginetan, Bas-relief, Bronze, Canephor(a), Canephore, Canephorus, Carve, Della-robbia, Figure, Mobile, Nude, Pergamene, Pieta, Relievo, Sc, Shape, STATUARY

**Sculptor** Artist, Bartholdi, Celline, Daedalus, Donatello, Gill, Landseer, Michelangelo, Myron, Nollekens, Phidias, Pisano, Praxiteles, Pygmalion, Rodin, Scopas, Stevens, Wheeler

**Scum** Confervoid, Dregs, Dross, Kish, Legge, Mantle, Mother, Rabble, Sandiver, Slag, Slime, Spume, Sullage

**Scupper** Drain, Ruin, Scuttle, Sink

**Scurf, Scurvy** Dander, Dandriff, Dandruff, Furfur, Horson, Lepidote, Leprose, Scabrous, Scall, Scorbutic, Whoreson, Yaws, Yaw(e)y

**Scurrilous** Fescennine, Profane, Ribald, Sotadic, Thersites, Vulgar

**Scurry** Hurry, Scamper, Scutter, Skedaddle

**Scut** Fud, Tail

**Scute** Plate

**Scuttle** Abandon, Dan, Hod, Purdonium, Scoop, Scrattle, Scupper, Sink, Wreck

**Scythe** Bushwhacker, Cut, Hook, Sickle, Sieth, Snath(e), Snead, Sneath, Sned

**Sea** Adriatic, Aegean, Andaman, Aral, Azov, Baltic, Barents, Beaufort, Benthos, Bering, Billow, Biscay, Black, Blue, Bosp(h)orus, Brine, Briny, Caribbean, Caspian, Celebes, Channel, Dead, Ditch, Drink, Euripus, Euxine, Galilee, Herring-pond, Hudson Bay, Ionian, Laptev, Ler, Main, Mare, Marmara, Med, North, OCEAN, Oggin, Pelagic, Polynya, Quantity, Red, Ross, Sargasso, Strand, Sulu, Tethys, Thalassic, Tiberias, Tide, Timor, Water, Weddell, White, Yellow, Zee

**Sea-anemone** Actinia, Zoantharia

**Sea-bear** Fur-seal, Otary, Seal, Seecatchie

**Sea-beast** Ellops, Manatee

**Sea-bream** Carp, Fish, Porgie, Porgy

**Sea-cow** Dugong, Rhytina, Sirenian

**Sea-cucumber** Bêche-de-mer, Trepang

**Sea-dog** Salt, Tar

**Sea-ear** Abalone, Paua

**Sea-fight** Naumachy

**Sea-front, Seaside** Beach, Coast(line), Littoral, Orarian, Prom(enade)

**Sea-god** Neptune, Triton

**Sea-green** Glaucous, Incorruptible, Robespierre

**Sea-horse** Hippocampus, Hippodame, Lophobranchiate, Morse, Tangie

**Seal(s), Seal box** Airtight, Appose, Bachelor, Bull(a), Cachet, Caulk, Chesterfield, Chop, Clinch, Cocket, Consign, Crab-eater, Elephant, Emblem, Fob, Gasket, Harp, Hermetic, Impress, Jark, Lute, Obsign, Otary, Phoca, Pinnipedia, Pintadera, Pod, Privy, Proof, Rookery, Sea-bear, Sealch, Sealgh, Seecatch(ie), Selkie, Sigil, Signet, Silkie, Silky, Size, Skippet, Solomon, Sphragistic, Stamp, Wafer, Washer, Weddell, Womb, Zalophus

**Sea-legs** Balance, Pleons

**Sea-lily** Crinoid, Palmatozoa

**Seam** Commissure, Fell, Furrow, Join, Layer, Sew, Suture, Welt

**Seaman, Seamen** AB, Crew, Jack, Lascar, Lubber, Mariner, OD, Ordinary, PO, RN, SAILOR, Salt, Tar

**Sea-mat** Flustra

**Sea-matiness** Gam

**Sea-monster** Kraken, Merman, Wasserman

**Sea-mouse** Bristle-worm

**Séance** Communication, Session, Sitting

**Sea-parrot** Puffin

**Sear** Brand, Burn, Catch, Cauterise, Frizzle, Parch, Scath(e), Scorch, Singe, Wither

**Search(ing)** Beat, Comb, Dragnet, Examine, Ferret, FORAGE, Fossick, Frisk, Grope, Home, Hunt, Indagate, Inquire, Jerk, Jerque, Kemb, Probe, Proll, Prospect, Proul, Prowl, Quest, Rake, Rancel, Ransack, Ransel, Ranzel, Ravel, Ripe, Root, Rummage, Scan, Scour, Scur, Sker, Skirr, Snoop, Thumb, Trace, Zotetic

**Sea-rover** Norseman, Viking

**Sea-serpent, Sea-snake** Ellops, Hydrophidae, Phoca

> **Seaside** See SEA-FRONT

**Sea-slug** Beche-de-mer, Trepang

**Sea-snail** Neritidae

**Season(able), Seasonal, Seasoned** Accustom, Aggrace, Autumn, Betimes, Christmas, Condiment, Devil, Dress, Duxelles, Easter, Enure, Etesian, Fennel, Flavour, Garlic, Hiems, In, Inure, Lent, Marjoram, Master, Mature, Nutmeg, Paprika, Pepper, Powellise, Practised, Ripen, Salt, Sar, Seal, Seel, Sele, Silly, Solstice, Spice, Spring, Summer(y), Ticket, Tide, Time, Winter

**Sea-squirt** Ascidian

**Seat** Backside, Banc, Banquette, Bench, Bleacher, Borne, Bottom, Bum, Buttocks, Canapé, Centre, Chair, Couch, Creepie, Croup(e), Croupon,

Cushion, Davenport, Deckchair, Dick(e)y, Ejector, Epicentre, Faldistory, Faldstool, Foundation, Fud, Fundament, Gradin, Hall, Home, Houdah, Howdah, Humpty, Hurdies, Knifeboard, Marginal, Marquise, Misericord, Natch, Nates, Ottoman, Palfrey, Perch, Pew, Pillion, Pit, Pouffe, Ringside, Rumble, Rump, Saddle, Sedes, Sedilium, See, Sell, Settee, Settle, Siege, Sofa, Squab, Stool, Strapontin, Subsellium, Sunk(ie), Synthronus, Throne, Woolsack

**Sea-urchin** Echinus, Pluteus, Whore's egg

**Sea-vampire** Manta

**Sea-wall** Bulwark, Dyke, Groyne

**Sea-weed** Agar, Alga(e), Arame, Badderlock, Bladderwort, Carrag(h)een, Conferva, Coralline, Chondrus, Cystocarp, Desmid, Diatom, Dulse, Enteromorpha, Fucus, Heterocontae, Kelp, Kilp, Kombu, Laminaria, Laver, Nori, Nullipore, Ore, Porphyra, Sargasso, Seabottle, Sea-tangle, Tang, Varec(h), Vraic, Wakane, Ware, Wrack

**Sea-worm** Palolo, Spunculid

**Secede, Secession(ist)** Adullamite, Antiburgher, Defy, Desert, Dissident, Flamingant, Sever, Splinter

**Seclude, Seclusion** Cloister, Incommunicado, Isolate, Maroon, Nook, Privacy, Purdah, Retreat, Secret, Sequester, Solitude

**Second(ary), Seconds** Abet, Alternative, Another (guess), Assist, Back(er), Coming, Comprimario, Flash, Friend, Imperfect, Indirect, Inferior, Instant, Jiffy, Latter, Lesser, Minor, Mo(ment), Nature, Other, Pig's-whisper, Runner-up, Sec, Shake, Share, Side(r), Sight, Silver, Support, Tick, Trice, Twinkling, Wind

**Second-best** Worsted

> **Second-class** see SECOND-RATE

**Second-hand** Hearsay, Re-paint, Tralatitious, Used

**Second-rate, Second-class** B, Inferior, Mediocre

**Second-sight** Deuteroscopy, Divination, Tais(c)h

**Second tine** Bay, Bez

**Second-year student** Semi(e)(-bajan), Sophomore

**Secrecy, Secret(s), Secretive** Apocrypha, Arcana, Arcane, Arcanum, Backstairs, Cagey, Clam, Clandestine, Closet, Code, Conventicle, Covert, Cryptadia, Cryptic, Crypto, Dark, Dearn, Dern, Deep, Esoteric, Hidden, Hidling, Hugger-mugger, Hush-hush, Inly, Inmost, Latent, Mysterious, Mystical, Mystique, Oyster, Petto, PRIVATE, Privity, Privy, QT, Rune, Scytale, Shelta, Silent, Sly, Stealth, Sub rosa, Unbeknown, Underhand, Undescried, Unre(a)d, Unrevealed, Untold

**Secretary** Aide, Amanuensis, Chancellor, Chronicler, CIS, Desk, Dcssc, Famulus, Minuteman, Moonshee, Munshi, Notary, Scrive, Stenotyper, Temp

**Secretary-bird** Messenger, Serpent-eater

**Secrete, Secretion** Aequorin, Cache, Castor, Chalone, Discharge, Emanation, Exude, Hide, Hormone, Juice, Lac, Lerp, Mucus, Musk, Osmidrosis, Resin, Rheum, Saliva, Sebum, Secern, Smegma, Spit(tle), Trypsin

**Sect(arian), Secret society** Abelite, Adamite, Amish, Anabaptist, Assassin, Babee, Babi, Bahai, Brahmin, Cabal, Cainite, Calixtine, Camorra, Cathar, Clan, Crypto, Cult, Danite, Darbyite, Dissenter, Docate(s), Donatist, Druse, Druze, Dunkard, Dunker, Ebionite, Essene, Gheber, Ghebre, Giaour, Gnostic, Group, Gueber, Guebre, Gymnosophist, Harmonist, Hillmen, Illuminati, Jacobite, Jansenist, Karaite, Karmathian, Lollard, Macedonian, Macmillanite, Mandaean, Marcionite, Maronite, Monothelite, Montanist, Mormon, Mucker, Muggletonian, Nazarine, Order, Partisan, Perfectionist, Pharisee, Philadelphian, Phrygian, Picard, Porch, Rappist, Sabbatian, Sabian, Sadducee, School, Seekers, Sex, Shia(h), Therapeutae, Tunker, Unitarian, Valdenses, Wahabee, Wahabi(i)te, Waldenses, Yezdi, Yezidee, Yezidi, Zen, Zezidee

**Section** Chapter, Classify, Conic, Cut, Division, Ellipse, Eyalet, Gau, Hyperbola, Lith, Metamere, Mortice, Movement, Outlier, Passus, PIECE, Platoon, Segment, Severy, Slice, Ungula, Unit, Zone

**Secular** Earthly, Laic, Non-CE, Profane, Temporal, Worldly

**Secure** Anchor, Bag, Bail, Band, Bar, Belay, Bolt, Calm, Catch, Cement, Chain, Cinch, Clamp, Clasp, Clinch, Close, Dunnage, Engage, Ensure, Establishment, Fasten, Fortify, Frap, Guy, Immune, Invest, Lace, Land, Lash, Latch, Lock, Nail, Obtain, Patte, Pin, Pledge, Pot, Pre-empt, Protect, Quad, Rope, Rug, SAFE, Settle, Snell, Snug, Sound, Stable, Stanchion, Staple, Staylace, Strap, Sure, Tack, Take, Tie, Tight, Trap, Trice, Wedge, Win

**Security** Assurance, Bail, Chain, Cheka, Collateral, Consols, Debenture, Equity, Fastness, Gilt, Hypothec, Indemnity, Investment, Lien, Lock, Longs, Mortgage, Pledge, Preference, Safe(ty), Stock, Surety, Warrant

**Sedan** Battle, Brougham, Chair, Jampan(i), Jampanee, Litter, Palanquin, Palkee, Palki, Saloon

**Sedate** Calm, Cool, Decorous, Dope, Douce, Drug, Serene, Staid, Stand

**Sedative** Amytal, Anodyne, Aspirin, Barbitone, Bromide, Chloral, Depressant, Hypnic, Lenitive, Lupulin, Meprobamate, Metopryl, Miltown, Narcotic, Nembutal, Opiate, Scopolamine, Soothing, Thridace, Veronal

**Sedentary** Inactive, Sessile, Stationary

**Sedge** Carex, Chufa, Seg, Xyris

**Sediment** Deposit, Dregs, F(a)eces, Fecula, Foots, Grounds, Lees, Molasse, Residue, Salt, Sapropel, Silt, Sludge, Varve, Warp

**Sedition, Seditious** Incitement, Insurrection, Revolt, Riot, Treason

**Seduce(r), Seductive** Allure, Betray, Bewitch, Bribe, Cuckold-maker, Debauch, Entice, Honeyed, Honied, Lothario, Luring, Mislead, Siren, Tempt, Trepan, Undo, Wrong

> **Seduce** may indicate one word inside another

**See(ing)** Acknow, Barchester, Behold, Bishopric, C, Consider, Deek, Descry, Diocesan, Discern, Durham, Ecce, Ely, Episcopal, Eye, Glimpse, La, Lo, Meet, Norwich, Notice, Observe, Papal, Perceive, Realise, Remark, Rumble, Sodor and Man, Spot, Spy, Truro, Twig, Understand, V, Vatican, Vid(e), View, Vision, Visit, Voila, Witness, York

**Seed(y)** Achene, Argan, Arilli, Arillode, Bean, Ben, Best, Bonduc, Cacoon, Caraway, Carvy, Coriander, Cum(m)in, Dragon's teeth, Embryo, Endosperm, Germ, Grain, Gritty, Issue, Lomentum, Mangy, Nut, Ovule, Pea, Pinon, Pip, Poorly, Sabadilla, Semen, Seminal, Sesame, Shabby, Sorus, Sow, Sperm, Spore, Zoosperm

**Seed-case** Aril, Bur(r), Husk, Pea(s)cod, Pod, Testa, Theca

**Seed-leaf** Cotyledon

**Seedsman** Driller, Nurseryman, Sower

**Seek(er)** Ask, Beg, Busk, Court, Endeavour, Pursue, Quest, Scur, Search, Skirr, Solicit, Suitor

**Seem(ingly)** Appear, Look, Ostensible, Purport, Quasi

**Seemly** Comely, Decent, Decorous, Fit, Suitable

**Seep** Dribble, Exude, Leak, Ooze, Osmose, Percolate

**Seer** Auspex, Eye, Melampus, Nahum, Observer, Oculiform, Onlooker, Prescience, Prophet, Sage, Sibyl, Soothsayer, T(e)iresias, Witness, Zoroaster

**Seesaw** Bascule, Teeter(-totter), Tilt, Vacillate, Wild mare

**Seethe(d)** Boil, Bubble, Churn, Ferment, Simmer, Smoulder, Sod

**Segment** Arthromere, Cut, Division, Intron, Lacinate, Lobe, Merome, Merosome, Metamere, Pig, Prothorax, Share, Shie, Somite, Split, Sternite, Tagma, Telson, Urite, Uromere

**Segregate, Segregation** Apartheid, Exile, Insulate, Intern, ISOLATE, Jim Crow, Seclude, Separate

**Seidlitz** Powder, Rochelle

**Seismic** Terremotive

**Seismograph** Tromometer

**Seize, Seizure** Angary, Apprehend, Arrest, Attach(ment), Bag, Bone, Capture, Claw, Cleek, Cly, Collar, Commandeer, Confiscate, Distrain, Distress, For(e)hent, GRAB, Grip, Hend, Impound, Maverick, Na(a)m, Nab, Nap, Nim, Possess, Sequestrate, Smug, Tackle

**Seldom** Infrequent, Rare, Unoften

**Select(ing), Selection, Selector** Assortment, Bla(u)d, Cap, Casting, Choice, Choose, Classy, Cull, Discriminate, Draw, Eclectic, Edit, Elite, Excerpt, Exclusive, Extract, Favour, Garble, Nap, PICK, Pot-pourri, Prefer, Recherché, Sample, Seed, Single, Sort, Stream, Tipster, Triage, UCCA

**Selenium** Se, Zorgite

**Self** Atman, Auto, Character, Ego, Person, Psyche, Seity, Sel, Soul

**Self-confidence** Aplomb, Ego

**Self-contained**  Absolute, Reticent, SC, Taciturn

**Self-contradictory**  Absurd, Irish

**Self-control**  Encraty, Modesty, Patience, Restraint, Temper(ance)

**Self-esteem**  Amour-propre, Conceit, Confidence, Egoism, Pride

**Self-evident**  Axiom, Manifest, Obvious, Patent, Truism, Truth

**Self-existence**  Solipsism

**Self-fertilisation, Self-origination**  Aseity, Autogamy

**Self-governing**  Autonomy, Idior(r)hythmic, Kabele, Kebel, Puritanism, Swaraj

**Self-help**  Smiles

**Self-important, Self-indulgent**  Aristippus, Arrogant, Conceited, Immoderate, Jack-in-office, Licentious, Pompous, Pragmatic, Profligate, Sybarite

**Selfish(ness)**  Avaricious, Egoist, Greedy, Hedonist, Mean, Solipsism

**Selfless**  Non-ego

**Self-limiting**  Kenotic

> **Self-origination**  see SELF-FERTILISATION

**Self-pollinating**  Cl(e)istogamic

**Self-possession**  Aplomb, Composure, Cool, Nonchalant

**Self-satisfied**  Complacent, Smug, Tranquil

**Self-service**  Automat, Buffet, Cafeteria, Supermarket

**Self-sufficiency**  Absolute, Autarky, Complete

**Self-taught**  Autodidact

**Sell(er), Selling**  Apprize, Auction, Barter, Catch, Chant, Chaunt, Cope, Dispose, Flog, Go, Have, Hawk, Hustle, Inertia, Market, Menage, Merchant, Peddle, Purvey, Push, Pyramid, Realise, Rep, Retail, Ruse, Simony, Stall-man, Sug, TRADE, Vend

**Selvage**  Border, Edge, Roon

**Semaphore**  Signal

**Semblance**  Aspect, Likeness, Sign

**Seminar**  Class, Group, Tutorial

**Semi-paralysis**  Dyaesthesia

**Semitic**  Accadian, Akkadian, Arab, Aramaic, Geez, Jewish

**Senate**  Council, Seanad (Eireann)

**Senator**  Antiani, Cicero, Elder, Legislator, Solon

**Send, Sent**  Consign, DESPATCH, Disperse, Emit, Entrance, Issue, Launch, Order, Post, Rapt, Ship, Transmit, Transport

**Send back**  Refer, Remit, Remand, Return

**Send down**  Lower, Rusticate

**Send up**  Chal(l)an, Lampoon, Promote

**Senegal**  SN

**Senescence**  Age

**Senile, Senility**  Dementia, Disoriented, Doddery, Doitit, Dotage, Eild, Eld, Gaga, Nostology

**Senior**  Aîné, Doyen, Elder, Father, Grecian, Mayor, Père, Primus, Superior, Upper

**Senor(a)**  Caballero, Don(a), Hidalga, Hidalgo

**Sensation(al)**  Acolouthite, Anoesis, Aura, Blood, Commotion, Empfindung, Feeling, Gas, Lurid, Melodrama, Shocker, Splash, Stir, Styre, Thrill, Tingle, Vibes, Wow, Yellow

**Sense, Sensual**  Acumen, Aura, Carnal, Coherence, Dress, Feel, Gross, Gumption, Gustation, Hearing, Idea, Import, Instinct, Intelligence, Lewd, Meaning, Olfactory, Palate, Rational, Rumble-gumption, Rumgumption, Rum(m)el-gumption, Rum(m)le-gumption, Sight, Slinky, Smell, Sybarite, Synesis, Taste, Touch, Voluptuary, Voluptuous, Wisdom, Wit

**Senseless**  Absurd, Anosmia, Illogical, Mad, Numb, Stupid, Stupor, Unconscious, Unwise

**Sensible**  Aware, Dianoetic, Prudent, Raisonné, Rational, Sane, Solid

**Sensitive**  Algesia, Alive, Allergic, Atopy, Delicate, Erogenous, Keen, Nesh, Passible, Sympathetic, Tender, Ticklish

**Sensor**  Palpi

**Sentence**  Assize, Bird, Carpet, Clause, Commit, Condemn, Custodial, Decree(t), Doom, Judgement, Period, Rap, Rune, Stretch, Suspended

**Sententious**  Concise, Gnomic, Laconic, Pithy, Pompous, Terse

**Sentiment(al)**  Corn, Drip, Feeling, Govey, Gush, Maudlin, Mind, Mush, Opinion, Romantic, Rosewater, Schmaltzy, Sloppy, Soppy, Tear-jerker, Traveller, Twee, View, Weepy

**Sentry**  Custodian, Guard, Picket, Sentinel, Vedette, Vidette, Watch

**Separate(d), Separation**  Abstract, Asunder, Atmolysis, Avulsion, Cull, Cut, Decompose, Decouple, Deglutinate, Detach, Dialyse, Diastasis, Diazeuxis, Diremption, Disally, Discerp, Discrete, Dissociate, Distance, Distinct, Disunite, Divide, Divorce, Eloi(g)n, Elute, Elutriate, Esloin, Estrange, Filter, Insulate, Intervene, Isolate, Lease, Part, Piece, Prescind, Ramify, Red(d), Scatter, Schism, Screen, Scutch, Secern, Sever, Shed, Shore, Shorn, Sift, Sleave, Sle(i)ded, Sort, SPLIT, Stream, Sunder, Sundry, Tems(e), Tmesis, Try, Twin(e), Unclasp, Winnow, Wrench, Yandy

**Sepia**  Cuttle, Ink

**Seppuku**  Hara-kiri, Hari-kari

**Septic**  Poisonous, Rotting

**Septimus**  Small

**Septum**  Mediastinum

**Sepulchral, Sepulchre**  Bier, Cenotaph, Charnel, Crypt, Funeral, Monument, Pyramid, Tomb, Vault, Whited

**Sequel** After-clap, Consequence, Effect, Outcome, Suite

**Sequence** Byte, Chronological, Fibonacci, Line, Order, Program(me), Run, Seriatim, Series, Succession, Suit, Suite, Train

**Sequester, Sequestrate** Confiscate, Esloin, Esloyne, Impound, Isolate, Retire, Seclude, Separate

**Sequin** Paillette

**Sequoia** Redwood

**Seraph** Abdiel, ANGEL

**Sere** Arid, DRY, Scorch, Wither

**Serenade(r)** Aubade, Charivari, Horning, Minstrel, Nocturne, Shivaree, Sing-song, Wait, Wake

**Serene, Serenity** Calm, Composed, Placid, Repose, Sangfroid, Sedate, Smooth, TRANQUIL

**Serf(dom)** Adscript, Bondman, Ceorl, Churl, Helot, Manred, SLAVE, Thete, Thrall, Vassal, Velle(i)nage

**Serge** Russian, Say

**Sergeant** Buzfuz, Cuff, Havildar, Kite, NCO, RSM, Sarge, SL, SM, Troy

**Serial** Episode, Feuilleton, Heft, Livraison

**Series** Catena, Chain, Concatenation, Continuum, Course, Cycle, Cyclus, Enfilade, Engrenage, Episode, Fibonacci, Line, Links, PROGRESSION, Rubber, Run, Sequence, Ser, String, Suit, Train

**Serious** Critical, Earnest, Grave, Important, Major, Momentous, Pensive, Sad, Serpentine, Sober, Solemn, Sombre, Staid

**Sermon** Address, Discourse, Homily, Lecture, Spital

**Serow** Goral, Thar

**Serpent(ine)** Adder, Amphisbaena, Anguine, Apepi, Apophis, Asp, Aspic(k), Basilisk, Boa, Cockatrice, Dipsas, Firedrake, Midgard, Nagas, Ouroboros, Peridotite, Retinalite, Sea-snake, Shesha, SNAKE, Traitor, Uraeus, Viper

**Serrate(d)** Diprionidian, Saw, Scallop, Serried

**Serum** Antilymphocyte, Antitoxin, ATS, Fluid, Opsonin, Senega

**Serval** Bush-cat

**Servant, Server** Attendant, Ayah, Batman, Bearer, Bedder, Bedmaker, Boots, Butler, Boy, Caddie, Chaprassi, Cook, Chuprassy, Daily, Domestic, Dromio, Drudge, Employee, Factotum, Famulus, Flunkey, Friday, Gehazi, G(h)illie, Gip, Gully, Gyp, Handmaid, Henchman, Iras, Jack, Khansama(h), Lackey, Maid, Man, Menial, Minion, Myrmidon, Nethinim, Obedient, Page, Pantler, Postman, Retainer, Scout, Scrub, Servitor, Skip, Soubrette, Steward, Tapsman, Tendance, Theow, Thete, Tiger, Tweeny, Vails, Vales, Valet, Varlet, Vassal, Waiter, Weller

**Serve, Service** Ace, Amenity, Answer, Arriage, Asperges, Assist, ATS, Attendance, Avail, Benediction, Candlemas, Cannonball, Ceefax, China, Communion, Complin(e), Credo, Dinnerset, Dish, Do, Dow, Duty, Employ,

Evensong, Fault, Fee, Forward, FUNCTION, Further, Go, Help, Hour, Ka(e), Let, Line, Ling, Litany, Liturgy, Mass, Mat(t)ins, Memorial, Minister, Ministry, Missa, Nocturn, Nones, Oblige, Office, Oracle, Overhaul, Pass, Pay, Prime, Proper, RAF, Requiem, Rite, RN, Sacrament, Senior, Sext, Sorb, Stead, Sted, Sue, Tenebrae, Trental, Uncork, Use, Utility, Vespers, Wait, Waiterage, Watch-night, Worship

**Service-book** Hymnal, Hymnary, Missal, Triodion

> **Serviceman** may indicate a churchman

**Servile, Servility** Abasement, Crawling, Knee, Lickspittle, Menial, Slavish, Slimy, Sycophantic

**Serving** Helping, Heuristic, Portion

**Servitude** Bondage, Domination, Peonism, Slavery, Yoke

**Sesame** Gingelly, Gingili, Jinjilli, Semsem, Til

**Session** Bout, Meeting, Round, Séance, Sederunt, Settle, Sitting, Term

**Set(ting) (down; in; off; up)** Adjust, Appoint, Arrange, Batch, Bent, Bezel, Cake, Case, Cast, Class, Clique, Cliveden, Coagulate, Cock, Cockshy, Collection, Comp(ositor), Compose, Congeal, Context, Coterie, Crew, Crystal, Decline, Decor, Diorama, Dispose, Earth, Environment, Establish, Fit, Flagstone, Found, Garniture, Geal, Gel, Genome, Group, Harden, Ilk, Incut, Jeel, Jell(y), Kit, Laid, Land, Lay, Leg, Locale, Locate, Lot, Milieu, Monture, Mournival, Nest, Occident, Ordinate, Parure, Physique, Pitch, Place(ment), Plant, Plaste, Ply, Posed, Posit, Put, Radio, Ready, Receiver, Relay, Rigid, Rooted, Rubber, Scenery, Series, Sink, Solidify, Squad, Stand, Stationed, Stede, Stell, Stick, Stiffen, Still, Stream, Suit, Surround, Tar, Team, Teeth, Telly, Till, Trigger, Venn, Weather, Yplast

**Setback** Checkmate, Hiccup, Jolt, Relapse, Retreat, Reversal, Scarcement, Tes, Vicissitude

**Setter** Cement, Comp, Dog, Gundog, Irish, Pectin, Red, Smoot, Sphinx, Trend

**Settle(d), Settler, Settlement** Adjust, Agree, Alight, Appoint, Arrange, Ascertain, Ausgleich, Avenge, Balance, Bandobast, Bed, Bench, Boer, Bundobust, Bustee, Clear, Clench, Clinch, Colonial, Colonise, Colony, Compose, Compound, Compromise, Decide, Defray, Determine, Diktat, Discharge, Dowry, Ekistics, Encamp, Endow, Ensconce, Entail, Feeze, Fix, Gravitate, Gridironer, Guilder, Illegitimate, Jointure, Kibbutz, Land, Ledge, Light, Lyte, Mission, Moshav, Nahal, Nest, Nestle, Oecist, Oikist, Opt, Pa(h), Pakka, Patroon, Pay, Pheazar, Peise, Penal, Perch, Pheese, Pheeze, Phese, Pilgrim, Pioneer, Placate, Planter, Populate, Pucka, Pueblo, Pukka, Readjust, Reduction, Reimburse, Remit, Reside, Resolve, Rest, Satisfaction, Secure, Sedimentary, Shagroon, Smoot, Sofa, Solve, Square, State, Still, Subside, Township, Ujamaa, Utu, Vested, Voortrekker

> **Settlement** may indicate an anagram

> **Settler** may indicate a coin

**Set upon** Attack, Sick

**Seven** Ages, Days, Dials, Great Bear, Hebdomad, Pleiad(es), S, Sages, Seas, Septimal, Sisters, Sleepers, Wonders

**Seventy** S

**Sever** Amputate, Cut, Detach, Divide, Sunder

**Several** Divers, Many, Multiple, Some, Sundry

**Severe(ly), Severity** Acute, Bad, Chronic, Cruel, Dour, Draconian, Drastic, Eager, Extreme, Grave, Grievous, Gruel(ling) Hard, HARSH, Ill, Inclement, Morose, Penal, Rhadamanthine, Rigor, Serious, Snelly, Sore, Spartan, Stern, Strict

**Sew(ing)** Baste, Embroider, Fell, Machine, Mitre, Run, Seam, Seel, Stitch, Tack, Whip

**Sewage, Sewer** Cesspool, Cloaca, Culvert, Dorcas, DRAIN, Effluence, Jaw-box, Jaw-hole, Mimi, Needle, Privy, Shore, Soil, Sough, Soughing-tile, Waste

**Sex(y)** Coupling, Erotic, Female, Gamic, Gender, Intercourse, Kind, Lingam, Male, Nookie, Oomph, Priapean, Race, Rut(ish), Screw, Sect, Steamy, Sultry, Venereal, VI

**Sex appeal** It, Oomph, SA

**Sexcentenarian** Shem

**Sexless** Agamogenetic, N, Neuter

**Sextet** Over, Six

**Sexton** Blake, Fossor, Sacristan, Shammes, Warden

**Sh** P, Quiet

**Shabby** Base, Buckeen, Dog-eared, Mean, Moth-eaten, Oobit, Oorie, Oubit, Ourie, Outworn, Owrie, Scaly, Scruffy, Seedy, Shoddy, Squalid, Tatty, Worn, Woubit

**Shack** Hideout, Hut

**Shackle(s)** Bilboes, Bind, Bracelet, Chain, Entrammel, Fetter(lock), Irons, Manacle, Restrict, Tie, Trammel, Yoke

**Shad** Allice, Allis, Fish, Twait(e)

**Shaddock** Grapefruit, Pomelo

**Shade(d), Shades, Shadow, Shady** Adumbrate, Arbour, Awning, Blend, Blind, Bongrace, Bowery, Buff, Cast, Chiaroscuro, Chroma, Cloche, Cloud, Degree, Dis, Dog, Dubious, Eclipse, Five o'clock, Galanty, Gamp, Ghost, Gradate, Gray, Hachure, Hell, Herbar, Hint, Hue, Inumbrate, Larva, Lee, Mezzotint, Nuance, Opaque, Overtone, Parasol, Phantom, Presence, Satellite, Screen, Shroud, Sienna, Silhouette, Silvan, Skia-, Spectre, Spirit, Stag, Sunglasses, Swale, Swaly, Tail, Tinge, Tint, Tone, Ugly, Umbra(tile), Underhand, Velamen, Velar(ium), Velum, Visor

**Shadowless** Ascian

**Shaft** Arbor, Arrow, Barb, Barrow-train, Beam, Column, Crank, Cue, Disselboom, Dolly, Fil(l), Fust, Incline, Journal, Limber, Loom, Mandrel, Mandril, Moulin, Parthian, Passage, Pit, Pole, Ray, Scape, Scapus, Shank,

Snead, Spindle, Staff, Steal(e), Steel, Stele, Stulm, Sunbeam, Thill, Tige, Trave, Upcast, Winze, Winning

**Shag**  Cronet, Hair, Intercourse, Nap, Pile, Scart(h), Skart(h), Tire, Tobacco

**Shaggy**  Ainu, Comate, Hairy, Hearie, Hirsute, Horrid, Horror, Rough, Rugged, Shock, Shough, Tatty, Untidy

**Shah**  Ruler, Sophi, Sophy

**Shake(n), Shakes, Shaky**  Ague(-fit), Astonish, Brandish, Coggle, Concuss, Dabble, Dick(e)y, Didder, Dither, Dodder, DT, Feeble, Groggy, Hod, Hotch, Jar, Jiggle, Jolt, Jounce, Jumble, Mo, Nid-nod, Quake, Quiver, Quooke, Rattle, Rickety, Rickle, ROCK, Rouse, Shimmer, Shiver, Shock, Shog, Shoogle, Shudder, Succuss(ation), Tremble, Tremolo, Tremor, Tremulous, Trill(o), Undulate, Vibrate, Vibrato, Wag, Wobble, Wonky

> **Shake**  may indicate an anagram

**Shakedown**  Blackmail, Chantage, Pallet

**Shakespeare**  Bard, Will, WS

**Shale**  Blaes, Fa(i)kes, Kerogen, Rock, Torbanite

**Shall**  Sal

**Shallot**  C(h)ibol, Onion, Scallion, Sybo(e), Sybow

**Shallow(s)**  Ebb, Flat, Fleet, Flew, Flue, Justice, Neritic, Shoal, Slight, Superficial

**Sham**  Apocryphal, Bluff, Bogus, Braide, Counterfeit, Deceit, Fake, FALSE, Hoax, Impostor, Mimic, Mock, Phony, Pinchbeck, Postiche, Pretence, Pseudo, Repro, Snide, Spurious

**Shamble(s)**  Abattoir, Butchery, Mess, Shuffle, Totter, Tripple

**Shame(ful), Shame-faced**  Abash, Aidos, Contempt, Crying, Degrade, Discredit, Disgrace, Dishonour, Embarrass, Fie, Gross, Hangdog, Honi, Humiliate, Ignominy, Infamy, Inglorious, Modesty, Mortify, Pity, Pudor, Pugh, Shend, Sin, Slander, Stain, Stigma, Yshend

**Shameless**  Audacious, Brash, Immodest, Ithyphallic

**Shampoo(ing)**  Massage, Tripsis, Wash

**Shandy**  Drink, Sterne, Tristram

**Shanghai**  Abduct, Kidnap, Trick

**Shank**  Leg, Shaft, Steal(e), Steel, Steil, Stele, Strike

**Shanty, Shanty town**  Boatsong, Bothy, Bustee, Cabin, Favela, Forebitter, Hutment, Lean-to, Pondok, Shack, Song

**Shape(d), Shaping**  Blancmange, Boast, Bruting, Cast, Contour, Face, Figure, Form, Format, Headquarters, Hew, Jello, Model, MOULD, Ream, Scabble, Sculpt, Spile, Tromino, Whittle, Wrought

**Shapeless**  Amorphous, Chaos, Dumpy, Vague

**Shard**  Fragment, Sliver, Splinter

**Share(d), Shares**  Allocation, Allotment, Apportion, Cahoots, Co, Cohabit, Coho(e), Common, Contango, Culter, Cut, Divi(dend), Divide,

Divvy, Dole, Dutch, Equity, Finger, Impart, Interest, Kaffer, Kaf(f)ir, Lion's, Moiety, Parcener, PART, Partake, Participate, Plough, Portion, Prebend, Pref(erred), Preference, Pro rata, Quarter, Quota, Ration, Rug, Scrip, Security, Shr, Slice, Snack, Snap, Sock, Split, Teene, Tranche, Whack

**Shareholder** Stag

**Shark** Basking, Beagle, Carpet, Cestracion, Demoiselle, Dog(fish), Huss, Mako, Nurse, Penny-dog, Plagiostomi, Porbeagle, Requiem, Rhin(e)odon, Rigg, Sail-fish, Sea-ape, Sharp, Shovelhead, Squaloid, Swindler, Thrasher, Thresher, Tope, Usurer, Wobbegong, Zygaena

**Sharkskin** Shagreen

**Sharp(er), Sharpen(er), Sharpness** Abrupt, Accidental, Acidulous, Acrid, Acumen, Acuminate, Acute, Alert, Angular, Arris, Bateless, Becky, Bitter, Brisk, Cacuminous, Cheat, Clear, Coticular, Dital, Edge(r), Fine, Grind, Hone, Hot, Keen, Kurtosis, Massé, Oilstone, Peracute, Piquant, Poignant, Pronto, Pungent, Razor, Rogue, Rook, Set, Shrewd, Snap, Snell, Sour, Spicate, Strop, Swindler, Tart, Vivid, Volable, Whet

**Sharpshooter** Bersaglier, Franc-tireur, Sniper, Tirailleur, Voltigeur

**Shatter(ing)** Astone, Break, Brisance, Craze, Dash, Explode, Shiver, Smash, Splinter, Unnerve

**Shave(r), Shaving** Barb(er), Grain, Moslings, Pare, Plane, Pogonotomy, Poll, Raze, Scrape, Skive, Splinter, Swarf, Todd, Tonsure, Whittle

**Shaw** Artie, Green, Spinn(e)y, Wood

**Shawl** Afghan, Cashmere, Chuddah, Chuddar, Fichu, Kaffiyeh, Mantilla, Maud, Paisley, Partlet, Serape, Stole, Tallith, Tonnag, Tozie, Whittle, Wrapper, Zephyr

**She** A

**Sheaf** Aplustre, Bundle, Folder, Gait, Garb(e), Gerbe, Shock, Thr(e)ave

**Shear(er)** Clip, Cut, Fleece, Poll, Ring(er), Shave, Trim

**Sheath** Case, Cocoon, Coleorhiza, Cover, Glume, Myelin, Neurilemma, Neurolemma, Oc(h)rea, Quiver, Scabbard, Spathe, Thecal, Vagina, Volva

**Sheave** Bee, Clevis

**Shed(der)** Barn, Cast, Cho(u)ltry, Depot, Discard, Doff, Drop, Effuse, Exuviate, Hangar, Hovel, Hut, Infuse, Lair, Lean-to, Linhay, Linny, Mew, Moult, Pent, Salmon, Shippen, Shippon, Shuck, Skeo, Skillion, Skio, Slough, Sow, Spend, Spent, Spill, Tilt

**Sheen** Glaze, Gloss, Luminance, Lustre, Patina, Schiller, Shine

**Sheep(ish)** Ammon, Ancon(es), Aoudad, Argali, Bharal, Bident, Bighorn, Black, Blackface, Blate, Broadtail, Burhel, Berrel(l), Caracul, Cheviots, Cotswold, Coy, Crone, Dinmont, Embarrassed, Ewe, Fank, Flock, Fold, Hangdog, Herdwick, Hidder, Hirsel, Hog(g), Jacob, Jemmy, Jumbuck, Karakul, Kent, Lamb, Lanigerous, Leicester, Lo(a)ghtan, Loghtyn, Marco Polo, Merino, Mor(t)ling, Mouf(f)lon, Muflon, Mug, Mus(i)mon, Mutton, Oorial, Ovine, Ram, Rosella, Shearling, Shorthorn, SHY, Soay, Southdown, Suffolk, Sumph, Teg(g), Texel, Theave, Trip, Tup, Udad,

Urial, Wensleydale, Wether, Woollyback, Yow(e)

**Sheep disease** Braxy, Dunt, Gid, Hoove, Louping-ill, Rubbers, Scrapie, Sturdy, Swayback, Variola, Wildfire

**Sheepfold** Fank, Pen

**Sheepskin** Basan, Caracul, Karakul, Roan, Wool

**Sheer** Absolute, Clear, Main, Mere, Peekaboo, Plumb, Pure, Simple, Stark, Steep, Swerve, Thin, Utter

**Sheet(s)** Balance, Cere-cloth, Cerement, Chart, Cutch, Expanse, Film, Folio, Foolscap, Heft, Leaf, Membrane, Nappe, Out-hauler, Page, Pot(t), Pour, Prospectus, Ream, Rope, Sail, Shroud, Stern, Stratus, Taggers, Tarpaulin(g), Tentorium, Terne

**Sheet-anchor** Letter-weight, Paperweight

**Sheet-iron** Taggers, Terne(plate)

**Sheikdom** Bahrein, Dubai

**Shekel** Sickle

**Sheldrake** Bergander

**Shelf, Shelve** Bank, Bar, Bracket, Counter, Credence, Delay, Ledge, Mantle, Postpone, Rack, Retable, Sidetrack, Sill, Spinsterhood, Whatnot

**Shell(ed), Shellfish** Abalone, Acorn-shell, Ambulacrum, Argonaut, Balanus, Bivalve, Blitz, Boat, Bombard, Buckie, Capiz, Capsid, Carapace, Cartridge, Casing, Chank, Chelonia, Chitin, Clam, Clio, Cockle, Cohog, Conch, Copepoda, Cover, Cowrie, Cowry, Crab, Crustacea, Dariole, Deerhorn, Dop, Drill, Escallop, Foraminifer, Framework, Frustule, Haliotis, Husk, Hyoplastron, Isopoda, Limacel, Limpet, Lyre, Malacostraca, Mollusc, Mussel, Murex, Nacre, Nautilus, Ormer, Ostracod, Ostrea, Oyster, Paua, Pawa, Peag, Peak, Pea(s)cod, Pecten, Pereia, Periostracum, Periwinkle, Pipi, Pipsqueak, Pod, Projectile, Purple, Putamen, Quahog, Sal, Scalarium, Scallop, Scollop, Sea-ear, Sea-pen, Shale, Sheal, Sheel, Shiel, Shill, Shock, Shot, Shrapnel, Sial, Spend, Stonk, Straddle, Strafe, Stromb(us), Swan-mussel, Test(a), Toheroa, Top, Torpedo, Turbo, Turritella, Univalve, Wakiki, Wampum, Whelk, Whizz-bang, Winkle, Xenophya, Yabbie, Yabby, Zimbi

**Shelled** Cracked, Kernel

> **Shelled** may indicate an anagram

**Shell money** Wakiki, Wampum, Zimbi

**Shelter** Abri, Anderson, Asylum, Awn, Belee, Bender, Bield, Booth, Bunker, Butt, Cab, Casemate, Cot(e), Cove, Covert, Defence, Dripstone, Dug-out, Fall-out, Garage, Gunyah, Harbour, Haven, Hithe, Hospice, Hostel, House, Hovel, Humpy, Hut, Kipsie, Lee, Lownd, Morrison, REFUGE, Retreat, Roof, Sanctuary, Scog, Sconce, Scoog, Scoug, Screen, Scug, Shiel(ing), Shroud, Skug, Tent, Testudo, Tortoise, Tupik, Umbrage, Weather, Wi(c)kiup, Wickyup, Wil(t)ja

**Shemozzle** Debacle

**Shenanigan** Antic

**Shepherd(ess)**   Abel, Acis, Amaryllis, Amos, Bergère, Bo-peep, Chloe, Clorin, Conduct, Corin, Corydon, Cuddy, Daphnis, Dorcas, Drover, Endymion, Escort, Ettrick, Grubbinol, Gyges, Herdsman, Hobbinol, Lindor, Marshal, Menalcas, Padre, Pastor(al), Pastorella, Phebe, Strephon, Tar-box, Thenot, Thyrsis, Tityrus

**Sheriff**   Bailiff, Deputy, Grieve, Land-dros(t), Shirra, Shrievalty, Viscount

**Sherry**   Amoroso, Cobbler, Cyprus, Doctor, Fino, Gladstone, Jerez, Manzanilla, Oloroso, Sack, Solera, Xeres

**Sherwood**   Anderson, Forest

**Shibboleth**   Password

**Shield(-shaped)**   Ablator, Aegis, Ancile, Armour, Arms, Bodyguard, Box, Buckler, Cartouche, Clypeus, Defend, Escutcheon, Fence, Gobo, Guard, Gyron, Hielaman, Pavis(e), Pelta, Protect, Rondache, Screen, Scute, Scutum, Targe(t), Thyroid

**Shift(y)**   Amove, Astatic, Budge, Change, Chemise, Core, Cymar, Devious, Displace, Doppler, Evasive, Expedient, Fend, Hedging, Landslide, Linen, Move, Night, Nighty, Relay, Remove, Ruse, Scorch, Shirt, Shunt, Simar(re), Slippery, Spell, Stint, Tour, Transfer, Tunic, Turn, Vary, Veer, Warp

> **Shift(ing)**   may indicate an anagram

**Shilling**   Bob, Deaner, Falkiner, Hog, S, Teston

**Shimmer**   Glint, Glitter, Iridescence, Shine

> **Shimmering**   may indicate an anagram

**Shin**   Clamber, Climb, Leg, Shank, Skink, Swarm

**Shindig, Shindy**   Bobbery, Row, Rumpus, Shivoo, Uproar

**Shine(r), Shining, Shiny**   Aglow, Beam, Buff, Burnish, Deneb, Effulge, Excel, Flash, Gleam, Glisten, Gloss, GLOW, Irradiant, Japan, Leam, Leme, Lucent, Luminous, Lustre, Mouse, Nitid, Phosphoresce, Polish, Radiator, Relucent, Resplend, Rutilant, Skyre, Sleek, Twinkle, Varnish

**Shingle(s), Shingly**   Beach, Chesil, Cut, Dartre, Dartrous, Gravel, Herpes, Herpetic, Shale, Stone, Zoster

**Shinpad**   Greave

**Shinty**   Caman, Camanachd

> **Shiny**   may indicate a star

**Ship(ping)**   Acapullo, Argo(sy), Ark, Aviso, Banker, Barge, Bark, Barque, Bateau, Bawley, Beagle, Bellerophon, Berthon-boat, Bethel, Bidarka, Bilander, Billyboy, Bireme, Boat, Borley, Bounty, Brig(antine), Broke, Bucentaur, Bumboat, Buss, Cabotage, Caique, Camel, Canoe, Capital, Caravel, Carrack, Carvel, Castle, Cat(boat), Clipper, Coaler, Coaster, Cob(b)le, Cock, Cockleshell, Cog, Collier, Convoy, Cooper, Coper, Coracle, Corocore, Corocoro, Corvette, Cot, Counter, Crare, Crayer, Currach, Curragh, Cutter, Cutty Sark, Dahabeeah, Dahabieh, Dahabiyah, Dahabiyeh, Dandy, Decker, Dhow, Ding(e)y, Dinghy, DISPATCH,

Dogger, Dory, Dow, Dreadnought, Dredger, Drifter, Drog(h)er, Dromedary, Dromon(d), Drover, Duck, Dugout, Embark, Export, Faldboat, Felucca, Ferry, Foldboat, Fore-and-after, First-rate, Freighter, Frigate, Frigatoon, Frigot, Funny, Gabbard, Gabbart, Galiot, Galleon, Galley, Galliot, Gallivat, Galloon, Gay-you, Golden Hind, Gondola, Grab, Gravy, Great Eastern, Gunboat, Her, Hooker, Hoveller, Hoy, Hulk, Hydrofoil, Hydroplane, Icebreaker, Indiaman, Ironclad, Jigger, Jolly, Keel, Ketch, Koff, Lapstreak, Launch, Leviathan, Liberty, Liner, Lorcha, Lugger, Lymphad, Mackinaw, Man, Marie Celeste, Masoolah, Massoola, Masula, Mayflower, Mistico, Monitor, Monohull, Moses, Mudscow, MV, Nina, Nuggar, Oiler, Oomiack, Outrigger, Packet, Patamar, Pedalo, Pelican, Penteconter, Pequod, Pinafore, Pink, Pinnace, Pinto, Pitpan, Piragua, Pirogue, Polacca, Polacre, Post, Pram, Prau, Privateer, Prize, Proa, Prore, Prow, Pulwar, Puteli, Q, Quadrireme, Ram, Randan, Razee, Revenge, Ro-ro, Saic, Sail, Sandal, Santa Maria, Savannah, Schooner, Schuit, Schuyt, Scoot, Scow, Scull, Settee, Shallop, Shanghai, She, Shell, Side-wheeler, Skidbladnir, Skiff, Slaver, Sloop, Snow, SS, Steamboat, Steamer, Stern-wheeler, Stew-can, Tartan(e), Tender, Tern, Three-master, Titanic, Torpid, Tramp, Trekschuit, Triaconter, Trireme, Trader, Tub, U-boat, Umiak, Vaporetto, Vedette, Vessel, Vidette, Whale-back, Whaler, Wherry, Whiff, Windjammer, Xebec, Yacht, Yawl, Zabra, Zebec(k), Zulu

**Shipmate** Crew, Hearty, Sailor

**Shipping line** P and O

**Ship's biscuit** Dandyfunk, Dunderfunk

**Shipshape** Apple-pie, Neat, Orderly, Tidy, Trim

**Shipwreck** Split

**Shire** County

**Shirk(er)** Cuthbert, Dodge, Evade, Funk, Malinger, Mike, Pike, Poler, Scrimshank, Skive, Skrimshank, Slack, Soldier

**Shirt** Camese, Camise, Chemise, Cilice, Dasheki, Dashiki, Dick(e)y, Hair, Kaftan, Kaross, K(h)urta, Nessus, Non-iron, Parka, Partlet, Sark, Serk, Shift, Smock, Stuffed, Subucula, T

**Shiva** Destroyer

**Shiver(ing), Shivers, Shivery** Aguish, Break, Chitter, Crumble, Dash, Dither, Fragile, Frisson, Grew, Grue, Malaria, Oorie, Ourie, Owrie, Quake, Quiver, SHAKE, Shatter, Shrug, Shudder, Smither, Smithereens, Splinter, Timbers, Tremble

> **Shiver(ed)** may indicate an anagram

**Shoal** Bar, Fish, Quantity, Reef, Run, School, Shallows, Shelf, Tail

**Shock(er), Shocking** Agitate, Appal, Astound, Awhape, Bombshell, Brunt, Bunch, Consternate, Disgust, Dorlach, Dreadful, Drop, Earthquake, Egregious, Epiphenomenon, Fleg, Floccus, Gait, Galvanism, Hair, Horrify, Impact, Infamous, Jar, Jolt, Live, Mane, Mop, Outrage, Putrid, Recoil, Revolt, Rick(er), Scandal(ise), Seismic, Shaghaired, Shake, Sheaf, Shilling, Shook, Stagger, Start(le), Stitch, Stook, Stun, Trauma, Turn

**Shock-absorber** Buffer, Oleo, Snubber

> **Shocked** may indicate an anagram

**Shod** Calced

**Shoddy** Cagmag, Catchpenny, Cheapjack, Cheap, Cloth, Gimcrack, Imitation, Oorie, Ourie, Owrie, Ropy, Schlock, SHABBY, Tatty, Tawdry, Tinny

**Shoe** Arctic, Balmoral, Bauchle, Boot, Brogan, Brogue, Buskin, Calceate, Calk(er), Calkin, Casuals, Caulker, Cawker, Chopin(e), Clog, Creeper, Dap, Espadrille, Flattie, Galoche, Galosh, Ghillie, Golosh, Gumshoe, High-low, Hush-puppy, Kletterschue, Mocassin, Moccasin, Muil, Mule, Oxford, Oxonian, Panton, Patten, Peeptoe, Plate, Plimsole, Plimsoll, Poulaine, Pump, Rivlin, Rubbers, Rullion, Sabaton, Sabot, Sandal, Scarpetto, Skid, Slingback, Slipper, Sneaker, Sock, Solleret, Spike, Stoga, Stogy, Suede, Tie, Trainer, Upper, Vamper, Veld-schoen, Veldskoen, Vesskoen, Vibram, Vibs, Wedgie, Welt, Zori

**Shoeless** Barefoot, Discalced

**Shoemaker** Blacksmith, Cobbler, Cordiner, Cordwainer, Cosier, Cozier, Crispi(a)n, Leprechaun, Sacha, Snob, Soutar, Souter, Sowter, Sutor

**Shoe-string** Cheap, Lace, Pittance

**Shoe-toe** Poulaine

**Shoo** Away, Begone, Hoosh, Off, Scat(ter), Voetsek

**Shoot(er), Shooting** Ack-ack, Airgun, Arrow, Bine, Bostryx, Braird, Breer, Bud, Bulbil, Catapult, Chit, Cyme, Dart(le), Discharge, Drib, Elance, Eradiate, Film, Fire, Germ, Germain(e), Germen, Germin(ate), GUN, Gunsel, Head-reach, Imp, Layer, Limb, Pluff, Plug, Poot, Pop, Pot, Pout, Ramulus, Rapids, Ratoon, Riddle, Rod, Rove, Septembriser, Skeet, Snipe, Spire, Spirt, Spout, Spray, Sprout, Spurt, Spyre, Start, Stole, Stolon, Sucker, Tellar, Teller, Tendril, Tiller, Turion, Twelfth, Twig, Udo, Vimen, Wand, Weapon, Wildfowler

**Shop(s)** Atelier, Arcade, Betray, Boutique, Bucket, Buy, Chain, Closed, Co-op, Corner, Dairy, Delicatessen, Denounce, Emporium, Factory, Galleria, Inform, Lucken-booth, Mall, Market, Precinct, PX, Retail, RMA, Salon, Shebang, Store, Studio, Superette, Supermarket, Warehouse, Works

**Shopkeeper** British, Butcher, Chemist, Greengrocer, Grocer, Haberdasher, Hosier, Ironmonger, Merchant, Provisioner, Retailer, Stationer

**Shoplift(er)** Boost, Heist

**Shore** Bank, Beach, Buttress, Coast, Coste, Eustatic, Landfall, Littoral, Prop, Rance, Rivage, Seaboard, Strand, Support

**Short(en), Shortly** Abbreviate, Abridge, Abrupt, Anon, Apocope, Brief, Brusque, Commons, Compendious, Concise, Contract, Crisp, Cross, Curt, Curtail, Curtal, Diminish, Drink, Eftsoons, Epitomise, Ere-long, Inadequate, Lacking, Laconical, Light, Low, Mini, Near, Nip, Nutshell, Punch, Pyknic, Reduce, Reef, Scanty, Scarce, Shrift, Shy, Soon, Sparse, Spirit, Squab, Squat, Staccato, Stint, Stocky, Strapped, Stubby, Succinct,

Syncopate, Systole, Taciturn, Teen(s)y, Terse, Tight, Tot, Towards, Transient, Wee

**Shortage** Dearth, Deficit, Drought, Famine, Lack, Need, Paucity, Scarcity, Sparsity

**Short circuit** Varistor

**Shortcoming** Weakness

**Shorthand** Gregg, Outline, Pitman, Tachygraphy, Tironian, Triphone

**Short-headed** Brachycephal

**Short-lived** Ephemeral, Fragile, Meson, Transitory

**Shorts** Bermuda, Briefs, Culottes, Lederhosen, Plus-fours, Trunks

**Short-sight** Myopia, Myosis

**Short-winded** Breathless, Concise, Puffed, Purfled, Succinct

**Shot(s)** Aim, All-in, Ammo, Approach, Attempt, Ball, Barrage, Blank, Blast, Bull, Canna, Cartridge, Chatoyant, Chip, Crack, Dram, Exhausted, Gesse, Glance, Go, Grape, Guess, Gun-stone, Langrage, Langridge, Magpie, Marksman, Massé, Multi-coloured, Noddy, Parthian, Parting, Pelican, Pellet, Photo, Pop, Pot, Puff, Rid, Round, Salvo, Scratch, Shy, Sighter, Silk, Six, Slug, Sped, Spell, Spent, Stab, Still, Throw, Try, Turn, Volley

**Should** Ought

**Shoulder** Carry, Crossette, Epaule, Hump, Omoplate, Pick-a-back, Roadside, Scapula, Shouther, Spald, Spall, Spaul(d), Speal, Spule, Tote, Withers

**Shout(er), Shouting** Bawl, Boanerges, Call, Claim, Clamour, Cry, Exclaim, Heckle, Hey, Holler, Hollo, Hooch, Hosanna, Hue, Rah, Rant, Root, Round, Sa sa, Treat, Trumpet, Whoop, Yell(och), Yippee

**Shove** Barge, Birr, Elbow, Jostle, Push, Ram, Spoon, Thrust

**Shovel** Backhoe, Hat, Main, Peel, Scoop, Shool, Spade, Trowel, Van

**Show(ing), Shown, Showy** Anonyma, Appearance, Betray, Burlesque, Cabaret, Circus, Come, Con, Cruft's, Demonstrate, Depict, Diorama, Display, Do, Dressy, Endeictic, Epideictic, Establish, Evince, EXHIBIT, Expo, Extravaganza, Fair, Fangled, Farce, Flamboyant, Flash, Flaunt, Galanty, Garish, Gaudy, Gay, Give, Gloss, Indicate, Kismet, Loud, Manifest, Matinée, Meritricious, Musical, Naumachy, Ostensible, Ostentatious, Pageant, Pantomime, Parade, Performance, Phen(o), Point, Pomp, Portray, Pretence, Pride, Project, Prominence, Prove, Pseudery, Puff, Raree, Represent, Reveal, Revue, Screen, Sight, Sitcom, Slang, Soap, Specious, Spectacle, Splay, Stage, Stunt, Tamasha, Tattoo, Tawdry, Telethon, Theatrical, Uncover, Usher, Vain, Vaudeville, Veneer, Wear, Zarzuela

**Showdown** Confrontation, Crunch

**Shower** Douche, Exhibitor, Flurry, Indicant, Indicator, Party, Pelt, Pepper, Precipitation, Rain, Scat, Skit, Snow, Spat, Spet, Spit, Splatter, Spray, Sprinkle

> **Showers** may indicate an anagram

**Showgirl** Evita, Nanette

> **Showing, Shown in** may indicate a hidden word

**Showman** Bailey, Barnum, Goon, Lord Mayor, MC, Ringmaster

**Show-off** Exhibitionist, Extrovert, Sport, Swagger, Swank

**Showpiece** Flagship

**Show-place** Exhibition, Olympia, Pavilion, Theatre

**Shrapnel** Fragment, Shell, Splinter

**Shred** Clout, Filament, Grate, Mammock, Mince, Rag, Screed, Swarf, Tag, Ta(i)ver, Tatter, Thread, To-tear, Wisp

**Shrew** Bangsring, Banxring, Callet, Hellcat, Kate, Nag, Shrow, Solenodon, Sondeli, Sorex, Spitfire, Tana, Termagant, Trull, Tupaia, Virago, Vixen, Xant(h)ippe, Yankie

**Shrewd** Acute, Arch, Argute, Artful, Astucious, Astute, Callid, Canny, Cute, File, Gnostic, Gumptious, Judicious, Knowing, Politic, Sagacious, Sapient(al), Wily, Wise

**Shriek** Cry, Scream, Scrike, Shright, Shrike, Shrill, Shritch, Skirl, Yell

**Shrift** Attention, Penance

**Shrike** Bird, Butcher-bird

**Shrill** Argute, High, Keen, Reedy, Sharp, Treble

**Shrimp(s)** Krill, Midge, Potted, Prawn, Small, Squill(a), Stomatopod

**Shrine** Adytum, Altar, Delphi, Fatima, Feretory, Harem, Holy, Kaaba, Marabout, Naos, Pagoda, Reliquary, Scrine, Scryne, Stupa, Tabernacle, Temple, Tope, Vimana

**Shrink(ing), Shrunk** Alienist, Blanch, Blench, Cling, Constringe, Contract, Cour, Cower, Creep, Crine, Cringe, Dare, Decrew, Dwindle, Flinch, Funk, Gizzen, Less, Nirl, Psychiatrist, Quail, Recoil, Reduce, Sanforised, Shrivel, Shy, Sphacelate, Violet, Wince, Wizened

**Shrivel(led)** Cling, Desiccate, Nirl, Parch, Scorch, Scrump, Sear, Shrink, Skrimp, Skrump, Tabid, Welk, Wither

**Shroud(s)** Chuddah, Chuddar, Cloak, Cloud, Conceal, Cover, Grave-cloth, Rigging, Screen, Sheet, Sindon, Turin, Wrap

**Shrub** Aalii, Acacia, Alhagi, Andromeda, Arboret, Arbutus, Azalea, Barberry, Brere, Brush, Buaze, Buazi, Buckthorn, Buddleia, Bullace, BUSH, Caper, Cola, Cytisus, Epacris, Feijoa, Frutex, Fynbos, Gardenia, Garrya, Gorse, Hebe, Henna, Hop-tree, Horizontal, Jaborandi, Jasmine, Jessamine, Jojoba, Kat, Lantana, Laurustine, Lavender, Lignum, Manoao, Maqui(s), Matico, Monte, Myrica, Myrtle, Nabk, Ocotillo, Olea(cea), Patchouli, Pituri, Plant, Privet, Protea, Pyracantha, Qat, Rhatany, Rhododendron, Rhus, Romneya, Rue, Ruta, Salal, Savanna(h), Savin(e), Senna, Shallon, Skimmia, Spekboom, Supplejack, Tamarisk, Thyme, Titi, Tutu, Undergrowth, Wahoo, Waratah, Ya(u)pon, Yupon, Zamia

**Shrug**  Discard, Toss

**Shudder(ing)**  Abhor, Ashake, Grew, Grise, Grue, Jerk, Quake, Shake, Spasm, Tremble

**Shuffle**  Dodge, Drag, Hedge, Make, Mix, Palter, Riffle, Scuff, Shamble, Shauchle, Stack

**Shun**  Attention, Avoid, Eschew, Evade, Forbear, Ignore, Ostracise, Secede, SPURN

**Shunt**  Move, Shelve, Shuttle, Side-track

**Shut(s), Shut (down; in; out; up)**  Bar, Close, Confined, Coop, Debar, Embar, Emure, Fasten, Impale, Impound, Latch, Lay-off, Lock, Rid, Scram, Seal, Shet, Spar, Steek, Telescope, Tine, To

**Shutter(s)**  Blind, Dead-lights, Douser, Jalousie, Louvre, Shade

**Shuttle**  Alternate, Commute, Drawer, Flute, Go-between, Shoot, Shunt, Weave

**Shy**  Bashful, Blate, Blench, Cast, Catapult, Chary, Coy, Deficient, Demure, Farouche, Funk, Heave, Jerk, Jib, Laithfu', Lob, Mim, Rear, Recoil, Reserved, Sheepish, Shrinking, Skeigh, Start, Thraw, Throw, Timid, Toss, Try, Violet, Verecund, Willyard, Willyart

**Siamese**  Seal-point, T(h)ai

**Siberian**  Ostiak, Ostyak, Samo(y)ed, Tungus, Yakut

**Sibilant**  Hissing, Whistling

**Sibling**  Brother, Kin, Sister

**Sibyl**  Oracle, Prophetess, Seer, Soothsayer, Witch

**Sicilian**  Sicanian, Trinacrian

**Sick(en), Sickening, Sickly, Sickness**  Aegrotat, Affection, Ague, Ail, Bad, Cat, Chalky, Colic, Chunder, Crapulence, Crook, Delicate, Disorder, Donsie, Gag, Icky, Ill, Infection, Maid-pale, Mal, Mawkish, Morbid, Nauseous, Pale, Peaky, Pestilent, Plague, Puly, Puna, Queachy, Queasy, Queechy, Regorge, Repulsive, Retch, Shilpit, Soroche, Spue, Squeamish, Twee, Valetudinarian, Virus, Vomit, Wamble-cropped, Wan

**Sick bay**  San

**Sickle(-shaped)**  Falx, Hook, Scythe

**Side**  Abeam, Airs, Beam, Border, Camp, Distaff, Edge, Effect, Eleven, English, Facet, Flank, Gunnel, Hand, Iliac, Lateral, Left, Off, On, OP, Pane, Part, Partisan, Party, Port, Profile, Rave, Reveal, Right, Silver, Slip, Spear, Starboard, Swank, TEAM, Wing, XI

**Sideboard(s)**  Beauf(f)et, Buffet, Cellaret, Commode, Credence, Credenza, Dresser, Whiskers

**Side-issue**  Offshoot, Secondary

**Side-line**  Hobby, Lye, Siding, Spur

**Side-step**  Crab, Dodge, Evade, Hedge, Volt

**Side-track**  Distract, Divert, Shunt

**Sidewalk**  Crab, Footpath, Pavement

**Sideways**  Askance, Indirect, Laterally, Laterigrade, Oblique

**Siding**  Alliance, Byway, Lie, Lye, Spur

**Sidle**  Edge, Passage

**Siege (work)**  Alamo, Beleaguer, Beset, Blockade, Gherao, Investment, Ladysmith, Leaguer, Obsidional, Perilous, Poliorcetic, Ravelin, Surround

**Siesta**  Nap, Noonday, Nooning

**Sieve, Sift(ing)**  Analyse, Bolt(er), Boult(er), Bunting, Colander, Cribble, Cribrate, Cribrose, Cullender, Eratosthenes, Ethmoid, Filter, Riddle, Screen, Searce, Separate, Strain, Sye, Tamis, Tammy, Tems(e), Trommel, Try

**Sigh**  Exhale, Heave, Lackaday, Long, Moan, Sough, Suspire, Welladay

**Sight(ed)**  Aim, Barleycorn, Bead, Conspectuity, Eye(ful), Eyesore, Glimpse, Ken, Oculated, Prospect, Range, Scene, Second, See, Spectacle, Taish, Vane, VIEW, Visie, Vision, Vista

**Sight-screen**  Eyelid

**Sightseer, Sightseeing**  Lionise, Observer, Rubberneck, Tourist, Tripper, Viewer

**Sign**  Ache, Ale-stake, Ampassy, Ampersand, Aquarius, Archer, Aries, Arrow, Auspice, Autograph, Badge, Balance, Beck, Brand, Bull, Bush, Cancer, Capricorn, Caract, Caret, Chevron, Clue, Coronis, Crab, Cross, Cue, Diacritic, Di(a)eresis, Diphone, DS, Earmark, Emblem, Endeixis, Endorse, Endoss, Enlist, Evidence, Exit, Fascia, Fish, Gemini, Gesture, Goat, Grammalogue, Hallmark, Hamza(h), Harbinger, Hieroglyphic, Hint, Ideogram, Indicate, Indication, Initial, Inscribe, Leo, Libra, Logogram, Neume, Notice, Obelisk, Obelus, Omen, Pisces, Presage, Prodromus, Ram, Rest, Sagittarius, Sain, Scorpio, Segno, Semeion, Shingle, Show, Sigil, Sigla, Signal, Subscribe, Superscribe, Symbol, Syndrome, Tag, Taurus, Tic(k)tac(k), Tilde, Token, Trace, Twins, Umlaut, Virgo, Warning, Waymark, Word, Zodiac

**Signal(ler)**  Alarm, Aldis lamp, Amber, Assemble, Baud, Beacon, Bell, Bleep, Bugle, Buzz, Chamado, Compander, Compandor, Cone, Cue, Detonator, Diaphone, Distress, Earcon, Flag, Flare, Flash, Gantry, Gesticulate, Gong, Griffin, Gun, Herald, Hooter, Horse and hattock, Icon, Important, Mark, Mase, Megafog, Message, Modem, Morse, Notation, Noted, Output, Password, Peter, Pip, Pulsar, Radio, Renowned, Reveille, Robot, Salient, Semaphore, Semiology, Singular, Smoke, SOS, Taps, Target, Tchick, Telegraph, Teles(e)me, Thumb, Tic(k)-tac(k), Troop, Video, Very, Waff, Waft, Wave, Wigwag

**Signature**  Autograph, By-line, Hand, Mark, Specimen

**Signet**  Ring, Seal, Sigil

**Significance, Significant**  Cardinal, Consequence, Emblem, Impact, Important, Indicative, Matter, Meaningful, Moment(ous), Noted, Pith, Pregnant, Salient, Special, Telling

**Signify** Bemean, Denote, Imply, Indicate, Intimate, Matter, MEAN, Represent

**Sign language** Ameslan, Semaphore, Tic(k)tac(k)

**Sikh** Khalsa, Mazhbi

**Silas** Uncle, Wegg

**Silence(r), Silent** Amyclaean, Clam, Clamour, Conticent, Gag, Hist, Hush, Mim(budget), Mumchance, Mute, Obmutescent, Quench, QUIET, Reticence, Shtoom, Shush, Speechless, Still, Sulky, Tace(t), Tacit(urn), Throttle, Whis(h)t

**Silhouette** Contour, Outline, Profile, Shape, Skyline

**Silica(te)** Albite, Analcite, Chabazite, Chert, Cristobalite, Datolite, Dioptase, Humite, Kyanite, Opal, Saponite, Scapolite, Silex, Staurolite, Tridymite, Tripoli, Zeolite

**Silicon** Chip, Si

**Silk(y)** Alamode, Atlas, Barathea, Brocade, Bur(r), Charmeuse, Chenille, Chiffon, Cocoon, Dupion, Faille, Filoselle, Florence, Flosh, Floss, Flox, Foulard, Georgette, Gimp, Glossy, KC, Kincob, Lustrine, Lustring, Lutestring, Makimono, Marabou(t), Matelasse, Mercery, Ninon, Organza, Ottoman, Paduasoy, Parachute, Peaudesoie, Pongee, Prunella, Prunelle, Prunello, Pulu, Samite, Sars(e)net, Satin, Schappe, Sendal, Seric, Shalli, Shantung, Sien-tsan, Sleave, Sle(i)ded, Sleek, Smooth, Surah, Tabaret, Tabby, Taffeta, Tasar, Tiffany, Tram, Tulle, Tussah, Tusser, Tussore, Velvet

**Silkworm (eggs)** Bombyx, Eria, Graine, Sericulture

**Sill** Ledge, Threshold

**Silly, Silliness** Absurd, Anserine, Brainless, Buffer, Crass, Cuckoo, Daft, Dumb, Fatuous, Folly, Fool, Footling, Frivolous, Goopy, Gormless, Idiotic, Imbecile, Inane, Incpt, Infield(er), Liminal, Mopoke, Puerile, Season, Simple, Spoony, STUPID, Tripe

> **Silly** may indicate relating to a sill

**Silt** Alluvium, Deposit, Dregs, Land, Lees, Residue, Sullage, Varve

**Silver(skin)** Ag, Albata, Arg(ent), Argyria, Cardecue, Cerargyrite, Grey, Lunar, One-legged, Paktong, Pegleg, Piastre, Plate, Plateresque, Stephanite, Sterling, Sycee, Thaler

> **Silver** may indicate a coin

**Silversmith** Demetrius, Lamerie, Plater

**Simian** Apelike, Catar(r)hine

**Similar(ity)** Analog(ue), Analogical, Corresponding, Etc, Equivalent, Homonym, Kindred, LIKE, Parallel, Resemblance

**Simmer** Bubble, Seethe, Stew

**Simon** Bolivar, Cellarer, Magus, Peter, Pure, Simple

**Simper** Bridle, Giggle, Smirk

**Simple(r), Simplicity, Simply** Aefa(u)ld, Afa(w)ld, Arcadian, Artless,

Austere, Bald, Basic, Crude, Doddle, Doric, EASY, Eath(e), Elegant, ESN, Ethe, Fee, Folksy, Gomeral, Gotham, Green, Herb(alist), Herborist, Homespun, Incomposite, Inornate, Jaap, Japie, Mere, Moner(on), Naive(té), Naked, Niaiserie, One-fold, Ordinary, Pastoral, Peter, Plain, Pleon, Pure, Saikless, Semplice, Sheer, Silly, Simon, Spartan, Stupid

**Simpleton** Abderite, Cokes, Cuckoo, Duffer, Flat, Fool, Gomeral, Gomeril, Greenhorn, Juggins, Spoon, STUPID PERSON, Wiseacre, Zany

**Simulate, Simulating** Affect, Anti, Feign, Pretend

**Simultaneous** Coinstantaneous, Contemporaneous, Together

**Sin** Aberrant, Accidie, Acedia, Anger, Avarice, Bigamy, Covetousness, Crime, Deadly, Debt, Envy, Err, Folly, Gluttony, Harm, Hate, Lapse, Lust, Misdeed, Misdoing, Mortal, OFFENCE, Original, Peccadillo, Pride, Scape, Sine, Sloth, Transgress, Trespass, Venial, Vice, Wrath

**Sinai** Horeb, Mount

**Since** Ago, As, Meantime, Seeing, Sens, Sinsyne, Sith(en), Whereas

**Sincere(ly), Sincerity** Bona-fide, Candour, Earnest, Entire, Frank, Genuine, Heartfelt, Honest, Open, Real(ly), True, Verity

**Sinclair** Lewis, Upton

**Sinecure** Bludge, Commendam

**Sinew** Fibre, Ligament, Nerve, String, Tendon

**Sinful** Evil, Impious, Scarlet, Unrighteous, Wicked, Wrong

**Sing(ing)** Bel canto, Carol, Chant, Cheep, Chorus, Croon, Crow, Hum, Inform, Intone, Karaoke, Lilt, Pen(n)illion, Pipe, Rand, Rant, Scat, Tell, Thrum, Trill, Troll, Vocalese, Warble, Yodel

**Singe** Burn, Char, Scorch

**Singer** Alto, Bard, Baritone, Bass, Bird, Callas, Canary, Cantabank, Cantatrice, Cantor, Car, Caruso, Castrato, Chaliapin, Chanteuse, Chazan, Chorister, Comprimario, Crooner, Dawson, Diva, Dylan, Ella, Falsetto, Gleemaiden, Gleeman, Kettle, Lark, Lauder, Lead, Lind, Lorelei, Lulu, Mathis, Melba, Minstrel, Oscine, Patti, Pitti, Robeson, Sinatra, Siren, Songstress, Soprano, Soubrette, Succentor, Swan, Tatiana, Tenor, Torch, Treble, Vocalist, Voice, Wait, Warbler

**Single** Ace, Aefa(u)ld, Aefawld, Alone, Bachelor, Celibate, Discriminate, EP, Exclusive, Matchless, Monact, Mono, Odd, Only, Pick, Run, Sole, Solitary, Spinster, Uncoupled, Unique, Unwed, Versal, Yin

**Single-cell** Protista

**Single-chambered** Monothalamous

**Singlestick** Sword

**Singlet** Tunic, Vest

**Singular** Curious, Especial, Exceptional, Extraordinary, Ferly, Odd, Once, One, Peculiar, Queer(er), Rare, UNIQUE, Unusual

**Singultus** Hiccup

**Sinister** Bend, Dark, Dirke, Evil, L, Left, Lh, Louche, OMINOUS

**Sink(ing), Sunken** Basin, Bog, Cower, Depress, Descend, Devall, Dip, Down, Drain, Drink, Drop, Drown, Ebb, Flag, Founder, Gravitate, Hole, Immerse, Invest, Jawbox, Lagan, Ligan, Merger, Pot, Prolapse, Put(t), Relapse, Sag, Scupper, Scuttle, Set, Settle, Steep-to, Sty, Submerge, Subside, Swag, Swamp

**Sinner** Evildoer, Malefactor, Offender, Reprobate, Trespasser

**Sinuous** Curvy, Snaky, Wavy, Winding

**Sinus** Cavity, Recess

**Sip(ping)** Delibate, Haporth, Libant, Sample, Sowp, Sup, Taste, Tiff(ing)

**Siphon** Draw, Suck, Transfer

**Sir** Dan, Dom, K, Kt, Lord(ing), Sahib, Signor, Sirrah, Stir, Stirra(h), Tuan

**Sire** Beget, Father

**Siren** Alarm, Diaphone, Hooter, Houri, Leucosia, Ligea, Lorelei, Mermaid, Oceanides, Parthenope, Salamander, Teaser, Temptress, Vamp

**Sirenian** Dugong, Lamantin, Manatee, Manati

**Sirloin** Backsey

**Sirree** Bo

**Sisal** Agave

**Siskin** Aberdevine, Bird, Finch

**Sister** Anne, Beguine, Minim, NUN, Nurse, Religeuse, Sib, Sis, Sob, Swallow, Titty, Ursuline, Verse

**Sisyphean** Uphill

**Sit(ter), Sitting** Bestride, Clutch, Dharna, Duck, Gaper, Lit de justice, Model, MP, Perch, Pose, Reign, Represent, Roost, Séance, Sejant, Session, Squat

**Site** Area, Location, Lot, Pad, Place, Plot, Silo, Spot, Stance

**Situation** Berth, Cart, Case, Catch, Cliff-hanger, Cow, Galère, Hole, Job, Lie, Niche, Office, Position, Post, Set-up, Status quo, Strait, Where

**Six(th)** Digamma, Hexad, Senary, Sestette, Sextet, Sice, Size, Vau, VI

**Six counties** NI

**Six days** Hexameron

**Six feet** Fathom

**Sixpence** Bender, Kick, Slipper, Tanner, Tester(n), Testril(l), Tizzy, VID, VIP, Zack

**Sixteen** Sweet

**Sixty** Degree, Threescore

**Size(able)** Amplitude, Area, Bulk, Calibre, Countess, Demy, EXTENT, Format, Girth, Glair, Glue, Imperial, Measure, Pot(t), Princess, Proportion, Tempera, Tidy

**Sizzle** Fry, Hiss, Scorch

**Skate(r), Skating** Blade, Choctaw, Cousins, Curry, Dean, Orser, Fish,

Maid, Mohawk, Rocker, Roller, Runner

**Skedaddle** Shoo, Vamoose

**Skein** Hank, Hasp

**Skeleton, Skeletal** Anatomy, Atomy, Bones, Cadre, Cage, Corallum, Framework, Key, Ossify, Outline, Scenario, Sclere

**Sketch** Cameo, Charade, Croquis, Diagram, Draft, DRAW, Ebauche, Limn, Maquette, Modello, Outline, Playlet, Précis, Profile, Summary, Thumbnail, Trick, Vignette, Visual

**Skew** Oblique, Sheer, Squint, Swerve, Veer

**Skewer** Brochette, Prong, Spit, Transfix

**Ski(ing)** Glide, Glissade, Hot-dog, Langlauf, Nordic, Schuss, Telemark, Wedeln

**Skid** Jackknife, Side-slip, Slew, Slide, Slip, Slither

> **Skidding** may indicate an anagram

**Skiff** Canoe, Dinghy, Outrigger

**Skill(ed), Skilful** Ability, Able, Ace, Adept, Address, Adroit, Art, Canny, Chic, Competence, Craft, Deacon, Deft, Dextrous, Expertise, Feat, Finesse, Flair, Gleg, Hand, Handicraft, Handy, Hend, Hot, Ingenious, Knack, Know-how, Knowing, Lear(e), Leir, Lere, Masterly, Mean, Mistery, Mystery, Mystique, Practised, Prowess, Resource, Savvy, Science, Skeely, Sleight, Touch, Trade, Trick, Versed, Virtuoso

**Skim** Cream, Despumate, Flit, Glide, Ream, Scan, Scud, Scum, Skiff, Skitter ,

**Skimp** Restrict, Scamp, Scrimp, Stint

**Skin(s)** Agnail, Bark, Basan, Basil, Box-calf, Calf, Callus, Case, Chevrette, Coat, Corium, Cortex, Cuticle, Cutis, Deacon, Derm(a), Dermis, Dewlap, Disbark, Ectoderm, Enderon, Epicanthus, Epicarp, Epidermis, Eschar, Excoriate, Exterior, Fell, Film, Flaught, Flay, Flench, Flinch, Forel, Hide, Kip, Kirbeh, Leather, Membrane, Nebris, Pachyderm, Parfleche, Peel, Pell, Pellicle, Pelt, Plew, Plu(e), Prepuce, Pteryla, Rack, Rind, Serosa, Shell, Shoder, Spetch, Strip, Tulchan, Veneer, Water-bouget

**Skin disease, Skin trouble** Boba, Boil, Buba, Chloasma, Chloracne, Cyanosis, Dartre, Dermatitis, Dyschroa, Ecthyma, Erysipelas, Exanthem(a), Favus, Flay, Framboesia, Herpes, Hives, Ichthyosis, Impetigo, Mal del pinto, Mange, Miliaria, Morula, Pemphigus, Pinta, Pityriasis, Prurigo, Psoriasis, Rash, Ringworm, Rosacea, Rose-rash, Sclerodermia, Scurvy, Serpigo, Strophillus, Tetter, Tinea, Verruca, Verruga, Vitiligo, Xanthoma, Yaws, Yawy

**Skinflint** Dryfist, Miser, Niggard, Pinch-gut, Scrooge, Tightwad

**Skinful** Drunk, Sausage

**Skinhead** Not, Punk, Scalp

**Skink** Seps

**Skinny** Barebone, Bony, Dermal, Emaciate, Lean, Scraggy, Thin, Weed

**Skint**  Broke, Ghat, Penniless, Stony

**Skip(ped), Skipper**  Boss, Caper, Captain, Drakestone, Elater, Frisk, Hesperian, Jump, Jumping-mouse, Lamb, Luppen, Miss, Omit, Patroon, Ricochet, Saury, Scombresox, Spring, Tittup, Trounce(r)

**Skirl**  Humdudgeon, Pibroch, Pipe, Screigh

**Skirmish**  Brush, Dispute, Escarmouche, Fray, Pickeer, Spar, Velitation

**Skirt(ing)**  Bases, Border, Cheongsam, Circle, Coat, Crinoline, Culotte(s), Dado, Dirndl, Edge, Fringe, Fustanella, Fustanelle, Girl, Gore, Harem, Hobble, Hoop, Hug, Kilt, Lamboys, Lava-lava, Marge, Mini, Pareo, Pareu, Peplum, Plinth, Ra-ra, Rim, Sarong, Sidestep, Tace, Tail, Taslet, Tasse(t), Tonlet, Tutu

**Skit**  Lampoon, Parody, Sketch

**Skittish**  Curvetting, Frisky, Restless

**Skittle(s)**  Bayle, Bowl, Kail(s), Kingpin, Ninepin, Pin, Spare

**Skive**  Scrimshank, Shirk

**Skivvy**  Drudge, Slave

**Skrimshank**  Bludge, Skive

**Skulk**  Lurk, Mooch, Shool

**Skull**  Bregma(ta), Calvaria, Cranium, Head, Malar, Pannikell, Scalp

**Skullcap**  Ya(r)mulka, Yarmulke, Zucchetto

**Skunk**  Atoc, Atok, Polecat, Teledu, Zoril(lo)

**Sky(-high)**  Air, Azure, Blue, Canopy, Carry, E-layer, Element, Ether, Firmament, Heaven, Lift, Loft, Mackerel, Occident, Octa, Welkin

**Sky-diver**  Para

**Skylark**  Aerobatics, Bird

**Skylight**  Abat-jour, Aurora, Comet, Lunette, Star

**Skyline**  Horizon, Rooftops

**Sky-pilot**  Chaplain, Vicar

**Slab**  Briquette, Cake, Chunk, Dalle, Hawk, Ledger, Marver, Metope, Mihrab, Mud, Plank, Sclate, Sheave, Slate, Slice, Stela, Stelene, Tab, Tile

**Slack(en), Slackness**  Abate, Careless, Crank, Dilatory, Dross, Ease, Easy-going, Idle, Lax(ity), Loose, Malinger, Relax, Release, Remiss, Shirk, Slow, Surge, Veer

**Slag**  Calx, Cinder, Dross, Scoria, Sinter

**Slake**  Abate, Cool, Quench, Refresh, Satisfy

**Slam**  Crash, Criticise, Dad, Grand, Pan(dy), Sock, Swap, Swop, Vole, Wap

**Slander(ous)**  Asperse, Backbite, Calumny, Defame, Derogatory, Disparage, Libel, Malediction, Malign, Missay, Mud, Sclaunder, Smear, Traduce, Vilify, Vilipend

**Slang**  Abuse, Argot, Berate, Cant, Colloquial, Flash, Jargon, Lingo, Nadsat, Slate, Zowie

**Slant(ing)**  Angle, Asklent, Atilt, Bevel, Bias, Brae, Cant, Careen, Chamfer, Clinamen, Diagonal, Escarp, Oblique, Prejudice, Slew, SLOPE, Splay, Talus, Tilt, Virgule

**Slap**  Clatch, Clout, Cuff, Pandy, Sclaff, Scud, Skelp, Smack, Spat, Twank

**Slapdash**  Careless, Hurried, Random

**Slash(ed)**  Chive, Cut, Gash, Jag, Laciniate, Leak, Oblique, Rash, Rast, Reduce, Scorch, Scotch, Slit, Solidus, Wee

**Slat(s)**  Fish, Jalousie, Louvre

**Slate, Slaty**  Cam, Countess, Credit, Criticise, Decry, Double, Duchess, Duchy, Enter, Griseous, Imperial, Killas, Knotenschiefer, Lady, Pan, Peggy, Princess, Queen, Rag(g), Shingle, Slat, Small

**Slater**  Hellier, Insect

**Slattern**  Bag, Besom, Drab, Drazel, Frump, Mopsy, Sloven, Slummock, Traipse, Trapes, Trollop

**Slaughter(house)**  Abattoir, Bleed, Bloodshed, Butcher, Carnage, Decimate, Hal(l)al, Holocaust, Kill, MASSACRE, Sc(h)ehita(h), Scupper, Shambles, Shechita(h), Smite

**Slav**  Bohunk, Croat, Czech, Kulak, Polabian, Serb, Sorb, Wend(ic)

**Slave(ry), Slaves**  Addict, Aesop, Aida, Androcles, Barracoon, Blackbird, Bond, Bond(s)man, Bondswoman, Bordar, Boy, Caliban, Coffle, Contraband, Drudge, Drug, Dulocracy, Esne, Galley, Gibeonite, Helot, Hierodule, Mameluke, Maroon, Minion, Odali(s)que, Odalisk, Peasant, Pr(a)edial, Rhodope, Serf, Spartacus, Terence, Theow, Thersites, Thete, Thrall, Topsy, Vassal, Villein, Yoke

**Slave-owner**  Assam

**Slaver**  Dribble, Drivel, Drool, Slobber, Spawl

**Slay(er), Slaying**  Destroy, Execute, Ghazi, KILL, Mactation, Murder, Quell, Slaughter, Saul

**Sleazy**  Flimsy, Seamy, Sordid, Squalid, Thin

**Sled(ge), Sleigh**  Bob, Dray, Hurdle, Kibitka, Komatik, Luge, Polack, Pulk(h)(a), Pung, Skidoo, Slipe, Stoneboat, Toboggan

**Sleek**  Bright, Shine, Silky, Smooth, Smug

**Sleep(er), Sleeping, Sleepy**  Beauty, Bed, Bivouac, Blet, Car, Catnap, Coma, Crash, Cross-sill, Cross-tie, Dormant, Dormient, Doss, Doze, Drowse, Endymion, Epimenides, Gum, Hibernate, Hypnos, Kip, Lethargic, Lie, Morpheus, Nap, Nod, Over, Petal, Repose, Rest, Rip Van Winkle, Sandman, Shuteye, Skipper, Sloom, Slumber, Somnolent, Snooze, Sopor(ose), Sownd, Tie, Torpid, Twilight, Wink, Zizz

**Sleeping place**  Bed, Cot, Dormitory, Kang

**Sleepless**  Wake-rife, Wauk-rife

**Sleet**  Graupel, Hail

**Sleeve (opening)**  Armhole, Batwing, Bush, Collet, Cover, Gigot, Liner, Magyar, Manche, Querpo, Raglan, Sabot, Scye, Slashed

> **Sleigh**   see SLED

**Sleight**   Artifice, Conjury, Cunning, Dodge, Legerdemain, Trick

**Slender(ness)**   Asthenic, Exiguity, Fine, Flimsy, Gracile, Jimp, Skinny, Slight, Slim, Spindly, Svelte, Sylph, Tenuous

**Sleuth**   Bloodhound, Detective, Dick, Eye, Lyam(-hound), Lime-hound, Lyme(-hound)

**Slew**   Number, Skid, Slide, Twist

**Slice**   Cantle, Chip, Collop, Cut, Doorstep, Fade, Piece, Rasure, Round, Sector, Segment, Share, Sheave, Shive, Slab, Sliver, Tranche, Wafer, Whang

> **Slice of**   may indicate a hidden word

**Slick**   Glim, Oil, Smooth, Suave

**Slide**   Chute, Cursor, Drift, Glissando, Hirsle, Ice-run, Illapse, Lantern, Mount, Pulka, Schuss, Skid, Skite, Slip, Slither, Transparency

**Slight(ly)**   Affront, Belittle, Cut, Disparage, Disregard, Flimsy, Halfway, Neglect, Nominal, Pet, Petty, Rebuff, Remote, SLENDER, Slim, Slur, Small, Snub, Superficial, Thin, Tiny

**Slim**   Jimp, Macerate, Reduce, Slender, Slight, Sylph, Thin

**Slime, Slimy**   Glit, Mother, Mucous, Oily, Ooze, Sapropel, Slake, Sludge, Uliginous

**Sling**   Balista, Catapult, Drink, Fling, Hang, Parbuckle, Support, Toss, Trebuchet

**Slink**   Lurk, Skulk, Slope

**Slip(ped), Slipping, Slips**   Boner, Cutting, Disc, Docket, Drift, EE, Elapse, Elt, Engobe, Error, Fielder, Form, Freudian, Glide, Glissade, Label, Landslide, Lapse, Lath, Lauwine, Mistake, Muff, Nod, Oversight, Parapraxis, Petticoat, Ptosis, Relapse, Run, Scape, Sc(h)edule, Scoot, Set, Shim, Sin, Ski, Skid, Skin, Slade, Slidder, Slide, Slither, Slive, Spillican, Stumble, Ticket, Trip, Underskirt, Unleash

**Slipper**   Baboosh, Babouche, Babuche, Calceolate, Eel, Mocassin, Moccasin, Moyl, Mule, Pabouche, Pampootie, Pantable, Pantof(f)le, Panton, Pantoufle, Pump, Rullion, Runner, Ski, Sledge, Sneaker, Sock

**Slippery**   Glid, Icy, Lubric, Shifty, Slick

**Slipshod**   Careless, Hurried, Jerry, Lax, Slapdash, Sloppy, Toboggan

> **Slipshod**   may indicate an anagram

**Slit**   Cut, Cranny, Fent, Fissure, Gash, Loop, Pertus(at)e, Placket, Race, Rit, Spare, Speld(er), Vent

**Slithy**   Tove

**Sliver**   Flake, Fragment, Moslings, Rove, Shaving, Slice, Splinter, Trace

**Slob(ber)**   Drool, Slaver, Smarm, Wet

**Sloe**   Blackthorn, Slae

**Slog(ger)**   Drag, Strike, Swot, Traipse, Tramp, Trape, Trudge, Yacker,

Yakka, Yakker

**Slogan** Byword, Catchword, Mot(to), Phrase, Rallying-cry, Slughorn(e), Warcry, Watchword

**Sloop** Cutter, Hoy, Ship

**Slop(s)** Cop(per), Gardyloo, Jordeloo, Muck, Policeman, Rossers, Rozzers, Schmaltz, Sop, Spill, Swill

**Slope(s)** Acclivity, Angle, Bahada, Bajada, Bank, Batter, Bevel, Borrow, Borstal(l), Brae, Chamfer, Cuesta, Declivity, Diagonal, Fla(u)nch, Glacis, Grade, Gradient, Heel, Hill, Incline, Lean, Nursery, Oblique, Pent, Pitch, Rake, Ramp, Scarp, Schuss, Scrae, Scree, Shelve, Sideling, Slant, Slippery, Slipway, Splay, Steep, Talus, Tilt, Verge, Versant, Weather

**Sloppily, Sloppy** Lagrimoso, Lowse, Madid, Mushy, Slapdash, Slipshod, Sloven, Slushy, Untidy

> **Sloppy** may indicate an anagram

**Slosh(y)** Dowse, Fist, Splash, Wet

**Slot(ted)** Groove, Hasp, Hesp, Hole, Key, Mortice, Mortise, Seat, Slit, Swanmark

**Sloth(ful)** Accidie, Acedia, Ai, Edentate, Idle, Inaction, Indolent, Inertia, Lazy, Lie-abed, Megatherium, Mylodon, Slugabed, Sweer(t), Sweered, Sweir(t), Unau

**Slouch** Mooch, Mope, Slump

**Slough(ing)** Cast, Despond, Ecdysis, Eschar, Exuviae, Lerna, Marsh, Morass, Shed, Shuck, Swamp

**Sloven(ly)** Careless, D(r)aggle-tail, Grobian, Jack-hasty, Ratbag, Slaister, Slammakin, Slammerkin, Slattern, Sleazy, Slipshod, Slubberdegullion, Slubberingly, Untidy

**Slow(ing), Slowly** Adagio, Andante, Brady, Brake, Broad, Calando, Crawl, Dawdle, Deliberate, Dilatory, Dull, Dumka, ESN, Flag, Gradual, Inchmeal, Lag, Langram, Larghetto, Largo, Lash, Lassu, Late, Leisurely, Lentando, Lento, Lifeless, Loiter, Obtuse, Pedetentous, Rall(entando), Rein, Reluctant, Retard, Ribattuta, Slack, Slug, Sluggish, Snaily, Solid, Stem, Tardigrade, Tardive, Tardy

**Slow-match** Portfire

**Sludge** Gunge, Mire, Muck, Sapropel

**Slug(s)** Ammo, Bullet, Cosh, Drink, Limaces, Limax, Linotype, Mollusc, Nerita, Shot, Snail, Trepang

**Sluggard** Bêche-de-mer, Drone, Lazy, Lie-abed, Lusk, Unau

**Sluggish** Dilatory, Drumble, Inert, Jacent, Laesie, Languid, Lazy, Lentor, Lethargic, Lug, Phlegmatic, Saturnine, Sleepy, SLOW, Stagnant, Tardy, Torpid, Unalive

**Sluice** Aboideau, Aboiteau, Drain, Gutter, Koker, Penstock, Rinse, Sasse

**Slum** Ghetto, Rookery, Shanty, Slurb, Warren

**Slumber** Doze, Drowse, Nap, Nod, Sleep, Sloom, Snooze

**Slump** Decrease, Depression, Dip, Flop, Recession, Sink, Slouch

**Slur(ring)** Defame, Drawl, Opprobrium, Slight, Smear, Synaeresis, Tie

**Slush** Bathos, Boodle, Bribe, Drip, Money, Mush, Pap, Slop, Sposh, Swash

**Slut** Dollymop, Draggle-tail, Dratchell, Drazel, Floosie, Harlot, Slattern, Sow, Tart, Traipse, Trapes, Trollop

**Sly** Christopher, Coon, Covert, Cunning, Foxy, Leery, Peery, Reynard, Stealthy, Subtle, Tinker, Tod, Tricky, Weasel, Wily

> **Slyly** may indicate an anagram

**Smack(er)** Buss, Cuff, Flavour, Foretaste, Fragrance, Hooker, Kiss, Lander, Lips, Pra(h)u, Relish, Salt, Saut, Skelp, Slap, Slat, Smatch, Smouch, Soupçon, Spank, Spice, Tack, TANG, Taste, Thwack, Tincture, Trace, X

**Small (thing)** Ateleiosis, Atom, Bantam, Beer, Centesimal, Curn, Denier, Drib, Elfin, Fry, Grain, Haet, Ha'it, Handful, Holding, Ion, Leet, Limited, Lite, LITTLE, Low, Meagre, Midget, Miniature, Minikin, Minute, Mite, Modest, Modicum, Peerie, Petit(e), Petty, Pigmean, Pigmy, Pittance, Pocket, Poujadist, Rap, Reduction, Runt, Santilla, Scrump, Scrunt, Scut, Shrimp, Skerrick, Slight, Slim, Smidge(o)n, Smidgin, Soupçon, Spud, Stim, Stunted, Tad, Thin, Tidd(l)y, Tiny, Tittle, Tot(tie), Totty, Trace, Trivial, Unheroic, Wee, Whit

**Smallest** Least, Minimal

**Smallholder, Smallholding** Croft, Nursery, Rundale, Share-cropper, Stead

**Small-minded(ness)** Parvanimity, Petty

**Smallness** Exiguity, Paucity

**Smallpox** Alastrim, Variola

**Smarm** Oil

**Smart(en), Smartest** Ache, Acute, Alec, Astute, Best, Bite, Chic, Classy, Clever, Cute, Dandy, Dapper, Dressy, Elegant, Flash, Flip, Groom, Natty, Neat, Nifty, Nip, Nobby, Posh, Preen, Prink, Pusser, Ritzy, Slick, Sly, Smoke, Smug, Snappy, Spiff, Sprauncy, Sprightly, Spruce, Sprush, Spry, Sting, Swish, Tiddley, Tippy, Titivate, U

**Smash(ed), Smasher, Smashing** Atom, Brain, Break, Crush, Demolish, Devastate, Dish, Kaput, Kill, Lulu, Shatter, Shiver, Slam, Squabash, Super, Terrific, Tight, To-brake, WRECK

**Smear** Assoil, Besmirch, Blur, Clam, Daub, Defile, Denigrate, Discredit, Drabble, Enarm, Gaum, Gorm, Lick, Pay, Plaster, Slairg, Slaister, Slather, Slime, Slubber, Slur, Smalm, Smarm, Smudge, Sully, Teer, Traduce, Wax

**Smell(y)** Aroma, Asafoetida, BO, Caproate, Fetor, F(o)etid, Fug, Gale, Gamy, Hing, Honk, Hum, Mephitis, Miasm(a), Musk, Nidor, Niff, Nose, Odour, Olent, Olfact(ory), Perfume, Pong, Ponk, Rank, Reek, Sar, Savour, SCENT, Sniff, Snook, Steam, Stench, Stifle, Stink, Tang, Whiff

**Smelt(ing)** Atherinidae, Melt, Salmon, Scoria, Speiss

**Smile(s), Smiling** Agrin, Beam, Cheese, Favour, Gioconda, Grin, Rictus, Self-help, Simper, Smirk

**Smirk** Grimace, Simper

**Smite, Smitten** Assail, Enamoured, Hit, Strike, Strook

**Smith** Adam, Farrier, FE, Forger, Mighty, Stan, Wayland

**Smithy** Forge, Smiddy

**Smock** Blouse, Chemise, Drabbet, Gather, Shift, Smicket

**Smoke(r), Smoky** Blast, Bloat, Censer, Chillum, Cure, Fog, Fuliginous, Fume, Funk, Gasper, Hemp, Incense, Indian hemp, Inhale, Kipper, Latakia, Lum, Lunt, Manil(l)a, Nicotian, Pother, Pudder, Puff, Reech, Reek, Reest, Roke, Smeech, Smeek, Smoor, Smoulder, Smudge, Snout, Vapour, Viper, Whiff

**Smoke-hating** Misocapnic

**Smoking-room** Divan

**Smollett** Tobias

> **Smooch** see SMOUCH

**Smooth(e), Smoother, Smoothly** Bland, Brent, Buff, Clean, Clockwork, Dress, Dub, Easy, Even, Fettle, File, Flat, Fluent, Glassy, Glib, Goose, Iron, Legato, Level, Levigate, Mellifluous, Oil, Plane, Rake, Roll, Rub, Sleek, Slick, Slur, Smug, Snod, Sostenuto, Suave, Swimmingly, Terete, Terse, Trim, Urbane

**Smooth-haired** Lissotrichous

**Smother** Burke, Choke, Muffle, Oppress, Overlie, Smore, Stifle, Suppress

**Smouch** Cheat, Kiss, Lallygag, Lollygag, Neck

**Smoulder** Burn, Seethe

**Smudge** Blur, Dab, Slur, Smear, Stain

**Smug** Complacent, Conceited, Oily, Pi, Trim

**Smuggle(d), Smuggler** Bootleg, Contraband, Moonshine, Mule, Owler, Rum-runner, Run, Secrete, Steal, Traffic

**Smut(ty)** Bawdy, Blight, Blue, Brand, Coom, Filth, Grime, Speck

**Smut-fungus** Basidia, Ustilago

**Snack** Bever, Bite, Brunch, Canapé, Chack, Crudités, Elevenses, Entremets, Gorp, Nacket, Nibble, Nocket, Nooning, Rarebit, Refreshment, Samo(o)sa, Sandwich, Savoury, Tapa, Taste, Voidee, Zakuska

**Snaffle** Bit, Bridoon, Grab, Purloin

**Snag** Catch, Contretemps, Drawback, Hindrance, Hitch, Impediment, Knob, Nog, Remora, Rub, Snubbe, Stub

**Snail** Dodman, Escargot, Gasteropod, Helix, Hodmandod, Limnaea, Lymnaea, Nautilus, Nerite, Roman, Slow, Slug, Unicorn-shell, Univalve, Wallfish

**Snake** Adder, Amphisbaena, Anaconda, Anguine, Anguis, Apod(e), Asp, Berg-adder, Boa, Boma, Boomslang, Bush-master, Cerastes, Clotho,

Coachwhip, Cobra, Coluber, Constrictor, Copperhead, Cottonmouth, Cribo, Crotalidae, Dendrophis, Diamond-back, Dipsas, Elaps, Ellops, Fer-de-lance, Garter, Glass, Grass, Habu, Hamadryad, Hognose, Homorelaps, Hydra, Jararaca, Jararaka, Kaa, K(a)rait, Lachesis, Langaha, Mamba, Massasauga, Mocassin, Moccasin, Naga, Naia, Naja, Ophidian, Puff-adder, Python, Racer, Rattler, Reptile, Ringhals, Rinkhals, River-jack, Seps, SERPENT, Sidewinder, Squamata, Sucuruju, Surucucu, Taipan, Takshaka, Uraeus, Vasuki, Viper, Water-mocassin, Wind

**Snake-charmer** Lamia

**Snake-in-the-grass** Peacher, Rat, Traitor

**Snake-root** Senega

**Snap(per), Snappy** Autolycus, Bite, Break, Brittle, Camera, Click, Crack, Edgy, Girnie, Gnash, Hanch, Knacker, Knap, Photo, Photogene, Snack, Snatch, Spell, Still, Tetchy, Vigour

**Snare** Bait, Benet, Engine, Entrap, Gin, Grin, Hook, Illaqueate, Inveigle, Net, Noose, Rat-trap, Springe, Toil, TRAP, Trapen, Trepan, Web, Weel, Wire

**Snarl** Chide, Complicate, Enmesh, Gnar(l), Gnarr, Growl, Grumble, Knar, Knot, Snap, Tangle, Yirr

**Snatch** Claucht, Claught, Fragment, Grab, Kidnap, Pluck, Race, Rap, Rase, Raunch, Snippet, Song, Spell, Strain, Take, Tweak, Wrap, Wrest

> **Snatch** may indicate the first letter of a word

**Snazzy** Cat

**Snead** Snath

**Sneak** Area, Carry-tale, Inform, Lurk, Mumblenews, Nim, Peak, Skulk, Slyboots, Snoop, Split, Steal, Stoolie, Tell(-tale)

**Sneer(ing)** Critic, Cynical, Fleer, Gibe, Jeer, Scoff, Smirk, Snide

**Sneeze (at), Sneezing** Atishoo, Neese, Neeze, Ptarmic, Scorn, Sternutation

**Snick** Click, Cut, Edge, Glance

**Snicker** Snigger, Titter, Whinny

**Snide** Shand, Bitchy

**Sniff** Inhale, Nursle, Nuzzle, Scent, Smell, Snivel, Snort, Snuffle, Vent, Whiff

**Snigger** Giggle, Laugh, Snicker, Snirtle, Titter, Whicker

**Snip(pet)** Bargain, Cert, Clip, Cut, Piece, Sartor, Snatch, Snick, Tailor

**Snipe(r)** Bird, Bushwhacker, Criticise, Franc-tireur, Gutter, Heather-bleat(er), Heather-bluiter, Heather-blutter, Scape, Shoot, Walk, Wisp

**Snitch** Conk, Konk, Nose

**Snivel** Blubber, Snuffle, Weep, Whine

**Snob(bery)** Cobbler, Crispin, Scab, Side, Snooty, Soutar, Souter, Sowter,

Toffee-nose, Vain, Vamp

**Snooker** Pool, Stimie, Stimy, Stym(i)e

**Snoop(er)** Meddle, Nose, Pry, Tec

**Snooty** Bashaw, Snob(bish)

**Snooze** Caulk, Dove, Doze, Nap, Nod, Sleep

**Snore, Snoring** Rhonchus, Rout, Snort, Sterterous, Zz

**Snort(er)** Drink, Grunt, Nare, Nasal, Roncador, Snore, Toot

**Snot(ty)** Mucoid

**Snout** Bill, Boko, Cigar, Informer, Muzzle, Nose, Nozzle, Schnozzle, Tinker, Wall

**Snow(storm), Snowy** Brig, Buran, Cocaine, Coke, Crud, Firn, Flake, Flurry, Graupel, Heroin, Mogul, Neve, Nival, Niveous, Onding, Sastruga, Stall, White-out, Wintry, Wreath, Zastruga

**Snowball** Accelerate, Cramp-bark, Cumulative, Guelder-rose, Increase, Magnify, Opulus, Pelt, Rose

**Snowdrop** Avalanche

**Snowflake** Leucojum

**Snow-goose** Wav(e)y

**Snowman** Abominable, Eskimo, Junkie, Sherpa, Yeti

**Snub** Cut, Diss, Go-by, Lop, Pug, Quelch, Rebuff, Reproof, Retroussé, Short, Slap, Slight, Sloan, Sneap, Snool, Wither

**Snuff(le)** Asarabacca, Dout, Errhine, Extinguish, Maccaboy, Ptarmic, Pulvil, Rappee, Smother, Snaste, Sneesh(an), Sniff, Snift, Snush, Tobacco, Vent

**Snuffbox** Mill, Mull

**Snug(gle)** Burrow, Cose, COSY, Cubby, Cuddle, Embrace, Lion, Neat, Nestle, Nuzzle, Rug, Snod, Tight, Trim

**So** Ergo, Forthy, Hence, Sae, Sic(h), Sol, Therefore, This, Thus, True, Very, Yes

**Soak** Bath(e), Beath, Bewet, Bloat, Blot, Buck, Cree, Deluge, Drench, Drink, Drook, Drouk, Drunk, Dunk, Embay, Embrue, Grog, Imbrue, Lush, Macerate, Marinate, Mop, Oncome, Permeate, Rait, Rate, Ret(t), Saturate, Seep, Sipe, Sog, Sop, Souce, Souse, Sows(s)e, Steep, Sype, Thwaite, Toper, Wet

**Soap(y)** Carbolic, Castile, Flake, Flannel, Flattery, Lather, Moody, Pears (tdmk), Saponaceous, Sawder, Slime, Suds, Syndet, Tall-oil, Toheroa

**Soapstone** Steatite, Talc

**Soar(ing)** Ascend, Essorant, Fly, Glide, Hilum, Rise, Tower, Zoom

**Sob (stuff)** Blub(ber), Boohoo, Goo, Gulp, Lament, Singult, Wail, Weep, Yoop

**Sober(sides)** Abstemious, Calm, Demure, Pensive, Sedate, Staid, Steady, TT

**Sobriquet** Byname, Cognomen, Nickname, To-name

**So-called** Alleged, Nominal, Soi-disant

**Sociable** Affable, Chummy, Cosy, Folksy, Friendly, Genial, Gregarious

**Socialise** Hobnob, Mingle, Mix

**Socialism, Socialist** Chartist, Fabian, Fourierism, ILP, International, Lansbury, Left(y), Marxism, Nihilism, Owen(ist), Owenite, Red, Spartacist

**Socialite** Deb

**Society** Affluent, Association, Body, Camorra, Carbonari, Class, Club, College, Company, Co-op, Culture, Danite, Defenders, Dorcas, Eleutheri, Elks, Fabian, Foresters, Freemans, Freemasons, Friendly, Friends, Grotian, Group, Guilds, Hautmonde, Hetairia, Illuminati, Institute, Invincibles, Ku-klux-klan, Kyrle, Linnean, Mafia, Malone, Mau-mau, Oddfellows, Order, Permissive, Pop, Provident, Ribbonism, Rosicrucian, Rotary, S, School, Soc, Tammany, Toc H, Ton, Tong, Triad, U, World

**Sock(s)** Argyle, Argyll, Biff, Bobby, Bootee, Hose(n), Slosh, Strike, Tabi

**Socket** Acetabulum, Alveole, Budget, Hollow, Jack, Nave, Ouch, Strike

**Sock-eye** Nerka, Salmon

**Socrates, Socratic** Ironist, Maieutics, Sage

**Sod** Clump, Delf, Delph, Divot, Gazo(o)n, Mool, Mould, Mouls, Scraw, Sward, Turf

**Soda, Sodium** Arfvedsonite, Barilla, Bicarb, Caustic, La(u)rvikite, Na, Natrium, Natron, Reh, Splash, Trona

**Sofa** Canapé, Chesterfield, Couch, Daybed, Divan, Dos-à-dos, Dosi-do, Ottoman, Settee, Squab

**So far** As, Until, Yonder

**Soft(en), Softener, Softening, Softly** Amalgam, Anneal, B, BB, Blet, Boodle, Cedilla, Cree, Dim, Dolcemente, Doughy, Emolliate, Emollient, Flabby, Gentle, Hooly, Intenerate, Lash, Lax, Lenient, Limp, Low, Malacia, Mardarse, Mardie, Mease, Mellow, Melt, Mild, Milksop, Mitigate, Mollify, Mollities, Mulch, Mush(y), Mute, Neale, Nesh, Option, P, Palliate, Pastel, Piano, Plushy, Porous, Propitiate, Rait, Rate, Relent, Scumble, Sentimental, Silly, Slack, Sumph, Talcose, Temper, TENDER, Tone, Weak

**Softness** Lenity

**Software** Spreadsheet

**Sog(gy)** Sodden

**Soil(y)** Adscript, Bedraggle, Chernozem, Clay, Defile, Desecrate, Dinge, Dirt(y), Discolour, Earth, Edaphic, Glebe, Grey, Ground, Gumbo, Humus, Land, Loam, Loess, Lome, Loss, Mire, Mool, Mould, Mud, Peat, Ped, Pedalfer, Pedocal, Podsol, Podzol, Pure, Regar, Regur, Rendzina, Sal, Smudge, Smut, Solonchak, Solonetz, Solum, Soot, Stain, Stonebrash, Sully, Tarnish, Tash, Terrain, Tilth, Tschernosem, Udal, Yarfa, Yarpha

**Soirée** Drum, Levee, Musicale

**Sojourn** Abide, Respite, Stay, Tarry

**Sol** G, Soh, Sun

**Solace** Cheer, Comfort

**Solar(ium)** Heliacal, Tannery

**Sold** Had

**Solder** Blaze, Join, Spelter, Tin, Weld

**Soldier(s)** Alpini, Ant, Anzac, Army, Arna(o)ut, Askari, Atkins, ATS, Banner, Bashi-Bazouk, Bersaglier, Bluff, Bod, Bombardier, Borderer, Botha, Brave, Buff-coat, Buff-jerkin, Butter-nut, Cadet, Caimac(am), Campaigner, Car(a)bineer, Car(a)binier, Cataphract, Centinel(l), Centonel(l), Chindit, Choco, Cohort, Colours, Commando, Contingent, Cornet, Corp(s), Detail, Dog-face, Doughboy, Draftee, Dragoon, Dugout, Engineer, Enomoty, Evzone, Fag(g)ot, Federal, Fencibles, Fighter, Forlorn-hope, Fusilier, Fuzzy-wuzzy, Fyrd, Gallo(w)glass, Galoot, GI, Goorkha, Grenadier, Grunt, Guardsman, Guerilla, Gurkha, Hackbuteer, Hobbler, Hoplite, Hussar, Immortal, Impi, Infantry, Iron Duke, Ironside, Irregular, Janissary, Janizery, Jawan, Joe, Kaimakam, Kern(e), Kitchener, Lancer, Landsknecht, Lansquenet, Lashkar, Legionary, Line, Lobster, Maniple, Martinet, Men-at-arms, Militiaman, Miner, Minuteman, Musketeer, Nahal, Naik, Nasute, Nizam, Non-com, OR, Orderly, Palatine, Palikar, Pandoor, Pandour, Paratroop, Partisan, Peltast, Peon, Piou-piou, Poilu, Pongo, Private, Rank(er), Reb, Redcoat, Reformado, Regiment, Regular, Reiter, Reservist, Retread, Rifleman, Rutter, Sammy, Samurai, SAS, Sebundy, Sentinel, Sepoy, Signaller, Silladar, Snarler, So(d)ger, Soldado, Sowar(ee), Sowarry, Spearman, Squaddie, Squaddy, Stalhelm(er), Strelitz, Subaltern, Swad(dy), Sweat, Targeteer, Templar, Terrier, Timariot, Tin, Tommy, Train-band, Trencher, Trooper, Troops, Turco(pole), Uhlan, Velites, Vet(eran), Volunteer, Warhorse, Warrior, Zouave

**Sole, Solitaire, Solitary** Alone, Anchoret, Anchorite, Fish, Incommunicado, Lemon, Lonesome, Megrim, Merl, Meunière, Monkish, Only, Pad, Palm, Patience, Pelma, Planta(r), Plantigrade, Platform, Recluse, Scaldfish, Single(ton), Skate, Slip, Smear-dab, Thenar, Unique, Vola

**Solemn** Agelast, Austere, Devout, Earnest, Grave, Majestic, Po-faced, Sacred, Sedate, Serious, Sober

**Solent** Lee

**Solicit** Accost, Approach, Ask, Attract, Bash, BEG, Canvass, Cottage, Importun(at)e, Ply, Speer, Speir, Tout, Woo

**Solicitor** Attorney, Avoué, Beggar, Canvasser, Hallanshaker, Law-agent, Lawyer, Notary, SL, Tout, WS

**Solid(ify)** Cake, Compact, Concrete, Cone, Congeal, Consolidate, Cube, Dense, Enneahedron, Firm, Hard, Holosteric, Impervious, Octahedron, Pakka, Petrarchan, Platonic, Prism, Pucka, Pukka, Set, Substantial, Thick, Unanimous

**Solipsism** Egotism, Panegoism

**Solitude** Privacy, Seclusion

**Solo** Aria, Cadenza, Cavatine, Lone, Monodrama, Monody, Ombre,

One-man, Scena, Variation

**Solon** Sage

**So long** Cheerio, Ciao, Goodbye, Tata

**Solstice** Tropic

**Soluble** Alkaline

**Solution** Acetone, ANSWER, Austenite, Elixir, Emulsion, Key, Lye, Oleoresin, Rationale, Ringer's, Rinse, Saline, Solvent, Tincture, Titrate

> **Solution** may indicate an anagram

**Solve(d), Solver** Assoil, Casuist, Clear, Crack, Decode, Loast, Loose, Read(er), Unclew, Unriddle

**Solvent** Acetone, Alcahest, Alkahest, Aqua-regia, Cleanser, Decalin, Dioxan(e), Ether, Funded, Menstruum, Naphtha, Sound, Stripper, Toluene, Toluol, Trilene, Turpentine

**Sombre** Dark, Drear, Dull, Gloomy, Grave, Subfusc, Subfusk, Sullen

**Some** Any, Arrow, Ary, Certain, Few, Divers, One, Part, Portion, Quota, These, They

> **Some** may indicate a hidden word

**Somebody** Dignitary, Name, Notable, One, Person, Quidam, Someone, VIP

**Somehow** Somegate

> **Somehow** may indicate an anagram

**Somersault** Pitchpole, Pitchpoll

**Something** Aliquid, Chattel, Matter, Object, Whatnot

**Sometime(s)** Erstwhile, Former, Occasional, Off and on, Quondam

**Somewhat** Bit, -ish, Mite, Partly, Quasi, Quite, Rather

**Somewhere** Somegate

**Son** Boy, Epigon(e), Fitz, Lad, Lewis, Offspring, Prodigal, Progeny, Scion

**Song** Air, Anthem, Antistrophe, Aria, Aubade, Ayre, Ballad, Ballant, Ballata, Barcarol(l)e, Berceuse, Bhajan, Blues, Brindisi, Burden, Burthen, Calypso, Cancionero, Canticle, Cantilena, Canzona, Canzone, Carmagnole, Carol, Catch, Cavatina, Chanson, Cha(u)nt, Come-all-ye, Descant, Dirge, Dithyramb, Ditty, Epithalamion, Epithalamium, Fado, Fit, Flamenco, Forebitter, Glee, Gorgia, Gradual, Hillbilly, Hum, Hymn, Internationale, Lay, Lied(er), Lilt, Lullaby, Lyric, Madrigal, Magnificat, Marseillaise, Matin, Melic, Melisma, Melody, Mento, Noel, Number, Oat, Paean, Pane, Pennillion, Prothalamion, Prothalamium, Psalm, Rap, Recitativo, Relish, Rhapsody, Rispetto, Roulade, Roundelay, Rune, Scat, Secular, Serenade, Shanty, Sirvente, Skolion, Spiritual, Stave, Strain, Strophe, Swan, Tenebrae, Theme, Torch, Trill, Tune, Warble, Wassail, Yodel, Yodle

**Song-book** Hymnal, Kommersbuch, Libretto, Psalter

**Songsmith, Songwriter** Dowland, Espla, Foster, Minot

**Sonnet** Amoret

**Sonometer** Monochord

**Soon(er)** Anon, Directly, Erelong, OK, Oklahoma, Presently, Shortly, Tight, Timely, Tit(ely), Tite, Tyte

**Soot(y)** Coom, Crock, Fuliginous, Grime, Smut, Speck

**Soothe, Soothing** Accoy, Anetic, Appease, Assuage, Bucku, Calm, Compose, Demulcent, Emollient, Irenic, Lull, Pacific, Paregoric, Poultice, Quell, Rock

**Soothsayer** Astrologer, Augur, Calchas, Chaldee, Divine, Forecaster, Haruspex, Melampus, Oracle, Picus, Prophet, Pythoness, Shipton, Tiresias

**Sop** Appease, Berry, Douceur, Rait, Ret, Sponge

**Sophist(ic)** Casuist, Elenchic, Quibbler

**Sophisticate(d)** Blasé, Civilised, Cosmopolitan, Sative, Svelte, Urbane, Worldly

> **Sophoclean** may indicate Greek (alphabet, etc)

**Soporific** Barbiturate, Bromide, Drowsy, Halothane, Hypnotic, Lullaby, Narcotic, Opiate, Sedative, Tedious

**Soppiness, Soppy** Maudlin, Schwarmerei, Sloppy, Slushy

**Soprano** Castrato, Crespin, Descant, Lind, Treble

**Sorcerer, Sorceress, Sorcery** Angakok, Ashipu, Circe, Conjury, Diablerie, Lamia, Mage, Magic(ian), Magus, Medea, Merlin, Necromancer, Obi, Pishogue, Shaman, Sortilege, Voodoo, Warlock, Witch, Wizard

**Sordid** Base, Scungy, Seamy, Sleazy, Squalid, Vile

**Sore(ly), Sores** Abrasion, Bitter, Blain, Boil, Canker, Chancre, Chap, Chilblain, Dearnly, Felon, Gall, Impost(h)ume, Ireful, Kibe, Quitter, Quittor, Raw, Rupia(s), Sair, Shiver, Surbate, Ulcer(s), Whitlow, Wound

**Sore throat** Garget, Prunella, Quinsy, Tonsillitis

**Sorrel** Hetty, Oca, Soar(e), Sore, Sourock

**Sorrow** Affliction, Distress, Dole, GRIEF, Lament, Misery, Nepenthe, Penance, Pietà, Remorse, Rue, Wae, Waugh, Wirra, Woe, Yoop

**Sorry** Ashamed, Contrite, Miserable, Penitent, Pitiful, Poor, Regretful, Relent, Wretched

> **Sorry** may indicate an anagram

**Sort(ing)** Arrange, Breed, Brand, Category, Character, Classify, Drive, Grade, KIND, Pranck(e), Prank, Sift, Species, Triage, Type, Variety

**Sortie** Attack, Foray, Mission, Outfall, Raid, Sally

> **Sorts** see OUT OF SORTS

**So-so** Average, Indifferent, Mediocre, Middling

> **So to speak** may indicate 'sound of'

**Sotto voce** Murmur, Whisper

> **Soubriquet** see SOBRIQUET

**Sough** Rustle, Sigh

**Soul(ful)** Alma, Ame, Anima, Animist, Atman, Ba, Brevity, Expressive, Heart, Inscape, Larvae, Manes, Person, Psyche, Saul, Shade, Spirit

**Sound(ed), Soundness, Sound system** Accurate, Acoustic, Affricate, Amphoric, Bay, Blow, Cacophony, Chime, Chord, Clang, Dental, Euphony, Fast, Fathom, Fere, Fettle, Fit, Hale, Healthy, Hearty, Hi-fi, Inlet, Knell, Kyle, Lucid, Mouillé, Music, Narrow, NOISE, Orthodox, Palatal, Peal, Pectoriloquy, Phoneme, Phonetic, Plap, Plop, Plumb, Plummet, Probe, Rale, Real, Ring, Roach, Robust, Rong, Rumble, Rustle, Safe, Sane, Solid, Sonance, Sone, Souffle, Stereo, Strait, Swish, Tamber, Tannoy, Thorough, Timbre, Tone, Trig, Trumpet, Unharmed, Valid, Voice, Well, Whole(some)

**Sounder** Lead

**Soundproof** Deaden

**Sound-track** Stripe

**Soup** Argolemono, Bird's nest, Bisk, Bisque, Borsch, Bouillon, Brewis, Broth, Burgoo, Chowder, Cock-a-leekie, Consommé, Garbure, Gazpacho, Gomb(r)o, Gruel, Gumbo, Hoosh, Julienne, Kail, Kale, Madrilene, Marmite, Mess, Minestrone, Mulligatawny, Oxtail, Pot(t)age, Pot-au-feu, Puree, Rubaboo, Shchi, Shtchi, Skilligalee, Skilligolee, Skilly, Skink, Stock, Tattie-claw, Turtle, Vichysoisse

> **Soup** may indicate an anagram

**Soupçon** Thought, Touch

**Sour(puss)** Acerb, Acescent, Acid, Acidulate, Alegar, Bitter, Citric, Crab, Esile, Ferment, Moody, Stingy, TART, Turn, Verjuice, Vinegarish

**Source** Authority, Basis, Bottom, Centre, Database, Font, Fount, Fountain-head, Germ, Head-stream, Mine, Origin, Parent, Pi, Pion, Provenance, Reference, Rise, Root, Seat, Spring, Urn, Well, Ylem

**Sour milk** Curds, Smetana, Whey, Whig, Yogh(o)urt

**Souse** Duck, Immerse, Pickle, Plunge, Soak, Spree, Steep

**South(ern), Southerner** Austral, Dago, Decanal, Decani, Dixieland, Meridian, S

**South African** Bantu, Caper, Griqua, Hottentot, Kaf(f)ir, SA, Swahili, Xhosa, ZA, Zulu

**South American** Argentino, Bolivian, Chilean, Inca, SA

**Southwark** Boro'

**Souvenir** Keepsake, Memento, Relic, Scalp, Token, Trophy

**Sovereign(ty), Sovereign remedy** Anne, Autocrat, Couter, Dominant, ER, Goblin, Haemony, Harlequin, Imperial, Imperium, James, King, L, Liege, Nizam, Pound, Quid, Royalty, Ruler, Shiner, Supreme, Swaraj, Synarchy, Thin'un

**Soviet** Circassian, Council, Estonian, Russian, Volost

**Sow(ing)** Catchcrop, Elt, Foment, Gilt, Inseminate, Plant, Scatter, Seed, Sprue, Strew, Yelt

**Spa** Baden, Bath, Evian, Harrogate, Hydro, Kurhaus, Kursaal, Leamington

**Space(d), Space agency** Abyss, Acre, Area, Areola, Bay, Bracket, Cellule, Contline, Cubbyhole, Diastema, Distal, Distance, Elbow-room, Esplanade, Ether, Expanse, Extent, Gap, Glade, Goaf, Homaloid, Interstice, Killogie, Lacuna, Lebensraum, Logie, Lumen, Lung, Machicolation, Maidan, Metope, Muset, Musit, NASA, Orbit, Plenum, Pomoerium, Quad, ROOM, Ruelle, Sheets, Spandrel, Spandril, Step, Storage, Vacuum, Vast, Void

**Spacecraft, Spaceship** Apollo, Capsule, Explorer, MIR, Module, Probe, Shuttle, Sputnik, Tardis

**Space walk** EVA

**Spade** Breastplough, Caschrom, Cas crom, Detective, Graft, Loy, Negro, Paddle, Pattle, Pettle, Pick, S, Shovel, Slane, Spit, Suit, Tus(h)kar, Tus(h)ker, Twiscar

**Spain** E, Iberia

**Spalpeen** Sinner

**Span** Age, Arch, Bestride, Bridge, Chip, Ctesiphon, Extent, Range

**Spangle(d)** Avanturine, Aventurine, Glitter, Instar, O, Paillette, Sequin

**Spaniard, Spanish** Alguacil, Alguazil, Barrio, Basque, Cab, Caballero, Carlist, Castilian, Catalan, Chicano, Dago, Don, Fly, Grandee, Hidalgo, Hispanic, Jose, Main, Mozarab, Pablo, Señor, Spic(k), Spik

**Spaniel** Blenheim, Clumber, Cocker, Crawler, Dog, Fawner, Maltese, Papillon, Placebo, Skip-kennel, Springer, Toad-eater

**Spank(ing)** Cob, Rapid, Scud, Slap, Slipper, Sprack

**Spanner** Arc, Bridge, Clapper, Key, Wrench

**Spar** Barytes, Blue John, Boom, Bowsprit, Box, Cauk, Cawk, Fight, Gaff, Jib-boom, Mainyard, Mast, Rail, Ricker, Shearleg, Sheerleg, Snotter, Spathic, Sprit, Steeve, Triatic, Yard

**Spare, Sparing** Angular, Cast-off, Duplicate, Economical, Free, Frugal, Gash, Hain, Lean, Lenten, Pardon, Reserve, Rib, Save, Scant, Slender, Stint, Thin

**Spark** Animate, Arc, Beau, Blade, Bluette, Dandy, Flash, Flaught, Funk, Ignescent, Kindle, Life, Muriel, Scintilla, Smoulder, Spunk, Trigger, Zest

**Sparkle(r), Sparkling** Aerated, Coruscate, Diamanté, Effervesce, Elan, Emicate, Fire, Fizz, Flicker, Frizzante, Glint, Glisten, Glitter, Petillant, Scintillate, Seltzer, Seltzogene, Spangle, Spritzig, Twinkle, Verve, Witty, Zap

**Sparrow** Bird, Isaac, Junco, Passerine, Piaf, Prunella, Spadger, Speug, Sprug, Titling

**Sparrow-grass** Asparagus, Sprue

**Sparse** Meagre, Rare, Scant, Thin

**Spartan(s)** Austere, Enomoty, Hardy, Helot, Laconian, Lysander, Menelaus, Valiant

**Spasm(odic)** Blepharism, Clonus, Cramp, Crick, Fit(ful), Hiccup, Hippus,

Intermittent, Irregular, JERK, Laryngismus, Paroxysm, Periodical, Start, Tetany, Throe, Tonus, Trismus, Twinge, Twitch

> **Spasmodic** may indicate an anagram

**Spastic** Athetoid, Clonic, Jerky

**Spat(s)** Bicker, Brattle, Gaiters, Legging, Quarrel, Shower, Tiff

**Spate** Flood, Sluice, Torrent

**Spatter** Disject, Ja(u)p, Scatter, Splash, Spot, Sprinkle

> **Spattered** may indicate an anagram

**Spawn(ing), Spawning place** Anadromous, Blot, Fry, Progeny, Propagate, Redd, Roud, Seed, Spat, Spet, Spit

**Speak(er), Speaking** Address, Articulate, Chat, Cicero, Collocuter, Communicate, Converse, Declaim, Discourse, Diseur, Dwell, Effable, Elocution, Eloquent, Expatiate, Express, Extemporise, Intone, Inveigh, Jabber, Jaw, Lip, Loq, Mang, Mina, Mike, Mouth, Nark, Open, Orate, Orator, Palaver, Parlance, Parley, Prate, Preach, Prelector, Rhetor, SAY, Sayne, Spout, Spruik, Stump, Talk, Tongue, Trap, Tweeter, Utter, Voice, Witter, Word

**Speakeasy** Fluent, Shebeen

**Spear** Ash, Assagai, Assegai, Dart, Gad, Gavelock, Gig, Gungnir, Hastate, Javelin, Lance(gay), Launcegaye, Leister, Partisan, Pierce, Pike, Pilum, Skewer, Spike, Trident, Trisul(a), Waster

**Spear-rest** Feutre, Fewter

**Special** Ad hoc, Constable, Designer, Distinctive, Important, Notable, Notanda, Particular, Peculiar, Specific

**Specialise, Specialist** Authority, Concentrate, Connoisseur, Consultant, ENT, Expert, Maestro, Major

**Species** Class, Genre, Genus, Kind, Strain, Taxa

**Specific(ally), Specify** As, Ascribe, Assign, Cure, Define, Detail, Explicit, Itemise, Medicine, Namely, Precise, Remedy, Sp, Special, State, Stipulate, The, Trivial

**Specimen(s)** Example, Exempla, Imago, Model, Sample, Slide, Swab

**Specious** False, Hollow, Plausible, Spurious

**Speck(le)** Atom, Bit, Dot, Fleck, Freckle, Particle, Peep(e), Pip, Spreckle, Stud

**Spectacle(d), Spectacles, Spectacular** Arresting, Barnacles, Bifocals, Blazers, Blinks, Bossers, Cheaters, Colourful, Epic, Escolar, Giglamps, Glasses, Goggles, Nose-nippers, Oo, Optical, Outspeckle, Pageant, Pince-nez, Pomp, Preserves, Scene, Show, Sight, Tamasha, Tattoo

**Spectator(s)** Bystander, Dedans, Etagère, Eyer, Gallery, Gate, Kibitzer, Observer, Onlooker, Standerby, Witness

**Spectral, Spectre** Apparition, Bogy, Eidolon, Empusa, Ghost, Idola, Iridal, Malmag, Phantom, Phasma, Spirit, Spook, Tarsier, Walking-straw, Wraith

**Spectrum** Iris

**Speculate, Speculative, Speculator** Arbitrage, Bear, Better, Bull, Conjecture, Flier, Flyer, Gamble, Guess, Ideology, If, Meditate, Notional, Operate, Pinhooker, Shark, Stag, Theoretical, Theorise, Theory, Thought, Trade, Wonder

**Speech** Address, Argot, Articulation, Bunkum, Burr, Delivery, Dialect, Diatribe, Diction, Direct, English, Eulogy, Gab, Harangue, Idiom, Indirect, Jargon, Lallation, LANGUAGE, Lingua franca, Litany, Monologue, Oral, Oration, Parabasis, Peroration, Phasis, Philippic, Prolocution, Rhetoric, Sandhi, Screed, Sermon, Side, Slang, Soliloquy, Tirade, Tongue, Vach, Voice

**Speech defect, Speech disease** Echolalia, Palilalia, Paralalia, Pararthria, Psellism, Stammer, Stutter

**Speechless** Alogia, Dumb, Inarticulate, Mute, Silent

**Speed(ily), Speedy** Accelerate, Amain, Amphetamine, Apace, Bat, Belt, Breakneck, Celerity, Clip, Despatch, Dispatch, Expedite, Fast, Further, Gait, Goer, Gun, Haste, Hie, Hotfoot, Induce, Knot, Lick, Mach, Merchant, MPH, PACE, Pike, Post-haste, Pronto, Race, Rapidity, Rate, RPS, Scorch, Scud, Scurr, Skirr, Soon, Spank, Split, Stringendo, Supersonic, Swift, Tach, Tear, Tempo, V, Velocity, Whid, Wing

**Speedwell** Brooklime, Fluellin, Germander

**Spelaean** Troglodyte

**Spelk** Skelf, Splinter

**Spell(ing)** Abracadabra, Bewitch, Bout, Cantrip, Charm, Do, Elf-shoot, Enchantment, Entrance, Fit, Go, Gri(s)-gri(s), Hex, Incantation, Innings, Jettatura, Knur, MAGIC, Need-fire, Nomic, Period, Philter, Philtre, Pinyin, Relieve, Ride, Romaji, Run, Rune, Scat, Shot, Signify, Snap, Snatch, Sorcery, Sp, Splinter, Stretch, Tour, Trick, Turn, Weird, Witchcraft

**Spelling-book** ABC, Grimoire

**Spencer** Topcoat, Vest

**Spend(ing)** Anticipate, Birl, Blue, Boondoggling, Consume, Disburse, Exhaust, Fritter, Live, Outlay, Pass, Pay, Splash, Ware

**Spendthrift** Prodigal, Profligate, Profuser, Scattergood, Wastrel

**Spent** Consumed, Dead, Done, Expended, Stale, Tired, Used, Weak

**Sperm** Seed, Semen

**Spew** Eject, Emit, Gush, Spit, Vomit

**Sphagnum** Moss, Peat

**Sphere** Discipline, Element, Field, Firmament, Globe, Mound, Orb(it), Planet, Province, Realm, Theatre, Wheel

**Sphinx** Hawk-moth, Oracle, Riddler

**Spice, Spicy** Amomum, Anise, Aniseed, Aryl, Cardamom, Cassareep, Cassaripe, Cinnamon, Clove, Clow, Coriander, Cubeb, Cum(m)in, Dash, Ginger, Mace, Malaguetta, Marjoram, Myrrh, Nutmeg, Oregano,

Peppercorn, Pimento, Piperic, Piquant, Season, Stacte, Staragen, Tamal(e), Tamara, Tansy, Tarragon, Taste, Turmeric, Vanilla, Variety

**Spick**  Dink, Neat, Spike, Tidy

**Spicule**  Sclere, Tetract

**Spider(s)**  Anancy, Ananse, Arachnid, Aranea, Araneida, Arthropodal, Attercop, Citigrade, Epeira, Epeirid, Ethercap, Ettercap, Funnel-web, Harvester, Harvestman, Katipo, Lycosa, Mite, Mygale, Pan, Podogona, Pycnogonid, Redback, Rest, Ricinulei, Saltigrade, Solifugae, Solpuga, Spinner, Strap, Tarantula, Telary, Wolf

**Spiderwort**  Tradescantia

**Spiel**  Spruik

**Spignel**  Baldmoney, Meu

**Spigot**  Plug

**Spike(d)**  Barb, Brod, Calt(h)rop, Cloy, Crampon, Ear, Fid, Foil, Gad, Goad, Grama, Herissé, Impale, Lace, Locusta, Marlin(e), Nail, PIERCE, Point, Pricket, Prong, Puseyite, Rod, Sharp, Shod, Skewer, Spadix, Spear, Spicate, Spicule, Tang, Thorn, Tine

**Spill(age)**  Divulge, Drop, Fidibus, Jackstraw, Lamplighter, Leakage, Let, Overflow, Overset, Scail, Scale, Shed, Skail, Slop, Stillicide, Taper, Tumble

**Spin(ner), Spinning**  Arachne, Birl, Cribellum, Cut, Dextrorse, Gimp, Googly, Gymp, Gyrate, Gyre, Hurl, Lachesis, Nun, Peg-top, Pirouette, Prolong, Purl, Rev(olve), Ride, Rotate, Screw, Sinistrorse, Slide, Spider, Stator, Strobic, Swirl, Swivel, Throstle, Tirl, Toss, Twirl, Twist, Whirl, Work

**Spinach**  Florentine, Orach(e)

**Spinal (chord), Spine, Spiny**  Acromion, Aculeus, Areole, Backbone, Barb, Chine, Coccyx, Column, Epidural, Muricate, Myelon, Notochord, Ocotillo, Prickle, Quill, Rachial, Ray, R(h)achis, Thorn, Tragacanth

**Spindle(-shanks), Spindly**  Arbor, Bobbin, Fusee, Fusiform, Fusil, Pin, Scrag, Staff

> **Spine**  see SPINAL

**Spinel**  Picotite

**Spineless**  Muticous, Timid, Weak

**Spinn(e)y**  Shaw

**Spinning-wheel**  Chark(h)a

**Spinster**  Discovert, Old maid, Tabby

**Spiral**  Cochlea, Coil, Dextrorse, Gyrate, Helical, Helix, Logarithmic, Loxodromical, Screw, Scroll, Sinistrorse, Turbinate, Volute, Wind

**Spire**  Broach, Flèche, Peak, Shaft, Steeple

**Spirit(ed)**  Ahriman, Akvavit, Alcohol, Angel, Animation, Aquavit, Arak, Arch(a)eus, Ardent, Ariel, Arrack, Asmoday, Blithe, Bogle, Brandy, Bravura, Brio, Buggan(e), Buggin, Cant, Cherub, Courage, Creature, Crouse, Daemon, Dash, Deev, Deva, Distillation, Div, Djinn(i), Domdaniel,

DRINK, Dryad, Duende, Duppy, Dybbuk, Eblis, Eidolon, Elan, Element(al), Emit, Empusa, Esprit, Essence, Ethos, Faints, Familiar, Feints, Fetich(e), Fetish, Fettle, Fight, Firewater, Gamy, Geist, Geneva, Genie, Genius, GHOST, Ghoul, Ginger, Gism, Glendoveer, Go, Grappa, Gremlin, Grit, Grug, Gumption, Gytrash, Heart, Hollands, Imp, Incubus, Jann, Jinn(i), Jinnee, Jism, Ka, Kachina, Kelpie, Kirsch, Kobold, Larva, Lemur(e), Liquor, Lively, Loki, Manes, Manito(u), Marid, Metal, Meths, Methyl(ated), Mettle, Mobbie, Mobby, Morale, Nain rouge, Nis, Nix, Nobody, Numen, Ondine, Orenda, Panache, Pecker, Pep, Peri, Petrol, Phantom, Pluck(y), Pneuma, Poltergeist, Poteen, Psyche, Puck, Python, Racy, Rakshos(a), Rosicrucian, Ruin, Rye, Samshoo, Samshu, Seraph, Shade, Shadow, Shaitan, She'ol, Short, Smeddum, Spectre, Spright, Sprite, Spunk, Steam, Strunt, Sylph, Tafia, Tangie, Ton, Turps, Undine, Verve, Vigour, Vim, Vodka, Voodoo, Weltgeist, Wili, Wraith, Zeitgeist, Zephon

**Spiritless** Craven, Dowf, Insipid, Languid, Meek, Milksop, Tame, Vapid

**Spirit-level** Vial

**Spiritual** Aerie, Aery, Coon-song, Ecclesiastic, Ethereous, Eyrie, Eyry, Incorporeal

**Spirt** Gush, Jet, Rush

**Spit(ting), Spittle** Barbecue, Broach, Chersonese, Dribble, Drool, Emptysis, Eructate, Expectorate, Fuff, Gob, Grill, Hawk, Impale, Jack, Peninsula, Ras, Ringer, Rotisserie, Saliva, Skewer, Slag, Spade(ful), Spawl, Sputter, Sputum, Tombolo, Yesk, Yex

**Spite(ful)** Grimalkin, Harridan, Irrespective, Malevolent, Malgrado, Malice, Mau(l)gre, Petty, Pique, Rancour, Spleen, Venom, Waspish

**Spitfire** Cacafogo, Cacafuego, Wildcat

**Spittoon** Cuspidor(e)

**Spiv** Lair, Rorter

**Splash** Blash, Blue, Dabble, Dash, Dog, Drip, Feature, Flouse, Fl(o)ush, Gardyloo, Jabble, Jirble, Paddle, Plap, Plop, Sket, Soda, Sozzle, Spairge, Spat(ter), Spectacle, Splat(ch), Splatter, Splodge, Splosh, Splotch, Spray, Spree, Squatter, Swatter, Water, Wet

**Splay(ed)** Flew, Flue, Patte(e), Spread

**Spleen** Acrimony, Bite, Lien, Melt, Milt(z), Pip, Wrath

**Splendid, Splendour** Ah, Braw, Brilliant, Bully, Capital, Champion, Clinker, Dandy, Eclat, Effulgent, Excellent, Fine, Gallant, Garish, Glitterand, Glittering, Glorious, Glory, Gorgeous, Grand(eur), Grandiose, Ha, Heroic, Lustrous, Mooi, Noble, Panache, Pomp, Proud, Radiant, Rich, Ripping, Stunning, Super(b)

**Splice** Braid, Join, Knit, Wed

> **Spliced** may indicate an anagram

**Splint** Brace, Cal(l)iper, Splenial

**Splinter(s)** Bone-setter, Breakaway, Flinder, Fragment, Matchwood, Shatter, Shiver, Skelf, Sliver, Spale, Spall, Speel, Spelk, Spicula, Spill

**Split**  Axe, Banana, Bifid, Bisect, Break, Chasm, Chine, Chop, Clint, Clove(n), Crack, Crevasse, Cut, Disjoin, DIVIDE, Division, Divorce, End, Fissile, Fissure, Grass, Lacerate, Partition, Red(d), Rift(e), Rive, Ryve, Schism, Scissor, Separate, Sever, Share, Skive, Slit, Sliver, Spall, Spalt, Speld, Tattle, Tmesis, Told, To-rend, To-tear, Wedge

> **Split**  may indicate a word to become two; one word inside another; or a connection with Yugoslavia

**Splodge, Splotch**  Blot, Drop, Splash

**Splurge**  Binge, Indulge, Lavish, Spend, Splash, Spree

**Splutter**  Chug, Expectorate, Fizz, Gutter, Spray, Stammer

**Spoil(s), Spoilt**  Addle, Agrise, Agrize, Agryze, Blight, Blunk, Booty, Bribe, Coddle, Corrupt, DAMAGE, Dampen, Deface, Defect, Harm, Impair(ed), Indulge, Loot, Maderise, Maltreat, Mar, Mardy, Mutilate, Mux, Pamper, Pet, Pickings, Pie, Plunder, Prize, Queer, Rait, Ravage, Rot, Ruin, Spuly(i)e, Swag, Taint, Vitiate, Winnings

> **Spoil(ed), Spoilt**  may indicate an anagram

**Spoilsport**  Damper, Wowser

**Spoke(s)**  Concentric, Radius, Ray, Rung, Said, Sed, Strut

> **Spoken**  may indicate the sound of a word or letter

**Spokesman**  Foreman, Mouthpiece, Orator, Prophet, Representative

**Spoliation, Spoliative**  Devastation, Pillage, Plunder, Predatory, Reif

**Sponge(r), Spongy**  Ambatch, Argentine, Battenburg, Bum, Cadge, Diact, Diploe, Fozy, Free-loader, Hexact, Lithistad(a), Loofa(h), Madeira, Madeleine, Mooch, Mop, Mouch, Mump, Parasite, Parazoa, Pentact, Porifera(n), Quandong, Rhabdus, Sarcenchyme, Scambler, Schnorrer, Scrounge, Shark, Shool, Siphonophora, Smell-feast, Sooner, Sop, Sucker, Swab, Sycophant, Tetract, Tylote, Wangle, Wipe, Zimocca, Zoophyte

**Sponsor(ship)**  Aegis, Angel, Backer, Egis, Finance, Godfather, Godparent, Gossip, Guarantor, Patron, Surety

**Spontaneous**  Autonomic, Immediate, Impulsive, Instant, Intuitive, Natural, Ultroneus, Unasked

**Spoof**  Chouse, Cozenage, Deception, Delusion, Fallacy, HOAX, Imposture, Ramp, Swindle, Trick

**Spook(y)**  Eerie, Frightening, Ghost, Shade

**Spool**  Bobbin, Capstan, Pirn, Reel, Trundle

**Spoon(ful), Spoon-shaped**  Apostle, Canoodle, Cochlear, Dollop, Dose, Gibby, Labis, Ladle, Mote, Neck, Rat-tail, Runcible, Scoop, Scud, Server, Spatula, Sucket, Woo

**Spoonerism**  Marrowsky, Metathesis

**Spoor**  Trace, Track, Trail

**Sporadic**  Fitful, Isolated, Occasional, Patchy

**Spore (case)**  Conidium, Fungus, Glomerule, Lenticel, Seed, Sorus

**Sporran** Pock

**Sport(s), Sporting, Sportive** Aikido, Amusement, Blood, Bonspiel, Breakaway, Brick, By-form, Curling, Daff, Dalliance, Dally, Deviant, Freak, Frisky, Frolic, Fun, GAME, Gent, Gig, In, Joke, Karate, Korfball, Laik, Lake, Langlauf, Lark, Merimake, Merry, Morph, Mutagen, Pal, Polo, Recreate, Rogue, RU, Shinny, Shinty, Squash, Steeplechase, Tournament, Tourney, Toy, Wear, Wrestling

> **Sport(s)** may indicate an anagram

**Sportsman, Sportsmen** Athlete, Blue, Corinthian, Hunter, Nimrod, Shikaree, Shikari

**Spot(s), Spotted, Spotting, Spotty** Ace, Acne, Areola, Areole, Baily's beads, Bausond, Blain, Blemish, Blob, Blot, Blotch(ed), Blur, Brind(l)ed, Caruncle, Cash, Check, Cloud, Colon, Comedo, Curn, Cyst, Dance, Dapple(-bay), Dick, Discern, Discover, Dot, Drop, Eruption, Espy, Eye, Facula, Fleck, Freak, Furuncle, Gay, Guttate, Jam, Lentago, Location, Loran, Macle, Mackle, Macul(at)e, Mail, Meal, Measly, Microdot, Moil, Mole, Morbilli, Mote, Note, Ocellar, Ocellus, Paca, Papule, Pardal, Patch, Peep(e), Petechia, Pied, Pimple, Pin, Pip, Place, Plook, Plouk, Pock, Punctuate, Pustule, Quat, Radar, Recognise, Rose-drop, Scotoma, Skewbald, Smut, Speck(le), Speculum, Splodge, Stigma, Sully, Taint, Touch, X, Zit

**Spotless** Immaculate, Virginal

**Spotlight** Baby

**Spot on** To a t

**Spouse** Companion, Consort, F(i)ere, Hubby, Husband, Mate, Partner, Pheer, Pirrauru, Wife, Xant(h)ippe

**Spout(er)** Adjutage, Gargoyle, Geyser, Grampus, Gush, Impawn, Jet, Mouth, Nozzle, Orate, Pawn, Pourer, Raile, Rote, Spurt, Stream, Stroup, Talk, Tap, Vent

**Sprain(ed)** Crick, Reckan, Rick, Stave, Strain, Wrench

**Sprat** Brit, Fish, Garvies, Garvock

**Sprawl** Loll, Scramble, Sprangle, Spread, Stretch

**Spray** Aerosol, Aigrette, Atomiser, Corsage, Egret, Rose, Rosula, Shower, Sparge, Spindrift, Splash, Sprent, Sprig, Sprinkle, Strinkle, Syringe

> **Spray** may indicate an anagram

**Spread(ing), Spreader** Air, Apply, Banquet, Bestrew, Blow-out, Branch, Bush, Butter, Carpet, Contagious, Couch, Coverlet, Coverlid, Deploy, Dilate, Disperse, Dissemination, Distribute, Divulge, Drape, Dripping, Elongate, Expand, Extend, Fan, Feast, Flare, Jam, Lay, Marge, Multiply, Nutter, Oleo, Open, Overgrow, Paste, Pâté, Patent, Patulous, Picnic, Propagate, Radiate, Ran, Run, Scale, Set, Sheet, Smear, Smorgasbord, Sow, Speld, Splay, Sprawl, Spray, Straw, Stretch, Strew, Suffuse, Teer, Unfold, Unguent, Wildfire

> **Spread** may indicate an anagram

**Spree** Bat, Beano, Bender, Binge, Bum, Bust, Carousal, Frolic, Jags, Jamboree, Juncate, Junket, Lark, Loose, Randan, Rantan, Razzle(-dazzle), Revel, Rouse, Tear, Ups(e)y

**Sprig** Brad, Branch, Cyme, Nail, Sien, Spray, Syen, Twig, Youth

**Sprightly** Agile, Airy, Chipper, Jaunty, Mercurial

**Spring(s), Springtime, Springy** Aganippe, Alice, Arise, Bolt, Bounce, Bound, Bunt, Cabriole, Caper, Castalian, Cavort, Cee, Coil, Dance, Elastic, Eye, Fount(ain), Germinate, Geyser, Grass, Hippocrene, Hop, Jump, Leap, Lent, Lep, Low-water, May, Originate, Persephone, Pounce, Prance, Primavera, Resilient, Ribbon, Rise, Season, Skip, Snap, Spa, Spang, Spaw, Stem, Thermae, Thermal, Trampoline, Vault, Voar, Ware, Well(-head), Whip

> **Spring(y)** may indicate an anagram

**Springless** Telega

**Springtail** Apterygota

**Sprinkle(r)** Asperge, Aspergill(um), Bedash, Bedrop, Bescatter, Caster, Dredge, Dust, Hyssop, Pouncet, Rose, Scatter, Shower, Sow, Spa(i)rge, Spatter, Splash, Spray, Spritz, Strinkle

**Sprint(er)** Burst, Dash, Race, Rash, Run, Rush, Wells

**Sprite** Apsaras, Croquemitaine, Echo, Elf, Fairy, Fiend, Genie, Goblin, Gremlin, Hobgoblin, Ondine, Puck, Spirit, Troll, Trow, Umbriel, Undine

**Sprout** Braird, Breer, Bud, Burgeon, Chit, Crop, Eye, Germ(inate), Grow, Pullulate, Shoot, Spire, Tendron, Vegetate

**Spruce** Dapper, Natty, Neat, Picea, Pitch-tree, Prink, Shipshape, Sitka, Smart, Spiff, Tidy, Tree, Trim, Tsuga

**Spry** Active, Agile, Dapper, Nimble, Volable

**Spud** Murphy, Potato, Spade, Tater, Tatie

**Spume** Eject, Foam, Froth, Lather, Spet, Spit

**Spunk** Courage, Grit, Pluck, Tinder

**Spur** Activate, Calcar(ate), Encourage, Fame, Fire, Goad, Heel, Incite, Limb, Lye, Needle, Prick, Rippon, Rowel, Shoot, Spica, Stimulus, Strut, Stud, Tar, Urge

**Spurge (tree)** Candelilla, Euphorbia, Kamala, Poinsettia, Ricinus

**Spurious** Adulterine, Apocryphal, Bogus, Counterfeit, Dog, Phoney, Pseudo, Sciolism

> **Spurious** may indicate an anagram

**Spurn** Despise, Disdain, Ignore, Jilt, Reject, SCORN, Shun

**Spurt** Burst, Geyser, Jet, Outburst, Pump, Spout

**Sputter** Fizzle, Spit, Splutter, Stutter

**Spy, Spies** Agent, Beagle, Caleb, CIA, Dicker, Emissary, Fink, Informer, Keeker, MI, Mole, Mouchard, Nark, Nose, Operative, Pimp, Plant, Pry, Recce, Scout, See, Setter, Shadow, Sinon, Sleeper, Spetsnaz, Tout, Wait

**Spyhole** Eyelet, Judas-hole, Oillet, Peephole

**Squab** Chubby, Cushion, Obese

**Squabble** Argue, Bicker, Quarrel, Row, Scrap

**Squad(ron)** Band, Blue, Company, Crew, Escadrille, Nahal, Platoon, Red, Wing

**Squalid, Squalor** Abject, Colluvies, Dinge, Dingy, Filth, Frowsy, Poverty, Scuzzy, Seedy, Sleazy, Slum(my), Sordid

**Squall** Blast, Blow, Commotion, Cry, Drow, Flurry, Gust, Sumatra, Wail, Yell, Yowl

**Squander** Blow, Blue, Fritter, Frivol, Mucker, Splash, Splurge, Ware, WASTE

**Square(d), Squares** Agree, Anta, Ashlar, Ashler, Bang, Block, Bribe, Chequer, Compone, Compony, Corny, Deal, Dinkum, Even(s), Fair, Fog(e)y, Forty-nine, Fossil, Four, Gobony, Grosvenor, Leicester, Level, Meal, Nasik, Neandert(h)aler, Nine, Norma, Old-fashioned, Palm, Passé, Pay, Piazza, Place, Plaza, Platz, Quad(rangle), Quadrate, Quits, Rood, S, Sett, Sloane, Solid, Straight, T, Tee, Times, Trafalgar, Unhip

**Squash** Adpress, Conglomerate, Crush, Gourd, Kia-ora, Mash, Press, Pulp, Silence, Slay, Slew, Slue, Suppress, Torpedo

**Squat(ter)** Bywoner, Crouch, Croup(e), Dumpy, Fubby, Fubsy, Hunker, Pudsey, Pyknic, Rook, Ruck, Sit, Spud, Stubby, Swatter, Usucaption

**Squaw** Kloo(t)chman

**Squawk** Complain, Cry, Scrauch, Scraugh

**Squeak(er)** Cheep, Creak, Peep, Pip, Scroop, Shoat, Squeal

**Squeal(er)** Blow, Eek, Howl, Inform, Pig, Screech, Sing, Sneak, Tell, Wee

**Squeamish(ness)** Delicate, Disgust, Nervous, Prudish, Queasy, Reluctant

**Squeeze** Bleed, Chirt, Coll, Compress, Concertina, Constrict, Cram, Crowd, Crush, Dispunge, Exact, Express, Extort, Hug, Jam, Mangle, Milk, Preace, Press, Sandwich, Sap, Scrooge, Scrouge, Scrowdge, Scruze, Shoehorn, Sweat, Thrutch, Wring

**Squelch** Gurgle, Squash, Squish, Subdue

**Squib** Banger, Firework, Lampoon

**Squid** Calamary, Cephalopod, Loligo, Mortar, Octopus

**Squiffy** Drunk, Tiddley

> **Squiggle** may indicate an anagram

**Squint(ing)** Boss-eyed, Cast, Cock-eye, Cross-eye, Glance, Gledge, Glee, Gley, Heterophoria, Louche, Proptosis, Skellie, Skelly, Sken, Squin(n)y, Strabism, Wall-eye

**Squire** Armiger(o), Beau, Donzel, Escort, Hardcastle, Headlong, Land-owner, Scutiger, Swain, Western

**Squirm(ing)** Reptation, Twist, Wriggle, Writhe

**Squirrel, Squirrel's nest** Aye-aye, Boomer, Bun, Cage, Chickaree,

Chipmuck, Chipmunk, Dray, Drey, Flickertail, Gopher, Hackee, Meerkat, Petaurist, Phalanger, Sciuroid, Sewellel, Skug, S(o)uslik, Spermophile, Taguan, Vair, Zizel

**Squirt** Chirt, Cockalorum, Douche, Jet, Scoosh, Scoot, Skoosh, Spirt, Spout, Wet, Whiffet, Whippersnapper

**Sri Lanka** Ceylon, CL, Serendip, Vedda

**St** Saint, Street

**Stab** Bayonet, Crease, Creese, Effort, Go, Guess, Jab, Knife, Kreese, Kris, Pang, Pierce, Pink, Poniard, Prick, Prong, Stiletto, Wound

**Stabilise(r), Stability** Aileron, Balance, Emulsifier, Even, Maintain, Peg, Permanence, Plateau, Poise, Steady

**Stable** Balanced, Byre, Constant, Durable, Firm, Manger, Mews, Poise, Secure, Solid, Sound, Stall, Static(al), Steadfast, Steady, Stud, Sure

**Stableman** Groom, Lad, Ostler

**Stachys** Betony

**Stack** Accumulate, Chimney, Clamp, Cock, Heap, Lum, PILE, Rick, Shock, Staddle

**Stadium** Arena, Bowl, Circus, Coliseum

**Staff** Alpenstock, Ash-plant, Bato(o)n, Bourdon, Burden, Caduceus, Cane, Crook, Crosier, Cross, Crozier, Crutch, Cudgel, Entourage, Equerry, Etat-major, Ferula, Ferule, Flagpole, Linstock, Lituus, Mace, Omlah, Personnel, Pike, Pole, Rod, Runic, Stave, Stick, Tapsmen, Thyrsus, Truncheon, Verge, Wand, Workers

**Stag** Brocket, Buck, Deer, Imperial, Line, Male, Party, Royal, Ten-pointer, Wapiti

**Stage** Act, Anaphase, Apron, Arena, Bema, Boards, Catasta, Diligence, Dog-leg, Estrade, Fargo, Fit-up, Grade, Juncture, Landing, Leg, Level, Mount, Oidium, Phase, Phasis, Pier, Pin, Platform, Point, PS, Rostrum, Scene, Stadium, Step, Stor(e)y, Theatre, Transition, Trek

**Stage-coach** Diligence, Thoroughbrace

**Stagger(ed)** Alternate, Amaze, Astichous, Awhape, Falter, Lurch, Recoil, Reel, Rock, Shock, Stoiter, Stot(ter), Stumble, Sway, Teeter, Thunderstricken, Thunderstruck, Titubate, Tolter, Totter, Wintle

> **Staggered** may indicate an anagram

**Stagirite, Stagyrite** Aristotle

**Stagnant, Stagnation** Foul, Inert, Scummy, Stasis, Static

**Staid** Decorous, Demure, Formal, Grave, Prim, Sad, Sober

**Stain(er)** Aniline, Bedye, Blemish, Blot, Blotch, Discolour, Dishonour, Dye, Embrue, Ensanguine, Eosin, Fox, Grime, Imbrue, Iodophile, Keel, Meal, Mote, Slur, Smirch, Smit, Soil, Splotch, Stigma, Taint, Tarnish, Tinge, Tint

**Stair(case), Stairs** Apples, Cochlea, Companionway, Escalator, Flight, Perron, Rung, Step, Vice, Turnpike, Wapping

**Stake**  Ante, Bet, Claim, Gage, Holding, Impale, Impone, Interest, Loggat, Mark, Mise, Paal, Pale, Paling, Palisade, Peel, Peg, Picket, Pile, Play, Post, Pot, Punt, Rest, Revie, Risk, Septleva, Spike, Spile, Stang, Stob, Sweep, Tether, Vie, Wager

**Stale**  Aged, Banal, Flat, Fozy, Frowsty, Hackneyed, Handle, Hoary, Mouldy, Musty, Old, Pretext, Rancid, Worn

> **Stale**  may indicate an obsolete word

**Stalemate**  Deadlock, Dilemma, Hindrance, Impasse, Standoff

**Stalk(s)**  Bun, Cane, Follow, Funicle, Garb(e), Ha(u)lm, Keck(s), Kecksey, Keksye, Kex, Pedicel, Pedicle, Peduncle, Petiole, Pursue, Seta, Shaw, Spear, Spire, Stem, Sterigma, Stipe(s), Stride, Strig, Strut, Stump, Trail

**Stalking-horse**  Stale

**Stall**  Arrest, Bay, Booth, Box, Bulk, DELAY, Floor, Hedge, Kiosk, Loose-box, Pen, Pew, Prebendal, Seat, Shamble, Stand, Temporise, Trap, Traverse, Travis, Trevis(s)

**Stallion**  Cooser, Cuisser, Cusser, Entire, HORSE, Stag, Staig, Stud

**Stalwart**  Anchor-man, Buirdly, Firm, Manful, Robust, Sturdy, Valiant

**Stamen(ed)**  Octandria

**Stamina**  Endurance, Fibre, Fortitude, Guts, Last, Stamen, Stay, Steel

**Stammer(ing)**  Balbutient, Hesitate, Hum, Psellism, Stumble, STUTTER, Waffle

**Stamp(s)**  Appel, Character, Dater, Die, Enface, Frank, Impress, Imprint, Label, Mint, Pane, Perfin, Philately, Press, Seal, Seebeck, Spif, Strike, Swage, Touch, Trample, Tromp

**Stamp-collecting**  Philately, Timbrology, Timbrophily

**Stampede**  Debacle, Flight, Panic, Rampage, RUSH

**Stand(ing)**  Apron, Arraign, Attitude, Base, Bear, Bide, Binnacle, Bipod, Canterbury, Caste, Confrontation, Dais, Degree, Dock, Dree, Easel, Etagère, Face, Foothold, Freeze, Gantry, Gueridon, Hob, Insulator, Klinostat, Last, Lectern, Nef, Odour, One-night, Ovation, Place, Plant, Podium, Pose, Position, Prestige, Protest, Rack, Rank, Regent, Remain, Represent, Repute, Rise, Stall, Statant, Station, STATUS, Stay, Stillage, Stock, Stool, Straddle, Straphang, Stroddle, Strut, Table, Tantalus, Terrace, TREAT, Tree, Tripod, Trivet, Upright, Whatnot

**Standard(s)**  Banner, Base, Basic, Benchmark, Bogey, Canon, Classic(al), Criterion, Eagle, English, Ethics, Examplar, Example, Exemplar, Flag, Ga(u)ge, Gold, Gonfalon, Labarum, Level, Model, Norm(a), Normal, Numeraire, Old Glory, Par, Pennon, Principle, Rate, Regular, Rod, Rose, Routine, RULE, Staple, Sterling, Stock, Time, Tricolour, Troy, Usual, Valuta, Vexillum, Yardstick

**Standard-bearer**  Alferez, Cornet, Ensign, Vexillary

**Stand-by**  Adminicle, Reserve, Substitute, Support, Understudy

**Stand-in**  Double, Locum, Sub(stitute), Surrogate, Temp, Understudy

**Standish** Miles

**Stand-offish** Aloof, Remote, Reserved, Upstage

**Standpoint** Angle

**Standstill** Deadset, Halt, Jam

**Stanley** Baldwin, Knife, Rupert

**Stannic** Tin

**Stanza** Ottava, Poem, Sixaine, Spenserian, Staff, Stave, Verse

**Staple** Basic, Bread, Chief, Maize, Pin

**Star(s)** Achernar, Acrux, Agena, Aldebaran, Algol, Alioth, Alkaid, Alpha, Altair, Andromeda, Antares, Aquila, Arcturus, Argo, Aster(isk), Auriga, Bellatrix, Beta(crucis), Betelgeuse, Betelgeuze, Body, Bootes, Calaeno, Canopus, Capella, Carina, Cassiopeia, Castor, Celebrity, Centaurus, Cepheus, Chamber, Circinus, Columba, Comet, Constant, Constellation, Cygnus, Cynosure, Delphinus, Deneb(ola), Dolphin, Dorado, Draco, Dubhe, Dwarf, Equuleus, Esther, E(s)toile, Feature, Fixed, Fomalhaut, Fornax, Galaxy, Grus, Headline, Hero, Hesperus, Hexagram, Hyad(e)s, Indus, Lion, Lode, Lucifer, Lupus, Lyra, Megrez, Mensa, Merak, Merope, Meteor(ite), Mira, Mizar, Mullet, Neutron, Norma, Nova, Octans, Ophiuchus, Orion's belt, Pavo, Pegasean, Pentacle, Personality, Phecda, Phoenix, Phosphor(us), Pip, Pleiades, Plough, Pointer, Polaris, Pollux, Praesepe, Principal, Procyon, Proximo, Psyche, Pulsar, Puppis, Quasar, Radio, Red dwarf, Red giant, Regulus, Rigel, Rigil, Sabaism, Saturn, Serpens, Shine, Shooting, Sidereal, Sirius, Solomon's seal, Sothis, Spangle, Spica, Starn(ie), Stellar, Stern, Sterope, Supergiant, Supernova, Synasty, Theta, Top-liner, Triones, Uranus, Vedette, Vega, Vela, Venus, Vesper, Virgo, Volans, Whale, White dwarf, Zeta

**Starboard** Right

**Starch(y), Starch producer** Amyloid, Arrowroot, Cassava, Ceremony, Congee, Conjee, Coontie, Coonty, Cycad, Fecula, Formal, Glycogen, Maranta, Stamina, Statolith, Tous-les-mois

**Stare** Fisheye, Gape, Gawp, Gaze, Goggle, Look, Peer

**Starfish** Asterid, Asteroid(ea), Bipinnaria, Radiata

**Star-gazing** Astrodome, Astronomy

**Stark** Austere, Bald, Harsh, Naked, Nude, Sheer, Stiff, Utterly

**Starling** Bird, Murmuration, Pastor, Stare

**Star of Bethlehem** Chincherinchee, Chinkerinchee

**Start(ed), Starter** Ab ovo, Abrade, Abraid, Abray, Activate, Actuate, Begin, Broach, Chance, Commence, Crank, Create, Dart, Ean, Embryo, Fire, Flinch, Float, Flush, Found, Gambit, Gan, Genesis, Getaway, Gun, Handicap, Impetus, Incept(ion), Initiate, Instigate, Institute, Intro, Jerk, Jump, L, Lag, Launch, Lead, Off, Onset, Ope(n), Ord, Origin, Outset, Preliminary, Prelude, Proband, Put-up, Resume, Roll, Rouse, Scare, Set off, Shy, Slip, Snail, Spring, Spud, String, Wince

> **Start** may indicate an anagram or first letter(s)

**Startle, Startling** Alarm, Disturb, Frighten, Magical, Scare

**Starvation, Starve(d), Starving** Anorexia, Anoxic, Bant, Clem, Cold, Deprive, Diet, Famish, Inanition, Macerate, Perish, Pine, Undernourished

> **Starving** may indicate an 'o' in the middle of a word

**State(s)** Affirm, Alabama, Alaska, Alle(d)ge, Andorra, Aread, Arizona, Ark, Arrede, Assert, Assever, Attest, Aver, Bahar, Belize, Brunei, Carolina, Case, Chad, Cite, Colorado, Commonwealth, Condition, Confederate, Conn, Country, Dakota, Declare, Del(aware), Dependency, Dubai, Durango, Emirate, Federal, Fettle, Fla, Flap, Florida, Ga, Ghana, Humour, Ia, Idaho, Illinois, Indiana, Iowa, Jamahiriya(h), Kansas, Kentucky, Land, Madras, Maine, Malawi, Maryland, Mass, Md, Me, Mess, Mi, Minnesota, Montana, Mysore, Name, NC, Nebraska, Nevada, New Mexico, Nirvana, NY, Oman, Oregon, Pa, Palatinate, Parana, Plight, Police, Predicament, Predicate, Premise, Pronounce, Punjab, Realm, Reich, Republic, RI, Satellite, Say, Sikkim, Sorry, Sparta, Standing, Tabasco, Tamil Nadu, Tasmania, Togo, Travancore, Trucial, UK, Union, US, Ut, Utah, Va, Venezuela, Vermont, Victoria, Welfare, Wis(consin)

> **Stated** may indicate a similar sounding word

**Stately (home)** August, Dome, Grand, Imposing, Noble, Regal

**Statement** Account, Affidavit, Aphorism, Assertion, Attestation, Bill, Bulletin, Communiqué, Dictum, Diktat, Evidence, Invoice, Manifesto, Pleading, Profession, Pronouncement, Proposition, Quotation, Release, Report, Sentence, Sweeping, Utterance, Verb

**Stateroom** Bibby, Cabin

**Statesman** American, Attlee, Botha, Briand, Bright, Canning, Clarendon, Diplomat, Disraeli, Draco, Franklin, Georgian, Gladstone, Gracchi, Grotius, Guy, Kissinger, Kruger, Lafayette, Lie, North, Politician, Politico, Smuts, Stein, Talleyrand, Tasmanian, Thiers, Yankee

**Static** Electricity, Inert, Maginot-minded, Motionless, Stationary

**Station** Berth, Birth, Camp, Caste, CCS, Crewe, Deploy, Depot, Dressing, Euston, Garrison, Halt, Lay, Location, Marylebone, Outpost, Panic, Pitch, Place, Plant, Point, Post, Quarter, Rank, Relay, Rowme, Seat, Sit, Stance, Stand, Status, Stond, Tana, Tanna(h), Terminus, Thana(h), Thanna(h), Victoria, Waterloo, Waverley

**Stationary** Immobile, Fasten, Fixed, Parked, Stable, Static

**Stationery-case** Papeterie

**Statistic(ian)** Figure, Gradgrind, Graph, Number, Percentage, Vital

**Statuary, Statue(tte)** Acrolith, Bronze, Bust, Colossus, Discobolus, Effigy, Figure, Idol, Image, Galatea, Kore, Kouros, Liberty, Memnon, Monument, Oscar, Palladium, Pietà, Sculpture, Sphinx, Stonework, Tanagra, Torso, Xoanon

**Stature** Growth, Height, Inches, Rank

**Status** Caste, Class, POSITION, Quo, Rank, Standing

**Statute** Act, Capitular, Decree, Edict, Law

**Staunch** Amadou, Leal, Resolute, Steady, Stem, Stout, Styptic, Watertight

**Stave** Break, Dali, Forestall, Slat, Stanza, Ward

**Stay(s)** Alt, Avast, Bide, Bolster, Corselet, Corset, Embar, Endure, Fulcrum, Gest, Guy, Hawser, Indwell, Jump, Lie, Lig, Linger, Manet, Moratorium, Piers, Prop, REMAIN, Reprieve, Restrain, Settle, Sist, Sojourn, Stem, Strut, Sustain, Tarry

**Stay-at-home** Indoor, Tortoise

**STD** Aids, Herpes, Telephone, VD

**Steadfast** Constant, Firm, Resolute, Sad, Stable

**Steady** Andantino, Ballast, Beau, Boyfriend, Composer, Constant, Even, Faithful, Firm, Girlfriend, Measured, Regular, Stabilise, Stable

**Steak** Carpet-bag, Chateaubriand, Fillet, Garni, Mignon, Rump, Slice, T-bone, Tenderloin

**Steal(ing)** Abstract, Bag, Bandicoot, Bone, Boost, Cabbage, Cly, Condiddle, Convey, Creep, Crib, Duff, Embezzle, Filch, Glom, Grab, Heist, Kidnap, Knap, Lag, Liberate, Lift, Loot, Mag(g), Mahu, Mill, Naam, Nam, Nap, Nick, Nim, Nip, Nym, Peculate, Pilfer, Pillage, Pinch, Plagiarise, Plunder, Poach, Prig, Proll, Purloin, Rifle, Rob, Rustle, Scrump, Skrimp, Smug, Snaffle, Snatch, Sneak, Swipe, Take, Theft, Thieve, Tiptoe, TWOC, Whip

**Stealth(y)** Art, Catlike, Covert, Cunning, Furtive, Obreption, Surreptitious

**Steam(ed), Steamy** Boil, Condensation, Fume, Gaseous, Het, Humid, Mist, Radio, Roke, Sauna, Spout, Vapour

**Steamer** Kettle, Showboat, SS, Str

**Steam-hammer** Ram

**Steed** Charger, Horse, Mount

**Steel** Acierate, Bethlehem, Blade, Blister, Bloom, Brace, Metal, Ripon, Sword, Toledo, Wootz

**Steelyard** Bismar

**Steep** Abrupt, Arduous, Brent, Embay, Expensive, Hilly, Krans, Krantz, Kranz, Macerate, Marinade, Marinate, Mask, Precipice, Precipitous, Rapid, Rate, Ret, Saturate, Scarp, SHEER, Soak, Sog, Stey, Stickle

**Steeple** Spire, Turret

**Steer(er), Steering** Airt, Buffalo, Bullock, Cann, Con(n), Cox, Direct, GUIDE, Helm, Navaid, Navigate, Ox, Pilot, Ply, Rudder, Stot, Zebu

**Stem** Alexanders, Arrow, Axial, Bine, Bole, Caudex, Caulome, Check, Confront, Corm, Culm, Dam, Epicotyl, Ha(u)lm, Kex, Peduncle, Pin, Pseudaxis, Rachis, Rise, Scapus, Seta, Shaft, Sobole(s), Spring, Stalk, Staunch, Stipe, Stopple, Sympodium, Tail

**Stench** Fetor, Miasma, Odour, Smell, Stink, Whiff

**Stencil** Copy, Duplicate, Mimeograph, Pochoir

**Stenographer, Stenography** Amanuensis, Secretary, Shorthand, Typist

**Step(s)**  Act, Chassé, Choctaw, Dance, Echelon, Escalate, Flight, Gain, Gait, Grecian, Greece, Grees(e), Greesing, Grese, Gressing, Griece, Grise, Grize, Halfpace, Lavolt, Measure, Move, Notch, Pace, Pas, Phase, Raiser, Roundel, Roundle, Rung, Shuffle, Stage, Stair, Stalk, Stile, Stride, Toddle, Tread, Unison, Waddle, Walk

**Stephen**  Martyr, Stainless

**Stepmother**  Novercal

**Stepney**  Spare

**Steppe**  Llano, Plain

**Stereotype(d)**  Ritual

**Sterile, Sterilise(r), Sterility**  Acarpous, Aseptic, Atocia, Autoclave, Barren, Dead, Fruitless, Impotent, Pasteurise

**Sterling**  Excellent, Genuine, Pound, Silver, Sound

**Stern**  Aft, Austere, Counter, Dour, Grim, Hard, Implacable, Iron, Isaac, Nates, Poop, Rear, Relentless, Stark, Strict, Tailpiece

**Steroid**  Cortisone, Testosterone

**Stertorous**  Snore

**Stet**  Restore

**Stevedore**  Docker, Dockhand, Longshoreman, Stower, Wharfinger

**Stevenson**  RLS, Tusitala

**Stew(ed), Stews**  Bagnio, Blanquette, Boil, Bouillabaisse, Braise, Brothel, Burgoo, Carbonade, Casserole, Cassoulet, Cholent, Chowder, Coddle, Colcannon, Compot(e), Daube, Flap, Fuss, Goulash, Haricot, Hash, Hell, Irish, Jug, Lobscouse, Maconochie, Matapan, Matelote, Mulligan, Navarin, Olla podrida, Osso bucco, Paddy, Paella, Pepperpot, Pot-au-feu, Pot-pourri, Ragout, Ratatouille, Salmi, Sass, Scouse, Seethe, Simmer, Slumgullion, Squiffy, Stie, Stove, Stovies, Sty, Succotash, Sweat, Tajine, Tzimmes, Zarzuela

**Steward**  Butler, Cellarer, Chamberlain, Dewan, Factor, Hind, Malvolio, Manciple, Maormor, Mormaor, Official, Oswald, Panter, Purser, Reeve, Seneschal, Shop, Sommelier, Waiter

> **Stewed**  may indicate an anagram

**Stibnite**  Antimony, Kohl

**Stick(ing), Sticky, Stuck**  Adhere, Agglutinant, Aground, Ash, Atlatl, Attach, Bamboo, Bastinado, Bat, Baton, Bauble, Bayonet, Bludgeon, Bond, Boondocks, Caman, Cambrel, Cammock, Cane, Celery, Cement, Chalk, Clag, Clam(my), Clarty, Cleave, Cling, Clog, Club, Cohere, Coinhere, Crab, Crosier, Cross(e), Crozier, Crummack, Crummock, Cue, Distaff, Divining-rod, Dog, Dure, Endure, Fag(g)ot, Flak, Founder, Fuse, Gad(e), Gaid, Gelatine, Glair, Gliadin, Glue, Goad, Goo, Gore, Ground-ash, Gum, Gunge, Gunk, Harpoon, Hob, Immobile, Impale, Inhere, Isinglass, Jam, Kid, Kierie, Kip, Kiri, Knitch, Ko, Lance, Lathee, Lathi, Lentisk, Limy, Lug, Molinet, Parasitic, Paste, Penang-lawyer, Persist, Phasmid, Pierce, Plaster, Pogo, Pole, Posser, Quarterstaff, Rash, Ratten, Rhubarb, Rod,

Ropy, Shillela(g)h, Size, Smudge, Spear, Squail(er), Staff, Stang, Stob, Stodgy, Supplejack, Swagger, Switch, Swizzle, Tacamahac, Tack(y), Tally, Tar, Thick, Truncheon, Viscid, Viscous, Waddy, Wait, Wand, Woomera(ng)

**Sticker** Araldite (tdmk), Barnacle, Bur, Glue, Label, Limpet, Partisan, Poster, Slogan

**Stickler** Poser, Problem, Purist, Rigid, Rigorist, Tapist

**Stiff, Stiffen(er)** Anchylosis, Angular, Ankylosis, Baleen, Bandoline, Brace, Buckram, Budge, Corpse, Corpus, Dear, Defunct, Expensive, Formal, Frore(n), Frorn(e), Goner, Gut, Hard, Mort, Pokerish, Prim, Ramrod, Rigid, Rigor, Sad, Set, Shank-iron, Size, Solid, Starch, Stark, Stay, Steeve, Stieve, Stilty, Stoor, Stour, Stowre, Sture, Unbending, Whalebone, Wigan, Wooden

**Stifle** Crush, Dampen, Funk, Muffle, Scomfish, Smore, Smother, Stive, Strangle

**Stigma(tise)** Blemish, Brand, Discredit, Note, Slur, Smear, Spot, STAIN, Wound

**Stile** Gate, Steps, Sty

**Stiletto** Bodkin, Heel, Knife

**Still** Accoy, Airless, Alembic, Assuage, Becalm, Calm, Check, Current, Doggo, Ene, Even(ness), Howbe, However, Hush, Illicit, Inert, Kill, Languid, Limbec(k), Lull, Motionless, Nevertheless, Peaceful, Photograph, Placate, Placid, Pose, Quiescent, Quiet, Resting, Silent, Snapshot, Soothe, Static, Stationary, Yet

**Stilt** Avocet, Bird, Poaka, Prop, Scatch

**Stimulant, Stimulate, Stimulus** Activate, Adrenaline, Antigen, Arak, Arouse, Caffeine, Cinder, Clomiphene, Coca, Coramine, Dart, Egg, Energise, Fillip, Ginger, Goad, Hormone, Incite, Innerve, Jog, Key, Kick, Mneme, Nikethamide, Oestrus, Oxytocin, Pemoline, Pep, Philtre, Pick-me-up, Pituitrin, Prod, Promote, Provoke, Roborant, ROUSE, Rowel, Rub, Sassafras, Spur, Sting, Stir, Tannin, Tar, Theine, Tickle, Tone, Tonic, Upper, Whet(stone), Wintergreen

**Sting(ing)** Aculeate, Barb, Bite, Cheat, Cnida, Goad, Nematocyst, Nettle(tree), Overcharge, Perceant, Piercer, Poignant, Prick, Pungent, Rile, Scorpion, Sephen, Smart, Spice, Stang, Surcharge, Tang, Urent, Urtica

**Sting-ray** Sephen, Trygon

**Stingy** Close, Costive, Hard, Illiberal, Mean, Miserly, Narrow, Near, Nippy, Parsimonious, Snudge, Tight(wad)

> **Stingy** may indicate something that stings

**Stink(er), Stinking, Stinks** Abroma, Atoc, Atok, Brock, Cacodyl, Crepitate, Desman, Fetor, Foumart, Heel, Hellebore, Malodour, Mephitis, Miasma, Ming, Niff, Noisome, Rasse, Reck, Rich, Science, SMELL, Sondeli, Stench, Teledu

**Stinkbird** Hoa(c)tzin

**Stint** Chore, Economise, Limit, Scantle, Scamp, Scrimp, Share, Skimp

**Stipend** Ann(at), Annexure, Pay, Prebend, Remuneration, Salary, Wages

**Stipulate, Stipulation** Clause, Condition, Covenant, Insist, Provision, Proviso, Rider, Specify

**Stipule** Ocrea

**Stir(red), Stirring** Accite, Admix, Afoot, Agitate, Amo(o)ve, Animate, Annoy, Bother, Bustle, Buzz, Can, Churn, Cooler, Excite, Foment, Furore, Fuss, Gaol, Hectic, Impassion, Incense, Incite, Inflame, Insurrection, Jee, Jog, Kitty, Limbo, Live, MIX, Move, Noy, Poss, PRISON, Provoke, Quad, Quatch, Quetch, Quinche, Qui(t)ch, Quod, Rabble, Rear, Roil, Rouse, Roust, Rummage, Rustle, Sod, Steer, Styre, Upstart, Wake

> **Stir(red), Stirring** may indicate an anagram

**Stirrup (guard)** Bone, Footrest, Footstall, Iron, Stapes, Tapadera, Tapadero

**Stitch** Bargello, Baste, Blanket, Chain, Couching, Crochet, Embroider, Feather, Fell, Herringbone, Knit, Rag, Saddle, Satin, Sew, Spider, Steek, Sutile, Suture, Tack, Tent

**Stock(s), Stocky** Aerie, Aery, Amplosome, Blue-chip, Bouillon, Bree, Breech, Brompton, But(t), Carry, Cattle, Choker, Cippus, Congee, Conjee, Equip, Cravat, Debenture, Fund, Graft, Handpiece, He(a)rd, Hilt, Hoosh, Kin, Line, Little-ease, Omnium, Pigeonhole, Preferred, Pycnic, Race, Ranch, Rep(ertory), Replenish, Reserve, Rolling, Scrip, Seed, Shorts, Soup, Squat, Staple, Steale, Steelbow, Stirp(e)s, STORE, Strain, Stubby, Supply, Surplus, Talon, Team, Tie, Utility

**Stockade** Barrier, Eureka, Zare(e)ba, Zereba, Zeriba

**Stocking(s)** Fishnet, Hogger, Hose, Leather, Moggan, Netherlings, Nylons, Seamless, Sheer, Sock, Spattee, Tights

**Stockman** Broker, Neatherd

**Stodge, Stodgy** Dull, Filling, Heavy

**Stoic** Impassive, Logos, Patient, Seneca(n), Spartan, Stolid, Zeno

**Stoke(r), Stokes** Bram, Fire(man), Fuel, S, Shovel

**Stole(n)** Bent, Epitrachelion, Hot, Maino(u)r, Manner, Nam, Orarion, Orarium, Reft, Scarf, Staw, Tippet

**Stolid** Deadpan, Dull, Impassive, Po-faced, Thickset, Wooden

**Stomach(ic)** Abdomen, Abomasum, Accept, Appetite, Belly, Bible, Bing(e)y, Bonnet, Bread-basket, Brook, C(o)eliac, Corporation, Epiploon, Fardel-bag, Gizzard, Gut, Heart, Jejunum, King's-hood, Kite, Kyte, Manyplies, Mary, Maw, Mesaraic, Omasum, Paunch, Propodon, Psalterium, Pylorus, Read, Rennet, Reticulum, Rumen, Stick, SWALLOW, Tum, Urite, Vell, Venter, Wame, Wem, Zingiber

**Stomach-ache** Colic, Colitis, Collywobbles, Gripe, Mulligrubs

**Stone(d), Stones, Stony** Adamantine, Aerolite, Aerolith, Agate, Alabaster, Alectorian, Amazon, Amber, Amethyst, Aragonites, Ashlar, Ashler, Asparagus, Asteria, Asteroid, Avebury, Baetyl, Baguette, Balas, Beryl, Bezoar, Blotto, Bologna, Boulder, Breccia, Cabochon, Cairngorm, Calculus, Callais, Carnelian, Carton-pierre, Celt, Chalcedony, Chalk, Chert,

Cholelith, Chondrite, Cinnamon, Coade, Cobble, Coping, Cornelian, Cromlech, Dichroite, Dolmen, Draconites, Drunk, Drupe, Ebenezer, Elf-arrow, Endocarp, Enhydritic, Essonite, Flag, Flint, Flusch, Fossil, Gan(n)ister, Gem, Gibber, Girasol(e), Gooley, Goolie, Gooly, Granite, Gravel, Grey-wether, Hessonite, Hoarstone, Hog, Hone, Humite, Hyacine, Hyalite, Jargo(o)n, Jasp(er), Jewel, Kenne, Kerb, Kimberlite, Kingle, Lapidate, Lapis, Lherzolite, Lia-fail, Lias, Ligure, Lime, Lithoid, Logan, Megalith, Menah, Menamber, Menhir, Metal, Metate, Moabite, Mocha, Monolith, Muller, Nephrite, Niobe(an), Nutlet, Olivine, Omphalos, Onychite, Onyx, Opal, Paleolith, Parpane, Parpend, Parpent, Parpoint, Paste, Pebble, Pelt, Peridot, Perpend, Perpent, Petrosal, Petrous, Phengite, Pit, Plum, Portland, Pot-lid, Prase, Pudding, Pumice, Pumie, Purbeck, Putamen, Pyrene, Quern, Quoin, Quoit, Rag(g), Rhinestone, Rip-rap, Rollrich, Rosetta, Rubicelle, Rubin, Rufus, Rybat, Sapphire, Sard, Sardine, Sardonyx, Sarsden, Sarsen, Scaglia, Scagliola, Scarab, Schanse, Schan(t)ze, Scone, Scree, Sermon, Skew, Slab, Slate, Smaragd, Sneck, St, Stele, Summer, Tanist, Tektite, Telamon, Tonalite, Topaz, Trilithon, Tripoli, Turquoise, Ventifact, Voussoir, Wacke, Wyman

**Stone-crop**   Orpin(e), Sedum, Succulent

**Stone-pusher**   Sisyphus

**Stone-thrower**   Bal(lista), Catapult, David, Mangonel, Onager, Perrier, Sling, Trebuchet

**Stone-wall(er)**   Block, Mule, Revet

**Stone-worker**   Jeweller, Knapper, Sculptor

**Stooge**   Butt, Cat's-paw, Feed

**Stook(s)**   Sheaf, Stack, Thr(e)ave

**Stool**   Buffet, Coppy, Creepie, Cricket, Cucking, Curule, Cutty, Faeces, Hassock, Pouf(fe), Seat, Sir-reverence, Stercoral, Sunkie, Tripod, Turd

**Stoop**   Bend, Condescend, C(o)urb, Daine, Deign, Incline, Porch, Slouch

**Stop(page), Stopper**   Abort, An(n)icut, Arrest, Avast, Bait, Bide, Blin, Block, Brake, Buffer, Bung, Canting-coin, CEASE, Check, Cheese, Clarabella, Clarino, Clarion, Clog, Close, Colon, Comma, Conclude, Curk, Cremo(r)na, Cremorne, Cromorna, Cut, Debar, Demurral, Desist, Deter, Devall, Diaphone, Discontinue, Dit, Dolce, Dot, Embargo, End, Field, Fifteenth, Flute, Foreclose, Fr(a)enum, Freeze, Gag, Gamba, Gemshorn, Glottal, Gong, Halt, Hamza(h), Hartal, Hinder, Hitch, Ho, Hold, Hoy, Intermit, Ischuria, Jam, Kibosh, Let-up, Lill, Lin, Lute, Nasard, Oboe, Obturate, Occlude, Oppilate, Outspan, Pause, Period, Piccolo, Plug, Point, Poop, Prevent, Principal, Prorogue, Punctuate, Quint, Quit, Red, Refrain, Register, Rein, Remain, Salicet, Scotch, Screw-top, Semi-colon, Sese, Sesquialtera, Sext, Sist, Spigot, Stall, Stanch, Standstill, Stash, Stasis, Station, Staunch, Stay, Stive, Strike, Subbase, Subbass, Suppress, Tamp(ion), Tenuis, Terminate, Toby, Toho, Waldflute, Waldhorn, When, Whoa

**Stopgap**   Caretaker, Gasket, Gaskin, Interim, Makeshift, Temporary

**Store(house)** Accumulate, Arsenal, Barn, Bin, Bottle, Bunker, Buttery, Cache, Cell, Cellar, Clamp, Coop, Cupboard, Deli, Dene-hole, Department(al), Depository, Depot, Dolia, Emporium, Ensile, Entrepot, Etape, Fund, Garner, Genizah, Girnal, Go-down, Granary, Groceteria, HOARD, House, Humidor, Husband, Imbarn, Larder, Lazaretto, Mart, Mattamore, Memory, Morgue, Mow, Multiple, Nest-egg, Off-licence, Pantechnicon, Provision, RAM, Repertory, ROM, Shop, Silage, Silo, Spence, Stack, Stash, Stock, Stow, Supply, Tack-room, Tank, Thesaurus, Tithe-barn, Tommy-shop, Warehouse

> **Storey**   see STORY

**Stork** Adjutant, Argala, Bird, Jabiru, Marabou, Marg, Saddlebill, Wader

**Stork's bill** Erodium

**Storm(y)** Ablow, Adad, Assail, Attack, Baguio, Blizzard, Bluster, Bourasque, Buran, Charge, Cyclone, Devil, Enlil, Expugn, Furore, Gale, Haboob, Hurricane, Onset, Oragious, Rage(ful), Raid, Rampage, Rant, Rush, Shaitan, Snorter, Squall, Sumatra, Tea-cup, Tebbad, Tempest, Tornado, Unruly, Weather, Willy-willy, Zu

> **Stormy**   may indicate an anagram

**Story, Storey, Stories** Account, Allegory, Anecdote, Apocrypha, Arthuriana, Attic, Bar, Basement, Baur, Bawr, Chestnut, Clearstory, Clerestory, Conte, Decameron, Edda, Epic, Episode, Etage, Exclusive, Fable, Fib, Fiction, Flat, Floor, Gag, Geste, Hard-luck, Heptameron, Hitopadesa, Idyll, Iliad, Jataka, Lee, Legend, Lie, Mabinogion, Marchen, Mezzanine, Myth(os), Mythus, Narrative, Novel(la), Parable, Pentameron, Plot, Rede, Report, Romance, Rumour, Saga, Scoop, Script, Serial, SF, Shocker, Spiel, Splash, Stage, Tale, Tall, Tier, Upper, Version, Yarn

**Story-teller** Aesop, Fibber, Griot, Liar, Narrator, Raconteur, Tusitala

**Stoup** Benitier, Bucket, Vessel

**Stout(ness)** Ale, Burly, Chopping, Embonpoint, Endomorph, Entire, Fat, Hardy, Lusty, Manful, Obese, Overweight, Porter, Portly, Robust, Stalwart, Stalworth, Sta(u)nch, Strong, Stuggy, Sturdy, Tall

**Stove** Break, Calefactor, Cockle, Cooker, Furnace, Gasfire, Oven, Primus, Range

**Stow** Cram, Flemish, Load, Pack, Rummage, Stash, Steeve

**Strabismus** Squint

**Straddle** Bestride, Strodle

**Strafe** Bombard, Shell, Shoot

**Straggle(r)** Estray, Gad, Meander, Ramble, Rat-tail, Sprawl, Stray, Wander

**Straight(en), Straightness** Align, Beeline, Correct, Die, Direct, Downright, Dress, Frank, Gain, Het(ero), Honest, Lank, Legit, Level, Normal, Rectitude, Righten, Sheer, Slap, Tidy, True, Unbowed, Unlay, Upright, Virgate

**Straight edge** Lute, Ruler

**Straightforward** Candid, Direct, Easy, Honest, Level, Jannock, Pointblank, Simple

**Straight-haired** Leiotrichous

**Strain(ed), Strainer, Straining** Ancestry, Aria, Breed, Carol, Colander, Distend, Drawn, Effort, Exert, Filter, Filtrate, Fit, Fitt(e), Force, Fray, Fytt(e), Intense, Kind, Melody, Milsey, Molimen, Music, Note, Overtask, Passus, Percolate, Pressure, Pull, Raring, Reck(an), Rick, Seep, Seil(e), Set, Shear, Sieve, Sift, Sile, Stape, Start, Stock, Streak, Stress, Stretch, Sye, Tamis, Tammy, Tax, Tenesmus, Tense, Tension, Threnody, Try, Vein, Vice, Work, Wrick

**Strait(s)** Bass, Bering, Channel, Condition, Cook, Crisis, Cut, Formosa, Gat, Gibraltar, Gut, Hormuz, Kattegat, Kyle, Magellan, Menai, Messina, Narrow, Otranto, Palk, Predicament, Solent, Sound, St, Sunda, Torres

**Straiten(ed)** Impecunious, Impoverish, Poor, Restrict

**Strait-laced** Blue-nosed, Narrow, Primsie, Puritan, Stuffy

**Strand(ed)** Abandon, Aground, Bank, Beach, Fibre, Haugh, Hexarch, Isolate, Lock, Maroon, Neaped, Ply, Rope, Shore, Sliver, Thread, Three-ply, Tress, Wisp

**Strange(ness), Stranger** Alien, Aloof, Amphitryon, Curious, Eerie, Exotic, Foreign, Fraim, Frem(d), Fremit, Frenne, Funny, Guest, Malihini, New, Novel, Odd(ball), Outlandish, Outsider, Quare, Queer, Rum, S, Selcouth, Tea-leaf, Unco, Unked, Unket, Unkid, Unused, Unusual, Weird

> **Strange** may indicate an anagram

**Strangle** Choke, Garotte, Suppress, Throttle

**Strap(ping)** Band, Barber, Beat, Bowyangs, Brail, Braw, Breeching, Crupper, Cuir-bouilli, Curb, Girth, Harness, Jess, Larrup, Lash, Ligule, Lorate, Lore, Manly, Martingale, Rand, Rein, Robust, Sling, Spider, Strop, Surcingle, Tab, Taws(e), Thong, Trace, Wallop

**Stratagem, Strategist, Strategy** Artifice, Coup, Deceit, Device, Dodge, Fetch, Finesse, Fraud, Minimax, Plan, RUSE, Scheme, Sleight, Tactic(s), Tactician, Trick, Wile

**Stratum, Strata** Bed, Layer, Neogene, Permian, Schlieren, Seam

**Straw(s), Strawy** Balibuntal, Boater, Buntal, Chaff, Halm, Hat, Haulm, Hay, Insubstantial, Leghorn, Nugae, Oaten, Panama, Pedal, Stalk, Stramineous, Strammel, Strummel, Stubble, Trifles, Wisp, Ye(a)lm

**Strawberry** Birthmark, Fragaria, Hautboy, Potentilla

**Stray** Abandoned, Chance, Deviate, Digress, Err, Forwander, Foundling, Maverick, Misgo, Pye-dog, Ramble, Roam, Streel, Traik, Unowned, Waff, Waif, Wander

**Streak(ed), Streaker, Streaky** Archimedes, Bended, Brindle, Comet, Flaser, Flash, Fleck, Freak, Hawked, Lace, Layer, Leonid, Mark, Merle, Race, Run, Schlieren, Seam, Striate, Striga, Strip(e), Vein, Venose, Vibex, Waif, Wake, Wale

**Stream** Acheron, Anabranch, Arroyo, Beam, Beck, Bogan, Bourne, Burn,

Course, Current, Flow, Flower, Freshet, Gulf, Jet, Kill, Lade, Lane, Leet, Logan, Pour, Pow, Rill, River, Rubicon, Sike, Streel, Syke, Tide-race, Tributary, Trickle

**Streamer** Banderol(e), Bandrol, Banner(all), Bannerol, Pennon, Pinnet, Ribbon, Vane

**Streamline(d)** Clean, Fair, Simplify, Sleek, Slim

**Street** Alley, Ave(nue), Bowery, Broad, Carey, Carnaby, Cato, Causey, Cheapside, Close, Corso, Crescent, Downing, Drive, Easy, Fleet, Gate, Grub, High(way), Lane, Meuse, Mews, Parade, Paseo, Queer, Road, Sinister, St, Strand, Terrace, Thoroughfare, Threadneedle, Throgmorton, Wall, Wardour, Watling, Way, Whitehall

**Street arab** Mudlark

**Streetcar** Desire, Tram

**Strength(en)** Afforce, Bant, Beef, Brace, Brawn, Build, Confirm, Consolidate, Enable, Energy, Foison, Force, Forte, Fortify, Freshen, Grit, Horn, Intensity, Iron, Main, Man, Might, Munite, Muscle, Nerve, POWER, Prepotence, Pre-stress, Proof, Reinforce, Sinew, Spike, Stamina, Steel, Stoutness, Thews, Titration, Unity, Vim

**Strenuous** Arduous, Exhausting, Hard, Laborious, Vehement

**Strephon** Rustic, Wooer

**Stress** Accent, Arsis, Birr, Brunt, Emphasis, Ictus, Italicise, Marcato, Orthotonesis, RSI, Sforzando, Strain, Tense, TENSION, Try, Underline, Underscore, Urge

**Stretch(able), Stretched, Stretcher** Belt, Brick, Crane, Distend, Draw, Eke, Elastic, Elongate, Expanse, Extend, Extensile, Farthingale, Fib, Frame, Give, Gurney, Lengthen, Litter, Outreach, Pallet, Pandiculation, Porrect, Procrustes, Prolong, Protend, Pull, Rack, Rax, REACH, Sentence, Spell, Spread, Strain, Taut, Tend, Tense, Tensile, Tenter, Term, Time, Tract, Tree, Trolley

**Striate** Lineolate, Vein

**Stricken** Beset, Hurt, Overcome, Shattered

**Strict** Dour, Harsh, Literal, Medic, Narrow, Orthodox, Penal, Puritanical, Rigid, Severe, Spartan, Stern, Strait

**Stride** Gal(l)umph, Lope, March, Pace, Piano, Stalk, Sten, Straddle, Stroam, Strut, Stump

**Strident** Brassy, Grinding, Harsh, Raucous, Screech

**Strife** Bargain, Barrat, Colluctation, Conflict, Conteck, Contest, Discord, Disharmony, Dissension, Feud, Food, Friction, Ignoble, Scrap(ping), Sturt

**Strike(r), Striking** Affrap, Alight, Appulse, Attitude, Baff, Band, Bandh, Bang, Bash, Bat, Baton, Batsman, Batter, Beat, Belabour, Biff, Black, Bonanza, Buff, Buffet, Bund, Butt, Catch, Cane, Chime, Chip, Clap, Clash, Clatch, Clip, Clock, Clout, Club, Cob, Collide, Coup, Cuff, Dad, Dent, Dev(v)el, Ding, Dint, Distingué, Douse, Dowse, Dramatic, Drive, Dush, Eclat, Fet(ch), Fillip, Firk, Fist, Flail, Flog, Frap, Get, Gowf, Hail, Hartal,

HIT, Hour, Hunger, Ictus, Illision, Impact, Impinge, Impress, Jarp, Jaup, Jolc, Joll, Joule, Jowl, Knock, Lam, Lambast, Laser, Lay(-off), Lightning, Noticeable, Out, Pash, Pat(ter), Pean, Peen, Pein, Pene, Percuss, Picket, Pize, Plectrum, Pronounced, Pummel, Punch, Ram, Rap, Remarkable, Salient, Shank, Sitdown, Sit-in, Slam, Slap, Slat, Slog, Slosh, Smack, Smash, Smite, Sock, Spank, Stop(page), Stub, Swap, Swat, Swinge, Swipe, Swop, Tat, Thump, Tip, Tonk, Walk-out, Wallop, Wap, Whack, Whap, Whop, Wick, Wildcat, Wipe, Wondrous

**Strike-breaker** Blackleg, Fink, Scab

**String(s), Stringy** Band, Beads, Bowyang, Cello, Chalaza, Chanterelle, Cord, Creance, Cremaster, Fiddle, Fillis, G, Gut, Henequin, Heniquin, Hypate, Keyed, Lace, Lag, Lichanos, Mese, Necklace, Nete, Nicky-tam, Paramese, Pledget, Proviso, Quint, Ripcord, Rope, Series, Shoe(-tie), Sinewy, Straggle, Strand, Tendon, Thairm, Tough, Train, Trite, Viola, Violin

**String-course** Moulding, Table

**Stringent** Extreme, Rigid, Severe, Strict, Urgent

**Strip(ped), Stripper, Striptease** Airfield, Band, Bare, Bark, Batten, Belt, Bereave, Comic, Cote, Denude, Deprive, Derobe, Despoil, Devest, Disbark, Dismantle, Dismask, Divest, Ecdysis, Ecorché, Fiche, Flay, Fleece, Flench, Flense, Flinch, Flounce, Flype, Gaza, Infula, Label, Lardon, Ledge, Linter, List, Littoral, Mobius, Panhandle, Peel, Pillage, Pluck, Pull, Puttee, Puttie, Rand, Raunch, Raw, Ribbon, Roon, Royne, Rund, Screed, Shear, Shed, Shuck, Skin, Slat, Slit, Splat, Splent, Spline, Splint, Straik, Strake, Strap, Streak, Strop, Tack, Tee, Thong, Tirl, Tirr, Uncase, Undress, Unfrock, Unrig, Unrip, Unvaile, Zone

**Stripe(d)** Band, Bausond, Candy, Chevron, Lance-jack, Laticlave, Line, List, NCO, Pirnie, Pirnit, Slash, Straik, Strake, Streak, Stroke, Tabaret, Tabby, Tiger, Tragelaph(us), Vitta, Weal

**Strive, Striving** Aim, Aspire, ATTEMPT, Contend, Endeavour, Enter, Kemp, Labour, Nisus, Pingle, Press, Strain, Struggle, Toil, Try, Vie

**Stroke** Apoplex(y), Backhander, Bat, Blow, Breast, Caress, Carom, Chip, Chop, Coup, Coy, Crawl, Dash, Dint, Drear(e), Drere, Dropshot, Effleurage, Estramazone, Feat, Flick, Fondle, Glance, Hairline, Hand(er), Ictus, Inwick, Jenny, Jole, Joll, Joule, Jowl, Knell, Knock, Lash, Like, Line, Loft, Loser, Massé, Oarsman, Odd, Off-drive, Outlash, Palp, Paw, Pot-hook, Put(t), Roquet, Rub, Scart, Sclaff, Scoop, Seizure, Sixte, Smooth, Solidus, Strike, Stripe, Sweep, Swipe, Touk, Trait, Trudgen, Tuck, Virgule, Wale, Whang

**Stroll(er), Strolling** Ambulate, Dander, Daun(d)er, Dawner, Flanerie, Flaneur, Idle, Lounge, Ramble, Saunter, Stravaig, Stray, Toddle, Walk, Wander

**Strong** Able, Brawny, Doughty, Durable, F, Fit, Forceful, Forcible, Forte, Hale, Hercules, Humming, Intense, Mighty, Nappy, Pithy, Pollent, Potent, Powerful, Rank, Robust, Samson, Solid, Stalwart, Stark, Sthenic, Stiff, Stout, Str, Strapping, Sturdy, Suit, Thesis, Thickset, Trusty, Vegete, Vehement, Vigorous, Violent, Well-set, Ya(u)ld

**Stronghold** Acropolis, Aerie, Bastion, Castle, Citadel, Fastness, Fortress, Keep, Kremlin, Redoubt, Tower

**Strontium** Sr

**Strop** Leather, Sharpen, Strap

**Struck** Aghast, Raught, Smitten

**Structural, Structure** Anatomy, Building, Compage(s), Edifice, Erection, Formation, Frame, Ice-apron, Mole, Organic, Palmation, Pediment, Pergola, Shape, Skeleton, Sporocarp, Squinch, Stylobate, Syntax, Tectonic, Texas

**Struggle** Agon(ise), Buckle, Camp, Chore, Conflict, Contend, Contest, Cope, Debatement, Effort, Endeavour, Fight, Flounder, Grabble, Grapple, Kampf, Labour, Luctation, Mill, Pingle, Rat-race, Scrimmage, Scrummage, Scrum, Scuffle, STRIVE, Toil, Tug, Tussle, Vie, War(sle), Wrestle

> **Struggle** may indicate an anagram

**Strum** Thrum, Tweedle, Vamp

**Strumpet** Cocotte, Harlot, Hiren, Lorette, Paramour, Succubus, Wench

**Strut(ter), Strutting** Bracket, Brank, Cock, Flounce, Haught(y), Kingrod, Longeron, Member, Peacock, Pown, Prance, Prop, Scotch, Spur, Stalk, Stretcher, Strunt, Swagger, Swank, Tie-beam

**Stuart** Anne, James, Pretender

**Stub(by)** Butt, Counterfoil, Dout, Dowt, Dumpy, Squat, Stob, Stocky

**Stubble** Ar(r)ish, Bristle, Hair, Ill-shaven, Stump

**Stubborn** Adamant, Bigoted, Contumacious, Cussed, Entêté, Hard(-nosed), Hidebound, Inveterate, Moyl(e), Mulish, Obdurate, Obstinate, Ornery, Ortus, Pertinacious, Perverse, Reesty, Refractory, Rigwoodie, Stiff, Tenacious, Thrawn

**Stuck** Fast, Glued, Jammed, Set, Stopped, Wedged

**Stuck-up** Chesty, Highty-tighty, Hoity-toity, La(h)-di-da(h), Proud, Sealed, Vain

**Stud(ded)** Boss, He-man, Knob, Nail, Race, Rivet, Seg, Set, Sire

**Student(s)** Alphabetarian, Alumnus, Apprentice, Bajan, Bejant, Bursch(en), Cadet, Class, Coed, Commoner, Dig, Disciple, Extensionist, Form, Fresher, Freshman, Gownsman, Gyte, Kommers, Kyu, LEARNER, Magistrand, NUS, Opsimath, Ordinand, Oxonian, Pennal, Plebe, Poll, Preppy, Pupil, Reader, Sap, SCHOLAR, Self-taught, Semi, Seminar, Shark, Sizar, Sizer, Smug, Softa, Soph(omore), Sophister, Swot, Templar, Tosher, Tuft

**Studio** Atelier, Gallery, Pinewood, Workshop

**Study, Studied** Analyse, Brown, Carol, Con(ne), Consider, Cram, Den, Dig, Etude, Learn, Lucubrate, Mug, Mull, Muse, Perusal, Peruse, Pore, Probe, Read, Research, Reverie, Revise, Sanctum, Sap, Scan, Scrutinise, Specialize, Stew, Take, Typto, Voulu

**Stuff(iness), Stuffing, Stuffy** Airless, Canvas, Close, Cloth,

Codswallop, Cram, Crap, Dimity, Farce, Feast, Fiddlesticks, Fill, Force, Forcemeat, Frows(t)y, Frowzy, Fug, Gear, Gobble, Gorge, Guff, Havers, Hooey, Horsehair, Lard, Line, Linen, MATERIAL, Matter, No-meaning, Nonsense, Pad, Pang, Panne, Pompous, Ram, Replete, Rot, Sate, Scrap, Sob, Stap, Steeve, Stew, Taxidermy, Trig, Upholster, Wad, Youth

**Stultify** Repress, Ridicule, Smother

**Stumble** Blunder, Err, Falter, Flounder, Founder, Lurch, Peck, Snapper, Stoit, Titubate, Trip

**Stump(ed)** Butt, Clump, Fag-end, Floor, More, Nog, Nonplus, Orate, Runt, Scrag, Snag, Snooker, St, Staddle, Stob, Stock, Stub(ble), Stud, Tramp, Truncate

**Stun(ning)** Astonish, Astound, Awhape, Bludgeon, Cosh, Daze, Dazzle, Deafen, Dove, Glam, KO, Shock, Stoun, Stupefy

**Stunner** Belle, Bobby-dazzler, Cheese, Cosh, Peach

**Stunt(ed)** Aerobatics, Confine, Dwarf, Feat, Gimmick, Hot-dog, Hype, Jehad, Jihad, Loop, Nirl, Puny, Ront(e), Runt, Scroggy, Scrub(by), Scrunt(y), Stub, Trick, Wanthriven

**Stupefaction, Stupefy(ing)** Amaze(ment), Assot, Benumb, Dozen, Dumbfound, Etherise, Fuddle, Hocus, Narcoses, Numb, Stonne, Stun

**Stupid (person)** Abderian, Abderite, Airhead, Analphabet, Anserine, Asinico, Asinine, Ass, Auf, Baeotian, Bampot, Becasse, Beccaccia, Berk, Besotted, Bete, Blockhead, Bob, Bobb(y), Boeotian, Booby, Boodle, Bozo, Brute, Buffoon, Burk, Cake, Calf, Capocchia, Changeling, Charlie, Chick, Chipochia, Chump, Clod(pole), Clodpoll, Clot, Clunk, Cokes, Cony, Coof, Coot, Crackpot, Crass, Cretin, Cuckoo, Cuddie, Cuddy, Cully, Daft, Daw, Dense, Desipient, Dick(e)y, Dill, Dim(wit), Dizzard, Doat, Doddipoll, Doddypoll, Dodipoll, Dodkin, Dolt, Donkey, Donnard, Donnart, Donner(e)d, Donnert, Dote, Dotterel, Dottipoll, Dottle, Dottrell, Drongo, Dull(ard), Dunce, Dunderhead, Dunderpate, Dweeb, Flat, Flathead, Fog(e)y, Fon, Fool(ish), Gaby, Gaga, Galah, Gaupus, Geck, Git, Golem, Gomeral, Gomeril, Goof, Goon, Goop, Goose(-cap), Gormless, Gouk, Gowk, Gross, Gubbins, Gull, Gump, Gunsel, Half-wit, Hammerheaded, Hash, Haverel, Idiot, Ignaro, Ignoramus, Imbecile, Inane, Ingram, Ingrum, Insensate, Insipient, Insulse, Jackass, Jay, Jerk, Jobernowl, Juggins, Liripipe, Liripoop, Lob, Log, Looby, Loony, Lummox, Lunkhead, Lurdane, Lurden, Mafflin(g), Malt-horse, Meathead, Mindless, Mome, Moon-calf, Moron, Muggins, Mutt, Muttonhead, Nana, Natural, Neddy, Nerd, Nerk, Nidget, Nig-nog, Nincompoop, Nincum, Ninny(-hammer), Nit(wit), Noddy, Nong, Noodle, Numpty, Nurd, Oaf, Obtuse, Ocker, Omadhaun, Ouph(e), Owl, Oxhead, Palooka, Patch, Pea-brain, Pinhead, Plonker, Poop, Pot-head, Prat, Prune, Put(t), Rook, Sap, Schlemihl, Schmo(e), Schmock, Schmuck, Schnook, Scogan, Scoggin, Shot-clog, Silly, Simon, Simp(leton), Snipe, Sot, Spoon, Stock, Stupe, Sucker, Sumph, Ta(i)ver, Thick, Thimblewit, Tom-noddy, Tony, Torpid, Touchstone, Tumphy, Turnip, Twerp, Twit, Twp, Waldo, Wally, Want-wit, Warb, Wiseacre, Woodcock, Wooden(head), Yap, Zany, Zombie

**Stupidity**  Goosery, Hebetude, Thickness, Torpor

**Stupor**  Catatony, Coma, Daze, Dwa(u)m, Fog, Lethargy, Narcosis, Trance

**Sturdy**  Burly, Dunt, Gid, Hardy, Hefty, Lubber, Lusty, Stalwart, Staunch, Steeve, Strapping, Strong, Thickset, Turnsick, Vigorous

**Sturgeon**  Beluga, Ellops, Fish, Huso, Osseter, Savruga, Sterlet

**Stutter**  Hesitate, Stammer

**Sty**  Frank, Hovel, Pen

**Stye**  Eyesore, Hordeolum

**Style, Stylish**  Adam, A la, Band, Barocco, Barock, Baroque, Burin, Call, Chic, Class, Cultism, Cut, Dapper, Dash, Decor, Diction, Directoire, Dub, Elan, Elegance, Empire, Entitle, Execution, Face, Farand, FASHION, Finesse, Flossy, Form(at), Genre, Gnomon, Gongorism, Grace, Hair-do, Hand, Intitule, Manner, Mod(e), Modish, New, Nib, Nifty, Old, Panache, Pattern, Pen, Perm, Phrase, Pistil, Pointel, Port, Preponderent, Rank, Regency, Rococo, Romanesque, Swish, Taste, Term, Title, Ton, Tone, Touch, Tuscan, Vogue, Way

**Stymie**  Thwart

**Styptic**  Alum, Amadou, Sta(u)nch

**Suave**  Bland, Oily, Smooth, Unctuous, Urbane

**Sub**  Advance, Due, Submarine, Subordinate, Under

**Sub-atomic**  Mesic

**Subconscious**  Inner, Instinctive, Not-I, Subliminal, Suppressed

**Sub-continent**  India

**Subdivision**  Sanjak

**Subdominant**  Fah

**Subdue(d)**  Abate, Allay, Chasten, Conquer, Cow, Dant(on), Daunt(on), Dominate, Lick, Low-key, Master, Mate, Mute, QUELL, Quieten, Reduce, Refrain, Slow, Sober, Suppress, Under

**Subfusc, Subfusk**  Dim, Dressy, Dusky, Evening, Sombre

**Subject(s), Subjection, Subject to**  Amenable, Bethrall, Caitive, Case, Citizen, Cow, Enthrall, Gist, Hobby, Inflict, Liable, Liege(man), Matter, National, On, Overpower, People, Poser, Serf, Servient, Servitude, Slavery, Sitter, Snool, Submit, THEME, Thirl, Thrall, Topic, Under, Vassal

**Subjugate**  Enslave, Master, Oppress, Overcome, Repress, Suppress

**Sublieutenant**  Cornet

**Sublimate(r)**  Aludel, Cleanse, Suppress, Transfer

**Sublime**  August, Empyreal, Grand, Lofty, Majestic, Outstanding, Perfect, Porte, Splendid

**Submarine**  Diver, Innerspace, Nautilus, Pig-boat, Polaris, Sub, U-boat, Undersea

> **Submarine**  may indicate a fish

**Submerge(d)** Dip, Dive, Drown, Embathe, Engulf, Imbathe, Lemuria, Ria, Sink, Take, Whelm

**Submissive, Submit** Acquiesce, Bow, Capitulate, Comply, Defer, Docile, Knuckle, Meek, Obedient, Obtemperate, Passive, Pathetic, Refer, Render, Resign, Sool, Stoop, Succumb, Truckle, YIELD

**Subordinate** Adjunct, Dependent, Inferior, Junior, Minion, Myrmidon, Offsider, Postpone, Secondary, Servient, Subject, Subservient, Surrender, Under(ling), Under-strapper, Vassal

**Subscribe(r), Subscription** Abonnement, Approve, Assent, Conform, Due, Pay, Sign(atory), Signature, Undersign, Underwrite

**Subsequent(ly)** Anon, Consequential, Future, Later, Next, Postliminary, Since, Then

**Subservient** Kneel, Obedient, Obsequious

**Subside, Subsidence, Subsidy** Abate, Adaw, Aid, Assuage, Bonus, Diminish, Ebb, Grant, Sink, Sit, Swag

**Subsidiary** Auxiliar(y), By(e), Junior, Secondary, Side, Succursal

**Subsist(ence)** Batta, Bread-line, Dole, Keep, Live, Maintain, Rely, Survive

**Substance, Substantial** Ambergris, Antithrombin, Antitoxin, Body, Calyx, Chitin, Colloid, Considerable, Content, Elemi, Essential, Excipient, Fabric, Gist, Gluten, Gravamen, Guanazolo, Hearty, Hefty, Indol, Isatin(e), Isomer, Lecithin, Linin, Material, Matter, Meaning, Meat(y), Mineral, Mole, Orgone, Polymer, Protyl(e), Quid, Reality, Sense, Solid, Stuff, Sum, Tabasheer, Tabashir, Tangible, Tusche, Viricide

**Substandard** Off, Poor, Schlo(c)k, Second, Small

> **Substantial** see SUBSTANCE

**Substantiate** Confirm, Prove, Strengthen, Support

**Substantive** Direct, Noun

**Substitute** Acting, Carborundum, Change, Commute, Deputy, Dextran, Emergency, Ersatz, -ette, Euphemism, Exchange, Instead, Lieu(tenant), Locum, Makeshift, Proxy, Relieve, Replace, Represent, Reserve, Ringer, Stand-in, Stead, Stopgap, Subrogate, Succedaneum, Surrogate, Switch, Swop, Vicar(ial), Vicarious

**Substructure** Base, Foundation, Keelson, Platform, Podium

**Subterfuge** Artifice, Chicane, Evasion, Hole, Ruse, Strategy, Trick

**Subterranean** Concealed, Sunken, Underground, Weem

**Subtle(ty)** Abstruse, Alchemist, Crafty, Fine(spun), Finesse, Ingenious, Nice, Sly, Thin, Wily

**Subtle difference** Nuance

**Subtract(ion)** Commission, Deduct, Discount, Sum, Take, Tithe, Withdraw

**Suburb** Banlieue, Environs, Exurbia, Faubourg, Outskirts, Purlieu

**Subversion, Subvert** Overthrow, Reverse, Sabotage, Sedition,

Undermine, Upset

**Subway** Metro, Passage, Tube, Underground

**Succeed, Success(ful)** Accomplish, Achieve, Arrive, Breakthrough, Contrive, Eclat, Effective, Fadge, Felicity, Flourish, Follow, Fortune, Go, Hit, Inherit, Killing, Landslide, Luck, Manage, Mega, Offcome, Pass, Prevail, Prosper, Replace, Riot, Score, Seal, Seel, Sele, Speed, Tanistry, Triumph, Up, Vault, Weather, Win, Wow

**Succession** Apostolic, Chain, Line, Order, Reversion, Sequence, Series, Suite

**Successor** Co(m)arb, Deluge, Descendant, Ensuite, Epigon, Heir, Incomer, Inheritor, Khalifa, Next, Syen

**Succinct** Brief, Compact, Concise, Laconic

**Succour** Aid, Assist, Help, Minister, Relieve, Rescue, Sustain

**Succulent** Cactus, Echeveria, Juicy, Lush, Rich, Saguaro, Sappy, Spekboom, Tender, Toothy

**Succumb** Capitulate, Fall, Surrender, Yield

**Such** Like, Sae, Sike, Similar, That

**Suck(er)** Absorb, Acetabular, Acetabulum, Amphistomous, Antlia, Aphis, Aspirator, Ass, Bull's eye, Culicidae, Dracula, Drink, Dupe, Fawn, Gnat, Graff, Graft, Gull, Haustellum, Haustorium, Lamia, Lamprey, Leech, Liquorice, Mammal, Monotremata, Mouth, Mug, Osculum, Patsy, Remora, Rook, Shoot, Siphon, Smarm, Spire, Spyre, Surculus, Swig, Sycophant, Tellar, Teller, Tick, Tiller, Toad-eater, Turion, Vampire

**Suckle** Feed, Mother, Nourish, Nurse, Nurture

**Suction** Adhere, Pump, Siphon

**Sud(s)** Foam, Sapples

**Sudanese** Mahdi

**Sudden(ly)** Abrupt, Astart, Astert, Extempore, Ferly, Fleeting, Hasty, Headlong, Impulsive, Overnight, Rapid, Slap, Subitaneous, Swap, Swop, Unexpected

**Sue** Ask, Beseech, Dun, Entreat, Implead, Petition, Process, Prosecute, Woo

**Suffer(er), Suffering** Abide, Aby(e), Ache, Agonise, Auto, BEAR, Brook, Calvary, Die, Distress, Dree, Endurance, Endure, Feel, Gethsemane, Golgotha, Grief, Hardship, Have, Incur, Let, Luit, Pain, Passible, Passion, Passive, Patible, Patience, Permit, Pine, Plague, Stand, Stomach, Sustain, Thole, Tolerate, Toll, Torment, Trial, Undergo, Use, Victim

**Suffering remnant** Macmillanite

**Suffice, Sufficient** Adequate, Ample, Basta, Do, Due, Enow, Enough, Satisfy, Serve

**Suffocate** Asphyxiate, Choke, Smoor, Smore, Smother, Stifle, Strangle, Throttle

**Suffrage(tte)** Ballot, Feminist, Franchise, Vote

**Suffuse** Colour, Glow, Imbue, Saturate, Spread

**Sugar(y), Sugar cane** Aldose, Arabinose, Barley, Candy, Cane, Carn(e), Cassonade, Caster, Chaptalise, Daddy, Demerara, Disaccharide, Flattery, Fructose, Galactose, Gallise, Goo(r), Granulated, Gur, Hexose, Iced, Invert, Jaggery, Lactose, Laevulose, Lump, Maltose, Manna, Mannose, Maple, Money, Muscovado, Panocha, Pentose, Penuche, Raffinose, Ribose, Saccharine, Saccharoid, Sis, Sorbose, Sorg(h)o, Sorghum, Sparrow, Sweet

**Sugar-daddy** Lyle, Tate

**Suggest(ion), Suggestive** Advance, Advice, Advise, Cue, Hint, Idea, Imply, Innuendo, Insinuate, Intimate, Mention, Modicum, Moot, Prompt, Proposal, Propound, Provocative, Racy, Recommend, Redolent, Reminiscent, Risqué, Smacks, Suspicion, Touch, Trace, Wind, Wrinkle

**Suicide** Felo-de-se, Hara-kiri, Hari-kari, Kamikaze, Lemming, Lethal, Sati, Seppuku, Suttee

**Suit** Action, Adapt, Agree, Answer, Appropriate, Become, Befit, Beho(o)ve, Bequest, Beseem, Birthday, Boiler, Cards, Case, Clubs, Conform, Courtship, Diamonds, Dittos, Do, Effeir, Effere, Fadge, Fashion, Fit, Garb, Gee, Gree, Hearts, Hit, Jump, Long, Major, Match, Minor, Orison, Outcome, Petition, Plaint, Plea, Please, Point, Prayer, Process, Quarterdeck, Queme, Salopette, Samfoo, Samfu, Satisfy, Serve, Spades, Sunday, Supplicat, Track, Trouser, Trumps, Twin, Uniform, Zoot

**Suitable** Apposite, Appropriate, Apt, Becoming, Capable, Congenial, Consonant, Convenance, Convenient, Due, Expedient, FIT, Giusto, Keeping, Opportune, Relevant, Seasonal, Very, Worthy

**Suite** Allemande, Apartment, Chambers, Ensemble, Nutcracker, Partita, Retinue, Rooms, Serenade, Set, Tail, Train

**Suitor** Beau, John Doe, Gallant, Lover, Petitioner, Pretender, Suppli(c)ant, Swain

**Sulk(y)** B(r)oody, Dod, Dort, Gee, Glout(s), Glower, Glum, Grouty, Grumps, Huff, Hump, Jinker, Mardy, Mope, Mump, Pet, Pique, Pout, Spider, Strunt, Stunkard, Sullen, Tout(ie), Towt

**Sullen** Dour, Farouche, Glum(pish), Grim, Moody, Peevish, Stunkard, Sulky, Surly

**Sully** Assoil, Besmirch, Blot, Defile, Glaur(y), Smear, Smirch, Soil, Tarnish, Tar-wash

**Sulphate, Sulphide** Alum, Alunite, Bluestone, Bornite, Copperas, Coquimbite, Glance, Pyrites, Zarnec, Zarnich

**Sulphur** Baregine, Brimstone, Hepar, Oleum, S

**Sultan(a), Sultanate** Caliph, Emir, Hen, Kalif, Oman, Osman, Padishah, Roxane, Saladin, Soldan, Tippoo, Tipu

**Sultry** Humid, Sexy, Smouldering, Steamy

**Sum(s), Sum up** Add(end), Aggregate, Amount, Arsmetric, Bomb, Foot, Number, Perorate, Plumule, QUANTITY, Re-cap, Refund, Total

**Summarize, Summary** Abridge, Abstract, Aperçu, Bird's eye, Brief, Compendium, Condense, Digest, Docket, Epitome, Gist, Instant, Minute,

Precis, Recap, Resumé, Syllabus, Synopsis, Tabloid, Tabulate, Tabulation

**Summer(time)** Aestival, BST, Computer, Estival, Indian, Luke, Prime, Solstice, Totter

**Summerhouse** Belvedere, Chalet, Conservatory, Folly, Gazebo

**Summit** Acme, Acri-, Apex, Brow, Climax, Conference, CREST, Crown, Height, Jole, Peak, Pinnacle, Spire, Vertex, Vertical, Yalta

**Summon(s)** Accite, Arrière-ban, Azan, Beck(on), Call, Cist, Cital, Citation, Command, Convene, Drum, Evoke, Garnishment, Hail, Muster, Order, Page, Post, Preconise, Rechate, Recheat, Reveille, Signal, Sist, Ticket, Warn, Warrant, Writ

**Sumo** Makunouchi

**Sump** Bilge, Drain, Pool, Sink

**Sumpter** Led horse, Pack-horse

**Sumptuous** Expensive, Palatial, Rich(ly), Superb

**Sun(light), Sunny, Sunshine** Bright, Cheer, Day(star), Dry, Glory, Heater, Helio, New Mexico, Parhelion, Phoebean, Photosphere, Ra, Radiant, Rays, Re, Rising, Sol(ar), Soleil, Svastika, Swastika, Tabloid, Tan, Titan, UV

**Sunbathe** Apricate, Bask, Brown, Tan

**Sunbeam** Car, Ray

**Sunburn** Bronze, Combust, Peeling, Tan

**Sunday** Best, Cantate, Care, Carle, Carling, Dominical, Fig, Jubilate, Judica, Laetare, Lost, Low, Mid-Lent, Mothering, Orthodox, Palm, Passion, Quadragesima, Quasimodo, Quinquagesima, Refreshment, Remembrance, Rogation, Rose, Rush-bearing, S, Septuagesima, Sexagesima, Stir-up, Tap-up, Trinity, Whit

**Sunday school** SS

**Sunder** Divide, Divorce, Part, Separate, Sever, Split

**Sundew** Drosera, Eyebright

**Sundry** Divers, Several, Various

**Sunflower** Kansas, KS

**Sunglasses** Shades

**Sun-god** Ra, Surya

> **Sunken** see SINK

**Sunrise, Sun-up** Aurora, Dawn, East

**Sunshade** Awning, Canopy, Chi(c)k, Cloud, Parasol, Umbrella

**Sunspot** Facula, Freckle, Macula

**Sunstroke** Heliosis, Siriasis

**Sunwise** Deasi(u)l, Deasoil, Deis(h)eal, Eutropic

**Sun-worshipper** Heliolater

**Sup** Dine, Eat, Feast, Sample, Sip, Swallow

**Super**  A1, Arch, Extra, Fab(ulous), Great, Grouse, Ideal, Lulu, Paramount, Superb, Terrific, Tip-top, Tops, Walker-on, Wizard

**Superadded**  Advene

**Superb**  A1, Fine, Concours, Grand, Great, Majestic, Splendid

**Supercilious**  Aloof, Arrogant, Bashaw, Cavalier, Haughty, Lordly, Snide, Snooty, Snotty, Snouty, Superior

**Superficial**  Cosmetic, Cursenary, Cursory, Exterior, Facile, Glib, Outside, Outward, Overlying, Perfunctory, Shallow, Sketchy, Skindeep, Smattering, Veneer

> **Superficial(ly)**  may indicate a word outside another

**Superfluous, Superfluity**  Cheville, De trop, Extra, Lake, Mountain, Needless, Otiose, Pleonastic, Redundant, Spare, Unnecessary

**Superhuman**  Bionic, Herculean, Supernatural

**Superintend(ent)**  Boss, Director, Foreman, Guide, Janitor, Oversee(r), Preside, Surveillant, Warden, Zanjero

**Superior(ity)**  Abbess, Abeigh, Above, Advantage, Aloof, Atop, Better, Choice, Custos, De luxe, Dinger, Eminent, Excellent, Exceptional, Finer, Liege, Mastery, Nob, Over, Paramount, Predominance, Prestige, Pretentious, Superordinate, Swell, Top(-loftical), U, Udal, Upper(most), Uppish, Upstage

**Superlative**  Best, Exaggerated, Peerless, Supreme, Utmost

**Superman**  Batman, Bionic, Titan, Ubermensch

**Supermarket**  Co-op, GUM, Self service, Store

**Supernatural**  Divine, Eerie, Fly, Gothic, Mana, Paranormal, Sharp, Siddhi, Unearthly

**Supernumerary**  Additional, Corollary, Extra, Orra

**Supersede**  Replace, Stellenbosch, Supplant

**Superstition**  Aberglaube, Abessa, Fable, Myth, Uncertainty

**Superstructure**  Mastaba(h)

**Supertonic**  Ray

**Supervise(d), Supervisor**  Administer, Chaperone, Check, Direct, Engineer, Foreman, Handle, Manager, Officiate, Overman, Oversee(r), Targe, Under

**Supine**  Inactive, Inert, Lying, Protract

**Supper**  Dinner, Hockey, Meal, Nagmaal, Repast, Soirée

**Supplant**  Displace, Exchange, Replace, Substitute, Supersede

**Supple**  Compliant, Limber, Lissom(e), LITHE, Loose, Pliable, Souple, Wan(d)le, Wannel

**Supplement(ary)**  Addend(um), Addition, And, Annex(e), Appendix, Auxiliary, Eche, Eke, Extra, Parlipomena, Postscript, Ripienist, Ripieno

**Supplicant, Supplicate**  Beg, Entreat, Importune, Invoke, Petition, Request, Schnorr, Sue

**Supplier, Supply** Accommodate, Advance, Afford, Cache, Cater, Commissariat, Crop, Endue, Equip, Feed, Find, Fund, Furnish, Heel, Holp(en), Indue, Issue, Lend, Lithely, Mains, Plenish, Ply, PROVIDE, Purvey, RASC, Retailer, Serve, Source, Stake, Stock, STORE, Vintner, Yield

**Support(er), Supporting** Abacus, Abutment, Adherent, Adminicle, Advocate, Aid, Aliment(ative), Ally, Ammunition, Anchor, Anta, Appui, Arch, Assistant, Axle, Back(bone), Baluster, Banister, Barrack, Base, Batten, Bear, Belt, Bibb, Bier, Bolster, Boom, Bouclée, Bra, Brace, Bracket, Breadwinner, Breast-summer, Bridge, Buttress, Chair, Champion, Chaptrel, Clientele, Column, Confirm, Console, Corbel, Corbel-table, Cross-beam, Crutch, Dado, Diagrid, Dog-shore, Easel, Encourage, Endorse, Endow, Espouse, Fan, Favour, Fid, Finance, Fly-rail, Gamb, Gantry, Garter, Girder, Glia, Headrest, Help, Henchman, Horse, Hound, Idealogue, Impost, Ite, Jack, Jockstrap, Joist, Keep, Kingpost, Knee, Lectern, Leg, Lifebelt, Lifebuoy, Lobby, Loper, Mainstay, Maintain, Miserere, Misericord(e), Monial, Mortsafe, Neuroglia, -nik, Paranymph, Partisan, Partizan, Patronage, Pedestal, Pessary, Pier, Pillar, Plinth, Poppet, Post, Potent, Prop, Proponent, Prop-root, Purlin(e), Pylon, Raft, Reinforce, Relieve, Respond, Rest, Rind, Rod, Roof-plate, Root, Rynd, Sanction, Second, Shore, Skeg, Skewput, Skid, Sleeper, Sling, Snotter, Socle, Solidarity, Splat, Splint, Sponson, Sprag, Staddle, Staff, Staging, Stanchion, Stay, Steady, Stem(pel), Step, Stirrup, Stool, Strut, Stylobate, Subscribe, Subsidy, Succour, Suffragist, Summer, Suppedaneum, Suspender, Sustain, Tailskid, Tee, Telamon, Third, Tie, Tige, Torsel, Trabecula, Tress(el), Trestle, Trivet, Truss, Underpin, Understand, Uphold, Upkeep, Viva, Y-level, Zealot

**Suppose(d), Supposition** An, Assume, Believe, Expect, Guess, Hypothetical, Idea, If, Imagine, Imply, Opine, Presume, Putative, Sepad, Theory

**Suppress(ion)** Abolish, Adaw, Burke, Cancel, Censor, Crush, Ecthlipsis, Elision, Mob(b)le, Quash, Quell, Quench, Restrain, Silence, Smother, Squash, Stifle

**Suppurate, Suppuration** Diapyesis, Discharge, Exude, Fester, Maturate, Ooze, Pus, Pyorrhoea, Rankle

**Supreme, Supremo** Caudillo, Consummate, Kronos, Napoleon, Overlord, Paramount, Peerless, Regnant, Sovereign, Sublime, Top, Utmost

**Surcharge** Addition, Extra, Tax

**Surd** Voiceless

**Sure(ly)** Ay, Bound, Cert(ain), Confident, Definite, Doubtless, Firm, Know, Pardi(e), Pardy, Perdie, Positive, Poz, Safe, Secure, Sicker, Syker, Uh-huh, Yes

**Surety** Bail, Guarantee, Security, Sponsional

**Surf** Breach, Breaker, Rollers, Rote, Sea

**Surface** Appear, Area, Arise, Camber, Day, Dermal, Dermis, Emerge, Exterior, Face, Facet, Macadam, Outward, Patina, Pave, Plane, Rise,

Salband, Side, Skin, Soffit, Superficies, Tarmac, Toroid

**Surf-boat** Masoola(h), Masula

**Surfeit(ed)** Blasé, Cloy, Excess, Glut, Satiate, Stall, Staw

**Surge** Billow, Drive, Gush, Onrush, Seethe, Sway, Swell

**Surgeon** Abernethy, BCh, BS, CHB, CM, Doctor, Lister, Medic, Operator, Plastic, Sawbones, Tang, Vet

**Surgery** Keyhole, Knife, Medicine, Op, Open-heart, Osteoplasty, Prosthetics, Repair, Ta(g)liacotian

**Surly** Cantankerous, Chough, Chuffy, Churl(ish), Crusty, Cynic, Glum, Gruff, Grum, Grumpy, Rough, Sullen, Truculent

**Surmise** Guess, Imagine, Infer, Presume, Suppose

**Surmount** Beat, Climb, Conquer, Crest, Master, Overcome, Scan, Tide, Transcend

**Surname** Cognomen, Patronymic

**Surpass** Bang, Beat, Best, Cap, Ding, Eclipse, Efface, Exceed, Excel, Outdo, Out-Herod, Outshine, Outstrip, Overtop, Transcend

**Surplice** Cotta, Ephod, Rochet, Vakass

**Surplus** Excess, Extra, Glut, Lake, Mountain, Out-over, Over, Overcome, Remainder, Rest, Spare, Surfeit

**Surprise, Surprising** Alert, Amaze, Ambush, Astonish, Bewilder, Bombshell, Caramba, Catch, Confound, Coo, Cor, Crick(e)y, Crikey, Criminé, Cripes, Criv(v)ens, Dear, Eye-opener, Gadso, Gemini, Geminy, Gemony, Golly, Hallo, Hello, Ho, Jeepers, Lawks, Musha, My, Obreption, Och, Odso, Oops, Overtake, Really, Shock, Spot, Stagger, Startle, Stun, Sudden, Turn-up, Wonderment, Wrongfoot, Zowie

**Surrealist** Bizarre, Dali, Ernst, Grotesque, Miro

**Surrender** Capitulate, Cession, Enfeoff, Fall, Forfeit, Hulled, Kamerad, Naam, Recreant, Relinquish, Remise, Rendition, Submit, Succumb, YIELD

**Surreptitious** Clandestine, Covert, Fly, Furtive, Secret, Sly, Underhand

**Surrey** Carriage, Sy

**Surrogate** Agent, Depute, Deputy, Locum, Proxy

**Surround(ed), Surroundings** Ambient, Architrave, Background, Bathe, Bego, Beset, Circumvent, Compass, Embail, Encase, ENCIRCLE, Enclave, Enclose, Encompass, Enfold, Environ, Enwrap, Gird, Hedge, Invest, Mid, Orb, Orle, Outflank, Outside, Perimeter, Setting

**Surtees** Jorrocks, Sponge

**Surveillance, Survey(ing), Surveyor** Behold, Cadastre, Case, Conspectus, Domesday, Espial, Examination, Eye, Geodesy, Groma, Look-see, Once-over, Poll, Recce, Reconnaissance, Regard, Review, Scan, Scrutiny, Stakeout, Supervision, Terrier, Theodolite, Watch

**Survival, Survive, Surviving, Survivor** Cope, Endure, Extant, Hibakusha, Last, Leftover, Outdure, Outlast, Outlive, Outwear, Persist, Relic(t), Ride, Viability, Weather

**Susceptible, Susceptibility** Anaphylaxis, Liable, Receptive, Vulnerable

**Suspect, Suspicion, Suspicious** Askance, Breath, Doubt, Dubious, Fishy, Grain, Guess, Hint, Hunch, Jalouse, Jealous, Misdeem, Misdoubt, Misgiving, Mistrust, Modicum, Notion, Paranoia, Queer, Scent, Smatch, Soupçon, Thought, Tinge

> **Suspect, Suspicious** may indicate an anagram

**Suspend(ed), Suspense, Suspension** Abate, Abeyance, Adjourn, Anabiosis, Cliffhanger, Dangle, Defer, Delay, Freeze, HANG, Intermit, Mist, Moratorium, Pensile, Poise, Reprieve, Sol, Swing, Tenterhooks, Withhold

> **Suspended** may indicate 'ice' (on ice) at the end of a down light

**Sussex** Rape

**Sustain(ed), Sustaining, Sustenance** Abide, Aliment, Bear, Constant, Depend, Endure, Food, Keep, Last, Maintain, Nutriment, Pedal, Prolong, Succour, Support, Tenuto

**Sutler** Vivandière

**Suture** Lambda, Pterion, Stitch

**Suzanne, Suzie** Lenglen, Wong

**Svelte** Lithe, Slender, Slim

**Swab** Dossil, Dry, Mop, Scour, Sponge, Stupe, Tampon, Tompon, Squeegee, Wipe

**Swaddle** Bind, Envelop, Swathe, Wrap

**Swag** Booty, Encarpus, Festoon, Haul, Loot, Maino(u)r, Manner, Matilda, Shiralee, Toran(a)

**Swagger(er), Swaggering** Birkie, Bluster, Boast, Brag, Bragadisme, Bravado, Bucko, Cock, Crow, Matamore, Nounce, Panache, Pra(u)nce, Roll, Roist, Roul, Royster, Ruffle, Side, Strive, Swank, Swash(-buckler)

**Swain** Amoretti, Beau, Churl, Corin, Damon, Hind, Lover, Rustic, Shepherd, Strephon

**Swallow(able), Swallowing** Ariel, Bird, Bolt, Consume, Deglutition, Devour, Down, Drink, Eat, Endue, Englut, Engulf, Esculent, Gobble, Gula, Gulp, Hirundine, Ingest, Ingulf, Itys, Lap, Martin, Martlet, Progne, Quaff, Shift, Sister, Slug, Stomach, Swig, Take

**Swamp(y)** Bog, Bunyip, Deluge, Dismal, Drown, Engulf, Everglade, Flood, Inundate, Lentic, Lerna, Lerne, Mar(i)sh, Morass, Muskeg, Overrun, Overwhelm, Quagmire, Slash, Slough, Sudd, Urman, Vlei, Vly

**Swan(s)** Avon, Bewick's, Bird, Cob, Cygnet, Cygnus, Game, Leda, Lindor, Pen, Seven, Seward, Song, Stroll, Trumpeter, Whooper

**Swank(y)** Boast, Lugs, Pretentious, Side, Style

**Swan-song** Finale, Last air

**Swap, Swop** BARTER, Chop, Commute, Exchange, Scorse, Switch, Trade, Truck

> **Swap(ped)** may indicate an anagram

**Sward** Grass, Green, Lawn, Sod, Turf

**Swarm(ing)** Alive, Bike, Bink, Byke, Cloud, Crowd, Flood, Geminid, Host, Hotter, Infest, Rife, Shin, Shoal, Throng

**Swarthy** Dark, Dusky, Melanotic

**Swash** Swig, Swill

**Swash-buckler** Adventurer, Boaster, Braggart, Gascon, Swordsman

**Swastika** Filfot, Fylfot, Gamma(dion), Hakenkreuz

> **Swat** see SWOT

**Swathe** Bind, Enfold, Swaddle, Wrap

**Sway(ing)** Careen, Carry, Command, Diadrom, Domain, Flap, Fluctuate, Govern, Hegemony, Influence, Lilt, Oscillate, Prevail, Reel, Rock, Roll, Rule, Shog, Shoogle, Swale, Swee, Swing(e), Titter, Totter, Vacillate

**Swear(ing), Swear word** Attest, Avow, Curse, Cuss, Depose, Execrate, Jurant, Juratory, Oath, Pledge, Plight, Rail, Sessa, Tarnal, Tarnation, Vow

**Sweat(ing), Sweaty** Clammy, Diaphoresis, Exude, Forswatt, Glow, Hidrosis, Ooze, Osmidrosis, PERSPIRE, Secretion, Slave, Stew, Sudament, Sudamina, Sudate, Swelter

**Sweater** Circassian, Circassienne, Fair Isle, Guernsey, Jersey, Polo, Pullover, Siwash, Skivvy, Slop-pouch, Woolly

**Swede** Nordic, Rutabaga, Scandinavian, Turnip

**Sweeney** Police, Todd

**Sweep(er), Sweeping(s)** Besom, Broad, Broom, Brush, Clean, Curve, Debris, Detritus, Expanse, Extensive, Lash, Lottery, Net, Oars, Police-manure, Range, Scud, Sling, Soop, Stroke, Surge, Swathe, Vacuum, Waft, Wide

**Sweepstake** Draw, Gamble, Lottery, Raffle, Tattersall's, Tombola

**Sweet(s), Sweetener, Sweetmeat** Adeline, Afters, Alcorza, Aldose, Amabile, Aspartame, Bonbon, Bonus, Bribe, Bull's eye, Burnt-almonds, Butterscotch, Candy, Caramel, Chaptalise, Charming, Choc(olate), Comfit, Confect(ion), Confetti, Confit, Conserve, Crème, Cyclamate, Dessert, Dolce, Dolly, Douce(t), Dowset, Dragee, Dulcet, Elecampane, Flummery, Fondant, Fool, Fragrant, Fresh, Fudge, Glucose, Gob-stopper, Goody, Gum(drop), Gundy, Hal(a)vah, Honey(ed), Ice, Icky, Indican, Jujube, Lavender, Licorice, Liquorice, Lollipop, Lolly, Lozenge, Marchpane, Marshmallow, Marzipan, Melodious, Mint, Mousse, Nectared, Noisette, Nonpareil, Nougat, Pastille, Pea, Pie, Praline, Pud(ding), Redolent, Rock, Romic, Saccharin(e), Scroggin, Seventeen, Sillabub, Sixteen, Solanine, Soot(e), Sop, Sorbet, Split, Sucrose, Sugar, Syllabub, Syrupy, Tart, Thaumatin, Toffee, Torte, Trifle, Truffle, Twee, Uses, William, Winsome, Xylitol

**Sweetbread** Bur(r), Inchpin, Pancreas

**Sweetheart** Amoret, Amour, Beau, Dona(h), Dowsabell, Doxy, Dulcinea,

Flame, Follower, Honey(bunch), Jarta, Jo(e), Leman, Lover, Masher, Neaera, Peat, Romeo, Steady, Tootsy, True-love, Valentine, Yarta, Yarto

**Sweet-seller** Butcher, Confectioner

**Swell(ing)** Adenomata, Ague-cake, Aneurysm, Bag, Bellying, Berry, Billow, Blab, Blister, Bloat, Blow, Boil, Boll, Bolster, Braw, Bulb, Bulge, Bump, Bunion, Capellet, Carnosity, Cat, Chancre, Chilblain, Clour, Cratches, Cyst, Dandy, Diapason, Dilate, DISTEND, Dom, Don, Eger, Enhance, Entasis, Epulis, Excellent, Farcy-bud, Frog, Gall, Gent, Goiter, Goitre, Gout, Grandee, Ground, Haemaloma, Heave, Heighten, Hove, Increase, Inflate, Kibe, L, Lampas(se), Louden, Lump, Macaroni, Mouse, Nodule, Odontoma, Oedema, OK, Ox-warble, Parotitis, Plim, Plump, Protrude, Proud, Pulvinus, Rise, Scirrhus, Scleriasis, Sea, Splenomegaly, Strout, Struma, Stye, Surge, Teratoma, Toff, Torulose, Tuber(cle), Tumescence, Tumour, Tympany, Upsurge, Warble, Wen, Whelk, Windgall

> **Swelling** may indicate a word reversed

**Swelter(ing)** Perspire, Stew, Sweat, Tropical

**Swerve, Swerving** Bias, Deflect, Deviate, Lean, Sheer, Shy, Stray, Swing, Warp, Wheel

**Swift(ly)** Apace, Bird, Dean, Dromond, Fleet, Flock, Hasty, Martlet, Newt, Nimble, Presto, Prompt, Quick, RAPID, Slick, Spanking, Velocipede, Wight

**Swig** Drink, Gulp, Nip, Scour, Swill

**Swill** Guzzle, Leavings, Rubbish, Slosh, Swash

> **Swilling** may indicate an anagram

**Swim(ming)** Bathe, Crawl, Dip, Float, Naiant, Natatorial, Paddle, Reel, Run, Soom, Trudgen, Whirl

> **Swim** may indicate an anagram

**Swimmer** Bather, Cichlid, Duckbill, Duckmole, Dugong, Frogman, Leander, Pad(d)le, Paidle, Planula, Pleopod, Pobble, Terrapin, Trudgen, Webb

> **Swimmer** may indicate a fish

**Swimming costume** Bathers, Bikini, Cossie, One-piece, Tanga, Trunks

**Swindle(r)** Beat, Bucket-shop, Bunco, Bunkosteerer, Cajole, Champerty, CHEAT, Chouse, Con, Defraud, Diddle, Do, Escroc, Fiddle, Fineer, Fleece, Fraud, Gazump, Goose-trap, Gip, Graft, Grifter, Gyp, Hocus, Hustler, Leg, Leger, Longfirm, Magsman, Nobble, Peter Funk, Plant, Racket, Ramp, Rig, Rogue, Scam, Sell, Shark, Sharper, Shicer, Shyster, Skelder, Skin, Sting, Stumer, Suck, Swiz(z), Trick, Twist, Two-time

**Swine(herd)** Boar, Brute, Cad, Eumaeus, Gadarene, Hog, Peccary, Pig, Pork, Rotter, Sounder, Sow, Sybotic

**Swing(er), Swinging** Colt, Dangle, Flail, Hang, Hep, Kip(p), Lilt, Metronome, Mod, Music, Oscillate, Pendulate, Pendulum, Rock, Rope, Shoogie, Shuggy, Slew, Swale, Sway, Swee, Swerve, Swey, Swipe, Trapeze, Vibratile, Wave, Wheel, Whirl, Yaw

**Swipe(s)** Backhander, Beer, Haymaker, Steal, Strike, Tap-lash

**Swirl** Eddy, Purl, Swoosh, Tourbill(i)on, Twist, Whirl

> **Swirling** may indicate an anagram

**Swish** Cane, Rustle, Smart, Whir, Whisper

**Swiss** Genevese, Ladin, Roll, Tell, Vaudois

**Switch** Birch, Change, Convert, Exchange, Hairpiece, Replace, Retama, Rocker, Rod, Scutch, Thyristor, Twig, Wave, Zap

**Switzerland** CH, Helvetia

**Swivel** Caster, Pivot, Root, Rotate, Spin, Terret, Territ, Torret, Turret, Wedein

**Swiz** Chiz(z)

**Swollen** Blown, Bollen, Bulbous, Full, Gourdy, Gouty, Nodose, Tumid, Turgid, Varicose, Vesiculate

**Swoon** Blackout, Collapse, Deliquium, Dover, Dwa(l)m, Dwaum, Faint

**Swoop** Descend, Dive, Glide, Plummet, Souse

> **Swop** see SWAP

**Sword(-like)** Andrew Ferrara, Anelace, Angurvadel, Anlace, Arondight, Balisarda, Bilbo, Blade, Brand, Brandiron, Brond, Cemitare, Claymore, Curtal-ax, Curtana, Curtax, Cutlass, Daisho, Damascene, Damaskin, Damocles, Dance, Dirk, Duranda(l), Durindana, Ensate, Ensiform, Epée, Espada, Estoc, Excalibur, Falchion, Faulchi(o)n, Firangi, Foil, Fox, Gladius, Glaive, Gleave, Hanger, Joyeuse, Katana, Kendo, Kirpan, Kris, Kukri, Kusanagi, Mandau, Merveilleuse, Mimming, Morglay, Nothung, Rapier, Rosse, Sabre, Schiavone, Schlager, Scimitar, Semita(u)r, Shabble, Shamshir, Sigh, Simi, Skene-dhu, Spadroon, Spirtle, Spit, Spurtle(blade), Steel, Toasting-iron, Toledo, Tuck, Tulwar, Waster, White-arm

**Sword-bearer, Swordsman, Swordswoman** Aramis, Athos, Blade, Brenda(n), D'Artagnon, Fencer, Frog, Gladiator, Porthos, Selictar, Spadassin, Spartacus, Swashbuckler, Zorro

**Sword-dancer** Matachin

**Swordfish** Espada, Istiophorus, Xiphias

**Sword-swallower** Samite

**Swot** Dig, Grind, Kill, Mug, Smug, Stew, Strike, Swat

**Sybarite** Aristippus, Epicure, Hedonist, Voluptuary

**Sycamore** Acer, Maple, Plane, Tree

**Sycophant** Crawler, Creeper, Damocles, Fawner, Lickspittle, Parasite, Pickthank, Toad-eater, Toady, Yesman

**Syllabary** Katakana

**Syllable(s)** Acatalectic, Aretinian, Om

**Syllabus** Program(me), Prospectus, Résumé, Summary, Table

**Syllogism** Argument, Conclusion, Deduction, Epicheirema

**Sylph**  Ariel, Nymph

**Symbol(ic), Symbolism, Symbolist**  Acrophony, Agma, Allegory, Aniconic, Ankh, Apostrophus, Aramanth, Asterisk, Cachet, Character, Cipher, Clef, Crest, Daffodil, Decadent, Double-axe, Eagle, Emblem, Eng, Hieroglyph, Hierogram, Icon, Index, Kanji, Logo(gram), Mallarmé, Mandala, Mark, Metaphor, Mezuzah, Mystical, Nominal, Notation, One, Ouroborus, Pentacle, Pi, Presa, Rose, Rune, Semiotic, Shamrock, Sign, Status, Svastika, Swastika, Talisman, Thistle, Tilde, Token, Totem, Triskele, Triskelion, Uraeus, Yoni

**Symmetric(al), Symmetry**  Balance, Digonal, Diphycercal, Even, Harmony, Isobilateral, Regular

**Sympathetic, Sympathise(r), Sympathy**  Approval, Compassion, Condole(nce), Condone, Congenial, Crypto, Empathy, Fellow-traveller, Par, Pity, Rapport, Ruth, Side

**Symphony**  Concert, Eroica, Fifth, Music, Opus, Pastoral, Sinfonia, Unfinished

**Symposium**  Assembly, Conference, Synod

**Symptom(s)**  Feature, Indicia, Semeiotic, Sign, Syndrome, Trait

**Synagogue**  Shul, Temple

**Synchronise**  Coincide, Tune

**Syncopated**  Abridged, Revamp, Zoppo

**Syndicate**  Associate, Cartel, Combine, Mafioso, Pool, Ring

**Syndrome**  Characteristic, ME, Pattern, Reye's

**Synod**  Assembly, Conference, Convocation

**Synonym(ous)**  Comparison, Reciprocal

**Synopsis**  Abstract, Blurb, Conspectus, Digest, Outline, Résumé, Schema, SUMMARY

**Syntax**  Grammar

**Synthesis**  Amalgam, Fusion, Merger

**Synthesizer**  Vocoder

**Synthetic**  Ersatz, Fake, False, Mock, Spencerian

**Syphilis**  Lues

**Syrian**  Aramaean, Aramaic, Druse, Druz(e), Hittite, Levantine

**Syringe(s)**  Douche, Flutes, Harpoon, Hypo, Needle, Reeds, Spray, Squirt, Wash

**Syrup**  Capillaire, Cassis, Diacodion, Diacodium, Flattery, Grenadine, Linctus, Maple, Molasses, Moskonfyt, Orgeat, Rob, Sugar, Treacle

**System(atic)**  Binary, Braille, Code, Cosmos, Course, Decimal, Dewey, Economy, Eocene, Ergodic, Establishment, Feudal, Giorgi, Linear, Madras, METHOD, Metric, Miocene, Nervous, Network, Notation, Octal, Order, Organon, Permian, Pleiocene, Process, Regime, Regular, Scientific, SI, Solar, Structure, Theory, Tommy, Trias(sic), Universe

# Tt

**T** Bone, Junction, Tau-cross, Tango, Tee, Time

**Tab** Bill, Check, LABEL, Tally

**Tabby** Blabbermouth, Brindled, CAT, Gossip, Mottled, Spinster, Striped, Trout

**Tabitha** Gazelle

**Table(-like)** Alphonsine, Altar, Board, Bradshaw, Calendar, CHART, Counter, Credence, Desk, Diagram, Dolmen, Ephemeris, Food, Graph, Green-cloth, Gueridon, Index, Key, LIST, Mahogany, Mensa(l), Mesa, Monopode, Occasional, Pembroke, Periodic, Piecrust, Plane, Pythagoras, Reckoner, Roll, Round, Rudolphine, Slab, Spoon, Stall, Stone, Tabular, Te(a)poy, Trolley

**Table-land** Kar(r)oo, Mesa, Plateau, Puna

**Table-list** Memo, Menu

**Tablet** Abacus, Album, Aspirin, Caplet, Eugebine, Medallion, Osculatory, Ostracon, Ostrakon, PAD, PILL, Plaque, Slate, Stele, Stone, Tombstone, Torah, Triglyph, Triptych, Troche, Trochisk, Ugarit

**Table-talker** Deipnosophist

**Table-turner** Tartar

**Table-ware** China, Cutlery, Silver

**Taboo, Tabu** Ban(ned), Bar, Blackball, Forbidden

**Tacit, Taciturn(ity)** Implicit, Laconic, Mumps, Silent, Understood

**Tack** Baste, Beat, Cinch, Clubhaul, Cobble, Gybe, Leg, Martingale, Nail, Saddlery, Salt-horse, SEW, Sprig, Veer, White-seam, Yaw, Zigzag

**Tackle** Accost, Approach, Attempt, Beard, Bobstay, Burton, Claucht, Claught, Clevis, Clew-garnet, Collar, Dead-eye, Garnet, Gear, Haliard, Halyard, Harness, Jury-rig, Rig, Scrag

**Tact, Tactful** Delicacy, Diplomacy, Diplomatic, Discreet, Discretion, Savoir-faire

**Tactic(s)** Audible, Manoeuvre, Plan, Ploy, STRATEGY, Strong-arm

**Tactless(ness)** Blundering, Brash, Gaffe, Gauche

**Tadpole** Polliwig, Polliwog, Pollywig, Pollywog, Porwiggle

**Taffy** Thief, Toffee, Welshman

**Tag** Aglet, Cliché, End, Epithet, FOLLOW, Kabaddi, Label, Quote, Remnant, Tab, TICKET

**Tail, Tailpiece** Apocopate, APPENDAGE, Bob, Brush, Cercal, Cercus, Coda, Colophon, Cue, Dock, Empennage, Fan, Floccus, FOLLOW, Fud, Liripoop, Pole, PS, Queue, Rumple-bane, Seat, Scut, Stag, Stern, Telson,

TIP, Train, Uropygium, Uro(some), Women

**Tailless**  Acaudal, An(o)urous, Fee-simple

**Tail-lobes**  Anisocercal

**Tailor**  Bespoke, Bushel, Cabbager, Couturier, Cutter, Darzi, Durzi, Feeble, Nine, Outfitter, Pricklouse, Sartor, Seamster, Snip, Starveling, Whipcat

> **Tailor**  may indicate an anagram

**Taint(ed)**  Besmirch, Blemish, Fly-blown, High, Infect, Leper, Off, SPOIL, Stain, Stigma, Trace, Unwholesome

**Taiwan**  RC

**Take, Taken, Taking, Take over**  Absorb, ACCEPT, Adopt, Assume, Attract, Bag, Beg, Bite, Bone, Borrow, CAPTURE, Catch, Coup, Detract, Dishy, Distrain, Exact, Get, Grab, Haul, Hent, House, Incept, Ingest, Mess, Nick, Occupy, Pocket, Quote, R, Rec, Receipt, Recipe, Rob, Smitten, Snatch, Sneak, STEAL, Stomach, Subsume, Swallow, Sweet, Toll, Trump, Turnover, Usurp, Wan, Winsome, Wrest

**Take away, Take off**  Aph(a)eresis, Carry-out, Deduct, Dock, Doff, Esloin, Exenterate, Jato, Parody, Press-gang, Shanghai, Skit, Subtract, Vertical, VTO(L)

**Take care**  Guard, See, Tend, Watch

> **Taken up**  may indicate reversed

**Take part**  Act, Engage, Side

**Talbot House**  Toc H

**Talc**  Potstone, Rensselaerite, Soapstone, Steatite

**Tale(s)**  Allegory, Blood, Boccaccio, Conte, Decameron, Edda, Fable, Fabliau, Fiction, Gag, Geste, Hadith, Iliad, Jeremiad, Legend, Lie, Mabinogion, Maise, Ma(i)ze, Marchen, Mease, Milesian, Narrative, Odyssey, Pentameron, Rede, Saga, Sandabar, Score, Sinbad, Sind(a)bad, STORY, Tradition, Weird

**Tale-bearer, Tale-teller**  Gossip, Grass, Informer, Sneak, Tattler, Tusitala

**Talent(ed)**  Accomplishment, Aptitude, Bent, Dower, Faculty, Flair, Genius, Gift, Knack, Nous, Schtick, Versatile, Virtuoso

**Talion**  Reprisal

**Talisman**  Amulet, Charm, Saladin, Sampo, Telesm

**Talk, Talker, Talks**  Ana, Articulate, Bibble-babble, Blab, Blague, Blat, Blether-skate, Cant, Chat, Chinwag, Chirp, Circumlocution, Colloquy, Commune, Confabulate, Confer, Converse, Cross, Descant, Dialogue, Diatribe, Dilate, Discourse, Diseur, Earful, Express, Filibuster, Gab, Gabble, Gabnash, Gas, Gibber, Gossip, Grandiloquence, Harp, Imparl, Jabber, Jargon, Jaw, Jazz, Korero, Lip, Logorrhoea, Macrology, Mang, Maunder, Mince, Monologue, Nashgab, Omniana, Palabra, Palaver, Parlance, Parley, Patter, Pawaw, Perorate, Phraser, Pidgin, Pitch, Potter, Powwow, Prate, Prattle, Prose, Ramble, Rap, Rigmarole, Rote, SALT, Shop, Slang(-whang), Soliloquy, SPEAK, Spiel, Turkey, Twaddle, Twitter,

Unbosom, Up(s), Utter, Vocal, Waffle, Witter, Wongi, Wrangle, Yabber, Yack, Yak, Yap, Yalta, Yatter

**Talkative** Chatty, Fluent, Gabby, Garrulous, Gash, Glib, Voluble

**Tall** Exaggerated, Hie, High, Hye, Lanky, Lofty, Long, Procerity, Randle-tree, Tangle, Taunt, Tower

**Tallboy** Chest, Dresser

**Tallow** Greaves, Hatchettite, Wax

**Tally** AGREE, Census, Correspond, Count, Match, Notch, Record, SCORE, Stick, Stock, Tab, Tag

**Talon** Claw, Ogee, Single

**Talus** Scree

**Tamasha** Fuss, To-do

**Tame** Amenage, Break, Docile, Domesticate, Meek, Mild, Snool, Subdue

**Tamp, Tampon** Plug

**Tamper** Bishop, Cook, Doctor, Fake, Fiddle, Meddle, Monkey

**Tam-tam** Gong

**Tan(ned), Tanned skin, Tanning** Adust, Bablah, Babul, Bark, Basil, Beige, BROWN, Catechu, Insolate, Lambast, Leather, Neb-neb, Paste, Pipi, Puer, Pure, Spank, Sun, Umber, Valonea, Val(l)onia, Ybet

**Tandem** Duo, Random

**Tang** Relish, Smack, Taste

**Tangent** Ratio, Slope, Touching

**Tangible** Concrete, Palpable, Plain, Solid, Tactual

**Tangle** Alga, Badderlock, Burble, Dulse, Embroil, Entwine, Fank, Heap, Implication, Ket, KNOT, Labyrinth, Laminaria, Lutin, Mat, Mix, Nest, Ore, Pleach, RAVEL, Sea-girdle, Seaweed, Skean, Skein, Snarl, Taigle, Taut(it), Tawt, Thicket, Varec

> **Tangled** may indicate an anagram

**Tank** Amphibian, Aquarium, Centurion, Challenger, Chieftain, Cistern, Feedhead, Keir, Kier, Mouse, Panzer, Pod, RESERVOIR, Septic, Sherman, Sponson, Sump, Think, Tiger, Vat, Vivarium, Whippet

**Tankard** Blackjack, Pewter, Pot, Stein

**Tanker** Bowser, Lorry, Oiler

**Tanner(y)** Bender, Kick, Solarium, Sunbather, Sunshine, Tawery, Tester(n), 'VId', Zack

**Tannin** Catechu

**Tantalise** Entice, Tease, Tempt, Torture

**Tantalum** Ta

**Tantivy** Alew, Halloo

**Tantrum** Paddy, Pet, Rage, Scene, Tirrivee, Tirrivie

**Tap(ping), Taps** Accolade, Bibcock, Blip, Broach, Bug, Cock, Drum,

Faucet, Flick, Hack, Milk, Paracentesis, Pat, Percuss, Petcock, RAP, Spigot, Stopcock, Stroup, Tat, Tit, Touk, Tuck

**Tape** DAT, DRINK, Ferret, Finish, Incle, Inkle, Measure, Passe-partout

**Taper(ing)** Diminish, Fastigiate, Lanceolate, Narrow, Nose, Subulate, Tail

**Tapestry** Alentous, Arras(ene), Bayeux, Bergamot, Crewel-work, Dosser, Gobelin, Hanging, Oudenarde, Tapet

**Tapeworm** Hydatid, Measle, Scolex, Taenia

**Tapioca** Cassava, Yuca, Yucca

**Tapir** Anta

**Tar, Tar product** AB, Bitumen, Creosote, Egg, Gladwellise, Gob, Maltha, Matelot, Matlo, Naphtha, Needle, OS, Parcel, Pay, Picamar, Picene, Pitch, Rating, Retene, Sailor, Salt, Uintahite, Uintaite, Xylol

**Tardy** Behindhand, Dilatory, Late, SLOW

**Tare** Tine, Vetch

**Target** AIM, Blank, Butt, End, Hub, Magpie, Mark, OBJECT, Pelta, Pin, Prick, Quintain, Sitter, Tee

**Tariff** List, Rate, Zabeta

**Tarnish** Discolour, Soil, Stain, Sully, Taint

**Taro** Arum, Coc(c)o, Dasheen, Eddo

**Tarot** Arcana

**Tarragon** Staragen

**Tarry** Bide, Dally, Leng, LINGER, Stay, Sticky

**Tarsier** Malmag

**Tarsus** Saul

**Tart** Acetic, Acid, Broad, Charlotte, Cocotte, Cupid, Dariole, Doxy, Duff, Flam(m), Flan, Flawn, Harlot, Hussy, Jade, Lemony, Moll, Mort, Nana, PIE, Pinnace, Piquant, Pro, Quean, Quine, SHARP, Sour, Stew, Strumpet, Tatin, Tramp, Treacle, Trull

**Tartan** Maud, Plaid, Set(t), Trews

**Tartar** Argal, Argol, Beeswing, Crust, Plaque, Rough, Tam(b)erlane, Zenocrate

**Tashkent** Uzbek

**Task** Assignment, Aufgabe, CHORE, Duty, Errand, Exercise, Fag, Imposition, Mission, Ordeal, Pensum, Stint, Thankless, Vulgus

**Tasmania** Apple Isle

**Tassel** Pompom, Toorie, Tourie, Tuft

**Taste, Tasteful, Tasty** Aesthetic, Appetite, Degust, Discrimination, EAT, Fashion, Flavour, Form, Gout, Gust, Hint, Lick, Palate, Penchant, Pica, Pree, Refinement, Relish, SAMPLE, Sapor, Sar, Savour, Sc(h)meck, Sip, Smack, Snack, Stomach, Soupçon, Tang, Titbit, Toothsome, TRY, Vertu, Virtu

**Tasteless** Appal, Fade, Flat, Insipid, Vapid, Vulgar, Watery, Wearish, Wersh

**Tat, Tatter, Tatty** Rag, Ribbon, Roon, Scrap, Shred, Tag, Tan, Untidy

**Tattie-bogle** Scarecrow

**Tattle(r)** Blab, Chatter, GOSSIP, Prate, Rumour, Sneak, Snitch, Totanus, Willet

**Tattoo** Drum, Moko, Rataplan, Row-dow, Tat

**Taught** Up

**Taunt** Dig, Fling, Gibe, Gird, JEER, Rag, Ridicule, Twight, Twit

**Taut** Stiff, Tense

**Tavern** Bar, Bodega, Bousing-ken, Bush, Fonda, INN, Kiddleywink, Kneipe, Mermaid, Mitre, Mughouse, Pothouse, Shebeen, Taphouse

**Taw** Alley, Ally, Marble

**Tawdry** Catchpenny, CHEAP, Flashy, Gaudy, Sleazy, Tatty

**Tawny** Brindle, Dusky, Fawn, Mulatto, Port, Tan

**Tawse** Cat, Lash, Thong, Whip

**Tax(ing), Taxation** ACT, Aid, Agist, Alms-fee, Assess, Carucage, Cense, Cess, CHARGE, Custom, Danegeld, Direct, Duty, EPT, Escot, Escuage, Exact, Excise, Exercise, Gabelle, Geld, Hidage, Impose, Impost, Indirect, IR, Jaghir(e), Jagir, Levy, Likin, Lot, Murage, Octroi, Overwork, PAYE, Peter-pence, Poll, Poundage, PT, Rate, Rome-pence, Scat(t), Scot (and lot), Scutage, Sess, SET, Skat, Stent, Streetage, Taille, Tallage, Talliate, Task, Teind, Tithe, Toilsome, Toll, Tonnage, Try, VAT, Wattle, Window, Zakat

**Tax area** Tahsil, Talooka, Taluk(a)

**Tax-collector, Taxman** Amildar, Cheater, Farmer, Gabeller, Inspector, IR(S), Publican, Stento(u)r, Tithe-proctor, Tollman, Undertaker

**Taxi** Cab, Hackney, Samlor

**Taxidermist** Venus

> **Taxman** see TAX-COLLECTOR

**TE** Lawrence, Ross, Shaw

**Tea** Afternoon, Assam, Beef, Black, Bohea, Brew, Brick, Cambric, Camomile, Ceylon, Cha, Chamomile, Chanoyu, China, Chirping-cup, Congo(u), Cream, Cuppa, Darjeeling, Earl Grey, Grass, Green, Gunfire, Gunpowder, High, Hyson, Indian, K(h)at, Labrador, Lapsang, Leaves, Ledum, Marijuana, Maté, Oolong, Oulong, Pekoe, Qat, Red-root, Rooibos, Senna, Souchong, Switchel, Tay, Thea, Theophylline, Twankay, Yerba (de Maté)

**Teach(er), Teaching (material)** Acharya, Adjoint, Agrege, Apostle, Barbe, Beale, BEd, Buss, COACH, Con(ne), Didactic, Didascalic, Docent, Doctrine, Dogma, Dominie, Dressage, Edify, EDUCATE, EIS, ELT, Explain, Froebel, Gerund-grinder, Gooroo, Gospel, Governess, Guru, Head, Hodja, Inform, Instil, Instruct, Ism, Kho(d)ja, Lair, Lancasterian, Larn, Lear(e), Lecturer, Leir, Lere, Maam, Magister, Maharishi, Mallam, Marker,

Marm, Master, Maulvi, Mentor, Miss, Mistress, Molla(h), Monitor, Montessorian, Moola(h), Mufti, Mullah, Munshi, Pedagogue, Pedant, Preceptor, Prof, Privat-docent, Rabbi, Realia, Rhetor, Schoolman, Show, Sir, Smriti, Socrates, Sophist, Staff, Starets, Staretz, Sunna, Swami, Tantra, Train(er), Tutor, Usher

**Teach-in** Seminar

**Team** Colts, Crew, Ecurie, Eleven, Equipe, Outfit, Oxen, Panel, Possibles, Probables, Relay, Scrub, SIDE, Span, Squad, Staff, Troupe, Turnout, Unicorn, United, XI

**Tea-party** Bunfight, Drum, Kettledrum, Shine

**Teapot** Billycan, Cadogan, Samovar

**Tear(s), Tearable, Tearful, Tearing** Beano, Claw, Crocodile, Drop, Eye-drop, Eye-water, Greeting, Hurry, Lacerate, Laniary, Pelt, Ranch, Rash, REND, Rheum, Rip, Rive, Rume, Scag, Shred, Split, Spree, Tire, Wet, Worry, Wrench, Wrest

**Tearaway** Get, Hothead, Ned

**Tear-jerker** Onion

**Tear-pit** Crumen, Larmier

**Tease, Teasing** Arch, Backcomb, Badinage, Bait, Banter, Chap, Chiack, Chip, Chyack, Cod, Grig, Guy, Hank, Imp, Ironic, Itch, Josh, Kid, Mag, Nark, Persiflage, RAG, Rally, Rib, Rot, TANTALISE, Toaze, Torment(or), Twilly, Twit

**Teasel** Dipsacus, Valerian

**Teat** Dug, Dummy, Mamilla, Nipple, Pap, Tit

**Tea-time** Chat

**Teaze** Gig, Moze

**Technetium** Tc

**Technical, Technician, Technique** Adept, Artisan, College, Execution, Kiwi, Manner, METHOD, Operative, Science

**Ted(dy)** Bodgie, Dexter, Ducktail, Moult, Widgie

**Tedium, Tedious** Boring, Deadly, Drag, Dreich, Dull, Ennui, Long, Longspun, Monotony, Operose, Prosy, Soul-destroying, TIRING, Wearisome, Yawn

**Tee** Hub, Umbrella

**Teem(ing)** Abound, Bustling, Empty, Great, Pullulate, Swarm

**Teenager** Adolescent, Junior, Juvenile, Minor, Mod, Sharpie

> **Teeth** see TOOTH

**Teething ring** Coral

**Teetotal(ler)** Abdar, Blue Ribbon, Nephalist, Rechabite, Temperate, TT, Wowser

**Telegram, Telegraph** Cable, Ems, Grapevine, Greetings, Message, Telex, Wire

**Telepathy, Telepathic** Clairvoyance, ESP, Seer

**Telephone** Ameche, Bell, Blower, BT, Call, Dial, Grace, Handset, Horn, Intercom, Line, Mercury, Ring, STD

**Teleprinter** Creed

**Telescope** Binocle, Collimator, Glass, Palomar, Reflector, Refractor, Shorten, Spyglass, Stadia, Tube

**Television, Telly** Box, ITV, PAL, RTE, Set, Tube, TV, Video

**Tell** Acquaint, Announce, Apprise, Archer, Beads, Blab, Clipe, Clype, Compt, Direct, DISCLOSE, Divulge, Grass, Impart, Inform, NARRATE, Noise, Notify, Number, Recite, Recount, Relate, Report, Retail, Sneak, Snitch, Spin, Teach, William

**Tellurium** Te

**Temerity** Cheek, Gall, Impertinence, Imprudence, Impudence, Incaution, Rashness, Recklessness

**Temper, Temperate** Abstemious, Abstinent, Allay, Anneal, Assuage, Calm, Continent, Dander, Delay, Ease, Fireworks, Flaky, Irish, Leaven, MILD, Mitigate, Moderate, MOOD, Neal, Paddy, Pet, Rage, Season, Sober, Spitfire, Spleen, Swage, Tantrum, Techy, Teen, Teetotal, Tetchy, Tiff, Tone, Trim, Tune

**Temperament(al)** Bent, Blood, Crasis, Kidney, Mettle, Moody, NATURE, Over-sensitive

**Temperance** Moderation, Pledge, Rechabite

**Temperature** Absolute, Celsius, Centigrade, Chambré, Fahrenheit, Fever, Flashpoint, Heat, Kelvin, Regulo, Weed, Weid

**Tempest(uous)** Bourasque, Euroclydon, Gale, High, Marie, STORM(Y)

**Temple, Temple gate** Adytum, Capitol, Chapel, Church, Delphi, Delubrum, Ephesus, Fane, Gompa, Gurdwara, Haffet, Haffit, Heroon, Inner, Mandir(a), Masjid, Monopteron, Monopteros, Mosque, Museum, Naos, Pagod(a), Pantheon, Parthenon, SHRINE, Teocalli, Teopan, Torii, Vihara, Wat

**Tempo** Agoge, Rate, RHYTHM, Rubato

**Temporary** Acting, Caretaker, Cutcha, Ephemeral, Hobjob, Interim, Locum, Makeshift, Pro tem, Stopgap, Temp, Transient, Transitional

**Tempt(ation), Tempting, Tempter, Temptress** Allure, Apple, Bait, Beguile, Beset, Dalilah, Decoy, Delilah, ENTICE, Eve, Groundbait, Impube, Lure, Providence, Satan, Seduce, Siren, Snare, Tice, Test, Trial

**Ten** Commandments, Dectet, Denary, 10, Iota, Tera-, Tribes, X

**Tenacious, Tenacity** Clayey, Determined, Dogged, Fast, Guts, Hold, Persevering, Persistent, Resolute, Retentive, Sticky

**Tenancy, Tenant(s)** Cosherer, Cotter, Dreng, Fcuar, Feudatory, Homage, Ingo, Inhabit, Leaseholder, Lessee, LODGER, Metayer, Occupier, Rentaller, Renter, Socager, Socman, Sokeman, Suckener, Valvassor, Vassal, Vavasour, Visit

**Tend** Care, Dress, Herd, Incline, Lean, Liable, Nurse, Prone, Run, Shepherd, Verge

**Tendency** Apt, Bent, Bias, Conatus, Drift, Import, Penchant, Trend

**Tender(ness)** Affettuoso, Amoroso, Bid, Bill, Coin, Ding(h)y, Dingey, Fond, Frail, Gentle, Green, Humane, Jolly-boat, Nesh, Nurse, OFFER, Pinnace, Prefer, Present, Proffer, Proposal, Quotation, Red Cross, Sair, Shepherd, SOFT, Sore, SRN, Submit, Sympathy, Tendre

**Tenderfoot** Babe, Chechacho, Chechako, Cub, Greenhorn, Innocent

**Tenderloin** Psoas, Undercut

**Tendon** Achilles, Aponeurosis, Hamstring, Paxwax, Sinew, String, Vinculum, Whitleather

**Tendril(led)** Capreolate, Cirrose, Cirrus, Tentacle

**Tenement** Rook, Tack

**Tenet** Adiaphoron, Creed, DOCTRINE, Dogma

**Tenfold** Decuple

**Tennis** LTA, Set, Sphairistike, Wimbledon

**Tenor** Course, DRIFT, Effect, Gigli, Gist, T, Timbre, Trial, Vein

**Tense** Aor, Aorist, Case, Drawn, Edgy, Electric, Essive, Imperfect, Keyed up, Mood(y), Nervy, Overstrung, Past, Perfect, Pluperfect, Preterite, Rigid, Stiff, Strict, T, TAUT, Uptight

**Tensing** Sherpa

**Tension** Isometrics, STRAIN, Stress, Stretch, Tone, Yips

**Tent** Cabana, Douar, Duar, Kedar, Kibitka, Marquee, Pavilion, Probe, Shamiana(h), Tabernacle, Teepee, Tepee, Tipi, Top, Topek, Tupek, Tupik, Wigwam, Y(o)urt

**Tentacle** Actinal, Feeler

**Tentative** Empirical, Experimental, Gingerly

**Tent-dweller, Tent-maker** Camper, Indian, Kedar, Omar, St Paul

**Tenth** Disme, Teind, Tithe

**Ten Thousand** Toman

**Tenuous** Frail, Slender, Slight, Thin, Vague

**Tenure** Burgage, Copyhold, Cottier(ism), Drengage, Fee-farm, Feu, Frankalmoi(g)n(e), Gavelkind, Leasehold, Manorial, Occupation, Raiyatwari, Rundale, Runrig, Ryotwari, Socage, TERM, Venville, Zemindar

**Tepid** Laodicean, Lukewarm

**Terbium** Tb

**Term(s), Terminal, Termly** Anode, Buffer, Coast, Coste, Desinant, Distal, EPITHET, Expression, Final, Gnomon, Goal, Half, Hilary, Lent, Michaelmas, PERIOD, Sabbatical, Semester, Session, Stint, Stretch, Trimester, Trimestrial, Ultimatum, WORD, Zeroth

**Termagant**  Jade, Shrew, Shrow, Spitfire, Vixen

**Terminate, Termination, Terminus**  Abort, Axe, Conclude, Depot, Desinent, Earth, END, Expiry, FINISH, Goal, Naricorn, Suffix

**Termite**  Duck-ant

**Tern**  Egg-bird, Scray, Three

**Terrace**  Barbette, Beach, Bench, Linch, Lynchet, Perron, Shelf, Stoep, Tarras, Veranda(h)

**Terra-cotta**  Tanagra

**Terrain**  Area, Landscape, Tract

**Terrapin**  Diamondback, Emydes, Emys, Slider, Turtle

**Terrible, Terribly**  Awful, Deadly, Fell, Frightful, Ghastly, Horrible, Much, Odious, Very

**Terrible person**  Humgruffi(a)n, Ivan, Ogre

**Terrier**  Aberdeen, Airedale, Apsos, Boston, Bull, Catalogue, Griffon, Kerry blue, Maltese, Pinscher, Ratter, Register, Scottie, Sealyham, Skye, TA

**Terrific, Terrified, Terrify**  Aghast, Agrise, Agrize, Agryze, Appal, Awe, Enorm, Fear, Fine, Fley, Gast, Helluva, Huge, Overawe, PETRIFY, Scare, Superb, Unman, Yippee

**Territory**  Abthane, Ap(p)anage, Colony, Domain, Dominion, Emirate, Enclave, Exclave, Goa, Lebensraum, Manor, Panhandle, Protectorate, Province, Realm, REGION, Sphere, Sultanate, Ter(r)

**Terror**  Bugaboo, Bugbear, FEAR, Fright, Panic

**Terrorist**  Alarmist, Anarchist, Bogeyman, Bomber, Bully, Cagoulard, Desperado, Dynamitard, Eta, Hijacker, Mau-mau, Mountain, Nihilist, Pirate, PLO, Provo, Robespierre

**Terry**  Ellen, Towel

**Terse**  Abrupt, Brusque, Curt, Laconic, Pithy, Precise, Succinct

**Tertiary**  Cainozoic, Eocene, Miocene, Oligocene, Pliocene

**Test(er), Testing**  Acid, Appro, Assay, Bender, Candle, Canopy, Check, Cloze, Conn(er), Crucial, Crucible, Crunch, Docimastic, Dummy-run, Eprouvette, Examine, Exercise, Experiment, International, Means, MOT, Mug, Neckverse, Oral, Ordalian, ORDEAL, Pale, PH, Pilot, Pree, Preeve, Preif, Preve, Probe, Proof, Prove, Pyx, Quiz, Rally, Reagent, Rorschach, SAT, Schick's, Screen, Showdown, Shroff, Sixpence, Sound, Tempt, Touch, Trier, Trior, Try, Viva, Wasserman's, Zack

**Testament**  Bible, Heptateuch, Hexateuch, New, Old, Pentateuch, Scripture, Septuagint, Tanach, Targum, Will

**Testicle(s)**  Balls, Knackers, Nuts, Ridgel, Ridgil, Rig(gald), Rocks, Stone

**Testify, Testimonial, Testimony**  Character, Chit, Declare, Depone, Deposition, EVIDENCE, Rap, Scroll, Witness

**Testy, Tetchy**  Cross, Narky, Peevish, Ratty

**Tetanus**  Lockjaw

**Tête a tête**  Collogue, Confab, Hobnob, Twosome

**Tether**  Cord, Endurance, Noose, Picket, Seal, Stringhalt, TIE

**Tetrahedrite**  Fahlerz, Fahlore

**Tetrarchy**  Iturea

**Tetrasyllabic**  Paeon

**Teuton(ic)**  Erl-king, German, Goth, Herren, Vandal

**Texas**  Ranger

**Text(s), Textbook**  ABC, Body, Donat, Libretto, Octapla, Pyramid, Quran, Responsa, Rubric, Script, Shema, SUBJECT, Tetrapla, Thesis, Topic, Upanis(h)ad, Vulgate, Zohar

**Textile**  Cloth, Fabric, Mercy

**Texture**  Constitution, Feel, Fiber, Fibre, Grain, Wale, Woof

**Thailand**  Lao(s), Shan, Siam

**Thallium**  Tl

**Thames**  Father, Tamesis

**Thank(s), Thankful, Thanksgiving**  Appreciate, Collins, Gloria, Grace, Gramercy, Grateful, Gratitude, Kaddish, Mercy, Roofer

**Thankless**  Ingrate, Vain

**That (is), That one**  As, Cestui, Das heisst, Dh, Exists, How, Ie, Ille, Namely, Que, Sc, Such, Thence, Thon(der), What, Yon, Yt

**Thatch(er), Thatching**  At(t)ap, Hair, Heard, Hear(i)e, Hele, Hell, Mane, PM, Reed, Straw, Thack, Theek, Wig

**Thaw**  Debacle, Defrost, MELT(-water), Relax

> **Thaw**  may indicate 'ice' to be removed from a word

**The**  Der, El, Il, La, Le, Los, T', Ye, Ze

**Theatre, Theatrical(ity)**  Abbey, Adelphi, Broadway, Camp, Cinema, Coliseum, Criterion, Drama, Everyman, Field, Gaff, Gaiety, Globe, Grand Guignol, Haymarket, Hippodrome, Histrionic, House, Kabuki, Legitimate, Lyceum, Noh, Odeon, Odeum, OUDS, Palladium, Panache, Playhouse, Rep(ertory), Shaftesbury, Sheldonian, Shop, Stage, Stoll, Touring, Vic, Windmill

**Theatregoer**  Circle, Gallery, Gods, Pit, Stalls

**Theft**  Burglary, Heist, Kinchinlay, Larceny, Maino(u)r, Manner, Pilfery, Plunder, Robbery, Stealth, Stouth(rief), Touch

**Their**  Her

**Theist**  Believer, Unitarian

**Them**  'Em, Hem, Tho

**Theme**  Fugue, Idea, Leitmotiv, Lemma, Lemmata, MELODY, Motif, Peg, SUBJECT, Text, Topic, Topos

**Then(ce)**  Away, Next, Since, So, Syne, Thereupon, Tho

> **The northern**  may indicate t'

**Theodolite**  Groma

**Theologian, Theologist**  Abelard, Aquinas, Calvin, Colet, DD, Divine, Eusebius, Hase, Newman, Origen, Paley, Pelagius, Rabbi, Religious, Schoolman, Softa, STP, Ulema, Universalist

**Theorem, Theoretical, Theorist, Theory**  Academic, Binomial, Dictum, Einstein, Epigenesist, Guess, Holism, Hypothesis, Ideal, Ideology, Ism(y), Lamarckism, Lemma, Notion, Pure, Quantum, System, Tachyon, TOE, Vulcanist, Wolfian

**Therapeutic, Therapy**  Aversion, Curative, Dianetics, Osteopathy, Radio, Rolfing, Sanatory, Scientology, Shiatsu

**There, Thereby, Thereupon**  Ipso facto, Thither, Thon, Y, Yonder

**Therefore**  Argal, Ergo, Forthy, Hence, So, Why

**Thermometer**  Aethrioscope, Centesimal, Glass

**Thermoplastic**  Cel(luloid), Resin

**Thesaurus**  Dictionary, Lexicon, Roget, Treasury

**These**  Thir

**Theseus**  Champion

**Thesis**  Argument, Dissertation, Theme

**Thespian**  ACTOR, Ham, Performer

**Thessalonian**  Lapith

**They**  A

**Thick(en), Thickening, Thickness, Thickset**  Abundant, Burly, Bushy, Callosity, Callus, Cruddle, Curdle, Dense, Dumose, Engross, Grist, Grume, Guar, Gum, Incrassate, Inspissate, Liaison, Panada, Roux, SOLID, Squat, Stumpy, STUPID, Thieves, This, Wooden, Xantham

**Thick-coated**  Atheromatous

**Thicket**  Brake, Brush, Cane-brake, Chamisal, Copse, Dead-finish, Greve, Grove, Reedrand, Reedrond, Salicetum, Shola

**Thick-lipped**  Labrose

**Thick-skinned**  Armadillo, Callous, Pachyderm, Tough

**Thief, Thieves, Thievish**  Abactor, Autolycus, Blood, Coon, Corsair, Cutpurse, Dismas, Dysmas, Filcher, Flood, Footpad, Freebooter, Furacious, Ganef, Gestas, Huaquero, Heist, Iceman, Jackdaw, Kiddy, Larcener, Limmer, Mag, Montith, Nip(per), Pad, Peculator, Pilferer, Pirate, Plagiarist, Poacher, Prig, Raffles, River-rat, ROBBER, Rustler, Shark, Sneak, Taffy, Taker, Tea-leaf, Thick

**Thigh**  Femoral, Ham, Hock, Meros

**Thin(ner)**  Acetone, Attenuate, Bald, Bony, Cull, Dilute, Emaciated, Enseam, Fine, Fine-drawn, Flimsy, Gaunt, Hair('s-)breadth, Inseam, Lanky, Lean, Puny, Rangy, Rare, Rarefied, Reedy, Scant, Scrannel, Scrawny, Sheer, Sieve, Skeletal, Skimpy, Skinking, Slender, Slim, Slink, SPARE, Sparse, Spindly, Stilty, Subtle, Taper, Tenuous, Turps, Wafer, Washy, Waste, Watch, WEAK, Weedy, Wispy, Wraith

**Thing(s)** Alia, Article, Chattel, Chose, Doodah, Entia, Fetish, Fixation, It, Item, Job, Material, Matter, OBJECT, Obsession, Paraphernalia, Phobia, Res, Tool, Whatnot

**Thingummy** Dingbat, Dinges, Doodah, Doofer, Doohickey, Gubbins, Whatsit, Yoke

**Think(er), Thinking** Believe, Brain, Brood, Cogitate, Consider, Contemplant, CONTEMPLATE, Deem, Deliberate, Dianoetic, Fancy, Ghesse, Gnostic, Guess, Hegel, Hold, IMAGINE, Judge, Lateral, Meditate, Mentation, Muse, Opine, Pensive, Philosopher, Phrontistery, Ponder, Pore, Presume, Rational, Reckon, Reflect, Reminisce, Ruminate, Trow, Ween

**Thin-skinned** Sensitive

**Third, Third rate** Bronze, C, Gamma, Gooseberry, Interval, Mediant, Picardy, Tertia, Tierce, Trisect

**Third man** Abel, Lime

**Thirst(y)** CRAVE, Dives, Drought, Drouth, Dry, Pant, Thrist

**Thirteen** Baker's dozen, Riddle, Unlucky

**Thirty nine books** All-OT, OT

**This** Hic, Hoc, The, Thick, Thilk, Thir

**Thistle** Carduus, Carline, Cnicus, Echinops, Safflower, Thrissel, Thristle

**This year** Ha

**Thomas** Aquinas, Arnold, Christadelphian, De Quincey, Didymus, Doubting, Dylan, Erastus, Hardy, Loco, Parr, Rhymer, Tompion, True, Turbulent

**Thong** Babiche, Jandal, Lash, Latchet, Leather, Lore, Riem, Shoe-latchet, STRAP, Taws(e), Whang, Whip

**Thor** Thunderer

**Thorax** Chest, Peraeon, Pereion, Throat

**Thorium** Th

**Thorn(y)** Acantha, Bael, Bel, Bhel, Bramble, Briar, Doorn, Edh, Eth, Irritation, Mahonia, Mayflower, Nabk, Nebbuk, Nebe(c)k, NEEDLE, Prickle, Slae, Spine, Spinescent, Spinulate, Trial, Wagn'bietjie, Ye, Zare(e)ba, Zariba, Zeriba

**Thorn-apple** Jimpson-weed

**Thornless** Inerm

**Thorough(ly)** A fond, Complete, Even-down, Firm, Fully, Ingrained, Out, Painstaking, Pakka, Pucka, Pukka, Sound, Strict, Total, Up

**Thoroughbred** Arab, Bloodstock, Pedigree

**Thoroughfare** Avenue, Broadway, Causeway, Freeway, Highway, ROAD, Street

**Those** Thaim, Them, Tho, Yon

**Thou** M, Mil

**Though** Albe, Albeit, All-be, Ever, Tho, Whenas

**Thought(ful)** Avisandum, Broody, Cerebration, Concept, Considerate, Contemplation, Dianoetic, Idea, Innate, Maieutic, Mind, Musing, Opinion, Pensée, Pensive, Philosophy, Rumination

**Thoughtless** Careless, Heedless, Inconsiderate, RASH, Remiss, Reckless, Scatter-brained, Vacant

**Thousand(s)** Chiliad, Gorilla, K, Lac, Lakh, M, Millenium, Plum, Toman

**Thracian** Spartacus

**Thrall** Captive, Esne, Serf, Slave

**Thrash(ing)** BEAT, Belt, Binge, Cane, Dress, Drub, Flail, Flog, Jole, Joll, Joule, Jowl, Lace, Laldie, Laldy, Lambast, Larrup, Lather, Leather, Lick, Paste, Quilt, Slog, Smoke, Swat, Targe, Towel, Trim, Trounce, Whale, Whap

**Thread, Threadlike** Ariadne, Bottom, Clew, Clue, Cop(pin), Cord, Eel-worm, End, Fibre, Filament, File, Filose, Gossamer, Heddle, Ixtle, Lace, Lingel, Lingle, Link, Lisle, Meander, Mycellum, Nematode, Nematoid, Pearlin(g), Pick, Plasmodesm, Ravel, Reeve, Seton, STRAND, Suture, Thrid, Thrum, Tram, Trundle, Twine, Warp, Watap, Weft, Wick, WIND, Worm

**Threadbare** Hackneyed, Napless, Shabby, Worn

**Threadworm** Nemathelminth

**Threat(en), Threatened, Threatening** Comminate, Face, Fatwa, Fraught, Impend, Imperil, Loom, MENACE, Minacious, Minatory, Mint, Omen, Overcast, Parlous, Peril, Portent, Shore, Ugly, Veiled, Warning

**Three, Threefold, Three-wheeler** Leash, Musketeers, Pairial, Pair-royal, Prial, Ter, Tern, Terzetta, Thrice, Tierce, Tray, Trey, Triad, Tricar, Trifid, Trigon, Trilogy, Trinal, Trine, Trio, Triple, Triptote, Troika

**Three-D** Lenticular

**Threehalfpence** Dandiprat, Dandyprat

**Three-handed** Cutthroat

**Three hundred** B

**Three-legged** IOM, Triskele, Triskelion

**Threepence, Threepenny bit** Tickey, Tray, Trey

**Three-year old** Staggard

**Threnody** Dirge, Epicede, LAMENT

**Thresh** Beat, Flail, Separate

**Threshold** Cill, Doorstep, Limen, Sill, Verge

**Thrift(y)** Economy, Frugal, Husbandry, Oeconomy, Sea-grass, Sea-pink, Virtue

**Thrill, Thrilling** Atingle, Delight, Dindle, Dinnle, Dirl, Dread, Emotive, ENCHANT, Excite, Frisson, Gas, Jag, Kick, Perceant, Plangent, Pulse, Quiver, Sensation, Thirl, Tinglish, Tremor, Vibrant

**Thriller** Whodunit

**Thrive** Batten, Blossom, Boom, Do, Fl, FLOURISH, Flower, Grow, Mushroom, PROSPER, Succeed, Thee

**Throat(y)** Craw, Crop, Dewlap, Fauces, Gorge, Gular, Gullet, Guttural, Jugular, Maw, Pereion, Prunella, Quailpipe, Roopit, Roopy, Swallet, Thrapple, Thropple, Throttle, Weasand, Wesand, Whistle, Windpipe

**Throb** Beat, Palpitate, Pant, Pit-a-pat, Pulsate, Quop, Stang, Tingle

> **Throbbing** may indicate an anagram

**Throe(s)** Agony, Pang, Paroxysm

**Throne** Bed-of-justice, Cathedra, Episcopal, Gadi, Rule, Seat, See, Siege, Tribune

**Throng(ing)** Crowd, Flock, Host, Press, Resort, Swarm

**Throttle** CHOKE, Gar(r)otte, Gun, Mug, Scrag, Silence, Stifle, Strangle, We(a)sand

**Through, Throughout** Along, Ana, By, Dia-, During, Everywhere, Over, Passim, Per, Pr, Sempre, To, Trans, Via

> **Throw(n)** see TOSS

**Throwback** Atavism, Echo

**Throw-out, Throw-up** Bin, Cast-off, Chunder, Egesta, Jettison, Puke, Spew, Squirt, Squit

**Thrush** Aphtha, Bird, Chat, Fieldfare, Mavis, Missel, Pitta, Prunella, Redwing, Sprue, Veery

**Thrust, Thruster** Aventre, Bear, Boost, Botte, Burn, Detrude, Dig, Drive, Elbow, Exert, Extrude, Flanconade, Foin, FORCE, Hay, Imbroc(c)ata, Job, Lunge, Obtrude, Oust, Pass, Passado, Peg, Pitchfork, Poke, Potch(e), Pote, Propel, Pun, Punto, PUSH, Put, Remise, Repost, Run, Shove, Single-stock, Sock, Sorn, Stap, Stoccado, Stoccata, Stock, Thrutch, Tilt, Tuck

**Thud** Drum, Dump, Flump, Plod, Thump

**Thug(s)** Goon(da), Gorilla, Hoodlum, Ninja, Ockers, Phansigar, SS, Strangler, Ted, Tsotsi

**Thule** Ultima

**Thulium** Tm

**Thumb** Hitch, Midget, Ovolo, Pollex, Scan, Tom

**Thump** Blow, Bonk, Cob, Crump, Drub, Dub, Hammer, Knevell, Knock, Nevel, Oner, Paik, POUND, Pummel, Slam, Slosh, Swat, Thud, Tund

**Thunder(ing), Thunderstorm** Bolt, Boom, Clap, Donnerwetter, Foudroyant, Foulder, Fulminate, Intonate, Lei-king, Pil(l)an, Raiden, ROAR, Rumble, Summanus, Tempest, Thor, Tonant

**Thursday** Chare, Maundy, Sheer, Shere

**Thus** Ergo, Sic, So, Therefore

**Thwart** Baffle, Balk, CROSS, Dish, Foil, Frustrate, Hamstring, Hogtie, Obstruct, Outwit, Pip, Scotch, Spike, Spite, Stymie, Transverse

**Tiara** Cidaris, Crownet

**Tiberius** Gracchus

**Tibetan** Lamaist, Naga, Sherpa, Sitsang

**Tick, Tick off** Acarida, Acarus, Beat, CHIDE, Click, Cr, CREDIT, HP, Idle, Instant, Jar, Ked, Mattress, Mile, Mo, Moment, Ricinulei, Second, Strap, Worm

**Ticket** Billet, Bone, Brief, Complimentary, Coupon, Docket, Label, Pass, Platform, Return, Season, Single, Stub, TAG, Tempest, Tessera(l), Tyburn

**Ticket-seller** Scalper

**Tickle, Ticklish** Amuse, Delicate, Divert, Excite, Gratify, Gump, ITCH, Kittle, Queasy, Thrill, Titillate

**Tiddler** Brit, Tom

**Tide, Tidal** Current, Drift, Eagre, Easter, Eger, Estuary, Flood, Neap, Roost, Sea, Seiche, Spring, Wave

**Tide-gate** Aboideau, Aboiteau, Weir

**Tidings** Gospel, NEWS, Rumour, Word

**Tidy** Considerable, Curry, Fair, Fettle, Kempt, Large, Neat, ORDER, Pachyderm, Predy, Preen, Primp, Red(d), Snug, Sort, Spruce, Trim

**Tie** Ascot, Attach, Barcelona, Berth, Bind, BOND, Bow, Bowyang, Cable, Cope, Cravat, Dead-heat, Drag, Draw, Halter, Handicap, Harness, Holdfast, KNOT, Lash, Ligate, Ligature, Link, Match, Moor, Oblige, Obstriction, Oop, Oup, Overlay, Raffia, Restrain, Rod, Scarf, School, Shackle, Sleeper, Slur, Solitaire, Soubise, Splice, Stake, Strap, Tether, Trice, Truss, Unite

**Tier** Bank, Gradin(e), Rank, Stage

**Tierce** Leash, Tc

**Tiff** Bicker, Difference, Dispute, Feed, Feud, Huff, Miff, Skirmish, Spat, Squabble

**Tiger** Bengal, CAT, Clemenceau, Demoiselle, Lily, Machairodont, Machairodus, Paper, Sabre-tooth, Smilodon, Woods

**Tight(en), Tightness, Tights** Boozy, Bosky, Brace, Close(-hauled), Constriction, Cote-hardie, DRUNK, Fishnet, High, Hose, Jam, Leggings, Lit, Loaded, Maillot, Mean, Merry, Niggardly, Oiled, Pickled, Pinch(penny), Plastered, Prompt, Proof, Rigour, Squiffy, Stenosis, STINGY, Strict, Stringent, Swift, Swig, Taut, Tense, Tipsy, Trig, Woozy

**Tightrope-walker** Equilibrist, Funambulist

**Tightwad** Cheapskate, MISER, Scrooge

**Tile(d), Tiles** Azulejo, Dalle, Derby, Encaustic, HAT, Imbrex, Imbricate, Lid, Ostracon, Ostrakon, Peever, Quarrel, Quarry, Rag(g), Sclate, Shingle, Tegula, Tessella, Tessera, Totfer, Topper, Wall, Wally

**Till** Cashbox, Checkout, Coffer, Ear, Eulenspiegel, Farm, Hoe, Husband, Lob, Peter, PLOUGH, Set, Unto

**Tiller** Gardener, Helm, Ploughman, Wheel

**Tilt** Awning, Bank, Camber, Cant, Cock, Dip, Heel, Joust, Just, LIST, Quintain, Rock, Tip, Unbalance

**Timber** Batten, Beam, Carapa, Chess, Cross-tree, Cruck, Futchel, Futtock, Greenheart, Iroko, Joist, Lauan, Ligger, Lintel, Log, Lumber, Plank-sheer, Purlin(e), Putlock, Putlog, Pyengadu, Rib, Rung, Satinwood, Scantling, Sissoo, Softwood, Skeg, Souari, Stemson, Stere, Sternson, Stumpage, Summer, Transom, Wale, WOOD, Yang

**Timbre** Clang, Klang(farbe), TENOR, Tone

**Time(s), Timer** Agoge, Bird, BST, Chronic, Chronometer, Chronon, Clock, Date, Day, Decade, Dimension, Duple, Duration, Early, Egg-glass, Enemy, Eon, Epoch, Equinox, Era, Extra, Father, Forelock, Gest, Healer, Horologe, Hour, Hr, Innings, Instant, Interlude, Juncture, Kalpa, Lay-day, Lean, Leisure, Life, Lilac, Metronome, Multiple, Nonce, Nones, Occasion, Oft, ON TIME, Period, Porridge, Prime, Question, Reaper, Seal, SEASON, Seel, Semeion, Session, Sith(e), Spell, Standard, Stound, Stownd, Stretch, Sundown, Sythe, T, Tem, Tempo, Tempore, Tense, Thief, Thunderer, Tick, Tid, Tide, Two-four, Usance, While, X, Yonks, Zero

**Time-keeper** Ben, Clock, Hourglass, Ref, Sand-glass, Sundial, Ticker, Tompion, Watch

**Timeless** Eternal, Nd, Undying

**Timely** Appropriate, Apropos, Happy, Opportune, Pat, Prompt

**Time-server** Prisoner, Trimmer

**Timetable** Bradshaw, CHART, Schedule

**Timid, Timorous** Afraid, Aspen, Bashful, Blate, Chicken, Cowardly, Eerie, Eery, Hare, Hen-hearted, Milquetoast, Mouse, Pavid, Quaking, SHY, Shrinking, Skeary, Sook, Yellow

**Timothy** Cat's-tail, Grass, Phleum

**Tin(ny), Tinfoil** Argentine, Britannia metal, Can, Cash, Dixie, MONEY, Moola(h), Ochre, Plate, Sn, Stannary, Stannic, Tain, Tole

**Tincture** Arnica, Bufo, Chroma, Elixir, Fur, Infusion, Laudanum, Metal, Or, Sericon, Sol, Spice, Taint, Tenné, Vert

**Tinder** Amadou, Faggot, Fuel, Punk, Spark, Spunk, Touchwood

**Tine** Antler, Bay, Cusp, Grain, Prong, Surroyal, Trey

**Tinge** Dye, Eye, Flavour, Gild, HUE, Taint, Tincture, Tone, Touch

**Tingle, Tingling** Dinnle, Dirl, Prickle, Thrill, Throb, Tinkle

**Tinker** Bell, Caird, Coster, Didicoy, Didikoi, FIDDLE, Gypsy, Mender, Pedlar, Potter, Prig, Putter, Repair, Sly, Snout, Tamper, Tramp, Traveller

**Tinkle** Pink

**Tinsel(ly)** Clinquant, Gaudy, Glitter, O, Spangle,

**Tint** Colour, Henna, Hue, Pigment, STAIN, Tinct, Tinge, Woad

**Tiny** Atto-, Baby, Dwarf, Ha'it, Itsy-bitsy, Lilliputian, Minim, Mite, Negligible, Petite, Small, Teeny, Tim, Tine, Toy, Wee

**Tip, Tipping** Apex, Asparagus, Backshish, Baksheesh, Batta, Beer-money, B(u)onamono, Cant, Cert, Chape, Coup, Cowp, Crown, Cue, Cumshaw, Douceur, Dump, Extremity, Fee, Ferrule, Gratillity, Gratuity, Heel, HINT,

Inkle, Iridise, Lagniappe, Largess(e), Mess, Middenstead, Nap, Noop, Ord, Perk, Point, Pointer, Pour, Suggestion, Summit, Tag, Tail, Tilt, Toom, Touch, Tronc, Vail, Vales, Whisper, Wrinkle

**Tippet** Cape, Fur, Scarf

**Tipple** Bib, Booze, DRINK, Paint, Pot

**Tipster** Prophet, Tout

**Tipsy** Bleary, Boozy, Bosky, DRUNK, Elevated, Moony, Oiled, On, Rocky, Screwed, Squiffy, Wet

> **Tipsy** may indicate an anagram

**Tirade** Diatribe, Invective, Laisse, Philippic, Rand, Rant, Screed, Slang

**Tire(d), Tiredness, Tiring** All-in, Beat, Bore, Bushed, Caparison, Dress, Drowsy, EXHAUST, Fag, Fatigue, Flag, Fordid, Fordod, Forjeskit, Frazzle, Irk, Jade, Limp, ME, Poop, ROBE, Rubber, Sap, Shagged, Sicken, Sleepry, Sleepy, Swinkt, Tax, Tedious, Wappend, Weary

**Tiresome** Boring, Humdrum, Pill, Tedious

**Tirl** Rattle, Risp, Strip, Turn

> **Tiro** see TYRO

**Tissue** Adhesion, Aerenchyma, Cartilage, Chalaza, Coenosarc, Collenchyma, Diploe, Epithelium, Eschar, Fabric, Fascia, Flesh, Gamgee, Gauze, Glia, Heteroplasia, Histogen, Histoid, Infarct, Keloid, Lamina, Lies, Ligament, Luteal, MEMBRANE, Meristem, Myelin(e), Nucellus, Pack, Pannus, Paper, Parenchyma, Phellogen, Phloem, Pith, Plerome, Polyarch, Pulp, Sarcenet, Sars(e)net, Sclerenchyma, Stereome, Stroma, Tela, Tendon, Web, Xylem

**Tit, Tit-bit(s)** Analecta, Currie, Curry, Delicacy, Dug, Nag, Nipple, Pap, Quarry, Sample, Scrap, Snack, Teat, Tug, Twitch, Zakuska

**Titan(ic), Titaness** Atlas, Colossus, Cronos, Enormous, Giant, Huge, Hyperion, Kronos, Leviathan, Liner, Oceanus, Phoebe, Prometheus, Rhea, Themis, Vast

**Titanium** Sagenite, Ti

**Tit for tat** Deserts, Revenge, Talion

**Tithe** Disme, Dyzemas, Teind, Tenth

**Titian** Abram, Auburn

**Titillate** Delight, Excite, Tickle

**Titivate** Primp

**Title** Abbe, Ag(h)a, Bahadur, Baroness, Baronet, Bart, Bretwalda, Caption, Charta, Claim, Count(ess), Credit, Dan, Deeds, Devi, Dom, Don, Dowager, Dub, Duchess, Duke, Earl, Effendi, Epithet, Handle, Header, Heading, Headline, Hon, Interest, King, Lady, Lemma, LIEN, Lord, Marchesa, Marchese, Marquess, Marquis, Masthead, Memsahib, Mevrou, Mr(s), Name, Nomen, Peerage, Pir, Polemarch, Prefix, Prince(ss), Queen, RANK, RIGHT, Sahib, Sama, San, Sir, Sri, V

**Title-holder** Cartouche, Champion, Landlord, Noble

**Titmouse**  Bird, Mag, Reedling, Tit

**Titter**  Giggle, Snigger, Tehee

**Tittle**  Jot

**Titus**  Oates

**Tizz(y)**  Pother, Spin, Tanner, Testril, VId

**TNT**  Explosive, Trotyl

**To(wards)**  At, Beside, Inby, Onto, Shet, Shut, Till

**Toad(y)**  Bootlicker, Bufo, Clawback, Crawler, Fawn, Frog, Jackal, Jenkins, Lackey, Lickspittle, Midwife, Minion, Natterjack, Nototrema, Paddock, Parasite, Pipa, Placebo, Platanna, Puddock, Spade-foot, Sycophant, Tuft-hunter, Xenopus, Yesman

**Toadstool**  Amanita, Death-cap, FUNGUS, Paddock-stool

**Toast**  Bacchus, Bell, Birsle, Brindisi, BROWN, Bumper, Cheers, Chin-chin, Crouton, Gesundheit, Grace-cup, Grill, Health, Kiaora, Loyal, Melba, Pledge, Propose, Prosit, Round, Scouther, Scowder, Scowther, Skoal, Slainte, Sunbathe

**Toastmaster**  MC, Symposiarch

**Tobacco, Tobacco-field**  Alfalfa, Bacchi, Baccy, Bird's eye, Burley, Canaster, Capa, Caporal, Cavendish, Chew, Dottle, Honeydew, Killikinnick, Kinnikinick, Latakia, Mundungus, Nailrod, Navy-cut, Negro-head, Nicotine, Niggerhead, Perique, Pigtail, Plug, Quid, Régie, Returns, Shag, Snuff, Twist, Vega, Virginia, Weed

**Toboggan**  Sled(ge), Sleigh

**Toby**  Dog, Highwayman, Jug

**Tocsin**  Alarm, Siren

**Today**  Hodiernal, Now, Present

**Toddle(r)**  Bairn, Gangrel, Mite, Tot, Totter, Trot, Waddle

**Toddy**  Arrack, DRINK, Sura

**To-do**  Sensation, Stir

**Toe**  Dactyl, Digit, Hallux, Hammer, Pinky, Pointe, Poulaine, Prehallux

**Toff**  Nob, Nut, Swell

**Toffee**  Butterscotch, Caramel, Cracknel, Gundy, Hard-bake, Humbug, Tom-trot

**Together**  Among, At-one, Atone, Attone, Gathered, Infere, JOINT, Sam, Unison, Wed, Y, Yfere, Ysame

**Toggle**  Fastener, Netsuke

**Togs**  Clothes, Gear, Rig, Strip

**Toil(s)**  Drudge, Fag, Industry, LABOUR, Mesh, Net, Sisyphus, Swink, Tela, Tew, Trap, Travail, Tug, Wrest, WORK, Yacker, Yakka, Yakker

**Toilet**  Coiffure, John, Lat(rine), Lavatory, Loo, Pot, WC

**Token**  Counter, Coupon, Disc, Double-axe, Emblem, Indication,

MEMENTO, Nominal, Portend, Sign, Signal, Symbol, Symptom, Tessera

**Tolerable** Acceptable, Bearable, Mediocre, Passable, So-so

**Tolerant, Tolerate(d)** Abear, Abide, ALLOW, Bear, Brook, Endure, Had, LENIENT, Lump, Mercy, Permit, Stand, Stick, Stomach, Suffer, Support, Wear

**Toll** Chime, Customs, Due, Duty, Excise, Joll, Joule, Jowl, Octroi, Pierage, Pike, Pontage, Rates, RING, Scavage, Streetage, Tariff, Tax

**Tom(my)** Atkins, Bell, Bowling, Bread, Brown, CAT, Collins, Edgar, Gib, Grub, Gun, He-cat, Jerry, Jones, Mog(gy), Nosh, Peeping, Private, Pte, Puss, Ram-cat, Sawyer, Snout, Soldier, Stout, Thos, Thumb, Tiddler

**Tomato** Love-apple, Wolf's peach

**Tomb** Burial, Catacomb, Catafalque, Cenotaph, Cist, Coffin, Dargah, Durgah, Grave, Hypogeum, Kistvaen, Marmoreal, Mastaba, Mausoleum, Monument, Pyramid, SEPULCHRE, Sepulture, Serdab, Shrine, Speos, Tholos, Tholus, Treasury, Vault

**Tombola** Draw, Lottery, Raffle

**Tomboy** Gamine, Gilpey, Gilpy, Hoyden, Ramp, Romp

**Tome** BOOK, Volume

**Tomfoolery** Caper, Fandangle, Shenanigan

**Tomorrow** Future, Manana, Morrow

**Tompion** Watchman

**Tom Snout** Tinker

**Ton** C, Chic, Hundred, T

**Tone, Tonality** Brace, Fifth, Harmonic, Key, Klang, Ninth, Qualify, SOUND, Temper, Tenor, Timbre, Trite

**Tongue** Brogue, Burr, Clapper, Doab, Final, Glossa, Glossolalia, Jinglet, LANGUAGE, Langue(tte), Lap, Ligula, Lill, Lingo, Organ, Radula, Ranine, Rasp, Red rag, Spit, Tab, Voice

**Tongue-twister** Jaw-breaker, Shibboleth

**Tonic** Bracer, C(h)amomile, Doh, Key, Medicinal, Mishmee, Mishmi, Oporice, Pick-me-up, Quassia, Refresher, Roborant, Sarsaparilla, Solfa

> **Tonic** may indicate a musical note

**Tonsil, Tonsillitis** Amygdala, Antiaditis, Quinsy

**Tonsure(d)** Haircut, Pield

**Tony** Bête, Fool, Smart

**Too** Als(o), Besides, Eke, Excessive, Item, Likewise, Moreover, Oer, Over, Overly, Plus, Troppo

**Took** Naam, Nam, Set, Stole, Wan, Won

**Tool** Adze, Aiguille, Auger, Awl, Ax(e), Beetle, Bevel, Bit, Broach, Brog, Bur(r), Burin, Catspaw, Chisel, Dibble, Die, Dolly, Eatche, Elsin, Eolith, Facer, File, Float, Fraise, Gimlet, Go-devil, Grattoir, Graver, Hammer, Hob, Hoe, IMPLEMENT, Insculp, INSTRUMENT, Iron, Jemmy, Laster,

Loom, Lute, Microlith, Moon-knife, Muller, Oustiti, Outsiders, Pattle, Pawn, Penis, Pestle, Pick, Piton, Plane, Pliers, Property, Punch, Puncheon, Ripple, Router, Sander, Saw, Scauper, Scissors, Scorper, Screwdriver, Scriber, Seam-set, Shoder, Spanner, Spirit-level, Spitsticker, Strickle, Swage, Swingle, Swipple, Tjanting, Triblet, Trowel, Upright, Wimble, Wrench

**Toot(er)** Blow, Horn, Trumpet

**Tooth(y), Teeth** Bicuspid, Bit, Buck, Canine, Chactodon, Cog, Crena(te), Ctenoid, Cusp, Dentures, Eye, Fang, Gam, Gat, Grinder, Incisor, Ivory, Joggle, Laniary, Molar, Nipper, Odontoid, Pawl, Peristome, Phang, Plate, Pre-molar, Prong, Ratch, Secodont, Sectorial, Serration, Set, Sprocket, Trophi, Tush, Tusk, Uncinus, Upper, Wallies, Wang, Wiper, Zalambdodont

**Toothache, Tooth troubles** Caries, Odontalgia

**Toothless** Edentate, Gummy, Pangolin

**Top(drawer; hole; line; notcher), Topper** Ace, Acme, A1, Apex, Apical, Altissimo, Behead, Best, Big, Brow, Cacumen, Cap, Capstone, Ceiling, Coma, Cop, Coping, Corking, CREST, Crista, Crown, Culmen, Decollate, Diabolo, Dog, Dome, Drawer, Elite, Execute, Finial, Gentry, Gyroscope, Hat, HEAD, Height, Hummer, Imperial, Lid, Nun, One-er, Optimate, Orb, PEAK, Peerie, Peery, Pinnacle, Pitch, Replenish, Ridge, Sawyer, Secret, Shaw, Shirt, Skim, Slay, Star, Summit, Superate, Supreme, Supremo, Surface, Tambour, Targa, Teetotum, Texas, Tile, Trash, Turbinate, Up(most), Uppermost, V, Vertex

> **Top** may indicate first letter

**Topaz** Pycnite

**Topcoat** Finish, Overcoat, Ulster

**Tope(r)** Boozer, Bouser, Dagaba, Dagoba, DRUNK, Sot, Tosspot

**Topic(al)** Head, Item, Motion, Subject, Text, THEME

**Top-knot** Tuft

**Topping** Grand, Icing, Meringue, Piecrust

**Topple** Overbalance, Overturn, Tip, UPSET

**Topsy** Parentless

**Topsy-turvy** Cockeyed, Inverted, Summerset, Tapsalteerie, Tapsleteerie

**Torch** Brand, Cresset, Flambeau, Lamp, Lampad, Link, Tead(e), Wisp

**Torch-bearer** Usherette

**Toreador** Escamillo, Matador, Picador, Torero

**Torment, Tormentor** Agony, Anguish, Bait, Ballyrag, Bedevil, Cruciate, Crucify, Curse, Distress, Frab, Grill, Harass, Hell, Martyrdom, Nettle, Pang, Pine, Plague, RACK, Sadist, Tantalise

**Tornado** Twister

**Torpedo** Bomb, Ray, Weapon

**Torpedo-guard** Crinoline

**Torpid, Torpor** Comatose, Dormant, Languid, Lethargic, Sluggish, Slumbering

**Torrent** Flood, Spate

**Torrid** Hot, Sultry, Tropical

**Torsk** Cusk

**Tortilla** Pancake, Taco

**Tortoise** Chelonia, Emydes, Emys, Galapago, Hic(c)atee, Kurma, Terrapin, Timothy, Turtle

**Tortoiseshell** Epiplastra, Hawksbill, Testudo

**Tortuous** Ambagious, Twisty, Winding

> **Tortuous** may indicate an anagram

**Torture, Torture chamber, Torture instrument** Agonise, Auto-da-fé, Bastinade, Bastinado, Boot, Catasta, Crucify, Engine, Excruciate, Flageolet, Fry, Gadge, Gyp, Knee-cap, Naraka, Persecute, Pilliwinks, Pine, Pinniewinkle, Pinnywinkle, RACK, Sadism, Scaphism, Scarpines, Scavenger, Strappado, Thumbscrew, Wheel, Wrack

> **Tortured** may indicate an anagram

**Torturer** Torquemada

**Torus** Disc

**Tory** Blimp, Blue, C, Right, Tantivy, Unionist

**Toss, Throw** Abject, Bandy, Bounce, Buck, Bung, Cant, Canvass, Cast, Catapult, CHUCK, Crabs, Dad, Daud, Deal, Disconcert, Elance, Estrapade, Falcade, FLING, Flip, Flump, Flutter, Flying (head)-mare, Gollum, Haunch, Heave, Hipt, Hoy, HURL, Jact(it)ation, Jaculation, Jeff, Jump, Lance, Lob, Loft, Pitch, Purl, Shy, Slat, Sling, Unhorse, Unseat

**Toss-up** Cross and pile, Heads or tails

**Tot** Add, Babe, Bairn, CHILD, Dop, Dram, Infant, Mite, Nightcap, Nip(per), Nipperkin, Slug, Snifter, Snort, Tad

**Total, Toto** Absolute, Aggregate, All(-out), Amount, Balance, Be-all, COMPLETE, Entire, Gross, Sum, Tale, Tally, Utter, Whole

**Totalitarian** Autocrat, Despot, Etatiste, Fascist

**Tote** Bear, CARRY, Yomp

**Totem** Fetish, Icon, Image, Pole

**Tottenham** Hotspur

**Totter** Abacus, Daddle, Daidle, Didakai, Didakei, Didicoi, Did(d)icoy, Halt, Ragman, Rock, STAGGER, Swag, Sway, Topple, Waver

**Touch(ed), Touching, Touchy** Accolade, Adjoin, Anent, Barmy, Cadge, Captious, Carambole, Caress, Carom, Concern, Connivent, Contact, Contiguous, FEEL, Finger, Flick, Fondle, Haptic, Huffy, IN TOUCH, J'adoube, Liaison, Loan, Loco, Miffy, Nigh, Nudge, Pathetic, Potty, Re, Sense, Skiff, Sore, Spice, SPOT, Tactile, Tactual, Tag, Tap, Taste, Tat, Tickle, Tig, Trace, Trait, Vestige

**Touchline** Tangent

**Touchstone** Basanite, Criterion, Norm, Standard

**Touchwood** Monk, Punk, Spunk, Tinder

**Tough(en)** Anneal, Apache, Arduous, Burly, HARD, Hard-boiled, Hardy, He-man, Husky, Indurate, Knotty, Leathern, Leathery, Nut, Pesky, Rigwiddie, Rigwoodie, Roughneck, Sinewy, Spartan, Steely, Stiff, String, Sturdy, Teuch, Thewed, Tityre-tu, Virile

**Toupee** Hairpiece, Tour, WIG

**Tour(er), Tourist** Barnstorm, Circuit, Emmet, Excursion, Grand, Grockle, GT, Holiday-maker, Itinerate, JOURNEY, Lionise, Mystery, Outing, Rubberneck, Safari, TRAVEL, Trip(per), Viator, Whistle-stop

**Tourmaline** Schorl, Zeuxite

**Tournament** Basho, Carousel, Drive, Event, Joust, Just, Plate, Pro-am, Royal, Tilt, Tourney, Wimbledon

**Tourniquet** Garrot, Throttle, Torcular

**Tousle** Dishevel, Rumple

**Tout** Barker, Laud, Ply, Praise, Solicit, Toot

**Tow** Fibre, HAUL, Pull, ROPE, Track

> **Towards** see TO

**Towel** Dry, Nappy, Rub, Terry

**Tower** Ascend, Atalaya, Babel, Barbican, Barmkin, Bartisan, Bartizan, Bastille, Bastion, Belfry, Bloody, Brattice, Brettice, Brogh, Campanile, Donjon, Dungeon, Edifice, Eiffel, Fortress, Garret, Giralda, Gopura(m), Ivory, Keep, Leaning, Loom, Louver, Louvre, Martello, Minar(et), Monument, Mouse, Nuraghe, Nurhag, Overtop, Peel, Pinnacle, Pound, Pylon, Rear, Rise, Rolandseck, Sail, Shoot, Ski-lift, Spire, Steeple, Tête-de-pont, Tractor, Tugboat, Turret, Turriculate, Victoria, Ziggurat, Zikkurat

**Town, Township** Borgo, Borough, Bourg, Burg(h), City, Conurbation, Deme, Favella, Garrison, Ham(let), Intraurban, Municipal, Nasik, One-horse, Podunk, Pueblo, Tp, Urban, Wick

**Townee, Townsman** Cad, Cit(izen), Dude, Freeman, Oppidan, Philister, Resident

**Town hall** Prytaneum

**Toxaemia** Eclampsia

**Toxic, Toxin** Abrin, Antigen, Coumarin, Curare, Deadly, Dioxan, Lethal, Serology, Venin, Venomous

**Toy** Bauble, Bull-roarer, Dally, Dandle, Doll, Faddle, Finger, Gewgaw, Golly, Gonk, Kaleidoscope, Kickshaw, Knack, Pantine, Plaything, Praxinoscope, Rattle, Skipjack, Taste, Teddy, Thaumatrope, TRIFLE, Trinket, Tu(r)ndun, Whirligig, Yoyo

**Trace** Cast, Derive, Describe, Draft, Dreg, Draw, Echo, Footprint, Ghost, HINT, Mark, Outline, Relic, Relict, Remnant, Scintilla, Smack, Soupçon,

TOUCH, Track, Vestige, Whit

**Tracery** Filigree

**Track(er), Tracking** Band, Caterpillar, Circuit, Course, Dog, Ecliptic, El, Footing, Hunt, Ichnite, Ichnolite, Lane, Line, Loipe, Loopline, Monitor, Monza, PATH, Persue, Piste, Pug, Pursue, Race, Rake, Ridgeway, Route, Run, Rut, Siding, Sign, Slot, Sonar, Speedway, Spoor, Tan, TRAIL, Trajectory, Tram, Tread, Trode, Tug(boat), Wake, Way

**Tract(able)** Area, Belt, Bench, Clime, Dene, Enclave, Flysheet, Lande, Leaflet, Monte, Moor, PAMPHLET, Prairie, Province, Purlieu, Region, Taluk, Tawie, Terrain, Wold

**Tractarian(ism)** Newman, Oxford movement, Pusey(ism)

**Tractor** Cat, Caterpillar, Pedrail, Tower

**Trade, Trader, Tradesman, Trading** Banian, Banyan, Bargain, Barter, Burgher, Business, Cabotage, Calling, Chaffer, Chandler, Chapman, Cheapjack, Comanchero, COMMERCE, Coster, Costermonger, Crare, Crayer, Deal(er), Easterling, Errand, Exchange, Factor, Free, Handle, Hot, Importer, Indiaman, Industry, Jobber, Line, Merchant, Métier, Mister, Monger, Outfitter, Ply, Rag, Retailer, Sell, Stallenger, Stallinger, Stationer, Sutler, SWAP, Traffic, Trant, Truck, Union, Vend, Wind

**Trademark** Brand, Idiograph, Label, Logo

**Trading money, Trading post** Cabotage, Fort, Wampum

**Tradition(s), Traditional(ist)** Ancestral, Convention, Custom(ary), Hadith, Heritage, Legend, Lore, Misoneist, Old-school, Pharisee, Practice, Purist, Trad, Tralaticious, Tralatitious

**Traduce** Abuse, Asperse, Defame, Impugn, Malign, Vilify

**Traffic** Barter, Broke, Commerce, Deal, Negotiate, Run, Smuggle, Trade, Truck, Vehicular

**Tragedian, Tragedy, Tragic** Aeschylus, Buskin, Calamity, Cenci, Dire, DRAMA, Macready, Melpomene, Oedipean, Oresteia, Otway, Pathetic, Seneca, Sophoclean, Thespian, Thespis

**Trail(er), Trailing** Abature, Bedraggle, Caravan, Creep, Drag, Draggle, Follow, Ipomaea, Lag, Liana, Liane, Path, Persue, Preview, Promo(tion), Pursue, Repent, Scent, Shadow, Sign, Sleuth, Slot, Spoor, Stream, Streel, Trace, TRACK, Trade, Traipse, Trape, Trauchle, Trayne, Troad, Vapour, Vine, Virga, Wake

**Train(er), Training** Advanced, APT, BR, Breed, Caravan, Cavalcade, Coach, Commuter, Condition, Cortège, Direct, Discipline, Dressage, Drill, Educate, Entourage, Enure, Exercise, Fartlek, Flier, Freightliner, Fuse, Ghan, Gravy, GWS, Handle(r), Instruct, Jerkwater, Journey, Liner, Link, LMS, LNER, Loco, Longe, Lunge, Maglev, Mailcar, Mein(e)y, Meinie, Nurture, Nuzzle, Paddy, PE, Potty, Practise, PREPARE, Procession, PT, Puffer, Puff-puff, Rattler, Rehearse, Retinue, Rocket, Ry, Sack, SCHOOL, Series, Sinkansen, Sloid, Sloyd, Sowarree, Sowarry, Special, SR, String, Suite, Tail, TEACH, Tire, Tirocinium, Trail, Tube

> **Train(ed)** may indicate an anagram

**Trainee** APPRENTICE, Cadet, Learner, Rookie, Rooky

**Train-spotter** Gricer

**Trait** Characteristic, Feature, Knack, Ph(a)enotype, Thew, Trick

**Traitor** Betrayer, Casement, Joyce, Judas, Nithing, Proditor, Quisling, Renegade, Reptile, Tarpeian, Traditor, Treachetour, Turncoat, Viper, Wallydraigle

**Trajectory** Parabola, Track

> **Trammel** may indicate an anagram

**Tramp, Trample** Bog-trottrer, Bum, Caird, Clochard, Derelict, Dero, Dingbat, Dosser, Estragon, Footslog, Freighter, Gadling, Hike, Hobo, Overrun, Override, Pad, Piker, Poach, Potch(e), Rover, Scorn, Ship, Splodge, Sundowner, Swagman, TINKER, Toe-rag(ger), Track, Traipse, Tread, Trek, Trog, Truant, Trudge, Tub, Vagabond, Vagrant, Weary Willie

**Trance** Catalepsy, Cataplexy, Narcolepsy

**Tranquil(lity)** Ataraxy, Calm, Composure, Lee, Quietude, Sedate, SERENE

**Tranquillise(r)** Appease, Ataraxic, Ataractic, CALM, Diazepam, Downer, Hypnone, Hypnotic, Librium (tdmk), Nervine, Placate, Satisfy, Soothe, Still

**Transaction(s)** Affair, Brokerage, Deal, Escrow, Tr

**Transcend(ent), Transcendental(ist)** Excel, Mystic, Overtop, Surpass, Thoreau

**Transcribe, Transcript** Copy, Tenor, TRANSLATE

**Transfer** Alien, Alienate, ASSIGN, Attorn, Calk, Cede, Consign, Convey(ance), Decal, Demise, Exchange, Explant, Mancipation, Metathesis, Mortmain, On-lend, Pass, Reassign, Remit, Remove, Repot, Second, Uproot, Virement

> **Transferred** may indicate an anagram

**Transfix** Impale, Rivet, SKEWER, Spear, Spit

**Transform(ation), Transformer** Alter, Change, Metamorphism, Metamorphose, Metamorphosis, Permute, Rectifier, Tinct, Toupee, Transmogrify, Wig

> **Transform(ed)** may indicate an anagram

**Transgress(ion)** Encroach, Err, Infringe, Offend, Overstep, Peccancy, SIN, Violate

**Transient, Transit(ion), Transitory** Brief, Ephemeral, Fleeting, Fly-by-night, Hobo, Metabasis, Passage, Provisional, Temporary

**Translate, Translation, Translator** Crib, Construe, Convert, Coverdale, Explain, Free, Interpret, Key, Linguist, Metaphrase, Paraphrase, Pinyin, Polyglot, Reduce, Render, Rendition, Targum, Tr, Transcribe, Transform, Trot, Unseen, Version(al), Vulgate, Wycliffe

> **Translate(d)** may indicate an anagram

**Transmigrate, Transmigration** Exodus, Metempsychosis, Passage, Trek

**Transmit(ter), Transmitted, Transmission** Air, Band, Beacon, BROADCAST, CB, Communicate, Consign, Contagion, Convection, Convey, Forward, Gearbox, Gene, Heredity, Impart, Intelsat, Microphone, Modem, Nicol, Racon, Radiate, Radio, Receiver, Simulcast, Telecast, Telegony, Teleprinter, Telex, Tiros, Traduce, Tralaticious, Tralatitious, Uplink, Walkie-talkie

**Transparent, Transparency** Adularia, Clear, Crystal(line), Diaphanous, Dioptric, Glassy, Glazed, Hyaloid, Iolite, Leno, Limpid, Lucid, Luminous, Patent, Pellucid, Sheer, Slide

**Transpire** Happen, Occur

**Transplant** Anaplasty, Graft, Repot, Reset, Shift

**Transport(ed), Transporter, Transportation** Argo, Bear, Bike, Broomstick, BRS, Bus, Cargo, Carract, CARRY, Cart, Charm, Convey, Delight, Ecstasy, Eloin, Enrapt, Enravish, Esloin, Estro, Freight, Haul(age), Jerrican, Joy, Kurvey, Maglev, Monorail, Pantechnicon, Put, Rape, Rapine, Rapture, Roadster, Shuttle, Ship, Sledge, Tote, Trap, Tuktuk, Waft, Wheels, Wireway

**Transpose, Transposition** Anagram, Commute, Convert, Invert, Metathesis, Shift, Spoonerism, Switch, Tr

> **Transposed** may indicate an anagram

**Transubstantiate, Transubstantiation** Capernaite

**Transverse** Across, Diagonal, Obliquid, Thwart

**Transvestite** Berdache, Berdash, Eonist

**Tranter** Dolly

**Trap(s), Trapdoor, Trappings** Ambush, BAGGAGE, Bags, Belongings, Buckboard, Bunker, Carriage, Catch, Clapnet, Corner, Cru(i)ve, Deadfall, Decoy, Dogcart, Eelset, Emergent, Ensnare, Fall, Fly, Fyke, Gig, Gin, Gob, Grin, Hatch, Jinri(c)ksha(w), Keddah, Kettle, Kheda, Kiddle, Kidel, Kipe, Kisser, Knur(r), Lime, LUGGAGE, Lure, Mesh, Mouth, Net, Nur(r), Paraphernalia, Pitfall, Plant, Pot, Putcheon, Putcher, Quicksand, Regalia, Scruto, SNARE, Spell, Spider, Springe, Stake-net, Toil, Tonga, Trou-de-loup, U, Vampire, Weel, Weir, Wire

**Trapezist** Leotard

**Trapper** Carson

**Trash** Bosh, Deface, Dre(c)k, Garbage, Junk, Kitsch, Pulp, RUBBISH, Schlock, Scum, Worthless

**Trauma** Insult, Shock

**Travel(ler)** Bagman, Commute, Drive, Drummer, Fare, Fellow, Fly, Fogg, Gipsen, Gipsy, Gitano, Globe-trotter, Go, Gulliver, Gypsy, Hike, Itinerant, Journey, Marco Polo, Meve, Migrant, Motor, Move, Mush, Nomad, Passepartout, Peregrination, Pilgrim, Ply, Polo, Range, Rep, Ride, Rom(any), Rove, Sail, Salesman, Samaritan, TOUR, Trek, Tsigane, Viator, Voyage, Wayfarer, Wend, Wildfire, Zigan

**Traverse** Cross, Quest, Trace

**Travesty** Burlesque, Charade, Distortion, Parody, Skit

**Trawl** Drag-net, Hose-net, Net

**Tray** Antler, Carrier, Charger, Coaster, Galley, Joe, Plateau, SALVER, Trencher, Voider

**Treacherous, Treachery** Deceit, Delilah, Fickle, Ganelon, Guile, Insidious, Knife, Medism, Perfidious, Punic, Quicksands, Serpentine, Sleeky, Snaky, Trahison, Traitor, TREASON, Two-faced, Viper

**Treacle** Blackjack, Butter, Molasses

**Tread** Clamp, Clump, Dance, Pad, Step, Stramp, Track, Trample

**Treason** Betrayal, Insurrection, Lèse-majesté, Lese-majesty, Perduellion, Sedition, TREACHERY

**Treasure(r), Treasury** Banker, Bursar, Cache, Camerlengo, Camerlingo, Cherish, Chest, Cimelia, Coffer, Exchequer, Fisc(al), Fisk, Godolphin, Golden, Hoard, Montana, Palgrave, PRIZE, Procurator, Purser, Relic, Riches, Steward, Thesaurus, Trove

**Treat, Treatment** Action, Acupuncture, Antidote, Archilowe, Arenation, Beano, Besee, Capitulate, Care, Chemotherapy, Condition, Course, Cure, Deal, Do, DOCTOR, Dose, Dress, Enantiopathy, Entertain, Fango, Figuration, Foment, Handle, Manage, Medicate, Negotiate, Opotherapy, OUTING, Physic, Pie, Shout, Smile, STAND, Tebilise (tdmk), Therapy, Titbit, Traction, Usance, Use

> **Treated** may indicate an anagram

**Treatise** Almagest, Commentary, Didache, Discourse, Pandect, Summa, Tract(ate), Upanishad, Vedanta

**Treaty** Agreement, Alliance, Assiento, Concordat, Covenant, Entente, Lateran, PACT, Protocol, Utrecht

**Treble** Castrato, Choirboy, Chorister, Pairial, Soprano, TRIPLE, Triune

**Tree** Abele, Abies, Abroma, Acacia, Acer, Ackee, Actor, Afara, Agila-wood, Aguacate, Ailanto(us), Alamo, Albespine, Alder, Alerce, Algaroba, Alnus, Aloe, Amboina, Amla, ANCESTRY, Angico, Annona, Anona, Antiar, Appleringie, Aquillia, Arar, Arbor Vitae, Arbute, Arbutus, Areca, Argan, Arolla, Ash, Asp(en), Avodire, Axle, Azedarach, Bael, Banyan, Baobab, Basswood, Bay, Beam, Bebeeru, Beech, Bel, Belah, Ben, Benjamin, Bhel, Bilian, Bilimbi(ng), Bilsted, Birch, Bito, Blackboy, Blackbully, Blimbing, Bo, Bolletrie, Bombax, Bonsai, Boom, Boree, Bo-tree, Bountree, Bourtree, Box, Brigalow, Bubinga, Buck-eye, Bully-tree, Buriti, Burrawary, Bursera, Butea, Cabbage-palm, Cacao, Cade, Cajeput, Cajuput, Calabash, Calamondin, Caliatour, Caliature, Calliature, Candle-wood, Canella, Carambola, Carapa, Carica, Cashew, Casuarina, Catalpa, Cedar, Cembra, Cerris, Chamaerops, Champac, Champak, Chaulmougra, Chaulmugra, Chayote, Cheesewood, Chenar, Cherimoya, Cherry, China, Chinar, Chincapin, Chinkapin, Chinquapin, Coco(a), Cocoplum, Cocus, Cola, Conifer, Coolabah, Cordon, Cordyline, Cornel, Cornus, Corypha, Cottonwood, Cupressus, Daddock, Dagwood, Dali, Deciduous, Dendroid, Deodar, Descent, Dhak, Diana's, Dika, Dipterocarp,

Dita, Dogwood, Dracaena, Dryades, Durian, Durion, Durmast, Elder, Elm,
Emblic, Eriodendron, Espalier, Eucalyptus, Eugh, Evergreen, Fagus, Feijoa,
Fiddlewood, Fir, Flamboyant(e), Flindersia, Flittern, Fothergilla, Fraxinus,
Fustet, Fustic, Gallows, Gallus, Garcinia, Garjan, Gean, Geebung, Genipap,
Gidgee, Gidjee, Gingko, Ginkgo, Gnetales, Gnetum, Gopher, Gl(u)inap,
Green-heart, Greenwood, Grove, Guaiacum, Guango, Guava, Gum, Gurjun,
Gympie, Hackmatack, Hakea, Hang, Hazel, Hevea, Hickory, Holly,
Holm-oak, Hornbeam, Hule, Huon-pine, Ilang-ilang, Illipe, Illipi, Iroko, Ita,
Jacaranda, Ja(c)k, Jambu, Jarool, Jarrah, Jarul, Jelutong, Jesse, Jipyapa,
Kaki, Kamala, Karite, Karri, Kauri, Khaya, Kiri, Koa, Kokum, Kowhai,
Kurrajong, Kola, Laburnum, Lancewood, Lagetto, Larch, Laurel, Lebbek,
Lecythis, Lemon, Letter-wood, Lilac, Lime, Linden, Liquidambar,
Loblolly, Locust, Logwood, Longan, Loquat, Lote, Lotus, Lucuma,
Lumbang, Macadamia, Maceranduba, Macoya, Macrocarpa, Madrono,
Magnolia, Mahoe, Mahogany, Mahua, Mahwa, Mako(mako), Mallee,
Manchineel, Mangabeira, Mangosteen, Mangrove, Manjack, Manna-ash,
Manuka, Maple, Marasca, Margosa, Masseranduba, Melia, Mesquit(e),
Mopane, Moringa, Mot(t), Motte, Mowa, Mulberry, Mulga, Mvule, Myall,
Myrtle, Ngaio, Nim, Nipa, Nurse, Nutmeg, Nyssa, Oak, Obeche, Ocotilio,
Oiticica, Oleaceae, Oleaster, Ombu, Opepe, Orange, Padauk, Padouk,
Palas, Palay, Palisander, Palm, Palmetto, Paloverde, Panax, Papaya,
Paper-mulberry, Paulownia, Pawpaw, Pedigree, Peepul, Pereira,
Persimmon, Pichurim, Pimento, Pinaster, Pine, Pinon, Pipal, Pipul,
Pitch-pine, Plane, Platan(e), Plum, Pohutukawa, Pole, Pollard, Pomelo,
Ponderosa, Pontianac, Poon, Poplar, Populus, Protea, Puriri, Quandang,
Quandong, Quantong, Quassia, Quebrecho, Quercitron, Quicken,
Quillai(a), Quina, Quinain, Quince, Raintree, Rambutan, Ramin, Rampike,
Rata, Red-bud, Redwood, Rewa-rewa, Rhus, Ricker, Rimu, Roble, Rowan,
Sabal, Sabicu, Sago-palm, Saksaul, Sal, Sallow, Sama(a)n, Sandarac,
Sandbox, Santalum, Saouari, Sapele, Sapindus, Sapium, Sapling, Sapodilla,
Sapota, Sapucaia, Sassafras, Satinwood, Sawyer, Saxaul, Scrog, Sequoia,
Service, Shea, She-oak, Shittah, Shittimwood, Silva, Simaruba, Sinder,
Sitka spruce, Sloe, Sneezewood, Sorb, Souari, Soursop, Spindle, Spruce,
Staddle, Star-anise, Stemma, Stinkwood, Storax, Sumac(h), Sundari,
Sunder, Sundra, Sundri, Sweetsop, Sycamore, Sycomore, Tacamahac,
Tamanu, Tamarack, Tamarind, Tamarisk, Tawa, Taxodium, Taxus, Tea,
Teak, Teil, Terebinth, Tewart, Thorn, Thuja, Thuya, Ti, Til, Tilia, Timber,
Titoki, Tooart, Toon, Totara, Tsuga, Tuart, Tulip, Tupelo, Turpentine,
Tyburn, Ule, Upas, Vitex, Waboom, Wagenboom, Wahoo, Wallaba,
Wandoo, Washingtonia, Wicken, Wilga, Willet, Willow, Witchen,
Witch-hazel, Witgat(boom), WOOD, Woollybutt, Wych-elm, Xylem,
Xylopia, Yacca, Yang, Yarran, Yellowwood, Yew, Yg(g)drasil,
Ylang-ylang, Yulan, Zaman(g), Zamia

**Tree-climber, Tree-dweller** Monkey, Opossum, Sciurus, Squirrel, Unau

**Tree-man** Ent

**Tree-moss** Usnea

**Tree-paeony** Moutan

**Tree-pecker** Picus

**Tree-shrew** Tana

**Trefoil** Lotos, Lotus

**Trek** Hike, Journey, Odyssey, Safari, Yomp

**Trellis** Espalier, Lattice, Pergola, Treillage, Treille

**Tremble, Trembling, Tremor** Butterfly, Dither, Dodder, Hotter, Judder, Palpitate, Quail, Quake, Quaver, Quiver, Seismal, SHAKE, Shiver, Shock, Shudder, Stound, Trepid, Vibrate, Vibration, Vibratiuncle, Vibrato, Wobble, Wuther

**Tremendous** Big, Enormous, Howling, Immense, Marvellous

**Tremolo** Bebung, Trillo

> **Tremor** see TREMBLE

**Tremulous** Dithering, Hirrient, Shaky, Timorous

**Trench(er)** Boyau, Cunette, Cuvette, Delf, Delph, Dike(r), DITCH, Dyke(r), Encroach, Fleet, Foss(e), Foxhole, Fur(r), Furrow, Grip, Gutter, Leat, Line, Moat, Rill, Ring-dyke, Salient, Sap, Sod, Sondage

**Trenchant** Acid, Cutting

**Trend(y)** Bent, Bias, Chic, Drift, Fashion, Hep, In, Mainstream, Pop, Rage, Style, Swim, Tendency, Tendenz, Tenor, Tide, Tonnish

**Trespass(ing)** Encroach, Errant, Infringe, Offend, Peccancy, Sin, Trench, Wrong

**Tress(es)** Curl, Lock, Ringlet, Switch, Tallent

**Trial** Adversity, Affliction, Appro, Approbation, Approval, Assize, Attempt, Bout, Corsned, Cross, Court-martial, Cow, Dock, Essay, EXPERIMENT, Fitting, Hearing, Nuremberg, Pilot, Pree, Ordeal, Probation, Proof, Rehearsal, Scramble, Taste

**Triangle(d), Triangular** Cosec, Deltoid, Eternal, Gair, Gore, Gyronny, Isosceles, Pedimental, Pyramid, Rack, Scalene, Similar, Trigon, Tromino

**Trias(sic)** Bunter, Keuper, Muschelkalk, Rhaetic

**Tribe, Tribal, Tribesmen** Amelakite, Ashanti, Asher, Benjamin, Celt, Cherokee, Clan(nish), Dan, Dinka, Dynasty, Edomites, Family, Gad, Gens, Gentes, Goth, Hittite, Horde, Hottentot, Ibo, Iceni, Israelite, Jat, Kaffir, Kenite, Kurd, Lashkar, Levi, Masai, Moabite, Mongol, Moro, Naga, Naphtali, Nation, Nervii, Ngati, Ostrogoths, Pathan, Phyle, RACE, Reuben, Riff, Rod, Sakai, Salian, Senones, Senussi, Sept, Shawnee, Silures, Simeon, Tasaday, Teuton, Trinobantes, Vandals, Wolof, X(h)osa

**Tribune, Tribunal** Aeropagus, Bema, Bench, COURT, Divan, Forum, Hague, Leader, Platform, Rienzi, Rota, Star-chamber

**Tributary** Affluent, Bogan, Branch, Creek, Fork

**Tribute** Cain, Citation, Commemoration, Compliment, Deodate, DUE, Epitaph, Festschrift, Gavel, Homage, Kain, Memento, Ode, PRAISE, Rome-penny, Scat(t), Tax, Toast, Wreath, Wroth

**Trice** Flash, Instant

**Trichosanthin** Q

**Trick(s), Trickery, Trickster, Tricky** Antic, Art, Artifice, Attrap, Bamboozle, Begunk, Book, Cantrip, Capot, Catch, Cheat, Chicane(ry), Chouse, Cog, Coyote, Crook, Davenport, Deception, Deck, Delicate, Delude, Device, DO, DODGE, Dupe, Elf, Fard, Fetch, Fiddle, Finesse, Flam, Flim-flam, Fob, Fox, Fraud, Funs, Game, Gaud, Gleek, Glike, Guile, Hoax, Hocus(-pocus), Hoodwink, Hornswoggle, Hum, Illude, Illusion, Illywhacker, Jadery, Jockey, Kittle, Knack, Lark, Mislead, Nap, Palter, Parlour, Pawk, Pleasantry, Pliskie, Prank, Prestige, Ramp, Raven, Reak, Reik, Rex, Rig, Roughie, Ruse, Scam, Sell, Shanghai, Shavie, Shifty, Shill, Skin-game, Skite, Skylark, Sleight, Slight, Slinter, Spoof, Stall, Stint, Sug, Thimble-rig, Three-card, Trap, Tregetour, Trump, Turn, Undercraft, Vole, Wangle, Wheeze, Wile, Wrinkle

> **Trick** may indicate an anagram

**Trickle** Drib(ble), Driblet, Leak, Rill, Seep

**Trickless** Misère

**Triclinic** Anorthic

**Trident** Fork, Plane, Trisula

**Trifle(s), Trifling** Bagatelle, Banal, Baubee, Bibelot, Birdseed, Bit, Cent, Coquette, Dabble, Dalliance, DALLY, Denier, Desipient, Do, Doit, Falderal, Fallal, Fattrell, Fewtril, Fiddle, Fig, Fingle-fangle, Flamfew, Fleabite, Flirt, Folderol, Fool, Footle, Fribble, Frippery, Fritter, Frivol, Gewgaw, Idle, Iota, Kickshaw, Knick-knack, Luck-penny, Mite, Nick-nacket, Niff-naff, Nothing, Nugae, Nugatory, Nyaff, Palter, Peddle, Peppercorn, Petty, Philander, Piddle, Pin, Pittance, Play, Potty, Quiddity, Quiddle, Slight, Smatter, Song, Sport, Stiver, Straw, Sundry, Sweet Fanny Adams, Tiddle, Toy, Trinket, Trivia, Whim-wham, Whit

**Trig** Neat, Sech, Tosh, Trim

**Trigger** Detent, Instigate, Pawl, Start

**Trill(ed), Triller, Trilling** Burr, Churr, Hirrient, Quaver, Ribattuta, Roll, Staphyle, Trim, Twitter, Warble

**Trilobite** Olenellus, Olenus, Paradoxide

**Trim(mer), Trimming** Bleed, Braid, Bray, Chipper, Clip, Dapper, Dinky, Dress, Face, Falbala, Fettle, File, Garnish, Garniture, Gimp, Macramé, Macrami, Marabou, Neat, Net, Ornament, Pare, Passament, Passement(erie), Pipe, Plight, Posh, Preen, Proign, Pruin(e), Proyn(e), Prune, Robin, Ruche, Sax, Sett, Shipshape, Smirk, Smug, Snod, SPRUCE, Straddle, Stroddle, Strodle, Svelte, TIDY, Time-server, Torsade, Trick, Wig

**Trinidadian** Carib

**Trinitarian, Trinity** Mathurin(e), Triad, Trimurti, Triune

**Trinket** Bauble, Bijou(terie), Charm, Fallal, Nicknack, Toy, Trankum

**Trio** Catch, Graces, Skat

**Trip(per)** Cruise, Dance, Errand, FALL, Flight, Flip, High, Journey, Link,

Outing, Ride, Run, Sail, Sashay, Spin, Spurn, STUMBLE, Tour, Trek, Voyage

> **Trip**  may indicate an anagram

**Tripe**  Abracadabra, Bosh, Caen, Entrails, Rot

**Triple, Triplet**  Hemiol(i)a, Sdrucciola, Ternal, Tiercet, Treble, Trifecta, Trilling, Trin, Tripling

**Tripod**  Cat, Cortina, Oracle, Triangle, Trippet, Trivet

**Triptych**  Volet

**Trishaw**  Cycle

**Trite**  Banal, Corny, Hackneyed, Hoary, Novelettish, Stale, Stock, Time-worn

**Triton**  Eft, Evet, Ewt, Trumpet-shell

**Triumph(ant)**  Cock-a-hoop, Codille, Cowabunga, Crow, Exult, Glory, Impostor, Killing, Ovation, Palm, Victorious, WIN

**Trivet**  Tripod, Trippet

**Trivia(l)**  Bagatelle, Balaam, Bald, BANAL, Frippery, Frothy, Futile, Idle, Light, Paltry, Pap, Peppercorn, Pettifoggery, Petty, Picayune, Shallow, Small, Snippety, Squirt, Squit, Toy(s)

**Trochee**  Choree

**Troglodyte**  Ape, Caveman, Hermit, Spelean, Wren

**Trojan**  Agamemnon, Dardan, Iliac, Priam, Teucrian, Troic

**Troll**  Gnome, Rove, Trawl, Warble

**Trolley**  Brute, Cart, Dolly, Truck

> **Trollop**  see LOOSE WOMAN

**Trombone**  Posaune

**Troop(s), Trooper**  Band, BEF, Brigade, Company, Depot, Detachment, Guard, Horde, Midianite, Militia, Pultan, Pulton, Pultoon, Pultun, SAS, Sowar, Tp, Turm(e)

**Troopship**  Transport

**Trophy**  Adward, AWARD, Belt, Cup, Emmy, Memento, Palm, PRIZE, Scalp, Spoils

**Tropic(al)**  Cancer, Capricorn, Derris, Jungle, Neogaea, Sultry

**Trot(ter), Trot out**  Air, Crib, Crubeen, Job, Jog, Pettitoes, Piaffe, Pony, Ranke, Red(-shirt)

**Troth**  Troggs

**Trotsky**  Entr(y)ism

**Troubador**  Blondel, Griot, Manrico, Minstrel, Singer, Sordello

**Trouble(s), Troublemaker, Troublesome**  Ache, Ado, Affliction, Aggro, Agitate, Ail, Alarm, Annoy, Bale, Barrat, BOTHER, Burden, Care, Coil, Concern, Debate, Disaster, Disquiet, Distress, Disturb, Dolour, Eat, Esclandre, Fash, Firebrand, Fossick, Gram(e), Hag-ride, Harass, Harry, Hassle, Hatter, Heat, Heist, Hellion, Hot water, Howdyedo, Hydra,

Inconvenience, IN TROUBLE, Kiaugh, Mess, Moil, Molest, Noy, Perturb, Pester, Plague, Poke, Reck, Rub, Shake, Soup, Spiny, Stir, Storm, Sturt, Tartar, Teen, Teething, Thorny, Tine, Toil, Trial, Tsuris, Turn-up, Tyne, Unsettle, Vex, WORRY

**Trouble-shooter** Ombudsman

> **Troublesome** may indicate an anagram

**Trough** Back, Bed, Bucket, Buddle, Channel, Chute, Culvert, Graben, Hod, Hutch, Manger, Stock, Straik, Strake, Sycline, Troffer, Tye

**Trounce** BEAT, Hammer, Thump

**Trousers** Bags, Bloomers, Churidars, Continuations, Cords, Corduroys, Daks, Drainpipe, Drawers, Ducks, Eel-skins, Flannels, Flares, Galligaskins, Gaskins, Hipsters, Inexpressibles, Innominables, Jeans, Jodhpurs, Kaccha, Lederhosen, Longs, Loons, Moleskins, Pants, Pegtops, Plus-fours, Reach-me-downs, Salopettes, Shalwar, Slacks, Strides, Trews, Trouse, Unmentionables, Unutterables, Utterless

**Trout** Finnac(k), Finnock, Fish, Gillaroo, Herling, Hirling, Peal, Peel, Phinnock, Pogies, Quintet, Sewen, Splake, Steelhead, Togue

**Trow** Faith, Meseems

**Trowel** Float

**Troy** Ilium, Sergeant, T, Weight

**Truant** Absentee, Dodge, Hooky, Kip, Miche, Mooch, Mouch, Wag

**Truce** Armistice, Barley, Fains, Pax, Stillstand, Treague, Treaty

**Truck** Bogie, Business, Cocopan, Dealings, Dolly, Haul, LORRY, Tipper, Trolley, Ute, Van

**Trudge** Jog, Lumber, Pad, Plod, Stodge, Stramp, Taigle, Traipse, Trash, Trog, Vamp

**True** Accurate, Actual, Apodictic, Constant, Correct, Exact, Factual, Faithful, Genuine, Honest, Leal, Literal, Loyal, Platitude, Plumb, Pure, Real, Realistic, Sooth, Very

**Truffle** Tuber

**Trug** Basket, Wisket

**Truly** Certes, Fegs, Indeed, Verily, Yea

**Trump(s), Trumpet(er)** Agami, Alchemy, Alchymy, Blare, Blast, Bray, Buccina, Bugle(r), Call, Card, Clarion, Conch, Cornet, Corona, Daffodil, Elephant, Fanfare, Hallali, Honours, HORN, Invent, Jew's, Last, Lituus, Lur(e), Lurist, Manille, Megaphone, NO TRUMP, Proclaim, Ram's-horn, Resurrect, Ruff, Salpingian, Salpinx, Satchmo, Sennet, Shofar, Shophar, Slug-horn, Surpass, Tantara, Tantarara, Tar(at)antara, Theodomas, Tiddy, Triton

**Trumpery** Fattrels, Jimcrack, Paltry, Trashy

**Truncate(d)** Abrupt, Cut, Dock, Shorten

**Truncheon** Billie, Billy, Blackjack, Cosh

**Trundle** Hump, Trill, Troll

**Trunk(s)** Aorta(l), A-road, Bole, Body, Box, Bulk, But(t), Carcase, Chest, Coffer, Hose, Imperial, Log, Peduncle, Pollard, Portmanteau, Portmantle, Proboscis, Ricker, Road, Saratoga, Shorts, STD, Stock, Stud, Synangium, Torso, Valise

**Truss** BIND, Ligate, Oop, Oup, Sheaf, Tie, Upbind

**Trust(y), Trustworthy** Affy, Authentic, Belief, Care, Cartel, Charge, Combine, Confide, Credit, Dependable, FAITH, Hope, Leal, Lippen, Loyal, National, NT, Reliable, Reliance, Rely, Reputable, Staunch, Tick, Trojan, Trow, True, Trump, Unit

**Trustee** Agent, Executor, Fiduciary, Tr

**Truth(ful), Truism** Accuracy, Axiom, Bromide, Cliché, Cold turkey, FACT, Forsooth, Gospel, Honesty, Idea(l), Naked, Pravda, Reality, Sooth, Veridical, Verity

**Try(ing)** Aim, Approof, Assay, Attempt, Audition, Bash, Bid, Birl, Burden, Burl, Conative, Contend, Crack, Effort, Empiric(utic), ENDEAVOUR, Essay, Examine, Experiment, Fand, Fish, Fling, Foretaste, Go, Harass, Hard, Hear, Irk, Offer, Ordalium, Practise, Pree, Prieve, SAMPLE, Seek, Shot, Sip, Stab, Strain, Strive, Taste, Tax, Tempt, Test, Touchdown

**Tryst** Date, Rendezvous

**Tsar(ist)** Alexis, Emperor, Godunov, Octobrist, Ruler

**TT** Rechabite

**Tub, Tubbiness, Tub-thumper** Ash-leach, Back, Bath, Boanerges, Bran, Corf, Cowl, Dan, Diogenes, Endomorph Keeve, Kid, Kieve, Kit, Pin, Podge, Pudge, Pulpit, Tun, Vat, Wash

**Tuba** Bombardon, Euphonium

**Tube** Arteriole, Artery, Barrel, Bronchus, Burette, Calamus, Cannula, Casing, Catheter, Conduit, Crookes, Diode, Duct, Eustachian, Fallopian, Fistule, Geissler, Hose, Inner, Klystron, Macaroni, Matrass, Metro, Oval, Oviduct, Pentode, PIPE, Pipette, Pitot, Promethean, Salpinx, Saucisse, Saucisson, Schnorkel, Siphon, Siphonostele, Siphuncle, Skelp, Skiatron, Sleeve, Snorkel, Spaghetti, Spout, Swallet, Teletron, Tetrode, Tile, Trocar, Trunk, Tunnel, Tuppenny, U, Ureter, Vas, Vein, Vena, Venturi, Video

**Tuber(s)** Arnut, Arracacha, Bulb, Coc(c)o, Earth-nut, Eddoes, Oca, Potato, Salep, Taproot, Yam

**Tuberculosis** Consumption, Crewels, Cruel(l)s, Decline, Lupus, Phthisis, Scrofula

**Tuck** Dart, Friar, Gather, Grub, Kilt, Pleat, Scran

**Tuesday** Hock, Shrove

**Tuft(ed)** Amentum, Beard, Caespitose, Candlewick, Catkin, Cluster, Coma, Comb, Cowlick, Crest, Dollop, Floccus, Goatee, Hassock, Pappus, Penicillate, Quiff, Scopate, Shola, Tassel, Toorie, Toupee, Tussock, Tuzz, Whisk

**Tug** Drag, Haul, Jerk, Lug, Pug, PULL, Rive, Ship, Sole, Soole, Sowl(e), Tit, Tow, Yank

**Tui** Poebird

**Tully** Cicero

**Tumble, Tumbler** Acrobat, Cartwheel, Drier, Fall, GLASS, Pitch, Popple, Spill, Stumble, Topple, Twig, Voltigeur, Welter

> **Tumble** may indicate an anagram

**Tumbledown** Decrepit, Dilapidated, Ramshackle, Rickle, Ruinous

**Tumbril** Caisson

**Tummy** Belly, Colon, Mary, Paunch, Pod

**Tummy-ache** Colic, Gripe, Tormina

**Tumour** Adenoma, Anbury, Angioma, Cancer, Chrondoma, Crab(-yaws), Encanthis, Encephaloma, Enchondroma, Epulis, Exostosis, Fibroma, Ganglion, Glioma, Grape, Gumma, Lipoma, Mesothelioma, Mole, Myeloma, Myoma, Myxoma, Neuroma, -oma, Oncology, Osteoma, Papilloma, Polypus, Sarcoma, Steatoma, Talpa, Teratoma, Wart, Wen, Wilms, Windgall, Wolf, Xanthoma, Yaw

**Tumult** Brawl, Coil, Deray, Ferment, Fracas, Hubbub, Reird, Riot, ROAR, Romage, Rore, Stoor, Stour, Stowre, Stramash, Tew, UPROAR

**Tumulus** Barrow, Mote, Motte

**Tun** Cask, Keg

**Tune(ful)** Adjust, Air, Aria, Carillon, Catch, Choral, Dump, Etude, Harmony, Hornpipe, Jingle, Key, Maggot, Measure, Melisma, MELODY, OUT OF TUNE, Port, Raga, Rant, Ranz-des-vaches, Snatch, Song, Spring, Strain, Sweet, Syntonise, Tone

**Tungstate, Tungsten** Scheelite, W, Wolfram

**Tunic** Ao dai, Caftan, Chiton, Choroid, Cote-hardie, Dalmatic, Dashiki, Hauberk, Kabaya, Kaftan, Kameez, K(h)urta, SINGLET, Tabard, Toga

**Tunnel** Bore, Culvert, Cundy, Gallery, Head, Mine, Simplon, Stope, Subway, Syrinx, Tube

**Tunny** Bonito, Tuna

**Turban** Bandanna, Hat, Mitral, Pagri, Puggaree, Puggery, Puggree, Sash, Scarf

**Turbid** Cloudy, Dense, Drumly, Roily

**Turbulence, Turbulent** Becket, Bellicose, Buller, Factious, Fierce, Rapids, Stormy

> **Turbulent** may indicate an anagram

**Turf** Caespitose, Clod, Divot, Earth, Fail, Feal, Flaught, GRASS, Greensward, Peat, Scraw, SOD, Sward

**Turk(ish)** Anatolian, Bashaw, Bimbashi, Bostangi, Byzantine, Caimac(am), Crescent, Effendi, Gregory, Horse(tail), Irade, Kaimakam, Kazak(h), Mameluke, Mutessarif(at), Omar, Osman(li), Ottamite, Ottoman, Ottomite, Rayah, Scanderbeg, Selim, Seljuk(ian), Seraskier, Spahi, Tatar, Timariot, Usak, Uzbeg, Uzbek, Yakut

**Turkey, Turkey-like** Bubbly(-jock), Curassow, Gobbler, Norfolk,

Sultanate, Talegalla, TR

**Turmeric** Curcumine

**Turmoil** Chaos, Din, Ferment, Stoor, Stour, Tornado, Tracasserie, Tumult, UPROAR, Welter

> **Turn(ing)** may indicate an anagram

**Turn(ing), Turned away, Turned up** Acescent, Act, Advert, Antrorse, Apostrophe, Apotropaic, Avert, Bank, Become, Bend, Buggins, Canceleer, Cancelier, Caracol(e), Careen, Cartwheel, Cast, Chandelle, Change, Char(e), Chore, Christiana, Christie, Christy, Churn, Cock, Coil, Crank(le), Cuff, Curd(le), Curve, Defect, Deflect, Demi-volt(e), Detour, Deviate, Dig, Digress, Divert, Ear, Earn, Elbow, Evert, Flip, Go, Gruppetto, Hairpin, Hie, High, Hup, Immelmann, Influence, Innings, Invert, Jar, Jink, Keel, Laeotropic, Lot, Luff, Number, Obvert, Parry, Penchant, Pivot, Plough, Pronate, PTO, Quarter, Quersprung, Rebut, Refer, Refract, Remuage, Retroussé, Retrovert, Rev, Revolt, Ride, Rocker, Roll, Root, ROTATE, Rote, Roulade, Rout, Routine, Screw, Secund, Sheer, SHOT, Shout, Sicken, Slew, Slue, Solstice, Sour, SPELL, Spin, Sprain, Swash, Swing, Swivel, Telemark, Throw, Tirl, Torque, Transpose, Trend, Trick, Trochilic, Turtle, Twiddle, Twist, U, Uey, Up, Veer, Versed, Version, Vertigo, Volta, Volte-face, Wap, Warp, Wedein, Wend, Went, WHEEL, Whelm, Whirl, Whorl, Wind, Wrest, Zigzag

**Turn-coat** Apostate, Cato, Defector, Quisling, Rat, Renegade, Tergiversate, Traitor

**Turner** Axle, Lana, Lathe, Painter, Pivot, Rose-engine, Spanner, Worm, Wrench

**Turning point** Crisis, Crossroads, Landmark

**Turnip(-shaped)** Hunter, Napiform, Navew, Neep, Rutabaga, STUPID PERSON, Swede

**Turnkey** Gaoler, Jailer

**Turn-out** Evert, Fadge, Gathering, Product, Prove, Rig, Style

**Turn over** Capsize, Careen, Flip, Inversion, Production, PTO, Somersault, TO, Up-end

**Turnpike** Highway, Toll

**Turntable** Rota, Rotator

**Turpentine** Galipot, Rosin, Thinner, Turps

**Turquoise** Ligure, Odontolite

> **Turret** see TOWER

**Turtle, Turtle head** Calipash, Calipee, Chelone, Hawksbill, Inverted, Leatherback, Loggerhead, Matamata, Snapper, Terrapin, Thalassian

**Tusk** Gam, Horn, Ivory, Tooth, Tush

**Tusker** Dicynodont, Elephant, Mastodon

**Tussle** Giust, Joust, Mêlée, Scrimmage, Scrum, Scuffle, Skirmish, Touse, Touze, Towse, Towze, Wrestle

**Tussock** Hassock, Tuft

**Tut(-tut)** Och, Pooh

**Tutelary** Guardian, Protector

**Tutor** Abbé, Aristotle, Ascham, Bear, COACH, Don, Instruct, Leader, Preceptor, Teacher

**TV** Baird, Box, Lime Grove, Monitor, Tele, Telly, Video

**Twaddle** Blether, Drivel, Rot, Slip-slop, Tripe

**Twang** Nasal, Pluck, Plunk, Rhinolalia

**Tweak** Pluck, Twiddle, Twist, Twitch

**Tweed(y)** Harris, Homespun, Lovat, Raploch

**Tweet** Chirrup

**Twelfth, Twelve** Apostles, Dozen, Epiphany, Glorious, Grouse, Midday, N, Night, Noon, Ternion, Twal

**Twenty** Score, Vicenary, Vigesimal

**Twenty-five** Quartern

**Twerp** Pipsqueak

> **Twice** see TWO

**Twice-yearly** Biennial, Equinox

**Twig(s)** Besom, Birch, Cotton, Cow, Dig, Grasp, Kow, Osier, Reis, Rice, Rumble, Sarment, See, Sprig, Sticklac, Switch, Understand, Wand, Wattle, Wicker, Withe

**Twilight** Cockshut, Crepuscular, Demi-jour, Dusk, Gloam(ing), Gotterdämmerung

**Twill** Chino

**Twin(s)** Asvins, Castor, Coetaneous, Didymus, Dioscuri, Ditokous, Dizygotic, Double, Gemel, Identical, Kindred, Macle, Pigeon-pair, Pollux, Siamese

**Twine** Braid, Coil, Cord, Inosculate, Sisal, Snake, String, Twist, Wreathe

**Twinge** Pang, Scruple, Stab

**Twinkle, Twinkling** Glimmer, Glint, Mo(ment), SPARKLE, Starnie, Trice

**Twirl** Spin, Swivel, Tirl, Trill, Twiddle, Whirl

> **Twirling** may indicate an anagram

**Twist(ed), Twister, Twisting, Twisty** Askant, Askew, Becurl, Bought, Card-sharper, Chisel, Coil, Contort, Convolution, Crinkle, Crisp, Curl(icue), Cyclone, Deform, Detort, Distort, DODGE, Garrot, Helix, Kink, Mat, Möbius strip, Oliver, Pandanaceous, Plait, Quirk, Raddle, Ravel, Rick, Rogue, Rotate, Rove, Slew, Slub(b), Slue, Snarl, Spin, Spiral, Sprain, Squiggle, Squirm, Tendril, Torc, Tornado, Torque, Torsade, Torsion, Tortile, Turn, Tweak, Twiddle, Twine, Twirl, Valgus, Volvulus, Welkt, Wigwag, Wind, Wound-wrap, Wrast, Wreathe, Wrench, Wrest, Wrethe, Wrick, Wring, Writhe, Wry, Zigzag

> **Twisted, Twisting** may indicate an anagram

**Twit, Twitter** Chaff, Cherup, Chirrup, Dotterel, Gear(e), Giber, JEER, Stupid, Taunt, Warble

**Twitch(y)** Athetosis, Clonic, Grass, Jerk, Life-blood, Start, Tic, Tig, Tit, Twinge, Vellicate, Yips

**Two, Twice** Bice, Bis, Bisp, Both, Brace, Couple(t), Deuce, Double, Duad, Dual, Duet, Duo, Dyad, PAIR, Swy, Twain, Twins, Twinter

**Two-edged** Ancipitous

**Two-faced** Dihedral, Dorsiventral, Hypocritical, Janus, Redan

**Two-gallon** Peck

**Two-headed** Amphisbaenic, Dicephalous

**Two hundred** H

**Two hundred and fifty** E, K

**Two-master** Brig

**Two-rayed** Diactinal

**Two-sided** Bilateral, Equivocatory

**Two-up** Kip, Swy

**Tycoon** Baron, Magnate, Plutocrat, Shogun

**Type(s)** Agate, Antimony, Antique, Balaam, Baskerville, Bodoni, Body, Bold face, Bourgeois, Braille, Brand, Brevier, Brilliant, Canon, Caslon, Category, Character, Chase, Cicero, Clarendon, Class, Columbian, Cut, Egyptian, Elite, Elzevir, Em, Emblem, Emerald, English, Face, Font, Form(e), Fount, Fraktur, Fudge, Garamond, Gem, Genre, Gent, Gothic, Great primer, Gutenberg, Hair, Ilk, Image, Kern(e), Kind, Ligature, Long-primer, Minion, Modern, Moon, Mould, Non-pareil, Norm, Old-face, Paragon, Pattern, Pearl, Peculiar, Pi, Pica, Pie, Point, Print, Quadrat, Roman, Ronde, Ruby, Sanserif, Serif, SORT, Sp, Species, Stanhope, Style, Times, Version

> **Type of** may indicate an anagram

**Typewriter** Golfball, Portable

**Typhoon** Cyclone, Hurricane, Monsoon, Tornado, Wind

**Typical** Average, Characteristic, Classic, Normal, Representative, Standard, Symbolic, True-bred, Usual

**Typist** Audio, Printer, Temp

**Tyrant, Tyranny** Autocrat, Despot, Dictator, Drawcansir, Gelon, Herod, Nero, Oppressor, Pharaoh, Sardanapalus, Satrap, Totalitarian, Tsar, Yoke

**Tyrannise(d)** Domineer, Lord, Under

**Tyre** Cross-ply, Pericles, Radial, Remould, Retread, Slick, Tread, Tubeless, Whitewall

**Tyro** Beginner, Ham, NOVICE, Rabbit, Rookie, Rooky, Starter

**Tyrolese** R(h)aetian

# Uu

**U, U-type**   Gent, Unicorn, Universal, Uranium

**Ubiquitous**   Everywhere, Omnipresent

**Udder**   Bag, Dug

**Ugandan**   Obote

**Ugly**   Customer, Eyesore, Foul, Gorgon, Gruesome, Hideous, Loth, Mean, Ominous, Plain

**Ugrian**   Ostiak, Ostyak, Samo(y)ed, Vogul

**Ukase**   Decree

**Ulcer**   Abscess, Aphthae, Canker, Noma, Peptic, Rupia, Sore, Wolf

**Ulster**   NI, Overcoat, Raincoat, Ulad

**Ulterior**   External, Hidden

**Ultimate**   Absolute, Basic, Deterrent, Eventual, Final, Furthest, Last, Maximum, So, Supreme, Thule

**Ultra**   Drastic, Extreme, Radical

**Ultra-republican**   Leveller

**Ulysses**   Bloom, Grant, Odysseus

**Umbellifer**   Angelica, Arnut, Car(r)away, Dill, Pig-nut, Seseli

**Umbrage**   Offence, Pique, Resentment, Shade

**Umbrella(-shaped)**   Bumbershoot, Chatta, Gamp, Gingham, Gloria, Mush(room), Parasol, Sunshade, Tea

**Umbria**   Eugubine, Iguvine

**Umpire**   Arb(iter), Byrlawman, Daysman, Decider, Judge, Oddjobman, Odd(s)man, Overseer, Referee, Rule, Stickler

**Unabashed**   Bare-faced, Brazen, Shameless

**Unable**   Can't, Incapable

**Unaccented**   Atonic, Proclitic

**Unacceptable**   Not on, Out

**Unaccompanied**   A cappella, Alone, Secco, Single, Solo, Solus

**Unaccustomed**   New

**Unadulterated**   Sincere

**Unaffected**   Artless, Genuine, Homely, Natural, Plain, Sincere, Unattached

**Unaltered**   Constant, Same

**Unanswerable**   Erotema, Irrefutable

**Unarguable**   Erotema

**Unarmed**  Inerm, Naked, Vulnerable

**Unashamed**  Blatant

**Unassigned**  Adespota, Anonymous

**Unattractive**  Lemon, Plain, Rebarbative, Seamy, Ugly

**Unattributable**  Anon

**Unauthentic**  Plagal

> **Unauthentic**  may indicate an anagram

**Unavail(able), Unavailing**  Bootless, Futile, Lost, No use, Off, Vain

**Unavoidable**  Inevitable, Necessary, Perforce

**Unaware**  Heedless, Ignorant, Innocent

**Unbalanced**  Deranged, Doolalli, Doolally, Loco, Lopsided, Uneven

**Unbearable**  Bassington, Intolerable

**Unbeaten**  All-time

**Unbecoming, Unbefitting**  Improper, Infra dig, Shabby, Unfitting, Unseemly, Unsuitable, Unworthy

**Unbelievable, Unbeliever**  Agnostic, Atheist, Cassandra, Doubter, Giaour, Heathen, Incredible, Infidel, Pagan, Painim, Paynim, Sceptic, Tall, Zendik

**Unbent**  Relaxed

**Unbiased**  Fair, Impartial, Just, Neutral, Objective

**Unblemished**  Spotless, Vestal

**Unblinking**  Alert, Astare, Fearless

**Unborn**  Future, Unbred

**Unbowed**  In-kneed, Resolute

**Unbridled**  Fancy free, Footloose, Lawless, Uncurbed, Unrestricted, Unshackled, Untramelled

**Unburden**  Confide, Relieve, Unload

**Uncanny**  Eerie, Eldritch, Extraordinary, Geason, Rum, Spooky, Weird

**Uncastrated**  Stone

**Uncertain(ty)**  Broken, Chancy, Chary, Contingent, Delicate, Dither, Doubtful, Hesitant, Iffy, Indeterminate, Indistinct, Irresolute, Peradventure, Queasy, Risky, Slippery, Vor

> **Uncertain**  may indicate an anagram

**Unchangeable**  Enduring, Eternal, Stable

**Uncharged**  Neutral, Neutron

**Unchaste**  Corrupt, Immodest, Immoral, Impure, Lewd, Wanton

**Unchecked**  Rampant

**Uncivil(ised)**  Barbaric, Benighted, Boondocks, Discourteous, Giant-rude, Heathen, Impolite, Military, Rude

**Uncle**  Abbas, Afrikaner, Arly, Bob, Dutch, Eme, Nunky, Oom,

Pawnbroker, Pop-shop, Remus, Sam, Tio, Tom, Usurer, Vanya

**Unclean** Defiled, Dirty, Impure, Obscene, Squalid, T(e)refa(h)

**Unclear** Ambitty, Hazy, Obscure

**Unclothed** Bald, Nude

**Uncloven** Soliped

**Uncommon** Rare, Strange, Unusual

> **Uncommon(ly)** may indicate an anagram

**Uncompanionable** Threesome

**Uncomplimentary** Blunt

**Uncomprehending** Anan, Ignorant

**Uncompromising** Hardshell, Rigid, Strict

**Unconcealed** Open, Pert

**Unconcerned** Bland, Careless, Casual, Cold, Indifferent, Strange

**Unconditional** Absolute, Free, Pure

**Unconnected** Asyndetic, Detached, Disjointed

**Unconscious(ness)** Asleep, Cold, Comatose, Instinctive, Non-ego, Subliminal, Trance, Under

**Unconsidered** Impetuous, Rash

**Uncontrolled** Atactic, Free, Wild

**Unconventional** Beatnik, Bohemian, Drop-out, Heretic, Heterodox, Informal, Irregular, Offbeat, Original, Outré, Raffish

> **Unconventional** may indicate an anagram

**Unconverted** Neat

**Unconvincing** Lame, Thin

**Uncoordinated** Asynergia, Ataxic, Awkward, Clumsy

**Uncorrect** Stet

**Uncouth(ness)** Backwoodsman, Bear, Crude, Gothic, Inelegant, Rube, Rude, Rugged, Uncivil

**Uncover** Bare, Disclose, Expose, Open, Peel, Reveal, Shave, Shill, Shuck, Uncap

**Unction, Unctuous(ness)** Anele, Balm, Chrism, Extreme, Ointment, Oleaginous, Ooze, Smarm, Soapy

**Uncultivated, Uncultured** Artless, Fallow, Ignorant, Philistine, Rude, Wild

**Undamaged** Intact, Sound, Whole

**Undecided** Doubtful, Pending, Uncertain, Wavering

**Undefiled** Chaste, Clean, Pure, Virgin

**Undeniable** Fact, Incontestable, Irrefutable

**Under** Aneath, Below, Beneath, Hypnotized, Sotto, Sub-, Unconscious

**Underarm** Axilla

**Underburnt** Samel

**Under-butler** Bread-chipper

**Undercarriage** Bogie

**Undercoat** Base

**Undercooked** Rare, Raw, Samel

**Undercover** Espionage, Secret, Veiled

**Undercurrent** Acheron, Undertone, Undertow

**Underdevelopment** Ateleiosis

**Underdog** Cerberus, Loser, Victim

> **Undergarment** see UNDERWEAR

**Undergo** Bear, Dree, Endure, Sustain

**Undergraduate** Fresher, L, Pup, Sizar, Sophomore, Student, Subsizar

**Underground (group)** Basement, Catacomb, Cellar, Hell, Hypogaeous, Irgun, Kiva, Macchie, Maquis, Mattamore, Metro, Phreatic, Plutonia, Pothole, Secret, Subsoil, Subterranean, Subway, Tube

**Undergrowth** Brush, Chaparral, Scrub

**Underhand** Dirty, Haunch, Insidious, Lob, Oblique, Secret, Sinister, Sly, Sneaky

**Underlease** Subtack

**Underline** Emphasise, Insist

**Underling** Bottle-washer, Inferior, Jack, Menial, Munchkin, Subordinate

**Underlying** Subjacent

**Undermine** Fossick, Sap, Subvert, Tunnel, Weaken

**Undernourished** Puny, Starveling

**Underpass** Simplon, Subway

**Underside** Soffit

**Understand(able), Understanding** Accept, Acumen, Apprehend, Capeesh, Clear, Comprehend, Conceive, Concept, Cotton-on, Dig, Enlighten, Entente, Fathom, Follow, Gather, Gauge, Gaum, Gorm, Grasp, Have, Head, Heels, Insight, Ken, Kind, Knowhow, Learn, Pact, Rapport, Rapprochement, Realise, Savey, Savvy, See, Sole, Substance, Tumble, Twig, Uptak(e), Wisdom, Wit

**Understatement** Litotes, M(e)iosis

**Understood** Implicit, OK, Roger, Tacit, Unspoken

**Understudy** Deputy, Double, Stand-in, Sub

**Undertake, Undertaking** Attempt, Contract, Covenant, Enterprise, Guarantee, Pledge, Promise, Scheme, Shoulder

**Undertaker** Entrepreneur, Mortician, Obligor, Sponsor, Upholder

**Under-ten** Unit, Yarborough

**Undertone** Murmur, Rhubarb, Sotto voce

**Underwear** Balbriggan, Bloomers, Bodice, Body, Bra(ssiere), Briefs, Camiknickers, Camisole, Chemise, Combs, Dainties, Frillies, Girdle, Linen, Lingerie, Linings, Long Johns, Pantaloons, Panties, Petticoat, Scanties, Semmit, Slip, Smalls, Step-ins, Suspenders, Thermal, Undies, Vest, Wylie-coat

**Underworld** Chthonic, Criminal, Hell, Mafia, Tartar(e), Tartarus, Tartary

**Underwrite, Underwritten** Assure, Endorse, Guarantee, Insure, Lloyds, PS

**Undesirable** Kibitzer

**Undeveloped** Backward, Green, Inchoate, Latent, Ridgel, Ridgil, Ridgling, Riggald, Riglin(g), Seminal

**Undifferentiated** Thalliform, Thallus

**Undigested** Crude

**Undignified (end)** Disaster, Foot, Improper, Infra dig, Unseemly

**Undiluted** Neat, Pure, Sheer

**Undiminished** Entire, Intact, Whole

**Undisciplined** Rule-less, Rulesse, Sloppy, Unruly, Wanton

**Undisclosed** Hidden, In petto

**Undisguised** Apert, Clear, Plain

**Undistinguished** Plebeian

**Undivided** Aseptate, Complete, Entire

**Undo(ing)** Annul, Defeat, Destroy, Downfall, Dup, Poop, Poupe, Release, Ruin, Unravel

**Undoctored** Neat

**Undone** Arrears, Left, Postponed, Ran, Ruined

**Undoubtedly** Certes, Positively, Sure

**Undress(ed)** Bare, Expose, Négligé, Nude, Nue, Peel, Querpo, Raw, Rough, Spar, Strip, Unapparelled

**Undulate, Undulating** Billow, Nebule, Ripple, Roll, Wave

> **Unduly** may indicate an anagram

**Undyed** Greige

**Undying** Eternal

**Unearth(ly)** Astral, Dig, Discover, Disentomb, Exhumate, Indagate

**Unease, Uneasy** Angst, Anxious, Restive, Shy, Tense, Uptight, Womble-cropped

**Unedifying** Idle

**Unembarrassed** Blasé, Dégagé

**Unemotional** Cool, Sober, Stolid

**Unemployed, Unemployment** Drone, Idle, Latent, Lay-off, Redundant

**Unending** Chronic, Eternal, Lasting, Sempiternal

**Unenlightened** Ignorant, Nighted

**Unenthusiastic** Tepid

**Unenveloped** Achlamydeous

**Unequal** Aniso-, Disparate, Scalene, Unjust

**Unerring** Dead, Exact, Precise

**Unestablished** Free

**Unethical** Amoral, Corrupt, Immoral

**Uneven(ness)** Accident, Blotchy, Bumpy, Irregular, Ragged, Scratchy

> **Unevenly** may indicate an anagram

**Unexpected(ly)** Abrupt, Accidental, Fortuitous, Inopinate, Snap, Sodain(e), Sudden, Unawares, Unwary

**Unexperienced** Strange

**Unexplained** Obscure

**Unfading** Evergreen

**Unfailing** Sure

**Unfair** Bias(s)ed, Dirty, Inclement, Partial

**Unfaithful** Disloyal, Godless, Infidel, Traitor

**Unfamiliar** New, Quaint, Strange

**Unfashionable** Cube, Dowdy, Passe, Square

> **Unfashionable** may indicate 'in' to be removed

**Unfavourable** Adverse, Poor, Untoward

**Unfeeling** Adamant, Callous, Cold, Cruel, Dead, Hard, Inhuman

**Unfinished** Crude, Inchoate, Raw, Scabble, Scapple, Stickit

**Unfit(ting)** Disabled, Faulty, Ill, Inept, Outré, Tref(a), Unable

> **Unfit** may indicate an anagram

**Unfixed** Isotropic, Loose

**Unflinching** Fast, Staunch

**Unfold** Deploy, Display, Divulge, Evolve, Interpret, Open, Relate, Spread

**Unforced** Voluntary

**Unforeseen** Accident, Sudden

**Unfortunate(ly)** Accursed, Alack, Alas, Ill-starred, Luckless, Shameless, Unlucky

**Unfounded** Groundless

**Unfriendly** Aloof, Antagonistic, Asocial, Chill(y), Cold, Fraim, Fremd, Fremit, Hostile, Remote, Surly

**Unfruitful** Barren, Sterile

**Unfulfilled** Manqué

**Ungainly** Awkward, Gawkish

**Ungodliness, Ungodly** Impiety, Pagan, Perfidious, Profane

**Ungracious** Cold, Offhand, Rough, Rude

**Ungrammatical** Anacoluthia

**Ungrateful** Ingrate, Snaky

**Unguent** Nard, Pomade, Salve

**Ungulate** Antelope, Dinoceras, Eland, Equidae, Hoofed, Moose, Ruminantia, Takin, Tapir, Tylopoda

**Unhappily, Unhappy** Blue, Depressed, Disconsolate, Dismal, Doleful, Downcast, Glumpish, Miserable, Sad, Tearful, Unlief, Upset

> **Unhappily** may indicate an anagram

**Unharmed** Safe, Scatheless

**Unhealthy** Bad, Clinic, Diseased, Epinosic, Morbid, Noxious, Sickly

**Unholy** Profane, Wicked

**Unicorn** Coin, Monoceros, Moth, Myth, Narwhal

**Unidentified** Anon, Anonym(ous), Incognito, Ligure

**Uniform** Abolla, Consistent, Equable, Equal, Even, Flat, Forage-cap, Identical, Khaki, Kit, Livery, Regimentals, Regular, Rig, Robe, Same, Sole, Standard, Steady, Unvaried

**Unification, Unify(ing)** Henotic, Integrate, Risorgimento, Unite

**Unimaginative** Pedestrian

**Unimpaired** Intact, Sound

**Unimportant** Idle, Immaterial, Inconsequent, Inconsiderable, Insignificant, Petty, Small-time, Trifling, Trivia(l)

**Unimpressible** Cynical

**Uninformed** Ingram

**Uninhibited** Bold, Raunchy

**Uninspired** Humdrum, Pedestrian, Pompier, Tame

**Unintelligent** Dumb, Obtuse, Stupid

**Unintelligible** Arcane, Code, Greek

**Uninterested, Uninteresting** Apathetic, Bland, Dreary, Dry, Dull

**Uninterrupted** Constant, Incessant, Running, Steady

**Uninvited** Interloper, Intruder, Trespasser

**Union(ist)** Affiance, Allegiance, Alliance, Anschluss, Association, Bed, Bond, Combination, Concert, Covalency, Diphthong, Enosis, Ensemble, Equity, EU, Fasciation, Federal, Federation, Fusion, Group, Guild, Knight of labour, Liaison, Link-up, Marriage, Match, Merger, Nuptials, NUM, NUR, NUT, Pearl, Samiti, Sex, Sherman, Splice, Sponsal, Symphysis, Syngamy, Synizesis, Synostosis, Synthesis, TU, U, Uxorial, Verein, Wedding, Wedlock, Wield, Zollverein, Zygosis

**Unique** Alone, A-per-se, Inimitable, Lone, Matchless, Nonesuch, Nonpareil, Nonsuch, Only, One-off, Peerless, Rare, Singular, Sole

**Unisex(ual)** Epicene, Hermaphrodite

**Unison** Chorus, Harmony, One, Sync

**Unit** Abampere, Ace, Amp, Angstrom, Bar, Barn, Baud, Becquerel, Bit, Byte, Cadre, Candela, Cell, Chronon, Corps, Coulomb, Crith, Cusec, Daraf, Darcy, Debye, Degree, Denier, Detachment, Dioptre, Dobson, Dol, Dyne, Ecosystem, Electron, Element, Em, En, Energid, Ensuite, Erg, Farad, Fermi, Flight, Fresnel, Gal, Gauss, Gilbert, Glosseme, Gram, Gray, Hartree, Henry, Ion, Item, Jansky, Joule, Kelvin, Kilderkin, Kilerg, Kilowatt, Lambert, Lexeme, Lumen, Maxwell, Measure, Megawatt, Metre, Mho, Micella, Micelle, Mil, Module, Monad, Morpheme, Neper, Nepit, Nest, Newton, Nit, Octa, Oersted, Ohm, Okta, Organ, Pascal, Phot, Pixel, Poise, Poundal, Probit, RA, Radian, Remen, Rep, Ro(e)ntgen, Rutherford, Sabin, Second, SI, Siemens, Sievert, Singleton, Slug, Sone, Steradian, Stilb, Stokes, TA, Tagmeme, Tesla, Therblig, Therm, Tog, Token, Torr, Var, Watt, Weber, Wing, Yrneh

**Unitarian** Arian, Socinian

**Unite(d)** Accrete, Bind, Coalesce, Combine, Concordant, Connect, Consolidate, Covalent, Fay, Federal, Federate, Gene, Injoint, Join, Kingdom, Knit, Lap, Link, Marry, Meint, Meng, Ment, Merge, Meynt, Ming, Nations, Oop, Oup, Solid, States, Tie, WED, Weld, Yoke

**United Ireland** Fine Gael

**Unity** Harmony, One, Solidarity, Sympathy, Togetherness

**Univalent** Monatomic

**Universal, Universe** All, Catholic, Cosmos, Creation, Ecumenic(al), Emma, General, Global, Infinite, Maddala, Sphere, U, World(wide)

**University** Academe, Academy, Alma mater, Aston, Bonn, Campus, College, Cornell, Exeter, Gown, Harvard, Open, OU, Oxbridge, Princeton, Reading, Redbrick, St Andrews, Sorbonne, Varsity, Yale

**Unjustified** Groundless, Invalid

**Unkempt** Dishevelled, Shaggy

**Unknown** Agnostic, Anon, A.N.Other, Incog(nito), N, Nobody, Noumenon, Quantity, Secret, Soldier, Strange, Symbolic, Warrior, X, Y

**Unleavened** Azymous

**Unless** Nisi, Save, Without

**Unliable** Exempt

**Unlicensed** Illicit

**Unlike(ly)** Difform, Dubious, Improbable, Outsider, Remote, Tall

**Unlimited** Almighty, Boundless, Measureless, Nth, Vast

**Unload** Discharge, Drop, Dump, Jettison, Land

**Unlock(ed)** Bald

**Unlucky** Donsie, Hapless, Ill(-starred), Inauspicious, Infaust, Misfallen, S(c)hlimazel, Stiff, Thirteen, Untoward, Wanchancie, Wanchancy

**Unman** Castrate

**Unmannerly**   Crude, Discourteous, Impolite, Rude

**Unmarried**   Bachelor, Single, Spinster

**Unmask**   Expose, Rumble

**Unmatched**   Bye, Champion, Orra, Unique

**Unmentionable(s)**   Bra, Foul, UNDERWEAR, Undies

**Unmindful**   Heedless, Oblivious

**Unmistakable**   Clear, Manifest, Plain

**Unmitigated**   Absolute, Arrant, Sheer

**Unmixed**   Me(a)re, Neat, Nett, Pure, Raw, Straight

**Unmoved**   Adamant, Firm, Serene, Static, Stolid

**Unnamed**   Anon

**Unnatural**   Abnormal, Affected, Cataphysical, Contrived, Eerie, Flat, Irregular, Strange

> **Unnaturally**   may indicate an anagram

**Unnecessary**   Extra, Gash, Needless, Redundant, Superfluous

**Unnerve, Unnerving**   Discouraging, Eerie, Rattle

**Unobserved**   Backstage, Sly, Unseen

**Unoccupied**   Empty, Idle, Vacant, Void

**Unofficial**   Wildcat

**Unoriginal**   Banal, Copy, Derivative, Imitation, Plagiarised, Slavish

**Unorthodox**   Heretic, Unconventional

**Unpaid**   Amateur, Hon(orary), Voluntary

**Unpaired**   Azygous, Bye

**Unpalatable**   Acid, Bitter, Unsavoury

**Unparalleled**   Supreme, Unique

**Unpartitioned**   Aseptate

**Unperturbed**   Bland, Calm, Serene

**Unpleasant, Unpleasant person**   Grim, Horrible, Icky, Nasty, Obnoxious, Odious, Offensive, Pejorative, Shady, Sticky, Toerag, Wart

**Unpopular**   Hat(e)able

**Unpractical**   Futile, Orra

**Unpredictable**   Dicy, Erratic

**Unprepared**   Ad lib, Extempore, Impromptu, Unready

**Unpretentious**   Quiet

**Unprincipled**   Amoral, Dishonest, Reprobate

**Unproductive**   Arid, Atokal, Atokous, Barren, Dead-head, Fallow, Futile, Lean, Poor, Shy, Sterile, Yeld, Yell

**Unprofitable**   Bootless, Lean, Thankless

**Unprogressive**   Inert, Square

**Unprotected** Exposed, Nude, Vulnerable

**Unpunctual** Tardy

**Unqualified** Absolute, Entire, Outright, Pure, Quack, Sheer, Straight, Thorough, Total, Utter

**Unquestionably, Unquestioning** Absolute, Certain, Doubtless, Implicit

**Unravel** Construe, Disentangle, Solve

**Unready** Unripe

**Unreal(istic)** Eidetic, En l'air, Fake, Fancied, Illusory, Oneiric, Phantom, Pseudo, Romantic, Sham, Spurious

**Unreasonable, Unreasoning** Absurd, Bigot, Illogical, Irrational, Misguided, Perverse, Rabid

**Unrecognised** Incognito, Invalid, Unsung

**Unrefined** Coarse, Common, Crude, Earthy, Gur, Rude, Vul(g), Vulgar

**Unrehearsed** Extempore, Impromptu

**Unrelenting** Implacable, Remorseless, Severe, Stern

**Unreliable** Erratic, Fickle, Flighty, Unstable, Wankle

**Unremitting** Dogged, Intensive

**Unresponsive** Cold, Nastic

**Unrest** Ferment

**Unrestrained** Free, Immoderate, Lax, Lowsit, Rampant, Wanton, Wild

**Unreturnable** Ace

**Unrighteousness** Adharma

**Unromantic** Classic(al), Mundane

**Unruffled** Calm, Placid, Serene, Smooth, Tranquil

**Unruly** Anarchic, Buckie, Camstairy, Camsteary, Camsteerie, Exception, Obstreperous, Ragd(e), Raged, Ragged, Rattlebag, Riotous, Tartar, Turbulent, Turk, Wanton, Wayward

> **Unruly** may indicate an anagram

**Unsafe** Insecure, Perilous, Vulnerable

**Unsatisfactory, Unsatisfying** Bad, Lame, Lousy, Meagre, Rocky, Thin, Wanting

**Unsavoury** Epinosic

**Unscramble** Decode, Decrypt

**Unscrupulous** Rascally, Slippery

**Unseasonable, Unseasoned** Green, Murken, Raw, Untimely

**Unseat** Depose, Dethrone, Oust, Overset, Overthrow, Throw

**Unseemly** Coarse, Improper, Indecent, Untoward

**Unselfish** Altruist, Generous

**Unsent** Square

**Unsettled** Homeless, Hunky, Nervous, Outstanding, Queasy, Restive

> **Unsettled** may indicate an anagram

**Unsexy** N, Neuter

**Unsheltered** Bleak, Exposed, Homeless

**Unsightly** Hideous, Repulsive, Ugly

**Unsinning** Impeccable, Pure

**Unskilled** Awkward, Dilutee, Gauche, Green, Inexpert, Rude

**Unsociable** Anchoretic, Grouchy, Solitary

**Unsophisticated** Homespun, Naive

**Unsound** Barmy, Infirm, Invalid, Shaky, Wonky

> **Unsound** may indicate an anagram

**Unsparing** Severe

**Unspeakable** Dreadful, Ineffable

**Unspecific** General, Generic, Vague

**Unspoiled, Unspoilt** Innocent, Natural, Perfect, Pure

**Unspoken** Silent, Tacit

**Unstable** Astatic, Casual, Crank(y), Dicky, Erratic, Fluidal, Infirm, Insecure, Labile, Rickety, Shifty, Slippy, Tickle, Variable, Wankle

**Unstated** Concordat, Tacit, Unknown

**Unsteady** Dicky, Groggy, Tottery, Totty, Variable, Wambling, Wankle, Wobbly

> **Unstuck** may indicate an anagram

**Unsubstantial** Aeriform, Airy, Flimsy, Paltry, Shadowy, Slight, Thin, Yeasty

**Unsuccessful** Abortive, Futile, Manqué, Vain

**Unsuitable** Impair, Improper, Inapt, Incongruous, Inexpedient, Malapropos, Unfit

**Unsupported** Astylar, Floating, Unfounded

**Unsurpassed** All-time, Best, Supreme

**Unsuspecting** Credulous, Innocent

**Unsweetened** Brut, Natural

**Unsymmetrical** Heterauxesis(m), Irregular, Lopsided

**Unthinking** Mechanical

**Untidy** Daggy, Dowd(y), Ragged, Scruff(y), Slovenly, Tatty

> **Untidy** may indicate an anagram

**Untie** Free, Undo, Unlace

**Until** Hasta

**Untilled** Fallow

**Untold** Secret, Umpteen, Vast

**Untouchable** Burakumin, Harijan, Immune, Sealed

**Untouched** Intact, Pristine, Inviolate, Virgin

> **Untrained** may indicate 'BR' to be removed

**Untrue, Untruth** Apocryphal, Eccentric, Faithless, False(hood), Lie, Prefabrication, Unleal

**Untrustworthy** Dishonest, Fickle, Sleeky, Tricky

**Untypical** Isolated, Unusual

**Unused** New, Over

**Unusual(ly)** Abnormal, Atypical, Extra(ordinary), Freak, New, Novel, Odd, Particular, Rare, Remarkable, Singular, Special, STRANGE, Unique, Untypical, Unwonted

> **Unusual** may indicate an anagram

**Unvarying** Constant, Eternal, Stable, Static, Uniform

**Unveil** Expose, Honour

**Unvoiced** Surd

**Unwanted** De trop, Exile, Outcast, Sorn

**Unwed** Celibate, Single

**Unwelcome, Unwelcoming** Icy, Lulu, Obtrusive

**Unwell** Ailing, Crook, Dicky, Ill, Impure, Poorly, Toxic

**Unwholesome** Miasmous, Morbid, Noxious

**Unwieldy** Cumbersome

**Unwillingness** Averse, Disinclined, Intestate, Loth, Nolition, Nolo, Perforce, Reluctant

**Unwind** Relax, Straighten, Unreave, Unreeve

> **Unwind** may indicate an anagram

**Unwise** Foolish, Ill-advised, Imprudent

**Unwitting** Accidental, Nescient

**Unwonted** Inusitate

**Unworried** Carefree

**Unworthy** Below, Beneath, Indign, Inferior

**Unwritten** Verbal

**Unyielding** Adamant, Eild, Firm, Inexorable, Obdurate, Rigid, Stubborn, Tough

**Unyoke** Outspan

**Up(on), Upper, Uppish** A, Afoot, Antidepressant, Astir, Astray, Astride, Cloud-kissing, Heavenward, Hep, Horsed, Incitant, Off, On, Range, Ride, Riding, Skyward, Speed, Vamp, Ventral

**Up-anchor** Atrip, Weigh

**Upbeat** Anacrusis, Arsis

**Upbraid** Abuse, Rebuke, Reproach, Reprove, Scold, Twit

**Upcountry**   Anabasis, Inland

**Update**   Renew, Report

**Upheaval**   Cataclysm, Eruption, Seismic, Stir

> **Upheld**   may indicate 'up' in another word

**Uphill**   Arduous, Borstal, Sisyphean

**Uphold**   Assert, Defend, Maintain

**Upholstery**   Lampas, Moquette, Trim

**Upkeep**   Support

**Upland**   Downs, Wold

**Uplift**   Boost, Edify, Elate, Elevation, Exalt, Hoist, Levitation

**Upper class**   Aristocrat, County, Patrician, Top-hat, U

**Upright(s), Uprightness**   Aclinic, Anend, Apeak, Apeek, Arrect, Erect, Goalpost, Honest, Jamb, Joanna, Mullion, Perpendicular, Piano, Pilaster(s), Post, Rectitude, Roman, Splat, Stanchion, Stares, Stile, Stud, Vertical, Virtuous

**Uprising**   Incline, Intifada, Rebellion, Revolt, Tumulus

**Uproar(ious)**   Ballyhoo, Bedlam, Blatancy, Brouhaha, Charivari, Clamour, Collieshangie, Commotion, Cry, Din, Dirdam, Dirdum, Durdum, Emeute, Flaw, Fracas, Furore, Garboil, Hell, Hubbub(oo), Hullabaloo, Hurly(-burly), Katzenjammer, Noise, Noyes, Outcry, Pandemonium, Racket, Raird, Reird, Riotous, Ruckus, Roister, Romage, Rowdedow, Rowdydow(dy), Ruction, Rumpus, Stramash, Turmoil, Whoobub

**Uproot**   Eradicate, Evict, Supplant, Weed

**Upset(ting)**   Aggrieve, Bother, Capsize, Catastrophe, Choked, Coup, Cowp, Crank, Derange, Dip, Discomboberate, Discombobulate, Discomfit, Discomfort, Discommode, Disconcert, Dismay, Disquiet, Disturb, Dod, Eat, Fuss, Inversion, Keel, Miff, Nauseative, Offend, Overturn, Perturb, Pip, Pother, Purl, Rile, Ruffle, Rumple, Sad, Seel, Shake, Sore, Spill, Tapsalteerie, Tip, Topple, Trauma, Undo

> **Upset**   may indicate an anagram; a word upside down; or 'tes'

**Upshot**   Outcome, Result, Sequel

**Upside down**   Inverted, Resupinate, Tapsie-teerie, Topsy-turvy

**Upstart**   Buckeen, Jumped-up, Mushroom, Parvenu

> **Upstart**   may indicate 'u'

**Upstream**   Thermal

**Upsurge**   Thrust, Waste

**Uptake**   Shrewdness, Understanding, Wit

**Up to**   Till, Until

**Up-to-date**   Abreast, Current, Mod, Swinging, Topical

**Upwards**   Acclivious, Aloft, Antrorse, Cabré

**Uranium**   Pitchblende, U

**Urban** Civic, Megalopolis, Municipal, Town

**Urbane** Debonair, Townly

**Urchin** Arab, Brat, Crinoid, Crossfish, Cystoid, Echinoidea, Echinus, Gamin, Mudlark, Nipper, Sand-dollar, Sea-egg, Spatangoidea, Spatangus, Street-arab, Townskip

**Urge, Urgent** Admonish, Coax, Constrain, Crying, Drive, Egg, Enjoin, Exhort, Exigent, Goad, Hard, Hie, Hunger, Hurry, Id, Impel, Impulse, Incense, Incite, Insist(ent), Instance, Instigate, Itch, Kick, Libido, Nag, Peremptory, Persuade, Press(ing), Push, Set on, Spur, Strong, Whig, Yen

> **Urgent** may indicate 'Ur-gent', viz. Iraqi

**Uriah** Hittite, Humble, Umble

**Urinal** Bog, John, Jordan, LAVATORY, Loo

**Urinate, Urine** Chamber-lye, Emiction, Lant, Leak, Micturition, Pee, Piddle, Piss, Slash, Stale, Widdle

**Urn** Ewer, Grecian, Olla, Ossuary, Samovar, Storied, Vase

**Us** 's, UK, Uns, We

**Usage, Use(d), Utilise** Application, Apply, Avail, Boot, Consume, Custom, Dow, EMPLOY, Ex, Exercise, Exert, Exploit, Flesh, Habit, Manner, Ply, Practice, Spent, Tradition, Treat, Ure, With, Wont

**Useful** Asset, Availing, Commodity, Dow, Expedient

**Useless** Base, Cumber, Dud, Empty, Futile, Gewgaw, Idle, Inane, Ineffective, Lame, Lemon, Otiose, Plug, Sculpin, Sterile, US, Vain, Void, Wet

**Usher** Chobdar, Conduct(or), Doorman, Escort, Herald, Huissier, Macer, Rod, Show, Steward

**Usual** Common, Customary, Habit(ual), Natural, Normal, Ordinary, Rule, Solito, Typical, Wont

**Usurp(er)** Abator, Arrogate, Encroach, Invade

**Usurer, Usury** Gombeen, Moneylender, Note-shaver, Shark, Uncle

**Ut** As, Doh, Utah

**Utah** Ut

**Utensil** Chopsticks, Cookware, Fish-kettle, Fork, Gadget, Implement, Instrument, Knife, Ricer, Skillet, Spoon, Tool

> **Utilise** See USE

**Utilitarian** Benthamite, Mill, Practical, Useful

**Utility** Elec(tricity), Gas, Water

**Utmost** Best, Extreme, Farthest, Maximum

**Utopia(n)** Cloud-cuckoo-land, Ideal, Pantisocracy, Paradise, Perfect, Shangri-la

**Utter(ance), Utterly** Absolute, Accent, Agrapha, Agraphon, Arrant, Cry, Dead, Deliver, Dictum, Dog, Downright, Ejaculate, Enunciate, Express, Extreme, Issue, Judgement, Lenes, Lenis, Most, Oracle, Pass, Phonate,

Pronounce, Pure, Rank, Rattle, Remark, Saw, SAY, Sheer, Syllable, Tell, Vend, Vent, Very, Voice

**Uvula** Staphyle

# Vv

**V** Anti, Bomb, Five, See, Sign, Verb, Verse, Versus, Victor(y), Volt, Volume

**Vacancy, Vacant** Blank, Empty, Hole, Hollow, Inane, Place, Space, Vacuum

**Vacation** Holiday, Leave, Non-term, Outing, Recess, Trip, Voidance

**Vaccination, Vaccine** Antigen, Cure, Jenner, Sabin, Salk

**Vacillate, Vacillating** Dither, Feeble, Hesitate, Shilly-shally, Wabble, Wave(r)

**Vacuous** Blank, Empty, Toom, Vacant

**Vacuum** Blank, Cleaner, Emptiness, Nothing, Plenum, Thermos, Void

**Vade-mecum** Ench(e)iridion, Notebook

**Vagabond** Bergie, Gadling, GYPSY, Hobo, Landlo(u)per, Rapparee, Romany, Rover, Runagate, Tramp

**Vagrant** Bum, Caird, Gangrel, Gang-there-out, Goliard, Gypsy, Hobo, Landlo(u)per, Lazzarone, Nomad, Patercove, Rintnereout, Rogue, Romany, Scatterling, Strag, Stroll, Swagman, Tinker, TRAMP, Truant

**Vague(ness)** Blur, Confused, Dim, Hazy, Ill-headed, Indeterminate, Indistinct, Loose, Mist, Nebulous

> **Vaguely** may indicate an anagram

**Vain** Bootless, Coxcomb, Coxcomical, Egoistic, Empty, Fruitless, FUTILE, Hollow, Idle, Proud, Strutting, Useless, Vogie

**Vainglory** Panache

**Valance** Pand, Pelmet

**Vale** Addio, Adieu, Cheerio, Coomb, Dean, Dene, Ebbw, Enna, Glen, Tempé, Valley

**Valedictory** Apopemptic, Farewell

**Valentine** Card, Sweetheart

**Valerian** All-heal, Cetywall, Setwall

**Valet** Aid, Andrew, Jeeves, Man, Passepartout, Servant, Skip-kennel

**Valetudinarian** Hypochondriac, Invalid

**Valiant** Brave, Doughty, Resolute, Stalwart, Wight

**Valid(ate)** Confirm, Establish, Just, Legal, Sound

**Valise** Bag, Case, Dorlach, Satchel

**Valley** Ajalon, Aosta, Baca, Bekaa, Bobon, Clough, Comb(e), Coomb, Cwm, Dale, Dargle, Dean, Defile, Dell, Den, Dene, Dingle, Dip, Gehenna, Ghyll, Glen, Graben, Heuch, Hollow, Hope, Humiliation, Ladin, Lallan,

Nemean, Olympia, Ravine, Rhondda, Ria, Rift, Slack, Slade, Strath(spey), Tempe, Tophet, Trossachs, Umbria, Valdarno, Vale, Vallambrosa, Water

**Valour** Bravery, Courage, Heroism, Merit, Prowess

**Valuable, Valuation, Value** Appraise, Appreciate, Apprize, Assess(ment), Asset, Bargain, Cherish, Cop, Cost, CIF, Equity, Esteem, Estimate, Intrinsic, Limit, Nominal, Omnium, Ph, Precious, Price, Prize, Rarity, Rate, Rating, Regard, Respect, Salt, Set, Steem, Stent, Store, Treasure, WORTH

**Valueless** Bum, Orra, Useless, Worthless

**Valve** Cock, Dynatron, Magnetron, Mitral, Pentode, Petcock, Poppet, Resnatron, Sluice, Stopcock, Tap, Tetrode, Thermionic, Throttle, Thyratron, Triode, Ventil

**Vamoose** Abscond, Decamp, Scat, Scram

**Vamp** Adlib, Charm, Rehash, Seduce, Siren, Strum, Twiddle

**Vampire** Dracula, Ghoul, Lamia, Lilith, Pontianak

**Van(guard)** Advance, Box-car, Cart, Forefront, Foremost, Front, Head, Lead, Leader(s), Lorry, Pantechnicon, Removal, Spearhead, Truck, Wagon

**Vanadium** V

**Vandal(ise), Vandalism** Desecrate, Hooligan, Loot, Pillage, Ravage, Rough, Sab(oteur), Sack, Saracen, Skinhead, Slash, Trash

**Vandyke** Beard, Painter

**Vane** Fan, Web, Wing

**Vanessa** Butterfly

**Vanish(ed)** Cease, Disappear, Disperse, Dissolve, Evanesce(nt), Evaporate, Faint(ed), Mizzle, Slope, Unbe

**Vanity** Amour-propre, Arrogance, Ego, Esteem, Futility, Pomp, Pride, Self-esteem

**Vanquish** Beat, Conquer, Floor, Master, Overcome

**Vantage (point)** Ascendancy, Coign(e), Height

**Vaporise, Vapour** Boil, Cloud, Fog, Fume, Halitus, Iodine, Miasma, Mist, Reek, Roke, STEAM, Steme

**Variable** Amphoteric, Diverse, Fickle, Fluctuating, Inconstant, Omniform, Parametric, Protean, Versatile

> **Variance, Variant, Variation** see VARY

> **Varied, Variety** see VARY

> **Varied** may indicate an anagram

**Variegate(d)** Dappled, Flecked, Fretted, Motley, Pied, Rainbow, Skewbald, Tissue

> **Variety of** may indicate an anagram

**Various** Diverse, Manifold, Separate, Several, Sundry

**Various years** Vy

**Varlet** Cad, Knave

**Varnish(ing)** Bee-glue, Copal, Cowdie-gum, Dam(m)ar, Dope, Dragon's-blood, Japan, Lacquer, Lentisk, Nibs, Shellac, Tung-oil, Tung-tree, Vernissage

**Vary, Variance, Variant, Variation, Varied, Variety** Ablaut, Aelotropy, Alter, Assortment, Breed, Brew, Change, Chequered, Colour, Contrapuntal, Counterpoint, Daedal(e), Dedal, Discrepancy, Enigma, Farraginous, Isochor, Isopleth, Line, Medley, Morph, Mutable, Olio, Orthogenesis, Remedy, Sort, Species, Spice, Stirps, Strain, Tolerance, Var, Version, Vl, Wane, Wax

**Vase** Canopus, Diota, Hydria, Jardiniere, Kalpis, Murr(h)a, Portland, Pot, Potiche, Urn, Vessel

**Vassal** Client, Lackey, Liege, Man, Servant, Vavaso(u)r

**Vast(ness)** Big, Cosmic, Enormous, Epic, Huge(ous), Immense, Mighty, Ocean

**Vat** Back, Barrel, Blunger, Copper, Cowl, Cuvee, Fat, Keir, Kier, Tank, Tub, Tun

**Vatican** Rome

**Vaudeville** Zarzuela

**Vaughan** Silurist

**Vault(ing)** Arch, Cavern, Cellar, Clear, Crypt, Cul-de-four, Cupola, Dome, Dungeon, Firmament, Jump, Kiva, Leap(frog), Lierne, Pend, Safe, Sepulchre, Severy, Shade, Souterrain, Tomb, Weem

> **Vault** may indicate an anagram

**Vaunt** Boast, Brag, Crow

**Veal** Escalope, Fricandeau, Galantine, Scallop, Schnitzel

**Vector, Vector operator** Dyad, Nabla

**Veer** Boxhaul, Broach, Deviate, Gybe, Swerve, Tack, Turn, Wear, Yaw

**Vegetable(s)** Alexanders, Artichoke, Asparagus, Aubergine, Beans, Beetroot, Brassica, Broccoli, Cabbage, Calabrese, Carrot, Castock, Cauliflower, Celeriac, Celery, Chard, Choko, Chufa, Colcannon, Cole, Crout, Custock, Daikon, Endive, Escarole, Eschalot, Flora, Greens, Guar, Inert, Ingan, Kale, Kohlrabi, Kumara, Kumera, Lablab, Leek, Legume(n), Lettuce, Macedoine, Mangel(-wurzel), Mangold, Marrow(-squash), Mirepoix, Mooli, Navew, Neep, Oca, Okra, Okro, Olitory, Onion, Orach(e), Parsnip, Pea(se), Plant, Potato, Pottage, Pratie, Pulse, Pumpkin, Quinoa, Radicchio, Radish, Ratatouille, Rocambole, Rutabaga, Salad, Salsify, Samphire, Sauce, Sauerkraut, Savoy, Scorzonera, Shallot, Sium, Skirret, Spinach(-beet), Spinage, Sprouts, Spud, Squash, Succotash, Swede, Tomato, Tonka-bean, Triffid, Turnip, Yam

**Vegetable extract** Solanine

**Vegetarian** Herbivore, Meatless, Vegan

**Vegetate, Vegetator, Vegetation** Alga, Cover, Flora, Greenery, Herb,

Scrub, Stagnate, Transect

**Vehemence, Vehement(ly)** Amain, Ardent, Fervid, Frenzy, Heat, Hot, Intense, Violent

**Vehicle** Ambulance, Amtrack, Articulated, ATV, Brancard, Brake, Buggy, Bus, Car, Caravan, Carry-all, Cart, Channel, Chariot, Conveyance, Curricle, Cycle, Dog-cart, Dray, Fiacre, Float, Gharri, Gharry, Go-cart, Go-kart, Growler, Hansom, Jeep, Jeepney, Jingle, Jinker, Jitney, Juggernaut, Kago, Kart, Landau, LEM, Limber, Litter, Lorry, Machine, Means, Medium, Minibus, Minicab, Norimon, Pedicab, Penny-farthing, Phaeton, Pick-up, Ricksha(w), Runabout, Samlor, Sand-yacht, Scow, Shay, Skidoo, Sled(ge), Sleigh, Soyuz, Spider, Stanhope, Steam-car, Sulky, Surrey, Tarantas(s), Taxi, Tempera, Tipcart, Tip-up, Tonga, Trailer, Tram, Trap, Tricycle, Trishaw, Troika, Trolley, Tumbril, Vahana, Velocipede, Vespa, Volante, Wagon, Wheelbarrow

**Veil** Burk(h)a, Calyptra, Chad(d)ar, Chador, Chuddah, Chuddar, Cover, Curtain, Envelop, Kalyptra, Kiss-me, Lambrequin, Mantilla, Mist, Obscure, Purdah, Scene, Veale, Volet, Wimple, Yashmak

**Vein** Artery, Costa, Fahlband, Jugular, Ledge, Lode, Media, Mood, Precava, Rake, Rib, Saphena, Stockwork, Stringer, Style, Varix, Vena

**Vellum** Cutch, Kutch, Parchment

**Velocity** Rate, Speed, V

**Velvet** Chenille, National, Panné, Pile, Velour, Velure

**Venal** Corruptible, Mercenary, Sale

**Vend(or)** Hawk, Pedlar, Rep, Sell, Sutler

**Vendetta** Feud

**Veneer** Facade, Gloss, Varnish

**Venerable** Aged, August, Bede, Guru, Hoary, Sacred, Sage

**Venerate, Veneration** Adore, Awe, Douleia, Dulia, Hallow, Homage, Idolise, Latria, Revere, Worship

**Venereal** NSU, VD

**Venery** Chase

**Venetian** Blind, Gobbo, Polo

**Vengeance** Reprisal, Ultion, Wannion, Wrack, Wreak

**Venom(ous)** Gall, Gila, Jamestown-weed, Jim(p)son-weed, Poison, Rancour, Spite, Toxic, Virus

**Vent** Aperture, Belch, Chimney, Emit, Express, Fumarole, Issue, Ostiole, Outlet, Solfatara, Undercast, Wreak

**Venter** Uterus

**Ventilate, Ventilator** Air, Air-brick, Air-hole, Discuss, Express, Louvre, Shaft, Voice, Winze

**Venture(d)** Ante, Chance, Dare, Daur, Durst, Flutter, Foray, Handsel, Hazard, Opine, Presume, Promotion, Risk, Throw

**Venue**  Bout, Locale, Place, Tryst, Visne

**Venus**  Cohog, Cytherean, Hesper(us), Love, Lucifer, Morning-star, Primavera, Quahog, Rokeby, Vesper

**Venus fly-trap**  Dionaea

**Veracity, Veracious**  Accurate, Factual, Sincere, Truth(ful)

**Veranda(h)**  Balcony, Gallery, Patio, Porch, Stoep, Stoop, Terrace

**Verb**  Active, Copula, Irregular, Passive, Vb

**Verbascum**  Mullein

**Verbena**  Vervain

**Verbose, Verbosity**  Padding, Prolix, Talkative, Wordy

**Verdant**  Lush

**Verdict**  Decision, Judg(e)ment, Opinion, Resolution, Ruling

**Verdigris**  Aeruginous, Patina

**Verge**  Border, Brink, EDGE, Incline, Rim

**Verger**  Beadle, Pew-opener

**Verify**  Affirm, Ascertain, Check, Confirm, Prove, Validate

**Verily**  Yea

**Verisimilitude**  Artistic, Authenticity, Credibility

**Verity**  Fact, Truth

**Vermifuge**  Cow(h)age, Cowitch

**Vermilion**  Cinnabar, Minium, Red

**Vermin**  Carrion, Catawampus, Lice, Mice, RODENT, Scum

**Vermouth**  French, It(alian), Martini

**Vernacular**  Common, Dialect, Idiom, Jargon, Lingo, Native, Patois

**Veronica**  Hebe, Speedwell

**Verruca**  Wart

**Versatile**  Adaptable, All-rounder, Flexible, Handy, Protean, Resourceful

**Verse(s), Versed**  Alcaics, Alexandrine, Amphigouri, Archilochian, Asclepiad, Asynartete, Awdl, Ballad, Beatitude, Blad, Blaud, Burden, Canto, Cinquain, Comus, Dimiter, Dithyramb, Doggerel, Duan, Elegiac, Epic, Epigram, Epos, Fabliau, Fescennine, Fit, Ghazal, Gnomic, Goliardic, Haikai, Heroic, Hexameter, Hokku, Hudibrastic(s), Huitain, Hymn, Ionic, Jingle, Kyrielle, Laisse, Leonine, Lyric, Macaronic, Madrigal, Meter, Miurus, Monometer, Neck, Octastich, Pantoum, Pantun, Pennill(ion), Pentameter, Pindaric, Poem, Poesy, Prosody, Quatrain, Renga, Rhopalic, RHYME, Rime, Rondeau, Rondel, Rubaiyat, Sapphic, Saturnian, Scazon, Senarius, Septenarius, Serpentine, Sestina, Sestine, Sijo, Sirvente, Sixaine, Song, Spasm, Stanza, Stave, Stornello, Strain, Strophe, Tanka, Tercet, Terza rima, Terzetta, Tract, Triad, Trimeter, Tripody, Tristich, Up, V, Vers

**Versed sine**  Sagitta

**Versifier**  Lyricist, Poetaster, Rhymer, Rhymester

**Version** Account, Edition, Form, Paraphrase, Rendering, Revision, Translation

**Vertebra(e), Vertebrate** Amphioxus, Atlas, Axis, Bone, Centrum, Cervical, Chordae, Dorsal, Ichthyopsida, Lumbar, Sauropsida, Spondyl, Vermis

**Vertex** Apex, Crest, Crown, Summit, Zenith

**Vertical** Apeak, Apeek, Atrip, Erect, Lapse, Perpendicular, Plumb, Sheer, Standing, Stemmed, Upright

**Vertigo** Dinic, Dizziness, Fainting, Giddiness, Megrim, Nausea, Staggers, Whirling

**Verve** Dash, Energy, Go, Panache, Vigour

**Very (good)** A1, Ae, Assai, Awfully, Bonzer, Boshta, Boshter, Dashed, Def, Ever, Extreme(ly), Fell, Frightfully, Gey, Grouse, Heap, Hellova, Helluva, Jolly, Light, Mighty, Molto, Much, OK, Precious, Precise, Purler, Real, Self same, So, Sore, Stinking, Utter, V, VG

**Vesicle** Ampul, Bladder

**Vespers** Evensong, Placebo, Sicilian

**Vessel** Alcarraza, Aludel, Amphora, Ampulla, Aorta, Argyle, Argyll, Ark, Artery, Aspersorium, Autoclave, Barge, Bark, Beaker, Bicker, Bin, BOAT, Bouget, Bowl, Bucentaur, Buss, Calabash, Calandria, Canteen, Carafe, Carboy, Cask, Cat, Cauldron, Chalice, Chatty, Ciborium, Coaster, Cog(ue), Colander, Container, Coolamon, Copper, Corvette, Costrel, Cot(t), Cowl, Craft, Crare, Crayer, Cresset, Crewe, Crock, Crucible, Cruet, Cruiser, Cucurbit, Cullender, Cup, Cupel, Cyathus, Dandy, Decanter, Deep-sinker, Destroyer, D(h)ow, Dinghy, Dish, Dixie, Dolium, Dredger, Drifter, Elutor, Etna, Fat, Felucca, Figuline, Flagon, Flagship, Font, Frigate, Frigot, Galiot, Galleass, Galleon, Galley, Galliass, Galliot, Gallipot, Gallivat, Goblet, Goglet, Gourd, Grab, Hydrofoil, Jardinière, Jugular, Keel, Ketch, Kettle, Laver, Longboat, Lorcha, Lota(h), Mazer, Monteith, Mortar, Mudscow, Noggin, Obe, Oiler, Olpe, Pan(cheon), Panchion, Pannikin, Patamar, Pig, Pinnace, Pitcher, Pokal, Polacca, Privateer, Quart, Receptacle, Retort, Rumkin, Saic(k), Saique, Sampan, Scoop, Shell, SHIP, Shippo, Skin, Snow, Steamer, Stean(e), Steen, Stoop, Stoup, Tankard, Tanker, Tappit-hen, Tassie, Tazza, Terrene, Triaconter, Troopship, Trough, Tub, Tureen, Urn, Utensil, Varix, Vas(e), Vat, Vein, Vena, Vial, Wherry, Xebec, Zabra, Zulu

**Vest** Beset, Confer, Gilet, Modesty, Semmit, Singlet, Skivvy, Sticharion, Undercoat, Waistcoat

**Vestibule** Entry, Exedra, Foyer, Hall, Lobby, Narthex, Porch, Portico, Pronaos, Tambour

**Vestige** Hint, Mark, Mention, Shadow, Sign, Trace

**Vestment** Alb, Chasuble, Cotta, Dalmatic, Ephod, Fannel, Garb, GARMENT, Mantelletta, Omophorion, Pallium, Parament, Ph(a)elonian, Raiment, Rational, Rochet, Rocquet, Sakkos, Stole, Surplice, Tunic(le)

**Vestry** Sacristy

**Vet(ting), Vets** Check, Doctor, Examine, OK, Screen, Veteran, Zoiatria, Zootherapy

**Vetch** Ers, Fitch, Locoweed, Tare, Tine

**Veteran** BL, Expert, Master, Oldster, Old-timer, Retread, Seasoned, Soldier, Stager, Stalwart, Stalworth, Vet, War-horse

> **Veteran** may indicate 'obsolete'

**Veto** Ban, Debar, Negative, Reject, Taboo, Tabu

**Vex(ed)** Anger, Annoy, Bother, Chagrin, Debate, Fret, Gall, Grieve, Harass, Irritate, Mortify, Pester, Rankle, Rile, Sore, Tease, Torment, Trouble

**Vexation(s)** Barrator, Chagrin, Drat, Grief, Nuisance, Pique, Spite, Trouble

**Vexillum** Web

**Via** By, Per, Through

**Viable** Economic, Going, Healthy, Possible

**Viand** Cate

**Vibrant** Energetic, Plangent, Resonant

**Vibrate, Vibration(s)** Atmosphere, Diadrom, Dinnle, Dirl, Flutter, Fremitus, Hotter, Jar, Judder, Oscillate, Pulse, Quake, Resonance, Seiche, Shimmy, Shudder, Thrill, Throb, Tingle, Tremor, Trill, Twinkle, Whir(r)

**Viburnum** Opulus

**Vicar** Bray, Elton, Incumbent, Pastoral, Plenarty, Primrose, Rector, Rev(erend), Trimmer

**Vice** Clamp, Crime, Deputy, Eale, Evil, Greed, Iniquity, Instead, Jaws, Regent, Second (in command), SIN

**Vice-president** Croupier

**Viceroy** Khedive, Nawab, Provost, Satrap, Willingdon

**Vichy water** Eau

**Vicinity** Area, Environs, Locality, Neighbourhood, Region

**Vicious** Flagitious

**Victim** Abel, Butt, Casualty, Dupe, Frame, Host, Mark, Martyr, Nebbich, Neb(b)ish, Pathic, Patsy, Prey, Sacrifice, Scapegoat

**Victor(y)** Banzai, Beater, Cadmean, Captor, Champ(ion), Conqueror, Conquest, Epinicion, Epinikion, Flagship, Fool's mate, Gree, Gris, Hugo, Kobe, Landslide, Lepanto, Ludorum, Mature, Nike, Palm, Philippi, Pyrrhic, Runaway, Signal, Triumph, VE day, Vee, Vic, Walkover, Win(ner)

**Victoria(n)** Aussie, Plum, Station

**Victualler** Caterer, Grocer, Purveyor, Supplier

**Video** Promo, Vera

**Vie** Compete, Contend, Emulate, Strive

**Vienna** Wien

**View(er)** Aim, Angle, Aspect, Belief, Bird's eye, Cineaste, Consensus,

Consider, Dogma, Doxy, Eye, Facet, Gander, Glimpse, Grandstand, Idea, Introspect, Kaleidoscope, Landscape, Notion, Opinion, Outlook, Pan, Panorama, Profile, PROSPECT, Scan, Scape, Scene(ry), See, Sight, Slant, Specular, Stereoscope, Tenet, Thanatopsis, Theory, Veduta, Vista, Visto, Watch, Witness

**Viewpoint** Attitude, Belvedere, Perspective, Sight

**Vigil, Vigilant(e)** Awake, Aware, Eve, Wake, Wary, Watch, Whitecap

**Vignette** Print, Profile, Sketch

**Vigorous, Vigour** Athletic, Billy-o, Blooming, Drastic, Elan, Emphatic, Energetic, Flame, Forceful, Go, Green, Heart(y), Lustihood, Lusty, P, Pep, Pith, Potency, Punchy, Racy, Rank, Robust, Round, Rude, Spirit, Sprack, Sthenic, Stingo, Strength, Strong, Thews, Tireless, Tone, Trenchant, Vegete, Vim, Vitality, Vivid, Zip

> **Vigorously** may indicate an anagram

**Viking** Dane, Norseman, Rollo

**Vile** Base, Corrupt, Depraved, Dregs, Durance, Mean, Offensive, Scurvy, Vicious

**Vilify** Smear

**Villa** Bastide, Chalet, Dacha, House

**Village** Aldea, Auburn, Burg, Clachan, Dorp, Endship, Gram, Greenwich, Hamlet, Kampong, Kraal, Mir, Pueblo, Rancherie, Thorp(e), Vill, Wick

**Villain** Baddy, Bluebeard, Bravo, Dastard, Dog, Heavy, Iago, Knave, Macaire, Miscreant, Mohock, Nefarious, Ogre, Rogue, Scelerat, Scoundrel, Tearaway, Traitor

**Villein** Bordar, Churl, Serf

**Vim** Go, Vigour, Vitality, Zing

**Vincent** Van Gogh

**Vindicate, Vindication** Absolve, Acquit, Avenge, Clear, Compurgation, Darraign(e), Darrain(e), Darrayn, Defend, Deraign, Justify

**Vindictive** Hostile, Malevolent, Repay(ing), Spiteful

**Vine(yard)** Bine, Chateau, Clos, Colocynth, Cru, Cubeb, Dodder, Domaine, Grapery, Hop, Kudzu, Naboth's, Supplejack, Turpeth, Vitis, Yam

**Vinegar** Acetic, Alegar, Eisel(l), Esile, Oxymel, Tarragon

**Vintage** Classic, Crack, Cru, Old, Quality

**Viola, Violet** African, Alto, Amethyst, Archil, Dog's tooth, Gamba, Gentian, Gridelin, Ianthine, Indole, Kiss-me, Mauve, Orchil, Pansy, Parma, Prater, Tenor

**Violate, Violation** Abuse, Breach, Contravene, Defile, Fract, Infraction, INFRINGE, March-treason, Outrage, Rape, Ravish, Stuprate, Trespass

**Violence, Violent(ly)** Amain, Attentat, Berserk, Drastic, Extreme, Fierce, Flagrant, Frenzied, Furious, Heady, Het, High, Hot, Mighty, Onset, Rampant, Rough, Rude, Severe, Slap, Stormy, Tearaway, Vehement, Vie

**Violin(ist), Violin-maker, Violin-shaped** Alto, Amati, Cremona, Fiddle, Griddle, Gu(e), Guarneri(us), Kit, Kubelik, Leader, Nero, Paganini, Pandurate, Rebeck, Rote, Stradivarius

**VIP** Bigshot, Bigwig, Brass, Cheese, Cob, Effendi, Envoy, Magnate, Mugwump, Nabob, Nib, Nob, Pot, Snob, Someone, Swell, Tuft, Tycoon, Worthy

**Viper** Asp, SNAKE, Traitor, Villain

**Virago** Amazon, Battle-axe, Beldam(e), Harpy, Shrew

**Virgil** Maro

**Virgin(al), Virginity** Celibate, Chaste, Cherry, Intact, Maiden, New, Pietà, Pucel(l)age, Pucelle, Pure, Queen, Snood, Tarpeia, Vestal

**Virginia(n)** Creeper, Tuckahoe, Va, Wade

**Virile** Energetic, Macho, Manly

**Virtu** Curio

**Virtue, Virtuous** Angelic, Assay-piece, Attribute, Cardinal, Caritas, Charity, Chastity, Continent, Dharma, Efficacy, Ethical, Excellent, Faith, Fortitude, Good, Grace, Hope, Justice, Moral(ity), Patience, Plaster-saint, Prudence, Qua, Say-piece, Temperance, Upright, Worth

**Virtuosity, Virtuoso** Artist, Excellence, Executant, Maestro, Savant

**Virulent** Acrimonious, Deadly, Hostile, Malign, Noxious, Toxic, Vitriolic, Waspish

**Virus** Coxsackie, Germ, Lassa, Parvo

**Viscera** Bowels, Entrails, Giblets, Guts, Harigal(d)s, Haslet, Innards, Omentum, Umbles, Vitals

**Viscount** Vis

**Viscous (liquid), Viscosity** Glaireous, Gluey, Gummy, Slab, Sticky, Stoke, Tacky, Tar, Thick

**Visible** Clear, Conspicuous, Evident, Explicit, Obvious

**Visigoth** Asaric

**Vision(ary)** Apparition, Bourignian, Dream(er), Fancy, Idealist, Image, Moonshine, Mouse-sight, Mystic, Phantasm(a), Phantom, Pholism, Romantic, Seeing, Seer, Sight

**Visit(or)** Affliction, Alien, Caller, ET, Event, Frequent, Gam, Guest, Habitue, Haunt, Kursaal, See, Sightseer, Stranger, Take

**Visor, Vizor** Eyeshade, Mesail, Mezail, Umbrel, Umbr(i)ere, Umbril, Vent(ayle)

**Vista** Outlook, Scene, View

**Visual(ise)** Envisage, Ocular, Optical, Visible

**Vital(ity)** Critical, Crucial, Energy, Esprit, Essential, Existent, Foison, Gusto, Indispensable, Key, Kick, Linchpin, Lung, Mites, Momentous, Oomph, Organ, Salvation, Sap, Viable, Vigour, Zing, Zoetic

**Vitals** Numbles, Umbles, Viscera

**Vitamin(s)** A, Aneurin, Axerophthol, B, Biotin, C, Citrin, D, E, Inositol, Menadione, Niacin, Panthenol, Phytonadione, Retinol, Riboflavin, Ribose, Thiamin(e), Tocopherol, Torulin

**Vitreous** Glassy, Hyaline

**Vitriol(ic)** Acid, Acrimonious, Biting, Caustic, Mordant

**Vituperate** Abuse, Berate, Castigate, Censure, Defame, Inveigh, Lash, Rail, Scold

**Viva** Oral

**Vivacity** Animation, Brio, Esprit, Spirit, Verve

**Vivid** Bright, Brilliant, Dramatic, Eidectic, Fresh, Graphic, Keen, Live, Sharp

**Vixen** Catamaran, Harridan, Shrew, Virago

**Viz** Sc, Videlicet

**Vizier** Pheazar, Wazir

> **Vizor** See VISOR

**Vocabulary** Idioticon, Jargon, (Kata)kana, Lexicon, Lexis, Meta-language, Nomenclator, Wordbook

**Vocal(ist)** Articulate, Eloquent, Minstrel, Oral, Singer

**Vocation** Call, Métier, Mission, Profession, Shop

**Vociferous(ly)** Clamant, Loud, Ore rotundo, Strident

**Vogue** Chic, Day, FASHION, Mode, Rage, Style, Ton

**Vogul** Ugrian, Ugric

**Voice(d)** Active, Alto, Ancestral, Contralto, Edh, Emit, Eth, Express, Falsetto, Mouth, Opinion, Passive, Phonic, Pipe, Presa, Quill, Say, Sonant, Soprano, Speak, Steven, Syrinx, Tais(c)h, Tenor, Throat, Tone, TONGUE, Treble, Utter

**Voiceless** Aphonia, Aphony, Dumb, Edh, Eth, Mute, Silent, Tacit

**Void** Abyss, Annul, Belch, Defecate, Diriment, Empty, Evacuate, Gap, Hollow, Inane, Irritate, Lapse, Nullify, Quash, Space, Vacuum

**Volatile** Explosive, Live(ly), Temperamental, Terpene

**Volcanic, Volcano** Aa, Agglomerate, Amygdale, Andesite, Antisana, Aragats, Ararat, Askja, Aso(san), Chimborazo, Citlalepetl, Cone, Conic, Corcovado, Cotopaxi, Demavend, Egmont, El Misti, Erebus, Etna, Fumarole, Haleakala, Hekla, Hornito, Idocrase, Igneous, Iwo Jima, Katmai, Krakatoa, Mayon, Mofette, Obsidian, Pele(e), Pericutin, Popocatepetl, Pozz(u)olana, Pumice, Puy, Puzzolana, Ruapeho, Salse, Soffioni, Solfatara, Soufriere, Stromboli, Tambora, Thira, Tolima, Trass, Vesuvius

**Vole** Arvicola, Musquash, Ondatra

**Volition** Velleity, Will

**Volley** Barrage, Boom, Broadside, Platoon, Salvo, Tirade, Tire

**Volt(age)** HT

**Voltaire** Arouet

**Volte face** U-turn

**Voluble** Fluent, Glib

**Volume** Band, Book, Capacity, CC, Code(x), Content, Cubage, Hin, Loudness, Mass, Ml, Omnibus, Quart(o), Roll, Roul(e), Size, Space, Stere, Tome, Vol

**Voluntary, Volunteer** Enlist, Fencible, Free, Honorary, Offer, Postlude, Reformado, Tender, Tennessee, Terrier, TN, Ultroneous, Yeoman

**Voluptuary, Voluptuous** Carnal, Hedonist, Luscious, Sensuist, Sensuous, Sybarite

**Volute** Helix, Roll

**Vomit(ing)** Anecatharsis, Barf, Boak, Boke, Cascade, Cat, Chunder, Egist, Egurgitate, Haematemesis, Parbreak, Posset, Puke, Retch, Rolf, Spew

**Voodoo** Charm, Jettatura, Kurdaitcha, Obeah, Sorcery, Zombi(e)

**Voracious, Voracity** Bulimia, Edacity, Gluttony, Greed, Ravenous, Serrasalmo

**Vortex** Charybdis, Eddy, Whirlpool

**Votary** Adherent, Cenobite, Devotee, Disciple, Fan, Nun, Zealot

**Vote(r), Votes** Aye, Ballot, Choose, Colonist, Coopt, Cross, Division, Fag(g)ot, Franchise, Nay, No, People, Placet, Plebiscite, Plump, Poll, Pot-wabbler, Pot-waller, Pot-walloner, Pot-walloper, Pot-wobbler, PR, Referendum, Return, Scrutiny, Side, Straw(-poll), Suffrage, Ten-pounder, Theta, Ticket, Voice, X, Yea, Yes

**Vote-catcher** Pork

**Vouch(er), Vouchsafe** Accredit, Assure, Attest, Chit, Coupon, Endorse, Guarantee, Receipt, Ticket, Token, Warrant

**Voussoir** Quoin, Wedge

**Vow** Behight, Behot(e), Earnest, Ex voto, Hecht, Hest, Nuncupate, OATH, Pledge, Plight, Promise, Swear, Vum

**Vowel** Ablaut, Anaptyxis, Breve, S(c)hwa, Seg(h)ol, Svarabhakti

**Voyage(r)** Anson, Cruise, Launch, Passage, Peregrinate, Sinbad, Travel

**Voyeur** Scopophiliac

**Vulcan(ite)** Blacksmith, Ebonite, Fire, Mulciber, Wayland

**Vulgar(ian)** Banausic, Barbaric, Blatant, Blue, Brassy, Buffoon, Canaille, Cit, Coarse, Common, Crude, Demotic, Flash, Forward, Gaudy, General, Gent, Heel, Hussy, Ignorant, Indecent, Lewd, Low(-life), Obscene, Pandemian, Plebeian, Popular, Proletarian, Raffish, Riff-raff, Scaff, Tawdry, Tiger, Upstart, Vulg

**Vulnerable** Exposed, Open, Susceptible, Unguarded

**Vulture** Aasvogel, Bird, Buzzard, Condor, Falcon, Gallinazo, Gier, Gripe, Grype, Lammergeier, Lammergeyer, Predator, Urubu, Zopilote

# Ww

**W** Watt, West, Whisky, Women

**Wad(ding)** Batting, Lump, Pad, Pledget, Roll, Swab, Wodge

**Waddle** Toddle, Waggle

**Waddy** Club, Cowboy, Stick

**Wade(r)** Antigropelo(e)s, Egret, Gallae, Greenshank, Heron, Ibis, Jacksnipe, Limpkin, Paddle, Phalarope, Sarus, Seriema, Splodge, Stilt(bird), Terek, Virginia

**Waesucks** Ewhow, O(c)hone

**Wafer** Biscuit, Cracker, Crisp, Gaufer, Gaufre, Gofer, Gopher, Host, Seal

**Waff** Flap, Flutter, Wave

**Waffle** Adlib, Blather, Equivocate, Gaufer, Gaufre, Gofer, Gopher, Hedge, Poppycock, Prate, Rabbit

**Waft(ing)** Airborne, Aura, Blow, Drift, Float

**Wag(gish), Waggle** Arch, Card, Comedian, Joker, Lick, Nod, Rogue, Shake, Sway, Wit(snapper), Wobble

**Wage(s)** Ante, Fee, Hire, Meed, Pay, Practise, Prosecute, Salary, Screw

**Wage-earner** Breadwinner, Employee, Proletariat(e)

**Wager** Back, BET, Gamble, Lay, Stake, Wed

**Wagon(er)** Ar(a)ba, Aroba, Bootes, Boxcar, Brake, Buckboard, Buggy, Caisson, Carriage, Cart, Chuck, Cocopan, Corf, Covered, Dray, Flatcar, Fourgon, Hutch, Palabra, Plaustral, Rave, Rubberneck, Shandry, Station, Tartana, Telega, Trap, Trekker, Truck, Van, Wain

**Waif** Arab, Foundling, Jetsam, Stray

**Wail(er)** Banshee, Bawl, Blubber, Howl, Keen, Lament, Moan, Threnody, Threnos, Ululate, Yammer

**Wain** Cart, Dray, Wagon

**Waist(band)** Belt, Cummerbund, Girdlestead, Hour-glass, Middle, Midship, Obi, Sash, Shash, Zoster

**Waistcoat** Gilet, Jerkin, Lorica, MB, Sayon, Vest

**Wait(er)** Abid(e), Ambush, Bide, Butler, Buttle, Commis, Delay, Expect, Flunkey, Frist, Garçon, Hesitate, Hover, Interval, Khidmutgar, Linger, Lurch, Omnibus, Pannier, Pause, Serve(r), Stay, Steward, Suspense, Tarry, Tend(ance), Tray, Won

**Waitress** Hebe, Miss, Mousme(e), Nippy, Server

**Waive** Abandon, Defer, Overlook, Postpone, Relinquish, Renounce

**Wake(n)** Abrade, Abraid, Abray, Aftermath, Alert, Animate, Arouse,

Astern, Excite, Hereward, Keen, Prod, Rear, ROUSE, Train, Wash

**Waldo** Emerson

**Wale(r)** Prop, Ridge, Weal

**Wales** Cambria, Cymru, Dyfed, Principality

**Walk(er), Walking** Alameda, Alure, Amble, Arcade, Berceau, Birdcage, Cloister, Clump, Constitutional, Dander, Dauner, Esplanade, EVA, Expatiate, Frescade, Gait, Gallery, Ghost, Go, Gradient, Hike, Hump, Lambeth, Leg, Lumber, Mall, Mince, Pace, Pad, Pasear, Paseo, Path, Ped, Perambulate, Pergola, Prance, Prom(enade), Ramble, Rampart, Sashay, Sidle, Stalk, Step, Stroll, Strut, Stump, Terrace, Toddle, Tramp, Trash, Tread, Trog, Trudge, Turn, Wend, Xyst

**Walk-over** Doddle, Scratch

**Wall** Bail, Barrier, Dam, Dike, Epispore, Exine, Fronton, Gable, Hadrian's, Immure, Mahjongg, Mani, Merlon, Parapet, Parpane, Parpen(d), Parpent, Parpoint, Partition, Pericarp, Perpend, Perpent, Pleuron, Revet(ment), Roman, Roughcast, Severus, Side, Somatopleure, Spandrel, Spandril, Street, Trumeau, Vallum, Wailing, Zooecia

**Wallaby** Brusher, Kangaroo, Pademelon, Pad(d)ymelon, Quokka, Tammar

**Wallaroo** Euro

**Wall-covering** Anaglypta (tdmk), Arras, Burlap, Lincrusta, Paper, Tapestry, Tapet

**Waller** Fats, Mason

**Wallet** Billfold, Case, Notecase, Pochette, Purse, Scrip

**Wallflower** Crucifer, Dowd(y), Pariah

**Wall-game** Eton, Mahjongg

**Wallop** Bash, Baste, Beat, Biff, Clout, Cob, HIT, Lam, Lounder, Polt, Pound, Slog, Strap, Swinge, Tan, Tat, Trounce

**Wallow(ing)** Bask, Flounder, Luxuriate, Revel, Roll, Splash, Swelter, Tolter, Volutation, Welter

**Wall-painting** Fresco, Graffiti, Grisaille

**Wall-plate** Tassel, Torsel

**Wall-support** Beam, Foundation, Pier, Rear-arch, Rere-arch

**Walnut** Hickory, Juglans

**Walrus** Morse, Moustache, Pinniped, Rosmarine, Sea-horse, Tash

**Walter** Bruno, Mitty, Pater, Scott

**Waltz** Anniversary, Boston, Dance, Rotate, Valse

**Wampum** Peag, Shell-money

**Wan** Pale, Pallid, Pasty, Sanguine, Sorry

**Wanchancy** Unlucky

**Wand** Baton, Caduceus, Rod, Runic, Stick, Thyrse, Thyrsus, Vara, Vare

**Wander(er), Wandering** Aberrance, Bedouin, Berber, Bum, Caird,

Delirious, Deviate, Digress, Divagate, Drift, Errant, Estray, Evagation, Gad(about), Grope, Hobo, Jew, Landloper, Meander, Meandrian, Moon, Nomad(e), Odysseus, Pedder, Peregrine, Peripatetic, Ramble, Range, Ratch, Roamer, Romany, Room, Rove, Solivagant, Stooge, Straggle, Stravaig, Stray, Streel, Stroam, Stroll, Swan, Ta(i)ver, Tramp, Tuareg, Waif

> **Wandering** may indicate an anagram

**Wane** Decline, Decrease, Diminish, Ebb

**Wangle** Arrange, Finagle, Trick

**Want(ing)** Absence, Conative, Covet, Crave, Dearth, Defect, Deficient, Derth, DESIRE, Destitution, Envy, Hardship, Indigent, Itch, Lack, Long, Mental, Need, Penury, Require, Scarceness, Scarcity, Shy, Void, Wish, Yen

**Wanton** Bona-roba, Cadgy, Chamber, Cocotte, Deliberate, Demirep, Gammerstang, Giglet, Giglot, Hussy, Jay, Jezebel, Lewd, Licentious, Loose, Nice, Roué, Slut, Smicker, Sybarite, Toyish, Twigger, Unchaste, Wayward

**Wap** Blow, Knock, Strike

**War(fare)** Ares, Armageddon, Arms, Attrition, Bate, Battle, Bishop, Chemical, Clash, Cod, Combat, Conflict, Crescentade, Crimean, Crusade, Emergency, Feud, FIGHT, Food, Fray, Germ, Gigantomachy, Guer(r)illa, Hostilities, Jehad, Jenkin's ear, Jihad, Krieg, Mars, Opium, Peloponnesian, Peninsular, Punic, Roses, Spam, Stoush, Sword, Terrapin, Trench, Vietnam

**Warble(r)** Carol, Chiff-chaff, Chirl, Peggy, Rel(l)ish, Trill, Vibrate, Yodel, Yodle

**War-chant, War-cry** Alalagmos, Haka, Slogan

**Ward (off)** Artemus, Averruncate, Care, Casual, Charge, Defend, District, Fend, Guard, Maternity, Oppose, Parry, Protégé, Pupil, Soc, Soken, Vintry

**Warden** Carctaker, Concierge, Constable, Curator, Custodian, Guardian, Keeper, Ranger, Septimus, Spooner, Steward

**Warder** Beefeater, Gaoler, Guardian, Keeper, Screw, Turnkey, Twirl

**Wardrobe** Almirah, Closet, Clothes, Garderobe, Outfit, Vestuary

**Ware** Beware, China, Etruria, Faience, Goods, Merchandise, Palissy, Samian, Shippo

**Warehouse** Depository, Entrepôt, Freight-shed, Go-down, Hong, Store

> **Warfare** see WAR

**War-game** Kriegs(s)piel

**War-god** Ares, Mars, Tiu, Tiw, Tyr

**Warhead** Atomic, Supremo

**Warhorse** Charger, Destrier, Fighter

**Wariness, Wary** Ca'canny, Cagey, Careful, Cautel, Caution, Chary, Discreet, Distrust, Guarded, Leery, Prudent, Sceptical, Vigilant

**Warlike** Battailous, Bellicose, Martial, Militant

**Warlord** Haw-haw, Kitchener, Shogun

**Warm(er), Warming, Warmth** Abask, Admonish, Air, Ardour, Balmy, British, Calefacient, Calid(ity), Chambré, Cordial, Enchafe, Fervour, Foment, Genial, Glow, HEAT, Hot, Incalescent, Kang, Lew, Logie, Loving, Muff, Mull, Tepid, Thermal

**Warm-blooded** Homothermal, Homothermic, Homothermous, Idiothermous

**Warmonger** Hawk

**Warn(ing)** Admonish, Alarum, Alert, Amber, Aposematic, Apprise, Beacon, Bleep, Caution, Caveat, Cone, Document, Example, Fore, Gardyloo, Garnisheement, Hoot, Larum, Lesson, Light, Maroon, Nix, Nota bene, Notice, Omen, Pi-jaw, Premonitory, Portent, Presage, Prodromal, Scarborough, Sematic, Shore, Signal, Tattler, Threat, Tip-off, Token, Vigia, Vor

**Warner** Alarm, Fore, Plum, Siren

**Warp(ed)** Bias, Buckle, Cast, Distort, Kam, Kedge, Pandation, Twist, Weft

**Warpath** Rampage

> **Warped** may indicate an anagram

**Warrant** Able, Authorise, Caption, Certificate, Detainer, Distress, Guarantee, Justify, Mittimus, Permit, Precept, Sepad, Swear, Transire, Vouch

**Warren** Burrow, Colony, Hastings

**Warrior** Achilles, Agamemnon, Amazon, Anzac, Berserk(er), Brave, Crusader, Eorl, Fighter, Ghazi, Impi, Myrmidon, Nestor, Samurai, Soldier, Tatar, Unknown, Warhorse, Zulu

**Warship** Battleship, Castle, Cog, Corvette, Cruiser, Destroyer, Drake, Dromon(d), Invincible, Man-o-war, Monitor, Ram

**Wart(y)** Anbury, Blemish, Muricate, Verruca, Wen

**Warwick** Kingmaker

> **Wary** see WARINESS

**Was** Erat, Existed, Past

**Wash(ed), Washer, Washing, Wash out** Ablution, Affusion, Bath, Bay(e), Bur(r), Calcimine, Circlip, Clean(se), D, Dashwheel, Dele(te), Dip, Edulcorate, Elute, Enema, Fen, Flush, Freshen, Gargle, Grommet, Grummet, Irrigate, Kalsomine, Lap, LAUNDER, Lave, Leather, Lip, Lotion, Maundy, Mop, Nipter, Pan, Pigswill, Poss, Purify, Rinse, Scrub, Shampoo, Shim, Sind, Sluice, Soogee, Soojee, Soojey, Sujee, Swab, Synd, Tie, Tye, Wake

**Washbasin, Washtub** Copper, Lavabo

**Washerman, Washerwoman** Dhobi, Laundress

**Washington** Wa

**Wasn't** Nas, Wasna

**Wasp(ish)** Bembex, Bink, Bite, Cuckoo-fly, Cynipidae, Cynips, Fretful, Gall-fly, Hornet, Irritable, Marabunta, Peevish, Vespa

**Wasp's nest**  Bike, Bink, Byke

**Wassail**  Carouse, Pledge, Toast

**Wast**  Wert

**Wastage, Waste(d), Wasting**  Atrophy, Blue, Cirrhosis, Consume, Contabescent, Decay, Dejecta, Desert, Devastate, Dilapidate, Dissipate, Dross, Dung, Dwindle, Dwine, Dystrophy, Egesta, Emaciate, Erode, Estrepe, Exhaust, Expend, Flue, Forpine, Fritter, Garbage, Gash, Gunge, Haggard, Knub, Lavish, Loose, Lose, Loss, Marasmus, Misspent, Moor, Moulder, Muir, Mullock, Mungo, Novalia, Nub, Offal, Pellagra, Phthisis, Pine, Prodigalise, Ravage, Recrement, Red tape, REFUSE, Reif, Rubble, Schappe, Scissel, Scoria, Scrap, Sewage, Slag, Slurry, Spend, Spill, Spoil(age), Squander, Sullage, Syntexis, Tabes, Thin, Ureal, Urine, Uropoiesis, Vast, Wear, Wilderness, Yearn

> **Wasted**  may indicate an anagram

**Wastrel**  Profligate, Spend-all, Spendthrift, Stalko, Vagabond

**Watch(er)**  Albert, Analog(ue), Argus, Await, Bark, Clock, Coastguard, Cock-crow, Espy, Fob, Glom, Guard, Half-hunter, Huer, Hunter, Kettle, Latewake, Lo, Look, Nark, Note, Nuremberg egg, Observe, Patrol, Pernoctation, Posse, Regard, Repeater, Scout, Sentinel, Sentry, Shadow, Spotter, Stemwinder, Surveillance, Tend, Ticker, Timepiece, Timer, Tompion, Tout, Turnip, Vedette, VIGIL, Wait, Wake

**Watch-chain**  Albert, Slang

**Watch-control**  Escapement

**Watchful(ness)**  Alert, Aware, Care, Ira, Jealous, Vigilant, Wary

**Watchman**  Bellman, Charley, Charlie, Chok(e)y, Cho(w)kidar, Guard, Sentinel, Sentry, Speculator, Tompion, Viewer

**Watch-tower**  Atalaya, Barbican, Beacon, Mirador, Sentry-go

**Watchword**  Cry, Password, Shibboleth, Slogan

**Water(s), Watery**  Adam's ale, Amrit, Apollinaris, Aq(ua), Aquatic, Aqueous, Broads, Brook, Burn, Canal, Cancer, Chresard, Chuck, Dew, Dill, Dilute, Dribble, Eau, Ebb, Echard, Element, Epilimnion, Flood, Ford, Gallise, Gallize, Hectum, Hydatoid, Irrigate, Javel(le), Kuroshio, Lagoon, Lagune, Lake, Lant, Lavender, Lentic, Lode, Lotic, Lough, Lymph, Nappe, Oasis, Oedema, Pawnee, Pee, Perrier, Phreatic, Pisces, Polynia, Polynya, Rain, Rate, Rip, Riverine, Runny, Scorpio, Sea, Seltzer, Sera, Serum, Shower, Simpson, Soda, Sodden, Solent, Sound, Souse, Stream, Tarn, Thin, Tonic, Vadose, Vichy, Vlei, Vly, Wash(y), Weak, Whey

**Waterbaby**  Moses, Tom

**Water-boa**  Anaconda

**Water-boatman**  Notonecta

**Water-brash**  Pyrosis

**Water-buckets**  Noria

**Water-carrier**  Aqueduct, Bheestie, Bheesty, Bhistee, Bhisti, Bucket,

Carafe, Chatty, Furphy, Hose, Hydra, Kirbeh, Pail, Pitcher

**Water-chestnut** Saligot

**Water-colour** Aquarelle, Painting, Pastel, RI

**Water-course** Arroyo, Billabong, Canal, Ditch, Dyke, Falaj, Furrow, Gutter, Khor, Nala, Nulla, Rean, Rhine, Shott, Wadi

**Water-device** Shadoof, Shaduf

**Water-diviner** Dowser, Hydrostat

**Waterfall** Cataract, Chute, Force, Foss, Lasher, Lin(n), Rapid, Sault

**Water-fern** Marsilea, Salvinia

**Water-gate** Penstock, Sluice

**Water-god** Aleion, Aleyin, Alpheus

**Water-hen** Gallinule

**Water-hole** Bore, Gilgai, Oasis

**Water-lily** Lotus, Nenuphar, Nuphar, Spatterdock

**Waterloo** Rout

**Waterman** Aquarius, Bargee, Ferryman, Oarsman

**Water-monster** Nicker

**Water-nymph** Kelpie, Kelpy, Naiad, Ondine, Rusalka

**Water-parsnip** Sium, Skirret

**Water-plant** Alisma, Aquatic, Cress, Crowfoot, Elodea, Lace-leaf, Nelumbo, Nenuphar, Nuphar, Ouvirandra, Pontederia, Reate, Sea-mat, Sedge, Seg, Stratiotes, Urtricularia, Vallisneria

**Waterproof, Water-tight** Caulk, Cofferdam, Dubbin(g), Loden, Mac, Mino, Oilers, Oilskin, Stank, Sta(u)nch, Waders

**Water-rat** Arvicola, Musk-rat, Ratty, Vole

**Watershed** Divide

**Water-spout** Gargoyle, Geyser

**Water-sprite** Kelpie, Kelpy, Nix(ie), Nixy, Tangie, Undine, Water-nymph

**Water supply** H, Hydrant, Spring, Tank, Tap

**Waterway** Aqueduct, Canal, Channel, Culvert, Ditch, Igarapé, River, Sound, Straight, Suez

**Water-wheel** Noria, Pelton, Sakia, Saki(y)eh

**Wattle(s)** Acacia, Boree, Dewlap, Mimosa, Mulga, Sallow, Snot

**Wave(d), Waves, Wavy** Beachcomber, Beam, Beck, Billow, Bore, Brandish, Breaker, Clapotis, Comber, Crest, Crime, Crimp, Cymotrichous, Decuman, Dumper, Flap, Flaunt, Float, Flote, Gesticulate, Marcel, Nebule, Oundy, Perm(anent), Radiation, Repand, Ripple, Roller, Sastrugi, Sea, Seiche, Snaky, Soliton, Surf, Surge, Sway, Tabby, Tidal, Tsunami, Undate, Unde, Undulate, Waffle, Waft, Wag, Wash, Waw, Whitecap

> **Wave(s)** may indicate an anagram

**Wave-band**  Channel

**Wave-detector**  Coherer

**Wavelength**  Band

**Waver(ing)**  Dither, Falter, Flag, Gutter, Hesitate, Oscillate, Stagger, Sway, Swither, Teeter, Vacillate, Waffle, Wet

**Wax(y), Waxing**  A-bate, Adipocere, Ambergris, Appal, Candelilla, Carna(h)uba, Cere, Cutin, Effuse, Enseam, Grow, Heelball, Increase, Increscent, Inseam, Ire, Kiss, Lipide, Livid, Lyrical, Montan, Mummy, Ozocerite, Ozokerite, Paraffin, Parmacitie, Pela, Pruina, Rage, Seal, Spermaceti, Suberin, Tallow, Tantrum, Temper, Yielding

**Waxwing**  Cedar-bird, Icarus

**Way(s), Wayside**  Access, Appian, Autobahn, Avenue, Borstal(l), Bypass, Companion, Course, Crescent, Direction, Door, Draw, E, Each, Entrance, Family, Foss(e), Gate, Hatch, Hedge, High, Hither, How, Lane, Manner, Means, Method, Milky, Mode, N, Pass, Path, Permanent, Pilgrim's, Procedure, Railroad, Regimen, Ridge, ROAD, Route, S, Sallypost, St(reet), Style, Thoroughfare, Thus, Trace, Trail, Troade, Turnpike, Untrodden, Via, W, Wise

**Wayfarer**  Commuter, Piepowder, Pilgrim, Traveller, Voyager

**Waylay**  Accost, Ambuscade, Ambush, Beset, Buttonhole, Molest, Obstruct

**Way-out**  Advanced, Bizarre, Egress, Esoteric, Exit, Extreme, Offbeat, Trendy

**Wayward**  Capricious, Disobedient, Erratic, Loup-the-dyke, Perverse, Stray, Wilful

**Weak(er), Weaken(ing), Weakest, Weakness**  Antimnemonic, Arsis, Asthenia, Blot, Brickle, Brittle, Chink, Cripple(d), Debile, Debilitate, Delay, Dilute, Disable, Effete, Enervate, Enfeeble, Entender, Fade, Faible, Failing, Faint, Fatigue, Feeble, Flag, Flaw, Flimsy, Foible, Fragile, Frail(tee), Frailty, Give, Gone, Ham, Helpless, Honeycomb, Impair, Infirm, Knock-kneed, Lassitude, Low, Namby-pamby, Pale, Pall, Paresis, Puny, Push-over, Reckling, Reduce, Simp, Slack, Thesis, Thin, Tottery, Unable, Undermine, Unnerve, Unstable, Vapid, Vessel, W, Water(y), Wish(y)-wash(y)

**Weakling**  Drip, Milksop, Reed, Softie

**Weal**  Ridge, Stripe, Wealth, Welfare, Welt, Whelk

**Wealth(y)**  Abundance, Affluence, Bullion, Croesus, Fortune, Golconda, Loaded, Lolly, Mammon, Means, Mine, Moneyed, Nabob, Opulence, Ore, Pelf, Reich, Rich, Solid, Substance, Treasure, Untold

**Wean**  Ablactation, Bairn, Spain, Spane, Spean

**Weapon**  Arbalest, Arblast, Arm, Armalite, Arquebus(e), Arrow, Assegai, Ataghan, Backsword, Battleaxe, Bayonet, Bill, Bludgeon, Bondook, Broadsword, Caliver, Carbine, Catapult, Cestus, Club, Co(e)horn, Cosh, Cudgel, Culverin, Cutlass, Dag(ger), Derringer, Doodlebug, Dragoon, Elf-arrow, Enfield, Estoc, Excalibur, Flail, Flintlock, Forty-five, Fougade,

Fougasse, Gad(e), Gaid, Gingal(l), Gisarme, Glaive, Halberd, Harpoon, Harquebus, Hoplology, Howitzer, Javelin, Jingal, Kris, Life-preserver, Longbow, Machete, Mangonel, Matchet, Maurikigusari, Morgenstern, Mortar, Munition, Musket, Nuke, Nunchaku, Orgue, Partisan, Petronel, Pilum, Pistol, Quarterstaff, Revolver, Rifle, Sabre, Saker, Sandbag, Skean-dhu, Skene-dhu, Snickersnee, Sparke, Sparth, Spat, Spontoon, Sten, Stiletto, Sting, Sword, Taiaha, Taser, Tomboc, Torpedo, Trident, Truncheon, V1, Vou(l)ge, Whirl-bat, Whorl-bat

**Wear(ing), Wear Out** Abate, Ablative, Abrade, Chafe, Corrade, Corrode, Deteriorate, Detrition, Efface, Erode, Erosion, Fashion, For(e)spend, Fray, Frazzle, Fret, Garb, Impair, In, Scuff, Sport, Stand, Tedy

> **Wear** may indicate the NE (eg Sunderland)

**Weariness, Wearisome, Weary** Beat, Bejade, Bore, Cloy, Dog-tired, Ennui, Ennuyé, Exhaust, Fag, Fatigate, Fatigue, Harass, Hech, Jade, Lassitude, Pall, Ramfeezle, Sleepy, Spent, Tire, Trash, Try, Tucker, Wabbit

**Weasel** Beech-marten, Cane, Delundung, Ermine, Ferret, Grison, Marten, Mustela, Pekan, Polecat, Stoat, Taira, Tayra, Vermin, Whitrick, Whitterick, Whit(t)ret, Woodshock

**Weather, Weather forecast** Atmosphere, Cyclone, Elements, Endure, Met, Sky, Stand, Survive, Tiros, Undergo, Withstand

**Weathercock** Barometer, Fane, Vane

**Weave(r), Weaving** Cane, Complect, Entwine, Finch, Heald, Haddle, Interlace, Lace, Lion, Loom, Marner, Shuttle, Sparrow, Spider, Taha, Throstle, Tissue, Tweel, Twill, Twine, Wabster, Waggle, Webster, Zigzag

**Weaver-bird** Amadavat, Avadavat, Quelea, Rice-bird, Taha

**Web(bing), Web-footed** Aranea, Fourchette, Maze, Mesh(work), Palama, Palmate, Patagium, Skein, Snare, Tela, Tissue, Toil

**Webster** Spider, Weaver

**Wed(ding), Wedlock** Alliance, Diamond, Espousal, Golden, Hymen, Join, Knobstick, Marriage, Marry, Mate, Meng(e), Me(i)nt, Meynt, Ming, Nuptials, Pair, Penny, Ruby, Shotgun, Silver, Spousal, UNION, Unite, Y

**Wedge** Chock, Chunk, Cleat, Cotter, Cuneal, Gib, Jack, Jam, Key, Niblick, Prop, Quoin, Scotch, Shim, Sphenic, Stick, Trig, Vomerine

**Wedgwood** Benn, China

**Wednesday** Ash, Spy

**Wee** Leak, Little, Pee, Small, Tiny, Urinate

**Weed(y)** Adderwort, Alga, Allseed, Anacharis, Arenaria, Bedstraw, Bell-bind, Blinks, Burdock, Charlock, Chlorella, Cigar(ette), Cissy, Cockle, Colonist, Coltsfoot, Corncockle, Dallop, Darnel, Dock, Dollop, Dulse, Elodea, Ers, Fag, Femitar, Fenitar, Fucoid, Fumitory, Groundsel, Helodea, Hoe, Indian, Knapweed, Knawel, Knot-grass, Lemna, Mare's-tail, Marijuana, Matfelon, Nard, Nettle, Nostoc, Pearlwort, Pilewort, Piri-piri, Plantain, Potamogeton, Purslane, Ragi, Ragwort, Reate, Rest-harrow, Ruderal, Runch, Sagittaria, Sargasso, Scal(l)awag, Scallywag, Senecio,

Sorrel, Spurge, Sudd, Sun-spurge, Swine's-cress, Tansy, Tare, Tine, Tobacco, Tormentil, Twitch, Ulotrichale, Vetch, Wartcress, Widow's, Winnow, Yarr

**Weedkiller** Atrazine, Dalapon, Diquat, Paraquat

**Week(ly)** Hebdomadary, Holy, Ouk, Oulk, Periodical, Sennight

**Weekend** K, Sat, Sun

**Weep(er), Weepy, Wept** Bawl, Blubber, Cry, Grat, Greet, Lachrymose, Lament, Loser, Ooze, Pipe, Sob

**Weevil** Anthonomous, Bug, Curculio, Insect

**Weft** Roon, Shot, Texture, Warp, Woof

**Weigh(ing), Weigh down, Weight(y)** All-up, Arroba, Artal, As, Avoirdupois, Balance, Bantam, Bob, Bulk, Burden, Candie, Candy, Cantar, Carat, Catty, Cental, Centner, Clove, Consider, Count, Cruiser, Ct, Decagram(me), Deliberate, Derham, Dirham, Dirhem, Drail, Dumbbell, Emphasis, Feather, Fother, G, Gerah, Grain, Gram, Heft, Importance, Incumbent, Journey, Kandy, Kantar, Kat(i), Katti, Khat, Kin, Kip, Last, Libra, Lisp(o)und, Load, Mark, Massive, Maund, Metage, Mina, Molecular, Moment, Mouse, Nail, Obol, Oke, Onerous, Oppress, Ounce, Overpoise, Oz, Pease, Peaze, Peise, Peize, Perpend, Peyse, Pikul, Plummet, Poise, Ponderal, Pood, Prey, Pud, Quintal, Recul, Rotl, Rotolo, Scruple, Seer, Semuncia, Ser, Sit, Slang, Talent, Tare, Tical, Tod, Tola, Ton(nage), Tonne, Troy, Trutinate, Unce, Unmoor, Welter, Wey, Wt

**Weighing machine** Bismar, Scales, Steelyard, Tron(e)

**Weightless** Agravic

**Weight-lifter** Crane, Lewis, Windlass

**Weir** Dam, Garth, Kiddle, Kidel, Lasher, Pen, Watergate

**Weird** Bizarre, Curious, Dree, Eerie, Eery, Eldritch, Kookie, Spectral, Strange, Supernatural, Taisch, Uncanny, Zany

**Welch, Welsh** Abscond, Cheat, Default, Embezzle, Levant, Rat, Reneg(ue), Renig, Skedaddle, Weasel

**Welcome** Ave, Bel-accoyle, Ciao, Embrace, Entertain, Greet, Haeremai, Halse, Hallo, Hello, How, Hullo, Receive, Reception, Salute

**Weld** Join, Merge, Sinter, Unite

**Welfare** Advantage, Alms, Benison, Ha(y)le, Heal, Health, Sarvodaya, Weal

**Welkin** Firmament, Sky

**Well (done)** Artesian, Atweel, Aweel, Bien, Bore(hole), Bravo, Cenote, Euge, Famously, Fine, Fit, Gasser, Good, Gosh, Gusher, Hale, HEALTHY, Inkpot, Law, My, Odso, Oh, Phreatic, So, Source, Spa, Spring, Sump, Surge, Upflow, Zemzem

**Well-being** Atweel, Comfort, Euphoria, Euphory, Good, Health, Welfare

**Well-built** Sturdy, Tight

**Well-covered** Chubby, Padded

**Well-curb** Puteal

**Welles** Orson

**Wellington** Gumboot, Iron Duke, Nosey

**Well-known** Famous, Illustrious, Notorious, Notour

**Well-off** Affluent, Far, Rich, Wealthy

**Well part** Bucket, Shadoof, Shaduf

**Wells** Bombardier, Fargo

**Well-wisher** Friend

> **Welsh** see WELCH

**Welshman** Briton, Brittonic, Brython, Cake, Cambrian, Celtic, Cog, Cym(ric), Cymry, Dai, Emlyn, Evan, Fluellen, Gareth, Harp, Idris, Ifor, Keltic, P-Celtic, P-Keltic, Rabbit, Rarebit, Rhys, Taffy, Tudor, W

**Wen** Cyst, Talpa, Tumour, Wart

**Wench** Blowze, Court, Girl, Hussy, Maid, Ramp, Rig, Smock, Strumpet

**Wend** Meander, Sorb, Steer

**Wendy** Darling, House

**Werewolf** Lycanthrope, Nazi, Turnskin, Vampire

**Wesleyan** Epworth, Methodist

**West(ern)** Hesperian, Mae, Movie, Oater, Occidental, Ponent, Sunset, W, Wild

**West African** Kroo, Wolof

> **West end** may indicate 't' or 'W1'

**West Indian** Carib, Creole, Jamaican

**Westminster** SW1

**Wet** Bedabble, Bedraggled, Clammy, Daggle, Damp, Dank, Dew, Dip, Douse, Dowse, Drench, Drip(ping), Drook, Drouk, Embrue, Feeble, Humect, Humid, Hyetal, Imbue, Madefy, Madid, Marshy, Moil, Moist(en), Molly, Namby-pamby, Pee, Rainy, Ret(t), Roral, Roric, Runny, Saturate, Shower, Simp(leton), Sipe, Sluice, SOAK, Sodden, Sopping, Sour, Steep, Urinate, Wat, Wee, Wimpy

**Whack** Belt, Bemaul, Biff, Joll, Jo(ule, Jowl, Lambast, Lounder, Swish, Thump

**Whale(meat)** Baleen, Beluga, Blower, Blubber, Bottlehead, Bowhead, Cachalot, Cetacea(n), Cete, Cowfish, Dolphin, Finner, Gam, Glutton, Grampus, Humpback, Kreng, Leviathan, Manatee, Minke, Monodon, Paste, Physeter, Pod, Porpoise, Right, Rorqual, Scrag, Sea-canary, Sea-unicorn, Sei, Sperm, Thrasher, White, Zeuglodon(t)

> **Whale** may indicate an anagram

**Whaler** Ahab, Harpooner, Ship, Waister

**Whales' meat** Clio

**Wham** Bang, Collide

**Whang**  Blow, Flog, Thrash, Whack

**Wharf(inger)**  Dock(er), Jetty, Key, Landing, Pier, Quay, Roustabout, Rouster, Staith(e)

**What**  Anan, Eh, How, Pardon, Que-, Siccan, That, Which

**Whatnot, What's-its-name**  Dinges, Dingus, Doings, Etagère, Jiggamaree, Jiggumbob, Thingamy, Thingumajig, Thingumbob, Thingummy, Timenoguy

**Wheat**  Amelcorn, Blé, Bulg(h)er, Durum, Einkorn, Emmer, Fromenty, Frumenty, Furme(n)ty, Furmity, Grain, Mummy, Rivet, Sarrasin, Semolina, Sharps, Spelt, Triticum

**Wheatsheaf**  Bale, Gerbe, Stook

**Wheedle**  Banter, Barney, Blandish, Cajole, Coax, Cog, Cuiter, Cuittle, Flatter, Inveigle, Whilly(whaw)

**Wheel(er)**  Bedel, Bevel, Bogy, Caracol(e), Caster, Castor, Catherine, Circle, Cistern, Cycle, Felloe, Felly, Ferris, Gear, Helm, Hurl, Idle, Mortimer, Pedal, Pelton, Perambulator, Pinion, Pivot, Prayer, Pulley, Rhomb, Roll, Rotate, Roulette, Rowel, Sheave, Sprocket, Stepney, Trindle, Trochus, Trundle, TURN, Tympan(um), Zoetrope

**Wheelbarrow**  Monotroch

**Wheelhouse**  Caravan, Paddle-box

**Wheel-hub**  Axle, Nave

**Wheelman**  Cyclist, Ixion

**Wheelwright**  Spokesman

**Wheeze**  Asthma, Jape, Joke, Pant, Ploy, Rale, Reak, Reik, Rhonchus, Ruse, Stridor, Trick, Whaisle, Whaizle

**Whelk**  Limpet, Shellfish, Stromb, Triton

**Whelp**  Bear, Bra(t)chet, Pup

**When(ever)**  Although, As, If, Though, Time

**Where(abouts)**  Location, Neighbourhood, Place, Site, Vicinity, Whaur, Whither

**Wherefore**  Cause, Reason, Why

**Whereupon**  So, When

**Wherewithal**  Finance, Means, Money, Needful, Resources

**Wherry**  Barge, Rowboat

**Whet(stone)**  Coticular, Excite, Hone, Sharpen, Stimulate

**Whether**  Conditional, If

**Whey**  Whig

**Which(ever), Which is**  Anyway, As, QE, Whatna, Who

**Whiff**  Breath, Cigarette, Gust, Puff, Redolence, Smatch, Sniff, Trace, Waft

**Whig**  Adullamite, Jig, Rascal, Tory, Whey

**While**  Interim, Since, Space, Span, Though, Throw, Time, Whenas, Yet

**Whim(s), Whimsical, Whimsy** Bizarre, Caprice, Conceit, Crotchet, Fad, Fancy, Fey, Flisk, Kicksy-wicksy, Kink, Notion, Quaint, Quirk, Tick, Toy, Vagary

**Whimper** Cry, Grizzle, Pule, Snivel, Whine

**Whin** Furze, Gorse, Ulex

**Whine** Cant, Carp, Grumble, Kvetch, Mewl, Peenge, Pule, Snivel, Whimper, Yammer

**Whinny** Neigh, Nicker, Whicker

**Whip(ped), Whipping** Beat, Cat, Chabouk, Chantilly, Chastise, Cilium, Colt, Crop, Drive, Flagellate, Flagellum, Feague, Firk, Hide, Jambok, Knout, K(o)urbash, Larrup, LASH, Limber, Quirt, Rawhide, Riem, Scourge, Sjambok, Slash, Strap-oil, Swinge, Switch, Taw, Thong, Welt, Whap, Whop

**Whippersnapper** Dandiprat, Dandyprat, Pup, Squirt

**Whirl(ing)** Circumgyrate, Dervish, Eddy, Gyrate, IN A WHIRL, Pivot, Reel, Spin, Swing, Swirl, Vortex, Vortical

**Whirlpool** Eddy, Gulf, Gurge, Maelstrom, Swelchie, Vorago, Vortex, Weel, Wiel

**Whirlwind** Cyclone, Eddy, Tornado, Tourbillion, Typho(o)n, Vortex, Willy-willy

**Whisk** Chowri, Chowry, Swish, Switch, Whid, Whip

**Whisker(s)** Beard, Beater, Burnsides, Cat's, Dundreary, Hackle, Hair, Moustache, Mutton-chop, Samuel, Side-burns, Vibrissa

**Whisky** Alcohol, Barley-bree, Barley-broo, Barley-broth, Bond, Bourbon, Cape Smoke, Corn, Cratur, Creature, Fife, Firewater, Hoo(t)ch, Irish, Malt, Monongahela, Moonshine, Morning, Mountain dew, Nip, Peat-reek, Pot(h)een, Ragwater, Red eye, Rye, Scotch, Spunkie, Tanglefoot, Usquebaugh, Whiss

> **Whisky** may indicate an anagram

**Whisper** Breath(e), Burr, Hark, Hint, Innuendo, Murmur, Rumour, Round, Sigh, Susurrus, Tittle, Undertone

**Whist** Hush, Quiet, Sh

**Whistle(r)** Blow, Calliope, Hiss, Penny, Ping, Pipe, Ref, Siffle(ur), Sowf(f), Sowth, Stop, Stridor, Swab(ber), Toot, Tweedle, Tweet, Whew, Wolf

**Whit** Atom, Doit, Figo, Haet, Iota, Jot, Particle, Point, Red cent

**White(n), Whitener, Whiteness** Agene, Agenise, Alabaster, Albedo, Albescent, Albino, Albugineous, Albumen, Argent, Ashen, Blanch, Blanco, Bleach, Buckra, Cam, Calm, Camstone, Candid, Candour, Canescent, Canities, Caucasian, Caum, Chinese, Christmas, Cliffs, Collar, Company, Dealbate, Elephant, Ermine, European, Fang, Fard, Feather, Flag, Glair, Gwen(da), Hore, House, Ivory, Lie, Lily, Man, Mealy, Niveous, Opal, Pakeha, Pale(face), Pallor, Paper, Pearl, Russian, Selborne, Sheep, Snow(y), Wan, Wedding

**Whitefish**  Menominee

**Whitefriars**  Alsatia

**Whitehall**  Ministry

**White horses**  Skipper's daughters

**White man**  Backra, Buckra, Caucasian, Gub(bah), Honkie, Honky, Mzungu, Occidental, Ofay, Pakeha, Paleface, Redleg, Redneck

**Whitewash**  Calcimine, Excuse, Kalsomine, Lime

**Whitlow**  Ancome, Panaritium, Paronychia

**Whitsun**  Pinkster, Pinxter

**Whittle**  Carve, Pare, Sharpen

**Who**  As, Doctor

**Whodunit**  Mystery

**Whole, Wholly**  All, Entire(ty), Entity, Fully, Hale, Intact, Integer, Largely, Lot, Sum, Thoroughly, Total, Unbroken, Uncut

**Wholesale(r)**  Cutprice, En bloc, Engrosser, Jobber, Sweeping

**Wholesome**  Clean, Good, Healthy, Sound

**Whoop, Whooping cough**  Alew, Celebrate, Chincough, Cry, Excite, Kink(cough), Kink-hoast, Pertussis

**Whoopee**  Carouse, Evoe, Hey-go-mad, Roister

**Whoosh**  Birr, Swish

**Whopper, Whopping**  Bam, Crammer, Huge, Immense, Jumbo, Lie, Lig, Oner, Out and outer, Scrouger, Slapper, Slockdolager, Soc(k)dalager, Soc(k)dolager, Soc(k)doliger, Soc(k)dologer, Sogdolager, Sogdoliger, Sogdologer, Tale, Taradiddle

**Whore**  Drab, Harlot, Loose woman, Pinnace, Pro, Quail, Road, Strumpet, Tart

**Whorl**  Corolla, Eucyclic, Spiral, Swirl, Verticil, Volute

**Why**  Reason

**Wick**  Farm, Rush, Snaste, Vill(age)

**Wicked(ness)**  Atrocity, BAD, Candle, Criminal, Cru(i)sie, Crusy, Depravity, Devilish, Evil, Flagitious, Godless, Immoral, Impious, Improbity, Iniquity, Lantern, Nefarious, Night-light, Ponerology, Pravity, Rush, Satanic, Sin(ful), Taper, Turpitude, Unholy, Vile

> **Wicked** may indicate containing a wick

**Wicker(work)**  Basketry, Sale, Seal

**Wicket**  Gate, Hatch, Pitch, Square, Stool, Stump, Yate

**Wicket-keeper**  Stumper

**Wide, Widen(ing), Width**  Ample, Bay, Broad, Drib, Expand, Extend, Far, Flanch, Flange, Flare, Flaunch, Ga(u)ge, Miss, Roomy, Spacious, Spread, Sweeping, Vast

**Wide-awake**  Alert, Fly, Hat, Wary, Watchful

**Widespread** Diffuse, Epidemic, Extensive, General, Pandemic, Prevalent, Prolate, Routh(ie), Sweeping

**Widow(ed)** Dame, Dowager, Grass, Relict, Sati, Sneerwell, Suttee, Vidual, Viduous, Whydah-bird

**Wield** Brandish, Control, Exercise, Handle, MANIPULATE, Ply

**Wife, Wives** Concubine, Consort, Devi, Dutch, Enid, Feme, Fiere, Frau, Haram, Harem, Harim, Helpmate, Helpmeet, Hen, Kali, Kickie-wickie, Kicksy-wicksy, Lakshmi, Mate, Memsahib, Missis, Missus, Mrs, Mummer's, Pirrauru, Potiphar's, Rib, Seraglio, Spouse, Squaw, W

**Wig** Bob(wig), Brutus, Buzz-wig, Campaign, Carpet, Cauliflower, Caxon, Chevelure, Chide, Cockernony, Dalmahoy, Gizz, Gregorian, Hair(piece), Heare, Jas(e)y, Jazey, Jiz, Major, Periwig, Peruke, Postiche, Ramil(l)ie(s), Rate, Reprimand, Rug, Scold, Scratch, Spencer, Targe, Tie, Toupee, Toupet, Tour

**Wiggle, Wiggly** Jiggle, Scoleciform, Wobble, Wriggle

**Wight** Man, Vectis

**Wigwam** Te(e)pee

**Wild** Aberrant, Agrestal, Barbarous, Berserk, Bundu, Bush, Chimeric, Crazy, Earl, Errant, Erratic, Farouche, Feral, Frantic, Frenetic, Hectic, Lawless, Mad(cap), Manic, Meshugge, Myall, Rampant, Raver, Riotous, SAVAGE, Unmanageable, Unruly, Violent, Warrigal, West, Woolly

> **Wild(ly)** may indicate an anagram

**Wild beast** Eyra, Sapi-utan, Scrubber

**Wildcat** Lion, Manul, Ocelot, Strike, Tiger

**Wilderness** Bush, Desert, Ruderal, Sinai, Solitude, Waste

**Wild goose** Chase, Greylag

**Wild oats** Haver

**Wile** Art, Artifice, CUNNING, Deceit, Ruse, Stratagem, Trick

**Wilful** Deliberate, Headstrong, Heady, Obstinate, Wayward

**Will, Willing(ly)** Alsoon, Amenable, Bard, Bequeath, Bewildered, Bill(y), Complaint, Content, Desire, Devise, Fain, Game, Hay, Leave, Lief, Obedient, On, Please, Prone, Purpose, Ready, Scarlet, Soon, Spirit, Swan, Testament, Testate, Volition, Voluntary, Volunteer, Way, Wimble

> **Will** may indicate an anagram

**William(s)** Bill(y), Conqueror, Occam, Orange, Pear, Rufus, Silent, Sweet, Tell, Tennessee

**Will o'the wisp** Friar's lantern, Ignis-fatuus, Jack o'lantern, Nightfire, Rush

**Willow(ing), Willowy** Lissom(e), Lithe, Osier, Poplar, Pussy, Salix, Sallow, Sauch, Saugh, Supple, Twilly, Withy

**Willpower** Determination, Strength

**Willy-nilly** Nolens volens, Perforce

**Wilt**  Decline, Droop, Fade, Flag, Sap, Shalt, Wither

**Wiltshireman**  Moonraker

**Wily**  Artful, Astute, Braide, Cunning, Foxy, Peery, Shifty, Shrewd, Slee, SLY, Spider, Streetwise, Subtle, Versute, Wide

**Wimple**  Gorget, Meander, Ripple, Turn

> **Wimple**  may indicate an anagram

**Win(ner), Winning**  Achieve, BEAT, Champion, Conquer, Cup, Decider, Dormie, Dormy, First, Gain, Gammon, Hit, Land, Lead, Medallist, Motser, Motza, Nice, Pile, Pot, Prevail, Profit, Purler, Rubicon, Slam, Snip, Success, Take, TRIUMPH, Up, Vellet, Velvet, Victor(y), Vole, Wrest

**Wince**  Blench, Cringe, Flinch, Recoil

**Winch**  Crab, Crane, Jack, Windlass

**Winchester**  Rifle

**Wind(y)**  Aeolian, Air, Airstream, Anabatic, Anti-trade, Aquilo(n), Argestes, Auster, Baguio, Bend, Bergwind, Bise, Blore, Blow, Bluster, Bora, Boreas, Bourasque, Brass, Breeze, Brickfielder, Burp, Buster, Carminative, Caurus, Chili, Chill, Chinook, Coil, Corus, Crank, Curl, Cyclone, Draught, Draw, Easterly, Etesian, Euraquilo, Euroclydon, Eurus, Favonian, Favonius, Fearful, Flatulence, Flatus, Flaw, Fo(e)hn, Gale, Gas, Gregale, Gust, Heaves, Hurricane, Hurricano, Kamseen, K(h)amsin, Levant(er), Libecc(h)io, Libs, Meander, Meltemi, Mistral, Monsoon, Nervous, Noreast, Norther, Noser, Notus, Pampero, Ponent, Poop, Puna, Quill, Reeds, Reel, Rip-snorter, Roll, Samiel, Sciroc, Scirocco, Screw, Second, Serpentine, Shimaal, Simoom, Simoon, Sirocco, Slant, Snake, Snifter, Snorter, Solano, Sough, Spiral, Spool, Squall, Sumatra, Thread, Throw, Tornado, Tourbillon, Trade, Tramontana, Trend, Twaddle, Twine, Twister, Typhoon, Vayu, Ventose, Volturnus, Waffle, Weave, Williwaw, Willy-willy, Winch, Woold, Wrap, Wreathe, Wrest, Zephyr(us), Zonda

**Windbag**  Balloon, Drogue, Prattler, Zeppelin

**Windfall**  Bonanza, Buckshee, Fortune, Godsend, Manna

**Windflower**  Anemone

**Winding(s)**  Ambages, Anfractuous, Evagation, Link, Sinuous, Spiral, Tortuous, Twisty

**Windlass**  Whim, Winch

**Windmill**  Post, Smock

**Window(s)**  Bay, Bow, Casement, Catherine-wheel, Companion, Compass, Day, Deadlight, Dormer, Dream-hole, Eye, Eyelids, Fanlight, Fenestella, Fenestra, Glaze, Guichet, Jesse, Lancet, Lattice, Loop-light, Lucarne, Lunette, Luthern, Lychnoscope, Mezzanine, Monial, Mullion, Oeil-de-boeuf, Ogive, Orb, Oriel, Ox-eye, Pane, Porthole, Rosace, Rose, Sash, Transom, Ventana, Wicket, Windock, Winnock

**Window-bar, Window-fastening**  Astragal, Espagnolette

**Windpipe**  Bronchus, Throat, Trachea, Weasand

**Windscale**  Beaufort

**Windsock**  Drogue

**Windswept**  Scud

**Wind-up**  End, Fright, Liquidate, Span

**Windward**  Ahold, Aloof, Luff

**Wine**  Alicant, Amontillado, Amoroso, Anker, Asti, Auslese, Bacharach, Barsac, Bastard, Beaujolais, Beaune, Biddy, Bin, Bishop, Bombo, Bordeaux, Brut, Bubbly, Bucellas, Bull's blood, Burgundy, Canary, Catawba, Chablis, Chambertin, Champers, Chardonnay, Charneco, Chateau, Chianti, Claret, Comet, Constantia, Cowslip, Cuvée, Dao, Dubonnet, Espumoso, Essence, Essencia, Falernian, Genevrette, Gladstone, Gluhwein, Graves, Hermitage, Hippocras, Hoccamore, Hock, It, Jerepigo, Johannisberger, Languedoc, Liebfraumilch, Lisbon, Log-juice, Loll-shraub, Loll-shrob, Macon, Madeira, Malaga, Malmsey, Malvasia, Malvesie, Malvoisie, Manzanilla, Marcobrunner, Marsala, Medoc, Merlot, Mirin, Mocker, Montilla, Montrachet, Mosel(le), Mull, Muscadel, Muscadet, Muscadine, Muscat(el), Must, Negus, Niersteiner, Noisy, Oenology, Oenomel, Ordinaire, Orvieto, Peter-see-me, Piment, Pinot(age), Pipe, Plonk, Plotty, Pomerol, Pommard, Port, Prisage, Resinata, Retsina, Rhenish, Rhine, Riesling, Rioja, Rosé, Rosy, Rudesheimer, Sack, Sangaree, Sangria, Scuppernong, Sekt, Shiraz, Spatlese, Steinberger, Straw, Stum, Supernaculum, Syrah, Tarragona, Tent, Toddy, Tokay, Tun, Tutu, Vat, Verdelho, Vin(o), Xeres, Zinfandel

**Wine-cellar, Wine-shop**  Bistro, Bodega, Vault, Vaut(e)

**Wine-glass**  Flute

**Wine-making**  Gallising

**Wing(ed), Winger, Wings, Wing-like**  Aerofoil, Ala(r), Alula, Annexe, Appendage, Arm, Branch, Canard, Cellar, Coulisse, Delta, Dipteral, El(l), Elytral, Elytriform, Elytron, Elytrum, Flew, Flipper, Forward, Halteres, Hurt, Limb, Parascenia, Patagium, Pennate, Pennon, Pinero, Pinion, Pip, Pterygoid, Putto, Rogallo, Sail, Scent-scale, Segreant, Seraphim, Swift, Tectrix, Tegmen, Transept, Van, Vol(et), Wound(ed)

**Winged sandals**  Talaria

> **Winger**  may indicate a bird

**Wing-footed**  Aliped, Fleet, Swift

**Wingless**  Apteral

**Wink**  Bate, Condone, Connive, Flicker, Ignore, Instant, Nap, Nictitate, Pink, Twinkle

**Winnie**  Pooh

**Winnow**  Fan, Riddle, Separate, Sift, Van, Wecht

**Winsome**  Bonny, Engaging, Gay, Pleasant

**Winter, Wintry**  Bleak, Brumal, Cold, Dec, Fimbul, Frigid, Frore, Hibernate, Hiemal, Hiems, Hodiernal, Jasmine, Snowy

**Winter cherry** Chinese lantern

**Wintergreen** Sarcodes

**Winter pear** Nelis

**Winter-sport** Ski

**Wipe (out), Wiping** Abolish, Abrogate, Absterge, Amortise, Cancel, Cleanse, Demolish, Destroy, Deterge, Dicht, Dight, Expunge, Hanky, Mop, Nose-rag, Null, Raze, Sponge, Tersion, Tissue

**Wire(s), Wiry** Aerial, Barb(ed), Cable, Coil, Filament, Filar, File, Heald, Heddle, Lean, Lecher, Marconigram, Mil, Nichrome (tdmk), Nipper, Pickpocket, Sinewy, Snake, Spit, Strand, String, Stylet, Telegram, Thoth, Thread

**Wireless (operator), Wireless part** Baffle, Set, Sparks, Valve

**Wise(acre), Wisdom** Advisedly, Athene, Canny, Depth, Ernie, Gothamite, Hep, Hindsight, Judgement, Learned, Lore, Manner, Mimir, Minerva, Norman, Oracle, Owl, Philosopher, Philosophy, Politic, Polymath, Prajna, Profound, Prudence, Sagacity, Sage, Sapience, Savvy, Shrewd, Sophia, Smartie, Solon, Wice

**Wisecrack** One-liner

**Wise man** Caspar, Heptad, Nestor, Sage, Sapient, Solomon, Thales, Worldly

**Wish(es)** Crave, DESIRE, Hope, Long, Pleasure, Precatory, Regards, Want, Yearn

**Wishbone** Furcula, Marriage-bone, Merrythought, Skipjack

**Wishy-washy** Bland, Feeble, Insipid, Irresolute, Milksop, Weak, Wheyey

**Wisp(y)** Cirrate, Frail, Scrap, Shred, Virga, Wase

**Wit(s)** Acumen, Attic, Badinage, Brevity, Commonsense, Cunning, Dry, Esprit, Estimation, Eutrapelia, Eutrapely, Facetious, Fantasy, Hartford, Humour, Imagination, Intelligence, Irony, Marinism, Memory, Mind, Nous, Pawky, Repartee, Rogue, Sally, Salt, Saut, Sconce, SENSE, Shaft, Videlicet, Viz, Wag, Weet, Word-play

**Witch(craft)** Broomstick, Cantrip, Carline, Coven, Craigfluke, Crone, Cutty Sark, Ensorcell, Galdragon, Glamour, Goety, Gramary(e), Gyre-carlin, Hag, Hecate, Hex, Lamia, Magic, Medea, Myal(ism), Night-hag, Obeahism, Obiism, Salem, Selim, Sibyl, Sieve, Sorceress, Speller, Sycorax, Trout, Valkyrie, Vaudoo, Vilia, Voodoo, Weird, Wicca

**Witch-doctor** Boyla, Mganga, Pawaw, Powwow, Sangoma, Shaman

**Witch-hazel** Platan(e), Winter-bloom

**With** And, Con, Cum, Hereby, In, Mit, Of, W

**Withdraw(al), Withdrawn** Abdicate, Alienate, Aloof, Detach, Disengage, Distrait, Evacuate, Introvert, Offish, Palinode, Preserve, Recant, Recoil, Repair, Reticent, Retire, Retract(ion), Retreat, Revoke, Revulsion, Scratch, Secede, Sequester, Shrink, Shy, Subduct, Unreeve, Unsay

**Wither(ed), Withering, Withers** Arefy, Atrophy, Burn, Corky, Die,

Droop, Dry, Evanish, Fade, Forpine, Googie, Languish, Marcescent, Nose, Scram, Sere, Shrink, Shrivel, Welk, Welt

**Withershins** Eastlin(g)s

> **With gaucherie** may indicate an anagram

**Withhold(ing)** Abstain, Conceal, Curt, Deny, Detain, Detinue, Hide, Keep, RESERVE, Trover

**Within** Enclosed, Indoors, Inside, Interior, Intra

**With it** Hep, Hip, Syn, Trendy, W

**Without** Bar, Beyond, Ex, Lack(ing), Less, Minus, Orb, Outdoors, Outside, Sans, Save, Sen, Senza, Sine, X

> **Without** may indicate one word surrounding another

> **Without restraint** may indicate an anagram

**Without stimulus** Nastic

**Withstand** Brave, Contest, Defy, Endure, Oppose, Resist

**Witness** Attest, Bystander, Depose, Expert, Evidence, Jehovah's, Martyr, Material, Muggletonian, Observe, Obtest, Onlooker, Proof, SEE, Testament, Teste, Testify

**Witness-box** Peter, Stand

**Witticism** Banter, Epigram, Jest, Joke, Mot, Pun, Repartee, Wisecrack

**Wizard (priest)** Carpathian, Conjuror, Expert, Gandalf, Hex, Magician, Merlin, Oz, Prospero, Shaman, Sorcerer, Super, Warlock, WITCH-DOCTOR

**Wizen(ed)** Dehydrate, Dry, Sere, Shrivel, Sphacelate, Wither

**Woad** Anil, Dye, Indigo, Isatis, Pastel, Pastil

**Wobble, Wobbling** Chandler's, Coggle, Precess, Quaver, Rock, Totter, Tremble, Trillo, Wag, Walty, Waver

**Wodehouse** Plum

**Woe(ful)** Alack, Alas, Bale, Bane, Distress, Dule, Ewhow, Gram, Grief, Lack-a-day, Misery, Pain, SORROW, Tribulation

**Wolf(-like)** Akela, Assyrian, Cancer, Casanova, Coyote, Cram, Dangler, Fenrir, Fenris, Gorge, Ise(n)grim, Lobo, Lothario, Lupine, Luster, Lycanthrope, MI, Michigan, Pack, Rip, Roué, Scoff, Thylacine, Timber, Wanderer, Were, Whistler

**Wolfram** Tungsten

**Wolf's bane** Aconite, Friar's-cap

**Wolseley** Sir Garnet

**Woman(hood), Women** Anile, Bellibone, Bimbo, Bint, Boiler, Broad, Cailleach, Callet, Chai, Chapess, Citess, Crone, Cummer, Dame, Daughter, Doe, Dona(h), Dorcas, Drab, Eve, F, Fair, FEMALE, Feme, Frail, Frow, Gammer, Gimmer, Gin, Hen, Her, Jane, Lady, Lorette, Maenad, Mary, Miladi, Milady, Mob, Mort, Ms, Muliebrity, Pict, Piece, Placket, Popsy, Quean, Queen, Ramp, Rib, Ribibe, Ronyon, Rudas, Runnion, Sabine, Sakti,

Scarlet, Shakti, She, Skirt, Sort, Squaw, Tail, Tiring, Tit, Trot, Umfazi, Vahine, Wahine

**Womaniser** Casanova, Lady-killer, Poodle-faker, Wolf

**Womb** Belly, Matrix, Side, Uterus, Ventricle

**Women's club, Women's lib** S(h)akti, Soroptimist

**Won** Chon

**Wonder(s)** Admire, Agape, Amazement, AR, Arkansas, Arrah, Awe, Colossus, Ferly, Grape-seed, Marle, MARVEL, Meteor, Mirabilia, Miracle, Muse, Nine-day, Phenomenon, Prodigy, Speculate, Stupor, Suppose, Surprise, Wheugh, Whew

**Wonderful(ly)** Amazing, Fantastic, Geason, Glorious, Great, Lal(l)apalooza, Magic, Mirable, Old, Purely, Ripping

**Wonder-worker** Thaumaturgist, Thaumaturgus

**Wonky** Cockeyed

**Wont(ed)** Accustomed, Apt, Custom, Habit, Shan't, Used

**Woo(er)** Address, Beau, Court, Seduce, Suitor, Swain

**Wood(en), Woodland, Woody** Afrormosia, Agalloch, Agila, Alburnum, Alerce, Algum, Almug, Amboina, Ash, Balsa, Bamboo, Basswood, Batten, Beam, Beaver, Beech, Beef, Bent, Birnam, Board, Bocage, Boord(e), Boscage, Bowl, Box, Brassie, Brazil, Bushveld, Caatinga, Calamander, Caliature, Cam, Cambium, Campeachy, Canary, Carapa, Carr, Cask, Cedar, Channel, Chipboard, Clapboard, Conductor, Coppice, Copse, Cord, Coromandel, Dead, Deadpan, Deal, Drive, Dunnage, Duramen, Ebony, Elm, Eugh, Fathom, Fire, Firth, Fish, Forest, Frith, Funk, Furious, Fustet, Fustoc, Gambrel, Gantry, Gapó, Gauntree, Gopher, Green, Greenheart, Grove, Hanger, Harewood, Heben, Hickory, Holt, Hurst, Hyle, Igapó, Iroko, Iron, Isle, Joist, Kindling, Knee, Kokra, Laburnum, Lana, Lath, Lignum(-vitae), Log(gat), Lumber, Mad, Mazer, Meranti, Miombo, Myall, Nemoral, Nemorous, Nettle-tree, Obeche, Offcut, Orache, Orange, Pallet, Plane, Pyengadu, Quebracho, Raddle, Ramin, Rata, Red, Rock, Rowan, Sabele, Sabicu, Sandal, Sanders(wood), Sapan, Sapele, Sappan, Satinwood, Shaw, Shawnee, Shittim, Silvan, Sissoo, Slat, Slippery elm, Southern, Spinney, Sponge, Spoon, Stink, Stolid, Sylvan, Taiga, Tangle, Three-ply, Timber, Touch, Treen, Trees, Tulip, Twiggy, Vert, Wald, Wallaba, Wild, Xylem, Xyloid, Yang, Zante

> **Wood** may indicate an anagram (in sense of mad)

**Wood-carver** Bodger, Gibbons, Whittler

**Woodchuck** Bobac, Marmot

**Woodcock** Becasse, Beccaccia, Snipe

**Woodlouse** Isopod, Oniscus, Slater

**Woodman** Ali (Baba), Forester, Hewer, Logger, Lumberjack

**Woodpecker** Bird, Flicker, Hickwall, Picarian, Rainbird, Sapsucker, Saurognathae, Witwall, Woodwale, Yaffle

**Wood-pigeon**  Bird, Cushat, Que(e)st, Qu(o)ist

**Wood-sorrel**  Oca

**Wood-tar**  Furan, Furfuran

**Woodwind**  Bassoon, Clarinet, Cornet, Flute, Oboe, Piccolo, Pipe, Recorder, Reed

**Woodwork(er)**  Sloid, Sloyd, Tarsia, Termite

**Woodworm**  Gribble, Termes

**Wookey**  Stalactite

**Wool(len), Woolly**  Alpaca, Angora, Aran, Ardil, Bainin, Beige, Berlin, Botany, Calamanco, Cardi(gan), Cashmere, Clip, Doeskin, Dog, Doily, Doyley, Down, Drugget, Fadge, Fingering, Fleece, Flock, Frieze, Fuzz, Guernsey, Hank, Hause-lock, Indumentum, Jaeger, Jersey, Kashmir, Ket, Lanate, Lanigerous, Lock, Loden, Merino, Mortling, Moul, Mullein, Noil(s), Nun's-veiling, Offsorts, Oo, Pashm, Pelage, Qiviut, Rolag, Sagathy, Saxon, Say, Shalloon, Shetland, Shoddy, Skein, Slipe, Slub, Spencer, Staple, Tamise, Tammy, Thibet, Three-ply, Tod, Tricot, Tweed, Vicuna, Worcester, Yarn, Zephyr, Zibel(l)ine

**Wool-gatherer**  Argo, Dreamer

**Wool-holder, Woolsack**  Bale, Distatff

**Woolly-bear**  Tiger-moth, Woubit

**Wool-oil**  Yolk

**Wooster**  Bertie

**Woozy**  Drunk, Vague, Woolly

**Word(s), Wording, Wordy**  Appellative, Claptrap, Comment, Dick, Dit(t), Epos, Faith, Hint, IN A WORD, IN TWO WORDS, Lexeme, Lexicon, Lexis, Lyrics, Message, Morpheme, Mot, Neologism, News, Nonce, Noun, Oracle, Order, Palabra, Paragram, Parole, Perissology, Phrase, Pledge, Prolix, Promise, Rhematic, Rumour, Saying, Signal, Term, Tetragram, Text, Verb, Verbiage, Warcry, Wort

**Word-blindness**  Alexia, Dyslexia

**Word-play**  Charade, Paronomasia, Pun

**Work(er), Working(-class), Workman(ship), Works**  Act(ivate), Ant, Appliqué, Artefact, Artel, Artifact, Artisan, Beaver, Bee, Bohunk, Boondoggle, Business, Casual, Char, Claim, Clock, Coolie, Corvée, Darg, Dog, Dogsbody, Droil, Drudge, Drug, Dung, Earn, Effect, Erg(ataner), Ergatoid, Erg-nine, Ergon, Erg-ten, Ern, Eta, Evince, Exercise, Exploit, Factotum, Facture, Fat, Fret, FUNCTION, Fuller, Gastarbeiter, Gel, Go, Graft, Grind, Grisette, Hand, Harness, Hat, Hobo, Horse, Hunky, Industry, Innards, Job, Journeyman, Labour, Luddite, Lump, Man, Manipulate, Meng, Midinette, Mine, Ming, Moider, Moonlight, Movement, Navvy, Neuter, Oeuvre, On, Op, Opera(tion), Operative, Operator, Opus, Opusc(u)le, Ouvrier, Ox, Peasant, Peg, Pensum, Peon, Ply, Practise, Production, Prole(tariat), Prud'homme, Pursuit, Rep, Ride, Run, Scabble, Scapple, Serve, Service, Situation, Slogger, Staff, Stakhanovite, Stevedore,

Stint, Strive, Sweat, Swink, Take, Task, Tenail(le), Tenaillon, Termite, Tew, Tick, Till, Toccata, Toil, Toreutic, Travail, Treatise, Trojan, Tut, Typto, Uphill, Wallah, Wark, White-collar, Wobblies, Yacker, Yakka, Yakker

**Workable** Feasible, Practical

**Work-basket** Caba(s)

**Workhouse** Spike, Union

> **Working** may indicate an anagram

**Working-party** Bee, Quilting-bee, Sewing-bee, Squad

**Work(s), Workshop** Atelier, Engine, Factory, Forge, Foundry, Garage, Hacienda, Innards, Lab, Mill, Plant, Shed, Shop, Skylab, Smithy, Studio

**Workshy** Sweer(ed), Sweert, Sweir(t)

**World(ly)** Carnal, Chthonic, Cosmopolitan, Cosmos, Earth, Ge, Globe, Kingdom, Lay, Mappemond, Microcosm, Mondial, Mundane, Orb, Oyster, Planet, Secular, Sensual, Society, Sphere, Temporal, Terra, Terrene, Terrestrial, Universe, Vale, Welt

**Worm(-like), Worms, Wormy** Anguillula, Annelid, Apod(e), Apodous, Articulata, Ascarid, Bob, Brandling, Caddis, Cestode, Cestoid, Diet, Diplozoon, Enteropneust, Filander, Filaria, Fluke, Gilt-tail, Gordius, Hair-eel, Helminth, Hemichordata, Hookworm, Leech, Liver-fluke, Lumbricus, Lytta, Merosome, Nematoda, Nematode, Nemertea, Nereid, Oligochaete, Palolo, Paste-eel, Peripatus, Piper, Sabella, Schistosome, Scoleciform, Scolex, Serpula, Servile, Sipunculacea, Sipunculoidea, Strongyle, Taenia, Tagtail, Tenioid, Teredo, Termite, Toxocara, Trematode, Trichin(ell)a, Trichinosed, Tubifex, Turbellaria, Vermiform, Wheat-eel

**Wormwood** Absinth, Appleringie, Artemisia, Mugwort, Santonica

**Worn(-out)** Attrite, Bare, Decrepit, Detrition, Effete, Exhausted, Forfairn, Forfoughten, Forjaskit, Forjeskit, Frazzled, Old, On, Passé, Raddled, Rag, Shabby, Shot, Spent, Stale, Tired, Traikit, Trite, Used, Whacked

**Worried, Worrier, Worry** Agonise, Annoy, Anxiety, Badger, Bait, Bother, Care(worn), Cark, Chafe, Concern, Deave, Deeve, Distress, Disturb, Dog, Exercise, Feeze, Frab, Fret, Fuss, Harass, Harry, Hyp, Knag, Nag, Perturb, Pester, Pheese, Pheeze, Phese, Pingle, Pium, Rile, Sool, Stew, Tew, Touse, Towse, Trouble, Vex, Wherrit, Worn

> **Worried** may indicate an anagram

**Worse(n)** Adversely, Degenerate, Deteriorate, Exacerbate, Impair, Inflame, Pejorate, War(re), Waur

**Worship(per)** Adore, Adulation, Angelolatry, Autolatry, Bless, Churchgoer, Cult, Deify, Douleia, Dulia, Epeolatry, Fetish, Glorify, Gurdwara, Idolise, Latria, Lionise, Lordolatry, Mariolatry, Oncer, Orant, Praise, Puja, Revere, Sabaism, Sakta, Service, Shakta, Synaxis, Thiasus, Vaishnava, Venerate, Votary, Wodenism

**Worst** Beat, Best, Defeat, Get, Nadir, Outdo, Overpower, Rock-bottom, Scum, Severest, Throw, Trounce

**Worsted**  Caddis, Caddyss, Challis, Coburg, Genappe, Lea, Serge, Shalli, Tamin(e)

> **Worsted**  may indicate an anagram

**Wort**  Laser, Parkleaves, Plant, Tutsan

**Worth(while), Worthy**  Admirable, Asset, Deserving, Eligible, Estimable, MERIT, Substance, Tanti, Use, Value, Virtuous, Wealth

**Worthless (person)**  Base, Beggarly, Bootless, Bum, Catchpenny, Cypher, Damn, Dodkin, Doit, Draffish, Draffy, Dross, Fallal, Footra, Fouter, Foutre, Frippery, Gimcrack, Gingerbread, Javel, Jimcrack, Left, Lorel, Lorrell, Losel, Lozell, Mud, Nugatory, Nyaff, Obol, Orra, Paltry, Pin, Punk, Raca, Rap, Rubbishy, Scabby, Scum, Shinkin, Sorry, Straw, Tinhorn, Tinsel, Tittle, Trangam, Trashy, Trumpery, Tuppenny, Two-bit, Twopenny, Useless, Vain, Vile, Waff, Wanworthy, Wauff

**Wotchermean**  Anan

**Would be**  Assumed, Pseudo, Soi-disant

**Wouldn't**  Nould(e)

**Wound(ed)**  Battery, Bite, Bless, Blighty, Bruise, Chagrin, Coiled, Crepance, Cut, Dere, Engore, Ganch, Gash, Gaunch, Gore, Harm, Hurt, Injury, Lacerate, Lesion, Maim, Molest, Mortify, Pip, Sabre-cut, Scab, Scar, Scath, Scotch, Scratch, Shoot, Snaked, Snub, Sore, Stab, Sting, Trauma, Twined, Umbrage, Vuln, Wing

**Woven**  Knitted, Pirnit, Textile, Wattle

**Wow**  Howl, My, Success

**Wrack**  Destroy, Downfall, Kelp, Ore, Torment, Varec(h), Vengeance

**Wraith**  Apparition, Fetch, Ghost, Phantom, Shadow, Spectre

**Wrangle**  Argie-bargie, ARGUE, Altercate, Bandy, Bicker, Brangle, Broil, Dispute, Haggle, Mathematical, Rag

**Wrap(per), Wrapping, Wrap up**  Amice, Amis, Bind, Cellophane, Clingfilm, Cloak, Clothe, Cocoon, Conclude, Emboss, Enfold, Enroll, Ensheath(e), Envelop(e), Foil, Furl, Hap, Hem, Kimono, Lag, Lap, Mail, Negligee, Parcel, Roll, Rug, Sheath(e), Stole, Swaddle, Swathe, Tinfoil, Tsutsumu, Velamen, Wap, Wimple

**Wrasse**  Conner, Cunner, Parrot-fish

**Wrath**  Anger, Cape, Fury, Ire, Passion, Vengeance

**Wreak**  Avenge, Indulge, Inflict

**Wreath(e)**  Adorn, Anadem, Chaplet, Coronal, Crown, Entwine, Festoon, Garland, Laurel, Lei, Torse, Tortile, Twist

**Wreathe(d)**  Hederated

**Wreck(age)**  Crab, Debris, Demolish, Devastate, Flotsam, Founder, Goner, Hesperus, Hulk, Lagan, Ligan, Mutilate, Ruin(ate), Sabotage, Shambles, Shatter, Sink, Smash, Subvert, Torpedo, Wrack

> **Wrecked**  may indicate an anagram

**Wren** Architect, Bird, Hannah, Jenny, Kinglet, Rifleman-bird, Sailor

**Wrench** Fit, Jerk, Mole, Pull, Spanner, Sprain, Stillson, Strain, Tear, Twist, Windlass, Wrest

**Wrestle(r), Wrestling** All-in, Antaeus, Clinch, Grapple, Judo, Milo, Ozeki, Palaestral, Pancratium, Rikishi, Sambo, Struggle, Sumo, Tussle, Wraxle, Writhe, Yokozuna

**Wretch(ed)** Blackguard, Blue, Caitiff, Cullion, Forlorn, Git, Hapless, Measly, Miser, Miserable, Pipsqueak, Poltroon, Poor, Punk, Rat, Scoundrel, Scroyle, Seely, Snake, Unblest, Wo(e)

> **Wretched** may indicate an anagram

**Wriggle** Hirsle, Shimmy, Squirm, Twine, Wiggle, Writhe

**Wring(er)** Drain, Extort, Mangle, Screw, Squeeze, Twist

**Wrinkle(d)** Clue, Corrugate, Crease, Crow's-foot, Crumple, Fold, Frounce, Frumple, Furrow, Gen, Groove, Headline, Hint, Idea, Line, Lirk, Pucker, Purse, Ridge, Rivel, Ruck(le), Rugose, Rumple, Runkle, Seamy, Sulcus, Tip

**Wrist** Carpus, Radialia, Shackle-bone

**Writ(s)** Capias, Certiorari, Cursitor, Dedimus, Distringas, Elegit, Filacer, Habeas-corpus, Injunction, Latitat, Law-burrows, Mandamus, Mittimus, Noverint, Praemunire, Process, Replevin, Scirefacias, Significat, Subpoena, Summons, Supersedeas, Tolt, Venire, Warrant

**Write(r), Writing** Acton, Albee, Aldrich, Allograph, Ambler, Andersen, Annotator, Apocrypha, Aretino, Arnold, Artaud, Asch, Asimov, Auden, Austen, AUTHOR, Ballpoint, Balzac, Baring, Barrie, Bates, Beckett, Belloc, Bellow, Bennett, Biographer, Biro, Blackmore, Blake, Boileau, Bolt, Borrow, Boswell, Boustrophedon, Bronte, Browning, Buchan, Bunyan, Burroughs, Butler, Calligraphy, Camus, Carlyle, Caroline, Chandler, Chateaubriand, Chaucer, Chekhov, Chesterton, Cicero, Clerk, Cobbett, Colette, Collins, Columnist, Conrad, Coppard, Corelli, Corpus, Corvo, Cowper, Crane, Cranmer, Cree, Dahl, Defoe, De la Mare, Diarist, Dickens, Disraeli, Dite, Dos Passos, Dostoevsky, Doyle, Draft, Dreiser, Dryden, Edgeworth, Eliot, Elohist, Emerson, Endorse, Endoss, Engross, Epistle, Essayist, Faulkner, Fenelon, Fielding, Fist, Fitzgerald, Flaubert, Forester, Form, Forster, France, Freelance, Galsworthy, Genet, Ghost, Gide, Gogol, Golding, Goldsmith, Gongorism, Graffiti, Graphite, Graves, Greene, Greer, Grimm, Hack, Haggard, Hairline, Hand, Hardy, Hawthorne, Hemingway, Herbert, Hesse, Heyer, Hichens, Hiragana, Hobbes, Homer, Hughes, Hugo, Hunt, Huxley, Ibsen, Indite, Ink, Inkerman, Inkslinger, Innes, Inscribe, James, Jerome, Johnson, Join-hand, Jonson, Jot(tings), Journalese, Journalist, Joyce, Kafka, Kalakana, Kana, Kanji, Keelivine, Keelyvine, Kingsley, Kipling, Lamb, Lardner, Lawrence, Lee, Linklater, Lipogram, Longland, Loos, Lorca, Loti, Lucian, Lucubrate, Lyly, Mackenzie, Madariaga, Mailer, Malony, Mann, Marivaudage, Marryat, Mason, Maugham, Mérimée, Milton, Minoan, Moravia, More, Ms(s), Munro, Nabokov, Nash(e), Nerval, Nesk(h), Nib, Notary, Novelist, Opie, Oppenheim, Orwell, Ouida, Ovid, Pasigraphy, Pasternak, Pater, Pen, Pencil, Penne, Pentel (tdmk), Perrault, Planchette, Plutarch, Poe, Poet,

Pope, Pot-hook, Priestley, Proser, Proust, Pushkin, Quill, Quipu, Rabelais, Ransome, Reade, Remarque, Renan, Rilke, RLS, Rostand, Roundhand, Rousseau, Runyon, Ruskin, Saki, Salinger, Sanskrit, Santayana, Saroyan, Sayers, Sci-fi, Scissorer, Scott, Scratch, Screeve, Scribe, Scrip(t), Scripture, Scrow, Scytale, Secretary, Sewell, Shakespeare, Shaw, Shelley, Sholokhov, Simenon, Sitwell, Smiles, Smollett, Snow, Steele, Steinbeck, Stendhal, Sterne, Stevenson, Style, Surtees, Swift, Syngraph, Taffrail, Tantra, Terence, Thackeray, Thomas, Thoreau, Tolkien, Tolstoy, Travers, Treatise, Trollope, Turgenev, Twain, Verne, Virgil, Voltaire, Wallace, Walpole, Walton, Waugh, Wells, Wharton, Wilde, Wilder, Williams, Woolf, Yates, Yonge, Zola

**Write-off** Amortise, Annul, Cancel, Scrap

**Writhe** Contort, Curl, Scriggle, Squirm, Twist, Wriggle

> **Writhing** may indicate an anagram

**Writing-case** Kalamdan

**Writing-room** Scriptorium

**Wrong** Aggrieve, Agley, Amiss, Awry, Bad, Chout, Delict, Err, Fallacious, False, Harm, Ill, Immoral, Improper, Incorrect, Injury, Mischief, Misintelligence, Misled, Mistake(n), Misuse, Nocent, Offbase, Offend, Peccadillo, Perverse, Sin(ful), Tort, Transgress, Unethical, Unsuitable, Withershins, Wryly

**Wrong** may indicate an anagram

**Wrong opinion** Cacodoxy

**Wrought (up)** Agitated, Beaten, Carved, Created, Excited, Filigree, Freestone, Shaped

**Wrung** Twisted, Withers

**Wry** Askew, Contrary, Devious, Distort, Droll, Grimace, Ironic

**Wryneck** Iynx, Jynx, Torticollis, Yunx

**Wycliffian** Lollard

**Wyoming** Wy

# Xx

**X(-shaped)**  Buss, By, Chi, Christ, Cross, Decussate, Drawn, Kiss, Ten, Times, Unknown, X-ray

**Xant(h)ippe**  Battle-axe, Dragon

**Xenon**  Xe

**Xerophyte, Xerophytic**  Cactus, Cereus, Mesquite, Tamaricaceae, Tamarisk

**Ximenes**  Cardinal

**X-ray**  Fermi, Plate, Rem, Roentgen, Sciagram, Screening, Skiagram

**Xhosan**  Caffre, Kaf(f)ir

**Xylophone**  Marimba, Sticcado, Sticcato

**Xmas**  Noel, Yuletide

# Yy

**Y** Samian, Unknown, Yankee, Yard, Year, Yen, Yttrium

**Yacht** Britannia, Dragon, Keelboat, Maxi, Sailboat

**Yachtsman, Yachtsmen** Chichester, RYS

**Yak** Gup, Talk

**Yale** Key, Lock

**Yam** Batata, Camote, Dioscorea, Diosgenin, Kumara

**Yank(ee)** Carpetbagger, Hitch, Jerk, Jonathan, Lug, Northerner, Pluck, Pull, Rug, Schlep(p), So(o)le, Sowl(e), TUG, Tweak, Twitch, Wrench, Wrest

> **Yank** may indicate an anagram

**Yap** Bark, Yelp

**Yard** Area, CID, Close, Court, Garden, Hof, Kail, Mast, Measure, Patio, Ree(d), Scotland, Spar, Sprit, Steel, Stick, Stride, Y, Yd

**Yarn(s)** Abb, Berlin, Bouclé, Caddice, Caddis, Chenille, Clew, Clue, Cop, Cord, Crewel, Fib, Fibroline, Fingering, Genappe, Gimp, Gingham, Guimp(e), Gymp, Homespun, Jaw, Knittle, Knot, Lay, Lea, Ley, Line, Lisle, Merino, Nylon, Organzine, Rigmarole, Ripping, Saxony, Sennit, Sinnet, Skein, Story, Strand, Tale, Taradiddle, Thread, Thrid, Thrum(my), Tram, Warp, Weft, Woof, Wool, Worsted, Zephyr

**Yarrow** Milfoil

**Yashmak** Veil

**Yaw(s)** Boba, Buba, Deviate, Framboesia, Lean, Morula, Tack, Veer

**Yawn(ing)** Boredom, Chasmy, Fissure, Gant, Gape, Gaunt, Greys, Oscitation, Pandiculation, Rictus

**Yea** Certainly, Truly, Verily, Yes

**Year(ly), Years** A, Age, Anno, Annual, Dot, Julian, Leap, Light, PA, Platonic, Riper, Sabbatical, Sothic, Summer, Sun, Time, Towmon(d), Towmont, Twelvemonth

**Yearbook** Annual

**Yearling** Colt, Hogget, Stirk, Teg

**Yearn(ing)** Ache, Aspire, Brame, Burn, Crave, Curdle, Desire, Greed, Hanker, LONG, Nostalgia, Pant, Pine, Sigh

> **Yearning** may indicate an anagram

**Year's end** Dec

**Yeast** Barm, Bees, Ferment, Flor, Leaven, Saccharomyces, Torula

**Yell** Cry, Hue, Shout, Skelloch, Tiger, Waul

**Yellow(ish)** Abram, Amber, Anthoclore, Auburn, Back, Beige, Buff, Canary, Chicken, Chrome, Citrine, Cowardly, Craven, Etiolin, Fallow, Fever, Filemot, Flavescent, Flavin(e), Flaxen, Fulvous, Gamboge, Gold, Icteric, Isabel(le), Jack, Jaundiced, Lammer, Lupulin, Lutein, Lutescent, Mustard, Nankeen, Naples, Oaker, Ochery, Ochre(y), Or(eide), Oroide, Pages, Peril, Pink, River, Saffron, Sallow, Sear, Spineless, Tawny, Topaz, Weld, Yolk

**Yellow-wood** Gopher

**Yelp** Cry, Squeal, Whee, Ya(w)p

**Yemeni** Saba, Sabean, Sheba

**Yen** Desire, Itch, Longing, Urge, Y, Yearn

**Yeoman** Beefeater, Exon, Salvation

**Yep** OK, Yes

**Yes** Ay(e), Da, Indeed, Ja, Jokol, Nod, OK, Oke, Quite, Sure, Truly, Uh-huh, Wilco, Yea, Yokul

**Yesterday** Démodé, Eve, Hesternal, Pridian

**Yet** But, How-be, Moreover, Nay, Nevertheless, Now, Still, Though

**Yeti** Abominable snowman, Sasquatch

**Yew** Taxus

**Yibbles** A(i)blins

**Yield(ing)** Abandon, Afford, Bend, Bow, Breed, Capitulate, Catch, Cede, Come, Comply, Concede, Crack, Crop, Defer, Dividend, Docile, Ductile, Elastic, Facile, Flaccid, Flexible, Give, Harvest, Interest, Knuckle, Meek, Meltith, Mess, Output, Pan, Pay, Pliant, Produce, Relent, Render, Return, Sag, Soft, SUBMIT, Succumb, Surrender, Truckle

**Yodel** Song, Warble

**Yoghurt** Madzoon, Matzoon

**Yogi** Bear, Fakir, Sid(d)ha

**Yoke** Bow, Collar, Couple, Harness, Inspan, Jugal, Pair, Span

**Yokel** Boor, Bumpkin, Chaw(-bacon), Clumperton, Hayseed, Hick, Jake, Jock, Peasant, Rustic

**Yolk** Parablast, Vitellicle, Vitellus, Yellow

**Yon(der)** Distant, Further, O'erby, Thae, There, Thether, Thither

**Yore** Agone, Olden, Past

**Yorick** Sterne

**York(shire), Yorkshireman** Batter, Bowl, Ebor, Pudding, Ridings, Tyke
**Yorker** Tice

**You** One, Sic, Thee, Thou, Usted, Ye

**Young (person), Youngster, Youth** Adolescent, Amorino, Bodgie, Boy, Brigham, Bub, Ch, Chick, Child, Chile, Colt, Comsomol, Cornstalk, Cub, DJ, Early, Ephebe, Ephebus, Fledgling, Foetus, Fry, Gigolo, Girl,

Gunsel, Halfling, Hebe, Immature, Imp, Infant, Issue, **Junior, Juvenal,
Juvenile, Keral, Kid, Knave-bairn, Komsomol, Lad, Latter-day, Less,
Litter, Loretta, Minor, Misspent, Mod, Mormon, Nance, Neophyte, New,
Nipper, Nymph, Plant, Progeny, Pup, Sapling, Scent, Scion, Shaver,
Skinhead, Slip, Spawn, Sprig, Springal(d), Stripling, Swain, Syen, Ted,
Teenager, Teens, Whelp, Whippersnapper, Yippy, Yoof, Yopper, Younker,
Yumpie, Yuppie**

**Younger, Youngest**   Baby, Benjamin, Cadet, Less, Seneca, Wallydrag,
Wallydraigle, Yr

**Your(s)**   Thee, Thine, Thy

**Yo-yo**   Bandalore

**Ytterbium**   Yb

**Yttrium**   Y

**Yucky**   Gooey, Grooly, Sickly, Sticky

**Yugoslav**   Croat(ian), Serb, Slovene

**Yuletide**   Advent, Dec, Noel, Xmas

# Zz

**Z** Izzard, Izzet, Zambia, Zebra

**Zamenhof** Esperanto

**Zander** Fogash, Sander

**Zany** Bor(r)el, Comic, Cuckoo, Idiotic, Mad

**Zeal(ous)** Ardour, Bigotry, Devotion, Eager, Enthusiasm, Evangelic, Fervour, Perfervid, Study

**Zealot** Bigot, Devotee, Fan(atic), St Simon, Votary

**Zebra** Convict, Quagga

**Zenith** Acme, Apogee, Height, Pole, Summit

**Zeno** Colonnade, Stoic

**Zeolite** Analcime, Analcite

**Zephyr** Breeze, Wind

**Zeppelin** Airship, Balloon, Dirigible

**Zero** Absolute, Blob, Cipher, Nil, Nothing, Nought, O, Z

**Zest** Condiment, Crave, Elan, Gusto, Pep, Piquancy, Relish, Spice, Tang, Zap

**Ziegfeld** Flo

**Zigzag** Crémaillère, Dancette, Ric-rac, Slalom, Stagger, Tack, Traverse, Yaw

**Zinc** Blende, Gahnite, Sherardise, Spelter, Sphalerite, Tutenag, Tutty, Willemite, Wurtzite, Zn

**Zip(per)** Dash, Energy, Fastener, Fly, Go, Oomph, Presto, Stingo, Vim, Vivacity, Whirry

**Zircon** Hyacinth, Jacinth, Jargo(o)n

**Zirconium** Baddeleyite, Zr

**Zither** Cithara, Kantela, Kantele, Koto

**Zodiac(al)** Aquarius, Archer, Aries, Bull, Cancer, Capricorn, Counter-glow, Crab, Fish, Gemini, Gegenschein, Goat, Horoscope, Leo, Libra, Lion, Ophiuchus, Pisces, Ram, Sagittarius, Scales, Scorpio(n), Taurus, Twins, Virgin, Virgo, Watercarrier

**Zola** Budd, Emile, Nana, Realism

**Zombie** Catatonic, Dolt, Robot

**Zone** Anacoustic, Area, Band, Belt, Benioff, Precinct, REGION, Ring, Smokeless, Torrid, Tundra

**Zoo** Bedlam, Circus, Menagerie, Whipsnade

**Zoologist**  Biologist, Botanist, Naturalist

**Zoom**  Close-up, Speed

**Zoroastrian**  Gheber, Ghebre, Gueber, Guebre, Magus, Parsee

**Zulu**  Chaka, Impi, Matabele, Niger, Shaka, Warrior

**Zut**  Crimini

# The Crossword Club

If you are interested in crosswords. consider joining the Crossword Club. Membership is open to all who enjoy tackling challenging crosswords and who appreciate the finer points of clue-writing and grid-construction. The Club's magazine, Crossword, contains two prize puzzles each month. A sample issue and full details are available on request.

**The Crossword Club**
Coombe Farm
Awbridge,
Romsey, Hants,
SO51 0HN

Peter Collin Publishing, 1 Cambridge Road, Teddington, TW11 8DT, UK
fax: +44 181 943 1673   tel: +44 181 943 3386   email: info@pcp.co.uk

| Title | ISBN | Send Details |
|---|---|---|

## English Dictionaries

| | | |
|---|---|---|
| Accounting | 0-948549-27-0 | ❏ |
| Agriculture, 2nd ed | 0-948549-78-5 | ❏ |
| American Business | 0-948549-11-4 | ❏ |
| Automobile Engineering | 0-948549-66-1 | ❏ |
| Banking & Finance | 0-948549-12-2 | ❏ |
| Business, 2nd ed | 0-948549-51-3 | ❏ |
| Computing, 3rd ed | 1-901659-04-6 | ❏ |
| Ecology & Environment, 3ed | 0-948549-74-2 | ❏ |
| Government & Politics, 2ed | 0-948549-89-0 | ❏ |
| Hotel, Tourism, Catering Mg | 0-948549-40-8 | ❏ |
| Human Resource & Personnel, 2ed | 0-948549-79-3 | ❏ |
| Information Technology, 2nd ed | 0-948549-88-2 | ❏ |
| Law, 2nd ed | 0-948549-33-5 | ❏ |
| Library & Information Management | 0-948549-68-8 | ❏ |
| Marketing, 2nd ed | 0-948549-73-4 | ❏ |
| Medicine, 2nd ed | 0-948549-36-X | ❏ |
| Printing & Publishing, 2nd ed | 0-948549-99-8 | ❏ |
| Science & Technology | 0-948549-67-X | ❏ |

## Vocabulary Workbooks

| | | |
|---|---|---|
| Banking & Finance | 0-948549-96-3 | ❏ |
| Business | 0-948549-72-6 | ❏ |
| Computing | 0-948549-58-0 | ❏ |
| Colloquial English | 0-948549-97-1 | ❏ |
| Hotels, Tourism, Catering | 0-948549-75-0 | ❏ |
| Law | 0-948549-62-9 | ❏ |
| Medicine | 0-948549-59-9 | ❏ |

## Professional/General

| | | |
|---|---|---|
| Astronomy | 0-948549-43-2 | ❏ |
| Economics | 0-948549-91-2 | ❏ |
| Multimedia, 2nd ed | 1-901659-01-1 | ❏ |
| PC & the Internet | 0-948549-93-9 | ❏ |
| Bradford Crossword Solver, 3rd ed | 1-901659-03-8 | ❏ |

## Bilingual Dictionaries

| | |
|---|---|
| French-English/English-French Dictionaries | ❏ |
| German-English/English-German Dictionaries | ❏ |
| Spanish-English/English-Spanish Dictionaries | ❏ |
| Swedish-English/English-Swedish Dictionaries | ❏ |

Name: ............................................................................................

Address: ........................................................................................

......................................................................................................

...........................................................Postcode:.............................